T0134758

Lecture Notes in Computer Science 11547

Commenced Publication in 1973
Founding and Former Series Editors:
Gerhard Goos, Juris Hartmanis, and Jan van Leeuwen

More information about this series at http://www.springer.com/series/7410

Julian Jang-Jaccard · Fuchun Guo (Eds.)

Information Security and Privacy

24th Australasian Conference, ACISP 2019
Christchurch, New Zealand, July 3–5, 2019
Proceedings

Springer

Editors
Julian Jang-Jaccard (iD)
Massey University
Palmerston North, New Zealand

Fuchun Guo
University of Wollongong
Wollongong, NSW, Australia

ISSN 0302-9743 ISSN 1611-3349 (electronic)
Lecture Notes in Computer Science
ISBN 978-3-030-21547-7 ISBN 978-3-030-21548-4 (eBook)
https://doi.org/10.1007/978-3-030-21548-4

LNCS Sublibrary: SL4 – Security and Cryptology

This Springer imprint is published by the registered company Springer Nature Switzerland AG
The registered company address is: Gewerbestrasse 11, 6330 Cham, Switzerland

Preface

This volume contains the papers presented at the 24th Australasian Conference on Information Security and Privacy (ACISP 2019), which was held at the University of Canterbury during July 3–5, 2019, in Christchurch, New Zealand. ACISP is an annual international forum for international researchers and industry experts to present and discuss the latest research, trends, breakthroughs, and challenges in the domain of information security, privacy, and cybersecurity.

This year we received 129 submissions of excellent quality from 31 countries around the world. Submitted papers were initially screened based on the submission guidelines. Then, the papers were assigned to and evaluated by at least three Program Committee members. Further, the papers were scrutinized during an extensive discussion. Finally, we accepted 32 full papers and eight short papers to be included in the conference program a total of 40 papers. The revised papers were not subject to editorial review and the authors bear full responsibility for their content. The submission and review process was supported by the EasyChair conference submission server.

Among the accepted papers, the ACISP chairs selected two papers to be given the Best Paper Award based on their novelty and scores. Further, one paper was awarded the Best Student Paper.

The Best Paper Award went to:

- "Ciphertext-Delegatable CP-ABE for a Dynamic Credential: A Modular Approach" by Jongkil Kim, Willy Susilo, Joonsang Baek, Surya Nepal, and Dongxi Liu
- "Field Extension in Secret-Shared Form and Its Applications to Efficient Secure Computation" by Ryo Kikuchi, Nuttapong Attrapadung, Koki Hamada, Dai Ikarashi, Ai Ishida, Takahiro Matsuda, Yusuke Sakai, and Jacob Schuldt

The Best Student Paper was awarded to:

- "Fast-to-Finalize Nakamoto-Like Consensus Protocol" by Shuyang Tang, Sherman S. M. Chow, Zhiqiang Liu, and Joseph Liu

This year, we were very honoured to have the Jennifer Seberry Lecture delivered by Professor Jennifer Seberry herself (University of Wollongong, Australia). The program also included three invited talks by Professor Jong Sou Park (Korea Aerospace University, South Korea), Associate Professor Joseph K. Liu (Monash University, Australia), and Professor Zbigniew Kalbarczyk (University of Illinois at Urbana-Champaign, USA).

We would like to thank all authors who submitted their papers to ACISP 2019, and the conference attendees for their interest and support. We thank the Program Committee members and the external reviewers for their hard work in reviewing the submissions—the conference could not be successful without their expert reviews.

We thank the publication chairs, Mengmeng Ge and Hyoungshick Kim, for their hard work in preparing the proceedings. We also thank the Organizing Committee and all volunteers for their time and effort dedicated to managing the conference.

April 2019   Julian Jang-Jaccard
                                                                              Fuchun Guo

Organization

General Chairs

Dong Seong Kim   The University of Queensland, Australia
Jin B. Hong   University of Western Australia, Australia

Program Chairs

Julian Jang-Jaccard   Massey University, New Zealand
Fuchun Guo   University of Wollongong, Australia

Publication Chairs

Mengmeng Ge   Deakin University, Australia
Hyoungshick Kim   Sungkyunkwan University, South Korea

Publicity Chairs

William Liu   Auckland University of Technology, New Zealand
Simon Yusuf-Enoch   University of Canterbury, New Zealand

Financial Chairs

Miguel Morales   University of Canterbury, New Zealand

Program Committee

Cristina Alcaraz   University of Malaga, Spain
Muhammad Rizwan Asghar   The University of Auckland, New Zealand
Man Ho Au   The Hong Kong Polytechnic University, SAR China
Joonsang Baek   University of Wollongong, Australia
Shi Bai   Florida Atlantic University, USA
Zubair Baig   Edith Cowan University, Australia
Lynn Batten   Deakin University, Australia
Elisa Bertino   Purdue University, USA
Jinjun Chen   University of Technology, Sydney
Liqun Chen   University of Surrey, UK
Rongmao Chen   National University of Defense Technology, China
Shiping Chen   CSIRO, Australia
Xiaofeng Chen   Xidian University, China
Josep Domingo-Ferrer   Universitat Rovira i Virgili, Spain
Ernest Foo   Queensland University of Technology, Australia

Additional Reviewers

Anglès-Tafalla, Carles
Bamiloshin, Michael
Banegas, Gustavo
Banik, Subhadeep
Bemmann, Pascal
Bert, Pauline
Blanco Justicia, Alberto
Buriro, Attaullah
Castagnos, Guilhem
Chen, Haixia
Choudhuri, Arka Rai
Chu, Cheng-Kang
Chvojka, Peter
Cominetti, Eduardo
Cui, Shujie
Davies, Gareth
Dragan, Constantin
    Catalin
Du, Jiangyi
Duong, Dung Hoang
El Kassem, Nada
Fernandez, Carmen
Ferraris, Davide
Gao, Yansong
Gardham, Daniel
Gerault, David
González, Alonso
Granger, Robert
Gunasinghe, Hasini
Guo, Kaiwen
Guo, Qingwen
Hassan, Fadi
He, Jingnan

Herranz, Javier
Hu, Jingwei
Hu, Kexin
Hu, Qinwen
Hua, Zhen
Huang, Jianye
Hébant, Chloé
Inoue, Akiko
Isobe, Takanori
Iwata, Tetsu
Jiang, Shaoquan
Keller, Marcel
Kim, Intae
Kim, Jon-Lark
Komo, Andrea Erina
Kuchta, Veronika
Li, Bingbing
Li, Nan
Li, Yanan
Li, Yannan
Li, Zhe
Lin, Chengjun
Liu, Jia
Lu, Xingye
Lu, Zhenliang
Luo, Xiapu
Ma, Xu
Martinez, Sergio
Miller, Shaun
Niehues, David
Parra Arnau, Javier
Phuong, Tran Viet Xuan
Pryvalov, Ivan

Ramchen, Kim
Ruan, Ou
Sakzad, Amin
Santini, Paolo
Sarkar, Santanu
Shen, Hua
Silva, Marcos V. M.
Singla, Ankush
Soria-Comas, Jordi
Sun, Hung-Min
Sun, Shifeng
Suzuki, Daisuke
Takashima, Katsuyuki
Trinh, Viet Cuong
Tucker, Ida
Wang, Haoyang
Wang, Yilei
Wang, Yuanhao
Wen, Weiqiang
Xia, Zhe
Xu, Dongqing
Xue, Haiyang
Yamakawa, Takashi
Yamamoto, Takumi
Yang, S. J.
Yu, Jiangshan
Yuen, Tsz Hon
Zhang, Xiaoyu
Zhang, Yuexin
Zhao, Shengnan
Zhou, Yanwei

Contents

Cryptocurrency Related

Foundations

Encryption

Ciphertext-Delegatable CP-ABE for a Dynamic Credential: A Modular Approach

Jongkil Kim[1]([✉]), Willy Susilo[1], Joonsang Baek[1], Surya Nepal[2], and Dongxi Liu[2]

[1] School of Computing and Information Technology, University of Wollongong, Wollongong, Australia
{jongkil,wsusilo,baek}@uow.edu.au
[2] Data61, Commonwealth Scientific and Industrial Research Organisation, Marsfield, Australia
{surya.nepal,dongxi.liu}@data61.csiro.au

Abstract. We introduce a new technique converting Ciphertext-policy Attribute-based Encryption (CP-ABE) to Ciphertext-delegatable CP-ABE (CD-CP-ABE). Ciphertext delegation is an important technique to deal with dynamic credentials, which enable users to be joined and revoked at any time while the system is operating. The delegation of CD-CP-ABE allows third parties such as cloud or proxy servers to convert a ciphertext to the other one with a more restrictive policy. Therefore, it can be used to revoke users dynamically in an access control system. Prior to our work, a delegation algorithm of CD-CP-ABE is not generic and the completeness of the delegation is shown when the size of the delegated access structure increases quadratically with the sizes of original and revocation access structures. In this paper, we provide a generic delegation algorithm to reform CP-ABE to CD-CP-ABE. We generalize properties necessary for the ciphertext delegation using the syntax of encodings for the modularity and construct a generic delegation algorithm based on those properties. In our new technique, we build the delegated access structures, which generally determines the size of the ciphertext, in a defined way. The size of delegated access structures grows only *linearly* with those of original and revocation access structures. Through presenting instances, we show that our technique is readily applicable to existing CP-ABE schemes including CP-ABE scheme with non-monotonic access structures.

Keywords: Ciphertext-delegation · Revocation · Attribute-based Encryption · Dynamic access control

1 Introduction

Attribute-based Encryption (ABE) [22] is an encryption scheme that supports fine-grained access control. ABE is an effective solution to building up access

© Springer Nature Switzerland AG 2019
J. Jang-Jaccard and F. Guo (Eds.): ACISP 2019, LNCS 11547, pp. 3–20, 2019.
https://doi.org/10.1007/978-3-030-21548-4_1

control systems that need a flexible and complicated access policy such as a Boolean formula. There are two types of ABE schemes, Key-policy Attribute-based Encryption (KP-ABE) and Ciphertext-policy Attribute-based Encryption (CP-ABE) [11]. In particular, CP-ABE is known as a more intuitive and practical system because users have a key based on their attributes and a ciphertext is encrypted using an access policy.

An access control system realized by CP-ABE is often static rather than dynamic. In a static CP-ABE system, once ciphertexts are generated, they cannot be modified. For example, if *Alice* has lost her secret key, then a static access control system must decrypt and encrypt again all encrypted credentials that *Alice* can access to revoke her secret key from the system. This rather greedy technique puts a significant computational burden on the system because the decryption of ABE schemes usually requires computationally demanding operations such as pairing computations. Moreover, in the system, the decryption process can be permitted only by a centralized authority who can decrypt any ciphertexts.

Revocable ABE [4,5,16,24] enables revocation by either including a revocation policy in the ciphertext when the sender encrypts data or requiring a regular update of users' private keys to revoke users. The former is called direct revocation. Direct revocation cannot support dynamic credential. It needs a revocation list when the data is encrypted. The later is called indirect revocation. Indirect revocation supports a dynamic access control system, but updating users' private keys requires significant communication burdens on the system since it needs secure key distribution between a key generator and users for the update.

Ciphertext-delegation is also useful for the *dynamic access control*. Sahai, Seyalioglu and Waters [21] showed that ciphertexts of CP-ABE schemes based on Linear Secret Sharing Scheme (LSSS) can be updated through a delegation process. In particular, if an access structure $\mathbb{A}'$ can be spanned from another access structure $\mathbb{A}$ and a ciphertext satisfies several properties of replicating operations necessary for the span, the ciphertext encrypted under $\mathbb{A}'$ is delegated from the ciphertext encrypted under $\mathbb{A}$. However, their delegation algorithm is operation-wise. It is not clear how we construct $\mathbb{A}'$ when the revocation list is given and whether we can generically formulate a delegation algorithm.

Moreover, deriving the delegated access structure $\mathbb{A}'$ directly from the original access structure of $\mathbb{A}$ is not trivial according to Lewko and Waters [15]. Lewko and Waters state that it is not always possible even if $\mathbb{A}'$ is more restrictive than $\mathbb{A}$. Due to this, the completeness of the delegation over LSSS can be proved only by an inefficient composite of those two access structures. Moreover, the size of this composited access structure increases quadratically with the sizes of both $\mathbb{A}$ and $\mathbb{A}'$.

1.1 Our Contributions

We introduce a generic technique converting a CP-ABE scheme to a ciphertext-delegatable CP-ABE (CD-CP-ABE) scheme. In our work, a ciphertext encrypted under an access structure $\mathbb{A}$ can be reformed to a ciphertext under another access structure $\mathbb{A}'$ through a delegation process. Compared with the existing delegation techniques for *LSSS* suggested by Sahai et al. [21] and Lewko and Waters [15], ours has the following advantages:

- We provide a *generic* delegation algorithm using a novel encoding technique. We take a modular approach as suggested in the encoding techniques for ABE schemes [3,23]. We generalize properties commonly shared among CP-ABE schemes and provide a new delegation algorithm based on those properties. Therefore, our delegation algorithm for the resulting CP-ABE schemes is constructed in a modular way using the encryption algorithms of their original CP-ABE schemes.
- The size of a delegated access structure $\mathbb{A}'$ increases only *linearly* with the sizes of the original access structure $\mathbb{A}$ and the revocation access structure $\mathbb{A}^*$. In order to achieve this, we define a delegated access policy $\mathcal{T}'$ corresponding to $\mathbb{A}'$ as $\mathcal{T}' = (\mathcal{T} \ AND \ \mathcal{R})$ where $\mathcal{T}$ and $\mathcal{R}$ are Boolean access policies corresponding to $\mathbb{A}$ and $\mathbb{A}^*$, respectively. By defining the delegated access policy in this way, we can efficiently construct a delegated access structure $\mathbb{A}'$ by combining $\mathbb{A}$ and $\mathbb{A}^*$. We show the completeness of our proposed algorithm using the composition model suggested by Nikov and Nokova [18].
- Our technique applied to multiple existing CP-ABE schemes for *LSSS*. In particular, we applied our technique to CP-ABE schemes supporting different types of access policies, a monotonic access policy [13] and a non-monotonic access policy [25]. As results, we show that they proved that they are ciphertext delegatable. Notably, in our CD-CP-ABE scheme with a non-monotonic access policy, a sender dynamically revokes users based on their attributes by updating access policies with "NOT" gates through the delegation algorithm. For example, a ciphertext can be encrypted for whole university students (i.e. "The University" AND "Student"). Later, this ciphertext can be updated to a new ciphertext to revoke users in "CS group" by appending NOT "CS group" to the original policy (i.e. ("The University" AND "Student") AND NOT "CS group")).

1.2   Related Work

Revocation systems [10,14,17] are a type of broadcast encryption (BE) [9]. In revocation systems, revoked users cannot decrypt ciphertexts although all other users in the system can decrypt ciphertexts. More fine-grained access control is archived by ABE supporting a non-monotonic access structure [19,20,25]. Non-monotonic access structure allows NOT gates. Hence, revocation can be more expressively described by negating attributes in an access policy.

   Re-encryption is one of the techniques that efficiently support dynamic credentials. It can be used to revoke users without decryption by re-encrypting ciphertexts. Updating an access policy through re-encryption is faster since it saves the time taken to decrypt ciphertexts. Moreover, it enables to delegate re-encryption to third parties such as a proxy server without sharing the master key. Existing re-encryption techniques in the literature were introduced only for schemes whose access policies in ciphertexts are simple (e.g. Broadcast Encryption (BE), Hierarchical Identity-based Encryption (HIBE) and KP-ABE). Re-encrypting ciphertexts for CP-ABE is difficult since ciphertexts in CP-ABE are associated with a complex logic such as monotonic and non-monotonic boolean access policies.

Revocable Attribute-based Encryption [4,5,16,24] were introduced to revoke illegitimate users efficiently. They are conjunctive schemes which combine broadcast encryption (BE) and ABE. An access policy can be set using both users' attributes and identities. However, in those schemes, revocation can be archived through BE using users' identities, and Only "AND" gates allowed for revoked identities (i.e. all users in a revocation list must be revoked).

Delegation is widely used in Hierarchical Identity Based Encryption [8,15], Wildcarded Identity Based Encryption [1,2], and KP-ABE [15]. In those schemes, a user can delegate its access rights to the other users by issuing delegated keys from their keys. Although those schemes do not aim to revoke users in a ciphertext, there may be an interesting extension of our works since converting KP-ABE to CP-ABE is well researched in [6].

2 Preliminaries

2.1 Bilinear Maps

Let $\mathcal{G}$ be a group generator which takes a security parameter λ as input and outputs (p, G_1, G_2, G_T, e), G_1, G_2 and G_T are cyclic groups of prime order p, and $e : G_1 \times G_2 \rightarrow G_T$ is a map such that $e(g^a, h^b) = e(g, h)^{ab}$ for all $g \in G_1$ $h \in G_2$ and $a, b \in \mathbb{Z}_p$ and $e(g, h) \neq 1_{G_T} \in G_T$ whenever $g \neq 1_{G_1}$ and $h \neq 1_{G_2}$. We assume that the group operations in G_1, G_2 and G_T as well as the bilinear map e are all computable in polynomial time with respect to λ. It should be noted that the map e is symmetric if $G_1 = G_2$. If $G_1 \neq G_2$, the map e is asymmetric.

2.2 Monotonic and Non-monotonic Access Structure

Definition 1 (*Access Structure*) *[7]. Let $\{P_1, \ldots, P_n\}$ be a set of parties. A collection $\mathbb{A} \subset 2^{\{P_1,\ldots,P_n\}}$ is monotone if $\forall B, C$: if $B \in \mathbb{A}$ and $B \subset C$, then $C \in \mathbb{A}$. An monotonic access structure is a monotone collection $\mathbb{A}$ of non-empty subsets of $\{P_1, \ldots, P_n\}$, i.e., $\mathbb{A} \subset 2^{\{P_1,\ldots,P_n\}} \setminus \{\}$. The sets in $\mathbb{A}$ are called the authorized sets, and the sets not in $\mathbb{A}$ are called the unauthorized sets.*

Definition 2 (*Linear Secret-Sharing Schemes (LSSS)*) *[7]. A secret sharing scheme Π over a set of parties $\mathcal{P}$ is called linear (over $\mathbb{Z}_p$) if (1) The shares for each party form a vector over $\mathbb{Z}_p$. (2) There exists a matrix A called the share-generating matrix for Π. The matrix A has m rows and ℓ columns. For all $i = 1, \ldots, m$, the ith row of A is labeled by a party $\rho(x)$ (ρ is a function from $\{1, \ldots, m\}$ to $\mathcal{P}$). When we consider the column vector $v = (s, r_2, \ldots, r_\ell)$, where $s \in \mathbb{Z}_p$ is the shared secret and $r_2, \ldots, r_\ell \in \mathbb{Z}_p$ are randomly chosen, then Av is* *the vector of m shares of the secret s according to Π. The share $(Av)_i$ belongs to party $\rho(x)$.*

Definition 3 *(A valid access structure). A Linear Secret Sharing Scheme Π is valid iff there exists $\boldsymbol{\omega} = (\omega_1, \ldots, \omega_m) \in \mathbb{Z}_p^m$ such that $\sum_{x \in [1,m]} \omega_x A_x = (1, 0, \ldots, 0) \in \mathbb{Z}_p^n$.*

Our method is also applicable to CP-ABE schemes with non-monotonic access structures. For a non-monotonic access structure, we adopt a technique from Ostrovsky, Sahai and Waters [20].

Moving from Monotone to Non-monotonic Access Structure. They assume a family of linear secret sharing schemes $\{\Pi_\mathbb{A}\}_{\mathbb{A} \in \mathcal{A}}$ for a set of monotonic access structures $\mathbb{A} \in \mathcal{A}$. For each access structure $\mathbb{A} \in \mathcal{A}$, the set of parties $\mathcal{P}$ underlying the access structures has the following properties: The names of the parties may be of two types: either it is normal (like x) or negated (like $\bar{x}$), and if $x \in \mathcal{P}$ then $\bar{x} \notin \mathcal{P}$ and vice versa.

We let $\tilde{\mathcal{P}}$ denote the set of all normal parties in $\mathcal{P}$. For every set $\tilde{S} \subset \tilde{\mathcal{P}}$, $N(\tilde{S}) \subset \mathcal{P}$ is defined by $N(\tilde{S}) = \tilde{S} \cup \{\bar{x} | x \in \tilde{P} \setminus \tilde{S}\}$. For each access structure $\mathbb{A} \in \mathcal{A}$ over a set of parties $\mathcal{P}$, a non-monotonic access structure $NM(\mathbb{A})$ over the set of parties $\tilde{\mathcal{P}}$ is defined by specifying that $\tilde{S}$ is authorized in $NM(\mathbb{A})$ iff $N(\tilde{S})$ is authorized in $\mathbb{A}$. Therefore, the non-monotonic access structure $NM(\mathbb{A})$ will have only normal parties in its access sets. For each access set $X \in NM(\mathbb{A})$, there will be a set in $\mathbb{A}$ that has the elements in X and negated elements for each party not in X. Finally, a family of non-monotonic access structures $\tilde{\mathcal{A}}$ is defined by the set of these $NM(\mathbb{A})$ access structures.

2.3 Definition of CD-CP-ABE

Our CD-CP-ABE consists of the following five algorithms. In the algorithms, a user has a set of attributes S, and each encryption needs an access policy $\mathbb{A}$. Particularly, a delegation algorithm can convert a ciphertext $CT_\mathbb{A}$ to $CT_{\mathbb{A}'}$ only using public parameters pp.

- Setup(1^n) $\rightarrow$ (pp, msk): It takes as inputs the security parameter n and generate public parameters pp (which are shared among all users) and msk.
- KeyGen(S, msk) $\rightarrow$ SK$_S$: For a user who has a set of attributes S, It computes SK$_S$ using msk.
- Encrypt (pp, $\mathbb{A}$, M) $\rightarrow$ $CT_\mathbb{A}$: It takes as inputs the public parameters pp, an access policy $\mathbb{A}$ and a message $M \in \mathcal{M}$ to be encrypted. It outputs $CT_\mathbb{A}$
- Delegate (pp, $CT_\mathbb{A}$, $\mathbb{A}^*$) $\rightarrow$ $CT_{\mathbb{A}'}$: It takes as inputs the public parameters pp, a revocation access policy $\mathbb{A}^*$ and a ciphertext $CT_\mathbb{A}$. It outputs $CT_{\mathbb{A}'}$ for the delegated access structure $\mathbb{A}'$.
- Decrypt (SK$_S$, $CT_{\mathbb{A}'}$) $\rightarrow$ M: It takes as inputs the private key SK$_S$ and $CT_{\mathbb{A}'}$. If the set of attribute S of SK$_S$ satisfies the policy $\mathbb{A}'$ of the ciphertext $CT_{\mathbb{A}'}$, it outputs the message M encrypted in the ciphertext.

2.4   IND-CPA Security of the CD-CP-ABE

A CD-CP-ABE is selectively secure if there is no PPT adversary $\mathcal{A}$ who has a non-negligible advantage in the game between $\mathcal{A}$ and the challenge $\mathcal{C}$ defined below.

Init: $\mathcal{A}$ declares the access structure $\mathbb{A}'$ for the challenge ciphertext to $\mathcal{C}$.

Setup: $\mathcal{C}$ runs Setup(1^n) to create (pp, msk). pp is sent to $\mathcal{A}$.

Phase 1: $\mathcal{A}$ requests private keys corresponding to a set of attributes S_i. For each S_i, $\mathcal{C}$ returns SK_{S_i} created by running KeyGen(S_i, msk).

Challenge: When $\mathcal{A}$ requests the challenge ciphertext of $\mathbb{A}'$ such that S_i does not satisfy $\mathbb{A}'$ for $\forall i \in \{1, \ldots, q_1\}$, and submits two messages M_0 and M_1, $\mathcal{C}$ randomly selects b from $\{0, 1\}$ and returns the challenge ciphertext $CT_{\mathbb{A}'}$ created by 1) running Encrypt(pp, $\mathbb{A}'$, M_b) or 2) generating $CT_{\mathbb{A}}$ from Encrypt(pp, $\mathbb{A}$, M_b) for any $\mathbb{A}$ that can be delegated to $\mathbb{A}'$ through $\mathbb{A}^*$ and converting it to $CT_{\mathbb{A}'}$ using Delegate(pp, $CT_{\mathbb{A}}$, $\mathbb{A}^*$).

Phase 2: This is identical with **Phase 1** except for the additional restriction that S_i does not satisfy $\mathbb{A}'$ for $\forall i \in \{q_1 + 1, \ldots, q_t\}$

Guess: $\mathcal{A}$ outputs $b' \in \{0, 1\}$. If $b = b'$, then $\mathcal{A}$ wins.

We define an adversary $\mathcal{A}$'s advantage as $Adv_{\mathcal{A}}^{ABE}(\lambda) := |\Pr[b = b'] - 1/2|$.

We define adaptive security of CD-CP-ABE by removing **Init**. In the adaptive security model, the challenger cannot get any information of the challenge ciphertext before it sees the adversary's challenge ciphertext query.

3   Delegated Access Structures

Notation. For the rest of the discussion, we briefly explain the terms used in this paper. We use an *access policy* to denote the human-readable Boolean formula such as ("The University" AND "Student"). An access policy can be presented using an *access structure* of a linear secret sharing scheme. Each access structure consists of an *access matrix* and a *mapping function* ρ (i.e., $\mathbb{A} = (A, \rho)$). An *original access policy* means the access policy of the input ciphertext of the delegation algorithm. A *revocation access policy* is the access policy to revoke invalid users from the original access policy. The *delegated access policy* means that the resulting access policy where the invalid users are revoked from the original access policy by the revocation access policy. We often use $\mathcal{T}$, $\mathcal{R}$ and $\mathcal{T}'$ to an original access policy, a revocation policy and a delegated access policy, respectively. We also use $\mathbb{A}$, $\mathbb{A}^*$ and $\mathbb{A}'$ to denote the access structures corresponding to $\mathcal{T}$, $\mathcal{R}$ and $\mathcal{T}'$, respectively across the paper.

The delegation process only revokes attributes from $\mathcal{T}$. Hence, an access policy $\mathcal{T}'$ delegated from $\mathcal{T}$ is always equivalent or more restrictive than the original access policy $\mathcal{T}$ [15]. We define *equivalent or more restrictive* access policy as follows:

Definition 4 (*Equivalent or more restrictive access policy*) [15]. *For two boolean access policies $\mathcal{T}$ and $\mathcal{T}'$, $\mathcal{T}'$ is equivalent or more restrictive than $\mathcal{T}$ iff $\mathcal{T}' = \mathcal{T}$ AND $\mathcal{T}'$.*

3.1   Difficulty

Lewko and Waters [15] introduced a key-delegatable KP-ABE where the private key for an original access structure $\mathbb{A} = (\boldsymbol{A}, \rho)$ is delegated to the key for a delegated access structure $\mathbb{A}' = (\boldsymbol{A}', \rho')$ if $\mathcal{T}'$ is *equivalent or more restrictive* than $\mathcal{T}$ where $\mathcal{T}'$ and $\mathcal{T}$ are access policies corresponding to $\mathbb{A}'$ and $\mathbb{A}$. However, given $\mathbb{A}$ and $\mathbb{A}'$, the completeness of the delegation algorithm is only proved by an access matrix $(\boldsymbol{A}'', \rho'')$ where

$$
\boldsymbol{A}'' = \begin{pmatrix}
\boldsymbol{A} & \boldsymbol{E}_1 & \boldsymbol{E}_2 & \cdots & \boldsymbol{E}_m \\
0 & \boldsymbol{A}' & 0 & \cdots & 0 \\
0 & 0 & \boldsymbol{A}' & \cdots & 0 \\
\vdots & \vdots & \vdots & \ddots & \vdots \\
0 & 0 & 0 & \cdots & \boldsymbol{A}'
\end{pmatrix}.
$$

Here, $\boldsymbol{E}_i$ is a matrix of which the ith entry of the first column is 1 and the all others are 0. Therefore, the size of $\boldsymbol{A}''$ is quadratic to the sizes of $\boldsymbol{A}$ and $\boldsymbol{A}'$.

Later, Sahai et al. show that if a ciphertext supports several properties that support the spanning operations necessary to convert $\boldsymbol{A}$ to $\boldsymbol{A}'$, then, those CP-ABE schemes are also ciphertext-delegatable. Nevertheless, because their algorithm is also depending on spanning operations which are similar to Lewko and Waters' delegation technique, the complete delegation algorithm can be built only through the inefficient access structure of which the size increases quadratically in the sizes of an original access structure and a delegated access structure as shown above. Moreover, it is not clear whether we can construct the generic delegation algorithm using the properties they proposed.

3.2   Delegated Access Structures

In this paper, we show that there exists a more efficient way to construct a delegated access structure from an original access structure and a revocation access structure.

Delegated Access Policies. For the purpose of revocation, we specifically define a delegated access policy $\mathcal{T}'$ by combining a revocation policy $\mathcal{R}$ to an original policy $\mathcal{T}$. We use "AND" gate to set $\mathcal{T}'$ so that $\mathcal{T}' = \mathcal{T}$ AND $\mathcal{R}$. This combined access policy $\mathcal{T}'$ is always equivalent or more restrictive than $\mathcal{T}$ whatever the revocation policy $\mathcal{R}$ is. We prove it in Proposition 1 following:

Proposition 1. *For any boolean policy $\mathcal{T}$ and $\mathcal{R}$, $\mathcal{T}' = \mathcal{T}$ AND $\mathcal{R}$ is equivalent or more restrictive than $\mathcal{T}$.*

Proof: Proposition 1 is proved because $\mathcal{T}'$ AND $\mathcal{T} = (\mathcal{T}$ AND $\mathcal{R})$ AND $\mathcal{T} = \mathcal{T}$ AND $\mathcal{R} = \mathcal{T}'$. □

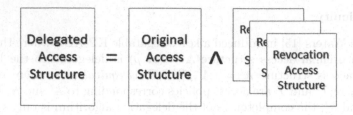

Fig. 1. A delegated access structure with multiple revocation access structures

The delegated access policy $T' = T$ AND R can be used to dynamically revoke users in an ABE scheme. For example, in ABE with a monotonic access policy which only uses "AND" and "OR" gates, if the original access policy was ("CS group" OR "Math group"). If all users have either "Student" or "Staff" as an attribute, we can revoke all students by appending "Staff" with an AND gate to the original access policy (i.e. $T =$ ("CS group" OR "Math group"), $R =$ "Staff", $T' =$ ("CS group" OR "Math Group") AND "Staff").

Delegated Access Structures. We let $\mathbb{A}$, $\mathbb{A}^*$ and $\mathbb{A}'$ be access structures corresponding respectively to the access policies T, R and T'. Using the composition model suggested by Nikov and Nokova [18], we can derive a compact delegated access structure $\mathbb{A}'$ using $\mathbb{A}$ and $\mathbb{A}^*$. Formally, we define a delegated access structure, $\mathbb{A}'$, for *LSSS* as follows:

Definition 5 *(Delegated Access Structure).* Given an $m \times n$ access structures $\mathbb{A} = (A, \rho)$ and an $\hat{m} \times \hat{n}$ access structure $\mathbb{A}^* = (A^*, \rho^*)$, the $(m + \hat{m}) \times (n + \hat{n})$ access policy $\mathbb{A}' = \mathbb{A} \wedge \mathbb{A}^*$ consisting of the following (A', ρ'):

$$A' = \left(\begin{array}{c|c|c} A & -a_1 & 0 \\ \hline 0 & & A^* \end{array} \right), \quad \rho'(i) = \left\{ \begin{array}{ll} \rho(i) & \text{if } i \leq m \\ \rho^*(i - m) & \text{if } i > m \end{array} \right.$$

where a_1 is the first column of A. We call $\mathbb{A}'$ the *delegated access structure* of $\mathbb{A}$ and $\mathbb{A}^*$.

Recursiveness. Revocations may be required repeatedly in the an dynamic access control system. In this case, our delegation algorithm also can be applied recursively to a ciphertext because the delegation of a ciphertext does not change the structure of ciphertext. We depict multiple revocation structures can be appended to, the original access structure repeatedly in Fig. 1.

Particularly, we let $\mathbb{A} = (A, \rho)$ and $\mathbb{A}^{\langle r_i \rangle} = (A^{\langle r_i \rangle}, \rho^{\langle r_i \rangle})$ denote access structures of T and R_i, respectively, and $\mathbb{A}^{[k]} = (A^{[k]}, \rho^{[k]})$ represents an access structure of a delegated access policy $T' = ((\ldots((T \text{ AND } R_1) \text{ AND } R_2) \text{ AND } \ldots)$ AND $R_k)$ where the revocation was permitted k times. Then, we can generate $\mathbb{A}^{[k]}$ by computing $\mathbb{A}^{[k]} = ((\ldots((\mathbb{A} \wedge \mathbb{A}^{\langle r_1 \rangle}) \wedge \mathbb{A}^{\langle r_2 \rangle}) \ldots) \wedge \mathbb{A}^{\langle r_k \rangle})$. $\mathbb{A}^{[k]}$ consists of the access matrix $A^{[k]}$ and the mapping function $\rho^{[k]}$) following:

$$A^{[k]} = \left(\begin{array}{c|cc} A^{[k-1]} & -a_1^{[k-1]} & 0 \\ \hline 0 & & A^{\langle r_k \rangle} \end{array} \right) = \begin{pmatrix} A & -a_1|0 & \cdots & -a_1|0 & -a_1|0 \\ 0 & A^{\langle r_1 \rangle} & \cdots & 0 & 0 \\ \vdots & \vdots & \ddots & \vdots & \vdots \\ 0 & 0 & \cdots & A^{\langle r_{k-1} \rangle} & 0 \\ 0 & 0 & \cdots & 0 & A^{\langle r_k \rangle} \end{pmatrix},$$

$$\rho^{[k]}(i) = \begin{cases} \rho(i) & \text{if } i \le m_0 \\ \rho^{\langle r_1 \rangle}(i - m_0) & \text{if } m_0 < i \le m_0 + m_1 \\ \quad \vdots & \quad \vdots \\ \rho^{\langle r_k \rangle}(i - \sum_{j \in [0,k-1]} m_j) & \text{if } \sum_{j \in [0,k-1]} m_j < i \le \sum_{j \in [0,k]} m_j \end{cases}.$$

Here, a_1 is a matrix of which the first column of A and $m_0 \times n_0$ and $m_i \times n_i$ denotes the sizes of A and $A^{\langle r_i \rangle}$, respectively. Table 1 compares the secrets shared by rows of $A^{[k-1]}$ and $A^{[k]}$ when the kth revocation access structure, $\mathbb{A}^{\langle r_k \rangle}$, is composited to the delegated access structure $\mathbb{A}^{[k-1]} = (A^{[k-1]}, \rho^{[k-1]})$.

In the table, s and $s^{\langle r_i \rangle}$ denote the first and the $(\sum_{j \in [0,i-1]} m_j + 1)$th elements of a random vector $s^{[k]}$ corresponding to $A^{[k]}$ and x is the index of rows for the access matrix. For example, the first m_0 rows of the access matrix $A^{[k-1]}$ are used to share $s - s^{\langle r_1 \rangle} - \ldots - s^{\langle r_{k-1} \rangle}$, but after the additional revocation, in the access matrix $A^{[k]}$, the first m_0 rows are updated to share $s - s^{\langle r_1 \rangle} - \ldots - s^{\langle r_{k-1} \rangle} - s^{\langle r_k \rangle}$.

Table 1. Shared secrets before and after the kth revocation

	$x \in [1, m_0]$	$: s - s^{\langle r_1 \rangle} - \ldots - s^{\langle r_{k-1} \rangle}$
	$x \in [m_0 + 1, m_0 + m_1]$	$: s^{\langle r_1 \rangle}$
$A^{[k-1]}$	$\vdots$	
	$x \in [(\sum_{j \in [0,k-2]} m_j) + 1, \sum_{j \in [0,k-1]} m_j] : s^{\langle r_{k-1} \rangle}$	
	$x \in [1, m_0]$	$: s - s^{\langle r_1 \rangle} - \ldots - s^{\langle r_{k-1} \rangle} - s^{\langle r_k \rangle}$
	$x \in [m_0 + 1, m_1]$	$: s^{\langle r_1 \rangle}$
$A^{[k]}$	$\vdots$	
	$x \in [(\sum_{j \in [0,k-2]} m_j) + 1, \sum_{j \in [0,k-1]} m_j] : s^{\langle r_{k-1} \rangle}$	
	$x \in [(\sum_{j \in [0,k-1]} m_j) + 1, \sum_{j \in [0,k]} m_j] \quad : s^{\langle r_k \rangle}$	

Completeness. The following Propositions 2 and 3 show that the *completeness* of the delegated access structure defined above. Those propositions are refined for *LSSS* from Nikov and Nokova's proofs in [18].

Proposition 2. *If an $m \times n$ sized $\mathbb{A} = (A, \rho)$ and an $\hat{m} \times \hat{n}$ sized $\mathbb{A}^* = (A^*, \rho^*)$ are valid LSSS access structures, $\mathbb{A}' := \mathbb{A} \wedge \mathbb{A}^* = (A', \rho')$, is also a valid LSSS access structure.*

Proof: Because $\mathbb{A}$ and $\mathbb{A}^*$ are valid access structures, there exist $\boldsymbol{\omega} = (\omega_1, \ldots, \omega_m) \in \mathbb{Z}_p^m$ and $\hat{\boldsymbol{\omega}} = (\hat{\omega}_1, \ldots, \hat{\omega}_{\hat{m}}) \in \mathbb{Z}_p^{\hat{m}}$ such that $\sum_{x \in [1,m]} \omega_x \boldsymbol{A}_x = (1, 0, \ldots, 0) \in \mathbb{Z}_p^n$ and $\sum_{x \in [1,\hat{m}]} \hat{\omega}_x \boldsymbol{A}_x^* = (1, 0, \ldots, 0) \in \mathbb{Z}_p^{\hat{n}}$ where $\boldsymbol{A}_x$ and $\boldsymbol{A}_x^*$ are the xth row of $\boldsymbol{A}$ and $\boldsymbol{A}^*$, respectively.

Then, the vector $\boldsymbol{\omega}' := (\omega_1', \ldots, \omega_{m'}') = (\omega_1, \ldots, \omega_m, \hat{\omega}_1, \ldots, \hat{\omega}_{\hat{m}})$ satisfies $\sum_{x \in [1,m']} \omega_x' \boldsymbol{A}_x' = (1, 0, \ldots, 0)$ where $m' = m + \hat{m}$ because

$$
\sum_{x \in [1,m']} \omega_x' \boldsymbol{A}_x' = \sum_{x \in [1,m]} \omega_x \boldsymbol{A}_x' + \sum_{x \in [1,\hat{m}]} \hat{\omega}_x \boldsymbol{A}_{x+m}'
$$

$$
= (\underbrace{1, 0, \ldots, 0}_{n}, \underbrace{-1, 0, \ldots, 0}_{\hat{n}}) + (\underbrace{0, 0, \ldots, 0}_{n}, \underbrace{1, 0, \ldots, 0}_{\hat{n}})
$$

$$
= (\underbrace{1, 0, \ldots, 0}_{n+\hat{n}}).
$$

Note that the $(n+1)$th coordinate of $\sum_{x \in [1,m]} \omega_x \boldsymbol{A}_x'$ equals to -1 since $\boldsymbol{\omega}^\top \boldsymbol{a}_1$ equals to the first entity of $\sum_{x \in [1,m]} \omega_x \boldsymbol{A}_x$ where $\boldsymbol{\omega} = (\omega_1, \ldots, \omega_m)$. $\qquad \square$

Proposition 3. If $\mathbb{A}' := \mathbb{A} \wedge \mathbb{A}^* = (\boldsymbol{A}', \rho')$ for an $m \times n$ sized $\mathbb{A} = (\boldsymbol{A}, \rho)$ and an $\hat{m} \times \hat{n}$ sized $\mathbb{A}^* = (\boldsymbol{A}^*, \rho^*)$ is a valid *LSSS* access structure, $\mathbb{A}$ and $\mathbb{A}^*$ are also valid *LSSS* access structures.

Proof: We let $\boldsymbol{a}_i$ and $\boldsymbol{a}_i'$ denote the ith column of $\boldsymbol{A}$ and $\boldsymbol{A}'$, respectively. Because $\mathbb{A}'$ is a valid access structure, there exist $\boldsymbol{\omega} = (\omega_1, \ldots, \omega_{m+\hat{m}}) \in \mathbb{Z}_p^{m+\hat{m}}$ such that $\sum_{x \in [1,m+\hat{m}]} \omega_x \boldsymbol{A}_x' = (1, 0, \ldots, 0) \in \mathbb{Z}_p^{n+\hat{n}}$. Therefore, $\boldsymbol{\omega}^\top \cdot \boldsymbol{a}_1' = 1$ and $\boldsymbol{\omega}^\top \cdot \boldsymbol{a}_i' = 0$ for all $i \in [2, n + \hat{n}]$.

We use $\boldsymbol{\omega}_1$ and $\boldsymbol{\omega}_2$ to write vectors consisting of the first m coordinators and the next $\hat{m}$ coordinator of $\boldsymbol{\omega}$, respectively (i.e. $\boldsymbol{\omega} = (\boldsymbol{\omega}_1, \boldsymbol{\omega}_2)$). Then,

$$
\boldsymbol{\omega}^\top \cdot \boldsymbol{A}' = (\boldsymbol{\omega}_1, \boldsymbol{\omega}_2)^\top \cdot \left(\begin{array}{c|c|c} \boldsymbol{A} & -\boldsymbol{a}_1 & \boldsymbol{0} \\ \hline \boldsymbol{0} & & \boldsymbol{A}^* \end{array} \right)
$$

$$
= (\underbrace{\boldsymbol{\omega}_1^\top \cdot \boldsymbol{A} + \boldsymbol{\omega}_2^\top \cdot \boldsymbol{0}}_{n}, \underbrace{-\hat{\boldsymbol{e}}_1 + \boldsymbol{\omega}_2^\top \cdot \boldsymbol{A}^*}_{\hat{n}})
$$

$$
= (\underbrace{\boldsymbol{e}_1}_{n}, \underbrace{\boldsymbol{0}}_{\hat{n}}).
$$

where an n sized vector $\boldsymbol{e}_1$ and an $\hat{n}$ sized vector $\hat{\boldsymbol{e}}_1$ has 1 as the first coordinator and 0 as the all other coordinates.

The first n columns of $\boldsymbol{\omega}^\top \cdot \boldsymbol{A}'$ is equivalent to $\boldsymbol{e}_1$. Therefore, $\boldsymbol{A}$ is a valid *LSSS* matrix since there exist $\boldsymbol{\omega}_1$ such that $\boldsymbol{\omega}_1^\top \cdot \boldsymbol{A} = \boldsymbol{e}_1 = (1, 0, \ldots, 0)$. Moreover, because $-\hat{\boldsymbol{e}}_1 + \boldsymbol{\omega}_2^\top \cdot \boldsymbol{A}^* = \boldsymbol{0}$ (i.e. $\boldsymbol{\omega}_2^\top \cdot \boldsymbol{A}^* = \hat{\boldsymbol{e}}_1$), $\boldsymbol{A}^*$ is a also valid access matrix. $\qquad \square$

Intuitively, Propositions 2 and 3 show that the delegated access structure $\mathbb{A}'$ is a share of secrets between two policies $\mathbb{A}$ and $\mathbb{A}^*$. If we set a random vector s' corresponding to the access matrix (A', ρ') to $(s'_1, \ldots, s'_{n+1}, \ldots)$. The first m rows of A' used to share $s'_1 - s'_{n+1}$ and the rest will share s'_{n+1}. This specific composition between A and A^* enables a ciphertext encrypted under (A, ρ) to be delegated to the other ciphertext encrypted under (A', ρ').[1]

4 Ciphertext Delegation

For our generic delegation algorithm, we use a notation of encoding frameworks [3,12,23]. Our algorithm does not require the full syntax of encoding frameworks. We only need to use encoding notations for ciphertexts and public parameters which are required for the delegation process.

Syntax. We define common values $h \in \mathbb{Z}_p^\kappa$ to denote exponents of public parameters (i.e. $\mathsf{pp} = g^h$) where κ is a parameter related with the size of public parameters. Then, we use a sequence of polynomials $c(\mathbb{A}, h; s, r)$ to denote the exponents of ciphertext $\mathsf{CT}_\mathbb{A}$ for an $m \times n$ access structure $\mathbb{A} = (A, \rho)$ (i.e. $\mathsf{CT}_\mathbb{A} = \{M \cdot e(g,g)^{\alpha s}, g^{c(\mathbb{A}, h; s, r)}\}$) where $s = s_1$ or s is a coordinate of r.

Therefore, each c_i of c is a linear combination of monomials $s_j, r_\ell, h_k s_j$ and $h_k r_\ell$ where s_j and r_ℓ are random variables which are only used to randomize ciphertexts. Specifically, $\{c_1, \ldots, c_{w_1}\}$ is defined by a set of coefficients $\{a_{i,j}, a'_{i,\ell}, a_{i,j,k}, a'_{i,\ell,k} : i \in [1, w_1], j \in [1, n], \ell \in [1, w_2], k \in [1, \kappa]\}$ as follows:

$$c_i(\mathbb{A}, h; s, r) = \sum_{j \in [1,n]} a_{i,j} s_j + \sum_{\ell \in [1,w_2]} a'_{i,\ell} r_\ell + \sum_{\substack{j \in [1,n] \\ k \in [1,\kappa]}} a_{i,j,k} h_k s_j + \sum_{\substack{\ell \in [1,w_2] \\ k \in [1,\kappa]}} a'_{i,\ell,k} h_k r_\ell$$

where w_2 represents the number of the random variables in r (i.e., the size of the vector r).

It is worth noting that we slightly change the notation of random variables from the pair encoding [3] to separately represent the variables which are used to share a secret for an *LSSS* access matrix from the other random variables. We use s to represent random variables to share the secret using A and r to present the other random variables.

4.1 Properties

We let $\mathbb{A}' = (A', \rho')$ be a delegated access structure of an access structure $\mathbb{A} = (A, \rho)$ and a revocation access structure $\mathbb{A}^* = (A^*, \rho^*)$ (i.e. $\mathbb{A}' = (\mathbb{A} \wedge \mathbb{A}^*)$) where $A \in \mathbb{Z}_p^{m \times n}$ and $A^* \in \mathbb{Z}_p^{\hat{m} \times \hat{n}}$. Also, we use $s = (s_1, \ldots, s_n) \in \mathbb{Z}_p^n$ and $r = (r_1, \ldots, r_{w_2}) \in \mathbb{Z}_p^{w_2}$ to denote randomization parameters. h is a vector of common variables used in $g^{c(\mathbb{A}, h; s, r)}$.

---

[1] We will explain the detailed properties required for this composition method in Sect. 4.

Property 1 *(Linearity)*. A ciphertext of an ABE scheme is *linear* iff

$$c(\mathbb{A}, h; s, r) + c(\mathbb{A}, h; s', r') = c(\mathbb{A}, h; s + s', r + r').$$

Property 2 *(Expandability)*. Given $g^{c(\mathbb{A}, h; s, r)}$ and $\mathbb{A}$, for any $\hat{m} \times \hat{n}$ sized access structure $\mathbb{A}^*$, $g^{c(\mathbb{A}', h; s', r')}$ is efficiently computable where $\mathbb{A}' = \mathbb{A} \wedge \mathbb{A}^*$, $s' = (s_1, \ldots, s_n, 0, \ldots, 0) \in \mathbb{Z}_p^{n+\hat{n}}$ and $r' = (r_1, \ldots, r_{w_2}, 0, \ldots, 0) \in \mathbb{Z}_p^{w_2'}$.

(Remark 1). In *Expandability*, we set random vectors $s' = (s_1, \ldots, s_n, 0, \ldots, 0) \in \mathbb{Z}_p^{n+\hat{n}}$ and $s = (s_1, \ldots, s_n) \in \mathbb{Z}_p^n$. Therefore,

$$A' \cdot s' = \left(\begin{array}{c|cc} A & -a_1 & 0 \\ \hline 0 & & A^* \end{array} \right) \cdot \left(\begin{array}{c} s \\ 0 \end{array} \right) = \left(\begin{array}{c} A \cdot s \\ 0 \end{array} \right).$$

This simple relation allows ABE schemes to compute $g^{A' \cdot s'}$ of the revoked ciphertext for any $\mathbb{A}^* = (A^*, \rho^*)$ without knowing the values of s when $g^{A \cdot s}$ is given in the original ciphertext where g is a group element. Particularly, *linearity* property is for re-randomization of s' so that the delegated ciphertext is also properly distributed.

4.2   Generic Delegation Algorithm

We present our delegation algorithm Delegate only using the two properties of a ciphertext defined in the previous subsection. Given a ciphertext $\mathsf{CT}_{\mathbb{A}}$ which satisfies Properties 1 and 2 and a revocation access structure $\mathbb{A}^*$, the following delegation algorithm can generate $\mathsf{CT}'_{\mathbb{A}'}$ for $\mathbb{A}' = \mathbb{A} \wedge \mathbb{A}^*$. Note that our delegation algorithm takes as an input a revocation access structure $\mathbb{A}^*$ instead of the delegated access structure $\mathbb{A}'$ for a notational convenience. This is acceptable since $\mathbb{A}'$ is clearly defined as $\mathbb{A} \wedge \mathbb{A}^*$.

Delegate($\mathsf{pp}, \mathsf{CT}_{\mathbb{A}}, \mathbb{A}^*) \to \mathsf{CT}'_{\mathbb{A}'}$: The algorithm takes as inputs public parameters pp, a ciphertext $\mathsf{CT}_{\mathbb{A}}$ with an access structure $\mathbb{A}$ and a revocation access structure $\mathbb{A}^*$ and outputs a new ciphertext $\mathsf{CT}'_{\mathbb{A}'}$ such that $\mathbb{A}' = \mathbb{A} \wedge \mathbb{A}^*$. First, the algorithm implicitly sets $\mathsf{CT}_{\mathbb{A}}$ to $\{C_M, g^{c(\mathbb{A}, h; s, r)}\}$. It, then, efficiently computes $g^{c(\mathbb{A}', h; s', r')}$ with $s' = (s_1, \ldots, s_n, 0, \ldots, 0)$ and $r' = (r_1, \ldots, r_{w_2}, 0, \ldots, 0)$ using *Expandability* property where $s = (s_1, \ldots, s_n)$ and $r = (r_1, \ldots, r_{w_2})$ are random values from $\mathsf{CT}_{\mathbb{A}}$. The algorithm computes a new ciphertext using Encrypt($\mathsf{pp}, 1_{G_T}, \mathbb{A}'$) to get $\mathsf{CT}''_{\mathbb{A}'} = \{C''_{1_{G_T}}, g^{c(\mathbb{A}', h; s'', r'')}\}$ where 1_{G_T} is the identity element of G_T. Using *Linearity* property, the algorithm outputs the following delegated $\mathsf{CT}'_{\mathbb{A}'}$:

$$\{C_M \cdot C''_{1_{G_T}}, \; g^{c(\mathbb{A}', h; s', r')} \cdot g^{c(\mathbb{A}', h; s'', r'')} = g^{c(\mathbb{A}', h; s'+s'', r'+r'')}\}.$$

Theorem 1. *A ciphertext-policy attribute-based encryption scheme which is (selectively or adaptively) IND-CPA secure and satisfies Properties 1 and 2 is ciphertext-delegatable.*

Proof: We already show that a delegated access policy is equivalent or more restrictive than an original policy, which means that, in the security model, the delegated ciphertext does not increase the advantage of the adversary $\mathcal{A}$. We additionally show that the delegated ciphertext of Delegate is secure from the newly revoked attributes by proving that the distribution of delegated ciphertext is statistically identical to that of the ciphertext generated by Encrypt in the following Lemma 1. Therefore, the security of the ciphertext-delegated is proved by the IND-CPA security of the original scheme.   □

Lemma 1 (*Delegation invariance*). $CT_{\mathbb{A}'}$ which is an output of Delegate(pp, $CT_{\mathbb{A}}$, $\mathbb{A}'$) is distributed identically to $CT'_{\mathbb{A}'}$ which is an output of Encrypt(pp, M, $\mathbb{A}'$).

Proof: In the Delegate process, due to the *Linearity* and *Expandability* properties, all randomization parameters in s and r used in the input ciphertext $CT_{\mathbb{A}}$ are properly re-randomized. We let s' and r' denote the randomized parameters of the output ciphertext $CT_{\mathbb{A}'}$. They are re-randomized by s'' and r'' (i.e., $s' = (s, 0) + s''$ and $r' = (r, 0) + r''$) in Delegate. Because all coordinates in s'' and r'' are random and being allocated uniquely to their corresponding variables in s' and r', the ciphertext $CT_{\mathbb{A}'}$ is identically distributed with the ciphertext $CT'_{\mathbb{A}'}$ generated by Encrypt(pp, M, $\mathbb{A}'$).   □

5 Instantiations

In this section, we will show that our delegation algorithm can be applied to existing CP-ABE schemes. We choose two popular CP-ABE schemes. The first CP-ABE scheme, as referred to as LOSTW, was introduced by Lewko et al. [13]. It is adaptively secure and supports a monotonic access structure. The second CP-ABE scheme, as referred to as YAHK, is from Yamada et al. [25]. This scheme is selectively secure and supports a non-monotonic access structure.

5.1 CD-CP-ABE

Theorem 2. *Lewko et al.'s CP-ABE scheme [13] is ciphertext-delegatable.*

Proof: To show that LOSTW is ciphertext-delegatable, we must show that a ciphertext of their scheme is *expandable* and *linear*. First, we denote the ciphertext $CT_{\mathbb{A}}$ and common variables h of public parameters pp in a encoding format where $A = (A, \rho)$ is $m \times n$ sized. We use A_x to denote the xth row of A.

Common variables (h)	$\{a, t_i : i \in \mathcal{U}\}$ where $\mathcal{U}$ is an attribute universe
An encoding of $\mathsf{CT}_{\mathbb{A}}$ (c)	Let $s = (s_1, \ldots, s_n)$, $r = (r_1, \ldots, r_m)$ and
	$c(\mathbb{A}, h; s, r) = (s_1, a\boldsymbol{A}_x s, -t_{\rho(x)} r_x, r_x; \forall x \in [1, m])$,
	Then $\mathsf{CT}_{\mathbb{A}} = \{M \cdot e(g, g)^{\alpha s_1}, g^{c(\mathbb{A}, h; s, r)}\}$

(*Linearity*). For all $s, s' \in \mathbb{Z}_N^n$ and $r, r' \in \mathbb{Z}_N^m$,

$$c(\mathbb{A}, h; s, r) + c(\mathbb{A}, h; s', r')$$
$$= (s_1, a\boldsymbol{A}_x s, -t_{\rho(x)} r_x, r_x) + (s_1', a\boldsymbol{A}_x s', -t_{\rho(x)} r_x', r_x')$$
$$= (s_1 + s_1', a\boldsymbol{A}_x(s + s'), -t_{\rho(x)}(r_x + r_x'), r_x + r_x')$$
$$= c(\mathbb{A}, h; s + s', r + r').$$

(*Expandability*). Given an access policy $\mathbb{A} = (\boldsymbol{A}, \rho)$ and $g^{c(\mathbb{A}, h; s, r)}$, we use $(s_1, \ldots, s_n) \in \mathbb{Z}_N^n$ and $(r_1, \ldots, r_m) \in \mathbb{Z}_N^m$ to denote s and r. We let $s' = (s_1, \ldots, s_n, 0, \ldots, 0) \in \mathbb{Z}_N^{n+\hat{n}}$ and $r' = (r_1, \ldots, r_m, 0, \ldots, 0) \in \mathbb{Z}_N^{m+\hat{m}}$. Then, for any $\hat{m} \times \hat{n}$ sized access policy $\mathbb{A}^* = (\boldsymbol{A}^*, \rho^*)$, we (implicitly) set $c(\mathbb{A}', h; s', r') = (s_1', a\boldsymbol{A}_x' s', -t_{\rho(x)} r_x', r_x')$ for $\mathbb{A}' = (\boldsymbol{A}', \rho')$ by setting $s_1' = s_1$,

$$a\boldsymbol{A}_x' s' = a\boldsymbol{A}_x s, \quad -t_{\rho(x)} r_x' = -t_{\rho(x)} r_x, \quad r_x' = r_x \quad \forall x \in [1, m]$$
$$a\boldsymbol{A}_x' s' = 0, \quad -t_{\rho(x)} r_x' = 0, \quad r_x' = 0 \qquad \forall x \in [m+1, m+\hat{m}]$$

where $\boldsymbol{A}' = \begin{pmatrix} \boldsymbol{A} & -\boldsymbol{a}_1 & \boldsymbol{0} \\ \boldsymbol{0} & & \boldsymbol{A}^* \end{pmatrix}$, $\rho'(x) = \begin{cases} \rho(x) & \text{if } x \leq m \\ \rho^*(x - m) & \text{if } x > m. \end{cases}$

Because $g^{c(\mathbb{A}, h; s, r)} = \{g^{s_1}, g^{a\boldsymbol{A}_x s}, g^{-t_{\rho(x)} r_x}, g^{r_x} : \forall x \in [1, m]\}$ is given, we can compute $g^{c(\mathbb{A}', h; s', r')}$ (without knowing the values of s and r) by setting

$$g^{s_1'} = g^{s_1}, \begin{cases} g^{a\boldsymbol{A}_x' s'} = g^{a\boldsymbol{A}_x s}, \ g^{-t_{\rho(x)} r_x'} = g^{-t_{\rho(x)} r_x}, \ g^{r_x'} = g^{r_x} \ \forall x \in [1, m] \\ g^{a\boldsymbol{A}_x' s'} = 1_{G_N}, \ g^{-t_{\rho(x)} r_x'} = 1_{G_N}, \ g^{r_x'} = 1_{G_N} \quad \forall x \in [m+1, m+\hat{m}]. \end{cases}$$

where 1_{G_N} is the identity matrix in G_N. $\square$

Dedicated Delegate algorithm for LOSTW [13]. We let $\mathbb{A}^* = (\boldsymbol{A}^*, \rho^*)$ and $\mathbb{A} = (\boldsymbol{A}, \rho)$ denote a revocation access structure and an original access policy of the ciphertext $\mathsf{CT}_{\mathbb{A}}$, respectively, where $\boldsymbol{A}^* \in \mathbb{Z}_N^{\hat{m} \times \hat{n}}$ and $\boldsymbol{A} \in \mathbb{Z}_N^{m \times n}$. Then, we can compute $\mathsf{CT}_{\mathbb{A}'}$ for $\mathbb{A}'(:= (\boldsymbol{A}', \rho')) = \mathbb{A} \wedge \mathbb{A}^*$ using the following Delegate algorithm.

Delegate ($\mathsf{pp}, \mathsf{CT}_{\mathbb{A}}, \mathbb{A}^*$): The algorithm takes as inputs public parameters pp, an original ciphertext $\mathsf{CT}_{\mathbb{A}}$, a revocation policy $\mathbb{A}^*$. It parses $\mathsf{CT}_{\mathbb{A}}$ to $\{C, C_0, C_x, D_x : \forall x \in [1, m]\}$. To expand $\mathsf{CT}_{\mathbb{A}}$ to $\mathsf{CT}_{\mathbb{A}'}$, it sets $s' = (s, s_2, \ldots, s_n, 0, \ldots, 0) \in \mathbb{Z}_N^{n+\hat{n}}$ and set $r' = (r_1, r_2, \ldots r_m, 0, \ldots, 0) \in \mathbb{Z}_N^{m+\hat{m}}$. Then, it sets $\mathsf{CT}_{\mathbb{A}'} = \{\hat{C}, \hat{C}_0, \hat{C}_x, \hat{D}_x : \forall x \in [1, m+\hat{m}]\}$ where $\hat{C} = C$, $\hat{C}_0 = C_0$,

$$\hat{C}_x = C_x, \hat{D}_x = D_x \quad \forall x \in [1, m]$$

$$\hat{C}_x = 1_{G_N}, \hat{D}_x = 1_{G_N} \quad \forall x \in [m+1, m+\hat{m}].$$

It then generates $\mathsf{CT}''_{\mathbb{A}'}$ from $\mathsf{Encrypt}(\mathsf{pp}, 1_{G_T}, \mathbb{A}')$. It parses $\mathsf{CT}''_{\mathbb{A}'}$ to C'', C''_0, C''_x, D''_x and computes $C' = \hat{C} \cdot C'', C'_0 = \hat{C}_0 \cdot C''_0, C'_x = \hat{C}_x \cdot C''_x, D'_x = \hat{D}_x \cdot D''_x$. It outputs $\mathsf{CT}'_{\mathbb{A}'} = \{C', C'_0, C'_x, D'_x : \forall x \in [1, m+\hat{m}]\}$.

5.2 CD-CP-ABE with Non-monotonic Access Structure

Yamada et al.'s scheme [25] is a CP-ABE scheme supporting "NOT" gates. We will show that this scheme is also ciphertext delegatable.

Theorem 3. *Yamada et al.'s scheme [25] is ciphertext delegatable.*

Proof: We show that Yamada et al.'s scheme is revocable by showing that their ciphertext is *expandable* and *linear*. It is worth noting that their scheme supports a non-monotonic access structure and "$\bar{}$" used to denote a negated attribute so that $\bar{x}_i$ is a negated attribute such as (NOT x_i). We let $\boldsymbol{A} = (\boldsymbol{A}, \rho)$ be $m \times n$ sized. We use $\boldsymbol{A}_i$ to denote the ith row of $\boldsymbol{A}$.

Common variables $(\boldsymbol{h})$	$\{b, y_h, y_u, y_v, y_w\}$
An encoding of CT (c)	Let $\boldsymbol{s} = (s_1, \ldots, s_n)$, $\boldsymbol{r} = (r_1, \ldots, r_m)$ and $c(\mathbb{A}, \boldsymbol{h}; \boldsymbol{s}, \boldsymbol{r}) = (s_1, y_w \boldsymbol{A}_i \boldsymbol{s} + f(r_i), -(y_u x_i + y_h) r_i, r_i)$ where $f(r_i) = \begin{cases} y_u r_i & \text{if } \rho(i) = x_i \\ b y_u r_i & \text{if } \rho(i) = \bar{x}_i \end{cases}$. Then, $\mathsf{CT}_{\mathbb{A}} = \{M \cdot e(g,g)^{\alpha s}, g^{c(\mathbb{A}, \boldsymbol{h}; \boldsymbol{s}, \boldsymbol{r})}\}$

(Linearity). For all $\boldsymbol{s}, \boldsymbol{s}' \in \mathbb{Z}^n$ and $\boldsymbol{r}, \boldsymbol{r}' \in \mathbb{Z}^m$,

$$c(\mathbb{A}, \boldsymbol{h}; \boldsymbol{s}, \boldsymbol{r}) + c(\mathbb{A}, \boldsymbol{h}; \boldsymbol{s}', \boldsymbol{r}')$$
$$= (s_1, y_w \boldsymbol{A}_i \boldsymbol{s} + f(r_i), -(y_u x_i + y_h) r_i, r_i) + (s'_1, y_w \boldsymbol{A}_i \boldsymbol{s}' + f(r'_i), -(y_u x_i + y_h) r'_i, r'_i)$$
$$= (s_1 + s'_1, y_w \boldsymbol{A}_i (\boldsymbol{s} + \boldsymbol{s}') + f(r_i + r'_i), -(y_u x_i + y_h)(r_i + r'_i), r_i + r'_i)$$
$$= c(\mathbb{A}, \boldsymbol{h}; \boldsymbol{s} + \boldsymbol{s}', \boldsymbol{r} + \boldsymbol{r}')$$

(Expandability). Given an access policy $\mathbb{A} = (\boldsymbol{A}, \rho)$ and $g^{c(\mathbb{A}, \boldsymbol{h}; \boldsymbol{s}, \boldsymbol{r})}$, we use $(s_1, \ldots, s_n) \in \mathbb{Z}_N^n$ and $(r_1, \ldots, r_m) \in \mathbb{Z}_N^m$ to denote $\boldsymbol{s}$ and $\boldsymbol{r}$. For any $\hat{m} \times \hat{n}$ sized access policy $\mathbb{A}^* = (\boldsymbol{A}^*, \rho^*)$, we set $\boldsymbol{s}' = (s_1, \ldots, s_n, 0, \ldots, 0) \in \mathbb{Z}_N^{n+\hat{n}}$ and $\boldsymbol{r}' = (r_1, \ldots, r_m, 0, \ldots, 0) \in \mathbb{Z}_N^{m+\hat{m}}$. Then, we (implicitly) set $c(\mathbb{A}', \boldsymbol{h}; \boldsymbol{s}', \boldsymbol{r}') = (s'_1, y_w \boldsymbol{A}_i \boldsymbol{s}' + f(r'_i), -(y_u x_i + y_h) r'_i, r'_i)$ for $\mathbb{A}' = (\boldsymbol{A}', \rho')$ by setting $s'_1 = s_1$,

$$y_w \boldsymbol{A}'_i \boldsymbol{s}' + f(r'_i) = y_w \boldsymbol{A}_i \boldsymbol{s} + f(r_i), \ -(y_u x_i + y_h) r'_i = -(y_u x_i + y_h) r_i, \ r'_i = r_i \ \forall x \in [1, m]$$

$$y_w \boldsymbol{A}'_i \boldsymbol{s}' + f(r'_i) = 0, \ -(y_u x_i + y_h) r'_i = 0, \ r'_i = 0 \quad \forall x \in [m+1, m+\hat{m}]$$

where $\boldsymbol{A}' = \begin{pmatrix} \boldsymbol{A} & -\boldsymbol{a}_1 & \boldsymbol{0} \\ \boldsymbol{0} & \boldsymbol{A}^* \end{pmatrix}$, $\rho'(i) = \begin{cases} \rho(i) & \text{if } x \leq m \\ \rho^*(i-m) & \text{if } x > m. \end{cases}$

Because $g^{c(\mathbb{A},h;s,r)} = \{g^{s_1}, g^{y_w A_i s + f(r_i)}, g^{-(y_u x_i + y_h) r_i}, g^{r_i} : \forall i \in [1, m]\}$ is given, we also can compute $g^{c(\mathbb{A}',h;s',r')}$ by setting $g^{s'_1} = g^{s_1}$,

$$g^{y_w A_i s' + f(r'_i)} = g^{y_w A_i s + f(r_i)}, \ g^{-(y_u x_i + y_h) r'_i} = g^{-(y_u x_i + y_h) r_i}, \ g^{r'_i} = g^{r_i} \ \forall x \in [1, m]$$

$$g^{y_w A_i s' + f(r'_i)} = 1_{G_p}, \ g^{-(y_u x_i + y_h) r'_i} = 1_{G_p}, \ g^{r'_i} = 1_{G_p} \qquad \forall x \in [m+1, m+\hat{m}].$$

$\square$

Dedicated Delegate Algorithm of YAHK [25]. We let $\mathbb{A}^* = (\boldsymbol{A}^*, \rho^*)$ and $\mathbb{A} = (\boldsymbol{A}, \rho)$ denote a revocation policy and an access policy of the original ciphertext, respectively, where $\boldsymbol{A}^* \in \mathbb{Z}_p^{\hat{m} \times \hat{n}}$ and $\boldsymbol{A} \in \mathbb{Z}_p^{m \times n}$. Then, we can compute $\mathsf{CT}'_{\mathbb{A}'}$ for $\mathbb{A}' = (\boldsymbol{A}', \rho') := \mathbb{A} \wedge \mathbb{A}^*$ using the following Delegate algorithm.

Delegate (pp, $\mathsf{CT}_{\mathbb{A}}$, $\mathbb{A}^*$): First, the algorithm parses $\mathsf{CT}_{\mathbb{A}}$ to $\{C_0, C_1, C_{i,1}, C_{i,2}, C_{i,3} : i \in [1, m]\}$. Then, it computes a delegated access structure $\mathbb{A}' = (\boldsymbol{A}', \rho')$ using $\mathbb{A}$ and $\mathbb{A}^*$ as defined in Definition 5. To delegate $\mathsf{CT}_{\mathbb{A}}$ to $\mathsf{CT}'_{\mathbb{A}'}$ encrypted under $\mathbb{A}'$, it implicitly sets $\boldsymbol{s}' = (s_1, \ldots, s_n, 0, \ldots, 0)$ and $\boldsymbol{r}' = (r_1, \ldots, r_\ell, 0, \ldots, 0)$ where $s_1, \ldots, s_n, r_1, \ldots, r_\ell$ is a random values used in $\mathsf{CT}_{\mathbb{A}}$. Then, it computes a new ciphertext $\mathsf{CT}_{\mathbb{A}'} = \{\tilde{C}_0, \tilde{C}_1, \tilde{C}_{i,1}, \tilde{C}_{i,2}, \tilde{C}_{i,3} : i \in [1, m+\hat{m}]\}$ by setting

$$\tilde{C}_0 = C_0, \ \tilde{C}_1 = C_1, \ \begin{cases} \tilde{C}_{i,1} = C_{i,1}, \ \tilde{C}_{i,2} = C_{i,2} \ \tilde{C}_{i,3} = C_{i,3} & \forall i \in [1, m], \\ \tilde{C}_{i,1} = \tilde{C}_{i,2} = \tilde{C}_{i,3} = 1_{G_2} & \forall i \in [m+1, m+\hat{m}]. \end{cases}$$

It, then, computes $\mathsf{CT}''_{\mathbb{A}'}$ by running Encrypt(pp, 1_{G_T}, $\mathbb{A}'$). It parses $\mathsf{CT}''_{\mathbb{A}'}$ to $\{C''_0, C''_1, C''_{i,1}, C''_{i,2}, C''_{i,3} ; i \in [1, m+\hat{m}]\}$ and sets

$$C'_0 = \tilde{C}_0 \cdot C''_0, C'_1 = \tilde{C}_1 \cdot C''_1,$$

$$C'_{i,1} = \tilde{C}_{i,1} \cdot C''_{i,1}, C'_{i,2} = \tilde{C}_{i,2} \cdot C''_{i,2}, C'_{i,3} = \tilde{C}_{i,3} \cdot C''_{i,3} \ \forall i \in [1, m+\hat{m}].$$

It outputs $\mathsf{CT}'_{\mathbb{A}'} = \{C'_0, C'_1, C'_{i,1}, C'_{i,2}, C'_{i,3} : \forall i \in [1, m+\hat{m}]\}$.

6   Conclusion

In this paper, we introduce a generic delegation algorithm for CP-ABE schemes. Our delegation technique directly revokes a group of users through updating a ciphertext without decryption. Therefore, it efficiently supports dynamic access control. We suggest a new composition method of access policies and their corresponding access structure where a ciphertext encrypted. Additionally, we generalize the structures and properties required for the ciphertext delegation of CP-ABE and formalize them using an encoding technique. We, then, present a new generic delegation algorithm converting CP-ABE to ciphertext-delegatable CP-ABE. We show that existing monotonic and non-monotonic CP-ABE schemes to CD-CP-ABE schemes using our technique.

References

1. Abdalla, M., et al.: Wildcarded identity-based encryption. J. Cryptol. **24**(1), 42–82 (2011)
2. Abdalla, M., De Caro, A., Phan, D.H.: Generalized key delegation for wildcarded identity-based and inner-product encryption. IEEE Trans. Inf. Forensics Secur. **7**(6), 1695–1706 (2012)
3. Attrapadung, N.: Dual system encryption via doubly selective security: framework, fully secure functional encryption for regular languages, and more. In: Nguyen, P.Q., Oswald, E. (eds.) EUROCRYPT 2014. LNCS, vol. 8441, pp. 557–577. Springer, Heidelberg (2014). https://doi.org/10.1007/978-3-642-55220-5_31
4. Attrapadung, N., Imai, H.: Attribute-based encryption supporting direct/indirect revocation modes. In: Parker, M.G. (ed.) IMACC 2009. LNCS, vol. 5921, pp. 278–300. Springer, Heidelberg (2009). https://doi.org/10.1007/978-3-642-10868-6_17
5. Attrapadung, N., Imai, H.: Conjunctive broadcast and attribute-based encryption. In: Shacham, H., Waters, B. (eds.) Pairing 2009. LNCS, vol. 5671, pp. 248–265. Springer, Heidelberg (2009). https://doi.org/10.1007/978-3-642-03298-1_16
6. Attrapadung, N., Yamada, S.: Duality in ABE: converting attribute based encryption for dual predicate and dual policy via computational encodings. In: Nyberg, K. (ed.) CT-RSA 2015. LNCS, vol. 9048, pp. 87–105. Springer, Cham (2015). https://doi.org/10.1007/978-3-319-16715-2_5
7. Beimel, A.: Secure schemes for secret sharing and key distribution. Ph.D. thesis, Israel Institute of Technology, Technion, Haifa, Israel (1996)
8. Boneh, D., Boyen, X., Goh, E.-J.: Hierarchical identity based encryption with constant size ciphertext. In: Cramer, R. (ed.) EUROCRYPT 2005. LNCS, vol. 3494, pp. 440–456. Springer, Heidelberg (2005). https://doi.org/10.1007/11426639_26
9. Fiat, A., Naor, M.: Broadcast encryption. In: Stinson, D.R. (ed.) CRYPTO 1993. LNCS, vol. 773, pp. 480–491. Springer, Heidelberg (1994). https://doi.org/10.1007/3-540-48329-2_40
10. Goodrich, M.T., Sun, J.Z., Tamassia, R.: Efficient tree-based revocation in groups of low-state devices. In: Franklin, M. (ed.) CRYPTO 2004. LNCS, vol. 3152, pp. 511–527. Springer, Heidelberg (2004). https://doi.org/10.1007/978-3-540-28628-8_31
11. Goyal, V., Pandey, O., Sahai, A., Waters, B.: Attribute-based encryption for fine-grained access control of encrypted data. In: Juels, A., Wright, R.N., De Capitani di Vimercati, S. (eds.) ACM Conference on Computer and Communications Security, pp. 89–98. ACM (2006)
12. Kim, J., Susilo, W., Guo, F., Au, M.H.: A tag based encoding: an efficient encoding for predicate encryption in prime order groups. In: Zikas, V., De Prisco, R. (eds.) SCN 2016. LNCS, vol. 9841, pp. 3–22. Springer, Cham (2016). https://doi.org/10.1007/978-3-319-44618-9_1
13. Lewko, A.B., Okamoto, T., Sahai, A., Takashima, K., Waters, B.: Fully secure functional encryption: attribute-based encryption and (hierarchical) inner product encryption. In: Gilbert, H. (ed.) EUROCRYPT 2010. LNCS, vol. 6110, pp. 62–91. Springer, Heidelberg (2010). https://doi.org/10.1007/978-3-642-13190-5_4
14. Lewko, A.B., Sahai, A., Waters, B.: Revocation systems with very small private keys. In: IEEE Symposium on Security and Privacy, pp. 273–285 (2010)
15. Lewko, A.B., Waters, B.: Unbounded HIBE and attribute-based encryption. In: Paterson, K.G. (ed.) EUROCRYPT 2011. LNCS, vol. 6632, pp. 547–567. Springer, Heidelberg (2011). https://doi.org/10.1007/978-3-642-20465-4_30

16. Liu, Z., Wong, D.S.: Practical ciphertext-policy attribute-based encryption: traitor tracing, revocation, and large universe. In: Malkin, T., Kolesnikov, V., Lewko, A.B., Polychronakis, M. (eds.) ACNS 2015. LNCS, vol. 9092, pp. 127–146. Springer, Cham (2015). https://doi.org/10.1007/978-3-319-28166-7_7
17. Naor, D., Naor, M., Lotspiech, J.: Revocation and tracing schemes for stateless receivers. In: Kilian, J. (ed.) CRYPTO 2001. LNCS, vol. 2139, pp. 41–62. Springer, Heidelberg (2001). https://doi.org/10.1007/3-540-44647-8_3
18. Nikov, V., Nikova, S.: New monotone span programs from old. IACR Cryptology ePrint Archive, 2004:282 (2004)
19. Okamoto, T., Takashima, K.: Fully secure unbounded inner-product and attribute-based encryption. In: Wang, X., Sako, K. (eds.) ASIACRYPT 2012. LNCS, vol. 7658, pp. 349–366. Springer, Heidelberg (2012). https://doi.org/10.1007/978-3-642-34961-4_22
20. Ostrovsky, R., Sahai, A., Waters, B.: Attribute-based encryption with non-monotonic access structures. In: Ning, P., De Capitani di Vimercati, S., Syverson, P.F. (eds.) ACM Conference on Computer and Communications Security, pp. 195–203. ACM (2007)
21. Sahai, A., Seyalioglu, H., Waters, B.: Dynamic credentials and ciphertext delegation for attribute-based encryption. In: Safavi-Naini, R., Canetti, R. (eds.) CRYPTO 2012. LNCS, vol. 7417, pp. 199–217. Springer, Heidelberg (2012). https://doi.org/10.1007/978-3-642-32009-5_13
22. Sahai, A., Waters, B.: Fuzzy identity-based encryption. In: Cramer, R. (ed.) EUROCRYPT 2005. LNCS, vol. 3494, pp. 457–473. Springer, Heidelberg (2005). https://doi.org/10.1007/11426639_27
23. Wee, H.: Dual system encryption via predicate encodings. In: Lindell, Y. (ed.) TCC 2014. LNCS, vol. 8349, pp. 616–637. Springer, Heidelberg (2014). https://doi.org/10.1007/978-3-642-54242-8_26
24. Yamada, K., Attrapadung, N., Emura, K., Hanaoka, G., Tanaka, K.: Generic constructions for fully secure revocable attribute-based encryption. In: Foley, S.N., Gollmann, D., Snekkenes, E. (eds.) ESORICS 2017. LNCS, vol. 10493, pp. 532–551. Springer, Cham (2017). https://doi.org/10.1007/978-3-319-66399-9_29
25. Yamada, S., Attrapadung, N., Hanaoka, G., Kunihiro, N.: A framework and compact constructions for non-monotonic attribute-based encryption. In: Krawczyk, H. (ed.) PKC 2014. LNCS, vol. 8383, pp. 275–292. Springer, Heidelberg (2014). https://doi.org/10.1007/978-3-642-54631-0_16

Location Based Encryption

Tran Viet Xuan Phuong[1,2]([✉]), Willy Susilo[1], Guomin Yang[1], Jun Yan[1], and Dongxi Liu[2]

[1] Institute of Cybersecurity and Cryptology,
School of Computing and Information Technology,
University of Wollongong, Wollongong, Australia
{txuan,wsusilo,gyang,jyang}@uow.edu.au
[2] Data61, CSIRO, Syndey, Australia
Dongxi.Liu@data61.csiro.au

Abstract. We first propose a 2D Location Based Encryption (LBE) scheme, where the setting includes a geography center system and the 2D triangle area including the set of locations. A user joining in the system is provided with a pre-arranged key, which belongs to her/his location. If the user's location is belonging to this area, he/she can decrypt the message. Our proposed scheme achieves a constant ciphertext size in encryption algorithm and decryption cost. Beyond the 2D-LBE scheme, we explore the 3D-LBE scheme; whereby the location is set up in the 3D dimensions. This proposed scheme is an extension of 2D-LBE scheme, which the ciphertext is also constant. Both two schemes are proved in the selective model under the decisional $\ell-$wBDHI assumption.

Keywords: 2D/3D · Location based encryption ·
Constant ciphertext size · w-lBDHI

1 Introduction

We consider the scenario where there is a geography center system and the 2D triangle area including the set of locations. Each location comprises the X and Y coordinator. When a user joining in the system, he/she is provided a pre-arranged key, which belongs to her/his location. At some point, the center wants to broadcast a message to a specific triangle area, which user's location belonging to this area can decrypt the message. In such a way, any other users located outside specific area cannot learn the information. In addition, according to Fig. 1, we require the user's X and Y coordinate to belong to the distance NE, NW respectively, in the NEWS triangle area if the decryption of message is processed.

The solution is that the center encrypts the message by embedding the set of locations from N to E, and from N to W, then it broadcast the ciphertext to the area NEWS. However, when the broadcasting is adjusted to cover larger area of triangle NESW, the size of the ciphertext will be increased. This requires a

© Springer Nature Switzerland AG 2019
J. Jang-Jaccard and F. Guo (Eds.): ACISP 2019, LNCS 11547, pp. 21–38, 2019.
https://doi.org/10.1007/978-3-030-21548-4_2

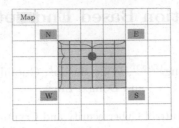

Fig. 1. Broadcasting encrypted message in the triangle area NESW. (Color figure online)

center system generating a ciphertext, which can reduce the size even the area of triangle is rescaled. Likewise, the ciphertext size is constant if the set of locations is increased or decreased.

Motivated from the above scenario, we present a solution which produces a constant ciphertext size. Even the set of locations is increased, the ciphertext size is constant. We also aim that the scheme should be computationally efficient. According Fig. 1, let's assume that the user is located in the red location p_1. If p_1 belongs to $[N, E]$, and $[N, W]$, he/she can decrypt the broadcasted message. There is an obvious solution from [9], which we consider the distance $[N, E]$, $[N, W]$ as the range queries, and the user location as the query. This approach can not deal with the reduce the ciphertext size, since the proposed scheme considers each encrypted data stored in the $(d \times l)$ matrix, and encrypts each data producing in each components in the ciphertext. In another approach, our scenario can be applied directly the Attribute-based encryption [1,5] and Predication Encryption [7]. In fact, a class of policies in Attribute Based Encryption expresses the distance $[N, E]$, $[N, W]$, attributes express user's location, and with the center system playing the role of attribute authority. However, in [1,5,7], the access policy embedded in ciphertext cannot be aggregated into one components, then ciphertext size increase linearly depending on the size of access policy generating by set of attributes. In order to construct a constant size of ciphertext even the resizing of the set of locations, we need to aggregate the ciphertext components corresponding to each location. Moreover, the scheme should guarantee that the successful decryption of one satisfied location belongs to the set of locations embedded in the ciphertext.

Contributions: We first propose a 2D Location Based Encryption (2D-LBE) scheme, which achieves the constant ciphertext size. We apply the Time Specific Encryption (TSE) scheme [6,8] to exploit the time interval properties to construct our idea. In TSE scheme, the decryption is processed when a time t falls into the specific distance time $[t_1, t_2]$. Consequently, we consider each distance $[p_1, p_2]$ as the interval $[t_1, t_2]$ in TSE scheme. We then produce our scheme by evaluating the location p belonging to the $[p_1, p_2]$, and $[p_3, p_4]$; achieving the constant ciphertext size in encryption algorithm and decryption cost. Beyond the 2D-LBE scheme, we explore the 3D-LBE scheme, where there are a center system and a 3D triangle area including the set of locations. Each location comprises the X, Y, and Z coordinator. Hence, the decryption is processed when a location p is belonging to the specific distance $[p_1, p_2]$, $[p_3, p_4]$, and $[p_5, p_6]$. This proposed scheme is an extension of the 2D-LBE scheme, which the ciphertext size is also constant.

We give a detailed comparison between the aforementioned obvious solution of Multi-Search Range Queries [9] and our proposed schemes in Table 1. The schemes are compared in terms of the order of the underlying group, ciphertext size, decryption cost, and security assumption. In the table, p denotes the pairing operation, (d, l) the dimension of the matrix.

Table 1. Performance comparison

Scheme	Ciphertext size	Decryption cost	Assumption
MQRED [9]	$(6 \times d \times l)|\mathbb{G}| + 1|\mathbb{G}_T|$	$5dp$	D-BDH
2D-LBE	$5|\mathbb{G}| + 1|\mathbb{G}_T|$	$5p$	$1\,\ell-\text{wBDHI}$
3D-LBE	$7|\mathbb{G}| + 1|\mathbb{G}_T|$	$7p$	$1\,\ell-\text{wBDHI}$

Related Works: In 2009, Chandran et al. [4] proposed a Position Based Cryptography scheme, which utilizes the geographic location to derive the user's identity. In addition, the scheme is position-secured to hide the user's position, however, the verifier still authenticates the location of the user. Buhrman et al. [2] constructed the position based cryptography in the quantum setting, which uses the geographical position of a party as its only credential. Extension in the mobile environment, You et al. [11] proposed a novel location-based encryption model based on a fuzzy vault scheme to protect the sensitive data and the location data. Recently, Yang et at. [10] constructed a secure positioning protocol with location privacy in the bounded retrieval model deploying in a fog computing environment.

2 Preliminaries

2.1 Bilinear Map on Prime Order Groups

Let $\mathbb{G}$ and $\mathbb{G}_T$ be two multiplicative cyclic groups of same prime order p, and g a generator of $\mathbb{G}$. Let $e : \mathbb{G} \times \mathbb{G} \to \mathbb{G}_T$ be a bilinear map with the following properties:

1. Bilinearity: $e(u^a, v^b) = e(u^b, v^a) = e(u, v)^{ab}$ for all $u, v \in \mathbb{G}$ and $a, b \in \mathbb{Z}_p$.
2. Non-degeneracy: $e(g, g) \neq 1$

Notice that the map e is symmetric since $e(g^a, g^b) = e(g, g)^{ab} = e(g^b, g^a)$.

2.2   The Decisional ℓ−wBDHI Assumption

The Decision ℓ-wBDHI problem in $\mathbb{G}$ is defined as follows: Let $\ell \in \mathbb{N}$, and $\mathbb{G}$ be a bilinear group of prime order p, and g, h two independent generators of $\mathbb{G}$. Denote $\overrightarrow{y}_{g,\alpha,\ell} = (g_1, g_2, \ldots, g_\ell) \in \mathbb{G}^\ell$ where $g_i = g^{\alpha^i}$ for some unknown $\alpha \in \mathbb{Z}_p^*$. We say that the ℓ-wBDHI assumption holds in $\mathbb{G}$ if for any probabilistic polynomial-time algorithm A

$$|\Pr[A(g, h, \overrightarrow{y}_{g,\alpha,\ell}, e(g_{\ell+1}, h)) = 1] - \Pr[A(g, h, \overrightarrow{y}_{g,\alpha,\ell}, W) = 1]| \leq \epsilon(k)$$

where the probability is over the random choive of g, h in $\mathbb{G}$, the random choice $\alpha \in \mathbb{Z}^*_p$, the random choice $W \in \mathbb{G}_T$, and $\epsilon(k)$ is negligible in the security parameter k.

2.3   Location Based Encryption

A Location Based Encryption (LBE) scheme consists of the following four probabilistic polynomial-time algorithms:

- **Setup**$(1^k, T = 2^\ell - 1)$: on input a security parameter 1^n, and the maximum $T = 2^\ell - 1$, the algorithm outputs a public key PK and a master secret key MSK.
- **Encrypt**$(PK, [t_{1N}, t_{2E}], [t_{2N}, t_{2W}], M)$: on input a public key PK, a message M, two distances $[t_{1N}, t_{2E}], [t_{2N}, t_{2W}]$, the algorithm outputs a ciphertext CT.
- **KeyGen**$(MSK, [t_1, t_2])$: on input a master secret key MSK, a location $[t_1, t_2]$, the algorithm outputs a decryption key SK.
- **Decrypt**(CT, SK): on input a ciphertext CT and a secret key SK, the algorithm outputs either a message M if $[t_1, t_2]$ belongs to $[t_{1N}, t_{2E}], [t_{2N}, t_{2W}]$, or a special symbol $\perp$.

2.4   Security Model

The security model for an LBE scheme is defined via the following game between an adversary A and a challenger B.

- **Setup**: The challenger B run **Setup**$(1^k, T = 2^\ell - 1)$ to generate the PK and MSK. PK is then passed to A.
- **Query Phase 1**: The challenger answers all location extraction queries t_{1_i}, t_{2_i} by generating $SK_{t_{1_i}, t_{2_i}}$ as in the KeyGen algorithm.
- **Challenge**: A submits two equal-length messages M_0 and M_1, challenge X-Y $[t_{1N}^*, t_{1E}^*][t_{2N}^*, t_{2W}^*]$ such that $t_{1_i} \notin [t_{1N}^*, t_{1E}^*], t_{2_i} \in [t_{2N}^*, t_{2W}^*]$ or $t_{1_i} \in [t_{1N}^*, t_{1E}^*], t_{2_i} \notin [t_{2N}^*, t_{2W}^*]$ that has been queried in Phase 1. The challenger then flips a coin $\beta \leftarrow \{0, 1\}$ and computes the challenge ciphertext CT^*, which is given to A.
- **Query Phase 2**: same as Query Phase 1
- **Output**: A outputs a bit β' as her guess for β.

Define the advantage of A as $\mathbf{Adv}_A^{\mathsf{LBE}}(k) = |\Pr[\beta' = \beta] - 1/2|$.

Selective Security. In the selective security model, the adversary A is required to submit the target challenge X-Y $[t_{1N}^*, t_{1E}^*][t_{2N}^*, t_{2W}^*]$ before the game setup, and A is only allowed to make private key queries for any $t_{1_i} \notin [t_{1N}^*, t_{1E}^*], t_{2_i} \in [t_{2N}^*, t_{2W}^*]$ or $t_{1_i} \in [t_{1N}^*, t_{1E}^*], t_{2_i} \notin [t_{2N}^*, t_{2W}^*]$ throughout the game.

3 2D Location Based Encryption

In this section, we propose a 2D Location Based Encryption scheme. Let $\ell \in \mathbb{N}$, we consider the binary tree B with $T = 2^\ell - 1$ nodes, where T will be the number of segments between the location N and E. By using the transformation [3], we map the distance location $[N.E]$ to the binary tree as the following:

We present the vector d_{X_t} and set $\{X_t\}$. d_{X_t} be a vector consisting of the indices corresponding to the root node of B as $2T + 1$.

Suppose that we balance a binary tree of depth $T = 2^\ell - 1$, which T segments in the specific distance from N and E. The root node is installed with $2T + 1$, and each node is labeled with a string in $\{0,1\}^{\leq \ell}$. In addition, the left and the right children of a node is assigned 0 and 1, Without loss of generality, from the root to E we view a binary string of length $m \leq \ell$ as an N-tuple of length m as $d_{X_{t_{1E+1}}} = \{N_0, \ldots, N_m\}$, and from the root to N we view a binary string of length $n \leq \ell$ as an E-tuple of length n as $d_{X_{2T-t_{1N}}} = \{E_0, E_1, \ldots E_n\}$. Therefore, when encrypting a message with a distance $[N, E]$, the algorithm will associate the $[N, E]$ into a binary tree, and construct the path way from the root tree to the $[N, E]$ by indexing two binary strings $(N_0, \ldots, N_m), (E_0, \ldots, E_n)$. Then to retrieve $t \in [N, E]$, the algorithm invoke as:

For $t \in [1, 2T]$, $X_t = \{d_{X_t}\}$, $X_{T+1} = \{d_{X_{T+1}}\}$. Recursively, for $t \in [1, 2T]\backslash\{1, T+1\}$, X_{t+1} is computed on X_t as: Let $s = \min\{u : X_u \in X_t\}$. If d_{X_s} is a leaf node, then X_{t+1} is retrieved by removing the vector d_{X_s} from the set X_t. Otherwise, let α_l, α_r be the index of the left, right node of node s respectively. X_{t+1} is the set obtained by removing d_{X_s} and adding $d_{X_{\alpha_l}}, d_{X_{\alpha_r}}$ to the set X_t (1). Hence, the setting of segments between the location N and W is similarly to the location N and E.

In addition, we should face another problem of a key generation when using master key $g^{\alpha\beta}$ to generate the user key securely. Hence, our idea is to share $\alpha\beta$, we re-generate r, z by randomly choosing and obtaining the re-share $(\alpha\beta + r - r), (z, -z)$, which r, z are also blinding factors. As a result, the extract keys are computed by the master key completely obviousness.

We elaborate the Setup, Encryption, Key Extraction, Decryption algorithms defined above. Let $\mathbb{G}, \mathbb{G}_T, e$ be bilinear maps, and $T = 2^\ell - 1$ ($\ell \in \mathbb{N}$) be a polynomial that indicates the segments of X and Y coordinate. Our 2D Location based scheme is presented in the following:

▶ Setup($1^k, T = 2^\ell - 1$): The algorithm first chooses randomly $\alpha, \beta \in \mathbb{Z}_p$, and chooses uniformly $g_{1N}, g_{1E}, g_{2N}, g_{2W}, h_0, \ldots, h_\ell \in \mathbb{G}$. Then it computes:

$$MSK = g^{\alpha\beta},$$
$$MPK = (g, g_1, g_{1N}, g_{1E}, g_{2N}, g_{2W}, h_0, \ldots, h_\ell, Y = e(g^\alpha, g^\beta)),$$

and returns MPK, MSK.

▶ Encryption($MPK, [t_{1N}, t_{2E}], [t_{2N}, t_{2W}], M$): Firstly, let

$$d_{X_{t_{1E}+1}} = (N_0, N_1, \ldots N_m), d_{X_{2T-t_{1N}}} = (E_0, E_1, \ldots E_n),$$

$$d_{Y_{t_{2W}+1}} = (\hat{N}_0, \hat{N}_1, \ldots \hat{N}_m), d_{Y_{2T-t_{2N}}} = (W_0, W_1, \ldots W_n),$$

with fixed numbers m, n. The algorithm then chooses randomly $s \in \mathbb{Z}_p$, and computes:

$$C_0 = Y^s \cdot M,$$
$$C_1 = g^s,$$
$$C_2 = (\prod_{i=0}^m h_i^{N_i} \cdot g_{1N})^s, C_3 = (\prod_{i=0}^n h_i^{E_i} \cdot g_{1E})^s$$
$$C_4 = (\prod_{i=0}^m h_i^{\hat{N}_i} \cdot g_{2N})^s, C_5 = (\prod_{i=0}^m h_i^{W_i} \cdot g_{2W})^s,$$

and returns $CT = (C_0, C_1, C_2, C_3, C_4, C_5, [t_{1N}, t_{1E}], [t_{2N}, t_{2W}])$.

▶ Extract($MSK, [t_1, t_2]$): The algorithm chooses randomly $r, z \in \mathbb{Z}_p$.

• For each $X_1 = (N_0, N_1, \ldots, N_m) \in X_{t_1+1}$, the algorithms picks randomly $r_{1N} \in \mathbb{Z}_p$, and computes:

$$d_{X_1} = (g^{\alpha\beta+r} \cdot (\prod_{i=0}^m h_i^{N_i} \cdot g_{1N})^{r_{1N}}, g^{r_{1N}}, h_{m+1}^{r_{1N}}, \ldots, h_\ell^{r_{1N}}).$$

• For each $X_2 = (E_0, E_1, \ldots, E_n) \in X_{2T-t_1}$, it picks randomly $r_{1E} \in \mathbb{Z}_p$. and computes:

$$d_{X_2} = (g^{-r} \cdot (\prod_{i=0}^n h_i^{E_i} \cdot g_{1E})^{r_{1E}}, g^{r_{1E}}, h_{n+1}^{r_{1E}}, \ldots, h_\ell^{r_{1E}}).$$

• For each $Y_1 = (\hat{N}_0, \hat{N}_1, \ldots, \hat{N}_m) \in Y_{t_2+1}$, it picks randomly $r_{2N} \in \mathbb{Z}_p$. and computes:

$$d_{Y_1} = (g^z \cdot (\prod_{i=0}^m h_i^{\hat{N}_i} \cdot g_{2N})^{r_{2N}}, g^{r_{2N}}, h_{m+1}^{r_{2N}}, \ldots, h_\ell^{r_{2N}}).$$

• For each $Y_2 = (W_0, W_1, \ldots, W_n) \in Y_{2T-t_2}$, it picks randomly $r_{2W} \in \mathbb{Z}_p$. and computes:

$$d_{Y_2} = (g^{-z} \cdot (\prod_{i=0}^n h_i^{W_i} \cdot g_{2W})^{r_{2W}}, g^{r_{2W}}, h_{n+1}^{r_{2W}}, \ldots, h_\ell^{r_{2W}}).$$

Finally, it sets:

$$SK_{t_1,1N} = \{d_{X_1}\}_{X_1 \in X_{t_1+1}}, SK_{t_1,1E} = \{d_{X_2}\}_{X_2 \in X_{2T-t_1}}$$
$$SK_{t_2,2N} = \{d_{Y_1}\}_{Y_1 \in Y_{t_2+1}}, SK_{t_2,2W} = \{d_{Y_2}\}_{Y_2 \in Y_{2T-t_2}},$$

and returns $SK_{t_1,t_2} = \{SK_{t_1,1N}, SK_{t_1,1E}, SK_{t_2,2N}, SK_{t_2,2W}, \{t_1, t_2\}\}$.

▶ Decryption(SK_{t_1,t_2}, CT): If $\{t_1, t_2\} \notin ([t_{1N}, t_{1E}], [t_{2N}, t_{2W}])$ return $\perp$. Otherwise, the algorithm retrieves:

$$d_{X_{t_{1E}+1}} = (N_1, N_2, \ldots), d_{X_{2T-t_{1N}}} = (E_1, E_2, \ldots),$$
$$d_{Y_{t_{2W}+1}} = (\hat{N}_1, \hat{N}_2, \ldots), d_{Y_{2T-t_{2N}}} = (W_1, W_2, \ldots),$$

Then, it computes:

$$\frac{C_0 \cdot e(d_{X_{12}}, C_2) \cdot e(d_{X_{22}}, C_3) \cdot e(d_{Y_{12}}, C_4) \cdot e(d_{Y_{22}}, C_5)}{e(d_{X_{11}} \cdot d_{X_{21}} \cdot d_{Y_{11}} \cdot d_{Y_{21}}, C_1)}$$

Let:

$$A = e(d_{X_{12}}, C_2) \cdot e(d_{X_{22}}, C_3) \cdot e(d_{Y_{12}}, C_4) \cdot e(d_{Y_{22}}, C_5)$$
$$= e(g^{r_{1N}}, (\prod_{i=0}^{m} h_i^{N_i} \cdot g_{1N})^s) \cdot e(g^{r_{1E}}, (\prod_{i=0}^{n} h_i^{E_i} \cdot g_{1E})^s)$$
$$\cdot e(g^{r_{2N}}, (\prod_{i=0}^{m} h_i^{\hat{N}_i} \cdot g_{2N})^s) \cdot e(g^{r_{2W}}, (\prod_{i=0}^{m} h_i^{W_i} \cdot g_{2W})^s)$$
$$B = e(d_{X_{11}} \cdot d_{X_{21}} \cdot d_{Y_{11}} \cdot d_{Y_{21}}, C_1)$$
$$= e(g^{\alpha\beta+r} \cdot (\prod_{i=0}^{m} h_i^{N_i} \cdot g_{1N})^{r_{1N}} \cdot g^{-r} \cdot (\prod_{i=0}^{n} h_i^{E_i} \cdot g_{1E})^{r_{1E}}$$
$$\cdot g^z \cdot (\prod_{i=0}^{m} h_i^{\hat{N}_i} \cdot g_{2N})^{r_{2N}} \cdot g^{-z} \cdot (\prod_{i=0}^{n} h_i^{W_i} \cdot g_{2W})^{r_{2W}}, g^s)$$

To recover message M:

$$\frac{Y^s \cdot M \cdot A}{B} = M$$

4   Security Proof

Theorem 1. *Assume that the ℓ-wBDHI assumption holds, then no polynomial-time adversary against our 2D Location based Encryption scheme can have a non-negligible advantage over random guess in the Selective IND-CPA security game.*

We assume our our 2D Location based Encryption with the size of X-Y coordinate which is polynomial in the security parameter k. We consider the selective adversary the decides the challenge X-Y $[t_{1N}^*, t_{1E}^*][t_{2N}^*, t_{2W}^*]$ at the beginning of the IND-CPA game.

Let $\mathcal{A}$ be any IND-CPA adversary that attacks our proposed scheme. We then build an algorithm $\mathcal{B}$ that solves the decisional ℓ-wBDHI problem in $(\mathbb{G}, \mathbb{G}_T, e)$ by using $\mathcal{A}$.

Let g, h choose uniformly in $\mathbb{G}$, randomly $\alpha \in \mathbb{Z}_p$, and sets $y_i = g^{\alpha^{i+1}}$. $\mathcal{B}$ is given as input $(g, h, y_0, y_1, \ldots, y_\ell, Y)$, where Y is $e(g, h)^{\alpha^{l+2}}$ or a random value in $\mathbb{G}_T$. $\mathcal{B}$ interacts with $\mathcal{A}$ as follows:

– **Setup:** $\mathcal{A}$ outputs the challenge X $[t_{1N}^*, t_{1E}^*]$, and Y $[t_{2N}^*, t_{2W}^*]$. Then lets:

$$d_{X_{t_{1E}^*+1}} = (N_0^*, N_1^*, \ldots N_m^*), d_{X_{2T-t_{1N}^*}} = (E_0^*, E_1^*, \ldots E_n^*),$$

$$d_{Y_{t_{2W}^*+1}} = (\hat{N}_0^*, \hat{N}_1^*, \ldots \hat{N}_m^*), d_{Y_{2T-t_{2N}^*}} = (W_0^*, W_1^*, \ldots W_n^*),$$

$\mathcal{B}$ picks randomly $\gamma, \gamma_0, \gamma_1, \ldots, \gamma_\ell, \alpha_N, \alpha_E, \alpha_{\hat{N}}, \alpha_W \in \mathbb{Z}_p$, and $g_1 = y_0$, then computes:

$$g_{1N} = g^{\alpha_N} \cdot \prod_{i=0}^m y_{\ell-1}^{N_i^*} g_{1E} = g^{\alpha_E} \cdot \prod_{i=0}^n y_{\ell-1}^{E_i^*}$$

$$g_{2N} = g^{\alpha_{\hat{N}}} \cdot \prod_{i=0}^m y_{\ell-1}^{\hat{N}_i^*} g_{2W} = g^{\alpha_W} \cdot \prod_{i=0}^n y_{\ell-1}^{W_i^*}$$

$$h_i = g^{\gamma_i} \cdot y_{\ell-i} = g^{\gamma_i - \alpha^{\ell-i+1}} Y = e(y_0, y_\ell g^\gamma),$$

where $\alpha^{\ell+1} + \gamma$ is implicitly setting as β. $\mathcal{B}$ then sets $MPK = (g, g_1, g_{1N}, g_{1E}, g_{2N}, g_{2W}, h_0, \ldots, h_\ell, Y = e(g^\alpha, g^\beta))$, and gives it to $\mathcal{A}$.

– **Phase 1:** If $\mathcal{A}$ submits a location extraction query t_{1_i}, t_{2_i}, $\mathcal{B}$ responds to each query by generating $SK_{t_{1_i}, t_{2_i}}$ as follows:

• **Case 1:** $t_{1_i} < t_{1N}^*, t_{2_i} \in [t_{2N}^*, t_{2W}^*]$
  $\mathcal{B}$ implicitly sets $r' = \alpha^{\ell+2} + r$, where r, z is chosen randomly from $\mathbb{Z}_p$, and r' is distributed uniformly in $\mathbb{Z}_p$. Then:
  * For each $X_1 = (N_0, N_1, \ldots, N_m) \in X_{t_{1_i}+1}$, $\mathcal{B}$ picks r_{1N} randomly in $\mathbb{Z}_p$, and computes:

$$d_{X_1} = \left(y_0^\gamma g^{r'} (\prod_{i=0}^m g^{\gamma_i - \alpha^{\ell-i+1}} g^{\alpha_N} \cdot \prod_{i=0}^m y_{\ell-1}^{N_i^*})^{r_{1N}}, g^{r_{1N}}, h_{m+1}^{r_{1N}}, \ldots, h_\ell^{r_{1N}} \right)$$

$$= \left(g^{\alpha^{\ell+2} + \gamma\alpha} \cdot g^{r' - \alpha^{\ell+2}} \cdot (\prod_{i=0}^m h_i^{N_i} \cdot g_{1N})^{r_{1N}}, g^{r_{1N}}, h_{m+1}^{r_{1N}}, \ldots, h_\ell^{r_{1N}} \right)$$

$$= \left(g^{\alpha\beta + r} \cdot (\prod_{i=0}^m h_i^{N_i} \cdot g_{1N})^{r_{1N}}, g^{r_{1N}}, h_{m+1}^{r_{1N}}, \ldots, h_\ell^{r_{1N}} \right).$$

  * We consider the secret keys of $X_2 \in X_{2T-t_{1_i}}$. For $X_2 = (E_0^*, \ldots, E_{d-1}^*, E_d, \ldots, E_n)$. $\mathcal{B}$ then generates the secret key of $(E_0^*, \ldots, E_{d-1}^*, E_d)$, and use this secret key to derive the secret key of X_2. $\mathcal{B}$ picks randomly r_{1E}', which implicitly sets $r_{1E}' = \alpha^{d+1} + r_{1E}(E_d^* - E_d)$. $\mathcal{B}$ computes:

$$d_{X_2} = \left(g^{r'} \cdot g^{\alpha^{\ell-d+1} r_{1E}'} \cdot \left\{ \left(\prod_{i=0}^{d-1} y_d^{\gamma_i E_i^*} \cdot y_d^{\gamma_d E_d} \cdot y_d^{\alpha_E} \cdot \prod_{j=d+1}^n y_{\ell-j+d+1}^{E_i^*} \right) \right. \right.$$

$$\left. \left. \cdot \left(\prod_{i=0}^{d-1} g^{\gamma_i E_i^*} \cdot g^{\gamma_d E_d} \cdot g^{\alpha_E} \cdot \prod_{j=d+1}^n (g^{\alpha^{\ell-j+d+1}})^{E_i^*} \right)^{-r_{1E}'} \right\}^{\frac{1}{E_d^* - E_d}}, \right.$$

$$\left(g^{r'_{1E}} \cdot y_d^{-1}\right)^{\frac{1}{E_d^* - E_d}}, \left(g^{\gamma_{d+1} r'_{1E}} \cdot y_d^{-\gamma_d+1} \cdot y_{\ell-d-1}^{r'_{1E}} \cdot y_\ell\right)^{\frac{1}{E_d^* - E_d}},$$

$$\left. h_{d+2}^{r_{1E}}, \ldots, h_\ell^{r_{1E}} \right)$$

$$= \left(g^{-r'} \cdot g^{\alpha^{\ell+2}} \cdot g^{\alpha^{\ell-d+1}(E_d^* - E_d)r_{1E}} \cdot \left(\prod_{i=0}^{d-1} g^{\gamma_i E_i^*} \cdot g^{\gamma_d E_d} \cdot g^{\alpha E} \cdot \right.\right.$$

$$\left. \prod_{j=d+1}^{n} (g^{\alpha^{\ell-j+d+1}})^{E_i^*} \right)^{r_{1E}},$$

$$g^{\frac{r'_{1E} - \alpha^{d+1}}{E_d^* - E_d}}, \left(g^{\gamma_{d+1} - \alpha^{\ell-d}}\right)^{\frac{r'_{1E} - \alpha^{d+1}}{E_d^* - E_d}}, h_{d+2}^{r_{1E}}, \ldots, h_\ell^{r_{1E}} \right)$$

$$= \left(g^{-r' + \alpha^{\ell+2}} \cdot \left(\prod_{i=0}^{d-1} g^{(\gamma_i - \alpha^{\ell-i+1})E_i^*} \cdot g^{(\gamma_d - \alpha^{\ell-d+1})E_d} \cdot g^{\alpha E}\right.\right.$$

$$\left. \cdot \prod_{j=0}^{n} (g^{\alpha^{\ell-j+1}})^{E_i^*} \right)^{r_{1E}},$$

$$\left. g^{r_{1E}}, h_{d+1}^{r_{1E}}, h_{d+2}^{r_{1E}}, \ldots, h_\ell^{r_{1E}} \right)$$

$$= \left(g^{-r} \cdot (\prod_{i=0}^{n} h_i^{E_i} \cdot g_{1E})^{r_{1E}}, g^{r_{1E}}, h_{n+1}^{r_{1E}}, \ldots, h_\ell^{r_{1E}} \right)$$

∗ For each $Y_1 = (\hat{N}_0, \hat{N}_1, \ldots, \hat{N}_m) \in Y_{t_2+1}$, $\mathcal{B}$ picks randomly $r_{2N} \in \mathbb{Z}_p$. and computes:

$$d_{Y_1} = (g^z \cdot (\prod_{i=0}^{m} h_i^{\hat{N}_i} \cdot g_{2N})^{r_{2N}}, g^{r_{2N}}, h_{m+1}^{r_{2N}}, \ldots, h_\ell^{r_{2N}}).$$

∗ For each $Y_2 = (W_0, W_1, \ldots, W_n) \in Y_{2T-t_2}$, $\mathcal{B}$ picks randomly $r_{2W} \in \mathbb{Z}_p$. and computes:

$$d_{Y_2} = (g^{-z} \cdot (\prod_{i=0}^{n} h_i^{W_i} \cdot g_{2W})^{r_{2W}}, g^{r_{2W}}, h_{n+1}^{r_{2W}}, \ldots, h_\ell^{r_{2W}}).$$

When simulating d_{X_2}, the components $h_{d+2}^{r_{1E}}, \ldots, h_\ell^{r_{1E}}$ are not involved a $\alpha^{\ell+2}$, then $\mathcal{B}$ can simulate these components similarly as in the main construction. Finally, $\mathcal{B}$ sets $SK_{t_{1_i}, t_{2_i}} = \{SK_{t_{1_i}, 1N}, SK_{t_{1_i}, 1E}, SK_{t_{2_i}, 2N}, SK_{t_{2_i}, 2W}, \{t_{1_i}, t_{2_i}\}$, and sends the $SK_{t_{1_i}, t_{2_i}}$ to $\mathcal{A}$.

– Case 2: $t_{2_i} > t_{1E}^*, t_{2_i} \in [t_{2N}^*, t_{2W}^*]$
$\mathcal{B}$ chooses r, z is chosen randomly from $\mathbb{Z}_p$. Then:

- For each $X_1 = (N_0, N_1, \ldots, N_m) \in X_{t_{1_i}+1}$, we consider the secret keys of $X_1 \in X_{t_{1_i}+1}$. For $X_1 = (N_0^*, \ldots, N_{d-1}^*, N_d, \ldots, N_m)$. $\mathcal{B}$ then generates the secret key of $(E_0^*, \ldots, E_{d-1}^*, E_d)$, and use this secret key to derive the secret key of X_1. $\mathcal{B}$ picks randomly r_{1N}', which implicitly sets $r_{1N}' = \alpha^{d+1} + r_{1N}(E_d^* - E_d)$. $\mathcal{B}$ computes:

$$
d_{X_1} = \left(y_0^\gamma g^r \cdot g^{\alpha^{\ell-d+1} r_{1N}'} \cdot \left\{ \left(\prod_{i=0}^{d-1} y_d^{\gamma_i N_i^*} \cdot y_d^{\gamma_d N_d} \cdot y_d^{\alpha N} \cdot \prod_{j=d+1}^{m} y_{\ell-j+d+1}^{N_i^*} \right) \right. \right.
$$

$$
\left. \cdot \left(\prod_{i=0}^{d-1} g^{\gamma_i N_i^*} \cdot g^{\gamma_d N_d} \cdot g^{\alpha N} \cdot \prod_{j=d+1}^{m} (g^{\alpha^{\ell-j+d+1}})^{N_i^*} \right)^{-r_{1N}'} \right\}^{\frac{1}{N_d^* - N_d}},
$$

$$
\left. (g^{r_{1N}'} \cdot y_d^{-1})^{\frac{1}{N_d^* - N_d}}, (g^{\gamma_{d+1} r_{1N}'} \cdot y_d^{-\gamma_{d+1}} \cdot y_{\ell-d-1}^{r_{1N}'} \cdot y_\ell)^{\frac{1}{N_d^* - N_d}}, h_{d+2}^{r_{1N}}, \ldots, h_\ell^{r_{1N}} \right)
$$

- For $X_2 \in X_{2T-t_{1_i}}$. For $X_2 = (E_0^*, \ldots, E_{d-1}^*, E_d, \ldots, E_n)$. $\mathcal{B}$ picks randomly r_{1E}, then computes:

$$
d_{X_2} = \left(g^{-r} \cdot (\prod_{i=0}^{n} h_i^{E_i} \cdot g_{1E})^{r_{1E}}, g^{r_{1E}}, h_{n+1}^{r_{1E}}, \ldots, h_\ell^{r_{1E}} \right)
$$

- For each $Y_1 = (\hat{N}_0, \hat{N}_1, \ldots, \hat{N}_m) \in Y_{t_2+1}$, $\mathcal{B}$ picks randomly $r_{2N} \in \mathbb{Z}_p$. and computes:

$$
d_{Y_1} = (g^z \cdot (\prod_{i=0}^{m} h_i^{\hat{N}_i} \cdot g_{2N})^{r_{2N}}, g^{r_{2N}}, h_{m+1}^{r_{2N}}, \ldots, h_\ell^{r_{2N}}).
$$

- For each $Y_2 = (W_0, W_1, \ldots, W_n) \in Y_{2T-t_2}$, $\mathcal{B}$ picks randomly $r_{2W} \in \mathbb{Z}_p$. and computes:

$$
d_{Y_2} = (g^{-z} \cdot (\prod_{i=0}^{n} h_i^{W_i} \cdot g_{2W})^{r_{2W}}, g^{r_{2W}}, h_{n+1}^{r_{2W}}, \ldots, h_\ell^{r_{2W}}).
$$

- Case 3: $t_{1_i} \in [t_{1N}^*, t_{1E}^*], t_{2_i} < t_{2N}^*$
  $\mathcal{B}$ chooses r, z is chosen randomly from $\mathbb{Z}_p$. Then:
  - For each $X_1 = (N_0, N_1, \ldots, N_m) \in X_{t_{1_i}+1}$, $\mathcal{B}$ picks r_{1N} randomly in $\mathbb{Z}_p$, and computes:

$$
d_{X_1} = \left(y_0^\gamma g^r (\prod_{i=0}^{m} g^{\gamma_i - \alpha^{\ell-i+1}} g^{\alpha N} \cdot \prod_{i=0}^{m} y_{\ell-1}^{N_i^*})^{r_{1N}}, g^{r_{1N}}, h_{m+1}^{r_{1N}}, \ldots, h_\ell^{r_{1N}} \right)
$$

  - For $X_2 \in X_{2T-t_{1_i}}$. For $X_2 = (E_0^*, \ldots, E_{d-1}^*, E_d, \ldots, E_n)$. $\mathcal{B}$ picks randomly r_{1E}, then computes:

$$
d_{X_2} = \left(g^{-r} \cdot (\prod_{i=0}^{n} h_i^{E_i} \cdot g_{1E})^{r_{1E}}, g^{r_{1E}}, h_{n+1}^{r_{1E}}, \ldots, h_\ell^{r_{1E}} \right)
$$

- For each $Y_1 = (\hat{N}_0, \hat{N}_1, \ldots, \hat{N}_m) \in Y_{t_2+1}$, $\mathcal{B}$ picks randomly $r_{2N} \in \mathbb{Z}_p$. and computes:

$$d_{Y_1} = (g^z \cdot (\prod_{i=0}^{m} h_i^{\hat{N}_i} \cdot g_{2N})^{r_{2N}}, g^{r_{2N}}, h_{m+1}^{r_{2N}}, \ldots, h_\ell^{r_{2N}}).$$

- We consider the secret keys of $Y_2 \in Y_{2T-t_{2_i}}$. For $Y_2 = (W_0^*, \ldots, W_{d-1}^*, W_d, \ldots, W_n)$. $\mathcal{B}$ then generates the secret key of $(W_0^*, \ldots, W_{d-1}^*, W_d)$, and use this secret key to derive the secret key of Y_2. $\mathcal{B}$ picks randomly r_{2W}', which implicitly sets $r_{2W}' = \alpha^{d+1} + r_{2W}(W_d^* - W_d)$. $\mathcal{B}$ computes:

$$d_{Y_2} = \left(g^{-z} \cdot g^{\alpha^{\ell-d+1} r_{2W}'} \cdot \left\{ \left(\prod_{i=0}^{d-1} y_d^{\gamma_i W_i^*} \cdot y_d^{\gamma_d W_d} \cdot y_d^{\alpha W} \cdot \prod_{j=d+1}^{n} y_{\ell-j+d+1}^{W_i^*} \right) \right.\right.$$
$$\left.\left. \cdot \left(\prod_{i=0}^{d-1} g^{\gamma_i W_i^*} \cdot g^{\gamma_d W_d} \cdot g^{\alpha W} \cdot \prod_{j=d+1}^{n} (g^{\alpha^{\ell-j+d+1}})^{W_i^*} \right)^{-r_{2W}'} \right\}^{\frac{1}{W_d^* - W_d}}, \right.$$
$$(g^{r_{2W}'} \cdot y_d^{-1})^{\frac{1}{W_d^* - W_d}}, (g^{\gamma_{d+1} r_{2W}'} \cdot y_d^{-\gamma_d+1} \cdot y_{\ell-d-1}^{r_{2W}'} \cdot y_\ell)^{\frac{1}{W_d^* - W_d}},$$
$$\left. h_{d+2}^{r_{2W}}, \ldots, h_\ell^{r_{2W}} \right)$$
$$= \left(g^{-z} \cdot (\prod_{i=0}^{n} h_i^{W_i} \cdot g_{2W})^{r_{2W}}, g^{r_{2W}}, h_{n+1}^{r_{2W}}, \ldots, h_\ell^{r_{2W}} \right)$$

- Case 4: $t_{1_i} \in [t_{1N}^*, t_{1E}^*], t_{2_i} > t_{2W}^*$

$\mathcal{B}$ chooses r, z is chosen randomly from $\mathbb{Z}_p$. Then:

- For each $X_1 = (N_0, N_1, \ldots, N_m) \in X_{t_{1_i}+1}$, $\mathcal{B}$ picks r_{1N} randomly in $\mathbb{Z}_p$, and computes:

$$d_{X_1} = \left(y_0^\gamma g^r (\prod_{i=0}^{m} g^{\gamma_i - \alpha^{\ell-i+1}} g^{\alpha N} \cdot \prod_{i=0}^{m} y_{\ell-1}^{N_i^*})^{r_{1N}}, g^{r_{1N}}, h_{m+1}^{r_{1N}}, \ldots, h_\ell^{r_{1N}} \right)$$

- For $X_2 \in X_{2T-t_{1_i}}$. For $X_2 = (E_0^*, \ldots, E_{d-1}^*, E_d, \ldots, E_n)$. $\mathcal{B}$ picks randomly r_{1E}, then computes:

$$d_{X_2} = \left(g^{-r} \cdot (\prod_{i=0}^{n} h_i^{E_i} \cdot g_{1E})^{r_{1E}}, g^{r_{1E}}, h_{n+1}^{r_{1E}}, \ldots, h_\ell^{r_{1E}} \right)$$

- We consider the secret keys of $Y_1 \in Y_{t_{2_i}+1}$. For $Y_1 = (\hat{N}_0^*, \ldots, \hat{N}_{d-1}^*, \hat{N}_d, \ldots, \hat{N}_m)$. $\mathcal{B}$ then generates the secret key of $(\hat{N}_0^*, \ldots, \hat{N}_{d-1}^*, \hat{N}_d)$, and use this secret key to derive the secret key of Y_1. $\mathcal{B}$ picks randomly $r_{2\hat{N}}'$, which implicitly sets $r_{2\hat{N}}' = \alpha^{d+1} + r_{1\hat{N}}(\hat{N}_d^* - \hat{N}_d)$. $\mathcal{B}$ computes:

$$d_{Y_1} = \left(g^z \cdot g^{\alpha^{\ell-d+1}r'_{2\hat{N}}} \cdot \left\{\left(\prod_{i=0}^{d-1} y_d^{\gamma_i \hat{N}_i^*} \cdot y_d^{\gamma_d \hat{N}_d} \cdot y_d^{\alpha_{\hat{N}}} \cdot \prod_{j=d+1}^{m} y_{\ell-j+d+1}^{\hat{N}_i^*}\right)\right.\right.$$

$$\left.\left.\cdot \left(\prod_{i=0}^{d-1} g^{\gamma_i \hat{N}_i^*} \cdot g^{\gamma_d \hat{N}_d} \cdot g^{\alpha_{\hat{N}}} \cdot \prod_{j=d+1}^{m} (g^{\alpha^{\ell-j+d+1}})^{\hat{N}_i^*}\right)^{-r'_{2\hat{N}}}\right\}^{\frac{1}{\hat{N}_d^* - \hat{N}_d}},\right.$$

$$(g^{r'_{2\hat{N}}} \cdot y_d^{-1})^{\frac{1}{\hat{N}_d^* - \hat{N}_d}}, (g^{\gamma_{d+1}r'_{2\hat{N}}} \cdot y_d^{-\gamma_d+1} \cdot y_{\ell-d-1}^{r'_{2\hat{N}}} \cdot y_\ell)^{\frac{1}{\hat{N}_d^* - \hat{N}_d}},$$

$$\left.h_{d+2}^{r_{2\hat{N}}}, \dots, h_\ell^{r_{2\hat{N}}}\right)$$

$$= \left(g^s \cdot (\prod_{i=0}^{m} h_i^{\hat{N}_i} \cdot g_{2\hat{N}})^{r_{2\hat{N}}}, g^{r_{2\hat{N}}}, h_{m+1}^{r_{2\hat{N}}}, \dots, h_\ell^{r_{2\hat{N}}}\right)$$

- For each $Y_2 = (W_0, W_1, \dots, W_n) \in Y_{2T-t_{2_i}}$, $\mathcal{B}$ picks randomly $r_{2W} \in \mathbb{Z}_p$. and computes:

$$d_{Y_2} = (g^{-z} \cdot (\prod_{i=0}^{n} h_i^{W_i} \cdot g_{2W})^{r_{2W}}, g^{r_{2W}}, h_{n+1}^{r_{2W}}, \dots, h_\ell^{r_{2W}}).$$

– **Challenge**: When $\mathcal{A}$ decides that Phase 1 is over, it outputs the challenge plaintexts M_0, M_1. $\mathcal{B}$ picks a random bit $b \in_U \{0, 1\}$, and computes the challenge ciphertext by

$$CT^* = (M_b \cdot T \cdot e(y_0, h^\gamma), h, h^{\alpha_N + \sum_{i=0}^{m} N_i^* \gamma_i}, h^{\alpha_E + \sum_{i=0}^{n} E_i^* \gamma_i}, h^{\alpha_{\hat{N}} + \sum_{i=0}^{m} \hat{N}_i^* \gamma_i},$$
$$h^{\alpha_W + \sum_{i=0}^{n} NW_{*i} \gamma_i}, [t_{1N}^*, t_{1E}^*][t_{2N}^*, t_{2W}^*])$$

If $T = e(g, h)^{\alpha^\ell + 2}$, then CT^* is of the following form by letting $\log_g h = s$

$$CT^* = (M_b \cdot e(g, h)^{\alpha^{\ell+2}s} \cdot e(g, g)^{\alpha\gamma s}, g^s, (g^{\alpha_N} \cdot \prod_{i=0}^{m} y_{\ell-1}^{N_i^*})^s, (g^{\alpha_E} \cdot \prod_{i=0}^{n} y_{\ell-1}^{E_i^*})^s,$$

$$(g^{\alpha_{\hat{N}}} \cdot \prod_{i=0}^{m} y_{\ell-1}^{\hat{N}_i^*})^s, (g^{\alpha_W} \cdot \prod_{i=0}^{n} y_{\ell-1}^{W_i^*})^s)$$

$\mathcal{B}$ sends the following challenge ciphertext to $\mathcal{A}$:

$$CT^* = (M_b T, C_1, C_2, C_3, C_4, C_5, [t_{1N}^*, t_{1E}^*][t_{2N}^*, t_{2W}^*]).$$

– **Phase II**: Same as Phase I.
– **Guess**: $\mathcal{A}$ outputs $b' \in \{0, 1\}$. If $b' = b$ then $\mathcal{B}$ outputs 1, otherwise outputs 0.
  Analysis: If $T = e(g, h)^{\alpha^{\ell+2}}$, then the simulation is the same as in the real game. Hence, $\mathcal{A}$ will have the probability $\frac{1}{2} + \epsilon$ to guess b correctly. If T is a random element of $\mathbb{G}_T$, then $\mathcal{A}$ will have probability $\frac{1}{2}$ to guess b correctly. Therefore, $\mathcal{B}$ can solve the Decisionℓ-wBDHI assumption also with advantage ϵ.   □

5   3D Location Based Encryption

We extend the 2D-LBE scheme to 3D-LBE scheme, where each location comprises the X, Y, and Z coordinator. Hence, the decryption is processed when a location t is belonging to the specific distance $[t_1, t_2]$, $[t_3, t_4]$, and $[t_5, t_6]$. In order to share $\alpha\beta$, we re-generate r, z, k by randomly choosing and obtaining the re-share $(\alpha\beta + r - r), (z, -z), (k, -k)$, which r, z, k are also blinding factors. We elaborate the Setup, Encryption, Key Extraction, Decryption algorithms defined above.

Let $\mathbb{G}, \mathbb{G}_{\mathbb{T}}, e$ be bilinear maps, and $T = 2^\ell - 1$ ($\ell \in \mathbb{N}$) be a polynomial that indicates the segments of X, Y and Z coordinate. Our 3D Location Based scheme is presented in the following:

▶ Setup($1^k, T = 2^\ell - 1$): The algorithm first chooses randomly $\alpha, \beta \in \mathbb{Z}_p$, and chooses uniformly $g_{1N}, g_{1E}, g_{2N}, g_{2W}, h_0, \ldots, h_\ell \in \mathbb{G}$. Then it computes:

$$MSK = g^{\alpha\beta},$$
$$MPK = (g, g_1, g_{1N}, g_{1E}, g_{2N}, g_{2W}, g_{3N}, g_{3E}, h_0, \ldots, h_\ell, Y = e(g^\alpha, g^\beta)),$$

and returns MPK, MSK.

▶ Encryption($MPK, [t_{1N}, t_{1E}], [t_{2N}, t_{2W}], [t_{3N}, t_{3E}], M$): Firstly, let

$$d_{X_{t_{1E}+1}} = (N_0, N_1, \ldots N_m), d_{X_{2T-t_{1N}}} = (E_0, E_1, \ldots E_n),$$
$$d_{Y_{t_{2W}+1}} = (\hat{N}_0, \hat{N}_1, \ldots \hat{N}_m), d_{Y_{2T-t_{2N}}} = (W_0, W_1, \ldots W_n),$$
$$d_{Z_{t_{3E}+1}} = (N'_0, N'_1, \ldots N'_m), d_{Z_{2T-t_{3N}}} = (E'_0, E'_1, \ldots E'_n),$$

with fixed numbers m, n. The algorithm then chooses randomly $s \in \mathbb{Z}_p$, and computes:

$$C_0 = Y^s \cdot M,$$
$$C_1 = g^s,$$
$$C_2 = (\prod_{i=0}^{m} h_i^{N_i} \cdot g_{1N})^s, C_3 = (\prod_{i=0}^{n} h_i^{E_i} \cdot g_{1E})^s$$
$$C_4 = (\prod_{i=0}^{m} h_i^{\hat{N}_i} \cdot g_{2N})^s, C_5 = (\prod_{i=0}^{m} h_i^{W_i} \cdot g_{2W})^s,$$
$$C_6 = (\prod_{i=0}^{m} h_i^{N'_i} \cdot g_{3N})^s, C_7 = (\prod_{i=0}^{m} h_i^{E'_i} \cdot g_{3E})^s,$$

and returns $CT = (C_0, C_1, C_2, C_3, C_4, C_5, C_6, C_7, [t_{1N}, t_{1E}], [t_{2N}, t_{2W}], [t_{3N}, t_{3E}])$.

▶ Extract($MSK, [t_1, t_2, t_3]$): The algorithm chooses randomly $r, z, k \in \mathbb{Z}_p$.
 • For each $X_1 = (N_0, N_1, \ldots, N_m) \in X_{t_1+1}$, the algorithms picks randomly $r_{1N} \in \mathbb{Z}_p$, and computes:

$$d_{X_1} = (g^{\alpha\beta+r} \cdot (\prod_{i=0}^{m} h_i^{N_i} \cdot g_{1N})^{r_{1N}}, g^{r_{1N}}, h_{m+1}^{r_{1N}}, \ldots, h_\ell^{r_{1N}}).$$

- For each $X_2 = (E_0, E_1, \ldots, E_n) \in X_{2T-t_1}$, it picks randomly $r_{1E} \in \mathbb{Z}_p$. and computes:

$$d_{X_2} = (g^{-r} \cdot (\prod_{i=0}^{n} h_i^{E_i} \cdot g_{1E})^{r_{1E}}, g^{r_{1E}}, h_{n+1}^{r_{1E}}, \ldots, h_\ell^{r_{1E}}).$$

- For each $Y_1 = (\hat{N}_0, \hat{N}_1, \ldots, \hat{N}_m) \in Y_{t_2+1}$, it picks randomly $r_{2N} \in \mathbb{Z}_p$. and computes:

$$d_{Y_1} = (g^z \cdot (\prod_{i=0}^{m} h_i^{\hat{N}_i} \cdot g_{2N})^{r_{2N}}, g^{r_{2N}}, h_{m+1}^{r_{2N}}, \ldots, h_\ell^{r_{2N}}).$$

- For each $Y_2 = (W_0, W_1, \ldots, W_n) \in Y_{2T-t_2}$, it picks randomly $r_{2W} \in \mathbb{Z}_p$. and computes:

$$d_{Y_2} = (g^{-z} \cdot (\prod_{i=0}^{n} h_i^{W_i} \cdot g_{2W})^{r_{2W}}, g^{r_{2W}}, h_{n+1}^{r_{2W}}, \ldots, h_\ell^{r_{2W}}).$$

- For each $Z_1 = (N'_0, N'_1, \ldots, N'_m) \in Z'_{t_3+1}$, the algorithms picks randomly $r_{3N} \in \mathbb{Z}_p$, and computes:

$$d_{Z_1} = (g^k \cdot (\prod_{i=0}^{m} h_i^{N'_i} \cdot g_{3N})^{r_{3N}}, g^{r_{3N}}, h_{m+1}^{r_{3N}}, \ldots, h_\ell^{r_{3N}}).$$

- For each $Z_2 = (E'_0, E'_1, \ldots, E'_n) \in Z'_{2T-t_3}$, it picks randomly $r_{3E} \in \mathbb{Z}_p$. and computes:

$$d_{Z_2} = (g^{-k} \cdot (\prod_{i=0}^{n} h_i^{E'_i} \cdot g_{3E})^{r_{3E}}, g^{r_{3E}}, h_{n+1}^{r_{3E}}, \ldots, h_\ell^{r_{3E}}).$$

Finally, it sets:

$$SK_{t_1,1N} = \{d_{X_1}\}_{X_1 \in X_{t_1+1}} SK_{t_1,1E} = \{d_{X_2}\}_{X_2 \in X_{2T-t_1}}$$
$$SK_{t_2,2N} = \{d_{Y_1}\}_{Y_1 \in Y_{t_2+1}} SK_{t_2,2W} = \{d_{Y_2}\}_{Y_2 \in Y_{2T-t_2}},$$
$$SK_{t_3,3N} = \{d_{Z_1}\}_{Z_1 \in X_{t_3+1}} SK_{t_3,3E} = \{d_{Z_2}\}_{Z_2 \in X_{2T-t_3}}$$

and returns $SK_{t_1,t_2} = \{SK_{t_1,1N}, SK_{t_1,1E}, SK_{t_2,2N}, SK_{t_2,2W}, SK_{t_3,3N}, SK_{t_3,3E}, \{t_1, t_2, t_3\}\}$.

▶ Decryption(SK_{t_1,t_2,t_3}, CT): If $\{t_1, t_2, t_3\} \notin ([t_{1N}, t_{1E}], [t_{2N}, t_{2W}], [t_{3N}, t_{3E}])$ return $\perp$. Otherwise, the algorithm retrieves:

$$d_{X_{t_{1E}+1}} = \{N_1, N_2, \ldots\}, d_{X_{2T-t_{1N}}} = \{E_1, E_2, \ldots\},$$
$$d_{Y_{t_{2W}+1}} = \{\hat{N}_1, \hat{N}_2, \ldots\}, d_{Y_{2T-t_{2N}}} = \{W_1, W_2, \ldots\},$$
$$d_{Z_{t_{3E}+1}} = \{N'_1, N'_2, \ldots\}, d_{Z_{2T-t_{3N}}} = \{E'_1, E'_2, \ldots\},$$

Then, it computes:

$$\frac{C_0 \cdot e(d_{X_{12}}, C_2) \cdot e(d_{X_{22}}, C_3) \cdot e(d_{Y_{12}}, C_4) \cdot e(d_{Y_{22}}, C_5) \cdot e(d_{Z_{12}}, C_6) \cdot e(d_{Z_{22}}, C_7)}{e(d_{X_{11}} \cdot d_{X_{21}} \cdot d_{Y_{11}} \cdot d_{Y_{21}} \cdot d_{Z_{11}} \cdot d_{Z_{21}}, C_1)}$$

Let:

$$A = e(d_{X_{12}}, C_2) \cdot e(d_{X_{22}}, C_3) \cdot e(d_{Y_{12}}, C_4) \cdot e(d_{Y_{22}}, C_5) \cdot e(d_{Z_{12}}, C_6) \cdot e(d_{Z_{22}}, C_7)$$

$$= e(g^{r_{1N}}, (\prod_{i=0}^{m} h_i^{N_i} \cdot g_{1N})^s) \cdot e(g^{r_{1E}}, (\prod_{i=0}^{n} h_i^{E_i} \cdot g_{1E})^s)$$

$$\cdot e(g^{r_{2N}}, (\prod_{i=0}^{m} h_i^{\hat{N}_i} \cdot g_{2N})^s) \cdot e(g^{r_{2W}}, (\prod_{i=0}^{m} h_i^{W_i} \cdot g_{2W})^s)$$

$$\cdot e(g^{r_{3N}}, (\prod_{i=0}^{m} h_i^{N'_i} \cdot g_{3N})^s) \cdot e(g^{r_{3E}}, (\prod_{i=0}^{n} h_i^{E'_i} \cdot g_{3E})^s)$$

$$B = e(d_{X_{11}} \cdot d_{X_{21}} \cdot d_{Y_{11}} \cdot d_{Y_{21}} \cdot d_{Z_{11}} \cdot d_{Z_{21}}, C_1)$$

$$= e(g^{\alpha\beta + r} \cdot (\prod_{i=0}^{m} h_i^{N_i} \cdot g_{1N})^{r_{1N}} \cdot g^{-r} \cdot (\prod_{i=0}^{n} h_i^{E_i} \cdot g_{1E})^{r_{1E}}$$

$$\cdot g^z \cdot (\prod_{i=0}^{m} h_i^{\hat{N}_i} \cdot g_{2N})^{r_{2N}} \cdot g^{-z} \cdot (\prod_{i=0}^{n} h_i^{W_i} \cdot g_{2W})^{r_{2W}}$$

$$\cdot e(g^k \cdot (\prod_{i=0}^{m} h_i^{N'_i} \cdot g_{3N})^{r_{3N}} \cdot g^{-k} \cdot (\prod_{i=0}^{n} h_i^{E'_i} \cdot g_{3E})^{r_{3E}}, g^s)$$

To recover message M:

$$\frac{Y^s \cdot M \cdot A}{B} = M$$

Security Proof

Theorem 2. *Assume that the ℓ-wBDHI assumption holds, then no polynomial-time adversary against our 3D Location Based Encryption scheme can have a non-negligible advantage over random guess in the Selective IND-CPA security game.*

We assume our 3D Location Based Encryption with the size of X,Y, and Z coordinate which is polynomial in the security parameter k. We consider the selective adversary the decides the challenge X,Y, and Z $[t^*_{1N}, t^*_{1E}][t^*_{2N}, t^*_{2W}][t^*_{3N}, t^*_{3E}]$ at the beginning of the IND-CPA game.

Let $\mathcal{A}$ be any IND-CPA adversary that attacks our proposed scheme. We then build an algorithm $\mathcal{B}$ that solves the decisional ℓ-wBDHI problem in $(\mathbb{G}, \mathbb{G}_T, e)$ by using $\mathcal{A}$ as in Theorem 1. Let g, h choose uniformly in $\mathbb{G}$, randomly $\alpha \in \mathbb{Z}_p$, and sets $y_i = g^{\alpha^{i+1}}$. $\mathcal{B}$ is given as input $(g, h, y_0, y_1, \ldots, y_\ell, Y)$, where Y is $e(g, h)^{\alpha^{l+2}}$ or a random value in $\mathbb{G}_T$. $\mathcal{B}$ interacts with $\mathcal{A}$ as follows:

- **Setup:** $\mathcal{A}$ outputs the challenge X $[t_{1N}^*, t_{1E}^*]$, and Y $[t_{2N}^*, t_{2W}^*]$. Then lets:

$$X_{t_{1E}^*+1} = (N_0^*, N_1^*, \ldots N_m^*), X_{2T-t_{1N}^*} = (E_0^*, E_1^*, \ldots E_n^*),$$
$$Y_{t_{2W}^*+1} = (\hat{N}_0^*, \hat{N}_1^*, \ldots \hat{N}_m^*), Y_{2T-t_{2N}^*} = (W_0^*, W_1^*, \ldots W_n^*),$$
$$Z_{t_{3E}^*+1} = (N_0'^*, N_1'^*, \ldots N_m'^*), Z_{2T-t_{3N}^*} = (E_0'^*, E_1'^*, \ldots E_n'^*),$$

$\mathcal{B}$ picks randomly $\gamma, \gamma_0, \gamma_1, \ldots, \gamma_\ell, \alpha_N, \alpha_E, \alpha_{\hat{N}}, \alpha_W, \alpha_N', \alpha_E', \in \mathbb{Z}_p$, and $g_1 = y_0$, then computes:

$$g_{1N} = g^{\alpha_N} \cdot \prod_{i=0}^{m} y_{\ell-1}^{N_i^*} g_{1E} = g^{\alpha_E} \cdot \prod_{i=0}^{n} y_{\ell-1}^{E_i^*}$$

$$g_{2N} = g^{\alpha_{\hat{N}}} \cdot \prod_{i=0}^{m} y_{\ell-1}^{\hat{N}_i^*} g_{2W} = g^{\alpha_W} \cdot \prod_{i=0}^{n} y_{\ell-1}^{W_i^*}$$

$$g_{3N} = g^{\alpha_N'} \cdot \prod_{i=0}^{m} y_{\ell-1}^{N_i'^*} g_{3E} = g^{\alpha_E'} \cdot \prod_{i=0}^{n} y_{\ell-1}^{E_i'^*}$$

$$h_i = g^{\gamma_i} \cdot y_{\ell-i} = g^{\gamma_i - \alpha^{\ell-i+1}}, Y = e(y_0, y_\ell g^\gamma),$$

where $\alpha^{\ell+1} + \gamma$ is implicitly setting as β. $\mathcal{B}$ then sets $MPK = (g, g_1, g_{1N}, g_{1E}, g_{2N}, g_{2W}, h_0, \ldots, h_\ell, Y = e(g^\alpha, g^\beta))$, and gives it to $\mathcal{A}$.

- **Phase 1:** If $\mathcal{A}$ submits a location extraction query $t_{1_i}, t_{2_i}, t_{3_i}$, $\mathcal{B}$ responds to each query by generating $SK_{t_{1_i}, t_{2_i}}$ as follows:
  - Case 1: $t_{1_i} < t_{1N}^*, t_{2_i} \in [t_{2N}^*, t_{2W}^*], t_{3_i} \in [t_{3N}^*, t_{3E}^*]$
  - Case 2: $t_{1_i} > t_{1E}^*, t_{2_i} \in [t_{2N}^*, t_{2W}^*], t_{3_i} \in [t_{3N}^*, t_{3E}^*]$
  - Case 3: $t_{1_i} \in [t_{1N}^*, t_{1E}^*], t_{2_i} < t_{2N}^*, t_{3_i} \in [t_{3N}^*, t_{3E}^*]$
  - Case 4: $t_{1_i} \in [t_{1N}^*, t_{1E}^*], t_{2_i} > t_{2W}^*, t_{3_i} \in [t_{3N}^*, t_{3E}^*]$
  - Case 5: $t_{1_i} \in [t_{1N}^*, t_{1E}^*], t_{2_i} \in [t_{2N}^*, t_{2W}^*], t_{3_i} < t_{3N}^*$
  - Case 6: $t_{1_i} \in [t_{1N}^*, t_{1E}^*], t_{2_i} \in [t_{2N}^*, t_{2W}^*], t_{3_i} > t_{3E}^*$

This query phase 1 is simulated similarly as in Phase 1.

- **Challenge:** When $\mathcal{A}$ decides that Phase 1 is over, it outputs the challenge plaintexts M_0, M_1. $\mathcal{B}$ picks a random bit $b \in_U \{0,1\}$, and computes the challenge ciphertext by

$$CT^* = (M_b \cdot T \cdot e(y_0, h^\gamma), h, h^{\alpha_N + \sum_{i=0}^{m} N_i^* \gamma_i}, h^{\alpha_E + \sum_{i=0}^{n} E_i^* \gamma_i}, h^{\alpha_{\hat{N}} + \sum_{i=0}^{m} \hat{N}_i^* \gamma_i},$$

$$h^{\alpha_W + \sum_{i=0}^{n} NW*_i \gamma_i}, h^{\alpha_N' + \sum_{i=0}^{m} N_i'^* \gamma_i}, h^{\alpha_E' + \sum_{i=0}^{n} E_i'^* \gamma_i}, [t_{1N}^*, t_{1E}^*][t_{2N}^*, t_{2W}^*][t_{3N}^*, t_{3E}^*])$$

If $T = e(g, h)^{\alpha^{\ell+2}}$, then CT^* is of the following form by letting $\log_g h = s$

$$CT^* = (M_b \cdot e(g, h)^{\alpha^{\ell+2} s} \cdot e(g, g)^{\alpha \gamma s}, g^s, (g^{\alpha_N} \cdot \prod_{i=0}^{m} y_{\ell-1}^{N_i^*})^s, (g^{\alpha_E} \cdot \prod_{i=0}^{n} y_{\ell-1}^{E_i^*})^s,$$

$$(g^{\alpha_{\hat{N}}} \cdot \prod_{i=0}^{m} y_{\ell-1}^{\hat{N}_i^*})^s, (g^{\alpha_W} \cdot \prod_{i=0}^{n} y_{\ell-1}^{W_i^*})^s, (g^{\alpha_N'} \cdot \prod_{i=0}^{m} y_{\ell-1}^{N_i'^*})^s, (g^{\alpha_E'} \cdot \prod_{i=0}^{n} y_{\ell-1}^{E_i'^*})^s)$$

$\mathcal{B}$ sends the following challenge ciphertext to $\mathcal{A}$:

$$CT^* = (M_b T, C_1, C_2, C_3, C_4, C_5, C_6, C_7, [t_{1N}^*, t_{1E}^*][t_{2N}^*, t_{2W}^*][t_{3N}^*, t_{3E}^*]).$$

- **Phase II**: Same as Phase I.
- **Guess**: $\mathcal{A}$ outputs $b' \in \{0, 1\}$. If $b' = b$ then $\mathcal{B}$ outputs 1, otherwise outputs 0.
  Analysis: If $T = e(g, h)^{\alpha^{\ell+2}}$, then the simulation is the same as in the real game. Hence, $\mathcal{A}$ will have the probability $\frac{1}{2} + \epsilon$ to guess b correctly. If T is a random element of $\mathbb{G}_T$, then $\mathcal{A}$ will have probability $\frac{1}{2}$ to guess b correctly. Therefore, $\mathcal{B}$ can solve the Decisionℓ-wBDHI assumption also with advantage ϵ. □

6   Conclusion

This work is the first endeavor to develop Location Based Encryption with constant ciphertext size. We proposed two new schemes, called 2D Location Based Encryption and 3D Location Based Encryption. Both of them are constant ciphertext size and are proven under in the selective model under the decisional $\ell-$wBDHI assumption. In future work, we will consider the privacy of the area purposed for encryption, since the ciphertext component can disclose the area information. This leads to a privacy preserving location scheme to protect the information encryption, and guarantee the user's location. Furthermore, we will deploy our proposed schemes on IoT devices to analyze the efficiency of transmitting message protocol in the practical scenario.

References

1. Bethencourt, J., Sahai, A., Waters, B.: Ciphertext-policy attribute-based encryption. In: 2007 IEEE Symposium on Security and Privacy (SP 2007), pp. 321–334 (2007)
2. Buhrman, H., et al.: Position-based quantum cryptography: impossibility and constructions. In: Rogaway, P. (ed.) CRYPTO 2011. LNCS, vol. 6841, pp. 429–446. Springer, Heidelberg (2011). https://doi.org/10.1007/978-3-642-22792-9_24
3. Canetti, R., Halevi, S., Katz, J.: Chosen-ciphertext security from identity-based encryption. In: Cachin, C., Camenisch, J.L. (eds.) EUROCRYPT 2004. LNCS, vol. 3027, pp. 207–222. Springer, Heidelberg (2004). https://doi.org/10.1007/978-3-540-24676-3_13
4. Chandran, N., Goyal, V., Moriarty, R., Ostrovsky, R.: Position based cryptography. In: Halevi, S. (ed.) CRYPTO 2009. LNCS, vol. 5677, pp. 391–407. Springer, Heidelberg (2009). https://doi.org/10.1007/978-3-642-03356-8_23
5. Goyal, V., Pandey, O., Sahai, A., Waters, B.: Attribute-based encryption for fine-grained access control of encrypted data. In: Proceedings of the 13th ACM Conference on Computer and Communications Security, CCS 2006, pp. 89–98 (2006)
6. Kasamatsu, K., Matsuda, T., Emura, K., Attrapadung, N., Hanaoka, G., Imai, H.: Time-specific encryption from forward-secure encryption. In: Visconti, I., De Prisco, R. (eds.) SCN 2012. LNCS, vol. 7485, pp. 184–204. Springer, Heidelberg (2012). https://doi.org/10.1007/978-3-642-32928-9_11

7. Katz, J., Sahai, A., Waters, B.: Predicate encryption supporting disjunctions, polynomial equations, and inner products. In: Smart, N. (ed.) EUROCRYPT 2008. LNCS, vol. 4965, pp. 146–162. Springer, Heidelberg (2008). https://doi.org/10.1007/978-3-540-78967-3_9

8. Paterson, K.G., Quaglia, E.A.: Time-specific encryption. In: Garay, J.A., De Prisco, R. (eds.) SCN 2010. LNCS, vol. 6280, pp. 1–16. Springer, Heidelberg (2010). https://doi.org/10.1007/978-3-642-15317-4_1

9. Shi, E., Bethencourt, J., Chan, T.H.H., Song, D., Perrig, A.: Multi-dimensional range query over encrypted data. In: Proceedings of the 2007 IEEE Symposium on Security and Privacy, SP 2007, pp. 350–364 (2007)

10. Yang, R., Xu, Q., Au, M.H., Yu, Z., Wang, H., Zhou, L.: Position based cryptography with location privacy: a step for fog computing. Future Gener. Comput. Syst. **78**, 799–806 (2018)

11. You, L., Chen, Y., Yan, B., Zhan, M.: A novel location-based encryption model using fuzzy vault scheme. Soft Comput. **22**, 3383–3393 (2018)

Group ID-Based Encryption
with Equality Test

Yunhao Ling, Sha Ma$^{(\boxtimes)}$, Qiong Huang, Ru Xiang, and Ximing Li

South China Agricultural University, Guangzhou, Guangdong, China
yunhaolingyy@163.com, shamahb@163.com, {qhuang,liximing}@scau.edu.cn,
xiangru327@163.com

Abstract. In era of cloud computing, how to search on encrypted data has been studied extensively. ID-based encryption with equality test (IBEET) as a type of searchable encryption allows a tester (insider) to check whether two ciphertexts encrypted under different identities contain the same message. Due to its equality test functionality, IBEET has many interesting applications, such as personal health record systems. In this paper, we first introduce group mechanism into IBEET and propose a new primitive, namely group ID-based encryption with equality test (G-IBEET). By the group mechanism, G-IBEET supports group granularity authorization. That is, a group administrator, who is trusted by group users, would issue the insider a group trapdoor to specify that it can only compare on ciphertexts of the group users but cannot compare with ciphertexts of any users other than them. Moreover, the workload of generation and management of trapdoors can be greatly reduced due to the group granularity authorization. For the insider attack which exists in most IBEET schemes with the goal of recovering the message from a ciphertext by mounting an offline message recovery attack, G-IBEET provides a nice solution for IBEET to resist it by the group mechanism. We propose a G-IBEET scheme in bilinear pairings, prove its security in the random oracle model and show that the proposed scheme has a more efficient test algorithm.

Keywords: ID-based encryption · Equality test · Group · Insider attack

1 Introduction

In era of cloud computing, how to search on encrypted data has been studied extensively. *Public key encryption with equality test* (PKEET) [27], which was introduced by Yang et al. in CT-RSA 2010, is a type of searchable encryption in multi-user environment that allows a tester (the insider) to check whether two ciphertexts encrypted under different public keys contain the same message without decrypting them. To simplify the certificate management for PKEET, Ma proposed *ID-based encryption with equality test* (IBEET) [12], integrating

© Springer Nature Switzerland AG 2019
J. Jang-Jaccard and F. Guo (Eds.): ACISP 2019, LNCS 11547, pp. 39–57, 2019.
https://doi.org/10.1007/978-3-030-21548-4_3

identity-based cryptosystem into PKEET. Due to its equality test functionality, IBEET has many interesting applications, such as personal health record systems. In this paper, we first introduce group mechanism into IBEET and propose a new primitive, namely *group ID-based encryption with equality test* (G-IBEET). By the group mechanism, G-IBEET supports group granularity authorization. That is, a group administrator, who is trusted by group users, would issue the insider a group trapdoor to specify that it can only compare on ciphertexts of the group users but cannot compare with ciphertexts of any users other than them. Moreover, the workload of generation and management of trapdoors can be greatly reduced due to the group granularity authorization. For the insider attack which exists in most IBEET schemes with the goal of recovering the message from a ciphertext by mounting an offline message recovery attack, G-IBEET provides a nice solution for IBEET to resist it by the group mechanism.

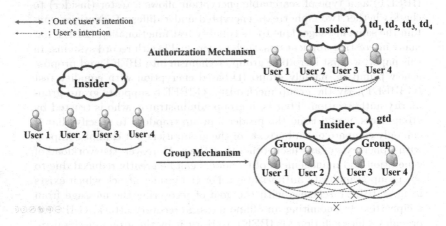

Fig. 1. A comparison with the group mechanism and authorization mechanism.

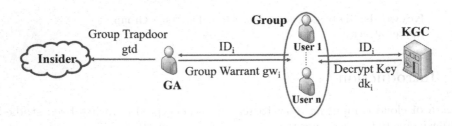

Fig. 2. A G-IBEET cryptosystem model

Group Granularity Authorization. The original PKEET scheme [27] only achieves *one-wayness under chosen-ciphertext attack* (OW-CCA) against any entity. For the improvement of security, [18] introduced authorization mechanism that allows users to specify who can perform the equality test between their ciphertexts into PKEET, which achieves OW-CCA against the adversary who has been authorized by the user and *indistinguishability under chosen-ciphertext attack* (IND-CCA) against the adversary who has not been authorized by the user. Then most PKEET and IBEET schemes and their variants [4,5,7,8,10,13, 16–20,22,25,28] with the authorization mechanism have been presented. But we argue that the authorization mechanism is probably not safe enough. That is, the insider who has been authorized by the users can compare ciphertexts of users arbitrarily, which may exceed the intention of the users. Using our example from Fig. 1, let U_1, U_2, U_3 and U_4 be users in a PKEET cryptosystem supporting authorization. If U_1 and U_2 want the insider to compare ciphertexts only for them, they should issue trapdoors td_1 and td_2 to the insider, respectively. If U_3 and U_4 want the insider to compare ciphertexts only for them, they also should issue trapdoors td_3 and td_4 to the insider, respectively. Then the insider obtaining td_1, td_2, td_3 and td_4 can not only compare U_1's ciphertexts with U_2's ciphertexts and compare U_3's ciphertexts with U_4's ciphertexts but also do other things such as comparing U_1's ciphertexts with U_3's ciphertexts, which exceeds the intention of U_1 and U_3. G-IBEET with granularity authorization can address this problem. Its cryptosystem model is illustrated in Fig. 2. There is a *group administrator* (GA) trusted by group users. GA should issue the insider a group trapdoor to specify that it can compare ciphertexts of group users. The insider can get the correct result of comparison if both the group trapoor and ciphertexts are from the same group. Therefore, insider who has been authorized by GA can only compare ciphertexts of the group users but cannot use their ciphertexts to compare with ciphertexts of any users other than them. From Fig. 2, if U_1, U_2 and U_3, U_4 are in different groups, the insider only compares U_1's ciphertexts with U_2's ciphertexts and U_3's ciphertexts with U_4's ciphertexts.

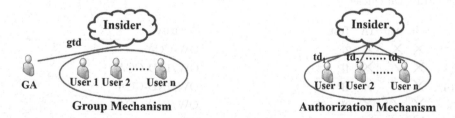

Fig. 3. A comparison with the group mechanism and authorization mechanism.

Group Trapdoor. From Fig. 3, to specify the insider to compare ciphertexts of n group users, GA would issue 1 group trapdoor to the insider under the group mechanism, but these users would issue n trapdoors to the insider under authorization mechanism. Obviously, the former costs much lower than the latter in the workload of generation and management of trapdoors.

Resistance Against Insider Attack. The insider can recover the message from a ciphertext due to the capability to access to user's trapdoor and public generation of PKEET ciphertexts, which was described by [19]. Roughly speaking, given a ciphertext $C = \mathsf{Enc}(pk_i, M)$, the insider can choose a guessing message M' from the message space $\mathcal{M}$ and then generate $C' = \mathsf{Enc}(pk_j, M')$, where pk_i and pk_j represent different public keys, respectively. Therefore, when the actual message space $\mathcal{M}$ is polynomial size, it can mount an offline message recovery attack by checking every $M' \in \mathcal{M}$ so that recover the message M. We call this type of attack *insider attack* (IA). Due to the desired equality test functionality, IA is inherent, which is similar to *inside keyword guessing attack* [1] (IKGA) in *public key encryption with keyword search* [3] (PEKS). One possible solution to against IA is to disable the public generation of ciphertexts. Therefore, the generation of ciphertexts should be embedded some secret information only known by the sender. We make the assumption that the insider plays the role of adversarial tester without having the group warrants for each group. In other words, there is no overlap between group users and the insider. From Fig. 3, GA should generate a group warrant, which is the secret information, for each group user, and then the each group user should embed own group warrant to generate ciphertexts. Due to lack of the group warrants, the insider cannot generate ciphertexts of group users for the guessing messages, so that it launches IA on them unsuccessfully. The detail about the generation of G-IBEET ciphertext will be introduced in Sect. 3.1.

Comparison. In Table 1, we compare relevant PKEET schemes [5,14,18,19,27] with G-IBEET scheme. It can be learnt from Table 1 that only G-IBEET supports the group mechanism. [5,13,14,18,19] support the authorization mechanism. G-IBEET and [19] can resist IA. Finally, G-IBEET scheme has more efficient test

Table 1. Comparison with relevant PKEET and IBEET schemes on properties and computational efficiency.

	Gr	Aut	IA	Test	Security
[27]	✗	✗	✗	2P	OW-CCA
[18]	✗	✓	✗	4P	OW/IND-CCA
[19]	✗	✓	✓	4P	OW/IND-CCA
[5]	✗	✓	✗	2P+6Exp	OW/IND-CCA
[14]	✗	✓	✗	2P+2Exp	OW/IND-CCA
[12]	✗	✓	✗	4P	OW-ID-CCA
[24]	✗	✓	✓	4P	SS-CKA/SS-KGA
[23]	✗	✓	✗	2P+2Exp	OW-ID-CCA
[9]	✗	✓	✓	2P/4P (Type-2, 3/Type-1)	OW-ID/IND-ID-CCA
[25]	✗	✗	✓	2P	W-IND-ID-CCA
Ours	✓	✗	✓	2P	W-IND-ID/IND-ID-CCA

Note: Gr: group mechanism. Aut: authorization mechanism. P: pairing computation. Exp: exponent computation.

algorithm compared with [5,13,14,18,19]. Then we compare IBEET schemes [9,12,23–25] with G-IBEET scheme. It can be learnt from Table 1 that only G-IBEET supports the group mechanism. [9,12,23,24] support the authorization mechanism. G-IBEET and [23–25] can resist IA. Compared with [9,12,23,24], G-IBEET scheme has more efficient test algorithm. With regard to the security, G-IBEET achieves W-IND-ID/IND-ID-CCA, which is more stronger than the security of [9,12,23–25].

1.1 Related Work

PKEET Supporting Authorization. [18] introduced the authorization mechanism into PKEET. Then [5] and [14] introduced different granularity authorization into PKEET, respectively. Their authorization mechanism, however, do not support the group granularity authorization.

IBEET. [12] first introduced IBEET. Then [23] improved the efficiency of [12]. [9] introduced the flexible authorization mechanism based on [14] into IBEET. In [9,14], there is a user-specific ciphertext level authorization. That is, a specific ciphertext of Alice could be only compared with a specific ciphertext of a specific receiver, for example, Bob, but could not be compared with any ciphertext of any receiver other than Bob. However, under user-specific ciphertext level authorization, the insider can only compare ciphertexts of two users, not more users such as three users. Hence [9,14] do not support the group granularity authorization. To resist IA, [24] extended the traditional single server to dual-server setting and proposed dual-server setting IBEET schemes. Under this setting, two servers need to work together to check whether two ciphertexts contain the same message. In other words, neither of them can independently run the test algorithm. Hence two servers cannot launch IA successfully if they do not collude. However, two servers setting generally is more time-consuming and complicated in communication compared with single server setting. [25] gave a better solution to resist IA. In the generation of their ciphertexts, a group user should embed a group token, which is secret information, shared by all group users, so that the insider cannot generate ciphertexts of group users without the knowledge of group token. But [25] does not has the authorization mechanism or group mechanism, and their scheme only achieves Weak-IND-ID-CCA.

Resistance Against IA/IKGA. To resist IA, [11,15,19,24] proposed dual-server setting PKEET or IBEET schemes, respectively. And then [25] gave a better solution to resist the attack (see above). To against IKGA, [1,2,21] used the dual-server setting, and [6] proposed the idea that the generation of trapdoor should take input sender's secret key. However, their schemes do not support the functionality of equality test.

1.2 Our Contributions

The contributions of this paper are as follows.

1. We propose a new primitive, namely G-IBEET, which is the first time to introduce group mechanism into IBEET. By the group mechanism, G-IBEET supports group granularity authorization. Moreover, the workload of generation and management of trapdoors can be greatly reduced due to the group granularity authorization.
2. For the insider attack, G-IBEET provides a nice solution for IBEET to resist it by the group mechanism.
3. We define G-IBEET security models and propose a concrete construction in bilinear pairings. We prove its security in the random oracle model and show that the proposed scheme has a more efficient test algorithm.

1.3 Paper Organization

In the next section we give preliminaries. Then we give the definition and security model of G-IBEET in Sect. 3 and its construction in Sect. 4. In Sect. 5, we give the security analysis of G-IBEET. Finally, we conclude this paper in Sect. 6.

2 Preliminaries

Bilinear Map. Let $\mathbb{G}_1 = \langle g_1 \rangle$, $\mathbb{G}_2 = \langle g_2 \rangle$ and $\mathbb{G}_T$ be cyclic groups of prime order p. A bilinear map $e : \mathbb{G}_1 \times \mathbb{G}_2 \to \mathbb{G}_T$ satisfies the following properties:

1. Bilinear: For any $g_1 \in \mathbb{G}_1$, $g_2 \in \mathbb{G}_2$ and $a, b \in \mathbb{Z}_p^*$, $e(g_1^a, g_2^b) = e(g_1, g_2)^{ab}$;
2. Non-degenerate: $e(g_1, g_2) \neq 1_{\mathbb{G}_T}$, where $1_{\mathbb{G}_T}$ is the generator of $\mathbb{G}_T$;
3. Computable: e is efficiently computable.

In this paper, our scheme is constructed by Type 3 (asymmetric) pairing, i.e., there exists no efficiently computable isomorphism from $\mathbb{G}_2$ to $\mathbb{G}_1$.

Bilinear Diffie-Hellman Assumption (BDH). Let $\mathbb{G} = \langle g \rangle$ and $\mathbb{G}_T$ be a cyclic group of prime order p, and let $e : \mathbb{G} \times \mathbb{G} \to \mathbb{G}_T$ be an admissible bilinear map. The BDH assumption states that given a tuple $(g, g^a, g^c, g^d) \in \mathbb{G}^4$, where $a, c, d \xleftarrow{R} \mathbb{Z}_p^*$, any *probabilistic polynomial-time* (PPT) algorithm has negligible advantage ε_{BDH} in computing $e(g, g)^{acd}$. Note that we denote by $\xleftarrow{R}$ the process of uniformly sampling a random element.

Variant Bilinear Diffie-Hellman Assumption (V-BDH). Our G-IBEET scheme uses a variant BDH assumption (V-BDH). Let $\mathbb{G}_1 = \langle g_1 \rangle$, $\mathbb{G}_2 = \langle g_2 \rangle$ and $\mathbb{G}_T$ be a cyclic group of prime order p, and let $e : \mathbb{G}_1 \times \mathbb{G}_2 \to \mathbb{G}_T$ be an admissible bilinear map. The V-BDH assumption states that given a tuple $(g_1, g_2, g_1^a, g_1^c, g_2^a, g_2^d) \in \mathbb{G}_1 \times \mathbb{G}_2 \times \mathbb{G}_1^2 \times \mathbb{G}_2^2$, where $a, c, d \xleftarrow{R} \mathbb{Z}_p^*$, any PPT algorithm has negligible advantage $\varepsilon_{\text{V-BDH}}$ in computing $e(g_1, g_2)^{acd}$. Similar to BDH $\Rightarrow$ CDH in [26], where $\Rightarrow$ denotes a polynomial Turing reduction, we also have V-BDH $\Rightarrow$ CDH. Because given oracle CDH input $(g_1, g_1^a, g_1^c) \in \mathbb{G}_1^3$ $((g_2, g_2^a, g_2^d) \in \mathbb{G}_1^3)$, and get back g_1^{ac} (g_2^{ad}), and then compute $e(g_1^{ac}, g_2^d) = e(g_1, g_2)^{acd}$ $(e(g_1^a, g_2^{ad}) = e(g_1, g_2)^{acd})$.

Decisional Diffie-Hellman Assumption (DDH). Let $\mathbb{G} = \langle g \rangle$ be a cyclic group of prime order p. The DDH assumption states that given a tuple $(g, g^a, g^b, g^r) \in \mathbb{G}^4$, where $a, b, r \xleftarrow{R} \mathbb{Z}_p^*$, any PPT algorithm has negligible advantage $\varepsilon_{\mathsf{ddh}}$ in deciding whether $g^{ab} = g^r$.

Symmetric eXternal Diffie-Hellman Assumption (SXDH). Let $\mathbb{G}_1 = \langle g_1 \rangle$ and $\mathbb{G}_2 = \langle g_2 \rangle$ and $\mathbb{G}_T$ be cyclic groups of prime order p and $e : \mathbb{G}_1 \times \mathbb{G}_2 \to \mathbb{G}_T$ be a Type 3 pairing. The SXDH assumption states that the DDH assumption holds in both groups $\mathbb{G}_1$ and $\mathbb{G}_2$.

3 Definition

3.1 Group ID-Based Encryption with Equality Test

A G-IBEET cryptosystem consists of the following algorithms (Setup, Key-Gen$_{group}$, Join, Extract, Enc, Dec, Aut, Test) operating over plaintext space $\mathcal{M}$, ciphertext space $\mathcal{C}$ and key space $\mathcal{K}$. Suppose that U_i, U_j, $\mathsf{U}_{i'}$ and $\mathsf{U}_{j'}$ are group users. We use $C_{i,j}$ to denote a G-IBEET ciphertext, where i and j refer to as a sender and a receiver, respectively.

- Setup(λ): On input a security parameter λ, this algorithm outputs a public system parameter PP and a master key msk.
- KeyGen$_{group}(PP)$: On input the public system parameter PP, this algorithm outputs a group key gsk. It is run by GA.
- Join(gsk, ID_i): On input the group key gsk and an identity ID_i, this algorithm outputs a group warrant gw_i for ID_i. It is run by GA.
- Extract(msk, ID_i): On input the master key msk and an identity ID_i, this algorithm outputs a private decryption key dk_{ID_i} for ID_i. It is run by KGC.
- Enc($PP, gw_i, \mathsf{ID}_i, \mathsf{ID}_j, M$): On input the PP, U_i's group warrant gw_i and identity ID_i, U_j's identity ID_j and a message M, this algorithm outputs a ciphertext $C_{i,j}$. *Note that the similarity between G-IBEET and IBEET is that a sender i uses the identity of receiver j to generate a ciphertext $C_{i,j}$, and $C_{i,j}$ can be only decrypted by receiver j. But their difference between them is that only group users can act as sender, not any user, which means that dishonest users cannot act as sender.*
- Dec($\mathsf{ID}_i, dk_{ID_j}, C_{i,j}$): On input U_i's identity ID_i, U_j's private decryption key dk_{ID_j} and a ciphertext $C_{i,j}$, this algorithm outputs a plaintext M.
- Aut(gsk): On input the group key gsk, this algorithm outputs a group trapdoor gtd. It is run by GA.
- Test($C_{i,j}, C_{i',j'}, gtd$): On input a ciphertext $C_{i,j}$ produced by U_i, a ciphertext $C_{i',j'}$ produced by $\mathsf{U}_{i'}$ and the group trapdoor gtd, this algorithm returns 1 if $C_{i,j}$ and $C_{i',j'}$ contain the same message and 0 otherwise.

Correctness. If a G-IBEET scheme is correct, these algorithms must satisfy the following three conditions. Note that $\forall M, M' \in \mathcal{M}$, where $M \neq M'$.

(1) If $PP \leftarrow \mathsf{Setup}(\lambda)$, $gw_i \leftarrow \mathsf{Join}(gsk, \mathsf{ID}_i)$ and $dk_{ID_j} \leftarrow \mathsf{Extract}(msk, \mathsf{ID}_j)$, then $\Pr[M \leftarrow \mathsf{Dec}(\mathsf{ID}_i, dk_{ID_j}, \mathsf{Enc}(PP, gw_i, \mathsf{ID}_i, \mathsf{ID}_j, M))] = 1$.

(2) If $PP \leftarrow \mathsf{Setup}(\lambda)$, $gw_i \leftarrow \mathsf{Join}(gsk, \mathsf{ID}_i)$, $gw_{i'} \leftarrow \mathsf{Join}(gsk, \mathsf{ID}_{i'})$, $gtd \leftarrow \mathsf{Aut}(gsk)$, $C_{i,j} \leftarrow \mathsf{Enc}(PP, gw_i, \mathsf{ID}_i, \mathsf{ID}_j, M)$ and $C_{i',j'} \leftarrow \mathsf{Enc}(PP, gw_{i'}, \mathsf{ID}_{i'}, \mathsf{ID}_{j'}, M)$, then $\Pr[\mathsf{Test}(C_{i,j}, C_{i',j'}, gtd) = 1] = 1$.

(3) If $PP \leftarrow \mathsf{Setup}(\lambda)$, $gw_i \leftarrow \mathsf{Join}(gsk, \mathsf{ID}_i)$, $gw_{i'} \leftarrow \mathsf{Join}(gsk, \mathsf{ID}_{i'})$, $gtd \leftarrow \mathsf{Aut}(gsk)$, $C_{i,j} \leftarrow \mathsf{Enc}(PP, gw_i, \mathsf{ID}_i, \mathsf{ID}_j, M)$ and $C_{i',j'} \leftarrow \mathsf{Enc}(PP, gw_{i'}, \mathsf{ID}_{i'}, \mathsf{ID}_{j'}, M')$, then $\Pr[\mathsf{Test}(C_{i,j}, C_{i',j'}, gtd) = 1]$ is negligible.

3.2 Security Models

We make the assumption that the insider plays the role of adversarial tester without having the group warrants for each group. In other words, there is no overlap between group users and the insider. We consider the following adversaries to define the security model for G-IBEET.

1. *Type-I adversary.* The attacker who has been authorized by GA, that is, the insider.
2. *Type-II adversary.* The attacker who has not been authorized by GA, including group user other than sender and receiver.

Weak Indistinguishability Under Chosen Ciphertext Attack Against a Non-adaptive Chosen Identity (W-IND-ID-CCA). Assume that $\mathcal{A}_1$ is the type-I adversary. We define W-IND-ID-CCA against the adversary for G-IBEET scheme by the following game. Furthermore, in the game, the adversary can obatin group warrants of all group users, which implies that even if it can obtain them, the G-IBEET ciphertext does not reveal any information about the underlying message to it. This provides somewhat worst-case security guarantee.

1. **Setup:** The challenger runs the Setup algorithm using a security parameter λ to generate the public system parameter PP. Then it runs the KeyGen_{group} algorithm to generate a group key gsk, runs the Join algorithm n times using ID_i to generate group warrants gw_i $(1 \leq i \leq n)$ of the group users and runs the Aut algorithm to generate a group trapdoor gtd. Finally, it randomly chooses a target sender U_{i^*} and a target receiver U_{j^*} $(1 \leq i^*, j^* \leq n)$, gives i^*, j^*, PP and gtd to the adversary $\mathcal{A}_1$.
2. **Phase 1:** $\mathcal{A}_1$ is allowed to issue the following queries. The constraint is that $\langle \mathsf{ID}_{j^*} \rangle$ does not appear in the $\mathcal{O}_{DK}$ oracle.
   - $\mathcal{O}_{gw}$ query $\langle i \rangle$. The challenger returns gw_i to $\mathcal{A}_1$.
   - $\mathcal{O}_{DK}$ query $\langle \mathsf{ID}_i \rangle$. The challenger returns $dk_{ID_i} \leftarrow \mathsf{Extract}(msk, \mathsf{ID}_i)$ to $\mathcal{A}_1$.
   - $\mathcal{O}_E$ query $\langle i, \mathsf{ID}_i, \mathsf{ID}_j, M \rangle$. The challenger issues the $\mathcal{O}_{gw}$ to obtain gw_i and then returns $C_{i,j} \leftarrow \mathsf{Enc}(PP, gw_i, \mathsf{ID}_i, \mathsf{ID}_j, M)$ to $\mathcal{A}_1$.

- $\mathcal{O}_D$ query $\langle j, \mathsf{ID}_i, \mathsf{ID}_j, C_{i,j} \rangle$. The challenger issues the $\mathcal{O}_{DK}$ to obtain dk_{ID_j} and then returns $M \leftarrow \mathsf{Dec}(\mathsf{ID}_i, dk_{ID_j}, C_{i,j})$ to $\mathcal{A}_1$.

3. **Challenge:** $\mathcal{A}_1$ randomly chooses $M_0, M_1 \in \mathcal{M}$ which have not appeared in encryption queries in **Phase 1** and sends them to the challenger. The challenger randomly chooses a bit $b \in \{0, 1\}$ and sets $C^*_{i^*, j^*} \leftarrow \mathsf{Enc}(PP, gw_{i^*}, \mathsf{ID}_{i^*}, \mathsf{ID}_{j^*}, M_b)$. Finally, it sends $C^*_{i^*, j^*}$ to $\mathcal{A}_1$.

4. **Phase 2:** $\mathcal{A}_1$ is able to issue queries in the same way as in **Phase 1**. But the constraint is that neither M_0 or M_1 does not appear in the $\mathcal{O}_E$ oracle and $\langle j^*, \mathsf{ID}_{i^*}, \mathsf{ID}_{j^*}, C^*_{i^*, j^*} \rangle$ does not appear in the $\mathcal{O}_D$ oracle.

5. **Guess:** $\mathcal{A}_1$ outputs b' and wins if $b' = b$.

We define $\mathcal{A}_1$'s advantage on breaking the G-IBEET scheme as

$$\mathbf{Adv}^{\text{W-IND-ID-CCA}}_{\text{G-IBEET}, \mathcal{A}_1}(\lambda) = |\Pr[b' = b] - 1/2|.$$

Indistinguishability Under Chosen Ciphertext Attack Against a Non-adaptive Chosen Identity (IND-ID-CCA). Assume that $\mathcal{A}_2$ is the type-II adversary. We define IND-ID-CCA against the adversary for G-IBEET scheme by the following game. The adversary would obtain group warrants of all group users as well.

1. **Setup:** The challenger runs the Setup algorithm using a security parameter λ to generate the public system parameter PP. Then it runs the KeyGen_{group} algorithm to generate a group key gsk, runs the Join algorithm n times using ID_i to generate group warrants gw_i $(1 \le i \le n)$ of the group users and runs the Aut algorithm to generate a group trapdoor gtd. Finally, it randomly chooses a target sender U_{i^*} and a target receiver U_{j^*} $(1 \le i^*, j^* \le n)$, gives i^*, j^* and PP to the adversary $\mathcal{A}_2$.

2. **Phase 1:** $\mathcal{A}_2$ is allowed to issue the following queries. The constraint is that $\langle \mathsf{ID}_{j^*} \rangle$ does not appear in the $\mathcal{O}_{DK}$ oracle.
   - $\mathcal{O}_{gw}$ query $\langle i \rangle$. The challenger returns gw_i to $\mathcal{A}_2$.
   - $\mathcal{O}_{DK}$ query $\langle \mathsf{ID}_i \rangle$. The challenger returns $dk_{ID_i} \leftarrow \mathsf{Extract}(msk, \mathsf{ID}_i)$ to $\mathcal{A}_2$.
   - $\mathcal{O}_E$ query $\langle i, \mathsf{ID}_i, \mathsf{ID}_j, M \rangle$. The challenger issues the $\mathcal{O}_{gw}$ to obtain gw_i and then returns $C_{i,j} \leftarrow \mathsf{Enc}(PP, gw_i, \mathsf{ID}_i, \mathsf{ID}_j, M)$ to $\mathcal{A}_2$.
   - $\mathcal{O}_D$ query $\langle j, \mathsf{ID}_i, \mathsf{ID}_j, C_{i,j} \rangle$. The challenger issues the $\mathcal{O}_{DK}$ to obtain dk_{ID_j} and then returns $M \leftarrow \mathsf{Dec}(\mathsf{ID}_i, dk_{ID_j}, C_{i,j})$ to $\mathcal{A}_2$.

3. **Challenge:** $\mathcal{A}_2$ randomly chooses $M_0, M_1 \in \mathcal{M}$ and sends them to the challenger. The challenger randomly chooses a bit $b \in \{0, 1\}$ and sets $C^*_{i^*, j^*} \leftarrow \mathsf{Enc}(PP, gw_{i^*}, \mathsf{ID}_{i^*}, \mathsf{ID}_{j^*}, M_b)$. Finally, it sends $C^*_{i^*, j^*}$ to $\mathcal{A}_2$.

4. **Phase 2:** $\mathcal{A}_2$ is able to issue queries in the same way as in **Phase 1**. But the constraint is that $\langle j^*, \mathsf{ID}_{i^*}, \mathsf{ID}_{j^*}, C^*_{i^*, j^*} \rangle$ does not appear in the $\mathcal{O}_D$ oracle.

5. **Guess:** $\mathcal{A}_2$ outputs b' and wins if $b' = b$.

Note that due to the lack of gtd, $\mathcal{A}_2$ is allowed to choose $M_0, M_1 \in \mathcal{M}$ which have appeared in encryption queries in **Phase 1**. We define $\mathcal{A}_2$'s advantage on breaking the G-IBEET scheme as

$$\mathbf{Adv}^{\text{IND-ID-CCA}}_{\text{G-IBEET}, \mathcal{A}_2}(\lambda) = |\Pr[b' = b] - 1/2|.$$

4   Construction

Our G-IBEET scheme is described as follows:

- Setup(λ): This algorithm outputs system parameter $PP = (\mathbb{G}_1, \mathbb{G}_2, \mathbb{G}_T, p,$
  $g_1, g_2, P_{pub}, e, H_1, H_2, H_3, H_4, H_5)$ as follows.
  Generate type 3 bilinear pairing parameters: group $\mathbb{G}_1$, $\mathbb{G}_2$ and $\mathbb{G}_T$ of prime
  order p, a bilinear map $e : \mathbb{G}_1 \times \mathbb{G}_2 \to \mathbb{G}_T$, a random generator g_1 of $\mathbb{G}_1$ and
  a random generator g_2 of $\mathbb{G}_2$. Select $msk = s \xleftarrow{R} \mathbb{Z}_p^*$ and set $P_{pub} = g_1^s$. Select
  five hash functions $H_1 : \{0,1\}^* \to \mathbb{G}_1$, $H_2 : \{0,1\}^* \to \mathbb{G}_2$, $H_3 : \{0,1\}^* \to \mathbb{G}_1$,
  $H_4 : \mathbb{G}_T \to \{0,1\}^{l_1+l_2}$ and $H_5 : \{0,1\}^* \to \{0,1\}^\lambda$, where l_1 and l_2 represent
  the length of messages and $\mathbb{Z}_p$, respectively, and λ is the security parameter.
- KeyGen$_{group}(PP)$: This algorithm randomly selects $x, y \xleftarrow{R} \mathbb{Z}_p^*$ and outputs a
  group key $gsk = (x, y)$.
- Join(gsk, ID_i): This algorithm computes $h_{1,i} = H_1(\mathsf{ID}_i)$ and outputs group
  warrant $gw_i = (h_{1,i}^x, y)$ for ID_i.
- Extract(msk, ID_i): This algorithm computes $h_{2,i} = H_2(\mathsf{ID}_i)$ and ouputs a
  private decryption key $dk_{ID_i} = h_{2,i}^s$ for the identity ID_i.
- Enc$(PP, gw_i, \mathsf{ID}_i, \mathsf{ID}_j, M)$: This algorithm randomly selects $\alpha_1, \alpha_2 \xleftarrow{R} \mathbb{Z}_p^*$,
  computes $h_{1,i} = H_1(\mathsf{ID}_i)$, $h_{2,j} = H_2(\mathsf{ID}_j)$ and outputs $C_{i,j} =$
  $(C_{i,j,1}, C_{i,j,2}, C_{i,j,3}, C_{i,j,4}, C_{i,j,5})$ as follows,

$$C_{i,j,1} = h_{1,i}^{\alpha_1}, C_{i,j,2} = h_{1,i}^{x\alpha_1} \cdot H_3(M)^y,$$

$$C_{i,j,3} = g_1^{\alpha_2}, C_{i,j,4} = H_4(e(P_{pub}, h_{2,j})^{\alpha_2}) \oplus (M\|\alpha_1),$$

$$C_{i,j,5} = H_5(C_{i,j,1}\|C_{i,j,2}\|C_{i,j,3}\|C_{i,j,4}\|M\|\alpha_1).$$

- Dec$(\mathsf{ID}_i, dk_{ID_j}, C_{i,j})$: This algorithm computes $h_{1,i} = H_1(\mathsf{ID}_i)$ and $(M\|\alpha_1) =$
  $C_{i,j,4} \oplus H_4(e(C_{i,j,3}, h_{2,j}^s))$. If

$$C_{i,j,1} = h_{1,i}^{\alpha_1}, C_{i,j,5} = H_5(C_{i,j,1}\|C_{i,j,2}\|C_{i,j,3}\|C_{i,j,4}\|M\|\alpha_1),$$

  return M; otherwise, return $\perp$.
- Aut(gsk): This algorithm randomly selects $\beta \xleftarrow{R} \mathbb{Z}_p^*$, and outputs a gtd,

$$gtd = (gtd_1, gtd_2) = (g_2^\beta, g_2^{x\beta}).$$

- Test$(C_{i,j}, C_{i',j'}, gtd)$: This algorithm outputs 1 if

$$e(\frac{C_{i,j,2}}{C_{i',j',2}}, gtd_1) = e(\frac{C_{i,j,1}}{C_{i',j',1}}, gtd_2),$$

otherwise returns 0.

Correctness. The G-IBEET scheme above satisfies the correctness.

(1) It is straightforward to be verified.

(2) For $M \in \mathcal{M}$, we have

$$e(\frac{C_{i,j,2}}{C_{i',j',2}}, gtd_1) = e(\frac{h_{1,i}^{x\alpha_1} \cdot H_3(M)^y}{h_{1,i'}^{x\alpha_1'} \cdot H_3(M)^y}, g_2^\beta) = e(\frac{h_{1,i}^{\alpha_1}}{h_{1,i'}^{\alpha_1'}}, g_2^{x\beta}) = e(\frac{C_{i,j,1}}{C_{i',j',1}}, gtd_2).$$

(3) For $\forall M, M' \in \mathcal{M}$ and $M \neq M'$, we have

$$e(\frac{C_{i,j,2}}{C_{i',j',2}}, gtd_1) \neq e(\frac{C_{i,j,1}}{C_{i',j',1}}, gtd_2).$$

5   Security Analysis

Theorem 1: G-IBEET scheme is W-IND-ID-CCA secure against type-I adversary in the random oracle model assuming both V-BDH and SXDH are intractable.

Proof. Let $\mathcal{A}_1$ be a PPT adversary attacking the W-IND-ID-CCA security of G-IBEET scheme. Suppose that $\mathcal{A}_1$ makes at most q_{H_1} H_1 hash queries, q_{H_2} H_2 hash queries, q_{H_3} H_3 hash queries, q_{H_4} H_4 hash queries, q_{H_5} H_5 hash queries, q_{gw} group warrant queries, q_{DK} decryption key queries, q_E encryption queries and q_D decryption queries. Let $\mathbf{Adv}_{\text{G-IBEET},\mathcal{A}_1}^{\text{W-IND-ID-CCA}}(\lambda)$ denotes the advantage of $\mathcal{A}_1$ in the W-IND-ID-CCA experiment. The analysis is done by a sequence of games.
Game 1.0. We consider the original game.

1. **Setup:** The challenger runs the Setup algorithm using a security parameter λ to generate the public system parameter PP. Then it runs the KeyGen$_{group}$ algorithm to generate a group key gsk and Aut algorithm to generate a group trapdoor gtd, respectively. It runs the Join algorithm using ID_i to generate group warrants gw_i respectively, as follows:
   (1) The challenger queries $\mathcal{O}_{H_1}$ (see below) on ID_i to obtain $h_{1,i}$;
   (2) Set $gw_i = (h_{1,i}^x, y)$. Add $(i, (h_{1,i}^x, y))$ into the W^{list}, which is initially empty.
   Finally, it chooses a target sender U_{i^*} and a target receiver U_{j^*}, gives i^*, j^*, PP and gtd to the adversary $\mathcal{A}_1$ and keeps msk and gsk by itself.
2. **Phase 1:** $\mathcal{A}_1$ is allowed to issue the following queries. The constraint is that $\langle \text{ID}_{j^*} \rangle$ does not appear in the $\mathcal{O}_{DK}$ oracle.
   - $\mathcal{O}_{H_1}$ query $\langle \text{ID}_i \rangle$. The challenger picks a random number $u_{i^*} \in \mathbb{Z}_q^*$, computes $h_{1,i^*} = g_1^{u_{i^*}} \in \mathbb{G}_1^*$ and adds the tuple $\langle \text{ID}_{i^*}, u_{i^*}, h_{1,i^*} \rangle$ to the H_1^{list}. It responds as follows:
     (1) If the query ID_i already appears on the H_1^{list} in a tuple $\langle \text{ID}_i, u_i, h_{1,i} \rangle$, the challenger responds with $h_{1,i} \in \mathbb{G}_1^*$.
     (2) Otherwise, the challenger picks a random number $u_i \in \mathbb{Z}_q^*$ and computes $h_{1,i} = g_1^{u_i} \in \mathbb{G}_1^*$. It adds the tuple $\langle \text{ID}_i, u_i, h_{1,i} \rangle$ to the H_1^{list}, which is initially empty, and responds to $\mathcal{A}_1$ with $H_1(\text{ID}_i) = h_{1,i}$.
   - $\mathcal{O}_{H_2}$ query $\langle \text{ID}_i \rangle$. The challenger picks a random number $v_{j^*} \in \mathbb{Z}_q^*$, computes $h_{2,j^*} = g_2^{v_{j^*}} \in \mathbb{G}_2^*$ and responds as follows:

(1) If the query ID_i already appears on the H_2^{list} in a tuple $\langle ID_i, v_i, h_{2,i} \rangle$, the challenger responds with $h_{2,i} \in \mathbb{G}_2^*$.

(2) Otherwise, it picks a random number $v_i \in \mathbb{Z}_q^*$ and computes $h_{2,i} = g_2^{v_i} \in \mathbb{G}_2^*$. The challenger adds the tuple $\langle ID_i, v_i, h_{2,i} \rangle$ to the H_2^{list}, which is initially empty, and responds to $\mathcal{A}_1$ with $H_2(ID_i) = h_{2,i}$.

- $\mathcal{O}_{H_3}$ query $\langle v_1 \rangle$. On input the tuple $v_1 \in \{0,1\}^*$, a compatible random value h_3 from $\mathbb{G}_1^*$ is returned, where by compatible we mean that if the same input is asked multiple times, the same answer will be returned. The challenger adds (v_1, h_3) into the H_3^{list}, which is initially empty.

- $\mathcal{O}_{H_4}$ query $\langle v_1 \rangle$. On input the tuple $v_1 \in \mathbb{G}_T^*$, a compatible random value h_4 from the set $\{0,1\}^{l_1+l_2}$ is returned. The challenger adds (v_1, h_4) into the H_4^{list}, which is initially empty.

- $\mathcal{O}_{H_5}$ query $\langle v_1 \rangle$. On input the tuple $v_1 \in \{0,1\}^*$, a compatible random value h_5 from the set $\{0,1\}^\lambda$ is returned. The challenger adds (v_1, h_5) into the H_5^{list}, which is initially empty.

- $\mathcal{O}_{gw}$ query $\langle i \rangle$. The challenger searches the W^{list} for i and responds $\mathcal{A}_1$ with $gw_i = (h_{1,i}^x, y)$.

- $\mathcal{O}_{DK}$ query $\langle ID_i \rangle$. The challenger responds as follows:
  (1) The challenger queries $\mathcal{O}_{H_2}$ on ID_i to obtain $h_{2,i}$. Let $\langle ID_i, v_i, h_{2,i} \rangle$ be the corresponding tuple in the H_2^{list}.
  (2) The challenger responds $\mathcal{A}_1$ with $dk_{ID_i} = g_2^{v_i s}$ by running Extract algorithm on $\langle ID_i \rangle$.

- $\mathcal{O}_E$ query $\langle i, ID_i, ID_j, M \rangle$. The challenger issues the $\mathcal{O}_{gw}$ to obtain gw_i and then returns $C_{i,j} \leftarrow \mathsf{Enc}(PP, gw_i, ID_i, ID_j, M)$ to $\mathcal{A}_1$.

- $\mathcal{O}_D$ query $\langle j, ID_i, ID_j, C_{i,j} \rangle$. The challenger issues the $\mathcal{O}_{DK}$ to obtain dk_{ID_j} and then returns $M \leftarrow \mathsf{Dec}(ID_i, dk_{ID_j}, C_{i,j})$ to $\mathcal{A}_1$.

3. **Challenge:** $\mathcal{A}_1$ randomly chooses $M_0, M_1 \in \mathcal{M}$ which have not appeared in encryption queries in **Phase 1** and sends them to the challenger. The challenger randomly chooses a bit $b \in \{0,1\}$ and $\alpha_1, \alpha_2 \xleftarrow{R} \mathbb{Z}_p^*$, queries $\mathcal{O}_{H_1}$ on ID_{i^*} to obtain h_{1,i^*}, queries $\mathcal{O}_{H_2}$ on ID_{j^*} to obtain h_{2,j^*} and sets C_{i^*,j^*}^* as follows.

$$C_{i^*,j^*,1} = h_{1,i^*}^{\alpha_1}, C_{i^*,j^*,2} = h_{1,i^*}^{x\alpha_1} \cdot H_3(M_b)^y,$$

$$C_{i^*,j^*,3} = g_1^{\alpha_2}, C_{i^*,j^*,4} = H_4(e(P_{pub}, h_{2,j^*})^{\alpha_2}) \oplus (M_b \| \alpha_1),$$

$$C_{i^*,j^*,5} = H_5(C_{i^*,j^*,1} \| C_{i^*,j^*,2} \| C_{i^*,j^*,3} \| C_{i^*,j^*,4} \| M_b \| \alpha_1).$$

Finally, it sends $C_{i^*,j^*}^* = (C_{i^*,j^*,1}, C_{i^*,j^*,2}, C_{i^*,j^*,3}, C_{i^*,j^*,4}, C_{i^*,j^*,5})$ to $\mathcal{A}_1$.

4. **Phase 2:** $\mathcal{A}_1$ is able to issue queries in the same way as in **Phase 1**. But the constraint is that neither M_0 or M_1 does not appear in the $\mathcal{O}_E$ oracle and $\langle j^*, ID_{i^*}, ID_{j^*}, C_{i^*,j^*}^* \rangle$ does not appear in the $\mathcal{O}_D$ oracle.

5. **Guess:** $\mathcal{A}_1$ outputs b' and wins if $b' = b$.

Let $\mathbf{S}_{1.0}$ be the event that $M' = M$ in Game 1.0. We have

$$\mathbf{Adv}_{\text{G-IBEET},\mathcal{A}_1}^{\text{W-IND-ID-CCA}}(q_{H_1}, q_{H_2}, q_{H_3}, q_{H_4}, q_{H_5}, q_{gw}, q_{DK}, q_E, q_D) = |\Pr[\mathbf{S}_{1.0}] - 1/2| \quad (1)$$

Game 1.1. In this game, the challenger performs identically to that in Game 1.0 except that the followings.

- $\mathcal{O}_E$ query $\langle i, \mathsf{ID}_i, \mathsf{ID}_j, M \rangle$. Same as that in Game 1.0, except that the challenger randomly selects $\alpha_1, \alpha_2 \xleftarrow{R} \mathbb{Z}_p^*$, queries $\mathcal{O}_{H_1}$ on ID_i to obtain $h_{1,i}$, queries $\mathcal{O}_{H_2}$ on ID_j to obtain $h_{2,j}$, queries $\mathcal{O}_{H_3}$ on M to obtain h_3 and queries $\mathcal{O}_{H_4}$ on $e(P_{pub}, h_{2,j})^{\alpha_2}$ to obtain h_4. Then it computes as follows:

$$C_{i,j,1} = h_{1,i}^{\alpha_1}, C_{i,j,2} = h_{1,i}^{x\alpha_1} \cdot h_3^y, C_{i,j,3} = g_1^{\alpha_2}, C_{i,j,4} = h_4 \oplus (M \| \alpha_1).$$

Finally, it queries $\mathcal{O}_{H_5}$ on $(C_{i,j,1} \| C_{i,j,2} \| C_{i,j,3} \| C_{i,j,4} \| M \| \alpha_1)$ to obtain h_5, sets $C_{i,j,5} = h_5$ and returns $C_{i,j} = (C_{i,j,1}, C_{i,j,2}, C_{i,j,3}, C_{i,j,4}, C_{i,j,5})$ to $\mathcal{A}_1$.

- $\mathcal{O}_D$ query $\langle j, \mathsf{ID}_i, \mathsf{ID}_j, C_{i,j} \rangle$. Same as that in Game 1.0, except that the challenger computes $(M \| \alpha_1) = C_{i,j,4} \oplus H_4(e(C_{i,j,3}, dk_{\mathsf{ID}_j}))$ and queries $\mathcal{O}_{H_1}$ on ID_i to obtain $h_{1,i}$, and verifies $C_{i,j,1} = h_{1,i}^{\alpha_1}$. If the verification fails, return $\perp$. Then the challenger checks whether there exists a tuple $(C_{i,j,1} \| C_{i,j,2} \| C_{i,j,3} \| C_{i,j,4} \| M \| \alpha_1, h_5)$ in the H_5^{list} that satisfies $C_{i,j,5} = h_5$. If so, return M; otherwise return $\perp$. Denoted by $\mathbf{E}_1$ event that in some $C_{i,j}$, a fresh input $(C_{i,j,1} \| C_{i,j,2} \| C_{i,j,3} \| C_{i,j,4} \| M \| \alpha_1)$ to H_5 results in $C_{i,j,5}$.

Let $\mathbf{S}_{1.1}$ be the event that $M' = M$ in Game 1.1. We have

$$|\mathrm{Pr}[\mathbf{S}_{1.1}] - \mathrm{Pr}[\mathbf{S}_{1.0}]| \leq \mathrm{Pr}[\mathbf{E}_1]. \tag{2}$$

Game 1.2. In this game, the challenger performs identically to that in Game 1.1 except that it randomly chooses $W_{2.1}^* \leftarrow \{0,1\}^{l_1+l_2}$ and sets C_{i^*,j^*}^* as follows.

$$C_{i^*,j^*,1} = h_{1,i^*}^{\alpha_1}, C_{i^*,j^*,2} = h_{1,i^*}^{x\alpha_1} \cdot H_3(M_b)^y, C_{i^*,j^*,3} = g_1^{\alpha_2}, C_{i^*,j^*,4} = W_{2.1}^* \oplus (M_b \| \alpha_1),$$

$$C_{i^*,j^*,5} = H_5(C_{i^*,j^*,1} \| C_{i^*,j^*,2} \| C_{i^*,j^*,3} \| C_{i^*,j^*,4} \| M_b \| \alpha_1).$$

Finally, it adds $(e(P_{pub}, h_{2,j^*})^{\alpha_2}, W_{2.1}^*)$ into the H_4^{list}.

Let $\mathbf{S}_{1.2}$ be the event that $M' = M$ in Game 1.2. Since the idealness of the random oracle, Game 1.2 is identical to Game 1.1. We have

$$\mathrm{Pr}[\mathbf{S}_{1.2}] = \mathrm{Pr}[\mathbf{S}_{1.1}]. \tag{3}$$

Game 1.3. In this game, the challenger performs identically to that in Game 1.2 except that the followings.

- $\mathcal{O}_{H_4}$ query $\langle v_1 \rangle$. Same as that in Game 1.2, except that if $\mathcal{A}_1$ asks $e(P_{pub}, h_{2,j^*})^{\alpha_2}$, the game is aborted. We denote the event by $\mathbf{E}_2$.
- $\mathcal{O}_D$ query $\langle j, \mathsf{ID}_i, \mathsf{ID}_j, C_{i,j} \rangle$. Same as that in Game 1.2, except that if $\mathcal{A}_1$ asks for decryption of $C_{i^*,j^*}^* = (C_{i^*,j^*,1}, C_{i^*,j^*,2}, C_{i^*,j^*,3}, C_{i^*,j^*,4}', C_{i^*,j^*,5})$ after obtaining the challenge ciphertext C_{i^*,j^*}^* (see below), where $C_{i^*,j^*,4}' \neq C_{i^*,j^*,4}$, $\perp$ is returned.

The challenger randomly chooses $W_{3.1}^* \leftarrow \{0,1\}^{l_1+l_2}$ and sets C_{i^*,j^*}^* as follows.

$$C_{i^*,j^*,1} = h_{1,i^*}^{\alpha_1}, C_{i^*,j^*,2} = h_{1,i^*}^{x\alpha_1} \cdot H_3(M_b)^y, C_{i^*,j^*,3} = g_1^{\alpha_2}, C_{i^*,j^*,4} = W_{3.1}^*,$$

$$C_{i^*,j^*,5} = H_5(C_{i^*,j^*,1} \| C_{i^*,j^*,2} \| C_{i^*,j^*,3} \| C_{i^*,j^*,4} \| M_b \| \alpha_1).$$

Finally, it adds $(e(P_{pub}, h_{2,j^*})^{\alpha_2}, W_{3.1}^* \oplus (M_b||\alpha_1))$ into the H_4^{list}.

Let $\mathbf{S}_{1.3}$ be the event that $M' = M$ in Game 1.3. Since $C_{i^*,j^*,4}$ is a random value in both Game 1.3 and Game 1.2, the challenge ciphertext generated in Game 1.3 is identically distributed to that in Game 1.2. Hence if event $\mathbf{E}_2$ does not occur, Game 1.3 is identical to Game 1.2. We have

$$|\Pr[\mathbf{S}_{1.3}] - \Pr[\mathbf{S}_{1.2}]| \leq \Pr[\mathbf{E}_2]. \tag{4}$$

Next, we show that the event $\mathbf{E}_2$ occurs with negligible probability.

Lemma 1: Event $\mathbf{E}_2$ happens in Game 1.3 with negligible probability if V-BDH is intractable.

$$\Pr[\mathbf{E}_2] \leq \mathbf{Adv}^{\text{V-BDH}} + \frac{q_D}{2^{l_1+l_2}}. \tag{5}$$

where $\mathbf{Adv}^{\text{V-BDH}}$ is the maximal advantage of a PPT adversary $\mathcal{B}_1$ in breaking the V-BDH assumption.

Proof. Suppose that $\Pr[\mathbf{E}_2]$ is non-negligible. We construct a PPT algorithm $\mathcal{B}_2$ to break the V-BDH problem. Given a tuple $(g_1', g_2', g_1'^a, g_1'^c, g_2'^a, g_2'^d) \in \mathbb{G}_1^* \times \mathbb{G}_2^* \times (\mathbb{G}_1^*)^2 \times (\mathbb{G}_2^*)^2$. $\mathcal{B}_2$ generates $PP' = (\mathbb{G}_1, \mathbb{G}_2, \mathbb{G}_T, p, g_1, g_2, e, H_1, H_2, H_3, H_4, H_5)$: Generate type 3 bilinear pairing parameters: group $\mathbb{G}_1$, $\mathbb{G}_2$ and $\mathbb{G}_T$ of prime order p, a bilinear map $e : \mathbb{G}_1 \times \mathbb{G}_2 \to \mathbb{G}_T$, a random generator g_1 of $\mathbb{G}_1$ and a random generator g_2 of $\mathbb{G}_2$. Select five functions $H_1 : \{0,1\}^* \to \mathbb{G}_1$, $H_2 : \{0,1\}^* \to \mathbb{G}_2$, $H_3 : \{0,1\}^* \to \mathbb{G}_1$, $H_4 : \mathbb{G}_T \to \{0,1\}^{l_1+l_2}$ and $H_5 : \{0,1\}^* \to \{0,1\}^\lambda$, where l_1 and l_2 represent the length of messages and the length of $\mathbb{Z}_p$, respectively.

It sets $P_{pub1} = g_1'^a$, $P_{pub2} = g_2'^a$ and adds $\langle \mathsf{ID}_{j^*}, \top, g_2'^d \rangle$ to H_2^{list}, where $\top$ means that the value is unknown yet. This implicitly sets $msk = a$ and $h_{1,j^*} = g_2'^d$. Note that the P_{pub2} is used to answer the oracle $\mathcal{O}_{DK}$ here, but it is unnecessary for the challenger in the above games because the challenger has the master key $msk = a$ and can generate the decryption keys without P_{pub2}. $\mathcal{B}_2$ performs identically to that in Game 1.3 except that the followings. The generation of challenge ciphertext $C_{i^*,j^*}^* = (C_{i^*,j^*,1}, C_{i^*,j^*,2}, C_{i^*,j^*,3}, C_{i^*,j^*,4}, C_{i^*,j^*,5})$ for M is defined as follows:

$$C_{i^*,j^*,1} = h_{1,i^*}^{\alpha_1}, C_{i^*,j^*,2} = h_{1,i^*}^{x\alpha_1} \cdot H_3(M_b)^y, C_{i^*,j^*,3} = g_1'^c, C_{i^*,j^*,4} = W_{3.1}^*,$$

$$C_{i^*,j^*,5} = H_5(C_{i^*,j^*,1}||C_{i^*,j^*,2}||C_{i^*,j^*,3}||C_{i^*,j^*,4}||M_b||\alpha_1).$$

It adds the $(\top, W_{3.1}^* \oplus (M_b||\alpha_1))$ into the H_4^{list}. The following oracles are simulated as follows.

- $\mathcal{O}_{DK}$ query $\langle \mathsf{ID}_i \rangle$. Same as that in Game 1.3, except that the challenger responds $\mathcal{A}_1$ with $dk_{ID_i} = P_{pub2}^{v_i}$ by running Extract algorithm on $\langle \mathsf{ID}_i \rangle$.
- $\mathcal{O}_E$ query $\langle i, \mathsf{ID}_i, \mathsf{ID}_j, M \rangle$. Same as that in Game 1.3, except that the challenger queries $\mathcal{O}_{H_4}$ on $e(P_{pub1}, h_{2,j})^{\alpha_2}$ to obtain h_4.

– $\mathcal{O}_D$ query $\langle j, \mathsf{ID}_i, \mathsf{ID}_j, C_{i,j} \rangle$. Same as that in Game 1.3, except that if $\mathcal{A}_1$ asks for the decryption of $C^*_{i^*,j^*} = (C_{i^*,j^*,1}, C_{i^*,j^*,2}, C_{i^*,j^*,3}, C'_{i^*,j^*,4}, C_{i^*,j^*,5})$ after obtaining $C^*_{i^*,j^*}$, where $C'_{i^*,j^*,4} \neq C_{i^*,j^*,4}$, $\perp$ is returned. Otherwise, $\mathcal{B}_1$ searches H_4^{list} to get h_4. For each tuple (v_1, h_4), $\mathcal{B}_1$ computes $(M \| \alpha_1) = C_{i,j,4} \oplus h_4$ and checks if $C_{i,j,1} = h_{1,i}^{\alpha_1}$ and $C_{i,j,5} = H_5(C_{i,j,1} \| C_{i,j,2} \| C_{i,j,3} \| C_{i,j,4} \| M \| \alpha_1)$. If so, $\mathcal{B}_1$ returns M; otherwise, $\perp$ is returned.

Denote $\mathbf{E}'_2$ the event that $\mathcal{A}_1$ asks $\mathcal{O}_{H_4}$ for $e(P_{pub1}, h_{2,j^*})^{\alpha_2}$. If $\mathbf{E}'_2$ does not occur, $\mathcal{B}_1$ aborts with failure. Next we prove that Game 1.3 and the simulation above are indistinguishable. We only focus on the simulation of $\mathcal{O}_D$. We distinguish the following two cases.

(1) $e(g'_1, g'_2)^{acd}$ has been queried to $\mathcal{O}_{H_4}$ before a decryption query $(C_{i,j,1}, C_{i,j,2}, C_{i,j,3}, C_{i,j,4}, C_{i,j,5})$ is issued. In this case, $C_{i,j,4}$ is uniquely determined after $e(g'_1, g'_2)^{acd}$ is queried to $\mathcal{O}_{H_4}$. Therefore, $\mathcal{O}_{Dec}$ is simulated perfectly.

(2) $e(g'_1, g'_2)^{acd}$ has never been queried to $\mathcal{O}_{H_4}$ before a decryption query $(C_{i,j,1}, C_{i,j,2}, C_{i,j,3}, C_{i,j,4}, C_{i,j,5})$ is issued. In this case, $\perp$ is returned by the $\mathcal{O}_D$. The simulation fails if $(C_{i,j,1}, C_{i,j,2}, C_{i,j,3}, C_{i,j,4}, C_{i,j,5})$ is a valid ciphertext. However, due to the idealness of the random oracle, it occurs with probability at most $1/2^{l_1+l_2}$.

Denote by $\mathbf{D}$ the event that a valid ciphertext is rejected in the simulation, and then we have $\Pr[\mathbf{D}] \leq 1/2^{l_1+l_2}$. If $\mathbf{D}$ does not occur, the simulation is identical to Game 1.3. Thus, $\Pr[\mathbf{E}'_2 | \neg \mathbf{D}] = \Pr[\mathbf{E}_2]$. We have

$$\Pr[\mathbf{E}'_2] = \Pr[\mathbf{E}'_2 | \mathbf{D}]\Pr[\mathbf{D}] + \Pr[\mathbf{E}'_2 | \neg \mathbf{D}]\Pr[\neg \mathbf{D}] \geq \Pr[\mathbf{E}'_2 | \neg \mathbf{D}]\Pr[\neg \mathbf{D}]$$
$$= \Pr[\mathbf{E}'_2 | \neg \mathbf{D}](1 - \Pr[\mathbf{D}]) \geq \Pr[\mathbf{E}'_2 | \neg \mathbf{D}] - \Pr[\mathbf{D}]$$

Therefore, we have $\Pr[\mathbf{E}'_2] = \mathbf{Adv}^{\text{V-BDH}} \geq \Pr[\mathbf{E}_2] - q_D/2^{l_1+l_2}$. If $\Pr[\mathbf{E}_2]$ is non-negligible, the probability of breaking the V-BDH problem is non-negligible as well. The proof of Lemma 1 is completed.

Game 1.4. In this game, the challenger performs identically to that in Game 1.3 except that the followings.

– $\mathcal{O}_{H_5}$ query $\langle v_1 \rangle$. Same as that in Game 1.3, except that if $\mathcal{A}_1$ asks $(C_{i^*,j^*,1} \| C_{i^*,j^*,2} \| C_{i^*,j^*,3} \| C_{i^*,j^*,4} \| M_b \| \alpha_1)$, the game is aborted. We denote the event by $\mathbf{E}_3$.
– $\mathcal{O}_D$ query $\langle j, \mathsf{ID}_i, \mathsf{ID}_j, C_{i,j} \rangle$. Same as that in Game 1.3, except that if $\mathcal{A}_1$ asks for decryption of $C^*_{i^*,j^*} = (C_{i^*,j^*,1}, C_{i^*,j^*,2}, C_{i^*,j^*,3}, C'_{i^*,j^*,4}, C'_{i^*,j^*,5})$ after obtaining the challenge ciphertext $C^*_{i^*,j^*}$ (see below), where $C'_{i^*,j^*,4} \neq C_{i^*,j^*,4}$ and $C'_{i^*,j^*,5} \neq C_{i^*,j^*,5}$, $\perp$ is returned.

The challenger randomly chooses $W^*_{4.1} \leftarrow \{0,1\}^{l_1+l_2}$ and $W^*_{4.2} \leftarrow \{0,1\}^{\lambda}$ and sets $C^*_{i^*,j^*}$ as follows.

$$C_{i^*,j^*,1} = h_{1,i^*}^{\alpha_1}, C_{i^*,j^*,2} = h_{1,i^*}^{x\alpha_1} \cdot H_3(M_b)^y, C_{i^*,j^*,3} = g_1^{\alpha_2}, C_{i^*,j^*,4} = W^*_{4.1},$$

$$C_{i^*,j^*,5} = W_{4.2}^*.$$

Finally, it adds $(e(P_{pub}, h_{2,j^*})^{\alpha_2}, W_{4.1}^* \oplus (M_b||\alpha_1))$ and $(C_{i^*,j^*,1}||C_{i^*,j^*,2}|| C_{i^*,j^*,3}||C_{i^*,j^*,4}||M_b||\alpha_1, W_{4.2}^*)$ into the H_4^{list} and H_5^{list}, respectively.

Let $\mathbf{S}_{1.4}$ be the event that $b' = b$ in Game 1.4. Since the idealness of the random oracle, $\Pr[\mathbf{E}_3]$ is negligible. If event $\mathbf{E}_3$ does not occur, Game 1.4 is identical to Game 1.3. We have

$$|\Pr[\mathbf{S}_{1.4}] - \Pr[\mathbf{S}_{1.3}]| \leq \Pr[\mathbf{E}_3]. \tag{6}$$

Game 1.5. In this game, the challenger performs identically to that in Game 1.4 except that the following.

- $\mathcal{O}_E$ query $\langle i, \mathsf{ID}_i, \mathsf{ID}_j, M\rangle$. Same as that in Game 1.4, except that if α_1 which equals to the random vale in the challenge step is chosen for answering encryption queries, the game is aborted. We denote the event by $\mathbf{E}_4$.

Let $\mathbf{S}_{1.5}$ be the event that $b' = b$ in Game 1.5. It is straightforward to know that $\Pr[\mathbf{E}_4]$ is negligible. If event E_4 does not occur, Game 1.5 is identical to Game 1.4. We have

$$|\Pr[\mathbf{S}_{1.5}] - \Pr[\mathbf{S}_{1.4}]| \leq \Pr[\mathbf{E}_4]. \tag{7}$$

Game 1.6. In this game, the challenger performs identically to that in Game 1.5, except that it randomly chooses $W_{6.1}^* \leftarrow \{0,1\}^{l_1+l_2}$, $W_{6.2}^* \leftarrow \{0,1\}^{\lambda}$ and $W_{6.3}^* \leftarrow \mathbb{G}_1^*$ and then sets C_{i^*,j^*}^* as follows.

$$C_{i^*,j^*,1} = h_{1,i^*}^{\alpha_1}, C_{i^*,j^*,2} = W_{6.3}^* \cdot H_3(M_b)^y, C_{i^*,j^*,3} = g_1^{\alpha_2}, C_{i^*,j^*,4} = W_{6.1}^*,$$

$$C_{i^*,j^*,5} = W_{6.2}^*.$$

Finally, it adds $(e(P_{pub}, h_{2,j^*})^{\alpha_2}, W_{6.1}^* \oplus (M_b||\alpha_1))$ and $(C_{i^*,j^*,1}||C_{i^*,j^*,2}|| C_{i^*,j^*,3}||C_{i^*,j^*,4}||M_b||\alpha_1, W_{6.2}^*)$ into the H_4^{list} and H_5^{list}, respectively.

Let $\mathbf{S}_{1.6}$ be the event that $b' = b$ in Game 1.6. If the adversary $\mathcal{A}_1$ cannot distinguish $h_{1,i}^{x,\alpha_1}$ ($\mathcal{A}_1$ can obtain $h_{1,i^*}^{\alpha_1} = C_{i^*,j^*,1}$ and $gw_i = h_{1,i^*}^x$) from the random value $W_{6.3}^*$ in $C_{i^*,j^*,2}$, Game 1.6 is identical to Game 1.5. We have

$$|\Pr[\mathbf{S}_{1.6}] - \Pr[\mathbf{S}_{1.5}]| \leq \mathbf{Adv}^{\mathsf{SXDH}}. \tag{8}$$

Game 1.7. In this game, the challenger performs identically to that in Game 1.6 except that it randomly chooses $W_{7.1}^* \leftarrow \{0,1\}^{l_1+l_2}$, $W_{7.2}^* \leftarrow \{0,1\}^{\lambda}$ and $W_{7.3}^* \leftarrow \mathbb{G}_1^*$, and then sets C_{i^*,j^*}^* as follows.

$$C_{i^*,j^*,1} = h_{1,i^*}^{\alpha_1}, C_{i^*,j^*,2} = W_{7.3}^*, C_{i^*,j^*,3} = g_1^{\alpha_2}, C_{i^*,j^*,4} = W_{7.1}^*,$$

$$C_{i^*,j^*,5} = W_{7.2}^*.$$

It adds $(M_b, (W_{7.3}^*/h_{1,i^*}^{x\alpha_1})^{-y})$, $(e(P_{pub}, h_{2,j^*})^{\alpha_2}, W_{7.1}^* \oplus (M_b||\alpha_1))$ and $(C_{i^*,j^*,1}|| C_{i^*,j^*,2}||C_{i^*,j^*,3}||C_{i^*,j^*,4}||M_b||\alpha_1, W_{7.2}^*)$ into the H_3^{list}, H_4^{list} and H_5^{list}, respectively.

Let $\mathbf{S}_{1.7}$ be the event that $b' = b$ in Game 1.7. It is straightforward to know that Game 1.7 is identical to Game 1.6. We have

$$\Pr[\mathbf{S}_{1.7}] = \Pr[\mathbf{S}_{1.6}]. \tag{9}$$

Finally, it is evident that all the five components in the challenge ciphertext of Game 1.7 are independent of the M_b, so $\mathcal{A}_1$ is able to make a correct guess $b' = b$ in Game 1.7 with probability at most $1/2$. That is,

$$\Pr[\mathbf{S}_{1.7}] = 1/2. \tag{10}$$

Combining (1)–(10), we have that

$$\mathbf{Adv}_{\text{G-IBEET},\mathcal{A}_1}^{\text{W-IND-ID-CCA}}(q_{H_1}, q_{H_2}, q_{H_3}, q_{H_4}, q_{H_5}, q_{gw}, q_{DK}, q_E, q_D)$$

$$\leq \Pr[\mathbf{E}_1] + \Pr[\mathbf{E}_3] + \Pr[\mathbf{E}_4] + \mathbf{Adv}^{\text{SXDH}} + \mathbf{Adv}^{\text{V-BDH}} + \frac{q_D}{2^{l_1+l_2}}.$$

Since $\Pr[\mathbf{E}_1]$, $\Pr[\mathbf{E}_3]$, $\Pr[\mathbf{E}_4]$, $\mathbf{Adv}^{\text{SXDH}}$, $\mathbf{Adv}^{\text{V-BDH}}$ and $q_D/2^{l_1+l_2}$ are negligible, we also have $\mathbf{Adv}_{\text{G-IBEET},\mathcal{A}_1}^{\text{W-IND-ID-CCA}}(q_{H_1}, q_{H_2}, q_{H_3}, q_{H_4}, q_{H_5}, q_{gw}, q_{DK}, q_E, q_D)$ is negligible, which completes the proof.

Theorem 2: G-IBEET scheme is IND-ID-CCA secure against type-II adversary in the random oracle model assuming both V-BDH and SXDH are intractable.

Proof. The proof of Theorem 2 can be easily obtained by above the proof of Theorem 1, and hence we omitted it.

6   Conclusion

In this paper, we introduced the group mechanism into IBEET and proposed G-IBEET. By the group mechanism, G-IBEET supports group granularity authorization. Moreover, the workload of generation and management of trapdoors can be greatly reduced due to the group granularity authorization. For the insider attack, G-IBEET provides a nice solution for IBEET to resist it by the group mechanism. We proved its security in the random oracle and showed that the proposed scheme has a more efficient test algorithm.

Acknowledgement. This work is supported by National Natural Science Foundation of China (No. 61872409, 61872152), Pearl River Nova Program of Guangzhou (No. 201610010037), Guangdong Natural Science Funds for Distinguished Young Scholar (No. 2014A030306021) and Guangdong Program for Special Support of Topnotch Young Professionals (No. 2015TQ01X796).

References

1. Chen, R., Mu, Y., Yang, G., Guo, F., Wang, X.: A new general framework for secure public key encryption with keyword search. In: Foo, E., Stebila, D. (eds.) ACISP 2015. LNCS, vol. 9144, pp. 59–76. Springer, Cham (2015). https://doi.org/10.1007/978-3-319-19962-7_4
2. Chen, R., Mu, Y., Yang, G., Guo, F., Wang, X.: Dual-server public-key encryption with keyword search for secure cloud storage. IEEE Transa. Inf. Forensics Secur. **11**(4), 789–798 (2016)
3. Boneh, D., Di Crescenzo, G., Ostrovsky, R., Persiano, G.: Public key encryption with keyword search. In: Cachin, C., Camenisch, J.L. (eds.) EUROCRYPT 2004. LNCS, vol. 3027, pp. 506–522. Springer, Heidelberg (2004). https://doi.org/10.1007/978-3-540-24676-3_30
4. Huang, K., Tso, R., Chen, Y.-C., Li, W., Sun, H.-M.: A new public key encryption with equality test. In: Au, M.H., Carminati, B., Kuo, C.-C.J. (eds.) NSS 2014. LNCS, vol. 8792, pp. 550–557. Springer, Cham (2014). https://doi.org/10.1007/978-3-319-11698-3_45
5. Huang, K., Tso, R., Chen, Y.C., Rahman, S.M.M., Almogren, A., Alamri, A.: Pke-aet: public key encryption with authorized equality test. Comput. J. **58**(10), 2686–2697 (2015)
6. Huang, Q., Li, H.: An efficient public-key searchable encryption scheme secure against inside keyword guessing attacks. Inf. Sci. **403**, 1–14 (2017)
7. Lee, H.T., Ling, S., Seo, J.H., Wang, H.: Semi-generic construction of public key encryption and identity-based encryption with equality test. Inf. Sci. **373**, 419–440 (2016)
8. Lee, H.T., Ling, S., Seo, J.H., Wang, H., Youn, T.Y.: Public key encryption with equality test in the standard model. IACR Cryptology ePrint Archive 2016, 1182 (2016)
9. Li, H., Huang, Q., Ma, S., Shen, J., Susilo, W.: Authorized equality test on identity-based ciphertexts for secret data sharing via cloud storage. IEEE Access (Early Access) **7**, 1 (2019)
10. Lin, X.J., Qu, H., Zhang, X.: Public key encryption supporting equality test and flexible authorization without bilinear pairings. IACR Cryptology ePrint Archive 2016, 277 (2016)
11. Ling, Y., Ma, S., Huang, Q., Li, X.: A general two-server framework for ciphertext-checkable encryption against offline message recovery attack. In: Sun, X., Pan, Z., Bertino, E. (eds.) ICCCS 2018. LNCS, vol. 11065, pp. 370–382. Springer, Cham (2018). https://doi.org/10.1007/978-3-030-00012-7_34
12. Ma, S.: Identity-based encryption with outsourced equality test in cloud computing. Inf. Sci. **328**, 389–402 (2016)
13. Ma, S.: Authorized equality test of encrypted data for secure cloud databases. In: 2018 17th IEEE International Conference on Trust, Security and Privacy in Computing and Communications/12th IEEE International Conference on Big Data Science and Engineering (TrustCom/BigDataSE), pp. 223–230 (2018)
14. Ma, S., Huang, Q., Zhang, M., Yang, B.: Efficient public key encryption with equality test supporting flexible authorization. IEEE Trans. Inf. Forensics Secur. **10**(3), 458–470 (2015)
15. Ma, S., Ling, Y.: A general two-server cryptosystem supporting complex queries. In: Kang, B.B.H., Kim, T. (eds.) WISA 2017. LNCS, vol. 10763, pp. 249–260. Springer, Cham (2018). https://doi.org/10.1007/978-3-319-93563-8_21

16. Ma, S., Zhang, M., Huang, Q., Yang, B.: Public key encryption with delegated equality test in a multi-user setting. Comput. J. **58**(4), 986–1002 (2015)
17. Qu, H., Yan, Z., Lin, X.J., Zhang, Q., Sun, L.: Certificateless public key encryption with equality test. Inf. Sci. **462**, 76–92 (2018)
18. Tang, Q.: Towards public key encryption scheme supporting equality test with fine-grained authorization. In: Parampalli, U., Hawkes, P. (eds.) ACISP 2011. LNCS, vol. 6812, pp. 389–406. Springer, Heidelberg (2011). https://doi.org/10.1007/978-3-642-22497-3_25
19. Tang, Q.: Public key encryption schemes supporting equality test with authorisation of different granularity. Int. J. Appl. Crypt. **2**(4), 304–321 (2012)
20. Tang, Q.: Public key encryption supporting plaintext equality test and user-specified authorization. Secur. Commun. Netw. **5**(12), 1351–1362 (2012)
21. Wang, C.H., Tai-Yuan, T.U.: Keyword search encryption scheme resistant against keyword-guessing attack by the untrusted server. J. Shanghai Jiaotong Univ. (Sci.) **19**(4), 440–442 (2014)
22. Wang, Y., Pang, H.: Probabilistic public key encryption for controlled equijoin in relational databases. Comput. J. **60**(4), 600–612 (2017)
23. Wu, L., Zhang, Y., Choo, K.K.R., He, D.: Efficient and secure identity-based encryption scheme with equality test in cloud computing. Future Gener. Comput. Syst. **73**, 22–31 (2017)
24. Wu, L., Zhang, Y., He, D.: Dual server identity-based encryption with equality test for cloud computing. J. Comput. Res. Dev. **54**(10), 2232–2243 (2017)
25. Wu, T., Ma, S., Mu, Y., Zeng, S.: ID-based encryption with equality test against insider attack. In: Pieprzyk, J., Suriadi, S. (eds.) ACISP 2017. LNCS, vol. 10342, pp. 168–183. Springer, Cham (2017). https://doi.org/10.1007/978-3-319-60055-0_9
26. Yacobi, Y.: A note on the bilinear Diffie-Hellman assumption. IACR Cryptology ePrint Archive 2002, 113 (2002)
27. Yang, G., Tan, C.H., Huang, Q., Wong, D.S.: Probabilistic public key encryption with equality test. In: Pieprzyk, J. (ed.) CT-RSA 2010. LNCS, vol. 5985, pp. 119–131. Springer, Heidelberg (2010). https://doi.org/10.1007/978-3-642-11925-5_9
28. Zhang, K., Chen, J., Lee, H.T., Qian, H., Wang, H.: Efficient public key encryption with equality test in the standard model. Theor. Comput. Sci. **755**, 65–80 (2019). https://doi.org/10.1016/j.tcs.2018.06.048

Strong Post-Compromise Secure Proxy Re-Encryption

Alex Davidson[1,2], Amit Deo[1], Ela Lee[1(✉)], and Keith Martin[1]

[1] ISG, Royal Holloway University of London, Egham, UK
Ela.Lee.2010@live.rhul.ac.uk
[2] Cloudflare, London, UK

Abstract. Proxy Re-Encryption (PRE) allows a ciphertext encrypted using a key pk_i to be re-encrypted by a third party so that it is an encryption of the same message under a new key pk_j, without revealing the message. We define Post-Compromise Security (PCS) in the context of PRE. This ensures that an adversary cannot distinguish which of two adversarially chosen ciphertexts a re-encryption was created from even when given the old secret key and the update token used to perform the re-encryption. We give separating examples demonstrating how PCS is stronger than existing security definitions for PRE achieving similar goals, before showing that PCS can be achieved using a combination of existing security properties from the literature. In doing so, we show there are existing PRE schemes satisfying PCS. Finally, we give a construction demonstrating that natural modifications of practical PRE schemes provably have PCS directly, without incurring overheads from the security reductions we have shown, and from weaker assumptions than existing schemes.

1 Introduction

Cloud storage has become increasingly popular in recent years, evolving from acting as a source of backup data to becoming the default storage for many applications and systems. For example, popular media streaming platforms such as Netflix and Spotify allow clients to subscribe to on-demand access for media files as opposed to storing them locally. This also incentivises the design of devices with small local storage, but high connectivity.

Since the cloud is usually a third party, clients must encrypt their files to ensure data confidentiality. This poses problems when a client wants to change the key for their encrypted files as a means of satisfying compliance directives [2,17,18] or to enforce access control policies. One trivial solution has the client download, decrypt, encrypt using the new key, then re-upload the file. However,

---

A. Davidson, A. Deo and E. Lee—These authors are supported by the EPSRC and the UK government as part of the Centre for Doctoral Training in Cyber Security at Royal Holloway, University of London (EP/K035584/1).

J. Jang-Jaccard and F. Guo (Eds.): ACISP 2019, LNCS 11547, pp. 58–77, 2019.
https://doi.org/10.1007/978-3-030-21548-4_4

this can be very expensive, particularly for modern applications involving large databases, or if the client has limited processing capability.

The primitive of Proxy Re-Encryption (PRE), introduced by Blaze et al. [3], presents a more elegant solution. In a PRE scheme, the client creates an *update token* $\Delta_{i,j}$ using the current secret key sk_i and a new public key pk_j. The server can then use this token to re-encrypt the ciphertext, transforming it into an encryption of the same message which can now be decrypted using sk_j. The most basic security notion for PRE states that the server performing the re-encryption learns nothing about the underlying message.

Post-Compromise Security. The notion of Post-Compromise Security (PCS) was first defined in [8] for messaging protocols, and informally states that security guarantees can still exist after the compromise of past secrets. This differs from *forward security*, which conveys that the compromise of future states does not affect the security of those in the past.

Motivation for PCS PRE. A common approach to PRE is to use a hybrid model where the message is encrypted under one static key and a ciphertext header is formed by encrypting this key with a PRE key. When the key changes, the header is re-encrypted while the body remains unchanged. Whilst this approach succeeds at granting access, the use of a static key is not appropriate for key rotation (key life-cycles) or access revocation. PCS therefore has clear applications for key rotation and dynamic access control schemes where keys are shared amongst groups and removing a user requires re-encrypting files.

One particular application of post-compromise PRE of interest is to complement PCS of messages in transit, by giving PCS security to backed up messages stored in the cloud. The Signal Protocol for encrypting messages in transit between two devices provides PCS [8]. However, popular Signal implementations such as WhatsApp back up client messages to cloud services, by encrypting using a static encryption key. This means that while messages in transit have PCS, it is lost once messages are backed up. Ideally, the user should have a means of mitigating a compromise by re-encrypting the backup to an uncompromised key. If the entire message history were stored locally, updated message history could be encrypted under a new key and re-uploaded at regular time intervals, but this will have a huge cost both in terms of computation and bandwidth, particularly as much messaging is done via smart-phones. A PRE scheme with PCS could be used instead, so the PCS of messages in transit is extended to message backups.

1.1 Contributions

In this paper we set out the first formalisation of PCS for PRE schemes. In our model, the adversary cannot distinguish a re-encrypted ciphertext given the old key, old ciphertexts and the token used to perform the re-encryption. In other words, we view a compromise as the loss of all previous public and secret states associated with a given ciphertext, and limit the information that must remain secret to the current secret key alone. To date there is no security definition that gives the adversary the update token used in the challenge re-encryption. Our definition implies unidirectionality (as opposed to treating unidirectional and bidirectional schemes differently), and that additional randomness beyond that given in the update token is added upon re-encryption. Since we do not make as many assumptions on which algorithms are deterministic or on the flow of re-encryption operations, our security model can be applied to more general PRE schemes and applications than similar definitions in the literature (see Sect. 3).

We analyse our model, proving several results that associate PCS with existing security models for PRE and related primitives such as updatable encryption [13], and provide separating examples that distinguish PCS as a separate security characteristic in its own right. One of our major contributions is to show how a combination of existing security notions leads to PCS, meaning that some of the PRE schemes given by Fuchsbauer et al. [11] immediately satisfy PCS. However, these schemes were designed with different goals in mind and do not necessarily lead to the most practical lattice-based PREs with PCS. We therefore give a new PRE scheme, pcBV-PRE, adapted from BV-PRE – the practical RLWE-based scheme of Polyakov et al. [19]. This new scheme leverages the speed of the original construction with minimal changes, implying efficiency. We prove that our adaptation achieves PCS and IND-CPA-security via a tighter reduction than using the combination of properties previously mentioned, meaning this combination is sufficient, but not necessary for achieving PCS.

Paper Structure. We begin by reviewing necessary preliminaries in Sect. 2 before reviewing related work in Sect. 3. In Sect. 4 we define PCS and show how our definition relates to those already in the literature. We then give an explicit construction of a PRE scheme satisfying PCS in Sect. 5.

2   Preliminaries

We introduce Proxy Re-Encryption and some related definitions and conventions. Whilst we stick to the asymmetric setting in the body of this work, we present symmetric variants in the full version [9] for easier comparison with related work in the symmetric setting such as key rotation and updatable encryption.

Definition 1. *A* Proxy Re-Encryption (PRE) *scheme consists of the following algorithms:*

- Setup(1^λ) → *params: Outputs a set of public parameters, including the message space and ciphertext space. Note that params is input to every subsequent algorithm, but we leave it out for compactness of notation. We often omit the* Setup *algorithm for the same reason.*
- KeyGen(1^λ) → (pk, sk): *Generates a public-private key pair.*
- Enc(pk, m) → C: *Encrypts a message m using a public key* pk, *producing a ciphertext C.*[1]

---

[1] Note that some definitions of a PRE scheme have an additional input ℓ to indicate a *level* the ciphertext should be at. In this work, we leave out ℓ unless discussing schemes and results that use levelling explicitly.

- $\mathsf{Dec}(\mathsf{sk}, C) \to m' \cup \perp$: *Decrypts a ciphertext C to produce either an element of the message space m' or an error symbol $\perp$.*
- $\mathsf{ReKeyGen}(\mathsf{sk}_i, \mathsf{pk}_j) \to \Delta_{i,j} \cup \perp$: *Takes a secret key sk_i and public key pk_j and outputs an update token $\Delta_{i,j}$, or $\perp$ when $i = j$. This last condition is often left out of constructions for compactness.*
- $\mathsf{ReEnc}(\Delta_{i,j}, C) \to C'$: *Takes a ciphertext C under pk_i and outputs a new ciphertext C' under pk_j.*

A PRE scheme is correct *if, for all* $m \in \mathcal{M}, (\mathsf{pk}, \mathsf{sk}) \xleftarrow{\$} \mathsf{KeyGen}(1^\lambda)$, *then:*

$$\mathsf{Dec}(\mathsf{sk}, \mathsf{Enc}(\mathsf{pk}, m)) \to m$$

and if, for all $C \in \mathcal{C}$ *such that* $\mathsf{Dec}(\mathsf{sk}_i, C) \to m$, *then:*

$$\mathsf{Dec}(\mathsf{sk}_j, \mathsf{ReEnc}(\Delta_{i,j}, C)) \to m$$

where $(\mathsf{pk}_i, \mathsf{sk}_i), (\mathsf{pk}_j, \mathsf{sk}_j) \xleftarrow{\$} \mathsf{KeyGen}(1^\lambda)$ *and* $\Delta_{i,j} \leftarrow \mathsf{ReKeyGen}(\mathsf{sk}_i, \mathsf{pk}_j)$.

Some PRE constructions have a *correctness bound, L* – a limit on the number of re-encryptions possible before the resulting ciphertext fails to decrypt properly.

A common approach to PRE is the *key encapsulation approach*. Encryption involves generating a symmetric key k for a symmetric encryption scheme $\mathcal{SE}$ and computing $C_1 \xleftarrow{\$} \mathcal{SE}.\mathsf{Enc}(k, m)$, before encrypting k using a public-key PRE scheme $\mathcal{PRE}$ to obtain $C_0 \leftarrow \mathcal{PRE}.\mathsf{Enc}(\mathsf{pk}, k)$. For re-encryption, the ciphertext header C_0 is re-encrypted so it is now an encryption of k under some specified pk', whilst C_1 remains unchanged. We describe why this approach is not sufficient for PCS in Sect. 3.2.

Definition 2. *If an update token* $\Delta_{i,j} \xleftarrow{\$} \mathcal{PRE}.\mathsf{ReKeyGen}(\mathsf{sk}_i, \mathsf{pk}_j)$ *computed using a PRE scheme* $\mathcal{PRE}$ *can be used to derive a token* $\Delta_{j,i}$ *that can re-encrypt ciphertexts from* pk_j *to* pk_i *then we say the scheme* $\mathcal{PRE}$ *is* bidirectional. *If* $\mathcal{PRE}$ *is not bidirectional then it is* unidirectional.

Directionality is often used in security games to determine the adversary's limitations.

We now move on to giving definitions for message confidentiality in PRE. IND-CPA-security is a well-known notion in public-key encryption which states that given a ciphertext, an adversary cannot distinguish which of two messages it is an encryption of. We refer to this as PKE-CPA security for PRE schemes, defining it as a separate notion to IND-CPA to avoid confusion and for easier comparison between definitions.

Definition 3. *A PRE scheme* $\mathcal{PRE}$ *is* ϵ-*PKE-CPA secure if the Public Key Encryption (PKE) scheme given by* $\mathcal{PKE} = \{\mathcal{PRE}.\mathsf{KeyGen}, \mathcal{PRE}.\mathsf{Enc}, \mathcal{PRE}.\mathsf{Dec}\}$ *is* ϵ-*IND-CPA-secure, where* ϵ *is the advantage over random guessing the adversary has in winning the game.*

If ϵ *is negligible as parameterised by the security parameter, then we say* $\mathcal{PRE}$ *is* PKE-CPA-secure.

2.1   Re-encryption Graphs

We often use a directed re-encryption graph (DRG) when discussing the security of PRE schemes. A DRG tracks queries the adversary $\mathcal{A}$ makes during a security game to represent re-encryptions that $\mathcal{A}$ can make locally – nodes v_i represent key pairs whilst directed[2] edges $\vec{e}_{i,j}$ represent update tokens The DRG is often used to enforce the condition that $\mathcal{A}$ cannot query oracles in such a way that reveals a challenge under a corrupted key.

Re-encryption graphs often reflect applications. For example, for simply rotating keys the resulting graph will be a chain, as is assumed in *updatable encryption* [4,13] and *key rotation for authenticated encryption* [10], whereas some access control hierarchies may lead to trees. Some results such as those given in [11] between selective and adaptive security mainly apply to some types of graph. Throughout this paper, we assume DRGs are acyclic.

2.2   Common Oracles

Most definitions use the same oracles, which we define in Fig. 1 for compactness. The main variations between definitions are how the challenge oracle $O_{\text{challenge}}$ is defined, and sometimes whether O_{ReEnc} affects the DRG. We therefore define these in each individual game. Games often keep track of lists updated by the oracles, namely a list of challenge keys $\mathcal{K}_{\text{chal}}$, corrupted keys $\mathcal{K}_{\text{corrupted}}$, oracle-generated ciphertexts $\mathcal{C}_{\text{honest}}$, challenge ciphertexts $\mathcal{C}_{\text{chal}}$ and oracle-generated tokens $\mathcal{T}_{\text{honest}}$.

$O_{\text{KeyGen}}(1^\lambda)$	$O_{\text{Corrupt}}(i)$	$O_{\text{Enc}}(i,m)$	$O_{\text{ReKeyGen}}(i,j)$
$\kappa = \kappa + 1$	$\mathcal{K}_{\text{corrupted}}.\text{add }(\text{sk}_i)$	$C \xleftarrow{\$} \text{Enc}(\text{pk}_i, m)$	if $\mathcal{DRG} \cup \vec{e}_{i,j}$ is cyclic:
$(\text{pk}_\kappa, \text{sk}_\kappa) \xleftarrow{\$} \text{KeyGen}(1^\lambda)$	**return** sk_i	$\boxed{\mathcal{C}_{\text{honest}}.\text{add }(i, C)}$	$\quad$ **return** $\perp$
$\mathcal{DRG}.\text{add }(v_\kappa)$		$\boxed{\mathcal{C}_{\text{msg}}[(i, C)] = m}$	$\Delta_{i,j} \xleftarrow{\$} \text{ReKeyGen}(\text{sk}_i, \text{pk}_j)$
return pk_κ		**return** C	$\mathcal{T}_{\text{honest}}.\text{add }(i, j, \Delta_{i,j})$
			$\mathcal{DRG}.\text{add }(\vec{e}_{i,j})$
			return $\Delta_{i,j}$

Fig. 1. Common oracles used in security games for PRE. κ is the number of keys in the game. Boxed values indicate steps to update lists that may not be used depending on the game. The lists a particular game uses are indicated in the game's setup phase.

In our syntax, the restrictions on what tokens the adversary is allowed to learn is not enforced by oracles (as in other work), but instead by the list of challenge keys $\mathcal{K}_{\text{chal}}$ being updated using the graph $\mathcal{DRG}$ at the end of the game. It is a winning condition in all PRE security definitions considering key

---

[2] If a scheme is bidirectional, then edges added would be directionless. In this work we mainly focus on unidirectional schemes.

corruption that the adversary cannot have queried oracles in such a way that reveals a challenge ciphertext under a corrupted key. We refer to this as the *trivial win condition.*

If the adversary has learned a series of update tokens that allow them to re-encrypt the challenge ciphertext, then the keys that tokens re-encrypt to are also considered challenge keys as the adversary can re-encrypt the challenge ciphertext locally. We therefore use the following function to update the set of challenge keys:

UpdateChallengeKeys($\mathcal{K}_{chal}, \mathcal{DRG}$)

$\forall i$ such that $sk_i \in \mathcal{K}_{chal}$:

   $\forall j$ such that $\exists$ a path from v_i to v_j in $\mathcal{DRG}$:

      $\mathcal{K}_{chal}$.add sk_j

  return $\mathcal{K}_{chal}$

We enforce the trivial win condition by calling UpdateChallengeKeys at the end of the game, and checking that $\mathcal{K}_{chal} \cap \mathcal{K}_{corrupted} = \emptyset$.

3   Related Work

3.1   Confidentiality Definitions

The basic security definition for PRE was first given in [3] for bidirectional schemes. Informally, it states the scheme should still be IND-CPA-secure when given the additional functionality of re-encryption. This means the proxy should not learn the message during the re-encryption process. Unidirectional PRE schemes were introduced by Ateniese et al. [1] together with an equivalent security definition. Similar definitions conveying this notion appear in all work on PRE. We refer to such notions as PRE-CPA as opposed to IND-CPA, to avoid confusion with IND-CPA (for PKE schemes) and PKE-CPA (for PRE schemes).

Definition 4. *A PRE scheme* $\mathcal{PRE}$ *is said to be* (selectively) ϵ-*PRE-Indistinguishable against Chosen Plaintext Attacks* (ϵ-*PRE-CPA-secure*) *if for all Probabilistic Polynomial-Time* (PPT) *adversaries* $\mathcal{A} = (\mathcal{A}_0, \mathcal{A}_1)$:

$$\left| \Pr\left[\mathsf{PRE\text{-}CPA}_{\mathcal{A}}^{0,\mathcal{PRE}}(1^\lambda) = 1 \right] - \Pr\left[\mathsf{PRE\text{-}CPA}_{\mathcal{A}}^{1,\mathcal{PRE}}(1^\lambda) = 1 \right] \right| \leq \epsilon,$$

where $\mathsf{PRE\text{-}CPA}_{\mathcal{A}}^{b,\mathcal{PRE}}$ *is defined in Fig. 2.*

If ϵ *is negligible as parameterised by the security parameter, then we say the scheme is* PRE-Indistinguishable against Chosen Plaintext Attacks *(PRE-CPAsecure).*

Whilst the above definition is based on the one given in [11], our formulation is slightly different as we account for there being multiple possible tokens per key pair, meaning O_{ReEnc} allows $\mathcal{A}$ to input an honestly-generated update token

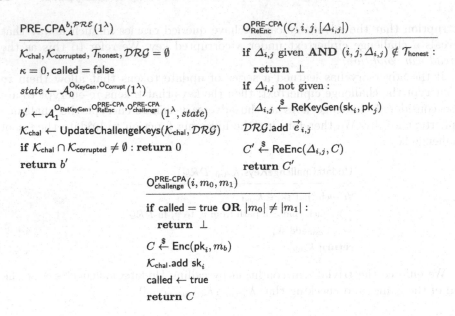

Fig. 2. The PRE-CPA game – an extension of PKE-CPA which accounts for re-encryption. $O_{KeyGen}, O_{Enc}, O_{ReKeyGen}$ are as defined in Fig. 1.

as opposed to only having indexes as input. Note that the $\mathcal{DRG}$ is created by adding an edge whenever O_{ReEnc} is called.

A definition of IND-CCA security for PRE first appears in [6] for bidirectional single-hop (ciphertexts can only be re-encrypted once) schemes. This allows the adversary to adaptively corrupt secret keys. A definition of IND-CCA security for unidirectional schemes is given in [14].

Honest Re-encryption Attacks. Recently, a stronger notion was introduced which allows the adversary to re-encrypt non-challenge ciphertexts to any key, as long as they were honestly generated. Cohen formalised these as *Honest Re-encryption Attacks (HRA)* [7] but the same idea is also used elsewhere [13]. We base our formulation of security against Honest Re-encryption Attacks on IND-ENC-security [13], IND-HRA-security [7] and IND-CPA-security [19].

Definition 5. *A PRE scheme $\mathcal{PRE}$ is said to be (selectively) ϵ-Indistinguishable against Honest Re-encryption Attacks (ϵ-IND-HRA-secure) if for all PPT adversaries $\mathcal{A} = (\mathcal{A}_0, \mathcal{A}_1)$:*

$$\left| \Pr\left[\text{IND-HRA}_{\mathcal{A}}^{0,\mathcal{PRE}}(1^\lambda) = 1 \right] - \Pr\left[\text{IND-HRA}_{\mathcal{A}}^{1,\mathcal{PRE}}(1^\lambda) = 1 \right] \right| \le \epsilon,$$

where $\text{IND-HRA}_{\mathcal{A}}^{b,\mathcal{PRE}}$ is defined in Fig. 3.

If ϵ is negligible as parameterised by the security parameter, then we say the scheme is (selectively) Indistinguishable against Honest Re-encryption Attacks (IND-HRA-secure).

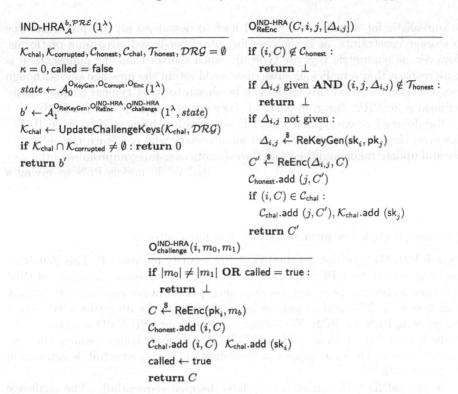

Fig. 3. The IND-HRA game. Like the IND-HRA model [7], it allows re-encryptions of non-challenge ciphertexts to compromised keys using O_{ReEnc}.

We discuss security with respect to adaptive key corruptions in the full version [9].

Theorem 1. *IND-HRA $\implies$ PRE-CPA $\implies$ PKE-CPA.*

As each game builds directly on the last but gives the adversary access to more information, proof of this theorem follows trivially.

Cohen also defines *re-encryption simulatability* [7] and demonstrates that PRE-CPA-secure schemes which have this property are IND-HRA-secure. We leave out the definition of re-encryption simulatability for brevity.

3.2 Ciphertext Re-randomisation

Thus far we have not considered key revocation explicitly. In this case, stronger definitions requiring re-encryption to re-randomise the ciphertext are required, as is demonstrated in the key encapsulation approach discussed in Sect. 1. Whilst this method grants the benefits of hybrid encryption, key-scraping attacks are possible: a malicious user simply retains the message encryption key k and can derive the message regardless of how often the ciphertext is re-encrypted. It may be unrealistic for a malicious revoked user to download all the plaintexts due to storage constraints, as is the case for subscriber-based streaming platforms. However, as symmetric keys are typically much shorter than the plaintexts, it is more realistic that a malicious subscriber could retain the message key. Although constructions based on this model can be shown to meet typical confidentiality definitions for PRE shown in Sect. 3.1, they are not appropriate for PCS.

Randomised re-encryption for PRE schemes has been studied in [6,10,13]. However, these works do not consider an adversary who can learn the old secret key and update token and therefore they do not cover full compromise of the user who generated the update token. Other related work models PCS by giving a bound on the amount of information the adversary retains about a the ciphertext prior to re-encryption [12,16]. Such definitions do not account for the possibility of revoked users storing parts of the original ciphertexts colluding, and lead to more complicated, less intuitive proofs than our approach.

IND-UPD. We now discuss the IND-UPD security notion [13]. This definition was created to convey PCS for *updatable encryption schemes* - a variant of PRE that uses symmetric keys and where re-encryption always happens sequentially from k_i to k_{i+1}. This is the most relevant definition in the literature with respect to achieving PCS for PRE. We consider a version of IND-UPD adapted to the public key setting which we call pkIND-UPD, for easier comparison to our definitions. We give the main points of the definition here, and a full description in the full version [9].

In the pkIND-UPD game, key updates happen sequentially. The challenge oracle outputs a re-encrypted ciphertext and the adversary must guess which ciphertext it is a re-encryption of. Challenge ciphertexts are updated whenever a new key is generated, but only given to the adversary if the oracle $O_{\mathsf{LearnChal}}^{\mathsf{pkIU}}$ is called. One of the winning conditions given in $O_{\mathsf{ReEnc}}^{\mathsf{pkIU}}$ is that when ReEnc is deterministic, the adversary $\mathcal{A}$ cannot have re-encrypted either of the challenge input ciphertexts $\bar{C}_0, \bar{C}_1$. Another notable condition is $\mathcal{A}$ cannot learn the token updating to the key that the first challenge is given under, as enforced by a condition in $O_{\mathsf{LearnTok}}^{\mathsf{pkIU}}$. The final constraint relates to directionality; if the scheme is bidirectional then $\mathcal{A}$ cannot have learned any tokens leading from corrupted keys to challenge keys. We will readdress these points in Sect. 4.

Source-Hiding. Fuchsbauer et al. [11] define *source-hiding* as a component for demonstrating that PRE security with selective key corruptions can imply security with adaptive key corruptions in restricted re-encryption circumstances. Informally, in a source-hiding scheme it is possible to create a fresh encryption of a message that is indistinguishable from a re-encrypted ciphertext that is an encryption of the same message. This means re-encrypted ciphertexts reveal no history as to the keys they were previously encrypted under, or similarities between components of previous ciphertexts.

We give a formal description of the game defining the source-hiding property in Fig. 4. Our formulation generalises the original definition in [11] by allowing the adversary to receive κ keypairs rather than 1. Moreover, as before, we allow the adversary to query multiple re-key tokens between any key pairs of their choice.

$SH_{\mathcal{A}}^{b,\mathcal{PRE}}(1^\lambda, 1^\kappa, 1^L)$	$O_{\text{challenge}}^{SH}(i, j, \Delta_{i,j}^*, m^*, \ell^*)$
$\{(pk_\iota, sk_\iota) \xleftarrow{\$} \text{KeyGen}(1^\lambda)\}_{\iota \in [\kappa]}$	**if** $[(i, j, \Delta_{i,j}^*) \notin \mathcal{T}_{\text{honest}}$ **OR** $\ell^* + 1 > L]$:
$\mathcal{T}_{\text{honest}} = \emptyset$	**return** $\perp$
$b' \leftarrow \mathcal{A}^{O_{\text{challenge}}^{SH}, O_{\text{ReKeyGen}}}(1^\lambda, \{(pk_\iota, sk_\iota)\}_{\iota \in [\kappa]})$	$C^* \leftarrow \text{Enc}(pk_i, m^*, \ell^*)$
return b'	$C^{(0)} \xleftarrow{\$} \text{ReEnc}(\Delta^*, C^*)$
	$C^{(1)} \xleftarrow{\$} \text{Enc}(pk_j, m^*, \ell^* + 1)$
	return $(C^*, C^{(b)})$

Fig. 4. Experiments for the source-hiding property. Here, ℓ denotes a *level* for the ciphertext to be encrypted at – essentially the number of times C has been re-encrypted. This is important for noisy PRE schemes, but ignored for PRE schemes without levelling. L is the number of times a ciphertext can be re-encrypted without breaking the correctness conditions (the correctness bound).

Definition 6. *A PRE scheme* $\mathcal{PRE}$ *is said to be* ϵ-*source-hiding* (ϵ-SH) *if for all* PPT *adversaries* $\mathcal{A} = (\mathcal{A}_0, \mathcal{A}_1)$:

$$\left| \Pr\left[SH_{\mathcal{A}}^{0,\mathcal{PRE}}(1^\lambda, 1^\kappa, 1^L) = 1\right] - \Pr\left[SH_{\mathcal{A}}^{1,\mathcal{PRE}}(1^\lambda, 1^\kappa, 1^L) = 1\right] \right| \leq \epsilon$$

where $SH_{\mathcal{A}}^{b,\mathcal{PRE}}$ *is defined in Fig. 4.*

If ϵ *is negligible as parameterised by the security parameter, then we say the scheme is* source-hiding (SH).

4   Strong PCS for PRE

We have two main motivations for creating a new definition of PCS in the PRE context. The first is that there is currently no definition that implies unidirectionality and ciphertext re-randomisation. These properties are vital in the post-compromise scenario to model the corruption of used update tokens. The second motivation is to remove assumptions as to which algorithms in the PRE scheme are probabilistic. By addressing these concerns, we formalise a provably stronger definition of PCS in the PRE setting.

Explicit Unidirectionality. IND-UPD places restrictions based on inferable information, defined by the following notions of directionality [13]:

– When sk_j cannot be derived from sk_i and $\Delta_{i,j}$ (LT-unidirectional)[3]

---

[3] The general understanding of unidirectionality is not so strong - the new key does not necessarily have to be derivable, but the token and old key should lead to the message being learned.

– When sk_j can be derived from sk_i and $\Delta_{i,j}$ (LT-bidirectional).

In the LT-unidirectional case, the adversary can acquire re-encryption tokens from a corrupted key to a challenge key, but not the other way around. In the LT-bidirectional case, the adversary is additionally prevented, by definition, from learning tokens from challenge keys to corrupted keys or vice versa. This means that for bidirectional schemes, the adversary queries tokens in such a way that the resulting re-encryption graphs form disjoint sub-graphs – one containing corrupted keys and the other containing challenge keys. Proving security is therefore reduced to proving that unrelated, randomly-generated keys cannot be used to infer information about an encrypted message. We consider this too restrictive for the intuition of PCS.

Assuming Probabilistic Algorithms. There appear to be only two existing security definitions explicitly considering re-randomisation of re-encryption, [10,13]. The [10] definition of a *key rotation scheme* assumes that ReKeyGen is randomised but ReEnc is deterministic. This leads to a necessary condition that the update token used to create the challenge re-encryption cannot be learned by the adversary, otherwise the adversary could use it to re-encrypt the input ciphertexts locally and compare this to the challenge to win the game. For this reason, it is important that new randomness is not just introduced via the update token to prevent trivial downgrading of the challenge ciphertext if the adversary compromises the update token used, but also in ReEnc. As such, UP-REENC [10] does not model compromise of the update token used.

In the [13] definition of an updatable encryption scheme, the opposite assumption is made – that ReEnc is randomised and ReKeyGen is deterministic. This means that for keys $\mathsf{sk}_i, \mathsf{pk}_j$, there is only one update token $\Delta_{i,j}$. This is reflected in the IND-UPD security game (and pkIND-UPD) by having all tokens generated at the start of the game and later having oracles reveal tokens for the adversary. More importantly, such an assumption rules out the possibility that secret keys are masked in the update token, which is important for PCS. The BV-PRE scheme is an example of this, where knowledge of the key 'pk_j' together with $\Delta_{i,j}$ can be used to derive sk_i. Another example are ElGamal-based symmetric PRE schemes (e.g. [3,13]) where update tokens have the form $\Delta_{i,j} = \mathsf{sk}_j/\mathsf{sk}_i$. Clearly, given the update token, compromise of the old key leads to compromise of the new key. Introducing extra randomness also means the client no longer solely relies on the proxy for adding new randomness during the re-encryption process. This may be more appropriate for some trust scenarios.

For constructions where randomness is added in both ReKeyGen and ReEnc, neither definition is suitable. It is therefore of interest to create a security notion for PCS which factors in the possibility that both the ReKeyGen and ReEnc algorithms are probabilistic.

4.1   Post-Compromise Security

We model Post-Compromise Security (PCS) using an adversary $\mathcal{A}$ who chooses two ciphertexts (whose decryption key can be known) and a re-encryption token, and receives a challenge ciphertext which is a re-encryption of one of the original ciphertexts created using the specified token. $\mathcal{A}$ attempts to distinguish which ciphertext was re-encrypted. This models the compromise of all key-related material prior to the challenge re-encryption.

As in IND-HRA security, we also allow $\mathcal{A}$ to re-encrypt oracle-generated non-challenge ciphertexts to corrupted keys, and oracle-generated update tokens. In the first stage, $\mathcal{A}_0$ can access a key corruption oracle O_{Corrupt}; in the second stage $\mathcal{A}_1$ can access the challenge oracle $O^{\text{PC}}_{\text{challenge}}$ and re-encryption oracle O_{ReKeyGen}.

$\mathsf{PostComp}^{b,\mathcal{PRE}}_{\mathcal{A}}(1^\lambda)$

$\mathcal{K}_{\text{chal}}, \mathcal{K}_{\text{corrupted}}, \mathcal{C}_{\text{honest}}, \mathcal{C}_{\text{chal}}, \mathcal{C}_{\text{msg}}, \mathcal{T}_{\text{honest}}, \mathcal{DRG} = \emptyset$

$\kappa = 0, \text{called} = \text{false}$

$state \leftarrow \mathcal{A}_0^{O_{\text{KeyGen}}, O_{\text{Corrupt}}, O_{\text{Enc}}}(1^\lambda)$

$b' \leftarrow \mathcal{A}_1^{O_{\text{ReKeyGen}}, O^{\text{PC}}_{\text{ReEnc}}, O^{\text{PC}}_{\text{challenge}}}(1^\lambda, state)$

$\mathcal{K}_{\text{chal}} \leftarrow \mathsf{UpdateChallengeKeys}(\mathcal{K}_{\text{chal}}, \mathcal{DRG})$

if $\mathcal{K}_{\text{chal}} \cap \mathcal{K}_{\text{corrupted}} \neq \emptyset$: return 0

return b'

$O^{\text{PC}}_{\text{ReEnc}}(C, i, j, [\Delta_{i,j}])$

---

if $\Delta_{i,j}$ given :

 if $(i, j, \Delta_{i,j}) \notin \mathcal{T}_{\text{honest}}$: return $\bot$

else : $\Delta_{i,j} \leftarrow \mathsf{ReKeyGen}(\mathsf{sk}_i, \mathsf{pk}_j)$

if $(i, C) \notin \mathcal{C}_{\text{honest}}$: return $\bot$

$C' \xleftarrow{\$} \mathsf{ReEnc}(\Delta_{i,j}, C)$

$\mathcal{C}_{\text{honest}}.\mathsf{add}\ (j, C')$

$\mathcal{C}_{\text{msg}}[(j, C')] = \mathcal{C}_{\text{msg}}[(i, C)]$

if $(i, C) \in \mathcal{C}_{\text{chal}}$:

 $\mathcal{C}_{\text{chal}}.\mathsf{add}\ (j, C'), \mathcal{K}_{\text{chal}}.\mathsf{add}\ (\mathsf{sk}_j)$

 return C'

$O^{\text{PC}}_{\text{challenge}}(C_0, C_1, i, j, \Delta_{i,j})$

---

if $|C_0| \neq |C_1|$ **OR** called = true : return $\bot$

if $(i, C_0), (i, C_1) \notin \mathcal{C}_{\text{honest}}$ **OR** $(i, j, \Delta_{i,j}) \notin \mathcal{T}_{\text{honest}}$: return $\bot$

$C' \xleftarrow{\$} \mathsf{ReEnc}(\Delta_{i,j}, C_b)$

$\mathcal{C}_{\text{msg}}[(j, C')] = \mathcal{C}_{\text{msg}}[(i, C_b)]$

$\mathcal{C}_{\text{honest}}.\mathsf{add}\ (j, C'), \mathcal{C}_{\text{chal}}.\mathsf{add}\ (j, C'), \mathcal{K}_{\text{chal}}.\mathsf{add}\ (\mathsf{sk}_j)$

called $\leftarrow$ true

return C'

Fig. 5. The PostComp game. This reflects full compromise of the old secret key and update token used to perform the re-encryption.

Definition 7. *A PRE scheme $\mathcal{PRE}$ is said to have (selective) ϵ-Post-Compromise Security (ϵ-PCS) if for all PPT adversaries $\mathcal{A} = (\mathcal{A}_0, \mathcal{A}_1)$:*

$$\left| \Pr\left[\mathsf{PostComp}^{0,\mathcal{PRE}}_{\mathcal{A}}(1^\lambda) = 1\right] - \Pr\left[\mathsf{PostComp}^{1,\mathcal{PRE}}_{\mathcal{A}}(1^\lambda) = 1\right]\right| \leq \epsilon,$$

where $\mathsf{PostComp}^{b,\mathcal{PRE}}_{\mathcal{A}}$ is defined in Fig. 5. If ϵ is negligible as parameterised by the security parameter, then we say the scheme achieves (selective) PCS.

Definitions of PCS for symmetric PRE schemes and adaptive key corruptions can be found in the full version [9].

4.2   Basic Observations

Lemma 1. *No PRE scheme where* ReEnc *is deterministic has PCS.*

Proof. If ReEnc is deterministic then $\mathcal{A}$ can submit $(C_0, C_1, i, j, \Delta_{i,j})$ to $O_{\text{challenge}}$ to learn challenge C'. Then $\mathcal{A}$ can locally compute $C'_0 \leftarrow$ ReEnc$(\Delta_{i,j}, C_0)$ and compare this with C' – if they match then output $b' = 0$, otherwise output $b' = 1$.

Lemma 2. *PCS* $\implies$ *unidirectional.*

Proof. We show that if a scheme is bidirectional then it cannot have PCS. Bidirectionality implies that an update token $\Delta_{i,j}$, can be used to derive $\Delta_{j,i}$. Therefore $\mathcal{A}$ can corrupt sk_i, and calculate $\Delta_{j,i}$ for challenge query $(C_0, C_1, i, j, \Delta_{i,j})$, where C_0 and C_1 are encryptions of different messages. $\mathcal{A}$ can then re-encrypt the challenge ciphertext back to its original key and decrypt to win the game.

4.3   Separating Examples

We now demonstrate the relationship between PCS and existing security notions and constructions via a number of separating examples.

Lemma 3. *pkIND-UPD-security* $\not\Longrightarrow$ *PCS.*

Proof. Let $\mathcal{PRE}$ be a pkIND-UPD-secure PRE scheme where ReEnc is deterministic. By Lemma 1, this scheme is not post-compromise secure.

Lemma 4. *Let* $\mathcal{PRE}$ *be a PRE scheme where* ReKeyGen *is deterministic. If* $\mathcal{PRE}$ *has PCS, then it is pkIND-UPD-secure.*

Proof Sketch. The PostComp adversary $\mathcal{A}$ can simulate the pkIND-UPD game. It begins by generating enough keys to cover the number of epochs in pkIND-UPD. Before the challenge is issued, O_{Next} can be easily simulated by generating a new keypair, corrupting the old secret key and creating an update token between the old key and the new. The adversary replaces the challenge ciphertext with the output from $O^{PC}_{\text{challenge}}(C_0, C_1, \tilde{e} - 1, \tilde{e})$. The PostComp adversary $\mathcal{A}_0$ must guess the remaining keys which the pkIND-UPD will corrupt, which will result in a sub-exponential loss of security as the challenge graph will be a chain. The simulator can update both challenge and honest ciphertexts using O_{ReEnc}, and ReKeyGen can be simulated with calls O_{ReKeyGen}. Re-encrypting a challenge ciphertext directly to the requested key as opposed to going through all previous keys in the chain first will go unnoticed, as if the number of times a ciphertext has been re-encrypted could be detected then this could be use to win the PostComp game.

Lemma 5. *IND-HRA-security* $\not\Longrightarrow$ *PCS.*

Proof. Consider the key encapsulation approach, where the ciphertext header is an encryption of the message key using an IND-HRA-secure PRE scheme, and the message is encrypted using a PRE-CPA-secure encryption. This scheme is also IND-HRA-secure, but is not PCS, as the ciphertext body does not change.

Lemma 6. *PCS* $\not\Rightarrow$ *IND-HRA-security.*

Proof. Let $\overline{\mathcal{PRE}}$ be a PRE scheme that is IND-HRA-secure and has PCS. We use it to construct the following PRE scheme:

- KeyGen(1^λ) : $(\mathsf{pk}, \mathsf{sk}) \leftarrow \overline{\mathsf{KeyGen}}(1^\lambda)$
- Enc(pk, m) : $C \leftarrow (m, \overline{\mathsf{Enc}}(\mathsf{pk}, m))$
- Dec(sk, C) : $m' \leftarrow \overline{\mathsf{Dec}}(\mathsf{sk}, C_1)$
- ReKeyGen$(\mathsf{sk}_i, \mathsf{pk}_j)$: $\Delta_{i,j} \leftarrow \overline{\mathsf{ReKeyGen}}(\mathsf{sk}_i, \mathsf{pk}_j)$
- ReEnc$(\Delta_{i,j}, C)$: $C'_0 \leftarrow \overline{\mathsf{Enc}}(\mathsf{pk}_j, 0), C'_1 \leftarrow \overline{\mathsf{ReEnc}}(\Delta_{i,j}, C_1)$

Clearly this scheme is not IND-HRA-secure, as fresh ciphertexts contain the plaintext. However the scheme has PCS, as re-encryptions C'_1 will be unrelated to C_1 since $\overline{\mathcal{PRE}}$ has PCS, and C'_0 is created independently of both C_0 and $\Delta_{i,j}$.

Since PCS does not imply any security notion concerning confidentiality of the message, confidentiality definitions must be proven separately for in order to demonstrate that a PRE scheme is useful in practice.

4.4 PCS via Source-Hiding and IND-HRA

In this section we show that a PRE scheme that is both source-hiding and IND-HRA-secure also has PCS.

Theorem 2. *Let $\mathcal{PRE}$ be a PRE scheme that satisfies ϵ_1-IND-HRA-security and is ϵ_2-SH. Let $\mathcal{A}$, $\mathcal{B}$ and $\mathcal{C}$ be PPT algorithms that are attempting to succeed in the $\mathsf{PostComp}_{\mathcal{A}}^{\mathcal{PRE}}$, $\mathsf{SH}_{\mathcal{B}}^{\mathcal{PRE}}$ and $\mathsf{IND\text{-}HRA}_{\mathcal{C}}^{\mathcal{PRE}}$ security games, respectively. Let $\mathcal{A}$ have advantage ϵ in $\mathsf{PostComp}_{\mathcal{A}}^{\mathcal{PRE}}$. Then:*

$$\epsilon \leq 2\epsilon_2 + \epsilon_1 < \mathsf{negl}(n),$$

for a negligible function $\mathsf{negl}(n)$, and thus $\mathcal{PRE}$ has PCS.

We prove this theorem using a sequence of hybrid steps as described below. The full proof is deferred to the full version [9].

Proof. Let $\mathsf{PostComp}_{\mathcal{A}}^{\mathcal{PRE},b}$ refer to the experiment in Fig. 5, where the choice of b is made explicit. We start with the execution of $\mathcal{PRE}$ in $\mathsf{PostComp}_{\mathcal{A}}^{\mathcal{PRE},0}$ and show via a sequence of security reductions that this situation is computationally indistinguishable from the case where $\mathcal{A}$ witnesses the execution in $b = 1$. We define a new oracle:

$$\overline{O_{\text{challenge}}}(C_0, C_1, i, j, \Delta_{i,j})$$

---

if $|C_0| \neq |C_1|$ **OR** called $=$ true : **return** $\perp$

if $(i, C_0), (i, C_1) \notin \mathcal{C}_{\text{honest}}$ **OR** $(i, j, \Delta_{i,j}) \notin \mathcal{T}_{\text{honest}}$: **return** $\perp$

$(m_0, m_1) \leftarrow (\mathcal{C}_{\text{msg}}[(i, C_0)], \mathcal{C}_{\text{msg}}[(i, C_1)])$

if $(i, j, \Delta_{i,j}) \notin \mathcal{T}_{\text{honest}}$ **OR** $\text{sk}_j \in \mathcal{K}_{\text{corrupted}}$: **return** $\perp$

$C' \xleftarrow{\$} \text{Enc}(\text{pk}_j, m_b)$

$\mathcal{C}_{\text{msg}}[(j, C')] = m_b$

$\mathcal{C}_{\text{honest}}.\text{add}\ (j, C'), \mathcal{C}_{\text{chal}}.\text{add}\ (j, C'), \mathcal{K}_{\text{chal}}.\text{add}\ (\text{sk}_j)$

called $\leftarrow$ true

return C'

Let $O_{\text{challenge},b}$ and $\overline{O_{\text{challenge},b}}$ be the executions of the oracles where the choice of $b \in \{0, 1\}$ is made explicit.

- Game$_0$: This is the original $\mathcal{PRE}$ construction in $\text{PostComp}_{\mathcal{A}}^{\mathcal{PRE},0}$.
- Game$_1$: Replace outputs from the oracle $O_{\text{challenge},0}$ with outputs from the oracle $\overline{O_{\text{challenge},0}}$.
- Game$_2$: Replace $\overline{O_{\text{challenge},0}}$ with $\overline{O_{\text{challenge},1}}$.
- Game$_3$: Replace $\overline{O_{\text{challenge},1}}$ with $O_{\text{challenge},1}$.

It is not hard to see that Game$_3$ is identical to the execution in the case of $\text{PostComp}_{\mathcal{A}}^{\mathcal{PRE},1}$. Therefore, if we can bound the advantage in distinguishing the game transitions above by a negligible function, then the probability of distinguishing in $\text{PostComp}_{\mathcal{A}}^{\mathcal{PRE},b}$ is also negligible.

For the sake of brevity, we complete the proof via the following observations:

- Distinguishing Game$_0$ from Game$_1$ or Game$_2$ from Game$_3$ with some advantage implies an adversary wins the source-hiding game with the same advantage.
- Distinguishing Game$_1$ from Game$_2$ with some advantage implies an adversary wins the IND-HRA game with the same advantage.

The advantage in distinguishing Game$_0$ and Game$_1$ is bounded by ϵ_2, and the advantage in distinguishing Game$_1$ and Game$_2$ is bounded by ϵ_1. Full details of this breakdown is given in the full version [9].

Theorem 3. *Let $\mathcal{PRE}$ be a PRE scheme which is both PKE-CPA-secure and source-hiding. Then $\mathcal{PRE}$ also has PCS.*

Proof. It has been shown that PKE-CPA-security and source-hiding imply IND-HRA-security [11, Theorem 6]. This, together with Theorem 2, gives us the result. A more precise security bound can be deduced from the results of [11].

Existing PRE Schemes that Satisfy PCS. The result of Theorem 2 means a number of existing PRE schemes satisfy PCS. This is advantageous, as it shows PCS is not a vacuous security model in the sense that it is achievable via well-known techniques. Specifically, any PRE scheme that satisfies PRE-CPA-security and is source-hiding is immediately a scheme that has PCS. Therefore, [11, Construction 2, Construction 4, Construction 7.b] all have PCS.

5   An Efficient Construction from Lattices

We introduce a natural construction with PCS, based on BV-PRE – the ring-LWE (RLWE) construction given in [19]. Whilst Theorem 3 shows that source-hiding can lead to PCS, the existing constructions with this property [11] make sub-optimal parameter choices that significantly impact the scheme's practicality. Our construction has PCS but is not source-hiding, implying that source-hiding is not necessary for PCS. This means that our construction can make much better parameter choices in terms of efficiency. We also achieve *transparency*, which means decryption is the same regardless of how many times the ciphertext has been re-encrypted, and the cost of decryption does not grow for repeatedly re-encrypted ciphertexts. This fits better with motivations for outsourcing re-encryption. Our construction makes some adaptations to BV-PRE to fit the workflow of PRE; making use of the key resampling technique of [5] to re-randomise the ciphertext. Any scheme that permits similar re-randomisation can be proven secure using related methods.

5.1   Lattice Preliminaries

We represent the set of integers modulo q as $\mathbb{Z}_q = \{\lfloor -q/2 \rfloor, \ldots, 0, \ldots, \lfloor q/2 \rfloor\}$. We will be working over power-of-two cyclotomic rings of the form $R_q = \mathbb{Z}_q[x]/(x^n + 1)$ where n is a power of two. We use the notation $s \xleftarrow{\$} D$ to denote that the element s is sampled according to distribution D. If D is a set, then we assume $s \xleftarrow{\$} D$ means that s is sampled uniformly from the set D. We denote the discrete Gaussian distribution over $\mathbb{Z}_q$ as χ_σ. The distribution χ_σ has its support restricted to $\mathbb{Z}_q$ and a probability mass function proportional to that of a Gaussian distribution with variance σ^2. Slightly abusing notation, we can sample a *polynomial* $s \xleftarrow{\$} \chi_\sigma$ by sampling each of the coefficients of s according to the distribution χ_σ.

We now informally introduce the *RLWE assumption* [15]. Let s be some secret polynomial in R_q. Samples from the $\mathrm{RLWE}_{n,q,\chi_e}(s)$ distribution take the form $(a, b = as + e) \in R_q \times R_q$ where $a \xleftarrow{\$} R_q$, $e \xleftarrow{\$} \chi_e$. Note that χ_e is referred to as the error distribution. The (normal form) $\mathrm{RLWE}_{n,q,\chi_e}$ problem is to distinguish between an oracle that outputs samples from $\mathrm{RLWE}_{n,q,\chi_e}(s)$ where $s \xleftarrow{\$} \chi_e$ and an oracle that outputs uniform elements in $R_q \times R_q$. The $\mathrm{RLWE}_{n,q,\chi_e}$ assumption states that no probabilistic polynomial-time algorithm can solve the $\mathrm{RLWE}_{n,q,\chi_e}$ problem with a non-negligible advantage. For details on secure parameter selection for the construction, see [19] or the full version [9].

5.2   Adapting BV-PRE for PCS

The underlying scheme, BV-PRE [19], is based on the BV-encryption scheme [5], which is based on RLWE. This scheme is parameterised by ciphertext modulus q, plaintext modulus $p \geq 2$, ring dimension n, polynomial ring $R_q = \mathbb{Z}_q[n]/\langle x^n + 1 \rangle$

and relinearisation window r. BV-PRE is not fully public-key, relying on an additional 'public' key 'pk'$_B$ for the target key s_B to generate update tokens. However, this key together with the token can be used to derive the old secret key. We get around this problem using the key resampling technique ReSample [5] shown in Fig. 6 which takes a public key pk$_B$ and outputs a fresh public key pk$'_B$ with the same underlying secret. We also use same relinearisation technique as [19] to reduce error growth.

$$
\begin{array}{l}
\hline
\textbf{ReSample(pk)} \\
\hline
(a, b) \leftarrow \text{pk} \\
v, e' \overset{\$}{\leftarrow} \chi_e \\
e'' \overset{\$}{\leftarrow} \chi_e \\
\bar{a} = av + pe' \\
\bar{b} = bv + pe'' \\
\textbf{return } \text{pk} = (\bar{a}, \bar{b}) \\
\hline
\end{array}
$$

Fig. 6. Key resampling technique given in [5] for re-randomizing public keys.

We give our construction, pcBV-PRE, in Fig. 7. It builds on BV-PRE in that randomness is also added by the proxy in the ReEnc operation. Recall that this is necessary for a scheme to have PCS, as otherwise an adversary could re-encrypt locally to obtain the same re-encryption. This additional randomness has minor implications for the correctness bound on multiple re-encryptions over that given in [19]. Note that pcBV-PRE inherits the IND-CPA-security proven in [19]. We defer further details including proof of correctness and correctness bound to the full version [9].

Theorem 4. pcBV-PRE *has Post-Compromise Security. In other words, any adversary $\mathcal{A}$ to the* PostComp *game,*

$$
\left| \Pr\left[\text{PostComp}_{\mathcal{A}}^{0, \mathcal{PRE}}(1^\lambda) = 1 \right] - \Pr\left[\text{PostComp}_{\mathcal{A}}^{1, \mathcal{PRE}}(1^\lambda) = 1 \right] \right| \leq \epsilon,
$$

for some $\epsilon = \text{negl}(n)$ under the $RLWE_{n,q,\chi_e}$ assumption.

We restrict ourselves to a proof overview of Theorem 4, giving the full proof in the full version [9], as the ideas are analogous to the proofs found in [19]. Recall that we do not leverage the result of Theorem 2 to prove PCS via source-hiding security, as pcBV-PRE is not source-hiding.

Proof Overview. The proof follows a sequence of game hops beginning with the PostComp$^{b,\mathcal{PRE}}$ security game where $b \overset{\$}{\leftarrow} \{0, 1\}$. In this game, the adversary is challenged to guess the bit b. Suppose that there are N honest entities who were not corrupted by the adversary. We make N game hops, each of which replaces:

KeyGen(1^λ)	Enc(pk, $m \in R_p$)	Dec(sk, c)
$a \xleftarrow{\$} R_q,$	$(a, b) \leftarrow \text{pk}$	$s \leftarrow \text{sk}$
$s, e \xleftarrow{\$} \chi_e \in R_q$	$v, e_0, e_1 \xleftarrow{\$} \chi_e$	$m' = c_0 - s \cdot c_1 \mod p$
$b = a \cdot s + pe \in R_q$	$c_0 = b \cdot v + pe_0 + m$	return m'
return (pk := (a, b), sk := s)	$c_1 = a \cdot v + pe_1$	
	return $c = (c_0, c_1)$	

ReKeyGen(sk_A, pk_B)	ReEnc($\Delta_{A \to B}, \text{pk}_B, c$)
for $i \in \{0, 1, \dots, \lfloor \log_2(q)/r \rfloor\}$:	$\{(\beta_i, \gamma_i)\}_{i=0}^{\lfloor \log_2(q)/r \rfloor} \leftarrow \Delta_{A \to B}$
$\quad (\beta_i, \theta_i) \xleftarrow{\$} \text{ReSample}(\text{pk}_B)$	$(c_0, c_1) \leftarrow c$
$\quad \gamma_i = \theta_i - \text{sk}_A \cdot (2^r)^i$	$(\beta^{\text{proxy}}, \theta^{\text{proxy}}) \leftarrow \text{ReSample}(\text{pk}_B)$
$\Delta_{A \to B} = \{(\beta_i, \gamma_i)\}_{i=0}^{\lfloor \log_2(q)/r \rfloor}$	$c_0' = c_0 + \displaystyle\sum_{i=0}^{\lfloor \log_2(q)/r \rfloor} (c_1^{(i)} \cdot \gamma_i) + \theta^{\text{proxy}}$
return $\Delta_{A \to B}$	$c_1' = \displaystyle\sum_{i=0}^{\lfloor \log_2(q)/r \rfloor} (c_1^{(i)} \cdot \beta_i) + \beta^{\text{proxy}}$
	return $c' = (c_0', c_1')$

Fig. 7. pcBV-PRE: an adaptation of the BV-PRE construction with Post-Compromise Security.ReSample is the key resampling algorithm described in [5]

1. the public key of a single honest (uncorrupted) entity with a uniform random value
2. the re-encryption keys created using the honest entity's public key with uniform random values.

In the final game hop, the challenge ciphertext given to the adversary is a uniformly sampled value and thus the adversary has no advantage in this game. This implies that $\text{PostComp}^{0, \mathcal{PRE}}$ and $\text{PostComp}^{1, \mathcal{PRE}}$ are indistinguishable.

6   Conclusions and Future Work

In this paper, we have formalised a provably stronger notion of Post-Compromise Security for PRE than existing and related security notions. We have shown PCS can be achieved via a number of existing PRE security notions which immediately shows that there are existing PRE schemes that satisfy PCS [11]. Finally, we give an efficient construction of a PCS secure PRE scheme based on lattices whose security can be proved directly without relying on the aforementioned existing and related security notions. We leave as future work the possibility of proving tighter bounds between security notions, and further investigating the relationship between selective and adaptive security for more generic graphs.

Acknowledgements. Special thanks to Katriel Cohn-Gordon for his help in motivating this work and providing the context for using PCS PRE to compliment the PCS messages in transit.

References

1. Ateniese, G., Fu, K., Green, M., Hohenberger, S.: Improved proxy re-encryption schemes with applications to secure distributed storage. ACM Trans. Inf. Syst. Secur. **9**(1), 1–30 (2006)
2. Barker, E., Barker, W., Burr, W., Polk, W., Smid, M.: Recommendation for key management part 1: general (revision 3). NIST Spec. Publ. **800**(57), 1–147 (2012)
3. Blaze, M., Bleumer, G., Strauss, M.: Divertible protocols and atomic proxy cryptography. In: Nyberg, K. (ed.) EUROCRYPT 1998. LNCS, vol. 1403, pp. 127–144. Springer, Heidelberg (1998). https://doi.org/10.1007/BFb0054122
4. Boneh, D., Lewi, K., Montgomery, H., Raghunathan, A.: Key homomorphic PRFs and their applications. In: Canetti, R., Garay, J.A. (eds.) CRYPTO 2013. LNCS, vol. 8042, pp. 410–428. Springer, Heidelberg (2013). https://doi.org/10.1007/978-3-642-40041-4_23
5. Brakerski, Z., Vaikuntanathan, V.: Fully homomorphic encryption from ring-LWE and security for key dependent messages. In: Rogaway, P. (ed.) CRYPTO 2011. LNCS, vol. 6841, pp. 505–524. Springer, Heidelberg (2011). https://doi.org/10.1007/978-3-642-22792-9_29
6. Canetti, R., Hohenberger, S.: Chosen-ciphertext secure proxy re-encryption. In: Ning, P., De Capitani di Vimercati, S., Syverson, P.F. (eds.) Proceedings of the 2007 ACM Conference on Computer and Communications Security, CCS 2007, pp. 185–194. ACM (2007)
7. Cohen, A.: What about bob? The inadequacy of CPA security for proxy reencryption. Cryptology ePrint Archive, Report 2017/785 (2017)
8. Cohn-Gordon, K., Cremers, C.J.F., Garratt, L.: On post-compromise security. In: IEEE 29th Computer Security Foundations Symposium, CSF 2016, pp. 164–178. IEEE Computer Society (2016)
9. Davidson, A., Deo, A., Lee, E., Martin, K.: Strong post-compromise secure proxy re-encryption. Cryptology ePrint Archive, Report 2019/368 (2019). https://eprint.iacr.org/2019/368
10. Everspaugh, A., Paterson, K.G., Ristenpart, T., Scott, S.: Key rotation for authenticated encryption. IACR Cryptology ePrint Archive, 2017:527 (2017)
11. Fuchsbauer, G., Kamath, C., Klein, K., Pietrzak, K.: Adaptively secure proxy re-encryption. Cryptology ePrint Archive, Report 2018/426 (2018)
12. Lee, E.: Improved security notions for proxy re-encryption to enforce access control. Cryptology ePrint Archive, Report 2017/824 (2017)
13. Lehmann, A., Tackmann, B.: Updatable encryption with post-compromise security. In: Nielsen, J.B., Rijmen, V. (eds.) EUROCRYPT 2018. LNCS, vol. 10822, pp. 685–716. Springer, Cham (2018). https://doi.org/10.1007/978-3-319-78372-7_22
14. Libert, B., Vergnaud, D.: Unidirectional chosen-ciphertext secure proxy re-encryption. In: Cramer, R. (ed.) PKC 2008. LNCS, vol. 4939, pp. 360–379. Springer, Heidelberg (2008). https://doi.org/10.1007/978-3-540-78440-1_21
15. Lyubashevsky, V., Peikert, C., Regev, O.: On ideal lattices and learning with errors over rings. In: Gilbert, H. (ed.) EUROCRYPT 2010. LNCS, vol. 6110, pp. 1–23. Springer, Heidelberg (2010). https://doi.org/10.1007/978-3-642-13190-5_1
16. Myers, S., Shull, A.: Efficient hybrid proxy re-encryption for practical revocation and key rotation. IACR Cryptology ePrint Archive, 2017:833 (2017)

17. OWASP. Cryptographic storage cheat sheet (2018). https://www.owasp.org/index. php/Cryptographic_Storage_Cheat_Sheet. Accessed 9 Oct 2018
18. PCI Security Standards Council. Payment card industry (PCI) data security standard (version 3.2.1) (2018)
19. Polyakov, Y., Rohloff, K., Sahu, G., Vaikuntanathan, V.: Fast proxy re-encryption for publish/subscribe systems. ACM Trans. Priv. Secur. **20**(4), 14:1–14:31 (2017)

Offline Witness Encryption from Witness PRF and Randomized Encoding in CRS Model

Tapas Pal$^{(\boxtimes)}$ and Ratna Dutta

Department of Mathematics, Indian Institute of Technology Kharagpur,
Kharagpur 721302, India
tapas.pal@iitkgp.ac.in, ratna@maths.iitkgp.ernet.in

Abstract. *Witness pseudorandom functions*, in short witness PRFs, (Zhandry, TCC 2016) and *witness encryption* (Garg et al., ACM 2013) are two powerful cryptographic primitives where the former produce a pseudorandom value corresponding to an instance of an NP language and the latter possesses the ability to encrypt a message with an NP problem. Mostly, these primitives are constructed using computationally expensive tools like obfuscation or multilinear maps. In this work, we build (single relation) witness PRFs using a puncturable pseudorandom function and a randomized encoding in common reference string (CRS) model. Next, we propose construction of an *offline witness encryption* having short ciphertexts from a public-key encryption scheme, an extractable witness PRF and a randomized encoding in CRS model. Furthermore, we show how to convert our single relation witness PRF into a *multi-relation* witness PRF and the offline witness encryption into an *offline functional witness encryption* scheme.

Keywords: Witness PRF · Offline witness encryption ·
Randomized encoding

1 Introduction

Witness PRF. Zhandry [15] generalizes the idea of witness encryption to initiate the study of a relatively modern and rich primitive *witness pseudorandom functions* (wPRFs). The power of wPRFs lie in the fact that it can be used in place of obfuscation to build many cryptographic tools that do not need to hide a programme P completely, like multiparty non-interactive key exchange without trusted setup, poly-many hardcore bits, re-usable witness encryption, Rudich secret sharing and fully distributed broadcast encryption.

Witness PRF for an NP language L is capable of computing a pseudorandom function F on an input statement x without the knowledge of secret key whenever a valid witness w for $x \in L$ is known and $F(x)$ can not be recognized in its domain if $x \notin L$, that is there does not exist a witness explaining $x \in L$. More specifically, wPRF first computes a pair of keys (fk, ek) depending on a relation

© Springer Nature Switzerland AG 2019
J. Jang-Jaccard and F. Guo (Eds.): ACISP 2019, LNCS 11547, pp. 78–96, 2019.
https://doi.org/10.1007/978-3-030-21548-4_5

circuit R corresponding to an NP language L where fk is the function secret key and ek is the function evaluation key. We note that $R(x, w) = 1$ if w is a valid witness for $x \in L$; otherwise 0. A user having the secret key fk generates a pseudorandom value $F(fk, x) \in \mathcal{Y}$ for any input x. The same pseudorandom value can be recovered using $Eval(ek, x, w)$ without the secret key fk if a valid witness w for $x \in L$ is known. From the adversary's point of view, the pseudorandom value $F(fk, x)$ is computationally indistinguishable from a uniformly chosen element in $\mathcal{Y}$ if there does not exist a witness w for $x \in L$. On the other hand, if $x \in L$ then, an adversary distinguishing $F(fk, x)$ from a random element in $\mathcal{Y}$ is to mean that there exists an efficient extractor that can be used to obtain a witness for $x \in L$. A wPRF processing this security assumption is called an *extractable witness pseudorandom function* (extractable wPRF). Another variant of wPRF is termed as *multi-relation* wPRF where one generates different function evaluation keys associated with many relation circuits of the same language L.

Witness Encryption. Garg et al. [8] introduced the notion of *witness encryption* (WE) which is closely related to wPRFs. In a plain public-key encryption (PKE), we encrypt data using a public key and decryption is possible if the corresponding secret key is known. WE enables us to encrypt a message with respect to an instance x of an NP language L. Only a witness holder can recover the original message from the ciphertext if he has a valid witness w for $x \in L$. The notion of *Functional witness encryption* was introduced by Boyle et al. [4] where a decrypter can only learn a function of the message if a valid witness for the instance is known.

Witness encryption consists of only two algorithms encryption and decryption. As a result, all the heavy-duty parts have been included in the encryption algorithm that makes WE more inefficient to use in small devices. Abusalah et al. [1] added a *Setup* phase which processes necessary tools to produce public parameters for encryption and decryption. Witness encryption with additional setup phase is called *offline witness encryption* (OWE).

Motivation. WEs and wPRFs are relatively new cryptographic primitives mostly built from either multilinear maps or obfuscation. As a result these primitives are experiencing inefficiency due to the existing noisy multilinear maps and impracticality of obfuscation. We aim to construct more efficient wPRF and OWE for any class of NP languages. Zhandry [15] used multilinear maps to construct wPRFs which are instance dependence and multilinearity level increases with respect to the size of relation circuits. The recent line of attacks on multilinear maps [3,5,6,9] is a threat to the cryptosystems where security is based on complexity assumptions related to multilinear maps. It was mentioned in [15] that wPRFs can be obtained from obfuscation but there was no explicit construction. In the same work, wPRFs were used to replace obfuscation from many cryptographic tools but those applications may not be fruitful in the practical sense as the existing multilinear maps are only approximate and encountered many non-trivial attacks.

The OWE scheme of [1] was realized using ElGamal public-key encryption and Gorth-Sahai proofs (GS-proofs) [12]. We note that GS-proofs are efficient non-interactive witness-indistinguishable proofs for some specific languages involving pairing product equations, multi-scaler multiplication equations or quadratic equations over some groups. The ElGamal ciphertexts can be represented in a way to get a set of pairing product equations so that a statistical simulation-sound non-interactive zero-knowledge (SSS-NIZK) proof can be ensured using the GS-proofs for those equations. Therefore, for practical use of the OWE scheme of [1], we need to carefully choose the PKE scheme so that a SSS-NIZK proof can be achieved through the GS-proofs. Otherwise, we need to use the transformation of [2,7] to achieve a SSS-NIZK proof that involves indistinguishability obfuscation and it may unnecessarily increase the size of OWE-ciphertexts. More specifically, for a given circuit C, an NIZK proof [11] for circuit satisfiability problem requires a size of $O(|C|k)$ where $O(k)$ is the size of common reference string and $|C|$ denotes size of circuit C. Therefore, the SSS-NIZK proof is of size at least linear in the size of the encryption circuit of the underlying PKE. We aim to get an OWE with relatively short ciphertexts where we do not require to generate such proofs and can use any PKE schemes as far as our requirement. Getting an efficient encryption algorithm producing short ciphertexts is a desirable property while constructing OWE so that one can use it in other cryptographic constructions.

Our Contribution. In this work we construct a single relation wPRF (Sect. 3) using a puncturable pseudorandom function and sub-exponentially secure randomized encoding scheme in CRS model. Our approach is to use the puncturable programming technique of [14] and incorporate the idea of getting obfuscation from randomized encoding (RE) scheme in common reference string (CRS) model [13]. A sub-exponentially secure randomized encoding scheme in CRS model can be achieved from a sub-exponentially secure public key functional encryption scheme and learning with error assumptions with sub-exponential hardness [13]. The security proof of our wPRF is independent of instances and does not rely on non-standard assumptions. We turn our single relation wPRF into a multi-relation wPRF (Remark 3) where one can use the scheme with a class of relations related to an NP language.

Furthermore, we build an OWE scheme (Sect. 4) utilizing an extractable wPRF. We replace SSS-NIZK by wPRF from the construction of [1] to reduce the size of ciphertext by at least linear to the size of encryption circuit of the elementary PKE scheme required in the building block. More precisely, our scheme is based on a public-key encryption, an extractable wPRF and employs a sub-exponentially secure randomized encoding scheme in CRS model. Consequently, the ciphertexts contain a pseudorandom string of fixed size instead of a SSS-NIZK proof. Using the same blueprint of [1], our OWE can be turned into an offline functional witness encryption (OFWE) scheme (Remark 4) where decryption releases a function of a message and witness as output. Inherently, our OFWE also possesses short ciphertext as compared to that of [1]. Unfortunately, the only extractable wPRF is known to be constructed from multilinear maps [15]. Our construction of OWE would be more interesting if wPRF with extracting feature can be built from standard assumptions without multilinear maps which is still an open problem.

2 Preliminaries

We use λ as the security parameter and follow the notations in Table 1 throughout this paper. We take $\perp$ as a distinguishing symbol.

Table 1. Notations

$a \leftarrow A$	a is an output of the procedure A
$a \xleftarrow{\$} X$	a is chosen uniformly at random from set X
Negligible function	$\mu : \mathbb{N} \rightarrow \mathbb{R}$ is a negligible function if $\mu(n) \leq \frac{1}{p(n)}$ holds for every polynomial $p(\cdot)$ and all sufficiently large $n \in \mathbb{N}$
$(\lambda_0, S(\cdot))$-indistinguishability	Two ensembles $\{X_\lambda\}$ and $\{Y_\lambda\}$ are $(\lambda_0, S(\cdot))$-indistinguishable means $|\Pr[x \xleftarrow{\$} X_\lambda : \mathcal{D}(x) = 1] - \Pr[y \xleftarrow{\$} Y_\lambda : \mathcal{D}(y) = 1]| \leq \frac{1}{S(\lambda)}$ for any security parameter $\lambda > \lambda_0$ and every $S(\lambda)$-size distinguisher $\mathcal{D}$, $S : \mathbb{N} \rightarrow \mathbb{N}$
δ-sub-exponential indistinguishability	Two ensembles $\{X_\lambda\}$ and $\{Y_\lambda\}$ are δ-sub-exponential indistinguishable means $|\Pr[x \xleftarrow{\$} X_\lambda : \mathcal{D}(x) = 1] - \Pr[y \xleftarrow{\$} Y_\lambda : \mathcal{D}(y) = 1]| < \delta(\lambda)^{\Omega(1)}$, for any security parameter λ and every poly-size distinguisher $\mathcal{D}$, where $\delta(\lambda) < 2^{\lambda^\epsilon}$, $0 < \epsilon < 1$.
$\text{Expt}(1^\lambda, 0) \approx_\delta \text{Expt}(1^\lambda, 1)$	For any polynomial size distinguisher $\mathcal{D}$, the advantage $\Delta = |\Pr[\mathcal{D}(\text{Expt}(1^\lambda, 0)) = 1] - \Pr[\mathcal{D}(\text{Expt}(1^\lambda, 1)) = 1]|$ is bounded by δ

Definition 1 (Puncturable pseudorandom function). A *puncturable pseudorandom function* (pPRF) consists of a tuple of algorithms pPRF = (Gen, Eval, Punc) over the domain $\mathcal{X}$ and range $\mathcal{Y}$ such that pPRF.Gen(1^λ) produces a secret key $K \in \{0, 1\}^\lambda$, pPRF.Eval(K', x) outputs a pseudorandom value $y \in \mathcal{Y}$ corresponding to $x \in \mathcal{X}$ using a key K' and pPRF.Punc($K, \mathcal{S}$) returns a punctured key $K\{\mathcal{S}\}$ for a polynomial size set $\mathcal{S} \subset \mathcal{X}$. The pPRF also satisfy the following properties:

- *Functionality preserving under puncturing.* For all polynomial-size subset $\mathcal{S}$ of $\mathcal{X}$, and for all $x \in \mathcal{X} \setminus \mathcal{S}$ we have

$$\Pr[\text{pPRF.Eval}(K, x) = \text{pPRF.Eval}(K\{\mathcal{S}\}, x)] = 1.$$

- *Pseudorandomness at punctured points.* For any PPT adversary $\mathcal{A}$ and polynomial size subset $\mathcal{S}$ of $\mathcal{X}$, where $K \leftarrow$ pPRF.Gen(1^λ), $K\{\mathcal{S}\} \leftarrow$ pPRF.Punc($K, \mathcal{S}$) we have

$$|\Pr[\mathcal{A}(K\{\mathcal{S}\}, \{\text{pPRF.Eval}(K, x)\}_{x \in \mathcal{S}}) = 1] - \Pr[\mathcal{A}(K\{\mathcal{S}\}, U^{|\mathcal{S}|}) = 1]| \leq \mu(\lambda)$$

where U denotes the uniform distribution over $\mathcal{Y}$ and μ is a negligible function in λ. The pPRF is said to be δ-secure for some specifies negligible function $\delta(\cdot)$ if the above indistinguishability gap $\mu(\lambda)$ is less than $\delta(\lambda)^{\Omega(1)}$.

(SK, PK) ← PKE.Gen(1^λ)	$x^* \leftarrow \mathcal{A}(1^\lambda)$	$(x, m_0, m_1, st) \leftarrow \mathcal{A}(1^\lambda)$
$(m_0, m_1, st) \leftarrow \mathcal{A}(1^\lambda, \text{PK})$	(fk, ek)← wPRF.Gen(1^λ, R)	$(pp_e, pp_d) \leftarrow$ OWE.Setup(1^λ, R)
$c_b \leftarrow$ PKE.Enc(PK, m_b; r)	$y_0 \leftarrow w\text{PRF.F(fk, } x^*), y_1 \xleftarrow{\$} \mathcal{Y}$	$c_b \leftarrow$ OWE.Enc(1^λ, x, m_b, pp_e)
$b' \leftarrow \mathcal{A}(c_b, st)$	$b' \leftarrow \mathcal{A}^{w\text{PRF.F(fk,}\cdot)}(\text{ek}, y_b)$	$b' \leftarrow \mathcal{A}(st, c_b, pp_e, pp_d)$
Return b' if $|m_0| = |m_1|$	Returns b' if $x^* \notin L$ and wPRF.F	Returns b' if $x \notin L$
	queries are distinct from x^*	

(a) $\mathbf{Expt}_\mathcal{A}^{\text{PKE}}(1^\lambda, b)$ (b) $\mathbf{Expt}_\mathcal{A}^{w\text{PRF}}(1^\lambda, b)$ (c) $\mathbf{Expt}_\mathcal{A}^{\text{OWE}}(1^\lambda, b)$

Fig. 1. Security experiments for PKE, wPRF and OWE

Definition 2 (Public-key encryption). A *public-key encryption* (PKE) scheme for a message space $\mathcal{M}$ is a tuple of PPT algorithms PKE = (Gen, Enc, Dec) where PKE.Gen(1^λ) generates a public key PK and a secret key SK, PKE.Enc (PK, m; r) outputs a ciphertext c for a message $m \in \mathcal{M}$ using a randomness r and PKE.Dec(SK, c) recovers the original message m if c is a valid ciphertext corresponding to the message, otherwise it returns $\perp$.

Definition 3 (Selectively secure PKE under chosen-plaintext attacks). We say that a public-key encryption scheme PKE = (Gen, Enc, Dec) is δ-selectively secure under chosen plaintext attacks (CPA) if

$$|\Pr[\mathbf{Expt}_\mathcal{A}^{\text{PKE}}(1^\lambda, 0) = 1] - \Pr[\mathbf{Expt}_\mathcal{A}^{\text{PKE}}(1^\lambda, 1) = 1]| \leq \mu(\lambda)$$

for any $\lambda \in \mathbb{N}$ and every PPT adversary $\mathcal{A}$ in the experiments $\mathbf{Expt}_\mathcal{A}^{\text{PKE}}(1^\lambda, b)$ defined in Fig. 1a where $b \in \{0, 1\}$ and μ is a negligible function of λ smaller than $\delta(\lambda)^{\Omega(1)}$.

Definition 4 (Witness PRF) [15]. A *witness PRF* (wPRF) for an NP language L with the witness relation $R : \chi \times W \rightarrow \{0, 1\}$ consists of three algorithms wPRF = (Gen, F, Eval) where wPRF.Gen(1^λ, R) generates a secret function key fk and a evaluation key ek, wPRF.F(fk, x) returns a pseudorandom value $y \in \mathcal{Y}$ corresponding to $x \in \mathcal{X}$ and wPRF.Eval(ek, x, w) deterministically recovers y if $x \in L$ and $R(x, w) = 1$, otherwise it returns $\perp$.

Definition 5 (Selectively secure witness PRF) [15]. We say that a witness PRF scheme wPRF = (Gen, F, Eval) for an NP language L, a relation $R : \chi \times W \rightarrow \{0, 1\}$, a set $\mathcal{Y}$, is δ-selectively secure if

$$\left|\Pr\left[\mathbf{Expt}_\mathcal{A}^{w\text{PRF}}(1^\lambda, 0) = 1\right] - \Pr\left[\mathbf{Expt}_\mathcal{A}^{w\text{PRF}}(1^\lambda, 1) = 1\right]\right| \leq \mu(\lambda)$$

for any $\lambda \in \mathbb{N}$ and every PPT adversary $\mathcal{A}$ in the experiments $\mathbf{Expt}_\mathcal{A}^{w\text{PRF}}(1^\lambda, b)$ defined in Fig. 1b where $b \in \{0, 1\}$ and μ is a negligible function of λ smaller than $\delta(\lambda)^{\Omega(1)}$.

Definition 6 (Extractable witness PRFs) [15]. A witness PRF scheme wPRF = (Gen, F, Eval) for an NP language L with relation R is said to be a secure *extractable witness PRF* if there exists a PPT adversary $\mathcal{A}$ having a non-negligible advantage $(1/2+1/p(\lambda))$, for a polynomial $p(\cdot)$, in the selective security experiment described in Fig. 1b with a small change that the challenge instance x^* may belong to L, then there is a polynomial time extractor $\mathcal{E}$ which on input $(\mathsf{ek}, x^*, \mathsf{Aux}, y^*, \{x_i\}, r)$ outputs a witness w^* satisfying $R(x^*, w^*) = 1$ with a significant probability greater than $1/q(\lambda)$ for a polynomial $q(\cdot)$ depending on $p(\cdot)$ where Aux is an auxiliary input, $\{x_i\}$ are the $w\mathsf{PRF.F}$ queries of $\mathcal{A}$ and r is a random coin.

Definition 7 (Offline witness encryption) [1]. An *offline witness encryption* (OWE) scheme for an NP language L with witness relation $R : \chi \times \mathcal{W} \rightarrow \{0, 1\}$ is a tuple of algorithms OWE $=$ (Setup, Enc, Dec) where $\mathsf{OWE.Setup}(1^\lambda, R)$ publishes a public parameter pp_e for encryption and a public parameter pp_d for decryption, $\mathsf{OWE.Enc}(1^\lambda, x, m, pp_e)$ outputs a ciphertext c corresponding to a message $m \in \mathcal{M}$ with an instance $x \in \chi$ and $\mathsf{OWE.Dec}(c, w, pp_d)$ recovers the original message m if $R(x, w) = 1$, otherwise it returns $\bot$.

Definition 8 (Selectively secure offline witness encryption) [1]. We say that an offline witness encryption OWE $=$ (Setup, Enc, Dec) for an NP language L and a relation $R : \chi \times \mathcal{W} \rightarrow \{0, 1\}$, is δ-selectively secure if

$$\left| \Pr\left[\mathrm{Expt}_{\mathcal{A}}^{\mathrm{OWE}}(1^\lambda, 0) = 1\right] - \Pr\left[\mathrm{Expt}_{\mathcal{A}}^{\mathrm{OWE}}(1^\lambda, 1) = 1\right] \right| \leq \mu(\lambda)$$

for any $\lambda \in \mathbb{N}$ and every PPT adversary $\mathcal{A}$ in the experiments $\mathrm{Expt}_{\mathcal{A}}^{\mathrm{OWE}}(1^\lambda, b)$ defined in Fig. 1c where $b \in \{0, 1\}$ and μ is a negligible function of λ smaller than $\delta(\lambda)^{\Omega(1)}$.

Remark 1. An *offline functional witness encryption* (OFWE) [1] scheme for an NP language L with witness relation $R : \chi \times \mathcal{W} \rightarrow \{0, 1\}$ and a class of functions $\{f_\lambda\}_{\lambda \in \mathbb{N}}$ is a tuple of algorithms OFWE $=$ (Setup, Enc, Dec) that follows the same syntax of Definition 7 except here Enc takes a message of the form $(f, m) \in f_\lambda \times \mathcal{M}$ instead of m. The security is defined similarly as in Definition 8.

Definition 9 (Randomized encoding schemes in CRS model) [13]. A randomized encoding (RE) scheme in CRS model for a class of Turing machines $\{\mathcal{M}_\lambda\}$ is a tuple of algorithms RE $=$ (Setup, Enc, Eval) where $\mathsf{RE.Setup}(1^\lambda, 1^m, 1^n, 1^T, 1^l)$ generates a common reference string crs and a public key pk, $\mathsf{RE.Enc}(pk, \Pi, x)$ outputs an encoding $\widehat{\Pi}_x$ corresponding to a Turing machine $\Pi \in \mathcal{M}_\lambda$ and $\mathsf{RE.Eval}(\widehat{\Pi}_x, \mathrm{crs})$ returns $\Pi^T(x)$ if $\widehat{\Pi}_x$ is a valid encoding of (Π, x). Here, $\Pi^T(x)$ denotes the output of the Turing machine Π on input x when run in at most T steps. The bounds on machine size, input length, time, output length are $m(\lambda), n(\lambda), T(\lambda), l(\lambda)$ respectively.

Definition 10 $((\lambda_0, S(\cdot))$-simulation security of randomized encoding in CRS model) [13]. We say that a randomized encoding scheme RE for a class of Turing machines $\{\mathcal{M}_\lambda\}$ in CRS model is $(\lambda_0, S(\cdot))$-simulation secure if there exists a

---

Hardwired: $\widetilde{\Pi}[\vec{pk}_1, C, \epsilon, \alpha]$, $\vec{crs}$
Input: an input $z = (z_1 z_2 \ldots z_n)$

1. $\widetilde{\Pi} \leftarrow \widetilde{\Pi}[\vec{pk}_1, C, \epsilon, \alpha]$, $i \leftarrow 0$
2. **while** $i \leqslant n$ **do**
3. $(\widetilde{\Pi}[\vec{pk}_{i+2}, C, z_1 z_2 \cdots z_i 0, \alpha_0^{i+1}], \widetilde{\Pi}[\vec{pk}_{i+2}, C, z_1 z_2 \cdots z_i 1, \alpha_1^{i+1}]) \leftarrow \text{RE.Eval}(\widetilde{\Pi}, \text{crs}_i)$
4. $\widetilde{\Pi} \leftarrow \widetilde{\Pi}[\vec{pk}_{i+2}, C, z_1 z_2 \cdots z_i z_{i+1}, \alpha_{z_{i+1}}^{i+1}]$
5. **end do**
6. **return** $\text{RE.Eval}(\widetilde{\Pi}, \text{crs}_i)$

Fig. 2. The special circuit $\mathcal{G}[\widetilde{\Pi}[\vec{pk}_1, C, \epsilon, \alpha], \vec{crs}]$

PPT algorithm Sim and a constant c such that for every $\{\Pi, x, m, n, l, T\}$ where $\Pi \in \mathcal{M}_\lambda$ and $|\Pi|, |x|, m, n, l, T \leq B(\lambda)$ for some polynomial B, the ensembles

$$\left\{ (\text{crs}, pk, \widehat{\Pi}_x) : (\text{crs}, pk) \leftarrow \text{RE.Setup}(1^\lambda, 1^m, 1^n, 1^T, 1^l), \widehat{\Pi}_x \leftarrow \text{RE.Enc}(pk, \Pi, x) \right\}$$

and $\left\{ (\text{crs}, pk, \widehat{\Pi}_x) : (\text{crs}, pk, \widehat{\Pi}_x) \leftarrow \text{Sim}(1^\lambda, \Pi^T(x), 1^{|\Pi|}, 1^{|x|}, 1^m, 1^n, 1^T, 1^l) \right\}$

are $(\lambda_0, S'(\lambda))$-indistinguishable (see Table 1), with $S'(\lambda) = S(\lambda) - B(\lambda)^c$ for all $\lambda \in \mathbb{N}$. The RE is said to be δ-simulation secure for some specific negligible function $\delta(\cdot)$ if $S'(\lambda)$ is greater than $\delta(\lambda)^{\Omega(1)}$. Also, we say that RE is δ-subexponential simulation secure if $\delta(\lambda) < 2^{\lambda^\epsilon}$, $0 < \epsilon < 1$.

Definition 11 (Sub-linear compactness of randomized encoding for Turing machines) [13]. A $(\lambda_0, S(\cdot))$-simulation secure randomized encoding scheme is said to be sub-linearly compact for a class of Turing machines $\{M_\lambda\}$ if we have $\text{Time}_{\text{RE.Enc}}(1^\lambda, \Pi, x, T) \leq \text{poly}(\lambda, |\Pi|, |x|) \cdot T^{1-\epsilon}$ for some $\epsilon \in (0, 1)$.

Remark 2. In [13], an $i\mathcal{O}$ is instantiated from a sub-exponentially secure and sub-linearly compact RE scheme in CRS model (Definition 11) and a sub-exponentially secure pseudorandom generator (PRG). They followed the technique of GGM construction [10] of building a PRF from a PRG using a tree. To get an $i\mathcal{O}$, the PRG in the GGM construction is replaced with a sub-exponentially secure sub-linear compact RE in CRS model. Let $\{\mathcal{C}_\lambda\}_{\lambda \in \mathbb{N}}$ be a circuit class with maximum size S, input size n, output size l and the running time bound T. The obfuscation procedure for a circuit $C \in \mathcal{C}_\lambda$ works as follows:

- We generate $(\text{crs}_i, pk_i) \leftarrow \text{RE.Setup}(1^\lambda, 1^S, 1^n, 1^T, 1^l)$, for $i \in \{0, 1, \ldots, n\}$, where crs_i is a common reference string and pk_i is an encoding key. Let $\vec{crs} = \{\text{crs}_i\}_{i=0}^n$, $\vec{pk}_i = \{pk_j\}_{j=i}^n$.
- We construct an input less Turing machine $\Pi[\vec{pk}_{i+1}, C, z, \alpha_{z_i}^i]$ where hardcoded entities are $\vec{pk}_{i+1}, C, z = z_1 z_2 \ldots z_i \in \{0, 1\}^i$ and a string $\alpha_{z_i}^i \in$

$\{0,1\}^{2p(\lambda,i)}$ (p being a polynomial depending on λ, i)[1] for all $i \in \{0, 1, \ldots, n-1\}$. When $i = 0$, z is the null string ϵ and $\alpha^i_{z_i}$ is a random string $\alpha \xleftarrow{\$} \{0,1\}^{2p(\lambda,0)}$. The Turing machine $\Pi[\vec{pk}_1, C, \epsilon, \alpha]$ computes randomized encodings of $\Pi[\vec{pk}_2, C, 0, \alpha^1_0]$ and $\Pi[\vec{pk}_2, C, 1, \alpha^1_1]$ where $(\alpha^1_0, \alpha^1_1) \leftarrow \mathrm{PRG}(\alpha)$ with $|\alpha^1_0| = |\alpha^1_1| = 2p(\lambda, 1)$, PRG being a sub-exponentially secure pseudorandom generator. To be more specific, the Turing machine $\Pi[\vec{pk}_1, C, \epsilon, \alpha]$ first generates $(\alpha^1_0, \alpha^1_1) \leftarrow \mathrm{PRG}(\alpha)$ and uses the randomness α^1_0 to compute encoding $\widetilde{\Pi}[\vec{pk}_2, C, 0, \alpha^1_0] \leftarrow \mathrm{RE.Enc}(pk_1, \Pi[\vec{pk}_2, C, 0, \alpha^1_0], \epsilon)$ and the randomness α^1_1 to compute the encoding $\widetilde{\Pi}[\vec{pk}_2, C, 1, \alpha^1_1] \leftarrow \mathrm{RE.Enc}(pk_1, \Pi[\vec{pk}_2, C, 1, \alpha^1_1], \epsilon)$. More generally, the Turing machine $\Pi[\vec{pk}_{i+1}, C, z, \alpha^i_{z_i}]$ computes randomized encodings $\widetilde{\Pi}[\vec{pk}_{i+2}, C, z0, \alpha^{i+1}_0] \leftarrow \mathrm{RE.Enc}(pk_{i+1}, \Pi[\vec{pk}_{i+2}, C, z0, \alpha^{i+1}_0], \epsilon)$ and $\widetilde{\Pi}[\vec{pk}_{i+2}, C, z1, \alpha^{i+1}_1] \leftarrow \mathrm{RE.Enc}(pk_{i+1}, \Pi[\vec{pk}_{i+2}, C, z1, \alpha^{i+1}_1], \epsilon)$, where $(\alpha^{i+1}_0, \alpha^{i+1}_1) \leftarrow \mathrm{PRG}(\alpha^i_{z_i})$ for $i \in \{1, 2, \ldots, n-1\}$. When $i = n$, the machine $\Pi[\vec{pk}_{i+1}, C, z, \alpha^i_{z_i}]$ outputs $C(z)$. We denote the class of all such Turing machines associated with the class of circuits $\{\mathcal{C}_\lambda\}$ as $\{\mathcal{M}_\lambda\}$.

- We compute an encoding $\widetilde{\Pi}[\vec{pk}_1, C, \epsilon, \alpha] \leftarrow \mathrm{RE.Enc}(pk_0, \Pi[\vec{pk}_1, C, \epsilon, \alpha], \epsilon)$. Next, we construct the special circuit $\mathcal{G}[\widetilde{\Pi}[\vec{pk}_1, C, \epsilon, \alpha], \vec{crs}]$ as described in Fig. 2 which takes input an n bit string $z = z_1 z_2 \cdots z_n$. For each $i \in \{0, 1, \ldots, n-1\}$, the circuit recursively computes $\mathrm{RE.Eval}(\widetilde{\Pi}[\vec{pk}_{i+1}, C, z_1 z_2 \cdots z_i, \alpha^i_{z_i}], crs_i)$ which by correctness of RE, is equal to the output of the Turing machine $\Pi[\vec{pk}_{i+1}, C, z_1 z_2 \cdots z_i, \alpha^i_{z_i}]$ i.e. two randomized encodings $\widetilde{\Pi}[\vec{pk}_{i+2}, C, z_1 z_2 \cdots z_i 0, \alpha^{i+1}_0]$ and $\widetilde{\Pi}[\vec{pk}_{i+2}, C, z_1 z_2 \cdots z_i 1, \alpha^{i+1}_1]$ (as in line 3 of Fig. 2). Finally, the circuit returns $\mathrm{RE.Eval}(\widetilde{\Pi}[\vec{pk}_{n+1}, C, z, \alpha^n_{z_n}], crs_n)$ which actually is equal to $C(z)$. The obfuscation of the circuit C is $i\mathcal{O}(1^\lambda, C) = \mathcal{G}[\widetilde{\Pi}[\vec{pk}_1, C, \epsilon, \alpha], \vec{crs}]$.

- To evaluate the circuit C for an input z, we compute $\mathcal{G}[\widetilde{\Pi}[\vec{pk}_1, C, \epsilon, \alpha], \vec{crs}](z)$.

Lin et al. [13] proved that for any pair of functionally equivalent circuits $C_0, C_1 \in \mathcal{C}_\lambda$, the joint distribution $(\widetilde{\Pi}[\vec{pk}_1, C_0, \epsilon, \alpha], \vec{crs})$ is indistinguishable from $(\widetilde{\Pi}[\vec{pk}_1, C_1, \epsilon, \alpha], \vec{crs})$. In particular, they have shown using the method of induction that for any label $i \in \{0, 1, \ldots, n\}$, $z \in \{0, 1\}^i$ the joint distributions $(\widetilde{\Pi}[\vec{pk}_{i+1}, C_0, z, \alpha^i_{z_i}], \vec{crs}_i, \vec{pk}_i)$ and $(\widetilde{\Pi}[\vec{pk}_{i+1}, C_1, z, \alpha^i_{z_i}], \vec{crs}_i, \vec{pk}_i)$ are indistinguishable. The indistinguishability was achieved by the simulation security of the RE scheme as described in the following theorem.

Theorem 1 [13]. *Assuming the existence of sub-exponentially secure one-way functions, if there exists a sublinearly compact randomized encoding scheme in*

---

[1] For every $\lambda \in \mathbb{N}, i \leq 2^\lambda$, $p(\lambda, i) = p(\lambda, i-1) + (2d\lambda)^{1/\epsilon}$ and $p(\lambda, -1) = \lambda$ where ϵ is a constant associated with the sub-exponential security of PRG, $d > 0$ is any constant strictly greater than c and the constant c represents the security loss associated with the indistinguishability security of RE (Sect. 4, [13]).

Hardwired: a pPRF key K.
Input: an instance $x \in \mathcal{X} = \{0,1\}^k$ and a witness $w \in \mathcal{W} = \{0,1\}^{n-k}$.
Padding: the circuit is padded to size pad $= \text{pad}(s, n, \lambda)$, determined in the analysis.

1. **if** $R(x, w) = 1$ **then**
2. $y \leftarrow$ pPRF.Eval(K, x).
3. **else** $y \leftarrow \perp$
4. **end if**
5. **return** y

Fig. 3. Evaluation circuit $E = \mathsf{EC}[K]$

the CRS model with sub-exponential simulation security, then there exists an bounded-input indistinguishability obfuscator for Turning machines.

We stress that RE.Enc$(pk_0, \Pi[\vec{pk}_1, C, \epsilon, \alpha], \epsilon)$ is actually a ciphertext obtained from the encryption algorithm of underlying PKFE that uses $(\Pi[\vec{pk}_1, C, \epsilon, \alpha], \epsilon, 0^{\lambda+1})$ as the plaintext. The size of the special circuit $\mathcal{G}$ is bounded by $\text{poly}(\lambda, |C|, T)$ and runtime of $\mathcal{G}$ on input z is bounded by $\text{poly}(\lambda, |z|, |C|, T)$. We will use the notation $\mathcal{G}[\widetilde{\Pi}[\vec{pk}_1, C, \epsilon, \alpha], \vec{crs}]$ for obfuscating a circuit C using a randomized encoding scheme in CRS model.

3 Our Witness PRF

Construction 1. We describe our construction of witness PRF (wPRF) that uses a puncturable pseudorandom function pPRF $=$ (Gen, Eval, Punc) with domain $\mathcal{X} = \{0,1\}^k$ and range $\mathcal{Y}$ and a randomized encoding scheme RE $=$ (Setup, Enc, Eval) which is a bounded input sub-linearly compact randomized encoding scheme in CRS model. Our scheme wPRF $=$ (Gen, F, Eval) for an NP language L with relation circuit $R : \mathcal{X} \times \mathcal{W} \rightarrow \{0,1\}$, $\mathcal{X} = \{0,1\}^k$, $\mathcal{W} = \{0,1\}^{n-k}$ and $|R| \leq s$, is given by the following algorithms.

- (fk, ek) $\leftarrow w$PRF.Gen$(1^\lambda, R)$: A trusted third party generates a secret function key fk and a public evaluation key ek for a relation R by executing the following steps where λ is a security parameter.
  - Choose a pPRF key $K \leftarrow$ pPRF.Gen(1^λ) where $K \in \{0,1\}^\lambda$.
  - Construct the circuit $E = \mathsf{EC}[K] \in \{E_\lambda\}$ as defined in Fig. 3. Let the circuit E be of size S with input size n, output size l and T is the runtime bound of the circuit.
  - Generate $(crs_i, pk_i) \leftarrow$ RE.Setup$(1^\lambda, 1^S, 1^n, 1^T, 1^l)$ for $i \in \{0, 1, \ldots, n\}$ where crs_i is a common reference string and pk_i is an encoding key. We define $\vec{crs} = \{crs\}_{i=0}^n$ and $\vec{pk}_i = \{pk_j\}_{j=i}^n$.
  - Compute the randomized encoding $\widetilde{\Pi}[\vec{pk}_1, E, \epsilon, \alpha] \leftarrow$ RE.Enc$(pk_0, \Pi[\vec{pk}_1, E, \epsilon, \alpha], \epsilon)$ where ϵ is a null string, α is a random binary string and $\Pi[\vec{pk}_1, E, \epsilon, \alpha]$ is a Turing machine defined in Remark 2.
  - Build the special circuit $\mathcal{G}[\widetilde{\Pi}[\vec{pk}_1, E, \epsilon, \alpha], \vec{crs}]$ as described in Fig. 2.

1. The adversary $\mathcal{A}$ submits a challenge statement $x^* \in \mathcal{X} \setminus L$.
2. The challenger generates (fk, ek) $\leftarrow$ wPRF.Gen(1^λ, R) as follows and sends ek to $\mathcal{A}$:
   2.1 Chose $K \leftarrow$ pPRF.Gen(1^λ) and set fk = K
   2.2 Construct the circuit $E = $ EC[K] as defined in Fig. 3
   2.3 Generate (crs$_i$, pk_i) $\leftarrow$RE.Setup(1^λ, 1^S, 1^n, 1^T, 1^l) for $i \in \{0, 1, \ldots, n\}$ where S, n, T, l are the same as in Construction 1 and set $\overrightarrow{\mathrm{crs}} = \{\mathrm{crs}\}_{i=0}^n$ and $\overrightarrow{pk_i} = \{pk_j\}_{j=i}^n$
   2.4 Build the special circuit $\mathcal{G}[\widetilde{\Pi}[\overrightarrow{pk}_1, E, \epsilon, \alpha], \overrightarrow{\mathrm{crs}}]$ as described in Fig. 2 where $\widetilde{\Pi}[\overrightarrow{pk}_1, E, \epsilon, \alpha] \leftarrow$ RE.Enc(pk_0, $\Pi[\overrightarrow{pk}_1, E, \epsilon, \alpha]$, ϵ) and $\Pi[\overrightarrow{pk}_1, E, \epsilon, \alpha]$ is a Turing machine defined in Rem. 2.
   2.5 Set ek = $\mathcal{G}[\widetilde{\Pi}[\overrightarrow{pk}_1, E, \epsilon, \alpha], \overrightarrow{\mathrm{crs}}]$
3. The challenger computes $y^* \leftarrow$ wPRF.F(fk, x^*) $\in \mathcal{Y}$ and sends it to $\mathcal{A}$.
4. The adversary $\mathcal{A}$ can make polynomial number of queries for wPRF.F on some $x \in \mathcal{X} \setminus \{x^*\}$ to the challenger and receives wPRF.F(fk, x).
5. The adversary $\mathcal{A}$ outputs a bit b'.

Fig. 4. Hybd$_0$ associated with our wPRF

- Set fk = K, ek = $\mathcal{G}$ $[\widetilde{\Pi}[\overrightarrow{pk}_1, E, \epsilon, \alpha], \overrightarrow{\mathrm{crs}}]$ and output (fk, ek). The secret function key fk is sent to a user over a secure channel and the evaluation key ek is made public.
- $y \leftarrow$ wPRF.F(fk, x): This algorithm is run by the user who has a secret function key fk and outputs a wPRF value $y \leftarrow$ pPRF.Eval(K, x) $\in \mathcal{Y}$ for an instance $x \in \mathcal{X}$ using the secret function key fk as a pPRF key K.
- wPRF.Eval(ek, x, w): An evaluator takes a witness $w \in \mathcal{W}$ for $x \in L$ and uses the public evaluation key ek = $\mathcal{G}[\widetilde{\Pi}[\overrightarrow{pk}_1, E, \epsilon, \alpha], \overrightarrow{\mathrm{crs}}]$ to get back the wPRF value as $\mathcal{G}[\widetilde{\Pi}[\overrightarrow{pk}_1, E, \epsilon, \alpha], \overrightarrow{\mathrm{crs}}](z)$ where $z = (x, w) \in \{0, 1\}^n$.

Correctness. By the correctness of randomized encoding scheme (Remark 2), we have $\mathcal{G}[\widetilde{\Pi}[\overrightarrow{pk}_1, E, \epsilon, \alpha], \overrightarrow{\mathrm{crs}}](z) = E(x, w)$. Therefore a valid witness-holder of $x \in L$ can recompute the wPRF value $y \in \mathcal{Y}$ associated with x using the witness w and the evaluation key ek = $\mathcal{G}[\widetilde{\Pi}[\overrightarrow{pk}_1, E, \epsilon, \alpha], \overrightarrow{\mathrm{crs}}]$. Note that, if w is not valid witness for $x \in L$ then the output of $E(x, w)$ is the distinguished symbol $\perp$.

Padding Parameter. The proof of security relies on the indistinguishability of randomized encodings of the machines $\Pi[\overrightarrow{pk}_1, E, \epsilon, \alpha]$ and $\Pi[\overrightarrow{pk}_1, E^*, \epsilon, \alpha]$ (where E and E^* are defined in Figs. 3 and 5 respectively). For this we set pad = max($|E|$, $|E^*|$). The circuits E and E^* compute the relation circuit R on an input (x, w) of size n and evaluate a puncturable PRF over the domain $\mathcal{X} = \{0, 1\}^k$ of size 2^k using a hardwired element which is a pPRF key for E or a punctured pPRF key for E^*. Thus, pad $\leq$ poly(λ, s, k) where s is the size of relation circuit R.

Efficiency. In this analysis, we discuss the size of wPRF.F and wPRF.Eval. The size of $\mathcal{X}$ is 2^k and wPRF.F includes a PRF evaluation over the domain $\mathcal{X}$. Therefore, size of wPRF.F is bounded by poly(λ, k). We note that, wPRF.Eval only runs the circuit $\mathcal{G}[\widetilde{\Pi}[\overrightarrow{pk}_1, E, \epsilon, \alpha], \overrightarrow{\mathrm{crs}}]$ over an input of size n. The running time of $\mathcal{G}[\widetilde{\Pi}[\overrightarrow{pk}_1, E, \epsilon, \alpha], \overrightarrow{\mathrm{crs}}]$ is poly($\lambda, n, |E|, T$) = poly(λ, n, k, s, T) and the size of $\mathcal{G}[\widetilde{\Pi}[\vec{pk}_1, E, \epsilon, \alpha], \vec{crs}]$ is $\mathrm{poly}(\lambda, |E|, T) = \mathrm{poly}(\lambda, k, s, T)$. In particular, the running time and size of wPRF.Eval are respectively $\mathrm{poly}(\lambda, n, k, s, T)$ and $\mathrm{poly}(\lambda, k, s, T)$. Here we note that the runtime T of the circuit E is bounded by the runtime of the relation R and the runtime of a pPRF evaluation. So, $T \leq T_R + \mathrm{poly}(\lambda, k)$ where T_R is the runtime of the relation circuit R on input (x, w) of size n. Hence, the runtime of wPRF.Eval is bounded by $\mathrm{poly}(\lambda, n, k, s, T_R)$ and size of wPRF.Eval is bounded by $\mathrm{poly}(\lambda, k, s, T_R)$.

Theorem 2. *Assume existence of δ-sub-exponentially secure one-way functions. Our construction 1 of wPRF = (Gen, F, Eval) is δ-selectively secure witness PRF if the pPRF is a δ-secure puncturable PRF and the RE is a bounded input sub-linearly compact randomized encoding scheme in CRS model with δ-sub-exponential simulation security for the class of Turing machines $\{\mathcal{M}_\lambda\}$ associated with the circuit class $\{E_\lambda\}$.*

Proof. We prove this by showing that for any non-uniform PPT adversary $\mathcal{A}$, the distinguishing advantage between the two experiments $\mathrm{Expt}_{\mathcal{A}}^{w\mathrm{PRF}}(1^\lambda, 0)$ and $\mathrm{Expt}_{\mathcal{A}}^{w\mathrm{PRF}}(1^\lambda, 1)$ (Fig. 1b) is negligible. Consider the following hybrid games:

Hybd$_0$. This is the standard experiment $\mathrm{Expt}_{\mathcal{A}}^{w\mathrm{PRF}}(1^\lambda, 0)$ described in Fig. 4.

Hybd$_1$. In this hybrid game we change $K \leftarrow$ pPRF.Gen(1^λ) into a punctured key $K\{x^*\} \leftarrow$ pPRF.Punc(K, x^*) and ek $= \mathcal{G}[\widetilde{\Pi}[\vec{pk}_1, E^*, \epsilon, \alpha], \vec{crs}]$ instead of $\mathcal{G}[\widetilde{\Pi}[\vec{pk}_1, E, \epsilon, \alpha], \vec{crs}]$ where $E^* = \mathsf{EC}[K\{x^*\}]$ is the circuit as defined in Fig. 5 and $y^* \leftarrow$ pPRF.Eval$(K, x^*) \in \mathcal{Y}$. We note that the functionality and running time of both the circuits E and E^* are the same. Also, the size of the two machines $\Pi[\vec{pk}_1, E, \epsilon, \alpha]$ and $\Pi[\vec{pk}_1, E^*, \epsilon, \alpha]$ is the same due to padding. Therefore, the joint distribution $(\widetilde{\Pi}[\vec{pk}_{i+1}, E, z, \alpha_{z_i}^i], \vec{crs}_i, \vec{pk}_i)$ is indistinguishable from $(\widetilde{\Pi}[\vec{pk}_{i+1}, E^*, z, \alpha_{z_i}^i], \vec{crs}_i, \vec{pk}_i)$ for every label $i \in \{0, 1, \ldots, n\}$ and $z \in \{0, 1\}^i$ (as discussed in Remark 2). Hence by simulation security of the RE scheme, we have Hybd$_0 \approx_\delta$ Hybd$_1$.

Hybd$_2$. This hybrid game is the same as previous one except that here we take y^* as a uniformly random element from $\mathcal{Y}$ instead of setting $y^* \leftarrow$ pPRF.Eval$(K, x^*) \in \mathcal{Y}$. From the pseudorandomness at punctured points (Definition 1) of the pPRF we have,

$$\mu(\lambda) \geq |\Pr[\mathcal{A}(K\{x^*\}, \mathrm{pPRF.Eval}(K, x^*)) = 1] - \Pr[\mathcal{A}(K\{x^*\}, U) = 1]| \geq |\Pr[\mathrm{Hybd}_1(\lambda) = 1] - \Pr[\mathrm{Hybd}_2(\lambda) = 1]|$$

for infinitely many λ and a negligible function μ where U denotes uniform distribution over the domain $\mathcal{Y}$ of pPRF.Eval. Since the pPRF is δ-secure, we have $\mu(\lambda) \leq \delta(\lambda)^{\omega(1)}$. Thus it holds that Hybd$_1 \approx_\delta$ Hybd$_2$.

Hybd$_3$. In this hybrid game, again we consider ek $= \mathcal{G}[\widetilde{\Pi}[\vec{pk}_1, E, \epsilon, \alpha], \vec{crs}]$ corresponding to the circuit $E = \mathsf{EC}[K]$ as in the original experiment Hybd$_0$. Everything else is the same as in Hybd$_2$. Following the similar argument as in Hybd$_1$, we have Hybd$_2 \approx_\delta$ Hybd$_3$.

```
Hardwired: a punctured key K{x*}.
Input: an instance x ∈ X and a witness w ∈ W

  1.  if R(x, w) = 1 then
  2.      if x = x* then
  3.          return y*
  4.      else return pPRF.Eval(K{x*}, x)
  5.  end if
  6.  return ⊥
```

Fig. 5. Evaluation circuit $E^* = \mathsf{EC}[K\{x^*\}]$

Note that Hybd_3 is actually the regular experiment $\mathrm{Expt}_{\mathcal{A}}^{w\mathrm{PRF}}(1^\lambda, 1)$. Hence, by the above sequence of hybrid arguments, $\mathrm{Expt}_{\mathcal{A}}^{w\mathrm{PRF}}(1^\lambda, 0)$ is indistinguishable from $\mathrm{Expt}_{\mathcal{A}}^{w\mathrm{PRF}}(1^\lambda, 1)$ and we write $\mathrm{Expt}_{\mathcal{A}}^{w\mathrm{PRF}}(1^\lambda, 0) \approx_\delta \mathrm{Expt}_{\mathcal{A}}^{w\mathrm{PRF}}(1^\lambda, 1)$. This completes the proof of Theorem 2.

Corollary 1. *Assuming* LWE *with sub-exponential hardness and the existence of δ-sub-exponentially secure one-way functions, if there exists a weakly sub-linear compact public key functional encryption scheme for* P/poly *with δ-sub-exponential security, then there exists a δ-secure witness* PRF *scheme. (The proof is available in the full version of this paper.)*

Remark 3. *A multi-relation wPRF* [15] *can be obtained from the above single-relation wPRF by generating evaluation keys for various relation circuits. This can be accomplished by splitting the key generation algorithm into two separate parts, one for function secret-key and the other is for function evaluation key. (We describe this in the full version of this paper.)*

4   Our Offline Witness Encryption

Construction 2. We now construct an offline witness encryption scheme OWE = (Setup, Enc, Dec) for any NP language L with relation circuit $R : \mathcal{X} \times \mathcal{W} \to \{0, 1\}$. The main ingredients are the following:

(i) A public-key encryption PKE = (Gen, Enc, Dec) semantically secure under chosen plaintext attack.

(ii) An extractable witness PRF $w\mathrm{PRF}$ = (Gen, F, Eval) for the NP language $L' = \{(c_1, c_2, \mathrm{PK}_1, \mathrm{PK}_2) : \exists \ (x, m, r_1, r_2) \text{ such that } c_i = \mathrm{PKE.Enc}(\mathrm{PK}_i, (x, m); r_i) \text{ for } i = 1, 2\}$ with the relation $R' : \mathcal{X}' \times \mathcal{W}' \to \{0, 1\}$. Therefore, $R'((c_1, c_2, \mathrm{PK}_1, \mathrm{PK}_2), (x, m, r_1, r_2)) = 1$ if c_1 and c_2 are both encryptions of the same message (x, m) using public keys $\mathrm{PK}_1, \mathrm{PK}_2$ and randomness r_1, r_2 respectively; otherwise 0. Here we assume that message, ciphertext of the PKE and the $w\mathrm{PRF}$ value can be represented as bit-strings.

(iii) A sub-linearly compact bounded input randomized encoding scheme RE = (Setup, Enc, Eval) in CRS model with δ-sub-exponential simulation security for Turing machines.

- $(pp_e, pp_d) \leftarrow$ OWE.Setup$(1^\lambda, R)$: This is run by a trusted authority to generate public parameters for both encryption and decryption where R is a relation circuit and λ is a security parameter. It works as follows:
  - Obtain two . pairs of PKE keys $(SK_1, PK_1) \leftarrow$ PKE.Gen(1^λ) and $(SK_2, PK_2) \leftarrow$ PKE.Gen(1^λ).
  - Generate $(fk, ek) \leftarrow w$PRF.Gen$(1^\lambda, R')$ for the relation circuit R'.
  - Construct the circuit $C_1 = \mathsf{MOC}[SK_1, fk] \in \{\mathcal{C}_\lambda\}$ as defined in Fig. 6. Let S be the size of the circuit C_1 with input size n, output size l and T is the runtime bound of the circuit on an input of size n.
  - Generate $(crs_i, pk_i) \leftarrow$ RE.Setup$(1^\lambda, 1^S, 1^n, 1^T, 1^l)$ for $i \in \{0, 1, \ldots, n\}$ where crs_i is a common reference string and pk_i is an encoding key. Set $\overrightarrow{crs} = \{crs\}_{i=0}^n$ and $\overrightarrow{pk_i} = \{pk_j\}_{j=i}^n$.
  - Compute the randomized encoding $\widetilde{\Pi}[\overrightarrow{pk}_1, C_1, \epsilon, \alpha] \leftarrow$ RE.Enc$(pk_0, \Pi$ $[\overrightarrow{pk}_1, C_1, \epsilon, \alpha], \epsilon)$ where ϵ is a null string, α is a random binary string and $\Pi[\overrightarrow{pk}_1, C_1, \epsilon, \alpha]$ is a Turing machine defined in Remark 2.
  - Build the special circuit $\mathcal{G}[\widetilde{\Pi}[\overrightarrow{pk}_1, C_1, \epsilon, \alpha], \overrightarrow{crs}]$ described in Fig. 2.
  - Set and output $(pp_e = (PK_1, PK_2, ek), pp_d = \mathcal{G}[\widetilde{\Pi}[\overrightarrow{pk}_1, C_1, \epsilon, \alpha], \overrightarrow{crs}])$.
- $c \leftarrow$ OWE.Enc$(1^\lambda, x, m, pp_e)$: An encrypter encrypts a message $m \in \mathcal{M}$ with respect to an NP statement $x \in \mathcal{X}$ using the public parameters for encryption pp_e and produces a ciphertext as follows:
  - Choose $r_1, r_2 \xleftarrow{\$} \{0, 1\}^{l_{\mathrm{PKE}}(\lambda)}$ where l_{PKE} is a polynomial in λ.
  - Compute two ciphertexts $c_i = $ PKE.Enc$(PK_i, (x, m); r_i)$ for $i = 1, 2$.
  - Generate a wPRF evaluation of the statement (c_1, c_2, PK_1, PK_2) with witness (x, m, r_1, r_2) as $y \leftarrow w$PRF.Eval$(ek, (c_1, c_2, PK_1, PK_2), (x, m, r_1, r_2))$ and output $c = (c_1, c_2, x, y)$ as ciphertext.
- OWE.Dec(c, w, pp_d): On receiving a ciphertext c, a receiver who has a witness w for $x \in L$, runs this algorithm using $pp_d = \mathcal{G}[\widetilde{\Pi}[\overrightarrow{pk}_1, C_1, \epsilon, \alpha], \overrightarrow{crs}]$ to learn the message by outputting $\mathcal{G}[\widetilde{\Pi}[\overrightarrow{pk}_1, C_1, \epsilon, \alpha], \overrightarrow{crs}](z)$ where $z = (c, w)$.

Correctness. If c_1, c_2 are the encryptions of the same message (x, m), then wPRF.Eval$(ek, (c_1, c_2, PK_1, PK_2), (x, m, r_1, r_2)) = w$PRF.F$(fk, (c_1, c_2, PK_1, PK_2))$. Since $w \in \mathcal{W}$ is a valid witness for the statement $x \in L$, then $R(x, w) = 1$ and by the correctness of RE scheme (Remark 2), we have $\mathcal{G}[\widetilde{\Pi}[\overrightarrow{pk}_1, C_1, \epsilon, \alpha], \overrightarrow{crs}](z) = C_1(z) = m$ where $z = (c, w)$.

Efficiency. The encryption algorithm OWE.Enc computes two public-key encryption on a message of size $(|x| + |m|)$ and one wPRF evaluation of an input of the form (c_1, c_2, PK_1, PK_2) with size-bound poly$(\lambda, |x| + |m|)$ using a witness of the form (x, m, r_1, r_2) with size-bound $(|x| + |m| + 2 . \mathrm{poly}(\lambda))$. Therefore, time of encryption is bounded by the time of PKE.Enc and evaluation time of wPRF and we have that $\mathsf{Time}_{\mathrm{OWE.Enc}} \leq 2 . \mathrm{poly}(\lambda, |x| + |m|) + \mathsf{Time}_{w\mathrm{PRF.Eval}}$. Also, the size of the ciphertext is $\mathsf{Size}_{\mathrm{OWE.c}} = 2 \, \mathsf{Size}_{\mathrm{PKE.c}} + |x| + |y|$ where $\mathsf{Size}_{\mathrm{PKE.c}}$ denotes the size of PKE-ciphertext. We note that $|y|$ can be bounded by a constant that does not depend on the PKE scheme.

Hardwired: a PKE secret key SK_j, a wPRF function key fk.
Input: a ciphertext c and a witness $w \in \mathcal{W}$

1. Parse $c = (c_1, c_2, x, y)$
2. if $(w\text{PRF.F}(\text{fk}, (c_1, c_2, PK_1, PK_2)) = y)$ then
3. $(\hat{x}, \hat{m}) \leftarrow \text{PKE.Dec}(SK_j, c_j)$
4.   if $((\hat{x} = x) \wedge (R(\hat{x}, w) = 1))$ then
5.   return $\hat{m}$
6.   end if
7. end if
8. return $\perp$

Fig. 6. Message output circuit $C_j = \text{MOC}[SK_j, \text{fk}]$, $j = 1, 2$

Theorem 3. *Assuming the existence of sub-exponentially secure one-way functions, our construction 2 of* OWE $=$ (Setup, Enc, Dec) *is δ-selectively secure offline witness encryption if the underlying* PKE *is a δ-secure public-key encryption under chosen plaintext attack (Definition 2), the* wPRF *is a δ-secure extractable witness* PRF *(Definition 6) and the* RE *is a bounded input δ-subexponential simulation secure (Definition 10) sub-linear compact randomized encoding scheme (Definition 11) in* CRS *model for the class of Turing machines* $\{\mathcal{M}_\lambda\}$ *associated with the class of circuits* $\{\mathcal{C}_\lambda\}$.

Proof. We show that the distinguishing advantage between two experiments $\text{Expt}_{\mathcal{A}}^{\text{OWE}}(1^\lambda, 0)$ and $\text{Expt}_{\mathcal{A}}^{\text{OWE}}(1^\lambda, 1)$ (Fig. 1c) for any PPT adversary $\mathcal{A}$ is negligible by defining the following sequence of hybrid games and proving the indistinguishability between them. Let the challenge messages be m_0 and m_1.

Hybd$_0$. The first game is the standard selective security experiment $\text{Expt}_{\mathcal{A}}^{\text{OWE}}(1^\lambda, 0)$ described in Fig. 7.

Hybd$_1$. In this hybrid game we choose y randomly from $\mathcal{Y}$ instead of computing $y \leftarrow w\text{PRF.Eval}(\text{ek}, (c_1, c_2, PK_1, PK_2), (x, m_0, r_1, r_2))$. The following claim shows that these games are indistinguishable in $\mathcal{A}$'s view.

Claim 1. *Assuming the* PKE *is a semantically secure public-key encryption[2] and the* wPRF *is an extractable witness* PRF, *Hybd$_0$ and Hybd$_1$ are δ-indistinguishable.*

Proof. Suppose the OWE-adversary $\mathcal{A}$ has a non-negligible advantage in distinguishing Hybd$_0$ and Hybd$_1$. Then $\mathcal{A}$ is now an adversary for wPRF relative to the relation R' and the security of extractable wPRF (Definition 6) implies that there is an extractor $\mathcal{E}$ that on input ek, (c_1, c_2, PK_1, PK_2), Aux, y, $\{x_i\}$, r, is able to find a witness $w' = (x, m_0, r_1, r_2)$, where Aux contains $st_\mathcal{A}$, the wPRF queries $\{x_i\}$ and r indicates the random coin used by $\mathcal{A}$. Therefore, $\mathcal{E}$ breaks the semantic security of the underlying PKE scheme used in our construction and we arrive at a contradiction. Hence, Hybd$_0 \approx_\delta$ Hybd$_1$.

---

[2] We know that indistinguishability security implies semanitc security for a public key encryption scheme.

1. The adversary chooses $(x, m_0, m_1, st) \leftarrow \mathcal{A}(1^\lambda)$ and sends it to the challenger. Here $x \notin L$, $|m_0| = |m_1|$ and st contains some auxiliary information.
2. The challenger generates public parameters $(pp_e, pp_d) \leftarrow$ OWE.Setup$(1^\lambda, R)$ as follows and sends it to $\mathcal{A}$:
    2.1 Generate $(SK_i, PK_i) \leftarrow$ PKE.Gen(1^λ) for $i = 1, 2$ and $(fk, ek) \leftarrow$ wPRF.Gen$(1^\lambda, R')$ where relation R' is the same as in Construction 2
    2.2 Set $pp_e = (PK_1, PK_2, ek)$
    2.3 Construct the message output circuit $C_1 = \text{MOC}[SK_1, fk]$ (see Fig. 6)
    2.4 Generate $(crs_i, pk_i) \leftarrow$ RE.Setup$(1^\lambda, 1^S, 1^n, 1^T, 1^l)$ for $i \in \{0, 1, \dots, n\}$ where S, n, T, l are the same as in Construction 2 and set $\overrightarrow{crs} = \{crs\}_{i=0}^n$ and $\overrightarrow{pk_i} = \{pk_j\}_{j=i}^n$
    2.5 Construct the special circuit $\mathcal{G}[\widetilde{\Pi}[\overrightarrow{pk}_1, C_1, \epsilon, \alpha], \overrightarrow{crs}]$ as described in Fig. 2, where $\widetilde{\Pi}[\overrightarrow{pk}_1, C_1, \epsilon, \alpha] \leftarrow$ RE.Enc$(pk_0, \Pi[\overrightarrow{pk}_1, C_1, \epsilon, \alpha], \epsilon)$ and $\Pi[\overrightarrow{pk}_1, C_1, \epsilon, \alpha]$ is a Turing machine defined in Rem. 2.
    2.6 Set $pp_d = \mathcal{G}[\widetilde{\Pi}[\overrightarrow{pk}_1, C_1, \epsilon, \alpha], \overrightarrow{crs}]$
3. The challenger produces the ciphertext $c \leftarrow$ OWE.Enc$(1^\lambda, x, m_0, pp_e)$ as follows and submits it to $\mathcal{A}$:
    3.1 Chose $r_1, r_2 \xleftarrow{\$} \{0, 1\}^{l_{PKE}(\lambda)}$
    3.2 Compute $c_1 \leftarrow$ PKE.Enc$(PK_1, (x, m_0); r_1)$, $c_2 \leftarrow$ PKE.Enc$(PK_2, (x, m_0); r_2)$
    3.3 Evaluate $y \leftarrow w$PRF.Eval$(ek, (c_1, c_2, PK_1, PK_2), (x, m_0, r_1, r_2))$
    3.4 Set $c \leftarrow (c_1, c_2, x, y)$
4. The adversary observing (st, c, pp_e, pp_d), outputs a bit $b' \leftarrow \mathcal{A}(st, c, pp_e, pp_d)$.

Fig. 7. Hybd$_0$ associated with our OWE

Hybd$_2$. In this hybrid game, we set $c_2 \leftarrow$ PKE.Enc$(PK_2, (x, m_1); r_2)$ instead of $c_2 \leftarrow$ PKE.Enc$(PK_2, (x, m_0); r_2)$. The distribution of ciphertexts in Hybd$_1$ and Hybd$_2$ are computationally indistinguishable due to the CPA-security of underlying PKE scheme (Definition 3). We prove this in the following claim.

Claim 2. *Assuming the* PKE *is a δ-secure public-key encryption under chosen plaintext attack,* Hybd$_1$ *and* Hybd$_2$ *are δ-indistinguishable.*

Proof. To prove this we construct a PKE-adversary $\mathcal{B}$ against the security (Definition 3) of PKE scheme for the key PK_2 as described in Fig. 8. From the construction we see that if $c'_b \leftarrow$ PKE.Enc$(PK_2, (x, m_0); r_2)$, then $\mathcal{B}$ simulates Hybd$_0$. If $c'_b \leftarrow$ PKE.Enc$(PK_2, (x, m_1); r_2)$, then $\mathcal{B}$ simulates Hybd$_1$. Therefore, the distinguishing advantage of $\mathcal{A}$ between Hybd$_0$ and Hybd$_1$ can be bounded as

$$|\Pr[\text{Hybd}_0(\lambda) = 1] - \Pr[\text{Hybd}_1(\lambda) = 1]|$$
$$\leq |\Pr[\text{Expt}_\mathcal{B}^{PKE}(1^\lambda, 0) = 1] - \Pr[\text{Expt}_\mathcal{B}^{PKE}(1^\lambda, 1) = 1]|.$$

Then, we can use the indistinguishability guarantee of the underlying PKE to make the above advantage less than a negligible function of λ. Therefore, we have Hybd$_1 \approx_\delta$ Hybd$_2$.

Hybd$_3$. This hybrid game is the same as the previous game except that we take pp_d as the circuit $\mathcal{G}[\widetilde{\Pi}[\overrightarrow{pk}_1, C_2, \epsilon, \alpha], \overrightarrow{crs}]$ instead of setting $pp_d \leftarrow \mathcal{G}[\widetilde{\Pi}[\overrightarrow{pk}_1, C_1, \epsilon, \alpha], \overrightarrow{crs}]$. We show indistinguishability in the following claim.

1. The PKE-challenger runs PKE.Gen(1^λ) → (SK$_2$, PK$_2$) and makes Pk$_2$ public.
2. The PKE-adversary $\mathcal{B}$ submits the challenge messages m_0', m_1' to the PKE-challenger as follows with some auxiliary information st and $|m_0'| = |m_1'|$:

   2.1 Invoke OWE-adversary $\mathcal{A}$ to obtain $(x, m_0, m_1, st_\mathcal{A}) \leftarrow \mathcal{A}(1^\lambda)$ where $x \notin L$ and $|m_0| = |m_1|$

   2.2 Genereate (SK$_1$, PK$_1$) ← PKE.Gen(1^λ)

   2.3 Compute (fk, ek)← wPRF.Gen(1^λ, R') for the relation R' defined in Construction 2

   2.4 Choose $r_1 \xleftarrow{\$} \{0, 1\}^{l_{\text{PKE}}(\lambda)}$

   2.5 Compute $c_1 = $ PKE.Enc(PK$_1$, (x, m_0); r_1)

   2.6 Set $m_0' = (x, m_0)$, $m_1' = (x, m_1)$ and $st = $ (SK$_1$, PK$_1$, fk, ek, c_1, r_1, x, m_0, m_1, $st_\mathcal{A}$)

3. The PKE-challenger chooses a random bit $b \in \{0, 1\}$ and sends the ciphertext $c_b' \leftarrow$ PKE.Enc(PK$_2$, $m_b' = (x, m_b)$; r_2) to $\mathcal{B}$, where $r_2 \xleftarrow{\$} \{0, 1\}^{l_{\text{PKE}}(\lambda)}$.

4. The PKE-adversary $\mathcal{B}$ simulates $\mathcal{A}$ to output a guess for b by observing (st, c_b') as foloows:

   4.1 Set $c_2 = c_b'$

   4.2 Compute $y \xleftarrow{\$} \mathcal{Y}$

   4.3 Construct the message output circuit $C_1 = $ MOC[SK$_1$, fk] (see Fig. 6)

   4.4 Generate (crs$_i$, pk_i) ← RE.Setup(1^λ, 1^S, 1^n, 1^T, 1^l) for $i \in \{0, 1, \ldots, n\}$ where S, n, T, l are the same as in Construction 2 and set $\overrightarrow{\text{crs}} = \{\text{crs}\}_{i=0}^n$ and $\overrightarrow{pk_i} = \{pk_j\}_{j=i}^n$

   4.5 Construct the special circuit $\mathcal{G}[\widetilde{\Pi}[\overrightarrow{pk}_1, C_1, \epsilon, \alpha], \overrightarrow{\text{crs}}]$ as described in Fig. 2, where $\widetilde{\Pi}[\overrightarrow{pk}_1, C_1, \epsilon, \alpha] \leftarrow$ RE.Enc(pk_0, $\Pi[\overrightarrow{pk}_1, C_1, \epsilon, \alpha]$, ϵ) and $\Pi[\overrightarrow{pk}_1, C_1, \epsilon, \alpha]$ is a Turing machine defined in Rem. 2.

   4.6 Set $c = (c_1, c_2, x, y)$, $pp_e = $ (PK$_1$, PK$_2$, ek), $pp_d = \mathcal{G}[\widetilde{\Pi}[\overrightarrow{pk}_1, C_1, \epsilon, \alpha], \overrightarrow{\text{crs}}]$ and send ($st_\mathcal{A}$, c, pp_e, pp_d) to the OWE-adversary $\mathcal{A}$

   4.7 Output a guess $b' \leftarrow \mathcal{A}(st_\mathcal{A}, c, pp_e, pp_d)$ for b

Fig. 8. The PKE-adversary $\mathcal{B}$ simulating **Hybd$_2$**

Claim 3. *Assuming the RE is a δ-sub-exponential simulation secure sub-linear compact randomized encoding scheme in CRS model for the class of Turing machines $\{\mathcal{M}_\lambda\}$ associated with the class of circuits $\{\mathcal{C}_\lambda\}$, Hybd$_2$ and Hybd$_3$ are δ-indistinguishable.*

Proof. We need to show that the joint distributions $(\widetilde{\Pi}[\overrightarrow{pk}_{i+1}, C_1, z, \alpha_{z_i}^i], \overrightarrow{\text{crs}}_i, \overrightarrow{pk}_i)$ and $(\widetilde{\Pi}[\overrightarrow{pk}_{i+1}, C_2, z, \alpha_{z_i}^i], \overrightarrow{\text{crs}}_i, \overrightarrow{pk}_i)$ for every label $i \in \{0, 1, \ldots, n\}$ and $z \in \{0, 1\}^i$, are indistinguishable. It will imply that the two hybrids Hybd$_2$, Hybd$_3$ are indistinguishable. If the functionality, runtime and size of two circuits C_1 and C_2 are the same then the above indistinguishability follows from the underlying simulation security of RE scheme in CRS model according to the discussion in Remark 2.

We define an RE-adversary $\mathcal{B}$ against the indistinguishability secure RE scheme in Fig. 9. We note RE is δ-indistinguishability secure implies that, if the two ensembles $\{\Pi_1(x_1), |\Pi_1|, |x_1|, T_1 : (\Pi_1, x_1, T_1) \xleftarrow{\$} X_{1,\lambda}\}$ and $\{\Pi_2(x_2), |\Pi_2|, |x_2|, T_2 : (\Pi_2, x_2, T_2) \xleftarrow{\$} X_{2,\lambda}\}$ are δ-indistinguishable then the two distributions $\{$RE.Enc(pk, Π_1, x_1): $(\Pi_1, x_1, T_1) \xleftarrow{\$} X_{1,\lambda}\}$ and $\{$RE.Enc(pk, Π_2, x_2): $(\Pi_2, x_2, T_2) \xleftarrow{\$} X_{2,\lambda}\}$ are also δ-indistinguishable, where $\Pi_j \in \mathcal{M}_\lambda$ and T_j denotes the runtime of Π_j on input x_j for $j = 1, 2$.

Therefore, if $pp_d = \mathcal{G}[\widetilde{\Pi}[\overrightarrow{pk}_1, C_1, \epsilon, \alpha], \overrightarrow{\text{crs}}]$ then $\mathcal{B}$ simulates Hybd$_1$ and if $pp_d = \mathcal{G}[\widetilde{\Pi}[\overrightarrow{pk}_1, C_2, \epsilon, \alpha], \overrightarrow{\text{crs}}]$ then $\mathcal{B}$ simulates Hybd$_2$. Now we show the functional

1. The OWE-adversary chooses $(\bar{x}, \bar{m}_0, \bar{m}_1, st) \leftarrow \mathcal{A}(1^\lambda)$ and sends it to the RE-adversary $\mathcal{B}$, where $\bar{x} \notin L$, $|\bar{m}_0| = |\bar{m}_1|$ and st contains some auxiliary information.
2. The RE-adversary $\mathcal{B}$ generates public parameters (pp_e, pp_d) as follows and sends it to $\mathcal{A}$:
   2.1 Generate $(\text{SK}_i, \text{PK}_i) \leftarrow \text{PKE.Gen}(1^\lambda)$ for $i = 1, 2$ and $(\text{fk}, \text{ek}) \leftarrow w\text{PRF.Gen}(1^\lambda, R')$ where relation R' is the same as in Construction 2
   2.2 Set $pp_e = (\text{PK}_1, \text{PK}_2, \text{ek})$
   2.3 Construct the message output circuits $C_j = \text{MOC}[\text{SK}_j, \text{fk}]$ for $j = 1, 2$ (see Fig. 6)
   2.4 Generate $(\text{crs}_i, pk_i) \leftarrow \text{RE.Setup}(1^\lambda, 1^S, 1^n, 1^T, 1^l)$ for $i \in \{0, 1, \ldots, n\}$ where S, n, T, l are the same as in Construction 2 and set $\overrightarrow{\text{crs}} = \{\text{crs}\}_{i=0}^n$ and $\overrightarrow{\text{pk}_i} = \{pk_i\}_{j=i}^n$
   2.5 Submit the circuits C_j to the RE-challenger for $j = 1, 2$
   2.6 The RE-challenger pick a random $j \xleftarrow{\$} \{1, 2\}$ and sends $\widetilde{\Pi}[\overrightarrow{pk}_1, C_j, \epsilon, \alpha] \leftarrow \text{RE.Enc}(pk_0, \Pi[\overrightarrow{pk}_1, C_j, \epsilon, \alpha], \epsilon)$ to $\mathcal{B}$ where $\Pi[\overrightarrow{pk}_1, C_j, \epsilon, \alpha]$ is a Turing machine defined in Rem. 2.
   2.7 Construct the special circuit $\mathcal{G}[\widetilde{\Pi}[\overrightarrow{pk}_1, C_j, \epsilon, \alpha], \overrightarrow{\text{crs}}]$ as described in Fig. 2.
   2.8 Set $pp_d = \mathcal{G}[\widetilde{\Pi}[\overrightarrow{pk}_1, C_1, \epsilon, \alpha], \overrightarrow{\text{crs}}]$
3. The RE-adversary $\mathcal{B}$ produces a OWE-ciphertext $\bar{c}$ as follows and submits it to the OWE-adversary $\mathcal{A}$:
   3.1 Chose $r_1, r_2 \xleftarrow{\$} \{0, 1\}^{l_{\text{PKE}}(\lambda)}$
   3.2 Compute $\bar{c}_1 \leftarrow \text{PKE.Enc}(\text{PK}_1, (\bar{x}, \bar{m}_0); r_1)$, $\bar{c}_2 \leftarrow \text{PKE.Enc}(\text{PK}_2, (\bar{x}, \bar{m}_1); r_2)$
   3.3 Choose $\bar{y} \xleftarrow{\$} \mathcal{Y}$
   3.4 Set $\bar{c} = (\bar{c}_1, \bar{c}_2, \bar{x}, \bar{y})$ and send it to the OWE-adversary $\mathcal{A}$
4. Output $b' \leftarrow \mathcal{A}(st, \bar{c}, pp_e, pp_d)$.

Fig. 9. The RE-adversary $\mathcal{B}$ simulating **Hybd$_3$**

equivalence of the circuits C_1 and C_2. Let (c, w) be any arbitrary input to the circuits C_j, $j = 1, 2$ where $c = (c_1, c_2, x, y)$.

Case 1. $(x = \bar{x}, c_1 = \bar{c}_1$ and $c_2 = \bar{c}_2)$: Since $\bar{x} \notin L$, we have $R(x, w) = 0$ in line 4 of C_j (Fig. 6), thus C_1 and C_2 both output $\bot$.

Case 2. $(x \neq \bar{x}, c_1 = \bar{c}_1$ and $c_2 = \bar{c}_2)$: Correctness of PKE scheme implies $\text{PKE.Dec}(\text{SK}_j, c_j) = (\bar{x}, \bar{m}_j)$ in line 3 of C_j (Fig. 6) and both the circuits returns $\bot$ as $x \neq \bar{x}$ in line 4.

Case 3. $(c_1 \neq \bar{c}_1$ or $c_2 \neq \bar{c}_2)$: If c_1 and c_2 are encryptions of the same message then we have $\text{PKE.Dec}(\text{SK}_1, c_1) = \text{PKE.Dec}(\text{SK}_2, c_2)$. Therefore, the behavior of both circuits C_1 and C_2 are the same as they differ only in line 3. If the decryptions of c_1 and c_2 not equal then $(c_1, c_2, \text{PK}_1, \text{PK}_2) \notin L'$ and by the correctness of $w\text{PRF}$ scheme we have $y \neq w\text{PRF.F}(\text{fk}, (c_1, c_2, \text{PK}_1, \text{PK}_2))$. Hence, the circuits C_1 and C_2 return $\bot$ due to line 2 (Fig. 6).

This shows that C_1 and C_2 are functionally equivalent. Also, we note that size and time bound for both the circuits are the same. Hence, we have $\text{Hybd}_2 \approx_\delta \text{Hybd}_3$. This completes the proof of Claim 3.

Hybd$_4$. The only difference of this hybrid from Hybd_3 is that we compute $c_1 \leftarrow \text{PKE.Enc}(\text{PK}_1, (x, m_1); r_1)$ instead of $c_1 \leftarrow \text{PKE.Enc}(\text{PK}_1, (x, m_0); r_1)$. Therefore, Hybd_3 and Hybd_4 are computationally indistinguishable by the CPA security of the underlying PKE scheme for the key PK_1.

Claim 4. Assuming the PKE is a δ-secure public-key encryption under chosen plaintext attack, Hybd_3 and Hybd_4 are δ-indistinguishable.

Hardwired: a PKE secret key SK_j, a wPRF function key fk.
Input: a ciphertext c and a witness $w \in \mathcal{W}$

1. Parse $c = (c_1, c_2, x, y)$
2. **if** $(w\text{PRF.F}(\text{fk}, (c_1, c_2, PK_1, PK_2)) = y)$ **then**
3. $\quad (\hat{x}, (\hat{f}, \hat{m})) \leftarrow \text{PKE.Dec}(SK_j, c_j)$
4. $\quad$ **if** $((\hat{x} = x) \wedge (R(\hat{x}, w) = 1))$ **then**
5. $\quad\quad$ **return** $\hat{f}(\hat{m}, w)$
6. $\quad$ **end if**
7. **end if**
8. **return** $\perp$

Fig. 10. Modified message output circuit $F_j = \text{MMOC}[SK_j, \text{fk}]$, $j = 1, 2$

Hybd$_5$. In this hybrid game we take pp_d as the circuit $\mathcal{G}[\widetilde{\Pi}[\overrightarrow{pk}_1, C_1, \epsilon, \alpha], \overrightarrow{\text{crs}}]$ instead of $\mathcal{G}[\widetilde{\Pi}[\overrightarrow{pk}_1, C_2, \epsilon, \alpha], \overrightarrow{\text{crs}}]$ as in the standard scheme. Therefore, by the underlying simulation secure RE scheme we have Hybd$_4$ and Hybd$_5$ are computationally indistinguishable as stated in the following claim.

Claim 5. *Assuming the* RE *is a* δ-*sub-exponential simulation secure sub-linear compact randomized encoding scheme in* CRS *model for the class of Turing machines* $\{\mathcal{M}_\lambda\}$ *associated with the class of circuits* $\{\mathcal{C}_\lambda\}$, Hybd$_4$ *and* Hybd$_5$ *are* δ-*indistinguishable.*

Hybd$_6$. In this hybrid we compute $y \leftarrow w\text{PRF.Eval}(\text{ek}, (c_1, c_2, PK_1, PK_2), (x, m_0, r_1, r_2))$ instead of choosing y randomly from $\mathcal{Y}$. The indistinguishability is guaranteed by the following claim.

Claim 6. *Assuming the* PKE *is a semantically secure public-key encryption and the* wPRF *is an extractable witness* PRF, Hybd$_5$ *and* Hybd$_6$ *are* δ-*indistinguishable.*

The proofs of Claims 4, 5, and 6 are analogous to that of Claims 2, 3, and 1 respectively. Observe that Hybd$_6$ is the experiment $\text{Expt}_{\mathcal{A}}^{\text{OWE}}(1^\lambda; 1)$. The indistinguishability between the above hybrid games implies that $\text{Expt}_{\mathcal{A}}^{\text{OWE}}(1^\lambda, 0) \approx_\delta \text{Expt}_{\mathcal{A}}^{\text{OWE}}(1^\lambda, 1)$ and the distinguishing advantage for the adversary $\mathcal{A}$ is strictly less than $\mu(\lambda)$, where μ is a negligible function of λ. This completes the proof.

Remark 4. We convert our OWE scheme into an offline functional witness encryption (OFWE) scheme for a class of functions $\{f_\lambda\}_{\lambda \in \mathbb{N}}$. The encryption algorithm of OFWE is the same as our OWE except that it takes an additional input a function $f \in f_\lambda$ and then encrypts the pair of the function f and a message m with the statement x using the PKE encryption to produce ciphertexts $c_i \leftarrow \text{PKE.Enc}(PK_i, (x, (f, m)); r_i)$ for $i = 1, 2$. In line 3 of the circuit C_j (Fig. 6), we will have $\text{PKE.Dec}(SK_j, c_j) = (\hat{x}, (\hat{f}, \hat{m}))$ and in line 5 it will return $\hat{f}(\hat{m}, w)$ instead of $\hat{m}$ (see circuit F_j in Fig. 10). Rest of the algorithms of OFWE.Setup and OFWE.Dec will be the same as that of our OWE scheme. The time of encryption of the OWEF is bounded by $\text{poly}(\lambda, |x| + |m| + |f|)$ where $|x|, |m|, |f|$ are the size of x, m, f respectively. The correctness and the security of the OFWE depend on the same assumptions as in the case of our OWE.

References

1. Abusalah, H., Fuchsbauer, G., Pietrzak, K.: Offline witness encryption. In: Manulis, M., Sadeghi, A.-R., Schneider, S. (eds.) ACNS 2016. LNCS, vol. 9696, pp. 285–303. Springer, Cham (2016). https://doi.org/10.1007/978-3-319-39555-5_16
2. Bitansky, N., Paneth, O.: ZAPs and non-interactive witness indistinguishability from indistinguishability obfuscation. In: Dodis, Y., Nielsen, J.B. (eds.) TCC 2015. LNCS, vol. 9015, pp. 401–427. Springer, Heidelberg (2015). https://doi.org/10. 1007/978-3-662-46497-7_16
3. Boneh, D., Wu, D.J., Zimmerman, J.: Immunizing multilinear maps against zeroizing attacks. Cryptology ePrint Archive, Report 2014/930 (2014). https://eprint. iacr.org/2014/930
4. Boyle, E., Chung, K.-M., Pass, R.: On extractability (aka differing-inputs) obfuscation. In: TCC (2014)
5. Cheon, J.H., Han, K., Lee, C., Ryu, H., Stehle, D.: Cryptanalysis on the multilinear map over the integers and its related problems. Cryptology ePrint Archive, Report 2014/906 (2014). https://eprint.iacr.org/2014/906
6. Coron, J.-S., Lepoint, T., Tibouchi, M.: Cryptanalysis of two candidate fixes of multilinear maps over the integers. IACR Cryptology ePrint Archive, 2014:975 (2014)
7. Garg, S., Gentry, C., Halevi, S., Raykova, M., Sahai, A., Waters, B.: Candidate indistinguishability obfuscation and functional encryption for all circuits. SIAM J. Comput. **45**(3), 882–929 (2016)
8. Garg, S., Gentry, C., Sahai, A., Waters, B.: Witness encryption and its applications. In: Proceedings of the Forty-Fifth Annual ACM Symposium on Theory of Computing, pp. 467–476. ACM (2013)
9. Gentry, C., Halevi, S., Maji, H.K., Sahai, A.: Zeroizing without zeroes: cryptanalyzing multilinear maps without encodings of zero. Cryptology ePrint Archive, Report 2014/929 (2014). https://eprint.iacr.org/2014/929
10. Goldreich, O., Goldwasser, S., Micali, S.: How to construct random functions. J. ACM **33**, 792–807 (1986)
11. Groth, J., Ostrovsky, R., Sahai, A.: Perfect non-interactive zero knowledge for NP. In: Vaudenay, S. (ed.) EUROCRYPT 2006. LNCS, vol. 4004, pp. 339–358. Springer, Heidelberg (2006). https://doi.org/10.1007/11761679_21
12. Groth, J., Sahai, A.: Efficient non-interactive proof systems for bilinear groups. In: Smart, N. (ed.) EUROCRYPT 2008. LNCS, vol. 4965, pp. 415–432. Springer, Heidelberg (2008). https://doi.org/10.1007/978-3-540-78967-3_24
13. Lin, H., Pass, R., Seth, K., Telang, S.: Output-compressing randomized encodings and applications. In: Kushilevitz, E., Malkin, T. (eds.) TCC 2016. LNCS, vol. 9562, pp. 96–124. Springer, Heidelberg (2016). https://doi.org/10.1007/978-3-662-49096-9_5
14. Sahai, A., Waters, B.: How to use indistinguishability obfuscation: deniable encryption, and more. In: Proceedings of the Forty-sixth Annual ACM Symposium on Theory of Computing, pp. 475–484. ACM (2014)
15. Zhandry, M.: How to avoid obfuscation using witness PRFs. In: Kushilevitz, E., Malkin, T. (eds.) TCC 2016. LNCS, vol. 9563, pp. 421–448. Springer, Heidelberg (2016). https://doi.org/10.1007/978-3-662-49099-0_16

Two-Client and Multi-client Functional Encryption for Set Intersection

Tim van de Kamp[✉] ⓘ, David Stritzl ⓘ, Willem Jonker, and Andreas Peter ⓘ

University of Twente, Enschede, The Netherlands
{t.r.vandekamp,w.jonker,a.peter}@utwente.nl,
d.l.stritzl@alumnus.utwente.nl

Abstract. We propose several functional encryption schemes for set intersection and variants on two or multiple sets. In these schemes, a party may learn the set intersection from the sets of two or more clients, without having to learn the plaintext set of each individual client. For the case of two clients, we construct efficient schemes for determining the set intersection and the cardinality of the intersection. To evaluate the cardinality of the intersection, no overhead is incurred when compared to operating on plaintext data. We also present other functionalities with a scheme for set intersection with data transfer and a threshold scheme that only discloses the intersection if both clients have at least t elements in common. Finally, we consider set intersection and set intersection cardinality schemes for the case of three or more clients from a theoretical perspective. Our proof-of-concept implementations show that the two-client constructions are efficient and scale linearly in the set sizes.

Keywords: Multi-client functional encryption · Non-interactive · Set intersection

1 Introduction

In functional encryption (FE) scheme, decryption keys are associated with a functionality f and the decryption of an encrypted message m returns the function applied to the message, $f(m)$, instead of the original message m. This concept can be extended to functions with more than one input, resulting in a multi-input functional encryption (MI-FE) scheme. Correspondingly, the decryption algorithm of an MI-FE scheme requires a decryption key, associated with an n-ary function f, and n encrypted values $x_1, \ldots, x_n$ to output $f(x_1, \ldots, x_n)$.

A strict subset of these MI-FE schemes are termed multi-*client* functional encryption (MC-FE) schemes [15]. In such an MC-FE scheme, the inputs for the n-ary function f are given by n distinct parties, termed *clients*. Each client encrypts their input using their own encryption key and a *time-step* or *session identifier*. This identifier is used to determine which ciphertexts from the various clients belong together. To evaluate a function f using the corresponding

© Springer Nature Switzerland AG 2019
J. Jang-Jaccard and F. Guo (Eds.): ACISP 2019, LNCS 11547, pp. 97–115, 2019.
https://doi.org/10.1007/978-3-030-21548-4_6

Table 1. Overview of the presented MC-FE schemes for set operations.

Functionality	Two-client	Multi-client
Set intersection	Sect. 6.2	Sect. 7.3
Set intersection cardinality	Sect. 6.1	Sects. 7.1, 7.2
Set intersection with data transfer	Sect. 6.3	Open problem
Threshold set intersection	Sect. 6.4	Open problem

decryption key, all inputted ciphertexts need to be associated with the same identifier or otherwise decryption will fail.

In this work, we explore the set intersection functionality and several variants. Inspired by the popularity of private set intersection (PSI) protocols [27], we define a scheme for determining the set intersection of two clients' sets in a *non-interactive* manner. Additionally, we propose several other non-interactive variants to interactive PSI protocols that were previously proposed in literature. We construct a two-client functional encryption (2C-FE) scheme for determining the cardinality of the intersection (i.e., $|\mathcal{S}_a \cap \mathcal{S}_b|$, where $\mathcal{S}_\gamma$ is the set belonging to client γ), similar to PSI cardinality [21]. We also consider a non-interactive 2C-FE version of the less common PSI with data transfer [9,16], where the common set elements are shared with associated data (i.e., $\{ (x_j, \varphi_a(x_j), \varphi_b(x_j)) \mid x_j \in \mathcal{S}_a \cap \mathcal{S}_b \}$, where $\varphi_\gamma(x_j)$ is the data associated with x_j by client γ). Finally, we construction a threshold scheme where the set intersection is only revealed if two clients have at least t set elements in common.

Following our 2C-FE schemes, we also explore the much harder multi-client case where we propose MC-FE schemes for determining the (cardinality of the) set intersection of more than two sets. While 2C-FE schemes could also be used to determine the intersection of multiple sets, doing so would leak information about the intersection of each pair of sets. To prevent this undesirable leakage and achieve secure MC-FE for set intersection, we require more involved constructions.

An overview of constructions for MC-FE for set intersection presented in this work is given in Table 1.

Although the functionalities for our MC-FE schemes are inspired by various PSI protocols, the usage scenario differs in a crucial way: We apply our MC-FE schemes in a scenario where a third party, termed the *evaluator*, learns the function outcome. In Sect. 5.1 we explain why non-interactive 2C-FE cannot be secure if one of the clients also serves as the evaluator. We highlight the difference between PSI and our MC-FE for set intersection in Fig. 1.

Using the functionalities provided by our constructions, it is possible to achieve privacy-preserving profiling. For example, consider a case where the police is looking for suspects which were both present at a concert and recently received a large sum of money on their bank account. Using a 2C-FE scheme

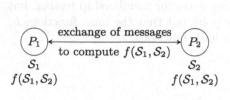

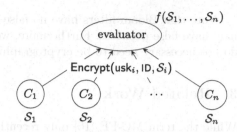

(a) A typical scenario of private set intersection (PSI). Both parties learn the output of the function evaluation, but not each others inputs.

(b) Our scenario of MC-FE for set intersection. The evaluator learns the function evaluation and nothing else about the clients' inputs.

Fig. 1. Fundamental difference between a private set intersection (PSI) protocol and our multi-client functional encryption (MC-FE) schemes for set intersection.

for determining the set intersection, the police will only learn about the suspects matching the two profiles, while learning nothing about the other visitors of the concert or other people that received an unusual amount of money. Another use case is privacy-preserving data mining, such as the computation of various set similarity scores. For example, by determining the cardinality of a set intersection we can compute the Jaccard index (i.e., $|\mathcal{S}_1 \cap \mathcal{S}_2|/|\mathcal{S}_1 \cup \mathcal{S}_2| = |\mathcal{S}_1 \cap \mathcal{S}_2|/(|\mathcal{S}_1| + |\mathcal{S}_2| - |\mathcal{S}_1 \cap \mathcal{S}_2|))$, without requiring the evaluator to learn the clients' sets themselves.

To asses the practicability of our constructions, we implemented several of our proposed schemes. Our 2C-FE constructions are quite efficient: Determining the cardinality of the set intersection of two encrypted sets is *as fast as any plaintext solution* and determining the set intersection of sets of 100 thousand elements in size can be done in just under a second.

2   Preliminaries

A t-OUT-OF-n Shamir's secret sharing scheme (SSSS) uses a t-degree polynomial f over a finite field $\mathbb{F}_p$. To share the secret s, pick a random polynomial with $f(0) = s$ and pick shares $(i, f(i))$ for distinct values i. To recover the secret from a set of at least t distinct shares $\{(i, f(i))\}_{i \in \mathcal{S}}$, Lagrange interpolation is used, $f(0) = \sum_{i \in \mathcal{S}} f(i) \cdot \Delta_{\mathcal{S},i}$, where $\Delta_{\mathcal{S},i} = \prod_{j \in \mathcal{S}, j \neq i} (j \cdot (j - i)^{-1})$.

A Bloom filter is a data structure that can be used for efficient set membership testing. An (m, k) Bloom filter consists of a bit string bs of length m (indexed using $bs[\ell]$ for $1 \leq \ell \leq m$) and is associated with k independent hash functions, $h_i \colon \{0,1\}^* \to \{1, \ldots, m\}$ for $1 \leq i \leq k$. The Bloom filter is initialized with the bit string of all zeros. To add an element x to the Bloom filter, we hash the element for each of the k hash functions to obtain $h_i(x)$ and set the $h_i(x)$th position in the bit string bs to 1, i.e., $bs[h_i(x)] = 1$ for $1 \leq i \leq k$. To test the membership of an element x^*, we simply check if $h_i(x^*) = 1$ for $1 \leq i \leq k$.

Note that Bloom filters have no false negatives for membership testing, but may have false positives. Furthermore, we point out that the hash functions h_i do not necessary need to be cryptographic hash functions.

3   Related Work

While the term MC-FE [15] only recently gained traction, a couple of MC-FE schemes have already been proposed several years ago. For example, for the functionality of summing inputs from distinct clients, Shi et al. [28] proposed a construction. Around the same time, Lewko and Waters [22] proposed a multiauthority attribute-based encryption scheme. Their construction can also be seen as MC-FE since the evaluated function only outputs a plaintext if the user has the right inputs (i.e., attributes) to the function (i.e., policy). More recently, MC-FE constructions for computing vector equality [30] and inner products [3,8] have been proposed. However, no MC-FE schemes for functionalities related to set operations have been proposed.

Despite being interactive by definition, PSI protocols are functionality-wise the closest related to our constructions. While the concept of PSI dates from the mid-80s [25], renewed interest in PSI protocols started in the beginning of the new millennium [13,21]. A comprehensive overview of various PSI constructions and techniques is given by Pinkas, Schneider, and Zohner [27]. While most PSI constructions achieve their functionality through techniques different from ours, Bloom filters have been used by interactive PSI protocols before [11,19].

The type of PSI protocols that are most related to our MC-FE schemes are termed *outsourced* PSI [1,2,17–19,23,31]. In outsourced PSI, a client may upload its encrypted set to a *service provider*, which will then engage in a PSI protocol on the client's behalf. Hence, in outsourced PSI the other client still learns the outcome of the evaluated set intersection, while in our definition of MC-FE for set intersection we require a dedicated evaluator to learn this outcome. This difference is typified by the difference in homomorphic encryption and FE: While both techniques allow us to compute over encrypted data, with homomorphic encryption we learn the *encrypted* output of the computation while with FE we learn the *plaintext* result. The two-client set intersection protocol by Kerschbaum [18] is a notable exception to regular outsourced PSI: In that construction the service provider also learns the outcome of the set intersection. However, besides their limited scope of considering only two-client set intersection, they consider a weaker security notion. Their construction is only collusion resistant if the two clients collude against the evaluator, not if the evaluator colludes with one client against the other client (something we show impossible in Sect. 5.1). As a consequence, their construction cannot be extended to a secure scheme in the multi-client case. Moreover, their proposed construction is malleable and thus does not provide any form of integrity.

4   Multi-client Functional Encryption for Set Operations

An MC-FE [15] scheme for a specific set operation consists of n parties, termed *clients*. Each of these clients encrypts their own set. Another party, which we term *evaluator*, having a decryption key and receiving these encrypted sets, can evaluate an n-ary set operation f over the clients' inputs.

To run the same functionality f multiple times without the possibility for the evaluator to mix old clients' inputs with newly received inputs, MC-FE schemes associate an identifier ID with every ciphertext. An evaluator is only able to evaluate the function if all ciphertexts use the same identifier ID.

The MC-FE schemes we propose support only a single functionality f (e.g., set intersection). Therefore, our schemes do not need to define a key generation algorithm to create a decryption key for each of the functionalities. Instead, we can suffice with the creation of a decryption key for the single functionality in Setup. This type of FE schemes is commonly referred to as *single key* [20]. However, to avoid confusion in our multi-client case – where we still have a key for each client – we refer to this setting as *single evaluation key* MC-FE.

Definition 1 (Multi-client Functional Encryption for Set Operations).
A single evaluation key MC-FE scheme for set operation f, consists of the following three polynomial time algorithms.

Setup$(1^\lambda, n) \to (\mathsf{pp}, \mathsf{esk}, \mathsf{usk}_1, \ldots, \mathsf{usk}_n)$. *On input of the security parameter λ and the number of clients, the algorithm outputs the public parameters pp, the evaluator's evaluation key esk, and the clients' secret keys usk_i for each client $1 \leq i \leq n$. The public parameters are implicitly used in the other algorithms.*

Encrypt$(\mathsf{usk}_i, \mathsf{ID}, \mathcal{S}_i) \to \mathsf{ct}_{\mathsf{ID},i}$. *For a client i to encrypt a set $\mathcal{S}_i$ for identifier ID, the client uses its secret key usk_i and outputs the ciphertext $\mathsf{ct}_{\mathsf{ID},i}$.*

Eval$(\mathsf{esk}, \mathsf{ct}_{\mathsf{ID},1}, \ldots, \mathsf{ct}_{\mathsf{ID},n}) \to f(\mathcal{S}_1, \ldots, \mathcal{S}_n)$. *An evaluator having the evaluation key esk and a ciphertext for identifier ID from every client, outputs the function evaluation $f(\mathcal{S}_1, \ldots, \mathcal{S}_n)$.*

4.1   Schemes Without an Evaluator Key

While having schemes with an evaluation secret key might be desirable in some cases, in other cases it is desirable that anyone may learn the outcome of the function, e.g., similar to property-revealing encryption [6,26]. However, observe that we can *always* adapt an MC-FE scheme without an evaluation key to the above defined single evaluation key MC-FE by using public key encryption. Indeed, instead of sending the ciphertexts resulting from the MC-FE scheme directly to the evaluator, we simply require the clients to encrypt these ciphertexts again, but now using the public key of the evaluator. This ensures that only the evaluator with the corresponding private key (used as an evaluation key) can evaluate the functionality f. An alternative solution is to require the clients to send their ciphertexts over a secure channel to the evaluator. This way, no other party has access to the ciphertexts.

We conclude that, since schemes without an evaluation key can be turned into a single evaluation key MC-FE scheme, MC-FE schemes without an evaluation key are at least as powerful as single evaluation key MC-FE. For this reason, *we construct only MC-FE schemes without an evaluation key* and stress that our resulting schemes can thus be used both *with* and *without* an evaluation key.

5 Security

We use the indistinguishability-based security notion from Goldwasser et al. [15, Sect. 3.2] for MC-FE. In this notion, the adversary's goal is to decide which of the two, by the adversary chosen, plaintexts is encrypted. The notion allows the adversary to adaptively query for the encryption of plaintext, while it can locally evaluate the received ciphertext using $\mathsf{Eval}(\mathsf{ct}_1, \ldots, \mathsf{ct}_n)$. Additionally, the adversary is allowed to statically corrupt the clients by announcing the corrupted clients before it receives the public parameters.

The adversary can thus be seen as a *malicious evaluator* that tries to learn information about the ciphertexts, other than what it should be allowed according to the functionality of the scheme. It its attempts, the malicious evaluator may collude with the clients in an effort to learn more about other clients' ciphertexts.

Let f be the supported function of the MC-FE scheme for n clients. This function has n inputs, one for every client. For a subset $I \subseteq \{1, \ldots, n\}$, we use the notation $f(\{x_i\}_{i \in I}, \cdot)$ to denote the function that has its inputs x_i, for $i \in I$, hardwired in the function.

Definition 2 (Adaptive IND-security of MC-FE [15]). *An MC-FE scheme without an evaluation key is secure if any probabilistic polynomial time (p.p.t.) adversary $\mathcal{A}$ has at most a negligible advantage in winning the following game.*

Corruptions. *The adversary sends a set of uncorrupted and corrupted clients to the challenger, I and $\bar{I}$, respectively.*

Setup. *The challenger $\mathcal{B}$ picks a bit $b \xleftarrow{R} \{0, 1\}$, and sends the public parameters pp along with the user keys of the corrupted clients $\{\mathsf{usk}_i\}_{i \in \bar{I}}$ to the adversary $\mathcal{A}$.*

Query 1. *The adversary may query the challenger for the encryption of sets $\mathcal{S}_i$ for uncorrupted clients $i \in I$ associated with an ID that has not been used before. For each uncorrupted client $i \in I$, the challenger returns the encrypted set $\mathsf{ct}_{\mathsf{ID},i} \leftarrow \mathsf{Encrypt}(\mathsf{usk}_i, \mathsf{ID}, \mathcal{S}_i)$.*

Challenge. *The adversary sends two equally sized sets $\mathcal{S}_{i,0}^*$, $\mathcal{S}_{i,1}^*$, $|\mathcal{S}_{i,0}^*| = |\mathcal{S}_{i,1}^*|$, for every uncorrupted client $i \in I$ together with an ID^* that has not been used before. The challenger checks if the challenge is allowed by checking if $f(\{\mathcal{S}_{i,0}^*\}_{i \in I}, \cdot) = f(\{\mathcal{S}_{i,1}^*\}_{i \in I}, \cdot)$. If this is not the case the challenger aborts the game. Otherwise, it returns the encrypted sets $\mathsf{Encrypt}(\mathsf{usk}_i, \mathsf{ID}, \mathcal{S}_{i,b}^*)$ for every uncorrupted client $i \in I$.*

Query 2. *Identical to Query 1.*

Guess. *The adversary outputs its guess b' for the challenger's bit b.*

Note that by definition, the ciphertext does not need to hide the set size. This is similar to the semantic security notion where the ciphertext does not need to hide the plaintext size. If this is undesirable, fixed-sized sets can easily be obtained by adding dummy elements to each set.

5.1 Corruptions in Two-Client Functional Encryption

We observe that *any* single evaluation key 2C-FE scheme can never be secure against corruptions for non-trivial functionalities. To see why this is the case, consider a 2C-FE scheme for the functionality $f(x, y)$. Assume, without loss of generality, that the adversary corrupts the client which determines the input y. By definition of the game for adaptive IND-security of MC-FE, the adversary submits two values x_0 and x_1 to the challenger. For the challenge inputs to be allowed, it is required that $f(x_0, \cdot) = f(x_1, \cdot)$, i.e., we require $f_{x_0}(y) = f_{x_1}(y)$ *for all possible* y. So, unless f is a constant function in y, we have to require that $x_0 = x_1$, for which it is trivial to see that the challenge will be indistinguishable.

Generalizing the result, we see that in an MC-FE scheme for n clients, at least two clients need to remain uncorrupted. Phrased differently, this means that for MC-FE with n clients, we can allow for at most $n - 2$ corruptions.

6 Two-Client Constructions for Set Intersections

We propose several 2C-FE schemes for various set operations: computing the cardinality of the set intersection, computing the set intersection itself, computing the set intersection with data transfer or projection, and computing the set intersection only if a threshold is reached. We discuss constructions supporting more than two clients in Sect. 7.

6.1 Two-Client Set Intersection Cardinality

To compute the cardinality of a set intersection from two clients, we can suffice with a simple scheme using a pseudorandom function (PRF) (e.g., see [29, Sect. 11.2]). The two clients encrypt each set element individually using a PRF under the same key. Since a PRF has a deterministic output, the evaluator can now use *any* algorithm for determining the cardinality of the intersection, even algorithms that only operate on plaintext data (e.g., see [10] for an overview).

Setup(1^λ) $\to$ (pp, usk$_1$, usk$_2$). Let $\Phi = \{\phi_\kappa\}$ be a PRF ensemble for functions $\phi_\kappa \colon \mathcal{ID} \times \{0,1\}^* \to \{0,1\}^{\geq \lambda}$. Pick a PRF ϕ_{msk}. The public parameters are pp $= (\Phi)$ and the clients' keys usk$_1 =$ usk$_2 = (\phi_{\mathsf{msk}})$.

Encrypt$(\mathsf{usk}_i, \mathsf{ID}, \mathcal{S}_i) \to \mathsf{ct}_{\mathsf{ID},i}$. For a client i to encrypt its set $\mathcal{S}_i$ for an identifier $\mathsf{ID} \in \mathcal{ID}$, the client computes the PRF for each set element $x_j \in \mathcal{S}_i$. It outputs the set $\mathsf{ct}_{\mathsf{ID},i} = \{\, \phi_{\mathsf{msk}}(\mathsf{ID}, x_j) \mid x_j \in \mathcal{S}_i \,\}$.

Eval$(\mathsf{ct}_{\mathsf{ID},1}, \mathsf{ct}_{\mathsf{ID},2}) \to |\mathcal{S}_1 \cap \mathcal{S}_2|$. To evaluate the cardinality of the set intersection, output $|\mathsf{ct}_{\mathsf{ID},1} \cap \mathsf{ct}_{\mathsf{ID},2}|$.

We can use a block cipher, keyed-hash function, hash-based message authentication code, or a similar function as the PRF.

Theorem 1. *The two-client set intersection cardinality scheme defined above is secure under the assumption that the PRF is indistinguishable from a random function.*

Proof. This directly follows from the security of the PRF. Note that the evaluator only learns whether two set elements $x_{1,j} \in \mathcal{S}_1$ and $x_{2,j'} \in \mathcal{S}_2$ equal or not. Nothing else is revealed about the set elements $x_{1,j}$ and $x_{2,j'}$.

6.2   Two-Client Set Intersection

In case of two-client set intersection, we need not only to determine whether two encrypted set elements are the same, but also learn the plaintext set element if they are the same. We achieve this by adapting our construction for two-client set intersection cardinality with a combination of convergent encryption [12] (cf. message-locked encryption [4]) and secret sharing: We encrypt the set element under a key derived from the message itself and secret share the encryption key. If both clients encrypted the same message, the decryption key can be recovered from the secret shares and the ciphertext can be decrypted. To encrypt the set element itself, we use an authenticated encryption (AE) scheme [5].

Setup$(1^\lambda) \to (\mathsf{pp}, \mathsf{usk}_1, \mathsf{usk}_2)$. Let $\langle g \rangle = \mathbb{G}$ be a group of prime order p and let $\Phi = \{\phi_\kappa\}$ be a PRF ensemble for functions $\phi_\kappa \colon \mathcal{ID} \times \{0,1\}^* \to \mathbb{G}$ and AE an AE scheme. Define a mapping from the group to the key space of the AE scheme, $H \colon \mathbb{G} \to \mathcal{K}_{\mathsf{AE}}$. Pick a PRF ϕ_{msk} and pick $\sigma_1 \xleftarrow{R} \mathbb{Z}_p$ to set $\sigma_2 = 1 - \sigma_1 \pmod p$. The public parameters are $\mathsf{pp} = (\mathbb{G}, \Phi, H, \mathsf{AE})$ and the clients' keys $\mathsf{usk}_1 = (\phi_{\mathsf{msk}}, \sigma_1)$ and $\mathsf{usk}_2 = (\phi_{\mathsf{msk}}, \sigma_2)$.

Encrypt$(\mathsf{usk}_i, \mathsf{ID}, \mathcal{S}_i) \to \mathsf{ct}_{\mathsf{ID},i}$. For a client i to encrypt its set $\mathcal{S}_i$ for an identifier $\mathsf{ID} \in \mathcal{ID}$, the client computes the PRF for each set element $x_j \in \mathcal{S}_i$. It outputs the set of tuples $\{(\mathsf{ct}_{\mathsf{ID},i,j,1}, \mathsf{ct}_{\mathsf{ID},i,j,2})\}_{1 \leq j \leq |\mathcal{S}_i|}$,

$$\mathsf{ct}_{\mathsf{ID},i} = \{\, \big(k_{\mathsf{ID},j}^{\sigma_i}, \mathsf{AE}.\mathsf{Enc}_{H(k_{\mathsf{ID},j})}(x_j)\big) \mid k_{\mathsf{ID},j} = \phi_{\mathsf{msk}}(\mathsf{ID}, x_j), x_j \in \mathcal{S}_i \,\} \; .$$

Eval$(\mathsf{ct}_{\mathsf{ID},1}, \mathsf{ct}_{\mathsf{ID},2}) \to \mathcal{S}_1 \cap \mathcal{S}_2$. For all $\mathsf{ct}_{\mathsf{ID},1,j,2} = \mathsf{ct}_{\mathsf{ID},2,k,2}$ (and hence $x = x_{1,j} = x_{2,k}$), determine

$$k_{\mathsf{ID},x} = \mathsf{ct}_{\mathsf{ID},1,j,1} \cdot \mathsf{ct}_{\mathsf{ID},2,k,1}$$
$$= \phi_{\mathsf{msk}}(\mathsf{ID}, x)^{\sigma_1} \cdot \phi_{\mathsf{msk}}(\mathsf{ID}, x)^{\sigma_2} = \phi_{\mathsf{msk}}(\mathsf{ID}, x)^{\sigma_1 + \sigma_2} = \phi_{\mathsf{msk}}(\mathsf{ID}, x) \; ,$$

to decrypt $\mathsf{ct}_{\mathsf{ID},i,j,2}$ using $\mathsf{AE}.\mathsf{Dec}_{H(k_{\mathsf{ID},x})}(\mathsf{ct}_{\mathsf{ID},i,j,2})$ for $i = 1$ or, equivalently, $i = 2$.

Theorem 2. *The two-client set intersection scheme defined above is secure under the decisional Diffie-Hellman (DDH) assumption, a secure PRF, and a secure AE scheme.*

Proof. We construct an algorithm that is able to break the DDH problem if a p.p.t. adversary $\mathcal{A}$ has a non-negligible advantage in winning the game.

Setup. The challenger $\mathcal{B}$ receives the DDH tuple (g, g^a, g^b, T) from the group $\mathbb{G}$ of prime order p. It defines a PRF ensemble $\Phi = \{\phi_\kappa\}$ and mapping $H \colon \mathbb{G} \to \mathcal{K}_{\mathsf{AE}}$ according to the scheme. The public parameters $\mathsf{pp} = (\mathbb{G}, \Phi, H, \mathsf{AE})$ are sent to the adversary. The challenger indirectly sets $\sigma_1 = a$ and $\sigma_2 = 1 - a$, i.e., $g^{\sigma_1} = g^a$ and $g^{\sigma_2} = g \cdot (g^a)^{-1}$.

Query. Upon receiving an allowed encryption query for $(i, \mathsf{ID}, \mathcal{S})$, the challenger encrypts the elements of the set $\mathcal{S}$ as follows. It models the PRF as follows: On input (ID, x_j), output $g^{r_{\mathsf{ID}, x_j}}$, where, if the input has not been queried before, $r_{\mathsf{ID}, x_j} \xleftarrow{R} \mathbb{Z}_p$. The challenger encrypts an element $x_j \in \mathcal{S}$ as

$$\mathsf{ct}_{\mathsf{ID},i,j} = \begin{cases} \left((g^a)^{r_{\mathsf{ID},x_j}}, \mathsf{AE.Enc}_k(x_j)\right) & \text{if } i = 1; \\ \left((g \cdot (g^a)^{-1})^{r_{\mathsf{ID},x_j}}, \mathsf{AE.Enc}_k(x_j)\right) & \text{if } i = 2, \end{cases} \quad \text{where } k = H(g^{r_{\mathsf{ID},x_j}}).$$

It outputs the encrypted set $\mathsf{ct}_{\mathsf{ID},i}$ to the adversary.

Challenge. An allowed challenge request from the adversary for the sets $\mathcal{S}^*_{1,0}$, $\mathcal{S}^*_{1,1}$, $\mathcal{S}^*_{2,0}$, and $\mathcal{S}^*_{2,1}$ with identifier ID^*, is answered by the challenger by sending the encrypted sets $\mathcal{S}^*_{1,b}$ and $\mathcal{S}^*_{2,b}$ back to the adversary. An element $x_j \notin (\mathcal{S}_{1,b} \cap \mathcal{S}_{2,b})$ is encrypted as

$$\mathsf{ct}_{\mathsf{ID},i,j} = \begin{cases} \left(T^{r_{\mathsf{ID}^*,x_j}}, \mathsf{AE.Enc}_k(x_j)\right) & \text{if } i = 1; \\ \left((g^b \cdot T^{-1})^{r_{\mathsf{ID}^*,x_j}}, \mathsf{AE.Enc}_k(x_j)\right) & \text{if } i = 2, \end{cases} \quad \text{where } k = H\left((g^b)^{r_{\mathsf{ID},x_j}}\right).$$

Note that this indirectly sets the output of the PRF to $g^{b r_{\mathsf{ID}^*,x_j}}$ for $x_j \notin (\mathcal{S}_{1,b} \cap \mathcal{S}_{2,b})$. The elements $x_j \in (\mathcal{S}_{1,b} \cap \mathcal{S}_{2,b})$ are encrypted as in the query phase.

If the adversary $\mathcal{A}$ outputs a correct guess $b' = b$, the challenger outputs the guess that $T = g^{ab}$, otherwise, it outputs its guess $T \in_R \mathbb{G}$.

6.3 Two-Client Set Intersection with Data Transfer or Projection

The two-client set intersection scheme described above can be extended into a two-client set intersection scheme with data transfer (analogous to *PSI with data transfer* [9,16]). Instead of only encrypting the set element x_j itself, $\mathsf{ct}_{\mathsf{ID},i,j,2} = \mathsf{AE.Enc}_k(x_j)$, we can also choose to encrypt both the element itself and the data associated to the set element $\rho(x_j)$. The security of the scheme is the same as before since we rely on the security of the AE scheme.

Moreover, the proposed scheme also allows for a two-client set intersection projection scheme (analogous to *PSI with projection* [7]). We construct such a scheme by encrypting only the associated data $\rho(x_j)$, $ct_{\mathsf{ID},i,j,2} = \mathsf{AE.Enc}_k(\rho(x_j))$, not the set element x_j itself. Security follows from the fact that the AE decryption key $k = H(\phi_{\mathsf{msk}}(\mathsf{ID}, x_j))$ does not reveal any information about the set element x_j, assuming the security of the used PRF. However, the evaluator does learn that the projections of both clients correspond to the same set element.

6.4 Two-Client Threshold Set Intersection

To allow the evaluator to learn the cardinality of the intersection, but only the set elements in the intersection if the clients have at least t set elements in common, we propose a two-client threshold set intersection scheme. We achieve this by encrypting the share of the decryption key for the AE ciphertext $k_{\mathsf{ID},j}^{\sigma_i}$ using another encryption key. This newly added encryption key can only be obtained by the evaluator if the clients have at least t set elements in common.

Although the construction is based on the previous scheme, the precise construction is quite technical. We therefore state the complete scheme below.

Setup$(1^\lambda, t) \rightarrow (\mathsf{pp}, \mathsf{usk}_1, \mathsf{usk}_2)$. Let AE an AE scheme and $\langle g \rangle = \mathbb{G}$ be a group and $\mathbb{F}_p$ be a field, both of prime order p. Let $\Phi = \{\phi_\kappa\}$ and $\Psi = \{\psi_\kappa\}$ be PRF ensembles for functions $\phi_\kappa \colon \mathcal{ID} \times \{0,1\}^* \rightarrow \mathbb{G}$ and $\psi_\kappa \colon \mathcal{ID} \times \{0,1\}^* \rightarrow \mathbb{F}_p$, respectively. Define a mapping from the group to the key space of the AE scheme, $H \colon \mathbb{G} \rightarrow \mathcal{K}_{\mathsf{AE}}$. Pick three PRFs $\phi \in \Phi$, $\psi_1, \psi_2 \in \Psi$ and $\sigma_1 \xleftarrow{R} \mathbb{Z}_p, \rho_1 \xleftarrow{R} \mathbb{Z}_{p-1}$, setting $\sigma_2 = 1 - \sigma_1 \pmod{p}$ and $\rho_2 = 1 - \rho_1 \pmod{p-1}$.

The public parameters are $\mathsf{pp} = (\mathbb{G}, \Phi, \Psi, H, \mathsf{AE}, t)$ and the clients' keys $\mathsf{usk}_1 = (\phi, \psi_1, \psi_2, \sigma_1, \rho_1)$ and $\mathsf{usk}_2 = (\phi, \psi_1, \psi_2, \sigma_2, \rho_2)$.

Encrypt$(\mathsf{usk}_i, \mathsf{ID}, \mathcal{S}_i) \rightarrow ct_{\mathsf{ID},i}$. For a client i to encrypt its set $\mathcal{S}_i$ for an identifier $\mathsf{ID} \in \mathcal{ID}$, the client computes the PRF for each set element $x_j \in \mathcal{S}_i$. It defines the $(t-1)$th degree polynomial f_{ID} by setting the coefficients $c_i = \psi_2(\mathsf{ID}, i)$, for $0 \leq i < t$, to obtain the polynomial $f_{\mathsf{ID}}(x) = c_{t-1}x^{t-1} + \cdots + c_1 x + c_0$.

The client outputs the set

$$ct_{\mathsf{ID},i} = \big\{ \big(k_{\mathsf{ID},j,2}, f(k_{\mathsf{ID},j,2})^{\rho_i}, \mathsf{AE.Enc}_{H(c_0)}(k_{\mathsf{ID},j,1}^{\sigma_i}), \mathsf{AE.Enc}_{H(k_{\mathsf{ID},j,1})}(x_j)\big)$$

$$\mid k_{\mathsf{ID},j,1} = \phi(\mathsf{ID}, x_j), k_{\mathsf{ID},j,2} = \psi_1(\mathsf{ID}, x_j), x_j \in \mathcal{S}_i \big\} \ .$$

Eval$(ct_{\mathsf{ID},1}, ct_{\mathsf{ID},2}) \rightarrow (|\mathcal{S}_1 \cap \mathcal{S}_2|, \{x_j \mid x_j \in \mathcal{S}_1 \cap \mathcal{S}_2, |\mathcal{S}_1 \cap \mathcal{S}_2| \geq t\})$. The evaluation algorithm consists of two stages; the second stage is only executed if $|\mathcal{S}_1 \cap \mathcal{S}_2| \geq t$.

1. To determine the cardinality of the set intersection $|\mathcal{S}_1 \cap \mathcal{S}_2|$, the evaluator counts the number of times a value $k_{\mathsf{ID},j,2}$ occurs both in $ct_{\mathsf{ID},1}$ and $ct_{\mathsf{ID},2}$.
2. If $|\mathcal{S}_1 \cap \mathcal{S}_2| \geq t$, the evaluator uses Lagrange interpolation to compute the value $c_0 = f(0)$. It can do so by taking t distinct tuples $(k_{\mathsf{ID},j,2}, f(k_{\mathsf{ID},j,2}))$, where $f(k_{\mathsf{ID},j,2}) = f(k_{\mathsf{ID},j,2})^{\rho_1} \cdot f(k_{\mathsf{ID},j,2})^{\rho_2}$. Now, when the secret c_0 has been recovered from the shares, the evaluator can use it to decrypt the values $\mathsf{AE.Enc}_{H(c_0)}(k_{\mathsf{ID},j,1}^{\sigma_i})$. So, the evaluator obtains $k_{\mathsf{ID},j,1}^{\sigma_i}$ for *every* set element

in $x_j \in S_i$ if $|S_1 \cap S_2| \geq t$. Observe that for the elements in the intersection, the evaluator has both $k_{\text{ID},j,1}^{\sigma_1}$ and $k_{\text{ID},j,1}^{\sigma_2}$, and can compute $k_{\text{ID},j,1} = k_{\text{ID},j,1}^{\sigma_1} \cdot k_{\text{ID},j,1}^{\sigma_2}$. Finally, using $H(k_{\text{ID},j,1})$, it can decrypt $\text{AE.Enc}_{H(k_{\text{ID},j,1})}(x_j)$ to obtain $x_j \in S_1 \cap S_2$.

Since the construction above builds upon the set intersection scheme, which can be modified into a set intersection with data transfer scheme or a set intersection with projection scheme, we similarly obtain both threshold set intersection with data transfer and projection.

Theorem 3. *The two-client threshold set intersection scheme defined above is secure under the DDH assumption, a secure PRF, and a secure AE scheme.*

Proof. We only have to prove that the values $k_{\text{ID},j,1}^{\sigma_i}$ can only be obtained if $|S_1 \cap S_2| \geq t$, as the rest of the proof directly follows from Theorem 2. Since the values $k_{\text{ID},j,1}^{\sigma_i}$ are encrypted using an AE scheme using the key $H(c_0)$, the values are only know to the evaluator if it has the key $H(c_0)$ (under the assumption of a secure AE scheme). The fact that c_0 (and hence $H(c_0)$) can only be obtained from the secret shares follows from the information-theoretic security of SSSS if a random polynomial f_{ID} was used. Note that the $(t-1)$th degree polynomial is random under the assumption of a secure PRF. Finally, using a similar argument as in Theorem 2, we can show that, under the DDH assumption, $f(k_{\text{ID},j,2})^{\rho_1}$ or $f(k_{\text{ID},j,2})^{\rho_2}$ does not reveal any information about $f(k_{\text{ID},j,2})$ if $f(k_{\text{ID},j,2})^{\rho_2}$ or $f(k_{\text{ID},j,2})^{\rho_1}$, respectively, is unknown.

7   Multi-client Constructions for Set Intersections

While the 2C-FE constructions from Sect. 6 could be used in a multi-client case, this would leak information about each pair of sets. For the same reason, deterministic encryption cannot be used in secure MC-FE constructions, which makes it much harder to develop efficient MC-FE schemes.

7.1   Multi-client Set Intersection Cardinality

We construct an MC-FE scheme for testing the set intersection using only a hash function and secret sharing. The proposed scheme incurs no additional leakage and is proven adaptive IND-secure. While our scheme has an evaluation algorithm which does not rely on heavy cryptographic machinery and runs in polynomial time (for a fixed number of clients n), it is not very efficient. The running time of evaluation algorithm grows in the product of the cardinality of the individual clients' set size. However, for relatively small sets or a small number of clients this scheme might still be efficient enough to use in practice.

Setup$(1^\lambda, n) \rightarrow (\text{pp}, \text{usk}_1, \ldots, \text{usk}_n)$. Let $\langle g \rangle = \mathbb{G}$ be a group of prime order p and let $H \colon \mathcal{ID} \times \{0,1\}^* \rightarrow \mathbb{G}$ be a hash function. Create random shares of 0 by picking $\sigma_i \xleftarrow{R} \mathbb{Z}_p$, for all $2 \leq i \leq n$, and setting $\sigma_1 = -\sum_{i=2}^n \sigma_i \pmod{p}$. The public parameters are $\text{pp} = (H)$ and the clients' keys $\text{usk}_i = (\sigma_i)$.

Encrypt$(\mathsf{usk}_i, \mathsf{ID}, \mathcal{S}_i) \to \mathsf{ct}_{\mathsf{ID},i}$. For a client i to encrypt its set $\mathcal{S}_i$ using an identifier $\mathsf{ID} \in \mathcal{ID}$, the client encrypts each set element $x_j \in \mathcal{S}_i$ individually. It outputs the set $\mathsf{ct}_{\mathsf{ID},i} = \{ H(\mathsf{ID}, x_j)^{\sigma_i} \mid x_j \in \mathcal{S}_i \}$.

Eval$(\mathsf{ct}_{\mathsf{ID},1}, \ldots, \mathsf{ct}_{\mathsf{ID},n}) \to |\bigcap_{i=1}^{n} \mathcal{S}_i|$. For each n-tuple $(c_{\mathsf{ID},1}, \ldots, c_{\mathsf{ID},n}) \in \mathsf{ct}_{\mathsf{ID},1} \times \cdots \times \mathsf{ct}_{\mathsf{ID},n}$, the evaluator evaluates $\prod_{i=1}^{n} c_{\mathsf{ID},i} \stackrel{?}{=} 1$. The evaluator outputs the count for the number of times the expression above evaluates to TRUE.

We will prove the construction secure under selective corruptions, but we note that it is also possible to achieve a proof under dynamic corruptions (although less tight) by adapting the proofs from [28].

Theorem 4. *The improved multi-client set intersection cardinality scheme defined above is secure up to* $(n - 2)$ *corruptions under the DDH assumption in the random oracle model (ROM).*

Proof. Let $\mathcal{A}$ be a p.p.t. adversary playing the adaptive IND-security game for MC-FE. We will show how to use $\mathcal{A}$ as a distinguisher for a DDH tuple, winning with a non-negligible advantage if $\mathcal{A}$ has a non-negligible advantage in winning the security game.

Random Oracle. On input of a tuple (ID, x_j) the oracle checks if it has answered the query before. If not, it picks a value $\beta_{\mathsf{ID},x_j} \stackrel{R}{\leftarrow} \mathbb{Z}_p$. Next, the challenger $\mathcal{B}$ guesses whether the query is for the challenge ID. If so, the oracle outputs $(g^b)^{\beta_{\mathsf{ID},x_j}}$, otherwise, it outputs $g^{\beta_{\mathsf{ID},x_j}}$. If the guess turns out to be wrong later, $\mathcal{B}$ can simply abort the game.

Corruptions. The adversary $\mathcal{A}$ announces the set of uncorrupted and corrupted clients, I and $\bar{I}$, respectively.

Setup. For $i \in \bar{I}$, the challenger $\mathcal{B}$ picks $\sigma_i \stackrel{R}{\leftarrow} \mathbb{Z}_p$ and sends the values to the adversary $\mathcal{A}$. Let $i' \in I$, for $i \in I \setminus \{i'\}$, $\mathcal{B}$ indirectly sets $\sigma_i = a \cdot \alpha_i$, where $\alpha_i \stackrel{R}{\leftarrow} \mathbb{Z}_p$, by setting $g^{\sigma_i} = (g^a)^{\alpha_i}$. For i', it indirectly sets $\sigma_{i'} = -\sum_{i \neq i'} \sigma_i$,

$$g^{\sigma_{i'}} = \prod_{i \in \bar{I}} g^{-\sigma_i} \cdot \prod_{i \in I, i \neq i'} (g^a)^{-\alpha_i} .$$

Query. To answer an encryption query $\mathcal{S}_i$ for an uncorrupted client $i \in I$, the challenger uses the oracle to obtain $\{ \beta_{\mathsf{ID},x_j} \mid x_j \in \mathcal{S}_i \}$ and construct the ciphertext as $\mathsf{ct}_{\mathsf{ID},i} = \{ (g^{\sigma_i})^{\beta_{\mathsf{ID},x_j}} \mid x_j \in \mathcal{S}_i \}$.

Challenge. Upon receiving the challenge sets $\{ (\mathcal{S}_{i,0}^*, \mathcal{S}_{i,1}^*) \mid i \in I \}$ and an ID^* from the adversary, the challenger picks $b \stackrel{R}{\leftarrow} \{0, 1\}$. The challenger returns the ciphertexts

$$\mathsf{ct}_{\mathsf{ID}^*,i'} = \left\{ \prod_{i \in \bar{I}} (g^b)^{-\sigma_i \cdot \beta_{\mathsf{ID}^*,x_j}} \cdot \prod_{i \in I, i \neq i'} T^{-\alpha_i \cdot \beta_{\mathsf{ID}^*,x_j}} \mid x_j \in \mathcal{S}_{i,b}^* \right\} \quad \text{and}$$

$$\mathsf{ct}_{\mathsf{ID}^*,i} = \left\{ T^{\alpha_i \beta_{\mathsf{ID}^*,x_j}} \mid x_j \in \mathcal{S}_{i,b}^* \right\} \quad \text{for } i \neq i'.$$

Note that if $T = g^{ab}$, the ciphertext is distributed properly according the scheme. If $T \in_R \mathbb{G}$, the challenger returns a ciphertext of a randomly distributed set element. So, the challenger $\mathcal{B}$ guesses that $T = g^{ab}$ if $\mathcal{A}$ correctly guessed $b' = b$ and otherwise, $\mathcal{B}$ guesses that $T \in_R \mathbb{G}$.

We remark that while the security of the two-client schemes could be proven in the standard model, our multi-client constructions can only be proven in the ROM. The difference in the constructions is that in the two-client case, no corruptions are taken place, and thus we can use a programmable PRF instead of a programmable random oracle.

7.2   Efficient Multi-client Set Intersection Cardinality

A drawback of the multi-client set intersection cardinality scheme might be that the computational complexity for the evaluator grows quickly in the total number of set elements (i.e., $\prod_{i=1}^{n} |\mathcal{S}_i|$). To address this problem, we propose an alternative scheme using Bloom filters. In this scheme, we first combine the Bloom filter representation of every client's set in the encrypted domain, resulting in an encrypted Bloom filter representing the intersection of all clients' sets. Next, the evaluator uses the encrypted set elements of *any* client to determine the cardinality of the intersection. This method used by the evaluator to determine the cardinality of the intersection can be seen as computing $|\mathcal{S}_i \cap (\bigcap_{i=1}^{n} \mathcal{S}_i)| = |\bigcap_{i=1}^{n} \mathcal{S}_i|$. The theoretical efficiency of $\mathcal{O}(n + \min_{i=1}^{n} |\mathcal{S}_i|)$ ciphertext operations is much better than the other scheme. However, the proposed scheme is only secure if no corruptions are taking place.

Setup$(1^\lambda, n, m, k) \rightarrow (\mathsf{pp}, \mathsf{usk}_1, \ldots, \mathsf{usk}_n)$. Let $\langle g \rangle = \mathbb{G}$ be a group of prime order p and let BF be a specification for an (m, k) Bloom filter. Let $\Phi = \{\phi_\kappa\}$ be a PRF ensemble for functions $\phi_\kappa \colon \{0,1\}^* \rightarrow \{0,1\}^{\geq \lambda}$ and let $H \colon \mathcal{ID} \times \{0,1\}^* \rightarrow \mathbb{G}$ be a hash function. Pick a PRF $\phi \in \Phi$. Additionally, pick for $1 \leq i \leq n$, values $c_i \xleftarrow{R} \mathbb{Z}_p$ and define the n-degree polynomial $f(x) = c_n x^n + \cdots + c_1 x$ over the field $\mathbb{F}_p$. The public parameters are $\mathsf{pp} = (\mathsf{BF}, \Phi, H)$ and the clients' secret keys are $\mathsf{usk}_i = (\phi, f(i), f(n + i))$ for $1 \leq i \leq n$. Note that every client receives the same PRF ϕ, but different secret shares $f(i)$ and $f(n + i)$.

Encrypt$(\mathsf{usk}_i, \mathsf{ID}, \mathcal{S}_i) \rightarrow (\mathsf{ct}_{\mathsf{ID},i,\mathsf{bs}_S}, \mathsf{ct}_{\mathsf{ID},i,\mathcal{S}})$. First, the client initializes the Bloom filter to obtain bs_S. Next, it adds its encrypted set elements $\{ \phi(x_j) \mid x_j \in \mathcal{S}_i \}$ to the Bloom filter. For each $1 \leq \ell \leq m$, the client sets $r_{i,\ell} \xleftarrow{R} \mathbb{Z}_p$, if $\mathsf{bs}_S[\ell] = 0$, and $r_{i,\ell} = 0$, otherwise. The client encrypts the Bloom filter for bs_S as the ordered set

$$\mathsf{ct}_{\mathsf{bs}_S} = \left\{ H(\mathsf{ID}, \ell)^{f(i)} \cdot g^{r_{i,\ell}} \mid 1 \leq \ell \leq m \right\} .$$

Additionally, the client initializes a new bit string bs_j for every set element $x_j \in \mathcal{S}_i$. It encrypts each element x_j and adds $\phi(x_j)$ to the Bloom filter for bs_j. Let t_j denote the Hamming weight (i.e., the number of 1s) of the resulting bit string bs_j. For the resulting bit string bs_j pick $r_{i,j,\ell} \xleftarrow{R} \mathbb{Z}_p$ for $1 \leq \ell \leq m$. Additionally, set

$\rho_{i,j,\ell} \xleftarrow{R} \mathbb{Z}_p$ if $\mathsf{bs}_j[\ell] = 0$, and $\rho_{i,j,\ell} = t_j \cdot r_{i,j,\ell}$, otherwise. It encrypts the Bloom filter for bs_j as

$$ \mathsf{ct}_{\mathsf{bs}_j} = \left(\left\{ H(\mathsf{ID}, \ell)^{f(n+i)} \cdot g^{\rho_{i,j,\ell}}, g^{r_{i,j,\ell}} \mid 1 \le \ell \le m \right\} \right) . $$

Finally, the client outputs the ciphertext $\left(\mathsf{ct}_{\mathsf{bs}_S}, \left\{ \mathsf{ct}_{\mathsf{bs}_j} \mid x_j \in \mathcal{S}_i \right\} \right)$.

Eval$(\mathsf{ct}_{\mathsf{ID},1}, \ldots, \mathsf{ct}_{\mathsf{ID},n}) \to |\bigcap_{i=1}^n \mathcal{S}_i|$. Since the clients' ciphertext are encryptions of the individual set elements, we can determine a client with the smallest (encrypted) set. Let γ be such a client. Now, for $1 \le \ell \le m$, compute the partial Lagrange interpolation

$$ a_\ell = \prod_{i=1}^n \left(\mathsf{ct}_{\mathsf{ID},i,\mathsf{bs}_S[\ell]} \right)^{\Delta_{\{1,\ldots,n,n+\gamma\},i}} . $$

Set $d = 0$. Next, to determine if an encrypted set element $x_j \in \mathcal{S}_\gamma$ (represented by a tuple $(\mathsf{ct}_{\mathsf{ID},\gamma,\mathsf{bs}_j}, g^{r_{\gamma,j,\ell}}) \in \mathsf{ct}_{\mathsf{ID},\gamma,\mathcal{S}}$) is in the intersection of all sets, check for each $1 \le \ell \le m$, if

$$ \left(\mathsf{ct}_{\mathsf{ID},\gamma,\mathsf{bs}_j[\ell]} \right)^{\Delta_{\{1,\ldots,n,n+\gamma\},n+\gamma}} \cdot a_\ell \stackrel{?}{=} \left(g^{r_{\gamma,j,\ell}} \right)^{t_{j,\ell} \cdot \Delta_{\{1,\ldots,n,n+\gamma\},n+\gamma}} $$

for values $1 \le t_{j,\ell} \le k$. If the value $t_{j,\ell}$ occurs $t_{j,\ell}$ times for the values $1 \le \ell \le m$, increase the value d by one.

After all encrypted set element $x_j \in \mathcal{S}_\gamma$ have been checked, output the cardinality of the set intersection d.

Correctness. To see that the above defined scheme is correct, observe that if a set element $x_j \in \mathcal{S}_i$ is in the intersection of all clients' sets, the values $r_{i,j,\ell}$ equal 0 for the same values of ℓ in the encrypted Bloom filters $\mathsf{ct}_{\mathsf{ID},i,\mathsf{bs}_S}$. Hence, by using the Lagrange interpolation on these elements (corresponding to a_ℓ) together with an encrypted Bloom filter for a single set element $x_j \in \mathcal{S}_\gamma$ (corresponding to $\mathsf{ct}_{\mathsf{ID},\gamma,\mathsf{bs}_j}$), we obtain $H(\mathsf{ID}, \ell)^{f(0)} \cdot g^{r_{i,j,\ell} \cdot \Delta_{\{1,\ldots,n,n+\gamma\},n+\gamma}} = g^{r_{i,j,\ell} \cdot \Delta_{\{1,\ldots,n,n+\gamma\},n+\gamma}}$. Now, note that we set $\rho_{i,j,\ell} = t_j \cdot r_{i,j,\ell}$ if the bit string value $\mathsf{bs}_j[\ell] = 1$. So, if exactly t_j bit string values in the set intersection are set to 1, we know that the element is a member of the set intersection.

Theorem 5. *The improved multi-client set intersection cardinality scheme defined above is secure without corruptions under the DDH assumption in the ROM.*

Proof. We construct an algorithm that is able to break the DDH problem if a p.p.t adversary $\mathcal{A}$ has a non-negligible advantage in winning the game.

Random Oracle. On input of a tuple (ID, ℓ) the oracle checks if it has answered the query before. If not, it picks a value $\beta_{\mathsf{ID},\ell} \xleftarrow{R} \mathbb{Z}_p$. Next, the challenger $\mathcal{B}$ guesses whether the query is for the challenge ID. If so, the oracle outputs $(g^b)^{\beta_{\mathsf{ID},\ell}}$, otherwise, it outputs $g^{\beta_{\mathsf{ID},\ell}}$. If the guess turns out to be wrong later, $\mathcal{B}$ can simply abort the game.

Setup. The challenger $\mathcal{B}$ receives the DDH tuple (g, g^a, g^b, T) from the group $\mathbb{G}$ of prime order p. It defines a PRF ensemble $\Phi = \{\phi_\kappa\}$ and the Bloom filter BF according to the scheme. Pick for $1 \le i \le n$, values $c_i \xleftarrow{R} \mathbb{Z}_p$ and define the n-degree polynomial $f'(x) = c_n x^n + \cdots + c_1 x$ over the field $\mathbb{F}_p$. The challenger uses $f(x) = a \cdot f'(x)$ to indirectly define the secret shares. Note that this still allows $\mathcal{B}$ to compute $g^{f(x)} = (g^a)^{f'(x)}$ for all values of x.

Query. To answer an encryption query $\mathcal{S}_i$ for a client i, the challenger uses the oracle to obtain $\{\, \beta_{\mathsf{ID},\ell} \mid x_j \in \mathcal{S}_i \,\}$ and construct the ciphertext as in the scheme, but using $H(\mathsf{ID}, \ell)^{f(x)} = (g^a)^{\beta_{\mathsf{ID},\ell} f'(x)}$.

Challenge. Upon receiving the challenge sets $(\mathcal{S}_{i,0}^*, \mathcal{S}_{i,1}^*)$ for $1 \le i \le n$ and an ID^* from the adversary, the challenger picks $b \xleftarrow{R} \{0, 1\}$. The challenger returns the encryptions of the sets $\mathcal{S}_{i,b}^*$ using the scheme's encrypt algorithm, but replacing $H(\mathsf{ID}^*, \ell)^{f(x)}$ by $T^{\beta_{\mathsf{ID}^*,\ell} f'(x)}$. Note that if $T = g^{ab}$, the ciphertext is distributed properly according the scheme. If $T \in_R \mathbb{G}$, the challenger returns a ciphertext of a randomly distributed set element. So, the challenger $\mathcal{B}$ guesses that $T = g^{ab}$ if $\mathcal{A}$ correctly guessed $b' = b$ and otherwise, $\mathcal{B}$ guesses that $T \in_R \mathbb{G}$.

To construct efficient multi-client functional encryption schemes for set operations that resist corruptions, we need to be able to check the membership of an encrypted set element against the encrypted intersection of the clients' sets. The above construction fails to be secure against corruptions as it (partially) reveals the individual bits in the bit string of a Bloom filter for a set element, i.e., the adversary learns (part of) the bit string representation of the set element.

7.3 Multi-client Set Intersection

The set intersection can be computed using a notion similar to non-interactive distributed encryption (DE) schemes [14,24]. A DE scheme is characterized by two distinctive features. Firstly, we have that multiple clients can encrypt a plaintext under their own secret key. Secondly, if enough clients have encrypted the same plaintext, anyone can recover this plaintext from the clients' ciphertexts.

We construct an MC-FE scheme for set intersection from a DE scheme.

Setup$(1^\lambda, n)$ $\rightarrow$ $(\mathsf{pp}, \mathsf{usk}_1, \ldots, \mathsf{usk}_n)$. Run $\mathsf{DE.Gen}(1^\lambda, n, n)$ to generate an n-OUT-OF-n DE scheme defined by pp and obtain the encryption keys $(\mathsf{usk}_1, \ldots, \mathsf{usk}_n)$.

Encrypt$(\mathsf{usk}_i, \mathsf{ID}, \mathcal{S}_i)$ $\rightarrow$ $\mathsf{ct}_{\mathsf{ID},i}$. To encrypt the set $\mathcal{S}_i$, encrypt the identifier ID together with each set element $x_j \in \mathcal{S}_i$ individually,

$$\mathsf{ct}_{\mathsf{ID},i} = \{\, \mathsf{DE.Enc}(\mathsf{usk}_i, \mathsf{ID} \parallel x_j) \mid x_j \in \mathcal{S}_i \,\},$$

where ID has a fixed length (e.g., by applying padding). The algorithm's output is a random ordering of the set $\mathsf{ct}_{\mathsf{ID},i}$.

$\mathsf{Eval}(\mathsf{ct}_{\mathsf{ID},1}, \ldots, \mathsf{ct}_{\mathsf{ID},n}) \rightarrow \bigcap_{i=1}^{n} \mathcal{S}_i$. For each n-tuple $(c_{\mathsf{ID},1}, \ldots, c_{\mathsf{ID},n}) \in \mathsf{ct}_{\mathsf{ID},1} \times \cdots \times \mathsf{ct}_{\mathsf{ID},n}$, the evaluator uses $\mathsf{DE}.\mathsf{Comb}(c_{\mathsf{ID},1}, \ldots, c_{\mathsf{ID},n})$ to obtain either the message $\mathsf{ID} \parallel x_j$ or $\perp$. If the message starts with the expected ID, it adds x_j to the initially empty set $\mathcal{R}$.

After evaluating all tuples, the evaluator outputs the set $\mathcal{R}$.

Theorem 6. *The multi-client set intersection scheme defined above is secure under the security of the DE scheme.*

Proof. For $b \in \{0, 1\}$, we consider for every set element $x_{j,b} \in \bigcup_{i \in I} \mathcal{S}_{i,b}^*$ two cases:

– if $x_{j,b} \in \bigcap_{i \in I} \mathcal{S}_{i,b}^*$, $x_{j,b}$ is also contained in every client i's set $\mathcal{S}_{i,1-b}^*$;
– if $x_{j,b} \notin \bigcap_{i \in I} \mathcal{S}_{i,b}^*$, there is at least one set $\mathcal{S}_{k,1-b}^*$ which does not contain $x_{j,b}$, but an element $x_{j,1-b} \notin \bigcap_{i \in I} \mathcal{S}_{i,1-b}^*$ (and hence $x_{j,1-b} \notin \bigcap_{i \in I} \mathcal{S}_{i,b}^*$) instead.

For the elements x_j satisfying the first case, the adversary does not learn anything about b since for every client i we have that $x_j \in \mathcal{S}_{i,b}^*$ and $x_j \in \mathcal{S}_{i,1-b}^*$, while $|\mathcal{S}_{i,b}^*| = |\mathcal{S}_{i,1-b}^*|$ (remember that the set elements are randomly ordered).

For the elements $x_{j,b}$ satisfying the second case, we claim that the adversary does not learn anything about b by the security of the DE scheme. To see this, note that there exist at least two uncorrupted clients, with at least one client which did not encrypt the plaintext $\mathsf{ID}^* \parallel x_{j,b}$. Observe that the security of the DE scheme gives us that one cannot distinguish an encryption of a plaintext m_0 from an encryption of a plaintext m_1 as long as at most $t-1$ uncorrupted clients have encrypted the same plaintext. Combined with the fact that in our scheme we have set $t = n$ and the fact that we know that at least one uncorrupted client did not encrypt the message $\mathsf{ID}^* \parallel x_{j,b}$ and also that at least one uncorrupted client did not encrypt the message $\mathsf{ID}^* \parallel x_{j,1-b}$, we know that the encryption of the message $\mathsf{ID}^* \parallel x_{j,b}$ is indistinguishable from the encryption of the message $\mathsf{ID}^* \parallel x_{j,1-b}$.

To improve efficiency, we can combine the above multi-client set intersection scheme with the efficient multi-client set intersection cardinality scheme. The construction for determining the cardinality can be used first to identify which ciphertext elements correspond to set elements that are in the set intersection. Next, we only have to use the evaluation algorithm of the multi-client set intersection scheme on these elements from which we know that they belong to the set intersection.

8   Evaluation

We created proof-of-concept implementations[1] of the proposed 2C-FE schemes and the two MC-FE schemes for determining the cardinality of the intersection. The implementations are done in Python using the Charm library at a

---

[1] Available at https://github.com/CRIPTIM/nipsi.

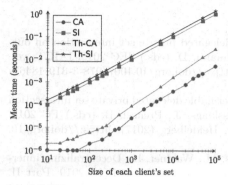
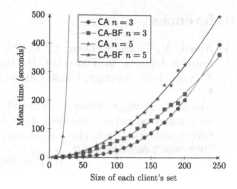

(a) 2C-FE timings; for the threshold scheme $t = 5$ is used.

(b) MC-FE timings, with interpolation on the domain $[0, 250]$.

Fig. 2. Evaluations for determining the cardinality (CA); set intersection (SI); and cardinality (Th-CA) and set intersection (Th-SI) in the threshold scheme.

128 bit security level. The evaluations are done on a commodity laptop (i5-4210U@1.7GHz, 8 GB RAM) using only a single core. In Fig. 2 we show the time it took to run Eval on encrypted sets of varying sizes. Each client encrypted a set of the same size and had 10% of their set in common with the other clients.

We see that the 2C-FE constructions can be evaluated in under a second, even for sets of 100 thousand elements in size. A lower bound of the timings is given by the 2C-FE cardinality scheme, CA, since it uses the same built-in Python algorithm that is used on plaintext data. The MC-FE constructions are polynomial in the set sizes. We evaluated the Bloom filter (BF) construction with a worst-case false positive rate of 0.001. While it scales linear for fixed Bloom filter sizes, the length of the bit strings have to increase linearly for larger sets, resulting in quadratic efficiency of the Eval algorithm.

9 Conclusion

We initiated the study of non-interactive two-client functional encryption (2C-FE) and multi-client functional encryption (MC-FE) schemes for set intersection. We show that very efficient 2C-FE schemes can be constructed for set intersection and related set operations. Additionally, the problem of constructing non-interactive set intersection schemes for three or more clients is addressed by our MC-FE schemes from a theoretical perspective. Finally, we show the practicability of the proposed schemes using proof-of-concept implementations.

Acknowledgments. This work was supported by the Netherlands Organisation for Scientific Research (Nederlandse Organisatie voor Wetenschappelijk Onderzoek, NWO) in the context of the CRIPTIM project.

References

1. Abadi, A., Terzis, S., Dong, C.: O-PSI: delegated private set intersection on outsourced datasets. In: Federrath, H., Gollmann, D. (eds.) SEC 2015. IAICT, vol. 455, pp. 3–17. Springer, Cham (2015). https://doi.org/10.1007/978-3-319-18467-8_1
2. Abadi, A., Terzis, S., Dong, C.: VD-PSI: verifiable delegated private set intersection on outsourced private datasets. In: Grossklags, J., Preneel, B. (eds.) FC 2016. LNCS, vol. 9603, pp. 149–168. Springer, Heidelberg (2017). https://doi.org/10.1007/978-3-662-54970-4_9
3. Abdalla, M., Benhamouda, F., Kohlweiss, M., Waldner, H.: Decentralizing inner-product functional encryption. In: Lin, D., Sako, K. (eds.) PKC 2019, Part II. LNCS, vol. 11443, pp. 128–157. Springer, Cham (2019). https://doi.org/10.1007/978-3-030-17259-6_5
4. Bellare, M., Keelveedhi, S., Ristenpart, T.: Message-locked encryption and secure deduplication. In: Johansson, T., Nguyen, P.Q. (eds.) EUROCRYPT 2013. LNCS, vol. 7881, pp. 296–312. Springer, Heidelberg (2013). https://doi.org/10.1007/978-3-642-38348-9_18
5. Bellare, M., Namprempre, C.: Authenticated encryption: relations among notions and analysis of the generic composition paradigm. In: Okamoto, T. (ed.) ASIACRYPT 2000. LNCS, vol. 1976, pp. 531–545. Springer, Heidelberg (2000). https://doi.org/10.1007/3-540-44448-3_41
6. Boneh, D., Lewi, K., Raykova, M., Sahai, A., Zhandry, M., Zimmerman, J.: Semantically secure order-revealing encryption: multi-input functional encryption without obfuscation. In: Oswald, E., Fischlin, M. (eds.) EUROCRYPT 2015, Part II. LNCS, vol. 9057, pp. 563–594. Springer, Heidelberg (2015). https://doi.org/10.1007/978-3-662-46803-6_19
7. Carpent, X., Faber, S., Sander, T., Tsudik, G.: Private set projections & variants. In: WPES. ACM (2017). https://doi.org/10.1145/3139550.3139554
8. Chotard, J., Dufour Sans, E., Gay, R., Phan, D.H., Pointcheval, D.: Decentralized multi-client functional encryption for inner product. In: Peyrin, T., Galbraith, S. (eds.) ASIACRYPT 2018. LNCS, vol. 11273, pp. 703–732. Springer, Cham (2018). https://doi.org/10.1007/978-3-030-03329-3_24
9. De Cristofaro, E., Tsudik, G.: Practical private set intersection protocols with linear complexity. In: Sion, R. (ed.) FC 2010. LNCS, vol. 6052, pp. 143–159. Springer, Heidelberg (2010). https://doi.org/10.1007/978-3-642-14577-3_13
10. Ding, B., König, A.C.: Fast set intersection in memory. In: Jagadish, H.V., Koudas, N. (ed.) Proceedings of the VLDB Endowment 4.4, pp. 255–266, January 2011. ISSN: 2150–8097. https://doi.org/10.14778/1938545.1938550
11. Dong, C., Chen, L., Wen, Z.: When private set intersection meets big data: an efficient and scalable protocol. In: CCS. ACM (2013). https://doi.org/10.1145/2508859.2516701
12. Douceur, J.R., Adya, A., Bolosky, W.J., Simon, D., Theimer, M.: Reclaiming space from duplicate files in a serverless distributed file system. In: ICDCS. IEEE (2002). https://doi.org/10.1109/ICDCS.2002.1022312
13. Freedman, M.J., Nissim, K., Pinkas, B.: Efficient private matching and set intersection. In: Cachin, C., Camenisch, J.L. (eds.) EUROCRYPT 2004. LNCS, vol. 3027, pp. 1–19. Springer, Heidelberg (2004). https://doi.org/10.1007/978-3-540-24676-3_1
14. Galindo, D., Hoepman, J.-H.: Non-interactive distributed encryption: a new primitive for revocable privacy. In: WPES. ACM (2011). https://doi.org/10.1145/2046556.2046567

15. Goldwasser, S., et al.: Multi-input functional encryption. In: Nguyen, P.Q., Oswald, E. (eds.) EUROCRYPT 2014. LNCS, vol. 8441, pp. 578–602. Springer, Heidelberg (2014). https://doi.org/10.1007/978-3-642-55220-5_32
16. Jarecki, S., Liu, X.: Fast secure computation of set intersection. In: Garay, J.A., De Prisco, R. (eds.) SCN 2010. LNCS, vol. 6280, pp. 418–435. Springer, Heidelberg (2010). https://doi.org/10.1007/978-3-642-15317-4_26
17. Kamara, S., Mohassel, P., Raykova, M., Sadeghian, S.: Scaling private set intersection to billion-element sets. In: Christin, N., Safavi-Naini, R. (eds.) FC 2014. LNCS, vol. 8437, pp. 195–215. Springer, Heidelberg (2014). https://doi.org/10.1007/978-3-662-45472-5_13
18. Kerschbaum, F.: Collusion-resistant outsourcing of private set intersection. In: SAC. ACM (2012). https://doi.org/10.1145/2245276.2232008
19. Kerschbaum, F.: Outsourced private set intersection using homomorphic encryption. In: ASIACCS. ACM (2012). https://doi.org/10.1145/2414456.2414506
20. Kim, S., Lewi, K., Mandal, A., Montgomery, H., Roy, A., Wu, D.J.: Function-hiding inner product encryption is practical. In: Catalano, D., De Prisco, R. (eds.) SCN 2018. LNCS, vol. 11035, pp. 544–562. Springer, Cham (2018). https://doi.org/10.1007/978-3-319-98113-0_29
21. Kissner, L., Song, D.: Privacy-preserving set operations. In: Shoup, V. (ed.) CRYPTO 2005. LNCS, vol. 3621, pp. 241–257. Springer, Heidelberg (2005). https://doi.org/10.1007/11535218_15
22. Lewko, A., Waters, B.: Decentralizing attribute-based encryption. In: Paterson, K.G. (ed.) EUROCRYPT 2011. LNCS, vol. 6632, pp. 568–588. Springer, Heidelberg (2011). https://doi.org/10.1007/978-3-642-20465-4_31
23. Liu, F., Ng, W.K., Zhang, W., Giang, D.H., Han, S.: Encrypted set intersection protocol for outsourced datasets. In: IC2E. IEEE (2014). https://doi.org/10.1109/IC2E.2014.18
24. Lueks, W., Hoepman, J.-H., Kursawe, K.: Forward-secure distributed encryption. In: De Cristofaro, E., Murdoch, S.J. (eds.) PETS 2014. LNCS, vol. 8555, pp. 123–142. Springer, Cham (2014). https://doi.org/10.1007/978-3-319-08506-7_7
25. Meadows, C.: A more efficient cryptographic matchmaking protocol for use in the absence of a continuously available third party. In: S&P. IEEE (1986). https://doi.org/10.1109/SP.1986.10022
26. Pandey, O., Rouselakis, Y.: Property preserving symmetric encryption. In: Pointcheval, D., Johansson, T. (eds.) EUROCRYPT 2012. LNCS, vol. 7237, pp. 375–391. Springer, Heidelberg (2012). https://doi.org/10.1007/978-3-642-29011-4_23
27. Pinkas, B., Schneider, T., Zohner, M.: Faster private set intersection based on OT extension. In: USENIX Security. USENIX Association (2014)
28. Shi, E., Chan, T.H., Rieffel, E.G., Chow, R., Song, D.: Privacy-preserving aggregation of time-series data. In: NDSS. The Internet Society (2011)
29. Smart, N.P.: Cryptography Made Simple. Information Security and Cryptography. Springer, Cham (2016). https://doi.org/10.1007/978-3-319-21936-3. ISBN: 978-3-319-21936-3. Ed. by D. Basin and K. Paterson
30. van de Kamp, T., Peter, A., Everts, M.H., Jonker, W.: Multi-client predicate-only encryption for conjunctive equality tests. In: Capkun, S., Chow, S.S.M. (eds.) CANS 2017. LNCS, vol. 11261, pp. 135–157. Springer, Cham (2018). https://doi.org/10.1007/978-3-030-02641-7_7
31. Zheng, Q., Xu, S.: Verifiable delegated set intersection operations on outsourced encrypted data. In: IC2E. IEEE (2015). https://doi.org/10.1109/IC2E.2015.38

Post-quantum Security

Improving the Security of the DRS Scheme with Uniformly Chosen Random Noise

Arnaud Sipasseuth[✉], Thomas Plantard, and Willy Susilo

iC²: Institute of Cybersecurity and Cryptology,
School of Computing and Information Technology, University of Wollongong,
Wollongong, Australia
{as447,thomaspl}@uowmail.edu.au, wsusilo@uow.edu.au

Abstract. At PKC 2008, Plantard et al. published a theoretical framework for a lattice-based signature scheme. Recently, after ten years, a new signature scheme dubbed as the Diagonal Reduction Signature (DRS) scheme was presented in the NIST PQC Standardization as a concrete instantiation of the initial work. Unfortunately, the initial submission was challenged by Yu and Ducas using the structure that is present on the secret key noise. In this paper, we are proposing a new method to generate random noise in the DRS scheme to elimite the aforementioned attack, and all subsequent potential variants.

Keywords: Lattice-based cryptography · DRS ·
Lattice-based signatures · NIST PQC · Diagonal dominant

1 Introduction

The popularity of post-quantum cryptography has increased significantly after the formal announcement by the National Institute of Standards and Technology (NIST) to move away from classical cryptography [18]. This is due to the potential threat that will be brought by the upcoming large scale quantum computers, which theoretically break the underlying traditional hard problem by using Shor's algorithm [25]. There are currently three main families in post-quantum cryptology, namely code-based cryptography, multivariate cryptography, and lattice-based cryptography. This work primarily concerns with lattice-based cryptography. First introduced by Minkowski in a pioneering work [15] to solve various number problems, lattices have the advantage to often base their security on worst-case assumptions [1] rather than the average case, and to be highly parallelizable and algorithmically simple enough to compete with traditional schemes in terms of computing speed. Inspired by this, Goldreich, Goldwasser and Halevi (GGH) [7] proposed an efficient way to use lattices to build a public-key encryption scheme. Their practical scheme has been broken using lattice reduction techniques [16], however the central idea remains viable

© Springer Nature Switzerland AG 2019
J. Jang-Jaccard and F. Guo (Eds.): ACISP 2019, LNCS 11547, pp. 119–137, 2019.
https://doi.org/10.1007/978-3-030-21548-4_7

and it has enabled a wide array of applications and improvements, such as using tensor products [5], Hermite Normal Forms [14], polynomial representations [19], rotations [26], and the most popular one being Learning With Errors [23] or its variants.

More recently, the NIST attempt at standardizing post-quantum cryptography [17] received a lot of interest from the community and the vast majority of the lattice-based submissions for "Round 1" are actually based on LWE [17]. One of the few lattice-based submissions which is not using LWE or ideal lattices is the Diagonal Reduction Signature Scheme (DRS) [20], which uses a diagonal dominant matrix that can be seen as a sum between a diagonal matrix with very big coefficients and a random matrix with low coefficients. DRS was based on a paper from PKC 2008 [21] however the original paper had mostly a theoretical interest and did not provide an explicit way to construct the random matrix with low values, rather than merely stating conditions on norm bounds it should respect for the signature scheme to be proven functioning. The NIST submission however provides a more straight-forward way to generate the noise, using another proof and condition to ensure the functionality of the scheme. This new way to generate the noise, however, is shown to be insecure: soon after DRS was made public, Yu and Ducas used machine learning techniques to severely reduce the security parameters [30]. Although according to Ducas' comments on the NIST forum [17], the attack was not devastating as it still seems asymptotically secure, however its concrete security was significantly decreased. On the same work, Yu and Ducas also provided several suggestions in order to fix those issues and one of those comments suggested using a statistical analysis. Another more recent attack from Li, Liu, Nitaj and Pan [11] on a randomized version of the initial scheme proposed by Plantard, Susilo and Win [21] can also be indirectly considered an attack to the DRS scheme, although this attack does not seem as important as Yu and Ducas's one.

In the following work, we do follow some of those suggestions and we aim to provide a new noise generation method to eliminate the aforementioned attack and restore some of the DRS' concrete security. We will present some statistical heuristics and remove some of the structure that allow the initial DRS scheme to be attacked.

Our Contribution and Paper Organization.
The rest of the paper is organized as follows. We first present some relevant background on lattice theory and re-introduce the DRS scheme from Plantard et al. Subsequently, we will comment on the attack of Li, Liu, Nitaj and Pan [11] and explain why it is not applicable. Then we discuss the weakness found by Yu and Ducas and our idea to correct this. We finally present the detail algorithms about our security patch and raise some open questions.

2   Background

In this section, we briefly recall the basics of lattice theory.

2.1 Lattice Theory

Definition 1. *We call lattice a discrete subgroup of $\mathbb{R}^n$ where n is a positive integer. We say a lattice is an integer lattice when it is a subgroup of $\mathbb{Z}^n$. A basis of the lattice is a basis as a $\mathbb{Z}-$ module. If M is a matrix, we define $\mathcal{L}(M)$ the lattice generated by the rows of M.*

In this work we only consider full-rank integer lattices, i.e., such that their basis can be represented by a $n \times n$ non-singular integer matrix.

Theorem 1 (Determinant). *For any lattice $\mathcal{L}$, there exists a real value we call* determinant, *denoted $det(\mathcal{L})$, such that for any basis B, $det(\mathcal{L}) = \sqrt{det(BB^T)}$.*

The literature sometimes call $det(\mathcal{L})$ as the **volume** of $\mathcal{L}$ [15].

Definition 2. *We say a lattice is a diagonally dominant type lattice if it admits a basis of the form $D + R$ where $D = d \times Id, d \in \mathbb{Z}$, and R is a "noise" matrix whose diagonal entries are zeroes and the absolute sum of each entry is lower than d per each row separately.*

We note that the definition is similar to the one which can be found in fundamental mathematics books [3] for diagonal dominant matrices. We will just adapt the lattice to its diagonal dominant basis.

Definition 3 (Minima). *We note $\lambda_i(\mathcal{L})$ the $i-th$ minimum of a lattice $\mathcal{L}$. It is the radius of the smallest zero-centered ball containing at least i linearly independant elements of $\mathcal{L}$.*

Definition 4 (Lattice gap). *We note $\delta_i(\mathcal{L})$ the ratio $\frac{\lambda_{i+1}(\mathcal{L})}{\lambda_i(\mathcal{L})}$ and call that a lattice gap. When mentioned without index and called "the" gap, the index is implied to be $i = 1$.*

In practice, only the case $i = 1$ is used, but other values are sometimes useful to consider [29]. We also define the "root lattice gap", i.e., elevated to the power $\frac{1}{n}$ where n is the dimension of the lattice.

Definition 5. *We say a lattice is a diagonally dominant type lattice (of dimension n) if it admits a diagonal dominant matrix as a basis B as in [3], i.e.,*

$$\forall i \in [1,n], B_{i,i} \geq \sum_{j=1, i \neq j}^{n} |B_{i,j}|$$

We can also see a diagonally dominant matrix B as a sum $B = D + R$ where D is diagonal and $D_{i,i} > \|R_i\|_1$. In our scheme, we use a diagonal dominant lattice as our secret key, and will refer to it as our "reduction matrix" (as we use this basis to "reduce" our vectors).

Definition 6. *Let F be a subfield of $\mathbb{C}$, V a vector space over F^k, and p a positive integer or ∞. We call l_p norm over V the norm:*

- $\forall x \in V, \|x\|_p = \sqrt[p]{\sum_{i=1}^{k} |x_i|^p}$
- $\forall x \in V, \|x\|_\infty = \max_{i \in [1,k]} |x_i|$

l_1 and l_2 are commonly used and are often called taxicab norm and euclidean norm, respectively. We note that we also define the maximum matrix norm as the biggest value among the sums of the absolute values in a single column.

The norm that was used by Plantard et al. for their signature validity is the maximum norm. However, as far as the security heuristics are concerned the euclidean norm (l_2) is used, and as far as the reduction termination proof is concerned the taxicab norm (l_1) is used.

2.2　Lattice Problems

The most famous problems on lattice are the Shortest Vector Problem (SVP) and the Closest Vector Problem (CVP). We tend to approximatively solving CVP by solving heuristically SVP in an expanded lattice [7].

Definition 7 (CVP: Closest Vector Problem). *Given a basis B of a lattice $\mathcal{L}$ of dimension n and $t \in \mathbb{R}^n$, find $v \in \mathcal{L}$ such that $\forall w \in \mathcal{L}, \|t - v\| \leq \|t - w\|$.*

Definition 8 (SVP: Shortest Vector Problem). *Given a basis B of a lattice $\mathcal{L}$ of dimension n, find $v \in \mathcal{L}$ such that $\forall w \in \mathcal{L}, v \neq w, \|v\| \leq \|w - v\|$, i.e $\|v\| = \lambda_1(B)$.*

In cryptography, we rely on the "easier" versions of those problems:

Definition 9 (uSVP$_\delta$: δ-unique Shortest Vector Problem). *Given a basis of a lattice $\mathcal{L}$ with its lattice gap $\delta > 1$, solve SVP.*

Since $\lambda_1(\mathcal{L})$ is also hard to determine (it is indeed another lattice problem we do not state here), measuring the efficiency of an algorithm is another challenge by itself. Therefore, to measure algorithm efficiency we must be able to define a problem with easily computable parameters, which is where the Hermite factor is originated from:

Definition 10 (HSVP$_\gamma$: γ-Hermite Shortest Vector Problem). *Given a basis B of a lattice $\mathcal{L}$ of dimension n and a factor γ we call Hermite Factor, find $y \in \mathcal{L}$ such that $\|y\| \leq \gamma \det(\mathcal{L})^{1/n}$.*

Some cryptosystems are based on worst-case hardness on uSVP with polynomial gap as [2] and [23]. The practical hardness of uSVP depends on its gap compared to a fraction of the Hermite factor, where the constant in front of the factor depends of the lattice and the algorithm used [6]. There exists an attack that was specifically built to exploit high gaps [12].

Definition 11 (BDD$_\gamma$: γ-Bounded Distance Decoding). *Given a basis B of a lattice $\mathcal{L}$, a point x and a approximation factor γ ensuring $d(x, \mathcal{L}) < \gamma \lambda_1(B)$ find the lattice vector $v \in \mathcal{L}$ closest to x.*

It has been proved that $\mathbf{BDD}_{1/(2\gamma)}$ reduces itself to $\mathbf{uSVP}_\gamma$ in polynomial time and the same goes from $\mathbf{uSVP}_\gamma$ to $\mathbf{BDD}_{1/\gamma}$ when γ is polynomially bounded by n [13], in cryptography the gap is polynomial the target point x must be polynomially bounded therefore solving one or the other is relatively the same in our case. To solve those problems, we usually use an embedding technique that extends a basis matrix by one column and one row vector that are full of zeroes except for one position where the value is set to 1 at the intersection of those newly added spaces, and then apply lattice reduction techniques on these. As far as their signature scheme is concerned, the $\mathbf{GDD}_\gamma$ is more relevant:

Definition 12 ($\mathbf{GDD}_\gamma$: γ-Guaranteed Distance Decoding). *Given a basis B of a lattice $\mathcal{L}$, any point x and a approximation factor γ, find $v \in \mathcal{L}$ such that $\|x - v\| \leq \gamma$.*

3   The Initial DRS Scheme and Its Security Pitfall

We will briefly summarize the DRS scheme below, which can be considered a fork of the theoretical framework of PKC 2008 [21]. The DRS scheme uses the maximum norm to check if a vector is reduced. To achieve that purpose, they use a diagonal dominant basis, where every substraction from a diagonally dominant basis vector reduces a coefficient by a lot more than it potentially adds to the other coefficients. By repeating those steps for each coefficient, we end up reducing the vector. The initial DRS scheme requires multiple parameters to be preset (see the file *api.h* in their NIST submission), which we give here the main ones describing their choice for a secret key: D, a big diagonal coefficient, N_B, the number of occurences per vector of the "big" noise $\{-B, B\}$, and is the lowest positive number such that $2^{N_B} \binom{n}{N_b} \geq 2^\lambda$, B, the value of the "big" noise, and is equal to $D/(2N_B)$, and N_1, the number of occurences per vector of the small noise $\{-1, 1\}$, and is equal to $D - (N_B B) - \Delta$. As we will see by discussing previous work, this structure directly impact the security.

3.1   The Original DRS Scheme

Setup. Using the same notation as the report given in [20], we briefly restate their initial algorithm. Those parameters are chosen such that the secret key matrix stays diagonal dominant as per the definition written previously. From our understanding, the large coefficients B were used to increase the euclidean norm, as an attempt to enhance its security against lattice reduction attacks. Algorithm 1 is the original secret key computation.

The public key is obtained by successive additions/substractions of pair of vectors (see Algorithm 2). Note that the only difference with the original scheme is that we do not store the $\log_2$ of the maximum norm. We estimate this information to be easily computed at will.

This is equivalent to a multiplication of random pairs of vectors (a $2 \times n$ matrix) by a square invertible matrix of dimension 2 and maximum norm of

```
Input: - all initial parameters;
- another extra random seed x₂;
Output: - x, S the secret key;
// Initialization
S ← 0;
t ∈ ℤⁿ;
// Algorithm start
InitiateRdmSeed(x₂);
// Set t[1] to D, N_B elements to B, N₁ to 1, the rest to 0
t ← [D,B,...,B,1,...,1,0,...,0];
        _____/  \____/
          N_B       N₁
// Randomly permute values of t with a function RdmPmtn
// RdmPmtn leaves t[1] unchanged
t ← RdmPmtn(t);
for i = 1 ; i ≤ n ; i = i + 1 do
    S[i][i] ← t[1];
    // Apply a circular permutation and randomly flip signs
    for j = 2 ; j ≤ n ; j = j + 1 do
        S[i][((i + j)  mod n) + 1] ← t[j] * RdnSgn();
    end
end
return x, S;
```

Algorithm 1. Secret key generation (square matrix of dimension n)

```
Input: - S the reduction matrix of dimension n, obtained previously;
- a random seed x;
Output: - P the public key, and p₂ a power of two;
// Initialization
P ← S;
// Algorithm start
InitiateRdmSeed(x);
// Apply R rounds
for i = 1 ; i < R ; i = i + 1 do
    P ← RdmPmtn(P);
    for j = 1 ; j ≤ n - 1 ; j = j + 2 do
        t ← RdmSgn();
        P[j] = P[j] + t * P[j + 1];
        P[j + 1] = P[j + 1] + t * P[j];
    end
end
P ← RdmPmtn(P);
return P, p₂;
```

Algorithm 2. Public key generation

2. In their case, every vector go through exactly one matrix multiplication per round, for a total of R rounds where R is defined by the system. The number of rounds R is decided upon security consideration but also efficiency reasons as the authors of DRS wanted to fit every computation within 64-bits. For more details we refer again to [20]. From our understanding, the power of 2 p_2 has no security impact, and is used mostly for the verification process to make sure intermediate computation results stay within 64-bits. This type of public key is very different from the Hermite Normal Form proposed in [21], however the computation time of a Hermite Normal Form is non-negligible. As we will see later this directly impact the signature.

Signature. Given the fact that the secret key is a diagonally dominant matrix, Algorithm 3 is guaranteed to complete. The proof can be seen in [20]. Plantard et al. did not have a second vector k to output in their initial scheme and thus only had to deal with the reduction part [21].

Input: - A vector $v \in \mathbb{Z}^n$;
- S the secret key matrix, with diagonal coefficient d;
- s a seed value;
Output: - w with $v \equiv w$ $[\mathcal{L}(S)]$, $\|w\|_\infty < d$ and k with $kP = v - w$;
// Initialization
$w \leftarrow v,\ i \leftarrow 0,\ k \leftarrow [0, ..., 0]$;
// Algorithm start
// Reduce until all coefficients are low enough
while $\|w\|_\infty < d$ do
| $q \leftarrow \frac{w_i}{d},\ k_i \leftarrow k_i + q,\ w \leftarrow w - qS[i],\ i \leftarrow i + 1$ mod n;
end
// Use the seed to modify k such that $kP = v - w$
// The seed defines the output of RdmPmtn and RdmSgn
$InitiateRdmSeed(x)$;
for $i = 1\ ;\ i \leq R\ ;\ i = i + 1$ do
| $k \leftarrow$ **RdmPmtn**(k);
| for $j = 1\ ;\ j \leq n - 1\ ;\ j = j + 2$ do
| | $t \leftarrow$ **RdmSgn**$()$;
| | $k[j + 1] = k[j + 1] - t * k[j]$;
| | $k[j] = k[j] - t * k[j + 1]$;
| end
end
$k \leftarrow$ **RdmPmtn**(k);
return k, v, w;

Algorithm 3. Sign: coefficient reduction first, validity vector then

Verification. Algorithm 4 checks if the vector v is reduced enough i.e $\|v\|_\infty < D$ where D is the diagonal coefficient of the secret key matrix S. Then it tries to check the validity of $kP = v - w$. By using the power p_2, the authors of DRS want to ensure the computations stay within 64-bits. If multiprecision integers were used (as GMP), we note it would not take a while loop with multiple rounds to check. Whether this is more efficient or not remains to be tested.

Input: - A vector $v \in \mathbb{Z}^n$;
- P, p_2 the public key matrix and the log_2 of its maximum norm;
- w the reduced form of v;
- k the extra information vector;
Output: - w a reduced vector, with $v \equiv w \ [\mathcal{L}(P)]$;
// Test for max norm first
if $\|w\|_\infty >= D$ then return *FALSE*;
// Loop Initialization
$q \leftarrow k, \ t \leftarrow v - w$;
while $q \neq 0 \wedge t \neq 0$ do
    $\quad r \leftarrow q \mod p_2, \ t \leftarrow rP - t$;
    $\quad$ // Check correctness
    $\quad$ if $t \neq 0 \mod y$ then return *FALSE*;
    $\quad t \leftarrow t/p_2, \ q \leftarrow (q - r)/p_2$;
    $\quad$ if $(t = 0) \veebar (q = 0)$ then return *FALSE*;
end
return *TRUE*;

Algorithm 4. Verify

3.2   Li, Liu, Nitaj and Pan's Attack on a Randomized Version of the Initial PKC'08

In ACISP 2018, Li, Liu, Nitaj and Pan [11] presented an attack that makes use of short signatures to recover the secret key. Their observation is that two different signatures from the same message is also a short vector of the lattice. Then, gathering sufficient number of short vectors enable easier recovery of the secret key using lattice reduction algorithms with the vectors generated. Their suggestion to fix this issue is to either store previous signed messages to avoid having different signatures, or padding a random noise in the hash function. We should note that the initial DRS scheme is not randomized as the algorithm is deterministic and produce a unique signature per vector.

We do note that the authors of DRS suggested in their report [20] to use a random permutation to decide the order of the coefficient reduction, and thus Li, Liu, Nitaj and Pan's attack might apply to their suggestion. However, the order of the coefficient reduction could also be decided deterministically by the hashed message itself, and therefore, Li, Liu, Nitaj and Pan's attack is not fully applicable, as this method would produce an unique signature per message. They can still generate a set of relatively short vectors $(r_1, ..., r_2) \in \mathcal{L}^n$ of the lattice $\mathcal{L}$, however it is unclear whether the specialized version of their attack using vectors $s, (v_1, ..., v_n)$ where $s - v_i \in \mathcal{L}$ is still applicable. It seems to be easier to recover the key when using multiple signatures from the same message as a lattice basis when using lattice reduction algorithms rather than using random small vectors of the lattice: this could imply that diagonal dominant basis have inner weaknesses beyond the simple instantiation of DRS. From our understanding, the secret key matrices they generated for their tests used a noise matrix with coefficients within $\{-1, 0, 1\}$, which could have had an impact in their experimentations. It is still unknown if other noise types such as the ones in DRS or the type of noise we are about to propose are affected: to the best of our knowledge, DRS was not quoted in their work.

We stress that we do not claim the new setup to be perfectly secure against Li, Liu, Nitaj and Pan's attack, we merely claim more experimentations would need to be done as of now. Furthermore, the countermeasures proposed by Li, Liu, Nitaj and Pan also apply to those new keys, and should be applied if one wishes for a more concrete security. The next attack however does not have clear known countermeasures as of now and is the main focus of this paper.

3.3   Yu and Ducas's Attack on the DRS Instantiation of the Initial Scheme of PKC'08

We explained in the previous section about the security of DRS against Li, Liu, Nitaj and Pan's attack. On the other hand, it is unclear if such a modification would add an extra weakness against Yu and Ducas's heuristic attack. Their attack work in two steps. The first one is based on recovering certain coefficients of a secret key vector using machine learning and statistical analysis. The second is classical lattice-reduction attack to recover the rest of the secret key.

For the first step, Yu and Ducas noticed that the coefficients B of the secret key and the 1 could be distinguished via machine learning techniques [30], noticing for one part that the non-diagonal coefficients follow an "absolute-circulant" structure, and the fact that only two types of non-zero values exist. Based on this information, a surprisingly small amount of selected "features" to specialize a "least-square fit" method allowed them to recover both positions and signs of all if not most coefficients B of a secret vector. We note they did not conduct a exhaustive search on all possible methods according to their paper thus stressing that their method might not be the best. We did not conduct much research on the related machine learning techniques therefore we cannot comment much on this part as of now.

On the second step, the recovered coefficients and their positions and signs allowed them to apply the Kannan embedding attack on a lattice with the exact same volume as the original public key but of a much lower dimension than the original authors of DRS based their security on, by scrapping the known B noise coefficients. Strictly speaking, using the same notation as in the previous description of DRS and assuming the diagonal coefficient is equal to the dimension, the initial search of a shortest vector of length $\sqrt{B^2 N_b + N_1 + 1}$ in a lattice of dimension n of determinant n^n becomes a search of a shortest vector of length

$\sqrt{N_1 + 1}$ in a lattice of dimension $n - N_b$ of determinant n^n. The efficiency of lattice reduction techniques then affects the evaluation of the security strength of the original DRS scheme.

Yu and Ducas conducted experiments and validated their claims, reducing the security of the initial submission of DRS from 128-bits to maybe at most 80-bits, using BKZ-138. The original concept (not the instantiation) from [21], however, still seems to be safe for now: although it has no security proof, to the best of our knowledge, no severe weaknesses have been found so far. Furthermore, Yu and Ducas advised of some potential countermeasures to fix DRS, i.e breaking the structure of the particular instance that was submitted: the deterministic approach of the number of B, 1, being limited to those 2 values (5 if we consider zeroes and signs), and the "absolute-circulant" structure. They also pointed that a lack of security proof could be problematic and gave some opinions about how one can potentially find provable security for the DRS scheme.

In the following section, we provide a countermeasure which follows some of the recommendations given by Yu and Ducas as breaking the secret key noise structure and giving some statistical heuristic, while still preserving the original idea given in PKC 2008 [21].

4   New Setup

We do not change any algorithm here aside the setup of the secret key: the public key generation method is left unchanged, along with the signature and verification. Compared to the old scheme, this new version is now determined by less parameters, which leave 6 of them using the previous DRS: the dimension n, a random generator seed s, a signature bound D, a max norm for hashed messages δ, a sparsity parameter Δ that we always set to one, and R a security parameter determining the number of multiplication rounds to generate the public key.

We choose random noise among all the possible noises vectors which would still respect the diagonal dominant property of the secret key. This choice is following Yu and Ducas's suggestions on breaking the set of secret coefficients, the "absolute-circulant" structure of the secret key, and allowing us to provide statistical evidence.

Although we want to have random noise, we must ensure we can still sign every message and thus guarantee the diagonal dominant structure of our secret key. Hence, the set of noise vectors we need to keep are all the vectors $v \in \mathbb{Z}^n$ that have a taxicab norm of $\|v\|_1 \leq D - 1$. Let us call that set V_n.

This new setup will also change the bounds used for the public key, as the original DRS authors linked several parameters together to ensure computations stay within $64-$bits. However, our paper has a more theoretical approach and we do not focus on the technical implementations yet, which could be left for further work.

4.1   Picking the Random Vectors

We are aiming to build the new noise matrix M, which is a $n \times n$ matrix such that $M \in V_n^n$. In that regard, we construct a table we will call T with D entries such that

$$T[i] = \#\text{vectors } v \in V_n \text{ with } i \text{ zeroes.}$$

This table is relatively easy to build and does not take much time, one can for example use the formulas derived from [24] and [10].

From this table, we construct another table T_S such that $T_S[k] = \sum_{i=0}^{k} T[i]$.

The generation algorithm of the table T_S, which we will use as a precomputation for our new setup algorithm can be seen in Algorithm 5.

Input: - all initial parameters;
Output: - T_S the table sum;
// Initialization
$m \leftarrow \mathbf{min}(dimension, diagonal\ value\ D)$;
$T \leftarrow \{1\}^{m+1}$;
$T_S \leftarrow \{1\}^{m+1}$;
// Construct array T
// Construct array T : loop over the norm
for $j = 2$; $j \leq D$; $j = j + 1$ **do**
    // Construct array T : loop over the number of non-zeroes
        elements in each possibility
    for $i = 2$; $i \leq m + 1$; $i = i + 1$ **do**
        $x \leftarrow 2^{i-1} \binom{n}{i-1} \binom{j-1}{i-2}$;
        $T[m + 1 - i] \leftarrow T[m + 1 - i] + x$;
    end
end
// Construct array T_S from T
for $i = 1$; $i \leq m$; $i = i + 1$ **do**
    $T[i + 1] \leftarrow T[i + 1] + T[i]$;
end
$T_S \leftarrow T$;
return T_S;

Algorithm 5. Secret key table precomputation

Let us denote the function $Z(x) \rightarrow y$ such that $T_S[y - 1] < x \leq T_S[y]$.

Since T_S is trivially sorted in increasing order $Z(x)$ is nothing more than a dichotomy search inside an ordered table.

If we pick randomly x from $[0; T_S[D - 1]]$ from a generator with uniform distribution $g() \rightarrow x$ then we got $Zero() \rightarrow Z(g(x))$ a function that selects uniformly an amount of zeroes amount all vectors of the set V_n, i.e.

$$Zero() \rightarrow \#\text{zeroes in a random } v \in V_n$$

Now that we can generate uniformly the number of zeroes we have to determine the coefficients of the non-zero values randomly, while making sure the final noise vector is still part of V_n. A method to give such a vector with chosen taxicab norm is given in [27] as a correction of the Kraemer algorithm. As we do not want to choose the taxicab norm M directly but rather wants to have any random norm available, we add a slight modification: the method in [27] takes k non-zero elements $x_1, ..., x_k$ such that $x_i \leq x_{i+1}$ and forces the last coefficient to be equal to the taxicab norm chosen, i.e $x_k = M$. By removing the restriction and using $x_k \leq D$, giving the amount of non-zero values, we modify the method to be able to take over any vector values in V_n with the help of a function we will call

$$\mathbf{KraemerBis}(z) \rightarrow \text{random } v \in V_n$$

such that v has z zeroes which is described in Algorithm 6

Input: - all initial parameters;
- a number of zeroes z;
Output: - a vector v with z zeroes and a random norm inferior or equal to D;
// Algorithm start
$v \in \mathbb{N}^n$;
Pick randomly $n - z + 1$ elements such that $0 \leq x_0 < x_1 < ... < x_{n-z} \leq D$;
for $i = 1$; $i \leq n - z$; $i = i + 1$ **do**
  $\quad | \quad v[i] \leftarrow x_i - x_{i-1}$;
end
for $i = n - z + 1$; $i \leq n$; $i = i + 1$ **do**
  $\quad | \quad v[i] \leftarrow 0$;
end
return v;

Algorithm 6. KraemerBis

With both those new parts, the new setup algorithm we construct is presented in Algorithm 7 using Kraemer bis. We note that in our algorithm, the diagonal coefficient in the secret key is not guaranteed to be equal to the bound used for the maximum norm of the signatures. Nevertheless, we will show that the termination is still ensured in Sect. 4.2. This heavy setup naturally affects the speed of the DRS setup, as we noticed in our experiments as shown in Sect. 4.3.

4.2   A Slightly More General Termination Proof

The proof stated in the DRS report on the NIST website [20] was considering that the diagonal coefficient of $S = d * I_d + M$ stayed equal to the signature bound, which is not our case. We show here that the reduction is still guaranteed nevertheless. Suppose that some coefficients of the noise matrix M are non-zero on the diagonal. Re-using for the most part notations of the original report, where:

Input: - all initial parameters;
- another extra random seed x_2;
Output: - x, S the secret key;
$S \leftarrow D \times Id_n$;
$t \in \mathbb{Z}^n$;
$InitiateRdmSeed(x_2)$;
for $i = 1$; $i \leq n$; $i = i + 1$ **do**
$\quad$ $Z \leftarrow Zero()$;
$\quad$ $t \leftarrow$ **KraemerBis**(Z);
$\quad$ **for** $j = 1$; $j \leq n - Z$; $j = j + 1$ **do**
$\quad\quad$ $\mid$ $t[j] \leftarrow t[j] \times$ **RdmSgn**$()$
$\quad$ **end**
$\quad$ $t \leftarrow$ **RdmPmtn**(t);
$\quad$ $S[i] \leftarrow S[i] + t$;
end
return x, S;

Algorithm 7. New secret key generation (square matrix of dimension n)

– m is the message we want to reduce, which we update step by step.
– M is the noise matrix (so M_i is the i-th noise row vector).
– d is the signature bound for which the condition $\|m\|_\infty < d$ has to be verified.
We note d_i the i-th diagonal coefficient of the secret key S.

Obviously, the matrix will still be diagonal dominant in any case. Let us denote d_i the diagonal coefficient $S_{i,i}$ of $S = D - M$.

If $d > d_i$ we can use the previous reasoning and reduce $|m_i|$ to $|m_i| < d_i < d$, but keep in mind we stop the reduction at $|m_i| < d$ to ensure we do not leak information about the noise distribution.

Now $d_i > d$ for some i: reducing to $|m_i| < d_i$ is guaranteed but not sufficient anymore as we can reach $d < |m_i| < d_i \leq d + \Delta < 2d$. Let us remind that $\Delta = d - \sum_{j=1}^{n} |M_{i,j}|$, where Δ is strictly positive as an initial condition of the DRS signature scheme (both on the original submission and this paper), $d_i = d + c$ where $c = |M_{i,i}|$.

Without loss of generality as we can flip signs, let us set $m_i = d + k < d_i = d + c$ with $k \geq 0$ the coefficient to reduce. Substracting by S_i transforms

$$m_i \leftarrow (d + k) - d_i = (d + k) - (d + c) = k - c < 0$$

with $d > c > k \geq 0$. Therefore the reduction of $\|m\|_1$ without the noise is

$$\|m\|_1 \leftarrow \|m\|_1 - (d + k) + (c - k) = \|m\|_1 - (d - c) - 2k.$$

but the noise contribution on other coefficients is at worst $(d - \Delta) - c$ thus

$$\|m\|_1 \leftarrow \|m\|_1 - (d - c) - 2k + (d - c - \Delta).$$
$$\|m\|_1 \leftarrow \|m\|_1 - 2k - \Delta = \|m\|_1 - (2k + \Delta).$$

where $2k + \Delta > 0$. Therefore the reduction is also ensured in the case $d_i > d$.

4.3 Setup Performance

Compared to the initial NIST submission where the code was seemingly made for clarity and not so much for performance, we wrote our own version of DRS using NIST specifications and managed to have much higher performance. However, most of the performance upgrade from the initial code have nothing much to do with the algorithms of the DRS scheme: we did notice that most of the time taken by the DRS initial code was used for the conversion from the character arrays to integer matrices and vice-versa, which they had to do to respect the NIST specifications: the algebraic computations themselves were actually reasonably fast, considering the size of the objects manipulated.

This is the reason why we decided to isolate the secret matrix generation code from the rest of the initial original DRS code, in order to have a fair comparison between our own secret key generation algorithm to theirs. In that regard we choose to compare similar matrix sizes instead of similar security, as initial security estimates for the DRS submission were severely undermined by Yu and Ducas's recent discoveries and thus would lead to comparing efficiency on matrices with massively different sizes. Therefore we are making tests on the initial parameters of the DRS scheme. Looking purely at the secret key generation, we are indeed much slower, as shown in Table 1.

Table 1. Secret key generation time in seconds for 10^4 keys

Dimension	912	1160	1518
OldDRS	28.71	44.15	79.57
NewDRS	317.45	631.89	993.92

Note that we use the options $-march = native$ and $-Ofast$ which led us to use $AVX512$ instructions and other gcc optimization tweaks. The new setup is barely parallelizable as there is almost no code that can be vectorized which also explains the huge difference.

5   Security Estimates

5.1   BDD-based attack

The security is based on what is known as the currently most efficient way to attack the scheme, a **BDD**-based attack as described in Algorithm 8.

Input: public key Pk of full rank n, diagonal coefficient d, $\mathbf{BDD}_\gamma$ solver ϕ
Output: secret key $Sk = (D - M)$
$Sk \leftarrow d * Id_n$;
foreach $\{i \in [1..n]\}$ **do**
$\quad \mid \quad r \leftarrow \phi(\mathcal{L}(Pk), Sk[i]),\ Sk[i] \leftarrow Sk[i] + r;;$
end
return Sk;

Algorithm 8. Diagonal Dominant Key recovery attack

Currently, the most efficient way to perform this attack will be, first, to transform a **BDD** problem into a Unique Shortest Vector Problem (**uSVP**) (Kannan's Embedding Technique [9]), assuming $v = (0, ...0, d, 0, ..., 0)$, and use lattice reduction techniques on the lattice spanned by $[v|1]$ and the rows of $[B|0]$. By using this method, we obtain a **uSVP** with a gap

$$\gamma \approx \frac{\Gamma\left(\frac{n+3}{2}\right)^{\frac{1}{n+1}} Det(\mathcal{L})^{\frac{1}{n+1}}}{\sqrt{\pi}\|M_1\|_2} \approx \frac{\Gamma\left(\frac{n+3}{2}\right)^{\frac{1}{n+1}} d^{n\frac{1}{n+1}}}{\sqrt{\pi}\|M_1\|_2}. \tag{1}$$

Lattice reduction methods are well studied and their strength are evaluated using the Hermite factor. Let $\mathcal{L}$ a d–dimensional lattice, the Hermite factor of a basis B of $\mathcal{L}$ is given by $\|B[1]\|_2/det(\mathcal{L})^{\frac{1}{n}}$. Consequently, lattice reduction algorithms strengths are given by the Hermite factor of their expected output basis. In [6], it was estimated that lattice reduction methods solve uSVP$_\gamma$ with γ a fraction of the Hermite factor. We will use a conservative bound of $\frac{1}{4}$ for the ratio of the uSVP gap to the Hermite factor. As we do not have a fixed euclidean norm for our secret vectors we have to rely on the approximates given to us by our new random method in sampling noise vectors M_i. In our case, we know that for any vector $v \in \mathbb{Z}^n$ we have $\|v\|_2 \geq \frac{\|v\|_1}{\sqrt{n}}$, and our experiments (as seen below) allow us to use a higher bound $\|v\|_2 \gtrsim \sqrt{2}\frac{\|v\|_1}{\sqrt{n}}$.

5.2 Expected Security Strength

Different papers are giving some relations between the Hermite factor and the security parameter λ [8,22] often using BKZ simulation [4]. Aiming to be conservative, we are to assume a security of $2^{128}, 2^{192}, 2^{256}$ for a Hermite factor of $1.006^d, 1.005^d, 1.004^d$, respectively. We set $D = n$, pick hashed messages $h(m)$ such that $\log_2(\|h(m)\|_\infty) = 28$, $R = 24$ and $\Delta = 1$.

Table 2 parameters have been choosen to obtain a uSVP gap (Eq. 1) with $\gamma < \frac{\delta^{d+1}}{4}$ for $\delta = 1.006, 1.005, 1.004$. Our experiments show us that the distribution of zeroes among sampled noise vectors form a Gaussian and so does the euclidean norm of noise vectors when picking our random elements x, x_i uniformly. Here we include below the distribution of 10^6 randomly generated noise vectors v with the x-axis representing $f(v) = \lfloor 100\sqrt{\frac{\|v\|_2^2}{D}} \rfloor$ where D is the signature bound (see Fig. 1).

Table 2. Parameter sets.

Dimension	Δ	R	δ	γ	2^λ
1108	1	24	28	$< \frac{1}{4}(1.006)^{d+1}$	2^{128}
1372	1	24	28	$< \frac{1}{4}(1.005)^{d+1}$	2^{192}
1779	1	24	28	$< \frac{1}{4}(1.004)^{d+1}$	2^{256}

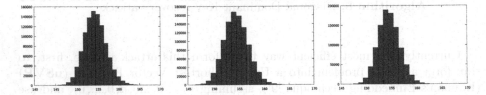

Fig. 1. $f(v)$ distribution for $n = 1108, 1372, 1779$ and $D = n - 1$ over 10^6 samples

We can see that the generated noise vectors follow a Gaussian distribution as far as their norms are concerned, and we believe it makes guessing values much harder for an attacker should they choose to focus on finding specific values or vectors (as it was the case in the original attack from Yu and Ducas [30]). We also conducted experiments, using BKZ20 from the fplll library [28] (see Fig. 2). Without any surprise we notice our new setup is seemingly resistant around dimension 400, where conservative bounds led us to believe the break happen until approximately dimension 445. However the sample size is relatively small

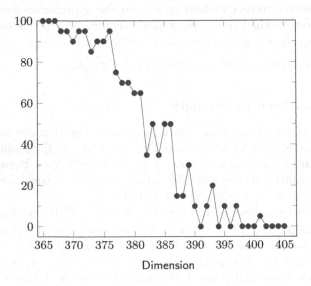

Fig. 2. Percentage of key recoveries of BKZ20 (20 sample keys/dim)

(yet computationally expensive to obtain) and thus should not be taken as a proof value, but rather as a heuristic support against heuristic attacks.

6 Conclusion and Open Questions

We presented in this paper a new method to generate secret keys for the DRS scheme, providing experimental results on the statistical distribution of the keys generated. We demonstrate that our new approach is sufficient to improve DRS to be secure against machine learning attacks as reported earlier in the literature. However, the secret matrix is still diagonal dominant and it remains an open question whether there exists a tight security proof to a well-known problem or if there is any unforeseen weaknesses to diagonal dominant lattices as both Li, Liu, Nitaj and Pan's [11] and Yu and Ducas's attacks [30] could lead to. The open questions for improvement stated in the original DRS report are also still applicable to our proposed iteration.

On the technical side, our method to generate random samples is also slow and might need improvement. It also impacts the setup as mentioned earlier, as keeping the current DRS parameters one can see the possibility to overflow and go over $64-$bits, even though the probability is extremely low, thus changing the public key generation is also left as an open question. The initial DRS scheme was very conservative not only on their security but also the manipulated integer size bounds: one might use heuristics to drastically increase the memory efficiency of the scheme.

Acknowledgements. We would like to thank Yang Yu, Léo Ducas and the anonymous reviewers for useful comments and suggestions.

References

1. Ajtai, M.: Generating hard instances of lattice problems. In: STOC 1996, pp. 99–108. ACM (1996)
2. Ajtai, M., Dwork, C.: A public-key cryptosystem with worst-case/average-case equivalence. In: STOC 1997, pp. 284–293. ACM (1997)
3. Brualdi, R.A., Ryser, H.J.: Combinatorial Matrix Theory, vol. 39. Cambridge University Press, Cambridge (1991)
4. Chen, Y., Nguyen, P.Q.: BKZ 2.0: better lattice security estimates. In: Lee, D.H., Wang, X. (eds.) ASIACRYPT 2011. LNCS, vol. 7073, pp. 1–20. Springer, Heidelberg (2011). https://doi.org/10.1007/978-3-642-25385-0_1
5. Fischlin, R., Seifert, J.-P.: Tensor-based trapdoors for CVP and their application to public key cryptography (extended abstract). In: Walker, M. (ed.) Cryptography and Coding 1999. LNCS, vol. 1746, pp. 244–257. Springer, Heidelberg (1999). https://doi.org/10.1007/3-540-46665-7_29
6. Gama, N., Nguyen, P.Q.: Predicting lattice reduction. In: Smart, N. (ed.) EURO-CRYPT 2008. LNCS, vol. 4965, pp. 31–51. Springer, Heidelberg (2008). https://doi.org/10.1007/978-3-540-78967-3_3

7. Goldreich, O., Goldwasser, S., Halevi, S.: Public-key cryptosystems from lattice reduction problems. In: Kaliski, B.S. (ed.) CRYPTO 1997. LNCS, vol. 1294, pp. 112–131. Springer, Heidelberg (1997). https://doi.org/10.1007/BFb0052231

8. Hoffstein, J., Pipher, J., Schanck, J.M., Silverman, J.H., Whyte, W., Zhang, Z.: Choosing parameters for NTRUEncrypt. In: Handschuh, H. (ed.) CT-RSA 2017. LNCS, vol. 10159, pp. 3–18. Springer, Cham (2017). https://doi.org/10.1007/978-3-319-52153-4_1

9. Kannan, R.: Minkowski's convex body theorem and integer programming. Math. Oper. Res. 12(3), 415–440 (1987)

10. Knuth, D.E., Graham, R.L., Patashnik, O., et al.: Concrete Mathematics. Addison Wesley, Boston (1989)

11. Li, H., Liu, R., Nitaj, A., Pan, Y.: Cryptanalysis of the randomized version of a lattice-based signature scheme from PKC '08. In: Susilo, W., Yang, G. (eds.) ACISP 2018. LNCS, vol. 10946, pp. 455–466. Springer, Cham (2018). https://doi.org/10.1007/978-3-319-93638-3_26

12. Liu, M., Wang, X., Xu, G., Zheng, X.: Shortest lattice vectors in the presence of gaps. IACR Cryptology ePrint Archive 2011/139 (2011)

13. Lyubashevsky, V., Micciancio, D.: On bounded distance decoding, unique shortest vectors, and the minimum distance problem. In: Halevi, S. (ed.) CRYPTO 2009. LNCS, vol. 5677, pp. 577–594. Springer, Heidelberg (2009). https://doi.org/10.1007/978-3-642-03356-8_34

14. Micciancio, D.: Improving lattice based cryptosystems using the hermite normal form. In: Silverman, J.H. (ed.) CaLC 2001. LNCS, vol. 2146, pp. 126–145. Springer, Heidelberg (2001). https://doi.org/10.1007/3-540-44670-2_11

15. Minkowski, H.: Geometrie der Zahlen. B.G. Teubner, Leipzig (1896)

16. Nguyen, P.: Cryptanalysis of the Goldreich-Goldwasser-Halevi cryptosystem from crypto '97. In: Wiener, M. (ed.) CRYPTO 1999. LNCS, vol. 1666, pp. 288–304. Springer, Heidelberg (1999). https://doi.org/10.1007/3-540-48405-1_18

17. NIST: Post-quantum cryptography standardization (2018). https://csrc.nist.gov/Projects/Post-Quantum-Cryptography

18. NIST: Nist kicks off effort to defend encrypted data from quantum computer threat, 28 April 2016. www.nist.gov/news-events/news-updates/

19. Paeng, S.-H., Jung, B.E., Ha, K.-C.: A lattice based public key cryptosystem using polynomial representations. In: Desmedt, Y.G. (ed.) PKC 2003. LNCS, vol. 2567, pp. 292–308. Springer, Heidelberg (2003). https://doi.org/10.1007/3-540-36288-6_22

20. Plantard, T., Sipasseuth, A., Dumondelle, C., Susilo, W.: DRS: diagonal dominant reduction for lattice-based signature. In: PQC Standardization Conference, Round 1 submissions (2018). https://csrc.nist.gov/CSRC/media/Projects/Post-Quantum-Cryptography/documents/round-1/submissions/DRS.zip

21. Plantard, T., Susilo, W., Win, K.T.: A digital signature scheme based on CVP_∞. In: Cramer, R. (ed.) PKC 2008. LNCS, vol. 4939, pp. 288–307. Springer, Heidelberg (2008). https://doi.org/10.1007/978-3-540-78440-1_17

22. van de Pol, J., Smart, N.P.: Estimating key sizes for high dimensional lattice-based systems. In: Stam, M. (ed.) IMACC 2013. LNCS, vol. 8308, pp. 290–303. Springer, Heidelberg (2013). https://doi.org/10.1007/978-3-642-45239-0_17

23. Regev, O.: New lattice-based cryptographic constructions. J. ACM (JACM) 51(6), 899–942 (2004)

24. Serra-Sagristà, J.: Enumeration of lattice points in l1 norm. Inf. Process. Lett. 76(1–2), 39–44 (2000)

25. Shor, P.W.: Polynomial-time algorithms for prime factorization and discrete logarithms on a quantum computer. SIAM J. Comput. **26**(5), 1484–1509 (1997)
26. Sloane, N.J.A.: Encrypting by random rotations. In: Beth, T. (ed.) EUROCRYPT 1982. LNCS, vol. 149, pp. 71–128. Springer, Heidelberg (1983). https://doi.org/10.1007/3-540-39466-4_6
27. Smith, N.A., Tromble, R.W.: Sampling uniformly from the unit simplex (2004)
28. The FPLLL team: FPLLL, a lattice reduction library. https://github.com/fplll
29. Wei, W., Liu, M., Wang, X.: Finding shortest lattice vectors in the presence of gaps. In: Nyberg, K. (ed.) CT-RSA 2015. LNCS, vol. 9048, pp. 239–257. Springer, Cham (2015). https://doi.org/10.1007/978-3-319-16715-2_13
30. Yu, Y., Ducas, L.: Learning strikes again: the case of the DRS signature scheme. In: Peyrin, T., Galbraith, S. (eds.) ASIACRYPT 2018. LNCS, vol. 11273, pp. 525–543. Springer, Cham (2018). https://doi.org/10.1007/978-3-030-03329-3_18

A Lattice-Based Public Key Encryption with Equality Test in Standard Model

Dung Hoang Duong[1(✉)], Kazuhide Fukushima[2], Shinsaku Kiyomoto[2], Partha Sarathi Roy[2(✉)], and Willy Susilo[1]

[1] Institute of Cybersecurity and Cryptology,
School of Computing and Information Technology, University of Wollongong,
Northfields Avenue, Wollongong, NSW 2522, Australia
{hduong,wsusilo}@uow.edu.au
[2] Information Security Laboratory, KDDI Research, Inc.,
2-1-15 Ohara, Fujimino-shi, Saitama 356-8502, Japan
{ka-fukushima,kiyomoto,pa-roy}@kddi-research.jp

Abstract. Public key encryption with equality test (PKEET) allows testing whether two ciphertexts are generated by the same message or not. PKEET is a potential candidate for many practical applications like efficient data management on encrypted databases. Potential applicability of PKEET leads to intensive research from its first instantiation by Yang et al. (CT-RSA 2010). Most of the followup constructions are secure in the random oracle model. Moreover, the security of all the concrete constructions is based on number-theoretic hardness assumptions which are vulnerable in the post-quantum era. Recently, Lee et al. (ePrint 2016) proposed a generic construction of PKEET schemes in the standard model and hence it is possible to yield the first instantiation of PKEET schemes based on lattices. Their method is to use a 2-level hierarchical identity-based encryption (HIBE) scheme together with a one-time signature scheme. In this paper, we propose, for the first time, a direct construction of a PKEET scheme based on the hardness assumption of lattices in the standard model. More specifically, the security of the proposed scheme is reduces to the hardness of the *Learning With Errors* problem. We have used the idea of the full identity-based encryption scheme by Agrawal et al. (EUROCRYPT 2010) to construct the proposed PKEET.

1 Introduction

Public key encryption with equality test (PKEET), which was first introduced by Yang et al. [21], is a special kind of public key encryption that allows anyone with a given trapdoor to test whether two ciphertexts are generated by the same message. This property is of use in various practical applications, such as keyword search on encrypted data, encrypted data partitioning for efficient encrypted data management, personal health record systems, spam filtering in encrypted email systems and so on. Due to its numerous practical applications,

© Springer Nature Switzerland AG 2019
J. Jang-Jaccard and F. Guo (Eds.): ACISP 2019, LNCS 11547, pp. 138–155, 2019.
https://doi.org/10.1007/978-3-030-21548-4_8

there have been intensive researches in this direction with the appearance of improved schemes or ones with additional functionalities [9,12,16–18]. However, they are all proven to be secure in the random oracle model which does not exist in reality. Therefore it is necessary to construct such a scheme in the standard model.

Up to the present, there are only a few PKEET schemes in the standard model. Lee et al. [8] first proposed a generic construction of a PKEET scheme. Their method is to use a 2-level hierarchical identity-based encryption (HIBE) scheme together with a one-time signature scheme. The HIBE scheme is used for generating an encryption scheme and for equality test, and the signature scheme is used for making the scheme CCA2-secure, based on the method of transforming an identity-based encryption (IBE) scheme to a CCA2-secure encryption scheme of Canetti et al. [4]. As a result, they obtain a CCA2-secure PKEET scheme given that the underlying HIBE scheme is IND-sID-CPA secure and the one-time signature scheme is strongly unforgeable. From their generic construction, it is possible to obtain a PKEET in standard model under many hard assumptions via instantiations. In a very recent paper, Zhang et al. [22] proposed a direct construction of a CCA2-secure PKEET scheme based on pairings without employing strong cryptographic primitives such as HIBE schemes and strongly secure signatures as the generic construction of Lee et al. [8]. Their technique comes from a CCA2-secure public key encryption scheme by [7] which was directly constructed by an idea from IBE. A comparison with an instantiation from Lee et al. [8] on pairings shows that their direct construction is much more efficient than the instantiated one.

All aforementioned existing schemes base their security on the hardness of some number-theoretic assumptions which will be efficiently solved in the quantum era [14]. The generic construction by Lee et al. [8] is the first one with the possibility of yielding a post-quantum instantiation based on lattices, since lattice cryptography is the only one among other post-quantum areas up to present offers HIBE primitives, e.g., [1]. It is then still a question of either yielding an efficient instantiation or directly constructing a PKEET based on lattices.

Our Contribution: In this paper, we give a direct construction of a PKEET scheme based on lattices from IBE. According to the best of our knowledge, this is the first construction of a PKEET scheme based on lattices. We first employ the multi-bit full IBE by Agrawal et al. [1] and then directly transform it into a PKEET scheme. In our scheme, a ciphertext is of the form $\mathsf{CT} = (\mathsf{CT}_1, \mathsf{CT}_2, \mathsf{CT}_3, \mathsf{CT}_4)$ where $(\mathsf{CT}_1, \mathsf{CT}_3)$ is the encryption of the message $\mathbf{m}$, as in the original IBE scheme, and $(\mathsf{CT}_2, \mathsf{CT}_4)$ is the encryption of $H(\mathbf{m})$ in which H is a hash function. In order to utilize the IBE scheme, we employ a second hash function H' and create the *identity* $H'(\mathsf{CT}_1, \mathsf{CT}_2)$ before computing CT_3 and CT_4; see Sect. 3 for more details. Finally, we have proved that the proposed PKEET scheme is CCA2-secure. As compared to the previous constructions, the proposed one is computationally efficient due to the absence of exponentiation. But, the size of the public parameters is more.

2   Preliminaries

2.1   Public Key Encryption with Equality Test (PKEET)

In this section, we will recall the model of PKEET and its security model.

We remark that a PKEET system is a multi-user setting. Hence we assume that in our system throughout the paper, each user is assigned with an index i with $1 \leq i \leq N$ where N is the number of users in the system.

Definition 1 (PKEET). *Public key encryption with equality test (PKEET) consists of the following polynomial-time algorithms:*

- Setup(λ): *On input a security parameter λ and set of parameters, it outputs the a pair of a user's public key* PK *and secret key* SK.
- Enc(PK, **m**): *On input the public key* PK *and a message* **m**, *it outputs a ciphertext* CT.
- Dec(SK, CT): *On input the secret key* SK *and a ciphertext* CT, *it outputs a message* **m'** *or* $\perp$.
- Td(SK_i): *On input the secret key* SK_i *for the user* U_i, *it outputs a trapdoor* td_i.
- Test(td_i, td_j, CT_i, CT_j): *On input two trapdoors* td_i, td_j *and two ciphertexts* CT_i, CT_j *for users* U_i *and* U_j *respectively, it outputs* 1 *or* 0.

Correctness. We say that a PKEET scheme is *correct* if the following three condition hold:

(1) For any security parameter λ, any user U_i and any message **m**, it holds that

$$\Pr\left[\text{Dec}(SK_i, CT_i) = \mathbf{m} \,\middle|\, \begin{array}{l} (PK_i, SK_i) \leftarrow \text{Setup}(\lambda) \\ CT_i \leftarrow \text{Enc}(PK_i, \mathbf{m}) \end{array} \right] = 1.$$

(2) For any security parameter λ, any users U_i, U_j and any messages $\mathbf{m}_i, \mathbf{m}_j$, it holds that:

$$\Pr\left[\text{Test}\begin{pmatrix} td_i \\ td_j \\ CT_i \\ CT_j \end{pmatrix} = 1 \,\middle|\, \begin{array}{l} (PK_i, SK_i) \leftarrow \text{Setup}(\lambda) \\ CT_i \leftarrow \text{Enc}(PK_i, \mathbf{m}_i) \\ td_i \leftarrow \text{Td}(SK_i) \\ (PK_j, SK_j) \leftarrow \text{Setup}(\lambda) \\ CT_j \leftarrow \text{Enc}(PK_j, \mathbf{m}_j) \\ td_j \leftarrow \text{Td}(SK_j) \end{array} \right] = 1$$

if $\mathbf{m}_i = \mathbf{m}_j$ regardless of whether $i = j$.

(3) For any security parameter λ, any users U_i, U_j and any messages $\mathbf{m}_i, \mathbf{m}_j$, it holds that

$$\Pr\left[\text{Test}\begin{pmatrix} td_i \\ td_j \\ CT_i \\ CT_j \end{pmatrix} = 1 \,\middle|\, \begin{array}{l} (PK_i, SK_i) \leftarrow \text{Setup}(\lambda) \\ CT_i \leftarrow \text{Enc}(PK_i, \mathbf{m}_i) \\ td_i \leftarrow \text{Td}(SK_i) \\ (PK_j, SK_j) \leftarrow \text{Setup}(\lambda) \\ CT_j \leftarrow \text{Enc}(PK_j, \mathbf{m}_j) \\ td_j \leftarrow \text{Td}(SK_j) \end{array} \right]$$

is negligible in λ for any ciphertexts CT_i, CT_j such that $Dec(SK_i, CT_i) \neq Dec(SK_j, CT_j)$ regardless of whether $i = j$.

Security Model of PKEET. For the security model of PKEET, we consider two types of adversaries:

- Type-I adversary: for this type, the adversary can request to issue a trapdoor for the target user and thus can perform equality tests on the challenge ciphertext. The aim of this type of adversaries is to reveal the message in the challenge ciphertext.
- Type-II adversary: for this type, the adversary cannot request to issue a trapdoor for the target user and thus cannot perform equality tests on the challenge ciphertext. The aim of this type of adversaries is to distinguish which message is in the challenge ciphertext between two candidates.

The security model of a PKEET scheme against two types of adversaries above is described in the following.

OW-CCA2 Security Against Type-I Adversaries. We illustrate the game between a challenger $\mathcal{C}$ and a Type-I adversary $\mathcal{A}$ who can have a trapdoor for all ciphertexts of the target user, say U_θ, that he wants to attack, as follows:

1. **Setup:** The challenger $\mathcal{C}$ runs $Setup(\lambda)$ to generate the key pairs (PK_i, SK_i) for all users with $i = 1, \cdots, N$, and gives $\{PK_i\}_{i=1}^N$ to $\mathcal{A}$.
2. **Phase 1:** The adversary $\mathcal{A}$ may make queries polynomially many times adaptively and in any order to the following oracles:
   - $\mathcal{O}^{SK}$: an oracle that on input an index i (different from θ), returns the U_i's secret key SK_i.
   - $\mathcal{O}^{Dec}$: an oracle that on input a pair of an index i and a ciphertext CT_i, returns the output of $Dec(SK_i, CT_i)$ using the secret key of the user U_i.
   - $\mathcal{O}^{Td}$: an oracle that on input an index i, return td_i by running $td_i \leftarrow Td(SK_i)$ using the secret key SK_i of the user U_i.
3. **Challenge:** $\mathcal{C}$ chooses a random message $\mathbf{m}$ in the message space and run $CT_\theta^* \leftarrow Enc(PK_\theta, \mathbf{m})$, and sends CT_θ^* to $\mathcal{A}$.
4. **Phase 2:** $\mathcal{A}$ can query as in Phase 1 with the following constraints:
   - The index θ cannot be queried to the key generation oracle $\mathcal{O}^{SK}$;
   - The pair of the index θ and the ciphertext CT_θ^* cannot be queried to the decryption oracle $\mathcal{O}^{Dec}$.
5. **Guess:** $\mathcal{A}$ output $\mathbf{m}'$.

The adversary $\mathcal{A}$ wins the above game if $\mathbf{m} = \mathbf{m}'$ and the success probability of $\mathcal{A}$ is defined as

$$\mathsf{Adv}_{\mathcal{A}, \mathrm{PKEET}}^{\mathrm{OW\text{-}CCA2}}(\lambda) := \Pr[\mathbf{m} = \mathbf{m}'].$$

Remark 2. *If the message space is polynomial in the security parameter or the min-entropy of the message distribution is much lower than the security parameter then a Type-I adversary $\mathcal{A}$ with a trapdoor for the challenge ciphertext can reveal the message in polynomial-time or small exponential time in the security parameter, by performing the equality tests with the challenge ciphertext and all other ciphertexts of all messages generated by himself. Hence to prevent this attack, we assume that the size of the message space $\mathcal{M}$ is exponential in the security parameter and the min-entropy of the message distribution is sufficiently higher than the security parameter.*

IND-CCA2 Security Against Type-II Adversaries. We present the game between a challenger $\mathcal{C}$ and a Type-II adversary $\mathcal{A}$ who cannot have a trapdoor for all ciphertexts of the target user U_θ as follows:

1. **Setup:** The challenger $\mathcal{C}$ runs $\mathsf{Setup}(\lambda)$ to generate the key pairs $(\mathsf{PK}_i, \mathsf{SK}_i)$ for all users with $i = 1, \cdots, N$, and gives $\{\mathsf{PK}_i\}_{i=1}^N$ to $\mathcal{A}$.
2. **Phase 1:** The adversary $\mathcal{A}$ may make queries polynomially many times adaptively and in any order to the following oracles:
   - $\mathcal{O}^{\mathsf{SK}}$: an oracle that on input an index i (different from t), returns the U_i's secret key SK_i.
   - $\mathcal{O}^{\mathsf{Dec}}$: an oracle that on input a pair of an index i and a ciphertext CT_i, returns the output of $\mathsf{Dec}(\mathsf{SK}_i, \mathsf{CT}_i)$ using the secret key of the user U_i.
   - $\mathcal{O}^{\mathsf{Td}}$: an oracle that on input an index i (different from t), return td_i by running $\mathsf{td}_i \leftarrow \mathsf{Td}(\mathsf{SK}_i)$ using the secret key SK_i of the user U_i.
3. **Challenge:** $\mathcal{A}$ chooses two messages $\mathbf{m}_0$ $\mathbf{m}_1$ of same length and pass to $\mathcal{C}$, who then selects a random bit $b \in \{0, 1\}$, runs $\mathsf{CT}^*_{\theta,b} \leftarrow \mathsf{Enc}(\mathsf{PK}_\theta, \mathbf{m}_b)$ and sends $\mathsf{CT}^*_{\theta,b}$ to $\mathcal{A}$.
4. **Phase 2:** $\mathcal{A}$ can query as in Phase 1 with the following constraints:
   - The index t cannot be queried to the key generation oracle $\mathcal{O}^{\mathsf{SK}}$ and the trapdoor generation oracle $\mathcal{O}^{\mathsf{Td}}$;
   - The pair of the index θ and the ciphertext $\mathsf{CT}^*_{\theta,b}$ cannot be queried to the decryption oracle $\mathcal{O}^{\mathsf{Dec}}$.
5. **Guess:** $\mathcal{A}$ output b'.

The adversary $\mathcal{A}$ wins the above game if $b = b'$ and the advantage of $\mathcal{A}$ is defined as

$$\mathsf{Adv}^{\mathsf{IND\text{-}CCA2}}_{\mathcal{A},\mathsf{PKEET}} := \left| \Pr[b = b'] - \frac{1}{2} \right|.$$

2.2 Lattices

Throughout the paper, we will mainly focus on integer lattices, which are discrete subgroups of $\mathbb{Z}^m$. Specially, a lattice Λ in $\mathbb{Z}^m$ with basis $B = [\mathbf{b}_1, \cdots, \mathbf{b}_n] \in \mathbb{Z}^{m \times n}$, where each $\mathbf{b}_i$ is written in column form, is defined as

$$\Lambda := \left\{ \sum_{i=1}^n \mathbf{b}_i x_i \,\middle|\, x_i \in \mathbb{Z} \ \forall i = 1, \cdots, n \right\} \subseteq \mathbb{Z}^m.$$

We call n the rank of Λ and if $n = m$ we say that Λ is a full rank lattice. In this paper, we mainly consider full rank lattices containing $q\mathbb{Z}^m$, called q-ary lattices, defined as the following, for a given matrix $A \in \mathbb{Z}^{n \times m}$ and $\mathbf{u} \in \mathbb{Z}_q^n$

$$\Lambda_q(A) := \{\mathbf{e} \in \mathbb{Z}^m \text{ s.t. } \exists \mathbf{s} \in \mathbb{Z}_q^n \text{ where } A^\mathsf{T}\mathbf{s} = \mathbf{e} \mod q\}$$
$$\Lambda_q^\perp(A) := \{\mathbf{e} \in \mathbb{Z}^m \text{ s.t. } A\mathbf{e} = 0 \mod q\}$$
$$\Lambda_q^\mathbf{u}(A) := \{\mathbf{e} \in \mathbb{Z}^m \text{ s.t. } A\mathbf{e} = \mathbf{u} \mod q\}$$

Note that if $\mathbf{t} \in \Lambda_q^\mathbf{u}(A)$ then $\Lambda_q^\mathbf{u}(A) = \Lambda_q^\perp(A) + \mathbf{t}$.

Let $S = \{\mathbf{s}_1, \cdots, \mathbf{s}_k\}$ be a set of vectors in $\mathbb{R}^m$. We denote by $\|S\| := \max_i \|\mathbf{s}_i\|$ for $i = 1, \cdots, k$, the maximum l_2 length of the vectors in S. We also denote $\tilde{S} := \{\tilde{\mathbf{s}}_1, \cdots, \tilde{\mathbf{s}}_k\}$ the Gram-Schmidt orthogonalization of the vectors $\mathbf{s}_1, \cdots, \mathbf{s}_k$ in that order. We refer to $\|\tilde{S}\|$ the Gram-Schmidt norm of S.

Ajtai [2] first proposed how to sample a uniform matrix $A \in \mathbb{Z}_q^{n \times m}$ with an associated basis S_A of $\Lambda_q^\perp(A)$ with low Gram-Schmidt norm. It is improved later by Alwen and Peikert [3] in the following Theorem.

Theorem 1. Let $q \geq 3$ be odd and $m := \lceil 6n \log q \rceil$. There is a probabilistic polynomial-time algorithm $\mathsf{TrapGen}(q, n)$ that outputs a pair $(A \in \mathbb{Z}_q^{n \times m}, S \in \mathbb{Z}^{m \times m})$ such that A is statistically close to a uniform matrix in $\mathbb{Z}_q^{n \times m}$ and S is a basis for $\Lambda_q^\perp(A)$ satisfying

$$\|\tilde{S}\| \leq O(\sqrt{n \log q}) \quad and \quad \|S\| \leq O(n \log q)$$

with all but negligible probability in n.

Definition 1 (Gaussian distribution). Let $\Lambda \subseteq \mathbb{Z}^m$ be a lattice. For a vector $\mathbf{c} \in \mathbb{R}^m$ and a positive parameter $\sigma \in \mathbb{R}$, define:

$$\rho_{\sigma,\mathbf{c}}(\mathbf{x}) = \exp\left(\pi \frac{\|\mathbf{x} - \mathbf{c}\|^2}{\sigma^2}\right) \quad and \quad \rho_{\sigma,\mathbf{c}}(\Lambda) = \sum_{\mathbf{x} \in \Lambda} \rho_{\sigma,\mathbf{c}}(\mathbf{x}).$$

The discrete Gaussian distribution over Λ with center $\mathbf{c}$ and parameter σ is

$$\forall \boldsymbol{y} \in \Lambda, \quad \mathcal{D}_{\Lambda,\sigma,\mathbf{c}}(\boldsymbol{y}) = \frac{\rho_{\sigma,\mathbf{c}}(\boldsymbol{y})}{\rho_{\sigma,\mathbf{c}}(\Lambda)}.$$

For convenience, we will denote by ρ_σ and $\mathcal{D}_{\Lambda,\sigma}$ for $\rho_{0,\sigma}$ and $\mathcal{D}_{\Lambda,\sigma,0}$ respectively. When $\sigma = 1$ we will write ρ instead of ρ_1. We recall below in Theorem 2 some useful results. The first one comes from [11, Lemma 4.4]. The second one is from [5] and formulated in [1, Theorem 17] and the last one is from [1, Theorem 19].

Theorem 2. Let $q > 2$ and let A, B be a matrix in $\mathbb{Z}_q^{n \times m}$ with $m > n$ and B is rank n. Let T_A, T_B be a basis for $\Lambda_q^\perp(A)$ and $\Lambda_q^\perp(B)$ respectively. Then for $c \in \mathbb{R}^m$ and $U \in \mathbb{Z}_q^{n \times t}$:

1. Let M be a matrix in $\mathbb{Z}_q^{n \times m_1}$ and $\sigma \geq \|\widetilde{T_A}\|\omega(\sqrt{\log(m + m_1)})$. Then there exists a PPT algorithm SampleLeft(A, M, T_A, U, σ) that outputs a matrix $\mathbf{e} \in \mathbb{Z}^{(m+m_1) \times t}$ distributed statistically close to $\mathcal{D}_{\Lambda_q^U(F_1), \sigma}$ where $F_1 := (A \mid M)$. In particular $\mathbf{e} \in \Lambda_q^U(F_1)$, i.e., $F_1 \cdot \mathbf{e} = U \mod q$.

2. Let R be a matrix in $\mathbb{Z}^{k \times m}$ and let $s_R := \sup_{\|\mathbf{x}\|=1} \|R\mathbf{x}\|$. Let $F_2 := (A \mid AR + B)$. Then for $\sigma \geq \|\widetilde{T_B}\| s_R \omega(\sqrt{\log m})$, there exists a PPT algorithm SampleRight$(A, B, R, T_B, U, \sigma)$ that outputs a matrix $\mathbf{e} \in \mathbb{Z}^{(m+k) \times t}$ distributed statistically close to $\mathcal{D}_{\Lambda_q^U(F_2), \sigma}$. In particular $\mathbf{e} \in \Lambda_q^\mathbf{u}(F_2)$, i.e., $F_2 \cdot \mathbf{e} = U \mod q$.

Note that when R is a random matrix in $\{-1, 1\}^{m \times m}$ then $s_R < O(\sqrt{m})$ with overwhelming probability (cf. [1, Lemma 15]).

The security of our construction reduces to the LWE (Learning With Errors) problem introduced by Regev [13].

Definition 2 (LWE problem). *Consider publicly a prime q, a positive integer n, and a distribution χ over $\mathbb{Z}_q$. An $(\mathbb{Z}_q, n, \chi)$-LWE problem instance consists of access to an unspecified challenge oracle $\mathcal{O}$, being either a noisy pseudorandom sampler $\mathcal{O}_\mathbf{s}$ associated with a secret $\mathbf{s} \in \mathbb{Z}_q^n$, or a truly random sampler $\mathcal{O}_\$$ who behaviors are as follows:*

$\mathcal{O}_\mathbf{s}$: *samples of the form $(\mathbf{u}_i, v_i) = (\mathbf{u}_i, \mathbf{u}_i^T \mathbf{s} + x_i) \in \mathbb{Z}_q^n \times \mathbb{Z}_q$ where $\mathbf{s} \in \mathbb{Z}_q^n$ is a uniform secret key, $\mathbf{u}_i \in \mathbb{Z}_q^n$ is uniform and $x_i \in \mathbb{Z}_q$ is a noise withdrawn from χ.*

$\mathcal{O}_\$$: *samples are uniform pairs in $\mathbb{Z}_q^n \times \mathbb{Z}_q$.*

The $(\mathbb{Z}_q, n, \chi)$-LWE problem allows responds queries to the challenge oracle $\mathcal{O}$. We say that an algorithm $\mathcal{A}$ decides the $(\mathbb{Z}_q, n, \chi)$-LWE problem if

$$\mathsf{Adv}_\mathcal{A}^{\mathsf{LWE}} := \left| \Pr[\mathcal{A}^{\mathcal{O}_\mathbf{s}} = 1] - \Pr[\mathcal{A}^{\mathcal{O}_\$} = 1] \right|$$

is non-negligible for a random $\mathbf{s} \in \mathbb{Z}_q^n$.

Regev [13] showed that (see Theorem 3 below) when χ is the distribution $\overline{\Psi}_\alpha$ of the random variable $\lfloor qX \rceil \mod q$ where $\alpha \in (0, 1)$ and X is a normal random variable with mean 0 and standard deviation $\alpha/\sqrt{2\pi}$ then the LWE problem is hard.

Theorem 3. *If there exists an efficient, possibly quantum, algorithm for deciding the $(\mathbb{Z}_q, n, \overline{\Psi}_\alpha)$-LWE problem for $q > 2\sqrt{n}/\alpha$ then there is an efficient quantum algorithm for approximating the SIVP and GapSVP problems, to within $\tilde{O}(n/\alpha)$ factors in the l_2 norm, in the worst case.*

Hence if we assume the hardness of approximating the SIVP and GapSVP problems in lattices of dimension n to within polynomial (in n) factors, then it follows from Theorem 3 that deciding the LWE problem is hard when n/α is a polynomial in n.

3   Our PKEET Construction

3.1   Construction

Setup(λ): On input a security parameter λ, set the parameters q, n, m, σ, α as in Sect. 3.2

1. Use TrapGen(q, n) to generate uniformly random $n \times m$-matrices $A, A' \in \mathbb{Z}_q^{n \times m}$ together with trapdoors T_A and $T_{A'}$ respectively.
2. Select $l + 1$ uniformly random $n \times m$ matrices $A_1, \cdots, A_l, B \in \mathbb{Z}_q^{n \times m}$.
3. Let $H : \{0,1\}^* \to \{0,1\}^t$ and $H' : \{0,1\}^* \to \{-1,1\}^l$ be hash functions.
4. Select a uniformly random matrix $U \in \mathbb{Z}_q^{n \times t}$.
5. Output the public key and the secret key

$$\mathsf{PK} = (A, A', A_1, \cdots, A_l, B, U), \quad \mathsf{SK} = (T_A, T_{A'}).$$

Encrypt($\mathsf{PK}, \mathbf{m}$): On input the public key PK and a message $\mathbf{m} \in \{0,1\}^t$, do:
1. Choose a uniformly random $\mathbf{s}_1, \mathbf{s}_2 \in \mathbb{Z}_q^n$
2. Choose $\mathbf{x}_1, \mathbf{x}_2 \in \overline{\Psi}_\alpha^t$ and compute[1]

$$\mathbf{c}_1 = U^T \mathbf{s}_1 + \mathbf{x}_1 + \mathbf{m} \lfloor \frac{q}{2} \rfloor, \quad \mathbf{c}_2 = U^T \mathbf{s}_2 + \mathbf{x}_2 + H(\mathbf{m}) \lfloor \frac{q}{2} \rfloor \in \mathbb{Z}_q^t.$$

3. Compute $\mathbf{b} = H'(\mathbf{c}_1 \| \mathbf{c}_2) \in \{-1,1\}^l$, and set

$$F_1 = (A|B + \sum_{i=1}^l b_i A_i), \quad F_2 = (A'|B + \sum_{i=1}^l b_i A_i).$$

4. Choose l uniformly random matrices $R_i \in \{-1,1\}^{m \times m}$ for $i = 1, \cdots, l$ and define $R = \sum_{i=1}^l b_i R_i \in \{-l, \cdots, l\}^{m \times m}$.
5. Choose $\mathbf{y}_1, \mathbf{y}_2 \in \overline{\Psi}_\alpha^m$ and set $\mathbf{z}_1 = R^T \mathbf{y}_1, \mathbf{z}_2 = R^T \mathbf{y}_2 \in \mathbb{Z}_q^m$.
6. Compute

$$\mathbf{c}_3 = F_1^T \mathbf{s}_1 + [\mathbf{y}_1^T | \mathbf{z}_1^T]^T, \mathbf{c}_4 = F_2^T \mathbf{s}_2 + [\mathbf{y}_2^T | \mathbf{z}_2^T]^T \in \mathbb{Z}_q^{2m}.$$

7. The ciphertext is

$$\mathsf{CT} = (\mathbf{c}_1, \mathbf{c}_2, \mathbf{c}_3, \mathbf{c}_4) \in \mathbb{Z}_q^{2t+4m}.$$

Decrypt($\mathsf{PK}, \mathsf{SK}, \mathsf{CT}$): On input public key PK, private key SK and a ciphertext $\mathsf{CT} = (\mathbf{c}_1, \mathbf{c}_2, \mathbf{c}_3, \mathbf{c}_4)$, do:
1. Compute $\mathbf{b} = H'(\mathbf{c}_1 \| \mathbf{c}_2) \in \{-1,1\}^l$ and sample $\mathbf{e} \in \mathbb{Z}^{2m \times t}$ from

$$\mathbf{e} \leftarrow \mathsf{SampleLeft}(A, B + \sum_{i=1}^l b_i A_i, T_A, U, \sigma).$$

Note that $F_1 \cdot \mathbf{e} = U$ in $\mathbb{Z}_q^{n \times t}$.

---

[1] Note that for a message $\mathbf{m} \in \{0,1\}^t$, we choose a random binary string $\mathbf{m}'$ of fixed length t' large enough and by abusing of notation, we write $H(\mathbf{m})$ for $H(\mathbf{m}' \| \mathbf{m})$.

2. Compute $\mathbf{w} \leftarrow \mathbf{c}_1 - \mathbf{e}^T \mathbf{c}_3 \in \mathbb{Z}_q^t$.
3. For each $i = 1, \cdots, t$, compare w_i and $\lfloor \frac{q}{2} \rfloor$. If they are close, output $m_i = 1$ and otherwise output $m_i = 0$. We then obtain the message $\mathbf{m}$.
4. Sample $\mathbf{e}' \in \mathbb{Z}^{2m \times t}$ from

$$\mathbf{e}' \leftarrow \mathsf{SampleLeft}(A', B + \sum_{i=1}^{l} b_i A_i, T_{A'}, U, \sigma).$$

5. Compute $\mathbf{w}' \leftarrow \mathbf{c}_2 - (\mathbf{e}')^T \mathbf{c}_4 \in \mathbb{Z}_q^t$.
6. For each $i = 1, \cdots, t$, compare w_i' and $\lfloor \frac{q}{2} \rfloor$. If they are close, output $h_i = 1$ and otherwise output $h_i = 0$. We then obtain the vector $\mathbf{h}$.
7. If $\mathbf{h} = H(\mathbf{m})$ then output $\mathbf{m}$, otherwise output $\perp$.

Trapdoor(SK_i): On input a user U_i's secret key $\mathsf{SK}_i = (K_{i,1}, K_{i,2})$, it outputs a trapdoor $\mathsf{td}_i = K_{i,2}$.

Test($\mathsf{td}_i, \mathsf{td}_j, \mathsf{CT}_i, \mathsf{CT}_j$): On input trapdoors $\mathsf{td}_i, \mathsf{td}_j$ and ciphertexts $\mathsf{CT}_i, \mathsf{CT}_j$ for users U_i, U_j respectively, computes

1. For each i (resp. j), do the following:
   - Compute $\mathbf{b}_i = H'(\mathbf{c}_{i1} \| \mathbf{c}_{i2}) = (b_{i1}, \cdots, b_{il})$ and sample $\mathbf{e}_i \in \mathbb{Z}^{2m \times t}$ from

$$\mathbf{e_i} \leftarrow \mathsf{SampleLeft}(A_i', B_i + \sum_{k=1}^{l} b_{ik} A_{ik}, T_{A_i'}, U_i, \sigma).$$

   Note that $F_{i2} \cdot \mathbf{e}_i = U_i$ in $\mathbb{Z}_q^{n \times t}$.
   - Compute $\mathbf{w}_i \leftarrow \mathbf{c_{i2}} - \mathbf{e}_i^T \mathbf{c}_{i4} \in \mathbb{Z}_q^t$. For each $k = 1, \cdots, t$, compare each coordinate w_{ik} with $\lfloor \frac{q}{w} \rfloor$ and output $\mathbf{h}_{ik} = 1$ if they are close, and 0 otherwise. At the end, we obtain the vector $\mathbf{h}_i$ (resp. $\mathbf{h}_j$).
2. Output 1 if $\mathbf{h}_i = \mathbf{h}_j$ and 0 otherwise.

Theorem 4. *Our PKEET construction above is correct if H is a collision-resistant hash function.*

Proof. It is easy to see that if CT is a valid ciphertext of $\mathbf{m}$ then the decryption will always output $\mathbf{m}$. Moreover, if CT_i and CT_j are valid ciphertext of $\mathbf{m}$ and $\mathbf{m}'$ of user U_i and U_j respectively. Then the Test process checks whether $H(\mathbf{m}) = H(\mathbf{m}')$. If so then it outputs 1, meaning that $\mathbf{m} = \mathbf{m}'$, which is always correct with overwhelming probability since H is collision resistant. Hence our PKEET described above is correct. $\square$

3.2   Parameters

We follow [1, Section 7.3] for choosing parameters for our scheme. Now for the system to work correctly we need to ensure

- the error term in decryption is less than $q/5$ with high probability, i.e., $q = \Omega(\sigma m^{3/2})$ and $\alpha < [\sigma l m \omega(\sqrt{\log m})]^{-1}$,
- that the TrapGen can operate, i.e., $m > 6n \log q$,

- that σ is large enough for SampleLeft and SampleRight, i.e., $\sigma > lm\omega(\sqrt{\log m})$,
- that Regev's reduction applies, i.e., $q > 2\sqrt{n}/\alpha$,
- that our security reduction applies (i.e., $q > 2Q$ where Q is the number of identity queries from the adversary).

Hence the following choice of parameters (q, m, σ, α) from [1] satisfies all of the above conditions, taking n to be the security parameter:

$$m = 6n^{1+\delta}, \quad q = \max(2Q, m^{2.5}\omega(\sqrt{\log n}))$$
$$\sigma = ml\omega(\sqrt{\log n}), \quad \alpha = [l^2 m^2 \omega(\sqrt{\log n})]^{-1} \tag{1}$$

and round up m to the nearest larger integer and q to the nearest larger prime. Here we assume that δ is such that $n^{\delta} > \lceil \log q \rceil = O(\log n)$.

3.3   Security Analysis

In this section, we will prove that our proposed scheme is OW-CCA2 secure against Type-I adversaries (cf. Theorem 5) and IND-CCA2 secure against Type-II adversaries (cf. Theorem 6).

Theorem 5. *The PKEET with parameters $(q, n, m, \sigma, \alpha)$ as in (1) is OW-CCA2 secure provided that H is a one-way hash function, H' is a collision-resistant hash function, and the $(\mathbb{Z}_q, n, \bar{\Psi}_\alpha)$-LWE assumption holds. In particular, suppose there exists a probabilistic algorithm $\mathcal{A}$ that wins the OW-CCA2 game with advantage ϵ, then there is a probabilistic algorithm $\mathcal{B}$ that solves the $(\mathbb{Z}_q, n, \bar{\Psi}_\alpha)$-LWE problem with advantage ϵ' such that*

$$\epsilon' \geq \frac{1}{2q}\left(\epsilon - \frac{1}{2}\epsilon_{H',\text{CR}} - \epsilon_{H,\text{OW}}\right).$$

Here $\epsilon_{H',\text{CR}}$ is the advantage of breaking the collision resistance of H' and $\epsilon_{H,\text{OW}}$ is the advantage of breaking the one-wayness of H.

Proof. The proof is similar to that of [1, Theorem 25]. Assume that there is a Type-I adversary $\mathcal{A}$ who breaks the OW-CCA2 security of the PKKET scheme with non-negligible probability ϵ. We construct an algorithm $\mathcal{B}$ who solves the LWE problem using $\mathcal{A}$. Assume again that there are N users in our PKEET system. We now describe the behaviors of $\mathcal{B}$. Assume that θ is the target index of the adversary $\mathcal{A}$ and the challenge ciphertext is $\text{CT}^*_\theta = (\text{CT}^*_{\theta,1}, \text{CT}^*_{\theta,2}, \text{CT}^*_{\theta,3}, \text{CT}^*_{\theta,4})$.

We will proceed the proof in a sequence of games. In game i, let W_i denote the event that the adversary $\mathcal{A}$ win the game. The adversary's advantage in Game i is $\Pr[W_i]$.

Game 0. This is the original OW-CCA2 game between the attacker $\mathcal{A}$ against the scheme and the OW-CCA2 challenger.

Game 1. This is similar to Game 0 except that in Phase 2 of Game 1, if the adversary queries the decryption oracel $\mathcal{O}^{\mathsf{Dec}}(\theta)$ of a ciphertext $\mathsf{CT}_\theta = (\mathsf{CT}_{\theta,1}, \mathsf{CT}_{\theta,2}, \mathsf{CT}_{\theta,3}, \mathsf{CT}_{\theta,4})$ such that $H'(\mathsf{CT}_{\theta,1} \| \mathsf{CT}_{\theta,2}) = \mathbf{b}^*$, where $\mathbf{b}^* = H'(\mathsf{CT}^*_{\theta,1} \| \mathsf{CT}^*_{\theta,2})$, but $\mathsf{CT}_\theta \neq \mathsf{CT}^*_\theta$ then the challenger aborts the game and returns a random guess. We denote this event by E_1. In this event, the adversary has found a collision for the hash function H' and so

$$\Pr[E_1] \leq \epsilon_{H',\mathsf{CR}}$$

where $\epsilon_{H'CR}$ is the advantage of the adversary $\mathcal{A}$ against the collision resistance of H'. Now the advantage of $\mathcal{A}$ in Game 1 is

$$\begin{aligned}
\Pr[W_1] &= \Pr[W_1|E_1]\Pr[E_1] + \Pr[W_1|\neg E_1]\Pr[\neg E_1] \\
&= \frac{1}{2}\Pr[E_1] + \Pr[W_0 \cap \neg E_1] \\
&= \frac{1}{2}\Pr[E_1] + \Pr[W_0] - \Pr[W_0 \cap E_1] \\
&\geq \Pr[W_0] - \frac{1}{2}\Pr[E_1] \\
&\geq \Pr[W_0] - \frac{1}{2}\epsilon_{H',\mathsf{CR}}
\end{aligned}$$

and hence
$$\Pr[W_0] - \Pr[W_1] \leq \frac{1}{2}\epsilon_{H',\mathsf{CR}}.$$

Game 2. This is similar to Game 1 except that at the challenge phase, $\mathcal{B}$ chooses two message $\mathbf{m}$ and $\mathbf{m}'$ in the message space and encrypt $\mathbf{m}$ in $\mathsf{CT}_{\theta,1}$ and $H(\mathbf{m}')$ in $\mathsf{CT}_{\theta,2}$. Other steps are similar to Game 1. Here we can not expect the behavior of $\mathcal{A}$. And since $\mathcal{A}$ has a trapdoor $T_{A'}$ and he can obtain $H(\mathbf{m}')$. At the end if $\mathcal{A}$ outputs $\mathbf{m}'$, call this event E_2, then $\mathcal{A}$ has broken the one-wayness of the hash function H. Thus

$$\Pr[E_2] \leq \epsilon_{H,\mathsf{OW}}$$

where $\epsilon_{H,\mathsf{OW}}$ is the advantage of $\mathcal{A}$ in breaking the one-wayness of H. Therefore we have

$$\begin{aligned}
\Pr[W_2] &= \Pr[W_2|E_2]\Pr[E_2] + \Pr[W_2|\neg E_2]\Pr[\neg E_2] \\
&= \Pr[W_2|E_2]\Pr[E_2] + \Pr[W_1]\Pr[\neg E_2] \\
&\geq \frac{1}{|\mathcal{M}|}\Pr[E_2] + \Pr[W_1] - \Pr[W_1]\Pr[E_2] \\
&\geq \Pr[W_1] - \Pr[E_2] \\
&\geq \Pr[W_1] - \epsilon_{H,\mathsf{OW}}
\end{aligned}$$

and hence
$$\Pr[W_1] - \Pr[W_2] \leq \epsilon_{H,\mathsf{OW}}.$$

Game 3. This is similar to Game 2 except the way the challenger $\mathcal{B}$ generates the public key for the user with index θ, as the following. Let $R_i^* \in \{-1,1\}^{m \times m}$ for $i = 1, \cdots, l$ be the ephemeral random matrices generated for the creation of the ciphertext CT_θ^*. In this game, the challenger chooses l matrices R_i^* uniformly random in $\{-1,1\}^{m \times m}$ and chooses l random scalars $h_i \in \mathbb{Z}_q$ for $i = 1, \cdots, l$. Then it generates A, A' and B as in Game 1 and constructs the matrices A_i for $i = 1, \cdots, l$ as

$$A_i \leftarrow A \cdot R_i^* - h_i \cdot B \in \mathbb{Z}_q^{n \times m}.$$

The remainder of the game is unchanged with R_i^*, $i = 1, \cdots, l$, used to generate the challenge ciphertext. Similar to the proof of [1, Theorem 25] we have that the A_i are close to uniform and hence they are random independent matrices in the view of the adversary as in Game 0. Therefore

$$\Pr[W_3] = \Pr[W_2].$$

Game 4. Game 4 is similar to Game 3 except that we add an abort that is independent of adversary's view. The challenger behaves as follows:
  - The setup phase is identical to Game 3 except that the challenger also chooses random $h_i \in \mathbb{Z}_q$, $i = 1, \cdots, l$ and keeps it to itself.
  - In the final guess phase, the adversary outputs a guest $\mathbf{m}'$ for $\mathbf{m}$. The challenger now does the following:
    1. **Abort check:** for all queries $\mathsf{CT} = (\mathsf{CT}_1, \mathsf{CT}_2, \mathsf{CT}_3, \mathsf{CT}_4)$ to the decryption oracle $\mathcal{O}^{\mathsf{Dec}}$, the challenger checks whether $\mathbf{b} = H'(\mathsf{CT}_1 \| \mathsf{CT}_2)$ satisfies $1 + \sum_{i=1}^h b_i h_i \neq 0$ and $1 + \sum_{i=1}^h b_i^* h_i = 0$ where $\mathbf{b}^* = H'(\mathsf{CT}_{\theta,1}^* \| \mathsf{CT}_{\theta,2}^*)$. If not then the challenger overwrites $\mathbf{m}'$ with a fresh random message and aborts the game.
    2. **Artificial abort:** the challenger samples a message Γ such that $\Pr[\Gamma = 1]$ is calculated through a function $\mathcal{G}$ (defined as in [1]) evaluated through all the queries of $\mathcal{A}$. If $\Gamma = 1$ the challenger overwrites $\mathbf{m}'$ with a fresh random message and we say that the challenger aborted the game due to artificial abort; see [1] for more details.

A similar proof as in that of [1, Theorem 25] yields that

$$\Pr[W_4] \geq \frac{1}{2q}\Pr[W_3].$$

Game 5. We now change the way how A and B are generated in Game 4. In Game 5, A is a random matrix in $\mathbb{Z}_q^{n \times m}$ and B is generated through $\mathsf{TrapGen}(q,n)$ together with an associated trapdoor T_B for $\Lambda_q^\perp(B)$. The construction of A_i for $i = 1, \cdots, l$ remains the same as in Game 3, i.e., $A_i = AR_i^* - h_i B$. When $\mathcal{A}$ queries $\mathcal{O}^{\mathsf{Dec}}(\theta, \mathsf{CT}_\theta)$ where $\mathsf{CT}_\theta = (\mathsf{CT}_{\theta,1}, \mathsf{CT}_{\theta,2}, \mathsf{CT}_{\theta,3}, \mathsf{CT}_{\theta,4})$, $\mathcal{B}$ performs as follows:
  - $\mathcal{B}$ computes $\mathbf{b} = H'(\mathsf{CT}_{\theta,1} \| \mathsf{CT}_{\theta,2}) \in \{-1,1\}^l$ and set

$$F_\theta := (A|B + \sum_{i=1}^l A_i) = (A|AR + h_\theta B)$$

where

$$R \leftarrow \sum_{i=1}^{l} b_i R_i^* \in \mathbb{Z}_q^{n \times m} \quad \text{and} \quad h_\theta \leftarrow 1 + \sum_{i=1}^{l} b_i h_i \in \mathbb{Z}_q. \tag{2}$$

- If $h_\theta = 0$ then abort the game and pretend that the adversary outputs a random bit γ' as in Game 3.
- Set $\mathbf{e} \leftarrow \mathsf{SampleRight}(A, h_\theta B, R, T_B, U, \sigma) \in \mathbb{Z}_q^{2m \times t}$. Note that since h_θ is non-zero, and so T_B is also a trapdoor for $h_\theta B$. And hence the output $\mathbf{e}$ satisfies $F_\theta \cdot \mathbf{e} = U$ in $\mathbb{Z}_q^t$. Moreover, Theorem 2 shows that when $\sigma > \|\widetilde{T_B}\| s_R \omega(\sqrt{m})$ with $s_R := \|R\|$, the generated $\mathbf{e}$ is distributed close to $\mathcal{D}_{A_q^U}(F_\theta)$ as in Game 3.
- Compute $\mathbf{w} \leftarrow \mathsf{CT}_{\theta,1} - \mathbf{e}^T \mathsf{CT}_{\theta,3} \in \mathbb{Z}_q^t$. For each $i = 1, \cdots, t$, compare w_i with $\lfloor \frac{q}{2} \rfloor$, and output 1 if they are close, and output 0 otherwise. Then $\mathcal{B}$ can answer the decryption query $\mathcal{O}^{\mathsf{Dec}}(\theta, \mathsf{CT}_\theta)$ made by $\mathcal{A}$.

Game 5 is otherwise the same as Game 4. In particular, in the challenge phase, the challenger checks if b^* satisfies $1 + \sum_{i=1}^{l} b_i h_i = 0$. If not, the challenger aborts the game as in Game 4. Similarly, in Game 5, the challenger also implements an artificial abort in the guess phase. Since Game 4 and Game 5 are identical in the adversary's view, we have that

$$\Pr[W_5] = \Pr[W_4].$$

Game 6. Game 6 is identical to Game 5, except that the challenge ciphertext is always chosen randomly. And thus the advantage of $\mathcal{A}$ is always 0.

We now show that Game 5 and Game 6 are computationally indistinguishable. If the abort event happens then the games are clearly indistinguishable. We, therefore, consider only the queries that do not cause an abort.

Suppose now $\mathcal{A}$ has a non-negligible advantage in distinguishing Game 5 and Game 6. We use $\mathcal{A}$ to construct $\mathcal{B}$ to solve the LWE problem as follows.

Setup. First of all, $\mathcal{B}$ requests from $\mathcal{O}$ and receives, for each $j = 1, \cdots, t$ a fresh pair $(\mathbf{a}_i, d_i) \in \mathbb{Z}_q^n \times \mathbb{Z}_q$ and for each $i = 1, \cdots, m$, a fresh pair $(\mathbf{u}_i, v_i) \in \mathbb{Z}_q^n \times \mathbb{Z}_q$. $\mathcal{A}$ announces an index θ for the target user. $\mathcal{B}$ executes $(\mathsf{PK}_i, \mathsf{SK}_i) \leftarrow \mathsf{Setup}(\lambda)$ for $1 \leq i \neq \theta \leq N$. Then $\mathcal{B}$ constructs the public key for user of index θ as follows:

1. Assemble the random matrix $A \in \mathbb{Z}_q^{n \times m}$ from m of previously given LWE samples by letting the i-th column of A to be the n-vector $\mathbf{u}_i$ for all $i = 1, \cdots, m$.
2. Assemble the first t unused the samples $\mathbf{a}_1, \cdots, \mathbf{a}_t$ to become a public random matrix $U \in \mathbb{Z}_q^{n \times t}$.
3. Run $\mathsf{TrapGen}(q, \sigma)$ to generate uniformly random matrices $A', B \in \mathbb{Z}_q^{n \times m}$ together with their trapdoor $T_{A'}$ and T_B respectively.
4. Choose l random matrices $R_i^* \in \{-1, 1\}^{m \times m}$ for $i = 1, \cdots, l$ and l random scalars $h_i \in \mathbb{Z}_q$ for $i = 1, \cdots, l$. Next it constructs the matrices A_i for $i = 1, \cdots, l$ as

$$A_i \leftarrow AR_i^* - h_i B \in \mathbb{Z}_q^{n \times m}.$$

Note that it follows from the leftover hash lemma [15, Theorem 8.38] that $A_1, \cdots, A_l$ are statistically close to uniform.

5. Set $\mathsf{PK}_\theta := (A, A', A_1, \cdots, A_l, B, U)$ to $\mathcal{A}$.

Then $\mathcal{B}$ sends the public keys $\{\mathsf{PK}_i\}_{i=1}^N$ to the adversary $\mathcal{A}$.

Queries. $\mathcal{B}$ answers the queries as in Game 4, including aborting the game if needed.

Challenge. Now $\mathcal{B}$ chooses random messages $\mathbf{m}^*$ and computes the challenge ciphertext $\mathsf{CT}_\theta^* = (\mathsf{CT}_{\theta,1}^*, \mathsf{CT}_{\theta,2}^*, \mathsf{CT}_{\theta,3}^*, \mathsf{CT}_{\theta,4}^*)$ as follows:

1. Assemble $d_1, \cdots, d_t, v_1, \cdots, v_m$ from the entries of the samples to form $\mathbf{d}^* = [d_1, \cdots, d_t]^T \in \mathbb{Z}_q^t$ and $\mathbf{v}^* = [v_1, \cdots, v_m]^T \in \mathbb{Z}_q^m$.
2. Set $\mathsf{CT}_{\theta,1}^* \leftarrow \mathbf{d}^* + \mathbf{m}^* \lfloor \frac{q}{2} \rfloor \in \mathbb{Z}_q^t$.
3. Choose a uniformly random $\mathbf{s}_2 \in \mathbb{Z}_q^n$ and $\mathbf{x}_2 \leftarrow \overline{\Psi}_\alpha^t$, compute

$$\mathsf{CT}_{\theta,2}^* \leftarrow U^T \mathbf{s}_2 + \mathbf{x}_2 + H(\mathbf{m}^*) \lfloor \frac{q}{2} \rfloor \in \mathbb{Z}_q^t.$$

4. Compute $\mathbf{b}^* = H'(\mathsf{CT}_{\theta,1}^* \| \mathsf{CT}_{\theta,2}^*) \in \{-1,1\}^l$ and $R^* := \sum_{i=1}^l b_i^* R_i^* \in \{-l, \cdots, l\}^{m \times m}$.
5. Set

$$\mathsf{CT}_{\theta,3}^* := \begin{bmatrix} \mathbf{v}^* \\ (R^*)^T \mathbf{v}^* \end{bmatrix} \in \mathbb{Z}_q^{2m}.$$

6. Choose $\mathbf{y}_2 \leftarrow \overline{\Psi}_\alpha^m$ and set

$$\mathsf{CT}_{\theta,4}^* := \begin{bmatrix} (A')^T \mathbf{s}_2 + \mathbf{y}_2 \\ (AR^*)^T \mathbf{s}_2 + (R^*)^T \mathbf{y}_2 \end{bmatrix} \in \mathbb{Z}_q^{2m}.$$

Then $\mathcal{B}$ sends $\mathsf{CT}_\theta^* = (\mathsf{CT}_{\theta,1}^*, \mathsf{CT}_{\theta,2}^*, \mathsf{CT}_{\theta,3}^*, \mathsf{CT}_{\theta,4}^*)$ to $\mathcal{A}$.

Note that in case of no abort, one has $h_\theta = 0$ and so $F_\theta = (A|AR^*)$. When the LWE oracle is pseudorandom, i.e., $\mathcal{O} = \mathcal{O}_\mathbf{s}$ then $\mathbf{v}^* = A^T \mathbf{s} + \mathbf{y}$ for some random noise vector $\mathbf{y} \leftarrow \overline{\Psi}_\alpha^m$. Therefore $\mathsf{CT}_{\theta,3}^*$ in Step 5 satisfies:

$$\mathsf{CT}_{\theta,3}^* := \begin{bmatrix} A^T \mathbf{s} + \mathbf{y} \\ (AR^*)^T \mathbf{s} + (R^*)^T \mathbf{y} \end{bmatrix} = (F_\theta)^T \mathbf{s} + \begin{bmatrix} \mathbf{y} \\ (R^*)^T \mathbf{y} \end{bmatrix}.$$

Moreover, $\mathbf{d}^* = U^T \mathbf{s} + \mathbf{x}$ for some $\mathbf{x} \leftarrow \overline{\Psi}_\alpha^t$ and therefore

$$\mathsf{CT}_{\theta,1}^* = U^T \mathbf{s} + \mathbf{x} + \mathbf{m}^* \lfloor \frac{q}{2} \rfloor.$$

One can easily see that

$$\mathsf{CT}_{\theta,4}^* = [A'|AR^*]^T \mathbf{s}_2 + [\mathbf{y}_2 (R^*)^T \mathbf{y}_2].$$

Therefore CT_θ^* is a valid ciphertext.

When $\mathcal{O} = \mathcal{O}_\$$ we have that $\mathbf{d}^*$ is uniform in $\mathbb{Z}_q^t$ and $\mathbf{v}^*$ is uniform in $\mathbb{Z}_q^m$. Then obviously $\mathsf{CT}_{\theta,1}^*$ is uniform. It follows also from the leftover hash lemma (cf. [15, Theorem 8.38]) that $\mathsf{CT}_{\theta,3}^*$ is also uniform.

Guess. After Phase 2, $\mathcal{A}$ guesses if it is interacting with a Game 5 or Game 6. The simulator also implements the artificial abort from Game 5 and Game 6 and output the final guess as the answer to the LWE problem.

We have seen above that when $\mathcal{O} = \mathcal{O}_\mathbf{s}$ then the adversary's view is as in Game 5. When $\mathcal{O} = \mathcal{O}_\$$ then the view of adversary is as in Game 6. Hence the advantage ϵ' of $\mathcal{B}$ in solving the LWE problem is the same as the advantage of $\mathcal{A}$ in distinguishing Game 5 and Game 6. Since $\Pr[W_6] = 0$, we have

$$\Pr[W_5] = \Pr[W_5] - \Pr[W_6] \le \epsilon'.$$

Hence combining the above results, we obtain that

$$\epsilon = \Pr[W_0] \le \frac{1}{2}\epsilon_{H',\mathsf{CR}} + \epsilon_{H,\mathsf{OW}} + 2q\epsilon'$$

which implies

$$\epsilon' \ge \frac{1}{2q}\left(\epsilon - \frac{1}{2}\epsilon_{H',\mathsf{CR}} - \epsilon_{H,\mathsf{OW}}\right)$$

as desired. $\qquad\qquad\square$

Theorem 6. *The PKEET with parameters $(q, n, m, \sigma, \alpha)$ as in (1) is IND-CCA2 secure provided that H' is a collision-resistant hash function, and the $(\mathbb{Z}_q, n, \bar{\Psi}_\alpha)$-LWE assumption holds. In particular, suppose there exists a probabilistic algorithm $\mathcal{A}$ that wins the IND-CCA2 game with advantage ϵ, then there is a probabilistic algorithm $\mathcal{B}$ that solves the $(\mathbb{Z}_q, n, \bar{\Psi}_\alpha)$-LWE problem with advantage ϵ' such that*

$$\epsilon' \ge \frac{1}{4q}\left(\epsilon - \frac{1}{2}\epsilon_{H',\mathsf{CR}}\right)$$

where $\epsilon_{H',\mathsf{CR}}$ is the advantage of $\mathcal{A}$ in breaking the collision resistance of H'.

Proof. The proof is similar to that of Theorem 5. Assume that there is a Type-II adversary $\mathcal{A}$ who breaks the IND-CCA2 security of the PKKET scheme with non-negligible probability ϵ. We construct an algorithm $\mathcal{B}$ who solves the LWE problem using $\mathcal{A}$. Assume again that there are N users in our PKEET system. We now describe the behavior of $\mathcal{B}$. Assume that θ is the target index of the adversary $\mathcal{A}$ and the challenge ciphertext is $\mathsf{CT}_\theta^* = (\mathsf{CT}_{\theta,1}^*, \mathsf{CT}_{\theta,2}^*, \mathsf{CT}_{\theta,3}^*, \mathsf{CT}_{\theta,4}^*)$.

We will proceed the proof in a sequence of games. In game i, let W_i denote the event that the adversary $\mathcal{A}$ correctly guesses the challenge bit. The adversary's advantage in Game i is $\left|\Pr[W_i] - \frac{1}{2}\right|$.

Game 0. This is the original IND-CCA2 game between the attacker $\mathcal{A}$ against the scheme and the IND-CCA2 challenger.

Game 1. This is similar to Game 1 in the proof of Theorem 5. Thus the advantage of $\mathcal{A}$ in Game 1 is

$$\left|\Pr[W_0] - \frac{1}{2}\right| - \left|\Pr[W_1] - \frac{1}{2}\right| \le \frac{1}{2}\epsilon_{H',\mathsf{CR}}.$$

Game 2. This is similar to Game 3 in the proof of Theorem 5 and we have

$$\Pr[W_2] = \Pr[W_1].$$

Game 3. Game 3 is similar to Game 2 except that we add an abort as in the proof of Theorem 5. It follows from the proof of [1, Theorem 25] that

$$\left| \Pr[W_3] - \frac{1}{2} \right| \geq \frac{1}{4q} \left| \Pr[W_2] - \frac{1}{2} \right|.$$

Game 4. This game is similar to Game 5 in the proof of Theorem 5, and we have

$$\Pr[W_3] = \Pr[W_4].$$

Game 5. Game 5 is identical to Game 4, except that the challenge ciphertext is always chosen randomly. And thus the advantage of $\mathcal{A}$ is always 0.

We now show that Game 4 and Game 5 are computationally indistinguishable. If the abort event happens then the games are clearly indistinguishable. We, therefore, consider only the queries that do not cause an abort.

Suppose now $\mathcal{A}$ has a non-negligible advantage in distinguishing Game 4 and Game 5. We use $\mathcal{A}$ to construct $\mathcal{B}$ to solve the LWE problem similar to the proof of Theorem 5. Note that in the IND-CCA2 game, we allow the adversary to query the trapdoor oracle $\mathcal{O}^{\mathsf{Td}}$. And since we generate A' together with $T_{A'}$ from $\mathsf{TrapGen}(q, n)$ and we can answer $T_{A'}$ to such queries.

We have seen above that when $\mathcal{O} = \mathcal{O}_\mathbf{s}$ then the adversary's view is as in Game 4. When $\mathcal{O} = \mathcal{O}_\$$ then the view of the adversary is as in Game 5. Hence the advantage ϵ' of $\mathcal{B}$ in solving the LWE problem is the same as the advantage of $\mathcal{A}$ in distinguishing Game 4 and Game 5. Since $\Pr[W_5] = \frac{1}{2}$, we have

$$\left| \Pr[W_4] - \frac{1}{2} \right| = |\Pr[W_4] - \Pr[W_5]| \leq \epsilon'.$$

Hence combining the above results, we obtain that

$$\epsilon = \left| \Pr[W_0] - \frac{1}{2} \right| \leq \frac{1}{2} \epsilon_{H',\mathsf{CR}} + 4q\epsilon'$$

which implies

$$\epsilon' \geq \frac{1}{4q} \left(\epsilon - \frac{1}{2} \epsilon_{H',\mathsf{CR}} \right)$$

as desired.   □

4   Conclusion

In this paper, we propose a direct construction of PKEET based on the hardness of Learning With Errors problem. Efficiency is the reason to avoid the instantiation of lattice-based PKEET from the generic construction by Lee et al. [8]. A concrete instantiation from [8] and comparative study are left for the complete version. In addition, our PKEET scheme can be further improved by utilizing improved IBE schemes [19,20] together with the efficient trapdoor generation [10] and faster Gaussian sampling technique [6], which we leave as future work.

Acknowledgement. The authors acknowledge the useful comments and suggestions of the referees. The first author would like to thank Hyung Tae Lee for sending him a copy of [22] and useful discussions, and acknowledges the support of the Start-Up Grant from University of Wollongong.

References

1. Agrawal, S., Boneh, D., Boyen, X.: Efficient lattice (H)IBE in the standard model. In: Gilbert, H. (ed.) EUROCRYPT 2010. LNCS, vol. 6110, pp. 553–572. Springer, Heidelberg (2010). https://doi.org/10.1007/978-3-642-13190-5_28
2. Ajtai, M.: Generating hard instances of the short basis problem. In: Wiedermann, J., van Emde Boas, P., Nielsen, M. (eds.) ICALP 1999. LNCS, vol. 1644, pp. 1–9. Springer, Heidelberg (1999). https://doi.org/10.1007/3-540-48523-6_1
3. Alwen, J., Peikert, C.: Generating shorter bases for hard random lattices. In 26th International Symposium on Theoretical Aspects of Computer Science, STACS 2009, Proceedings, 26–28 February 2009, Freiburg, Germany, pp. 75–86 (2009)
4. Canetti, R., Halevi, S., Katz, J.: Chosen-ciphertext security from identity-based encryption. In: Cachin, C., Camenisch, J.L. (eds.) EUROCRYPT 2004. LNCS, vol. 3027, pp. 207–222. Springer, Heidelberg (2004). https://doi.org/10.1007/978-3-540-24676-3_13
5. Cash, D., Hofheinz, D., Kiltz, E., Peikert, C.: Bonsai trees, or how to delegate a lattice basis. In: Gilbert, H. (ed.) EUROCRYPT 2010. LNCS, vol. 6110, pp. 523–552. Springer, Heidelberg (2010). https://doi.org/10.1007/978-3-642-13190-5_27
6. Genise, N., Micciancio, D.: Faster Gaussian sampling for trapdoor lattices with arbitrary modulus. In: Nielsen, J.B., Rijmen, V. (eds.) EUROCRYPT 2018. LNCS, vol. 10820, pp. 174–203. Springer, Cham (2018). https://doi.org/10.1007/978-3-319-78381-9_7
7. Lai, J., Deng, R.H., Liu, S., Kou, W.: Efficient CCA-secure PKE from identity-based techniques. In: Pieprzyk, J. (ed.) CT-RSA 2010. LNCS, vol. 5985, pp. 132–147. Springer, Heidelberg (2010). https://doi.org/10.1007/978-3-642-11925-5_10
8. Lee, H.T., Ling, S., Seo, J.H., Wang, H., Youn, T.Y.: Public key encryption with equality test in the standard model. Cryptology ePrint Archive, Report 2016/1182 (2016)
9. Lee, H.T., Ling, S., Seo, J.H., Wang, H.: Semi-generic construction of public key encryption and identity-based encryption with equality test. Inf. Sci. **373**, 419–440 (2016)
10. Micciancio, D., Peikert, C.: Trapdoors for lattices: simpler, tighter, faster, smaller. In: Pointcheval, D., Johansson, T. (eds.) EUROCRYPT 2012. LNCS, vol. 7237, pp. 700–718. Springer, Heidelberg (2012). https://doi.org/10.1007/978-3-642-29011-4_41
11. Micciancio, D., Regev, O.: Worst-case to average-case reductions based on Gaussian measures. In 45th Symposium on Foundations of Computer Science (FOCS 2004), Proceedings, 17–19 October 2004, Rome, Italy, pp. 372–381 (2004)

12. Ma, S., Zhang, M., Huang, Q., Yang, B.: Public key encryption with delegated equality test in a multi-user setting. Comput. J. **58**(4), 986–1002 (2015)
13. Regev, O.: On lattices, learning with errors, random linear codes, and cryptography. In: Proceedings of the 37th Annual ACM Symposium on Theory of Computing, Baltimore, MD, USA, 22–24 May 2005, pp. 84–93 (2005)
14. Shor, P.W.: Polynomial-time algorithms for prime factorization and discrete logarithms on a quantum computer. SIAM J. Comput. **26**(5), 1484–1509 (1997)
15. Shoup, V.: A Computational Introduction to Number Theory and Algebra, 2nd edn. Cambridge University Press, Cambridge (2008)
16. Tang, Q.: Towards public key encryption scheme supporting equality test with fine-grained authorization. In: Parampalli, U., Hawkes, P. (eds.) ACISP 2011. LNCS, vol. 6812, pp. 389–406. Springer, Heidelberg (2011). https://doi.org/10.1007/978-3-642-22497-3_25
17. Tang, Q.: Public key encryption schemes supporting equality test with authorisation of different granularity. IJACT **2**(4), 304–321 (2012)
18. Tang, Q.: Public key encryption supporting plaintext equality test and user-specified authorization. Secur. Commun. Netw. **5**(12), 1351–1362 (2012)
19. Yamada, S.: Adaptively secure identity-based encryption from lattices with asymptotically shorter public parameters. In: Fischlin, M., Coron, J.-S. (eds.) EUROCRYPT 2016. LNCS, vol. 9666, pp. 32–62. Springer, Heidelberg (2016). https://doi.org/10.1007/978-3-662-49896-5_2
20. Yamada, S.: Asymptotically compact adaptively secure lattice IBEs and verifiable random functions via generalized partitioning techniques. In: Katz, J., Shacham, H. (eds.) CRYPTO 2017. LNCS, vol. 10403, pp. 161–193. Springer, Cham (2017). https://doi.org/10.1007/978-3-319-63697-9_6
21. Yang, G., Tan, C.H., Huang, Q., Wong, D.S.: Probabilistic public key encryption with equality test. In: Pieprzyk, J. (ed.) CT-RSA 2010. LNCS, vol. 5985, pp. 119–131. Springer, Heidelberg (2010). https://doi.org/10.1007/978-3-642-11925-5_9
22. Zhang, K., Chen, J., Lee, H.T., Qian, H., Wang, H.: Efficient public key encryption with equality test in the standard model. Theor. Comput. **755**, 65–80 (2019)

Lattice RingCT V2.0 with Multiple Input and Multiple Output Wallets

Wilson Alberto Torres[1], Veronika Kuchta[1], Ron Steinfeld[1], Amin Sakzad[1], Joseph K. Liu[1(✉)], and Jacob Cheng[2]

[1] Faculty of IT, Monash University, Melbourne, Australia
{Wilson.Torres,Veronika.Kuchta,Ron.Steinfeld,
Amin.Sakzad,Joseph.Liu}@monash.edu
[2] Collinstar Capital, Melbourne, Australia
jacob@collinstar.com

Abstract. This paper presents the Lattice-based Ring Confidential Transactions "*Lattice RingCT v2.0*" protocol. Unlike the previous Lattice RingCT v1.0 (LRCT v1.0) protocol, the new protocol supports Multiple-Input and Multiple-Output (MIMO) wallets in transactions, and it is a fully functional protocol construction for cryptocurrency applications such as *Hcash*. Since the MIMO cryptocurrency setting introduces new balance security requirements (and in particular, security against *out-of-range* amount attacks), we give a refined balance security model to capture such attacks, as well as a refined anonymity model to capture amount privacy attacks. Our protocol extends a previously proposed ring signature scheme in the LRCT v1.0 protocol, to support the MIMO requirements while preserving the post-quantum security guarantees, and uses a lattice-based zero-knowledge range proof to achieve security against *out-of-range* attacks. Preliminary parameter estimates and signature sizes are proposed as a point of reference for future studies.

Keywords: Cryptocurrencies · Lattice-based cryptography · Post-quantum cryptography · RingCT

1 Introduction

In the current digital age, cryptocurrencies are applications that use virtual assets and cryptographic mechanisms to conduct e-commerce operations such as electronic payments or money transfers. Those payments can be carried out among accounts or wallets, independently of a central party [10]. Cryptocurrencies lead to some advantages like lower transaction fees, theft resistance and anonymous transactions. Bitcoin [24] is by far the most widely known and decentralised cryptocurrency to date, having its three underlying building blocks: transactions, blockchain and consensus protocol. Contrary to the traditional banking model, Bitcoin allows electronic financial operations in a decentralised Peer-to-Peer (P2P) network. Although Bitcoin was intended to achieve the security properties of privacy and anonymity by using pseudonyms, some analyses

© Springer Nature Switzerland AG 2019
J. Jang-Jaccard and F. Guo (Eds.): ACISP 2019, LNCS 11547, pp. 156–175, 2019.
https://doi.org/10.1007/978-3-030-21548-4_9

[16,28] show that these security properties can be compromised, therefore information about the payers, payees and transactions can be revealed. Thus Bitcoin is only a pseudo-anonymous cryptocurrency.

Nonetheless, since its creation, Bitcoin has revolutionised the field of digital currency and motivated the invention of new cryptocurrencies, also known as alcoins. As an example, CryptoNote [31] was proposed to address the privacy weaknesses of Bitcoin, as it also offers a framework that can be extended by other cryptocurrencies such Bytecoin [6] and Monero [23]. CryptoNote uses *traceable ring signatures* [15] as a fundamental component to achieve true anonymity, where any member of the ring (or group) can create a signature, but it is infeasible by a verifier to identify the real signer. This type of signature hides information about the sender and receiver, and it also has a *linking tag* to prevent double spending coins. Further enhancements to this framework have resulted in an extended protocol called Ring Confidential Transactions "RingCT" [25]. The RingCT protocol uses three techniques: a new type of ring signature *Linkable Ring Signatures* [18], a *homomorphic commitment* and a *range proof*, to preserve the privacy of the sender and the receiver as well as the transaction amounts.

However, the security of this RingCT protocol relies on classical number-theory assumptions, such as the hardness of discrete logarithms [13]. As a consequence, this protocol will be vulnerable in the event of powerful quantum computers [29]. This situation has motivated researchers in the area of post-quantum cryptography to construct secure approaches against quantum attacks. Among the alternatives, lattice-based cryptography has attracted attention due to its distinguishing features and robust security guarantees [8,22].

To the best of our knowledge, the first *post-quantum RingCT* scheme using Lattice-based cryptography was proposed in [2]. However, this proposal is limited. Firstly, it only enables transfers from a single input wallet to a single output wallet (SISO). In the RingCT model, signatures are *one-time*, then if one needs to receive change after making a payment or transfer, a new output wallet is required, so this points out the importance of supporting multiple input and output wallets. Secondly, having more than one output wallet also introduces a new security problem like the negative output amount (or out-of-range) attack [5], where an adversary is capable of creating extra coins. This attack is addressed in the previous RingCT [25] by using a range proof technique; however, this technique is not post-quantum secure.

1.1   Contributions

- We construct the Lattice-based Ring Confidential Transactions (LRCT) for Multiple-Input and Multiple-Output wallets (MIMO). This construction is a generalisation of the SISO.LRCT scheme in [2] where we changed its underlying framework (L2RS signature) to be compatible. Our MIMO.LRCT inherits the post-quantum security guarantees, like the hardness of lattice mathematical assumptions as well as unconditional anonymity.
- We improve the MIMO.LRCT's security model, in particular, the balance and anonymity properties. We explicitly define a balance model that considers out-of-range attacks [5], and we prove the security of our protocol which

previous RingCT's proposals [2,30] did not address. User anonymity is only addressed in [30], while we include the analysis of both user anonymity and amount privacy.

- We show how to incorporate a lattice-based range proof into our MIMO.LRCT protocol, which was a missing ingredient in former proposals [2,30]. To begin with, our protocol deals with the difficulties of the imperfection of lattice-based zero-knowledge proofs, Sect. 5.1 discusses more on this. In particular, range proofs follow the approach based on 1-of-2 OR-proofs, but our analysis shows that directly applying lattice-based OR-proofs from [11] does not provide soundness for the range proof. This argument leads us to carefully select the challenge space as we describe in Lemma 3. Although these challenges are smaller (in norm) than the ones used in the OR-proofs, they are still larger than the challenges in [17]. In this framework, we achieve lower soundness error than the previous lattice-based range proof [17]. We also provide a thorough concrete analysis of the MIMO.LRCT protocol by including this range proof analysis.
- We apply our concrete bounds to derive preliminary scheme parameters for regular RingCT transactions that support 64-bit amounts along with fewer Multiple Input and Output wallets. This analysis serves as a benchmark for future practical implementations.

The organisation of this work is as follows. Section 1.2 presents CryptoNote and RingCT protocols literature. After introducing the notation and concepts used in our work in Sect. 2, we define the MIMO.LRCT as well as its security model in Sect. 3. Section 4 involves the concrete construction of the homomorphic commitment and the MIMO.L2RS signature schemes, then Sect. 5 illustrates the construction of MIMO.LRCT. Sections 6 and 7 point out the MIMO.LRCT's security and performance analyses, respectively. We note that all proofs of this paper are shown in the full version which is in [1].

1.2   Related Work

Evaluations [20,26] of CryptoNote have discovered serious vulnerabilities which impact the privacy of the involved parties in the transactions. Therefore, the Ring Confidential Transactions RingCT [25] protocol was devised to address these issues. The RingCT extends the CryptoNote scheme by using a new class of linkable ring signature called *Multi-layered Linkable Spontaneous Anonymous Group Signature* (MLSAG) [18]. This signature is spontaneous (or *ad-hoc*), which removes the dependency of a trusted third party and group members are unaware of belonging to a determined group, thereby enhancing the *anonymity* property. It is also multilayered, meaning that it enables multiple input and output wallets in transactions. The security of RingCT is ameliorated by introducing the Confidential Transactions [21], which enables amounts to be hidden by using the *Pedersen Commitment* [27] technique. This cryptographic primitive enables a party to commit to a chosen secret value while keeping it hidden to other parties, where this commitment can later be opened. Such a primitive offers homomorphic properties allowing parties to prove the account balance by computing homomorphically input and output accounts to show that their result is zero. RingCT added another verification mechanism for the committed output amounts which was called *range proof*, guaranteeing that this amount lies in a range of *non-negative* values and avoiding the creation of *free money*. Bulletproofs [5] is an efficient technique for this range preservation.

RingCT v2.0 [30] was later proposed. It provided sound security analysis of the (RingCT) protocol as well as improved the size of the signature by using one-way accumulators [3] along with signatures of knowledge "SoK" [7]. However, it requires a trusted setup for its accumulator to achieve the signature constant size. The first post-quantum RingCT protocol was proposed in [2], where the authors named it *Lattice RingCT v1.0*. This construction uses lattice-based cryptography to design a new *Linkable Ring Signature*, which is called *Lattice-based Linkable Ring Signature* (L2RS). The L2RS follows the well known Fiat-Shamir [14] transformation signature: *Bimodal Lattice Signature Scheme* (BLISS) [12], a practical and secure lattice-based signature scheme. The L2RS offers computational security as per the hardness of lattice assumptions for *unforgeability, linkability* and *non-slanderability*, it also achieves unconditional *anonymity*. However, the proposed *Lattice RingCT v1.0* showed no security definition or proofs, and transactions were restricted to Single Input and Single Output wallets.

2   Preliminaries

The polynomial ring $\mathcal{R} = \mathbb{Z}[x]/f(x)$, where $f(x) = x^n + 1$ with n being a power of 2. The ring $\mathcal{R}_q$ is then defined to be the quotient ring $\mathcal{R}_q = \mathcal{R}/(q\mathcal{R}) = \mathbb{Z}_q[x]/f(x)$, where $\mathbb{Z}_q$ denotes the set of all positive integers modulo q (a prime number $q = 1 \bmod 2n$) in the interval $[-q/2, q/2]$. The challenge space $\mathcal{S}_{n,\kappa}$, is the set of all binary vectors of length n and weight κ. A hash function modeled as Random Oracle Model (ROM), H_1 with range $\mathcal{S}_{n,\kappa} \subseteq \mathcal{R}_{2q}$. When we use $x \leftarrow D$, it means that x is chosen uniformly from the distribution D. The discrete Gaussian distribution over $\mathbb{Z}^m$ with standard deviation $\sigma \in \mathbb{R}$ and center at zero, is defined by $D_\sigma^m(\mathbf{x}) = \rho_\sigma(\mathbf{x})/\rho_\sigma(\mathbb{Z}^m)$, where ρ_σ is the m-dimensional Gaussian function $\rho_\sigma(\mathbf{x}) = \exp(-\|\mathbf{x}\|^2/(2\sigma^2))$. Vector transposition is denoted by $\mathbf{v}^T$. The hardness assumption of this work is the Module-SIS (Short Integer Solution) problem and is defined as follows.

Definition 1 ($MSIS_{q,m,k,\beta}^{\mathcal{K}}$ problem). *Let $\mathcal{K}$ be some uniform distribution over the ring $\mathcal{R}_q^{k \times m}$. Given a random matrix $\mathbf{A} \in \mathcal{R}_q^{k \times m}$ sampled from $\mathcal{K}$ distribution, find a non-zero vector $\mathbf{v} \in \mathcal{R}_q^{m \times 1}$ such that $\mathbf{Av} = 0$ and $\|\mathbf{v}\|_2 \leq \beta$, where $\|\cdot\|_2$ denotes the Euclidean norm.*

Lemma 1 (Rejection Sampling). *(Based on [12], Lemma 2.1). Let V be an arbitrary set, and $h : V \to \mathbb{R}$ and $f : \mathbb{Z}^m \to R$ be probability distributions. If $g_v : \mathbb{Z}^m \to R$ is a family of probability distributions indexed by $v \in V$ with the property that there exists a $M \in \mathbb{R}$ such that $\forall v \in V, \forall \mathbf{v} \in \mathbb{Z}^m, M \cdot g_v(\mathbf{z}) \geq f(\mathbf{z})$. Then the output distributions of the following two algorithms are identical:*

1. $v \leftarrow h, \mathbf{z} \leftarrow g_v, output(\mathbf{z}, v)$ *with probability* $f(\mathbf{z})/(M \cdot g_v(\mathbf{z}))$.
2. $v \leftarrow h, \mathbf{z} \leftarrow f, output(\mathbf{z}, v)$ *with probability* $1/M$.

Lemma 2 (Based on [4]). *Let $\mathcal{R} = \mathbb{Z}[X]/(X^n + 1)$ where $n > 1$ is a power of 2 and $0 < i, j < 2n - 1$. Then all the coefficients of $2(X^i - X^j)^{-1} \in \mathcal{R}$ are in $\{-1, 0, 1\}$. This implies that $\|2(X^i - X^j)^{-1}\| \leq \sqrt{n}$.*

Lemma 3. *For $a, b \in \mathcal{R}_q = \mathbb{Z}_q[X]/(X^n + 1)$ the following relations hold $\|a\| \leq \sqrt{n}\|a\|_\infty$, $\|a \cdot b\| \leq \sqrt{n}\|a\|_\infty \cdot \|b\|_\infty$, $\|a \cdot b\|_\infty \leq \|a\| \cdot \|b\|$.*

For detailed definitions of the homomorphic commitment scheme and the Fiat-Shamir non-interactive zero-knowledge proof, we refer the reader to full version of this paper in [1].

3 Ring Confidential Transaction Protocol (RCT)

The RCT protocol is defined based on the former RingCT 2.0 protocol in [30].

Definition 2 (Account or wallet). *A wallet has a public component "act" and a private component "ask". The act is composed of the user's pk (or a valid address) and the coin cn, while the ask is formed of the user's sk along with the coin-key ck.*

The RCT protocol has five PPT algorithms (RCT.Setup, RCT.KeyGen, RCT.Mint, RCT.Spend, RCT.Verify) as well as the correctness (RCT.Correctness). The RCT's algorithms are defined as follows:

- RCT.Setup: this PPT algorithm takes the security parameter λ and outputs the public parameters Pub-Params.
- RCT.KeyGen: this PPT algorithm uses the Pub-Params to produce a pair of keys, the public-key pk and the private-key sk.
- RCT.Mint: a PPT algorithm generating new coins by receiving Pub-Params and the amount \$. This algorithm outputs a coin **cn** and a coin-key **ck**.
- RCT.Spend: a PPT algorithm that receives the Pub-Params, a set of input wallets $\{IW_i\}_{i \in [w]}$ with w being the size of the ring, a user π's input wallets IW_π along with its set of secret keys K_π, a set of output addresses OA, some transaction string $\mu \in \{0, 1\}^*$, the output amount \$ and the set of output wallets OW. Then, this algorithm outputs: the transaction $TX = (\mu, IW, OW)$, the signature sig and a set of transaction/serial numbers TN, which is used to prevent the double spending coins.
- RCT.Verify: a deterministic PPT algorithm that takes as input the Pub-Params, the signature sig, the TX, and the TN and verifies if the transaction was legitimately generated and outputs either: Accept or Reject.

TRANSACTION CORRECTNESS REQUIREMENTS: RCT.Correctness ensures that an honest user (payer) is able to spend or transfer any of his accounts (wallets) into a group of destination accounts (payee), where this transaction is accepted with overwhelming probability by a verifier. Thus the correctness of RCT is guaranteed if for all PPT adversaries $\mathcal{A}$, if Pub-Params $\leftarrow$ RCT.Setup(1^λ), $(\mu, IW, OA) \leftarrow \mathcal{A}(\text{Pub-Params}, IW_\pi, K_\pi)$, with (IW_π, K_π), (pk, sk) $\leftarrow$ RCT.KeyGen(Pub-Params), (**cn**, **ck**) $\leftarrow$ RCT.Mint(Pub-Params, \$), and $(TX, \text{sig}, TN) \leftarrow$ RCT.Spend(μ, Pub-Params, $IW_\pi, K_\pi, IW, OA, \$_{(out)}$), it holds that: $\Pr[\text{RCT.Verify}(\text{sig}, TX, TN) = 1] = 1$.

3.1 Oracles for Adversaries

We now list all the adversarial oracles used in RCT, and we define them as:

- AddGen(i): on input a query number i, this oracle picks randomness τ_i, runs algorithm $(\mathsf{pk}_i, \mathsf{sk}_i) \leftarrow$ RCT.KeyGen(Pub-Params, τ_i), and returns the public-key or one-time address pk_i.
- ActGen($i, \$_i$): on input a query number i and an amount $\$_i$, it runs $(\mathbf{cn}_i, \mathbf{ck}_i) \leftarrow$ RCT.Mint(Pub-Params, $\$_i$). Then, ActGen adds i and the account $act_i = (\mathsf{pk}_i, \mathbf{cn}_i)$ to empty lists $\mathcal{I}$ and IW, respectively. ActGen outputs $(act_i, \mathbf{ck}_i)$ for the one-time address pk_i, where these addresses are added to a list $\mathcal{PK}$. The associated secret key with account act_i is defined as $ask_i \triangleq (\mathsf{sk}_i, \mathbf{ck}_i)$. With this ask_i, the challenger calls MIMO.L2RS.SigGen($\mathsf{sk}_i, \cdot, \cdot, \cdot$) to determine the transaction number TN_i of act_i and adds it to a list $\mathcal{TN}$.
- O-Spend($\mu, IW, IW_\pi, OA, \$_{(out)},$ Pub-Params): on input the transaction string μ, input accounts (wallets) IW containing IW_π and output addresses OA, it runs $(TX, \mathsf{sig}, TN) \leftarrow$ RCT.Spend($\mu, K_\pi, IW, IW_\pi, OA, \$_{(out)},$ Pub-Params) and adds the outputs to $\mathcal{T}$, where $IW_\pi \in IW$. We assume that at least one account/address in IW_π has not been corrupted. We define the set of transaction numbers in the RCT.Spend queries as $\mathcal{TN}^*$.
- Corrupt(i): on input query number $i \in \mathcal{I}$, uses account key ask_i to determine the transaction/serial number TN_i of account act_i with address pk_i, then adds TN_i and $(TN_i, \$_i)$ to lists $\mathcal{C}$ and $\mathcal{B}$ respectively and finally returns τ_i.

3.2 Threat Model

The protocol RCT is modeled in terms of *balance, anonymity* and *non-slanderability* for security analysis purposes, which are defined as follows.

Definition 3 (Balance). *This property requires that any malicious user cannot spend any account without her control and spend her own/controllable accounts with a larger output amount. This security property is guaranteed if for all PPT adversaries $\mathcal{A}$, if Pub-Params $\leftarrow$ RCT.Setup(1^λ) and $(\{IW_i^{(k)}\}_{i \in [w], k \in [N_{in}]}, \mathcal{T}) \leftarrow \mathcal{A}^{\mathsf{AddGen,ActGen,O\text{-}Spend,Corrupt}}($Pub-Params$)$, it holds that: $\Pr[\mathcal{A} \text{ wins}] = negl(\lambda)$, where adversaries' oracles are defined in Sect. 3.1. We have that $IW_i^{(k)} = \{\mathsf{pk}_{(in),i}^{(k)}, \mathbf{cn}_{(in),i}^{(k)}\}_{i \in [w], k \in [N_{in}]}$ and $\mathcal{T} = (TX, \mathsf{sig}, TN)$. These spends can be transferred to the challenger with the account address $\mathsf{pk}_{(out)} = \{\mathsf{pk}_{(out)}^{(j)}\}_{j \in [N_{out}]}$, where we assume not all of them are corrupted, and at least one of them is honest. This $\mathsf{pk}_{(out)}$ has been created by the AddGen oracle, so the challenger knows all balances of the spent accounts and output accounts involved in the adversarial spends $\mathcal{T}$. This means that $TX = (\mu, IW, OW)$ with $OW = \{OW^{(j)}\}_{j \in [N_{out}]} = \{\mathsf{pk}_{(out)}^{(j)}, \mathbf{cn}_{(out)}^{(j)}\}_{j \in [N_{out}]}$ being the output wallet corresponding to output account $\mathsf{pk}_{(out)}$. The adversary $\mathcal{A}$ wins this experiment if her outputs satisfy the following conditions: (a) RCT.Verify(TX, sig, TN) = 1, (b) $\sum_{k \in E_{(in)}} \$_{(in),\pi}^{(k)} < \sum_{j \in G_{(out)}} \$_{(out)}^{(j)}$, where we Let $\pi \in [w]$ s.t. π's row $\{\mathsf{pk}_{(in),\pi}^{(1)}, \ldots, \mathsf{pk}_{(in),\pi}^{(N_{in})}\}$ are* the ones that have $\{TN_\pi^{(1)}, \ldots, TN_\pi^{(N_{in})}\}$ which are found in ActGen, $E_{(in)}$ are the corrupted inputs, and $G_{(out)}$ are the not corrupted outputs in $\mathcal{T}$. For each $TN^{(k)}$ let $\$_{(in)}^{(k)}$ be the amount queried to ActGen at query i^* such that $TN_{i_k} = TN^{(k)}$ s.t. TN_{i_k} exist because $TN \subseteq \mathcal{TN}$, $\$_{(in)}^{(k)}$ is also defined as equal to zero if $IW_i^{(k)}$ is equal to some input wallet IW queried to O-Spend, using same TN, meaning that $IW_i^{(k)}$ has been spent; otherwise, it is defined as the amount queried to ActGen. (c) TN cannot be the output of previous queries to the O-Spend($\cdot$) (i.e. $TN \cap \mathcal{TN}^* = \emptyset$), and (d) $PK \subseteq \mathcal{PK}$, where $PK \triangleq \{pk_{(in),i}^{(k)}\}_{i\in[w],k\in[N_{in}]}$.

Our extended *anonymity* property captures two types of attacks (compared to one type in [30]) that depend on the adversary's choices for users $\pi_0, \pi_1 \in [w]$ and output amounts $\$_{(out),0}, \$_{(out),1}$. It starts with the user anonymity attack where the adversary selects $\pi_0 \neq \pi_1$ with $\$_{(out),0} = \$_{(out),1}$, while in the amount privacy attack this adversary chooses $\pi_0 = \pi_1$ with $\$_{(out),0} \neq \$_{(out),1}$. We formally define this property as:

Definition 4 (Anonymity). *This property requires that two proofs of knowledge with the same transaction string μ, input accounts IW, output addresses OA, distinct both output amounts ($\$_{(out),0}, \$_{(out),1}$) and spent accounts $IW_{\pi_0}, IW_{\pi_1} \in IW$ are indistinguishable, meaning that the spender's accounts and amounts are successfully hidden among all the honestly generated accounts. The protocol RCT is called anonymous if for all PPT adversaries $\mathcal{A} = (\mathcal{A}_1, \mathcal{A}_2)$, if Pub-Param $\leftarrow$ Setup(1^λ), $(\mu, IW_{\pi_0}, IW_{\pi_1}, IW, OA, \$_{(out),0}, \$_{(out),1}) \leftarrow \mathcal{A}_1^{AddGen,ActGen,O\text{-}Spend,Corrupt}$(Pub-Params), $b \leftarrow \{0,1\}$, $(TX^*, sig_b^*, TN^*) \leftarrow$ RCT.Spend($\mu, K_{\pi_b}, IW_{\pi_b}, IW, OA, \$_{(out)_b}$Pub-Params), and $b' \leftarrow \mathcal{A}_2^{O\text{-}Spend,Corrupt}$(Pub-Params, (TX^*, sig_b^*, TN^*)) it holds that: $\left|\Pr[b' = b :] - \frac{1}{2}\right|$, is negl($\lambda$), where adversaries' oracles are defined in Sect. 3.1. In addition, the following restrictions should be satisfied: (a) For all $b \in \{0,1\}$, any account in IW_{π_i} has not been corrupted and (b) Any query in the form of $(\cdot, IW_\pi, \cdot, \cdot)$, such that $IW_\pi \cap IW_{\pi_i} \neq \emptyset$ has not been issued to O-Spend oracle.*

Definition 5 (Non-slanderability). *This property requires that a malicious user cannot slander any honest user after observing an honestly generated spending. That is, it is infeasible for any malicious user to produce a valid spending that shares at least one transaction/serial number with a previously generated honest spending. The protocol RCT is non-slanderable if for all PPT adversaries $\mathcal{A}$, if Pub-Params $\leftarrow$ RCT.Setup(1^λ) and $((TX, sig, TN), (TX^*, sig^*, TN^*)) \leftarrow \mathcal{A}^{AddGen,ActGen,O\text{-}Spend,Corrupt}$(Pub-Params) it holds that: $\Pr[\mathcal{A} \text{ wins}] = negl(\lambda)$, where adversaries' oracles are defined in Sect. 3.1, and (TX, sig, TN) is one output of the oracle O-Spend for some (μ, IW_π, IW, OA). We say $\mathcal{A}$ succeeds if the output satisfies: (a) RCT.Verify(TX^*, sig^*, TN^*) = 1, (b) $(TX^*, sig^*, TN^*) \notin \mathcal{T}$, and (c) $TN \cap \mathcal{C} = \emptyset$ but $TN \cap TN^* \neq \emptyset$.*

4   Building Blocks Construction

In this section, we summarize the underlying lattice-based primitives that will be used in the construction of MIMO.LRCT. This includes a lattice-based homomorphic commitment scheme and a MIMO version of L2RS specified in [1].

4.1   Lattice-Based Commitment Construction

The MIMO.LRCT protocol requires a non-interactive homomorphic commitment (Com) as an essential primitive. We construct the three algorithms: (KeyGen, Com, Open), using the MIMO.L2RS scheme [1]:

- $\mathbf{A} \leftarrow$ KeyGen(1^λ): A PPT algorithm that produces a public commitment parameter $\mathbf{A} \in \mathcal{R}_q^{2 \times (m-1)}$ after receiving the security parameter (λ). In doing so, we call the MIMO.L2RS.Setup (from [1]) to generate $\mathbf{A} \in \mathcal{R}_q^{2 \times (m-1)}$.
- $\mathbf{c} \leftarrow$ Com$_\mathbf{A}$(m, sk): A PPT algorithm that receives the public parameter $\mathbf{A}$ (from KeyGen), the randomness sk and the message formed as $\overline{m} = (0, m)^T \in \mathcal{R}_q^{1 \times 2}$. This algorithm generates the commitment $\mathbf{c} \in \mathcal{R}_q^2$. The randomness sk $\in$ Dom$_{sk} \subseteq \mathcal{R}_q^{(m-1) \times 1}$ with every component chosen uniformly and independently with coefficients in $(-2^\gamma, 2^\gamma)$, is produced by calling the MIMO.L2RS.KeyGen (Algorithm 1) and the message m $\in$ Dom$_m = \mathcal{R}_q$, then the commitment $\mathbf{c} = $ Com$_\mathbf{A}$(m, sk) $= \mathbf{A} \cdot$ sk $+ \overline{m} \in \mathcal{R}_q^2$.
- $m' \leftarrow$ Open$_\mathbf{A}$(c, sk): A PPT algorithm receiving commitment $\mathbf{c}$ and randomness sk, and it outputs m'. A valid $\mathbf{c}$ is opened if ($m' = m$). This algorithm computes $\overline{m}' = (0, m')^T = $ Open$_\mathbf{A}$(c, sk) $= \mathbf{c} - \mathbf{A} \cdot$ sk.

Remark 1. Dom$_m$ is full and not a small subset $\mathcal{R}_q$, whereas Dom$_{sk}$ is only a small domain versus q. These adjustments help us to obtain better parameters than SISO.LRCT and security against out-of-range attacks.

This homomorphic commitment scheme performs the following operations:

$$\text{Com}_\mathbf{A}(m, sk) \boxed{\pm} \text{Com}_\mathbf{A}(m', sk') \triangleq \text{Com}_\mathbf{A}(m, sk) \pm \text{Com}_\mathbf{A}(m', sk') \bmod q$$
$$\triangleq \text{Com}_\mathbf{A}(m \pm m', sk \pm sk') \bmod q. \quad (1)$$

Theorem 1 (Hiding). *If $\frac{1}{2}\sqrt{\frac{q^{2n}}{2^{(\gamma+1)\cdot(m-1)\cdot n}}}$ is negligible in security parameter λ, then the above Com is information theoretically hiding.*

Theorem 2 (β–Binding). *The described Commitment Scheme is computationally β–binding if the $\mathbf{MSIS}_{q,m,k,2\beta}^\mathcal{K}$ problem is hard.*

4.2   Multiple-input Multiple-output Wallets L2RS (MIMO.L2RS)

We adapt all the notations from [2] into our MIMO.L2RS. The MIMO.L2RS signs a signature for multiple wallets, which means that it signs N_{in} L2RS signatures in parallel. This MIMO.L2RS is an extension of the single-input and single-output proposal from [2]. In such extension, we needed to modify the Lattice-based Linkable Ring Signature (L2RS) to be capable of signing multiple wallets. Precisely, we adjusted the key generation, the signature generation and the verification algorithms to sign the total number of input wallets that a user wants to transfer to some output wallets. We call these algorithms: MIMO.L2RS.KeyGen, MIMO.L2RS.SigGen and MIMO.L2RS.SigVer, and we describe them in Algorithms 1, 2 and 3, respectively.

Algorithm 1. MIMO.L2RS.KeyGen - Key-pair Generation $(\mathbf{a}, \mathbf{S})$

Input: Pub-Param: $\mathbf{A} \in \mathcal{R}_q^{2 \times (m-1)}$.
Output: $(\mathbf{a}, \mathbf{S})$, being the public-key and the private-key, respectively.
1: **procedure** MIMO.L2RS.KeyGen$(\mathbf{A})$
2:     Let $\mathbf{S}^T = (\mathbf{s}_1, \ldots, \mathbf{s}_{m-1}) \in \mathcal{R}_q^{1 \times (m-1)}$, where $\mathbf{s}_i \leftarrow (-2^\gamma, 2^\gamma)^n$, for $1 \leq i \leq m-1$
3:     Compute $\mathbf{a} = (\mathbf{a}_1, \mathbf{a}_2)^T = \mathbf{A} \cdot \mathbf{S} \bmod q \in \mathcal{R}_q^2$.
4:     **return** $(\mathbf{a}, \mathbf{S})$.

Algorithm 2. MIMO.L2RS.SigGen - MIMO Signature Generation $\sigma_{L'}(\mu)$

Input: $\{\mathbf{S}_{(in),\pi}^{(k)}\}_{k \in [N_{in}+1]}, \mu, L'$ as in (5), and Pub-Params.
Output: $\sigma_{L'}(\mu) = \left(\mathbf{c}_1, \{\mathbf{t}_1^{(k)}, \ldots, \mathbf{t}_w^{(k)}\}_{k \in [N_{in}+1]}, \{\mathbf{h}^{(k)}\}_{k \in [N_{in}]} \right)$
1: **procedure** MIMO.L2RS.SigGen$(\mathbf{S}_{(in),\pi}^{(k)}, \mu, L', \text{Pub-Params})$
2:     **for** $(1 \leq k \leq N_{in}+1)$ **do**
3:         Set $\mathbf{H}_{2q}^{(k)} = (2 \cdot \mathbf{H}, -2 \cdot \mathbf{h}^{(k)} + \mathbf{q}) \in \mathcal{R}_{2q}^{2 \times m}$, where $\mathbf{h}^{(k)} = \mathbf{H} \cdot \mathbf{S}_{(in),\pi}^{(k)} \in \mathcal{R}_q^2$.
4:         Call L2RS.Lift$(\mathbf{A}, \mathbf{a}_{(in),\pi}^{(k)})$ to obtain $\mathbf{A}_{2q,\pi}^{(k)} = (2 \cdot \mathbf{A}, -2 \cdot \mathbf{a}_{(in),\pi}^{(k)} + \mathbf{q}) \in \mathcal{R}_{2q}^{2 \times m}$.
5:         Let $\mathbf{u}^{(k)} = (u_1, \ldots, u_m)^T$, where $u_i \leftarrow D_\sigma^n$, for $1 \leq i \leq m$.
6:         Compute $\mathbf{c}_{\pi+1} = H_1 \left(L', \{\mathbf{H}_{2q}^{(k)}\}_{k \in [N_{in}+1]}, \mu, \{\mathbf{A}_{2q,\pi}^{(k)} \cdot \mathbf{u}^{(k)}\}_{k \in [N_{in}+1]}, \{\mathbf{H}_{2q}^{(k)} \cdot \mathbf{u}^{(k)}\}_{k \in [N_{in}+1]} \right)$.
7:         **for** $(i = \pi+1, \pi+2, \ldots, w, 1, 2, \ldots, \pi-1)$ **do**
8:             **for** $(1 \leq k \leq N_{in}+1)$ **do**
9:                 Call L2RS.Lift$(\mathbf{A}, \mathbf{a}_{(in),i}^{(k)})$ to obtain $\mathbf{A}_{2q,i}^{(k)} = (2 \cdot \mathbf{A}, -2 \cdot \mathbf{a}_{(in),i}^{(k)} + \mathbf{q}) \in \mathcal{R}_{2q}^{2 \times m}$.
10:                Let $\mathbf{t}_i^{(k)} = (t_{i,1}, \ldots, t_{i,m})^T$, where $t_{i,j} \leftarrow D_\sigma^n$, for $1 \leq j \leq m$.
11:                Compute $\mathbf{c}_{i+1} = H_1 \left(L', \{\mathbf{H}_{2q}^{(k)}\}_{k \in [N_{in}+1]}, \mu, \{\mathbf{A}_{2q,i}^{(k)} \cdot \mathbf{t}_i^{(k)} + \mathbf{q} \cdot \mathbf{c}_i\}_{k \in [N_{in}+1]}, \{\mathbf{H}_{2q}^{(k)} \cdot \mathbf{t}_i^{(k)} + \mathbf{q} \cdot \mathbf{c}_i\}_{k \in [N_{in}+1]} \right)$.
12:        **for** $(1 \leq k \leq N_{in}+1)$ **do**
13:            Choose $b^{(k)} \leftarrow \{0,1\}$.
14:            Let $\mathbf{t}_\pi^{(k)} \leftarrow \mathbf{u}^{(k)} + \mathbf{S}_{2q,\pi}^{(k)} \cdot \mathbf{c}_\pi \cdot (-1)^{b^{(k)}}$, where $\mathbf{S}_{2q,\pi}^{(k)} = [(\mathbf{S}_\pi^{(k)})^T, 1]^T$.
15:            **Continue** with prob. $\left(M \exp \left(-\frac{\|\mathbf{S}_{2q,\pi}^{(k)} \cdot \mathbf{c}_\pi\|^2}{2\sigma^2} \right) \cosh \left(\frac{\langle \mathbf{t}_\pi^{(k)}, \mathbf{S}_{2q,\pi}^{(k)} \cdot \mathbf{c}_\pi \rangle}{\sigma^2} \right) \right)^{-1}$ otherwise **Restart**.
16:    **return** $\sigma_{L'}(\mu) = \left(\mathbf{c}_1, \{\mathbf{t}_1^{(k)}, \ldots, \mathbf{t}_w^{(k)}\}_{k \in [N_{in}+1]}, \{\mathbf{h}^{(k)}\}_{k \in [N_{in}]} \right)$.

Algorithm 3. MIMO.L2RS.SigVer - MIMO Signature Verification

Input: $\sigma_{L'}(\mu)$ as in (8), L' as in (5), μ, and Pub-Params.
Output: Accept or Reject
1: **procedure** MIMO.L2RS.SIGVER($\sigma_{L'}(\mu)$, L', Pub-Params)
2:     **for** $(1 \leq k \leq N_{in} + 1)$ **do**
3:         **if** $\mathbf{H}_{2q}^{(k)} = (2 \cdot \mathbf{H}, -2 \cdot \mathbf{h}^{(k)} + \mathbf{q}) \in \mathcal{R}_{2q}^{2 \times m}$ **then** Continue
4:     **for** $(i = 1, \ldots, w)$ **do**
5:         **for** $(1 \leq k \leq N_{in} + 1)$ **do**
6:             Call L2RS.Lift$(\mathbf{A}, \mathbf{a}_{(in),i}^{(k)})$ to obtain $\mathbf{A}_{2q,i}^{(k)} = (2 \cdot \mathbf{A}, -2 \cdot \mathbf{a}_i^{(k)} + \mathbf{q}) \in \mathcal{R}_{2q}^{2 \times m}$.
7:         **if** $c_{i+1} = H_1\left(L', \{\mathbf{H}_{2q}^{(k)}\}_{k \in [N_{in}+1]}, \mu, \{\mathbf{A}_{2q,i}^{(k)} \cdot \mathbf{t}_i^{(k)} + \mathbf{q} \cdot c_i\}_{k \in [N_{in}+1]}, \{\mathbf{H}_{2q}^{(k)} \cdot \mathbf{t}_i^{(k)} + \mathbf{q} \cdot c_i\}_{k \in [N_{in}+1]}\right)$ **then** Continue
8:             **else if** $\|\mathbf{t}_i^{(k)}\|_2 \leq \beta_v$ (the acceptance bound based on [12]) **then** Continue
9:             **else if** $\|\mathbf{t}_i^{(k)}\|_\infty < q/4$ **then** Continue
10:     **if** $c_1 = H_1\left(L', \{\mathbf{H}_{2q}^{(k)}\}_{k \in [N_{in}+1]}, \mu, \{\mathbf{A}_{2q,w}^{(k)} \cdot \mathbf{t}_i^{(k)} + \mathbf{q} \cdot c_w\}_{k \in [N_{in}+1]}, \{\mathbf{h}_{2q}^{(k)} \cdot \mathbf{t}_w^{(k)} + \mathbf{q} \cdot c_w\}_{k \in [N_{in}+1]}\right)$ **then** Accept
11:     **else** Reject
12:     **return** Accept or Reject

4.3 MIMO.L2RS Security Properties

The security properties of the MIMO.L2RS are inherited from the L2RS' security analysis. By appropriately modifying these analysis, we can obtain the same results for unforgeability, anonymity, linkability and non-slanderability, which are shown in Theorems (2, 3, 4, 5 from [2]), respectively. The following proposition summarises these inherited properties:

Proposition 1. *If* $\mathbf{MSIS}_{q,m,k,\beta}^{\mathcal{K}}$ *problem (with* $\beta = 2\beta_v$*) is hard and* $\sqrt{\frac{q^{4n}}{2^{(\gamma+1) \cdot (m-1) \cdot n}}}$ *is negligible in* n*, then the MIMO.L2RS achieves one-time unforgeability, anonymity, linkability and non-slanderability as in Definitions (3, 4, 5, 6 from [2]).*

We also use the MIMO.L2RS signature scheme as a Proof of Knowledge (PoK) to accomplish, in part, the MIMO.LRCT's balance property. This proof is formalised, namely as:

Proposition 2. *The MIMO.L2RS.SigGen and MIMO.L2RS.SigVer which are described in Algorithms 2 and 3, respectively, are a Fiat-Shamir Non-Interactive Proof of Knowledge in the Random Oracle Model (from [1]) for the relations* R_{PoK} *and* R'_{PoK} *that we represent as:*

$$R_{PoK} \triangleq \left\{ \begin{array}{l} \{\mathbf{a}_{(in),i}^{(k)}, \mathbf{cn}_{(in),i}^{(k)}, \mathbf{cn}_{(out)}^{(j)}, \mu\}; \{\mathbf{S}_{(in),i}^{(k)}, \mathbf{ck}_{(in),i}^{(k)}, \mathbf{ck}_{(out)}^{(j)}, \$_{in}, \$_{out}\} : \\ \exists i \in [w] \; s.t. \; \mathbf{a}_{(in),i}^{(N_{in}+1)} = \mathsf{Com}_{\mathbf{A}}(0, \mathbf{S}_{(in),i}^{(N_{in}+1)}); \|\mathbf{S}_{(in),i}^{(N_{in}+1)}\| \leq \beta_{wit} \end{array} \right\}$$

$$R'_{PoK} \triangleq \left\{ \begin{array}{l} \{\mathbf{a}_{(in),i}^{(k)}, \mathbf{cn}_{(in),i}^{(k)}, \mathbf{cn}_{(out)}^{(j)}, \mu'\}; \{\mathbf{S}_{(in),i}^{(k)}, \mathbf{ck}_{(in),i}^{(k)}, \mathbf{ck}_{(out)}^{(j)}, \$_{in}, \$_{out}\} : \\ \exists z \in [w] \; s.t. \; \mathbf{v}_z^{(N_{in}+1)} = (\mathbf{v}_{z,(1)}^{(N_{in}+1)}, \mathbf{v}_{z,(2)}^{(N_{in}+1)})^T; \\ \mathbf{a}_{(in),z}^{(N_{in}+1)} \cdot \mathbf{v}_{z,(2)}^{N_{in}+1} = \mathsf{Com}_{\mathbf{A}}(0, \mathbf{v}_{z,(1)}^{(N_{in}+1)}); \|\mathbf{v}_z^{(N_{in}+1)}\| \leq \beta'_{wit} \end{array} \right\}$$

where $\beta_{wit} = 3 \cdot 2^{\gamma}$ is said to be the honest prover's witness norm and $\beta'_{wit} = 2 \cdot \beta_v$ being the extracted malicious prover's witness norm. β_v is the acceptance bound of $\mathbf{t}$ from Algorithm 3 and $\mathbf{a}_{(in),i}^{(N_{in}+1)}$ is defined in (6).

5   MIMO Lattice-Based RingCT Construction

In this section, we construct the MIMO Lattice-based RingCT (MIMO.LRCT) protocol (Table 1 shows the MIMO.LRCT's notations), where one is allowed to have multiple (IW) and to spend them into multiple (OW). Furthermore, two sub-protocols are needed to support the MIMO.LRCT's threat model, which are: MIMO.L2RS security properties (Subsect. 4.3) and range preservation (Subsect. 5.1). MIMO scheme works using a set of algorithms MIMO.LRCT = (MIMO.LRCT.Setup, MIMO.LRCT.KeyGen, MIMO.LRCT.Mint, MIMO.LRCT.Spend, MIMO.LRCT.Verify) and they are listed as:

1. (Pub-Params) $\leftarrow$ MIMO.LRCT.Setup(λ): On input the security parameter λ, this algorithm calls MIMO.L2RS.Setup (from [1]) and outputs the public parameters $\mathbf{A} \in \mathcal{R}_q^{2 \times (m-1)}$ and $\mathbf{H} \in \mathcal{R}_q^{2 \times (m-1)}$.

Table 1. Notation of the Lattice RingCT v2.0

Notation	Description
act	Account or Wallet "Public part" $= (\mathsf{pk}, \mathbf{cn}) \in \mathcal{R}_q^2 \times \mathcal{R}_q^2$
ask	Account or Wallet "Private part" $= (\mathsf{sk}, \mathbf{ck}) \in \mathcal{R}_q^2 \times \mathcal{R}_q^2$
$\mathcal{S}_{n,\kappa}$	Binary vectors of length n of weight κ
$\$$	Amount $\in \mathcal{S}_{n,\kappa}$
$\$_{(in)}$	Group of input amounts $\$_{(in)}^{(k)}$ for $k \in [N_{in}]$
$\$_{(out)}$	Group of output amounts $\$_{(out)}^{(j)}$ for $j \in [N_{out}]$
$\ell_{\$}$	The bit-length of $\$$
w	Number of users in the ring
N_{in}	Number of input wallets of a user
IW_i	Input wallet of the i-th user $act_i = \left\{ \mathsf{pk}_{(in),i}^{(k)}, \mathbf{cn}_{(in),i}^{(k)} \right\}_{k \in [N_{in}]}$
IW	Set of input wallet $= \{IW_i\}_{i \in [w]}$
IW_π	Input wallet of user $\pi = \left\{ \mathsf{pk}_{(in),\pi}^{(k)}, \mathbf{cn}_{(in),\pi}^{(k)} \right\}_{k \in [N_{in}]}$
K_π	User π's private-keys $= ask_\pi = \left\{ \mathsf{sk}_{(in),\pi}^{(k)}, \mathbf{ck}_{(in),\pi}^{(k)} \right\}_{k \in [N_{in}]}$
N_{out}	Number of output wallets
OW	Set of output wallet $= \{OW^{(j)}\}_{j \in [N_{out}]} = \{\mathsf{pk}_{(out)}^{(j)}, \mathbf{cn}_{(out)}^{(j)}\}_{j \in [N_{out}]}$
OA	Set of output addresses $= \left\{ \mathsf{pk}_{(out)}^{(j)} \right\}_{j \in [N_{out}]}$
TX	Transaction $= (\mu, IW, OW)$
TN	Set of serial/transaction numbers (linking tag)

In this work, we consider that all users have a fixed number of input wallets N_{in}.

2. $(\mathbf{a}, \mathbf{S}) \leftarrow$ MIMO.LRCT.KeyGen($\mathbf{A}$): Given the public parameter $\mathbf{A} \in \mathcal{R}_q^{2 \times (m-1)}$, it runs MIMO.L2RS.KeyGen (Algorithm 1) and outputs a pair of keys, the public-key or one-time address pk as $\mathbf{a} \in \mathcal{R}_q^2$ and the private-key sk as $\mathbf{S} \in \mathcal{R}_q^{(m-1) \times 1}$. A homomorphic commitment is generated as $\mathbf{a} = \mathsf{Com}_\mathbf{A}(\mathbf{0}, \mathbf{S}) = \mathbf{A} \cdot \mathbf{S} + \mathbf{0} \bmod q \in \mathcal{R}_q^2$.

3. $(\mathbf{cn}, \mathbf{ck}) \leftarrow$ MIMO.LRCT.Mint($\mathbf{A}, \$$): It receives the public parameter $\mathbf{A}$ and input amount $\$ \in [0, 2^{\ell_\$} - 1]$. It computes a coin $\mathbf{cn}$, by choosing a coin-key $\mathbf{ck} \in \mathsf{Dom}_\mathbf{S}$, where every component of $\mathbf{ck}$ is chosen uniformly and independently, then compute $\mathbf{cn}$ (as below) and this algorithm returns $(\mathbf{cn}, \mathbf{ck})$:

$$\mathbf{cn} \triangleq \mathsf{Com}_\mathbf{A}(\$, \mathbf{ck}) = \mathbf{A} \cdot \mathbf{ck} + \overline{\$} \bmod q \in \mathcal{R}_q^2 \text{ with } \overline{\$} = (0, \$)^T \in \mathcal{R}_q^{1 \times 2}. \quad (2)$$

4. $(TX, \mathsf{sig}, TN) \leftarrow$ MIMO.LRCT.Spend($\mu, IW, IW_\pi, K_\pi, OA, \$_{(out)}^{(j)}$, Pub-Params):
   This algorithm spends/transfers amounts from the user π's input wallets to some output wallets. We denote the user π who successfully created its input wallets IW_π, based on determine amounts $\$_{(in)}$. Note that notation of these parameters are defined in Table 1, and this spend algorithm is briefly described in Algorithm 4. Then, π selects the recipients' valid public keys or output addresses OA where π wants to spend his/her amount. To do so π performs the following steps:

   (a) π receives $\{\$_{(out)}^{(j)}\}_{j \in [N_{out}]}$, with $\$_{(out)}^{(j)} \in [0, \ldots, 2^{\ell_\$} - 1]$, for $j \in [N_{out}]$, such balance satisfies, we call this condition *amount preservation*. This checks that input amounts are equal to output amounts, by checking if the following equality holds:

   $$\sum_{k=1}^{N_{in}} \$_{(in),\pi}^{(k)} = \sum_{j=1}^{N_{out}} \$_{(out)}^{(j)}. \quad (3)$$

   π then runs MIMO.LRCT.Mint($\mathbf{A}, \$_{(out)}^{(j)}$) for $j \in [N_{out}]$ and obtain $(\mathbf{cn}_{(out)}^{(j)}, \mathbf{ck}_{(out)}^{(j)})_{j \in [N_{out}]}$, which define the output wallets as

   $$OW = \{OW^{(j)}\}_{j \in [N_{out}]} = \{\mathbf{a}_{(out)}^{(j)}, \mathbf{cn}_{(out)}^{(j)}\}_{j \in [N_{out}]}. \quad (4)$$

   Then, the output coin-keys and amounts $\{\mathbf{ck}_{(out)}^{(j)}, \$_{(out)}^{(j)}\}_{j \in [N_{out}]}$ are securely sent to users with valid $OA^j = \{\mathbf{a}_{(out)}^{(j)}\}_{j \in [N_{out}]}$.

   (b) User π selects $(w - 1)$ input wallets from the blockchain which he/she uses to anonymously transfer her/his input wallets $\{IW_\pi^{(k)}\}_{k \in [N_{in}]}$. Then, a preliminary ring signature list is built as $IW = \{IW_i\}_{i \in [w]} = \{\mathbf{a}_{(in),i}^{(k)}, \mathbf{cn}_{(in),i}^{(k)}\}_{i \in [w], k \in [N_{in}]}$.

   (c) π adds a record to IW_i in order to homomorphically compute and verify the *amount preservation*; this uses the homomorphic commitment scheme (defined in Sect. 4). The result of this computation is a commitment to zero, where the user π is only able to obtain since he/she knows both

IW_π and OW. This new record is placed in the position $(N_{in} + 1)$ and then a list L' is defined as:

$$L' = \left\{ \mathbf{a}_{(in),i}^{(k)} \right\}_{i \in [w], k \in [N_{in}+1]}, \tag{5}$$

with $\mathbf{a}_{(in),i}^{(N_{in}+1)} \triangleq \mathsf{Com_A}\left(\sum_{k=1}^{N_{in}} \$_{(in),i}^{(k)} - \sum_{j=1}^{N_{out}} \$_{(out)}^{(j)}, \mathbf{S}_{(in),i}^{(N_{in}+1)} \right)$, where $\mathbf{S}_{(in),i}^{(N_{in}+1)} \triangleq \sum_{k=1}^{N_{in}} \mathbf{S}_{(in),i}^{(k)} + \mathbf{ck}_{(in),i}^{(k)} - \sum_{j=1}^{N_{out}} \mathbf{ck}_{(out)}^{(j)} \in \mathcal{R}_q^{(m-1) \times 1}$. This implies that

$$\mathbf{a}_{(in),i}^{(N_{in}+1)} = \sum_{k=1}^{N_{in}} \mathbf{a}_{(in),i}^{(k)} + \mathbf{cn}_{(in),i}^{(k)} - \sum_{j=1}^{N_{out}} \mathbf{cn}_{(out)}^{(j)}. \tag{6}$$

Note that if the *amount preservation* conditions (3) and (7) (for every $k \in [N_{in}]$) are achieved, then $\mathbf{a}_{(in),i}^{(N_{in}+1)} = \mathsf{Com_A}(0, \mathbf{S}_{(in),i}^{(N_{in}+1)})$.

$$\mathbf{a}_{(in),i}^{(k)} = \mathsf{Com_A}(0, \mathbf{S}_{(in),i}^{(k)}) = \mathbf{A} \cdot \mathbf{S}_{(in),i}^{(k)} + \mathbf{0} \quad \mathrm{mod}\ q \in \mathcal{R}_q^2. \tag{7}$$

(d) To sign the transaction, we use the π's private-keys: $\{\mathbf{S}_{(in),\pi}^{(k)}\}_{k \in [N_{in}+1]}$, the list L' and a transaction string $\mu \in \{0,1\}^*$. Then, we run MIMO.L2RS.SigGen (Algorithm 2) which outputs:

$$\sigma_{L'}(\mu) = \left(\mathbf{c}_1, \{\mathbf{t}_1^{(k)}, \ldots, \mathbf{t}_w^{(k)}\}_{k \in [N_{in}+1]}, \{\mathbf{h}^{(k)}\}_{k \in [N_{in}]} \right). \tag{8}$$

(e) Decompose $\$_{(out)}^{(j)}$ into its binary representation, i.e. $\$_{(out)}^{(j)} = (b_0^{(j)}, \ldots, b_{l_\$}^{(j)})$ and run MIMO.LRCT.Mint$(\mathbf{A}, b_i^{(j)})$ for each $i \in [0, l_\$]$ to obtain $\mathbf{ck}_{(out),i}^{(j)}$ and $\mathbf{cn}_{(out),i}^{(j)}$.

(f) We show that the output amount lies in a non-zero range value, by running a *range proof* (see Sect. 5.1). This proof outputs: $\sigma_{range}^{(j)} = \mathcal{P}_{range}\left(\mathbf{cn}_{(out)}^{(j)}, \{b_{(out),i}^{(j)}, \mathbf{ck}_{(out),i}^{(j)}\}_{i=0}^{l_\$ - 1}, \$_{(out)}^{(j)}, \mathbf{ck}_{(out)}^{(j)}, \right)$, with $\sigma_{range}^{(j)} = \left(\{\sigma_{OR}^{(j)}, \mathbf{cn}_{(out),i}^{(j)}, \sigma_{PoK^*}^{(j)}\}_{j \in [N_{out}], i \in [0, l_\$ - 1]} \right)$.

(g) We set the transaction TX as (μ, IW, OW) and $TN = \{\mathbf{h}^{(k)}\}_{k \in [N_{in}]}$. This algorithm outputs TX, TN, $\mathrm{sig}_\pi = (\sigma_{L'}(\mu), \{\sigma_{range}^{(j)}\}_{j \in [N_{out}]})$.

5. (*Accept/Reject*) $\leftarrow$ MIMO.LRCT.Verify$(TX, \mathrm{sig}_\pi, TN)$: This algorithm calls MIMO.L2RS.SigVer$(\mathrm{sig}_{\pi,1}, L', \mathsf{Pub\text{-}Params})$ (Algorithm 3) with $\mathrm{sig}_{\pi,1} = \sigma_{L'}(\mu)$, and on input $\mathrm{sig}_{\pi,2} = \{\sigma_{range}^{(j)}\}_{j \in [N_{out}]}$, it runs $\mathcal{V}_{range}$ (Sect. 5.1). This MIMO.LRCT.Verify outputs *Accept* if both MIMO.L2RS.SigVer and $\mathcal{V}_{range}$ output *Accept*, else it outputs *Reject*.

Algorithm 4. MIMO.LRCT.Spend

Input: $(\mu, IW, IW_\pi, K_\pi, OA, \$_{(out)}^{(j)}, \text{Pub-Params})$, being the message, the input wallets, π's input wallet, π's private keys, the output addresses, the output amount and the public parameter, respectively.

Output: $(TX, \sigma_{L'}(\mu), TN)$

1: **procedure** MIMO.LRCT.SPEND$(\mu, IW, IW_\pi, K_\pi, OA, \$_{(out)}^{(j)}, \text{Pub-Params})$

2:     User π selects $\{\$_{(out)}^{(j)}\}_{j \in [N_{out}]}$ such that (3) is satisfied.

3:     User π runs MIMO.LRCT.Mint$\left(\mathbf{A}, \$_{(out)}^{(j)}\right)$ for $j \in [N_{out}]$ to generate $(\mathbf{cn}_{(out)}^{(j)}, \mathbf{ck}_{(out)}^{(j)})$ and sets OW as in (4).

4:     User π sends securely coin-keys and amounts $\{\mathbf{ck}_{(out)}^{(j)}, \$_{(out)}^{(j)}\}_{j \in [N_{out}]}$ to user's $OA^j = \mathbf{a}_{(out)}^{(j)}$ for $j \in [N_{out}]$.

5:     Create the list of input wallets $IW = \{IW_i\}_{i \in [w]} = \{\mathbf{a}_{(in),i}^{(k)}, \mathbf{cn}_{(in),i}^{(k)}\}_{i \in [w], k \in [N_{in}]}$.

6:     Let $L' = \{\mathbf{a}_{(in),i}^{(k)}\}_{i \in [w], k \in [N_{in}+1]}$, where $\mathbf{a}_{(in),i}^{(k)}$ are defined in (7) and (6) for $1 \leq k \leq N_{in}$ and $k = N_{in} + 1$, respectively.

7:     Call MIMO.L2RS.SigGen$\left(\{\mathbf{S}_{(in),\pi}^{(k)}\}_{k \in [N_{in}+1]}, L', \mu, \text{Pub-Params}\right)$ and obtain $\sigma_{L'}(\mu)$ as in (8).

8:     Decompose $\$_{(out)}^{(j)} = (b_0^{(j)}, \ldots, b_{l_\$}^{(j)})$ and run MIMO.LRCT.Mint$(\mathbf{A}, b_i^{(j)})$ for each $i \in [0, l_\$]$ to obtain $\mathbf{ck}_{out,i}^{(j)}$ and $\mathbf{cn}_{(out),i}^{(j)}$.

9:     Run $\sigma_{range}^{(j)} \leftarrow \mathcal{P}_{range}\left(\mathbf{cn}_{(out)}^{(j)}, \{b_{(out),i}^{(j)}, \mathbf{ck}_{(out),i}^{(j)}\}_{i=0}^{l_\$-1}, \$_{(out)}^{(j)}, \mathbf{ck}_{(out)}^{(j)},\right)$ for $j \in [N_{out}]$.

10:     Set $\mathbf{sig}_\pi = (\sigma_{L'}(\mu), \{\sigma_{range}^{(j)}\}_{j \in [N_{out}]})$.

11:     Let $TX = (\mu, IW, OW)$ and $TN = \{\mathbf{h}^{(k)}\}_{k \in [N_{in}+1]}$.

12:     **return** $(TX, \mathbf{sig}_\pi, TN)$

5.1 Range Preservation

In this section, we present a range proof for the statement that an amount $\$ \in \mathcal{S}_{n,\kappa}$ belongs to $[0, 2^{\ell_\$} - 1]$. To do so, we need first to prove that $\$$ has the following binary representation $\$ = \sum_{i=0}^{\ell_\$-1} 2^i b_i$, where $b_i \in \{0, 1\}$. To prove that b_i, for $1 \leq i \leq \ell_\$ - 1$, is binary, we use an OR proof introduced by [11] but adapted to our commitment scheme, defined in Sect. 4.

Binary Proof [11] We want to prove $R_{OR} \triangleq R_0 \lor R_1$ and the corresponding relaxed relation $R'_{OR} \triangleq R'_0 \lor R'_1$, where

$$R_0 \triangleq \{(\mathbf{cn}, \mathbf{ck}) \in \mathcal{R}_q^2 \times \mathcal{R}_q^{(m-1)\times 1}, \mathbf{cn} = \mathbf{A} \cdot \mathbf{ck} + 0, \|\mathbf{ck}\| \leq B_{OR}\},$$

$$R_1 \triangleq \{(\mathbf{cn}, \mathbf{ck}) \in \mathcal{R}_q^2 \times \mathcal{R}_q^{(m-1)\times 1}, \mathbf{cn} = \mathbf{A} \cdot \mathbf{ck} + 1, \|\mathbf{ck}\| \leq B_{OR}\},$$

$$R'_0 \triangleq \{(\mathbf{cn}, \mathbf{ck}, f), f \cdot \mathbf{cn} = \mathbf{A} \cdot \mathbf{ck} + 0 \cdot f, \|\mathbf{ck}\| \leq B'_{OR}, \|f\| \leq 2\sqrt{\kappa}\},$$

$$R'_1 \triangleq \{(\mathbf{cn}, \mathbf{ck}, f), f \cdot \mathbf{cn} = \mathbf{A} \cdot \mathbf{ck} + 1 \cdot f, \|\mathbf{ck}\| \leq B'_{OR}, \|f\| \leq 2\sqrt{\kappa}\},$$

for a public parameter $\mathbf{A} \in \mathcal{R}_q^{2\times(m-1)}$. We further let:

$$\mathcal{C}_0 \triangleq \{X^i \in \mathcal{R}_q, i = 0, \ldots, 2n-1\}, \tag{9}$$

with all the coefficients of $(X^i - X^j)^{-1}$ in $\{-1, 0, 1\}$ according to Lemma 2. The challenge space $\mathfrak{P}$ consists of the set of all permutations of dimension n, $\mathtt{Perm}(n)$, and a vector of κ bits, i.e. $\mathfrak{P} \triangleq \{p = (s, \mathbf{c}) \in \mathtt{Perm}(n) \times \{0, 1\}\}$. Each $p \in \mathfrak{P}$ permutes the exponents of a polynomial in $\mathcal{C}_0$ according to the permutation s as follows: Let $f, g \in \mathcal{C}_0$ be two monomials. In particular, if $f = X^{i_f}, g = X^{i_g}$ and $s(i_f) - i_g$, then we denote such a permutation $s(f) = g$. It holds $\Pr[p(f) = g] = 1/|\mathcal{C}_0|$. Let σ_{OR} and B_{OR} be two positive real numbers. We also need a collision resistant hash function H, mapping arbitrary inputs to the uniform distribution over the challenge space $\mathfrak{P}$. Note that the digit \$ can be encoded into a coefficient vector $\mathbf{b} = (b_0, \ldots, b_{\ell_\$-1}) \in \{0, 1\}^{\ell_\$}$ Our OR proof is defined in R'_{b_i} protocol in Table 2.

Table 2. ZKP- OR-Composition Π_{OR}-Protocol

$\mathcal{P}_{OR}(\mathbf{ck}, b \in \{0,1\})$	$\mathcal{V}_{OR}(\mathbf{cn} = (\mathbf{cn}^{(1)} \ldots \mathbf{cn}^{(\theta)}))$
for $j \in [\theta]$ compute $\quad f^{(j)}_{1-b} \leftarrow \mathcal{C}_0, \mathbf{r}^{(j)}_{1-b} \leftarrow D^{n(m-1)}_{\sigma_{OR}}$ $\quad \mathbf{u}^{(j)} \leftarrow D^{n(m-1)}_{\sigma_{OR}}$ $\quad \mathbf{a}^{(j)}_b = \mathbf{A} \cdot \mathbf{u}^{(j)}$ $\quad \mathbf{a}^{(j)}_{1-b} = \mathbf{A} \cdot \mathbf{r}^{(j)}_{1-b} - f^{(j)}_{1-b} \cdot \mathbf{cn}^{(j)} + f_{1-b}(1-b)$ $\quad p \triangleq H\left(\{\mathbf{cn}^{(j)}, \mathbf{a}^{(j)}_b, \mathbf{a}^{(j)}_{1-b}\}^\theta_{j=1}\right) \leftarrow \mathfrak{P}$ $\quad f^{(j)}_b = p^{2b-1}(f^{(j)}_{1-b})$ $\quad \mathbf{r}^{(j)}_b = \mathbf{u}^{(j)} + f^{(j)}_b \cdot \mathbf{ck}^{(j)}$ Let $\mathbf{u}_{||} = \left(\mathbf{u}^{(1)}, \ldots, \mathbf{u}^{(\theta)}\right)$ Let $(f \cdot \mathbf{ck})_{||} = \left(f^{(1)}_b \cdot \mathbf{ck}^{(1)}, \ldots, f^{(\theta)}_b \cdot \mathbf{ck}^{(\theta)}\right)$ $\mathbf{r}_{||} = \mathbf{u}_{||} + (f \cdot \mathbf{ck})_{||}$ Abort with prob. ρ_b as in (10)	
	$\xrightarrow{\{f^{(j)}_0, f^{(j)}_1, \mathbf{r}^{(j)}_0, \mathbf{r}^{(j)}_1\}^\theta_{j=1}}$
	for $j \in [\theta]$ compute $\quad \mathbf{a}^{(j)}_0 = \mathbf{A} \cdot \mathbf{r}^{(j)}_0 - f^{(j)}_0 \cdot \mathbf{cn}^{(j)}$ $\quad \mathbf{a}^{(j)}_1 = \mathbf{A} \cdot \mathbf{r}^{(j)}_1 + f^{(j)}_1 \cdot (1 - \mathbf{cn}^{(j)})$ Let $p = H(\{\mathbf{cn}^{(j)}, \mathbf{a}^{(j)}_0, \mathbf{a}^{(j)}_1\}^\theta_{j=1})$ Check $\|\mathbf{r}^{(j)}_0\| \leq B'_{OR} \wedge \|\mathbf{r}^{(j)}_1\| \leq B_{OR}$ Check $f^{(j)}_0 \in \mathcal{C}_0 \wedge f^{(j)}_1 = p(f^{(j)}_0)$

Based on Lemma 1, note that the abort probability used in the protocol is defined as

$$\rho_b(\mathbf{r}_{||}) \triangleq 1 - \min\left\{\frac{D^{n(m-1)\theta}_{\sigma_{OR}}(\mathbf{r}_{||})}{M \cdot D^{n(m-1)\theta}_{(f \cdot \mathbf{ck})_{||}, \sigma_{OR}}(\mathbf{r}_{||})}, 1\right\}, \tag{10}$$

for $b \in \{0, 1\}$. We let $\sigma_{OR} = 2^{\gamma+1}\sqrt{\kappa\theta n(m-1)}$ since $\|(f \cdot \mathbf{ck})_{||}\| \leq \sqrt{\theta}\|f_{||}\|_\infty\|\mathbf{ck}_{||}\|_\infty \leq 2\sqrt{\theta\kappa} \cdot 2^\gamma\sqrt{n(m-1)} = 2^{\gamma+1}\sqrt{\kappa\theta n(m-1)}$.

Range Proof Construction. We define a range proof $\Pi_{range}(\mathcal{P}_{range}, \mathcal{V}_{range})$ with common input $(\mathbf{cn} = \{\mathbf{cn}_i\}^{\ell_\$-1}_{i=0}, \{\mathbf{cn}^{(j)}\}_{j \in [N_{out}]})$ and prover's input $(\$, \{b_i\}^{\ell_\$-1}_{i=0}, \mathbf{r}, \{\mathbf{ck}_i\}^{\ell_\$-1}_{i=0})$ for the following relations:

$$
R_{range} \triangleq
\left\{
\begin{array}{c}
\{\mathbf{cn}_i^{(j)}, \mathbf{cn}^{(j)}\}, \{\$, b_i^{(j)}, \mathbf{ck}_i^{(j)}, \mathbf{r}^{(j)}\} : \exists i \in [0, \ell_\$ - 1] \ s.t. \\
(b_i^{(j)} = 0 \vee b_i^{(j)} = 1) \wedge \mathbf{cn}_i^{(j)} = \mathsf{Com_A}(b_i, \mathbf{ck}_i^{(j)}) \wedge \forall j \in [N_{(out)}] \\
s.t. \mathbf{cn}^{(j)} = \mathsf{Com_A}(\$^{(j)}, \mathbf{r}^{(j)}) \wedge \$^{(j)} \in [0, 2^{\ell_\$} - 1] \\
\wedge \|\mathbf{r}^{(j)}\| \le 2\beta, \|\mathbf{ck}_i^{(j)}\| \le B_{OR}
\end{array}
\right\}
$$

$$
R'_{range} \triangleq
\left\{
\begin{array}{c}
\{\mathbf{cn}_i^{(j)}, \mathbf{cn}^{(j)}\}, \{\$, b_i^{(j)}, \mathbf{ck}_i^{(j)}, \mathbf{r}^{(j)'}, f, f_i\} : \exists i \in [0, \ell_\$ - 1] \ s.t. \\
(b_i^{(j)} = 0 \vee b_i^{(j)} = 1) \ \wedge f_i \cdot \mathbf{cn}_i^{(j)} = \mathsf{Com_A}(f_i \cdot b_i^{(j)}, \mathbf{ck}_i^{(j)}) \wedge \\
\forall j \in [N_{(out)}] \ s.t. f \cdot \mathbf{cn}^{(j)} = \mathsf{Com_A}(f \cdot \$^{(j)}, \mathbf{r}^{(j)'}) \wedge \\
\$^{(j)} \in [0, 2^{\ell_\$} - 1] \wedge \|\mathbf{r}^{(j)'}\| \le \beta_{range}, \|\mathbf{ck}_i^{(j)}\| \le B'_{OR} \wedge \\
\|f_i\| \le 2\sqrt{\kappa}, \|f\| \le 4\sqrt{\kappa}
\end{array}
\right\}
$$

The range prove is defined for each output amount $\$_{(out)}^{(j)}, j \in [N_{out}]$, i.e, for the sum of output amounts $\$_{out}^{(j)}$ over N_{out} output wallets, the prover runs in parallel the R'_{range} protocols for all $j \in [N_{out}]$: In the last step of the range proof protocol in Table 3 we use the proof of knowledge (PoK^*) of opening a zero-commitment from [19] with

$$
\rho_0 := 1 - \min\left\{ \frac{D_{\sigma_0}^{n(m-1)}(\overline{\mathbf{r}})}{M \cdot D_{(f' \cdot \mathbf{r}), \sigma_0}^{n(m-1)}(\overline{\mathbf{r}})}, 1 \right\} \tag{11}
$$

Table 3. ZK-Range Proof Π_{range}-Protocol

$\mathcal{P}_{range}(\{\mathbf{ck}_i^{(j)}, b_i^{(j)}\}_{i \in [\ell_\$]}, \mathbf{r}^{(j)}, \mathbf{cn}^{(j)}, \$^{(j)})$	$\mathcal{V}_{range}(\mathbf{cn}^{(j)})$
For all $j \in N_{out}$ and all $i \in [0, l_\$ - 1]$:	
Run $\mathcal{P}_{OR}(\mathbf{ck}_i^{(j)}, b_i^{(j)})$	
Output $\{\sigma_{OR}^{(j)}, \mathbf{cn}_i^{(j)}\}_{j \in N_{out}}$	
Compute $D^{(j)} := \sum_{i=0}^{\ell_\$ - 1} 2^i \mathbf{cn}_i^{(j)} - \mathbf{cn}^{(j)}$	
$= \mathsf{Com_A}(0, \mathbf{r}^{(j)})$	
Run $\mathcal{P}_{PoK^*}(D^{(j)}, \mathbf{r}^{(j)})$:	
Pick $\mathbf{r}_0 \in D_{\sigma_0}^{m(n-1)}$	
Compute $U := \mathbf{A} \cdot \mathbf{r}_0$	
Set $f' := H(\mathbf{A} \cdot \mathbf{r}_0)$	
Compute $\mathbf{r}^{(j)} := f' \mathbf{r}^{(j)} + \mathbf{r}_0$	
Abort with prob. ρ_0 from (11)	
Output $\sigma_{PoK^*}^{(j)} = \{(f', \overline{\mathbf{r}}^{(j)})\}_{j \in [N_{out}]}, \{D^{(j)}\}$	
	$\xrightarrow{\{\sigma_{OR}^{(j)}, \mathbf{cn}_i^{(j)}, \sigma_{PoK^*}{}^{(j)}\}_{j \in [N_{out}]}}$
	For all $j \in [N_{out}]$:
	Run $\mathcal{V}_{OR}(\sigma_{OR}^{(j)}, \mathbf{cn}_i^{(j)})$
	Compute $D^{(j)} := \sum_{i=0}^{\ell_\$ - 1} 2^i \mathbf{cn}_i^{(j)} - \mathbf{cn}^{(j)}$
	Run $\mathcal{V}_{PoK}(\{\sigma_{PoK^*}^{(j)}, D^{(j)}\}_j)$:
	Check $f' := H(\mathbf{A}\overline{\mathbf{r}}^{(j)} - f' D^{(j)})$

and $\sigma_0 = 12n\sqrt{n(m-1)}$. The prover's inputs of this proof of knowledge are given by a randomness $\mathbf{r}^{(j)}$, while the verifier's input is a commitment $D^{(j)}$ of zero. The proof in [19] allows us to use the same relaxation factor f' in each of the parallel runs of our range proof protocol in Table 3, which is significant for the proof of balance of our MIMO.LRCT.

Remark 2. The main difference between our OR proof and the OR proof from [11] is the size of the challenges. As we cannot achieve soundness of our range proof using the same challenge space as in [11], we adapt their protocol to another challenge space which we call $\mathcal{C}_0$ (this space was introduced in [4]). It consists of monomials in $\mathcal{R}_q$ as defined in (9). Because of these relatively small challenges, we need to repeat R'_b-protocol θ times, where the rejection sampling as defined in Lemma 1, returns something after $\theta - 1$ repeats. With this new space $\mathcal{C}_0$ we are now able to prove soundness of our relaxed range proof to the relaxed relation R'_{range}. In practice, we only need a relatively small $\theta < 20$, whereas previous lattice based range proofs [17] need much larger $\theta > 100$ for the same soundness level.

Theorem 3. *If $\sigma_{OR} \geq 22\sqrt{\kappa}B_{OR}$ and $B'_{OR} \geq 2\sqrt{n}\sigma_{OR}$, then the protocol in Table 2 is a R'_b-Protocol complete for relation R_{OR} and sound for relation R'_{OR}.*

Theorem 4. *The protocol described in Step 2 of the range proof is a proof of knowledge (from [19]) complete for relation R_{range} and sound for relation R'_{range} with $\beta_{range} = 2^{\ell_s+2}n\sqrt{\kappa n(m-1)}\sigma_{OR} + 2^2\sqrt{n}\beta_v$.*

6   Security Analysis

Theorem 5 (Balance). *If MIMO.L2RS is unforgeable, linkable and Com$_A$ is β-binding with $\beta = 4\sqrt{\kappa(2\beta_v)^2 + \kappa(2\beta_v)^2n(m-1)((2N_{in}+N_{out})2^\gamma)^2} + 2\beta_v N_{out}(2^{\ell_s+2}n\sqrt{\kappa n(m-1)}\sigma_{OR} + 2^2\sqrt{n}\beta_v)$, then MIMO.LRCT satisfies balance.*

Remark 3. In the balance proof, we only need zero-time unforgeability, meaning that in the reduction the attacker produces a forgery without seeing any signatures. Secondly, we do not need the message part of the signature, and thus this is treated as a Proof of Knowledge.

Theorem 6 (LRCT-Anonymity). *If the MIMO.L2RS scheme is unconditionally anonymous as Proposition 1 and the homomorphic commitment scheme is hiding, then MIMO.LRCT achieves anonymity. Hence, the unconditional anonymity of MIMO.LRCT can also be reduced from unconditional anonymity of MIMO.L2RS.*

Theorem 7 (LRCT-Non-Slanderability). *If MIMO.LRCT satisfies balance, then it satisfies non-slanderability as in Definition 5. In addition, the non-slanderability of MIMO.LRCT can be reduced to the non-slanderability of MIMO.L2RS.*

7   Performance Analysis

In this section, we propose a set of parameters for the MIMO.LRCT scheme. This construction is secure against direct lattice attacks in terms of the BKZ algorithm Hermite factor δ, using the value of $\delta = 1.007$, based on the BKZ 2.0 complexity estimates with pruning enumeration-based Shortest Vector Problem (SVP) [9]. We let $n = 1024$, $m = 132$, $\log q = 196$, $\kappa = 14$, $\eta = 1.1$, $\alpha = 0.5$, $\sigma = 22010$, $\sigma_{OR} = 277350$ and $\ell_\$ = 64$ to achieve the security parameter $\lambda = 100$, with α being the rejection sampling parameter determined in ([12] Sect. 3.2). Signature sizes of this analysis are illustrated in Table 4, where regular numbers for N_{in} and N_{out} were taken from Monero blockchain network[1].

Table 4. Size estimation for MIMO.LRCT

MIMO.LRCT	$(N_{in}, N_{out}) = (1,2)$	$(N_{in}, N_{out}) = (2,2)$	$(N_{in}, N_{out}) = (3,2)$
$\log(\beta)$ (Theorem 5)	≈ 126.3	≈ 126.3	≈ 126.3
Signature size ($w = 1$)	≈ 4.8 MB	≈ 5.1 MB	≈ 5.4 MB
Signature size ($w = 5$)	≈ 6.7 MB	≈ 8 MB	≈ 9.2 MB
Private-key size	≈ 49 KB	≈ 73 KB	≈ 98 KB
Public-key size	≈ 97 KB	≈ 146 KB	≈ 195 KB

Acknowledgement. This research project was supported by the Monash-HKPU (Hong Kong Polytechnic University)-Collinstar Blockchain Research Lab, whereas the work of Ron Steinfeld and Amin Sakzad was supported in part by ARC Discovery Project grant DP150100285. The work of Ron Steinfeld and Joseph K. Liu were also supported in part by ARC Discovery Project grant DP180102199.

References

1. Alberto Torres, W., Kuchta, V., Steinfeld, R., Sakzad, A., Liu, J.K., Cheng, J.: Lattice RingCT v2.0 with Multiple Input and Output Wallets. https://eprint.iacr.org/2019/ (2019)
2. Alberto Torres, W.A., et al.: Post-quantum one-time linkable ring signature and application to ring confidential transactions in blockchain (lattice RingCT v1.0). In: Susilo, W., Yang, G. (eds.) ACISP 2018. LNCS, vol. 10946, pp. 558–576. Springer, Cham (2018). https://doi.org/10.1007/978-3-319-93638-3_32
3. Benaloh, J., de Mare, M.: One-way accumulators: a decentralized alternative to digital signatures. In: Helleseth, T. (ed.) EUROCRYPT 1993. LNCS, vol. 765, pp. 274–285. Springer, Heidelberg (1994). https://doi.org/10.1007/3-540-48285-7_24
4. Benhamouda, F., Camenisch, J., Krenn, S., Lyubashevsky, V., Neven, G.: Better zero-knowledge proofs for lattice encryption and their application to group signatures. In: Sarkar, P., Iwata, T. (eds.) ASIACRYPT 2014. LNCS, vol. 8873, pp. 551–572. Springer, Heidelberg (2014). https://doi.org/10.1007/978-3-662-45611-8_29
5. Bunz, B., Bootle, J., Boneh, D., Poelstra, A., Wuille, P., Maxwell, G.: Bulletproofs: short proofs for confidential transactions and more. In: IEEE Symposium on Security and Privacy. IEEE (2018)
6. Bytecoin Team: Aggregate Addresses in CryptoNote: Towards Efficient Privacy (2015). https://bytecoin.org/static/files/docs/aggregate-addresses.pdf

---

[1] https://moneroblocks.info/.

7. Chase, M., Lysyanskaya, A.: On signatures of knowledge. In: Dwork, C. (ed.) CRYPTO 2006. LNCS, vol. 4117, pp. 78–96. Springer, Heidelberg (2006). https://doi.org/10.1007/11818175_5

8. Chen, L., et al.: Report on Post-Quantum Cryptography. NIST (2016)

9. Chen, Y., Nguyen, P.Q.: BKZ 2.0: better lattice security estimates. In: Lee, D.H., Wang, X. (eds.) ASIACRYPT 2011. LNCS, vol. 7073, pp. 1–20. Springer, Heidelberg (2011). https://doi.org/10.1007/978-3-642-25385-0_1

10. Conti, M., Kumar, E.S., Lal, C., Ruj, S.: A survey on security and privacy issues of bitcoin. IEEE Commun. Surv. Tutorials 20, 3416–3452 (2018)

11. del Pino, R., Lyubashevsky, V., Neven, G., Seiler, G.: Practical quantum-safe voting from lattices. In: CCS, pp. 1565–1581. ACM Press (2017)

12. Ducas, L., Durmus, A., Lepoint, T., Lyubashevsky, V.: Lattice signatures and bimodal Gaussians. In: Canetti, R., Garay, J.A. (eds.) CRYPTO 2013. LNCS, vol. 8042, pp. 40–56. Springer, Heidelberg (2013). https://doi.org/10.1007/978-3-642-40041-4_3

13. Elgamal, T.: A public key cryptosystem and a signature scheme based on discrete logarithms. IEEE Trans. Inf. Theor. 31(4), 469–472 (1985)

14. Fiat, A., Shamir, A.: How to prove yourself: practical solutions to identification and signature problems. In: Odlyzko, A.M. (ed.) CRYPTO 1986. LNCS, vol. 263, pp. 186–194. Springer, Heidelberg (1987). https://doi.org/10.1007/3-540-47721-7_12

15. Fujisaki, E., Suzuki, K.: Traceable ring signature. In: Okamoto, T., Wang, X. (eds.) PKC 2007. LNCS, vol. 4450, pp. 181–200. Springer, Heidelberg (2007). https://doi.org/10.1007/978-3-540-71677-8_13

16. Koshy, P., Koshy, D., McDaniel, P.: An analysis of anonymity in bitcoin using P2P network traffic. In: Christin, N., Safavi-Naini, R. (eds.) FC 2014. LNCS, vol. 8437, pp. 469–485. Springer, Heidelberg (2014). https://doi.org/10.1007/978-3-662-45472-5_30

17. Libert, B., Ling, S., Nguyen, K., Wang, H.: Lattice-based zero-knowledge arguments for integer relations. In: Shacham, H., Boldyreva, A. (eds.) CRYPTO 2018. LNCS, vol. 10992, pp. 700–732. Springer, Cham (2018). https://doi.org/10.1007/978-3-319-96881-0_24

18. Liu, J.K., Wei, V.K., Wong, D.S.: Linkable spontaneous anonymous group signature for ad hoc groups. In: Wang, H., Pieprzyk, J., Varadharajan, V. (eds.) ACISP 2004. LNCS, vol. 3108, pp. 325–335. Springer, Heidelberg (2004). https://doi.org/10.1007/978-3-540-27800-9_28

19. Lyubashevsky, V.: Lattice signatures without trapdoors. In: Pointcheval, D., Johansson, T. (eds.) EUROCRYPT 2012. LNCS, vol. 7237, pp. 738–755. Springer, Heidelberg (2012). https://doi.org/10.1007/978-3-642-29011-4_43

20. Mackenzie, A., Noether, S., Team, M.C.: Improving obfuscation in the CryptoNote protocol (2015). https://lab.getmonero.org/pubs/MRL-0004.pdf

21. Maxwell, G.: Confidential Transactions (2015). https://xiph.org/confidential_values.txt

22. Micciancio, D., Regev, O.: Lattice-based cryptography. In: Bernstein, D.J., Buchmann, J., Dahmen, E. (eds.) Post-Quantum Cryptography, pp. 147–191. Springer, Berlin (2009). https://doi.org/10.1007/978-3-540-88702-7_5

23. Monero: About Monero — Monero - secure, private, untraceable (2014). https://getmonero.org/resources/about/

24. Nakamoto, S.: Bitcoin: A Peer-to-Peer Electronic Cash System (2009). https://bitcoin.org/bitcoin.pdf

25. Noether, S.: Ring Signature Confidential Transactions for Monero (2015). https://eprint.iacr.org/2015/1098

26. Noether, S., Noether, S., Mackenzie, A.: A Note on Chain Reactions in Traceability in CryptoNote 2.0 (2014). https://lab.getmonero.org/pubs/MRL-0001.pdf

27. Pedersen, T.P.: Non-interactive and information-theoretic secure verifiable secret sharing. In: Feigenbaum, J. (ed.) CRYPTO 1991. LNCS, vol. 576, pp. 129–140. Springer, Heidelberg (1992). https://doi.org/10.1007/3-540-46766-1_9

28. Ron, D., Shamir, A.: Quantitative analysis of the full bitcoin transaction graph. In: Sadeghi, A.-R. (ed.) FC 2013. LNCS, vol. 7859, pp. 6–24. Springer, Heidelberg (2013). https://doi.org/10.1007/978-3-642-39884-1_2

29. Shor, P.W.: Polynomial-time algorithms for prime factorization and discrete logarithms on a quantum computer. SIAM Rev. **41**(2), 303–332 (1999)

30. Sun, S.-F., Au, M.H., Liu, J.K., Yuen, T.H.: RingCT 2.0: a compact accumulator-based (linkable ring signature) protocol for blockchain cryptocurrency Monero. In: Foley, S.N., Gollmann, D., Snekkenes, E. (eds.) ESORICS 2017. LNCS, vol. 10493, pp. 456–474. Springer, Cham (2017). https://doi.org/10.1007/978-3-319-66399-9_25

31. Van Saberhagen, N.: CryptoNote v 2.0 (2013). https://cryptonote.org/whitepaper.pdf

Two New Module-Code-Based KEMs with Rank Metric

Li-Ping Wang[1,2($\boxtimes$)] and Jingwei Hu[3]

[1] Institute of Information Engineering, Chinese Academy of Sciences, Beijing, China
wangliping@iie.ac.cn
[2] School of Cyber Security, University of Chinese Academy of Sciences,
Beijing, China
[3] School of Physical and Mathematical Sciences, Nanyang Technological University,
Singapore, Singapore
davidhu@ntu.edu.sg

Abstract. In this paper, we use a class of module codes to construct a suite of code-based public-key schemes—Piglet, which includes a new IND-CPA-secure public-key encryption scheme Piglet-1.CPAPKE and an IND-CCA-secure key encapsulation mechanism (KEM for short) Piglet-1.CCAKEM by applying the KEM variant of Fujisaki-Okamoto transform to Piglet-1.CPAPKE. We also put a new IND-CPA-secure KEM Piglet-2.CPAKEM into Piglet. Then, we present the parameters comparison between our schemes and some code-based NIST submissions. The results show that our schemes are good long-term-secure candidates for post-quantum cryptography.

Keywords: Code-based post-quantum cryptography ·
Rank syndrome decoding problem · Quasi-cyclic codes ·
Gabidulin codes · LRPC codes

1 Introduction

1.1 Background

Perceivable advances in quantum computers render Shor's quantum algorithm a threat to the widely used public key cryptosystems based on integer factoring and discrete logarithm problems [43]. As a consequence, NIST develops a post-quantum cryptography standardization project to solicit, evaluate, and standardize one or more quantum-resistant public cryptographic algorithms in recent years [38]. The cryptographic research community is stimulated by this initiation to construct practicable cryptographic systems that are secure against both quantum and classic computers, and can incorporate with existing communications protocols and networks. It is commonly thought that code-based cryptosystems can be resistant to quantum computing attack and so they are still becoming a hot topic even if NIST has ended the call.

© Springer Nature Switzerland AG 2019
J. Jang-Jaccard and F. Guo (Eds.): ACISP 2019, LNCS 11547, pp. 176–191, 2019.
https://doi.org/10.1007/978-3-030-21548-4_10

The first code-based cryptosystem was proposed by McEliece in 1978 by hiding a generator matrix of a Goppa code [33]. Another equivalent Niederreiter-type code-based scheme is constructed by scrambling a parity-check matrix of a Goppa code [35]. They are still secure under approximate parameters. However, the size of public keys in above schemes using Goppa codes is very huge. In order to reduce the size of public keys, LDPC (Low Density Parity Check) codes, convolutional codes, Gabidulin codes, Reed-Muller codes, and generalized Reed-Solomon codes were used to replace Goppa codes in the above cryptosystems framework, however, all were proven to be insecure [7,27,36,45,46].

As we all know, there are significant analogies between lattices and coding theory and the difference mainly consists in the use of different metrics (Euclidean metric for lattices, Hamming metric or rank metric for codes). Recently, inspired by the merits of lattices such as ideal rings and ring-LWE [2,32,39,40], diverse code-based public-key schemes such as RQC, HQC, BIKE, LOCKER, and Ouroboros-R, were proposed by using specific quasi-cyclic codes so that the size of public key is significantly reduced [1,4,5,17]. Those quasi-cyclic codes, i.e., we called one-dimensional module codes here, are also used in the many other code-based cryptosystems to advance compact key size [8,9,34]. However, the added quasi-cyclic structure may be exploited to initiate an algebraic attack and therefore brings about less confidence in the underlying security [18,41,42].

In lattice-based public key cryptosystems, Kyber which employs module lattices was proposed to thwart attacks from exploiting the algebraic structure of cyclotomic ideal lattices [11–15]. However, in code-based cryptosystems, there are no similar schemes.

In this paper, motivated by Kyber based on module lattices, we use the concept of module codes to redefine quasi-cyclic codes and propose an alternative assumption that rank module syndrome decoding (RMSD for short) problem is difficult so that our schemes are distinguishable from those so-called quasi-cyclic-code-based cryptosystems. It is worth mentioning that a handful of cryptosystems using rank codes exist in literature due to nice properties of rank metric such as RQC, Ouroboros-R, GPT's variant [31]. Therefore, based on the hardness of RMSD problem, we construct a suite of code-based public-key schemes—Piglet, which includes a new IND-CPA-secure public-key encryption scheme Piglet-1.CPAPKE and an IND-CCA-secure key encapsulation mechanism (KEM for short) Piglet-1.CCAKEM by applying the KEM variant of Fujisaki-Okamoto transform to Piglet-1.CPAPKE. We also put a new IND-CPA-secure KEM Piglet-2.CPAKEM into this suite. Then, we present the parameters comparison between our schemes and some code-based NIST submissions. The results show that our schemes are good long-term-secure candidates for post-quantum cryptography.

1.2   Our Contribution and Techniques

In this paper, the main contribution is that we propose a semantically secure public-key encryption scheme Piglet-1.CPAPKE and a new IND-CPA-secure

KEM Piglet-2.CPAKEM based on the hardness of rank module syndrome decoding problem. We believe that our schemes would be good candidates for post-quantum public-key cryptosystems with long-term security. The following are some advantages:

Security. The security of our schemes is established on the hardness of RMSD problem with two dimensions, while current code-based schemes are built upon rank quasi-cyclic syndrome decoding (RQCSD) problem which is RMSD problem with one dimension. In [42], the authors used the quasi-cyclic algebraic structure to propose a generic decoding attack. It shows that higher dimension of a module code can diminish the impact that possible attacks introduce. Furthermore, it cannot be excluded that some fatal attacks which exploits the quasi-cyclic structure embedded in the code might be proposed in the future. Therefore, we use module codes with two dimensions to construct new schemes, which would be good candidates for post-quantum public-key cryptosystems with long-term security.

More Plaintext Bits. In kyber, the size of plaintext is fixed to 256 bits, however, in our schemes, the size of plaintext depends on the extension degree of the finite field and the dimension of the auxiliary code in our scheme Piglet-1. So the sizes of plaintexts in Piglet-1 in 128, 192, and 256 bits security level are 267, 447, and 447 bits, respectively.

Efficiency. Although the operations in our schemes are implemented in large finite fields, it is also efficient in practice.

Decoding Failure. There is no decoding failure in Piglet-1.CPAKE and Piglet-1.CCAKEM since we use the decoding algorithm for Gabidulin codes. As to Piglet-2.CPAKEM, the decoding failure rate is extremely low and tolerable.

1.3   Road Map

The rest of the paper is organized as follows. Section 2 introduces some basic concepts and some results needed in our paper. In Sect. 3, we describe a difficult problem on which the security of our schemes is based. In Sect. 4, we propose Piglet-1.CPAPKE and give the security proof. Then, we apply Fujisaki-Okamoto transform to Piglet-1.CPAPKE and then construct Piglet-1.CCAKEM with CCA security. Next, we give three parameter sets achieving 128, 192 and 256 bits of security, and make comparison on parameters between our schemes and some NIST candidates. In Sect. 5, we present Piglet-2.CPAKEM, whose session key is the hash value of error vectors without encrypting plaintexts. In Sect. 6, we provide analysis on the existing attacks to our schemes. Finally, Sect. 7 is devoted to our conclusions.

2   Preliminaries

2.1   Results on Rank Codes

We represent vectors by lower-case bold letters and matrices by upper-case letters, and all vectors will be assumed to be row vectors. Let $\mathbb{F}_{q^m}^n$ be an n-

dimensional vector space over a finite field $\mathbb{F}_{q^m}$ where q is a prime power, and n, m are positive integers.

Let $\beta = \{\beta_1, \ldots, \beta_m\}$ be a basis of $\mathbb{F}_{q^m}$ over $\mathbb{F}_q$. Let $\mathcal{F}_i$ be the map from $\mathbb{F}_{q^m}$ to $\mathbb{F}_q$ where $\mathcal{F}_i(u)$ is the i-th coordinate of an element $u \in \mathbb{F}_{q^m}$ in the basis representation with β. To any $\mathbf{u} = (u_1, \ldots, u_n)$ in $\mathbb{F}_{q^m}^n$, we associate the $m \times n$ matrix $(\mathcal{F}_i(u_j))_{1 \leq i \leq m, 1 \leq j \leq n}$ over $\mathbb{F}_q$. The rank weight of a vector $\mathbf{u}$ can be defined as the rank of its associated matrix, denoted by $w_R(\mathbf{u})$. We refer to [29] for more details on rank codes.

For integers $1 \leq k \leq n$, an $[n, k]$ linear rank code C over $\mathbb{F}_{q^m}$ is a subspace of dimension k of $\mathbb{F}_{q^m}^n$ embedded with the rank metric. The minimum rank distance of the code C, denoted by $d_R(C)$, is the minimum rank weight of the non-zero codewords in C. A $k \times n$ matrix is called a generator matrix of C if its rows span the code. The dual code of C is the orthogonal complement of the subspace C of $\mathbb{F}_{q^m}^n$, denoted by $C^\perp$. A parity-check matrix H for a linear code C is a generator matrix for $C^\perp$.

For any vector $\mathbf{x} = (x_1, \ldots, x_n)$ in $\mathbb{F}_{q^m}^n$, the support of $\mathbf{x}$, denoted by $\mathrm{Supp}(\mathbf{x})$, is the $\mathbb{F}_q$-linear subspace of $\mathbb{F}_{q^m}$ spanned by the coordinates of $\mathbf{x}$, that is, $\mathrm{Supp}(\mathbf{x}) = <x_1, \ldots, x_n>_{\mathbb{F}_q}$. So we have $w_R(\mathbf{x}) = \dim(\mathrm{Supp}(\mathbf{x}))$.

Let r be a positive integer and a vector $\mathbf{v} = (v_1, \ldots, v_r) \in \mathbb{F}_{q^m}^r$. The circulant matrix $\mathrm{rot}(\mathbf{v})$ induced by $\mathbf{v}$ is defined as follows:

$$\mathrm{rot}(\mathbf{v}) = \begin{pmatrix} v_1 & v_r & \cdots & v_2 \\ v_2 & v_1 & \cdots & v_3 \\ \vdots & \vdots & \ddots & \vdots \\ v_r & v_{r-1} & \cdots & v_1 \end{pmatrix} \in \mathbb{F}_{q^m}^{r \times r},$$

where $\mathbb{F}_{q^m}^{r \times r}$ denotes the set of all matrices of size $r \times r$ over $\mathbb{F}_{q^m}$.

For any two vectors $\mathbf{u}, \mathbf{v} \in \mathbb{F}_{q^m}^r$, $\mathbf{u} \cdot \mathbf{v}$ can be expressed to vector-matrix product as follows.

$$\mathbf{u} \cdot \mathbf{v} = \mathbf{u} \times \mathrm{rot}(\mathbf{v})^T = (\mathrm{rot}(\mathbf{u}) \times \mathbf{v}^T)^T = \mathbf{v} \times \mathrm{rot}(\mathbf{u})^T = \mathbf{v} \cdot \mathbf{u}.$$

Let $\mathcal{R} = \mathbb{F}_{q^m}[x]/(x^r - 1)$. Then $\mathbb{F}_{q^m}^r$ is an $\mathbb{F}_{q^m}$-algebra isomorphic to $\mathcal{R}$ defined by $(v_1, v_2, \ldots, v_r) \mapsto \sum_{i=1}^r v_i x^i$.

Definition 1. *An $[n, k]$-linear block code $C \in \mathbb{F}_{q^m}^n$ is a quasi-cyclic with index s if for any $\mathbf{c} = (\mathbf{c}_1, \ldots, \mathbf{c}_s) \in C$ with $s | n$, the vector obtained after applying a simultaneous circulant shift to every block $\mathbf{c}_1, \ldots, \mathbf{c}_s$ is also a codeword.*

When $n = sr$, it is convenient to have parity-check matrices composed by $r \times r$ circulant blocks. In this paper, we use another viewpoint to describe quasi-cyclic codes so that it is clear to distinguish the quasi-cyclic codes used in our schemes from the many other quasi-cyclic-code-based cryptosystems.

Definition 2. *An $[n, k]$-linear block code C over $\mathcal{R}$ is called an $\mathcal{R}$-module code if C is a k-dimensional $\mathcal{R}$-submodule of $\mathcal{R}^n$.*

Remark 1. 1. The module code C over $\mathcal{R}$ is also quasi-cyclic over $\mathbb{F}_{q^m}$ since $(xc_1, \cdots, xc_n)$ is also a codeword of C for any $(c_1, \cdots, c_n) \in C$.
2. The quasi-cyclic codes over $\mathbb{F}_{q^m}$ used in RQC, HQC, Ouroboros-R, BIKE, etc, are module codes over $\mathcal{R}$ with dimension $k = 1$.
3. The module codes are reduced to a general linear cyclic code if $n = 1$.
4. The module codes are a general linear code if $r = 1$.

Definition 3. *A systematic $[n, k]$ module code over $\mathcal{R}$ has the form of a parity-check matrix as $H = (I|A)$, where A is an $(n - k) \times k$ matrix over $\mathcal{R}$.*

For example, in our schemes we use a systematic $[4, 2]$ module code over $\mathcal{R}$ and A has the form $\begin{pmatrix} a_{1,1} & a_{1,2} \\ a_{2,1} & a_{2,2} \end{pmatrix}$, where $a_{ij} \in \mathcal{R}$, $i = 1, 2, j = 1, 2$, and so a_{ij} can also be seen a circulant matrix over $\mathbb{F}_{q^m}$. In fact, the systematic cyclic codes used in RQC, HQC, Ouroboros-R, BIKE are $[2, 1]$ module codes over $\mathcal{R}$ and have such forms $A = (a)$, where $a \in \mathcal{R}$.

Next, we generalize the rank weight of a vector in $\mathbb{F}_{q^m}^n$ to $\mathcal{R}^n$.

Definition 4. *Let $\mathbf{v} = (v_1, \ldots, v_n) \in \mathcal{R}^n$, where $v_i = \sum_{j=0}^{r-1} a_{ij} x^j$ for $1 \leq i \leq n$. The support of $\mathbf{v}$ is defined by $Supp(\mathbf{v}) = \langle a_{1,0}, \ldots, a_{1,r-1}, \ldots, a_{n,0}, \ldots, a_{n,r-1} \rangle_{\mathbb{F}_q}$. The rank weight of $\mathbf{v}$ is defined to be the dimension of the support of $\mathbf{v}$, also denoted by $w_R(\mathbf{v})$.*

2.2 Gabidulin Codes and Their Decoding Technique

Gabidulin codes were introduced by Gabidulin in [20] and independently by Delsarte in [16]. They exploit linearized polynomials instead of regular ones, which was introduced in [37].

A q-linearized polynomial over $\mathbb{F}_{q^m}$ is defined to be a polynomial of the form

$$L(x) = \sum_{i=0}^{d} a_i x^{q^i}, a_i \in \mathbb{F}_{q^m}, a_d \neq 0$$

where d is called the q-degree of $f(x)$, denoted by $\deg_q(f(x))$. Denote the set of all q-linearized polynomials over $\mathbb{F}_{q^m}$ by $\mathcal{L}_q(x, \mathbb{F}_{q^m})$.

Let $g_1, \ldots, g_n \in \mathbb{F}_{q^m}$ be linearly independent over $\mathbb{F}_q$ and the Gabidulin code $\mathcal{G}$ is defined by

$$\mathcal{G} = \{(L(g_1), \ldots, L(g_n)) \in \mathbb{F}_{q^m}^n \mid L(x) \in \mathcal{L}_q(x, \mathbb{F}_{q^m}) \text{ and } \deg_q(L(x)) < k\}.$$

The Gabidulin code $\mathcal{G}$ with length n has dimension k over $\mathbb{F}_{q^m}$ and the generator matrix of $\mathcal{G}$ is

$$G = \begin{pmatrix} g_1 & \cdots & g_n \\ g_1^q & \cdots & g_n^q \\ \vdots & \ddots & \vdots \\ g_1^{q^{k-1}} & \cdots & g_n^{q^{k-1}} \end{pmatrix}. \tag{1}$$

The minimum rank distance of Gabidulin code $\mathcal{G}$ is $n - k + 1$, and so it can efficiently decode up to $\frac{n-k}{2}$ rank errors [20]. The decoding algorithm employed in our scheme was proposed in [44], which is the generalization of Berlekamp-Massey algorithm and its computational complexity is $O(n^2)$, see details in [44].

2.3 Low Rank Parity Check Codes and Their Decoding Algorithm

The Low Rank Parity Check (LRPC) codes have been introduced in [24]. LRPC codes are widely used in code-based cryptosystems because they have a weak algebraic structure and efficient decoding algorithms.

An LRPC code of rank d, length n and dimension k is an $[n, k]$-linear block code over $\mathbb{F}_{q^m}$ that has its parity-check matrix $H = (h_{ij})_{1 \leq i \leq n-k, 1 \leq j \leq n}$ such that the dimension of the subspace spanned by all h_{ij} is d.

The rank syndrome decoding for an LRPC code is that given a parity-check matrix $H \in \mathbb{F}_{q^m}^{(n-k) \times n}$ of an LRPC code of rank d and a syndrome $\mathbf{s} \in \mathbb{F}_{q^m}^{n-k}$, the goal is to find a vector $\mathbf{x} \in \mathbb{F}_{q^m}^n$ with $w_R(\mathbf{x}) \leq r$ such that $H\mathbf{x}^T = \mathbf{s}^T$.

In fact, what we want in Piglet-2.CPAKEM is just to recover the subspace E spanned by $\mathbf{x}$ instead of $\mathbf{x}$, which is called rank support recovery problem. The rank support recovery algorithm was provided in [17], which combines the general decoding algorithm of LRPC codes in [21] and a tweak of the improved algorithm in [3]. The following is the rank support recovery algorithm in detail (RS-Recover for short).

In the following algorithm, S and E are the vector spaces generated by the coordinates of the syndrome $\mathbf{s} = (s_1, \cdots, s_{n-k})$ and of the vector $\mathbf{x}$, respectively. S_i is defined by $S_i = F_i^{-1}.S = \langle F_1^{-1}s_1, F_1^{-1}s_2, \cdots, F_d^{-1}s_{n-k} \rangle$, with F_i an element of a basis of H, and $S_{ij} = S_i \cap S_j$.

RS-recover$(H, \mathbf{s}, r)$

Input: $H = \langle F_1, F_1, \ldots F_d \rangle$, $\mathbf{s} = (s_1, \ldots, s_{n-k})$, r (the dimension of E)
Output: The vector space E
// Part 1: Compute the vector space $E.F$
1 Compute $S = \langle s_1, \ldots, s_{n-k} \rangle$
2 Precompute every S_i for $i = 1$ to d
3 Precompute every $S_{i,i+1}$ for $i = 1$ to $d - 1$
4 for i from 1 to $d - 2$ do
5   tmp $\leftarrow S + F.(S_{i,i+1} \oplus S_{i_1,i+2} \oplus S_{i,i+2})$
6   if dim(tmp) $\leq rd$ then
7         $S \leftarrow tmp$
8   end
9 end
// Part 2: Recover the vector space E
10 $E \leftarrow F_1^{-1}.S \cap \ldots \cap F_d^{-1}.S$
11 return E

The above algorithm will probably fail in some cases and the decode failure probability is given in Ouroboros-R [17].

Proposition 1. *The probability of failure of the above algorithm is* $\max(q^{(2-r)(d-2)} \times q^{-(n-k-rd+1)}, q^{-2(n-k-rd+2)})$, *where r is the rank weight of the error vector.*

3   Difficult Problems for Code-Based Cryptography

In this section, we describe some difficult problems which are used in code-based cryptography. In particular, we introduce a difficult problem, i.e., rank module syndrome decoding (RMSD for short) problem, which is the security assumption for our schemes.

Definition 5 (Rank Syndrome Decoding (RSD for short) Problem). *Given a parity-check matrix $H = (I_{n-k} | A_{(n-k) \times k}) \in \mathbb{F}_{q^m}^{(n-k) \times n}$ of a random linear code, and $\mathbf{y} \in \mathbb{F}_{q^m}^{n-k}$, the goal is to find $\mathbf{x} \in \mathbb{F}_{q^m}^n$ with $w_R(\mathbf{x}) \le w$ such that $H\mathbf{x}^T = \mathbf{y}^T$.*

The RSD problem has recently been proven difficult with a probabilistic reduction to the Hamming setting in [22]. As we all know, syndrome decoding problem in Hamming metric is NP-hard [10]. Most of QC-code-based cryptosystems in rank metric are built upon the following difficult problem.

Definition 6 (Rank Quasi-Cyclic Syndrome Decoding (RQCSD) Problem). *Given a parity-check matrix $H = (I_{n-1} | A_{(n-1) \times 1}) \in \mathcal{R}^{(n-1) \times n}$ of a systematic random module code over $\mathcal{R}$ and a syndrome $\mathbf{y} \in \mathcal{R}^{n-1}$, to find a word $\mathbf{x} \in \mathcal{R}^n$ with $\omega_R(\mathbf{x}) \le w$ such that $\mathbf{y}^T = H\mathbf{x}^T$.*

RQCSD problem is not proven to be NP-hard, however, the size of public-key is much shorter of variant code-based cryptosystems constructed on this problem such as RQC, Ouroboros-R, LOCKER. As for Hamming metric, one use quasi-cyclic syndrome decoding (QCSD for short) problem as security assumption [8], [34]. We give a new difficult problem as follows:

Definition 7 (Rank Module Syndrome Decoding (RMSD) Problem). *Given a parity-check matrix $H = (I_{n-k} | A_{(n-k) \times k}) \in \mathcal{R}^{(n-k) \times n}$ of a systematic random module code over $\mathcal{R}$ and a syndrome $\mathbf{y} \in \mathcal{R}^{n-k}$, to find a word $\mathbf{x} \in \mathcal{R}^n$ with $\omega_R(\mathbf{x}) \le w$ such that $\mathbf{y}^T = H\mathbf{x}^T$.*
Simply denote the above problem by the (n, k, w, r)-RMSD problem over $\mathcal{R}$.

Remark 2. 1. If $k = 1$, the (n, k, w, r)-RMSD problem over $\mathcal{R}$ is the RQCSD problem, which is used in some NIST submissions such as RQC, Ouroboros-R, LOCKER. The result holds for the Hamming metic.

2. If $r = 1$, the (n, k, w, r)-RMSD problem over $\mathcal{R}$ is the usual RSD problem over $\mathbb{F}_{q^m}$.

3. The RSD problem is proved to be NP-hard [22], however, the RQCSD and the RMSD problem are still not yet proven to be NP-hard. Furthermore, smaller k implies more algebraic structure makes the scheme potentially susceptible to more avenues of attacks. Therefore, the security of RMSD-based schemes ($k \ge 2$ by default) is supposed to be in between RSD and RQCSD based cryptosystems.

The above problem is also called the search version of RMSD problem. We also give the definition of the decisional rank module syndrome decoding problem (DRMSD). Since the best known attacks on the (n, k, w, r)-DRMSD problem consist in solving the same instance of the (n, k, w, r)-RMSD problem, we make the assumption that the (n, k, w, r)-DRMSD problem is difficult.

Definition 8. *Given input* $(H, \mathbf{y}) \in \mathcal{R}^{(n-k) \times n} \times \mathcal{R}^{n-k}$, *the decisional RMSD problem asks to decide with non-negligible advantage whether* $(H, \mathbf{y}^T)$ *came from the RMSD distribution or the uniform distribution over* $\mathcal{R}^{(n-k) \times n} \times \mathcal{R}^{n-k}$.

The above problem is simply denoted as (n, k, w, r)-DRMSD problem.

4   Piglet-1: A New Module-Code-Based Public-Key Scheme

4.1   Piglet-1.CPAPKE

In this subsection, we first present a new IND-CPA-secure public-key encryption, i.e., Piglet-1.CPAPKE, in which $\text{XOF}(\cdot)$ denotes an extendable output function and $S := \text{XOF}(x)$ denotes the output of the function is distributed uniformly over a set S while x is as input.

In this scheme, we exploit an $[r, l]$-Gabidulin code $\mathcal{G}$, since the Gabidulin code is a unique rank code family with an efficient decoding algorithm. The minimum distance is $r - l + 1$ and so one can efficiently decode up to $\frac{r-l}{2}$ rank errors. The plaintext $\mathbf{m}$ is chosen from the plaintext space $\mathbb{F}_{q^m}^l$.

Piglet-1.CPAPKE.keyGen(): key generation

1. $\rho \xleftarrow{\$} \{0, 1\}^{256}$, $\sigma \xleftarrow{\$} \{0, 1\}^{320}$
2. $H \in \mathcal{R}^{k \times k} := \text{XOF}(\rho)$
3. $(\mathbf{x}, \mathbf{y}) \in \mathcal{R}^k \times \mathcal{R}^k := \text{XOF}(\sigma)$ with $w_R(\mathbf{x}) = w_R(\mathbf{y}) = w$
4. $\mathbf{s} := \mathbf{x}H + \mathbf{y}$
5. return $(pk := (H, \mathbf{s}), sk := \mathbf{x})$

Piglet-1.CPAPKE.Enc($\rho, \mathbf{s}, \mathbf{m} \in \mathbb{F}_{q^m}^l$): encryption

1. $\tau \xleftarrow{\$} \{0, 1\}^{320}$
2. $H \in \mathcal{R}^{k \times k} := \text{XOF}(\rho)$
3. $(\mathbf{r}, \mathbf{e}, \mathbf{e}') \in \mathcal{R}^k \times \mathcal{R}^k \times \mathcal{R} := \text{XOF}(\tau)$ with $w_R(\mathbf{r}) = w_R(\mathbf{e}) = w_R(\mathbf{e}') = w_e$
4. $\mathbf{u} := H\mathbf{r}^T + \mathbf{e}^T$
5. $\mathbf{v} := \mathbf{s}\mathbf{r}^T + \mathbf{e}' + \mathbf{m}G$, where G is an $l \times r$ generator matrix over $\mathbb{F}_{q^m}$ of a Gabidulin code $\mathcal{G}$.
6. return a ciphertext pair $\mathbf{c} := (\mathbf{u}, \mathbf{v})$

Piglet-1.CPAPKE.Dec($sk = \mathbf{x}, \mathbf{c} = (\mathbf{u}, \mathbf{v})$): decryption

1. Compute $\mathbf{v} - \mathbf{x}\mathbf{u} := \mathbf{m}G + \mathbf{y}\mathbf{r}^T + \mathbf{e}' - \mathbf{x}\mathbf{e}^T$

2. $\mathbf{m} := \mathcal{D}_G(\mathbf{v} - \mathbf{x}\mathbf{u})$, where $\mathcal{D}_G(\cdot)$ is a decoding algorithm for the Gabidulin code $\mathcal{G}$.

Remark 3. 1. The secret key $\mathbf{x}$ and $\mathbf{y}$ share the same support including 1 with dimension w. The $\mathbf{r}$, $\mathbf{e}$ and $\mathbf{e}'$ share the same support with dimension w_e. So that the rank weight of overall error vector $\mathbf{yr}^T + \mathbf{e}' - \mathbf{xe}^T$ is less than or equal to ww_e.
2. The plaintext $\mathbf{m}$ can be obtained by decoding algorithm of the Gabidulin code $\mathcal{G}$ if $w_R(\mathbf{yr}^T + \mathbf{e}' - \mathbf{xe}^T) = ww_e \leq \frac{r-l}{2}$.

4.2   Proof of Security

In this subsection, we show that Piglet-1.CPAPKE is IND-CPA secure under the RMSD hardness assumption.

Theorem 1. *For any adversary A, there exists an adversary B such that*
$$Adv^{CPA}_{Piglet-1.CPAPKE}(A) \leq Adv^{DRMSD}_{2k,k,w,r}(B) + Adv^{DRMSD}_{2k+1,k,w_e,r}(B).$$

Proof. Let A be an adversary that is executed in the IND-CPA security experiment which we call game G_1, i.e.,

$$Adv^{CPA}_{Piglet-1.CPAPKE}(A) = |Pr[b = b' \text{ in game } G_1] - 1/2|,$$

In game G_2, the view of $\mathbf{s} = \mathbf{x}H + \mathbf{y}$ generated in KeyGen is replaced by a uniform random matrix. It is possible to verify that there exists an adversary B with the same running time as that of A such that

$$|Pr[b = b' \text{ in game } G_1] - Pr[b = b' \text{ in game } G_2]| \leq Adv^{DMRSD}_{2k,k,w,r}(B),$$

since $(I \; H^T)\begin{pmatrix} \mathbf{y}^T \\ \mathbf{x}^T \end{pmatrix} = \mathbf{s}^T$, where $(I \; H^T)$ is a systematic parity-check matrix of a module code over $\mathcal{R}$ while $\mathbf{x}$ and $\mathbf{y}$ are drawn randomly with low rank weight w.

In game G_3, the values of $\mathbf{u} = H\mathbf{r}^T + \mathbf{e}^T$ and $\mathbf{v} = \mathbf{s}\mathbf{r}^T + \mathbf{e}' + \mathbf{m}G$ used in the generation of the challenge ciphertext are simultaneously substituted with uniform random values. Again, there exists an adversary B with the same running time as that of A such that

$$|Pr[b = b' \text{ in game } G_2] - Pr[b = b' \text{ in game } G_3]| \leq Adv^{DMRSD}_{2k+1,k,w_e,r}(B),$$

since $\begin{pmatrix} I_k & H \\ I_1 & \mathbf{s} \end{pmatrix}\begin{pmatrix} \mathbf{e}^T \\ \mathbf{e}' \\ \mathbf{r}^T \end{pmatrix} = \begin{pmatrix} \mathbf{u} \\ \mathbf{v} - \mathbf{m}G \end{pmatrix}$, where $\begin{pmatrix} I_k & H \\ I_1 & \mathbf{s} \end{pmatrix}$ is a systematic parity-check matrix of a module code while H, $\mathbf{s}$ are uniform and $\mathbf{r}, \mathbf{e}, \mathbf{e}'$ are drawn randomly with low rank weight w_e.

Note that in game G_3, the value $\mathbf{v}$ from the challenge ciphertext is independent of b and therefore $Pr[b = b' \text{ in game } G_3] = \frac{1}{2} + \epsilon$, in which ϵ is arbitrarily small. We build a sequence of games allowing a simulator to transform a ciphertext of a message $\mathbf{m}_0$ to a ciphertext of a message $\mathbf{m}_1$. Hence the result is required.   □

4.3 Piglet-1.CCAKEM: A New IND-CCA-Secure KEM

In this subsection, let $G : \{0,1\}^* \to \{0,1\}^{3 \times 256}$ and $H : \{0,1\}^* \to \{0,1\}^{2 \times 256}$ be hash functions, and z is a random, secret seed. Then, we apply the KEM variant of Fujisaki-Okamoto transform to Piglet-1.CPAPKE to construct an IND-CCA-secure KEM, i.e., Piglet-1.CCAKEM when the hash functions G and H are modeled random oracle.

Piglet-1.CCAKEM.Keygen() is the same as Piglet-1.CPAPKE. Keygen()
Piglet-1.CCAKEM.Encaps(pk $= (\rho, \mathbf{s})$)

1. $\mathbf{m} \leftarrow \mathbb{F}_{q^m}^l$
2. $(\hat{K}, \sigma, d) := G(pk, \mathbf{m})$
3. $(\mathbf{u}, \mathbf{v}) := $ Piglet-1.CPAPKE.Enc$((\rho, \mathbf{s}), \mathbf{m}; \sigma)$
4. $\mathbf{c} := (\mathbf{u}, \mathbf{v}, d)$
5. $K := H(\hat{K}, \mathbf{c})$
6. return$(\mathbf{c}, K)$

Piglet-1.CCAKEM.Decaps(sk $= (\mathbf{x}, z, \rho, \mathbf{s}), \mathbf{c} = (\mathbf{u}, \mathbf{v}, d)$)

1. $\mathbf{m}' := $ Piglet-1.CPAKEM.Dec$(\mathbf{x}, (\mathbf{u}, \mathbf{v}))$
2. $(\hat{K}', \sigma', d') := G(pk, \mathbf{m}')$
3. $(\mathbf{u}', \mathbf{v}') := $ Piglet-1.CPAKEM.Enc$((\rho, \mathbf{s}), \mathbf{m}'; \sigma')$
4. if $(\mathbf{u}', \mathbf{v}', d') = (\mathbf{u}, \mathbf{v}, d)$ then
5. return $K := H(\hat{K}', \mathbf{c})$
6. else
7. return $K := H(z, \mathbf{c})$
8. end if

4.4 Parameter Sets

In this subsection, we give three sets of parameters for Piglet-1.CCAKEM, achieving 128, 192 and 256 bits of security, respectively.

First we choose the dimension of the module code used in our schemes $k = 2$ so that the size of public key is as small as possible. In this case, we consider $1 \in \text{Supp}(\mathbf{x}, \mathbf{y})$, since finding a small weight codeword of weight w with support containing 1 is harder than finding a small weight codeword of $w - 1$. Therefore, the security of the $(2k, k, w, r)$-RMSD over $\mathcal{R}$ in our scheme can be reduced to decoding $[4r, 2r]$-linear codes over $\mathbb{F}_{q^m}$ with rank weight $w - 1$. The security of the $(2k + 1, k, w_e, r)$-RMSD over $\mathcal{R}$ can be reduced to decoding $[5r, 2r]$-linear codes over $\mathbb{F}_{q^m}$ with rank weight w_e. One can use the best combinatorial attack algorithm in [22] to determine the choice of parameters such as m, r, w, w_e. Furthermore, we can determine l since $w w_e \leq \frac{r-l}{2}$. Those parameters also need to resist the algebraic attacks which are presented in Sect. 6. The concrete parameters are listed in Table 1.

Table 1. Parameter sets of Piglet-1.CCAKEM

Instance	k	q	m	r	w	w_e	l	Security level
Piglet-1.CCAKEM-I	2	2	89	53	5	5	3	128
Piglet-1.CCAKEM-II	2	2	149	53	5	5	3	192
Piglet-1.CCAKEM-III	2	2	149	75	6	6	3	256

Table 2. The theoretical sizes in bytes for Piglet-1.CCAKEM

Instance	pk size	sk size	ct size	ss size	Security level
Piglet-1.CCAKEM-I	1212	40	1801	64	128
Piglet-1.CCAKEM-II	2007	40	2994	64	192
Piglet-1.CCAKEM-III	2826	40	4223	64	256

Table 2 presents the theoretical sizes in bytes for Piglet-1.CCAKEM. The size of pk is $kmr + 256$ bits, i.e., $\frac{2mr+256}{8}$ bytes. The size of sk is 256 bits, i.e., 32 bytes. The size of ciphertext is $3mr + 256$ bits, i.e., $3mr/8 + 32$ bytes. The size of ss (session secret) is 2×256 bits, i.e., 64 bytes.

Table 3. Comparison on sizes of public keys (in bytes)

Instance	128 bits	192 bits	256 bits
Classic McEliece	368,282		1,046,737
NTS-kem	319,488	929,760	1,419,704
Piglet-1.CCAKEM	1212	2007	2826
Piglet-2.CPAKEM	1212	2007	2826
RQC	786	1411	1795
HQC	2819	5115	7417
LEDAKem	3,480	7,200	12,384
BIKE-I	2541	5474	8181
BIKE-II	1271	2737	4094
BIKE-III	2757	5421	9033
Ouroboros-R	676	807	1112
LOCKER	737	1048	1191

Table 3 presents parameters comparison between our scheme and some NIST submissions which proceed the second round of NIST PQC standardization process. As we have analyzed in Sect. 3, it shows that the size of public key in our schemes is slightly larger than those in RQC, Ouroboros-R and LOCKER, which are based RQCSD hardness problem. The size of public key in our schemes is better than those in HQC, LEDAkem, BIKE which are based on the QCSD hardness problem. And it is much better than those in Classic McEliece and NTS-kem which are original McEliece cryptosystems.

5   Piglet-2: A New Module-Code-Based KEM

In this section, we propose a new IND-CPA-secure KEM Piglet-2.CPAKEM. The difference lies in choice of the auxiliary codes we use (LRPC codes for Piglet-2.CPAKEM, Gabidulin codes for Piglet-1.CPAPKE). The session key is the hash value of error vectors without encrypting a plaintext. As for LRPC codes, we introduced them in Sect. 2. In addition, $G : \{0,1\}^* \to \{0,1\}^{2\times 256}$ denotes a hash function.

Piglet-2.CPAKEM.Keygen(): key generation

1. $\rho \xleftarrow{\$} \{0,1\}^{256}$, $\sigma \xleftarrow{\$} \{0,1\}^{320}$
2. $H \in \mathcal{R}^{k\times k} := \mathrm{XOF}(\rho)$
3. $(\mathbf{x}, \mathbf{y}) \in \mathcal{R}^k \times \mathcal{R}^k := \mathrm{XOF}(\sigma)$ with $w_R(\mathbf{x}) = w_R(\mathbf{y}) = w$
4. $\mathbf{s} := \mathbf{x}H + \mathbf{y}$
5. return $(pk := (H, \mathbf{s}), sk := (\mathbf{x}, \mathbf{y}))$

Piglet-2.CPAKEM.Encaps($\rho, \mathbf{s}$): encapsulation

1. $\tau \xleftarrow{\$} \{0,1\}^{320}$
2. $H \in \mathcal{R}^{k\times k} := \mathrm{XOF}(\rho)$
3. $(\mathbf{r}, \mathbf{e}, \mathbf{e}') \in \mathcal{R}^k \times \mathcal{R}^k \times \mathcal{R} := \mathrm{XOF}(\tau)$ with $w_R(\mathbf{r}) = w_R(\mathbf{e}) = w_R(\mathbf{e}') = w_e$
4. $E := \mathrm{Supp}(\mathbf{r}, \mathbf{e}, \mathbf{e}')$ and $K := G(E)$
5. $\mathbf{u} := H\mathbf{r}^T + \mathbf{e}^T$
6. $\mathbf{v} := \mathbf{s}\mathbf{r}^T + \mathbf{e}'$
7. return a ciphertext pair $\mathbf{c} := (\mathbf{u}, \mathbf{v})$

Piglet-2.CPAKEM.Decaps($sk = (\mathbf{x}, \mathbf{y}), \mathbf{c} = (\mathbf{u}, \mathbf{v})$): decapsulation

1. $F := \mathrm{Supp}(\mathbf{x}, \mathbf{y})$
2. Compute $\mathbf{v} - \mathbf{x}\mathbf{u} := \mathbf{y}\mathbf{r}^T + \mathbf{e}' - \mathbf{x}\mathbf{e}^T$
3. $E := \mathrm{RS\text{-}recover}(F, \mathbf{v} - \mathbf{x}\mathbf{u}, w_e)$
4. $K := G(E)$

Remark 4. 1. In the above scheme, $E = \mathrm{RS\text{-}recover}(F, \mathbf{v} - \mathbf{x}\mathbf{u}, w_e)$ denotes that the decoding algorithm outputs the support E of error vectors $\mathbf{r}, \mathbf{e}$ and $\mathbf{e}'$ with dimension w_e given the support F of $\mathbf{x}$ and $\mathbf{y}$ and the syndrome $\mathbf{v} - \mathbf{x}\mathbf{u}$.
2. The security proof of Piglet-2.CPAKEM is the same as that of Piglet-1.CPAPKE and so we omit it here.
3. The choice of parameter sets for Piglet-2.CPAKEM are the same as that for Piglet-1.CCAKEM.

4. The rank support recovery algorithm is probabilistic and the decoding failure probability can be computed by Proposition 1. So in our case the result is $\max(q^{(2-w)(w_e-2)} \times q^{-(r-ww_e+1)}, q^{-2(r-ww_e+2)}) = 2^{-38}$ for both 128 and 192 bits security levels, and 2^{-52} for 256 bits security level.

5. Since rank support recovery decoding techniques do not attain a negligible decoding failure rate, this makes it challenge to achieve higher security notions such as IND-CCA.

6   Known Attacks

There are two types of generic attacks on our schemes, which play an important role in choice of parameter sets in our schemes. One is general combinatorial decoding attack and the other is algebraic attack using Gröbner basis.

The decoding algorithm was proposed in [3,21] and the best result is as follows.

For an $[n, k]$ rank code $\mathcal{C}$ over $\mathbb{F}_{q^m}$, the time complexity of the known best combinatorial attack to decode a word with rank weight d is

$$O((nm)^3 q^{d\lceil \frac{m(k+1)}{n}\rceil - m}). \tag{2}$$

As for algebraic attack, the time complexity is much greater than the decoding attack when $q = 2$. The complexity of the above problem is $q^{d\lceil \frac{d(k+1)-(n+1)}{d}\rceil}$ [28].

Next, the general attacks from [42] which use the cyclic structure of the code have less impact on module codes than quasi-cyclic codes in RQC, Ouroboros-R, LOCKER, etc.

In addition, as for the choice of r, no attacks of quasi-cyclicity of a code are known if there are only two factors of $x^r - 1 \mod q$ [26]. Therefore, r should be prime, and q is a generator of the multiplicative group of $(\mathbb{Z}/r\mathbb{Z})^*$.

7   Conclusions

In this paper, we propose an IND-CCA-secure KEM Piglet-1.CCAKEM and an IND-CPA-secure Piglet-2.CPAKEM, both of which are based on the RMSD difficult problem. More importantly, the size of public key in our schemes is much shorter than those of NIST submissions which entered the second round except the candidates based on RQCSD hardness problem. The shorter keys from the RQCSD-problem related candidates are due to simple quasi-cyclic structure used. However, the advantage of our new construction is the elimination of possible quasi-cyclic attacks and thus makes our schemes strong and robust. The parameter comparison between Piglet and other NIST proposals shows that our schemes would be good candidates for post-quantum cryptosystems with long-term security. Moreover, we expect to further reduce the public key size by using similar Kyber's approach in our future work.

Acknowledgment. The author would like to thank the anonymous reviewers for their valuable comments and suggestions which improved the quality of this paper. The work of L.-P. Wang was supported in part by the National Natural Science Foundation of China (Grant No. 61872355) and National Cryptography Development Fund (MMJJ 20170124).

References

1. Aguilar-Melchor, C., Blazy, O., Deneuville, J.-C., Gaborit, P., Zémor, G.: Efficient encryption from random quasi-cyclic codes. IEEE Trans. Inf. Theory **64**(5), 3927–3943 (2018)
2. Alekhnovich, M.: More on average case vs approximation complexity. Comput. Complex. **20**(4), 755–786 (2011)
3. Aragon, N., Gaborit, P., Hautevile, A., Tillich, J.-P.: Improvement of generic attacks on the rank syndrome decoding problem (2017). Pre-print https://www.unilim.fr/pages_perso/philippe.gaborit/newGRS.pdf
4. Aragon, N., Barreto, P., Bettaieb, S., Bidoux, L., Blazy, O., et al.: BIKE: bit flipping key encapsulation. Submission to the NIST Post Quantum Standardization Process (2017)
5. Aragon, N., Blazy, O., Deneuville, J.-C., Gaborit, P., Hauteville, A., et al.: LOCKER: low rank parity check codes encryption. Submission to the NIST Post Quantum Standardization Process (2017)
6. Albrecht, M.R., Player, R., Scott, S.: On the concrete hardness of learning with errors. J. Math. Cryptol. **9**(3), 169–203 (2015)
7. Baldi, M.: QC-LDPC Code-Based Cryptography. Springer Briefs in Electrical and Computer Engineering. Springer, Cham (2014). https://doi.org/10.1007/978-3-319-02556-8
8. Baldi, M., Barenghi, A., Chiaraluce, F., Pelosi, G., Santini, P.: LEDAkem: a post-quantum key encapsulation mechanism based on QC-LDPC codes. In: Lange, T., Steinwandt, R. (eds.) PQCrypto 2018. LNCS, vol. 10786, pp. 3–24. Springer, Cham (2018). https://doi.org/10.1007/978-3-319-79063-3_1
9. Barreto, P.S.L.M., Lindner, R., Misoczki, R.: Monoidic codes in cryptography. In: Yang, B.-Y. (ed.) PQCrypto 2011. LNCS, vol. 7071, pp. 179–199. Springer, Heidelberg (2011). https://doi.org/10.1007/978-3-642-25405-5_12
10. Berlekamp, E., McEliece, R., Van Tilborg, H.: On the inherent intractability of certain coding problems. IEEE Trans. Inf. Theory **24**(3), 384–386 (1978)
11. Biasse, J.-F., Song, F.: Efficient quantum algorithms for computing class groups and solving the principal ideal problem in arbitrary degree number fields. In: Krauthgamer, R. (ed.) 27th SODA, pp. 893–902. ACM-SIAM (2016)
12. Bos, J.W., et al.: CRYSTALS- Kyber: a CCA-secure module-lattice-based KEM. In: EuroS&P 2018, pp. 353–367 (2018)
13. Campbell, P., Groves, M., Shepherd, D.: Soliloquy: a cautionary tale. In: ETSI 2nd Quantum-Safe Crypto Workshop, pp. 1–9 (2014)
14. Cramer, R., Ducas, L., Peikert, C., Regev, O.: Recovering short generators of principal ideals in cyclotomic rings. In: Fischlin, M., Coron, J.-S. (eds.) EUROCRYPT 2016. LNCS, vol. 9666, pp. 559–585. Springer, Heidelberg (2016). https://doi.org/10.1007/978-3-662-49896-5_20

15. Cramer, R., Ducas, L., Wesolowski, B.: Short stickelberger class relations and application to ideal-SVP. In: Coron, J.-S., Nielsen, J.B. (eds.) EUROCRYPT 2017. LNCS, vol. 10210, pp. 324–348. Springer, Cham (2017). https://doi.org/10.1007/978-3-319-56620-7_12

16. Delsarte, P.: Bilinear forms over a finite field, with applications to coding theory. J. Comb. Theory Ser. A **25**(3), 226–241 (1978)

17. Deneuville, J.-C., Gaborit, P., Zémor, G.: Ouroboros: a simple, secure and efficient key exchange protocol based on coding theory. In: Lange, T., Takagi, T. (eds.) PQCrypto 2017. LNCS, vol. 10346, pp. 18–34. Springer, Cham (2017). https://doi.org/10.1007/978-3-319-59879-6_2

18. Faugère, J.-C., Otmani, A., Perret, L., Tillich, J.-P.: Algebraic cryptanalysis of McEliece variants with compact keys. In: Gilbert, H. (ed.) EUROCRYPT 2010. LNCS, vol. 6110, pp. 279–298. Springer, Heidelberg (2010). https://doi.org/10.1007/978-3-642-13190-5_14

19. Fujisaki, E., Okamoto, T.: Secure integration of asymmetric and symmetric encryption schemes. In: Wiener, M. (ed.) CRYPTO 1999. LNCS, vol. 1666, pp. 537–554. Springer, Heidelberg (1999). https://doi.org/10.1007/3-540-48405-1_34

20. Gabidulin, E.M.: Theory of codes with maximum rank distance. Probl. Inf. Transm. **21**(1), 3–16 (1985)

21. Gaborit, P., Ruatta, O., Schrek, J.: On the complexity of the rank syndrome decoding problem. IEEE Trans. Inf. Theory **62**(2), 1006–1019 (2016)

22. Gaborit, P., Zémor, G.: On the hardness of the decoding and the minimum distance problem for rank codes. IEEE Trans. Inf. Theory **62**(12), 7245–7252 (2016)

23. Gaborit, P., Hauteville, A., Phan, D.H., Tillich, J.-P.: Identity-based encryption from codes with rank metric. In: Katz, J., Shacham, H. (eds.) CRYPTO 2017. LNCS, vol. 10403, pp. 194–224. Springer, Cham (2017). https://doi.org/10.1007/978-3-319-63697-9_7

24. Gaborit, P., Murat, G., Ruatta, O., Zémor, G.: Low rank parity check codes and their application to cryptography. In: Proceedings of the Workshop on Coding and Cryptography WCC 2013, Bergen, Norway (2013)

25. Gabidulin, E.M., Paramonov, A.V., Tretjakov, O.V.: Ideals over a noncommutative ring and their application in cryptology. In: Davies, D.W. (ed.) EUROCRYPT 1991. LNCS, vol. 547, pp. 482–489. Springer, Heidelberg (1991). https://doi.org/10.1007/3-540-46416-6_41

26. Hauteville, A., Tillich, J.-P.: New algorithms for decoding in the rank metric and an attack on the LRPC cryptosystem. In: 2015 IEEE International Symposium on Information Theory (ISIT), pp. 2747–2751 (2015)

27. Landais, G., Tillich, J.-P.: An Efficient attack of a McEliece cryptosystem variant based on convolutional codes. In: Gaborit, P. (ed.) PQCrypto 2013. LNCS, vol. 7932, pp. 102–117. Springer, Heidelberg (2013). https://doi.org/10.1007/978-3-642-38616-9_7

28. Levy-dit-Vehel, F., Perret, L.: Algebraic decoding of rank metric codes. In: Proceedings of YACC 2006 (2006)

29. Loidreau, P.: Properties of codes in rank metric. http://arxiv.org/abs/cs/0610057

30. Loidreau, P.: A Welch–Berlekamp like algorithm for decoding Gabidulin codes. In: Ytrehus, Ø. (ed.) WCC 2005. LNCS, vol. 3969, pp. 36–45. Springer, Heidelberg (2006). https://doi.org/10.1007/11779360_4

31. Loidreau, P.: A new rank metric codes based encryption scheme. In: Lange, T., Takagi, T. (eds.) PQCrypto 2017. LNCS, vol. 10346, pp. 3–17. Springer, Cham (2017). https://doi.org/10.1007/978-3-319-59879-6_1

32. Lyubashevsky, V., Peikert, C., Regev, O.: On ideal lattices and learning with errors over rings. In: Gilbert, H. (ed.) EUROCRYPT 2010. LNCS, vol. 6110, pp. 1–23. Springer, Heidelberg (2010). https://doi.org/10.1007/978-3-642-13190-5_1

33. McEliece, R.J.: A public key crytosystem based on algebraic coding theory. DSN progress report 44, pp. 114–116 (1978)

34. Misoczki, R., Tillich, J.-P., Sendrier, N., Barreto, P.S.L.M.: MDPCMcEliece: new McEliece variants from moderate density parity-check codes. In: Proceedings of the IEEE International Symposium on Information Theory - ISIT 2013, pp. 2069–2073 (2013)

35. Niederreiter, H.: Knapsack-type cryptosystems and algebraic coding theory. Probl. Control. Inf. Theory **15**, 159–166 (1986)

36. Overbeck, R.: Structural attacks for public key cryptosystems based on Gabidulin codes. J. Cryptol. **21**, 280–301 (2008)

37. Ore, O.: Theory of non-commutative polynomials. Ann. Math. **34**(3), 480–508 (1933)

38. NIST. Post Quantum Crypto Project (2017). http://csrc.nist.gov/groups/ST/post-quantum-crypto. Available at https://csrc.nist.gov/Projects/Post-Quantum-for-Cryptography/Post-Quantum-Cryptography-Standardization/call-for-Proposalls. List of First Round candidates available at https://csrc.nist.gov/projects/post-quantum-cryptography/round-1-submissions

39. Pietrzak, K.: Cryptography from learning parity with noise. In: Bieliková, M., Friedrich, G., Gottlob, G., Katzenbeisser, S., Turán, G. (eds.) SOFSEM 2012. LNCS, vol. 7147, pp. 99–114. Springer, Heidelberg (2012). https://doi.org/10.1007/978-3-642-27660-6_9

40. Regev, O.: On lattices, learning with errors, random linear codes, and cryptography. In: STOC 2005, pp. 84–93 (2005)

41. Santini, P., Baldi, M., Cancellieri, G., Chiaraluce, F.: Hindering reaction attacks by using monomial codes in the McEliece cryptosystem. In: IEEE International Symposium on Information Theory (ISIT) 2018, pp. 951–955 (2018)

42. Sendrier, N.: Decoding one out of many. In: Yang, B.-Y. (ed.) PQCrypto 2011. LNCS, vol. 7071, pp. 51–67. Springer, Heidelberg (2011). https://doi.org/10.1007/978-3-642-25405-5_4

43. Shor, P.: Polynomial-time algorithms for prime factorization and discrete logarithms on a quantum computer. SIAM J. Comput. **26**(5), 1484–1509 (1997)

44. Sidorenko, V., Richter, G., Bossert, M.: Linearized shift-register synthesis. IEEE Trans. Inf. Theory **57**(9), 6025–6032 (2011)

45. Sidelnikov, V.M.: A public-key cryptosystem based on binary Reed-Muller codes. Discrete Math. Appl. **4**, 191–207 (1994)

46. Sidelnikov, V.M., Shestakov, S.O.: On insecurity of cryptosystems based on generalized Reed-Solomon codes. Discrete Math. Appl. **2**, 439–444 (1992)

Adding Distributed Decryption and Key Generation to a Ring-LWE Based CCA Encryption Scheme

Michael Kraitsberg[3], Yehuda Lindell[1,3], Valery Osheter[3],
Nigel P. Smart[2,4(✉)], and Younes Talibi Alaoui[2]

[1] Bar-Ilan University, Ramat Gan, Israel
yehuda.lindell@biu.ac.il
[2] KU Leuven, Leuven, Belgium
{nigel.smart,younes.talibialaoui}@kuleuven.be
[3] Unbound Technology, Petah Tikva, Israel
{michael.kraitsberg,valery.osheter}@unboundtech.com
[4] University of Bristol, Bristol, UK

Abstract. We show how to build distributed key generation and distributed decryption procedures for the LIMA Ring-LWE based post-quantum cryptosystem. Our protocols implement the CCA variants of distributed decryption and are actively secure (with abort) in the case of three parties and honest majority. Our protocols make use of a combination of problem specific MPC protocols, generic garbled circuit based MPC and generic Linear Secret Sharing based MPC. We also, as a by-product, report on the first run-times for the execution of the SHA-3 function in an MPC system.

1 Introduction

Distributed decryption enables a set of parties to decrypt a ciphertext under a shared (i.e. distributed) secret key. Distributed decryption protocols for traditional public key encryption and signature schemes have had a long history of innovation [9–12,14,16,19,20,25,26]. But the research on such protocols for schemes based on Ring-LWE (Learning-With-Errors) has only been started quite recently.

Despite research on Ring-LWE, and Fully/Somewhat Homormorphic Encryption (FHE/SHE) schemes derived from Ring-LWE being relatively new, applications of distributed decryption have found numerous applications already. One of the earliest applications we could find is the two-round passively secure FHE-based multiparty computation (MPC) protocol of Gentry [13]. In this MPC protocol, n parties encrypt their inputs to the MPC computation via an FHE scheme, and broadcast the ciphertexts. All parties can then homomorphically compute the desired function, with the result finally obtained via a distributed decryption. A similar methodology is applied in the multi-key FHE techniques of Asharov et al. [4]. These two works only aim for passive security, whereas

© Springer Nature Switzerland AG 2019
J. Jang-Jaccard and F. Guo (Eds.): ACISP 2019, LNCS 11547, pp. 192–210, 2019.
https://doi.org/10.1007/978-3-030-21548-4_11

a similar technique is applied in [21] to obtain low-round MPC via the BMR methodology [5], and in [7] to utilize Gentry's technique via an SHE scheme (and not an FHE scheme) for non-full-threshold access structures (such as the ones considered in this paper). Despite the overal protocols obtaining active security, the distributed decryption procedures in [7,21] are only required to be actively secure up to additive errors. A similar situation occurs in the SPDZ protocol [8] in which an actively secure (up to additive errors) distributed decryption protocol is required to produce the multiplication triples in the offline phase. The same technique is used in the High Gear variant of the Overdrive [17] offline phase for SPDZ.

The application of such distributed decryption protocols is however not just restricted to usage in MPC protocols. It is well established in the side-channel community that such key-splitting techniques can form the basis of various defences based on 'masking'; see for example a recent initiative of NIST in this area [6]. However, every masking technique requires a recombination technique, which is exactly what distributed decryption provides.

More importantly, the interest in standard Ring-LWE schemes due to the need to find suitable Post-Quantum Crypto (PQC) algorithms, as evidenced by the current NIST "competition", means that PQC schemes which can support distributed decryption will become of more interest. However there is a major issue with prior techniques to this problem. Firstly the methods require "noise-flooding" to ensure that no information leaks about the underlying secret key during decryption. This requires that the ciphertext modulus q needs to be made much larger than in a standard system which does not support distributed decryption. Secondly, the methods are only actively secure up to additive error (i.e. they are not fully actively secure) and they only allow distributed decryption of the IND-CPA versions of the underlying encryption schemes.

In this paper we present efficient methods to perform actively secure distributed decryption for IND-CCA versions of Ring-LWE based encryption in the case of three party honest majority protocols. This is done by combining in a novel manner traditional garbled circuit based MPC, with bespoke protocols for the specific functionality we require. On the way we also provide, to our knowledge, the first MPC implementation of the evaluation of the SHA-3 function; previously in [28] an MPC-optimized circuit was given, but no execution times for an actual MPC evaluation of SHA-3 has been presented. We also show how to utilize secret sharing based protocols such as embodied in the SCALE-MAMBA system [3] to produce an efficient distributed key generation procedure suitable for our underlying distributed decryption procedure.

Prior work on CCA secure distributed decryption protocols, even for encryption schemes based on "traditional" assumptions (such as RSA or Discrete Logarithms), such as those in [11,19,26], have looked at designing special purposes encryption procedures which are both CCA secure, and which enable an efficient distributed decryption procedure. In this work we instead take an off-the-shelf CCA secure encryption scheme and show how it can be made into a scheme which supports both distributed decryption and distributed key generation. This brings added challenges as the method for ciphertext checking is not immediately "MPC-friendly". Despite this drawback we show that such schemes can be implemented via MPC.

In total we use *four* different types of secret sharing between the three parties in order to obtain efficient protocols for the various sub-steps:

1. INS-sharing [15] modulo q of the Ring-LWE secret key.
2. Shamir secret sharing modulo q to generate the INS secret key via SCALE-MAMBA.
3. An additive 3-party binary sharing of the output of the Round function, before we pass it to the KMAC operation. This additive sharing is non-standard and looks like a cross between INS and replicated sharing.
4. An additive sharing modulo q of the output of the KMAC operation between two of the parties S_1 and S_2.

To illustrate our methods in terms of a concrete Ring-LWE system we take the LIMA submission [1] to the PQC contest. We take the latest version of this submission (version 1.1 at the time of writing). However, almost all our techniques will apply, with minor changes to the specific definitions of usage of SHA-3 etc, to a number of the other Ring-LWE systems under submission. A major advantage of the LIMA proposal versus a proposal such as say NTRU is that key generation and encryption are essentially linear operations; thus providing a distributed actively secure protocol for key generation and re-encryption becomes easy. For NTRU the key generation method, for example, needs to generate polynomials with distributions which cannot be generated in a linear fashion; in particular distributions with given coefficients with a given weight of -1 and $+1$ coefficients.

We end this section by noting that running our distributed decryption protocol using two as opposed to three parties, and using traditional passively secure Yao protocols, results in a passively secure distributed decryption protocol. For the two party case of the key generation protocol we could utilize the SPDZ [8] implementation within the SCALE-MAMBA framework. The two-party key generation would be actively secure and, more importantly, is possible since the modulus $q = 40961$ used in the LIMA v1.1 scheme is "FHE-Friendly" and hence can be used as the plaintext modulus for the SPDZ-offline phase.

2   Preliminaries

To focus our discussion we pick a specific Ring-LWE submission to the NIST PQC "competition"; in particular v1.1 of LIMA [1]. This was selected as it utilizes a relatively standard transform for ciphertext validity checking; namely randomness recovery followed by re-encryption which could pose a particular problem for a distributed decryption protocol. In addition the encryption and key generation procedures are also relatively linear, allowing one to utilize simple MPC protocols to perform re-encryption and distributed key generation.

We will focus on the main parameter sets in the LIMA proposal. In particular $N = 1024$ and $q = 40961$. However, our protocol can be easily adapted to the other parameter sets (in fact the protocol stays the same, all that needs to change is the specific implementation of the underlying garbled and arithmetic circuits).

In this section we summarize the LIMA construction and also summarize some tools from the MPC literature which we will be using. Our focus in the MPC literature will be on three party honest majority protocols which offer active security *with abort*.

2.1   The LIMA IND-CCA Encryption Scheme

Here we summarize the LIMA v1.1 construction. For more details readers are referred to [1]. As explained above we use the latest version of the proposal which avoids the rejection sampling in encryption of the first proposal and has, as a result, smaller parameters.

Cycloctomic Rings: LIMA makes use of two types of cyclotomic rings, in this paper we will concentrate on only the first type (minor modifications in what follows are needed to support the second type proposed in LIMA). We select N to be power of two, q to be a prime such that $q \equiv 1 \pmod{2 \cdot N}$. The scheme makes use of the following rings $R = \mathbb{Z}[X]/(X^N + 1)$, $R_2 = \mathbb{Z}_2[X]/(X^N + 1)$, and $R_q = \mathbb{Z}_q[X]/(X^N + 1)$. Note that $\Phi_{2 \cdot N}(X) = X^N + 1$ in this case. Elements of these rings are degree $(N - 1)$ polynomials with coefficients from $\mathbb{Z}, \mathbb{Z}_2, \mathbb{Z}_q$, respectively. Equivalently, these are represented as vectors of length N, with elements in $\mathbb{Z}, \mathbb{Z}_2, \mathbb{Z}_q$, respectively.

LIMA makes a lot of use of the number theoretic FFT algorithm to enable fast multiplication of ring elements. We will denote this operation in this paper by $\mathbf{f} \leftarrow \mathsf{FFT}(f)$ for the forward FFT, and $f \leftarrow \mathsf{FFT}^{-1}(\mathbf{f})$ for the inverse FFT operation. The forward direction maps a polynomial of degree $N - 1$ into a vector of length N over the same finite field $\mathbb{F}_q$ (by choice of q). For our MPC operations it is important to note that the FFT operation is a linear operation, i.e. $\mathsf{FFT}(f + g) = \mathsf{FFT}(f) + \mathsf{FFT}(g)$.

Use of SHA-3 in KMAC256: LIMA makes use of KMAC256, to create an XOF (Extendable Output Function) and a KDF (Key Derivation Function). The algorithm KMAC256 is itself derived from the SHA-3 hash function and is defined in NIST SP 800 185 [24]. Following the LIMA specification we use the following notation for the various uses of KMAC256. When called in the form $\mathsf{XOF} \leftarrow \mathsf{KMAC}(\mathsf{key}, \mathsf{data}, 0)$ the output is an XOF object, and when called in the form $K \leftarrow \mathsf{KMAC}(\mathsf{key}, \mathsf{data}, L)$ the output is a string of L bits in length. In both cases the input is a key key (of length at least 256 bits), a (one-byte) data string data, and a length field L in bits. The data string data is a diversifier and corresponds to the *domain separation* field in the KMAC standard. Different values of data will specify different uses of the KMAC construction. In the case when $L = 0$ we shall let $a \leftarrow \mathsf{XOF}[n]$ denote the process of obtaining n bytes from the XOF object returned by the call to KMAC. The KDF in LIMA is given by the notation $\mathsf{KDF}^{[n]}(k)$, which outputs the result of computing $\mathsf{KMAC}(k, 0x00, n)$.

KeyGen(N)

1. $a = (a_0, \ldots, a_{N-1}) \xleftarrow{\text{XOF}} \mathbb{F}_q^N$.
2. For $i = 0$ to $N - 1$ do $s_i \leftarrow$ GenerateGaussianNoise$_{\text{XOF}}(\sigma)$.
3. For $i = 0$ to $N - 1$ do $e'_i \leftarrow$ GenerateGaussianNoise$_{\text{XOF}}(\sigma)$.
4. $\mathbf{a} \leftarrow$ FFT(a), $\mathbf{s} \leftarrow$ FFT(s), $\mathbf{e}' \leftarrow$ FFT(e').
5. $\mathbf{b} \leftarrow (\mathbf{a} \otimes \mathbf{s}) \oplus \mathbf{e}'$,
6. $\mathfrak{st} \leftarrow (\mathbf{s}, \mathbf{a}, \mathbf{b})$.
7. $\mathfrak{pt} \leftarrow (\mathbf{a}, \mathbf{b})$.
8. Return ($\mathfrak{pt}, \mathfrak{st}$)

Fig. 1. LIMA key generation

In the full version we describe how LIMA uses the XOF to generate random values in different domains and with different distributions. These are $a \xleftarrow{\text{XOF}} \mathbb{F}_q$ to generate uniformly random single finite field element, $\mathbf{a} \xleftarrow{\text{XOF}} \mathbb{F}_q^n$ to generate a vector of such elements, and GenerateGaussianNoise$_{\text{XOF}}(\sigma)$ to generate elements in $\mathbb{F}_q$ from a distribution which is an approximation to a discrete Gaussian with standard deviation σ. It will turn out their method here is particularly well suited to enabling distributed key generation. In particular the LIMA algorithm uses the method of approximating a Discrete Gaussian via a centred binomial distribution given in [2], to produce a Gaussian with standard deviation $\sigma \approx 3.19$.

LIMA Key Generation: The specification of LIMA details that the private component of a public/private key pair is generated from the KMAC256 XOF. However, in practice this component can come from any source of random bits, thus the XOF output in lines 2 and 3 of Fig. 1 can be replaced by *any* source of random bits known to the secret key creator. We will make use of this fact in our distributed key generation procedure later on. Key Generation proceeds as in Fig. 1, where we assume a XOF has already been initiated and the operations $\otimes$ and $\oplus$ denote pointwise multiplication and addition (mod q).

Encryption and Decryption: Both the CCA encryption and decryption operations make use of a sub-procedure, called Enc-CPA-Sub($\mathbf{m}, \mathfrak{pt}, \text{XOF}$) which takes as input a message in $\mathbf{m} \in \{0,1\}^\ell$, a public key and an initialized XOF object XOF, and outputs a ciphertext $\mathfrak{c}$. The associated inverse operation is denoted Dec-CPA($\mathbf{c}, \mathfrak{st}$). These algorithms are defined in the full version. The operations make use of three sub-routines:

- Trunc denotes a procedure which throws away unnecessary coefficients of c_0, retaining only the ℓ elements corresponding to message component.
- BV-2-RE is a procedure which takes a bit string of length at most N and maps it into R_2.
- RE-2-BV is the inverse operation to BV-2-RE.

We can then define the CCA LIMA encryption, decryption, encapsulation and decapsulation operations as in Fig. 2.

Enc-CCA($\mathbf{m}, \mathfrak{pe}, \mathbf{r}$):

1. If $|\mathbf{r}| \neq 256$ or $|\mathbf{m}| \geq N - 256$ then return $\perp$.
2. $\mu \leftarrow \mathbf{m}\|\mathbf{r}$.
3. XOF $\leftarrow$ KMAC($\mu, 0x03, 0$).
4. $\mathbf{c} \leftarrow$ Enc-CPA-Sub($\mu, \mathfrak{pe}, $ XOF).
5. Return $\mathbf{c}$.

Dec-CCA($\mathbf{c}, \mathfrak{se}$):

1. $\mu \leftarrow$ Dec-CPA($\mathbf{c}, \mathfrak{se}$).
2. If $|\mu| < 256$ then return $\perp$.
3. XOF $\leftarrow$ KMAC($\mu, 0x03, 0$).
4. $\mathbf{c}' \leftarrow$ Enc-CPA-Sub($\mu, \mathfrak{pe}, $ XOF).
5. If $\mathbf{c} \neq \mathbf{c}'$ then return $\perp$.
6. $\mathbf{m}\|\mathbf{r} \leftarrow \mu$, where $\mathbf{r}$ is 256 bits long.
7. Return $\mathbf{m}$.

Encap-CCA($\ell, \mathfrak{pe}, \mathbf{s}$):

1. If $|\mathbf{r}| < 384$ or $|\mathbf{r}| > N$ then return $\perp$.
2. XOF $\leftarrow$ KMAC($\mathbf{r}, 0x05, 0$).
3. $\mathbf{c} \leftarrow$ Enc-CPA-Sub($\mathbf{r}, \mathfrak{pe}, $ XOF).
4. $\mathbf{k} \leftarrow$ KDF$^{[\ell]}(\mathbf{r})$.
5. Return ($\mathbf{c} = (c_0, \mathbf{c}_1), \mathbf{k}$).

Decap-CCA($\ell, \mathbf{c}, \mathfrak{se}$):

1. $\mathbf{r} \leftarrow$ Dec-CPA($\mathbf{c}, \mathfrak{se}$).
2. If $|\mathbf{r}| < 384$ then return $\perp$.
3. XOF $\leftarrow$ KMAC($\mathbf{r}, 0x05, 0$).
4. $\mathbf{c}' \leftarrow$ Enc-CPA-Sub($\mathbf{r}, \mathfrak{pe}, $ XOF).
5. If $\mathbf{c} \neq \mathbf{c}'$ then return $\perp$.
6. $\mathbf{k} \leftarrow$ KDF$^{[\ell]}(\mathbf{r})$.

Fig. 2. CCA secure encryption, decryption, encapsulation and decapsulation algorithms for LIMA

2.2 Three Party Honest Majority MPC Using Garbled Circuits

Our protocols make use of actively secure garbled circuit based MPC for honest majority in the three party setting. In this situation we use the techniques from [23]. The basic protocol to evaluate a function F on inputs x_1, x_2 and x_3 from parties P_1, P_2 and P_3 is as follows. Parties P_1 and P_2 agree on a random seed s and then use s to generate a garbled circuit. Party P_3 acts as evaluator. If P_1 or P_2 cheats then this is detected by P_3 as they will obtain different circuits, where as if P_3 cheats in sending output tables values incorrectly back to P_1 or P_2 (for their output), then the table values will not decode correctly. The overall protocol is described in Fig. 3. Thus we cheaply obtain active security with abort in this scenario.

1. Denote the inputs of S_1, S_2 and S_3 by x_1, x_2 and x_3, respectively.
2. Let $f(x_1, x_2, x_3)$ be the function to be computed and let $C(x_1, x_2, x_3)$ be a circuit that computes f.
3. Party S_1 chooses a random seed s and generates a garbled circuit GC computing C and the output translation tables O_1, O_2 and O_3 for the three parties outputs), using seed s.
4. Party S_3 chooses a random $x_3^a \leftarrow \{0,1\}^\ell$, where $\ell = |x_3|$, and sets $x_3^b \leftarrow x_3^a \oplus x_3$ and it sends x_3^a to S_1, and sends x_3^b to S_2.
5. Party S_1 sends (GC, O_3) to S_3. For every wire w associated with the input x_3 in the circuit, the garbled circuit definition is assumed to include $(H(k_w^0), H(k_w^1))$ in this order (where the keys on that wire are k_w^0, k_w^1).
6. Party S_1 sends s to S_2.
7. Party S_2 computes GC from s and sends $h = H(GC)$ to S_3.
8. S_3 checks that $h = H(GC)$ where h is the value it received from S_2, and GC is as received from S_1. If not, it aborts.
9. Party S_1 sends S_3 the keys associated with its own input x_1 and with x_3^a.
10. Party S_2 sends S_3 the keys associated with its own input x_2 and with x_3^b.
11. Parties S_1 and S_2 run a secure coind tossing protocol to generate random strings $R_1, \ldots, R_{|x_3|}$.
12. Denote the bits of x_3^a by $x_3^a[1], \ldots, x_3^a[\ell]$, denote the bits of x_3^b by $x_3^b[1], \ldots, x_3^b[\ell]$, and denote the wires associated with x_3 by $w_1, \ldots, w_\ell$.
13. For every $i = 1, \ldots, \ell$, party S_1 sends $k_i' \leftarrow k_{w_i}^0 \oplus x_3^a[i] \cdot \Delta \oplus R_i$ to S_3. We use the "free-XOR" trick so we have $k_{w_i}^1 = k_{w_i}^0 \oplus \Delta$.
14. For every $i = 1, \ldots, \ell$, party S_2 sends $k_i'' \leftarrow x_3^b[i] \cdot \Delta \oplus R_i$ to S_3.
15. For every $i = 1, \ldots, \ell$, party S_3 computes $k_{w_i}^{x_3[i]} \leftarrow k_i' \oplus k_i''$ and checks that this is consistent with the appropriate hash. That is, if $x_3[i] = 0$ then the hash of the key equals the first value in the appropriate pair; otherwise the second value. If not then S_3 aborts.
16. S_3 computes the garbled circuit GC and obtains their output using the table O_3.
17. S_3 sends the garbled outputs corresponding to S_1 and S_2's output wires to S_1 and S_2 respectively.
18. S_1 and S_2 decode their output using the translation tables O_1 and O_2.

Fig. 3. Garbled circuit based three party computation

2.3   Three Party Honest Majority MPC Using Shamir Secret Sharing

We also require honest majority three party actively secure MPC with abort based on linear secret sharing over the finite field $\mathbb{F}_q$. For this we use a protocol based on Shamir secret sharing implemented in the SCALE-MAMBA system [3]. This uses an offline phase to produce multiplication triples and shared random bits (using Maurer's multiplication protocol [22]) and then an online phase which checks for correctness by using the error detection properties of the underlying Reed-Solomon codes. See [18,27] for precise details of how this protocol works. This arithmetic circuit based MPC protocol is used in our distributed key generation phase, and we make crucial use of the ability of the SCALE-MAMBA system to generate shared random bits in the offline phase; as then our online phase becomes essentially a local operation.

We denote secret shared values over $\mathbb{F}_q$ by the notation $[a]$. In this notation linear operations, such as $[z] \leftarrow \alpha \cdot [x] + \beta \cdot [y] + \gamma$ are local operations, and hence essentially for free. Where as non-linear operations, such as $[z] \leftarrow [x] \cdot [y]$ require interaction. In the SCALE-MAMBA system these are done using a pre-processed set of Beaver triples $([a], [b], [c])$ with $c = a \cdot b$.

Output/opening values to all players will be denoted by $\mathsf{Output}([a])$ by which we mean all players learn the value of a, and abort if the value is not output correctly. Outputing to a specific player we will denote by $\mathsf{Output\text{-}To}(i, [a])$, in which case player i will learn the value of a, and abort if the value is not correct.

One can also use these pre-processed Beaver triples to generate random shared elements (by taking a triple and using $[a]$ and $[b]$ as the random elements. Of course when using Shamir sharing one could also generate such sharings using a PRSS, however the SCALE-MAMBA system does not currently support this functionality. So when generating random elements in the online phase we simply consume the first two components of a Beaver triple, and we will write $([a], [b], [c]) \leftarrow \mathsf{Triples}$, this is secure as long as $[c]$ is never used later. The offline phase also produced shared random bits, namely sharings of the form $[b]$ with $b \in \{0, 1\}$. We will denote this operation in what follows as $[b] \leftarrow \mathsf{Bits}$.

3   SHA3 in MPC

The TinyGarble compiler [28] has been reported to produce a circuit for the SHA-3 core internal Keccak-f function of 38,400 AND gates (160,054 total gates). Using similar techniques to the TinyGarble paper we compiled our own circuit for Keccak-f, finding a circuit with the same number of gates and 193,686 wires. This function takes as input, a sequence of 1600 bit values, and returns a 1600 bit value. The output is either then passed into the next round, during the absorption phase where it is combined with additional input, or part of the output is used as the output of SHA-3, in the squeezing phase.

Using our garbled circuit based protocol for honest majority computation amongst three parties, we were able to execute the Keccak-f function with a latency of 16ms per operation. With the testing being conducted on a set of three Linux RHEL servers running on AWS of type t2.small, which correspond to one "virtual CPU" and 2 GB of RAM.

4   Distributed Decryption for CCA-Secure Ring-LWE Encryption

Recall that a public key is a pair $(\mathbf{a}, \mathbf{b})$ and a secret key is a value $\mathbf{s}$, where $\mathbf{a}, \mathbf{b}, \mathbf{s} \in \mathbb{Z}_q^N$. Given our three servers, of which we assume at least two are honest, we share the secret key using Ito–Nishizeki–Saito sharing [15]. In particular S_1 is assumed to hold $(\mathbf{s}_1^{1,2}, \mathbf{s}_1^{1,3}) \in \mathbb{Z}_q^N$, S_2 is assumed to hold $(\mathbf{s}_2^{1,2}, \mathbf{s}_1^{2,3}) \in \mathbb{Z}_q^N$, and S_3 is assumed to hold $(\mathbf{s}_2^{1,3}, \mathbf{s}_2^{2,3}) \in \mathbb{Z}_q^N$ such that

$$\mathbf{s}_1^{1,2} + \mathbf{s}_2^{1,2} = \mathbf{s}_1^{1,3} + \mathbf{s}_2^{1,3} = \mathbf{s}_1^{2,3} + \mathbf{s}_2^{2,3} = \mathbf{s}.$$

How one generates a valid secret key satisfying this secret sharing we discuss in the next section. We call such a sharing an INS-sharing of s. Our overall distributed decryption and decapsulation protocols are then build out of a number of special protocols which either utilize our generic 3-party garbled circuit based protocol from earlier, or utilize special purpose MPC protocols built on top the ISN-sharing of inputs or other sharings of inputs. Thus in this protocol we combine a variety of MPC techniques together in a novel manner.

4.1 Sub-protocol: Round Function

We first require a protocol which takes an ISN-sharing of a vector $\mathbf{f}$ and produces the output of the function

$$\mu \leftarrow \left\| \left\lfloor \frac{2}{q} f \right\rceil \right\|$$

from the procedure Dec-CPA($\mathbf{c}, \mathfrak{st}$). In particular it needs to evaluate the functionality given in Fig. 4, which we do via the protocol given in Fig. 5.

We note that this protocol is secure by definition since the only thing defined here is the circuit, and a protocol that is secure for malicious adversaries is used to compute it. Let $|q|$ denote the number of bits needed to represent q and recall that addition and each less-than-comparison can be computed using a single AND gate per bit. Thus, $a + b \bmod q$ can be computed using exactly $4 \cdot |q|$ AND gates, and all the initial additions require $12 \cdot |q|$ AND gates. Next, the bitwise NOR of v, w requires $2 \cdot |q| - 1$ AND gates, each of the 2 less-than-comparisons (and greater-than etc.) of x are computed using $|q|$ AND gates, and there is 1 more AND gate. Overall, we therefore have a cost of $12 \cdot |q| + 2 \cdot |q| - 1 + 2 \cdot |q| + 1 = 16 \cdot |q|$ AND gates. In our experiments we used the parameter set of LIMA with $q = 40961$ and thus $|q| = 16$. Hence, each execution of this protocol for an individual coefficient requires 256 AND gates. When iterated over the 1024 coefficients we end up with a total of $262, 144$ AND gates.

4.2 Sub-protocol: Secure Evaluation of the Enc-CPA-Sub Function

Our next sub-protocol is to evaluate the Enc-CPA-Sub function on inputs which have been INS-shared. The protocol is given in Fig. 7 but from a high level works as follows: Firstly the three parties execute the KMAC function on their suitably padded inputs (which have been shared via a different secret sharing scheme), from this S_1 and S_2 obtain an additive $\mathbb{F}_q$-sharing of the output bits. This operation utilizes the SHA-3 implementation given earlier as a sub-procedure, and to aid readability we separate this operation into a sub-protocol in Fig. 6. In this protocol the parties have as input a sharing of a bit string μ defined as follows: S_1 holds (μ_1, ν_1), S_2 holds (μ_1, ν_2), and S_3 holds (μ_2, ν_1) such that $\mu = \mu_1 \oplus \mu_2 = \nu_1 \oplus \nu_2$. The output of the function will be an $\mathbb{F}_q$-sharing between S_1 and S_2 of the XOF applied to this input with diversifier D. The diversifier will be 0x03 for decryption and 0x05 for decapsulation). Note, that the first thing the circuit does is to ensure the input values are consistent, i.e. $\mu_1 \oplus \mu_2 = \nu_1 \oplus \nu_2$.

Input:

1. S_1 has $f_1^{1,2}, f_1^{1,3} \in \mathbb{Z}_q^\ell$, S_2 has $f_2^{1,2}, f_1^{2,3} \in \mathbb{Z}_q^\ell$, S_3 has $f_2^{1,3}, f_2^{2,3} \in \mathbb{Z}_q^\ell$.

Computation:

1. Compute $f^{1,2} \leftarrow f_1^{1,2} + f_2^{1,2} \bmod q$, $f^{1,3} \leftarrow f_1^{1,3} + f_2^{1,3} \bmod q$, $f^{2,3} \leftarrow f_1^{2,3} + f_2^{2,3} \bmod q$.
2. Set $b \leftarrow 1$ if $f^{1,2} = f^{1,3} = f^{2,3}$ and $b \leftarrow 0$ otherwise.
3. Convert f into centered representation.
4. Compute $\mu \leftarrow \left| \left| \left\lfloor \frac{2}{q} f \right\rceil \right| \right|$.
5. Choose random $\mu_1, \nu_1 \leftarrow \{0,1\}^\ell$ and set $\mu_2 \leftarrow \mu_1 \oplus \mu$ and $\nu_2 \leftarrow \nu_1 \oplus \mu$ (where here we mean bitwise XOR).

Output:

1. All parties S_1, S_2, S_3 receive b.
2. If $b = 1$ then S_1 receives μ_1, ν_1, S_2 receives μ_2, ν_2, and S_3 receives μ_2, ν_1.

Fig. 4. The functionality: $\mathcal{F}_{\mathsf{Round}}$

Also note that only party S_2 obtains output from this step. Since the number of AND gates in the permutation function is 38,400 and we have 114 rounds, then the total number of AND gates needed to execute this step is *approximately* $114 \cdot 38,400 = 4,377,600$, plus the number of AND gates needed to create S_2's output (which is approximately $3 \cdot 40 \cdot N \cdot \log_2 q \approx 1,966,080$).

The additive $\mathbb{F}_q$-sharing between S_1 and S_2 output from Fig. 6 is then used in a completely local manner by S_1 and S_2 to obtain a modulo q additive sharing of the supposed ciphertext. The fact we can perform mainly local operations is because the method to generate approximate Gaussian noise is completely linear and the FFT algorithm is itself linear. This is then revealed to players S_1 and S_2, via means of a garbled circuit computation between the three players. See Fig. 7 for details.

The privacy of the protocol to evaluate Enc-CPA-Sub is inherent in the fact we use secure actively secure protocols to evaluate the two required garbled circuits. The only place that an active adversary could therefore deviate is by entering incorrect values into the evaluation of the Trunc function; e.g. S_1 could enter the incorrect value for μ_1 or $y^{(1)}$. Any incorrect adversarial behaviour here will result in an incorrect value of c_0', which will be detected by the calling algorithm.

4.3   Secure Evaluation of Dec-CCA$(\mathbf{c}, \mathfrak{sk})$

We can now give the method for decryption for the CCA public key encryption algorithm, see Fig. 8. The secret key $\mathfrak{sk}$ is shared as described earlier, with the ciphertext $\mathbf{c} = (c_0, \mathbf{c}_1)$ being public.

We first, define a boolean circuit C that receives for input bit α, β and six elements $a, b, c, d, e, f \in \mathbb{Z}_q$, and works as follows:

1. Compute $x = a + b \bmod q$, $y = c + d \bmod q$ and $z = e + f \bmod q$. Observe that addition modulo q inside a circuit works by first adding two numbers (into a value that is larger by one bit) and then subtracting q if the comparison of the result with q is returns a value one. In a circuit this looks like:

$$a + b - (LT(a + b, q) \wedge q)$$

where $LT(r, s) = 0$ if and only if $r < s$ (as integers). Note that we compute the AND of a single bit $LT(a + b, q)$ and a value q; our meaning is to compute the AND of each bit of q.

2. Compute $v = x \oplus y$ and $w = x \oplus z$. Denote by γ the bitwise NOR of all the bits of v and w (i.e., $\gamma = 1$ if and only if *all* the bits of v and w equal 0, meaning that $x = y$ and $x = z$ and so $x = y = z$).

3. Let δ be the bit that satisfies the following Boolean formula:

$$\delta = \left[\left(x \geq \frac{q-1}{4} \right) \wedge \left(x < \frac{3(q-1)}{4} \right) \right]$$

4. Output β on the first output wire.
5. Output γ on the second output wire.
6. Output $\gamma \wedge (\alpha \oplus \delta)$ on the third output wire.
7. Output $\gamma \wedge (\beta \oplus \delta)$ on the fourth output wire.

Now, the function Round can be computed securely, as follows:

1. S_1 chooses random $\mu_1, \nu_1 \leftarrow \{0, 1\}^{\ell}$; denote the ith bit of μ_1 by μ_1^i and the ith bit of ν_1 by ν_1^i.
2. For every $i = 1, \ldots, \ell$:
   (a) Denote by $f[i]$ the ith element of $f \in \mathbb{Z}_q^{\ell}$.
   (b) S_1, S_2 and S_3 securely compute $C\left(\mu_1^i, \nu_1^i, f_1^{1,2}, f_2^{1,2}, f_1^{1,3}, f_2^{1,3}, f_1^{2,3}, f_2^{2,3}\right)$ using the previous 3-party garbled circuit protocol. Note that S_1 provides input $\left(\mu_1^i, \nu_1^i, f_1^{1,2}, f_1^{1,3}\right)$, S_2 provides input $\left(f_2^{1,2}, f_2^{2,3}\right)$, and S_3 provides input $\left(f_2^{1,3}, f_2^{2,3}\right)$. The secure protocol provides outputs as follows:
      i. S_3 *only* receives the output bit β on the first output wire. S_3 denotes this output by ν_1^i.
      ii. *All* parties receive the output bit γ on the second output wire. They denote the output bit by γ.
      iii. S_2 and S_3 *only* receive the output bit on the third output wire. S_2 and S_3 denote this output by μ_2^i.
      iv. S_2 *only* receives the output bit on the fourth output wire. S_2 denotes this output by ν_2^i.
   (c) If any party receives output bit $\gamma = 0$, it aborts.
3. S_1 outputs $\mu_1 = \mu_1^1, \ldots, \mu_1^{\ell}$ and $\nu_1 = \nu_1^1, \ldots, \nu_1^{\ell}$.
4. S_2 outputs $\mu_2 = \mu_2^1, \ldots, \mu_2^{\ell}$ and $\nu_2 = \nu_2^1, \ldots, \nu_2^{\ell}$.
5. S_3 outputs $\mu_2 = \mu_2^1, \ldots, \mu_2^{\ell}$ and $\nu_1 = \nu_1^1, \ldots, \nu_1^{\ell}$.

Fig. 5. The protocol: Π_{Round}

The parties using the 3-party garbled circuit protocol from earlier securely compute the application of KMAC (with diversifer D) on the values $\mu = \mu_1 \oplus \mu_2 = \nu_1 \oplus \nu_2$ as follows. In addition party S_1 enters a random value $b_i^{(1)} \in \mathbb{F}_q$ for each output bit.

Padding: The parties first defin: $\bar{\mu}_1 = \mu_1 || 1 || 0^{r-|\mu_1|-2} || 1$, $\bar{\mu}_2 = \mu_2 || 0^{r-|\mu_2|}$, $\bar{\nu}_1 = \nu_1 || 1 || 0^{r-|\nu_1|-2} || 1$ and $\bar{\nu}_2 = \nu_2 || 0^{r-|\nu_2|}$ where $r = 1088$.
The parties then run the following circuit:

1. Compute $u \leftarrow \bar{\mu}_1 \oplus \bar{\mu}_2$, $v \leftarrow \bar{\nu}_1 \oplus \bar{\nu}_2$.
2. Check that $u = v$, if not, abort. i.e. output 1 on a special abort wire and 0 on all others; if no abort, then the abort wire should hold 0.
3. Compute KMAC(u): We need one absorbtion round, and for the squeezing we repeatedly apply the garbled round function for SHA-3, so as to obtain $3 \cdot 40 \cdot N$ bits of shared output. Thus we need to execute $3 \cdot 40 \cdot N/r$ rounds of squeezing, when $N = 1024$ and $r = 1088$, so we require 113 rounds of squeezing.
   Specifically: Let $p(x, y)$ denote the permutation function of SHA-3, with domain size of 1600 bits
   (a) Set $R_0 \leftarrow 0^{1088}$, $C_0 \leftarrow 0^{512}$
   (b) $(R_0', C_0') \leftarrow p(u, 0^{512})$
   (c) For $i = 1$ to 113: $(R_i', C_i') \leftarrow p(R_{i-1}', C_{i-1}')$.
   (d) The values $(R_1', \ldots, R_{113}')$ are then used (combined with the respected $b_i^{(1)}$ input from S_1) to produce the output for S_2. In particular if bit k of R_j' corresponds to output bit b_i then we set $b_i^{(2)}$ to $b_i - b_i^{(1)} \pmod{q}$.

Fig. 6. Protocol to securely evaluate KMAC on shared inputs

Security of the Protocol: The Round function is computed by a protocol that is secure against malicious adversaries. Intuitively, this means that the view of each party can be trivially simulated since S_1, S_2 and S_3 receive nothing but random shares as output from this subprotocol and no other messages are even sent. However, the parties *can* provide incorrect values at all steps of the protocol. Specifically, a corrupt S_1 can input an incorrect f_1 into Round, similarly a corrupt S_2 can input an incorrect f_2 into Round, etc. We resolve this problem by adding redundancy into the computation.

First, we compute the initial f values three times; once between each different pair or parties. Since at least one of these pairs is guaranteed to be honest, we have that the output of the operation $c_0 - \mathsf{Trunc}(\mathsf{FFT}^{-1}(\mathbf{s} \otimes \mathbf{c}_1))$ will be correct for this pair. Since the Round function computation verifies that all these values are equal (or else $\gamma = 0$ in the output and the parties learn nothing and abort), we have that this must be correct.

The parties then the protocol to evaluate Enc-CPA-Sub from Fig. 7 to obtain the re-encryption $(c_0', \mathbf{c}_1')$. Note, that for this to be correct, and so the equality check to pass, the servers must act honestly. Otherwise an invalid ciphertext is produced. Finally, the output message is obtained, and checked for correctness, using the redundancy inherent in the output of the Round function.

---

1. Using Figure 6 party S_1 and S_2 obtain an additive sharing over $\mathbb{F}_q$ of the output bits from the KMAC operation applied to $\mu = \mu_1 \oplus \mu_2 = \nu_1 \oplus \nu_2$.
2. Parties S_1 and S_2 now locally compute additive sharings modulo q of the random Gaussian values v_i, e_i and d_i from the Enc-Sub-CPA algorithm of LIMA. This is done by locally applying the algorithm to produce Gaussian values, GenerateGaussianNoise since it is a linear function of the input random bits. Thus party S_1 obtains three ring elements $(v^{(1)}, e^{(1)}, d^{(1)})$, and party S_2 obtains three ring elements $(v^{(2)}, e^{(2)}, d^{(2)})$ such that $v = v^{(1)} + v^{(2)}$, $e = e^{(1)} + e^{(2)}$ and $d = d^{(1)} + d^{(2)}$.
3. Party S_1 locally computes the values $\mathbf{v}^{(1)} \leftarrow \mathsf{FFT}(v^{(1)})$, $\mathbf{e}^{(1)} \leftarrow \mathsf{FFT}(e^{(1)})$, $s^{(1)} \leftarrow \mathsf{FFT}^{-1}(\mathbf{b} \otimes \mathbf{v}^{(1)})$, $\mathbf{c}_1^{(1)} \leftarrow (\mathbf{a} \otimes \mathbf{v}^{(1)}) \oplus \mathbf{e}^{(1)}$.
4. Party S_2 locally computes the values $\mathbf{v}^{(2)} \leftarrow \mathsf{FFT}(v^{(2)})$, $\mathbf{e}^{(2)} \leftarrow \mathsf{FFT}(e^{(2)})$, $s^{(2)} \leftarrow \mathsf{FFT}^{-1}(\mathbf{b} \otimes \mathbf{v}^{(2)})$, $\mathbf{c}_1^{(2)} \leftarrow (\mathbf{a} \otimes \mathbf{v}^{(2)}) \oplus \mathbf{e}^{(2)}$.
5. Parties S_1 and S_2 locally compute sharing of $y = y^{(1)} + y^{(2)} = s + d$ by computing $y^{(1)} \leftarrow s^{(1)} + d^{(1)}$ and $y^{(2)} \leftarrow s^{(2)} + d^{(2)}$.
6. The parties S_1 and S_2 open $\mathbf{c}_1^{(1)}$ and $\mathbf{c}_1^{(2)}$ to each other, so they can obtain $\mathbf{c}_1'$.
7. With private input $(y^{(1)}, \mu_1)$ and $(y^{(2)}, \mu_2)$ from S_1 and S_2 the three parties compute (using a secure Garbled Circuit based secure computation protocol) the value

$$c_0' = \mathsf{Trunc}\left(y^{(1)} + y^{(2)} + \Delta_q \cdot \mathsf{BV\text{-}2\text{-}RE}(\mu_1 \oplus \mu_2), \ell\right).$$

with S_1 and S_2 obtaining the output.

Fig. 7. Protocol to securely evaluate Enc-CPA-Sub$((\mu_1, \nu_1), (\mu_1, \nu_2), (\mu_2, \nu_1), \mathsf{pk}, D)$

We prove the security of the protocol via simulation by constructing a simulator $\mathcal{S}$ for the adversary $\mathcal{A}$. The simulator $\mathcal{S}$ knows the shares of the key held by each party, and works as follows:

- If S_1 is corrupted by $\mathcal{A}$, then the simulator $\mathcal{S}$ sends $c_0, \mathbf{c}_1$ to the trusted party computing the functionality and receives back $m = x \| s$. Then, $\mathcal{S}$ invokes $\mathcal{A}$ and receives the inputs $(f_1^{1,2}, f_1^{1,3})$ that $\mathcal{A}$ inputs to the Round function. Since $\mathcal{S}$ knows $\mathbf{s}_1^{1,2}$ and $\mathbf{s}_1^{1,3}$, it can verify if $\mathcal{A}$ computed these correctly. If not, then $\mathcal{S}$ sends $\bot$ to the trusted party, simulates the output of Round providing $\gamma = 0$ at the appropriate places and halts. (All other outputs of Round are given as random.) Else, $\mathcal{S}$ provides output of Round to be $\gamma = 1$ and the μ^2, ν^2 values as random.
  The simulation of the application of KMAC via a Garbled Circuit can be done, assuming an ideal functionality for the secure computation of KMAC, in the standard way. Note, that if S_1 lies about its input into the KMAC algorithm, or lies about its value $(y^{(1)}, \mu_1)$ input into the Trunc evaluation, then with overwhelming probability party S_2 will abort when checking $c_0' = c_1'$ or $\mathbf{c}_1' = \mathbf{c}_1$.
  The view of $\mathcal{A}$ in the simulation is clearly identical to its view in a hybrid execution where the function Round, Trunc and a function to perform secure computation are ideal functionalities. Thus, the output distributions are computationally indistinguishable, as required.
- The simulation for S_2 and S_3 is similar; with S_3 being a little simpler.

1. Let ℓ denote the length of c_0, abort if $\ell \neq 0 \pmod 8$.
2. Party S_1 locally computes

$$f_1^{1,2} \leftarrow c_0 - \mathsf{Trunc}(\mathsf{FFT}^{-1}(\mathbf{s}_1^{1,2} \otimes \mathbf{c}_1), \ell) \text{ and } f_1^{1,3} \leftarrow c_0 - \mathsf{Trunc}(\mathsf{FFT}^{-1}(\mathbf{s}_1^{1,3} \otimes \mathbf{c}_1), \ell).$$

3. Party S_2 locally computes

$$f_2^{1,2} \leftarrow \mathsf{Trunc}(\mathsf{FFT}^{-1}(\mathbf{s}_2^{1,2} \otimes \mathbf{c}_1), \ell) \text{ and } f_1^{2,3} \leftarrow c_0 - \mathsf{Trunc}(\mathsf{FFT}^{-1}(\mathbf{s}_1^{2,3} \otimes \mathbf{c}_1), \ell).$$

4. Party S_3 locally computes

$$f_2^{1,3} \leftarrow \mathsf{Trunc}(\mathsf{FFT}^{-1}(\mathbf{s}_2^{1,3} \otimes \mathbf{c}_1), \ell) \text{ and } f_2^{2,3} \leftarrow \mathsf{Trunc}(\mathsf{FFT}^{-1}(\mathbf{s}_2^{2,3} \otimes \mathbf{c}_1), \ell).$$

5. Note that after these operations we have $f_1^{1,2} + f_2^{1,2} = f_1^{1,3} + f_2^{1,3} = f_1^{2,3} + f_2^{2,3} = c_0 - \mathsf{Trunc}(\mathsf{FFT}^{-1}(\mathbf{s} \otimes \mathbf{c}_1), \ell)$.
6. S_1, S_2 and S_3 securely compute $\mathsf{Round}\,((f_1^{1,2}, f_1^{1,3}), (f_2^{1,2}, f_1^{2,3}), (f_2^{1,3}, f_2^{2,3}), \ell)$, as given above in Figure 5. Denote the output of S_1 from this computation by μ_1, ν_1, the output of S_2 by μ_2, ν_2, and the output of S_3 by μ_2, ν_1, with $\mu_1, \nu_1, \mu_2, \nu_2 \in \{0, 1\}^\ell$. If any party received an abort in the Round function computation, then it does not proceed.
7. The parties now run $\mathsf{Enc\text{-}CPA\text{-}Sub}(\mu_1, \mu_2, \nu_1, \nu_2, \mathfrak{pk}, 0x03)$ using the protocol in Figure 7, so that parties S_1 and S_2 obtain c_0' and $\mathbf{c}_1'$.
8. If S_1 or S_2 detect that $c_0 \neq c_0'$ or $\mathbf{c}_1 \neq \mathbf{c}_1'$ then the parties abort.
9. All three parties reveal the first $\ell - 256$ bits of μ_1, μ_2, ν_1 and ν_2 to each other using a broadcast channel (ensuring a sending party cannot send different values to different players). Call these values μ_1', μ_2', ν_1' and ν_2'. A party now aborts if any value it receives, which it owns, does not equal what they expected, i.e. S_1 aborts if ν_1' that they hold does not equal the ν_1' that was sent from party S_3.
10. The parties compute $m = \mu_1' \oplus \mu_2'$ and $m' = \nu_1' \oplus \nu_2'$ and abort if $m \neq m'$.
11. The parties output m.

Fig. 8. Secure evaluation of Dec-CCA$(\mathbf{c}, \mathfrak{sk})$

4.4 Secure Evaluation of Decap-CCA$(\mathbf{c}, \mathfrak{sk})$

The distributed decapsulation routine works much like the distributed decryption routine. However, to obtain the same ideal functionality of a real decapsulation routine we need to evaluate the KDF computation within a secure computation. This can be done using the same method we use to evaluate the KMAC needed in the XOF computation; since in LIMA both are based on different modes of the SHA-3 based KMAC operation. The overal protocol is similar and is given in the full version.

4.5 Experimental Results

Using the basic LIMA parameters of $q = 40961$ and $N = 1024$ we implemented the above protocol, and run it on a set of three Linux RHEL servers running on AWS of type t2.small with 2 GB of RAM. The total run time for distributed decryption was 4280 ms. The main cost was the need to perform the initial decryption, and then re-encrypt, without recovering the message in plaintext. This is inherent in the methodology adopted by LIMA, and many other of the PQC candidate algorithms, for producing a chosen ciphertext secure encryption algorithm. More MPC friendly methods to obtain CCA security could reduce this run time considerably, but that does not seem to have been a design goal for any of the candidate submissions. For distributed decapsulation in the KEM algorithm we achieved an execution time of 4342 ms.

5   Distributed Key Generation for Ring-LWE Encryption

Distributed key generation can be performed relatively straightforwardly using a generic MPC system based on linear secret sharing which supports two-out-of-three threshold access structures and gives active security with abort. As explained earlier we selected SCALE-MAMBA to do this, as we could use an off-the-shelf system.

SecGauss()

1. $[a] \leftarrow 0$.
2. For $i \in [0, \dots, 19]$ do
   (a) $[b] \leftarrow$ Bits, $[b'] \leftarrow$ Bits.
   (b) $[a] \leftarrow [a] + [b] - [b']$.
3. Return $[a]$.

Fig. 9. Securely generating approximate Gaussians

The main difficulty in key generation would appear to be the need to generate the approximate Gaussian distributions needed for LIMA. However, the specific distribution method chosen in LIMA dovetails nicely with the offline preprocessing found in SCALE-MAMBA. This results in the method to securely generate approximate Gaussian distributions given in Fig. 9, which we note becomes a completely local operation in the online phase of the MPC protocol.

From this it is easy to produce the key generation procedure which we give in terms of an inner MPC-core of the algorithm (which mainly consists of local operations and opening values to different players which is implemented in SCALE-MAMBA) (lines 3 to 5 of Fig. 10). plus non-interactive local operations which are purely about placing data into the correct formats. We make extensive use of the fact that the FFT operation is linear. In our algorithms we utilize vectors/polynomials of secret shared values which we will write as $[\underline{f}]$ which we use to represent the element in R given by $[\underline{f}]_0 + [\underline{f}]_1 \cdot X + \dots + [\underline{f}]_{N-1} \cdot X^{N-1}$.

KeyGen()

1. All players agree on a key for a XOF, XOF.
2. $\underline{a} \xleftarrow{\text{XOF}} \mathbb{F}_q^N$.
3. For $i \in [0, \ldots, N-1]$ do
   (a) $[\underline{s}]_i \leftarrow \mathsf{SecGauss}()$, $[\underline{e}]_i \leftarrow \mathsf{SecGauss}()$.
   (b) $([\underline{s}_1^{1,2}]_i, [\underline{s}_1^{1,3}]_i, [c]) \leftarrow \mathsf{Triples}$, $([\underline{s}_1^{2,3}]_i, [b], [c]) \leftarrow \mathsf{Triples}$.
   (c) $[\underline{s}_2^{1,2}]_i \leftarrow [\underline{s}]_i - [\underline{s}_1^{1,2}]_i$, $[\underline{s}_2^{1,3}]_i \leftarrow [\underline{s}]_i - [\underline{s}_1^{1,3}]_i$, $[\underline{s}_2^{2,3}]_i \leftarrow [\underline{s}]_i - [\underline{s}_1^{2,3}]_i$.
   (d) Output-To$(1, [\underline{s}_1^{1,2}]_i)$, Output-To$(1, [\underline{s}_1^{1,3}]_i)$.
   (e) Output-To$(2, [\underline{s}_1^{2,3}]_i)$, Output-To$(2, [\underline{s}_2^{1,2}]_i)$.
   (f) Output-To$(3, [\underline{s}_2^{1,3}]_i)$, Output-To$(3, [\underline{s}_2^{2,3}]_i)$.
4. $[\underline{b}] \leftarrow \underline{a} \cdot [\underline{s}] + [\underline{e}] \pmod{\Phi_{2 \cdot N}(X)}$.
   This is a completely local operation as $\underline{a}$ is public. For $k = 0, \ldots, N-1$ we compute:
   (a) $[\underline{b}]_k \leftarrow \left(\sum_{i+j=k} \underline{a}_i \cdot [\underline{s}]_j\right) - \left(\sum_{i+j=k+N} \underline{a}_i \cdot [\underline{s}]_j\right) + [\underline{e}]_k$.
5. For $i \in [0, \ldots, N-1]$ execute Output$([\underline{b}]_i)$.
6. $\mathbf{a} \leftarrow \mathsf{FFT}(\underline{a})$, $\mathbf{b} \leftarrow \mathsf{FFT}(\underline{b})$, $\mathfrak{pt} \leftarrow (\mathbf{a}, \mathbf{b})$.
7. Player S_1 executes $\mathbf{s}_1^{1,2} \leftarrow \mathsf{FFT}(\underline{s}_1^{1,2})$ and $\mathbf{s}_1^{1,3} \leftarrow \mathsf{FFT}(\underline{s}_1^{1,3})$.
8. Player S_2 executes $\mathbf{s}_2^{1,2} \leftarrow \mathsf{FFT}(\underline{s}_2^{1,2})$ and $\mathbf{s}_1^{2,3} \leftarrow \mathsf{FFT}(\underline{s}_1^{2,3})$.
9. Player S_3 executes $\mathbf{s}_2^{1,3} \leftarrow \mathsf{FFT}(\underline{s}_2^{1,3})$ and $\mathbf{s}_2^{2,3} \leftarrow \mathsf{FFT}(\underline{s}_2^{2,3})$.

Fig. 10. Main key generation routine

5.1 Experimental Results

We implemented the above key generation phase within the SCALE-MAMBA framework for the parameters $N = 1024$ and $q = 40961$ of LIMA. We used the settings of Shamir secret sharing and the Maurer [22] based offline settings of SCALE-MAMBA. Our experiments for this component were executed on three Linux Ubuntu machines with Intel i7-7700K processors running at 4.20 GHz, and with 8192 KB cache and 32 GB RAM.

The SCALE-MAMBA system runs in an integrated offline–online manner, however one can program it so as to obtain estimates for the execution times of both the offline and the online phases. Within the system there is a statistical security parameter secp which defines the probability that an adversary can get the pre-processing to invalid data. The variable $s = \mathtt{sacrifice\_stat\_sec}$ in the system defines the value of secp via the equation

$$\mathsf{secp} = \lceil \log_2 q \rceil \cdot \left\lceil \frac{s}{\lceil \log_2 q \rceil} \right\rceil.$$

When q is large (i.e. $q > 2^{128}$), as it is in most envisioned executions of SCALE-MAMBA the default value of $s = 40$ results in a suitable security parameter. However, for our small value of q we needed to modify s so as to obtain a suitable value of secp. We note, that this setting only affects the runtime for the offline phase; and as can be seen the effect on the run times in Table 1 is marginal.

The online run time takes 1.22 s, although roughly one second of this is used in performing the 6144 output operations. On further investigation we found this

Table 1. Times to produce the offline data for the Key Generation operation. This is essentially producing 81920 shared random bits, 2048 multiplication triples and enough shared randomness to enable the output of the shared keys.

s	secp	Time (Seconds)
40	48	20.2
80	80	20.7
128	128	23.1

was because SCALE-MAMBA performs all the reveals in a sequential as opposed to batch manner (requiring 6144 rounds of communication as opposed to one). We suspect a more careful tuned implementation could reduce the online time down to less than a quarter of a second. However, our implementation of the Key Generation method in SCALE-MAMBA took about a day of programmers time; thus using a general system (even if inefficient) can be more efficient on the development time.

Acknowledgements. This work has been supported in part by ERC Advanced Grant ERC-2015-AdG-IMPaCT and by the Defense Advanced Research Projects Agency (DARPA) and Space and Naval Warfare Systems Center, Pacific (SSC Pacific) under contract No. N66001-15-C-4070, and by the FWO under an Odysseus project GOH9718N.

References

1. Albrecht, M.R., et al.: LIMA-1.1: a PQC encryption scheme (2018). https://lima-pq.github.io/
2. Alkim, E., Ducas, L., Pöppelmann, T., Schwabe, P.: Post-quantum key exchange - a new hope. In: Holz, T., Savage, S. (eds.) 25th USENIX Security Symposium, USENIX Security 2016, Austin, TX, USA, 10–12 August 2016, pp. 327–343. USENIX Association (2016). https://www.usenix.org/conference/usenixsecurity16/technical-sessions/presentation/alkim
3. Aly, A., et al.: SCALE and MAMBA documentation (2018). https://homes.esat.kuleuven.be/~nsmart/SCALE/
4. Asharov, G., Jain, A., López-Alt, A., Tromer, E., Vaikuntanathan, V., Wichs, D.: Multiparty computation with low communication, computation and interaction via threshold FHE. In: Pointcheval, D., Johansson, T. (eds.) EUROCRYPT 2012. LNCS, vol. 7237, pp. 483–501. Springer, Heidelberg (2012). https://doi.org/10.1007/978-3-642-29011-4_29
5. Beaver, D., Micali, S., Rogaway, P.: The round complexity of secure protocols (extended abstract). In: 22nd ACM STOC, pp. 503–513. ACM Press, May 1990
6. Brandao, L.T.A.N., Mouha, N., Vassilev, A.: Threshold schemes for cryptographic primitives: challenges and opportunities in standardization and validation of threshold cryptography (2018). https://csrc.nist.gov/publications/detail/nistir/8214/draft

7. Choudhury, A., Loftus, J., Orsini, E., Patra, A., Smart, N.P.: Between a rock and a hard place: interpolating between MPC and FHE. In: Sako, K., Sarkar, P. (eds.) ASIACRYPT 2013. LNCS, vol. 8270, pp. 221–240. Springer, Heidelberg (2013). https://doi.org/10.1007/978-3-642-42045-0_12

8. Damgård, I., Pastro, V., Smart, N., Zakarias, S.: Multiparty computation from somewhat homomorphic encryption. In: Safavi-Naini, R., Canetti, R. (eds.) CRYPTO 2012. LNCS, vol. 7417, pp. 643–662. Springer, Heidelberg (2012). https://doi.org/10.1007/978-3-642-32009-5_38

9. Desmedt, Y.: Society and group oriented cryptography: a new concept. In: Pomerance, C. (ed.) CRYPTO 1987. LNCS, vol. 293, pp. 120–127. Springer, Heidelberg (1988). https://doi.org/10.1007/3-540-48184-2_8

10. Desmedt, Y., Frankel, Y.: Threshold cryptosystems. In: Brassard, G. (ed.) CRYPTO 1989. LNCS, vol. 435, pp. 307–315. Springer, New York (1990). https://doi.org/10.1007/0-387-34805-0_28

11. Fouque, P.-A., Pointcheval, D.: Threshold cryptosystems secure against chosen-ciphertext attacks. In: Boyd, C. (ed.) ASIACRYPT 2001. LNCS, vol. 2248, pp. 351–368. Springer, Heidelberg (2001). https://doi.org/10.1007/3-540-45682-1_21

12. Frederiksen, T.K., Lindell, Y., Osheter, V., Pinkas, B.: Fast distributed RSA key generation for semi-honest and malicious adversaries. In: Shacham, H., Boldyreva, A. (eds.) CRYPTO 2018. LNCS, vol. 10992, pp. 331–361. Springer, Cham (2018). https://doi.org/10.1007/978-3-319-96881-0_12

13. Gentry, C.: A fully homomorphic encryption scheme. Ph.D. thesis, Stanford University (2009). http://crypto.stanford.edu/craig

14. Hazay, C., Mikkelsen, G.L., Rabin, T., Toft, T.: Efficient RSA key generation and threshold paillier in the two-party setting. In: Dunkelman, O. (ed.) CT-RSA 2012. LNCS, vol. 7178, pp. 313–331. Springer, Heidelberg (2012). https://doi.org/10.1007/978-3-642-27954-6_20

15. Ito, M., Nishizeki, T., Saito, A.: Secret sharing scheme realizing general access structure. Electron. Commun. Jpn. (Part III: Fundam. Electron. Sci.) **72**, 56–64 (1989)

16. Katz, J., Yung, M.: Threshold cryptosystems based on factoring. In: Zheng, Y. (ed.) ASIACRYPT 2002. LNCS, vol. 2501, pp. 192–205. Springer, Heidelberg (2002). https://doi.org/10.1007/3-540-36178-2_12

17. Keller, M., Pastro, V., Rotaru, D.: Overdrive: making SPDZ great again. In: Nielsen, J.B., Rijmen, V. (eds.) EUROCRYPT 2018. LNCS, vol. 10822, pp. 158–189. Springer, Cham (2018). https://doi.org/10.1007/978-3-319-78372-7_6

18. Keller, M., Rotaru, D., Smart, N.P., Wood, T.: Reducing communication channels in MPC. In: Catalano, D., De Prisco, R. (eds.) SCN 2018. LNCS, vol. 11035, pp. 181–199. Springer, Cham (2018). https://doi.org/10.1007/978-3-319-98113-0_10

19. Libert, B., Yung, M.: Non-interactive CCA-secure threshold cryptosystems with adaptive security: new framework and constructions. In: Cramer, R. (ed.) TCC 2012. LNCS, vol. 7194, pp. 75–93. Springer, Heidelberg (2012). https://doi.org/10.1007/978-3-642-28914-9_5

20. Lindell, Y.: Fast secure two-party ECDSA signing. In: Katz, J., Shacham, H. (eds.) CRYPTO 2017. LNCS, vol. 10402, pp. 613–644. Springer, Cham (2017). https://doi.org/10.1007/978-3-319-63715-0_21

21. Lindell, Y., Smart, N.P., Soria-Vazquez, E.: More efficient constant-round multi-party computation from BMR and SHE. In: Hirt, M., Smith, A. (eds.) TCC 2016. LNCS, vol. 9985, pp. 554–581. Springer, Heidelberg (2016). https://doi.org/10.1007/978-3-662-53641-4_21

22. Maurer, U.: Secure multi-party computation made simple. Discrete Appl. Math. **154**(2), 370–381 (2006)
23. Mohassel, P., Rosulek, M., Zhang, Y.: Fast and secure three-party computation: the garbled circuit approach. In: Ray, I., Li, N., Kruegel, C. (eds.) ACM CCS 2015, pp. 591–602. ACM Press, October 2015
24. NIST National Institute for Standards and Technology: SHA-3 derived functions: cSHAKE, KMAC, TupleHash and ParallelHash (2016). http://nvlpubs.nist.gov/nistpubs/SpecialPublications/NIST.SP.800-185.pdf
25. Shoup, V.: Practical threshold signatures. In: Preneel, B. (ed.) EUROCRYPT 2000. LNCS, vol. 1807, pp. 207–220. Springer, Heidelberg (2000). https://doi.org/10.1007/3-540-45539-6_15
26. Shoup, V., Gennaro, R.: Securing threshold cryptosystems against chosen ciphertext attack. In: Nyberg, K. (ed.) EUROCRYPT 1998. LNCS, vol. 1403, pp. 1–16. Springer, Heidelberg (1998). https://doi.org/10.1007/BFb0054113
27. Smart, N.P., Wood, T.: Error detection in monotone span programs with application to communication-efficient multi-party computation. In: Matsui, M. (ed.) CT-RSA 2019. LNCS, vol. 11405, pp. 210–229. Springer, Cham (2019). https://doi.org/10.1007/978-3-030-12612-4_11
28. Songhori, E.M., Hussain, S.U., Sadeghi, A.R., Schneider, T., Koushanfar, F.: TinyGarble: highly compressed and scalable sequential garbled circuits. In: 2015 IEEE Symposium on Security and Privacy, pp. 411–428. IEEE Computer Society Press, May 2015

Cryptanalysis on CCA2-Secured LRPC-Kronecker Cryptosystem

Terry Shue Chien Lau$^{(\boxtimes)}$ and Chik How Tan

Temasek Laboratories, National University of Singapore,
5A Engineering Drive 1, #09-02, Singapore 117411, Singapore
{tsltlsc,tsltch}@nus.edu.sg

Abstract. Recently, a new rank metric code, namely LRPC-Kronecker Product codes was proposed in APKC 2018 Workshop, and adapted into a construction of a new cryptosystem, namely the LRPC-Kronecker cryptosystem. The LRPC-Kronecker cryptosystem has compact key size, with their parameters achieve 256-bit security with key size (9,768 bits) smaller than the RSA's key size (15,360 bits). It was also shown that the LRPC-Kronecker cryptosystem is CCA2-secured via the Kobara-Imai conversion. In this paper, we point out some errors in the original LRPC-Kronecker cryptosystem and suggest a reparation for the errors. We show that the LRPC-Kronecker cryptosystem in fact is equivalent to the LRPC cryptosystem. With this equivalence shown, we suggest alternative encryption and decryption, namely AKron for the LRPC-Kronecker cryptosystem. Furthermore, we show that there exists design weakness in the LRPC-Kronecker cryptosystem. We exploit this weakness and successfully cryptanalyze all the suggested parameters for $k_1 = n_1$. We are able to recover secret key for all the proposed parameters within the claimed security level.

Keywords: Code-based cryptography · McEliece ·
Kronecker Product · Key recovery attack · Public-key encryption ·
Rank metric codes · LRPC codes

1 Introduction

Code-based cryptography was first introduced by McEliece [15] using Goppa codes in Hamming metric. In particular, the McEliece cryptosystem generates a public key matrix $G_{\mathsf{pub}} = SGQ$ where S is a random $k \times k$ invertible matrix over $\mathbb{F}_q$, G is a generator matrix for a random decodable Goppa code, Q is a random $n \times n$ permutation matrix, with the secret key (S, G, Q). The sender first encrypts the message by multiplying the plaintext $m \in \mathbb{F}_q^k$ with G_{pub} and adds a random error vector $e \in \mathbb{F}_q^n$ of weight at most r, producing $c = mG_{\mathsf{pub}} + e$. The recipient decrypts the ciphertext by computing $cQ^{-1} = mSGQQ^{-1} + eQ^{-1}$ and perform decoding of G on cQ^{-1} to recover mS. Finally, the plaintext can be recovered by computing $m = (mS)S^{-1}$. Although McEliece cryptosystem is

© Springer Nature Switzerland AG 2019
J. Jang-Jaccard and F. Guo (Eds.): ACISP 2019, LNCS 11547, pp. 211–228, 2019.
https://doi.org/10.1007/978-3-030-21548-4_12

secured up to date, its key size of 1 MB for 256-bit security level is significantly larger than RSA.

To reduce the key size of code-based cryptography, an alternative metric, called the rank metric was introduced. Up to date, there are only two classes of rank metrics codes with efficient decoding algorithms, namely the Gabidulin codes [4] (and its variants such as generalized Gabidulin codes [2], λ-Gabidulin codes [14]), and the Low Rank Parity Check (LRPC) codes [6] that are used in the rank metric code-based cryptosystem. In the Asia PKC Workshop 2018, Kim et al. [10] proposed a new variant of the LRPC codes, namely the LRPC-Kronecker Product code, $\mathcal{C}$ generated by $G = G_1 \otimes G_2$ where $\otimes$ is the Kronecker product for two matrices, and G_1 and G_2 are generator matrices for codes $\mathcal{C}_1$ and $\mathcal{C}_2$. Kim et al. employed this code and proposed a new McEliece-type cryptosystem, namely an LRPC-Kronecker cryptosystem. They claimed that their crytosystem provides compact key size of 4,692 bits, 7,656 bits and 9,768 bits for 128-bit, 192-bit and 256-bit security level respectively. Moreover, the γ-conversion proposed by Kobarai and Imai [11] was used to convert the LRPC-Kronecker cryptosystem into a CCA2-secured encryption scheme.

In order to optimize the size of public key $G_{\mathsf{pub}} = SGQ$ for LRPC-Kronecker cryptosystem, Kim et al. employed double circulant LRPC codes for the $\mathcal{C}_2$ used in the Kronecker product, i.e., $\mathcal{C}_2$ is an $[n_2, \frac{n_2}{2}, d_2]$-LRPC code. For $\mathcal{C}_1$, they consider two constructions, i.e., $[2, 2]$-$\mathcal{C}_1$ where $n_1 = k_1 = 2$ and $[3, 2]$-$\mathcal{C}_1$ where $n_1 = 3$ and $k_1 = 2$. Furthermore, the matrix S and Q were chosen such that they are block circulant matrices and G_{pub} is of the systematic block circulant form. For the first set of parameters where $[2, 2]$-$\mathcal{C}_1$ is used, Kim et al. claimed that their proposal achieved 128-bit, 192-bit and 256-bit security level with key size of 4,692 bits, 7,656 bits and 9,768 bits respectively. For the second set of parameters where $[3, 2]$-$\mathcal{C}_1$ is used, they claimed that their proposal achieved 128-bit, 192-bit and 256-bit security level with key size of 9,568 bits, 13,920 bits and 17,760 bits respectively.

Our Contribution. In this paper, we point out some errors in the original LRPC-Kronecker cryptosystem and suggest a reparation for the errors. We show that the LRPC-Kronecker cryptosystem is equivalent to the LRPC cryptosystem by suitable algebraic manipulations. With this equivalence, we suggest alternative encryption and decryption, namely AKron for the LRPC-Kronecker cryptosystem. Furthermore, we show that there exists design weakness in the LRPC-Kronecker cryptosystem for $k_1 = n_1$ when choosing $[n_1, k_1]$-$\mathcal{C}_1$ for the Kronecker product code. We exploit this weakness and successfully cryptanalyze all the suggested parameters for $k_1 = n_1$. Our cryptanalysis is able to recover secret key for all the proposed parameters within the claimed security level.

Organization of the Paper. The rest of the paper is organized as follows: we first review in Sect. 2 some preliminaries for rank metric and the hard problems in rank metric code-based cryptography. We also review the definitions and properties of LRPC codes, LRPC-Kronecker Product codes, and the LRPC-Kronecker cryptosystem. In Sect. 3, we point out some errors in the original LRPC-Kronecker cryptosystem and make reparations in the encryption and update the parameters. In Sect. 4, we show that the LRPC-Kronecker cryptosystem is equivalent to the LRPC cryptosystem and propose an alternative LRPC-Kronecker cryptosystem called AKron. We also make some comparisons in terms of secret key, decoding failure probability and decoding complexity between AKron and the corrected LRPC-Kronecker cryptosystem (KronF). In Sect. 5, we discuss design weakness for LRPC-Kronecker cryptosystem when $k_1 = n_1$. We exploit this weakness to cryptanalyze the proposed DC-LRPC-Kronecker cryptosystem for $k_1 = n_1$ by recovering the support basis for H_2 and recovering secret key within the claimed security level. Finally, we give our final considerations of this paper in Sect. 6.

2   Preliminaries

In this section we recall the backgrounds for rank metric code. We also include the hard problems in coding theory, namely the Rank Syndrome Decoding (RSD) problem which LRPC-Kronecker cryptosystem is based on and give the complexity for existing generic attacks on the RSD problem. Furthermore, we recall some definitions and results related to the LRPC-Kronecker Product codes.

2.1   Rank Metric Background

Let $\mathbb{F}_{q^m}$ be a finite field with q^m elements and let $\{\beta_1, \ldots, \beta_m\}$ be a basis of $\mathbb{F}_{q^m}$ over the base field $\mathbb{F}_q$.

Definition 1. A *linear code* of length n and dimension k is a linear subspace $\mathcal{C}$ of the vector space $\mathbb{F}_{q^m}^n$.

Given a matrix M over a field $\mathbf{F}$, the rank of M, $\mathrm{rk}(M)$ is the dimension of the row span of M as a vector space over $\mathbf{F}$. The row span of a matrix M over $\mathbf{F}$ is denoted as $\langle M \rangle_{\mathbf{F}}$. We define the rank metric of a vector on $\mathbb{F}_{q^m}^n$:

Definition 2. Let $x = (x_1, \ldots, x_n) \in \mathbb{F}_{q^m}^n$ and $M \in \mathbb{F}_{q^m}^{k \times n}$. The *rank* of x in $\mathbb{F}_q$, denoted by $\mathrm{rk}(x)$ is the rank of the matrix $X = [x_{ij}] \in \mathbb{F}_q^{m \times n}$ where $x_j = \sum_{i=1}^m x_{ij}\beta_i$.

Lemma 1 [9, Proposition 3.1]. *Let $x \in \mathbb{F}_{q^m}^n$ such that $rk(x) = r$. Then there exists $\hat{x} \in \mathbb{F}_{q^m}^r$ with $rk(\hat{x}) = r$ and $U \in \mathbb{F}_q^{r \times n}$ with $rk(U) = r$ such that $x = \hat{x}U$. We call such $\hat{x}$ and U as a* support basis *and a* support matrix *for x respectively.*

We now define circulant matrix induced by x:

Definition 3. Let $x = (x_0, \ldots, x_{n-1}) \in \mathbb{F}_{q^m}^n$. The *circulant matrix*, $\mathrm{Cir}_n(x)$ induced by x is defined as $\mathrm{Cir}_n(x) = [x_{\langle i-j \rangle_n}] \in \mathbb{F}_{q^m}^{n \times n}$, where $\langle i - j \rangle_n := i - j \bmod n$.

Definition 4. An $[m'n, s'n]$ *block circulant* matrix $M \in \mathbb{F}_{q^m}^{m'n \times s'n}$ is a matrix of

the form $M = \begin{bmatrix} M_{11} & \cdots & M_{1s'} \\ \vdots & \ddots & \vdots \\ M_{m'1} & \cdots & M_{m's'} \end{bmatrix}$ where each M_{ij} is an $n \times n$ circulant matrix for

$1 \leq i \leq m'$, $1 \leq j \leq s'$. Let $m' \leq s'$, a *systematic block circulant matrix* $M_{sys} \in$

$\mathbb{F}_{q^m}^{m'n \times s'n}$ is a matrix of the form $M_{sys} = \begin{bmatrix} I_n & & 0 & M_{11} & \cdots & M_{1,s'-m'} \\ & \ddots & & \vdots & \ddots & \vdots \\ 0 & & I_n & M_{m'1} & \cdots & M_{m',s'-m'} \end{bmatrix}$ where

each M_{ij} is an $n \times n$ circulant matrix for $1 \leq i \leq m'$, $1 \leq j \leq s' - m'$.

2.2 Hard Problems in Coding Theory

We describe the hard problems which rank metric code-based cryptosystem is based on.

Definition 5. (Rank Syndrome Decoding (RSD) Problem). Let $H \in \mathbb{F}_{q^m}^{(n-k) \times n}$ of full rank, $s \in \mathbb{F}_{q^m}^{n-k}$ and an integer, w. The *Rank Syndrome Decoding Problem* $\mathrm{RSD}(q, m, n, k, w)$ needs to determine $x \in \mathbb{F}_{q^m}^n$ with $\mathrm{rk}(x) = w$ and $Hx^T = s^T$.

Recently, the RSD problem has been proven to be NP-complete with a probabilistic reduction to the Hamming setting [7]. Nevertheless, there are two approaches for practical attacks on a generic RSD problem. The combinatorial approach depends on counting the number of possible support basis of size r or support matrix of rank r for a rank code of length n over $\mathbb{F}_{q^m}$, which corresponds to the number of subspaces of dimension r in $\mathbb{F}_{q^m}$. On the other hand, the nature of the rank metric favors algebraic attacks using Gröbner bases and became efficient when q increases. There are mainly three methods to translate the notion of rank into algebraic setting: considering directly the RSD problem [12]; reducing RSD problem into MinRank [3]; using linearized q-polynomials [5].

[13, Tables 1 and 2] summarizes the best attacks on RSD with their conditions and complexities (Table 1):

Table 1. Conditions and complexities of the best combinatorial and algebraic attacks on RSD

Attacks	Conditions	Complexity
AGHT-Combi [1]		$O\left((n-k)^3 m^3 q^{r\frac{(k+1)m}{n}-m}\right)$
GRS-Combi [5]		$O\left((n-k)^3 m^3 q^{(r-1)k}\right)$
OJ-Combi [16]		$O\left(r^3 m^3 q^{(r-1)(k+1)}\right)$
CG-Kernel [8]		$O\left(k^3 m^3 q^{r\lceil\frac{km}{n}\rceil}\right)$
GRS-Basic [5]	$n \geq (r+1)(k+1) - 1$	$O\left(((r+1)(k+1)-1)^3\right)$
GRS-Hybrid [5]	$\left\lceil\frac{(r+1)(k+1)-(n+1)}{r}\right\rceil \leq k$	$O\left(r^3 k^3 q^{r\lceil\frac{(r+1)(k+1)-(n+1)}{r}\rceil}\right)$

2.3 LRPC Codes and LRPC-Kronecker Product Codes

We now give the definitions for LRPC codes, Quasi-Cyclic codes and Quasi-Cyclic LRPC codes. Then, we give the definitions of LRPC-Kronecker Product codes and state the block decoding algorithm for LRPC-Kronecker Product codes.

Definition 6 (Low Rank Parity Check (LRPC) Codes). An $[n, k, d]$-Low Rank Parity Check (LRPC) code of rank d, length n and dimension k over $\mathbb{F}_{q^m}$ is a code such that the code has for parity check matrix, an $(n - k) \times n$ matrix $H = [h_{ij}]$ such that the coefficients h_{ij} generate a vector subspace, V of $\mathbb{F}_{q^m}$ with dimension at most d. We call this dimension the weight of H. We denote one of V's bases by $\{F_1, \ldots, F_d\}$.

There exists efficient probabilistic decoding algorithm for $[n, k, d]$-LRPC codes, with error correcting capabilities of $r \leq \lfloor \frac{n-k}{d} \rfloor$. Gaborit et al. proposed a decoding algorithm, [6, Algorithm 1] to decode an $[n, k, d]$-LRPC codes, with $q^{-(n-k+1-rd)}$ probability of decoding failure and $r^2(4d^2m + n^2)$ decoding complexity.

Definition 7 (Quasi-Cyclic Codes). An $[n, k]$ linear code is an $[n, k]$-*Quasi-Cyclic* code if there is some integer n_0 such that every cyclic shift of a codeword by n_0 places is again a codeword.

When $n = n_0 p$ for some integer p, it is possible to have both the generator and parity check matrices composed by $p \times p$ circulant blocks.

Definition 8 (Quasi-Cyclic LRPC). An $[n, k, d]$-*Quasi-Cyclic Low Rank Parity Check* (QC LRPC) code of rank d, is an $[n, k]$-Quasi-Cyclic code which has for parity check matrix, an $(n - k) \times n$ matrix $H = [h_{ij}]$ such that the coefficients h_{ij} generate a vector subspace, V of $\mathbb{F}_{q^m}$ with dimension at most d.

Now, we give the definition for LRPC-Kronecker Product codes:

Definition 9 (LRPC-Kronecker Product Codes [10]). Let $\mathcal{C}_1$ be an $[n_1, k_1]$-linear code generated by the matrix $G_1 = [a_{ij}] \in \mathbb{F}_{q^m}^{k_1 \times n_1}$ and $\mathcal{C}_2$ be an $[n_2, k_2, d_2]$-LRPC code generated by matrix $G_2 \in \mathbb{F}_{q^m}^{k_2 \times n_2}$ with error correcting capability r_2. Then an $[n, k]$-LRPC-Kronecker Product code, $\mathcal{C}$ is generated by the matrix

$$G = G_1 \otimes G_2 = \begin{bmatrix} a_{11}G_2 & \cdots & a_{1n_1}G_2 \\ \vdots & \ddots & \vdots \\ a_{k_11}G_2 & \cdots & a_{k_1n_1}G_2 \end{bmatrix} \in \mathbb{F}_{q^m}^{k \times n}$$

where $n = n_1 n_2$ and $k = k_1 k_2$.

Decoding LRPC-Kronecker Codes. Kim et al. [10] proposed a decoding algorithm, namely the block decoding algorithm for LRPC-Kronecker Product codes when the error vector e satisfies certain properties. In particular, let

$\boldsymbol{y} = \boldsymbol{c} + \boldsymbol{e}$ where $\boldsymbol{c} = \boldsymbol{x}G$ and $\boldsymbol{e} = (\boldsymbol{e}_1, \ldots, \boldsymbol{e}_{n_1})$ with each $\boldsymbol{e}_i \in \mathbb{F}_{q^m}^{n_2}$ and $\mathrm{rk}(\boldsymbol{e}_i) \leq r_2$. Let $\boldsymbol{x} = (\boldsymbol{x}_1, \ldots, \boldsymbol{x}_{k_1})$ where each $\boldsymbol{x}_i \in \mathbb{F}_{q^m}^{k_2}$, the vector $\boldsymbol{y}$ can be rewritten in blockwise form:

$$\boldsymbol{y} = (\boldsymbol{y}_1, \ldots, \boldsymbol{y}_{n_1}) \quad \text{where} \quad \boldsymbol{y}_j = \sum_{i=1}^{k_1} a_{ij} \boldsymbol{x}_i G_2 + \boldsymbol{e}_j \in \mathbb{F}_{q^m}^{n_2}.$$

Let $I = \{d_{j_1}, \ldots, d_{j_{k_1}}\}$. We can perform LRPC decoding on each $\boldsymbol{y}_j$ for each $j \in I$ to recover $\sum_{i=1}^{k_1} a_{i,j} \boldsymbol{x}_i G_2$, since $\mathrm{rk}(\boldsymbol{e}_j) \leq r_2$. Then, the vectors $\boldsymbol{x}_i$ can be recovered from this system of equations, since a_{ij} are known.

2.4   LRPC-Kronecker Cryptosystem

In this section, we describe briefly the LRPC-Kronecker cryptosystem. Let n, n_1, n_2, k, k_1, k_2, r, r_2, d_1 and d_2 be integers such that $k = k_1 k_2$ and $n = n_1 n_2$. The steps in the algorithm is outlined as follows:

1. $\mathcal{K}^{\mathrm{Kron}}(n, n_1, n_2, k, k_1, k_2, r, r_2)$:
   (a) Randomly choose an $[n_1, k_1, d_1]$-LRPC codes $\mathcal{C}_1$ with parity check matrix $H_1 \in \mathbb{F}_{q^m}^{(n_1 - k_1) \times n_1}$ of weight d_1. Construct generator matrix G_1 for $\mathcal{C}_1$.
   (b) Randomly choose an $[n_2, k_2, d_2]$-LRPC codes $\mathcal{C}_2$ with parity check matrix $H_2 \in \mathbb{F}_{q^m}^{(n_2 - k_2) \times n_1}$ of weight d_2 such that $\mathcal{C}_2$ can correct errors of rank r_2. Construct generator matrix G_2 for $\mathcal{C}_2$.
   (c) Construct the matrix $G = G_1 \otimes G_2$.
   (d) Randomly generate a vector $\boldsymbol{a} \in \mathbb{F}_{q^m}^k$ such that $S = \mathrm{Cir}_k(\boldsymbol{a})$ is invertible.
   (e) Randomly generate a vector $\boldsymbol{b} \in \mathbb{F}_q^n$ such that $Q = \mathrm{Cir}_n(\boldsymbol{b})$ is invertible.
   (f) Compute the public matrix $G_{\mathrm{pub}} = SGQ$.
   Output: $\mathrm{pk} = G_{\mathrm{pub}}$, $\mathrm{sk} = (S^{-1}, Q^{-1}, G_1, H_2)$.
2. $\mathcal{E}^{\mathrm{Kron}}(\boldsymbol{m}, e, \mathrm{pk} = G_{\mathrm{pub}})$: let $\boldsymbol{m}$ be a plaintext to be encrypted
   (a) Randomly generate vector $\boldsymbol{e} \in \mathbb{F}_{q^m}^n$ with $\mathrm{rk}(\boldsymbol{e}) \leq r = n_1 r_2$, where r_2 is the number of errors that can be corrected by $\mathcal{C}_2$.
   (b) Compute $\boldsymbol{c} = \boldsymbol{m}G_{\mathrm{pub}} + \boldsymbol{e}$.
   Output: ciphertext $\boldsymbol{c}$.
3. $\mathcal{D}^{\mathrm{Kron}}(\boldsymbol{c}, \mathrm{sk} = (Q^{-1}, S^{-1}, G_1, H_2))$: let $\boldsymbol{c}$ be the received ciphertext
   (a) Compute $\boldsymbol{c}' = \boldsymbol{c}Q^{-1} = \boldsymbol{m}SG + \boldsymbol{e}Q^{-1}$.
   (b) Determine $\boldsymbol{m}' = \boldsymbol{m}S$ by correcting the errors in $\boldsymbol{c}'$ using the LRPC Block decoding algorithm.
   (c) Compute $\boldsymbol{m} = \boldsymbol{m}'S^{-1}$.
   Output: plaintext $\boldsymbol{m}$.

To reduce the key size, Kim et al. [10] employed double circulant LRPC (DC-LRPC) codes and used the fact that the sum and product of circulant square matrices are also circulant. In particular, they choose n_2 to be even and $k_2 = \frac{n_2}{2}$. Then the generator matrix for $\mathcal{C}_2$ is of the form $G_2 = [A_1 \mid A_2]$ where A_1 and A_2 are $\frac{n_2}{2} \times \frac{n_2}{2}$ circulant matrices. They also consider the matrix Q to be invertible block circulant matrix in the form of $Q = \begin{bmatrix} Q_{11} & \cdots & Q_{1,2n_1} \\ \vdots & \ddots & \vdots \\ Q_{2n_1,1} & \cdots & Q_{2n_1,2n_1} \end{bmatrix}$ where each Q_{ij}

is an $\frac{n_2}{2} \times \frac{n_2}{2}$ circulant matrix over $\mathbb{F}_q$. Then the product GQ is a block circulant

matrix of the form $GQ = \begin{bmatrix} B_{11} & \cdots & B_{1,2n_1} \\ \vdots & \ddots & \vdots \\ B_{k_1,1} & \cdots & B_{k_1,2n_1} \end{bmatrix}$ where each B_{ij} is an $\frac{n_2}{2} \times \frac{n_2}{2}$

circulant matrix over $\mathbb{F}_q$. Finally, the matrix S is an invertible block circulant matrix such that

$$S = \begin{bmatrix} S_{11} & \cdots & S_{1,k_1} \\ \vdots & \ddots & \vdots \\ S_{k_1,1} & \cdots & S_{k_1,k_1} \end{bmatrix} \Rightarrow G_{\mathsf{pub}} = \begin{bmatrix} I_{\frac{n_2}{2}} & & 0 & B'_{11} & \cdots & B'_{1,(2n_1-k_1)} \\ \vdots & \ddots & \vdots & \vdots & \ddots & \vdots \\ 0 & & I_{\frac{n_2}{2}} & B'_{k_1,1} & \cdots & B'_{k_1,(2n_1-k_1)} \end{bmatrix}$$

where S_{ij} and B'_{ij} are $\frac{n_2}{2} \times \frac{n_2}{2}$ circulant matrices. The suggested parameters for LRPC-Kronecker cryptosystem will be shown in Sect. 3, Table 2.

3 Errors in LRPC-Kronecker Cryptosystem and Its Reparations

In this section, we identify some errors in the original encryption $\mathcal{E}^{\mathrm{Kron}}(m, e, \mathrm{pk})$ and decryption $\mathcal{D}^{\mathrm{Kron}}(c, \mathrm{sk})$.[1] Then, we repair the cryptosystem and update the correct parameters at the end of this section.

3.1 Some Errors in LRPC-Kronecker Cryptosystem

In the $\mathcal{E}^{\mathrm{Kron}}(m, e, \mathrm{pk})$, an error vector e with $\mathrm{rk}(e) \leq r = n_1 r_2$ is randomly generated, where r_2 is the number of errors that can be corrected by $\mathcal{C}_2$.

Suppose that $\mathrm{rk}(e) = r = n_1 r_2$. In the $\mathcal{D}^{\mathrm{Kron}}(c)$, $c' = cQ^{-1} = mSG + eQ^{-1}$ is computed. Let $e' = eQ^{-1} = (e'_1, \ldots, e'_{n_1})$, where each $e'_j \in \mathbb{F}_{q^m}^{n_2}$ for $1 \leq j \leq n_1$. Since $Q \in \mathrm{GL}_n(\mathbb{F}_q)$, we have $\mathrm{rk}(e') = \mathrm{rk}(e) = r$.

To apply the LRPC Block decoding algorithm [10, Sect. 3.1], it is required that the vector $\mathrm{rk}(e'_j) \leq r_2$. However, $\mathrm{rk}(e'_1, \ldots, e'_{n_1}) = n_1 r_2$ does not necessarily imply that $\mathrm{rk}(e'_j) = r_2$ for each $1 \leq j \leq n_1$. In fact, it is very likely that $\mathrm{rk}(e'_j) = r > r_2$, which creates problem in applying the LRPC Block decoding algorithm. The recipient may not be able to decode correctly and recover the vector e'. Thus, the decryption $\mathcal{D}^{\mathrm{Kron}}(c, \mathrm{sk})$ will fail.

In [10, Table 2], the values for the columns of "block decoding" (LRPC block decoding complexity), "failure" (decryption failure) and security (RSD complexity) were calculated based on the parameters in [10, Table 2]. The following is the list of the formula for the mentioned calculations:

---

[1] We have pointed out the errors mentioned in this section to the authors of [10]. They have recognized these errors and our suggestions to fix the errors as in Table 3.

block decoding : $k_1^6 + k_1 r_2^2 (4 d_2^2 m + n_2^2),$ (1)

failure : $\sum_{i=1}^{k_1} \binom{k_1}{i} q^{-i(n_2 - k_2 + 1 - r_2 d_2)} \left(1 - q^{-(n_2 - k_2 + 1 - r_2 d_2)}\right)^{k_1 - i},$ (2)

$\mathsf{RSD}(q, m, n, k, r)$: $\min\left\{(n - k)^3 m^3 q^{r \frac{(k+1)m}{n} - m}, r^3 k^3 q^{r \left\lceil \frac{r(k+1) - (n+1)}{r} \right\rceil}\right\}.$ (3)

Remark 1. From the description of LRPC-Kronecker cryptosystem, we notice that there are errors in the general $\mathcal{D}^{Kron}(c, \mathrm{sk})$. However, when choosing the parameters for LRPC-Kronecker cryptosystem, instead of choosing $\mathrm{rk}(e) \leq r = n_1 r_2$ as described in $\mathcal{E}^{Kron}(m, e, \mathrm{pk})$, Kim et al. chose the error vector e with $\mathrm{rk}(e) \leq r_2 = \frac{n_2 - k_2}{d_2}$ such that the decoding would be successful. For example, the error vector in $[2, 2]$-Kron-I has rank $\mathrm{rk}(eQ^{-1}) = \mathrm{rk}(e) = 6 \leq \frac{46 - 23}{3}$. Thus the LRPC block decoding can be applied. As a consequence, the value of $\mathrm{rk}(e) = r$ should be replaced with r_2.

3.2　Reparation for LRPC-Kronecker Cryptosystem

To fix the problem during decoding, we need to ensure the vector e_j' has rank at most r_2. This could be achieved by restricting the error e to have $\mathrm{rk}(e) \leq r_2$. We propose the following reparation, **KronF** for the original LRPC-Kronecker cryptosystem. Note that the key generation $\mathcal{K}^{KronF}$ is the same as the original $\mathcal{K}^{Kron}$. We underline the reparation for the encryption $\mathcal{E}^{KronF}(m, e, \mathrm{pk} = G_{\mathsf{pub}})$ and decryption $\mathcal{D}^{KronF}(c, \mathrm{sk} = (Q^{-1}, S^{-1}, G_1, H_2))$ of KronF:

2. $\mathcal{E}^{KronF}(m, e, \mathrm{pk} = G_{\mathsf{pub}})$: let m be a plaintext to be encrypted
   (a) Randomly generate vector $e \in \mathbb{F}_{q^m}^n$ with $\mathrm{rk}(e) \leq r_2$, where r_2 is the num-ber of errors that can be corrected by $\mathcal{C}_2$.
   (b) Compute $c = m G_{\mathsf{pub}} + e$.
   Output: ciphertext c.

3. $\mathcal{D}^{KronF}(c, \mathrm{sk} = (Q^{-1}, S^{-1}, G_1, H_2))$: let c be the received ciphertext
   (a) Compute $c' = cQ^{-1} = mSG + eQ^{-1}$.
   (b) Determine $m' = mS$ by correcting the errors in c' using the LRPC Block decoding algorithm.
   (c) Compute $m = m'S^{-1}$.
   Output: plaintext m.

Table 2 is the original parameters for LRPC-Kronecker cryptosystem taken from [10, Table 2]. Notice that r_2 is inaccurate, as it should be $r_2 \leq \frac{n_2 - k_2}{d_2}$. By Remark 1, we consider the same parameters for $(n_1, k_1, n_2, k_2, m, q, d_2)$ and update r, r_2, "block decoding", "failure" and "security" in Table 3. The value for "block decoding" and "failure" is calculated using formula (1) and (2) respectively. While the value for security is calculated using $\min\left\{q^{r_2 \left\lceil \frac{r_2(k+1) - (n+1)}{r_2} \right\rceil}, (n - k)^3 m^3 q^{r_2 \frac{(k+1)m}{n} - m}\right\}.$
Comparing Tables 2 and 3, notice that the parameters, key size and decoding failure for both Kron and KronF are the same, except for the values r_2.

Table 2. Suggested parameters for LRPC-Kronecker cryptosystem

Schemes	C_1		C_2		C		m	q	r	d_2	r_2
	n_1	k_1	n_2	k_2	n	k					
[2, 2]-Kron-I	2	2	46	23	92	46	17	8	6	3	3
[2, 2]-Kron-II	2	2	44	22	88	44	29	8	6	3	3
[2, 2]-Kron-III	2	2	44	22	88	44	37	8	6	3	3
[3, 2]-Kron-I	3	2	52	26	156	52	23	4	9	2	3
[3, 2]-Kron-II	3	2	40	20	120	40	29	8	9	2	3
[3, 2]-Kron-III	3	2	40	20	120	40	37	8	9	2	3

Schemes	decryption complexity	decoding failure	key size (bits)	security
[2, 2]-Kron-I	$2^{15.6}$	2^{-44}	4692	128
[2, 2]-Kron-II	$2^{15.7}$	2^{-41}	7656	192
[2, 2]-Kron-III	$2^{15.8}$	2^{-41}	9768	256
[3, 2]-Kron-I	$2^{15.8}$	2^{-41}	9568	128
[3, 2]-Kron-II	$2^{15.2}$	2^{-44}	13920	192
[3, 2]-Kron-III	$2^{15.3}$	2^{-44}	17760	256

Table 3. Suggested parameters corrected for KronF

Schemes	C_1		C_2		C		m	q	d_2	r_2
	n_1	k_1	n_2	k_2	n	k				
[2, 2]-KronF-I	2	2	46	23	92	46	17	8	3	6
[2, 2]-KronF-II	2	2	44	22	88	44	29	8	3	6
[2, 2]-KronF-III	2	2	44	22	88	44	37	8	3	6
[3, 2]-KronF-I	3	2	52	26	156	52	23	4	2	9
[3, 2]-KronF-II	3	2	40	20	120	40	29	8	2	9
[3, 2]-KronF-III	3	2	40	20	120	40	37	8	2	9

Schemes	decryption complexity	decoding failure	key size (bits)	security
[2, 2]-KronF-I	$2^{15.6}$	2^{-44}	4692	128
[2, 2]-KronF-II	$2^{15.7}$	2^{-41}	7656	192
[2, 2]-KronF-III	$2^{15.8}$	2^{-41}	9768	256
[3, 2]-KronF-I	$2^{15.8}$	2^{-41}	9568	128
[3, 2]-KronF-II	$2^{15.2}$	2^{-44}	13920	192
[3, 2]-KronF-III	$2^{15.3}$	2^{-44}	17760	256

4 Equivalence of LRPC-Kronecker Cryptosystem and LRPC Cryptosystem

In this section, we first show that the LRPC-Kronecker cryptosystem and KronF cryptosystem is equivalent to the LRPC cryptosystem [6]. With this equivalence, we give an alternative encryption and decryption algorithm for the KronF cryptosystem.

4.1 General Idea for Equivalence

For a general C_1 and C_2 generated by G_1 and G_2 respectively, we can rewrite the matrix

$$
G = G_1 \otimes G_2 = \begin{bmatrix} a_{11}G_2 & \cdots & a_{1n_1}G_2 \\ \vdots & \ddots & \vdots \\ a_{k_11}G_2 & \cdots & a_{k_1n_1}G_2 \end{bmatrix} = \underbrace{\begin{bmatrix} a_{11}I_{k_2} & \cdots & a_{1n_1}I_{k_2} \\ \vdots & \ddots & \vdots \\ a_{k_11}I_{k_2} & \cdots & a_{k_1n_1}I_{k_2} \end{bmatrix}}_{k_1k_2 \times n_1k_2} \underbrace{\begin{bmatrix} G_2 & & 0 \\ & \ddots & \\ 0 & & G_2 \end{bmatrix}}_{n_1k_2 \times n_1n_2}
$$

$$
= \begin{bmatrix} D_{11} & \cdots & D_{1n_1} \\ \vdots & \ddots & \vdots \\ D_{k_11} & \cdots & D_{k_1n_1} \end{bmatrix} \begin{bmatrix} G_2 & & 0 \\ & \ddots & \\ 0 & & G_2 \end{bmatrix} = \mathcal{D}\mathcal{G}_2
$$

where $D_{ij} = a_{ij}I_{k_2}$ is a diagonal matrix with its entries equal to a_{ij} for $1 \leq i \leq k_1$, $1 \leq j \leq n_1$. Recall that $S \in \mathrm{GL}_k(\mathbb{F}_{q^m})$ and $Q \in \mathrm{GL}_n(\mathbb{F}_q)$, we rewrite

$$
G_{\mathsf{pub}} = SGQ = \underbrace{S\mathcal{D}}_{S'} \underbrace{\mathcal{G}_2 Q}_{G'} = S'G'.
$$
$$
\underset{k \times n_1k_2}{} \underset{n_1k_2 \times n}{}
$$

Let H_2 be the low rank parity check matrix of G_2 with weight d_2, then the matrix G' has parity check matrix

$$
H' = \begin{bmatrix} H_2 & & 0 \\ & \ddots & \\ 0 & & H_2 \end{bmatrix} [Q^{-1}]^T.
$$

The matrix G' generates an $[n, n_1k_2, d_2]$-LRPC, C' with a low rank parity check matrix H', which can correct error up to $\left\lfloor \frac{n-n_1k_2}{d_2} \right\rfloor = \left\lfloor \frac{n_1n_2-n_1k_2}{d_2} \right\rfloor = n_1r_2$.

In an LRPC-Kronecker cryptosystem, a message $\boldsymbol{m} \in \mathbb{F}_{q^m}^k$ is encrypted into $\boldsymbol{c} = \boldsymbol{m}G_{\mathsf{pub}} + \boldsymbol{e}$ where $\mathrm{rk}(\boldsymbol{e}) \leq n_1r_2$. Note that this can be viewed as an LRPC cryptosystem, as $\boldsymbol{c} = \boldsymbol{m}S'G' + \boldsymbol{e}$. Therefore, once the low rank parity check matrix H' is known, then we can perform LRPC decoding algorithm [6, Algorithm 1] on $\boldsymbol{c}[H']^T = \boldsymbol{e}[H']^T$ and thus recover the error vector $\boldsymbol{e}$, as long as $\mathrm{rk}(\boldsymbol{e}) \times n \leq (n-k)m$. Finally, substitute $\boldsymbol{e}$ into the equation $\boldsymbol{c} = \boldsymbol{m}G_{\mathsf{pub}} + \boldsymbol{e}$ and solve for the plaintext $\boldsymbol{m}$.

4.2 Alternative Encryption and Decryption for KronF Cryptosystem

By the equivalence shown in Sect. 4.1, we can view the LRPC-Kronecker cryptosystem as an LRPC cryptosystem. In particular, since $\boldsymbol{c} = \boldsymbol{m}G_{\mathsf{pub}} + \boldsymbol{e} = \boldsymbol{m}SGQ + \boldsymbol{e} = \boldsymbol{m}S'G' + \boldsymbol{e}$, the recipient can deduce the low rank parity check matrix H' of G', since he has information on H_2 and Q^{-1}. Then he can perform LRPC decoding algorithm on $c\,[H']^T$ and recover the vector e. Finally, the vector e could be substituted into $c = mG_{\mathsf{pub}} + e$ and solve for the plaintext m.

We now give an alternative encryption and decryption for KronF cryptosystem to convert it into an LRPC cryptosystem, namely AKron. Note that the key generation $\mathcal{K}^{\mathrm{AKron}}$ is the same as the original $\mathcal{K}^{\mathrm{Kron}}$, except that the encryption and decryption are different. The followings are the encryption and decryption of AKron:

2. $\mathcal{E}^{\mathrm{AKron}}(m, e, \mathrm{pk} = G_{\mathsf{pub}})$: let m be a plaintext to be encrypted
   (a) Randomly generate vector $e \in \mathbb{F}_{q^m}^n$ with $\mathrm{rk}(e) \le r = n_1 r_2$, where r_2 is the number of errors that can be corrected by $\mathcal{C}_2$.
   (b) Compute $c = mG_{\mathsf{pub}} + e$.
   Output: ciphertext c.
3. $\mathcal{D}^{\mathrm{AKron}}(c, \mathrm{sk} = (Q^{-1}, H_2))$: let c be the received ciphertext
   (a) Compute $c' = c\,[H']^T = mS'G'\,[H']^T + e\,[H']^T = e\,[H']^T$.
   (b) Determine e by correcting the errors in c' using LRPC decoding algorithm for $[n, n_1 k_2, d_2]$-LRPC, $\mathcal{C}'$.
   (c) Compute $c - e = mG_{\mathsf{pub}}$ and solve for m.
   Output: plaintext m.

Correctness of AKron: Since the LRPC decoding algorithm for $\mathcal{C}'$ can correct errors up to $r = n_1 r_2$, the error vector e with $\mathrm{rk}(e) \le r$ can be recovered. Note that the matrix G_{pub} is of dimension $k \times n$. Since $k \le n$, by linear algebra we can solve for a unique m from $c - e$.

Remark 2. Since an LRPC-Kronecker cryptosystem is equivalent to an LRPC cryptosystem (AKron), we do not suggest new parameters for AKron. Instead, we compare the codes used, secret key, the rank of error vector, decoding failure probability and decoding complexity for KronF (the corrected LRPC-Kronecker cryptosystem) and AKron. Table 4 summarizes the comparison between KronF and AKron.

Notice the secret key size of AKron is smaller than the secret key size of KronF. Moreover, since $r \ge r_2$, there are more choices for e in AKron as compared to KronF. AKron has lower decoding failure probability as compared to KronF. On the other hand, the decoding complexity for AKron is higher than the decoding complexity for KronF. We conclude that an LRPC-Kronecker cryptosystem (KronF) can be viewed as an LRPC cryptosystem (AKron).

5   Cryptanalysis on DC-LRPC-Kronecker Cryptosystem

We show that there are some design weaknesses in LRPC-Kronecker cryptosystem using double circulant LRPC (DC-LRPC) codes. In particular, if $[n_1, k_1]$-linear code $\mathcal{C}_1$ and $[n_2, k_2, d_2]$-LRPC codes $\mathcal{C}_2$ satisfying $k_1 = n_1$ and $k_2 = n_2/2$, then the security of LRPC-Kronecker cryptosystem would be reduced. We cryptanalyze the proposed QC-LRPC-Kronecker cryptosystem with all the parameters for $[2, 2]$-$\mathcal{C}_1$ proposed in [10].

Table 4. Comparing KronF and AKron

	KronF	AKron (as LRPC cryptosystem)
Code $\mathcal{C}$	$\mathcal{C} = \mathcal{C}_1 \otimes \mathcal{C}_2$, $\mathcal{C}_2$ is $[n_2, k_2, d_2]$-LRPC	$\mathcal{C} = \mathcal{C}_1 \otimes \mathcal{C}_2$, $\mathcal{C}_2$ is $[n_2, k_2, d_2]$-LRPC
Secret key	$(Q^{-1}, S^{-1}, G_1, H_2)$	(Q^{-1}, H_2)
Error vector	$\mathrm{rk}(e) \leq r_2$	$\mathrm{rk}(e) \leq r = n_1 r_2$
Decoding	LRPC Block decoding	LRPC decoding
Decoding failure probability	$\sum_{i=1}^{k_1} \binom{k_1}{i} a^i (1-a)^{k_1-i}$, $a = q^{-(n_2-k_2+1-r_2 d_2)}$	$q^{-(n-k+1-rd_2)}$
Decoding complexity	$k_1^6 + k_1 r_2^2 (4d_2^2 m + n_2^2)$	$r^2 (4d_2^2 m + n^2)$

5.1 Simplication of DC-LRPC-Kronecker Cryptosystem

Consider $k_2 = n_2/2$ and an $[n_2, k_2, d_2]$-DC-LRPC code $\mathcal{C}_2$ as proposed in [10].
There exists $\frac{n_2}{2} \times \frac{n_2}{2}$ circulant matrices A_1 and A_2 such that $G_2 = [A_1 \mid A_2]$.
Since the matrix G_2 has low rank parity check matrix H_2 of rank d_2, there exists
$\frac{n_2}{2} \times \frac{n_2}{2}$ circulant matrices L_1 and L_2 of low rank d_2 such that

$$G_2 H_2^T = [A_1 \mid A_2] \begin{bmatrix} L_1 \\ L_2 \end{bmatrix} = \mathbf{0}.$$

Assume that L_1 is invertible (which happens at high probability), we can rewrite
$A_1 L_1 + A_2 L_2 = \mathbf{0} \Leftrightarrow A_1 = -A_2 L_2 L_1^{-1}$. Let $R = A_2 L_1^{-1}$, then G_2 can be
expressed as

$$G_2 = [A_1 \mid A_2] = [-A_2 L_2 L_1^{-1} \mid A_2] = A_2 L_1^{-1} [-L_2 \mid L_1] = R[-L_2 \mid L_1].$$

Rewrite G as

$$G = G_1 \otimes G_2 = \begin{bmatrix} a_{11} G_2 & \cdots & a_{1n_1} G_2 \\ \vdots & \ddots & \vdots \\ a_{k_1 1} G_2 & \cdots & a_{k_1 n_1} G_2 \end{bmatrix} = \begin{bmatrix} a_{11} I_{k_2} & \cdots & a_{1n_1} I_{k_2} \\ \vdots & \ddots & \vdots \\ a_{k_1 1} I_{k_2} & \cdots & a_{k_1 n_1} I_{k_2} \end{bmatrix} \begin{bmatrix} G_2 & & \mathbf{0} \\ & \ddots & \\ \mathbf{0} & & G_2 \end{bmatrix}$$

$$= \begin{bmatrix} D_{11} & \cdots & D_{1n_1} \\ \vdots & \ddots & \vdots \\ D_{k_1 1} & \cdots & D_{k_1 n_1} \end{bmatrix} \begin{bmatrix} -RL_2 \mid RL_1 & & \mathbf{0} \\ & \ddots & \\ \mathbf{0} & & -RL_2 \mid RL_1 \end{bmatrix}$$

$$= \begin{bmatrix} D_{11} & \cdots & D_{1n_1} \\ \vdots & \ddots & \vdots \\ D_{k_1 1} & \cdots & D_{k_1 n_1} \end{bmatrix} \begin{bmatrix} R & \cdots & 0 \\ \vdots & \ddots & \vdots \\ 0 & \cdots & R \end{bmatrix} \begin{bmatrix} -L_2 \mid L_1 & & \mathbf{0} \\ & \ddots & \\ \mathbf{0} & & -L_2 \mid L_1 \end{bmatrix}$$

$$= \underbrace{\mathcal{D}}_{k_1 k_2 \times n_1 k_2} \underbrace{\mathcal{R}}_{n_1 k_2 \times n_1 k_2} \underbrace{\mathcal{L}}_{n_1 k_2 \times n_1 n_2}$$

where $D_{ij} = a_{ij} I_{k_2}$ is a diagonal matrix with its entries equal to a_{ij} for $1 \leq i, j \leq n_1$.

Note that $S = \begin{bmatrix} S_{11} & \cdots & S_{1k_1} \\ \vdots & \ddots & \vdots \\ S_{k_11} & \cdots & S_{k_1k_1} \end{bmatrix}$ is a block circulant matrix with each S_{ij} is $\frac{n_2}{2} \times \frac{n_2}{2}$ circulant matrices for $1 \leq i,j \leq k_1$. Let $T = S\mathcal{D}\mathcal{R}$, then T is a block circulant matrix such that

$$T = \begin{bmatrix} T_{11} & \cdots & T_{1n_1} \\ \vdots & \ddots & \vdots \\ T_{k_11} & \cdots & T_{k_1n_1} \end{bmatrix} = \begin{bmatrix} S_{11} & \cdots & S_{1k_1} \\ \vdots & \ddots & \vdots \\ S_{k_11} & \cdots & S_{k_1k_1} \end{bmatrix} \begin{bmatrix} D_{11} & \cdots & D_{1n_1} \\ \vdots & \ddots & \vdots \\ D_{k_11} & \cdots & D_{k_1n_1} \end{bmatrix} \begin{bmatrix} R & \cdots & 0 \\ \vdots & \ddots & \vdots \\ 0 & \cdots & R \end{bmatrix}$$

where T_{ij} is a $\frac{n_2}{2} \times \frac{n_2}{2}$ circulant matrix for $1 \leq i \leq k_1$, $1 \leq j \leq n_1$. We can now rewrite G_{pub} as

$$G_{\mathsf{pub}} = SGQ = S(\mathcal{D}\mathcal{R}\mathcal{L})Q = T \begin{bmatrix} -L_2 \mid L_1 & & \mathbf{0} \\ & \ddots & \\ \mathbf{0} & & -L_2 \mid L_1 \end{bmatrix} \begin{bmatrix} Q_{11} & \cdots & Q_{1,2n_1} \\ \vdots & \ddots & \vdots \\ Q_{2n_1,1} & \cdots & Q_{2n_1,2n_1} \end{bmatrix}$$

where each Q_{ij} is an $\frac{n_2}{2} \times \frac{n_2}{2}$ circulant matrix over $\mathbb{F}_q$ for $1 \leq i,j \leq n_1$. Since L_1, L_2 and Q_{ij} are $\frac{n_2}{2} \times \frac{n_2}{2}$ circulant matrices, for $1 \leq a \leq n_1$ and $1 \leq b \leq 2n_1$, there exists $\frac{n_2}{2} \times \frac{n_2}{2}$ circulant matrices L'_{ab} such that

$$\mathcal{L}' = \mathcal{L}Q = \begin{bmatrix} L'_{11} & L'_{12} & \cdots & L'_{1,2n_1-1} & L'_{1,2n_1} \\ \vdots & \vdots & \ddots & \vdots & \vdots \\ L'_{n_11} & L'_{n_12} & \cdots & L'_{n_1,2n_1-1} & L'_{n_1,2n_1} \end{bmatrix} \tag{4}$$

where each L'_{ab} is of low rank d_2. Finally, G_{pub} can be simplified into

$$G_{\mathsf{pub}} = T\mathcal{L}Q = T\mathcal{L}' = \begin{bmatrix} T_{11} & \cdots & T_{1n_1} \\ \vdots & \ddots & \vdots \\ T_{k_11} & \cdots & T_{k_1n_1} \end{bmatrix} \begin{bmatrix} L'_{11} & L'_{12} & \cdots & L'_{1,2n_1-1} & L'_{1,2n_1} \\ \vdots & \vdots & \ddots & \vdots & \vdots \\ L'_{n_11} & L'_{n_12} & \cdots & L'_{n_1,2n_1-1} & L'_{n_1,2n_1} \end{bmatrix}$$

$$= \begin{bmatrix} I_{k_2} & & \mathbf{0} & B'_{11} & \cdots & B'_{1,(2n_1-k_1)} \\ & \ddots & & \vdots & \ddots & \vdots \\ \mathbf{0} & & I_{k_2} & B'_{k_11} & \cdots & B'_{k_1,(2n_1-k_1)} \end{bmatrix} \tag{5}$$

where the last equation is the form of G_{pub} which [10] considered, with each B'_{ij} are $\frac{n_2}{2} \times \frac{n_2}{2}$ circulant matrices for $1 \leq i \leq k_1$ and $1 \leq j \leq 2n_1 - k_1$.

5.2 Recover Support Basis for H_2 when $k_1 = n_1$

Now, suppose that $k_1 = n_1$, then $2n_1 - k_1 = n_1$. From (5) we have

$$
\begin{bmatrix} I_{k_2} & & 0 \\ & \ddots & \\ 0 & & I_{k_2} \end{bmatrix} = \begin{bmatrix} T_{11} & \cdots & T_{1n_1} \\ \vdots & \ddots & \vdots \\ T_{n_11} & \cdots & T_{n_1n_1} \end{bmatrix} \begin{bmatrix} L'_{11} & \cdots & L'_{1n_1} \\ \vdots & \ddots & \vdots \\ L'_{n_11} & \cdots & L'_{n_1n_1} \end{bmatrix}, \tag{6}
$$

$$
\begin{bmatrix} B'_{11} & \cdots & B'_{1n_1} \\ \vdots & \ddots & \vdots \\ B'_{n_11} & \cdots & B'_{n_1n_1} \end{bmatrix} = \begin{bmatrix} T_{11} & \cdots & T_{1n_1} \\ \vdots & \ddots & \vdots \\ T_{n_11} & \cdots & T_{n_1n_1} \end{bmatrix} \begin{bmatrix} L'_{1,n_1+1} & \cdots & L'_{1,2n_1} \\ \vdots & \ddots & \vdots \\ L'_{n_1,n_1+1} & \cdots & L'_{n_1,2n_1} \end{bmatrix}. \tag{7}
$$

Substituting (6) into (7),

$$
\begin{bmatrix} T_{11} & \cdots & T_{1n_1} \\ \vdots & \ddots & \vdots \\ T_{n_11} & \cdots & T_{n_1n_1} \end{bmatrix} = \begin{bmatrix} L'_{11} & \cdots & L'_{1n_1} \\ \vdots & \ddots & \vdots \\ L'_{n_11} & \cdots & L'_{n_1n_1} \end{bmatrix}^{-1}
$$

$$
\Rightarrow \begin{bmatrix} L'_{11} & \cdots & L'_{1n_1} \\ \vdots & \ddots & \vdots \\ L'_{n_11} & \cdots & L'_{n_1n_1} \end{bmatrix} \begin{bmatrix} B'_{11} & \cdots & B'_{1n_1} \\ \vdots & \ddots & \vdots \\ B'_{n_11} & \cdots & B'_{n_1n_1} \end{bmatrix} = \begin{bmatrix} L'_{1,n_1+1} & \cdots & L'_{1,2n_1} \\ \vdots & \ddots & \vdots \\ L'_{n_1,n_1+1} & \cdots & L'_{n_1,2n_1} \end{bmatrix}. \tag{8}
$$

Let $B' = \begin{bmatrix} B'_{11} & \cdots & B'_{1n_1} \\ \vdots & \ddots & \vdots \\ B'_{n_11} & \cdots & B'_{n_1n_1} \end{bmatrix}$. Since all the matrices L'_{ab} are circulant matrices induced by vectors $l_{ab} \in \mathbb{F}_{q^m}^{\frac{n_2}{2}}$, we can view (8) in vector form, i.e., for $1 \le a \le n_1$,

$$
(l_{a,1}, \ldots, l_{a,n_1})B' = (l_{a,n_1+1}, \ldots, l_{a,2n_1})
$$

$$
\Rightarrow (l_{a,1}, \ldots, l_{a,n_1}, l_{a,n_1+1}, \ldots, l_{a,2n_1}) \begin{bmatrix} -B' \\ I_{\frac{n_1n_2}{2}} \end{bmatrix} = 0. \tag{9}
$$

Let $F = \begin{bmatrix} -B' \\ I_{\frac{n_1n_2}{2}} \end{bmatrix}$ and $l_a = (l_{a,1}, \ldots, l_{a,2n_1})$. Note that $\mathrm{rk}(l_a) = d_2$ of low rank, therefore solving for l_a from (9) is equivalent to solve $\mathrm{RSD}_F(q, m, n_1n_2, \frac{n_1n_2}{2}, d_2)$ problem. Note that a basis for $\mathcal{L}'$ is also a basis for $\mathcal{L}$, which is also a support basis for H_2. Once l_a is determined, we are able to determine $\mathcal{L}'$ and recover a support basis $\mathcal{F}_2$ for the low rank parity check matrix H_2.

5.3 Recover Alternative Secret Key for DC-LRPC-Kronecker Cryptosystem

Although $\mathcal{L}'$ is known, we do not know a low rank parity check matrix for $\mathcal{L}'$. We are required to compute an alternative low rank parity check matrix for $\mathcal{L}'$.

First of all, we rewrite

$$P_{ij} := \left[\begin{array}{c|c} Q_{2i-1,2j-1} & Q_{2i-1,2j} \\ \hline Q_{2i,2j-1} & Q_{2i,2j} \end{array} \right] \quad \Rightarrow \quad Q = \begin{bmatrix} P_{11} & \cdots & P_{1,n_1} \\ \vdots & \ddots & \vdots \\ P_{n_1,1} & \cdots & P_{n_1,n_1} \end{bmatrix}.$$

for $1 \leq i, j \leq n_1$. Then we have

$$
Q = \begin{bmatrix} P_{11} & & & 0 \\ & P_{11} & & \\ & & \ddots & \\ 0 & & & P_{11} \end{bmatrix} \begin{bmatrix} I_{n_2} & P_{11}^{-1}P_{12} & \cdots & P_{11}^{-1}P_{1,n_1} \\ P_{11}^{-1}P_{21} & P_{11}^{-1}P_{22} & \cdots & P_{11}^{-1}P_{2,n_1} \\ \vdots & \vdots & \ddots & \vdots \\ P_{11}^{-1}P_{n_1,1} & P_{11}^{-1}P_{n_1,2} & \cdots & P_{11}^{-1}P_{n_1,n_1} \end{bmatrix}
$$

$$
= \begin{bmatrix} P_{11} & & & 0 \\ & P_{11} & & \\ & & \ddots & \\ 0 & & & P_{11} \end{bmatrix} \begin{bmatrix} I_{n_2} & W_{12} & \cdots & W_{1,n_1} \\ W_{21} & W_{22} & \cdots & W_{2,n_1} \\ \vdots & \vdots & \ddots & \vdots \\ W_{n_1,1} & W_{n_1,2} & \cdots & W_{n_1,n_1} \end{bmatrix} = \mathcal{P}W
$$

where $\mathcal{P} = \begin{bmatrix} P_{11} & & & 0 \\ & P_{11} & & \\ & & \ddots & \\ 0 & & & P_{11} \end{bmatrix}$, $W = \begin{bmatrix} I_{n_2} & W_{12} & \cdots & W_{1,n_1} \\ W_{21} & W_{22} & \cdots & W_{2,n_1} \\ \vdots & \vdots & \ddots & \vdots \\ W_{n_1,1} & W_{n_1,2} & \cdots & W_{n_1,n_1} \end{bmatrix}$ and $W_{ij} =$

$P_{11}^{-1}P_{ij}$. From (4), we have $[L'_{11} \mid L'_{12}] = [-L_2 \mid L_1] \begin{bmatrix} Q_{11} & Q_{12} \\ Q_{21} & Q_{22} \end{bmatrix}$. Let $\mathcal{L}' = \mathcal{L}Q$ as in (4), then

$$
\mathcal{L}' = \begin{bmatrix} L'_{11} & L'_{12} & \cdots & L'_{1,2n_1-1} & L'_{1,2n_1} \\ \vdots & \vdots & \ddots & \vdots & \vdots \\ L'_{n_1 1} & L'_{n_1 2} & \cdots & L'_{n_1,2n_1-1} & L'_{n_1,2n_1} \end{bmatrix} \tag{10}
$$

$$
\mathcal{L}Q = \begin{bmatrix} -L_2 \mid L_1 & & 0 \\ & \ddots & \\ 0 & & -L_2 \mid L_1 \end{bmatrix} \mathcal{P}W = \begin{bmatrix} L'_{11} \mid L'_{12} & & 0 \\ & \ddots & \\ 0 & & L'_{11} \mid L'_{12} \end{bmatrix} W. \tag{11}
$$

Consider the system (10)=(11) over $\mathbb{F}_q$, we have $m(n_1^2 - 1)n_2$ equations with $2(n_1^2 - 1)n_2$ unknown variables for W_{ij}. Since $m > 2$, we have $m(n_1^2 - 1)n_2 > 2(n_1^2 - 1)n_2$, thus W could be solved uniquely in $(2(n_1^2 - 1)n_2)^3$ operations. Once W is computed, we can compute an alternative low rank parity check matrix, $H_{\mathcal{L}'}$ for $\mathcal{L}'$:

$$H_{\mathcal{L}'} = \begin{bmatrix} -[L'_{12}]^T \mid [L'_{11}]^T & & 0 \\ & \ddots & \\ 0 & & -[L'_{12}]^T \mid [L'_{12}]^T \end{bmatrix} [W^{-1}]^T$$

$$\Rightarrow \quad \mathcal{L}'[H_{\mathcal{L}'}]^T = \begin{bmatrix} L'_{11} \mid L'_{12} & & 0 \\ & \ddots & \\ 0 & & L'_{11} \mid L'_{12} \end{bmatrix} WW^{-1} \begin{bmatrix} -L'_{12} & & 0 \\ L'_{11} & & \\ & \ddots & \\ & & -L'_{12} \\ 0 & & L'_{11} \end{bmatrix} = 0.$$

Finally, compute

$$c[H_{\mathcal{L}'}]^T = mG_{\mathsf{pub}}[H_{\mathcal{L}'}]^T + e[H_{\mathcal{L}'}]^T = mS\mathcal{DRL}'[H_{\mathcal{L}'}]^T + e[H_{\mathcal{L}'}]^T = e[H_{\mathcal{L}'}]^T.$$

As the basis $\mathcal{F}_2$ is known and $\mathrm{rk}(e) \leq r_2$, we can apply decoding algorithm of LRPC and recover e and thus solve for the plaintext m.

5.4   Cryptanalysis on DC-LRPC-Kronecker Cryptosystem for $\mathcal{C}_1$ of Dimension $[2, 2]$

By the cryptanalysis in Sect. 5.2, we first solve the $\mathrm{RSD}_F(q, m, 2n_2, n_2, d_2)$ for all the parameters in [10, Table 2] which $\mathcal{C}_1$ is of dimension $[2, 2]$. Then we determine an alternative low rank parity check matrix with the strategies in Sect. 5.3 in $(6n_2)^3$ operations. Table 5 shows the complexity to recover the plaintext of the LRPC-Kronecker cryptosystem. In other words, for all the original parameters with $\mathcal{C}_1$ of dimension $[2, 2]$, our cryptanalysis is able to recover alternative secret key $H_{\mathcal{L}'}$ within the claimed security level. We denote the complexity to solve the $\mathrm{RSD}_F(q, m, 2n_2, n_2, d_2)$ and alternative low rank parity check matrix as "CO1" and "CO2" respectively. We calculate the total complexity of our attack by "CO1+CO2" and denote it as "TO".

From Table 5, we can observe that the LRPC-Kronecker cryptosystem with $\mathcal{C}_1$ of dimension $[2, 2]$ in fact does not achieve the required security level. Our attack can recover all the secret key for the all parameters set with $k_1 = n_1$. As a consequence, the parameters need to be adjusted to achieve the required security level, which will result in larger public key size. We conclude that the design of $\mathcal{C}_1$ with $k_1 = n_1$ in fact is insecure against our attack.

Table 5. Complexity to recover alternative secret key $H_{\mathcal{L}'}$ of LRPC-Kronecker cryptosystem with $\mathcal{C}_1$ of dimension $[2, 2]$

Schemes	q	m	n_2	d_2	CO1	CO2	TO	Claimed security
$[2, 2]$-KronF-I	8	17	46	3	56	24	80	128
$[2, 2]$-KronF-II	8	29	44	3	77	24	101	192
$[2, 2]$-KronF-III	8	37	44	3	91	24	115	256

5.5   Limitations of Our Attack

Our attack in this section may not work well on the case where $k_1 \neq n_1$. For instance, when $k_1 = 2 < 3 = n_1$, from (5) we have

$$\begin{bmatrix} T_{11} & T_{12} & T_{13} \\ T_{21} & T_{22} & T_{23} \end{bmatrix} \begin{bmatrix} L'_{11} & L'_{12} & L'_{13} & L'_{14} & L'_{15} & L'_{16} \\ L'_{21} & L'_{22} & L'_{23} & L'_{24} & L'_{25} & L'_{26} \\ L'_{31} & L'_{32} & L'_{33} & L'_{34} & L'_{35} & L'_{36} \end{bmatrix} = \begin{bmatrix} I_{k_2} & 0 & B'_{11} & B'_{12} & B'_{13} & B'_{14} \\ 0 & I_{k_2} & B'_{21} & B'_{22} & B'_{23} & B'_{24} \end{bmatrix}.$$

Let $\mathcal{L}'_1 = \begin{bmatrix} L'_{11} & L'_{12} & L'_{13} \\ L'_{21} & L'_{22} & L'_{23} \\ L'_{31} & L'_{32} & L'_{33} \end{bmatrix}$ and $\mathcal{L}'_2 = \begin{bmatrix} L'_{14} & L'_{15} & L'_{16} \\ L'_{24} & L'_{25} & L'_{26} \\ L'_{34} & L'_{35} & L'_{36} \end{bmatrix}$, we have

$$\begin{bmatrix} T_{11} & T_{12} & T_{13} \\ T_{21} & T_{22} & T_{23} \end{bmatrix} \mathcal{L}'_1 = \begin{bmatrix} I_{k_2} & 0 & B'_{11} \\ 0 & I_{k_2} & B'_{21} \end{bmatrix}, \quad \begin{bmatrix} T_{11} & T_{12} & T_{13} \\ T_{21} & T_{22} & T_{23} \end{bmatrix} \mathcal{L}'_2 = \begin{bmatrix} B'_{12} & B'_{13} & B'_{14} \\ B'_{22} & B'_{23} & B'_{24} \end{bmatrix}$$

$$\Rightarrow \quad \begin{bmatrix} T_{11} & T_{12} & T_{13} \\ T_{21} & T_{22} & T_{23} \end{bmatrix} = \begin{bmatrix} I_{k_2} & 0 & B'_{11} \\ 0 & I_{k_2} & B'_{21} \end{bmatrix} [\mathcal{L}'_1]^{-1}$$

$$\Rightarrow \quad \begin{bmatrix} T_{11} & T_{12} & T_{13} \\ T_{21} & T_{22} & T_{23} \end{bmatrix} \mathcal{L}'_2 = \begin{bmatrix} I_{k_2} & 0 & B'_{11} \\ 0 & I_{k_2} & B'_{21} \end{bmatrix} [\mathcal{L}'_1]^{-1} \mathcal{L}'_2 = \begin{bmatrix} B'_{12} & B'_{13} & B'_{14} \\ B'_{22} & B'_{23} & B'_{24} \end{bmatrix}.$$

Here, the matrices $[\mathcal{L}'_1]^{-1}$ and $\mathcal{L}'_2$ do not commute, we are not able to rewrite the system in the form of (8). Therefore this attack fails.

6   Conclusion

We point out some errors in the original LRPC-Kronecker cryptosystem and repair the errors and parameters as KronF cryptosystem. We also show that an LRPC-Kronecker cryptosystem is equivalent to an LRPC cryptosystem (AKron) by modifying the encryption and decryption of the original LRPC-Kronecker cryptosystem. Furthermore, we show that KronF cryptosystem in fact has design weakness when $k_1 = n_1$ for $\mathcal{C}_1$. In particular, we are able to cryptanalyze the KronF cryptosystem whenever $k_1 = n_1$ and successfully recover secret key for all the proposed parameters. In other words, although KronF with $k_1 = n_1 = 2$ promises compact key size of $4,692$ bits, $7,656$ bits and $9,768$ bits, in fact the schemes only achieve 80-bit, 101-bit and 115-bit security level. As a consequence, Kim et al.'s claim that their parameters for $[2,2]$-$\mathcal{C}_1$ could achieve 128-bit, 192-bit and 256-bit security level has to be revised.

Acknowledgments. The authors would like to thank the Galvez et al. (the authors of [10]) for their feedback on our identification of the errors in the original proposal.

References

1. Aragon, N., Gaborit, P., Hauteville, A., Tillich, J.-P.: A new algorithm for solving the rank syndrome decoding problem. In: Proceedings of IEEE International Symposium on Information Theory (ISIT 2018), pp. 2421–2425 (2018)
2. Augot, D., Loidreau, P., Robert, G.: Generalized Gabidulin codes over fields of any characteristic. Des. Codes Crypt. **86**(8), 1807–1848 (2018)
3. Faugère, J.-C., Levy-dit-Vehel, F., Perret, L.: Cryptanalysis of MinRank. In: Wagner, D. (ed.) CRYPTO 2008. LNCS, vol. 5157, pp. 280–296. Springer, Heidelberg (2008). https://doi.org/10.1007/978-3-540-85174-5_16
4. Gabidulin, E.M.: Theory of codes with maximum rank distance. Probl. Peredachi Informatsii **21**(1), 3–16 (1985)
5. Gaborit, P., Ruatta, O., Schrek, J.: On the complexity of the rank syndrome decoding problem. IEEE Trans. Inf. Theory **62**(2), 1006–1019 (2016)
6. Gaborit, P., Ruatta, O., Schrek, J., Zémor, G.: New results for rank-based cryptography. In: Pointcheval, D., Vergnaud, D. (eds.) AFRICACRYPT 2014. LNCS, vol. 8469, pp. 1–12. Springer, Cham (2014). https://doi.org/10.1007/978-3-319-06734-6_1
7. Gaborit, P., Zémor, G.: On the hardness of the decoding and the minimum distance problems for rank codes. IEEE Trans. Inf. Theory **62**(12), 7245–7252 (2016)
8. Goubin, L., Courtois, N.T.: Cryptanalysis of the TTM cryptosystem. In: Okamoto, T. (ed.) ASIACRYPT 2000. LNCS, vol. 1976, pp. 44–57. Springer, Heidelberg (2000). https://doi.org/10.1007/3-540-44448-3_4
9. Horlemann-Trautmann, A., Marshall, K., Rosenthal, J.: Extension of overbeck's attack for Gabidulin based cryptosystems. Des. Codes Crypt. **86**(2), 319–340 (2018)
10. Kim, J.-L., Galvez, L., Kim, Y.-S., Lee, N.: A new LRPC-Kronecker product codes based public-key cryptography. In: Proceedings of the 5th ACM on ASIA Public-Key Cryptography Workshop (APKC 2018), pp. 25–33 (2018)
11. Kobara, K., Imai, H.: Semantically secure McEliece public-key cryptosystems - conversions for McEliece PKC. In: Kim, K. (ed.) PKC 2001. LNCS, vol. 1992, pp. 19–35. Springer, Heidelberg (2001). https://doi.org/10.1007/3-540-44586-2_2
12. Levy-dit-Vehel, F., Perret, L.: Algebraic decoding of rank metric codes. In: Proceedings of Yet Another Conference on Cryptography (YACC 2006), pp. 142–152 (2006)
13. Lau, T.S.C., Tan, C.H.: A new technique in rank metric code-based encryption. Cryptography **2**, 32 (2018)
14. Lau, T.S.C., Tan, C.H.: A new Gabidulin-like code and its application in cryptography. In: Carlet, C., Guilley, S., Nitaj, A., Souidi, E.M. (eds.) C2SI 2019. LNCS, vol. 11445, pp. 269–287. Springer, Cham (2019). https://doi.org/10.1007/978-3-030-16458-4_16
15. McEliece, R.J.: A public-key cryptosystem based on algebraic coding theory. The Deep Space Network Progress Report 42-44, pp. 114–116. Jet Propulsion Laboratory, Pasedena, CA (1978)
16. Ourivski, A.V., Johansson, T.: New technique for decoding codes in the rank metric and its cryptography applications. Probl. Inf. Transm. **38**(3), 237–246 (2002)

Pseudorandom Functions from LWE: RKA Security and Application

Nan Cui[1,2], Shengli Liu[1,2,3(✉)], Yunhua Wen[1], and Dawu Gu[1]

[1] Department of Computer Science and Engineering,
Shanghai Jiao Tong University, Shanghai 200240, China
{cuinan913,slliu,happyle8,dwgu}@sjtu.edu.cn
[2] State Key Laboratory of Cryptology, P.O. Box 5159, Beijing 100878, China
[3] Westone Cryptologic Research Center, Beijing 100070, China

Abstract. Pseudorandom Functions (PRF) is a basic primitive in cryptography. In this paper, we study related key attacks (RKA) with which the adversary is able to choose function ϕ and observe the behavior of the PRF under the modified secret key $\phi(k)$. We focus on the PRF from the *Learning with Errors* (LWE) assumption by Banerjee and Peikert in CRYPTO 2014. We prove that the PRF is secure against unique-input key shift attacks and restricted affine attacks. After that, we use this RKA-secure PRF to construct a robustly reusable fuzzy extractor, which enjoys higher efficiency and better error correction rate.

Keywords: PRF · Related key attacks ·
Robustly reusable fuzzy extractor

1 Introduction

As an essential cryptographic primitive, pseudorandom function (PRF) family plays an important role in modern cryptography. A pseudorandom function [1] $F : \mathcal{K} \times \mathcal{X} \rightarrow \mathcal{Y}$ requires that the output of $F(k, \cdot)$ is pseudorandom when k is uniform. In other words, the behavior of function $F(k, \cdot)$ is computationally indistinguishable from that of a truly random function $\mathsf{U} : \mathcal{X} \rightarrow \mathcal{Y}$. Research on construction of PRF can be founded in [1,2].

Traditionally, pseudorandomness of PRF is always studied under the assumption that the key k is uniformly distributed and unchanged in the function evaluations. However, recent research showed that the key in cryptography device may suffer from leaking or tampering, for instance, fault injection attacks [3], side-channel attacks [4], etc. In this case, the key might not be uniform to the adversary, then the pseudorandomness of the PRF may not be guaranteed in case of such attacks. To solve this problem of key tampering, researchers developed the notion of related-key attack (RKA) security. RKA security for PRF captures the computational indistinguishability between the $F(\phi(k), x)$ and $\mathsf{U}(\phi(k), x)$, where $\mathsf{U}(\cdot, \cdot)$ is the keyed truly random function, and the tampering function ϕ together with input x are adaptively designated by the adversary. A RKA-secure

© Springer Nature Switzerland AG 2019
J. Jang-Jaccard and F. Guo (Eds.): ACISP 2019, LNCS 11547, pp. 229–250, 2019.
https://doi.org/10.1007/978-3-030-21548-4_13

PRF enjoys a wide range of applications. It can be used to construct many other RKA-secure primitives like signature, identity-based encryption, chosen ciphertext secure encryption scheme [5] and fuzzy extractor [6].

In 2000, Bellare and Cash [7] presented the first RKA-secure PRF under standard assumption. Besides, they developed a framework to build RKA-secure PRFs and presented instantiations under DDH, DLIN assumptions. Later, Boneh et al. [8] constructed the first key-homomorphic PRF without random oracle and Lewi et al. [9] proved that this key-homomorphic PRF [8] is RKA secure for restricted affine functions under a strong LWE assumption. In 2014, Peikert et al. [10] proposed an improved key homomorphic PRF which is more efficient and rely on a weaker LWE assumption compared with [8]. Natural questions arise:

Is this improved key-homomorphic PRF RKA secure?
If yes, what RKA function set does this PRF support?

In this paper, we will answer these questions. We will prove the RKA security of the improved PRF [10] and show the supported RKA function set. Moreover, we construct a more efficient robustly reusable fuzzy extractor based on this improved RKA secure PRF.

1.1   Our Contribution

- **Unique-input RKA security against key-shift family.** We prove the key-homomorphic PRF in [10] is unique-input RKA secure against the key-shift family $\Phi_{\mathsf{shift}} = \{\psi_{\mathbf{b}} : \psi_{\mathbf{b}}(\mathbf{k}) = \mathbf{k} + \mathbf{b}\}$, where $\mathbf{b}$ is an arbitrary vector in $\mathbb{Z}_q^n$.
- **Unique-input RKA security against restricted affine family.** We extend the PRF to a matrix version $F(\mathbf{K}, x) := \lfloor \mathbf{K} \cdot \mathbf{A}_T(x) \rceil_p$, then prove the PRF is unique-input RKA secure against affine function family $\Phi_{\mathsf{raff}} = \{\phi_{\mathbf{C},\mathbf{B}} : \phi_{\mathbf{C},\mathbf{B}}(\mathbf{K}) = \mathbf{C}\mathbf{K} + \mathbf{B}\}$, where $\mathbf{C}$ is a full rank matrix with low norm and $\mathbf{B}$ is an arbitrary matrix in $\mathbb{Z}_q^{n \times n}$.
- **Robustly Reusable Fuzzy Extractor.** We use this RKA-secure PRF to construct a robustly reusable fuzzy extractor of higher efficiency and better error correction rate.

2   Preliminaries

2.1   Notation

We use normal, bold and capital bold letters like $x, \mathbf{x}, \mathbf{X}$ to denote element, column vector and matrix, respectively. For a set $\mathcal{X}$, $x \leftarrow_\$ \mathcal{X}$ means randomly choosing an element x from set $\mathcal{X}$. For a distribution X over set $\mathcal{X}$, let $x \leftarrow X$ denotes sampling x according to X. For two random variables X and Y over the same set $\mathcal{X}$, let $H_\infty(X) = -\log_2 \max_{x \in \mathcal{X}} \Pr[X = x]$ denotes the min-entropy of X, $\tilde{H}_\infty(X|Y) = -\log(\mathbb{E}_{y \leftarrow Y}[2^{-H_\infty(X|Y=y)}])$ denotes the conditional min-entropy. $X \approx_c Y$ means that the distributions X and Y are computationally indistinguishable. For a bit string x of length at least i, we use $x_{(i)}$ to denote the first i bits of string x while $x^{(i)}$ denote the remainder. Let ε denote the empty string. Then, for a bit string x of length ℓ, $x^{(\ell)} = \varepsilon$.

For real number x, let $\lfloor x \rfloor$ denote rounding x to the largest integer which does not exceed it. For an integer $q \geq 1$, $\mathbb{Z}_q = \mathbb{Z}/q\mathbb{Z}$ denotes the quotient ring of integers modulo q. For integers p, q where $q \geq p \geq 2$, define rounding function $\lfloor \cdot \rceil : \mathbb{Z}_q \to \mathbb{Z}_p$ as $\lfloor x \rceil_p = \lfloor \frac{p}{q} \cdot x \rceil$. For a vector $\mathbf{x} \in \mathbb{Z}_q^n$, we define $\lfloor \mathbf{x} \rceil_p$ as the vector in $\mathbb{Z}_p^n$ obtained by rounding each coordinate of $\mathbf{x}$ individually. For an algorithm Alg, we denote by $y \leftarrow \mathsf{Alg}(x)$ the operation of running Alg with input x (possibly together with randomness r) and assigning y as the output of Alg. A function $f(\lambda)$ is *negligible* if it is $o(\lambda^{-c})$ for all $c > 0$. We use $\mathsf{negl}(\lambda)$ to denote a negligible function of λ and PPT to denote probabilistic polynomial-time.

Remark 1. In this paper, we concentrate on Hamming metric space $\mathcal{M} = \{0,1\}^*$ with $\mathsf{dis}(w_1, w_2)$ the number of positions in which the strings w_1 and w_2 differ.

2.2   Related Key Attack (RKA) Secure PRFs

Before introducing related key attack (RKA) secure PRFs, we review the security definition of pseudorandom functions (PRF) in [9] which considers the PRF with public parameters pp. Let $\mathsf{U}(x)$ denote a truly random function.

Definition 1 (PRF). *PRF consists of two algorithms* PRF.Setup *and* PRF.Eval. *The setup algorithm* PRF.Setup *takes security parameter λ as input and outputs a public parameter* pp, *namely* pp $\leftarrow$ *PRF.Setup(λ). The public parameter* pp *defines a family of keyed functions* $F_{\mathsf{pp}} : \mathcal{K} \times \mathcal{X} \to \mathcal{Y}$. *The evaluation algorithm* PRF.Eval *takes k, x as input and calculates $F_{\mathsf{pp}}(k, x)$. The PRF $F_{\mathsf{pp}} : \mathcal{K} \times \mathcal{X} \to \mathcal{Y}$ is secure if* $\mathbf{Adv}_{\mathcal{A},F}^{\mathsf{PRF}}(\lambda) := |\Pr[\mathbf{Exp}_{\mathcal{A},F}^{\mathsf{PRF}}(0) \Rightarrow 1] - \Pr[\mathbf{Exp}_{\mathcal{A},F}^{\mathsf{PRF}}(1) \Rightarrow 1]|$ *is negligible for any PPT adversary $\mathcal{A}$, where the experiment* $\mathbf{Exp}_{\mathcal{A},F}^{\mathsf{PRF}}(b), b \in \{0,1\}$, *is formalized in Fig. 1.*

$\mathbf{Exp}_{\mathcal{A},F}^{\mathsf{PRF}}(0)$:	$\mathbf{Exp}_{\mathcal{A},F}^{\mathsf{PRF}}(1)$:
pp $\leftarrow$ PRF.Setup(λ). $k \leftarrow_\$ \mathcal{K}$; $b' \leftarrow \mathcal{A}^{\mathcal{O}(\cdot)}$. Return b'.	$b' \leftarrow \mathcal{A}^{\mathcal{O}(\cdot)}$. Return b'.
$\mathcal{O}(x)$: $y := F_{\mathsf{pp}}(k, \cdot)$. Return y.	$\mathcal{O}(x)$: $y := \mathsf{U}(x)$. Return y.

Fig. 1. The security game $\mathbf{Exp}_{\mathcal{A},F}^{\mathsf{PRF}}(b)$ of PRF.

Φ-RKA security of PRF deals with Φ-RKA attacks where the adversary is able to choose a function ϕ from $\Phi = \{\phi : \mathcal{K} \to \mathcal{K}\}$ and observe the output of the PRF under the modified secret key $\phi(k)$. Φ-RKA security asks for the pseudorandomness of PRF under $\phi(k)$. Formally, we define the Φ-RKA security for a pseudorandom function $F : \mathcal{K} \times \mathcal{X} \to \mathcal{Y}$ in Definition 2. Let $\mathsf{U}(k, x)$ denote a keyed random function.

Definition 2 (Φ-RKA Security). *A PRF* $F : \mathcal{K} \times \mathcal{X} \to \mathcal{Y}$ *is RKA-secure with respect to function class* $\Phi = \{\phi : \mathcal{K} \to \mathcal{K}\}$ *if* $\mathbf{Adv}^{\mathsf{RKA}}_{\Phi,F,\mathcal{A}}(\lambda) :=$ $|\Pr[\mathbf{Exp}^{\mathsf{RKA}}_{\Phi,F,\mathcal{A}}(0) \Rightarrow 1] - \Pr[\mathbf{Exp}^{\mathsf{RKA}}_{\Phi,F,\mathcal{A}}(1) \Rightarrow 1]|$ *is negligible for any PPT adversary* $\mathcal{A}$, *where the experiment* $\mathbf{Exp}^{\mathsf{RKA}}_{\Phi,F,\mathcal{A}}(b), b \in \{0, 1\}$, *is formalized in Fig. 2.*

$\mathbf{Exp}^{\mathsf{RKA}}_{\Phi,F,\mathcal{A}}(0):$	$\mathbf{Exp}^{\mathsf{RKA}}_{\Phi,F,\mathcal{A}}(1):$
$\mathsf{pp} \leftarrow \mathsf{PRF.Setup}(\lambda).$	$k \leftarrow_\$ \mathcal{K}.$
$k \leftarrow_\$ \mathcal{K}.$	$b' \leftarrow \mathcal{A}^{\mathcal{O}^{\mathsf{RKA}}_k(\cdot,\cdot)}.$
$b' \leftarrow \mathcal{A}^{\mathcal{O}^{\mathsf{RKA}}_k(\cdot,\cdot)}.$	Return b'.
Return b'.	
$\mathcal{O}^{\mathsf{RKA}}_k(\phi, x):$	$\mathcal{O}^{\mathsf{RKA}}_k(\phi, x):$
$y := F_{\mathsf{pp}}(\phi(k), \cdot).$	$y := \mathsf{U}(\phi(k), x).$
Return y.	Return y.

Fig. 2. The Φ-RKA security game $\mathbf{Exp}^{\mathsf{RKA}}_{\Phi,F,\mathcal{A}}(b)$ of PRF.

Unique-input Φ-RKA security is a weaker notion of RKA security defined in Definition 2, and it only deals with unique-input adversaries. For a unique-input adversary, it is required that $x_1, \cdots, x_Q$ are distinct in queries $(\phi_1, x_1), \cdots, (\phi_Q, x_Q)$, which are submitted by the adversary to oracle $\mathcal{O}^{\mathsf{RKA}}_k(\cdot, \cdot)$ in $\mathbf{Exp}^{\mathsf{RKA}}_{\Phi,F,\mathcal{A}}(b)$.

Definition 3 (Unique-input RKA Security) [7]. *A PRF is unique-input Φ-RKA secure if it is Φ-RKA secure against unique-input adversaries, who are required to submit distinct* $x_1, \cdots, x_Q$ *in queries* $(\phi_1, x_1), \cdots, (\phi_Q, x_Q)$ *to oracle* $\mathcal{O}^{\mathsf{RKA}}_k(\cdot, \cdot)$ *in* $\mathbf{Exp}^{\mathsf{RKA}}_{\Phi,F,\mathcal{A}}(b)$.

2.3   The Learning with Errors (LWE) Assumption

The learning with errors (LWE) problem was introduced by Regev in [11,12].

Definition 4 (LWE Assumption). *Let* $n = n(\lambda)$, $m = m(\lambda)$, $q \geq 2$, *and let* χ *denote a distribution over* $\mathbb{Z}_q$. *The* $\mathsf{LWE}_{n,m,q,\chi}$ *problem is to distinguish the following distributions*

$$(\mathbf{A}, \mathbf{s}^\top \mathbf{A} + \mathbf{e}^\top) \quad and \quad (\mathbf{A}, \mathbf{u}^\top),$$

where $\mathbf{A} \leftarrow_{\$} \mathbb{Z}_q^{n \times m}$, $\mathbf{s} \leftarrow_{\$} \mathbb{Z}_q^n$, $\mathbf{e} \leftarrow \chi^m$, *and* $\mathbf{u} \leftarrow_{\$} \mathbb{Z}_q^m$. *The* $\mathsf{LWE}_{n,m,q,\chi}$ *assumption means that* $\mathsf{Adv}_{\mathsf{LWE},\mathcal{A}}^{n,m,q,\chi}(\lambda)$ *is negligible for any PPT adversary* $\mathcal{A}$, *i.e.,*

$$\mathsf{Adv}_{\mathsf{LWE},\mathcal{A}}^{n,m,q,\chi}(\lambda) := |\Pr[\mathbf{A} \leftarrow_{\$} \mathbb{Z}_q^{n \times m}, \mathbf{s} \leftarrow_{\$} \mathbb{Z}_q^n, \mathbf{e} \leftarrow \chi^m : \mathcal{A}(\mathbf{A}, \mathbf{s}^\top \mathbf{A} + \mathbf{e}^\top) \Rightarrow 1]$$
$$- \Pr[\mathbf{A} \leftarrow_{\$} \mathbb{Z}_q^{n \times m}, \mathbf{u} \leftarrow_{\$} \mathbb{Z}_q^m : \mathcal{A}(\mathbf{A}, \mathbf{u}^\top) \Rightarrow 1]| = \mathsf{negl}(\lambda). \quad (1)$$

The $\mathsf{LWE}_{n,m,\ell,q,\chi}$ *assumption means that* $\mathsf{Adv}_{\mathsf{LWE},\mathcal{A}}^{n,m,\ell,q,\chi}(\lambda)$ *is negligible for any PPT adversary* $\mathcal{A}$, *i.e.,*

$$\mathsf{Adv}_{\mathsf{LWE},\mathcal{A}}^{n,m,\ell,q,\chi}(\lambda) := |\Pr[\mathbf{S} \leftarrow_{\$} \mathbb{Z}_q^{\ell \times n}, \mathbf{A} \leftarrow_{\$} \mathbb{Z}_q^{n \times m}, \mathbf{E} \leftarrow \chi^{\ell \times m} : \mathcal{A}(\mathbf{A}, \mathbf{SA} + \mathbf{E}) \Rightarrow 1]$$
$$- \Pr[\mathbf{A} \leftarrow_{\$} \mathbb{Z}_q^{n \times m}, \mathbf{U} \leftarrow_{\$} \mathbb{Z}_q^{\ell \times m} : \mathcal{A}(\mathbf{A}, \mathbf{U}) \Rightarrow 1]| = \mathsf{negl}(\lambda). \quad (2)$$

A simple hybrid argument [9] implies $\mathsf{Adv}_{\mathsf{LWE},\mathcal{A}}^{n,m,\ell,q,\chi}(\lambda) \leq \ell \cdot \mathsf{Adv}_{\mathsf{LWE},\mathcal{A}}^{n,m,q,\chi}(\lambda)$.

For a parameter $r > 0$ and a prime q, let Φ_r denote the distribution over $\mathbb{Z}_q$ of a random variable $X \mod q$ where X follows the discrete Gaussian distribution $D_{\mathbb{Z},r}$ with mean 0 and standard deviation $r/\sqrt{2\pi}$ for each $z \in \mathbb{Z}$. We have the following lemma.

Lemma 1 [11]. *For* $r > 0$, n *is an integer and* q *is a prime such that* $r \geq 3\sqrt{n}$. *If there exists an efficient algorithm that solves the decisional* $\mathsf{LWE}_{n,m,q,\Phi_r}$ *problem, then there exists an efficient quantum algorithm that approximates the shortest vector problem (SVP) and the shortest independent vectors problem (SIVP) to within* $\tilde{O}(n \cdot q/r)$ *in the wost case.*

3   Unique-Input RKA Secure Pseudorandom Function

In this section, we recall the PRF in [10] and prove the unique-input RKA security of it. In Sect. 3.1, we recall the construction of the PRF and review some relevant definitions in [10]. In Sect. 3.2, we prove that the PRF is unique-input Φ_{shift}-RKA secure against key-shift attacks. And in Sect. 3.3, we extend the construction of the PRF to a matrix version and prove the matrix version is unique-input Φ_{raff}-RKA secure against restricted affine attacks.

First of all, we present some notations. For $q \geq 1$, let $\ell = \lfloor \log q \rfloor$ and gadget vector $\mathbf{g}^\top = (1, 2, 4, \cdots, 2^{\ell-1}) \in \mathbb{Z}_q^\ell$. Define the deterministic binary decomposition function $\mathbf{g}^{-1} : \mathbb{Z}_q \to \{0,1\}^\ell$ as $\mathbf{g}^{-1}(a) = (x_0, x_1, \cdots, x_{\ell-1})^\top$, where $x_i \in \{0,1\}$, and $a = \sum_{i=0}^{\ell-1} x_i 2^i$ is the binary representation of a. Clearly, we have $\mathbf{g}^\top \cdot \mathbf{g}^{-1}(\mathbf{a}) = \mathbf{a}$. Similarly, we can extend the gadget vector $\mathbf{g}$ to matrix $\mathbf{G} = \mathrm{diag}(\mathbf{g}^\top, \cdots, \mathbf{g}^\top) = \mathbf{I}_n \otimes \mathbf{g}_n^\top \in \mathbb{Z}_q^{n \times n\ell}$. Define function $\mathbf{G}^{-1} : \mathbb{Z}_q^{n \times m} \to \{0,1\}^{n\ell \times m}$ as follows: for any matrix $\mathbf{A} = (a_{ij}) \in \mathbb{Z}_q^{n \times m}$, let $a_{ij} = \sum_{w=0}^{\ell-1} a_{ij,w} 2^w$ be the binary representation of a_{ij}, and $\hat{\mathbf{a}}_{\mathbf{ij}} := (a_{ij,0}, \cdots, a_{ij,\ell-1})^\top$. Then,

$$\mathbf{G}^{-1}(\mathbf{A}) := \begin{bmatrix} \hat{\mathbf{a}}_{\mathbf{11}} & \cdots & \hat{\mathbf{a}}_{\mathbf{1m}} \\ \vdots & \ddots & \vdots \\ \hat{\mathbf{a}}_{\mathbf{n1}} & \cdots & \hat{\mathbf{a}}_{\mathbf{nm}} \end{bmatrix}.$$

Clearly, it holds that $\mathbf{G} \cdot \mathbf{G}^{-1}(\mathbf{A}) = \mathbf{A}$.

A fully binary tree T (not necessarily complete) means that each non-leaf node has two children. Let $|T|$ denote the number of leaves, and let $T.l$, $T.r$ respectively denote the left and right subtrees of T if $|T| \geq 1$.

3.1 Construction

Before presenting the construction of PRF, we review some definitions related to the pseudorandom functions in [10] in this subsection.

Definition 5 (Pruning) [10]. *For a full binary tree T, $\mathsf{pr}(T)$ removes its left-most leaf x_1 of T and replaces the subtree rooted at x_1's parent (if it exists) with the subtree rooted at x_1's sibling (i.e., Figs. 3 and 4). It can be formalized inductively as follows:*

$$T' = \mathsf{pr}(\mathsf{T}) := \begin{cases} T' = T.r & \text{if } |T.l| \leq 1 \\ T'.l = \mathsf{pr}(T.l),\ T'.r = T.r & \text{otherwise.} \end{cases}$$

Let $T^{(i)}$ denote the resulting tree after the i-th successive pruning of T, then $T^{(0)} = T$ and $T^{(i)} = \mathsf{pr}(T^{(i-1)})$.

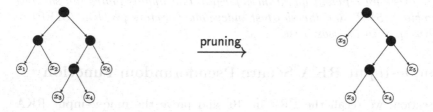

Fig. 3. A full binary tree T **Fig. 4.** The pruning tree $T' = \mathsf{pr}(T)$

Definition 6 ($\mathbf{A}_T(x)$ Function) [10]. *For a full binary tree T of at least one node and $\mathbf{A}_0, \mathbf{A}_1 \in \mathbb{Z}_q^{n \times n\ell}$, the function $\mathbf{A}_T(x) : \{0,1\}^{|T|} \to \mathbb{Z}_q^{n \times n\ell}$ is defined as*

$$\mathbf{A}_T(x) := \begin{cases} \mathbf{A}_x & \text{if } |T| = 1 \\ \mathbf{A}_{T.l}(x_l) \cdot \mathbf{G}^{-1}(\mathbf{A}_{T.r}(x_r)) & \text{otherwise,} \end{cases}$$

where $x = x_l || x_r$, $x_l \in \{0,1\}^{|T.l|}$ denotes the leaves of left subtree $T.l$, and $x_r \in \{0,1\}^{|T.r|}$ denotes the leaves of right subtrees $T.r$.

Remark 2. For an empty tree, $\mathbf{A}_\varepsilon(\varepsilon) := \mathbf{G}$.

Definition 7 ($\mathbf{S}_T(x)$ Function) [10]. *For a full binary tree T of at least one node and $\mathbf{A}_0, \mathbf{A}_1 \in \mathbb{Z}_q^{n \times n\ell}$, the function $\mathbf{S}_T(x) : \{0,1\}^{|T|-1} \to \mathbb{Z}_q^{n\ell \times n\ell}$ is defined as*

$$\mathbf{S}_T(x) := \begin{cases} \mathbf{I}\ \textit{(the identity matrix)} & \text{if } |T| = 1 \\ \mathbf{S}_{T.l}(x_l) \cdot \mathbf{G}^{-1}(\mathbf{A}_{T.r}(x_r)) & \text{otherwise.} \end{cases}$$

Given a full binary tree T with leaves $x \in \{0,1\}^{|T|}$, for any subtree T' of T, let $x'_{T'}$ denote the leaves of the subtree T'. Suppose that d is the depth of the leftmost leaf $x_1 \in \{0,1\}$, and subtree T_i is the right child of x_1's ith ancestor. Then $x = x_1 \| x' = x_1 \| \underbrace{x'_{T_1} \| \cdots , \| x'_{T_d}}_{x'}$ with $x_1 \in \{0,1\}$, $x'_{T_i} \in \{0,1\}^{|T_i|}$. Let $T' := \mathsf{pr}(T)$, then we can rewrite the function $\mathbf{A}_T(x)$ and $\mathbf{S}_T(x)$ as

$$\mathbf{A}_T(x) := \mathbf{A}_{x_1} \cdot \underbrace{\prod_{i=1}^{d} \mathbf{G}^{-1}(\mathbf{A}_{T_i}(x'_{T_i}))}_{\mathbf{S}_T(x')}. \tag{3}$$

$$\mathbf{S}_T(x') := \mathbf{G}^{-1}(\mathbf{A}_{T_1}(x'_{T_1})) \cdot \underbrace{\prod_{i=2}^{d} \mathbf{G}^{-1}(\mathbf{A}_{T_i}(x'_{T_i}))}_{\mathbf{S}_{T'}(x')}. \tag{4}$$

Based on Eqs. (3) and (4), we can obtain

$$\mathbf{A}_T(x) = \mathbf{A}_{x_1} \cdot \mathbf{S}_T(x'), \tag{5}$$
$$\mathbf{G} \cdot \mathbf{S}_T(x') = \mathbf{A}_{T'}(x'), \tag{6}$$

where $x = x_1 \| x' \in \{0,1\}^{|T|}$ with $x_1 \in \{0,1\}$, and $x' \in \{0,1\}^{|T|-1}$.

Definition 8 (Expansion $e(T)$ and Sequentiality $s(T)$) [10]. *Let T be a full binary tree, the expansion $e(T)$ is the maximum number of terms of the form $\mathbf{G}^{-1}(\cdot)$ that are ever consecutively multiplied together in function $\mathbf{A}_T(x)$. It can be defined inductively as*

$$e(T) := \begin{cases} 0 & \text{if } |T| = 1 \\ \max\{e(T.l) + 1, \ e(T.r)\} & \text{otherwise.} \end{cases}$$

The sequentiality $s(T)$ is the maximum nesting depth of $\mathbf{G}^{-1}(\cdot)$ expression in function $\mathbf{A}_T(x)$. It can be defined inductively as

$$s(T) := \begin{cases} 0 & \text{if } |T| = 1 \\ \max\{e(T.l), \ e(T.r) + 1\} & \text{otherwise.} \end{cases}$$

Definition 9 (Error Functions for Vector) [10]. *Let T be a full binary tree, matrix $\mathbf{A}_0, \mathbf{A}_1 \in \mathbb{Z}_q^{n \times n\ell}$, and distribution $\chi = \Phi_r$ (see Sect. 2.3). The error function family $\mathcal{E} = \mathcal{E}_{\mathbf{A}_0,\mathbf{A}_1,T}(x) : \{0,1\}^{|T|} \to \mathbb{Z}_q^{n\ell}$ can be defined inductively as follows:*

- *Set the error function $E(\varepsilon) = 0$ if $|T| = 0$.*
- *If $|T| > 0$, set $T' = \mathsf{pr}(T)$, and $x = x_1 \| x' \in \{0,1\}^{|T|}$ with $x_1 \in \{0,1\}$, $x' \in \{0,1\}^{|T|-1}$. An error function $E(x)$ is sampled from $\mathcal{E}$ as follows $(E(x) \leftarrow \mathcal{E}$ is defined inductively):*

$$E_{\mathbf{e}_0,\mathbf{e}_1,E'_0,E'_1}(x) := \mathbf{e}_{x_1}^{\top} \cdot \mathbf{S}_T(x') + E'_{x_1}(x'),$$

where $\mathbf{e}_0, \mathbf{e}_1 \leftarrow \chi^{n\ell}$, $E'_0, E'_1 \leftarrow \mathcal{E}_{\mathbf{A}_0,\mathbf{A}_1,T'}$, and $\mathbf{S}_T(x')$ is defined in Definition 7.

Construction 1 (Construction of PRF) [10]. *Let λ denote the security parameter. The PRF family $\mathcal{G}_{\mathbf{A}_0,\mathbf{A}_1,T}$ is a set of functions $F(\mathbf{k},x) : \{0,1\}^\lambda \to \mathbb{Z}_q^{n\ell}$ with public parameter $\mathsf{pp} = (\mathbf{A}_0, \mathbf{A}_1, T)$. It consists of the following two algorithms.*

- PRF.Setup(λ)*: On input λ, choose $\mathbf{A}_0, \mathbf{A}_1 \leftarrow_\$ \mathbb{Z}_q^{n \times n\ell}$, and set $e = s = \lceil \log_4(\lambda) \rceil$. Next, do the following:*
  1. *Check if $\binom{e+s}{e} \geq \lambda$. If yes, go to the next step. Else, set $e := e + 1$ and $s := s + 1$ until $\binom{e+s}{e} \geq \lambda$.*
  2. *Let $t(e,s)$ denote the size of the binary tree and construct the full binary tree T by using the recurrence equation:*

$$t(e,s) := \begin{cases} 1 & \text{if } e = 0 \text{ or } s = 0. \\ t(e-1,s) + t(e,s-1) & \text{otherwise.} \end{cases} \tag{7}$$

  Finally, output $\mathsf{pp} = (\mathbf{A}_0, \mathbf{A}_1, T)$.
- PRF.Eval($\mathbf{k},x$)*: On input a secret key $\mathbf{k} \in \mathbb{Z}_q^n$, $x \in \{0,1\}^\lambda$, the algorithm computes*

$$F(\mathbf{k},x) := \lfloor \mathbf{k}^\top \cdot \mathbf{A}_T(x) \rceil_p.$$

Remark 3. Indeed, we know that the real domain set of the PRF in Construction 1 is as large as $\{0,1\}^{|T|}$, where $|T| = \binom{e+s}{e} \geq \lambda$. Hence, we acquiesce that the domain set of the PRF is $\{0,1\}^{|T|}$ in the later proof.

Lemma 2 [10]. *Let matrix $\mathbf{A}_0, \mathbf{A}_1 \in \mathbb{Z}^{n \times n\ell}$, T be a full binary tree and distribution $\chi = \Phi_r$. Then for any $x \in \{0,1\}^{|T|}$, sampling an error function $E \in \mathcal{E}$ according to Definition 9, it holds that*

$$\Pr[E(x) \in [-R,R]^{n\ell}] \geq 1 - \mathsf{negl}(\lambda)$$

for $R = r\sqrt{|T|} \cdot (n\ell)^{e(T)} \cdot \omega(\sqrt{\log \lambda})$.

Lemma 3 [10]. *Let $n, q \geq 1$, distribution $\chi = \Phi_r$, and T be a full binary tree. Then for any PPT adversary $\mathcal{A}$, we have*

$$|\Pr[\mathbf{k} \leftarrow_\$ \mathbb{Z}_q^n, \mathbf{A}_0, \mathbf{A}_1 \leftarrow_\$ \mathbb{Z}_q^{n \times n\ell}, E(x) \leftarrow \mathcal{E} : \mathcal{A}^{\mathcal{O}_T(\cdot)} \Rightarrow 1] - \Pr[\mathcal{A}^{\mathcal{O}_\mathsf{U}(\cdot)} \Rightarrow 1]| \leq |T| \cdot \mathsf{Adv}^{n,Q,2n\ell,q,\chi}_{\mathsf{LWE},\mathcal{A}}(\lambda),$$

where $\mathcal{O}_T(x)$ returns $\mathbf{k}^\top \cdot \mathbf{A}_T(x) + E(x)$, $\mathcal{O}_\mathsf{U}(x)$ returns the output of the truly random function $\mathsf{U}(x)$, and $\mathbf{A}_T(x)$ is defined as in Definition 6. Here $\ell = \lfloor \log q \rfloor$, and Q denotes the number of oracle queries.

3.2 Unique-Input RKA Security for Key-Shift Function Family

In this section, we prove the pseudorandom function in Construction 1 is unique-input Φ_shift-RKA secure against the key-shift family $\Phi_\mathsf{shift} = \{\psi_\mathbf{b} : \psi_\mathbf{b}(\mathbf{k}) = \mathbf{k} + \mathbf{b}, \mathbf{b} \in \mathbb{Z}_q^n\}$.

Theorem 1. *For $F(\mathbf{k}, x) := \lfloor \mathbf{k}^\top \cdot \mathbf{A}_T(x) \rceil_p$ in Construction 1 with respect to* $pp = (\mathbf{A}_0, \mathbf{A}_1, T)$, *if distribution* $\chi = \Phi_r$, $r \geq 3\sqrt{n}$ *and* p, q *satisfies*

$$q \geq p \cdot r\sqrt{|T|} \cdot (n\ell)^{e(T)} \cdot \lambda^{\omega(1)},$$

then for any PPT adversary $\mathcal{A}$,

$$\mathbf{Adv}^{\mathsf{RKA}}_{\Phi,F,\mathcal{A}}(\lambda) \leq 2|T| \cdot \mathsf{Adv}^{n,Q,2n\ell,q,\chi}_{\mathsf{LWE},\mathcal{A}}(\lambda) + (2R+1) \cdot 2n\ell \cdot p/q + \mathsf{negl}(\lambda),$$

for class Φ_{shift}, where $R = r\sqrt{|T|} \cdot (n\ell)^{e(T)} \cdot \omega(\sqrt{\log \lambda})$, $e(T)$ is the expansion of T and Q is the number of RKA oracle queries.

Proof. We will prove the unique-input RKA security via a series of games. Let $\Pr[\mathbf{G}_j]$ denote the probability that $\mathcal{A}$ wins in game $\mathbf{G}_j$.

Game $\mathbf{G}_0$: $\mathbf{G}_0$ is the unique-input RKA attack game $\mathbf{Exp}^{\mathsf{RKA}}_{\Phi,F,\mathcal{A}}(0)$ played between the challenger and a PPT adversary $\mathcal{A}$. More precisely,

1. The challenger chooses $\mathbf{A}_0, \mathbf{A}_1 \leftarrow_\$ \mathbb{Z}_q^{n \times n\ell}$, a binary tree T and $\mathbf{k} \leftarrow_\$ \mathbb{Z}_q^n$, and sends $pp = (\mathbf{A}_0, \mathbf{A}_1, T)$ to $\mathcal{A}$.
2. Upon receiving the query $(\psi_\mathbf{b}, x)$ from $\mathcal{A}$, the challenger invokes $\mathcal{O}^{\mathsf{RKA}}_k(\psi_\mathbf{b}, x)$ to calculate $\mathbf{y} = (\mathbf{k} + \mathbf{b})^\top \cdot \mathbf{A}_T(x)$ and returns $\lfloor \mathbf{y} \rceil_p$ to $\mathcal{A}$.
3. As long as the adversary $\mathcal{A}$ outputs a bit $b' \in \{0,1\}$, the game returns b'.

Clearly, we have

$$\Pr[\mathbf{G}_0] = \Pr[\mathcal{A} \Rightarrow 1 | b = 0]. \tag{8}$$

Game $\mathbf{G}_1$: $\mathbf{G}_1$ is identical to $\mathbf{G}_0$ except for the way of answering $\mathcal{A}$'s oracle queries in step 2. More precisely, the challenger answers each query $(\psi_\mathbf{b}, x)$ as follows:

2.
   - Compute $\mathbf{y} = (\mathbf{k}^\top \cdot \mathbf{A}_T(x) + E(x)) + \mathbf{b}^\top \cdot \mathbf{A}_T(x)$.
   - Check whether $\lfloor \mathbf{y} + [-R, R]^{n\ell} \rceil_p \neq \lfloor \mathbf{y} \rceil_p$. If yes, game aborts. Else, return $\lfloor \mathbf{y} \rceil_p$.

Recall that $E(x)$ is defined in Definition 9 and $R = r\sqrt{|T|} \cdot (n\ell)^{e(T)} \cdot \omega(\sqrt{\log\lambda})$. Based on Lemma 2, we know that $E[x] \in [-R, R]^{n\ell}$ with overwhelming probability $1 - \mathsf{negl}(\lambda)$. Define event bad_i as $\lfloor \mathbf{y} + [-R, R]^{n\ell} \rceil_p \neq \lfloor \mathbf{y} \rceil_p$ in Game i. Then, as long as bad_1 does not happen, we have

$$\lfloor (\mathbf{k}^\top \cdot \mathbf{A}_T(x) + [-R, R]^{n\ell}) + \mathbf{b}^\top \cdot \mathbf{A}_T(x) \rceil_p = \lfloor (\mathbf{k} + \mathbf{b})^\top \cdot \mathbf{A}_T(x) \rceil_p,$$

so

$$|\Pr[\mathbf{G}_1] - \Pr[\mathbf{G}_0]| \leq \Pr[\mathsf{bad}_1]. \tag{9}$$

The analysis is complicated, so we defer it to later games.

Game $\mathbf{G}_2$: $\mathbf{G}_2$ is almost the same as $\mathbf{G}_1$, but the reply of query $(\psi_\mathbf{b}, x)$ is changed as follows:

2. • Compute $\mathbf{y} = \mathsf{U}(\mathsf{x}) + \mathbf{b}^\top \cdot \mathbf{A}_{\mathsf{T}(\mathsf{x})}$, where $\mathsf{U}(\cdot) : \{0,1\}^{|T|} \to \mathbb{Z}_q^{n\ell}$ is a truly random function.
    • Check whether $\lfloor \mathbf{y} + [-R, R]^{n\ell} \rceil_p \neq \lfloor \mathbf{y} \rceil_p$, If yes, game aborts. Else, return $\lfloor \mathbf{y} \rceil_p$.

Based on Lemma 3, we get

$$| \Pr[\mathbf{G}_2] - \Pr[\mathbf{G}_1]| \leq |T| \cdot \mathsf{Adv}_{\mathsf{LWE},\mathcal{A}}^{n,Q,2n\ell,q,\chi}(\lambda). \tag{10}$$

Consequently, we have

$$| \Pr[\mathsf{bad}_2] - \Pr[\mathsf{bad}_1]| \leq |T| \cdot \mathsf{Adv}_{\mathsf{LWE},\mathcal{A}}^{n,Q,2n\ell,q,\chi}(\lambda). \tag{11}$$

Game $\mathbf{G}_3$: $\mathbf{G}_3$ is almost the same as $\mathbf{G}_2$, but the reply of query (ψ_b, x) is changed again.

2. • Compute $\mathbf{y} = \mathsf{U}(\mathsf{x})$.
    • Check whether $\lfloor \mathbf{y} + [-R, R]^{n\ell} \rceil_p \neq \lfloor \mathbf{y} \rceil_p$. If yes, game aborts. Else, return $\lfloor \mathbf{y} \rceil_p$.

Owing to the fact that $\mathsf{U}(\mathsf{x}) + \mathbf{b}^\top \cdot \mathbf{A}_{\mathsf{T}(\mathsf{x})}$ and $\mathsf{U}(\mathsf{x})$ are both independently and uniformly distributed over the same set for distinct x, we have

$$\Pr[\mathbf{G}_3] = \Pr[\mathbf{G}_2], \tag{12}$$

$$\Pr[\mathsf{bad}_3] = \Pr[\mathsf{bad}_2]. \tag{13}$$

Lemma 4 [10]. $\Pr[\mathsf{bad}_3] \leq (2R+1) \cdot n\ell \cdot p/q$.

Proof. For $\mathbf{y} \in \mathbb{Z}_q^{n\ell}$, define $\mathbf{z} := \mathbf{y} + [-R, R]^{n\ell}$. Then event bad_3 means $\lfloor \mathbf{y} \rceil_p \neq \lfloor \mathbf{z} \rceil_p$. Since $q/p \gg R$, then bad_3 happens if and only if there exists a coordinate y in $\mathbf{y}$ such that $\lfloor y - R \rceil_p \neq \lfloor y + R \rceil_p$. In $\mathbf{G}_3$, $\mathbf{y}$ is uniform over $\mathbb{Z}_q^{n\ell}$. Clearly,

$$\Pr[\mathsf{bad}_3] \leq (2R+1) \cdot n\ell \cdot p/q = \mathsf{negl}(\lambda), \tag{14}$$

since $R = r\sqrt{|T|} \cdot (n\ell)^{e(T)} \cdot \omega(\sqrt{\log \lambda})$ and $q \geq p \cdot r\sqrt{|T|} \cdot (n\ell)^{e(T)} \cdot \lambda^{\omega(1)}$. $\square$

If bad_3 does not happen, **Game $\mathbf{G}_3$** is identical to $\mathbf{Exp}_{\Phi,F,\mathcal{A}}^{\mathsf{RKA}}(1)$. Thus, we have

$$| \Pr[\mathcal{A} \Rightarrow 1 | b = 1] - \Pr[\mathbf{G}_3]| \leq \Pr[\mathsf{bad}_3] \leq (2R+1) \cdot n\ell \cdot p/q. \tag{15}$$

Consequently,

$$\begin{aligned} | \Pr[\mathbf{G}_1] - \Pr[\mathbf{G}_0]| &\leq \Pr[\mathsf{bad}_1] \leq \Pr[\mathsf{bad}_2] + |T| \cdot \mathsf{Adv}_{\mathsf{LWE},\mathcal{A}}^{n,Q,2n\ell,q,\chi}(\lambda) \\ &\leq \Pr[\mathsf{bad}_3] + |T| \cdot \mathsf{Adv}_{\mathsf{LWE},\mathcal{A}}^{n,Q,2n\ell,q,\chi}(\lambda) \\ &\leq (2R+1) \cdot n\ell \cdot p/q + |T| \cdot \mathsf{Adv}_{\mathsf{LWE},\mathcal{A}}^{n,Q,2n\ell,q,\chi}(\lambda), \end{aligned} \tag{16}$$

according to Eqs. (9), (13), and (14).

Finally, taking Eqs. (8), (12), (15), and (16) together, Theorem 1 follows. $\square$

3.3 Unique-Input RKA Security for Restricted Affine Function Family

Construction 1 can be extended to a matrix version

$$F(\mathbf{K}, x) := \lfloor \mathbf{K} \cdot \mathbf{A}_T(x) \rceil_p, \tag{17}$$

where $\mathbf{K} \in \mathbb{Z}_q^{n \times n}$. Now, we prove the unique-input RKA security for this matrix version of PRF with respect to the restricted affine function family. Beforehand, we present some definitions which will be used in the proof.

Definition 10 (Error Functions for Matrix). *Let T be a full binary tree, matrix $\mathbf{A}_0, \mathbf{A}_1 \in \mathbb{Z}_q^{n \times n\ell}$, and distribution $\chi = \Phi_r$ (see Sect. 2.3). The error function family $\mathcal{E} = \mathcal{E}_{\mathbf{A}_0, \mathbf{A}_1, T}(x) : \{0,1\}^{|T|} \to \mathbb{Z}_q^{n \times n\ell}$ can be defined inductively as follows:*

- *Set the error function $E(x) = 0$ if $|T| = 0$.*
- *If $|T| > 0$, set $T' = \mathsf{pr}(T)$, and $x = x_1 \| x' \in \{0,1\}^{|T|}$ with $x_1 \in \{0,1\}$, $x' \in \{0,1\}^{|T|-1}$. The error function $E(x) \in \mathcal{E}$ is defined inductively as*

$$E_{\mathbf{E_0}, \mathbf{E_1}, E_0', E_1'}(x) := \mathbf{E}_{x_1} \cdot \mathbf{S}_T(x') + E_{x_1}'(x').$$

where $\mathbf{E_0}, \mathbf{E_1} \leftarrow \chi^{n \times n\ell}$, $E_0', E_1' \in \mathcal{E}_{\mathbf{A}_0, \mathbf{A}_1, T'}$, and $\mathbf{S}_T(x')$ is defined in Definition 7.

$(\star)$ Algorithm **Sample**$(\mathcal{E})$ independently chooses $\mathbf{E_0}, \mathbf{E_1}$ according to $\chi^{n \times n\ell}$ and E_0', E_1' from $\mathcal{E}_{\mathbf{A}_0, \mathbf{A}_1, T'}$, and outputs $E_{\mathbf{E_0}, \mathbf{E_1}, E_0', E_1'}(x)$.

$(\star)$ Though $\mathcal{E}$ is indexed by exponentially matrices, $E(x)$ only depends on matrices $\mathbf{E}_{x(i)}, i \in [0, |T|]$ when x is determined. Hence, **Sample**$(\mathcal{E})$ can be conducted in polynomial time for a given x.

$(\star)$ For error function family, we use $\mathcal{E}^{(i)}$ to denote $\mathcal{E}_{\mathbf{A}_0, \mathbf{A}_1, T^{(i)}}$.

Definition 11 (Auxiliary Functions) [10]. *Let T be a full binary tree of at least one node, matrix $\mathbf{A}_0, \mathbf{A}_1 \in \mathbb{Z}_q^{n \times n\ell}$, and $\mathcal{P} \subset \mathbb{Z}_q^{n \times n\ell}$ denote a set of representatives of the quotient group $\mathbb{Z}_q^{n \times n\ell}/(\mathbb{Z}_q^{n \times n} \cdot \mathbf{G})$. The auxiliary function family $\mathcal{V}^{(i)} = \mathcal{V}_{\mathbf{A}_0, \mathbf{A}_1, T^{(i-1)}}^{(i)}$ consists of functions from $\{0,1\}^{|T|}$ to $\mathbb{Z}_q^{n \times n\ell}$ for $0 \le i \le |T|$. And the sampling algorithm **Sample**$(\mathcal{V}^{(i)})$ performs as follows:*

- *If $i = 0$, **Sample**$(\mathcal{V}^{(0)})$ outputs zero function.*
- *If $i > 0$, for each $x \in \{0,1\}^{|T|}$, **Sample**$(\mathcal{V}^{(i)})$ outputs a function $\mathbf{V}_{x(i)}(\cdot)$ which behaves as follows:*
  1. *Choose $\mathbf{W}_{x(i)} \leftarrow_\$ \mathcal{P}$.*
  2. *Invoke $\mathbf{V}_{x(i-1)} \leftarrow \textbf{Sample}(\mathcal{V}^{(i-1)})$.*
  3. *Compute $\mathbf{V}_{x(i)}(x^{(i)}) := \mathbf{W}_{x(i)} \cdot \mathbf{S}_{T^{(i-1)}}(x^{(i)}) + \mathbf{V}_{x(i-1)}(x^{(i-1)})$, where $\mathbf{S}_{T^{(i-1)}}(x^{(i)})$ is defined in Definition 7, and $T^{(i)}$ denotes the i-th successive pruning of T, i.e., $T^{(i)} = \mathsf{pr}(T^{(i-1)})$.*

Remark 4. Though $\mathcal{V}^{(i)}$ is indexed by exponentially matrices, $\mathbf{V}_{x_{(i)}}(x^{(i)})$ only depends on matrices $\mathbf{W}_{x_{(i)}}, i \in [0, |T|]$ when x is determined. Hence, **Sample**$(\mathcal{V}^{(i)})$ can be conducted in polynomial time for a given x.

Remark 5. Based on the fact that $\mathbb{Z}_q^{n \times n} \cdot \mathbf{G}$ is a subgroup of $\mathbb{Z}_q^{n \times n\ell}$, then for $\mathbf{U}_{x_{(i)}} \leftarrow_{\$} \mathbb{Z}_q^{n \times n\ell}$, we can rewrite it as $\mathbf{U}_{x_{(i)}} = \mathbf{K}_{x_{(i)}} \cdot \mathbf{G} + \mathbf{W}_{x_{(i)}}$ where $\mathbf{K}_{x_{(i)}} \in \mathbb{Z}_q^{n \times n}$, $\mathbf{W}_{x_{(i)}} \in \mathcal{P}$. Moreover, we can construct a bijection from $\mathbf{U}_{x_{(i)}}$ to the pair $(\mathbf{K}_{x_{(i)}}, \mathbf{W}_{x_{(i)}})$. Because $\mathbf{U}_{x_{(i)}}$ is uniform, then $\mathbf{K}_{x_{(i)}}$ and $\mathbf{W}_{x_{(i)}}$ are independent of each other, and uniformly distributed over $\mathbb{Z}_q^{n \times n}$ and $\mathbb{Z}_q^{n \times n\ell}$, respectively.

Definition 12 [10]. *Let T be a full binary tree of at least one node, two matrices $\mathbf{A}_0, \mathbf{A}_1 \in \mathbb{Z}_q^{n \times n\ell}$, and $\mathcal{H}^{(i)} = \mathcal{H}_{\mathbf{A}_0, \mathbf{A}_1, T^{(i)}}$ be a set of functions $H_{\mathbf{K}_{x_{(i)}}}(x^{(i)})$: $\{0,1\}^{|T|} \to \mathbb{Z}_q^{n \times n\ell}$ indexed by $\mathbf{K}_{x_{(i)}} \in \mathbb{Z}_q^{n \times n}$. Given x, **Sample**$(\mathcal{H}^{(i)})$ outputs a function $H_{\mathbf{K}_{x_{(i)}}}(x^{(i)})$ which behaves as follows:*

- *Choose $\mathbf{K}_{x_{(i)}} \leftarrow_{\$} \mathbb{Z}_q^{n \times n}$.*
- *Compute $H_{\mathbf{K}_{x_{(i)}}}(x^{(i)}) := \mathbf{K}_{x_{(i)}} \cdot \mathbf{A}_{T^{(i)}}(x^{(i)})$, where $\mathbf{A}_T(x)$ is defined in Definition 6.*

With the above definitions, we will prove following theorem.

Theorem 2. *For $F(\mathbf{K}, x) := \lfloor \mathbf{K} \cdot \mathbf{A}_T(x) \rceil_p$ defined in Eq. (17) with respect to $\mathsf{pp} = (\mathbf{A}_0, \mathbf{A}_1, T)$, if distribution $\chi = \Phi_r$, $r \geq 3\sqrt{n}$ and p, q satisfies*

$$q \geq u \cdot p \cdot r\sqrt{|T|} \cdot (n\ell)^{e(T)} \cdot n^3 l \cdot \lambda^{\omega(1)},$$

then for any PPT adversary $\mathcal{A}$,

$$\mathbf{Adv}_{\Phi_{\mathsf{raff}}, F, \mathcal{A}}^{\mathsf{RKA}}(\lambda) \leq 2|T| \cdot \mathbf{Adv}_{\mathsf{LWE}, \mathcal{A}}^{n, Qn, 2n\ell, q, \chi}(\lambda) + (2nuR + 1) \cdot 2n^2 l \cdot p/q + \mathsf{negl}(\lambda),$$

where $R = r\sqrt{|T|} \cdot (n\ell)^{e(T)} \cdot \omega(\sqrt{\log \lambda})$, $e(T)$ is the expansion of T and Q denotes the number of RKA oracle queries. Meanwhile, $\Phi_{\mathsf{raff}} = \{\phi_{\mathbf{C}, \mathbf{B}} : \phi_{\mathbf{C}, \mathbf{B}}(\mathbf{K}) = \mathbf{CK} + \mathbf{B}, \mathbf{C} \in [-u, u]^{n \times n}, rank(\mathbf{C}) = n, \mathbf{B} \in \mathbb{Z}_q^{n \times n}\}$, where u is a small constant such that $(2nuR + 1) \cdot n^2 l \cdot p/q$ is negligible.

Proof. We will prove the unique-input RKA security via a series of games.

Game $\mathbf{G}_0$: $\mathbf{G}_0$ is the unique-input RKA attack experiment $\mathbf{Exp}_{\Phi, F, \mathcal{A}}^{\mathsf{RKA}}(0)$ played between the challenger and a PPT adversary $\mathcal{A}$. More precisely,

1. The challenger chooses $\mathbf{A}_0, \mathbf{A}_1 \leftarrow_{\$} \mathbb{Z}_q^{n \times n\ell}$, a binary tree T and $\mathbf{K} \leftarrow_{\$} \mathbb{Z}_q^{n \times n}$, and sends $\mathsf{pp} = (\mathbf{A}_0, \mathbf{A}_1, T)$ to $\mathcal{A}$.
2. Upon receiving the query $(\phi_{\mathbf{C}, \mathbf{B}}, x)$ from $\mathcal{A}$, the challenger invokes $\mathcal{O}_{\mathbf{k}}^{\mathsf{RKA}}(\phi_{\mathbf{C}, \mathbf{B}}, x)$ to calculate $\mathbf{Y} = (\mathbf{CK} + \mathbf{B}) \cdot \mathbf{A}_T(x)$ and returns $\lfloor \mathbf{Y} \rceil_p$ to $\mathcal{A}$.
3. As long as the adversary $\mathcal{A}$ outputs a bit $b' \in \{0,1\}$, the game returns b'.

Clearly,
$$\Pr[\mathbf{G}_0] = \Pr[\mathcal{A} \Rightarrow 1 | b = 0]. \tag{18}$$

Game $\mathbf{G}_1$: $\mathbf{G}_1$ is identical to $\mathbf{G}_0$ except for the way of answering $\mathcal{A}$'s oracle queries in step 2. More precisely, the challenger answers each query $(\phi_{\mathbf{C},\mathbf{B}}, x)$ as follows:

2.   • Compute $\mathbf{Y} = \mathbf{C}(\mathbf{K} \cdot \mathbf{A}_T(x) + E(x)) + \mathbf{B} \cdot \mathbf{A}_T(x)$.
     • Check whether $\lfloor \mathbf{Y} + \mathbf{C}[-R, R]^{n \times n\ell} \rfloor_p \neq \lfloor \mathbf{Y} \rfloor_p$. If yes, game aborts. Else, return $\lfloor \mathbf{Y} \rfloor_p$.

Recall $E(x) \leftarrow \mathbf{Sample}(\mathcal{E})$ is defined in Definition 10 and $R = r\sqrt{|T|} \cdot (n\ell)^{e(T)} \cdot \omega(\sqrt{\log\lambda})$. Based on Lemma 5 (see below), we know that $E[x] \in [-R, R]^{n \times n\ell}$ with overwhelming probability $1 - \mathsf{negl}(\lambda)$. Define event bad_i as $\lfloor \mathbf{Y} + \mathbf{C}[-R, R]^{n \times n\ell} \rfloor_p \neq \lfloor \mathbf{Y} \rfloor_p$ in Game i. As long as bad_1 does not happen, we have

$$\lfloor \mathbf{C}(\mathbf{K} \cdot \mathbf{A}_T(x) + [-R, R]^{n \times n\ell}) + \mathbf{B} \cdot \mathbf{A}_T(x) \rfloor_p = \lfloor (\mathbf{CK} + \mathbf{B}) \cdot \mathbf{A}_T(x) \rfloor_p.$$

So
$$|\Pr[\mathbf{G}_1] - \Pr[\mathbf{G}_0]| \leq \Pr[\mathsf{bad}_1]. \tag{19}$$

The analysis is complicated, so we defer it to later games.

Lemma 5. *Let matrix $\mathbf{A}_0, \mathbf{A}_1 \in \mathbb{Z}_q^{n \times n\ell}$, T be a full binary tree and distribution $\chi = \Phi_r$. Then for any $x \in \{0,1\}^{|T|}$, sampling an error function $E \in \mathcal{E}$ according to Definition 10, it holds that*

$$\Pr[E(x) \in [-R, R]^{n \times n\ell}] \geq 1 - \mathsf{negl}(\lambda)$$

for $R = r\sqrt{|T|} \cdot (n\ell)^{e(T)} \cdot \omega(\sqrt{\log\lambda})$.

Proof. $E(x) \in \mathbb{Z}^{n \times n\ell}$ can be regarded as a matrix composed of n row vectors $\mathbf{e}(x)^\top$ of dimensional $n\ell$, where $\mathbf{e}(x)$ is defined in Definition 9. Then by Lemma 2, each $\mathbf{e}(x) \in [-R, R]^{n\ell}$ except with $\mathsf{negl}(\lambda)$ probability for $R = r\sqrt{|T|} \cdot (n\ell)^{e(T)} \cdot \omega(\sqrt{\log\lambda})$. Hence, $E(x) \in [-R, R]^{n \times n\ell}$ holds with probability $1 - \mathsf{negl}(\lambda)$.   □

Game $\mathbf{G}_2$: $\mathbf{G}_2$ is almost the same as $\mathbf{G}_1$, but the reply of query $(\phi_{\mathbf{C},\mathbf{B}}, x)$ is changed as follows:

2.   • Compute $\mathbf{Y} = \mathbf{C} \cdot \mathsf{U}(x) + \mathbf{B} \cdot \mathbf{A}_T(x)$.
     • Check whether $\lfloor \mathbf{Y} + \mathbf{C}[-R, R]^{n \times n\ell} \rfloor_p \neq \lfloor \mathbf{Y} \rfloor_p$, If yes, game aborts. Else, return $\lfloor \mathbf{y} \rfloor_p$.

where $\mathsf{U}(x) : \{0,1\}^{|T|} \to \mathbb{Z}_q^{n \times n\ell}$ is a truly random function.

Lemma 6. $|\Pr[\mathbf{G}_1] - \Pr[\mathbf{G}_2]| \leq |T| \cdot \mathsf{Adv}_{\mathsf{LWE},\mathcal{A}}^{n, Qn, 2n\ell, q, \chi}(\lambda)$.

Proof. We will prove this lemma by a series of games $\mathbf{G}_{1.i}$.

Game $\mathbf{G}_{1.i}$: $\mathbf{G}_{1.i}$ is identical to $\mathbf{G}_1$, but the reply of query $(\phi_{\mathbf{C},\mathbf{B}}, x)$ is changed as follows:

2.   • For each x, run $E_{x_{(i)}}(x^{(i)}) \leftarrow \mathbf{Sample}(\mathcal{E}^{(i)})$, $\mathbf{V}_{x_{(i)}}(x^{(i)}) \leftarrow \mathbf{Sample}(\mathcal{V}^{(i)})$, $H_{\mathbf{K}_{x_{(i)}}}(x^{(i)}) \leftarrow \mathbf{Sample}(\mathcal{H}^{(i)})$.
   • Compute $\mathbf{Y} = \mathbf{C}(H_{\mathbf{K}_{x_{(i)}}}(x^{(i)}) + E_{x_{(i)}}(x^{(i)}) + \mathbf{V}_{x_{(i)}}(x^{(i)})) + \mathbf{B} \cdot \mathbf{A}_T(x)$.
   • Check whether $\lfloor \mathbf{Y} + \mathbf{C}[-R, R]^{n \times n\ell} \rfloor_p \neq \lfloor \mathbf{Y} \rfloor_p$. If yes, game aborts. Else, return $\lfloor \mathbf{Y} \rfloor_p$.

Lemma 7. $\Pr[\mathbf{G}_{1.0}] = \Pr[\mathbf{G}_1]$.

Proof. In $\mathbf{G}_{1.0}$, based on $\mathcal{V}^{(0)} = \{$zero function$\}$, $x_{(0)} = \varepsilon$, and $x^{(0)} = x$, we have

$$\mathbf{Y} = \mathbf{C}(H_{\mathbf{K}_{x_{(0)}}}(x^{(0)}) + E_{x_{(0)}}(x^{(0)}) + \mathbf{V}_{x_{(0)}}(x^{(0)})) + \mathbf{B} \cdot \mathbf{A}_T(x)$$
$$= \mathbf{C}(\mathbf{K}_{x_{(0)}} \cdot \mathbf{A}_{T^{(0)}}(x^{(0)}) + E_{x_{(0)}}(x^{(0)}) + \mathbf{V}_{x_{(0)}}(x^{(0)})) + \mathbf{B} \cdot \mathbf{A}_T(x)$$
$$= \mathbf{C}(\mathbf{K}_\varepsilon \cdot \mathbf{A}_T(x) + E_\varepsilon(x)) + \mathbf{B} \cdot \mathbf{A}_T(x),$$

which is the same as in $\mathbf{G}_1$. Hence, $\Pr[\mathbf{G}_{1.0}] = \Pr[\mathbf{G}_1]$.   □

Lemma 8. $|\Pr[\mathbf{G}_{1.i}] - \Pr[\mathbf{G}_{1.i+1}]| \leq \mathsf{Adv}_{\mathsf{LWE},\mathcal{A}}^{n,Qn,2n\ell,q,\chi}(\lambda)$ *for* $i \in [0, |T| - 1]$.

Proof. We define games named $\mathbf{G}_{1.i^*}$ and prove $\mathbf{G}_{1.i} \approx_c \mathbf{G}_{1.i^*}$ and $\mathbf{G}_{1.i^*} = \mathbf{G}_{1.i+1}$.
Game $\mathbf{G}_{1.i^*}$: $\mathbf{G}_{1.i^*}$ is identical to $\mathbf{G}_{1.i}$ but the reply of query $(\phi_{\mathbf{C},\mathbf{B}}, x)$ is changed as follows:

2.   • For each x, run $E_{x_{(i+1)}}(x^{(i+1)}) \leftarrow \mathbf{Sample}(\mathcal{E}^{(i+1)})$, $\mathbf{V}_{x_{(i)}}(x^{(i)}) \leftarrow \mathbf{Sample}(\mathcal{V}^{(i)})$ and choose $\mathbf{U}_{x_{(i+1)}} \leftarrow_{\$} \mathbb{Z}_q^{n \times n\ell}$.
   • Compute $\mathbf{Y} = \mathbf{C}(\mathbf{U}_{x_{(i+1)}} \cdot \mathbf{S}_{T^{(i)}}(x^{(i+1)}) + E_{x_{(i+1)}}(x^{(i+1)}) + \mathbf{V}_{x_{(i)}}(x^{(i)})) + \mathbf{B} \cdot \mathbf{A}_T(x)$.
   • Check whether $\lfloor \mathbf{Y} + \mathbf{C}[-R, R]^{n \times n\ell} \rfloor_p \neq \lfloor \mathbf{Y} \rfloor_p$. If yes, game aborts. Else, return $\lfloor \mathbf{Y} \rfloor_p$.

We prove $\mathbf{G}_{1.i} \approx_c \mathbf{G}_{1.i^*}$ by showing that if there exists a PPT adversary $\mathcal{A}$ such that $|\Pr[\mathbf{G}_{1.i^*}] - \Pr[\mathbf{G}_{1.i}]| = \varepsilon$, then we can construct a PPT algorithm $\mathcal{A}'$, which can solve the decisional $\mathsf{LWE}_{n,Qn,2n\ell,q,\chi}$ problem with the same probability ε. Algorithm $\mathcal{A}'$ simulates $\mathbf{G}_{1.i^*}/\mathbf{G}_{1.i}$ as follows.

- $\mathcal{A}'$ queries its own oracle to obtain $(\mathbf{A}, \mathbf{D}) \in \mathbb{Z}_q^{n \times 2n\ell} \times \mathbb{Z}_q^{Qn \times 2n\ell}$, where Q denotes the number of queries of $\mathcal{A}$.
- $\mathcal{A}'$ creates an empty table $L : \{0,1\}^i \times \mathbb{Z}_q^{n \times 2n\ell}$, and initializes it to empty. Besides, $\mathcal{A}'$ creates a list of matrices $\mathbf{List} \in (\mathbb{Z}_q^{n \times 2n\ell})^Q$ such that $\mathbf{List} = \{\mathbf{D}_i\}_{i \in [1,Q]}$ where $\mathbf{D}_i$ contains the $(i-1)n$-th row to the in-th row of $\mathbf{D}$. Clearly, $\mathbf{D}^\top = [\mathbf{D}_1^\top | \mathbf{D}_2^\top | \cdots | \mathbf{D}_Q^\top]$
- $\mathcal{A}'$ constructs a full binary tree T, parses $\mathbf{A} = [\mathbf{A}_0 | \mathbf{A}_1]$ where $\mathbf{A}_0, \mathbf{A}_1 \in \mathbb{Z}_q^{n \times n\ell}$, and returns $pp = (\mathbf{A}_0, \mathbf{A}_1, T)$ to $\mathcal{A}$.
- Upon receiving a query $(\phi_{\mathbf{C},\mathbf{B}}, x) = (\mathbf{C}, \mathbf{B}, x)$ from $\mathcal{A}$, algorithm $\mathcal{A}'$ does following.

- $\mathcal{A}'$ runs $E_{x_{(i+1)}}(x^{(i+1)}) \leftarrow \mathbf{Sample}(\mathcal{E}^{(i+1)})$ and $\mathbf{V}_{x_{(i)}}(x^{(i)}) \leftarrow \mathbf{Sample}$ $(\mathcal{V}^{(i)})$ for each x.
- $\mathcal{A}'$ checks whether $x_{(i)}$ is in L. If no, choose an unused $\mathbf{D}_i$, parse it as $[\mathbf{D}_{x_{(i)}\|0}|\mathbf{D}_{x_{(i)}\|1}]$ and add $(x_{(i)}, \mathbf{D}_i)$ to L. Else, pick the corresponding $\mathbf{D}_i$ and parse it as $[\mathbf{D}_{x_{(i)}\|0}|\mathbf{D}_{x_{(i)}\|1}]$.
- $\mathcal{A}'$ computes $\mathbf{Y} = \mathbf{C}(\mathbf{D}_{x_{(i+1)}} \cdot \mathbf{S}_{T^{(i)}}(x^{(i+1)}) + E_{x_{(i+1)}}(x^{(i+1)}) + \mathbf{V}_{x_{(i)}}(x^{(i)})) + \mathbf{B} \cdot \mathbf{A}_T(x)$ where if $x_{i+1} = 0$, $\mathbf{D}_{x_{(i+1)}} = \mathbf{D}_{x_{(i)}\|0}$, else $\mathbf{D}_{x_{(i+1)}} = \mathbf{D}_{x_{(i)}\|1}$.
- $\mathcal{A}'$ checks whether $\lfloor \mathbf{Y} + \mathbf{C}[-R, R]^{n \times n\ell} \rfloor_p \neq \lfloor \mathbf{Y} \rfloor_p$. If yes, game aborts. Else, return $\lfloor \mathbf{Y} \rfloor_p$ to $\mathcal{A}$.
- As long as $\mathcal{A}$ outputs a guessing bit b', $\mathcal{A}'$ outputs b' as its own guess.

Now we analyze the advantage of $\mathcal{A}'$.

- If $\mathbf{D}$ is a uniform sample, i.e., $\mathbf{D} \leftarrow_\$ \mathbb{Z}_q^{Qn \times 2n\ell}$, then $\mathbf{Y} = \mathbf{C}(\mathbf{D}_{x_{(i+1)}} \cdot \mathbf{S}_{T^{(i)}}(x^{(i+1)}) + E_{x_{(i+1)}}(x^{(i+1)}) + \mathbf{V}_{x_{(i)}}(x^{(i)})) + \mathbf{B} \cdot \mathbf{A}_T(x)$ enjoys the same distribution as in $\mathbf{G}_{1,i^*}$. In this case, algorithm $\mathcal{A}'$ perfectly simulates $\mathbf{G}_{1,i^*}$ for $\mathcal{A}$.
- If $\mathbf{D} = \mathbf{K}' \cdot \mathbf{A} + \mathbf{E}$ where $\mathbf{A} \leftarrow_\$ \mathbb{Z}_q^{n \times 2n\ell}$, $\mathbf{K}' \leftarrow_\$ \mathbb{Z}_q^{Qn \times n}$, and $\mathbf{E} \leftarrow \chi^{Qn \times 2n\ell}$, we parse $\mathbf{K}'$ as $\mathbf{K}'^\top = [\mathbf{K}'^\top_1 | \mathbf{K}'^\top_2 | \cdots | \mathbf{K}'^\top_Q]$ where $\mathbf{K}'_j \in \mathbb{Z}_q^{n \times n} (j \in [1, Q])$, and $\mathbf{E}^\top = [\mathbf{E}^\top_1 | \mathbf{E}^\top_2 | \cdots | \mathbf{E}^\top_Q]$ where $\mathbf{E}_j \in \mathbb{Z}_q^{n \times 2n\ell} (j \in [1, Q])$. Therefore, $\mathbf{D}_j = \mathbf{K}'_j \cdot \mathbf{A} + \mathbf{E}_j$. Furthermore, for each $\mathbf{E}_j$, we can parse it as $\mathbf{E}_j = [\mathbf{E}_{j\|0}|\mathbf{E}_{j\|1}]$. Hence, $\mathbf{D}_{j\|0} = \mathbf{K}'_j \cdot \mathbf{A}_0 + \mathbf{E}_{j\|0}$ and $\mathbf{D}_{j\|1} = \mathbf{K}'_j \cdot \mathbf{A}_1 + \mathbf{E}_{j\|1}$. If $[\mathbf{D}_{x_{(i)}\|0}|\mathbf{D}_{x_{(i)}\|1}] = \mathbf{D}_j$, let $[\mathbf{E}_{x_{(i)}\|0}|\mathbf{E}_{x_{(i)}\|1}] := [\mathbf{E}_{j\|0}|\mathbf{E}_{j\|1}]$ and $\mathbf{K}_{x_{(i)}} := \mathbf{K}'_j$. As a result, $\mathbf{D}_{x_{(i+1)}} = \mathbf{K}_{x_{(i)}} \cdot \mathbf{A}_1 + \mathbf{E}_{x_{(i)}\|1}$ if $x_{i+1} = 1$, and $\mathbf{D}_{x_{(i+1)}} = \mathbf{K}_{x_{(i)}} \cdot \mathbf{A}_0 + \mathbf{E}_{x_{(i)}\|0}$ if $x_{i+1} = 0$. Hence, we can rewrite algorithm $\mathcal{A}'$'s answer as

$$\mathbf{Y} = \mathbf{C}(\mathbf{D}_{x_{(i+1)}} \cdot \mathbf{S}_{T^{(i)}}(x^{(i+1)}) + E_{x_{(i+1)}}(x^{(i+1)}) + \mathbf{V}_{x_{(i)}}(x^{(i)})) + \mathbf{B} \cdot \mathbf{A}_T(x)$$

$$= \mathbf{C}((\mathbf{K}_{x_{(i)}} \cdot \mathbf{A}_{x+1} + \mathbf{E}_{x_{(i)}\|x_{i+1}}) \cdot \mathbf{S}_{T^{(i)}}(x^{(i+1)}) + E_{x_{(i+1)}}(x^{(i+1)}) + \mathbf{V}_{x_{(i)}}(x^{(i)})) + \mathbf{B} \cdot \mathbf{A}_T(x)$$

$$= \mathbf{C}((\mathbf{K}_{x_{(i)}} \cdot \mathbf{A}_{x+1} \cdot \mathbf{S}_{T^{(i)}}(x^{(i+1)}) + \mathbf{E}_{x_{(i)}\|x_{i+1}} \cdot \mathbf{S}_{T^{(i)}}(x^{(i+1)}) + E_{x_{(i+1)}}(x^{(i+1)}) + \mathbf{V}_{x_{(i)}}(x^{(i)})))$$
$$+ \mathbf{B} \cdot \mathbf{A}_T(x) \tag{20}$$

$$= \mathbf{C}(\mathbf{K}_{x_{(i)}} \cdot \mathbf{A}_{T^{(i)}}(x^{(i)})) + E_{x_{(i)}}(x^{(i)}) + \mathbf{V}_{x_{(i)}}(x^{(i)})) + \mathbf{B} \cdot \mathbf{A}_T(x). \tag{21}$$

Note that Eq. (20) follows from Eqs. (5), and (21) is the same as in $\mathbf{G}_{1,i}$. Hence, in this case, algorithm $\mathcal{A}'$ perfectly simulates $\mathbf{G}_{1,i}$ for $\mathcal{A}$.

Consequently,

$$|\Pr[\mathbf{G}_{1.i}] - \Pr[\mathbf{G}_{1.i^*}]| \leq \mathsf{Adv}^{n,Qn,2n\ell,q,\chi}_{\mathsf{LWE},\mathcal{A}}(\lambda) \text{ for } i \in [0, |T|]. \tag{22}$$

Next we prove that $\mathbf{G}_{1.i^*} = \mathbf{G}_{1.i+1}$ for $1 \leq i \leq |T| - 1$. For $\mathbf{U}_{x_{(i)}} \leftarrow_\$ \mathbb{Z}_q^{n \times n\ell}$, we can rewrite it as $\mathbf{U}_{x_{(i)}} = \mathbf{K}_{x_{(i)}} \cdot \mathbf{G} + \mathbf{W}_{x_{(i)}}$ where $\mathbf{K}_{x_{(i)}} \in \mathbb{Z}_q^{n \times n}$ and $\mathbf{W}_{x_{(i)}} \in \mathcal{P}$ are independent and uniformly distributed according to Definition 11. Hence,

$$\mathbf{Y} = \mathbf{C}(\mathbf{U}_{x_{(i+1)}} \cdot \mathbf{S}_{T^{(i)}}(x^{(i+1)}) + E_{x_{(i+1)}}(x^{(i+1)}) + \mathbf{V}_{x_{(i)}}(x^{(i)})) + \mathbf{B} \cdot \mathbf{A}_T(x) \tag{23}$$

$$= \mathbf{C}((\mathbf{K}_{x_{(i+1)}} \cdot \mathbf{G} + \mathbf{W}_{x_{(i+1)}}) \cdot \mathbf{S}_{T^{(i)}}(x^{(i+1)}) + E_{x_{(i+1)}}(x^{(i+1)}) + \mathbf{V}_{x_{(i)}}(x^{(i)})) + \mathbf{B} \cdot \mathbf{A}_T(x)$$

$$= \mathbf{C}(\mathbf{K}_{x_{(i+1)}} \cdot \mathbf{A}_{T^{(i+1)}}(x^{(i+1)}) + E_{x_{(i+1)}}(x^{(i+1)}) + \mathbf{W}_{x_{(i+1)}} \cdot \mathbf{S}_{T^{(i)}}(x^{(i+1)}) + \mathbf{V}_{x_{(i)}}(x^{(i)})) + \mathbf{B} \cdot \mathbf{A}_T(x) \tag{24}$$

$$= \mathbf{C}(H_{\mathbf{K}_{x_{(i+1)}}}(x^{(i+1)}) + E_{x_{(i+1)}}(x^{(i+1)}) + \mathbf{V}_{x_{(i+1)}}(x^{(i+1)})) + \mathbf{B} \cdot \mathbf{A}_T(x) \tag{25}$$

Note that Eq. (23) is the same as $\mathbf{G}_{1.i^*}$, Eq. (24) follows from Eqs. (6), and (25) is the same as in $\mathbf{G}_{1.i+1}$. Consequently,

$$\Pr[\mathbf{G}_{1.i^*}] = \Pr[\mathbf{G}_{1.i+1}] \quad \text{for} \quad i \in [0, |T| - 1]. \tag{26}$$

Taking Eqs. (22) and (26) together, Lemma 8 follows. □

Lemma 9. $\Pr[\mathbf{G}_{1.|T|}] = \Pr[\mathbf{G}_2]$.

Proof. If $i = |T|$, $\mathcal{A}'$'s answer is

$$\mathbf{Y} = \mathbf{C}(H_{\mathbf{K}_{x_{(|T|)}}}(x^{(|T|)}) + E_{x_{(|T|)}}(x^{(|T|)}) + \mathbf{V}_{x_{(|T|)}}(x^{(|T|)})) + \mathbf{B} \cdot \mathbf{A}_T(x),$$

where $x_{(|T|)} = x$, $x^{(|T|)} = \varepsilon$. Then $E_x(\varepsilon) = 0$ according to Definition 10. $\mathbf{V}_{x_{(|T|)}}(x^{(|T|)}) = \mathbf{W}_x + \mathbf{V}_{x_{(|T|-1)}}(x^{(|T|-1)})$ according to Definition 11. $H_{\mathbf{K}_{x_{(|T|)}}}(x^{(|T|)}) = \mathbf{K}_x \cdot \mathbf{G}$ according to Definitions 1 and 12. Thus, we have

$$\mathbf{Y} = \mathbf{C}(\mathbf{K}_x \cdot \mathbf{G} + \mathbf{W}_x + \mathbf{V}_{x_{(|T|-1)}}(x^{(|T|-1)})) + \mathbf{B} \cdot \mathbf{A}_T(x). \tag{27}$$

In Eq. (27), $\mathbf{K}_x$ and $\mathbf{W}_x$ are uniformly distributed, so $\mathbf{K}_x \cdot \mathbf{G} + \mathbf{W}_x$ is uniform according to Remark 5. Recall that $\mathbf{C}$ is full rank, and $\mathbf{V}_{x_{(|T|-1)}}(x^{(|T|-1)})$ and $\mathbf{B} \cdot \mathbf{A}_T(x)$ are both independent of $(\mathbf{K}_x, \mathbf{W}_x)$. Therefore, $\mathbf{Y}$ is uniformly distributed in $\mathbf{G}_{1.|T|}$, and Lemma 9 follows. □

Based on Lemmas 7, 8, 9, Lemma 6 follows. □
    Consequently, we have

$$|\Pr[\mathsf{bad}_2] - \Pr[\mathsf{bad}_1]| \leq |T| \cdot \mathsf{Adv}_{\mathsf{LWE},\mathcal{A}}^{n,Qn,2n\ell,q,\chi}(\lambda). \tag{28}$$

Game $\mathbf{G}_3$: $\mathbf{G}_3$ is almost the same as $\mathbf{G}_2$, but the reply of query $(\phi_{\mathbf{C},\mathbf{B}}, x)$ is changed again.

2. • Compute $\mathbf{Y} = \mathsf{U}(x)$.
    • Check whether $\lfloor \mathbf{Y} + \mathbf{C}[-R, R]^{n \times n\ell} \rfloor_p \neq \lfloor \mathbf{Y} \rfloor_p$. If yes, game aborts. Else, return $\lfloor \mathbf{Y} \rfloor_p$.

Owing to the fact that $\mathbf{C}$ is full rank, and $\mathbf{C} \cdot \mathsf{U}(x) + \mathbf{B} \cdot \mathbf{A}_T(x)$ and $\mathsf{U}(x)$ are both uniformly distributed over the same set for distinct x, we have

$$\Pr[\mathbf{G}_3] = \Pr[\mathbf{G}_2]. \tag{29}$$

$$\Pr[\mathsf{bad}_3] = \Pr[\mathsf{bad}_2]. \tag{30}$$

Lemma 10. $\Pr[\mathsf{bad}_3] \leq (2nuR + 1) \cdot n^2 l \cdot p/q$.

Proof. For $\mathbf{Y} \in \mathbb{Z}_q^{n \times n\ell}$, define $\mathbf{Z} := \mathbf{Y} + \mathbf{C}[-R, R]^{n \times n\ell}$. Then bad_3 means $\lfloor \mathbf{Y} \rfloor_p \neq \lfloor \mathbf{Z} \rfloor_p$. Since $q/p \gg R$, $\mathbf{C}$ is a full rank matrix in $[-u, u]^{n \times n}$, then bad_3 happens if and only if there exists a coordinate y in $\mathbf{Y}$ such that

$$\lfloor y - (nuR) \rceil_p \neq \lfloor y + (nuR) \rceil_p.$$

In $\mathbf{G}_3$, $\mathbf{Y}$ is uniform over $\mathbb{Z}_q^{n \times n\ell}$. Clearly,

$$\Pr[\mathsf{bad}_3] \leq (2nuR + 1) \cdot n^2\ell \cdot p/q = \mathsf{negl}(\lambda), \tag{31}$$

since $R = r\sqrt{|T|} \cdot (n\ell)^{e(T)} \cdot \omega(\sqrt{\log\lambda})$ and $q \geq up \cdot r\sqrt{|T|} \cdot (n\ell)^{e(T)} \cdot n^3\ell \cdot \lambda^{\omega(1)}$. □

If bad$_3$ does not happen, **Game G$_3$** is identical to $\mathbf{Exp}^{RKA}_{\Phi,F,\mathcal{A}}(1)$. Thus, we have

$$|\Pr[\mathcal{A} \Rightarrow 1 | b = 1] - \Pr[\mathbf{G}_3]| \leq \Pr[\mathsf{bad}_3] \leq (2nuR + 1) \cdot n^2 \ell \cdot p/q. \qquad (32)$$

Meanwhile,

$$\begin{aligned}
|\Pr[\mathbf{G}_1] - \Pr[\mathbf{G}_0]| &\leq \Pr[\mathsf{bad}_1] \leq \Pr[\mathsf{bad}_2] + |T| \cdot \mathsf{Adv}^{n,Q,2n\ell,q,\chi}_{\mathsf{LWE},\mathcal{A}}(\lambda) \\
&\leq \Pr[\mathsf{bad}_3] + |T| \cdot \mathsf{Adv}^{n,Q,2n\ell,q,\chi}_{\mathsf{LWE},\mathcal{A}}(\lambda) \\
&\leq (2nuR + 1) \cdot n^2 \ell \cdot p/q + |T| \cdot \mathsf{Adv}^{n,Q,2n\ell,q,\chi}_{\mathsf{LWE},\mathcal{A}}(\lambda). \qquad (33)
\end{aligned}$$

according to Eqs. (19), (28), (30) and (31).
Taking Eqs. (18), (29), (33) and Lemma 6 together, Theorem 2 follows.   □

3.4 Comparsion to the PRF in [8]

In [9], Lewi et al. proved the unique-input Φ_{raff}-RKA security for the PRF proposed by Boneh et al. [8] in Crypto13. In comparison, we prove the unique-input Φ_{raff}-RKA security for the PRF proposed by Banerjee et al. [10] in Crypto14. With the same security parameter λ and under the same unique-input Φ_{raff}-RKA security, the PRF in [10] is more efficient than [8] according to [10]. More precisely, by omitting $\log^{O(1)} \lambda$, the key size is reduced from λ^3 to λ bits, the pp size is reduced from λ^6 to λ^2 bits, and the best known runtime of the PRF.Eval is decreased from λ^5 per output bit to λ^ω where $\omega \in [2, 2.373]$. See Fig. 5 for more details.

PRF Schemes	Bit-length of Key	Bit-length of pp	Runtime	Bit-length of Output
BLMR13[8]	λ^3	λ^6	λ^5	λ
BP14[10]	λ	λ^2	$\lambda^\omega, \omega \in [2, 2.373]$	λ^2

Fig. 5. Comparison of BP14 [10] with BLMR13 [13] in running time, parameter's size, key size and output size. All values omit $\log^{O(1)} \lambda$. "Bit-length of Key" denote the bit length of the PRF key. "Runtime" denote the best known runtime of PRF, where $\omega \in [2, 2.373]$. "Bit-length of pp" denotes the length of public parameter pp. "Bit length of Output" denotes the length of PRF output.

4 Application to Robustly Reusable Fuzzy Extractor

In this section, we will use this Φ-RKA secure PRF to construct a robustly reusable fuzzy extractor (rrFE).

Most recently, Wen, Liu and Gu (denoted by WLG19) [6] proposed a framework of establishing a robustly reusable fuzzy extractor with unique-input RKA secure PRF, Secure Sketch (denoted by SS = SS.Gen, SS.Rec) and Universal Hash

($\mathcal{H}_\mathcal{I} = \{H_i : \mathcal{X} \to \mathcal{Y}\}_{i\in\mathcal{I}}$) in PKC 2019. See Fig. 6 for extraction in the framework. In the concrete construction, the authors instantiated the PRF with the unique-input RKA secure PRF proposed in [9]. Now we can replace this PRF with the one in Construction 1, then a more efficient rrFE is obtained, following the framework in Fig. 6.

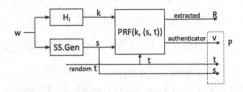

Fig. 6. The extraction in the framework.

Before introducing our more efficient rrFE, we recall the definitions of robustly reusable fuzzy extractor.

Definition 13 (Robustly Reusable Fuzzy Extractor). *An* $(\mathcal{M}, m, \mathcal{R}, t, \varepsilon_1, \varepsilon_2)$*-robustly reusable Fuzzy Extractor* (rrFE) *consists of three algorithms* rrFE = (Init, Gen, Rep).

- Init(1^λ) $\to$ crs. *The* Init *algorithm takes the security parameter as input and outputs the common reference string* crs.
- Gen(crs, w) $\to$ (P, R). *The* Gen *algorithm takes the common reference string* crs *and an element* $w \in \mathcal{M}$ *as input. It outputs a public helper string* P *and an extracted string* $R \in \mathcal{R}$.
- Rep(crs, w', P) $\to$ R/$\perp$. *The* Rep *algorithm takes the common reference string* crs, *an element* $w' \in \mathcal{M}$ *and the public helper string* P *as input. It outputs an extracted string* R *or* $\perp$.

The Correctness, Reusability and Robustness of rrFE are defined below.

- **Correctness.** *If* dis(w, w') $< t$, *then for all* crs $\leftarrow$ Init(λ) *and* (P, R) $\leftarrow$ Gen(crs, w), R = Rep(crs, w', P).
- **Reusability.** *For any PPT adversary* $\mathcal{A}$ *and any distribution* W *over* $\mathcal{M}$ *such that* $H_\infty(W) \geq m$, *the advantage function* $\mathsf{Adv}^{reu}_{\mathcal{A},rrFE}(\lambda) := |\Pr[\mathbf{Exp}^{reu}_{\mathcal{A},rrFE}(\lambda) \Rightarrow 1] - 1/2| \leq \varepsilon_1$ *where experiment* $\mathbf{Exp}^{reu}_{\mathcal{A},rrFE}(\lambda)$ *is specified in the left side of Fig. 7.*
- **Robustness.** *For any PPT adversary* $\mathcal{A}$ *and any distribution* W *over* $\mathcal{M}$ *such that* $H_\infty(W) \geq m$, *the advantage function* $\mathsf{Adv}^{rob}_{\mathcal{A},rrFE}(\lambda) := \Pr[\mathbf{Exp}^{rob}_{\mathcal{A},rrFE}(\lambda) \Rightarrow 1] \leq \varepsilon_2$ *where experiment* $\mathbf{Exp}^{rob}_{\mathcal{A},rrFE}(\lambda)$ *is specified in the right side of Fig. 7.*

$\mathbf{Exp}^{\mathsf{reu}}_{\mathcal{A},\mathsf{rrFE}}(\lambda)$:	$\mathbf{Exp}^{\mathsf{rob}}_{\mathcal{A},\mathsf{rrFE}}(\lambda)$:
$\mathsf{crs} \leftarrow \mathsf{Init}(1^\lambda)$.	$\mathsf{crs} \leftarrow \mathsf{Init}(1^\lambda)$.
$b \leftarrow_{\$} \{0,1\}$, $\mathsf{w} \leftarrow W$.	$\mathsf{w} \leftarrow W$, $\mathcal{Q} = \emptyset$.
Return crs.	Return crs.
$b^* \leftarrow \mathcal{A}^{\mathcal{O}^{\mathsf{ch}}(\cdot)}$.	$(P^*, \delta^*) \leftarrow \mathcal{A}^{\mathcal{O}^{\mathsf{Gen}}(\cdot)}$.
If $b = b^*$, Return 1.	If $\mathsf{dis}(\delta^*) > t$, Return 0.
Else, Return 0.	If $P^* \in \mathcal{Q}$, Return 0.
	Return $(\mathsf{Rep}(\mathsf{crs}, \mathsf{w} + \delta^*, P^*) \neq \bot)$.
$\mathcal{O}^{\mathsf{ch}}(\delta)$:	$\mathcal{O}^{\mathsf{Gen}}(\delta)$:
If $\mathsf{dis}(\delta) > t$, Return $\bot$.	If $\mathsf{dis}(\delta) > t$, Return $\bot$.
$(P, R) \leftarrow \mathsf{Gen}(\mathsf{crs}, \mathsf{w} + \delta)$.	$(P, R) \leftarrow \mathsf{Gen}(\mathsf{crs}, \mathsf{w} + \delta)$.
If $b = 1$, Return (P, R).	$\mathcal{Q} = \mathcal{Q} \cup \{P\}$.
Else, $U \leftarrow_{\$} \mathcal{R}$, Return (P, U).	Return (P, R).

Fig. 7. Left: The experiment for defining the reusability game $\mathbf{Exp}^{\mathsf{reu}}_{\mathcal{A},\mathsf{rrFE}}(\lambda)$ for a rrFE. Right: The experiment for defining the robustness game $\mathbf{Exp}^{\mathsf{rob}}_{\mathcal{A},\mathsf{rrFE}}(\lambda)$ for a rrFE.

4.1   New Construction of rrFE

According to [6], the rrFE is composed of three building blocks, i.e., the syndrome-based secure sketch $\mathsf{SS} = (\mathsf{SS.Gen}, \mathsf{SS.Rec})$, the homomorphic universal hash $\mathcal{H}_{\mathcal{I}} = \{H_i : \mathcal{M} \to \mathcal{K}\}_{i \in \mathcal{I}}$, and the Φ_{shift}-RKA secure PRF with key space $\mathcal{K}$. By using the PRF in Construction 1, we obtain a specific new construction of rrFE as shown in Fig. 8.

$\mathsf{crs} \leftarrow \mathsf{Init}(1^\lambda)$:	$(P, R) \leftarrow \mathsf{Gen}(\mathsf{crs}, \mathsf{w})$:	$R \leftarrow \mathsf{Rep}(\mathsf{crs}, P, \mathsf{w}')$:
$i \leftarrow_{\$} \mathcal{I}$ (i.e., $H_i \leftarrow_{\$} \mathcal{H}_{\mathcal{I}}$).	$s \leftarrow \mathsf{SS.Gen}(\mathsf{w})$.	Parse $P = (s, t, v)$.
$\mathbf{A}_0, \mathbf{A}_1 \leftarrow \mathbb{Z}_q^{n \times n\ell}$.	$k \leftarrow H_i(\mathsf{w})$.	$\tilde{\mathsf{w}} \leftarrow \mathsf{SS.Rec}(\mathsf{w}', s)$.
Construct a full binary tree T.	$t \leftarrow_{\$} \mathcal{T}$. $x = (s, t)$.	$\tilde{k} \leftarrow H_i(\tilde{\mathsf{w}})$. $x = (s, t)$.
$\mathsf{crs} = (H_i, \mathbf{A}_0, \mathbf{A}_1, T)$.	$F(k, x) := \lfloor k^\top \cdot \mathbf{A}_T(x) \rceil_p = (r, v)$.	$F(k, x) := \lfloor \tilde{k}^\top \cdot \mathbf{A}_T(x) \rceil_p = (\tilde{r}, \tilde{v})$.
Return crs.	$P := (s, t, v)$, $R := r$.	If $\tilde{v} = v$, Return $R := \tilde{r}$.
		Else, Return $\bot$.

Fig. 8. New construction of rrFE.

For the PRF function $F(\cdot, \cdot) : \{0,1\}^\lambda \to \mathbb{Z}_q^{n\ell}$ in Construction 1, to obtain provable 2^λ security against the best known lattice algorithms, choose $n = e(T) \cdot \lambda \log^{O(1)} \lambda$, $\log q = e(T) \cdot \log^{O(1)} \lambda$ as suggested in [10]. Moreover, according to Theorem 1, to achieve the unique-input Φ_{shift}-RKA security, set $e(T) = s(T) = \log_4 \lambda$ (so that $|T| \approx \lambda$), $r_f = 3\sqrt{n}$, $p = \omega(\log \lambda)$ such that $q \geq p \cdot r_f \sqrt{|T|} \cdot (n\ell)^{e(T)} \cdot \lambda^{\omega(1)}$. Then, the PRF $F(\cdot, \cdot)$ is unique-input RKA secure against key-shift family $\Phi_{\mathsf{shift}} = \{\psi_{\mathbf{b}} : \psi_{\mathbf{b}}(k) = k + \mathbf{b}, k \in \mathcal{K} = \mathbb{Z}_q^n\}$.

In the new construction, the input of $F(k, \cdot)$ is $x = (s, t)$, and we set $|s| = |t| = \lambda/2$ where $t \in \mathcal{T} = \{0,1\}^{\lambda/2}$. We parse the output of the PRF as (r, v) where $r \in \mathcal{R} = \mathbb{Z}_p^{n(\ell-1)}$, $v \in \mathcal{V} = \mathbb{Z}_p^n$.

According to [6], we have the following theorem.

Theorem 3. *For the rrFE scheme in Fig. 8, let* $n = e(T) \cdot \lambda \log^{O(1)} \lambda$, $\log q = e(T) \cdot \log^{O(1)} \lambda$ *with* $e(T) = s(T) = \log_4 \lambda$. *Let* $\chi = \Phi_{r_f}$ *with* $r_f = 3\sqrt{n}$, $p = \omega(\log \lambda)$, $\mathcal{T} = \{0,1\}^{\lambda/2}$ *and* $\mathcal{V} = \mathbb{Z}_p^n$ *such that* $\log |\mathcal{T}| \geq \omega(\log \lambda)$ *and* $\log |\mathcal{V}| \geq \omega(\log \lambda)$. *If* $\mathsf{SS} = (\mathsf{SS.Gen}, \mathsf{SS.Rec})$ *is instantiated with a homomorphic* $(\mathcal{M}, m, \tilde{m}, 2t)$-*secure sketch with linearity property and* $\mathcal{H}_\mathcal{I} = \{H_i : \mathcal{M} \to \mathcal{K}\}_{i \in \mathcal{I}}$ *is instantiated with a family of homomorphic universal hash functions such that* $\tilde{m} - \log |\mathcal{K}| \geq \omega(\log \lambda)$[1], *then the rrFE scheme in Fig. 8 is an* $(\mathcal{M}, m, \mathcal{R}, t, \varepsilon_1, \varepsilon_2)$-*robustly reusable Fuzzy Extractor with* $\varepsilon_1 = 2\mathbf{Adv}^{\mathsf{RKA}}_{\Phi_{\mathsf{shift}}, F, \mathcal{A}}(\lambda) + 2^{-\omega(\log \lambda)}$ *and* $\varepsilon_2 = 2\mathbf{Adv}^{\mathsf{RKA}}_{\Phi_{\mathsf{shift}}, F, \mathcal{A}}(\lambda) + 2^{-\omega(\log \lambda)}$ *where* $\mathbf{Adv}^{\mathsf{RKA}}_{\Phi_{\mathsf{shift}}, F, \mathcal{A}}(\lambda)$ *is defined in Theorem 1.*

Similarly to the LWE-based rrFE in WLG19 [6], our construction enjoys both robustness and reusability, both of which are based on LWE assumption (see Fig. 9).

FE Schemes	Robustness?	Reusability?	Standard Assumption?	Quantum Resistance?
DRS08[13]	✗	✗	–	✗
BDKOS05[14]	✔	✗	✗	✗
ACEK17[15]	✗	✔	✔	✗
WL18[16]	✔	✔	✔	✗
WLG19[6]	✔	✔	✔	✔
rrFE in this paper	✔	✔	✔	✔

Fig. 9. Comparison with known FE schemes [6,13–16].

We compare our scheme in property and the underlying assumption with others in Fig. 9. Besides, we analyze the runtime and error correction rate of our scheme.

- The running time of Gen, Rep are dominated by the evaluation of the underlying PRF, so we compare the computational efficiency of the PRF in the scheme. In our scheme, the output length of the PRF is $n\ell \log p = n \log q \log p = \lambda (\log_4 \lambda)^2 (\log^{O(1)} \lambda) \cdot \log \log \lambda = \lambda \cdot \log^{O(1)} \lambda \cdot \log \log \lambda$, the best runtime per output bit is $\lambda^\omega \log^{O(1)} \lambda$ where $\omega \in [2, 2.373]$ according to [10], and the length of extracted string R is $n(\ell-1) \log p = \lambda \cdot \log^{O(1)} \lambda \cdot \log \log \lambda$. Hence, the runtime per extracted bit is $(n\ell \log p \cdot \lambda^\omega \log^{O(1)} \lambda)/n(\ell-1) \log p) \approx \lambda^\omega \log^{O(1)} \lambda$. With a similar analysis, their runtime per extracted bit is λ^5.
- For error correction rate, our construction could support higher error correction rate. In WLG19 [6]'s construction, the length of s is $\omega(\log \lambda)$ so the error correction rate is $\omega(\log \lambda)/|\mathsf{w}|$ while ours is $\Theta(\lambda)/|\mathsf{w}|$ (since the length of $|s| = \Theta(\lambda)$) (Fig. 10).

---

[1] See [6] for the definitions and instantiations of SS and $\mathcal{H}_\mathcal{I}$.

FE Schemes	Runtime per Extracted Bit	Error Correction Rate
WLG19[6]	λ^5	$\omega(\log \lambda)/|w|$
Ours	$\lambda^\omega \log^{O(1)} \lambda, \omega \in [2, 2.373]$	$\Theta(\lambda)/|w|$

Fig. 10. Comparison with WLG19 [6].

Acknowledgments. This work is supported by the National Natural Science Foundation of China (NSFC Nos.61672346 and U1636217) and National Key R&D Program of China (No. 2016YFB0801201).

References

1. Goldreich, O., Goldwasser, S., Micali, S.: How to construct random functions. J. ACM **33**(4), 792–807 (1986)
2. Naor, M., Reingold, O.: Synthesizers and their application to the parallel construction of psuedo-random functions. In 36th Annual Symposium on Foundations of Computer Science, Milwaukee, Wisconsin, USA, 23–25 October 1995, pp. 170–181 (1995)
3. Boneh, D., DeMillo, R.A., Lipton, R.J.: On the importance of checking cryptographic protocols for faults. In: Fumy, W. (ed.) EUROCRYPT 1997. LNCS, vol. 1233, pp. 37–51. Springer, Heidelberg (1997). https://doi.org/10.1007/3-540-69053-0_4
4. Bonneau, J., Mironov, I.: Cache-collision timing attacks against AES. In: Goubin, L., Matsui, M. (eds.) CHES 2006. LNCS, vol. 4249, pp. 201–215. Springer, Heidelberg (2006). https://doi.org/10.1007/11894063_16
5. Bellare, M., Cash, D., Miller, R.: Cryptography secure against related-key attacks and tampering. In: Lee, D.H., Wang, X. (eds.) ASIACRYPT 2011. LNCS, vol. 7073, pp. 486–503. Springer, Heidelberg (2011). https://doi.org/10.1007/978-3-642-25385-0_26
6. Wen, Y., Liu, S., Gu, D.: Generic constructions of robustly reusable fuzzy extractor. In: Public-Key Cryptography - PKC 2019 - 22nd IACR International Conference on Practice and Theory of Public-Key Cryptography, Beijing, China, April 14–17, 2019, Proceedings, Part II, pp. 349–378 (2019). https://doi.org/10.1007/978-3-030-17259-6_12
7. Bellare, M., Cash, D.: Pseudorandom functions and permutations provably secure against related-key attacks. In: Rabin, T. (ed.) CRYPTO 2010. LNCS, vol. 6223, pp. 666–684. Springer, Heidelberg (2010). https://doi.org/10.1007/978-3-642-14623-7_36
8. Boneh, D., Lewi, K., Montgomery, H., Raghunathan, A.: Key homomorphic prfs and their applications. In: Canetti, R., Garay, J.A. (eds.) CRYPTO 2013. LNCS, vol. 8042, pp. 410–428. Springer, Heidelberg (2013). https://doi.org/10.1007/978-3-642-40041-4_23
9. Lewi, K., Montgomery, H., Raghunathan, A.: Improved constructions of PRFs secure against related-key attacks. In: Boureanu, I., Owesarski, P., Vaudenay, S. (eds.) ACNS 2014. LNCS, vol. 8479, pp. 44–61. Springer, Cham (2014). https://doi.org/10.1007/978-3-319-07536-5_4

10. Banerjee, A., Peikert, C.: New and improved key-homomorphic pseudorandom functions. In: Garay, J.A., Gennaro, R. (eds.) CRYPTO 2014. LNCS, vol. 8616, pp. 353–370. Springer, Heidelberg (2014). https://doi.org/10.1007/978-3-662-44371-2_20

11. Regev, O.: On lattices, learning with errors, random linear codes, and cryptography. In: Proceedings of the 37th Annual ACM Symposium on Theory of Computing, Baltimore, MD, USA, 22–24 May 2005, pp. 84–93 (2005)

12. Regev, O.: The learning with errors problem (invited survey). In: Proceedings of the 25th Annual IEEE Conference on Computational Complexity, CCC 2010, Cambridge, Massachusetts, USA, 9–12 June 2010, pp. 191–204 (2010)

13. Dodis, Y., Ostrovsky, R., Reyzin, L., Smith, A.D.: Fuzzy extractors: how to generate strong keys from biometrics and other noisy data. SIAM J. Comput. $38(1)$, 97–139 (2008)

14. Boyen, X., Dodis, Y., Katz, J., Ostrovsky, R., Smith, A.: Secure remote authentication using biometric data. In: Cramer, R. (ed.) EUROCRYPT 2005. LNCS, vol. 3494, pp. 147–163. Springer, Heidelberg (2005). https://doi.org/10.1007/11426639_9

15. Apon, D., Cho, C., Eldefrawy, K., Katz, J.: Efficient, reusable fuzzy extractors from LWE. In: Dolev, S., Lodha, S. (eds.) CSCML 2017. LNCS, vol. 10332, pp. 1–18. Springer, Cham (2017). https://doi.org/10.1007/978-3-319-60080-2_1

16. Wen, Y., Liu, S.: Robustly reusable fuzzy extractor from standard assumptions. In: Peyrin, T., Galbraith, S. (eds.) ASIACRYPT 2018. LNCS, vol. 11274, pp. 459–489. Springer, Cham (2018). https://doi.org/10.1007/978-3-030-03332-3_17

δ-subgaussian Random Variables in Cryptography

Sean Murphy and Rachel Player$^{(\boxtimes)}$

Royal Holloway, University of London, Egham, UK
{s.murphy,rachel.player}@rhul.ac.uk

Abstract. In the Ring-LWE literature, there are several works that use a statistical framework based on δ-subgaussian random variables. These were introduced by Miccancio and Peikert (Eurocrypt 2012) as a relaxation of subgaussian random variables. In this paper, we completely characterise δ-subgaussian random variables. In particular, we show that this relaxation from a subgaussian random variable corresponds only to the shifting of the mean. Next, we give an alternative noncentral formulation for a δ-subgaussian random variable, which we argue is more statistically natural. This formulation enables us to extend prior results on sums of δ-subgaussian random variables, and on their discretisation.

Keywords: Ring Learning with Errors · Subgaussian random variable

1 Introduction

A subgaussian random variable [4] is a random variable that is bounded in a particular technical sense by a Normal random variable. Subgaussian random variables cover a wide class of random variables: for example is well known that any centred and bounded random variable is subgaussian [17]. They have many of the attractive properties of Normal random variables: for example, they form a linear space and their tails that are bounded by the tails of a Normal random variable [15]. Subgaussian random variables have been used widely in cryptography [2].

In [7], Micciancio and Peikert introduced the notion of a δ-subgaussian random variable, where δ can take a value $\delta \geq 0$, as a relaxation of a subgaussian random variable. In the formulation of [7], the case $\delta = 0$ gives a 0-subgaussian random variable, which is exactly a subgaussian random variable. Statistical arguments based on δ-subgaussian random variables have been used in Ring-LWE cryptography in many application settings including signature schemes [7], key exchange [10] and homomorphic encryption [6].

In this paper, we re-examine the relaxation in [7] of subgaussian random variables to give δ-subgaussian random variables. We completely characterise δ-subgaussian random variables by showing that this relaxation corresponds only to the shifting of the mean. This enables us to give a noncentral formulation for δ-subgaussian random variables which we argue is more statistically natural.

J. Jang-Jaccard and F. Guo (Eds.): ACISP 2019, LNCS 11547, pp. 251–268, 2019.
https://doi.org/10.1007/978-3-030-21548-4_14

Amongst the prior literature using δ-subgaussian random variables, perhaps the prominent work is *A Toolkit for Ring-LWE Cryptography* [6]. This work gives an algebraic and statistical framework for Ring-LWE cryptography that is widely applicable. Using our noncentral formulation for δ-subgaussian random variables, we extend results presented in the *Toolkit* on sums of δ-subgaussian random variables, and on their discretisation.

1.1 Contributions

The first main contribution of this paper is to give a full and particularly simple characterisation of δ-subgaussian random variables. We show in Lemma 5 that any δ-subgaussian random variable with mean 0 must be a 0-subgaussian random variable. We then show in Lemma 6 that shifting a δ-subgaussian random variable by its mean gives a 0-subgaussian random variable. Finally, we show in Lemma 7 that any shift of a 0-subgaussian random variable is a δ-subgaussian random variable for some $\delta \geq 0$. These results give our main result in this section, Proposition 1, that the relaxation from 0-subgaussian random variables to δ-subgaussian random variables corresponds only to a shifting of the mean.

The second main contribution of this paper is to generalise results about δ-subgaussian random variables that have previously appeared in the literature. Firstly, we give an alternative noncentral formulation for a δ-subgaussian random variable which enables us in Theorem 1 to generalise the results in [6,10] for sums of δ-subgaussian random variables. Secondly, in Theorem 2 we improve the result of the *Toolkit* [6] for the δ-subgaussian standard parameter of the coordinatewise randomised rounding discretisation (termed *CRR-discretisation* in our paper) of the *Toolkit* [6, Sect. 2.4.2] of a δ-subgaussian random variable.

1.2 Structure

We review the necessary background in Sect. 2. We analyse and characterise δ-subgaussian random variables in Sect. 3. We give a noncentral formulation for δ-subgaussian random variables in Sect. 4. We consider the discretisations of random variables arising in Ring-LWE in Sect. 5.

2 Background

2.1 Algebraic Background

This section mainly follows [6]. We consider the ring $R = \mathbb{Z}[X]/(\Phi_m(X))$, where $\Phi_m(X)$ is the mth cyclotomic polynomial of degree n, and we let R_a denote R/aR for an integer a. For simplicity, we only consider the case where m is a large prime, so $n = \phi(m) = m - 1$, though our arguments apply more generally.

Let ζ_m denote a (primitive) m^{th} root of unity, which has minimal polynomial $\Phi_m(X) = 1 + X + \ldots + X^n$. The mth *cyclotomic number field* $K = \mathbb{Q}(\zeta_m)$ is the field extension of the rational numbers $\mathbb{Q}$ obtained by adjoining this m^{th} root of unity ζ_m, so K has degree n.

There are n *ring embeddings* $\sigma_1, \ldots, \sigma_n \colon K \to \mathbb{C}$ that fix every element of $\mathbb{Q}$. Such a ring embedding σ_k (for $1 \leq k \leq n$) is defined by $\zeta_m \mapsto \zeta_m^k$, so $\sum_{j=1}^n a_j \zeta_m^j \mapsto \sum_{j=1}^n a_j \zeta_m^{kj}$. The *canonical embedding* $\sigma \colon K \to \mathbb{C}^n$ is defined by

$$a \mapsto (\sigma_1(a), \ldots, \sigma_n(a))^T.$$

The *ring of integers* $\mathcal{O}_K$ of a number field is the ring of all elements of the number field which are roots of some monic polynomial with coefficients in $\mathbb{Z}$. The ring of integers of the mth cyclotomic number field K is

$$R = \mathbb{Z}[\zeta_m] \cong \mathbb{Z}[x]/(\Phi_m).$$

The canonical embedding σ embeds R as a lattice $\sigma(R)$. The conjugate dual of this lattice corresponds to the embedding of the dual fractional ideal

$$R^\vee = \{a \in K \mid \mathrm{Tr}(aR) \subset \mathbb{Z}\}.$$

The ring embeddings $\sigma_1, \ldots, \sigma_n$ occur in conjugate pairs, and much of the analysis of Ring-LWE takes place in a space H of conjugate pairs of complex numbers. The conjugate pairs matrix T gives a basis for H that we call the T-basis.

Definition 1. The *conjugate pair matrix* is the $n \times n$ complex matrix T, so $T \colon \mathbb{C}^n \to \mathbb{C}^n$, given by

$$T = 2^{-\frac{1}{2}} \begin{pmatrix} 1 & 0 & \ldots & 0 & 0 & \ldots & 0 & i \\ 0 & 1 & \ldots & 0 & 0 & \ldots & i & 0 \\ \vdots & \vdots & \ddots & \vdots & \vdots & & \vdots & \vdots \\ 0 & 0 & \ldots & 1 & i & \ldots & 0 & 0 \\ 0 & 0 & \ldots & 1 & -i & \ldots & 0 & 0 \\ \vdots & \vdots & & \vdots & \vdots & \ddots & \vdots & \vdots \\ 0 & 1 & \ldots & 0 & 0 & \ldots & -i & 0 \\ 1 & 0 & \ldots & 0 & 0 & \ldots & 0 & -i \end{pmatrix}.$$

□

Definition 2. The *complex conjugate pair space* H is given by $H = T(\mathbb{R}^n)$, where T is the conjugate pairs matrix. □

Our results on discretisation will rely on the spectral norm of the basis for H being considered. We note that the spectral norm for the T-basis is 1.

Definition 3. Suppose that the lattice Λ has (column) basis matrix B. The *Gram matrix* of the basis matrix B is $B^\dagger B$, where $B^\dagger = \overline{B}^T$ is the complex conjugate of B. The *spectral norm* $\lambda(B) > 0$ of the basis matrix B is the square root of largest eigenvalue of the Gram matrix $B^\dagger B$. □

2.2   The Ring-LWE Problem

The Learning with Errors (LWE) problem [13,14] has become a standard hard problem in cryptology that is at the heart of lattice-based cryptography [8,11]. The Ring Learning with Errors (Ring-LWE) problem [5,16] is a generalisation of the LWE problem from the ring of integers to certain other number field rings. Both the LWE problem and the Ring-LWE problem are related to well-studied lattice problems that are believed to be hard [1,5,6,9,12,13].

Definition 4 ([5,16]). Let R be the ring of integers of a number field K. Let $q \geq 2$ be an integer modulus. Let $R^\vee$ be the dual fractional ideal of R. Let $R_q = R/qR$ and $R_q^\vee = R^\vee/qR^\vee$. Let $K_\mathbb{R} = K \otimes_\mathbb{Q} \mathbb{R}$.

Let χ be a distribution over $K_\mathbb{R}$. Let $s \in R_q^\vee$ be a secret. A sample from the *Ring-LWE distribution* $A_{s,\chi}$ over $R_q \times K_\mathbb{R}/qR^\vee$ is generated by choosing $a \leftarrow R_q$ uniformly at random, choosing $e \leftarrow \chi$ and outputting

$$(a, b = (a \cdot s)/q + e \mod qR^\vee).$$

Let Ψ be a family of distributions over $K_\mathbb{R}$. The *Search Ring-LWE* problem is defined as follows: given access to arbitrarily many independent samples from $A_{s,\chi}$ for some arbitrary $s \in R_q^\vee$ and $\chi \in \Psi$, find s.

Let Υ be a distribution over a family of error distributions, each over $K_\mathbb{R}$. The *average-case Decision Ring-LWE* problem is to distinguish with non-negligible advantage between arbitrarily many independent samples from $A_{s,\chi}$ for a random choice of $(s, \chi) \leftarrow \mathcal{U}\left(R_q^\vee\right) \times \Upsilon$, and the same number of uniformly random samples from $R_q \times K_\mathbb{R}/qR^\vee$.   □

2.3   Moment Generating Functions

The moment generating function is a basic tool of probability theory, and we first give a definition for a univariate random variable.

Definition 5. The *moment generating function* M_W of a real-valued univariate random variable W is the function from a subset of $\mathbb{R}$ to $\mathbb{R}$ defined by

$$M_W(t) = \mathbf{E}\left(\exp(tW)\right) \quad \text{for } t \in \mathbb{R} \text{ whenever this expectation exists.}$$

□

Fundamental results underlying the utility of the moment generating function are given in Lemma 1.

Lemma 1 ([3]). If M_W is the moment generating function of a real-valued univariate random variable W, then M_W is a continuous function within its radius of convergence and the kth moment of W is given by $\mathbf{E}(W^k) = M_W^{(k)}(0)$ when the kth derivative of the moment generating function exists at 0. In particular, (i) $M_W(0) = 1$, (ii) $\mathbf{E}(W) = M_W'(0)$ and (iii) $\text{Var}(W) = M_W''(0) - M_W'(0)^2$, where these derivatives exist.   □

More generally, the statistical properties of a random variable W can be determined from its moment generating function M_W, and in particular from the behaviour of this moment generating function M_W in a neighbourhood of 0 as its Taylor series expansion (where it exists) is given by

$$M_W(t) = 1 + M_W'(0)\, t + \tfrac{1}{2} M_W''(0)\, t^2 + \ldots + \tfrac{1}{k!} M_W^{(k)}(0)\, t^k + \ldots$$
$$= 1 + \mathbf{E}(W)\, t + \tfrac{1}{2}\mathbf{E}(W^2)\, t^2 + \ldots + \tfrac{1}{k!}\mathbf{E}(W^k)\, t^k + \ldots.$$

The definition of a moment generating function for a real-valued univariate random variable generalises to multivariate random variables and to random variables on H, and the above results also generalise in the appropriate way.

Definition 6. The *moment generating function M_W* of a multivariate random variable W on $\mathbb{R}^l$ is the function from a subset of $\mathbb{R}^l$ to $\mathbb{R}$ defined by

$$M_W(t) = \mathbf{E}\left(\exp(\langle t, W\rangle)\right) = \mathbf{E}\left(\exp\left(t^T W\right)\right) \text{ whenever this expectation exists.}$$

□

Definition 7. The *moment generating function M_W* of a multivariate random variable W on H is the function from a subset of H to $\mathbb{R}$ defined by

$$M_{W(t)} = \mathbf{E}\left(\exp(\langle t, W\rangle)\right) = \mathbf{E}\left(\exp\left(t^\dagger W\right)\right) \text{ whenever this expectation exists.}$$

□

2.4 Subgaussian Random Variables

In Lemma 2 we recall the standard result for the moment generating function of a Normal random variable with mean 0.

Lemma 2 ([3]). If $W \sim \mathrm{N}(0, b^2)$ is a Normal random variable with mean 0 and standard deviation $b \geq 0$, then W has moment generating function

$$M_W(t) = \mathbf{E}\left(\exp(tW)\right) = \exp(\tfrac{1}{2}b^2 t^2) \qquad \text{for all } t \in \mathbb{R}.$$

□

Lemma 2 gives rise to the idea of considering random variables with mean 0 whose moment generating function is dominated everywhere by the moment generating function of an appropriate Normal random variable with mean 0. Such a random variable is known as a *subgaussian* random variable [15] and is specified in Definition 8.

Definition 8. A real-valued random variable W is *subgaussian* with *standard parameter* $b \geq 0$ if its moment generating function M_W satisfies

$$M_W(t) = \mathbf{E}(\exp(tW)) \leq \exp(\tfrac{1}{2}b^2 t^2) \qquad \text{for all } t \in \mathbb{R}.$$

□

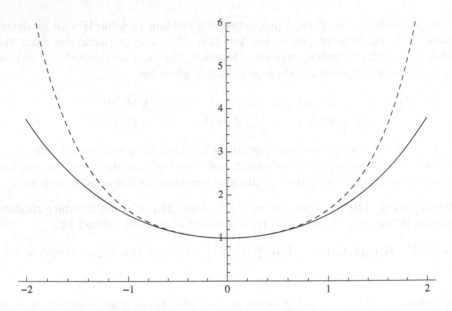

Fig. 1. Moment generating function $M_X(t) = \cosh t$ for the random variable X taking values ± 1 with probability $\frac{1}{2}$ (solid line) and subgaussian bounding function $\exp(\frac{1}{2}t^2)$ (dashed line).

An example of a subgaussian random variable is illustrated in Fig. 1, which shows the moment generating function $M_X(t) = \cosh t$ for the subgaussian random variable X taking values ± 1 with probability $\frac{1}{2}$ (so $\mathbf{E}(X) = 0$ and $\mathrm{Var}(X) = 1$), together with its corresponding bounding function $\exp(\frac{1}{2}t^2)$, which is the moment generating function of a standard Normal $N(0,1)$ random variable having the same mean and variance.

3 δ-subgaussian Random Variables

In this section, we give a complete and particularly simple characterisation of δ-subgaussian random variables. Statistical arguments based on δ-subgaussian random variables have been widely used in Ring-LWE [6,7,10], as noted in Sect. 1. Our main result, Proposition 1, shows that a δ-subgaussian random variable (for $\delta \geq 0$) is simply a translation of some 0-subgaussian random variable.

3.1   Defining a δ-subgaussian Random Variable

A δ-subgaussian random variable is a generalisation of a subgaussian random variable in the following sense: δ is allowed to be any value $\delta \geq 0$, and taking the case $\delta = 0$ gives a subgaussian random variable. In other words, what is termed a 0-subgaussian random variable for example in [6,7] is exactly a subgaussian random variable.

We now give two definitions for a univariate δ-subgaussian random variable to make this generalisation precise. Definition 9 corresponds with the usual probability theory of moment generating functions [3]. Definition 10 is used for example in [6]. Lemma 3 shows that these definitions are equivalent.

Definition 9. A real-valued random variable W is *δ-subgaussian* ($\delta \geq 0$) with *standard parameter* $b \geq 0$ if its moment generating function M_W satisfies

$$M_W(t) = \mathbf{E}(\exp(tW)) \leq \exp(\delta)\exp(\tfrac{1}{2}b^2 t^2) \qquad \text{for all } t \in \mathbb{R}.$$

□

Definition 10. A real-valued random variable W is *δ-subgaussian* ($\delta \geq 0$) with *scaled parameter* $s \geq 0$ if its moment generating function M_W satisfies

$$M_W(2\pi t) = \mathbf{E}(\exp(2\pi tW)) \leq \exp(\delta)\exp(\pi s^2 t^2). \qquad \text{for all } t \in \mathbb{R}.$$

□

Lemma 3. A real-valued univariate random variable is δ-subgaussian with standard parameter b if and only if it is δ-subgaussian with scaled parameter $(2\pi)^{\frac{1}{2}}b$.

The definition of a univariate δ-subgaussian random variable generalises to a multivariate δ-subgaussian random variable and a δ-subgaussian random variable on H in the obvious way.

Definition 11. A multivariate random variable W on $\mathbb{R}^l$ is *δ-subgaussian* ($\delta \geq 0$) with *standard parameter* $b \geq 0$ if its moment generating function M_W satisfies

$$M_W(t) = \mathbf{E}\left(\exp\left(t^T W\right)\right) \leq \exp(\delta)\exp(\tfrac{1}{2}b^2 |t|^2) \qquad \text{for all } t \in \mathbb{R}^l.$$

□

Definition 12. A random variable W on H is *δ-subgaussian* ($\delta \geq 0$) with *standard parameter* $b \geq 0$ if its moment generating function M_W satisfies

$$M_W(t) = \mathbf{E}\left(\exp\left(t^\dagger W\right)\right) \leq \exp(\delta)\exp(\tfrac{1}{2}b^2 |t|^2) \qquad \text{for all } t \in H.$$

□

3.2   Characterisation of Univariate δ-subgaussian Random Variables

In this section, we give a complete characterisation of a univariate δ-subgaussian random variable. We show that the relaxation of the 0-subgaussian condition to give the δ-subgaussian condition for a univariate random variable does not correspond to any relaxation in the fundamental statistical conditions on the random variable except for the location of its mean.

We firstly recall in Lemma 4 a property of 0-subgaussian random variables proved in [15], namely that their mean is 0. This can be heuristically explained

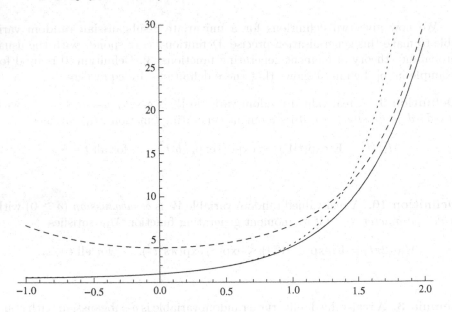

Fig. 2. Moment generating function $M_{X+1}(t) = \frac{1}{2}(1+\exp(2t))$ for the random variable $X + 1$ (for $X \sim \mathrm{Uni}(\{-1, 1\})$ of Fig. 1) taking values 0 and 2 with probability $\frac{1}{2}$ and having mean 1 (solid line), δ-subgaussian bounding function $\exp(\frac{7}{5} + \frac{1}{2}t^2)$ (dashed line), and "noncentral" subgaussian bounding function $\exp(t + \frac{1}{2}t^2)$ (dotted line).

as follows. Lemma 1 (i) shows that any moment generating function must pass through $(0, 1)$. However, a 0-subgaussian bounding function $\exp(\frac{1}{2}b^2t^2)$ also passes through $(0, 1)$ and has derivative 0 at 0. Thus any moment generating function bounded by $\exp(\frac{1}{2}b^2t^2)$ must have derivative 0 at 0. Lemma 1 (ii) then shows that such a 0-subgaussian random variable with moment generating function bounded by $\exp(\frac{1}{2}b^2t^2)$ must have mean 0.

Lemma 4 ([15]). *If W is a univariate real-valued 0-subgaussian random variable, then $\mathbf{E}(W) = 0$.* $\square$

We now give some results to show that the relaxation of the 0-subgaussian condition to the δ-subgaussian condition (for $\delta \geq 0$) corresponds exactly to the relaxation of the condition that the mean of the random variable is 0. These results are illustrated in Fig. 2 for a random variable with mean 1.

Intuitively, relaxing the constraint that $\delta = 0$ in the δ-subgaussian bounding function $\exp(\delta)\exp(\frac{1}{2}b^2t^2)$ essentially shifts the bounding function "up the y-axis", and in particular away from the point $(0, 1)$. However, a moment generating function must pass through the point $(0, 1)$. This relaxation essentially permits us to "tilt" the moment generating function of a 0-subgaussian random variable, pivoting about the point $(0, 1)$, so that the moment generating function has a nonzero derivative at 0. This allows random variables with nonzero mean potentially to be δ-subgaussian random variables.

We now make the intuition described above and illustrated by Fig. 2 more precise in a number of ways. First, Lemma 5 shows that any δ-subgaussian random variable with mean 0 must be a 0-subgaussian random variable.

Lemma 5. If W is a univariate real-valued δ-subgaussian random variable ($\delta \geq 0$) with mean $\mathbf{E}(W) = 0$, then W is a 0-subgaussian random variable. $\square$

Proof. The δ-subgaussian bounding function $\exp(\delta)\exp(\frac{1}{2}b^2t^2)$ is bounded above and away from 1 when $\delta > 0$. However, the moment generating function M_W of W is continuous at 0 with $M_W(0) = 1$, so the δ-subgaussian bounding function $\exp(\delta)\exp(\frac{1}{2}b^2t^2)$ is neccesarily always a redundant bounding function for any moment generating function in some open neighbourhood of 0. The proof therefore proceeds by considering the moment generating function M_W of W in two separate regions: an open neighbourhood containing 0 and the region away from this open neighbourhood.

We first consider a region that is some open neighbourhood of 0. Taylor's Theorem (about 0) shows that the moment generating function M_W of W can be expressed in this open neighbourhood of 0 as

$$M_W(t) = \mathbf{E}\left(\exp(tW)\right) = 1 + \mathbf{E}(W)t + \tfrac{1}{2}\mathbf{E}\left(W^2\right)t^2 + o(t^2)$$
$$= 1 + \tfrac{1}{2}\mathbf{E}\left(W^2\right)t^2 + o(t^2),$$

where a function $g(t) = o(t^2)$ in the infinitesimal sense near 0 if $t^{-2}g(t) \to 0$ as $t \to 0$. Similarly we can write $\exp(\frac{1}{2}c^2t^2) = 1 + \frac{1}{2}c^2t^2 + o(t^2)$, so we have

$$\frac{M_W(t) - \exp(\frac{1}{2}c^2t^2)}{t^2} = \tfrac{1}{2}\left(\mathbf{E}\left(W^2\right) - c^2\right) + \frac{o(t^2)}{t^2}.$$

Thus for values of c such that $c^2 > \mathbf{E}\left(W^2\right)$ we have

$$\lim_{t \to 0} \frac{M_W(t) - \exp(\frac{1}{2}c^2t^2)}{t^2} = \tfrac{1}{2}\left(\mathbf{E}\left(W^2\right) - c^2\right) < 0,$$

in which case there exists an open neighbourhood $(-\nu, \nu)$ of 0 ($\nu > 0$) such that

$$\frac{M_W(t) - \exp(\frac{1}{2}c^2t^2)}{t^2} < 0$$

in this neighbourhood, so

$$M_W(t) \leq \exp(\tfrac{1}{2}c^2t^2) \quad [|t| < \nu].$$

We now consider the complementary region away from the open neighbourhood $(-\nu, \nu)$ of 0. If W is δ-subgaussian with standard parameter $b \geq 0$, then its moment generating function satisfies $M_W(t) \leq \exp(\delta)\exp(\frac{1}{2}b^2t^2)$ for all $t \in \mathbb{R}$, and in particular for $|t| \geq \nu$. If we let $d^2 = b^2 + 2\nu^{-2}\delta$, then in this other region the moment generating function M_W of W satisfies

$$M_W(t) \leq \exp(\delta)\exp(\tfrac{1}{2}b^2t^2) = \exp(\delta)\exp(\tfrac{1}{2}d^2t^2)\exp(-\delta\nu^{-2}t^2)$$
$$\leq \exp(\delta(1 - \nu^{-2}t^2))\exp(\tfrac{1}{2}d^2t^2) \leq \exp(\tfrac{1}{2}d^2t^2) \qquad [|t| \geq \nu].$$

Taking the two regions together shows that the moment generating function M_W of W satisfies

$$M_W(t) \leq \exp\left(\tfrac{1}{2} \max\{c^2, d^2\} \, t^2 \right) \qquad \text{for all } t \in \mathbb{R}.$$

Thus W is a 0-subgaussian random variable. □

Next, Lemma 6 shows that shifting a δ-subgaussian random variable by its mean results in a 0-subgaussian random variable.

Lemma 6. If W is a univariate real-valued δ-subgaussian random variable ($\delta \geq 0$), then the centred random variable $W_0 = W - \mathbf{E}(W)$ is a 0-subgaussian random variable. □

Proof. If W is a δ-subgaussian random variable with standard parameter b, then its moment generating function M_W satisifies

$$M_W(t) \leq \exp(\delta) \exp(\tfrac{1}{2} b^2 t^2) \qquad \text{for all } t \in \mathbb{R}.$$

The centred random variable $W_0 = W - \mathbf{E}(W)$ with mean $\mathbf{E}(W_0) = 0$ has moment generating function M_{W_0} given by

$$
\begin{aligned}
M_{W_0}(t) &= \mathbf{E}\left(\exp(tW_0) \right) = \mathbf{E}\left(\exp(t(W - \mathbf{E}(W))) \right) \\
&= \exp(-\mathbf{E}(W)t) \, \mathbf{E}\left(\exp(tW) \right) \\
&= \exp(-\mathbf{E}(W)t) \, M_W(t).
\end{aligned}
$$

The required result can be obtained by noting that for $c > b > 0$, the inequality

$$\left(\delta + (\tfrac{1}{2} b^2 t^2 - \mathbf{E}(W)t)\right) \leq \left(\left(\delta + \frac{1}{2} \frac{\mathbf{E}(W)^2}{c^2 - b^2}\right) + \tfrac{1}{2} c^2 t^2\right)$$

holds, which can be demonstrated as

$$\left(\left(\delta + \frac{1}{2} \frac{\mathbf{E}(W)^2}{c^2 - b^2}\right) + \tfrac{1}{2} c^2 t^2\right) - \left(\delta + (\tfrac{1}{2} b^2 t^2 - \mathbf{E}(W)t)\right) = \frac{c^2 - b^2}{2} \left(t + \frac{\mathbf{E}(W)}{c^2 - b^2}\right)^2$$

is non-negative for $c > b > 0$. This inequality means that the moment generating function M_{W_0} of W_0 satisfies

$$
\begin{aligned}
M_{W_0}(t) &= \exp(-\mathbf{E}(W)t) \, M_W(t) \\
&\leq \exp(-\mathbf{E}(W)t) \exp(\delta) \exp(\tfrac{1}{2} b^2 t^2) \\
&\leq \exp\left(\delta + (\tfrac{1}{2} b^2 t^2 - \mathbf{E}(W)t) \right) \\
&\leq \exp\left(\delta + \frac{1}{2} \frac{\mathbf{E}(W)^2}{c^2 - b^2} \right) \exp(\tfrac{1}{2} c^2 t^2).
\end{aligned}
$$

Thus W_0 is a $\left(\delta + \frac{1}{2} \frac{\mathbf{E}(W)^2}{c^2 - b^2}\right)$-subgaussian random variable. As W_0 has mean $\mathbf{E}(W_0) = 0$, Lemma 5 therefore shows that $W_0 = W - \mathbf{E}(W)$ is a 0-subgaussian random variable. □

Finally, Lemma 7 shows that any shift of a δ_0-subgaussian random variable with mean 0 is a δ-subgaussian random variable for some $\delta \geq 0$.

Lemma 7. If W_0 is a univariate real-valued δ_0-subgaussian random variable with mean $\mathbf{E}(W_0) = 0$, then for $\beta \in \mathbb{R}$ the real-valued shifted random variable $W = W_0 + \beta$ is a δ-subgaussian random variable for some $\delta \geq 0$.   □

Proof. If W_0 is a δ_0-subgaussian random variable with mean 0, then Lemma 5 shows that W_0 is a 0-subgaussian random variable with some standard parameter $c \geq 0$. The moment generating function M_{W_0} of W_0 is therefore bounded as $M_{W_0}(t) \leq \exp(\frac{1}{2}c^2t^2)$. If $b > c \geq 0$ and $\delta \geq \dfrac{\beta^2}{2(b^2 - c^2)}$, then we note that

$$\left(\tfrac{1}{2}b^2t^2 + \delta\right) - \left(\tfrac{1}{2}c^2t^2 + \beta t\right) = \frac{(b^2 - c^2)}{2}\left(t - \frac{\beta}{b^2 - c^2}\right)^2 + \delta - \frac{\beta^2}{2(b^2 - c^2)} \geq 0.$$

In this case, the moment generating function M_W of $W = W_0 + \beta$ satisfies

$$M_W(t) = \exp(\beta t)M_{W_0}(t) \leq \exp(\tfrac{1}{2}c^2t^2 + \beta t) \leq \exp(\delta)\exp(\tfrac{1}{2}b^2t^2).$$

Thus $W = W_0 + \beta$ is δ-subgaussian with standard parameter b.   □

Lemmas 5, 6 and 7 collectively give the main result Proposition 1 of this section. Proposition 1 precisely characterises δ-subgaussian random variables as shifts of 0-subgaussian random variables, which must have mean 0.

Proposition 1. A real-valued univariate δ-subgaussian random variable can essentially be described in terms of a 0-subgaussian random variable (which must have mean 0) as:

δ-subgaussian univariate RV = 0-subgaussian univariate RV + constant.

□

3.3   Properties of δ-subgaussian Random Variables

In this section, we give some basic properties of δ-subgaussian random variables. These are analogous to well-known properties of subgaussian random variables, given for example in [15].

Lemma 8. Suppose that W is a univariate real-valued δ-subgaussian random variable ($\delta \geq 0$) with standard parameter $b \geq 0$. Such a random variable W satisfies: (a) $\mathrm{Var}(W) \leq b^2$, (b) $\mathbf{P}\left(|W - \mathbf{E}(W)| > \alpha\right) \leq 2\exp\left(-\tfrac{1}{2}b^{-2}\alpha^2\right)$ and (c) $\mathbf{E}\left(\exp(a(W - \mathbf{E}(W))^2)\right) \leq 2$ for some $a > 0$.   □

Lemma 9. The set of δ-subgaussian random variables form a linear space.   □

Lemma 10. If W is a bounded univariate real-valued random variable, then W is a δ-subgaussian random variable for some $\delta \geq 0$.   □

Proof. If W is a bounded random variable, then $W_0 = W - \mathbf{E}(W)$ is a bounded random variable with mean 0. However, Theorem 2.5 of [15] or Theorem 9.9 of [17] shows that a bounded random variable with mean 0, such as W_0, is a 0-subgaussian random variable. Thus Lemma 7 shows that $W = W_0 + \mathbf{E}(W)$ is a δ-subgaussian random variable for some $\delta \geq 0$. $\square$

4   Noncentral Subgaussian Random Variables

Proposition 1 shows that the class of δ-subgaussian random variables are precisely those random variables that can be obtained as shifts of 0-subgaussian random variables. In this section, we use this characterisation to give an alternative noncentral formulation for a δ-subgaussian random variable. We then use this formulation to analyse sums and products of δ-subgaussian random variables. Our main result is Theorem 1, which generalises a result of [6] on sums of δ-subgaussian random variables.

4.1   A Noncentral Formulation for δ-subgaussian Random Variables

Proposition 1 enables us to see a δ-subgaussian random variable as a shifted 0-subgaussian random variable. This motivates the following definition.

Definition 13. A random variable Z (on $\mathbb{R}^l$ or H) is a *noncentral subgaussian* random variable with *standard parameter* $d \geq 0$ if the centred random variable $Z - \mathbf{E}(Z)$ is a 0-subgaussian random variable with standard parameter d. $\square$

Lemma 11 establishes the equivalence of the δ-subgaussian and noncentral subgaussian definitions. Lemma 11 also gives a basic property of noncentral subgaussian random variables, which follows from Lemma 9.

Lemma 11. A noncentral subgaussian random variable Z (on $\mathbb{R}^l$ or H) is a δ-subgaussian random variable and vice versa, and the set of noncentral subgaussian random variables (on $\mathbb{R}^l$ or H) is a linear space. $\square$

4.2   Motivation for the Noncentral Formulation

In this section, we motivate the alternative noncentral formulation. We begin by specifying a noncentral subgaussian random variable in terms of its moment generating function.

Lemma 12. The random variable Z is a noncentral subgaussian random variable (on $\mathbb{R}^l$ or H) with standard parameter d if and only if the moment generating function M_Z of Z satisfies $M_Z(t) \leq \exp\left(\langle t, \mathbf{E}(Z)\rangle\right)\exp(\frac{1}{2}d^2|t|^2)$. $\square$

Proof. If Z is a noncentral subgaussian random variable, then $Z - \mathbf{E}(Z)$ is a 0-subgaussian random variable with standard parameter d and so has moment generating function $M_{Z-\mathbf{E}(Z)}$ satisfying $M_{Z-\mathbf{E}(Z)}(t) \leq \exp(\frac{1}{2}d^2|t|^2)$. Thus M_Z satisfies $M_Z(t) = M_{\mathbf{E}(Z)}(t)\,M_{Z-\mathbf{E}(Z)}(t) \leq \mathbf{E}(\exp(\langle t, \mathbf{E}(Z)\rangle))\,\exp(\frac{1}{2}d^2|t|^2)$.

Conversely, if $M_Z(t) \leq \exp(\langle t, \mathbf{E}(Z) \rangle) \exp(\frac{1}{2} d^2 |t|^2) = M_{\mathbf{E}(Z)}(t) \exp(\frac{1}{2} d^2 |t|^2)$, then $Z - \mathbf{E}(Z)$ has moment generating function $M_{Z - \mathbf{E}(Z)} = M_Z M_{-\mathbf{E}(Z)}$ satisfying $M_{Z-\mathbf{E}(Z)}(t) = M_{\mathbf{E}(Z)}(t) \exp(\frac{1}{2} d^2 |t|^2) M_{-\mathbf{E}(Z)}(t) \leq \exp(\frac{1}{2} d^2 |t|^2)$. Thus $Z - \mathbf{E}(Z)$ is a 0-subgaussian random variable with standard parameter d, and so Z is a noncentral subgaussian random variable with standard parameter d.
□

We now argue that the noncentral subgaussian formulation is more natural from a statistical point of view, for the following reasons.

Firstly, the bounding function of Lemma 12 allows us to directly compare such a noncentral subgaussian random variable with a corresponding Normal random variable. Figure 2 illustrates an example of a noncentral subgaussian bounding function and a δ-subgaussian bounding function. It can be seen that this noncentral subgaussian bounding function is a tight bounding function to the moment generating function at 0, and hence captures better the behaviour at 0. Moreover, the noncentral subgaussian bounding function is actually a moment generating function of some Normal random variable.

Secondly, the standard parameter of a noncentral subgaussian random variable is invariant under translation of the random variable, mirroring a fundamental property of standard deviation. By contrast, in Example 1 we show that the standard parameter of a δ-subgaussian random variable is not necessarily invariant under translation.

Example 1. Suppose that $W \sim \mathrm{N}(0, \sigma^2)$ is a Normal random variable with mean 0 and variance σ^2, so has moment generating function $M_W(t) = \exp(\frac{1}{2} \sigma^2 t^2)$. In terms of Definition 13, it is clear that W is a noncentral subgaussian random variable with mean 0 and standard parameter σ. Similarly, the translated random variable $W + a \sim \mathrm{N}(a, \sigma^2)$ is by definition a noncentral random variable with mean a and standard parameter σ.

In terms of Definition 9, W is a 0-subgaussian random variable with standard parameter σ. If $W + a$ is a δ-subgaussian random variable with the same standard parameter σ, then $M_{W+a}(t) = \exp(\frac{1}{2} \sigma t^2 + at) \leq \exp(\delta + \frac{1}{2} \sigma^2 t^2)$ so $at \leq \delta$ for all t, which is impossible for $a \neq 0$. Thus even though $W + a$ is a Normal random variable with standard deviation σ, it is not a δ-subgaussian random variable with standard parameter σ when $a \neq 0$.
□

4.3   Sums of Univariate Noncentral Subgaussian Random Variables

In this section, we give our main result, Theorem 1, on sums of noncentral subgaussian (equivalently δ-subgaussian) random variables. This a far more general result than previous results [6,10] on sums of δ-subgaussian random variables, which apply only in restricted settings. For example, [10, Fact 2.1] applies when the summands are independent, and [6, Claim 2.1] applies in a martingale-like setting.

Theorem 1. Suppose that $W_1, \ldots, W_l$ are noncentral subgaussian, or equivalently δ-subgaussian, random variables where W_j has standard parameter $d_j \geq 0$ for $j = 1, \ldots, l$.

(i) The sum $\sum_{j=1}^{l} W_j$ is a noncentral subgaussian random variable with mean $\sum_{j=1}^{l} \mathbf{E}(W_j)$ and standard parameter $\sum_{j=1}^{l} d_j$.

(ii) If $W_1, \ldots, W_l$ are independent, then the standard parameter of the sum $\sum_{j=1}^{l} W_j$ can be improved to $\left(\sum_{j=1}^{l} d_j^2 \right)^{\frac{1}{2}}$. □

Proof. If W_j is a noncentral subgaussian random variable with standard parameter $d_j \geq 0$, then $W_j' = W_j - \mathbf{E}(W_j)$ is a 0-subgaussian random variable with standard parameter d_j. Theorem 2.7 of [15] therefore shows that $\sum_{j=1}^{l} W_j' = \sum_{j=1}^{l} W_j - \sum_{j=1}^{l} \mathbf{E}(W_j)$ is a 0-subgaussian random variable with standard parameter $\sum_{j=1}^{l} d_j$. Thus $\sum_{j=1}^{l} W_j$ is a noncentral subgaussian random variable with mean $\sum_{j=1}^{l} \mathbf{E}(W_j)$ and standard parameter $\sum_{j=1}^{l} d_j$. The second (independence) result similarly follows from the independence result of Theorem 2.7 of [15]. □

5   Discretisation

Discretisation is a fundamental part of Ring-LWE cryptography in which a point is "rounded" to a nearby point in a lattice coset. In fact, such a discretisation process usually involves randomisation, so discretisation typically gives rise to a random variable on the elements of the coset. We consider the coordinate-wise randomised rounding method of discretisation [6, Sect. 2.4.2] or *CRR-discretisation*, as an illustration of a discretisation process, though most of our comments apply more generally.

We begin by giving a formal definition of CRR-discretisation in terms of a Balanced Reduction function. This allows us to establish general results about the CRR-discretisation of δ-subgaussian random variables. In particular, our main result is Theorem 2, which improves prior results [6] for the δ-subgaussian standard parameter of the CRR-discretisation of a δ-subgaussian random variable.

5.1   Coordinate-Wise Randomised Rounding Discretisation

In this section we describe the coordinate-wise randomised rounding discretisation method of the first bullet point of [6, Sect. 2.4.2], which we term CRR-discretisation. We first introduce the Balanced Reduction function in Definition 14, and give its basic properties in Lemma 13.

Definition 14. The univariate *Balanced Reduction* function $\mathcal{R}$ on $\mathbb{R}$ is the random function with support on $[-1, 1]$ given by

$$\mathcal{R}(a) = \begin{cases} 1 - (\lceil a \rceil - a) & \text{with probability} \quad \lceil a \rceil - a \\ -(\lceil a \rceil - a) & \text{with probability} \quad 1 - (\lceil a \rceil - a). \end{cases}$$

The multivariate *Balanced Reduction* function $\mathcal{R}$ on $\mathbb{R}^l$ with support on $[-1, 1]^l$ is the random function $\mathcal{R} = (\mathcal{R}_1, \ldots, \mathcal{R}_l)$ with component functions $\mathcal{R}_1, \ldots, \mathcal{R}_l$ that are independent univariate Balanced Reduction functions. □

Lemma 13. The random variable $\mathcal{R}(a) + (\lceil a \rceil - a) \sim \text{Bern}(\lceil a \rceil - a)$ has a Bernoulli distribution for any $a \in \mathbb{R}$, and the random variable $\mathcal{R}(a)$ satisifies (i) $\mathbf{E}(\mathcal{R}(a)) = 0$, (iii) $\text{Var}(\mathcal{R}(a)) \leq \frac{1}{4}$ and (iii) $a - \mathcal{R}(a) \in \{\lfloor a \rfloor, \lceil a \rceil\} \subset \mathbb{Z}$. $\quad\square$

We are now in a position to define CRR-discretisation in terms of the Balanced Reduction function.

Definition 15. Suppose B is a (column) basis matrix for the n-dimensional lattice Λ in H. If $\mathcal{R}$ is the Balanced Reduction function, then the *coordinate-wise randomised rounding discretisation* or *CRR-discretisation* $\lfloor X \rceil_{\Lambda+c}^{B}$ of the random variable X to the lattice coset $\Lambda + c$ with respect to the basis matrix B is the random variable

$$\lfloor X \rceil_{\Lambda+c}^{B} = X + B\,\mathcal{R}\left(B^{-1}(c - X)\right).$$

$\quad\square$

In Lemma 14 we show that the specification of coordinate-wise randomised rounding in Definition 15 is well-defined.

Lemma 14. The CRR-discretisation $\lfloor X \rceil_{\Lambda+c}^{B}$ of the random variable X with resect to the (column) basis B is (i) a random variable on the lattice coset $\Lambda + c$, (ii) is *valid* (does not depend on the chosen coset representative c) and (iii) has mean $\mathbf{E}(\lfloor X \rceil_{\Lambda+c}^{B}) = \mathbf{E}(X)$. $\quad\square$

Proof. For part (i), the CRR-discretisation can be expressed as

$$\begin{aligned}\lfloor X \rceil_{\Lambda+c}^{B} &= X + B\mathcal{R}\left(B^{-1}(c - X)\right) = B\left(B^{-1}X + \mathcal{R}\left(B^{-1}(c - X)\right)\right) \\ &= c - B\left(B^{-1}(c - X) - \mathcal{R}\left(B^{-1}(c - X)\right)\right) \\ &\in \Lambda + c,\end{aligned}$$

as Lemma 13 (iii) shows that $B^{-1}(c - X) - \mathcal{R}\left(B^{-1}(c - X)\right)$ is a random variable on $\mathbb{Z}^n$. For part (ii), if $c' \in \Lambda + c$, so $c - c' \in \Lambda$, then there exists an integer vector z such that $c - c' = Bz$, so $B^{-1}(c - X) - B^{-1}(c' - X) = z$, that is to say $B^{-1}(c - X)$ and $B^{-1}(c' - X)$ differ by an integer vector. Thus $\mathcal{R}\left(B^{-1}(c - X)\right)$ and $\mathcal{R}\left(B^{-1}(c' - X)\right)$ have identical distributions. The distribution of $\lfloor X \rceil_{\Lambda+c}^{B}$ on the lattice coset $\Lambda + c$ does not therefore depend on the chosen coset representative c, and so the discretisation is *valid*. Finally, for part (iii), Lemma 13 (i) shows that $\mathbf{E}(\lfloor X \rceil_{\Lambda+c}^{B}) = \mathbf{E}(X) + B\mathbf{E}\left(\mathcal{R}\left(B^{-1}(c - X)\right)\right) = \mathbf{E}(X)$. $\quad\square$

5.2 The CRR-Discretisation of δ-Subgaussian Random Variables

In this section we examine the subgaussian properties of the CRR-discretisation of a noncentral subgaussian random variable. Our main result is Theorem 2, which gives a subgaussian standard parameter for such a CRR-discretisation arising in Ring-LWE, that is to say discretisation for a lattice in H. Theorem 2 uses a factor of $\frac{1}{2}$ with the standard parameter of a random variable obtained by such a CRR-discretisation. By contrast, any comparable result in [6] uses a factor of 1 (see for example the first bullet point of [6, Sect. 2.4.2]). Thus the results of this Section improve and extend any comparable result in [6] about a CRR-discretisation of a δ-subgaussian random variable.

We first give in Lemma 15 the subgaussian property of the (multivariate) Balanced Reduction function.

Lemma 15. The (multivariate) Balanced Reduction $\mathcal{R}(v)$ (Definition 14) is a 0-subgaussian random variable with standard parameter $\frac{1}{2}$ for all $v \in \mathbb{R}^l$. $\quad\square$

Proof. We first consider the univariate random variable $R_j = \mathcal{R}(p)$ given by the Balanced Reduction of the constant p, where $0 \le p \le 1$ without loss of generality. Thus R_j takes the value p with probability $1 - p$ and the value $p - 1$ with probability p, so has moment generating function

$$M_{R_j}(t) = \mathbf{E}(\exp(tR_j)) = (1 - p)\exp(pt) + p\exp((p - 1)t) = \exp(pt)h(t),$$

where $h(t) = (1 - p) + p\exp(-t)$. We consider the logarithm of the moment generating function given by the function

$$g(t) = \log M_{R_j}(t) = pt + \log h(t).$$

The first three derivatives of g are given by

$$g'(t) = \frac{p(1 - p)(1 - \exp(-t))}{h(t)}, \qquad g''(t) = \frac{p(1 - p)\exp(-t)}{h(t)^2}$$

$$\text{and } g'''(t) = \frac{-p(1 - p)\exp(-t)\left((1 - p) - p\exp(-t)\right)}{h(t)^3}.$$

We see that $g''(t) \ge 0$ and that solving $g'''(t) = 0$ shows that the maximum of g'' occurs at $t_0 = \log\left(\frac{p}{1-p}\right)$ with a maximum value of $g''(t_0) = \frac{1}{4}$, so $0 \le g''(t) \le \frac{1}{4}$ for all $t \in \mathbb{R}$, and we also note that $g(0) = g'(0) = 0$. The Lagrange remainder form of Taylor's Theorem shows that there exists ξ between 0 and t such that $g(t) = \frac{1}{2}g''(\xi)t^2$, so $0 \le g(t) \le \frac{1}{8}t^2$. Thus $M_{R_j}(t) = \exp(g(t)) \le \exp(\frac{1}{2}(\frac{1}{2})^2t^2)$, so R_j is a 0-subgaussian random variable with standard parameter $\frac{1}{2}$.

We now consider the multivariate random variable $R = (R_1, \ldots, R_l)^T$ given by the Balanced Reduction of a vector, which has moment generating function M_R satisfying

$$M_R(t) = \mathbf{E}(\exp(t^T R)) = \mathbf{E}\left(\exp\left(\sum_{j=1}^l t_j R_j\right)\right) = \mathbf{E}\left(\prod_{j=1}^l \exp(t_j R_j)\right)$$

$$= \prod_{j=1}^l \mathbf{E}(\exp(t_j R_j)) = \prod_{j=1}^l M_{R_j}(t_j)$$

$$\le \prod_{j=1}^l \exp(\tfrac{1}{2}(\tfrac{1}{2})^2 t_j^2) = \exp\left(\tfrac{1}{2}(\tfrac{1}{2})^2 \sum_{j=1}^l t_j^2\right) = \exp(\tfrac{1}{2}(\tfrac{1}{2})^2|t|^2).$$

Thus R is a 0-subgaussian random variable with standard parameter $\frac{1}{2}$. $\quad\square$

We now give in Theorem 2 a subgaussian standard parameter for a CRR-discretisation. The details of the CRR-discretisation depend on the lattice basis used, and in particular on the spectral norm of a lattice basis matrix.

Theorem 2. Suppose that B is a (column) basis matrix for a lattice Λ in H with spectral norm $\lambda(B)$. If Z is a noncentral subgaussian random variable with standard parameter b, then its CRR-discretisation $\lfloor Z \rceil_{\Lambda+c}^{B}$ is a noncentral subgaussian random variable with mean $\mathbf{E}(Z)$ and standard parameter $\left(b^2 + (\frac{1}{2}\lambda(B))^2\right)^{\frac{1}{2}}$. □

Proof. Lemma 14 (iii) shows that $\lfloor Z \rceil_{\Lambda+c}^{B} = Z + B\mathcal{R}(B^{-1}(c-Z))$ has mean $\mathbf{E}(Z)$. For $v \in H$, Lemma 15 allows us to bound the relevant conditional expectation as

$$
\begin{aligned}
\mathbf{E}\left(\exp\left(v^\dagger \lfloor Z \rceil_{\Lambda+c}^{B}\right)\mid Z = z\right) &= \mathbf{E}\left(\exp\left(v^\dagger \left(z + B\mathcal{R}(B^{-1}(c-z))\right)\right)\right) \\
&= \exp(v^\dagger z)\,\mathbf{E}\left(\exp\left(v^\dagger B\mathcal{R}(B^{-1}(c-z))\right)\right) \\
&= \exp(v^\dagger z)\,\mathbf{E}\left(\exp\left((B^\dagger v)^\dagger \mathcal{R}(B^{-1}(c-z))\right)\right) \\
&= \exp(v^\dagger z)\, M_{\mathcal{R}(B^{-1}(c-z))}\left(B^\dagger v\right) \\
&\le \exp(v^\dagger z)\,\exp\left(\tfrac{1}{2}(\tfrac{1}{2})^2|B^\dagger v|^2\right) \\
&\le \exp(v^\dagger z)\,\exp\left(\tfrac{1}{2}(\tfrac{1}{2}\lambda(B))^2|v|^2\right),
\end{aligned}
$$

so the corresponding conditional expectation random variable is bounded as

$$
\mathbf{E}\left(\exp\left(v^\dagger \lfloor Z \rceil_{\Lambda+c}^{B}\right)\mid Z\right) \le \exp(v^\dagger Z)\,\exp\left(\tfrac{1}{2}(\tfrac{1}{2}\lambda(B))^2|v|^2\right).
$$

Thus the Law of Total Expectation shows that the moment generating function $M_{\lfloor Z \rceil_{\Lambda+c}^{B}}$ of the discretisation $\lfloor Z \rceil_{\Lambda+c}^{B}$ is bounded by

$$
\begin{aligned}
M_{\lfloor Z \rceil_{\Lambda+c}^{B}}(v) &= \mathbf{E}\left(\exp\left(v^\dagger \lfloor Z \rceil_{\Lambda+c}^{B}\right)\right) = \mathbf{E}\left(\mathbf{E}\left(\exp\left(v^\dagger \lfloor Z \rceil_{\Lambda+c}^{B}\right)\mid Z\right)\right) \\
&\le \exp\left(\tfrac{1}{2}(\tfrac{1}{2}\lambda(B))^2|v|^2\right)\mathbf{E}\left(\exp(v^\dagger Z)\right) \\
&= \exp\left(\tfrac{1}{2}(\tfrac{1}{2}\lambda(B))^2|v|^2\right) M_Z(v) \\
&\le \exp\left(\tfrac{1}{2}(\tfrac{1}{2}\lambda(B))^2|v|^2\right)\exp(v^\dagger \mathbf{E}(Z))\exp(\tfrac{1}{2}b^2|v|^2) \\
&\le \exp(v^\dagger \mathbf{E}(Z))\exp\left(\tfrac{1}{2}\left(b^2 + (\tfrac{1}{2}\lambda(B))^2\right)\right)
\end{aligned}
$$

as Z is a noncentral subgaussian random variable with standard parameter b. Thus its discretisation $\lfloor Z \rceil_{\Lambda+c}^{B}$ is a noncentral subgaussian random variable with standard parameter $\left(b^2 + (\frac{1}{2}\lambda(B))^2\right)^{\frac{1}{2}}$. □

Acknowledgements. We thank the anonymous referees for their comments on previous versions of this paper, and we thank Carlos Cid for his interesting discussions about this paper. Rachel Player was supported by an ACE-CSR Ph.D. grant, by the French Programme d'Investissement d'Avenir under national project RISQ P141580, and by the European Union PROMETHEUS project (Horizon 2020 Research and Innovation Program, grant 780701).

References

1. Brakerski, Z., Langlois, A., Peikert, C., Regev, O., Stehlé, D.: Classical hardness of learning with errors. In: Boneh, D., Roughgarden, T., Feigenbaum, J. (eds.) 45th Annual ACM Symposium on Theory of Computing (2013)
2. Genise, N., Micciancio, D., Polyakov, Y.: Building an efficient lattice gadget toolkit: subgaussian sampling and more. In: Ishai, Y., Rijmen, V. (eds.) EUROCRYPT 2019. LNCS, vol. 11477, 655–684. Springer, Cham (2019). https://doi.org/10.1007/978-3-030-17656-3
3. Grimmett, G., Stirzaker, D.: Probability And Random Processes, 3rd edn. Oxford University Press, Oxford (2001)
4. Kahane, J.: Propriétés locales des fonctions à séries de Fourier aléatoires. Stud. Math. **19**, 1–25 (1960)
5. Lyubashevsky, V., Peikert, C., Regev, O.: On Ideal Lattices and Learning with Errors Over Rings. IACR Cryptology ePrint Archive 2012:230 (2012)
6. Lyubashevsky, V., Peikert, C., Regev, O.: A Toolkit for Ring-LWE Cryptography. IACR Cryptology ePrint Archive 2013:293 (2013)
7. Micciancio, D., Peikert, C.: Trapdoors for lattices: simpler, tighter, faster, smaller. In: Pointcheval, D., Johansson, T. (eds.) EUROCRYPT 2012. LNCS, vol. 7237, pp. 700–718. Springer, Heidelberg (2012). https://doi.org/10.1007/978-3-642-29011-4_41
8. Micciancio, D., Regev, O.: Lattice-based cryptography. In: Bernstein, D.J., Buchmann, J., Dahmen, E. (eds.) Post-Quantum Cryptography, pp. 147–191. Springer, Heidelberg (2009). https://doi.org/10.1007/978-3-540-88702-7_5
9. Peikert, C.: Public-key cryptosystems from the worst-case shortest vector problem. In: Mitzenmacher, M. (ed.), 41st Annual ACM Symposium on Theory of Computing (2009)
10. Peikert, C.: Lattice cryptography for the Internet. In: Mosca, M. (ed.) PQCrypto 2014. LNCS, vol. 8772, pp. 197–219. Springer, Cham (2014). https://doi.org/10.1007/978-3-319-11659-4_12
11. Peikert, C.: A Decade of Lattice Cryptography. IACR Cryptology ePrint Archive 2015:939 (2016)
12. Peikert, C., Regev, O., Stephens-Davidowitz, N.: Pseudorandomness of ring-LWE for any ring and modulus. In: Hatami, H., McKenzie, P., King, V. (eds.), Proceedings of the 49th Annual ACM SIGACT Symposium on Theory of Computing, STOC 2017, pp. 461–473 (2017)
13. Regev, O.: On lattices, learning with errors, random linear codes and cryptography. In: Gabow, H., Fagin, R. (eds.), 37th Annual ACM Symposium of Theory of Computing (2005)
14. Regev, O.: The learning with errors problem (invited survey). In: IEEE Conference on Computational Complexity, pp. 191–204 (2010)
15. Rivasplata, O.: Subgaussian Random Variables: An Expository Note. http://www.stat.cmu.edu/~arinaldo/36788/subgaussians.pdf (2015)
16. Stehlé, D., Steinfeld, R., Tanaka, K., Xagawa, K.: Efficient public key encryption based on ideal lattices. In: Matsui, M. (ed.) ASIACRYPT 2009. LNCS, vol. 5912, pp. 617–635. Springer, Heidelberg (2009). https://doi.org/10.1007/978-3-642-10366-7_36
17. Stromberg, K.R.: Probability for Analysts. Chapman and Hall (1994)

Cryptocurrency Related

Fast-to-Finalize Nakamoto-Like Consensus

Shuyang Tang[1], Sherman S. M. Chow[2] (ORCID), Zhiqiang Liu[1,3](✉),
and Joseph K. Liu[4](✉)

[1] Department of Computer Science and Engineering, Shanghai Jiao Tong University,
Shanghai, China
ilu_zq@sjtu.edu.cn
[2] Department of Information Engineering, The Chinese University of Hong Kong,
Shatin, N.T., Hong Kong
[3] Shanghai Viewsource Information Science and Technology Co., Ltd,
Shanghai, China
[4] Faculty of Information Technology, Monash University, Clayton, VIC, Australia
Joseph.Liu@monash.edu

Abstract. As the fundamental component of blockchains, proof-of-work
(PoW) scheme has been widely leveraged to provide consensus for maintaining a distributed public ledger. However, the long confirmation time,
and hence the slow finality rate, is far from satisfactory. Alternative
paradigms with performance improvement emerge. Nevertheless, there
are fewer attempts in modifying the PoW mechanism itself.

We find that the slow finality rate in PoW is caused by using only one
bit to measure the computational power, namely, whether the attained
hash value is smaller than a given target. In this paper, we first propose
Demo-of-Work (DoW), a generalized PoW which assigns the computational work with a score depending on the hash value. We also treat the
bitcoin blockchain as a global "clock" to attain synchronization for ensuring that each participant takes part in DoW for roughly the same time
interval for ensuring fairness. With these two tools, we construct an alternative blockchain called AB-chain which provides a significantly faster
finality rate when compared with the existing PoW-based blockchains,
without sacrificing communication complexity or fairness.

Keywords: Blockchain · Consensus · Cryptocurrency · Proof-of-work

1 Introduction

Since 2008, the blockchain mechanism has been providing a consensus protocol
for maintaining a distributed ledger in a decentralized manner. The blockchain

Part of the work was done while the first author was a research intern in CUHK.
The second author is supported by General Research Funds (CUHK 14210217) of the
Research Grants Council, Hong Kong. The third author is supported by the National
Natural Science Foundation of China (Grant No. 61672347). A preliminary version
appeared as "Fast-to-Converge PoW-like Consensus Protocol" in China Blockchain
Conference 2018.

© Springer Nature Switzerland AG 2019
J. Jang-Jaccard and F. Guo (Eds.): ACISP 2019, LNCS 11547, pp. 271–288, 2019.
https://doi.org/10.1007/978-3-030-21548-4_15

structure is a chain of blocks, each of which contains transactions in the ledger. To generate a block, participants called miners perform a *proof-of-work* (PoW) [11,16] by brute force to find an admissible *nonce*. A nonce is an admissible solution when the hash of the nonce concatenating with the necessary information is smaller than a predetermined value governing the *difficulty* of PoW. The information includes the hash of the previous block header, (the root of a Merkle tree of) transactions, and other auxiliary data. When such a nonce is found, a block is assembled and appended to the end of the blockchain, i.e., it extends the ledger. This process is referred to as *mining* due to the award of proposing a block. Such a consensus scheme is referred to as *Nakamoto* or *bitcoin blockchain* [20].

A fork emerges when two sets of blocks are mined after the same previous block, due to malicious purposes or by coincidence. Fork resolution is needed to converge the branches into one. In Nakamoto blockchain, honest miners always mine on the longest valid branch, hence malicious forking attempt for tampering the ledger requires significant work to outrace these honest miners. When any given block is followed by a sufficient number of new blocks, it is considered as *finalized* (or *confirmed*) since it will never be outraced except for a (sufficiently) small probability. We say that such resolution ensures *secure finality*.

Existing blockchain mechanism requires a long confirmation time to reach secure finality. It is a serious constraint of applications which rely on blockchains (e.g., see [19])[1]. To address this issue, a possible approach is to replace PoW by alternative mechanisms such as the proof-of-stake (PoS) or its generalization [18] that transfer the decision power from miners to stakeholders, e.g., Algorand [15] and Ouroboros Praos [10]. However, they require utter reconstructions of the consensus mechanism, which may be harder to deploy in practice. Moreover, recent results have shown the necessity of PoW [23] in the presence of late spawning.Optimizations at an application level on top of blockchain are also considered, such as the lightning network [24] for rapid micropayments, and blockchain fabrics [1,22,26] that also leverage a permissioned Byzantine fault-tolerance protocol.

In this paper, we adopt the third approach [6] which modifies the blockchain itself. In principle, it can be used with any application-layer optimizations. Although there are alternative blockchains [12,21] or attempts which extend the linked list in blockchain to directed acyclic graph (DAG) [7,25], for a greater throughput or better fairness, improving the finality rate by an alternative blockchain principle is seldom considered.

1.1   Roadmap

To the best of our knowledge, we provide the first formal study of improving the finality rate of a Nakamoto-like blockchain by replacing the underlying PoW principle. The roadmap of our fast-to-finalize blockchain is as follows.

---

[1] For improving throughput, many sharding protocols are also proposed (e.g., see [9]).

Demo-of-Work. We observe (to be justified later) that the finality of PoW is slow since it assesses the computational power via only one bit of information of whether attaining a hash value smaller than a target. We propose *Demo-of-Work* (DoW) which utilizes a potential function[2] to assign a score to each block according to the block hash, without a hard target of the hash puzzle.

Blockchain as a Global Clock. Blockchain has been leveraged for various purposes, for example, publicly verifiable source of randomness [2,4,8] or penalty mechanism (e.g. in the context of secure multiparty computations [3,5,17]). Inspired by these usages, here we leverage the bitcoin blockchain as a global clock. To the best of our knowledge, this treatment is the first in the research literature.

AB-Chain with Fast Finality. Based on the two tools above, we build an alternative blockchain which we call AB-chain. Similar to bitcoin, it consists of a linear order of blocks, but now each block has a *block weight* assigned by its hash according to a potential function. When there is ambiguity, honest miners always build blocks onto the chain branch with the greatest the *total weight* – the sum of all block weights on the branch, as the *score* in our DoW. However, apart from the previous block, each block should also refer to the last block on the longest chain of the underlying (bitcoin) blockchain. In case the underlying blockchain has a fork with multiple newest blocks, any one of them can be chosen.

We use blockchain as a synchronization mechanism, for assuring that each participant performs DoW for roughly the same time when they are attempting to assemble each block. A round starts from the generation of the newest block and ends with the generation of the next block. During a round, each miner tries to compose a block and find a proper nonce to lessen the block hash as far as possible. It broadcasts the block if the hash is "competitive" (with a positive block weight no less than that of existing blocks in its view of this round). All the participating peer nodes take part only in the forwarding of competitive blocks.

1.2 Evaluation of the Improvement

The *finality rate* indicates the speed of reaching a secure finality on a new block. With our round-based mechanism, we aim to lessen the number of rounds expected to reach confidence that one block remains on the chain forever except for a small probability q. The *finality rate* varies with different potential function $\mathcal{L}$. To analyze the finality rate, we propose a novel finality model and evaluate it experimentally under some selected potential functions.

We prove that the general bound of the *communication cost*, i.e., the total amount of all communications during the protocol execution, is at most

---

[2] Potential function is a term borrowed from the Physics literature. The existing PoW is a special case of DoW, whose potential function assigns one to all hashes smaller than a predetermined parameter, and zero to others.

$O(N \log N)$, where N stands for the total number of network nodes[3]. Finally, we pick a potential function with an $O(N)$ communication cost as bitcoin.

Our protocol should also be fair. *Fairness* in this paper is defined as the property that the most competitive block of each round with the greatest weight is generated by each party with a probability according to its proportion of hash power. The fairness is guaranteed as long as the potential function is *valid* (monotonously non-increasing regarding the input hash)[4].

Organization. We first describe our notations and assumptions as well as our protocol framework in the next section. In Sect. 3, we build a model to study the rate of secure finality. In Sect. 4, the communication cost is analyzed and the fairness is shown to be reached under our finality model, then we suggest one potential function to instantiate our AB-chain protocol.

2   AB-Chain: DoW-Based Blockchain with Fast Finality

2.1   Notations and Assumptions

Table 1 lists the major notations. We regard the range of the hash function $H(\cdot)$ as $[M]$ where the notation $[M] := \{1, 2, \ldots, M\}$ is defined to be all positive integers no greater than M. We denote the global hash rate by T, which is the total number of hash attempts taken by all participants in one round. We assume that T is significantly smaller than M and its value is accessible to all participants.

For easier exposition, multiplying a ratio (α, β, δ) with T results in integers. We use B to denote a block. $\boxed{B.\text{nonce}}$ is the nonce solution provided by the proposer and $\boxed{B.\text{hash}}$ is the hash of B. $B.\text{preBlock}^1$ (or just $B.\text{preBlock}$) is the previous block that B follows (or B itself in case that it is the genesis block, i.e., the first block of the chain). $B.\text{preBlock}^k$ ($k \in \mathbb{N}^+ \setminus \{1\}$) is defined recursively,

$$\boxed{B.\text{preBlock}^k} := \begin{cases} B & , \text{isGenesisBlock}(B) \\ (B.\text{preBlock}^{k-1}).\text{preBlock}^1 & , \text{otherwise} \end{cases},$$

where isGenesisBlock($\cdot$) is a predicate of whether one block is the genesis block. The notation $\boxed{B.\text{preBlocks} := \cup_{i=1}^{\infty} \{B.\text{preBlock}^i\}}$ denotes the set of all "ancestor" blocks of B (include all $B.\text{preBlock}^k$'s). For an AB-chain block, $\boxed{B.\text{btcBlock}}$ is the block of the underlying (bitcoin) blockchain it refers.

---

[3] The cost is hard to be measured by any specific quantity, so we measure it with complexity.

[4] There are other works which analyze or evaluate blockchain or blockchain-based cryptocurrencies. For example, *Bitcoin backbone* [13] has shown common prefix and chain quality, two basic properties of the bitcoin protocol. There is also model for formally analyzing the security and performance of various cryptocurrencies [14].

We assume a peer-to-peer network where each node forwards only competitive nodes in its view, i.e., any block forwarding is aborted if $\mathcal{L}(B.\text{hash}) \leq 0$. When receiving a block B following an AB-chain block B_{-1} that is already followed by B', each node forwards B only if $\mathcal{L}(B.\text{hash}) \geq \mathcal{L}(B'.\text{hash}) > 0$. We consider that the network is robust, hence any newly generated block on the bitcoin blockchain is revealed to all nodes of AB-chain almost simultaneously. We assume that each round is long enough and omitted network issues such as latency. For simplicity, we regard that all participants mining on a chain branch that is finally overrun by another branch during a fork are controlled by an adversary.

2.2   The Incentive Problem

With an improper establishment of $\mathcal{L}(\cdot)$, miners may tend to deviate from the standard mining protocol to maximize their profits. In the discussion below, $\varphi_{\mathcal{L}}(t)$ denotes the expected value of the maximal block weight that one party with hash rate t achieves in one round. Suppose the global hash rate is T.

Table 1. Table of notations

Notation	Description
N	The total number of nodes participating in the network
T	The global hash rate, the number of hash attempts taken by all participants in one round
M	The cardinality of the range of $H(\cdot)$, for example, $M = 2^{256}$ for SHA-256
D	The difficulty parameter defined by $D := M/T$
α	The fraction of the adversary hash power within the global rate
$\mathcal{L}(\cdot)$	A potential function that returns the block weight of a hash value input
q	The small probability that a confirmed branch is later outraced
$\Gamma_{\mathcal{L},q}^{\alpha,T}$	The (α, T, q)-trust gap, see Definition 6
$\Lambda_{\mathcal{L},q}^{\alpha,T}$	The inverse of the (α, T, q)-finality rate, see Definition 7
$\mathcal{H}_{\min}^{T}$	An oracle that returns the minimal hash value for T hash attempts
$\text{Rev}(y)$	The inverse function of $y = x \ln \frac{M}{x}$, well-defined for $0 < x < M/e$
$\text{sgn}(x)$	A function that returns 1 for positive x, -1 for negative x, and 0 for 0
e, γ	The natural constant $e \approx 2.718$ and Euler's constant $\gamma \approx 0.577$

1. In case of a too-convex establishment that $\varphi_{\mathcal{L}}((\alpha+\beta)T) < \varphi_{\mathcal{L}}(\alpha T) + \varphi_{\mathcal{L}}(\beta T)$ happens with a considerable gap[5] for any two parties with α, β fraction of global hash power respectively, miners are lured to maximize their total profits by node spawning and hash power splitting. In this case, massively spawned nodes may cause a significant burden to the network. Honest nodes then are less likely to receive their deserved profits without massive spawning. Even worse, nodes may perform block-splitting by dividing their total power for a long sequence of blocks and cause selfish mining. That is why we use the bitcoin blockchain as a global clock to avoid such a block splitting.

---

[5] $|\varphi_{\mathcal{L}}((\alpha + \beta)T) - (\varphi_{\mathcal{L}}(\alpha T) + \varphi_{\mathcal{L}}(\beta T))|$ is non-negligible for certain $0 < \alpha, \beta < 1$.

2. In case of a too-concave establishment that $\varphi_{\mathcal{L}}((\alpha+\beta)T) > \varphi_{\mathcal{L}}(\alpha T) + \varphi_{\mathcal{L}}(\beta T)$ happens with a considerable gap for any two parties with α, β fraction of global hash power, miners tend to aggregate their hash power. Thereby, existing mining pools are lured to combine their resource and become one or few unified pools. This is a serious centralization which is likely to lead to a pool controlling more than a half total hash power.

Both cases cause a loss of *fairness*. However, most $\varphi_{\mathcal{L}}(\cdot)$ under sensible establishments of $\mathcal{L}(\cdot)$ are somewhat convex (but not too convex, including the Nakamoto case) so all terrifying ending mentioned above would not happen. We assume that all our chosen $\mathcal{L}(\cdot)$ are neither too convex or too concave in this paper. A more formal and thorough treatment of fairness is left as future work.

2.3   Our Demo-of-Work and AB-Chain Framework

Demo-of-Work. We apply our finality model (to be formalized in the next section) to formulate the notion of Demo-of-Work (DoW). In this scheme, we evaluate computation work by using the potential function instead of checking whether the attained hash value is smaller than a given target or not. Specifically, we assign a score (the weight) to each block according to the block hash and the potential function. This allows exploiting more information related to hash powers, which more accurately measures the work accumulated over a chain via the total weight of the chain. Furthermore, the accumulation of work in DoW scheme grows faster than that in the original PoW protocol if a nice potential function is adopted. The hope is that it can lead to a faster finality rate.

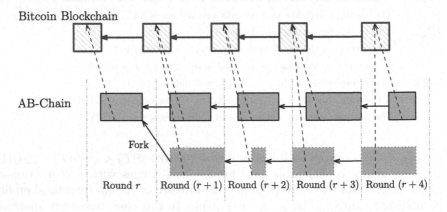

Fig. 1. Outline of The AB-Chain (the length in the graph indicates the block weight)

Chain Structures. The AB-chain structure is similar to the blockchain structure of bitcoin, except for a few differences (see Fig. 1). First, each block contains a weight corresponding to the block hash. Specifically, the weight of block

B equals $\boxed{\mathcal{L}(B.\text{hash})}$, where $\mathcal{L}(\cdot)$ is the potential function that maps a hash value to a specific block weight. No block with non-positive weight will survive. Second, each AB-chain block B refers to both the previous block $B.\text{preBlock}$ and a bitcoin block $B.\text{btcBlock}$ that

$$(B.\text{preBlock}).\text{btcBlock} = (B.\text{btcBlock}).\text{preBlock}.$$

Mining. At the beginning of each round, each miner packs hashes of the previous block of AB-chain and the newest block of bitcoin blockchain, its collected transactions, along with other auxiliary information into the block record. Afterwards, it tries to find a proper nonce value $B.\text{nonce}$ to minimize (as far as possible) the block hash. At the same time, the miner takes part in the forwarding of blocks from others and records the block with the greatest weight w that refers to the same previous block as its. It broadcasts its own block if it finds a nonce that leads to a competitive block weight no less than w. It is possible that no block of positive weight is proposed in a few rounds, so not necessarily every round has a block. In this case, we regard that this round has a block of zero weight.

Fork Resolutions. When multiple blocks are built following the same block, the fork happens. Each honest node builds blocks following the valid branch with the largest total weight. The branch with a total weight greater than others by a "trust gap" is considered to be confirmed. A block might suddenly appear in the view, so fork may happen anytime before the finality. No matter forks happen or not in the current view, it is a must to wait for our notion of "trust gap" to form before reaching the block finality. In our analysis, we assume the worst case that fork is likely to happen for every block generation, without explicitly considering the probability of forking. The next section formally defines the notion of trust gap and explains its role in fork resolution.

3 Rate of Secure Finality

We build a model to describe the finality rate of all AB-chains with different potential functions.

3.1 Finality Model

To facilitate the description of our finality model, we propose the notion of "minimal hash value oracle", which provides an equivalent simulation of the mining process of each participant. Specifically, this oracle inputs the number of hash attempts T_0, and returns which is the least value among T_0 uniform random selections from the range of the cryptographic hash function $H(\cdot)$. This simulates the mining since the event of "mining an AB-block" is essentially "having the least hash value of T_0 hash attempts small". Now we formalize this definition.

Definition 1 (Minimal Hash Value Oracle). *For a positive integer T_0, oracle $\boxed{\mathcal{H}_{\min}^{T_0}}$ outputs the minimal hash value in T_0 hash attempts. For a fixed T_0, $\forall i \in [M]$, it is equivalent to a discrete probabilistic distribution with*

$$\Pr\left[h \leftarrow \mathcal{H}_{\min}^{T_0} \Big| h \leq i\right] = 1 - (1 - \frac{i}{M})^{T_0}.$$

Then, we define the potential function $\mathcal{L}(\cdot)$ which assigns a weight to each block regarding the block hash h, to measure the work required to reach a hash value no greater than h. In addition, we ask for each potential function $\mathcal{L}(\cdot)$ to be *valid*, i.e., $\mathcal{L}(h)$ should be monotonously non-increasing by h, since smaller the least hash value is, more hash attempts are done in expectation.

Definition 2 (Valid Potential Function). *In the AB-chain consensus, a potential function $\mathcal{L} : [M] \rightarrow \mathbb{R}^+$ is called valid if and only if for all integer $1 \leq i < M$, $\mathcal{L}(i) \geq \mathcal{L}(i+1)$.*

Now we describe definition regarding the study of finality (i.e., resolving of chain forks) one-by-one. To begin, we define the chain weight and formally discuss the chain competition criteria.

Definition 3 (The Total Weight of A Chain). *For a chain of blocks chain $= (B_0, B_1, \ldots, B_\ell)$ (from the genesis block to the newest valid block), with $B_{i-1} = B_i$.preBlock[1] for all $i \in [\ell]$, its total weight is weight(chain) $:= \sum_{i=1}^{\ell} \mathcal{L}(B_i.hash)$.*

Figure 2 depicts the fork resolutions. For finality, we require that one chain branch has a total weight greater than all others by a "gap" to be defined below.

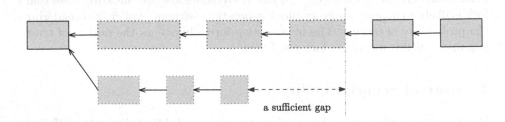

Fig. 2. AB-Chain with Fork Resolutions

Definition 4 (The Chain Competition). *When two chains of blocks chain$_1$ $= (B_0, B_1, \ldots, B_\ell)$ and chain$_2$ $= (B_0', B_1', \ldots, B_{\ell'}')$ cause a chain fork, where the fork starts from the kth block (i.e., $B_i = B_i'$ for all natural number $i < k$), chain$_1$ outraces chain$_2$ if and only if*

$$\sum_{i=k}^{\ell} \mathcal{L}(B_i.hash) - \sum_{j=k}^{\ell'} \mathcal{L}(B_j'.hash) > \Gamma,$$

which is equivalent to

$$weight(chain_1) - weight(chain_2) > \Gamma,$$

for a certain gap Γ (to be determined in Definition 6).

Definition 5 ($(R, \Delta, \alpha, T, q)$-Confidence). *For an AB-chain consensus with potential function $\mathcal{L}(\cdot)$ and round number R, it achieves $(R, \Delta, \alpha, T, q)$-confidence if*

$$\Pr \left[\begin{array}{c} x_1, x_2, \ldots, x_R \leftarrow \mathcal{H}_{\min}^{\alpha \cdot T} \\ y_1, y_2, \ldots, y_R \leftarrow \mathcal{H}_{\min}^{(1-\alpha)T} \end{array} \middle| \sum_{i=1}^{R} \mathcal{L}(x_i) - \sum_{j=1}^{R} \mathcal{L}(y_j) > \Delta \right] \leq q.$$

To measure the finality rate regarding the establishment of a potential function $\mathcal{L}(\cdot)$, we introduce the notion of the trust gap parameterized by the proportion of the hash rate of the adversary α, the global hash rate T, a probability q. As long as one chain branch has a total weight greater than all others' with a sufficiently large enough gap Γ, we have the confidence that this branch reaches a secure finality, i.e., will never be outraced except for a small probability q.

Definition 6 ((α, T, q)-Trust Gap). *For an AB-chain with potential function $\mathcal{L}(\cdot)$, we denote (α, T, q)-trust gap $\boxed{\Gamma_{\mathcal{L}, q}^{\alpha, T}}$ as the least Δ satisfying its $(R, \Delta, \alpha, T, q)$-confidence for all $R \in \mathbb{N}$.*

Once such a trust gap is achieved by one chain branch over others, the fork is resolved and the secure finality is reached. The quicker chain competitions are concluded (i.e., fewer rounds expected to attain such a trust gap), the better a finality rate is reached. Finally, the finality rate is the inverse of the expected[6] number of rounds required to reach a safety gap.

Definition 7 ($\boxed{(\alpha, T, q)\text{-Finality Rate}}$). *For an AB-chain consensus with potential function $\mathcal{L}(\cdot)$, its (α, T, q)-finality rate is $\boxed{1/\Lambda_{\mathcal{L}, q}^{\alpha, T}}$ with*

$$\Lambda_{\mathcal{L}, q}^{\alpha, T} := \frac{\Gamma_{\mathcal{L}, q}^{\alpha, T}}{\mathbb{E}\left[\begin{array}{c} x \leftarrow \mathcal{H}_{\min}^{\alpha \cdot T} \\ y \leftarrow \mathcal{H}_{\min}^{(1-\alpha)T} \end{array} \middle| \mathcal{L}(y) - \mathcal{L}(x) \right]},$$

where the denominator is the expected gap formed in one round.

To facilitate comparisons, we will only use $\Lambda_{\mathcal{L}, q}^{\alpha, T}$ (which is essentially the inverse of the finality rate) to signify the finality rate in later parts. The greater $\Lambda_{\mathcal{L}, q}^{\alpha, T}$ is, a slower finality rate is attained. $\Lambda_{\mathcal{L}, q}^{\alpha, T}$ is denoted by $\boxed{\Lambda_\alpha}$ when no ambiguity exists (in which case $1/\Lambda_\alpha$ is the finality rate).

---

[6] It is not exactly the mathematical expectation, but it simplifies descriptions.

3.2 Testimony of Our Finality Model

With a slight difference[7], we view the Nakamoto blockchain as an AB-chain with potential function

$$\mathcal{L}(h) = \begin{cases} 1, & h \leq D \\ 0, & \text{otherwise} \end{cases}.$$

The difficulty parameter D here is determined to have one block with the weight of 1 mined in expectation for one round, i.e., $T \cdot (D/M) = 1$. Mining a bitcoin block corresponds to mining an AB-chain block with the weight 1.

To show this claim and also the reliability of our model, a Monte Carlo experiment (Appendix A) is conducted to calculate the finality rate under different assumptions on the adversary hash rate with the above $\mathcal{L}(h)$.[8] We set $q = 0.001$. For the results in Table 2, the first column reflects the adversary hash rate, the second and the third columns are the numbers of rounds needed to confirm a block provided by two independent Monte Carlo experiments of our model. We can observe from the fourth and fifth columns that the experimental result is coherent with that of Nakamoto in 2008 [20].

Table 2. Experimental results for finality rate on Nakamoto Blockchain

Adversary hash rate α	Experiment I	Experiment II	Average result	Result of Bbitcoin [20]
0.10	4.0258	4.0128	4.0193	5
0.15	6.9477	7.0094	6.9785	8
0.20	10.2896	8.1600	9.2248	11
0.25	16.1332	15.1540	15.6436	15
0.30	24.5419	25.2738	24.9079	24
0.35	44.1077	41.7835	42.9456	41
0.40	105.5780	89.7551	97.6666	89
0.45	363.5730	311.9380	337.7555	340

4   Communication Cost and Fairness

When devising a new protocol, communication cost and fairness need to be taken into account since they are vital for efficiency and security. In the following, we can also see that the choice of potential function $\mathcal{L}(\cdot)$ is closely related to the communication cost and fairness. Our analysis of these two factors gives the bounds of communication cost for valid potential functions, and proves that fairness always holds as long as the potential function is a monotonously non-increasing function. This gives a basis for determining a "good" potential function which balances the finality rate and communication cost without compromising fairness. We then choose a "good" potential function experimentally and come up with AB-chain accordingly.

---

[7] A coherence on experimental results even with "noise" from such a difference further justifies the reliability of our finality model and the experiment.

[8] We are showing that the Nakamoto chain can be regarded as one instantiation of our model. We are not competing with Nakamoto blockchain in this part.

4.1   Communication Cost

Since hashes of amount $O(1)$ can be found to satisfy $h < D$ by all participants each round ($T \cdot (D/M) = 1$), we can infer that as long as $\mathcal{L}(h) \leq 0$ holds for all $h > kD$ with some constant k, the communication cost should remain $O(kN) = O(N)$ (N is the total number of nodes of the network), since the expected number of proposed blocks will be no greater than k times that of bitcoin. For instance, for $\mathcal{L}(h)$ we eventually chose in Sect. 4.3, $\mathcal{L}(h) \leq 0$ holds for all $h > 2D$, and the overall communication cost is bounded by $O(2N) = O(N)$.

A General Bound. Although an $O(N)$ communication cost is guaranteed for certain cases, such complexity is not reached by all cases of the generalized model. As an analysis of the general model, we can prove that the overall communication cost will not exceed $O(N \log N)$.

We assume that each miner generates a block with a unique block hash, and their blocks are proposed in turn. Each block is successfully proposed (and cause an $O(N)$ communication burden to the network) only if its block has a hash smaller than all previously proposed blocks, or no node forwards its block.

Theorem 1. *For any valid potential function $\mathcal{L}(\cdot)$, assuming each node $i \in [N]$ has a nonce solution of hash value h_i, and proposes successfully (i.e., causing an $O(N)$ network burden) only if $\mathcal{L}(h_i) > \max_{j=1}^{i-1} \mathcal{L}(h_j)$. Then, the overall communication cost is bounded by the complexity $O(N \log N)$.*

Proof. Without a significant twist on results, we assume all nodes submit solutions with different hash values. We let indicator $\mathcal{I}_i$ be 1 if $\mathcal{L}(h_i) > \max_{j=1}^{i-1} \mathcal{L}(h_j)$, 0 otherwise. Similarly, we let indicator $\mathcal{J}_i$ be 1 if $h_i < \min_{j=1}^{i-1} h_j$, 0 otherwise. Since $\mathcal{L}(\cdot)$ is a valid potential function, we can infer that $\mathcal{L}(h_i) > \max_{j=1}^{i-1} \mathcal{L}(h_j) \Rightarrow h_i < \min_{j=1}^{i-1} h_j$, and hence $\mathcal{I}_i \leq \mathcal{J}_i$ for each $i \in [N]$.

The overall communication cost is $\sum_{i=1}^{N} \mathcal{I}_i$ times $O(N)$, which should be smaller than $\sum_{i=1}^{N} \mathcal{J}_i$ times $O(N)$. Let F_n be $\sum_{i=1}^{n} \mathcal{I}_i$ for each $n \in [N]$, we have

$$\mathbb{E}[F_n] = (\frac{1}{n} \cdot 0 + \frac{1}{n}\mathbb{E}[F_1] + \frac{1}{n}\mathbb{E}[F_2] + \cdots + \frac{1}{n}\mathbb{E}[F_{n-1}]) + 1$$

for each $n \in [N]$. Denoting $S_n := \sum_{i=1}^{n} \mathbb{E}[F_i]$, we have

$$S_n - S_{n-1} = \frac{1}{n}S_{n-1} + 1$$

for each $n \in [N] \setminus \{1\}$, and $S_1 = 1$. Denoting $T_n := \frac{S_n}{n+1}$, we next have

$$T_n = T_{n-1} + \frac{1}{n+1},$$

for each $n \in [N] \setminus \{1\}$, and $T_1 = \frac{S_1}{2} = \frac{1}{2}$. Thereby $T_n = \sum_{i=1}^{n} \frac{1}{i+1}$, and $S_n = (n+1) \sum_{i=1}^{n} \frac{1}{i+1}$. Finally,

$$\mathbb{E}[F_n] = S_n - S_{n-1} = (n+1)\sum_{i=1}^{n}\frac{1}{i+1} - n\sum_{i=1}^{n-1}\frac{1}{i+1}$$

$$= (n+1)\cdot\frac{1}{n+1} + \sum_{i=1}^{n-1}\frac{1}{i+1} = \sum_{i=1}^{n}\frac{1}{i} \approx \ln n - \gamma$$

for each $n \in [N]\setminus\{1\}$. To conclude, the overall communication cost is bounded by $O(N\log N)$.

4.2 Fairness

Fairness considers the most competitive block with the greatest weight for a single round is proposed by a participant according to its hash power.

Definition 8 (Fairness). *For an AB-chain consensus scheme with the potential function $\mathcal{L}(\cdot)$, it achieves fairness if and only if*

$$\Pr\left[x \leftarrow \mathcal{H}_{min}^{\beta\cdot T}, y \leftarrow \mathcal{H}_{min}^{(1-\beta)T}\Big|\mathcal{L}(x) \geq \mathcal{L}(y)\right] \geq \beta - \epsilon$$

holds for any party holding β rate of global hash power, where ($\epsilon = o(\frac{T}{M})$ is a negligible component,) T is the number of hash attempts done by all participants in one round.

We prove that if the potential function $\mathcal{L}(\cdot)$ is valid, fairness is achieved.

Theorem 2. *Basic fairness of an AB-chain consensus always holds as long as the potential function $\mathcal{L}(\cdot)$ is a monotonously non-increasing function.*

Proof. Suppose that $\mathcal{L}(\cdot)$ is monotonously non-increasing, then

$$x \leq y \Rightarrow \mathcal{L}(x) \geq \mathcal{L}(y).$$

Hence

$$\Pr\left[x \leftarrow \mathcal{H}_{min}^{\beta\cdot T}, y \leftarrow \mathcal{H}_{min}^{(1-\beta)T}\Big|\mathcal{L}(x) \geq \mathcal{L}(y)\right]$$

$$\geq \Pr\left[x \leftarrow \mathcal{H}_{min}^{\beta\cdot T}, y \leftarrow \mathcal{H}_{min}^{(1-\beta)T}\Big|x \leq y\right],$$

and

$$P_{inf} \leq \Pr\left[x \leftarrow \mathcal{H}_{min}^{\beta\cdot T}, y \leftarrow \mathcal{H}_{min}^{(1-\beta)T}\Big|x \leq y\right] \leq P_{sup},$$

where

$$P_{inf} = \sum_{i=1}^{M}\frac{1}{M}\cdot\beta T\cdot\left(\frac{M-i}{M}\right)^{\beta T-1}\cdot\left(\frac{M-i}{M}\right)^{(1-\beta)T}$$
$$= \frac{\beta T}{M^T}\sum_{i=1}^{M}(M-i)^{T-1} = \frac{\beta T}{M^T}\sum_{i=0}^{M-1}i^{T-1}$$
$$= \frac{\beta T}{M^T}\int_0^M x^{T-1}\mathrm{d}x - O\left(\left(\frac{T}{M}\right)^2\right)$$
$$= \frac{\beta T}{M^T}\cdot\frac{M^T}{T} - O\left(\left(\frac{T}{M}\right)^2\right)$$
$$= \beta - O\left(\left(\frac{T}{M}\right)^2\right),$$

and that

$$P_{sup} = \sum_{i=1}^{M} \frac{1}{M} \cdot \beta T \cdot \left(\frac{M-i+1}{M}\right)^{\beta T-1} \cdot \left(\frac{M-i+1}{M}\right)^{(1-\beta)T}$$
$$\lesssim \frac{\beta T}{M^T} \cdot \frac{(M+1)^T}{T}$$
$$= \beta \cdot \left(1 + \frac{1}{M}\right)^T \approx \beta \cdot e^{T/M}.$$

Since we may assume that $T \ll M$, we have

$$\Pr\left[x \leftarrow \mathcal{H}_{\min}^{\beta \cdot T}, y \leftarrow \mathcal{H}_{\min}^{(1-\beta)T} \middle| x \leq y\right] \gtrsim \beta - O\left(\left(\frac{T}{M}\right)^2\right),$$

and so forth

$$\Pr\left[x \leftarrow \mathcal{H}_{\min}^{\beta \cdot T}, y \leftarrow \mathcal{H}_{\min}^{(1-\beta)T} \middle| \mathcal{L}(x) \geq \mathcal{L}(y)\right] \geq \beta - O\left(\left(\frac{T}{M}\right)^2\right).$$

This achieves our defined fairness since $O\left((T/M)^2\right) = o(T/M)$ is negligible.

4.3 The Choice of Potential Function and the Resulting AB-Chain

With the above analysis, we have a rough direction in picking a potential function which reaches a "nice" balance between the finality rate and communication cost while not sacrificing fairness. We selected representatives of monotonously non-increasing functions according to the gross type of function curve, and run independent experiments for different types of potential functions via the Monte Carlo simulations under our finality model. For the adversary assumptions of 10%, 20%, 30%, and 40%, Table 3 in Appendix A shows the estimated communication complexity and the experimental results of the finality rate for each experimented potential function.

With a faster finality rate and $O(N)$ communication, we decide $\mathcal{L}(h)$ to be

$$\mathcal{L}(h) = \begin{cases} 2, & h \leq D \\ 1, & D < h \leq 2D \\ 0, & h > 2D \end{cases}.$$

For instance, according to the result of Table 3, for the adversary assumption of $\alpha = 10\%$, 4 rounds are sufficient for the safety of $q = 10^{-3}$, while it is 6 rounds for the bitcoin. For $\alpha = 30\%$, 15 rounds for AB-chain reaches roughly the same security as 25 rounds for bitcoin. Our experiments confirm that the finality rate in DoW is significantly improved when compared with that of Nakamoto.

5 Conclusion and Discussion

We proposed demo-of-work that assigns a weighting score to evaluate the computation work on each block more accurately by introducing potential functions. Further, we used the blockchain as a global clock that divides the protocol execution into rounds. Based on these two tools, we constructed a blockchain protocol with a faster finality rate as well as satisfactory communication cost and fairness.

This protocol changed the underlying mechanism of proof-of-work and could be applicable to any blockchains adopting proof-of-work.

This work spawns various future research directions, especially regarding the potential function. A systematic approach to finding an optimal potential function is desired. A formal analysis of incentives from the perspective of game theory is expected. More relationship between the potential function and the finality rate needs to be discovered. Finally, this model is expected to be put into practice and attested with real and empirical data.

With different establishments of the potential function $\mathcal{L}(\cdot)$ miners tend to adopt different mining strategies due to an alternative incentive model (especially when mining pools are also taken into consideration). So, we think that the mining behavior on AB-chain is unlikely to be identical to that of any existing blockchain and omitted an empirical analysis based on existing data from Bitcoin. Further study in this regard is left as future work.

A   Detailed Protocols of The Simulation Experiment

For each instantiation of the generalized model with a potential function $\mathcal{L}(\cdot)$, an experiment is performed to reveal its finality rate with a Monte Carlo method. In our experiment, $M = 2^{20}$, $T = D = 2^{10}$ and $q = 10^{-3}$ are chosen, the algorithms listed below are executed (starting from the main function, Algorithm 7). After the execution, the main function returns the expected number of rounds required to form the safety gap.

1. **Preparation(α, T)** prepares two arrays to provide outcomes of two discrete cumulative distribution functions. Specifically, aCDF$[i]$ is the probability of having a hash value no greater than i found by the adversary. hCDF$[i]$ is similarly the probability of having a hash value no greater than i found by honest nodes.
2. **GetH(CDF)** returns a random number according to a distribution of a cumulative distribution function recorded in the array CDF.
3. **SimAttack$(\Delta, \mathsf{aCDF}, \mathsf{hCDF})$** models the behaviour of the adversary attempt of forming a new chain of blocks with the total weight greater than the honest one by a certain gap Δ.
4. **Test$(\Delta, q, \mathsf{aCDF}, \mathsf{hCDF})$** performs "SimAttack" for sufficiently enough times, to show (via Monte Carlo method) whether the probability of adversary in successfully performing an attack (and overrunning the honest one by a total weight of Δ) is smaller than q.
5. **FindMinGap$(q, \mathsf{aCDF}, \mathsf{hCDF})$** utilizes a binary search to find the minimal gap δ such that the adversary can catch up with the honest chain by a total weight of δ only with a negligible probability q.
6. **Expc(CDF)** returns the expected block weight attained by either honest parties or the adversary by another Monte Carlo experiment.
7. **Main(α, T, q)** is the main function that returns (the inverse of) the finality rate Λ_α of the blockchain with potential function $\mathcal{L}(\cdot)$, i.e., the expected number of rounds required to form the safety gap.

In our final experiment, we execute the algorithms with NUM_TEST_SAMPLE = 100000, NUM_TEST_BLOCK = 200, and $\epsilon = 10^{-4}$.

Algorithm 1 Preparation(α, T)

1: aCDF[0] := 0
2: hCDF[0] := 0
3: **for** $i := 1$ to M **do**
4:   aCDF[i] := $1 - (1 - \frac{i}{M})^{\alpha T}$
5:   hCDF[i] := $1 - (1 - \frac{i}{M})^{(1-\alpha)T}$
6: **end for**
7: **return** (aCDF, hCDF)

Algorithm 2 GetH(CDF)

1: x := random($0, 1$)
2: **return** binary_search(CDF, x)

Algorithm   3
SimAttack(Δ, aCDF, hCDF)

1: $S_1, S_2 := 0$
2: **for** $i := 1$ to NUM_TEST_BLOCK **do**
3:   $S_1 := S_1 + \mathcal{L}(\text{GetH}(\text{aCDF}))$
4:   $S_2 := S_2 + \mathcal{L}(\text{GetH}(\text{hCDF}))$
5:   **if** $S_1 - S_2 > \Delta$ **then**
6:     **return** true
7:   **end if**
8: **end for**
9: **return** false

Algorithm 4 Test(Δ, q, aCDF, hCDF)

1: $succ := 0$
2: **for** $i := 1$ to NUM_TEST_SAMPLE **do**
3:   **if**   SimAttack(Δ, aCDF, hCDF) **then**
4:     $succ := succ + 1$
5:   **end if**
6: **end for**
7: **return** ($succ < q * $ NUM_TEST_SAMPLE)

Algorithm   5
FindMinGap(q, aCDF, hCDF)

1: $left := 0$
2: $right := $ SUFFICIENT_LARGE
3: **while** $right - left > \epsilon$ **do**
4:   $x := (left + right)/2$
5:   **if** Test(Δ, q, aCDF, hCDF) **then**
6:     $right := x$
7:   **else**
8:     $left := x$
9:   **end if**
10: **end while**
11: **return** $right$

Algorithm 6 Expc(CDF)

1: $S := 0$
2: **for** $i := 1$ to NUM_TEST_SAMPLE **do**
3:   $S := S + \mathcal{L}(\text{GetH}(\text{CDF}))$
4: **end for**
5: **return** $S/$NUM_TEST_SAMPLE

Algorithm 7 Main(α, T, q)

1: (aCDF, hCDF) := Preparation(α, T)
2: $\Delta_0 := (\text{Expc}(\text{hCDF}) - \text{Expc}(\text{aCDF}))$
3: finality   :=
   FindMinGap(q, aCDF, hCDF)$/\Delta_0$

4: **return** finality

Table 3. Experiments on few establishments of the potential function

Potential Function	Figure	$\Lambda_{0.1}$	$\Lambda_{0.2}$	$\Lambda_{0.3}$	$\Lambda_{0.4}$	Communication Complexity
$\mathcal{L}(h) = \frac{\pi}{2} - \arctan\frac{h-D}{2D}$		1.68	4.13	11.01	48.66	$O(N \log N)$
$\mathcal{L}(h) = \min\{\frac{M}{h}, \frac{M}{D}\}$		2.00	4.67	11.60	49.37	$O(N \log N)$
$\mathcal{L}(h) = 2\sqrt{D} - \text{sgn}(h-D) \cdot \sqrt{|h-D|}$		2.25	5.21	13.66	54.81	$O(N \log N)$
$\mathcal{L}(h) = \begin{cases} 2, & h \le D \\ 1, & D < h \le 2D \\ 0, & h > 2D \end{cases}$		2.63	6.09	14.83	66.17	$O(N)$
$\mathcal{L}(h) = \begin{cases} 1, & h \le D \\ 0, & h > D \end{cases}$		4.02	9.22	24.91	97.67	$O(N)$
$\mathcal{L}(h) = \begin{cases} 2, & h \le \frac{D}{2} \\ 1, & \frac{D}{2} < h \le D \\ 0, & h > D \end{cases}$		4.89	11.60	26.02	103.18	$O(N)$

References

1. Abraham, I., Malkhi, D., Nayak, K., Ren, L., Spiegelman, A.: Solidus: an incentive-compatible cryptocurrency based on permissionless byzantine consensus. arXiv CoRR abs/1612.02916 (2016)
2. Andrychowicz, M., Dziembowski, S.: PoW-based distributed cryptography with no trusted setup. In: Gennaro, R., Robshaw, M. (eds.) CRYPTO 2015. LNCS, vol. 9216, pp. 379–399. Springer, Heidelberg (2015). https://doi.org/10.1007/978-3-662-48000-7_19
3. Andrychowicz, M., Dziembowski, S., Malinowski, D., Mazurek, L.: Secure multi-party computations on bitcoin. In: 2014 IEEE Symposium on Security and Privacy, SP 2014, Berkeley, CA, USA, 18–21 May 2014, pp. 443–458 (2014)
4. Bentov, I., Gabizon, A., Zuckerman, D.: Bitcoin beacon. arXiv CoRR abs/1605.04559 (2016)
5. Bentov, I., Kumaresan, R.: How to use bitcoin to design fair protocols. In: Garay, J.A., Gennaro, R. (eds.) CRYPTO 2014. LNCS, vol. 8617, pp. 421–439. Springer, Heidelberg (2014). https://doi.org/10.1007/978-3-662-44381-1_24
6. Bissias, G., Levine, B.N.: Bobtail: a proof-of-work target that minimizes blockchain mining variance (draft). arXiv CoRR abs/1709.08750 (2017)
7. Boyen, X., Carr, C., Haines, T.: Blockchain-free cryptocurrencies: a framework for truly decentralised fast transactions. Cryptology ePrint Archive, Report 2016/871 (2016)
8. Bünz, B., Goldfeder, S., Bonneau, J.: Proofs-of-delay and randomness beacons in ethereum. In: IEEE Security & Privacy on the Blockchain (IEEE S&B) (2017)
9. Chow, S.S.M., Lai, Z., Liu, C., Lo, E., Zhao, Y.: Sharding blockchain (invited paper). In: The First IEEE International Workshop on Blockchain for the Internet of Things (BIoT) (2018, To appear)
10. David, B., Gaži, P., Kiayias, A., Russell, A.: Ouroboros praos: an adaptively-secure, semi-synchronous proof-of-stake blockchain. In: Nielsen, J.B., Rijmen, V. (eds.) EUROCRYPT 2018. LNCS, vol. 10821, pp. 66–98. Springer, Cham (2018). https://doi.org/10.1007/978-3-319-78375-8_3
11. Dwork, C., Naor, M.: Pricing via processing or combatting junk mail. In: Brickell, E.F. (ed.) CRYPTO 1992. LNCS, vol. 740, pp. 139–147. Springer, Heidelberg (1993). https://doi.org/10.1007/3-540-48071-4_10
12. Eyal, I., Gencer, A.E., Sirer, E.G., van Renesse, R.: Bitcoin-NG: a scalable blockchain protocol. In: 13th USENIX Symposium on Networked Systems Design and Implementation, NSDI 2016, Santa Clara, CA, USA, 16–18 March 2016, pp. 45–59 (2016)
13. Garay, J., Kiayias, A., Leonardos, N.: The bitcoin backbone protocol: analysis and applications. In: Oswald, E., Fischlin, M. (eds.) EUROCRYPT 2015. LNCS, vol. 9057, pp. 281–310. Springer, Heidelberg (2015). https://doi.org/10.1007/978-3-662-46803-6_10
14. Gervais, A., Karame, G.O., Wüst, K., Glykantzis, V., Ritzdorf, H., Capkun, S.: On the security and performance of proof of work blockchains. In: Proceedings of the 2016 ACM SIGSAC Conference on Computer and Communications Security, Vienna, Austria, 24–28 October 2016, pp. 3–16 (2016)
15. Gilad, Y., Hemo, R., Micali, S., Vlachos, G., Zeldovich, N.: Algorand: scaling byzantine agreements for cryptocurrencies. In: Proceedings of the 26th Symposium on Operating Systems Principles, Shanghai, China, 28–31 October 2017, pp. 51–68 (2017)

16. Jakobsson, M., Juels, A.: Proofs of work and bread pudding protocols. In: Secure Information Networks: Communications and Multimedia Security, IFIP TC6/TC11 Joint Working Conference on Communications and Multimedia Security (CMS 1999), 20–21 September 1999, Leuven, Belgium, pp. 258–272 (1999)
17. Kumaresan, R., Bentov, I.: Amortizing secure computation with penalties. In: Proceedings of the 2016 ACM SIGSAC Conference on Computer and Communications Security, Vienna, Austria, 24–28 October 2016, pp. 418–429 (2016)
18. Liu, Z., Tang, S., Chow, S.S.M., Liu, Z., Long, Y.: Fork-free hybrid consensus with flexible proof-of-activity. Future Gener. Comp. Syst. **96**, 515–524 (2019)
19. Meng, W., et al.: Position paper on blockchain technology: smart contract and applications. In: Au, M.H., et al. (eds.) NSS 2018. LNCS, vol. 11058, pp. 474–483. Springer, Cham (2018). https://doi.org/10.1007/978-3-030-02744-5_35
20. Nakamoto, S.: Bitcoin: a peer-to-peer electronic cash system (2008). www.bitcoin.org
21. Pass, R., Shi, E.: Fruitchains: a fair blockchain. In: Proceedings of the ACM Symposium on Principles of Distributed Computing, PODC 2017, Washington, DC, USA, 25–27 July 2017, pp. 315–324 (2017)
22. Pass, R., Shi, E.: Hybrid consensus: efficient consensus in the permissionless model. In: 31st International Symposium on Distributed Computing, DISC 2017, Vienna, Austria, 16–20 October 2017, pp. 39:1–39:16 (2017)
23. Pass, R., Shi, E.: Rethinking large-scale consensus. In: 30th IEEE Computer Security Foundations Symposium, CSF 2017, Santa Barbara, CA, USA, 21–25 August 2017, pp. 115–129 (2017)
24. Poon, J., Dryja, T.: The bitcoin lightning network: scalable off-chain instant payments (2016). https://lightning.network/lightning-network-paper.pdf
25. Sompolinsky, Y., Lewenberg, Y., Zohar, A.: Spectre: a fast and scalable cryptocurrency protocol. Cryptology ePrint Archive, Report 2016/1159 (2016)
26. Vukolic, M.: The quest for scalable blockchain fabric: Proof-of-work vs. BFT replication. In: Open Problems in Network Security - IFIP WG 11.4 International Workshop, iNetSec 2015, Zurich, Switzerland, 29 October 2015, pp. 112–125 (2015). Revised Selected Papers

A Flexible Instant Payment System Based on Blockchain

Lin Zhong[1,2], Huili Wang[3,4](✉), Jan Xie[5], Bo Qin[6], Joseph K. Liu[7], and Qianhong Wu[1,8](✉)

[1] School of Cyber Science and Technology, Beihang University, Beijing, China
{zhonglin,qianhong.wu}@buaa.edu.cn
[2] State Key Laboratory of Cryptology, P. O. Box 5159, Beijing 100878, China
[3] State Key Laboratory of Integrated Services Networks, Xidian University,
Xi'an 710071, China
[4] China Electronics Standardization Institute, Beijing 100100, China
wanghuili@cesi.cn
[5] Crytape Research, Cryptape Co., Ltd, Hangzhou 31000, China
jan@cryptape.com
[6] School of Information, Renmin University of China, Beijing 100872, China
bo.qin@ruc.edu.cn
[7] Faculty of Information Technology, Monash University,
Clayton, VIC 3800, Australia
joseph.liu@monash.edu
[8] Science and Technology on Information Assurance Laboratory,
Beijing 100000, China

Abstract. Improving the throughput of blockchain systems such as Bitcoin and Ethereum has been an important research problem. Off-chain payments are one of the most promising technologies to tackle this challenge. Once a payment channel, however, is established there exists a strict one-one correspondence between a payee and prepayments, which reduces the flexibility of off-chain payments. In this paper, we propose a flexible instant payment system (FIPS) based on blockchain to improve the flexibility of off-chain payments. In the FIPS system, there exists a depositor who locks enough amounts of tokens on the chain, and supervises payers to make off-chain payments. Therefore, payers can pay to multiple payees off-chain without double-spending. Even the depositor colludes with the payer, and performs double-spending attacks, payees will not suffer any losses as they can withdraw their tokens from the locked tokens of the depositor. Besides, payers can allocate flexibly the prepayments off-chain, and all transactions are settled off-chain. We present a formal generic construction for the FIPS system, prove its security strictly, analyze its related properties, and compare with related schemes in detail. Analyses show that our scheme is flexible and practical.

Keywords: Cryptocurrency · Blockchain · Off-chain payment · Flexibility · Double-spending

© Springer Nature Switzerland AG 2019
J. Jang-Jaccard and F. Guo (Eds.): ACISP 2019, LNCS 11547, pp. 289–306, 2019.
https://doi.org/10.1007/978-3-030-21548-4_16

1   Introduction

Bitcoin [1] and Ethereum [2] have become increasingly popular as fully decentralized cryptographic networks, which are widely adopted today as alternative monetary payment systems. These cryptocurrencies have a genius innovation, i.e., its consensus mechanism that allows each transaction to be recorded in the so-called blockchain (or ledger), which is a database maintained by a set of mutually distrusted peers around the world. Microtransaction [3] is one of the most interesting applications for blockchain systems, such as fair sharing of WiFi connection. However, the consensus mechanism of blockchain caused serious scaling issues, e.g., the throughput of the bitcoin blockchain is only 7 transactions per second as on every 10 min only a 1 MB blocks are added to the system, whereas the Visa payment networks can support peaks of up to 47,000 transactions per second [4]. Therefore, it impedes the emerge of many novel business models that need a high throughput. Fortunately, there are two solutions to solve these problems, which describe as follows.

One is to introduce new fast consensus mechanisms such as Byzantine agreement protocols. However, alternative consensus mechanisms typically introduce different trust assumptions [5–8], which completely change the consensus mechanisms, and incompatible with the current systems. In other words, it needs to construct a whole new system. On the other hand, a prominent tool for improving the scalability of blockchains is a second layer payment channel [9–12], which is compatible with most of the existing blockchain systems.

Payment channels can only be used for payment applications, which can be generalized as state channels [13]. State channels radically break through the limits of payment channels, and bring scalability benefits to other smart contract applications as well, such as auctions and online games [9]. In order to cater to a growing number of users and payments for state channels, many challenges must be overcome. Several contributions intend to enhance the performance characteristic of state channels. Especially some related payment schemes, e.g., credit networks [14,15] that a fully-fledged payment channel network must offer a solution to several issues, such as liquidity [16,17], network formation [18], routing scalability [19,20], concurrency [11], and privacy [11,21–23] among others.

As described above, until now there has not been any satisfactory schemes to improve the flexibility of off-chain state channels. The main contribution of this work is to address this shortcoming by providing the construction for building a flexible off-chain state channel with a formal definition and security analysis. Our construction (i) allows the payers to pay to multiple payees off-chain and offline without double-spending, and (ii) permits the payers to allocate flexibly the prepayments off-chain.

In summary, we make the following contributions:

– We propose a new FIPS system to improve the flexibility of off-chain payments of blockchain systems. The key method of our approach is to add a depositor who locks enough amounts of tokens on the chain, and supervises payers to make off-chain payments. As a result, payers can pay to multiple payees off-chain and offline without double-spending.

- We construct the FIPS system in a modular way by using a digital signature scheme. We prove that if the underlying blockchain system, smart contract, and digital signature all are secure, then the FIPS system is secure. Analyses show that the FIPS system has the properties of flexibility, high security, instant payment, scalability, and high efficiency.

Organization. The remainder of this paper is organized as follows. Section 2 discusses related work. Section 3 presents an overview of the system model. Section 4 gives assumptions, adversary models, and design goals of the system. Section 5 presents a formal generic construction. Section 7 analyzes the related properties, and compares with related schemes. Section 8 concludes the paper.

2   Related Work

Duplex Micropayment Channels [24]. Decker and Wattenhofer proposed the first duplex off-chain payment channel networks between payment service providers (PSPs), which are the equivalent autonomous systems on the Internet. Relying on the timelock functionality of modern Bitcoin transactions, the PSPs can route transactions between any two participants, possibly over multiple hops, guarantee end-to-end security, enable real-time transactions.

Lightning Network [25]. Similar to the duplex micropayment channels, the Lightning Network, which is the most prominent proposal for a payment channel network in Bitcoin, allows to perform off-chain payments between Bitcoin participants. The Lightning Network relies on a punishment mechanism to guarantee the behavior of users instead of timelocks. Other payment channel networks such as Thunder [26] and Eclair [27] for Bitcoin are being proposed as slight modifications of the Lightning Network. Flare [28] and SpeedyMurmurs [12] are two routing algorithms for these transaction networks.

Raiden Network [29]. The Raiden Network is an off-chain scaling solution on the Ethereum blockchain using smart contracts for performing transactions. It supports secure transactions between participants without the need for global consensus, which is achieved using digital signature and hash-locked mechanism, called balance proofs, fully collateralized by previously setup on-chain deposits. Besides, it supports the creation of custom exchangeable tokens, as the Raiden Network enables off-chain transactions with any kinds of tokens that follow the standard token API [2].

Teechain [10]. Teechain is a layer-two payment network that only requires asynchronous blockchain access by leveraging trusted platform module, which is a trusted execution environment in modern CPUs. However, it only focuses on a single payment channel and their extensions to support payment channel networks remain an open problem.

Sprites [13]. Sprites designed for Ethereum are a variant of payment channels that aim to reduce the worst-case collateral costs of indirect off-chain payments. It supports partial deposits and withdrawals, during which the channel can continue to operate without interruption. At the same time, Gervais et al. [30]

proposed the *Revive* protocol for allowing an arbitrary set of users in payment channel networks to securely rebalance their channels, according to the preferences of the channel owners.

Malavolta et al. [11] studied on concurrency and privacy in payment channel networks, and presented a formal definition in the universal composability framework as well as practical and provably secure solutions. Dziembowski et al. [31] further reduces latency and costs in complex channel networks by using the technology of channel virtualization. It further reduces latency and costs in complex channel networks by using the technology of channel virtualization.

In all above schemes, however, there exists a strict one-one correspondence between a payee and prepayments, which reduces the flexibility of off-chain payments. Therefore, we propose the FIPS system, which allows the payers to pay to multiple payees off-chain without double-spending, and permits the payers to allocate flexibly the prepayments off-chain.

3   Overview

In this section, we first present the FIPS system model, which includes an informal description and a formal definition. Then, we give its adversary models and design goals.

3.1   System Model

Generally, as shown in Fig. 1, the FIPS system consists of four types of participants including *nodes (or miners)*, a *depositor*, a *payer*, and multiple *payees*. The key characteristic of the FIPS system is that it adds a deposit procedure in the blockchain systems. In the FIPS system, the depositor locks enough amounts of tokens on the blockchain. Then he can act as a supervisor to supervise the payer for each transaction. He must guarantee that the payer does not double-spend in off-chain payments. If the payer double-spends, then payees can withdraw tokens from the locked tokens of the depositor.

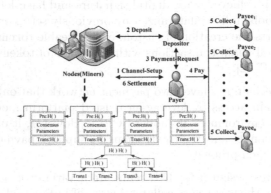

Fig. 1. The FIPS system model

   Payers can build a new channel, and lock some amounts of tokens, which he will pay to multiple payees off-chain. But before performing a transaction, the payer has to make a payment request to the depositor. The payment request contains the address of the payee and the amount of tokens. If the payer does not pay more than the prepayments, then the depositor will agree with the transaction. Payees can verify the validity of the locked tokens and payments, and accept if valid. There is no need to worry about double-spending attacks of the payer, as payees can also withdraw tokens from the locked tokens of the depositor. Finally, nodes (or miners) construct blocks, which contain valid locked transactions and settlement transactions, and add to the blockchain. After finishing all settlements, the locked tokens will be unlocked. It is reasonable that the depositor will charge a few transaction fees for each transaction.

   Formally, the FIPS system consists of six procedures, denoted as **Channel-Setup, Deposit, Payment-Request, Pay, Collect, Settlement**. The functionality of each procedure is as follows:

- **Channel-Setup.** This protocol is run between the payer and nodes.
  The payer takes as input his private key sk_0, an prepayment M, his account address ID_0, n payees $ID_1, ..., ID_n$, and some auxiliary information aux_0, returns a channel-setup signature σ_0

$$\sigma_0 \leftarrow \text{Channel}(sk_0, channel).$$

  Let $channel = (M, ID_0, ID_1, ..., ID_n, aux_0)$. The auxiliary information aux_0 includes the account address ID_D of a depositor, timestamps, etc.
  Nodes (or miners) of the system verify the validity of the channel-setup signature, and accept if valid

$$Valid/Invalid \leftarrow \text{ChannelVerify}(pk_0, channel, \sigma_0).$$

- **Deposit.** This protocol is run between the depositor and nodes.
  The depositor takes as input his private key sk_D, enough amounts of prelocked tokens $\tilde{M}$, his account ID_D, and some auxiliary information aux_D, returns a locked signature σ_1

$$\sigma_1 \leftarrow \text{Deposit}(sk_D, lock).$$

  Let $lock = (\tilde{M}, ID_D, aux_D)$. The auxiliary information aux_D includes the channel-setup signature of the payer, timestamps, etc. Note that $\tilde{M} \geq M * n$ must be satisfied.
  Nodes (or miners) of the system verify the validity of the locked signature, and accept if valid

$$Valid/Invalid \leftarrow \text{DepositVerify}(pk_D, lock, \sigma_1).$$

- **Payment-Request.** This protocol is run between the payer and depositor.
  The payer takes as input his private key sk_0, some tokens m, his account address ID_0, the account address of a payee ID_i, timestamps T, returns a payment-request signature $\sigma_{2,i}$. Let $pay_i = (m, ID_0, ID_i, T)$.

$$\sigma_{2,i} \leftarrow \text{Request}(sk_0, pay_i).$$

The depositor verifies the validity of the payment-request signature

$$Valid/Invalid \leftarrow \text{RequestVerify}(pk_0, pay_i, \sigma_{2,i}),$$

and returns a permission signature $\sigma_{3,i}$ if valid

$$\sigma_{3,i} \leftarrow \text{Permission}(sk_D, pay_i).$$

The payer verifies the validity of the permission signature $\sigma_{3,i}$

$$Valid/Invalid \leftarrow \text{PermissionVerify}(pk_D, pay_i, \sigma_{3,i}).$$

If valid, then accept, else reject.
- **Pay.** This procedure is run by payers.
  The payer takes as input his private key sk_0 and the permission signature $(pay_i, \sigma_{3,i})$, output a payment signature

$$\sigma_{4,i} \leftarrow \text{Pay}(sk_0, pay_i, \sigma_{3,i}).$$

He sends the permission signature $\sigma_{3,i}$ and the payment signature $\sigma_{4,i}$ to the payee ID_i.
- **Collect.** This procedure is run by payees.
  The payee ID_i verifies the validity of the permission signature $\sigma_{3,i}$ and the payment signature $\sigma_{4,i}$

$$Valid/Invalid \leftarrow \text{PermissionVerify}(pk_D, pay_i, \sigma_{3,i}),$$
$$Valid/Invalid \leftarrow \text{PayVerify}(pk_0, pay_i, \sigma_{3,i}, \sigma_{4,i}).$$

If all valid, $m \leq M$ and $\tilde{M} \geq M * n$ hold, then accept, else reject.
- **Settlement.** This protocol is run between the depositor and the payee.
  If the payee wants to settle accounts, then he and the depositor sign a final balance, which means that all of them accept the settlement

$$\sigma_{5,i} \leftarrow \text{Settlement}(sk_D, sk_i, balance_i).$$

Let $balance_i = (pay_i, \sigma_{3,i}, \sigma_{4,i}, pk_D, pk_0)$. The final balance must be impartial, else the depositor will suffer financial loss as the payees can withdraw deposits from the locked tokens. Besides, it is reasonable that the depositor will charge a few transaction fees for each transaction. Finally, the locked tokens will be unlocked after finishing all settlements.
As the depositor knows exactly the paying ability of the payer, he can sponsor a settlement on his own if the payer has spent all, and most of the payees have finished their settlements.

$$\sigma'_{5,i,...,n} \leftarrow \text{Settlement}(sk_D, balance_i, ..., balance_n).$$

But this unilateral settlement needs some time negotiated previously before it goes into effect.

4 Assumptions, Adversary Models, and Goals

In this section, we give the assumptions, adversary models, and goals of the FIPS system.

4.1 Assumptions

- The blockchain is secure. As the FIPS system is based on the blockchain system, we assume that the underlying blockchain system is secure in spite of its consensus mechanism, e.g., Proof of Work (PoW) [1], Proof of Stake (PoS) [32], Delegated Proof of Stake (DPoS) [33].
- The smart contract is secure. The FIPS system brings two kinds of special transactions, i.e., token lock/unlock transactions and channel setup/abolish transactions, to the blockchain system. Besides, the account bill should be settled off-chain. Therefore, it should be better to use smart contracts to achieve these transactions.
- The digital signature is secure. Locking/Unlocking tokens, building/abolishing channels, and taking transactions need to perform digital signature algorithms. Thus, the digital signature that the FIPS system used need to have a high security.

4.2 Adversary Models

As the FIPS system introduces new roles and interactive protocols to the blockchain system, it may suffer from active attacks and passive attacks. Active attacks, especially the double-spending attack, are key attacks in blockchain systems. It is the key problem, which needs to be resolved in the FIPS system.
Active attacks:

- **Channel double-building attacks.** An adversary builds two channels by using the same amounts of the prepayments. In other words, he wants to pay the same amounts of tokens to two different kinds of payees. Therefore, he can achieve double-spending in subsequent transactions.
- **Token double-locking attacks.** An adversary locks the same tokens into two different channels. In other words, the adversary locks the tokens twice. Thus, he can collude with the payer to double-spend without losing anything. Besides, the depositor can also lock some amounts of tokens, which are less than the product of prepayment times the amounts of payees. Therefore, if the depositor colludes with the payer, then the double-spending attacks will render payees to suffer financial loss.
- **Double-spending attacks.** After building a payment channel, the payer can pay to multiple payees. But the sum of all transactions is greater than his prepayments. In other extreme cases, the payer as an adversary colludes with the depositor, and performs transactions such that the product of prepayment times the amounts of payees is greater than the amounts of locked tokens.

- **Malicious settlement attacks.** In the settlement stage, the payer or the depositor or the payee is not online maliciously to postpone settlements. In other words, malicious participants want to decrease the efficiency of the settlement. Besides, they can also wind up an account with a wrong balance, such that some of the honest participants will suffer losses. For instance, the payer, the depositor, and part of payees collude with each other to achieve double-spending and malicious settlement, such that the malicious payees can withdraw all locked tokens.

Passive attacks: Passive attacks, e.g., eavesdropping attacks and traffic analysis, are also confronted by the FIPS system. For instance, adversaries can monitor the communication between the payer and the depositor. Besides, they can also analyze the traffic data between the payer and the payees. However, there exist no complicated Diffie-Hellman key exchange protocols in the FIPS system, which makes the FIPS system can be able to resist man-in-the-middle attacks. Besides, pseudonyms used in the FIPS system, make the adversaries can only count some pseudonymous transactions, which are almost useless. Therefore, passive attacks are not important problems that the FIPS system should concern.

4.3 Design Goals

The FIPS system is to achieve the following properties: flexibility, security, instant payment, scalability, and high efficiency.

- **Flexibility** is the most significant characteristic of the FIPS system, as in existing off-chain payment systems, there exists a strict one-one correspondence between a payee and prepayments, which reduces the flexibility of off-chain payments. Therefore, off-chain payments that pay to multiple payees are a very important means to improve the liquidity of tokens.
- **Security** is a basic requirement of the FIPS system, as blockchain systems are vulnerable to attacks such as double-spending, eavesdropping, and traffic analysis. The FIPS system should be able to defend against the adversary models described above.
- **Instant payment** is one of the key goals of the FIPS system, as current blockchain systems suffer from relatively low throughput. On the other hand, exist off-chain payments need either a costly on-chain settlement or a complicated off-chain routing algorithm, such as the Lightning Network. However, A shorter payment route is an advantage for any off-chain payment, as it can improve transaction speeds, and reduce costs.
- **Scalability** is an additional goal that the FIPS system should possess. Current blockchain systems such as Ethereum have run a few years, which means they have a high security and practicability. The FIPS system should deploy on these systems, and inherit their security and practicability. Therefore, the FIPS system should have a good scalability.
- **High efficiency** is the last but not least goal of the FIPS system, as the FIPS system should be used by mobile users, which have relatively low computational capabilities. Besides, mobile users also cannot use complicated routing

algorithms to find online intermediate users to achieve off-chain transactions. Therefore, the FIPS system should have a high efficiency.

5   Generic Construction

In this section, we demonstrate a formal generic construction.

Formally, in generic construction, we employ a digital signature $(Sign, Verify)$ to construct the FIPS system. The generic construction of the FIPS scheme **Channel-Setup, Deposit, Payment-Request, Pay, Collect, Settlement** is as follows:

Channel-Setup. The procedure **Channel-Setup** performs as follows:

i. A payer performs the signature algorithm $Sign$, takes as input his private key sk_0, an prepayment M, his account address ID_0, n payees $ID_1, ..., ID_n$, and some auxiliary information aux_0, returns a channel-setup signature σ_0

$$\sigma_0 \leftarrow Sign(sk_0, channel),$$

where $channel = (M, ID_0, ID_1, ..., ID_n, aux_0)$. The auxiliary information aux_0 includes the account address ID_D of a depositor, timestamps, etc. He broadcasts the channel-setup signature, which will be received and verified by nodes who maintain the system.

ii. Nodes perform the verification algorithm $Verify$, takes as input the channel-setup signature $(channel, \sigma_0)$ as well as the corresponding public key pk_0, and returns a judgment

$$Valid/Invalid \leftarrow Verify(pk_0, channel, \sigma_0).$$

If valid, then add it to the blockchain, else reject.

Deposit. The procedure **Deposit** performs as follows:

i. A depositor performs the signature algorithm $Sign$, takes as input his private key sk_D, enough amounts of prelocked tokens $\tilde{M}$, his account ID_D, and some auxiliary information aux_D, returns a locked signature

$$\sigma_1 \leftarrow Sign(sk_D, lock),$$

where $lock = (\tilde{M}, ID_D, aux_D)$. The auxiliary information aux_D includes the channel-setup signature of the payer, timestamps, etc. Note that $\tilde{M} \geq M * n$. He broadcasts the locked signature, which will be received and verified by nodes.

ii. Nodes perform the verification algorithm $Verify$, takes as input the locked signature $(lock, \sigma_1)$ as well as the corresponding public key pk_D, and returns a judgment

$$Valid/Invalid \leftarrow Verify(pk_D, lock, \sigma_1).$$

If valid, then add it to the blockchain, else reject.

Payment-Request. The procedure **Payment-Request** performs as follows:

i. The payer performs the signature algorithm $Sign$, takes as input his private key sk_0, some tokens m_i, his account address ID_0, the account address of a payee ID_i, timestamps T, returns a payment-request signature $\sigma_{2,i}$

$$\sigma_{2,i} \leftarrow Sign(sk_0, pay_i),$$

where $pay_i = (m_i, ID_0, ID_i, T)$. He sends the payment-request signature to the depositor.

ii. The depositor performs the verification algorithm $Verify$, takes as input the payment-request signature $(pay_i, \sigma_{2,i})$ as well as the corresponding public key pk_0, and outputs a judgment

$$Valid/Invalid \leftarrow Verify(pk_0, pay_i, \sigma_{2,i}).$$

If output valid, then performs the signature algorithm $Sign$, takes as input his private key sk_D, the content of a payment pay_i, returns a permission signature $\sigma_{3,i}$

$$\sigma_{3,i} \leftarrow Sign(sk_D, pay_i,).$$

iii. The payer performs the verification algorithm $Verify$, takes as input the permission signature $(pay_i, \sigma_{3,i})$ as well as the corresponding public key pk_D, and outputs a judgment

$$Valid/Invalid \leftarrow Verify(pk_D, pay_i, \sigma_{3,i}).$$

If valid, then accept, else reject.

Pay. The procedure **Pay** performs as follows:

i. The payer performs the signature algorithm $Sign$, takes as input his private key sk_0 and the permission signature $(pay_i, \sigma_{3,i})$, output a payment signature

$$\sigma_{4,i} \leftarrow Sign(sk_0, pay_i, \sigma_{3,i}).$$

He sends the permission signature $\sigma_{3,i}$ and the payment signature $\sigma_{4,i}$ to the payee ID_i.

Collect. The procedure **Collect** performs as follows:

i. The payee performs the verification algorithm $Verify$, takes as input the permission signature $\sigma_{3,i}$ and the payment signature $\sigma_{4,i}$ as well as the corresponding public keys pk_D, pk_0, and outputs a judgment

$$Valid/Invalid \leftarrow Verify(pk_D, pay_i, \sigma_{3,i}),$$
$$Valid/Invalid \leftarrow Verify(pk_0, pay_i, \sigma_{3,i}, \sigma_{4,i}).$$

If all valid, $\tilde{M} \geq M * n$ and $M \geq m_i * n$ hold, then accept, else reject.

Settlement. The procedure **Settlement** performs as follows:

i. After receiving the settlement request from a payee ID_i, the depositor performs the signature algorithm $Sign$, takes as input his private key sk_D, a balance $balance_i$ for payee ID_i, returns a settlement signature $\sigma_{5,i}$

$$\sigma_{5,i} \leftarrow Sign(sk_D, balance_i).$$

Let $balance_i = (ID_0, ID_i, pay_i, \sigma_{3,i}, \sigma_{4,i}, pk_D, pk_0)$. The balance includes the permission signature and the payment signature. He sends the settlement signature to the payee ID_i.

ii. The payee ID_i performs the verification algorithm $Verify$, takes as input the settlement signature $(balance_i, \sigma_{5,i}, pk_D)$, and outputs a judgment

$$Valid/Invalid \leftarrow Verify(pk_D, balance_i, \sigma_{5,i}).$$

If valid, then he performs the signature algorithm $Sign$, takes as input his private key sk_i, the settlement signature $(balance_i, \sigma_{5,i})$, returns a signature $\sigma_{6,i}$

$$\sigma_{6,i} \leftarrow Sign(sk_i, balance_i, \sigma_{5,i}),$$

and broadcasts $(balance_i, \sigma_{5,i}, \sigma_{6,i}, pk_i)$.

iii. Nodes verify these four signatures, i.e., the permission signature $\sigma_{3,i}$, the payment signature $\sigma_{4,i}$, the settlement signature of the depositor $\sigma_{5,i}$, and the settlement signature of the payee $\sigma_{6,i}$. And add them to the blockchain if all valid, $\tilde{M} \geq M * n$ and $M \geq m_i * n$ hold, else reject. And the locked tokens will be unlocked after finishing all settlements.

iv. If the payer has spent all, and most of the payees have finished their settlements, then the depositor can sponsor a settlement on his own. But this unilateral settlement needs some time negotiated previously before it goes into effect. The depositor performs the signature algorithm $Sign$, takes as input his private key sk_D, the balances $balance_i, ..., balance_n$ for payees $ID_i, ..., ID_n$, returns a settlement signature $\sigma'_{5,i,...,n}$

$$\sigma'_{5,i,...,n} \leftarrow Sign(sk_D, balance_i, ..., balance_n).$$

Let $balance_i = (ID_0, ID_i, pay_i, \sigma_{3,i}, \sigma_{4,i}, pk_D, pk_0)$. The permission signature $\sigma_{3,i}$, the payment signature $\sigma_{4,i}$, and the settlement signature $\sigma'_{5,i,...,n}$ will be verified by nodes.

Theorem 1. *The above generic construction of the FIPS system is secure, provided that (1) the underlying blockchain and smart contracts are secure, (2) the procedures, i.e., **Channel-Setup**, **Deposit**, **Payment-Request**, **Pay**, **Collect**, and **Settlement**, all are secure.*

6   Formal Security Analysis

Proof of Theorem 1. The **Channel-Setup** and **Deposit** procedures in smart contracts are two transactions of the underlying blockchains. As the blockchain has the property of strong consistency, the attack that an adversary wants to build two different channels by using the same amount of token or locks the same amount of token for different payment channels cannot be achieved. These kinds of behaviors will be rejected by the underlying blockchain. Therefore, the channel double-building attack and token double-locking attack will be defended against by the blockchain. In other words, if the **Channel-Setup** and **Deposit** procedures are not secure, then we can build an adversary to break the consistency of the blockchain, or break the smart contract. Therefore, the **Channel-Setup** and **Deposit** procedures are secure.

Before each transaction going into effect, it needs the permission signature of the depositor in the first place, and the payment signature of the payer in the second place, which is a new signing way. We use the following *payment model* to formalize its security. The functionality of the *payment model* is equivalent to the **Payment-Request**, **Pay**, and **Collect** procedures. The *payment model* assumes that there exists an adversary who wants to double spend. This is equivalent to the adversary running the **Payment-Request** and **Pay** procedures on his own. Assume that the adversary cannot get the private key from the depositor.

Formally, the *payment model* of the FIPS system is defined through a security game played between an adversary $\mathcal{A}$ and a challenger $\mathcal{C}$, both of which take as input a security parameter $\lambda \in N$.

Setup. The challenger $\mathcal{C}$ obtains a key pair $(SK_\mathcal{C}, PK_\mathcal{C})$, and sends the public key $PK_\mathcal{C}$ to the adversary $\mathcal{A}$.

Query. The adversary $\mathcal{A}$ adaptively queries the permission signature to the challenger $\mathcal{C}$. More specifically, the adversary $\mathcal{A}$ generates adaptively q transactions

$$\sigma_j \leftarrow Sign(SK_\mathcal{A}, pay_j),$$
$$pay_j = (m_j, ID_\mathcal{A}, ID_\mathcal{C}, T), 1 \leq j \leq q.$$

The adversary $\mathcal{A}$ sends $(pay_j, \sigma_j), 1 \leq j \leq q$ to the challenger $\mathcal{C}$. Without loss of generality, the adversary $\mathcal{A}$ would not query the same payment-request signature twice.

Challenge. The challenger $\mathcal{C}$ generates a permission signature for each submitted payment-request signature by executing the signature algorithm

$$\delta_j \leftarrow Sign(SK_\mathcal{C}, pay_j), 1 \leq j \leq q.$$

The challenger $\mathcal{C}$ gives to the adversary $\mathcal{A}$ each permission signature pair $(pay_j, \delta_j), 1 \leq j \leq q$.

Output. The adversary $\mathcal{A}$ generates a payment signature for each permission signature by executing the signature algorithm

$$\Upsilon_j \leftarrow Sign(SK_\mathcal{A}, pay_j, \delta_j), 1 \leq j \leq q.$$

The adversary $\mathcal{A}$ outputs a payment signature $(pay^*, \delta^*, \Upsilon^*)$ and wins the game if $pay^* \notin \{pay_j\}, 1 \leq j \leq q$, and

$$Valid = Verify(PK_C, pay^*, \delta^*),$$
$$Valid = Verify(PK_A, pay^*, \delta^*, \Upsilon^*).$$

We define $Adv_{\mathcal{A}}(\lambda)$ to be the probability that the adversary $\mathcal{A}$ wins in the above game, taken over the coin tosses made by $\mathcal{A}$ and the challenger $\mathcal{C}$. We say that the FIPS system satisfies *payment* security provided that $Adv_{\mathcal{A}}(\lambda)$ is negligible.

Lemma 1. *The payment model, i.e., the **Payment-Request, Pay,** and **Collect** procedures, is secure, provided that the digital signature algorithm satisfies unforgeability.*

Proof. Suppose that there exists a polynomial-time adversary $\mathcal{A}$ that can break the *payment model*. We construct a simulator $\mathcal{S}$ to break the unforgeability of the digital signature with a non-negligible probability with the help of the algorithm $\mathcal{A}$. The simulator $\mathcal{S}$ acts as the adversary for the original challenger, and as the challenger for the *payment model*. The simulation is run as follows.

Setup. After receiving the public key PK_C from the original challenger, the simulator $\mathcal{S}$ gives to the adversary $\mathcal{A}$.

Query. After receiving the payment-request signature $(pay_j, \sigma_j), 1 \leq j \leq q$ from the adversary $\mathcal{A}$, the simulator $\mathcal{S}$ performs the verification algorithm $Verify$, inputs the payment-request signature $(pay_j, \sigma_j), 1 \leq j \leq q$ as well as the corresponding public key PK_A, outputs a judgment $Valid/Invalid$

$$Valid/Invalid \leftarrow Verify(PK_A, pay_j, \sigma_j), 1 \leq j \leq q.$$

If valid, then send $(pay_j, \sigma_j), 1 \leq j \leq q$ to the original challenger, else reject.

Challenge. After receiving the permission signatures $(pay_j, \delta_j), 1 \leq j \leq q$ from the original challenger, the simulator $\mathcal{S}$ performs the verification algorithm $Verify$, inputs the permission signatures $(pay_j, \delta_j), 1 \leq j \leq q$ as well as the corresponding public key PK_C, outputs a judgment $Valid/Invalid$

$$Valid/Invalid \leftarrow Verify(PK_C, pay_j, \delta_j), 1 \leq j \leq q.$$

If valid, then send the permission signatures $(pay_j, \delta_j), 1 \leq j \leq q$ to the adversary $\mathcal{A}$, else reject.

Output. The adversary $\mathcal{A}$ outputs a payment permission signature $(pay^*, \delta^*, \Upsilon^*)$ and wins the game if $pay^* \notin \{pay_j\}, 1 \leq j \leq q$, and

$$Valid = Verify(PK_C, pay^*, \delta^*),$$
$$Valid = Verify(PK_A, pay^*, \delta^*, \Upsilon^*).$$

The simulator $\mathcal{S}$ also returns the pair $(pay^*, \delta^*, \Upsilon^*)$ as its own signature to the original challenger.

Therefore, if the adversary $\mathcal{A}$ can break the *payment model* to achieve double spend with a non-negligible advantage, then the simulator $\mathcal{S}$ can break the unforgeability of the digital signature with non-negligible probability. However, the digital signature defined in Sect. 4 satisfies unforgeability. Therefore, double-spending attacks cannot be achieved in the *payment model*. In other words, the **Payment-Request** and **Pay** procedures are secure. On the other hand, payees cannot forge signatures of both the payer and depositor to steal tokens from the payer or from the depositor. They can only verify correctly the validity of each payment signature. Therefore, the **Collect** procedure is secure. This completes the proof of Lemma 1.   ∎

In the **settlement** stage, the depositor and the payee are restraint mutually and mutually beneficial. For one thing, the payee cannot be able to forge signatures of the payer and the depositor to steal tokens from the payer or from the depositor. The depositor is restricted by the payee as the payee can use double-spending transactions to withdraw his locked tokens. For another, the payee needs help from the depositor to withdraw his tokens from the payment channel. But the depositor can only unlock his locked tokens, and get his transaction fees after all payees finishing their settlements. Thus, if they do not collaborate and win together, then all of them will suffer failure.

Furthermore, malicious collusion settlements, i.e., the settlement amount is greater than the prepayments, and the product of prepayment times the amounts of payees is greater than the amounts of locked tokens, will be defended against by the underlying blockchain system.

Finally, in order to defend against the attacks that malicious payees are not online maliciously to postpone settlements. The FIPS system permits that the depositor can sponsor a settlement on his own if the payer has spent all, and most of the payees have finished their settlements. But this unilateral settlement needs some time negotiated previously before it goes into effect. Therefore, malicious settlement attacks can be defended against, and only perform transactions honestly can they reap. Therefore, the **settlement** procedure is secure.

To sum up, the security of the **Channel-Setup** and **Deposit** procedures can be reduced to the security of the underlying blockchain and smart contracts. The security of the **Payment-Request**, **Pay**, **Collect**, and **Settlement** procedures can be reduced to the unforgeability of the digital signature. Thus, the FIPS system is secure if (1) the underlying blockchain and smart contracts are secure, (2) the procedures, **Channel-Setup**, **Deposit**, **Payment-Request**, **Pay**, **Collect**, and **Settlement**, all are secure. This completes the proof of Theorem 1.   ∎

7   Analysis and Comparision

In this section, we first analyze the properties of the FIPS system, including flexibility, security, instant payment, scalability, and efficiency. Then, we compare it with the related schemes.

- **Flexibility.** The prepayments locked in the off-chain channel can be paid to one of the n payees without double-spending attacks, which improves the flexibility of the FIPS system, as users need not have to decide in advance whom they will pay to, and how much they will spend, before building a channel. Besides, the payer can separate their payees into the subway, supermarket, online shopping, restaurant, hotel, and so on. The payer can lock these common public accounts in a payment channel. When it needs to take a transaction, the payer can pay to one of these public accounts, and then the public account pays to the specific address specified by the payer. Thus, completing a transaction usually requires only one-hop. Therefore, the FIPS has a high flexibility.
- **Security.** We demonstrate that the security of the FIPS system can be reduced to the security of the underlying blockchain, smart contracts, and digital signatures. Therefore, the FIPS system has a high security.
- **Instant payment.** After establishing payment channels users in the FIPS system can perform instant transactions flexibly. Besides, users need not have to use a complicated routing algorithm to find the shortest transaction route, as each payer has n payees such that completing a transaction usually requires only one-hop. As the FIPS system needs only one-hop to complete a transaction such that it has a faster payment speed comparing with existing off-chain payment systems which often need multiple hops to complete a transaction.
- **Scalability.** The FIPS system is characterized by high scalability. Firstly, if the depositor is a centralized trusted third party, then the FIPS system is a centralized digital currency system. Secondly, the FIPS system can be compatible with the channel rebalancing algorithm [30] friendly. Besides, it is easier to find reviving cycles in the FIPS system than the other off-chain systems, e.g., the Lightning Network and the Raiden Network. Finally, in the Payment-Request stage, two signatures that the payer sends the payment-request signature to the depositor, and the depositor sends permission signature to the payer, can be transmitted in an encrypted manner or in a secure channel. Besides, it can also use homomorphic encryption schemes or Pedersen commitments to hide the amounts for each transaction. Therefore, the FIPS system can also be compatible with privacy protection systems.
- **Efficiency.** Most of the common receivers such as subway, supermarket, online shopping, restaurant, hotel, and so on, can be locked in only one transaction when building an off-chain channel, as the FIPS system can lock n payees. Thus, it reduces the need for payment channels, and saves storage resources of the blockchain. Besides, as a payer has multiple payees such that an off-chain payment network usually only needs one-hop to complete a transaction, which reduces the complexity of the off-chain payment networks. Finally, the settlement is happening off-chain, which saves resources of the blockchain further, and has a faster settlement rate comparing with the existing off-chain payment systems.

In Table 1, we compare the FIPS scheme with the Raiden Network. The comparison can be classified in the following four aspects, i.e., the amount of payees, allotment of tokens, hops, and method of settlement. In the Raiden Network, a payer can only be able to lock only one payee in a payment channel while in the FIPS system a payer can lock n payees in a payment channel. Besides, before building a payment channel, the amounts of prepayments that paid to a payee have to be preallocated in the Raiden Network. However, in the FIPS system, the prepayments can be allocated allodially off-chain after building a payment channel. Thus, the FIPS system is more flexible than the Raiden Network.

Table 1. Comparison with the Raiden Network

	Amount-of-payees	Allotment-of-tokens	Hops	Settlement
Raiden	One	On-chain	Multiple	On-chain
FIPS	Multiple	Off-chain	One	Off-chain

The Raiden Network often needs multiple hops to achieve a transaction, which is relatively complicated, low-speed, and high-cost. However, the FIPS system only needs one-hop to complete a transaction, which is simpler, high-speed, and low-cost. Therefore, the FIPS system is more efficient than the Raiden Network.

Besides, in the settlement stage, the Raiden Network needs to settle on-chain while the FIPS system can be settled off-chain, which saves the storage resources of the blockchain, and leads to a rapid settlement. Furthermore, the FIPS system supports single payee settlement without double-spending attacks, as the locked token mechanism will prevent malicious behaviors of the payer and the depositor. But, the only complicated part of the FIPS system is that it adds a new role, i.e., the depositor, to the payment channel systems.

Finally, if we deploy the FIPS scheme on Bitcoin-like blockchain systems, then the underlying blockchain needs to add a lock (or lock) mechanism for depositors and payers. Therefore, it needs to make some changes in the underlying blockchain. However, if we deploy it on Ethereum-like blockchain systems, then it needs not to make any change, as the lock mechanism can be implemented in smart contracts. Besides, signatures used in the underlying blockchain systems are also suitable for the FIPS scheme, as it does not require any special property.

8   Conclusion

We presented a FIPS scheme to improve the flexibility of off-chain payment of blockchains. We proposed a generic construction for the FIPS system based on the digital signature. We manifested that the FIPS system is secure provided that the underlying blockchain, smart contract, and digital signature all are secure. In other words, if the basic tools, i.e., the blockchain, smart contracts, and the digital signature, are secure, then the FIPS system can defend against channel double-building attacks, token double-locking attacks, double-spending attacks, and malicious settlement attacks. Then, we analyzed its properties, and compared it with the related schemes. Analyses show that the FIPS system has the properties of flexibility, high security, instant payment, scalability, and high efficiency. Finally, comparison results demonstrate that the FIPS system is more flexible and efficient than the Raiden Network system.

Acknowledgements. This paper is supported by the National Key R&D Program of China through project 2017YFB0802500, by the National Cryptography Development Fund through project MMJJ20170106, by the foundation of Science and Technology on Information Assurance Laboratory through project 61421120305162112006, the Natural Science Foundation of China through projects 61772538, 61672083, 61532021, 61472429, 91646203 and 61402029. This paper is also partially funded by Cryptape.

References

1. Nakamoto, S.: Bitcoin: a peer-to-peer electronic cash system[/OL] (2008). http://digitalasc.com/download/blockchain_whitepaper.pdf
2. Wood, G.: Ethereum: a secure decentralised generalised transaction ledger. Ethereum Proj. Yellow Pap. **151**, 1–32 (2014)
3. Pass, R., et al.: Micropayments for decentralized currencies. In: Proceedings of the 22nd ACM SIGSAC Conference on Computer and Communications Security, pp. 207–218 (2015)
4. Trillo, M.: Stress test prepares VisaNet for the most wonderful time of the year[/OL] (2013). https://www.visa.com/blogarchives/us/2013/10/10/stress-test-prepares-visanet-for-the-most-wonderful-time-of-the-year/index.html
5. Luu L., Narayanan V., Baweja K, et al.: SCP: a computationally-scalable byzantine consensus protocol for blockchains, p. 1168 (2015)
6. Kogias, E.K., Jovanovic, P., Gailly, N., et al.: Enhancing bitcoin security and performance with strong consistency via collective signing. In: 25th USENIX Security Symposium (USENIX Security 16), pp. 279–296 (2016)
7. Eyal, I., Gencer, A.E., Sirer, E.G., et al.: Bitcoin-NG: a scalable blockchain protocol. In: NSDI, pp. 45–59 (2016)
8. Pass, R., Shi, E.: Hybrid consensus: efficient consensus in the permissionless model. In: LIPIcs-Leibniz International Proceedings in Informatics, vol. 91 (2017)
9. Bentov, I., Kumaresan, R., Miller, A.: Instantaneous decentralized poker. In: Takagi, T., Peyrin, T. (eds.) ASIACRYPT 2017. LNCS, vol. 10625, pp. 410–440. Springer, Cham (2017). https://doi.org/10.1007/978-3-319-70697-9_15
10. Lind, J., Eyal, I., Kelbert, F., et al.: Teechain: scalable blockchain payments using trusted execution environments. arXiv preprint arXiv:1707.05454 (2017)
11. Malavolta, G., Moreno-Sanchez, P., Kate, A., et al.: Concurrency and privacy with payment-channel networks. In: Proceedings of the 2017 ACM SIGSAC Conference on Computer and Communications Security, pp. 455–471 (2017)
12. Roos, S., Moreno-Sanchez, P., Kate, A., et al.: Settling payments fast and private: efficient decentralized routing for path-based transactions. arXiv preprint arXiv:1709.05748 (2017)
13. Miller, A., Bentov, I., Kumaresan, R., et al.: Sprites: payment channels that go faster than lightning. CoRR abs/1702.05812 (2017)

14. Anon: Ripple protocol[/OL]. https://ripple.com/
15. Anon: Stellar protocol[/OL]. https://www.stellar.org/
16. Dandekar, P., Goel, A., Govindan, R., et al.: Liquidity in credit networks: a little trust goes a long way. In: Proceedings of the 12th ACM Conference on Electronic Commerce, pp. 147–156 (2011)
17. Moreno-Sanchez, P., Modi, N., Songhela, R., et al.: Mind your credit: assessing the health of the ripple credit network. arXiv preprint arXiv:1706.02358 (2017)
18. Dandekar, P., Goel, A., Wellman, M.P., et al.: Strategic formation of credit networks. ACM Trans. Internet Technol. (TOIT) **15**(1), 3 (2015)
19. Post, A., Shah, V., Mislove, A.: Bazaar: strengthening user reputations in online marketplaces. In: Proceedings of NSDI 2011: 8th USENIX Symposium on Networked Systems Design and Implementation, p. 183 (2011)
20. Viswanath, B., Mondal, M., Gummadi, K.P., et al.: Canal: scaling social network-based sybil tolerance schemes. In: Proceedings of the 7th ACM European Conference on Computer Systems, pp. 309–322 (2012)
21. Moreno-Sanchez, P., Kate, A., Maffei, M., et al.: Privacy preserving payments in credit networks. In: Network and Distributed Security Symposium (2015)
22. Moreno-Sanchez, P., Zafar, M.B., Kate, A.: Listening to whispers of ripple: linking wallets and deanonymizing transactions in the ripple network. Proc. Priv. Enhancing Technol. **2016**(4), 436–453 (2016)
23. Sun, S.-F., Au, M.H., Liu, J.K., Yuen, T.H.: RingCT 2.0: a compact accumulator-based (linkable ring signature) protocol for blockchain cryptocurrency monero. In: Foley, S.N., Gollmann, D., Snekkenes, E. (eds.) ESORICS 2017. LNCS, vol. 10493, pp. 456–474. Springer, Cham (2017). https://doi.org/10.1007/978-3-319-66399-9_25
24. Decker, C., Wattenhofer, R.: A fast and scalable payment network with bitcoin duplex micropayment channels. In: Symposium on Self-Stabilizing Systems, pp. 3–18 (2015)
25. Poon, J., Dryja, T.: The bitcoin lightning network: scalable off-chain instant payments[/OL] (2016). https://lightning.network/lightning-network-paper.pdf
26. Anon: Thunder network[/OL]. https://github.com/blockchain/thunder
27. Anon: Eclair implementationof the lightning network[/OL]. https://github.com/ACINQ/eclair
28. Prihodko, P., Zhigulin, S., Sahno, M., et al.: Flare: an approach to routing in lightning network[/OL] (2016). https://bitfury.com/content/downloads/whitepaper_flare_an_approach_to_routing_in_lightning_network_7_7_2016.pdf
29. Anon: Raiden network[/OL]. https://raiden.network/
30. Khalil, R., Gervais, A.: Revive: rebalancing off-blockchain payment networks. In: Proceedings of the 2017 ACM SIGSAC Conference on Computer and Communications Security, pp. 439–453 (2017)
31. Dziembowski, S., Faust, S., Hostáková, K.: General state channel networks. In: Proceedings of the 2018 ACM SIGSAC Conference on Computer and Communications Security, pp. 949–966 (2018)
32. David, B., Gaži, P., Kiayias, A., Russell, A.: Ouroboros praos: an adaptively-secure, semi-synchronous proof-of-stake blockchain. In: Nielsen, J.B., Rijmen, V. (eds.) EUROCRYPT 2018. LNCS, vol. 10821, pp. 66–98. Springer, Cham (2018). https://doi.org/10.1007/978-3-319-78375-8_3
33. Larimer, D.: Delegated proof-of-stake (DPoS). Bitshare whitepaper (2014)

Risk of Asynchronous Protocol Update: Attacks to Monero Protocols

Dimaz Ankaa Wijaya[1(✉)], Joseph K. Liu[1], Ron Steinfeld[1], and Dongxi Liu[2]

[1] Monash University, Melbourne, Australia
{dimaz.wijaya,joseph.liu,ron.steinfeld}@monash.edu
[2] Data61, CSIRO, Sydney, Australia
dongxi.liu@data61.csiro.au

Abstract. In a cryptocurrency system, the protocol incorporated in the node application runs without human intervention. Cryptographic techniques are implemented to determine the ownership of the coins; they enable the owners to transfer the ownership of the coins to other users. Consensus protocols are employed to determine the source of the truth of the information contained in the public ledger called blockchain. When the protocol needs to be updated, all nodes need to replace the application with the newest release. We explore an event where an asynchronous protocol update opens a vulnerability in Monero nodes which have not yet updated to the newest software version. We show that a Denial of Service attack can be launched against the nodes running the outdated protocol, where the attack significantly reduces the system' performance. We also show that an attacker, given a sufficient access to cryptocurrency services, is able to utilise the Denial of Service attack to launch a traceability attack.

Keywords: Monero · Transaction pool · Traceability · Denial of Service

1 Introduction

One of the main ideas of applying a permissionless blockchain in cryptocurrencies is to remove the role of a central authority to control and run the whole system [16]. To replace the need for a central controller, a set of protocol is used an run by software systems without any human intervention [16]. Blockchain was first implemented in Bitcoin. The first block of Bitcoin, called genesis block, was created on 3 January 2009. Since then, the popularity of Bitcoin and other cryptocurrencies created after Bitcoin have increased significantly.

Monero is one of the most successful cryptocurrencies based on its market cap, with a total value of US$720 million[1]. It was developed based on CryptoNote protocol created by Nicolas van Saberhagen (pseudonym) [18]. Monero focuses on preserving the privacy of the transaction data such that the real sender is

---

[1] Based on Coinmarketcap.com as of 4 February 2019.

© Springer Nature Switzerland AG 2019
J. Jang-Jaccard and F. Guo (Eds.): ACISP 2019, LNCS 11547, pp. 307–321, 2019.
https://doi.org/10.1007/978-3-030-21548-4_17

indistinguishable over a set of senders (*untraceability*) and the transactions cannot be linked even if they are sent to the same receiver (*unlinkability*) [18]. The untraceability and unlinkability features are achieved by applying Linkable Ring Signature [11,12,17] and one-time public key [18].

There are usually two main applications in a cryptocurrency system, namely node application (node) and wallet application (wallet). Monero node stores and maintains the Monero blockchain. A Monero node is connected to other nodes through a peer-to-peer network. Monero node also stores unconfirmed transactions in its temporary database called transaction pool (txpool) located in the node's RAM. Monero's (txpool) is identical to memory pool (mempool) in other cryptocurrencies such as Bitcoin [1]. The unconfirmed transactions are stored in the txpool for at most three days, or (86400*3) seconds as defined in DEFAULT_TXPOOL_MAX_WEIGHT parameter in src/cryptonote_config.h [9].

Monero wallet is the application on the client side. It is used to help the client manage her private keys, track the Monero balance, detect incoming transactions, and create outgoing transactions to spend Monero. Monero wallet is a thin client; it does not store any information about the blockchain. Therefore, for any operations on the Monero wallet which require blockchain information, the Monero wallet will create a network connection to a Monero node.

Monero Classic emerged as the result of Monero hard fork in April 2018. While the Monero main chain upgraded to Monero protocol version seven, Monero Classic runs on Monero protocol version six. On 16 October 2018, Monero Classic announced a protocol upgrade [4]. The upgrade was intended to add more features in Monero Classic system [4]. Furthermore, at the same time Monero Classic increased the minimum ring size from five to eight. The change in minimum ring size impacted the protocol as it caused a **protocol reduction** [23], but due to its circumstances, no hard fork occurred after the event. Protocol reduction is a type of protocol change where the new protocol reduces the rules of the old protocol. Protocol reduction is usually followed up by a hard fork if both protocols are supported by miners with equal computing power.

In this paper, we propose attacks to the transaction pool of Monero nodes running an old protocol after a protocol reduction event. The transaction pool size can be inflated by launching a Denial of Service to the nodes which greatly reduces the quality of service of the attacked nodes. We also expose that the attack to the transaction pool might be utilised to reveal the users' traceability by double-spending the same coins in two different protocols.

2   Background

2.1   Monero Hard Fork

Unlike other cryptocurrencies, which always try to avoid hard fork, Monero has a scheduled semi-annual hard forks to improve the system. Prior to 2018, there were already five hard forks in Monero for the purpose of protocol upgrades [14]. The sixth protocol upgrade which occurred on 6 April 2018 split the Monero blockchain into two branches; the first branch ran Monero version six (the old protocol) and the second branch ran Monero version seven (the new protocol). While the latter branch became the main Monero branch, the other branch running Monero protocol version six were renamed into different names: Monero Original[2], Monero Classic[3], and Monero0[4] [13]. Although none of these brands is less popular compared to the Monero main branch, Monero Classic (XMC) and Monero Original (XMO) were traded in several cryptocurrency exchanges[5]. The April 2018 Monero hard fork is shown in Fig. 1.

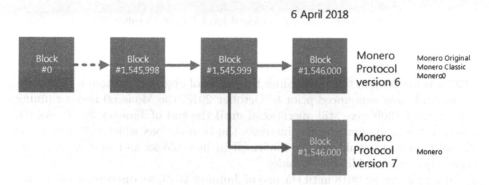

6 April 2018

Fig. 1. Monero hard fork in April 2018.

2.2 Monero Classic Protocol Upgrade

We define a Monero0 Protocol XMOP as the protocol which accepts transactions with a minimum ring size $r \geq 5$. The protocol XMOP is the same protocol as Monero Protocol version 6 before Monero Classic upgrade. We also define a Monero Classic Protocol XMCP as the new protocol which only accepts transactions with a minimum ring size $r \geq 8$. The protocol XMOP allows a new block b' from the protocol XMCP to be included in the blockchain C, but the new protocol XMCP does not allow a new block b the protocol XMOP to be in the blockchain C' such that $C \supset C'$ [23]. This occurs if the block b contains any transactions where $5 \leq r < 8$. Figure 2 shows how blocks created by using XMCP protocol is still compatible with XMOP and it shows that XMCP reduces the rules of XMOP.

Monero Classic claimed to acquire the majority of the miners, therefore the new protocol XMCP applies to the blockchain branch running Monero protocol

---

[2] https://monero-original.org.

[3] http://monero-classic.org.

[4] https://monero0.org.

[5] As of 12 February 2019, no cryptocurrency exchange trades XMO. However, the market price history provided by Coinmarketcap.com shows that XMO were traded until 1 February 2019. Based on Coinmarketcap.com, XMC is currently available in Gate.io, HitBTC, and TradeOgre.

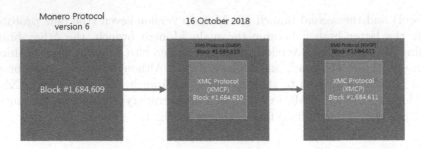

Fig. 2. Monero protocol version 6 hard fork in October 2018.

version six. The claim was confirmed by the fact that no transaction of protocol XMOP was included in the blocks since the protocol upgrade. Although the protocol upgrade was announced prior to October 2018, the Monero0 nodes running the protocol XMOP were still operational until the end of January 2019[6]. As the result of the minimum ring size increase, the transactions which had a ring size of less than eight could not be confirmed in new blocks and were kept in the transaction pool of Monero0's nodes.

From November 2018 until the end of January 2019, we discovered 115 transactions that contain 337 inputs and 1,865 ring members that were created by using a minimum ring size $5 \leq r < 8$ in Monero0's temporary storage. As the result of the incompatibility between Monero0's protocol XMOP and Monero Classic's protocol XMCP, these transactions were not found on Monero Classic node's temporary storage. Also, as there was no miner running the protocol XMOP, the 115 transactions were never included in the blocks and the blockchain hard fork did not happen. We also discovered that identical inputs were found on different transactions which contain different sets of mixins or decoys and a different ring size. From this occurrence, we discovered five traceable inputs.

2.3 Denial of Service Attack in Cryptocurrency

In cryptocurrency space, Denial of Service (DoS) attack is one of the challenges for cryptocurrencies [2]. DoS attacks target several services, such as cryptocurrency exchanges, mining pools, gambling services, financial services, wallet services, etc [19]. Not only attacking services, DoS attacks can also be launched on the cryptocurrency to disrupt the system, e.g. by creating a large number of transactions, each contains dust coins [1,3].

A DoS attack scenario to target Monero's txpool has been discussed in [5,6]. In the proposed scenario, the author described that transactions with the size of 360 kB could be created by modifying monero-wallet-rpc source codes [5,6]. These transactions were set to have a low priority but enough to be relayed.

---

[6] According to Monero0.org, the Monero0 nodes are: 159.65.227.38, 167.99.96.174, 159.65.113.142. Based on our investigation, all of these nodes were no longer accessible as of early February 2019.

However, due to median block size growth protocol, the author stated that the transactions could never be confirmed in the blocks, hence, it would be on Monero node's `txpool` for a maximum allowed time [5,6].

The problem was reported to Monero developers as a potential vulnerability, where the developers then responded the problem by providing an optional setting to limit the maximum `txpool` size[7]. However, when we further investigated the matter, we could not find the related codes in the newest Monero software. In this vulnerability report, the author did not provide further information on how the attack was done, what modification was conducted, nor whether the attack was successful.

3   Related Work

3.1   Cryptocurrency Protocol Change Classification

Zamyatin et al. [23] classified four types of protocol changes from the old protocol P associated with a blockchain C to the new protocol P' associated with a blockchain C'. These changes are: **protocol expansion**, **protocol reduction**, **protocol confliction**, and **conditional protocol reduction** [23]. The protocol expansion occurs if the new protocol P' increases the previous protocol P's scope such that the set of blocks V' of the new protocol P' expands the set of blocks V of the previous protocol P. On the other hand, a protocol reduction occurs if the new protocol P' reduces the previous protocol P's scope by adding more rules. Protocol confliction occurs if the new protocol P' is incompatible with the previous protocol P, while the conditional protocol reduction (velvet) is a protocol reduction on specific elements of the protocol, where no changes is supposedly to happen in the created blocks of both protocols P and P'.

3.2   Zero Mixin Transaction and Cascade Effect Analyses

The original CryptoNote protocol [18] describes that a ring signature can only be constructed by a set of outputs where all members of the output set contain the same amount of coins. However, the protocol does not further explain the method in a practical scenario such that there are many outputs that contain unique amount of coins. These outputs could not be paired with other outputs, and therefore the ring signature can only have one key in the set. These problems lead to zero mixin transaction problem, where the traceability of the inputs can be disclosed as well as the outputs that were spent in the transactions [10,15].

Cascade effect analysis expands the traceability analysis by exploiting the zero mixin transaction. In the cascade effect analysis, the spent output information were used to deduct the traceability of other inputs that does not have zero mixin issue. The combination of both analyses can trace 87% of all inputs in Monero [10]. However, this problem has been mitigated by enforcing a minimum

---

[7] https://github.com/monero-project/monero/pull/3205.

ring size $r \geq 2$. This protocol change was also strengthened by the implementation of **Ring Confidential Transaction (RingCT)**, where the amount of coins in every output is hidden. Additionally, the ring signature creation can be made easier, because a user can choose mixins/decoys from a larger pool of outputs.

3.3   Monero Traceability Attack

Monero Ring Attack (MRA) is a technique where an attacker create malicious transactions [20]. The malicious transactions are constructed such that all outputs in the attack are proven to be spent. In this case, whenever the attacker's outputs are used as mixins or decoys by other transactions, then the transactions will suffer anonymity reduction, or in a worst case scenario reveal its traceability.

This type of attack can be launched in a brute-force scenario by creating as many transactions as possible or in a targeted attack where the attacker controls online services such as cryptocurrency exchange or online wallets. Furthermore, an attacker can collaborate with other attackers without the need of trust to each other. Each attacker accumulates all malicious transactions created by other attackers whenever they find them in the public blockchain. An extension of this attack called **Monero Ring Attack Extended (MRAE)** was proposed such that the attack cannot be easily identified by other users by involving a large number of outputs and construct combinations of outputs [21]. An algorithm has been developed to search the occurrence on Monero blockchain, where 5,752 transactions are traceable [22].

3.4   Key Reuse Attack in Monero

The Monero fork which occurred on 6 April 2018 has created a new attack vector called key reuse [7]. A new traceability analysis called cross-chain analysis was developed and found that 5.22% of the transaction inputs created between 1 April 2018 and 31 August 2018 are traceable [8]. Although the result of the attack is insignificant compared to other attacks such as zero mixin attack, similar events in the future can occur, whenever certain conditions are met. The Monero developers have responded the issue by implementing **Shared Ringdb** feature in the default Monero wallets, including `monero-wallet-cli` and `monero-wallet-rpc`.

4   Threat Model

It is assumed that there exist two nodes, $Node_A$ and $Node_B$, running two different protocols, P and P'. The protocol P' is an upgrade from P, where the upgrade is a protocol reduction as described in [23]. It is also assumed that all miners have already updated their protocol from P and P' and connect to $Node_B$.

We propose the threat model as follows. An attacker owns sufficient funds and has the ability to create valid transactions under P but invalid under P'. The attacker launches Denial of Service attacks by creating a set of transactions T as many as possible such that the transactions T remain in the $Node_A$'s txpool. The attacker has access to two wallets: $Wallet_A$ and $Wallet_B$. $Wallet_A$ is connected to $Node_A$ and $Wallet_B$ is connected to $Node_B$. The attack is successful if the resource usage of $Node_A$ increases significantly compared to the $Node_B$ as the control.

It is also assumed that the attacker has a control over a cryptocurrency-related service such as a coin exchange. In this scenario, the attacker creates a set of transactions T' from the same coins that have been spent in T to be double-spent in T'. The purpose of this activity is to let any observers to conduct traceability analysis as described in [8] by comparing two sets of transactions T and T'.

5 Attacks to Monero Protocols

5.1 Overview

The attacks were developed based on the problem discovered in Sect. 2.2. In the attacks, the scale of the event is increased to creates a bigger damage to the node as well as to the anonymity of the transactions.

The attacks exploit the late update conducted by node maintainers when there is a change in the protocol where the software run by every node needs to be updated to the latest version. If the change is a protocol reduction, the old version of the protocol accepts new transactions. However, the new version of the protocol will not be able to confirm transactions that follow the old protocol. As the result, an old node keeps these incompatible transactions in the txpool for at least three days.

An attacker floods the txpool with incompatible transactions which will create a denial of service (DoS) to the nodes running the old protocol. The massive number of transaction creation and the large transaction storage requirement will reduce the performance of the nodes. Knowing that the transactions will not be confirmed in the blockchain, there will be no transaction fee to be paid by the attacker. However, the attacker needs to have sufficient funds in as many public keys as possible.

5.2 Attack Phases

The attack consists of three phases: preparation phase, Denial of Service (DoS) Attack phase, and traceability reveal attack phase. The last two phases can be done either separately or subsequently.

Preparation Phase. In the preparation phase, the attacker first prepares enough funds. Then, the funds will be sent to as many public keys (outputs) as possible by creating transactions to send the funds to the attacker's own address. The transactions need to be compatible with the new protocol; it will also be confirmed by the nodes running the old protocol.

Denial of Service Attack (DoS) Phase. In the attack phase, the attacker launches the attack against the old nodes. The attacker creates as many transactions as possible, where these transactions cannot be confirmed by the new protocol because it follows the old protocol which is not compatible with the new protocol. The transactions are likely to be discarded by the new nodes, but stored by the old nodes in the `txpool`. When the number of transactions is large, the `txpool` size will expand significantly and affect the system.

Traceability Reveal Attack Phase. If the attacker has a control over a cryptocurrency service, the attacker is able to create transactions to spend the same coins used in the DoS phase. Assuming that the transactions are created according to the business' best interest, the attacker would not need to worry about losing money for the transaction fees, as the fees will be paid by the customers.

5.3   Simulation

We simulated the protocol reduction event as described in Sect. 2.2 in a private testnet environment. The purpose of the simulation was to increase the scalability of the event such that the impact of a large scale event can be analysed. Instead of using Monero Classic and Monero0 nodes, we modified Monero *"Beryllium Bullet"* software[8]. The latest upgrade of Monero requires a mandatory bulletproofs feature for every transaction to be validated in the node to reduce the transaction size significantly. We also ran Monero blockchain explorers called `Onion Monero blockchain explorer` (`xmrblocks`)[9] to simplify the data extraction process from the nodes. The blockchain explorers were also used to monitor the size of the `txpools` of the nodes. The `xmrblocks` would only be run during data extraction process at the end of the simulation to reduce the extra workload that might affect the result.

Our simulations were executed on a `Ubuntu 18.04.1 LTS` virtual machine with 8 GB RAM and two processor cores. The virtual machine was hosted on a physical server equipped with two Intel® Xeon(R) CPU X5570@2.93GHz and 72 GB RAM. The virtual machine ran two `monerod` as the Monero nodes and two `xmrblocks` applications, each connected to a different node. A default RPC-based wallet, `monero-wallet-rpc`, was also used; it was connected to the target node. We wrote a Python script to automate the transaction creation with the help of Shoupn's `moneropy` library[10] to connect the script to `monero-wallet-rpc`.

Simulation Scenario. Two nodes, denoted as $Node_A$ and $Node_B$, were used to construct the Monero network where both nodes were synchronised with a

---

[8] The open source software is available in Monero's Github page https://github.com/monero-project/monero.

[9] https://github.com/moneroexamples/onion-monero-blockchain-explorer.

[10] https://github.com/shoupn/moneropy.

blockchain C. $Node_A$'s source code was modified such that the node could validate any transactions with a ring size $r \geq 7$, while $Node_B$'s protocol mimicked the latest Monero transaction requirement with the ring size $r = 11$. These two nodes imitated a situation of a **protocol reduction** from protocol P_A to protocol P_B, where the new protocol requires a higher ring size such that $r_A < r_B$

However, it is assumed that all miners have updated their software to follow the new protocol P_B. In this scenario, protocol P_A does not have enough mining power to compete with the new protocol P_B in creating blocks, however the node $Node_A$ still follows protocol P_A while the node $Node_B$ has updated to protocol P_B.

Simulation 1. The first simulation evaluated a key reuse attack which can potentially happen in the given scenario. Although a key reuse attack normally happens in two or more different blockchains, the given scenario can also create two "temporary" blockchains, where the `txpools` of the nodes pose as the temporary blockchains.

We created 9,353 transactions T_1 with the ring size $r = 8$, each contains 10 or 11 outputs (transactions who have 11 outputs contain one change address to send the change money back to the sender). There were a total of 18,688 inputs in transactions T_1 and the total size is 34.2 MB. The transaction fee required to create all transactions T_1 is 80.46XMR where the average transaction fee is 0.0086 per transaction. As a result, the transactions would be validated only by the $Node_A$ but not $Node_B$. The transactions T_1 were stored in $Node_A$'s `txpool`. However, none of the transactions T_1 were found in $Node_B$'s `txpool`. Figure 3 shows the linear relationship between `txpool` size and the number of transactions. Also, a similar linear relationship is found between transaction fee and the number of transactions.

A new set of transactions T_2 were created by using the protocol P_B from the same pool of coins. In this case, there is a possibility of sending the same coins in two different transactions t_1 and t_2 where $t_1 \in T_1$ and $t_2 \in T_2$ and $T_1 \neq T_2$, since none of the transactions in T_1 were confirmed in the blockchain. Transactions T_2 were accepted and confirmed by $Node_B$ as the miner and then $Node_A$ had the same information after synchronising with $Node_B$.

Simulation 2. In the second simulation, we flooded the $Node_A$ with transactions. We utilised a `monero-wallet-rpc` which was connected to $Node_A$ to programmatically created Monero transactions using a single thread. We ran the script simultaneously. We then evaluated the performance of $Node_A$. When the data was evaluated, there were 64,633 transactions in $Node_A$'s `txpool`.

6 Discussion

6.1 Shared Ringdb

During our first trial of **Simulation 1**, we were unable to recreate key reuse attack. All transactions T_2 which spent the same coins as T_1 were using the same

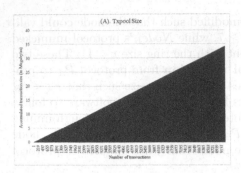 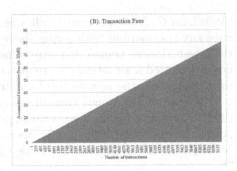

Fig. 3. Figure (A) shows the accumulated transaction size stored in `txpool`. Figure (B) shows the transaction fee paid by the attacker to create the transactions.

ring members as t_1 in addition to other outputs to satisfy the minimum ring size of the protocol P_2. We evaluated the occurrence and discovered that the newest version of Monero default desktop wallet took a preventive action by creating an additional database called `Shared Ringdb` located in $\sim$/.`shared-ringdb` folder. The wallet can detect the difference between two systems based on the protocols, where a transaction that tries to spend the coin that has been spent on another blockchain needs to maintain the anonymity set by using the identical ring members.

This result shows the effectiveness of `Shared Ringdb` for general users who run the Monero default desktop wallet and deserve a better anonymity in their cross-chain transactions. However, the feature might not be implemented on other wallets such as web wallet or smartphone wallet. An attacker can also simply remove the database since it is stored in the attacker's local storage.

6.2   Traceability Analysis

An input in Monero is traceable if an observer manages to guess the real spent output over a set of outputs in that input with the probability of **one**. Based on the specification given by the Linkable Ring Signature [12], each private key which can be used to create a ring signature is tagged with a unique value called **key image**. If a **key image** appears in two or more ring signatures, then it means that the same private key has been used to sign these signatures, and the associated public key must be a ring member of both ring signatures. Therefore, the public key has become traceable. This type of analysis has been discussed by Hinteregger et al. [8].

After the **Simulation 1** was completed, a traceability analysis was done by using the following algorithm.

1. For each input in $Node_A$'s `txpool`:
   (a) Identify the key image value.
   (b) Find the **key image** in the blockchain.

(c) If the `key image` is found in the blockchain, proceed to the next step. Otherwise, continue to the next input.
(d) Examine the related sets of outputs. If at most one identical output is found on multiple sets of outputs, then the input is traceable.
(e) Otherwise, the input is not traceable. However, the effective ring size (the term coined in [8]) is reduced to exactly the number of outputs found on both sets.
2. The result is the traceable inputs identified by the algorithm.

By using the above algorithm, we then evaluated the 9,353 transactions we created and managed to identify 95% of the transactions' inputs. The other 5% of the inputs suffer reduced effective ring size to a minimum of two. This shows the effectiveness of the method in revealing Monero transaction's traceability.

6.3   Denial of Service Analysis

We define a `Quality of Service` (QoS) of the cryptocurrency system (the node and the wallet) as the number of new transactions created by the wallet and received by the node. The QoS was measured to determine the impact of DoS attacks. We also measured the resource usage (CPU and RAM) of both $Node_A$ and $Node_B$.

$Node_A$'s Quality of Service Monitoring. Figure 4 shows the QoS of $Node_A$, measured by number of new transactions per hour. It shows that after the `txpool` of $Node_A$ exceeds 7,800 transactions, the QoS sharply declines from the peak, 3,000 transactions per hour (tph), to below 500 tph when there are at least 53,000 transactions in the node's `txpool` and the total size of these transactions is 190 MB. These 53,000 transactions requires 375.6XMR as the transaction fees. However, as these transactions will not be confirmed in the blockchain, the cost does not really incur.

Resource Usage Monitoring. We also ran a simple script to capture information from Ubuntu's `top` command every 60 s. Figure 6 shows the comparison of CPU usage (measured in percentage of usage compared to the system's CPU) between $Node_A$ and $Node_B$, where $Node_A$ was a target to the DoS attack and $Node_B$ was not. In this scenario, none of these nodes was mining new blocks. The result demonstrates an insignificant difference between both nodes in terms of CPU usage (Fig. 6).

Figure 7 shows the comparison of RAM usage between two nodes, where $Node_A$'s RAM utilisation was four times more than $Node_B$'s RAM utilisation. The highest RAM size used by $Node_A$ was near to 9% of the system's RAM, or roughly about 720 MB.

7   Limitation

In our experiment, we used one virtual machine to run multiple applications, such as node applications, wallets, blockchain explorers, and the monitoring script.

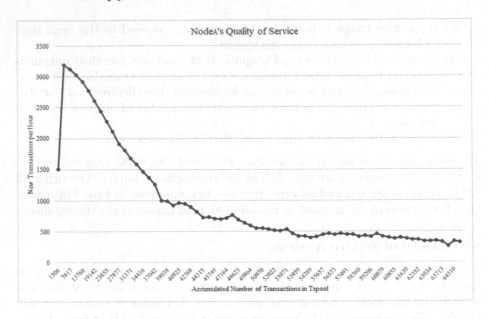

Fig. 4. The `Quality of Service` of $Node_A$ during the DoS attack.

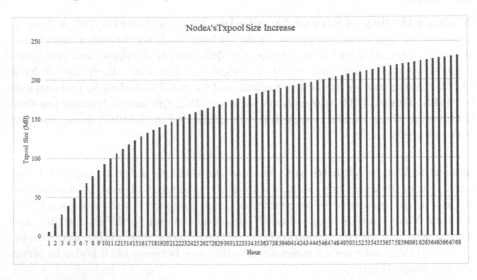

Fig. 5. The `txpool` size increase of $Node_A$ during the DoS attack.

This could have impacted the performance of the evaluated node. The results might differ if these applications are run on separate machines. Our experiments did not utilise the Monero version 6 source code (Monero Classic or Monero0), as we preferred to use the latest Monero applications. This may or may not impact the result, since the transaction size would be different compared to our result, including the fee structure.

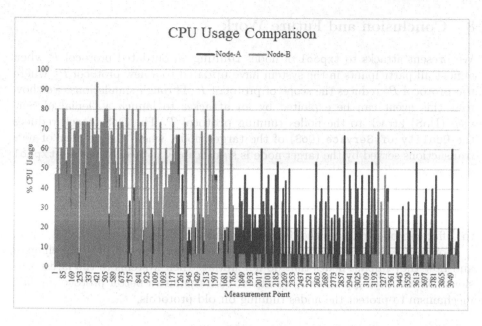

Fig. 6. The CPU usage comparison between $Node_A$ and $Node_B$.

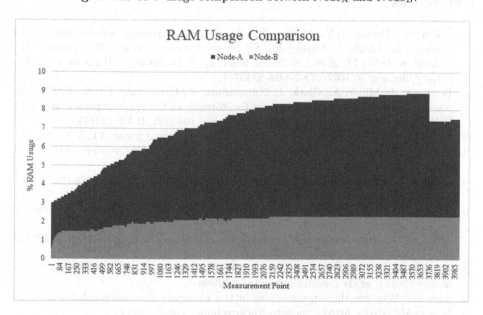

Fig. 7. The RAM usage comparison between $Node_A$ and $Node_B$.

8   Conclusion and Future Work

We present attacks to `txpool` of nodes running an outdated protocol P when almost all participants in the system have updated to a new protocol P', where the protocol P' reduces the scope of protocol P. Through simulations, we show that this event can be exploited by an attacker to launch a Denial of Service (DoS) attack to the nodes running protocol P. The DoS attack reduces the `Quality of Service` (QoS) of the target node, where the number of new transactions served by the target node is significantly reduced when the `txpool` increases.

The attack can be further expanded to reveal users' traceability if the attacker controls a cryptocurrency service such as coin exchanger. It is done by double-spending the coins, where two sets of transactions are created; each set is sent to different nodes running the protocol P and P'.

For future work, we plan to investigate the other types of protocol changes and how they impact nodes that do not update their systems to the latest versions. By identifying problems, we expect to formulate a better protocol update mechanism to protect the nodes running on old protocols.

References

1. Baqer, K., Huang, D.Y., McCoy, D., Weaver, N.: Stressing out: bitcoin "stress testing". In: Clark, J., Meiklejohn, S., Ryan, P.Y.A., Wallach, D., Brenner, M., Rohloff, K. (eds.) FC 2016. LNCS, vol. 9604, pp. 3–18. Springer, Heidelberg (2016). https://doi.org/10.1007/978-3-662-53357-4_1
2. Bonneau, J., Miller, A., Clark, J., Narayanan, A., Kroll, J.A., Felten, E.W.: Sok: research perspectives and challenges for bitcoin and cryptocurrencies. In: 2015 IEEE Symposium on Security and Privacy, pp. 104–121. IEEE (2015)
3. Bradbury, D.: The problem with bitcoin. Comput. Fraud Secur. **11**, 5–8 (2013)
4. Monero Classic. Upgrade announcement of xmc (2018). http://monero-classic.org/open/notice_en.html
5. cmaves. 0-conf possible attack using large transactions (2018). https://github.com/amiuhle/kasisto/issues/33
6. cmaves. Possible mempool spam attack (2018). https://github.com/monero-project/monero/issues/3189
7. dEBRYUNE. Pow change and key reuse (2018). https://ww.getmonero.org/2018/02/11/PoW-change-and-key-reuse.html
8. Hinteregger, A., Haslhofer, B.: An empirical analysis of monero cross-chain traceability (2018). arXiv preprint arXiv:1812.02808
9. jtgrassie. Why are there transactions in the mempool that are invalid or over 50 hours old? (2018). https://monero.stackexchange.com/a/8513
10. Kumar, A., Fischer, C., Tople, S., Saxena, P.: A traceability analysis of monero's blockchain. In: Foley, S.N., Gollmann, D., Snekkenes, E. (eds.) ESORICS 2017. LNCS, vol. 10493, pp. 153–173. Springer, Cham (2017). https://doi.org/10.1007/978-3-319-66399-9_9
11. Liu, J.K., Au, M.H., Susilo, W., Zhou, J.: Linkable ring signature with unconditional anonymity. IEEE Trans. Knowl. Data Eng. **26**(1), 157–165 (2014)

12. Liu, J.K., Wei, V.K., Wong, D.S.: Linkable spontaneous anonymous group signature for ad hoc groups. In: Wang, H., Pieprzyk, J., Varadharajan, V. (eds.) ACISP 2004. LNCS, vol. 3108, pp. 325–335. Springer, Heidelberg (2004). https://doi.org/10.1007/978-3-540-27800-9_28
13. Monero. Monero XMR forks & hard forks. https://monero.org/forks/. Accessed 4 February 2019
14. Monero. Monero project github page (2018). https://github.com/monero-project/monero. Accessed 4 February 2019
15. Möser, M., et al.: An empirical analysis of traceability in the monero blockchain. Proc. Priv. Enhancing Technol. **2018**(3), 143–163 (2018)
16. Nakamoto, S.: Bitcoin: a peer-to-peer electronic cash system (2008). http://bitcoin.org/bitcoin.pdf
17. Sun, S.-F., Au, M.H., Liu, J.K., Yuen, T.H.: RingCT 2.0: a compact accumulator-based (linkable ring signature) protocol for blockchain cryptocurrency monero. In: Foley, S.N., Gollmann, D., Snekkenes, E. (eds.) ESORICS 2017. LNCS, vol. 10493, pp. 456–474. Springer, Cham (2017). https://doi.org/10.1007/978-3-319-66399-9_25
18. Nicolas van Saberhagen. Cryptonote v 2.0 (2013) (2018). https://cryptonote.org/whitepaper.pdf
19. Vasek, M., Thornton, M., Moore, T.: Empirical analysis of denial-of-service attacks in the bitcoin ecosystem. In: Böhme, R., Brenner, M., Moore, T., Smith, M. (eds.) FC 2014. LNCS, vol. 8438, pp. 57–71. Springer, Heidelberg (2014). https://doi.org/10.1007/978-3-662-44774-1_5
20. Wijaya, D.A., Liu, J., Steinfeld, R., Liu, D.: Monero ring attack: recreating zero mixin transaction effect. In: 2018 17th IEEE International Conference On Trust, Security And Privacy In Computing And Communications/12th IEEE International Conference On Big Data Science And Engineering (TrustCom/BigDataSE), pp. 1196–1201. IEEE (2018)
21. Wijaya, D.A., Liu, J., Steinfeld, R., Liu, D., Yuen, T.H.: Anonymity reduction attacks to monero. In: Guo, F., Huang, X., Yung, M. (eds.) Inscrypt 2018. LNCS, vol. 11449, pp. 86–100. Springer, Cham (2019). https://doi.org/10.1007/978-3-030-14234-6_5
22. Yu, Z., Au, M.H., Yu, J., Yang, R., Xu, Q., Lau, W.F.: New empirical traceability analysis of cryptonote-style blockchains (2019)
23. Zamyatin, A., Stifter, N., Judmayer, A., Schindler, P., Weippl, E., Knottenbelt, W.J.: A wild velvet fork appears! inclusive blockchain protocol changes in practice. In: Zohar, A., Eyal, I., Teague, V., Clark, J., Bracciali, A., Pintore, F., Sala, M. (eds.) FC 2018. LNCS, vol. 10958, pp. 31–42. Springer, Heidelberg (2019). https://doi.org/10.1007/978-3-662-58820-8_3

A Combined Micro-block Chain Truncation Attack on Bitcoin-NG

Ziyu Wang[1,2], Jianwei Liu[1], Zongyang Zhang[1(✉)], Yanting Zhang[1,2],
Jiayuan Yin[1], Hui Yu[1], and Wenmao Liu[3]

[1] School of Cyber Science and Technology, Beihang University, Beijing, China
{wangziyu,liujianwei,zongyangzhang,
yantingzhang,yinjiayuan,yhsteven}@buaa.edu.cn
[2] Shenyuan Honors College, Beihang University, Beijing, China
[3] NSFOCUS Inc., Beijing, China
liuwenmao@nsfocus.com

Abstract. Bitcoin-NG, introduced by Eyal et al. in NSDI 2016, divides
a blockchain into key-blocks and micro-blocks to improve transaction
process efficiency. In this paper, we propose a novel attack on Bitcoin-
NG, called a micro-block chain truncation attack. Combined with key-
block selfish and stubborn mining, and an eclipse attack, this attack
is able to bring extra reward to attackers in Bitcoin-NG than in Bitcoin through a colluded strategy or a "destroyed if no stake" strategy. Our evaluation calculates the reward proportion of an attacker by
these attacks on both Bitcoin-NG and Bitcoin, which helps us figure
out whether Bitcoin-NG sacrifices security for efficiency promotion. We
also evaluate 18 strategy combinations by traversing different values of
computation power and practical truncation rate. In a setting with reasonable parameters, the optimal combined micro-block chain truncation
attack obtains at most 5.28% more reward proportion in Bitcoin-NG
than in Bitcoin.

Keywords: Blockchain security · Bitcoin-NG · Micro-block chain

1 Introduction

Since Bitcoin (BTC) is invented in 2008 [8], Bitcoin and other altcoins have been
faced with many research challenges and open questions.

Security. There are continuous concerns about various attacks on Bitcoin system
since its invention. These attacks are not only theoretically analyzed by academic
researchers, but also further launched in practice. Bitcoin could resist no more
than one half of computation power controlled by attackers as Nakamoto originally analyzed [8]. However, Eyal and Sirer reduce this security threshold to 0.25
by selfish mining (SM) [3]. This is a deviant strategy that an attacker tries to
spend more honest power on an abandoned block. The following work [9] ampli-
fies the reward of a selfish miner by advanced selfish mining strategies, which

© Springer Nature Switzerland AG 2019
J. Jang-Jaccard and F. Guo (Eds.): ACISP 2019, LNCS 11547, pp. 322–339, 2019.
https://doi.org/10.1007/978-3-030-21548-4_18

is named as stubborn mining (SBM). An attacker controlling part of network connections could eclipse a Bitcoin node. All information passing this node is blocked by this kind of attack, which is referred to as an eclipse attack (ECA) [4]. The selfish and stubborn mining strategies are combined with an eclipse attack in [9] by three eclipse strategies, i.e., destroyed strategy, colluded strategy and "destroyed if no stake" strategy.

Efficiency. Efficiency is another hot topic in Blockchain research. Bitcoin solves the Byzantine general problem by publishing all transaction details in blockchain. It encourages all nodes to recognize the longest chain as the valid chain. The Nakamoto consensus, also named as the proof of work (PoW) mechanism, depends on brute force searching for a preimage to avoid Sybil attacks. It has a relatively good scalability supporting ten thousands of nodes [10]. However, its efficiency is quite limited measured by the number of transaction per second (TPS). Bitcoin only provides at most 7 TPS in current parameters [1] (before activating Segwit). Bitcoin efficiency is less competitive compared to a centralized system, e.g., 256,000 TPS peak capacity of Alipay[1].

On-chain, off-chain and hybrid consensus are three main methods to improve blockchain efficiency. On-chain proposals usually directly increase the size limitation of each block, or reduce block interval to achieve higher throughput. However, a bigger block has longer propagation time. The more compact the block interval is, the more disagreements the system would have. These two consequences increase the risk of natural chain forking. Therefore, on-chain improvements are tradeoffs for security. Off-chain proposals mainly build another high speed *clearing* layer on top of an existing cryptocurrency, while a basic blockchain only focuses on *settlement*. Hybrid consensus mechanisms try to combine PoW with a classical Byzantine Fault Tolerance protocol or with proof of stake (PoS) to achieve the best of both worlds at the same time. Other proposals for an efficient blockchain refer to a multi-committees design [5,7].

Bitcoin-NG [2] (BNG), raised by Eyal et al. in NSDI 2016, has an overlap between a hybrid consensus mechanism and an on-chain proposal. On one hand, it decouples transactions serialization and leader election. It seems that Bitcoin-NG deploys a consensus committee policy. Every miner tries to become a valid creator of a key-block by PoW. The winner could be seen as the only one miner (leader) in an elected committee. On the other hand, Bitcoin-NG allows a valid leader to rapidly generate and sign micro-blocks in each epoch. This high-speed micro-block generation design is similar to an on-chain blockchain improvement.

The incentive mechanism of Bitcoin-NG encourages both a current miner to release signed micro-blocks as many as possible, and the next lucky leader to admit more valid micro-blocks created by the last leader. It aims to resist micro-block selfish mining. Bitcoin-NG [2] is claimed to be able to remit the impossible trinity of decentralization, security and efficiency. To the best of our knowledge, Bitcoin-NG is an improved cryptocurrency achieving the largest TPS only based on a single PoW consensus mechanism or Bitcoin parameter reconfiguration.

---

[1] https://www.techinasia.com/china-singles-day-2017-record-spending.

However, it is still unclear whether or how much Bitcoin-NG trades security for its efficiency promotion. The micro-block chain design is the most significant difference between Bitcoin and Bitcoin-NG. Its incentive mechanism indeed discourages micro-block selfish mining. However, the original paper [2] only discusses how to set the transaction fee distribution ratio as its secure analysis. For one thing, the analysis of the ratio ignores some details. This ratio is refined by Yin et al. [11]. For another thing, Bitcoin-NG partly follows Bitcoin and makes an innovation that adjusting an original blockchain into a key-block and micro-block mixed chain. Most of Bitcoin attacks could also be mounted on Bitcoin-NG. There is limited literature exhibiting whether micro-block chain manipulation affects the reward of an attacker, which is the main motivation of our work. In addition, we believe that a secure PoW-based blockchain is the basis of designing a secure and efficient hybrid consensus mechanism or a multi-committee in a cryptocurrency.

1.1 Our Contributions

We propose a quantitative analysis about Bitcoin-NG micro-block chain manipulation, which is named as a micro-block chain truncation (CT) attack. This novel attack is launched by a dishonest leader in a Bitcoin-NG epoch. We combine this attack with key-block selfish and stubborn mining, and an eclipse attack, in order to evaluate the security sacrifices of Bitcoin-NG compared with Bitcoin. Our main contributions are as follows.

1. We show that an attacker could earn more by launching a micro-block chain truncation attack with key-block selfish mining and an eclipse attack in a colluded strategy in Bitcoin-NG than the similar attack in Bitcoin. An attacker steals part of a colluded miner's reward by refusing some micro-blocks propagation. For a 0.1 truncation rate combined attack, it achieves 22.25% more reward proportion than she deserves in typical parameters. This attack also offers 2.87% extra reward proportion to a Bitcoin-NG attacker than the one in Bitcoin in the same setting. If an attacker truncates all micro-block chains between an eclipse victim and honest nodes, the increased reward proportion compared with Bitcoin is 38.62% at the same power distribution.
2. This combined attack also works in a "destroyed if no stake" strategy on Bitcoin-NG. For the same computation power distribution, a 0.9 truncation rate micro-block chain truncation attack in this strategy gives an attacker 18.05% extra reward proportion than honest mining by combining Lead stubborn mining and an eclipse attack. This advantage in Bitcoin-NG is 3.85% more than the one in Bitcoin.
3. To thoroughly evaluate the effect of these combined attacks, we traverse all combinations of the eight selfish and stubborn mining strategies and two eclipse attack strategies. Plus honest mining and a single eclipse attack, we find out the optimal combination in different values of all parties' computation power among these 18 combinations. To make a fair and clear comparison, practical truncation rate is introduced to calculate the total truncated transactions amount from a global view. In a practical truncation rate of 0.001,

a combined micro-block chain truncation attack in Bitcoin-NG adds at most 5.28% more reward proportion than the one in Bitcoin.

1.2 Related Work

The concept of insufficient majority is introduced by Eyal and Sirer [3]. A miner in a Bitcoin mining game is rational and selfish, which degrades the tolerated dishonest power threshold from 0.5 to 0.25 (0.33 in the best assumption). Nayak et al. [9] give a selfish miner more advantage in a computation power competition. It extends the previous selfish mining strategy to seven advanced strategies, which is concluded as stubborn mining.

For the basic Peer-to-Peer (P2P) network layer of a cryptocurrency, Croman et al. [1] measure the best performance by re-parameterizing block size and block interval. They emphasize that the original Bitcoin PoW-based blockchain has a natural weakness and blockchain redesigning may be unavoidable. Heilman et al. [4] provide an attacker with more chances to block or eclipse a Bitcoin node. By controlling the information propagation, this attack not only leads to dishonest income but also assists a double spending attack or selfish mining. Nayak et al. [9] also evaluate the reward of an attacker by combining selfish and stubborn mining with an abstract eclipse attack in Bitcoin.

Besides Bitcoin-NG [2], there are other blockchain efficiency improvements like ByzCoin [5], Omniledger [6] and Elastico [7]. The incentive mechanism of Bitcoin-NG is revisited by Yin et al. [11]. Byzcoin, Omniledger and Elastico all keep a PoW-based leader election setting, while Byzcoin [5] replaces the directly leader signature design with a special collective signature scheme. Concurrent transaction processing or multiple committee researches [6,7] are another kind of altcoins trying to parallel Bitcoin-NG or Byzcoin. It is noteworthy that the one-committee performance decides the limitation of a multi-committee scheme.

Organization. The following part of our work is structured as follows. In Sect. 2, we introduce some related backgrounds of Bitcoin and Bitcoin-NG. Section 3 proposes our attack model and some assumptions. We begin our formal evaluation in Sect. 4 for a colluded strategy and a "destroyed if no stake" strategy. The compared analysis is described in Sect. 5. We discuss our finding in Sect. 6 and conclude in Sect. 7.

2 Preliminaries

2.1 Notations

We first introduce some basic notations of the following analysis. Some of them are borrowed from the classical Bitcoin researches [3,9]. A dishonest miner Alice controls α proportion computation power. The mining power proportion of two parts of honest miners, named as Bob and Carol, are β and λ respectively. The total power proportion is $\alpha + \beta + \lambda = 1$. The proportion income of these three parties are denoted as R_{Alice}, R_{Bob} and R_{Carol}, and $R_{Alice} + R_{Bob} + R_{Carol} = 1$. If someone behaves honestly, the reward proportion of a miner equals to her power proportion. We use r_{Alice}, r_{Bob} and r_{Carol} to denote their absolute rewards.

Notations $R_{Alice,BNG}$ and $R_{Alice,BTC}$ denote the reward proportion of a Bitcoin-NG or Bitcoin attacker. The increased reward proportion compared with honest mining δ_H is $\delta_H = \frac{R_{Alice,BNG} - \alpha}{\alpha}$. Similarly, δ_{BTC} is a notation counting the increased reward proportion between Bitcoin-NG and Bitcoin as $\delta_{BTC} = \frac{R_{Alice,BNG} - R_{Alice,BTC}}{R_{Alice,BTC}}$. To avoid confusion, we only express the increased reward proportion (δ_H, δ_{BTC}) in percentage, and all other variables are in decimals.

In Bitcoin-NG, a key-block leader is able to sign several micro-blocks in one epoch. We count the number of micro-blocks in an epoch by n, and define k as the rate of truncated micro-blocks. $k = 0$ keeps an integrated micro-block chain, which makes the information propagation similar to Bitcoin. $k > 0$ is for various levels of a micro-block CT attack on Bitcoin-NG. We distinguish k_C and k_D for a colluded strategy combined attack and a "destroyed if no stake" strategy respectively. There are three cases where a combined micro-block chain truncation attack works in a "destroyed if no stake" strategy. We count the total times of these three cases by T_{3cs}. Additionally, practical truncation rate k_P is also introduced to globally measure the total amount of truncated transactions.

Bitcoin-NG divides one epoch reward to a current leader and the next one by proportion r and $1 - r$ respectively. We accept the revisited value $r = \frac{3}{11}$ from [11] in our calculations. An attacker could propagate her key-blocks faster than honest nodes. We follow [3] to describe the proportion of honest miners mining on a dishonest chain by γ. Note that this proportion does not includes an eclipsed victim. Main notations are concluded in Table 1.

2.2 Bitcoin and Bitcoin-NG Structure

Bitcoin. Bitcoin transactions are propagated by a gossip protocol. Miners collect transactions and validate them. They package several transactions and keep trying random nonces to search a preimage satisfying the system difficulty. When a lucky miner finds out a right answer, she propagates the valid block to other miners for agreement and she would be paid for minted reward and transaction fee. Every block has a number named blockheight to represent its order in history. If honest miners receive a new block having a larger blockheight, they would change their views to this new block; otherwise, they reject the new block.

Bitcoin-NG. Compared with Bitcoin, a miner in Bitcoin-NG [2] also follows a PoW-based hash preimage exhaustive searching method to compete for a key-block creator. In each round, a winner in a competition is responsible for a current epoch. Every client still floods transactions through a P2P network. A leader collects several transactions and packages them as a micro-block. After signing by her private key, a leader spreads her micro-blocks and repeats this process until another lucky miner becomes the next leader mining on top of the latest micro-block. The small size and high frequency of micro-blocks account

Table 1. Table of notations

Symbol	Description
α, β, λ	Power proportion of an attacker, honest nodes or a victim
R_{Alice}, R_{Bob}, R_{Carol} r_{Alice}, r_{Bob}, r_{Carol}	Reward proportion or absolute reward of an attacker, honest nodes or a victim
$R_{Alice,BNG}$, $R_{Alice,BTC}$	Reward proportion of an attacker in Bitcoin-NG or Bitcoin
$\delta_H = \frac{R_{Alice,BNG} - \alpha}{\alpha}$	Increased reward proportion compared with honest mining
$\delta_{BTC} = \frac{R_{Alice,BNG} - R_{Alice,BTC}}{R_{Alice,BTC}}$	Increased reward proportion compared with a similar attack in Bitcoin
n	Number of micro-blocks in a mining epoch
k (k_C, k_D)	Truncation rate of a combined micro-block chain truncation attack in a colluded strategy or a "destroyed if no stake" strategy
k_P	Practical truncation rate from a global view
T_{3cs}	Total times of three cases where a combined micro-block CT attack in a "destroyed if no stake" strategy works
γ	Proportion of honest miners mining on a dishonest chain
$r = 3/11$	Transaction fee distribution ratio to a current leader

for an efficiency improvement in Bitcoin-NG. In order to prevent a leader from withholding micro-blocks and encourage other miners to mine on top of the longest micro-block chain, Eyal et al. [2] distribute transaction fees of an epoch into two parts for a current leader and the next one. The distributed ratio is originally set as $r = 0.4$ by the security analysis of [2], and is revisited to $r = \frac{3}{11}$ by [11]. Note that Bitcoin-NG only includes transaction fee as miner incentive without minted reward in the original security analysis [2].

2.3 Selfish/Stubborn Mining and Eclipse Attack

Solo miners reduce their revenue volatility if they aggregate in a pool style. However, pool miners may deviate from the Bitcoin protocol to earn more dishonest mining reward. This dishonest mining strategy is analyzed in the Eyal and Sirer's work [3], which is named as selfish mining (SM). In general, a selfish miner mainly violates the longest-chain rule and secretly maintains a private fork chain. This strategy includes when and how to release a secret block as shown in Fig. 1(a).

A following work [9] extends this strategy after considering more complicated conditions. In the equal Fork stubborn (F-s) mining strategy, if an attacker successfully mines a valid block in a competition with honest nodes, she withholds it without declaration by hiding this block as in Fig. 1(b). The Trail stubborn (T-s) mining strategy helps a dishonest miner refuse to capitulate and accept the honest chain too earlier as in Fig. 1(c). If an attacker deploys the

Lead stubborn (L-s) mining strategy (Fig. 1(d)), she would always reveal only one block if she is in a leading position. For example, if an attacker's private chain is two-blocks longer than a public chain, she only reveals one block when honest nodes find out a block instead of revealing all blocks to cover the honest chain. It makes the system enter a competition more often. These three basic strategies and four hybrid ones (FT-s, LF-s, LT-s, LFT-s) based on them are generalized as stubborn mining by the previous work [9].

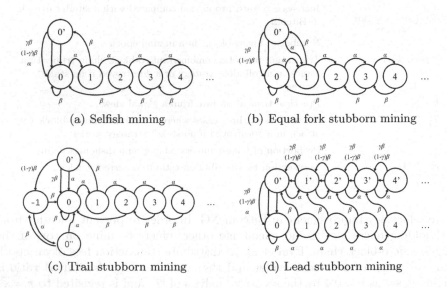

(a) Selfish mining   (b) Equal fork stubborn mining

(c) Trail stubborn mining   (d) Lead stubborn mining

Fig. 1. Selfish and stubborn mining strategies [3,9]. α: attacker power proportion. β: honest power proportion. γ: proportion of honest nodes mining on an attacking chain.

An attacker who has a powerful network strength is also able to increase her dishonest reward. Typical techniques include manipulating the incoming and outgoing information of a mining node. This method is named as an eclipse attack [4], which isolates a node from the public network and all information in the view of a victim is *filtered* by an eclipse attacker. The abstract eclipse attack modeled in [9] only depicts the strength of an eclipse attacker by the power proportion of a victim λ, while omits elaborate techniques from [4]. We review the three eclipse strategies from [9]. The reward proportion of an attacker who deploys a selfish or stubborn mining strategy is denoted as SelfReward(x) for the power proportion of an attacker x.

- **Destroyed (Dol.) strategy:** Equipped with this policy, an eclipse attacker would not propagate any blocks between honest nodes and a victim. The reward proportion is SelfReward($\frac{\alpha}{\alpha+\beta}$).
- **Colluded (Col.) strategy:** The practical power proportion of a colluded mining group is $\alpha + \beta$, which belongs to an attacker and a victim. Hence, the

attacker's reward proportion is her share of the total reward of this colluded group as $\frac{r_{Alice}}{r_{Alice}+r_{Carol}}$ SMReward$(\alpha + \lambda) = \frac{\alpha}{\alpha+\lambda}$ SelfReward$(\alpha + \lambda)$.

– **Destroyed if No Stake (DNS) strategy:** This strategy is a probabilistic combination of a destroyed strategy and a colluded one [9]. An attacker only propagates a victim block if this block is included by a colluded chain. However, the attacker's reward is relatively complex, which might not be able to generalized by an equation. The previous work [9] designs four zones for different DNS view situations as follows.

- Zone 1: An attacker, an eclipse victim and honest nodes mine on top of the same blockchain.
- Zone 2: An eclipse victim mines on top of an individual chain while others mine on another chain, which is similar to a destroyed strategy eclipse attack.
- Zone 3: An attacker shares her view with an eclipse victim while others mine on another chain, which is similar to a colluded strategy eclipse attack.
- Zone 4: The three parties mine on top of three individual chains.

3   Attack Model and Assumption

We introduce our model and assumptions for a micro-block chain truncation attack on Bitcoin-NG in this section.

3.1   Attack Model

The model of a micro-block CT attack partly follows the one in [9]. An attacker has the ability to block the information propagation of part of honest nodes. These eclipsed nodes are regarded as a victim. The power proportion of an attacker, a victim and remained honest nodes α, λ, β are three key parameters in this model. They also have names as Alice, Carol and Bob, respectively. In Bitcoin-NG, a micro-block CT attacker truncates a micro-block chain signed by an honest leader (Bob or Carol).

3.2   Assumptions

In order to reflect a clear and non-trivial evaluation on Bitcoin-NG, we list some assumptions for simplification as follows.

1. Transaction fees are assumed to be in proportion to the number of transactions and a micro-block has a certain amount of transactions. It means that transaction fees are in proportion to the number of micro-blocks.
2. We simplify the mining reward by following the assumption in [2], which only includes transaction fee without minted reward. Therefore, when a micro-block chain is truncated by a rate, the attacker's reward is decreased by this rate. Note that Bitcoin mining reward includes minted reward and transaction fee. If taking the minted reward of Bitcoin-NG into consideration, we

will come to a different result, which is still an open question. However, since the minted reward keeps decreasing, a single transaction fee driven cryptocurrency deserves much more attention.

4   A Combined Micro-block Chain Truncation Attack on Bitcoin-NG

We next present the formal attack analysis on Bitcoin-NG. An attacker is not able to increase her absolute reward through launching a single micro-block CT attack. However, she could add her absolute reward by combining this attack with selfish or stubborn mining and an eclipse attack. This combined attack works on two strategies, i.e., a colluded strategy and a "destroyed if no stake" strategy. Following our notations, the level of a micro-block CT attack is reflected by truncation rate k $(0 \leq k \leq 1)$. We use k_C and k_D to distinguish these two eclipse strategies in a combined attack.

4.1   The Colluded Strategy

Without loss of generality, we model a two-key-block scenario. Alice truncates Bob's and Carol's signing micro-blocks at k_C rate as in Fig. 2. It is straightforward to extend this to a multi-key-block scenario from this abstract model.

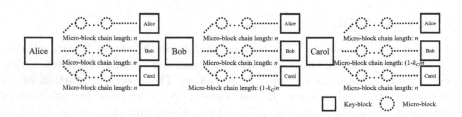

Fig. 2. A two-block abstract model for a micro-block CT attack on Bitcoin-NG.

For $\alpha + \beta + \lambda = 1$, if Alice mines honestly, the absolute reward (only transaction fees without minted reward) of three parties are

$$r_{\text{Alice}} = \alpha^2 n + r\alpha\beta n + r\alpha\lambda n + (1 - r)\beta\alpha n + (1 - r)\lambda\alpha n = \alpha^2 n + \alpha(\beta + \lambda)n,$$
$$r_{\text{Bob}} = \beta^2 n + r\beta\alpha n + r\beta\lambda n + (1 - r)\alpha\beta n + (1 - r)\lambda\beta n = \beta^2 n + \beta(\alpha + \lambda)n,$$
$$r_{\text{Carol}} = \lambda^2 n + r\lambda\alpha n + r\lambda\beta n + (1 - r)\alpha\lambda n + (1 - r)\beta\lambda n = \lambda^2 n + \lambda(\alpha + \beta)n.$$

If a dishonest miner launches a single micro-block CT attack, she could not directly increase her absolute reward. But she could reduce two victims' absolute reward as

$$R_{\text{Bob}} = \beta^2 n + \beta(\alpha + (1 - k_C)\lambda)n, \quad R_{\text{Carol}} = \lambda^2 n + \lambda(\alpha + (1 - k_C)\beta)n.$$

Hence, we turn to analyze a combined micro-block CT attack on Bitcoin-NG. The original selfish mining result in [3] is

$$\text{SelfReward}(\alpha) = \frac{\alpha(1-\alpha)^2(4\alpha + \gamma(1-2\alpha)) - \alpha^3}{1 - \alpha(1 + (2-\alpha)\alpha)}.$$

The attacker Alice launches an eclipse attack to the honest miner Carol in a colluded strategy. Alice controls the connections of Carol. It seems that Alice and Carol run the key-block selfish mining strategy as a whole. They share dishonest rewards with each other according to their practical rewards. By following the original colluded strategy result from [9] as described in Sect. 2.3, the reward proportion of a Bitcoin-NG attacker by mounting a combined micro-block CT attack in this setting is

$$R_{\text{Alice,BNG}} = \frac{r_{\text{Alice}}}{r_{\text{Alice}} + r_{\text{Carol}}} \text{SelfReward}(\alpha + \lambda)$$

$$= \frac{-(\alpha(\beta - 1)(2\beta - \beta^2\gamma + 2\beta^3\gamma + 3\beta^2 - 4\beta^3 - 1))}{((-\beta^3 + \beta^2 + 2\beta - 1)(\beta^2 k_C - \beta k_C - \beta + \alpha\beta k_C + 1))}.$$

We compute this reward proportion of Alice in Fig. 3(a) (the red line) in the setting where $\alpha = 0.20$, $\lambda = 0.15$. The truncation rate increases from $k_C = 0$ to $k_C = 1$. Note that $k_C = 0$ means selfish mining with an eclipse attack in a colluded strategy on Bitcoin (without truncation, the black line in Fig. 3(a)). $k_C > 0$ means Alice launches an extra micro-block CT attack on Bitcoin-NG, which she steals part of dishonest reward from a colluded miner Carol. $\gamma = 0.5$ is a typical setting in Bitcoin-NG and Bitcoin for the random tie breaking rule. Our result shows that this combined attack offers extra reward proportion to a combined micro-block CT attacker in Bitcoin-NG, which exposes a Bitcoin-NG vulnerability in contrast to Bitcoin. In addition, k_C also reflects the level of the stealing. Along with the rising of the truncation rate k_C, the reward proportion of an attacker is increasing.

As is shown in Table 2, in a configuration of typical parameters ($\alpha = 0.20$, $\lambda = 0.15$, $\gamma = 0.5$, $k_C = 0.1$), we get the increased reward proportion as $\delta_H = 22.25\%$ compared with honest mining, and $\delta_{\text{BTC}} = 2.87\%$ compared with the one in Bitcoin. Note that a micro-block CT attack for relative small levels, such as $k = 0.1$, is not so easy to be detected by a colluded miner. Carol would believe that the bad network environment causes a relatively shorter micro-block chain.

Additionally, there is another interesting observation that even Alice steals some rewards from Carol, a colluded miner Carol still gains more reward proportion, i.e., $R_{\text{Carol}} = 0.1783$ is more than her power proportion $\lambda = 0.15$. The blue line in Fig. 3(a) is over the green line if $k_C < 0.38$. It means that an attacker gives Carol an incentive to collude with Alice if the truncation rate is below this threshold in this setting. As for the same distribution of all parities' computation power, we get the optimal increased reward proportion for an attacker in $k_C = 1$ as $\delta_H = 64.75\%$ and $\delta_{\text{BTC}} = 38.62\%$.

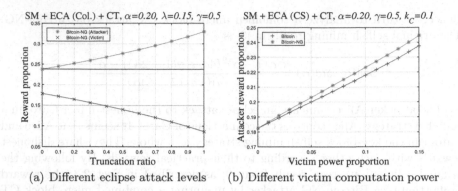

(a) Different eclipse attack levels   (b) Different victim computation power

Fig. 3. A micro-block chain truncation attack combined with key-block selfish mining and a colluded strategy eclipse attack on Bitcoin-NG. SM: key-block selfish mining. ECA (Col.): a colluded strategy eclipse attack. α, λ: power proportion of an attacker or a victim. γ: proportion of honest nodes mining on top of an attacking chain. k_C: truncation rate in a colluded strategy. (Color figure online)

Table 2. The reward proportion for three parties in different attacks when $\alpha = 0.20$, $\beta = 0.65$, $\lambda = 0.15$. SM: key-block selfish mining. CT: a micro-block chain truncation attack. ECA (Col.): a colluded strategy eclipse attack. α, β, λ: power proportion of an attacker, honest nodes and a victim. γ: proportion of honest nodes mining on top of an attacking chain. k_C: truncation rate in a colluded strategy.

Party Name(Power)	ECA (Col.)+SM, Bitcoin	ECA (Col.)+SM+CT Bitcoin-NG($k_C = 0.1$)	ECA (Col.)+SM+CT Bitcoin-NG($k_C = 1$)
Alice(0.20)	0.2377	0.2445	0.3295
Bob(0.65)	0.5840	0.5772	0.5840
Carol(0.15)	0.1783	0.1783	0.0865

4.2   Destroyed if No Stake Strategy

The Bitcoin-NG analysis for combining a "destroyed if no stake" strategy eclipse attack is also followed the similar attack in Bitcoin from [9]. Compared with a colluded strategy, this one is more complex for different attacking behaviors in various cases. As the name shows, this strategy means an attacker would recognize a victim chain only if this chain includes the stake of an attacker. A victim's block would be propagated to honest nodes only if the victim mines on top of an attacker's block.

We claim that a micro-block CT attack creates extra reward by combining a selfish or stubborn mining strategy (Fig. 1) and a DNS strategy eclipse attack. If an attacker truncates a micro-block chain between her and honest nodes, her interests are damaged, which is conflicted with her incentives. A victim block would be recognized only if it is behind an attacker's chain. Any victim's blocks which are mined on top of an honest nodes' block are not going to be concerned. It means that a micro-block CT attack also does not occur from honest nodes to a victim. Therefore, this combined micro-block CT attack only works from a victim to honest nodes. The Lead stubborn mining strategy assists an attacker more situations where this attack works. There are three worked cases as follows.

Case 1: Honest Nodes Mine Behind a Victim Block in Zone 1. This case, as is shown in Fig. 4(a), is a basic one that all three parties mine on top of the same chain. If the last block is mined by a victim, the attacker would launch a micro-block CT attack when the victim is blocked by this eclipse attacker. The attacker only propagates $1 - k_D$ proportion micro-blocks to honest nodes. Therefore, when the next valid block is mined by honest nodes, the reward of this block distributed to the victim and to honest nodes would decrease by $r \cdot k_D n$ and $(1 - r) \cdot k_D n$ proportion of transaction fees, respectively.

Case 2: Honest Nodes Win a Tie and Mine Behind a Victim Chain in Zone 3. In this case, honest nodes and a corrupted group (an attacker Alice and a victim Carol) are competing for the next block in a tie as shown in Fig. 4(b). Note that the latest block of a private chain belongs to a victim. The attacker also truncates the micro-block chain of the victim. Finally, honest nodes win this tie and mine on the top of the truncated victim's micro-block chain.

Case 3: Honest Nodes Mine Behind a Corrupt Chain, and the Father Block Belongs to a Victim in Zone 3. In the Lead stubborn strategy, an attacker always reveals one block and pushes the system into a competition at any leading time. Hence, it is rising for the possibility that honest nodes mine on top of a private chain which is withheld by an attacker and a victim. A micro-block CT attack works if honest nodes win in a temporary tie when an attacker is leading and the last block is created by a victim as shown in Fig. 4(c). An attack in this case has the similar effect to the one in Case 2. However, a Case 3 micro-block CT attack only works for one time when there are several Case 3 attacks during one leading chain, which is significant in its frequency calculation.

The reward of a victim and honest nodes also decrease by $r \cdot kn$ and $(1-r) \cdot kn$ respectively at one time of one case in Case 2 and 3. To calculate the extra reward proportion of this combined micro-block CT attack, we conduct an experiment to simulate 100,000 steps starting from zone 1 in Monte Carlo style. The simulation is repeated ten times to average the result for the reward proportion of an attacker.

If an attacker eclipses a $\lambda = 0.15$ victim in DNS strategy combining with a $k_D = 0.9$ micro-block CT attack and Lead stubborn mining, Fig. 5(a) shows the reward proportion of an attacker with different dishonest computation power. $\gamma = 0.5$ also reflects the random tie breaking rule. Note that $k_C = 0$ means a similar attack on Bitcoin (without truncation).

Table 3 indicates that the result of a $k_D = 0.9$ DNS strategy combined micro-block CT attack in the same setting as in Sect. 4.1, i.e., $\alpha = 0.2$, $\lambda = 0.15$, $\gamma = 0.5$. A $\alpha = 0.20$ computation power attacker obtains $R_{\text{Alice}} = 0.2453$ reward proportion by this combined attack. Her increased reward proportion is $\delta_H = 18.05\%$ more than honest mining, or $\delta_{\text{BTC}} = 3.85\%$ more than the one in Bitcoin. In addition, an $\alpha = 0.35$ attacker could obtain the optimal increased reward

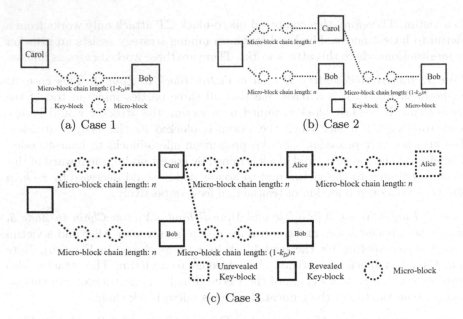

Fig. 4. Case 1, 2 and 3 for a worked combined micro-block chain truncation attack on Bitcoin-NG. k_D: truncation rate in a "destroyed if no stake" strategy.

proportion $\delta_H = 95.66\%$ when $R_{Alice} = 0.6848$. An $\alpha = 0.25$ attacker have the reward proportion $R_{Alice} = 0.3518$, which gets the best increased reward proportion than Bitcoin as $\delta_{BTC} = 3.90\%$.

As for the reward proportion of a victim, the situation is different from a combined micro-block attack in a colluded strategy as in Sect. 4.1. In Fig. 5(b), the victim's reward proportion is badly decreased by a DNS strategy eclipse attacker even in Bitcoin ($\alpha = 0.20$, $\lambda = 0.15$). However, a more powerful attacker would help a victim to earn more than honest mining.

Readers might wounder that the values of two truncation rates are different in Sects. 4.1 and 4.2 ($k_C = 0.1, k_D = 0.9$), which may result in an unfair comparison. However, even $k_D = 0.9$ is relatively large for one time micro-block CT attack, the times of those three cases where this attack works are quite rare compared with 100,000 simulation steps as Table 3 shows. We would make a comparison at the same level in Sect. 5.

5   The Comparison of Different Strategies in Unified Truncation Rate

In this section, we make a thorough comparison of these two combined attacks as Sect. 4 describes. Apart from the Lead stubborn strategy, selfish and other stubborn mining strategies are also introduced in our combined analysis from [3, 9] as described in Sect. 2.3.

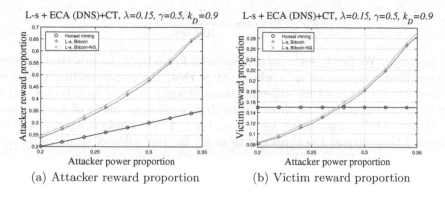

(a) Attacker reward proportion   (b) Victim reward proportion

Fig. 5. A micro-block chain truncation attack combined with key-block Lead stubborn mining and a "destroyed if no stake" strategy eclipse attack on Bitcoin-NG. L-s: key-block Lead stubborn mining. ECA (DNS): a "destroyed if no stake" strategy eclipse attack. λ: power proportion of a victim. γ: proportion of honest nodes mining on top of an attacking chain. k_D: truncation rate in a "destroyed if no stake" strategy.

Table 3. The attacker's reward proportion for $\lambda = 0.15$, $\gamma = 0.5$, $k_D = 0.9$ in different power proportions of an attacker. L-s: key-block Lead stubborn mining. CT: a micro-block chain truncation attack. ECA (DNS): a "destroyed if no stake" strategy eclipse attack. λ: power proportion of a victim. γ: proportion of honest nodes mining on top of an attacking chain. R_{Alice}, R_{Carol}: reward proportion of an attacker or a victim. k_D: truncation rate in a "destroyed if no stake" strategy.

Attacker's power proportion	ECA (DNS)+L-s, Bitcoin, R_{Alice}	ECA (DNS)+L-s+CT, Bitcoin-NG($k_D = 0.9$)		
		R_{Alice}	3 cases times	R_{Carol}
0.2000	0.2362	0.2453	2150	0.0836
0.2500	0.3386	0.3518	2130	0.1237
0.3000	0.4760	0.4890	1600	0.1864
0.3500	0.6752	0.6848	60	0.2906

5.1 Practical Truncation Rate

To make a fair and clear comparison, we introduce practical truncation rate k_P to model the absolute amount of all transactions truncated by a micro-block CT attacker. Every comparison in this section is unified for having the same value of practical truncation rate.

For a colluded strategy, an attacker always truncates the micro-block chains of a victim. From the two-blocks example in Fig. 2, it is clear that a truncation occurs in two situations where Bob mines behind Carol and otherwise. The possibility of these two events is $\beta\lambda + \lambda\beta$. For a "destroyed if no stake" strategy, there are three cases where a combined micro-block CT attack works as we describe above. The total times of these cases are T_{3cs}. Hence, we have the relations to map k_C or k_D to k_P as

$$k_P = 2\beta\gamma \cdot k_C = \frac{T_{3cs}}{100,000} \cdot k_D.$$

Methodology. We firstly set a specific value of k_P to limit the practical amount of truncated transactions as a whole. After that, the corresponding values of k_C and k_D are obtained for different computation powers of an attacker and a victim by the equations as above. Note that a too large value of k_P or a too small value of T_{3cs} may cause $k_C > 1$ or $k_D > 1$. We would assign $k_C = 1$ or $k_D = 1$ if they surpass the threshold to avoid an error value of truncation rate.

5.2 Simulation Results

We combined the selfish mining strategy and seven stubborn mining strategies (three basic ones F-s, T-s, L-s, and four hybrid ones FT-s, LF-s, LT-s, LFT-s) with two eclipse attack strategies (colluded, and "destroyed if no stake"). In addition to honest mining and an single eclipse attacking, there are 18 combinations for a micro-block CT attack in total. We traverse every value of computation power α, λ, in order to find out the best combined strategy in different practical truncation rate k_P.

The results in Fig. 6 shows that the effect of different combined micro-block attacks. Different colors reflect different optimal strategies for the largest reward proportion at a certain point. $k_P = 0$ corresponds to the attack in Bitcoin. A DNS strategy combined attack has a better reward proportion if k_P is relatively small. However, the total times of three working cases could not be increased. When k_P is rising, k_D still could not surpass the threshold. Hence, a colluded combined micro-block attack would take a prominent place eventually.

Table 4 also gives us a clear and overall view of the combinations. The optimal increased reward proportion than Bitcoin δ_{BTC} for a DNS strategy combined attack decreases if the value of k_P is rising. When k_P is small, it offers an attacker reasonable extra reward. At the same time, a colluded combined attack has a less impact on Bitcoin-NG compared with the DNS one. When we raise k_P, the optimal values of δ_{BTC} for colluded strategies are also rising. If $k_P = 0.015$, we could find out that collude strategies almost take place a prominent position from the proportion of their area.

6   Discussion

Plausible Choices for Parameters. $\alpha = 0.20$, $\lambda = 0.15$ is a typical value for a computation power distribution, which is comparable for current Bitcoin pools[2]. $\alpha + \lambda = 0.35$ is more than the classical security threshold (0.25) against selfish mining from [3]. The random tie breaking rule ($\gamma = 0.5$) has been deployed in many altcoins including Bitcoin-NG. Our simulation always keeps a practical truncation rate k_P no larger than 0.02, which may be intuitive for hiding this attack. However, Bitcoin unconfirmed transactions pool would not be empty if

---

[2] https://www.blockchain.com/en/pools.

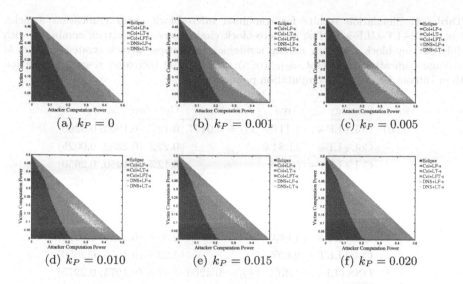

(a) $k_P = 0$ (b) $k_P = 0.001$ (c) $k_P = 0.005$

(d) $k_P = 0.010$ (e) $k_P = 0.015$ (f) $k_P = 0.020$

Fig. 6. Strategy combinations for a micro-block chain truncation attack. Eclipse: A single eclipse attack. Col./DNS+LT-s/LF-s/LFT-s: a micro-block chain truncation attack combined with different stubborn mining strategies and eclipse attack strategies. (Color figure online)

the transaction amount is quite large [12]. So for each node, it is not so surprised that part of transactions are not included in a micro-block chain.

Impact and Difficulty for Mounting a Combined Micro-Block CT Attack. The maximum increased reward proportion could even reach $\delta_{BTC} = 426.32\%$ when $\alpha = 0.01$, $\lambda = 0.09$, $k_C = 1$, which is not a very typical setting. Nevertheless, the goal of this work is to prove that the Bitcoin-NG indeed sacrifices security for efficiency instead of exploring a largest δ_{BTC} in an ideal setting. Considering the same distribution that $\alpha = 0.20$, $\lambda = 0.15$, the reward proportion of a $k_C = 1$ colluded strategy combined micro-block CT attack is $R_{Alice} = 0.3295$ and $\delta_{BTC} = 38.62\%$. This result is larger than the reward of a total destroyed eclipse attack $R_{Alice} = 0.2292$. However, the difficulty of truncating all micro-block chains between a victim and honest nodes is much smaller than that of blocking all information transiting to a node as a destroyed eclipse attack in [9].

Differences Between a Micro-Block CT Attack and Transactions Blocking. Bitcoin (Bitcoin-NG) nodes are quite concentrated in network topology. If a Bitcoin-NG node manages to become a valid key-block creator, she is the only miner of a consensus committee. She signs all valid micro-blocks in an epoch. It seems that the information stream of micro-block diffuses from a single point, which assists micro-block CT attacks from the P2P network level. On the contrary, a transaction is much smaller and is dispersed over the world by a gossip protocol. It is quite difficult to block a specific transaction in a P2P network.

Table 4. Simulation results for combined micro-block chain truncation attacks. Col./DNS+LT-s/LF-s/LFT-s: a micro-block chain truncation attack combined with different key-block stubborn mining strategies and eclipse attack strategies. Ave. k: average truncation rate. Opt. δ_{BTC} (α, λ): the optimal increased reward proportion than Bitcoin for α and λ computation power.

k_P	Strategy	Area	Ave. k	Opt. δ_{BTC} (α, λ)
0.001	Col.+LF-s	1.11%	$k_C = 0.0177$	0.12% (0.1000, 0.3200)
	Col.+LT-s	11.84%		0.22% (0.2250, 0.0025)
	Col.+LFT-s	5.92%		0.12% (0.1450, 0.2650)
	DNS+LF-s	5.58%	$k_D = 0.0906$	5.28% (0.1975, 0.2275)
	DNS+LT-s	2.98%	$k_D = 0.0217$	5.08% (0.1850, 0.2150)
0.010	Col.+LF-s	1.90%	$k_C = 0.1339$	1.22% (0.3875, 0.0275)
	Col.+LT-s	14.63%		2.30% (0.2150, 0.0075)
	Col.+LFT-s	9.69%		1.23% (0.1450, 0.2650)
	DNS+LF-s	1.40%	$k_D = 0.4200$	5.11% (0.1975, 0.2275)
	DNS+LT-s	0.98%	$k_D = 0.2227$	4.77% (0.2200, 0.2000)
0.015	Col.+LF-s	2.01%	$k_C = 0.1774$	1.84% (0.3875, 0.0275)
	Col.+LT-s	15.73%		3.57% (0.2025, 0.0150)
	Col.+LFT-s	10.82%		1.86% (0.1450, 0.2650)
	DNS+LF-s	0.39%	$k_D = 0.7982$	4.62% (0.2325, 0.1900)
	DNS+LT-s	0.24%	$k_D = 0.3174$	5.00% (0.2200, 0.2000)

The Assumption of None Minted Reward. The original Bitcoin-NG [2] analyses security in a situation where the reward for mining a block includes only transaction fee and ignores minted reward. We follow this assumption in this paper. However, minted reward indeed has an impact on the analysis when combining selfish mining and an eclipse attack, so we will extend this work by taking minted reward into consideration in future.

The Necessity of This Work. In this work, we evaluate the impact of a micro-block CT attack combined with selfish mining and an eclipse attack on Bitcoin-NG. Here, the attacking rate is modeled as the computation power of an attacker α, the level of an eclipse attack λ and truncation rate k_C or k_D. Nayak et al. [9] emphasizes the reason why selfish mining or stubborn mining is not observed in practice as the previous work [3] shows. The widespread awareness of various attacks improves the security of Bitcoin. Even this work may not be observed in practice, when designing a scalable and efficient cryptocurrency, our work would alarm researchers to focus more on security.

7   Conclusion

We analyze the utility of a combined micro-block chain truncation attack on Bitcoin-NG. This attack combines classical selfish and stubborn mining strategies and an eclipse attack in a colluded strategy or a "destroyed if no stake" strategy. Our results show that Bitcoin-NG indeed sacrifices security for efficiency improvement. We assume that mining reward only includes transaction fee. We left a more refined model which captures the real world very well and a game theory analysis in a multi-attackers scenario as future works.

Acknowledgment. This work is partly supported by the National Key R&D Program of China (2017YFB1400700), National Cryptography Development Fund (MMJJ20180215), and CCF-NSFOCUS KunPeng Research Fund (2018013).

References

1. Croman, K., et al.: On scaling decentralized blockchains. In: Clark, J., Meiklejohn, S., Ryan, P.Y.A., Wallach, D., Brenner, M., Rohloff, K. (eds.) FC 2016. LNCS, vol. 9604, pp. 106–125. Springer, Heidelberg (2016). https://doi.org/10.1007/978-3-662-53357-4_8
2. Eyal, I., Gencer, A.E., Sirer, E.G., van Renesse, R.: Bitcoin-NG: a scalable blockchain protocol. In: NSDI 2016, Santa Clara, CA, USA, 16–18 March 2016, pp. 45–59 (2016)
3. Eyal, I., Sirer, E.G.: Majority is not enough: bitcoin mining is vulnerable. In: Christin, N., Safavi-Naini, R. (eds.) FC 2014. LNCS, vol. 8437, pp. 436–454. Springer, Heidelberg (2014). https://doi.org/10.1007/978-3-662-45472-5_28
4. Heilman, E., Kendler, A., Zohar, A., Goldberg, S.: Eclipse attacks on bitcoin's peer-to-peer network. In: USENIX Security 2015, Washington, D.C., USA, 12–14 August 2015, pp. 129–144 (2015)
5. Kokoris-Kogias, E., Jovanovic, P., Gailly, N., Khoffi, I., Gasser, L., Ford, B.: Enhancing bitcoin security and performance with strong consistency via collective signing. In: USENIX Security 2016, Austin, TX, USA, 10–12 August 2016, pp. 279–296 (2016)
6. Kokoris-Kogias, E., Jovanovic, P., Gasser, L., Gailly, N., Syta, E., Ford, B.: Omniledger: a secure, scale-out, decentralized ledger via sharding. In: S&P 2018, San Francisco, California, USA, 21–23 May 2018, pp. 583–598 (2018)
7. Luu, L., Narayanan, V., Zheng, C., Baweja, K., Gilbert, S., Saxena, P.: A secure sharding protocol for open blockchains. In: Proceedings of the 2016 ACM SIGSAC Conference on Computer and Communications Security, Vienna, Austria, 24–28 October 2016, pp. 17–30 (2016)
8. Nakamoto, S.: Bitcoin: A peer-to-peer electronic cash system (2008). https://bitcoin.org/bitcoin.pdf
9. Nayak, K., Kumar, S., Miller, A., Shi, E.: Stubborn mining: generalizing selfish mining and combining with an eclipse attack. In: EuroS&P 2016, Saarbrücken, Germany, 21–24 March 2016, pp. 305–320 (2016)
10. Vukolić, M.: The quest for scalable blockchain fabric: proof-of-work vs. BFT replication. In: Camenisch, J., Kesdoğan, D. (eds.) iNetSec 2015. LNCS, vol. 9591, pp. 112–125. Springer, Cham (2016). https://doi.org/10.1007/978-3-319-39028-4_9
11. Yin, J., Wang, C., Zhang, Z., Liu, J.: Revisiting the incentive mechanism of bitcoin-NG. In: Susilo, W., Yang, G. (eds.) ACISP 2018. LNCS, vol. 10946, pp. 706–719. Springer, Cham (2018). https://doi.org/10.1007/978-3-319-93638-3_40
12. Yu, H., Zhang, Z., Liu, J.: Research on scaling technology of bitcoin blockchain. J. Comput. Res. Dev. **54**(10), 2390–2403 (2017)

Foundations

Field Extension in Secret-Shared Form and Its Applications to Efficient Secure Computation

Ryo Kikuchi[1(✉)], Nuttapong Attrapadung[2], Koki Hamada[1], Dai Ikarashi[1], Ai Ishida[2], Takahiro Matsuda[2], Yusuke Sakai[2], and Jacob C. N. Schuldt[2]

[1] NTT, Tokyo, Japan
kikuchi_ryo@fw.ipsj.or.jp, {koki.hamada.rb,dai.ikarashi.rd}@hco.ntt.co.jp
[2] National Institute of Advanced Industrial Science and Technology (AIST),
Tokyo, Japan
{n.attrapadung,a.ishida,t-matsuda,yusuke.sakai,jacob.schuldt}@aist.go.jp

Abstract. Secure computation enables participating parties to jointly compute a function over their inputs while keeping them private. Secret sharing plays an important role for maintaining privacy during the computation. In most schemes, secret sharing over the *same* finite field is normally utilized throughout all the steps in the secure computation. A major drawback of this "uniform" approach is that one has to set the size of the field to be as large as the maximum of all the lower bounds derived from all the steps in the protocol. This easily leads to a requirement for using a large field which, in turn, makes the protocol inefficient. In this paper, we propose a "non-uniform" approach: dynamically changing the fields so that they are suitable for each step of computation. At the core of our approach is a surprisingly simple method to extend the underlying field of a secret sharing scheme, in a non-interactive manner, while maintaining the secret being shared. Using our approach, default computations can hence be done in a small field, which allows better efficiency, while one would extend to a larger field only at the necessary steps. As the main application of our technique, we show an improvement upon the recent actively secure protocol proposed by Chida et al. (Crypto'18). The improved protocol can handle a binary field, which enables XOR-free computation of a boolean circuit. Other applications include efficient (batch) equality check and consistency check protocols, which are useful for, e.g., password-based threshold authentication.

Keywords: Secure computation · Secret sharing · Active security

1 Introduction

Secret-sharing-based secure computation enables parties to compute a function of a given set of inputs while keeping these secret. The inputs are distributed to several parties via a secret sharing scheme, and the parties then compute

© Springer Nature Switzerland AG 2019
J. Jang-Jaccard and F. Guo (Eds.): ACISP 2019, LNCS 11547, pp. 343–361, 2019.
https://doi.org/10.1007/978-3-030-21548-4_19

the function by interacting with each other. Throughout the above steps, any information except the output must be kept secret to the parties.

Secure computation should satisfy the security notions, such as privacy and correctness, in the presence of an adversary, which might compromise some of the parties participating in the computation. There are two classical adversary models capturing different adversarial behaviors: passive (i.e., semi-honest) and active (i.e., malicious). The latter provides a stronger security guarantee as an actively secure protocol will remain secure in the presence of an adversary following an arbitrary adversarial strategy. Another metric of security is the number of parties that an adversary can corrupt. The setting in which an adversary is allowed to corrupt up to half of the parties, is referred to as honest majority. Unconditionally secure protocols can only be realized in the honest majority setting [19].

Many secret-sharing-based secure computations are defined over a finite field, e.g., [4,6,7,10,12]. The choice of the underlying field greatly affects the efficiency of those protocols since field elements and field operations are the units of any processing, and the size of the field affects the size and efficiency of field elements and field operations, respectively. In other words, an unnecessarily large field incurs a large cost of storage, computation, and communication among parties. From this, a natural question arises: how small can the field size be?

Intuitively speaking, we can consider two lower bounds regarding the field size. The first is the range of values used in the computation. The field size should be large enough to contain any value that appears in all steps in the computation. For example, if one wants to store values that are less than 10, and compute the sum of 100 values, the field size should be larger than $10 \times 100 \approx 2^{10}$ to accommodate this computation, while if one wants to store binary values and compute a boolean circuit, a binary field is sufficient.

Another bound is derived from statistical errors which are typically a part of the computation, and which in turn provides an upper bound for the advantage of an adversary. These errors are typically dependent on the size of the field used in the computation. For example, consider a protocol for checking equality of secret shared values. Specifically, let $\mathbb{K}$ be a field, and let $[s]$ and $[s']$ be shares of $s, s' \in \mathbb{K}$. There is a straightforward way for the parties holding $[s]$ and $[s']$ to verify that $s = s'$ without revealing s and s' themselves: generate a random share $[r]$, securely compute $[r(s - s')]$, reconstruct this value, and verify whether the reconstructed value $r(s - s')$ is 0 or not. If $s \neq s'$, $r(s - s')$ will be a random value different from 0, except probability $1/|\mathbb{K}|$, where $|\mathbb{K}|$ denotes the size of $\mathbb{K}$. Therefore, if one wants to ensure that a statistical error probability is less than $2^{-\kappa}$, the field size must be larger than 2^{κ}.

The field size should be larger than these two lower bounds even if there is a gap between those. For example, if the parties securely compute statistics with a possible range from 0 to $1,000$ ($\approx 2^{10}$) with statistical error 2^{-40}, a field size larger than 2^{40} must be used (this comes from $\max(2^{10}, 2^{40})$).

Our Contribution. We propose a method to dynamically change the fields used in secure computation to improve efficiency. Note that a large field (e.g. chosen to lower the statistical error of a protocol) is not necessarily required in all stages of a secure computation. Often, a significant part of the computation can be done in a smaller field which is just sufficiently large to accommodate the values appearing in the computation, and only when verifying correctness, a much larger field is required to reduce the statistical error inherent in the used protocol, e.g. like the equality check described above.

Therefore, if we can dynamically change the underlying field, we can improve the efficiency of secure computation by using a field of an appropriate size for each stage of the computation. Note that for this approach to work, it is required that the parties can change the underlying field while a secret is shared over the field. In this paper, we propose a method that achieves this, which furthermore does not require the parties holding the shared secret to communicate. Hence, this allows the parties by default to use a small field over which computation is efficient, and only switch to a large (extended) field at the time of verification to achieve the desired statistical error.

Let us briefly recall standard construction of field extension. Let $\mathbb{K}$ be a base field and let $F \in \mathbb{K}[X]$ be an irreducible polynomial of degree $m - 1$. Then $\widehat{\mathbb{K}} := \mathbb{K}[X]/F$ is a field extension of $\mathbb{K}$ of size $|\mathbb{K}|^m$. An m-tuple of elements in $\mathbb{K}$, $(s_1, \ldots, s_m)$, can be regarded as a vector representation of a single element $\widehat{s} \in \widehat{\mathbb{K}}$ defined as $\widehat{s} = s_1 + s_2 X + \cdots + s_m X^{m-1}$. Note that a single element $s_1 \in \mathbb{K}$ can also be regarded as an element in $\widehat{\mathbb{K}}$ by setting $s_i = 0$ for $2 \leq i \leq m$.

We show that this kind of extension allows shares from a secret sharing scheme to be mapped into the extended field, as long as we use a t-out-of-n linear secret sharing scheme. Let $[s]$ (that is not necessarily in $\mathbb{K}$) be a share of $s \in \mathbb{K}$ and $[\![s']\!]$ be a share of $s' \in \widehat{\mathbb{K}}$. We show that, if the parties have an m-tuple of shares $[s_1], \ldots, [s_m]$, the parties can regard them as a single share, $[\![s']\!]$, where $s' := s_1 + s_2 X + \cdots + s_m X^{m-1}$. Similar to the above, this also implies that a single share $[s]$ can be regarded as a share of $[\![\widehat{s}]\!]$, where $\widehat{s} := s + 0X + \cdots + 0X^{m-1}$.

This technique is simple but useful for improving the efficiency of secure computation. Let us revisit the example of equality checking highlighted above. Assume that the parties have computed $[s]$ and $[s']$, where $s, s' \in \mathbb{K}$ and that to make the computation efficient $\mathbb{K}$ was chosen to be a small field, e.g., GF(2). Let $\widehat{\mathbb{K}}$ be the extended field of $\mathbb{K}$ with size larger than 2^κ. To check that $s = s'$, the parties extend $[s]$ and $[s']$ into $[\![\widehat{s}]\!]$ and $[\![\widehat{s'}]\!]$ using our technique, and generate a sharing $[\![r]\!]$ of randomness $r \in \widehat{\mathbb{K}}$. The parties then securely compute $[\![r(s - s')]\!]$, reconstruct the resulting value, and check whether this is 0 or not. Since the revealed value belongs to $\widehat{\mathbb{K}}$, the statistical error of the comparison, and thereby the advantage of an adversary, is bounded by $2^{-\kappa}$. Besides this, the parties can batch multiple equality checks by "packing" multiple secrets in $\mathbb{K}$ into a single secret in $\widehat{\mathbb{K}}$. If m secrets in a field are packed into a single element in an m-degree extended field, there is no extra cost with respect to communication compared to parallel executions of equality checks in $\mathbb{K}$. Similar scenarios appear in password-based threshold authentication [21] and batch consistency check [14,22], and we can apply this technique to the protocols for these.

As the main application of our technique, we show how to improve a recent protocol proposed by Chida et al. [10] which achieves fast large-scale honest-majority secure computation for active adversaries. Although Chida et al. proposed a protocol suitable for small fields, the protocol cannot be applied to a binary field, since the bound on the advantage of the adversary is given by $(3/|\mathbb{K}|)^\delta$, which is not meaningful for $|\mathbb{K}| = 2$. This, for example, prevents the use of XOR-free computation of a boolean circuit.[1] Informally, their protocol generates δ shared random values, computes δ "randomized" outputs in addition to the ordinary one, and verifies correctness of the computation by checking if the randomized outputs correspond to the ordinary outputs when the latter is randomized using the same randomnesses. Here, the shared random values and the randomized outputs are used for verification only. Hence, we can apply our technique to this protocol as follows. The (shared) random values and randomized outputs in $\mathbb{K}$ are replaced by a single random value and the randomized output in $\widehat{\mathbb{K}}$, and then the ordinary output in $\mathbb{K}$ is extended to $\widehat{\mathbb{K}}$ at the time of verification. The bound on the adversarial advantage in this modified protocol is $3/|\widehat{\mathbb{K}}|$. Therefore, we can choose a binary field as $\mathbb{K}$ (and an extension field $\widehat{\mathbb{K}}$ of appropriate size) in the protocol.

Related Work. There are several techniques to achieve active security even if the field size is small. Beaver [3] showed that one can securely compute a multiplication gate in the presence of active adversaries for any field/ring by sacrificing a multiplication triple. The SPDZ protocol [13] and subsequent studies generate the triples using cryptographic primitives, such as somewhat homomorphic encryption and oblivious transfer. Furukawa et al. [14] and subsequent works [1,22] used another approach to generate the triples using cut-and-choose technique in honest majority. Genkin et al. [16] introduced an algebraic manipulation detection (AMD) circuit that implies actively secure computation. Although their construction relies on a tamper-proof primitive if one uses a binary field, the later result [17] obtained a binary AMD circuit from a boolean one with polylog overhead with $2^{-\kappa}$ statistical error.

Cascudo et al. [9] employed different fields to offer a trade-off with the field size of the circuit. Their technique makes use of an encode between $\mathrm{GF}(2^k)$ and $(\mathrm{GF}(2))^m$ while maintaining the structure of multiplication of those ring and field in some sense. Since the motivation is different, our technique does not maintain the structure of multiplication, while our technique is space-efficient: we can embed several secrets in $\mathbb{K}$ into $\widehat{\mathbb{K}}$ without redundancy.

Paper Organization. The rest of the paper is organized as follows. In Sect. 2, we will recall linear secret sharing. In Sect. 3, we introduce our main technique of field extension in a secret-sharing form. In Sect. 4, we show several applications of our technique to secure computation based on threshold linear secret sharing: consistency check, equality check of multiple shares, and finally and as the main technical result, an efficient secure computation protocol for arithmetic circuits.

---

[1] Precisely, secure computation in $\mathrm{GF}(2^m)$ is XOR-free but redundant for a boolean circuit.

2 Linear Secret Sharing

In this section we give the definition of linear secret sharing [5]. Here, we consider general linear secret sharing with respect to an access structure.

Definition 2.1 (Secret Sharing). *Let $\mathbb{S}$ be a finite domain of secrets. Also, let $\mathcal{A}$ be an access structure of parties $P_1, \ldots, P_n$. A secret sharing scheme $\Pi = (\mathsf{Share}, \mathsf{Rec})$ realizing $\mathcal{A}$ satisfies the following two requirements:*

Reconstruction Requirement. *Let $\mathbb{S}_i$ be a finite domain of the party P_i's shares. For any set $G \in \mathcal{A}$ where $G = \{i_1, \ldots, i_{|G|}\}$, there exists a reconstruction function $\mathsf{Rec}_G : \mathbb{S}_{i_1} \times \cdots \times \mathbb{S}_{i_{|G|}} \to \mathbb{S}$ such that for any secret $s \in \mathbb{S}$, it holds that $\mathsf{Rec}_G([s]_{i_1}, \ldots, [s]_{i_{|G|}}) = s$ where $\mathsf{Share}(s) \to \langle [s]_1, \ldots, [s]_n \rangle$.*

Security Requirement. *For any set $B \notin \mathcal{A}$, any two secrets $\alpha, \beta \in \mathbb{S}$, and any elements $\mathsf{val}_i \in \mathbb{S}_i$ $(1 \leq i \leq n)$, it holds that*

$$\Pr\left[\bigwedge_{P_i \in B} \{[\alpha]_i = \mathsf{val}_i\} \right] = \Pr\left[\bigwedge_{P_i \in B} \{[\beta]_i = \mathsf{val}_i\} \right]$$

where the probabilities are taken over the randomness of the sharing algorithm.

Definition 2.2 (Linear Secret Sharing). *Let $\mathbb{K}$ be a finite field and Π a secret sharing scheme with a domain of secrets $\mathbb{S} \subseteq \mathbb{K}$ realizing an access structure $\mathcal{A}$ of parties $P_1, \ldots, P_n$. We say that Π is a linear secret sharing scheme over $\mathbb{K}$ if the following holds:*

1. *A share of each party consists of a vector over $\mathbb{K}$. More precisely for any index i, there exists a constant d_i such that the party P_i's share is taken from $\mathbb{K}^{d_i}$. We denote by $[s]_{ij}$ the j-th coordinate of the party P_i's share of a secret $s \in \mathbb{S}$.*
2. *For any set in $\mathcal{A}$, i.e., authorized set, its reconstruction function is linear. More precisely, for any set $G \in \mathcal{A}$, there exist constants $\{\alpha_{ij}\}_{P_i \in G, 1 \leq j \leq d_i}$ such that for any secret $s \in \mathbb{S}$, it holds that*

$$s = \sum_{P_i \in G} \sum_{1 \leq j \leq d_i} \alpha_{ij} \cdot [s]_{ij}$$

where the addition and multiplication are over the field $\mathbb{K}$.

If all shares consist of only one element in the field $\mathbb{K}$, Definition 2.2 implies that for any set $G \in \mathcal{A}$, there exist constants $\{\alpha_i\}_{P_i \in G}$ such that for any secret $s \in \mathbb{S}$, it holds that $s = \sum_{P_i \in G} \alpha_i \cdot [s]_i$.

3 Field Extension in Secret-Shared Form

In this section we propose a simple but highly useful method to extend a sharing of a secret over a field to a sharing of the same secret over an extended field, without requiring any communication between the parties which the secret is shared. This is the main mechanism we will exploit in our hybrid approach to protocol design, in which evaluation will be done over a smaller field, but verification is done over a large field to ensure a low statistical error, which in turn bounds the advantage of an adversary.

Let Π be a linear secret sharing scheme with a domain of secrets $\mathbb{S} \subseteq \mathbb{K}$ realizing an access structure $\mathcal{A}$ of parties $P_1, \ldots, P_n$. In the following, we consider a scenario in which these parties will be sharing m secrets $s_1, \ldots, s_m$.

Let $\widehat{\mathbb{K}} = \mathbb{K}[X]/F$ be the extended field of $\mathbb{K}$ where $F \in \mathbb{K}[X]$ is an irreducible polynomial of degree $m - 1$. Let f be the bijective function of natural extension i.e. $f : \mathbb{K}^m \to \widehat{\mathbb{K}}$ and $f(a_1, \ldots, a_m) = a_1 + a_2 X + \cdots + a_m X^{m-1}$.

The following theorem shows that if secrets in $\mathbb{K}$ are shared via a linear secret sharing scheme as $[s_1]_{ij}, \ldots, [s_m]_{ij}$ with coefficients $\{\alpha_{ij}\}_{P_i \in G, 1 \leq j \leq d_i}$ for some $G \in \mathcal{A}$, a "packed" share $f([s_1]_{ij}, \ldots, [s_m]_{ij})$ is in fact a share of $s_1 + s_2 X + \cdots + s_m X^{m-1} \in \widehat{\mathbb{K}}$ with coefficients $\{f(\alpha_{ij}, 0, \ldots, 0)\}_{P_i \in G, 1 \leq j \leq d_i}$. In other words, multiple shares can be embedded in the extended field $\widehat{\mathbb{K}}$ (which we will refer to as packing), and jointly reconstructed over $\widehat{\mathbb{K}}$. Since a party can locally compute $f([s_1]_{ij}, \ldots, [s_m]_{ij})$, the parties can obtain a share of $s_1 + s_2 X + \cdots + s_m X^{m-1} \in \widehat{\mathbb{K}}$ from shares of $s_1, \ldots, s_m \in \mathbb{K}$ without communicating. The theorem also implies that the parties can obtain a share of $s_1 + \cdots + s_\ell X^{\ell-1} + 0 X^\ell + \cdots + 0 X^{m-1} \in \widehat{\mathbb{K}}$ from shares of $\ell \ (< m)$ secrets by setting $[s_k]_{ij} = 0$ for $\ell < k \leq m$.

Theorem 3.1. *Let $[s_k]_{ij}$ be the j-th coordinate of P_i's share of a secret $s_k \in S$. Then for any set $G \in \mathcal{A}$, it holds that*

$$f^{-1}\left(\sum_{P_i \in G} \sum_{1 \leq j \leq d_i} f(\alpha_{ij}, 0, \ldots, 0) \cdot f([s_1]_{ij}, \ldots, [s_m]_{ij}) \right) = (s_1, \ldots, s_m)$$

where $\{\alpha_{ij}\}_{P_i \in G, 1 \leq j \leq d_i}$ are the constants defined in Definition 2.2.

[**Proof**] We have that

$$\sum_{P_i \in G} \sum_{1 \leq j \leq d_i} f(\alpha_{ij}, 0, \ldots, 0) \cdot f([s_1]_{ij}, \ldots, [s_m]_{ij})$$

$$= \sum_{P_i \in G} \sum_{1 \leq j \leq d_i} \alpha_{ij} \cdot \left([s_1]_{ij} + [s_2]_{ij} \cdot X + \cdots + [s_m]_{ij} \cdot X^{m-1} \right)$$

$$= \sum_{P_i \in G} \sum_{1 \leq j \leq d_i} \alpha_{ij} \cdot [s_1]_{ij} + \left(\sum_{P_i \in G} \sum_{1 \leq j \leq d_i} \alpha_{ij} \cdot [s_2]_{ij} \right) X$$

$$+ \cdots + \left(\sum_{P_i \in G} \sum_{1 \leq j \leq d_i} \alpha_{ij} \cdot [s_m]_{ij} \right) X^{m-1}$$

$$= s_1 + s_2 \cdot X + \cdots + s_m \cdot X^{m-1}.$$

Thus, we see that $f^{-1}\left(\sum_{P_i \in G} \sum_{1 \leq j \leq d_i} f(\alpha_{ij}, 0, \ldots, 0) \cdot f([s_1]_{ij}, \ldots, [s_m]_{ij}) \right) = f^{-1}(s_1 + s_2 \cdot X + \cdots + s_m \cdot X^{m-1}) = (s_1, \ldots, s_m)$. ∎

Induced Secret Sharing Scheme. The above theorem not only shows that shares from a secret sharing scheme over $\mathbb{K}$ can be embedded and reconstructed in the extension field $\widehat{\mathbb{K}}$, but in fact let us define an "induced" secret sharing scheme over $\widehat{\mathbb{K}}$ based on the secret sharing scheme over $\mathbb{K}$. More specifically, let $\Pi = (\mathsf{Share}, \mathsf{Rec})$ be a linear secret sharing scheme with a domain of secrets $S \subseteq \mathbb{K}$ realizing an access structure $\mathcal{A}$ of parties $P_1, \ldots, P_n$. We consider the induced scheme $\widehat{\Pi} = (\widehat{\mathsf{Share}}, \widehat{\mathsf{Rec}})$ with a domain of secrets $\widehat{S} \subseteq \widehat{\mathbb{K}} = \mathbb{K}[X]/F$ defined as follows.

$\widehat{\mathsf{Share}}(s)$:

1. Compute $(s_1, \ldots, s_m) \leftarrow f^{-1}(s)$
2. For $k \in [1, m]$: compute $\mathsf{Share}(s_k) \rightarrow \langle \{[s_k]_{1j}\}_{1 \leq j \leq d_1}, \ldots, \{[s_k]_{nj}\}_{1 \leq j \leq d_n} \rangle$
3. For $i \in [1, n]$ and $j \in [1, d_i]$: set $[\![s]\!]_{ij} \leftarrow f([s_1]_{ij}, \ldots, [s_m]_{ij})$
4. Output $\langle \{[\![s]\!]_{1j}\}_{1 \leq j \leq d_1}, \ldots, \{[\![s]\!]_{nj}\}_{1 \leq j \leq d_n} \rangle$

$\widehat{\mathsf{Rec}}_G(\{[\![s]\!]_{ij}\}_{P_i \in G, j \in [1, d_i]})$:

1. For $P_i \in G$ and $j \in [1, d_i]$: compute $\widehat{\alpha_{ij}} \leftarrow f(\alpha_{ij}, 0, \ldots, 0)$.
2. Output $s \leftarrow \sum_{P_i \in G, j \in [1, d_i]} \widehat{\alpha_{ij}} \cdot [\![s]\!]_{ij}$.

The linearity of the above secret sharing scheme follows directly from Theorem 3.1, and security likewise follows in a straightforward manner. We write this as the following corollary.

Corollary 3.2. *Assume that Π is a linear secret sharing scheme. Then the induced secret sharing scheme $\widehat{\Pi}$ is a linear secret sharing scheme.*

The ability of the parties to locally evaluate the embedding function f, means that the parties can locally construct a sharing $[\![\widehat{s}]\!]$ of the induced scheme $\widehat{\Pi}$ from sharings $[s_1], \ldots, [s_m]$ of Π, where $\widehat{s} = s_1 + s_2 X + \cdots + s_m X^{m-1} \in \widehat{\mathbb{K}}$ and $s_1, \ldots, s_m \in \mathbb{K}$.

Throughout the paper, we will adopt the notation used above. Specifically, for a secret sharing scheme $\Pi = (\mathsf{Share}, \mathsf{Rec})$ over $\mathbb{K}$, which we will also refer to as the *base* scheme, $\widehat{\Pi} = (\widehat{\mathsf{Share}}, \widehat{\mathsf{Rec}})$ denotes the *induced* secret sharing scheme defined above over the field extension $\widehat{\mathbb{K}} = \mathbb{K}[X]/F$. For values $s \in \mathbb{K}$ and $v \in \widehat{\mathbb{K}}$, we will use $[s]$ and $[\![v]\!]$ to denote sharings of the base and the induced secret sharing scheme, respectively. We will sometimes abuse this notation, and for a value $s \in \mathbb{K}$ use $[\![s]\!]$ to denote $[\![f(s, 0, \ldots, 0)]\!]$, and will also refer to this as an induced sharing.

4   Applications to Secure Computation

In this section, we show several applications for actively secure computation with abort and an honest majority. As preliminaries to these, in Sect. 4.1, we first give basic definitions, including threshold secret sharing and several protocols that are used as building blocks. Then, we present applications of our field extension technique to consistency check of shares in Sect. 4.2, equality check of multiple shares in Sect. 4.3, and computation of arithmetic circuits in Sect. 4.4.

4.1 Preliminaries

Threshold Linear Secret Sharing. A t-out-of-n secret sharing scheme [5] enables n parties to share a secret $v \in \mathbb{K}$ so that no subset of t parties can learn any information about it, while any subset of $t + 1$ parties can reconstruct it. In addition to being a linear secret sharing scheme, we require that the secret sharing scheme used in our protocol supports the following procedures:

- Share(v): We consider *non-interactive* secret sharing where there exists a probabilistic dealer D that receives a value v (and some randomness) and outputs shares $[v]_1, \ldots, [v]_n$. We denote the sharing of a value v by $[v]$. We use the notation $[v]_J$ to denote the shares held by a subset of parties $J \subset \{P_1, \ldots, P_n\}$. If the dealer is corrupted, then the shares received by the parties may not be correct. Nevertheless, we abuse notation and say that the parties hold shares $[v]$ even if these are not correct. We will define correctness of a sharing formally below.
- Share($v, [v]_J$): This non-interactive procedure is similar to the previous one, except that here the shares of a subset J of parties with $|J| \leq t$ are fixed in advance. We assume that there exists a probabilistic algorithm $\widetilde{D}$ that receives a value v and some values $[v]_J = \{\widetilde{[v]}_i\}_{P_i \in J}$ (and some randomness) and outputs shares $[v]_1, \ldots, [v]_n$ where $[v]_i = \widetilde{[v]}_i$ holds for every $P_i \in J$. We also assume that if $|J| = t$, then $[v]_J$ together with v *fully determine* all shares. This also means that any $t+1$ shares fully determine all shares. (This follows since with $t+1$ shares one can always obtain v. However, for the secret sharing schemes we use, this holds directly as well.)
- Reconstruct($[v], i$): Given a sharing of a value v and an index i held by the parties, this interactive protocol guarantees that if $[v]$ is not correct (see formal definition below), then P_i will output $\perp$ and abort. Otherwise, if $[v]$ is correct, then P_i will either output v or abort.
- Open($[v]$): Given a sharing of a value v held by the parties, this procedure guarantees that at the end of the execution, if $[v]$ is not correct, then *all* the honest parties will abort. Otherwise, if $[v]$ is correct, then each party will either output v or abort. Clearly, Open can be run by any subset of $t + 1$ or more parties. We require that if any subset J of $t + 1$ honest parties output a value v, then any superset of J will output either v or $\perp$ (but no other value).
- *Local Operations*: Given correct sharings $[u]$ and $[v]$, and a scalar $\alpha \in \mathbb{K}$, the parties can generate correct sharings of $[u + v]$, $[\alpha \cdot v]$ and $[v + \alpha]$ using local operations only (i.e., without any interaction). We denote these local operations by $[u] + [v], \alpha \cdot [v]$, and $[v] + \alpha$, respectively.

Standard secret sharing schemes like the Shamir scheme [23] and the replicated secret sharing scheme [11,20] support all of these procedures (with their required properties). Furthermore, if a base secret sharing scheme supports the above procedures, then the induced secret sharing scheme over a field extension likewise supports the above procedures. This easily follows from the one-to-one correspondence between a set of m shares $[s_1], \ldots, [s_m]$ of the base scheme and a share $[\![\hat{s}]\!]$ of the induced scheme, where $\hat{s} = s_1 + s_2 X + \cdots + s_m X^{m-1}$. Specifically, the above procedures for the induced scheme can be implemented by simply mapping the input shares to shares of the base scheme using f^{-1}, and running the corresponding procedure of the base scheme.

The following corollary regarding the security of an induced secret sharing scheme is a simple extension of Corollary 3.2 and follows from the one-to-one correspondence between a set of m shares in the base scheme and a share in the induced scheme.

Corollary 4.1. *Let Π be a secure threshold linear secret sharing scheme. Then the induced scheme $\widehat{\Pi}$ is a secure threshold linear secret sharing scheme.*

In the following, we set the threshold for the secret sharing scheme to be $\lfloor (n-1)/2 \rfloor$, and we denote by t the number of corrupted parties. Since we assume an honest majority, it holds that $t < n/2$, and so the corrupted parties can learn nothing about a shared secret.

We now define correctness for secret sharing. Do we need to add that correctness can be defined as shares being the output of the share algorithm for some value and random coins? This is to avoid the cyclic dependency regarding correctness and the opening algorithm. Let J be a subset of $t+1$ honest parties, and denote by $\mathsf{val}([v])_J$ the value obtained by these parties after running the Open procedure where no corrupted parties or additional honest parties participate. We note that $\mathsf{val}([v])_J$ may equal $\bot$ if the shares held by the honest parties are not valid. Informally, a secret sharing is correct if every subset of $t+1$ honest parties reconstruct the same value (which is not $\bot$). Formally:

Definition 4.2. *Let $H \subseteq \{P_1, \ldots, P_n\}$ denote the set of honest parties. A sharing $[v]$ is correct if there exists a value $\tilde{v} \in \mathbb{K}$ ($\tilde{v} \neq \bot$) such that for every $J \subseteq H$ with $|J| = t+1$ it holds that $\mathsf{val}([v])_J = \tilde{v}$.*

If a sharing $[v]$ is not correct, then either there exists a subset J of $t+1$ honest users such that $\mathsf{val}([v])_J = \bot$, or there exists two subsets J_1 and J_2 such that $\mathsf{val}([v])_{J_1} = v_1$ and $\mathsf{val}([v])_{J_2} = v_2$, where $v_1, v_2 \in \mathbb{K}$ and $v_1 \neq v_2$. We will refer to the former as an invalid sharing, and the latter as a value-inconsistent sharing. Note that a correct sharing in an induced secret sharing scheme corresponds to a set of m correct shares of the base scheme (and conversely, if a single sharing in the base scheme is incorrect, the sharing in the induced scheme will be incorrect).

Definition of Security for Secure Computation. We use the standard definition of security based on the ideal/real model paradigm [8,18], with security formalized for non-unanimous abort. This means that the adversary first receives the output, and then determines for each honest party whether they will receive abort or receive their correct output.

Definitions for Ideal Functionalities. Here, we recall the definitions of the ideal functionalities used in the paper, which are based on the ones used in [10]. These functionalities are associated with a threshold linear secret sharing scheme. Since in this paper we will utilize functionalities for both a secret sharing scheme for a base field $\mathbb{K}$ and those of the induced scheme for an extension field $\widehat{\mathbb{K}}$, we will use the style like $\mathcal{F}_x$ for the former, and the style like $\widehat{\mathcal{F}}_x$ for the latter. In the following, we only describe the functionalities for the base field $\mathbb{K}$; Those for the extension field $\widehat{\mathbb{K}}$ are defined in exactly the same way, with the correspondences that the sharing algorithm is of the induced scheme, and every value is of $\widehat{\mathbb{K}}$. We note that the protocols realizing these functionalities can be efficiently instantiated using standard secret sharing schemes [2,11,23]. (These protocols treat the underlying field and secret sharing scheme in a black-box manner, and hence can be naturally used for realizing the functionalities for the induced scheme.)

- $\mathcal{F}_{\text{coin}}$ – *Generating Random Coins:* When invoked, this functionality picks an element $r \in \mathbb{K}$ uniformly at random and sends it to all parties.
- $\mathcal{F}_{\text{rand}}$ – *Generating Random Shares:* This functionality generates a sharing of a random value in $\mathbb{K}$ unknown to the parties. The formal description is given in Functionality 4.3.
- $\mathcal{F}_{\text{input}}$ – *Secure Sharing of Inputs:* This functionality captures a secure sharing of the parties' inputs. The formal description is given in Functionality 4.4.
- $\mathcal{F}_{\text{checkZero}}$ – *Checking Equality to 0:* This functionality allows callers to check whether a given sharing is a sharing of 0 without revealing any further information on the shared value. The formal description is given in Functionality 4.5.
- $\mathcal{F}_{\text{mult}}$ – *Secure Multiplication up to Additive Attacks* [15,16]*:* This functionality captures a secure computation of a multiplication gate in an arithmetic circuit, but allows an adversary to mount the so-called *additive attacks*. Specifically, this functionality receives input sharings $[x]$ and $[y]$ from the honest parties and an additive value d from the adversary, and outputs a sharing of $x \cdot y + d$. The formal description is given in Functionality 4.6.
- $\mathcal{F}_{\text{product}}$ – *Secure Sum of Products up to Additive Attacks:* This functionality captures a secure computation for the inner product of two vectors of input sharings. As with $\mathcal{F}_{\text{mult}}$, security up to additive attacks is considered. The formal description is given in Functionality 4.7.

4.2   Share Consistency Check

In this section, we present a protocol for checking the correctness of a collection of shares $[x_1], \ldots, [x_l]$. The protocol outputs *reject* if there is an invalid or incorrect share in $[x_1], \ldots, [x_l]$, and outputs *accept* otherwise. The protocol is based on Protocol 3.1 from [22], and works by choosing random coefficients from the extension field, using these to compute a linear combination of the shares embedded in the extension field, and finally opening the resulting sharing. To ensure no information regarding the original shares is revealed, a sharing of a random value of the extension field is added to the linear combination of shares. The description of the protocol is shown in Protocol 4.10. Note that, unlike [22],

---

FUNCTIONALITY 4.3 ($\mathcal{F}_{rand}$ – Generating Random Shares)

Upon receiving $\{\alpha_i\}_{P_i \in \mathcal{C}}$ from the ideal adversary $\mathcal{S}$, $\mathcal{F}_{rand}$ chooses a random $r \in \mathbb{K}$, sets $[r]_{\mathcal{C}} = \{\alpha_i\}_{P_i \in \mathcal{C}}$, and runs $[r] = ([r]_1, \dots, [r]_n) \leftarrow \mathsf{Share}(r, [r]_{\mathcal{C}})$. Then, $\mathcal{F}_{rand}$ hands each honest party P_i (for $i \in H$) its share $[r]_i$.

FUNCTIONALITY 4.4 ($\mathcal{F}_{input}$- Sharing of Inputs)

1. $\mathcal{F}_{input}$ receives inputs $v_1, \dots, v_M \in \mathbb{K}$ from the parties. For each $k \in \{1, \dots, M\}$, $\mathcal{F}_{input}$ also receives from the ideal adversary $\mathcal{S}$ the corrupted parties' shares $[v_k]_{\mathcal{C}}$ for the k-th input.
2. For each $k \in \{1, \dots, M\}$, $\mathcal{F}_{input}$ runs $[v_k] = ([v_k]_1, \dots, [v_k]_n) \leftarrow \mathsf{Share}(v_k, [v_k]_{\mathcal{C}})$.
3. For each $i \in \{1, \dots, n\}$, $\mathcal{F}_{input}$ sends P_i the shares $([v_1]_i, \dots, [v_M]_i)$.

FUNCTIONALITY 4.5 ($\mathcal{F}_{checkZero}$ – Checking Equality to 0)

$\mathcal{F}_{checkZero}$ receives $[v]_H$ from the honest parties and uses it to compute v. Then:

- If $v = 0$, then $\mathcal{F}_{checkZero}$ sends 0 to the ideal adversary $\mathcal{S}$. Then, if $\mathcal{S}$ sends *reject* (resp. *accept*), then $\mathcal{F}_{checkZero}$ sends *reject* (resp. *accept*) to the honest parties.
- If $v \neq 0$, then $\mathcal{F}_{checkZero}$ proceeds as follows:
  - With probability $1/|\mathbb{K}|$, it sends *accept* to the honest parties and $\mathcal{S}$.
  - With probability $1 - 1/|\mathbb{K}|$, it sends *reject* to the honest parties and $\mathcal{S}$.

---

the coefficients for the linear combination are chosen from the full extension field, which allows an analysis with a better probability bound; while the original protocol from [22] will fail with probability $\frac{1}{|\mathbb{K}|-1}$, our protocol fails with probability $\frac{1}{|\widehat{\mathbb{K}}|}$. Hence, our protocol will, in addition to allowing the failure probability to be freely adjusted via the size of the extension field, also remain meaningful for binary fields, for which the original protocol cannot be used.

The protocol relies on the base secret sharing scheme to be *robustly-linear*, which is defined as follows.

Definition 4.8. *A secret sharing scheme is robustly-linear if for every pair of invalid shares $[u]$ and $[v]$, there exists a unique $\alpha \in \mathbb{K}$ such that $\alpha[u] + [v]$ is valid (when computed locally by the parties).*

Note that secret sharing schemes for which there are no invalid shares, like the Shamir secret sharing scheme, will trivially be robustly-linear.

The following lemma plays a central role in the analysis of Protocol 4.10.

Lemma 4.9. *Let $[u]$ be an incorrect sharing of a robustly-linear secret sharing scheme over $\mathbb{K}$, and let $[\![v]\!]$ be any sharing of the induced secret sharing scheme over $\widehat{\mathbb{K}}$. Then, for a randomly chosen $\alpha \in \widehat{\mathbb{K}}$, the probability that $\alpha \cdot f([u], 0, \dots, 0) + [\![v]\!]$ is a correct sharing, is at most $1/|\widehat{\mathbb{K}}|$.*

[Proof]. The proof proceeds by considering the possible combinations of validity, invalidity, and value-inconsistency of $[u]$ and $[\![v]\!]$, and for each combination, show

---

FUNCTIONALITY 4.6 ($\mathcal{F}_{\text{mult}}$ - Secure Mult. up to Additive Attacks)

1. Upon receiving $[x]_H$ and $[y]_H$ from the honest parties where $x, y \in \mathbb{K}$, $\mathcal{F}_{\text{mult}}$ computes x, y and the corrupted parties' shares $[x]_C$ and $[y]_C$.
2. $\mathcal{F}_{\text{mult}}$ hands $[x]_C$ and $[y]_C$ to the ideal adversary $\mathcal{S}$.
3. Upon receiving d and $\{\alpha_i\}_{P_i \in C}$ from $\mathcal{S}$, $\mathcal{F}_{\text{mult}}$ defines $z = x \cdot y + d$ and $[z]_C = \{\alpha_i\}_{P_i \in C}$. Then, $\mathcal{F}_{\text{mult}}$ runs $[z] = ([z]_1, \ldots, [z]_n) \leftarrow \mathsf{Share}(z, [z]_C)$.
4. $\mathcal{F}_{\text{mult}}$ hands each honest party P_i its share $[z]_i$.

FUNCTIONALITY 4.7 ($\mathcal{F}_{\text{product}}$ - Product up to Additive Attacks)

1. Upon receiving $\{[x_\ell]_H\}_{\ell=1}^L$ and $\{[y_\ell]_H\}_{\ell=1}^L$ from the honest parties where $x_\ell, y_\ell \in \mathbb{K}$, $\mathcal{F}_{\text{product}}$ computes x_ℓ and y_ℓ and the corrupted parties' shares $[x_\ell]_C$ and $[y_\ell]_C$, for each $\ell \in \{1, \ldots, L\}$.
2. $\mathcal{F}_{\text{product}}$ hands $\{[x_\ell]_C\}_{\ell=1}^L$ and $\{[y_\ell]_C\}_{\ell=1}^L$ to the ideal adversary $\mathcal{S}$.
3. Upon receiving d and $\{\alpha_i\}_{P_i \in C}$ from $\mathcal{S}$, $\mathcal{F}_{\text{product}}$ defines $z = \sum_{\ell=1}^L x_\ell \cdot y_\ell + d$ and $[z]_C = \{\alpha_i\}_{P_i \in C}$. Then, it runs $[z] = ([z]_1, \ldots, [z]_n) \leftarrow \mathsf{Share}(z, [z]_C)$.
4. $\mathcal{F}_{\text{product}}$ hands each honest party P_i its share $[z]_i$.

---

that only a single choice of $\alpha \in \widehat{\mathbb{K}}$ will make $[\![w]\!] = \alpha \cdot f([u], 0, \ldots, 0) + [\![v]\!]$ a valid sharing.

Firstly, recall that a value $w \in \widehat{\mathbb{K}}$ can be expressed as $w = w_1 + w_2 X + \cdots + w_m X^{m-1}$, where $w_i \in \mathbb{K}$, and a sharing $[\![w]\!]$ in the induced sharing scheme over $\widehat{\mathbb{K}}$ corresponds to $[\![w]\!] = [w_1] + [w_2]X + \cdots + [w_m]X^{m-1}$, where $[w_i]$ are shares over $\mathbb{K}$. Note that for a sharing $[\![w]\!]$ to be valid, each sharing $[w_i]$ for $1 \le i \le m$ must be valid.

Now consider $[\![w]\!] = \alpha f([u], 0, \ldots, 0) + [\![v]\!]$ for a value $\alpha \in \widehat{\mathbb{K}}$, and let $\alpha_i \in \mathbb{K}$ for $1 \le i \le m$ be the values defining α. Then, it must hold that $[w_i] = \alpha_i[u] + [v_i]$. In the following, we will argue about the validity of $[w_i]$. We consider the following cases.

- $[v_i]$ is valid. In this case, only $\alpha_i = 0$ will make $[w_i]$ valid. To see this, assume for the purpose of a contradiction, that $[w_i]$ is valid and $\alpha_i \ne 0$. Then $[u] = \alpha_i^{-1}([w_i] - [v_i])$ will be valid due to the validity of local computations, which contradicts the assumption in the lemma that $[u]$ is incorrect.
- $[v_i]$ is value-inconsistent. That is, there exist sets J_1 and J_2 of $t + 1$ users such that $\mathsf{val}([v_i])_{J_1} = v_i^{(1)}$, $\mathsf{val}([v_i])_{J_2} = v_i^{(2)}$, and $v_i^{(1)} \ne v_i^{(2)}$. There are two sub-cases to consider, $[u]$ being value-inconsistent or invalid (recall that the assumption in the lemma is that $[u]$ is incorrect).
  - $[u]$ is value-inconsistent. Let $\mathsf{val}([u])_{J_1} = u^{(1)}$ and $\mathsf{val}([u]))_{J_2} = u^{(2)}$. Note that $\mathsf{val}([w_i])_{J_1} = \alpha_i u^{(1)} + v_i^{(1)}$ and $\mathsf{val}([w_i])_{J_1} = \alpha_i u^{(1)} + v_i^{(1)}$ due to the correctness of local operations. Now, if $u^{(1)} = u^{(2)}$, it must hold that $\alpha_i u^{(1)} + v_i^{(1)} \ne \alpha_i u^{(2)} + v_i^{(2)}$, since $v_i^{(1)} \ne v_i^{(2)}$. Hence, $[w_i]$ is value-inconsistent. On the other hand, if $u^{(1)} \ne u^{(2)}$, only the unique value $\alpha_i = \frac{v_i^{(2)} - v_i^{(1)}}{u^{(1)} - u^{(2)}}$ will ensure that $\alpha_i u^{(1)} + v_i^{(1)} = \alpha_i u^{(2)} + v_i^{(2)}$, and thereby make $[w_i]$ valid.

- $[u]$ is invalid. Firstly, observe that $\alpha_i = 0$ implies that $[w_i] = [v_i]$, and as $[v_i]$ is value-inconsistent, so will be $[w_i]$. Hence, in the following analysis assumes that $\alpha_i \neq 0$. Since $[u]$ is invalid, there is a set J' satisfying $\mathsf{val}([u])_{J'} = \perp$. For this J' we claim that $\mathsf{val}([w_i])_{J'} = \perp$. To see this assume that $\mathsf{val}([w_i])_{J'} \neq \perp$. Since $[v_i]$ is value-inconsistent, $\mathsf{val}([v_i])_{J'} \neq \perp$. Thus we have that $\mathsf{val}(\alpha_i^{-1}([w_i] - [v_i]))_{J'} = \mathsf{val}([u])_{J'} \neq \perp$, which contradicts the definition of J'.

- $[v_i]$ is invalid. There are again two sub-cases to consider.

  - $[u]$ is value-inconsistent. This case is symmetric to the case where $[v_i]$ is value-inconsistent and $[u]$ is invalid. A similar analysis to the above yields that at most a single choice of α_i will make $[w_i]$ valid.

  - $[u]$ is invalid. That is, both $[u]$ and $[v_i]$ are invalid. As the secret sharing scheme over $\mathbb{K}$ is assumed to be robustly-linear, there is only a single value α_i that will make $[w_i] = \alpha_i[u] + [v_i]$ valid.

As shown in the above analysis, all possible combinations of validity, value-inconsistency, and invalidity of $[u]$ and $[v_i]$ lead to at most a single possible value α_i that will make $[w_i]$ valid. Since α is picked uniformly at random from $\widehat{\mathbb{K}}$, the α_i values are independent and uniformly distributed in $\mathbb{K}$. Hence, the probability that $[\![w]\!]$ is valid, which requires each $[w_i]$ to be valid, is bounded by $(1/|\mathbb{K}|)^m = 1/|\widehat{\mathbb{K}}|$. ∎

PROTOCOL 4.10 (Share Consistency Check)

Inputs: The parties hold l shares $[x_1], \ldots, [x_l]$.

Auxiliary Input: The parties hold the description of finite fields $\mathbb{K}$ and $\widehat{\mathbb{K}}$.

The Protocol:

1. For all $i \in [l]$, the parties compute $[\![x_i]\!] = f([x_i], 0, \ldots, 0)$.
2. The parties call $\widehat{\mathcal{F}}_{\text{coin}}$ to obtain random elements $\alpha_1, \ldots, \alpha_l \in \widehat{\mathbb{K}}$.
3. The parties call $\widehat{\mathcal{F}}_{\text{rand}}$ to obtain a sharing $[\![r]\!]$ for a random element $r \in \widehat{\mathbb{K}}$.
4. The parties locally compute

$$[\![w]\!] = \alpha_1 \cdot [\![x_1]\!] + \ldots + \alpha_l \cdot [\![x_l]\!] + [\![r]\!]$$

5. The parties run $\mathsf{Open}([\![w]\!])$.
6. If any party aborts, the parties output *reject*. Otherwise, the parties output *accept*.

With the above lemma in place, establishing the following result is straightforward.

Theorem 4.11. *Assume the sharing scheme over $\mathbb{K}$ is robustly-linear. Then, in Protocol 4.10, if one of the input shares $[x_1], \ldots, [x_l]$ is not correct, the honest parties in the protocol will output accept with probability at most $1/|\widehat{\mathbb{K}}|$.*

[**Proof**]. Assume that there is an index $i \in [l]$ such that $[x_i]$ is not correct, and note that $[v]$ can be expressed as $[w] = \alpha_i f([x_i], 0, \ldots, 0) + [v]$, where $[v] = \sum_{j \in [l] \setminus \{i\}} \alpha_j f([x_j], 0, \ldots, 0) + [r]$. Then, applying Lemma 4.9 yields that, when $\alpha_i \in \widehat{\mathbb{K}}$ is picked uniformly at random, as done in the protocol, the probability that $[w]$ is correct, is at most $1/|\widehat{\mathbb{K}}|$. As Open guarantees that the honest parties will output reject on input an incorrect share, the theorem follows. ∎

Similar to [22], we will not define the ideal functionality and show full security of Protocol 4.10, as this leads to complications. For example, defining the ideal functionality would require knowing how to generate the inconsistent messages caused by inconsistent shares. Instead, the protocol will have to be simulated directly when showing security of a larger protocol using Protocol 4.10 as a sub-protocol.

4.3   Equality Check of Multiple Shares

Here, we show a simple application of our field extension technique to a protocol for checking that multiple shared secrets $[v_1], \ldots, [v_m]$ of the base field elements $v_1, \ldots, v_m \in \mathbb{K}$ are all equal to 0. This functionality, which we denote by $\mathcal{F}_{\mathsf{mcheckZero}}$, is specified in Functionality 4.12. Our protocol uses the ideal functionality $\mathcal{F}_{\mathsf{checkZero}}$ (Functionality 4.5) in a straightforward way, and thus the definition of $\mathcal{F}_{\mathsf{mcheckZero}}$ incorporates an error probability from the false positive case, namely, even if some non-zero shared secret is contained in the inputs, the protocol outputs accept with probability at most $1/|\widehat{\mathbb{K}}|$, where $\widehat{\mathbb{K}}$ is the extension field. The formal description of our protocol appears in Protocol 4.13.

FUNCTIONALITY 4.12 ($\mathcal{F}_{\mathsf{mcheckZero}}$ — **Batch-Checking Equality to 0**)

$\mathcal{F}_{\mathsf{mcheckZero}}$ receives $[v_1]_H, \ldots, [v_m]_H$ from the honest parties and uses them to compute $v_1, \ldots, v_m$. Then,

1. If $v_1 = \cdots = v_m = 0$, then $\mathcal{F}_{\mathsf{mcheckZero}}$ sends 0 to the ideal adversary $\mathcal{S}$. Then, if $\mathcal{S}$ sends reject (resp., accept), then $\mathcal{F}_{\mathsf{mcheckZero}}$ sends reject (resp., accept) to the honest parties.
2. If $v_i \neq 0$ for some $i \in \{1, \ldots, m\}$, then $\mathcal{F}_{\mathsf{mcheckZero}}$ proceeds as follows:
   (a) With probability $1/|\widehat{\mathbb{K}}|$, it sends accept to the honest parties and $\mathcal{S}$.
   (b) With probability $1 - 1/|\widehat{\mathbb{K}}|$, it sends reject to the honest parties and $\mathcal{S}$.

PROTOCOL 4.13 (Batch-Checking Equality to 0)

Inputs: The parties hold a sharing $[v_1], \ldots, [v_m]$.

The protocol:

1. The parties locally compute a "packed" share $[\widehat{v}] = f([v_1], \ldots, [v_m])$.
2. The parties call $\widehat{\mathcal{F}}_{\mathsf{checkZero}}$ on input $[\widehat{v}]$, and output whatever $\widehat{\mathcal{F}}_{\mathsf{checkZero}}$ outputs.

The security of Protocol 4.13 is guaranteed by the following theorem. (We omit the proof since it is straightforward.)

Theorem 4.14. *Protocol 4.13 securely computes $\mathcal{F}_{\text{mcheckZero}}$ with abort in the $\widehat{\mathcal{F}}_{\text{checkZero}}$-hybrid model in the presence of active adversaries who control $t < n/2$ parties.*

Since the efficient protocol for checking equality to zero of a finite field $\mathbb{K}$ by Chida et al. [10, Protocol 3.7] in the $(\mathcal{F}_{\text{rand}}, \mathcal{F}_{\text{mult}})$-hybrid model uses the underlying secret sharing scheme and the finite field in a black-box manner, it can be used for checking equality to zero for an extension field $\widehat{\mathbb{K}}$ in the $(\widehat{\mathcal{F}}_{\text{rand}}, \widehat{\mathcal{F}}_{\text{mult}})$-hybrid model. Hence, by combining this protocol with Theorem 4.14, we also obtain an efficient protocol for checking equality to zero of multiple shared secrets in the base field $\mathbb{K}$ in the $(\widehat{\mathcal{F}}_{\text{rand}}, \widehat{\mathcal{F}}_{\text{mult}})$-hybrid model.

An obvious merit of our protocol is that it can be used even if the size of the base field $\mathbb{K}$ is small, i.e, $|\mathbb{K}| \leq 2^{\kappa}$ for an intended statistical error κ. On the contrary, Chida et al.'s original protocol [10, Protocol 3.7] cannot be used for small field elements. Another merit of our protocol is that by adjusting the size of the extension field $\widehat{\mathbb{K}}$, we can flexibly reduce the error probability (i.e. the false positive probability) that the protocol outputs *accept* even though some input shares contain a non-zero secret.

Application to Password-Based Authentication. We can apply our protocol to implement a password-based authentication protocol, such as [21]. Let us consider the following scenario. A password is stored among multiple backend servers in a linear secret sharing form. To log-in to the system the user splits his password into shares and sends each share to each server. The servers run Protocol 4.13 to determine whether the password sent from the user is correct (more precisely, the servers subtract the two shares, the one sent from the user and the one stored by themselves, and run Protocol 4.13 to determine whether the difference between two shares is zero).

We claim that the most space-efficient way to store the password is to store a password in a character-by-character manner. For example, if a password is encoded by the ASCII code (8-bit represents a single character), shares of a password is a sequence of $\text{GF}(2^8)$-shares. By running Protocol 4.13, the servers combine $\text{GF}(2^8)$-shares into a single induced share which contains the entire password, and check that the secret-shared bytes are all zeros. This approach has advantages over the following alternative choices regarding storage capacity. The first alternative is (1) to use a field sufficiently large both for storing the password and for providing statistical security, for example, a 320-bit field. This alternative is not efficient because we need to allocate 320 bits of storage for every password, which may include short, say, 8-byte passwords. Another alternative is (2) to use a field sufficiently large for statistical security but not necessarily large enough for storing the password, for example, a 40-bit field. In this case, the password will be stored by first dividing the password into a sequence of 40-bit blocks, and then share these among the servers in a block-by-block manner. This alternative is again not efficient, particularly in the case that the length of a password is not a multiple of the size of a block.

4.4   Secure Computation for Arithmetic Circuits

As mentioned earlier, the original highly efficient protocol for computing arithmetic circuits for a small finite field by Chida et al. [10, Protocol 5.3], in fact cannot be used for a field $\mathbb{K}$ with $|\mathbb{K}| \leq 3$ (e.g. computation for boolean circuits).

In this section, we show how to remove this restriction by using our field extension technique. Namely, we propose a variant of Chida et al.'s protocol that truly works for any finite field. The formal description of our protocol is given in Protocol 4.16. The simple idea employed in our protocol is to perform the computations for the randomized shares $[r \cdot x]$ and the equality check of the invariant done in the verification stage, over an extension field $\widehat{\mathbb{K}}$. In contrast, these operations are done over the base field $\mathbb{K}$ in Chida et al.'s original protocol. This allows us to perform the computation of the randomized shares using only a single element (of the extension field), while still achieving statistical security $3/|\widehat{\mathbb{K}}|$, which is a simplification compared to the protocol by Chida et al. Note that $3/|\widehat{\mathbb{K}}|$ can be chosen according to the desired statistical error by adjusting the degree m for the field extension.

The following theorem formally guarantees the security of our protocol.

Theorem 4.15. *Let κ be a statistical security parameter such that $3/|\widehat{\mathbb{K}}| \leq 2^{-\kappa}$. Let $\mathcal{F}$ be an n-party functionality over $\mathbb{K}$. Then, Protocol 4.16 securely computes $\mathcal{F}$ with abort in the $(\mathcal{F}_{\text{input}}, \mathcal{F}_{\text{mult}}, \widehat{\mathcal{F}}_{\text{mult}}, \widehat{\mathcal{F}}_{\text{product}}, \widehat{\mathcal{F}}_{\text{rand}}, \widehat{\mathcal{F}}_{\text{checkZero}})$-hybrid model with statistical error $2^{-\kappa}$, in the presence of active adversaries who control $t < n/2$ parties.*

Due to the space limitation, the formal proof of Theorem 4.15 is given in the full version.

PROTOCOL 4.16 (Computing Arithmetic Circuits over Any Finite $\mathbb{K}$)

Inputs: Each party P_i ($i \in \{1, \ldots, n\}$) holds an input $x_i \in \mathbb{K}^\ell$.

Auxiliary Input: The parties hold the description of finite fields $\mathbb{K}$ and $\widehat{\mathbb{K}}$ with $3/|\widehat{\mathbb{K}}| \leq 2^{-\kappa}$, and an arithmetic circuit C over $\mathbb{K}$ that computes $\mathcal{F}$ on inputs of length $M = \ell \cdot n$. Let N be the number of multiplication gates in C.

The Protocol:

1. *Secret sharing the inputs:* For each input v_j held by the party P_i, the party P_i sends v_j to $\mathcal{F}_{\text{input}}$. Each party P_i records its vector of shares $([v_1]_i, \ldots, [v_M]_i)$ of all inputs, as received from $\mathcal{F}_{\text{input}}$. If the party received $\perp$ from $\mathcal{F}_{\text{input}}$, then it sends abort to the other parties and halts.

2. *Generate a randomizing share:* The parties call $\widehat{\mathcal{F}}_{\text{rand}}$ to receive a sharing $[\![\widehat{r}]\!]$.

3. *Randomization of inputs:* For each input wire sharing $[v_j]$ (where $j \in \{1, \ldots, M\}$), the parties locally compute the induced share $[\![v_j]\!] = f([v_j], 0, \ldots, 0)$. Then, the parties call $\widehat{\mathcal{F}}_{\text{mult}}$ on $[\![\widehat{r}]\!]$ and $[\![v_j]\!]$ to receive $[\![\widehat{r} \cdot v_j]\!]$.

4. *Circuit emulation:* Let $G_1, \ldots, G_{|C|}$ be a predetermined topological ordering of the gates of the circuit C. For $j = 1, \ldots, |C|$ the parties proceed as follows:
    - If G_j *is an addition gate:* Given pairs $([x], [\![\widehat{r} \cdot x]\!])$ and $([y], [\![\widehat{r} \cdot y]\!])$ on the *left* and *right* input wires respectively, each party locally computes $([x + y], [\![\widehat{r} \cdot (x + y)]\!])$.
    - If G_j *is a multiplication-by-a-constant gate:* Given a pair $([x], [\![\widehat{r} \cdot x]\!])$ on the input wire and a constant $a \in \mathbb{K}$, each party locally computes $([a \cdot x], [\![\widehat{r} \cdot (a \cdot x)]\!])$.
    - If G_j *is a multiplication gate:* Given pairs $([x], [\![\widehat{r} \cdot x]\!])$ and $([y], [\![\widehat{r} \cdot y]\!])$ on the *left* and *right* input wires respectively, the parties compute $([x \cdot y], [\![\widehat{r} \cdot x \cdot y]\!])$ as follows:
        (a) The parties call $\mathcal{F}_{\text{mult}}$ on $[x]$ and $[y]$ to receive $[x \cdot y]$.
        (b) The parties locally compute the induced share $[\![y]\!] = f([y], 0, \ldots, 0)$.
        (c) The parties call $\widehat{\mathcal{F}}_{\text{mult}}$ on $[\![\widehat{r} \cdot x]\!]$ and $[\![y]\!]$ to receive $[\![\widehat{r} \cdot x \cdot y]\!]$.

5. *Verification stage:* Let $\{([z_k], [\![\widehat{r} \cdot z_k]\!])\}_{k=1}^{N}$ be the pairs on the output wires of the mult. gates, and $\{([v_j], [\![\widehat{r} \cdot v_j]\!])\}_{j=1}^{M}$ be the pairs on the input wires of $\dot{C}$.
    (a) For $k = 1, \ldots, N$, the parties call $\widehat{\mathcal{F}}_{\text{rand}}$ to receive $[\![\widehat{\alpha}_k]\!]$.
    (b) For $j = 1, \ldots, M$, the parties call $\widehat{\mathcal{F}}_{\text{rand}}$ to receive $[\![\widehat{\beta}_j]\!]$.
    (c) *Compute linear combinations:*
        i. The parties call $\widehat{\mathcal{F}}_{\text{product}}$ on vectors $([\![\widehat{\alpha}_1]\!], \ldots, [\![\widehat{\alpha}_N]\!], [\![\widehat{\beta}_1]\!], \ldots, [\![\widehat{\beta}_M]\!])$ and $([\![\widehat{r} \cdot z_1]\!], \ldots, [\![\widehat{r} \cdot z_N]\!], [\![\widehat{r} \cdot \widehat{v}_1]\!], \ldots, [\![\widehat{r} \cdot v_M]\!])$ to receive $[\![\widehat{u}]\!]$.
        ii. For each $k \in \{1, \ldots, N\}$, the parties locally compute the induced share $[\![z_k]\!] = f([z_k], 0, \ldots, 0)$ of the output wire of the k-th mult. gate. Then, the parties call $\widehat{\mathcal{F}}_{\text{product}}$ on vectors $([\![\widehat{\alpha}_1]\!], \ldots, [\![\widehat{\alpha}_N]\!], [\![\widehat{\beta}_1]\!], \ldots, [\![\widehat{\beta}_M]\!])$ and $([\![z_1]\!], \ldots, [\![z_N]\!], [\![v_1]\!], \ldots, [\![v_M]\!])$ to receive $[\![\widehat{w}]\!]$.
        iii. The parties run $\mathsf{Open}([\![\widehat{r}]\!])$ to receive $\widehat{r}$.
        iv. Each party locally computes $[\![\widehat{T}]\!] = [\![\widehat{u}]\!] - \widehat{r} \cdot [\![\widehat{w}]\!]$.
        v. The parties call $\widehat{\mathcal{F}}_{\text{checkZero}}$ on $[\![\widehat{T}]\!]$. If $\widehat{\mathcal{F}}_{\text{checkZero}}$ outputs *reject*, the parties output $\perp$ and abort. Else, if it outputs *accept*, they proceed.

6. *Output reconstruction:* For each output wire of C, the parties run $\mathsf{Reconstruct}([v], i)$ where $[v]$ is the sharing on the output wire, and P_i is the party whose output is on the wire. If a party received $\perp$ in any of the $\mathsf{Reconstruct}$ procedures, it sends $\perp$ to the other parties, outputs $\perp$, and halts.

Output: If a party has not aborted, it outputs the values received on its output wires.

Acknowledgement. A part of this work was supported by JST CREST grantnumber JPMJCR19F6.

References

1. Araki, T., et al.: Optimized honest-majority MPC for malicious adversaries - breaking the 1 billion-gate per second barrier. In: IEEE Symposium on Security and Privacy, SP 2017 (2017)
2. Araki, T., Furukawa, J., Lindell, Y., Nof, A., Ohara, K.: High-throughput semi-honest secure three-party computation with an honest majority. In: ACM CCS 2016, pp. 805–817 (2016)
3. Beaver, D.: Efficient multiparty protocols using circuit randomization. In: Feigenbaum, J. (ed.) CRYPTO 1991. LNCS, vol. 576, pp. 420–432. Springer, Heidelberg (1992). https://doi.org/10.1007/3-540-46766-1_34
4. Beerliová-Trubíniová, Z., Hirt, M.: Perfectly-secure MPC with linear communication complexity. In: Canetti, R. (ed.) TCC 2008. LNCS, vol. 4948, pp. 213–230. Springer, Heidelberg (2008). https://doi.org/10.1007/978-3-540-78524-8_13
5. Beimel, A.: Secure schemes for secret sharing and key distribution. Ph.D. thesis, Israel Institute of Technology (1996)
6. Ben-Or, M., Goldwasser, S., Wigderson, A.: Completeness theorems for non-cryptographic fault-tolerant distributed computation (extended abstract). In: STOC 1988, pp. 1–10 (1988)
7. Ben-Sasson, E., Fehr, S., Ostrovsky, R.: Near-linear unconditionally-secure multiparty computation with a dishonest minority. In: Safavi-Naini, R., Canetti, R. (eds.) CRYPTO 2012. LNCS, vol. 7417, pp. 663–680. Springer, Heidelberg (2012). https://doi.org/10.1007/978-3-642-32009-5_39
8. Canetti, R.: Universally composable security: a new paradigm for cryptographic protocols. In: FOCS 2001, pp. 136–145 (2001)
9. Cascudo, I., Cramer, R., Xing, C., Yuan, C.: Amortized complexity of information-theoretically secure MPC revisited. In: Shacham, H., Boldyreva, A. (eds.) CRYPTO 2018. LNCS, vol. 10993, pp. 395–426. Springer, Cham (2018). https://doi.org/10.1007/978-3-319-96878-0_14
10. Chida, K., et al.: Fast large-scale honest-majority MPC for malicious adversaries. In: Shacham, H., Boldyreva, A. (eds.) CRYPTO 2018. LNCS, vol. 10993, pp. 34–64. Springer, Cham (2018). https://doi.org/10.1007/978-3-319-96878-0_2
11. Cramer, R., Damgård, I., Ishai, Y.: Share conversion, pseudorandom secret-sharing and applications to secure computation. In: Kilian, J. (ed.) TCC 2005. LNCS, vol. 3378, pp. 342–362. Springer, Heidelberg (2005). https://doi.org/10.1007/978-3-540-30576-7_19
12. Damgård, I., Nielsen, J.B.: Scalable and unconditionally secure multiparty computation. In: Menezes, A. (ed.) CRYPTO 2007. LNCS, vol. 4622, pp. 572–590. Springer, Heidelberg (2007). https://doi.org/10.1007/978-3-540-74143-5_32
13. Damgård, I., Pastro, V., Smart, N., Zakarias, S.: Multiparty computation from somewhat homomorphic encryption. In: Safavi-Naini, R., Canetti, R. (eds.) CRYPTO 2012. LNCS, vol. 7417, pp. 643–662. Springer, Heidelberg (2012). https://doi.org/10.1007/978-3-642-32009-5_38
14. Furukawa, J., Lindell, Y., Nof, A., Weinstein, O.: High-throughput secure three-party computation for malicious adversaries and an honest majority. In: Coron, J.-S., Nielsen, J.B. (eds.) EUROCRYPT 2017. LNCS, vol. 10211, pp. 225–255. Springer, Cham (2017). https://doi.org/10.1007/978-3-319-56614-6_8
15. Genkin, D., Ishai, Y., Polychroniadou, A.: Efficient multi-party computation: from passive to active security via secure SIMD circuits. In: Gennaro, R., Robshaw, M. (eds.) CRYPTO 2015. LNCS, vol. 9216, pp. 721–741. Springer, Heidelberg (2015). https://doi.org/10.1007/978-3-662-48000-7_35

16. Genkin, D., Ishai, Y., Prabhakaran, M., Sahai, A., Tromer, E.: Circuits resilient to additive attacks with applications to secure computation. In: STOC 2014, pp. 495–504 (2014)
17. Genkin, D., Ishai, Y., Weiss, M.: Binary AMD circuits from secure multiparty computation. In: Hirt, M., Smith, A. (eds.) TCC 2016. LNCS, vol. 9985, pp. 336–366. Springer, Heidelberg (2016). https://doi.org/10.1007/978-3-662-53641-4_14
18. Goldreich, O.: The Foundations of Cryptography - Basic Applications, vol. 2. Cambridge University Press, Cambridge (2004)
19. Hirt, M.: Multi-party computation: efficient protocols, general adversaries, and voting. Ph.D. thesis, ETH Zurich (2001)
20. Ito, M., Saito, A., Nishizeki, T.: Secret sharing schemes realizing general access structure. Globecom **1987**, 99–102 (1987)
21. Kikuchi, R., Chida, K., Ikarashi, D., Hamada, K.: Password-based authentication protocol for secret-sharing-based multiparty computation. IEICE Trans. **101–A(1)**, 51–63 (2018)
22. Lindell, Y., Nof, A.: A framework for constructing fast MPC over arithmetic circuits with malicious adversaries and an honest-majority. In: ACM CCS 2017, pp. 259–276 (2017)
23. Shamir, A.: How to share a secret. Commun. ACM **22**(11), 612–613 (1979)

Efficient Secure Multi-Party Protocols for Decision Tree Classification

Atsunori Ichikawa[1]([✉]), Wakaha Ogata[2][iD], Koki Hamada[1][iD], and Ryo Kikuchi[1]

[1] NTT Secure Platform Laboratories, Tokyo 180-8585, Japan
{atsunori.ichikawa.nf,koki.hamada.rb}@hco.ntt.co.jp,
kikuchi_ryo@fw.ipsj.or.jp
[2] Tokyo Institute of Technology, Tokyo 152-8852, Japan
ogata.w.aa@m.titech.ac.jp

Abstract. We propose novel secure multi-party protocols for decision-tree classification. Our protocols hide not only an input vector and an output class but also the *structure* of the tree, which incurs an exponential communication complexity in terms of the maximum depth of the tree, d_{max}, for a naive construction. We tackle this problem by applying Oblivious RAM (ORAM) and obtain two efficient constructions with polynomial communication complexity (that counts the number of multiplications). The first protocol simulates ORAM in secure multi-party computation. The communication complexity of the first protocol is $O(d_{max}^3 \log d_{max})$ in the online phase and $O(d_{max}^4 \log d_{max})$ in total. We then improve this protocol by removing the position-map accesses, which is the most time-consuming parts in the ORAM. In the second protocol, we reduce the communication complexity to $O(d_{max}^2 \log d_{max})$ in the online phase and $O(d_{max}^3 \log d_{max})$ in total, and also reduce the number of rounds from $O(d_{max}^2)$ to $O(d_{max})$. We implemented the proposed two constructions and the naive one, and experimentally evaluated their performance.

Keywords: Multi-party computation · Decision tree · Oblivious RAM

1 Introduction

Machine-learning techniques are widespread, and the need for applying them to analyze personal information is increasing. Methods of *learning* a machine-learning model from personal training data have been developed. On the other hand, secure *usage* of the model to classify personal information is also an important issue. We focus on the secure usage of a learnt model. A model we deal with is a *decision tree*, which is the most common model because of its ease of handling and readability.

We assume an *outsourced* service that analyzes personal information, such as medical conditions and purchasing histories, by using a mathematical model, e.g., a decision tree, learnt from training data. Such a service consists of the following

J. Jang-Jaccard and F. Guo (Eds.): ACISP 2019, LNCS 11547, pp. 362–380, 2019.
https://doi.org/10.1007/978-3-030-21548-4_20

Table 1. Comparison of asymptotic running costs to execute a secure decision tree of each construction we investigated. On- denotes online phase of whole protocol and Off- denotes offline phase. d_{max} is the maximum depth of the decision tree. Complexity denotes the number of invocations of multiplication protocols in each construction. Rounds denote number of batch invocations of multiplication protocols in each construction when we can simultaneously invoke any number of multiplication protocols.

	On- Complexity	On- Rounds	Off- Complexity	Off- Rounds
Naive	$O(d_{max} \cdot 2^{d_{max}})$	$O(1)$	—	—
Applying ORAM	$O(d_{max}^3 \log d_{max})$	$O(d_{max}^2)$	$O(d_{max}^4 \log d_{max})$	$O(d_{max}^3)$
Daisy chain	$O(d_{max}^2 \log d_{max})$	$O(d_{max})$	$O(d_{max}^3 \log d_{max})$	$O(d_{max}^2)$

four steps. (1) The mathematical model owned by a *model holder* (*holder* for short) is passed to another entity called an *agent*. (2) A *client* sends its personal input, which is given as an *input vector*, to the agent. (3) The agent computes a class that matches the input vector based on the mathematical model. (4) Finally, the client receives the result from the agent. For privacy preservation, the client wishes to hide its input vector from the agent, whereas the holder wants to hide the model from the client and the agent as it is its intellectual property.

We approach this problem using *secure multi-party computation (MPC)*. MPC is a technique introduced by Yao [1] that enables multiple *parties* to cooperatively evaluate any function while keeping input and output values secret from each party. In the service as mentioned above, the set of parties in MPC plays the role of the agent.

Ignoring efficiency, we can solve this problem by using the following naive approach. We store the decision tree to a sufficiently large complete tree by padding. For evaluation, the parties privately evaluate *all* nodes regardless of the evaluation results of their ancestral nodes then privately aggregate all results to decide the leaf to which the input vector is classified. This naive approach incurs exponential communication cost in terms of the height d_{max} of the complete tree, which is intractable since d_{max} should be large to store any decision tree.

1.1   Our Contributions

We overcome this intractability using *Oblivious RAM (ORAM)* data structure. ORAM allows a user to access (read from or write to) an element in an external database stored in a server without disclosing the access pattern to the server. We use MPC protocols simulating ORAM [12] to efficiently and privately read nodes in the decision tree. As a result, we propose two constructions that run with polynomial communication cost in terms of d_{max}.

Our contributions are listed as follows:

- We first propose an efficient construction of secure multi-party protocols for decision-tree classification, which keeps both queries and decision trees secret from the parties of an MPC. In contrast to the naive construction, in this construction, the parties only evaluate the nodes located on a path from the root to a leaf corresponding to the input, yet evaluated nodes are hidden thanks to ORAM data structures. As a result, the communication complexity of the classification protocols is $O(d_{max}^4 \log d_{max})$, which is an exponential improvement from that of the naive construction. Communication cost is determined as the number of invocations of a multiplication protocol, which is one of the minimal operations in our setting.

- In this construction, the classification procedure is divided into online and offline parts. The communication complexity of the protocol for the online phase is $O(d_{max}^3 \log d_{max})$.
- We also propose *Daisy Chain* technique that improves the communication complexity and rounds for sequential invocations of multi-stage ORAM. This technique removes the position-map accesses, which are the most time-consuming parts in the ORAM access, from each ORAM. Applying this technique to our first construction, the communication complexity is reduced from $O(d_{max}^3 \log d_{max})$ to $O(d_{max}^2 \log d_{max})$ for the online phase. The communication rounds are also reduced from $O(d_{max}^2)$ to $O(d_{max})$ for the online phase.
- We implement the naive construction and the proposed constructions and experimentally evaluate their performances.

We give an overview of communication complexity and communication rounds of these constructions in Table 1.

1.2 Related Work

Recent studies [3,9,10,14] investigated algorithms that can be applied to decision-tree classification in MPC under a slightly different assumption from ours. They hide the input vector from the parties in MPC but the information about the decision tree is assumed to be public to the parties. Bost et al. investigated methods using homomorphic encryption to classify information securely by using a decision tree [14], and Wu et al. [3] and Backes et al. [10] each extended it for a random forest. Hamada et al. [9] converted Fisher's Exact Test to a form of a decision tree and proposed a method of computing it by using MPC.

In the context of privacy-preserving data mining, a secure-machine learning algorithm for a decision tree model was introduced by Lindell and Pinkas [17]. Our work is motivated by this but focused on how to use a constructed classifier securely, not how to construct a classifier.

2 Preliminary

2.1 Decision Tree

A decision tree is a tree-structured model used to classify a given *input vector* $X = (X_1, \ldots, X_n)$. Classification in this model is based on a tree, which is also called a *decision tree*, each internal node of which is assigned a test function, and each leaf node is assigned a class.

We assume that each test function is a predicate $[X_t =_? V]$ or $[X_t <_? V]$ for $t \in \{1, \ldots, n\}$. Each internal node is a tuple of values $((d, i), P, CL, CR, t, V, op)$: (d, i) means the node is the ith element at depth d. P, CL, and CR denote indices of the parent, left child, and right child nodes respectively. t denotes an index of the input vector to be compared. V denotes the threshold to be compared. op designates the operator where $op = 0$ means equality test and $op = 1$ means comparison test. When the left (resp. right) child of $N_{d,i}$ is a leaf L_j, CL (resp. CR) is set to j. For notational clarity, we often omit (d, i), P, CL, and CR if they are apparent.

Each leaf is a tuple of values $(j, P, Class)$: j is the index of the leaf L_j, P denotes the index of the parent, and Class denotes the class corresponding to the leaf. For the same reason as above, we often omit j and P.

We specify a decision tree Tree by a triple $(d_{max}, \mathcal{N}, \mathcal{L})$, where d_{max} is the maximum depth of internal nodes, $\mathcal{N}$ is a set of all internal nodes, and $\mathcal{L}$ is a set of all leaves. The *size* of a decision tree means the number of nodes $|\mathcal{N}|$.

Tree classifies an input vector $\boldsymbol{X}$ in the following manner. Test $\boldsymbol{X}$ at the root node $N_{0,0} = ((0, 0), \perp, (1, 0), (1, 1), t_{0,0}, V_{0,0}, op_{0,0})$ [1] and obtain the result of a test function: $z_0 \leftarrow [X_{t_{0,0}} =_? V_{0,0}]$ if $op_{0,0} = 0$; otherwise, $z_0 \leftarrow [X_{t_{0,0}} <_? V_{0,0}]$. If $z_0 = 0$, proceed to the left child node $N_{1,0}$; otherwise, proceed to the right child node $N_{1,1}$. After that, repeat the same procedures at the child node until reaching one of the leaf nodes. The output is an assigned Class of the leaf. We can obtain Class with at most $d_{max} + 1$ comparisons. We assume that all $V_{d,i}$ are integers, and can be expressed with a fixed length.

2.2   Secret Sharing Scheme

Secret Sharing Scheme (SSS), invented by Shamir [2] and Blakley [6], is a technique to share a secret and store it securely. In SSS, a dealer of a secret value s converts it to n fractions by function **share** (s). Each fraction is called a *secret-shared* value, or simply a *share*, and n shares are sent to n parties one by one. We use $[\![s]\!]$ to denote a list of n shares of s. When parties want to reconstruct s together, they can obtain it from (a subset of) n shares by function **Reveal**$([\![s]\!])$. When s is an element of a finite field and $[\![s]\!]$ is obtained from s and random elements of this field by linear mapping, this is called the *Linear* Secret Sharing Scheme (LSSS). Examples of the LSSS are given in previous studies [2,6,11].

2.3   Secure Multi-Party Computation

Secure Multi-Party Computation (MPC) enables us to compute any arithmetic function while hiding information of inputs. It is known that multi-party addition/multiplication protocols based on the LSSS can be constructed [15]. I.e., $[\![X]\!] + [\![Y]\!] \rightarrow [\![X + Y]\!]$ and $[\![X]\!] \cdot [\![Y]\!] \rightarrow [\![X \cdot Y]\!]$.

---

[1] $\perp$ means that there is no corresponding node, and the depth d starts from 0.

Building blocks. We assume the following secure protocols based on MPC:

- $[\![\bar{x}]\!] \to [\![1-x]\!]$ denotes the inverse for $x \in \{0,1\}$.
- $[\![x]\!] \vee [\![y]\!] \to [\![x \vee y]\!]$ denotes OR operation for $x, y \in \{0,1\}$.
- **Comp**$([\![X]\!], [\![Y]\!], [\![op]\!]) \to [\![b]\!]$ compares two secrets X and Y while hiding operator op. That is, $[\![b]\!] = [\![X =_? Y]\!] \cdot [\![\overline{op}]\!] + [\![X <_? Y]\!] \cdot [\![op]\!]$.
- **LinearAccess**$([\![T]\!], [\![U]\!]) \to [\![U_t]\!]$
  gets a secret element $[\![U_t]\!]$ from a secret vector $[\![U]\!] = ([\![U_1]\!], \ldots, [\![U_m]\!])$. Vector $T = (0, \ldots, 0, 1, 0, \ldots, 0)$, called *tag vector of* t, of length m indicates t, such that only the tth element is set to be 1.
- **IfElse**$([\![c]\!], [\![a]\!], [\![b]\!]) \to [\![x]\!]$ denotes branching for $c \in \{0,1\}$. It outputs a share $[\![x]\!]$ s.t. $x = a$ if $c = 1$; otherwise $x = b$. This protocol is implemented as $[\![a]\!] + [\![c]\!] \cdot ([\![b]\!] - [\![a]\!])$ [12].

Comp can be straightforwardly built from a known comparison protocol, e.g. [16]. If we assume that the sizes of X and Y is fixed, we can evaluate **Comp**$([\![X]\!], [\![Y]\!], [\![op]\!])$ by $O(1)$ multiplications. **LinearAccess** can be obtained from a simple inner product of $[\![T]\!]$ and $[\![U]\!]$, that is, parallel m multiplications.

We also assume **RandomPos**(Oram), Oram.**Init**, Oram.**Read**, and Oram.**Write** as building blocks. They are predicated in the following section.

2.4   Oblivious RAM

Oblivious RAM (ORAM), introduced by Goldreich and Ostrovsky [13], is a system that enables us to securely access an external storage. It can hide not only the data but also the access pattern queried by a user.

Path ORAM. The Path ORAM is an efficient ORAM proposed by Shi et al. [4] and improved by Stefanov et al. [5]. In the Path ORAM, the storage is assumed to have a binary tree structure, and some meta-data associated with a leaf of the tree are attached to data to be stored into the Path ORAM. We call a tuple composed of data and meta-data an Entry.

Keller et al. [12] proposed MPC protocols for maintaining a distributed storage that operates as the Path ORAM. In the following, we use a term "Path ORAM" or simply "ORAM" to indicate this MPC -based protocols.

The whole system of the Path ORAM Oram includes distributed memory structures $(\mathcal{B}, \mathcal{S}, \mathcal{P})$. Remember that all values in $\mathcal{B}, \mathcal{S}, \mathcal{P}$ are secret-shared between parties.

- $\mathcal{B}$ is storage having a binary tree structure, each node of which holds a certain number of entries. Each entry includes three types of meta-data: its index u, *position* p, and *empty flag*. The p indicates where the entry should be located in $\mathcal{B}$, i.e., p corresponds to a random path (or equivalently random leaf). *empty flag* indicates whether the entry is a dummy. We omit it since we do not use it in the summaries of our protocols. Thus, an entry is denoted as Entry $= ([\![u]\!], [\![Data]\!], [\![p]\!])$.

- $\mathcal{S}$ is an array that holds entries overflowed from $\mathcal{B}$.
- $\mathcal{P}$, called *position map*, is a structure that holds pairs $(\llbracket u_i \rrbracket, \llbracket p_i \rrbracket)$ for all $i \in \{1, \ldots, N\}$, where N is the number of entries. This structure is used to obtain the position p_i to access an entry of index u_i. There are two cases of setting up $\mathcal{P}$: *non-recursive* and *recursive* [5]. In the non-recursive case, $\mathcal{P}$ is an array of size N. In the recursive case, $\mathcal{P}$ is stored into other smaller Path ORAMs and can be accessed more efficiently. In this paper, we follow Keller et al. [12] and assume that the recursions occur $O(\log N)$ times, i.e., Oram has small $O(\log N)$ Path ORAMs as $\mathcal{P}$.

To handle these data structures, Oram has an initialization protocol and access protocols.

- Oram.**Init**(N) initializes Oram. For a given number of entries N, it first builds $\mathcal{B}$ as a complete binary tree of maximum depth $\lceil \log N \rceil - 2$ [2] and fills $\mathcal{B}$ and $\mathcal{S}$ by dummy entries. Then it constructs $\mathcal{P}$.

For an access procedure to the Path ORAM, **Access** was prepared [5]. Keller et al. [12] split it into two protocols **ReadAndRemove** and **Add**, that is, corresponding to the former and latter parts of **Access**. For simplicity, we recompose these protocols into **Read** and **Write** as follows.

- Oram.**Read**($\llbracket u \rrbracket$) pops Entry of index u and removes it from Oram. This consists of the following two subprotocols: **posRead**($\llbracket u \rrbracket$) that obtains a position $\llbracket p \rrbracket$ associated with $\llbracket u \rrbracket$ from $\mathcal{P}$, and **npRead**($\llbracket u \rrbracket, \llbracket p \rrbracket$) that explores the path indicated by p to obtain Entry.
- Oram.**Write**(Entry) stores Entry into Oram. This consists of the following two subprotocols: **posRenew**(Entry) that replaces the current $\llbracket p \rrbracket$ in both Entry and $\mathcal{P}$ with new $\llbracket p' \rrbracket$, which is randomly generated using subprotocol **RandomPos**(Oram), and **npWrite**(Entry) that stores Entry into the root of $\mathcal{B}$ and runs an eviction process. **RandomPos** can be obtained from a secure random number generator, e.g., described in [7].

3   System Model

There are three types of participants: *client* that has an input vector X to be classified, *holder* that has a decision tree $(d_{max}, \mathcal{N}, \mathcal{L})$, and *agent* that is delegated classification by the holder.

We consider a secure delegation for a decision tree classification. The client requires a classification result of the decision tree with its input. The holder provides classification service by using its decision tree, however, must delegate the service itself to the agent. If there is no privacy/secret information, it is easy to meet these requirements by sending the client's input and holder's tree to the

---

[2] In theory, we need the maximum depth $\lceil \log N \rceil - 1$, but in practice, $\lceil \log N \rceil - 2$ is sufficient, as in [5].

agent. However, both types of information can contain private information of the client and holder; therefore, they should be kept secret.

We use secret-sharing-based MPC to delegate the classification while both the input and decision tree are kept secret. We assume the agent consists of n servers[3] in this paper. Our approach to securely delegate the classification is as follows:

1. The holder secretly shares a decision tree to the (agent) servers.
2. The client secretly shares its input to the servers.
3. The servers securely compute shares of the classification result by using shares of the decision tree and the input.
4. The servers send the shares of the classification result to the client.
5. The client reconstructs the classification result from the sent shares.

We can easily confirm that privacy of the client's input is immediately reduced to the underlying secret sharing and MPC. However, the privacy of the decision tree is a bit complicated. The decision tree contains information about not only a test function, e.g., $[X_t < 10]$, but also the *structure* of the tree, e.g., the topology of the tree. Such a structure can contain secret information, for example, how many elements in an input vector are used for classification. Therefore, we try to hide not only a test function but also the structure of the tree.

3.1   Hiding Structure of Decision Tree

We try to hide information of a decision tree except the upper bound of the maximum depth $\tilde{d}_{max}$. Recall a decision tree consists of $(d_{max}, \mathcal{N}, \mathcal{L})$, and each node $N_{d,i}$ in $\mathcal{N}$ contains $((d,i), \mathsf{P}_{d,i}, \mathsf{CL}_{d,i}, \mathsf{CR}_{d,i}, t_{d,i}, V_{d,i}, op_{d,i})$. The holder can secretly share each Class in $\mathcal{L}$ and (t, V, op) node-by-node to hide the label and a test function straightforwardly. However, the holder cannot do the same for $((d,i), \mathsf{P}, \mathsf{CL}, \mathsf{CR})$ since they are essential for the servers to securely compute a decision tree; otherwise, the servers cannot specify which node they should securely compute in the next.

To prevent information leakage from $((d,i), \mathsf{P}, \mathsf{CL}, \mathsf{CR})$, a holder uses a padding algorithm. Let $\tilde{d}_{max}$ be an upper bound of the tree depth. In the padding algorithm, the holder generates the complete tree of size $2^{\tilde{d}_{max}+1} - 1$ while maintaining classification results. Figure 1 shows an example of $\tilde{d}_{max} = 2$. The non-existent nodes $\tilde{N}_{1,1}$, $\tilde{N}_{2,2}$, and $\tilde{N}_{2,3}$ are inserted in the complete tree. The holder sets $\tilde{N}_{1,1} = ((d,i), \mathsf{P}, \mathsf{CL}, \mathsf{CR}, t, V, op) = ((1,1), (0,0), (2,2), (2,3), 0, 0, 0)$, and sets $\tilde{N}_{2,2}$ and $\tilde{N}_{2,3}$ in the same manner. Finally, the holder replicates the leaf $L_4 = (4, (0,0), \mathsf{Class}_4)$ to leaves $\tilde{L}_j = (j, (2, \lfloor j/2 \rfloor), \mathsf{Class}_4)$ for $4 \leq j \leq 7$. Since all $\tilde{L}_j$ have the same Class_4, the classification results are maintained.

After generating the complete tree, the holder distributes the tree $(\tilde{d}_{max}, \mathcal{N}, \mathcal{L})$ to the servers via SSS. All (t, V, op) of nodes and Class of leaves are

---

[3] The holder can be one of the servers.

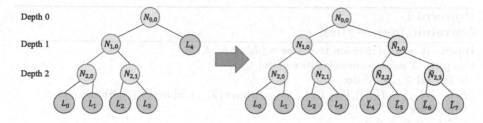

Fig. 1. An example of padding algorithm.

secret-shared, and $\widetilde{d}_{max}, (d, i), j, \mathsf{P}, \mathsf{CL}$ and CR are not. Since the tree is complete, these indices do not leak the tree structure except for an upper bound of depth $\widetilde{d}_{max}$.

3.2 Security Requirement

We consider security against passive adversaries. An adversary can corrupt up to $k - 1$ servers and either the client or holder. There are three cases according to which participant an adversary corrupts. If an adversary corrupts a client, information about the tree except for $\widetilde{d}_{max}$ and the classification result should be kept secret. If an adversary corrupts a holder, an input vector should be kept secret. If an adversary corrupts only servers, both the model except $\widetilde{d}_{max}$, and the input vector should be kept secret.

3.3 Complexity

Computational cost is affected by the number of multiplications because a secure multiplication protocol based on MPC requires communication. Thus, we indicate the cost of a protocol by *(communication) complexity* and *(communication) rounds*, that is, the number of invocations/batch invocations of multiplication protocols.

4 Naive Construction for Secure Classification

In this section, we discuss a naive construction for a secure decision tree classification. This consists of two protocols: a initialization protocol **NaiveInit** and a classification protocol **NaiveClassify**.

  NaiveInit described in Protocol 1 shares a padded decision tree of maximum depth d_{max} across servers. For all nodes $N_{d,i}$, $\boldsymbol{T}_{d,i}$ denotes a tag vector of $t_{d,i}$. All **Share**$(\cdot)$ are executed by the holder that has Tree. Note that the holder is involved in only initialization. For simplicity, we use **Share**(T) as a vector $\boldsymbol{T} = (t_1, t_2, \ldots)$ to obtain $(\llbracket t_1 \rrbracket, \llbracket t_2 \rrbracket, \ldots)$. We similarly use **Share**$(a, b, \ldots)$ to obtain $(\llbracket a \rrbracket, \llbracket b \rrbracket, \ldots)$, in the following.

Protocol 1
NaiveInit(Tree) $\to$ $[\![$Tree$]\!]$

Input: A padded decision tree Tree $= (d_{max}, \mathcal{N}, \mathcal{L})$.
Output: A naive secure classifier $[\![$Tree$]\!]$.
1: **for all** $N_{d,i} \in \mathcal{N}$ **do**
2:     $[\![N_{d,i}]\!] \leftarrow ((d,i), \mathsf{P}_{d,i}, \mathsf{CL}_{d,i}, \mathsf{CR}_{d,i}, \mathbf{Share}(T_{d,i}), \mathbf{Share}(V_{d,i}), \mathbf{Share}(op_{d,i}))$
3: **end for**
4: **for all** $L_j \in \mathcal{L}$ **do**
5:     $[\![L_j]\!] \leftarrow (j, \mathsf{P}_j, \mathbf{Share}(\mathsf{Class}))$
6: **end for**
7: $[\![\mathcal{N}]\!] \leftarrow ([\![N_{0,0}]\!], \ldots, [\![N_{d_{max},2^{d_{max}}-1}]\!])$
8: $[\![\mathcal{L}]\!] \leftarrow ([\![L_0]\!], \ldots, [\![L_{|\mathcal{L}|}]\!])$
9: **return** $[\![$Tree$]\!] \leftarrow (d_{max}, [\![\mathcal{N}]\!], [\![\mathcal{L}]\!])$

Protocol 2
NodeComp($[\![N]\!], [\![X]\!]$) $\to$ $[\![b]\!]$

Input: A secret node $[\![N]\!]$ and secret vector $[\![X]\!]$.
Output: A secret comparison result $[\![b]\!]$.
1: $[\![X_t]\!] \leftarrow \mathbf{LinearAccess}([\![T]\!], [\![X]\!])$
2: $[\![b]\!] \leftarrow \mathbf{Comp}([\![X_t]\!], [\![V]\!], [\![op]\!])$ $\triangleright$ Note that $[\![N]\!]$ includes $[\![T]\!], [\![V]\!], [\![op]\!]$.

When given a secret-shared input vector $[\![X]\!] = ([\![X_0]\!], \ldots, [\![X_m]\!])$, servers execute Protocol 3 to secretly compute the output. In this protocol, comparisons for all nodes of the decision tree are evaluated using subprotocol **NodeComp** in parallel (lines 1–3), and the comparison results are merged along paths from the root to each leaf (lines 4–15). In line 6 of $d = d_{max}$, for all leaves $L_j = (j, \mathsf{P}_j, [\![\mathsf{Class}_j]\!])$, we obtain the parent index $(d_{max}, i_{d_{max}}) = \mathsf{P}_j$. Next, we compare index j to $\mathsf{CL}_{d_{max}, i_{d_{max}}}$ for recognizing whether L_j is the left or right child of $N_{d_{max}, i_{d_{max}}}$. If $\mathsf{CL}_{d_{max}, i_{d_{max}}} = j$, then we have to hold the inverse of the comparison result as $[\![path_{j, d_{max}}]\!]$; otherwise, we hold the comparison result. We follow the path to $N_{0,0}$ in the same manner, and finally obtain the merged comparison result $[\![path_j]\!]$ for L_j, that is, the total product of $[\![path_{j,d}]\!]$.

We assume that the length of vector X is $O(d_{max})$, and thus **NodeComp** has $O(d_{max})$ complexity and $O(1)$ rounds. Protocol 3 has constant rounds since the total product can be evaluated in $O(1)$ rounds [8], which is the best in this sense. However, its complexity is exponential in d_{max}, i.e., $O(d_{max} \cdot 2^{d_{max}})$, since the size of a padded decision tree with maximum depth d_{max} is $O(2^{d_{max}})$.

Security. If the adversary corrupts:

the client, then only output Class is revealed.
the holder, then no information leaks because the holder does not observe anything except the tree.
the servers, it does not leak any information about both the input and tree because they only execute secure multiplications, **Comp**, and **LinearAccess**.

Therefore, this construction satisfies the security requirement.

Protocol 3

NaiveClassify($[\![\mathsf{Tree}]\!]$, $[\![\boldsymbol{X}]\!]$) $\rightarrow$ $[\![\mathsf{Class}]\!]$

Input: A secure classifier $[\![\mathsf{Tree}]\!]$ and a secret input vector $[\![\boldsymbol{X}]\!]$.

Output: A secret class $[\![\mathsf{Class}]\!]$.

1: **for all** $[\![N_{d,i}]\!] \in [\![\mathcal{N}]\!]$ **do**
2:     $[\![b_{d,i}]\!] \leftarrow \mathbf{NodeComp}([\![N_{d,i}]\!], [\![\boldsymbol{X}]\!])$
3: **end for**
4: **for all** $[\![L_j]\!] \in [\![\mathcal{L}]\!]$ **do**
5:     **for** $d = d_{max}$ **to** 0 **do**
6:         $(d, i_d) \leftarrow \mathsf{P}_{d+1,i_{d+1}}$ $\triangleright$ If $d = d_{max}$, use P_j of L_j instead of $\mathsf{P}_{d+1,i_{d+1}}$.
7:         **if** $\mathsf{CL}_{d,i_d} = (d+1, i_{d+1})$ **then** $\triangleright$ If $d = d_{max}$, use j instead of $(d+1, i_{d+1})$
8:             $[\![path_{j,d}]\!] \leftarrow [\![\overline{b_{d,i_d}}]\!]$
9:         **else**
10:            $[\![path_{j,d}]\!] \leftarrow [\![b_{d,i_d}]\!]$
11:        **end if**
12:    **end for**
13:    $[\![path_j]\!] \leftarrow \prod_d [\![path_{j,d}]\!]$
14:    $[\![\mathsf{Output}_j]\!] \leftarrow [\![\mathsf{Class}_j]\!] \cdot [\![path_j]\!]$
15: **end for**
16: **return** $[\![\mathsf{Class}]\!] \leftarrow \sum_j [\![\mathsf{Output}_j]\!]$

---

5 Applying the Path ORAM to Naive Construction

All nodes are compared to hide the actually used path, which makes the naive construction very inefficient. How can we overcome the exponential computations?

Our idea is applying ORAM to hide which node is actually evaluated at each depth. More precisely, we store the data (such as $\boldsymbol{T}_{d,i}, V_{d,i}, op_{d,i}$) of all nodes at the same depth into ORAM. Then, even if only one node is evaluated, servers have no information about which node is actually evaluated at this depth. We use the Path ORAM investigated by Keller et al. [12] as an instantiation of ORAM because of its expandability and efficiency.

We describe our first proposed construction protocols which use the Path ORAM as follows.

In Protocol 6, we show the initialization procedure that secret-shares Tree and stores it into $d_{max} - 1$ Path ORAMs, $\mathsf{Oram}_3, \ldots, \mathsf{Oram}_{d_{max}}$, and Oram_L. In this construction, we make nodes at depth < 3 to be a naive secure classifier because the Path ORAM is inefficient for a small data set. Note that we can change this depth arbitrarily.

All leaves L_j are first stored into Oram_L by using Protocol 4. Different from the naive construction, the indices j of L_j are secret-shared and assigned to the indices of Entry_j.

Next, by using Protocol 5, nodes $N_{d_{max},i}$ at depth d_{max} are stored in $\text{Oram}_{d_{max}}$. In this process, we need additional information, *next indices* $u^0_{d_{max},i}$ and $u^1_{d_{max},i}$. These indices correspond to $\text{CL}_{d_{max},i}$ and $\text{CR}_{d_{max},i}$, but secret-shared in this construction. Similarly, nodes $N_{d,i}$ at depth d are stored into Oram_d, depth-by-depth. Each $u^b_{d,i}$ can also be obtained from $2i + b$.

Protocol 4
OramInitLeaves$(\mathcal{L})$ $\rightarrow$ Oram_L

Input: Leaves $\mathcal{L}$ of a decision tree.
Output: The Path ORAM Oram_L that holds $\mathcal{L}$.
1: $\text{Oram}_\text{L}.\textbf{Init}(|\mathcal{L}|)$
2: **for all** $L_j \in \mathcal{L}$ **do**
3:     $[\![\text{Class}_j]\!] \leftarrow \textbf{Share}(\text{Class}_j)$
4:     $[\![j]\!] \leftarrow \textbf{Share}(j)$
5:     $\text{Entry}_j \leftarrow ([\![j]\!], [\![\text{Class}_j]\!], [\![0]\!])$
6:     $\text{Oram}_\text{L}.\textbf{Write}(\text{Entry}_j)$
7: **end for**
8: **return** Oram_L

Protocol 5
OramInitNodes$(\mathcal{N}_d)$ $\rightarrow$ Oram_d

Input: Nodes $\mathcal{N}$ of a decision tree.
Output: The Path ORAM Oram_d that holds $\mathcal{N}_d$.
1: $\text{Oram}_d.\textbf{Init}(|\mathcal{N}_d|)$
2: **for all** $N_{d,i} \in \mathcal{N}_d$ **do**
3:     $[\![N_{d,i}]\!] \leftarrow \textbf{Share}(T_{d,i}, V_{d,i}, op_{d,i}, u^0_{d,i}, u^1_{d,i})$ $\triangleright u^b_{d,i} = 2i + b$
4:     $[\![i]\!] \leftarrow \textbf{Share}(i)$
5:     $\text{Entry}_{d,i} \leftarrow ([\![i]\!], [\![N_{d,i}]\!], [\![0]\!])$
6:     $\text{Oram}_d.\textbf{Write}(\text{Entry}_{d,i})$
7: **end for**
8: **return** Oram_d

We finally construct a naive $[\![\text{Tree}_2]\!]$ of maximum depth 2 that classifies input into a class j, that is, the indices of $N_{3,j}$.

To make a response to clients faster, we split a classification protocol into two protocols: an online protocol that is run triggered by a client's input, and an offline one that runs a clearing up process after each execution of the online protocol. Remember that one data access in ORAM is divided into **Read** and **Write**. In the online protocol, we can obtain all required data before **Write** because each Path ORAM is accessed only once. Therefore, only **Read** is performed in the online protocol, and all **Write** is done after the classification result has been returned to the client.

Protocol 6
OramInit(Tree) → $[\![\text{Tree}]\!]_{\text{Oram}}$

Input: A decision tree Tree.
Output: A secure classifier $[\![\text{Tree}]\!]_{\text{Oram}}$ consisting of $d_{max} - 1$ Path ORAMs.
1: $\text{Oram}_L \leftarrow \textbf{OramInitLeaves}(\mathcal{L})$
2: **for** $d = d_{max}$ **to** 3 **do**
3:     $\text{Oram}_d \leftarrow \textbf{OramInitNodes}(\mathcal{N}_d)$ ▷ $\mathcal{N}_d \subseteq \mathcal{N}$ includes all $N_{d,i}$ at depth d.
4: **end for**
5: **for** $j = 0$ **to** 7 **do**   ▷ Convert indices of $N_{3,j}$ to leaves of the naive construction.
6:     $L_{3,j} \leftarrow (j, (2, \lfloor j/2 \rfloor), j)$ ▷ Done by the holder.
7: **end for**
8: $[\![\text{Tree}_2]\!] \leftarrow \textbf{NaiveInit}(2, (N_{d,i})_{0 \leq d \leq 2}, (L_{3,j})_{0 \leq j \leq 7})$
9: **return** $[\![\text{Tree}]\!]_{\text{Oram}} \leftarrow ([\![\text{Tree}_2]\!], (\text{Oram}_d)_{3 \leq d \leq d_{max}}, \text{Oram}_L)$

The online protocol is described in Protocol 7. It enables us to classify an input with only $d_{max} + 5$ comparisons, and $d_{max} - 1$ **Read** accesses of ORAM. These numbers come from that we can decide the needed one of two children from the comparison result b_d (line 7). Since $\text{Oram}_d.\textbf{Read}$ has $O(d^2 \log d)$ complexity and $O(d^2)$ rounds, we can find the complexity of Protocol 7 to be $O(d_{max}^3 \log d_{max})$, and the rounds to be $O(d_{max}^3)$.

Protocol 7
OramClassify-Online($[\![\text{Tree}]\!]_{\text{Oram}}, [\![X]\!]$) → $[\![\text{Class}_{\text{result}}]\!]$

Input: A secure classifier $[\![\text{Tree}]\!]_{\text{Oram}}$ and secret input vector $[\![X]\!]$.
Output: A secret class $[\![\text{Class}_{\text{result}}]\!]$.
1: $[\![u_2]\!] \leftarrow \textbf{NaiveClassify}([\![\text{Tree}_2]\!], [\![X]\!])$
2: **for** $d = 3$ **to** d_{max} **do**
3:     $\text{Entry}_d \leftarrow \text{Oram}_d.\textbf{Read}([\![u_{d-1}]\!])$ ▷ Entry_d includes $[\![N_d]\!]$
4:     $[\![b_d]\!] \leftarrow \textbf{NodeComp}([\![N_d]\!], [\![X]\!])$
5:     $[\![u_d]\!] \leftarrow \textbf{IfElse}([\![u_d^1]\!], [\![u_d^0]\!], [\![b_d]\!])$
6: **end for**
7: $\text{Entry}_{\text{result}} \leftarrow \text{Oram}_L.\textbf{Read}([\![u_{d_{max}}]\!])$ ▷ $\text{Entry}_{\text{result}}$ includes $[\![\text{Class}_{\text{result}}]\!]$
8: **return** $[\![\text{Class}_{\text{result}}]\!]$

The offline protocol is described in Protocol 8. In this protocol, all used data are restored in re-randomized positions of Path ORAMs to prepare for the next classification. This procedure must be executed after each execution of **OramClassify-Online**. The offline protocol has $O(d_{max}^4 \log d_{max})$ comprexity and $O(d_{max}^3)$ rounds because $\text{Oram}_d.\textbf{Write}$ has $O(d^3 \log d)$ complexity and $O(d^2)$ rounds.

Security. If the adversary corrupts:

the client, then only $[\![\text{Class}_{\text{result}}]\!]$ is revealed.

Protocol 8

OramClassify-Offline($[\![\text{Tree}]\!]_{\text{Oram}}$, $\text{Entry}_{\text{result}}$, $(\text{Entry}_d)_{3 \leq d \leq d_{max}}$) $\rightarrow$ $[\![\text{Tree}]\!]_{\text{Oram}}$

Input: $[\![\text{Tree}]\!]_{\text{Oram}}$ and entries of $\text{Oram}_3, \ldots, \text{Oram}_{d_{max}}$ and Oram_L.

Output: Refreshed $[\![\text{Tree}]\!]_{\text{Oram}}$.

1: $\text{Oram}_L.\textbf{Write}(\text{Entry}_{\text{result}})$
2: **for** $d = d_{max}$ **to** 3 **do**
3:     $\text{Oram}_d.\textbf{Write}(\text{Entry}_d)$
4: **end for**
5: **return** $[\![\text{Tree}]\!]_{\text{Oram}} \leftarrow ([\![\text{Tree}_2]\!], (\text{Oram}_d)_{3 \leq d \leq d_{max}}, \text{Oram}_L)$

---

the holder, then no information leaks because the holder does not observe anything except the tree.

the servers, it does not leak any information about both the input and tree because they only execute secure multiplications, **Comp**, **LinearAccess**, and access protocols for Oram.

Therefore, this construction satisfies the security requirement.

6   Efficient Construction for Secure Classification: Daisy Chain Construction

Though the construction shown in Sect. 5 reduces the exponential complexity of the naive classification protocol to polynomial, it is still inefficient. In this section, we discuss our second proposed construction, *Daisy Chain Construction* in which ORAMs are chained one after another. It can classify the input more efficiently than the previous ones.

6.1   Avoidance of Handling Position Maps

MPC simulating ORAM generally incurs massive communication cost, especially in handling a position map. Note, that the position map is necessary to satisfy obliviousness if we want to freely access the entire domain of ORAM. In decision tree classifications, however, we want to access one of two entries of Oram_d, that is, corresponding to the left or right child of the node we obtain from Oram_{d-1}. Therefore, instead of maintaining a position map as a large data structure, the position information of Oram_d can be distributed to each entry of Oram_{d-1}. This modification enables us to avoid handling position maps, and reduce complexity and rounds.

To implement this idea, we use three procedures: **npInit**, **npRead** and **npWrite**. I.e.,

$\text{Oram}.\textbf{npInit}(N)$: construct and initialize the Path ORAM as Oram $= (\mathcal{B}, \mathcal{S}, \text{NULL})$.

Oram.npRead($[\![u]\!]$, $[\![p]\!]$): read and remove an entry whose index is u and position is p. This is equal to the latter subprotocol of **Read**, and has $O(\log N \log \log N)$ complexity and $O(1)$ rounds where N entries stored into Oram.

Oram.npWrite(Entry): write back Entry into Oram without re-randomizing. This is equal to the latter subprotocol of **Write**, and has $O(\log^2 N \log \log N)$ complexity and $O(\log N)$ rounds.

To maintain the correctness of reading/writing, we have to control positions adequately by explicitly specifying and re-randomizing them.

6.2   Daisy Chain Construction

Daisy Chain Construction consists of three protocols: **DcInit** for initialization, **DcClassify-Online** for classification, and **DcClassify-Offline** for refreshing ORAMs.

Protocol 9
DcInitLeaves($\mathcal{L}$) $\rightarrow$ (Oram$_L$, $([\![p_j]\!])_{j<|\mathcal{L}|}$)

Input: Leaves $\mathcal{L}$ of a decision tree.
Output: The Path ORAM Oram$_L$ of $\mathcal{P} = $ NULL and an array $([\![p_j]\!])_{j<|\mathcal{L}|}$ of positions.
1: Oram$_L$.**npInit**($|\mathcal{L}|$)
2: **for all** $L_j \in \mathcal{L}$ **do**
3:     $[\![\text{Class}_j]\!] \leftarrow$ **Share**(Class_j)
4:     $[\![j]\!] \leftarrow$ **Share**(j)
5:     $[\![p_j]\!] \leftarrow$ **RandomPos**(Oram$_L$)   ▷ Choose a random position of Oram$_L$
6:     Entry$_j \leftarrow ([\![j]\!], [\![\text{Class}_j]\!], [\![p_j]\!])$
7:     Oram$_L$.**npWrite**(Entry$_j$)
8: **end for**
9: **return** (Oram$_L$, $([\![p_j]\!])_{j<|\mathcal{L}|}$)

DcInit, described in Protocol 11, stores a padded decision tree into Path ORAMs. This is different from **OramInit** regarding the following points:

- In subprotocols Protocols 9 and 10, the position of each leaf and inner node is explicitly chosen randomly because **npWrite** does not set a random position in each entry.
- The positions of Oram$_L$ chosen in Protocol 9 are not stored into a position map but in an entry associated with the parent node. More precisely, each entry of Oram$_{d_{max}}$ includes not only next indices u^0, u^1 but also additional information p^0, p^1 that we call *next positions*. If we assume the children of the node associated with this entry are leaves L_{u^0} and L_{u^1}, then class Class_{u^0} (resp. Class_{u^1}) is in position p^0 (resp. p^1) of Oram$_L$.
- Similarly, in lines 2–4 of Protocol 11, the position information of Oram$_{d+1}$ is added to the parent entry stored in Oram$_d$.

– The same as with Protocol 6, nodes at depth 2 or lower are shared as $[\![\mathsf{Tree}_2]\!]$, but each leaf includes the next position $p_{3,j}$.

We easily confirm that no position map is used in this procedure.

Protocol 10
DcInitNodes$(\mathcal{N}_d, ([\![p_j]\!])) \ \rightarrow (\mathsf{Oram}_d, ([\![p_{d,i}]\!]))$

Input: Nodes $\mathcal{N}_d$ of a decision tree and an array $([\![p_j]\!])$ of positions.
Output: The Path ORAM Oram_d and an array $([\![p_{d,i}]\!])$ of positions.
1: $\mathsf{Oram}_d.\mathbf{npInit}(|\mathcal{N}_d|)$
2: **for all** $N_{d,i} \in \mathcal{N}_d$ **do**
3:     $[\![N_{d,i}]\!] \leftarrow \mathbf{Share}(T_{d,i}, V_{d,i}, op_{d,i}, u^0_{d,i}, u^1_{d,i}, p^0_{d,i} = 0, p^1_{d,i} = 0)$ ▷ $u^b_{d,i} = 2i + b$
4:     replace $[\![p^b_{d,i}]\!]$ in $[\![N_{d,i}]\!]$ with $[\![p_{2i+b}]\!]$.   ▷ $[\![p_{2i+b}]\!]$ is an element of input $([\![p_j]\!])$.
5:     $[\![i]\!] \leftarrow \mathbf{Share}(i)$
6:     $[\![p_{d,i}]\!] \leftarrow \mathbf{RandomPos}(\mathsf{Oram}_d)$ ▷ Choose a random position of Oram_d.
7:     $\mathsf{Entry}_{d,i} \leftarrow ([\![i]\!], [\![N_{d,i}]\!], [\![p_{d,i}]\!])$
8:     $\mathsf{Oram}_d.\mathbf{npWrite}(\mathsf{Entry}_{d,i})$
9: **end for**
10: **return** $(\mathsf{Oram}_d, ([\![p_{d,i}]\!]))$

Protocol 11
DcInit$(\mathsf{Tree}) \ \rightarrow [\![\mathsf{Tree}]\!]_{\mathsf{DC}}$

Input: A decision tree Tree.
Output: A secure classifier $[\![\mathsf{Tree}]\!]_{\mathsf{DC}}$ consisting of *daisy-chained* Path ORAMs.
1: $(\mathsf{Oram}_{\mathsf{L}}, ([\![p_{\mathsf{L},j}]\!])_{j<|\mathcal{L}|}) \leftarrow \mathbf{DcInitLeaves}(\mathcal{L})$
2: **for** $d = d_{max}$ **to** 3 **do**   ▷ If $d = d_{max}$, then use $([\![p_{\mathsf{L},i}]\!])$ instead of $([\![p_{d+1,i}]\!])$.
3:     $(\mathsf{Oram}_d, ([\![p_{d,i}]\!])) \leftarrow \mathbf{DcInitNodes}(\mathcal{N}_d, ([\![p_{d+1,i}]\!]))$
4: **end for**
5: **for** $j = 0$ **to** 7 **do**   ▷ Convert indices and positions of $N_{3,j}$ to leaves.
6:     $L_{3,j} \leftarrow (j, (2, \lfloor j/2 \rfloor), (j, p_j = 0))$ ▷ Done by the holder.
7: **end for**
8: $[\![\mathsf{Tree}_2]\!] \leftarrow \mathbf{NaiveInit}(2, (N_{d,i})_{0 \leq d \leq 2}, (L_{3,j})_{0 \leq j \leq 7})$
9: replace each $[\![p_j]\!]$ of $[\![\mathsf{Tree}_2]\!]$ by $[\![p_{3,j}]\!]$.
10: **return** $[\![\mathsf{Tree}]\!]_{\mathsf{DC}} \leftarrow ([\![\mathsf{Tree}_2]\!], (\mathsf{Oram}_d)_{3 \leq d \leq d_{max}}, \mathsf{Oram}_{\mathsf{L}})$

The online protocol **DcClassify-Online** is described in Protocol 12. This is different from **OramClassify-Online** regarding the following point:

– In each access to ORAM, instead of searching the position map, we determine the position of the next (child) node by choosing one of two *next positions* in the parent entry (lines 4 and 9 of Protocol 12).

Protocol 12 has $O(d^2_{max} \log d_{max})$ complexity and $O(d_{max})$ rounds.
Protocol 13, the re-randomization process, is somewhat complicated.

Protocol 12
DcClassify-Online($[\![\text{Tree}]\!]_{\text{DC}}, [\![X]\!]$) → $[\![\text{Class}_{\text{result}}]\!]$

Input: A Daisy-Chained tree $[\![\text{Tree}]\!]_{\text{DC}}$ and secret input vector $[\![X]\!]$
Output: A secret class $[\![\text{Class}_{\text{result}}]\!]$
 1: $([\![u_2]\!], [\![p_2]\!]) \leftarrow$ **NaiveClassify**($[\![\text{Tree}_2]\!], [\![X]\!]$)
          ▷ In this process, servers hold each $[\![path_j]\!]$ ($0 \le j \le 7$) in **NaiveClassify**.
 2: **for** $d = 3$ **to** d_{max} **do**
 3:     $\text{Entry}_d \leftarrow \text{Oram}_d.\textbf{npRead}([\![u_{d-1}]\!], [\![p_{d-1}]\!])$
 4:     $[\![b_d]\!] \leftarrow \textbf{NodeComp}([\![N_d]\!], [\![X]\!])$ ▷ Servers hold each $[\![b_d]\!]$.
 5:     $[\![u_d]\!] \leftarrow \textbf{IfElse}([\![u_d^1]\!], [\![u_d^0]\!], [\![b_d]\!])$
 6:     $[\![p_d]\!] \leftarrow \textbf{IfElse}([\![p_d^1]\!], [\![p_d^0]\!], [\![b_d]\!])$
 7: **end for**
 8: $\text{Entry}_{\text{result}} \leftarrow \text{Oram}_L.\textbf{npRead}([\![u_{d_{max}}]\!], [\![p_{d_{max}}]\!])$
 9: **return** $[\![\text{Class}_{\text{result}}]\!]$

- Before writing back each entry by using **npWrite**, a new position is randomly chosen secretly, and the entry's position is renewed by the new one (lines 1 and 7).
- One of two *next positions* in the parent entry is also replaced with the new position of the child (lines 5–6).
- Finally, we must replace the first *next position*, that is, a leaf of $[\![\text{Tree}_2]\!]$ corresponding to $path_j = 1$ (lines 11–13).

Those procedures correspond to re-randomization of a position map on Path ORAM. Protocol 13 has $O(d_{max}^3 \log d_{max})$ complexity and $O(d_{max}^2)$ rounds.

6.3 Security

If we assume the existence of Oram, we can straightforwardly obtain secure **npInit**, **npRead** and **npWrite**. In this construction, if the adversary corrupts

the client, then only $[\![\text{Class}_{\text{result}}]\!]$ is revealed.
the holder, then no information leaks because the holder does not observe anything except the tree.
the servers, it does not leak any information about both the input and tree because they only execute secure multiplications, **Comp**, **LinearAccess**, **RandomPos**, **npRead**, and **npWrite**.

Therefore, this construction satisfies the security requirement.

7   Evaluation

We compared the efficiency of the naive construction (Sect. 4), one that uses the Path ORAM (Sect. 5), and Daisy Chain Construction (Sect. 6).

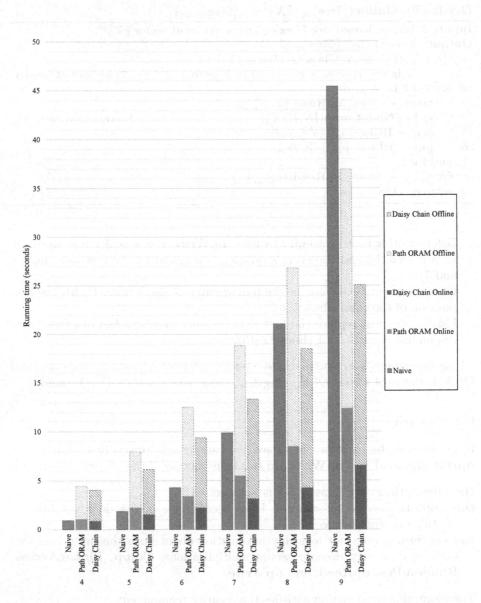

Fig. 2. Running time of three constructions for complete binary decision tree of depth d_{max}

Protocol 13

DcClassify-Offline$(\llbracket \text{Tree} \rrbracket_{\text{DC}}, \text{Entry}_{\text{result}}, (\text{Entry}_d), (\llbracket b_d \rrbracket), (\llbracket path_j \rrbracket)) \rightarrow \llbracket \text{Tree} \rrbracket_{\text{DC}}$

Input: $\llbracket \text{Tree} \rrbracket_{\text{DC}}$, each entries, $\llbracket b_d \rrbracket$ and $\llbracket path_j \rrbracket$ held in Protocol 12.

Output: Refreshed $\llbracket \text{Tree} \rrbracket_{\text{DC}}$.

  1: $\llbracket p'_{\text{result}} \rrbracket \leftarrow \textbf{RandomPos}(\text{Oram}_L)$ ▷ Re-randomize a position of $\text{Entry}_{\text{result}}$.

  2: replace $\llbracket p_{\text{result}} \rrbracket$ in $\text{Entry}_{\text{result}}$ with $\llbracket p'_{\text{result}} \rrbracket$.

  3: $\text{Oram}_L.\textbf{npWrite}(\text{Entry}_{\text{result}})$

  4: **for** $d = d_{max}$ **to** 3 **do**   ▷ Renew next positions then store Entry_d.

  5:     $\llbracket p_d^0 \rrbracket \leftarrow \textbf{IfElse}(\llbracket p_d^0 \rrbracket, \llbracket p'_{d+1} \rrbracket, \llbracket b_d \rrbracket)$

  6:     $\llbracket p_d^1 \rrbracket \leftarrow \textbf{IfElse}(\llbracket p'_{d+1} \rrbracket, \llbracket p_d^1 \rrbracket, \llbracket b_d \rrbracket)$

                                 ▷ If $d = d_{max}$ then use $\llbracket p'_{\text{result}} \rrbracket$ instead of $\llbracket p'_{d+1} \rrbracket$.

  7:     $\llbracket p'_d \rrbracket \leftarrow \textbf{RandomPos}(\text{Oram}_d)$

  8:     replace $\llbracket p_d \rrbracket$ in Entry_d with $\llbracket p'_d \rrbracket$.

  9:     $\text{Oram}_d.\textbf{npWrite}(\text{Entry}_d)$

10: **end for**

11: **for all** $\llbracket L_{3,j} \rrbracket$ of $\llbracket \text{Tree}_2 \rrbracket$ **do**

12:     $\llbracket p_j \rrbracket \leftarrow \textbf{IfElse}(\llbracket p' \rrbracket, \llbracket p_j \rrbracket, \llbracket path_j \rrbracket)$ ▷ Replace p_j that corresponds to $path_j = 1$.

13: **end for**

14: **return** $\llbracket \text{Tree} \rrbracket_{\text{DC}} \leftarrow (\llbracket \text{Tree}_2 \rrbracket, (\text{Oram}_d)_{3 \leq d \leq d_{max}}, \text{Oram}_L)$

All codes we implemented were compiled using gcc version 4.8.5 (C++14). We used three machines (CentOS Linux release 7.2.1511, Intel Core i7 6900K, 32 GB memory) connected to each other by a 1-Gbps LAN. All reported times of each protocol are the running times to classify one input vector.

We used the parameters of each Path ORAM shown in previous studies [5, 12]: the bucket size was 4, and the stash size was 12, which satisfy a security parameter 16. If we want to increase the security parameter, we need a larger stash, but this modification has little effects on running time.

Figure 2 shows the running times of the three constructions for each d_{max}. Recall that we focused on a complete binary decision tree. The number of nodes was $2^{d_{max}+1} - 1$ in each d_{max}. We assume that all elements in the input vector and values compared in each node are in $GF(2^8)$. We found that, in any $d_{max} \geq 4$, Daisy Chain Construction responded faster than the others. Furthermore, the entire protocol (online + offline) is more efficient than the naive construction in $d_{max} \geq 8$.

8 Conclusion

We proposed efficient, secure protocols for decision tree classification based on MPC. They enable a model holder to delegate a classification service to servers while hiding information about the decision tree and clients to demand classification while preserving privacy. They can classify the input in polynomial time, in contrast to the naive one that costs us exponential time. We evaluated the running times of the three constructions for secure classification. The simulation results indicate that Daisy Chain Construction is the most efficient for a complete binary decision tree that is enlarged to hide its topology.

References

1. Yao, A.C.: Protocols for secure computations. In: Proceedings of 23rd FOCS, pp. 160–164 (1982)
2. Shamir, A.: How to share a secret. Commun. ACM **22**(11), 612–613 (1979)
3. Wu, D.J., Feng, T., Naehrig, M., Lauter, K.E.: Privately evaluating decision trees and random forests. PoPETs **2016**(4), 335–355 (2016)
4. Shi, E., Chan, T.-H.H., Stefanov, E., Li, M.: Oblivious RAM with $O((\log N)^3)$ worst-case cost. In: Lee, D.H., Wang, X. (eds.) ASIACRYPT 2011. LNCS, vol. 7073, pp. 197–214. Springer, Heidelberg (2011). https://doi.org/10.1007/978-3-642-25385-0_11
5. Stefanov, E., et al.: Path ORAM: an extremely simple oblivious RAM protocol. In: CCS, pp. 299–310 (2013)
6. Blakley, G.R.: Safeguarding cryptographic keys. In: National Computer Conference, pp. 313–317. American Federation of Information Processing Societies Proceedings (1979)
7. Damgård, I., Nielsen, J.B.: Scalable and unconditionally secure multiparty computation. In: Menezes, A. (ed.) CRYPTO 2007. LNCS, vol. 4622, pp. 572–590. Springer, Heidelberg (2007). https://doi.org/10.1007/978-3-540-74143-5_32
8. Damgård, I., Fitzi, M., Kiltz, E., Nielsen, J.B., Toft, T.: Unconditionally secure constant-rounds multi-party computation for equality, comparison, bits and exponentiation. In: Halevi, S., Rabin, T. (eds.) TCC 2006. LNCS, vol. 3876, pp. 285–304. Springer, Heidelberg (2006). https://doi.org/10.1007/11681878_15
9. Hamada, K., Hasegawa, S., Misawa, K., Chida, K., Ogishima, S., Nagasaki, M.: Privacy-preserving fisher's exact test for genome-wide association study. In: International Workshop on Genome Privacy and Security (GenoPri) (2017)
10. Backes, M., et al.: Identifying personal DNA methylation profiles by genotype inference. In: IEEE Symposium on Security and Privacy (2017)
11. Ito, M., Saito, A., Nishizeki, T.: Secret sharing schemes realizing general access structures. In: Proceedings of the IEEE Global Telecommunication Conference, Globecom 1987, pp. 99–102 (1987)
12. Keller, M., Scholl, P.: Efficient, oblivious data structures for MPC. In: Sarkar, P., Iwata, T. (eds.) ASIACRYPT 2014. LNCS, vol. 8874, pp. 506–525. Springer, Heidelberg (2014). https://doi.org/10.1007/978-3-662-45608-8_27
13. Goldreich, O., Ostrovsky, R.: Software protection and simulation on oblivious RAMs. J. ACM **43**(3), 431–473 (1996)
14. Bost, R., Popa, R.A., Tu, S., Goldwasser, S.: Machine learning classification over encrypted data. In: NDSS (2015)
15. Cramer, R., Damgård, I., Maurer, U.: General secure multi-party computation from any linear secret-sharing scheme. In: Preneel, B. (ed.) EUROCRYPT 2000. LNCS, vol. 1807, pp. 316–334. Springer, Heidelberg (2000). https://doi.org/10.1007/3-540-45539-6_22
16. Nishide, T., Ohta, K.: Multiparty computation for interval, equality, and comparison without bit-decomposition protocol. In: Okamoto, T., Wang, X. (eds.) PKC 2007. LNCS, vol. 4450, pp. 343–360. Springer, Heidelberg (2007). https://doi.org/10.1007/978-3-540-71677-8_23
17. Lindell, Y., Pinkas, B.: Privacy preserving data mining. J. Cryptol. **15**, 177–206 (2000)

The Wiener Attack on RSA Revisited: A Quest for the Exact Bound

Willy Susilo, Joseph Tonien[✉], and Guomin Yang

Institute of Cybersecurity and Cryptology,
School of Computing and Information Technology,
University of Wollongong, Wollongong, Australia
{willy.susilo,joseph.tonien,guomin.yang}@uow.edu.au

Abstract. Since Wiener pointed out that the RSA can be broken if the private exponent d is relatively small compared to the modulus N (using the continued fraction technique), it has been a general belief that the Wiener attack works for $d < N^{\frac{1}{4}}$. On the contrary, in this work, we give an example where the Wiener attack fails with $d = \left\lfloor \frac{1}{2}N^{\frac{1}{4}} \right\rfloor + 1$, thus, showing that the bound $d < N^{\frac{1}{4}}$ is not accurate as it has been thought of. By using the classical Legendre Theorem on continued fractions, in 1999 Boneh provided the first rigorous proof which showed that the Wiener attack works for $d < \frac{1}{3}N^{\frac{1}{4}}$. However, the question remains whether $\frac{1}{3}N^{\frac{1}{4}}$ is the best bound for the Wiener attack. Additionally, the question whether another rigorous proof for a better bound exists remains an elusive research problem. In this paper, we attempt to answer the aforementioned problems by improving Boneh's bound after the two decades of research. By a new proof, we show that the Wiener continued fraction technique works for a wider range, namely, for $d \leq \frac{1}{\sqrt[4]{18}}N^{\frac{1}{4}} = \frac{1}{2.06...}N^{\frac{1}{4}}$. Our new analysis is supported by an experimental result where it is shown that the Wiener attack can successfully perform the factorization on the RSA modulus N and determine a private key d where $d = \left\lfloor \frac{1}{\sqrt[4]{18}}N^{\frac{1}{4}} \right\rfloor$.

Keywords: RSA · Continued fractions · Wiener technique · Small secret exponent

1 Introduction

The RSA cryptosystem is one of the most popular and de facto public-key systems used in practice today. It is among the most common ciphers used in the SSL/TLS protocol which allows sensitive information transmitted securely over the Internet.

© Springer Nature Switzerland AG 2019
J. Jang-Jaccard and F. Guo (Eds.): ACISP 2019, LNCS 11547, pp. 381–398, 2019.
https://doi.org/10.1007/978-3-030-21548-4_21

A simplified version of the RSA encryption algorithm works as follows. Two large primes of the same size p and q are selected to form a product $N = pq$ – which is called the *RSA modulus*. Two integers e and d are chosen so that

$$ed = 1 \pmod{\phi(N)},$$

where $\phi(N) = (p-1)(q-1)$ is the order of the multiplicative group $\mathbb{Z}_N^*$. The number e is called the *encryption exponent* and d is called the *decryption exponent*. This is because to encrypt a message $m \in \mathbb{Z}_N^*$, one calculates the exponentiation $c = m^e \pmod{N}$, and to decrypt a ciphertext $c \in \mathbb{Z}_N^*$, one performs the exponentiation $m = c^d \pmod{N}$. The pair (N, e) is called the *public key* and so that anyone can encrypt, whereas d is called the *private key* and only the owner of d can perform the decryption operation.

Since the modular exponentiation $m = c^d \pmod{N}$ takes $\mathcal{O}(\log d)$ time, to reduce decryption time, one may wish to use a relatively small value of d. However, in 1991, Wiener [20] showed that if the bit-length of d is *approximately one-quarter* of that of the modulus N, then it is possible to determine the private exponent d from the public-key (N, e), hence, a total break of the cryptosystem. Wiener's attack is based on continued fractions and the idea is as follows. Since $ed = 1 \pmod{\phi(N)}$, we have $ed - k\phi(N) = 1$ for some integer k, and thus,

$$\frac{k}{d} \approx \frac{e}{\phi(N)} \approx \frac{e}{N}.$$

Now one knows that the *convergents* of the continued fraction expansion of a number provide *rational approximations* to the number, so it is natural to search for the private fraction $\frac{k}{d}$ among the convergents of the public fraction $\frac{e}{N}$. Given Wiener's approximation analysis [20], it has been a general belief that the Wiener attack works for $d < N^{\frac{1}{4}}$ (see [1,4,13,17]). On the converse, in 2005, Steinfeld-Contini-Wang-Pieprzyk [17] showed that for any positive number ϵ, with an overwhelming probability, Wiener's attack will fail for a random choice $d \approx N^{\frac{1}{4}+\epsilon}$. Thus, the bound $d < N^{\frac{1}{4}}$ has since been believed to be the optimal bound for the Wiener attack.

There are other variants of Wiener's attack [8,10,11,18] that allow the RSA cryptosystem to be broken when d is a few bits longer than $N^{\frac{1}{4}}$. In 1997, Verheul and van Tilborg [18] proposed a method that works for $d < DN^{\frac{1}{4}}$ using an exhaustive search of about $2 \log D + 8$ bits. This method was later improved by Dujella [10,11]. In the Verheul and van Tilborg attack [18], the secret exponent is of the form $d = rb_{m+1} + sb_m$, where the b_i are the denominators of the convergents of the continued fraction. Calculation of the convergents needs a complexity of $O(\log N)$, and so searching through all possible pairs (r, s) at each convergent makes the running time increased by a factor of $O(D^2 A^2)$, where A is the maximum of the partial quotients $x_{m+1}, x_{m+2}, x_{m+3}$ of the continued fraction. The first Dujella method [10] improved this extra running time factor to $O(D^2 \log A)$ and $O(D^2 \log D)$, and the second Dujella method [11] improved it further to $O(D \log D)$ (with the space complexity of $O(D)$). In 2017, Bunder and Tonien [8] proposed another variant of Wiener's attack. Instead of considering the continued fraction of $\frac{e}{N}$ as in the original Wiener's attack, the Bunder and Tonien method uses the continued fraction of $\frac{e}{N'}$, where N' is a number depending on N. This new attack works for $d < 2^{(n+3-t)/2} N^{\frac{1}{4}}$ where $n = \log N$, $t = \log e$, and the running time is $O(\log N)$.

There are yet other variants of Wiener's attack that utilise more than just the public information (N, e). For example, the Weger attack [19] exploited the small distance between the two RSA's secret primes: if $|p - q| = N^\beta$ and $d = N^\delta$ then d can be recovered if $2 - 4\beta < \delta < 1 - \sqrt{2\beta - \frac{1}{2}}$ or $\delta < \frac{1}{6}(4\beta + 5) - \frac{1}{3}\sqrt{(4\beta + 5)(4\beta - 1)}$. The Blömer and May attack [2] assumed a linear relation between e and $\phi(N)$: $ex + y = 0 \mod \phi(N)$ with either $0 < x < \frac{1}{3}N^{\frac{1}{4}}$ and $y = \mathcal{O}(N^{-\frac{3}{4}}ex)$ or $x < \frac{1}{3}\sqrt{\frac{\phi(N)}{e}}\frac{N^{\frac{3}{4}}}{p-q}$ and $|y| \leq \frac{p-q}{\phi(N)N^{\frac{1}{4}}}ex$. The Nassr et al. attack [15] required an approximation $p_o \geq \sqrt{N}$ of the prime p.

In 1999, Boneh and Durfee [4] showed the first significant improvement over the Wiener's result. Based on the Coppersmith technique [9], exploiting a non-linear equation satisfied by the secret exponent, the Boneh-Durfee method can break the RSA when $d < N^{0.292}$. Using a somewhat more optimized lattice, Herrmann and May [13] also derived the same bound $d < N^{0.292}$, although their proof is more elementary. This bound $d < N^{0.292}$ remains as the best bound to date.

Our Contributions. In this paper, we revisit Wiener's original attack based on continued fraction technique. In research literature, there have been two different bounds reported for this attack, one is $d < N^{\frac{1}{4}}$ (for example, in [1,4,13,17]) and another one is $d < \frac{1}{3}N^{\frac{1}{4}}$ (for example, in [3,5–8]). The second bound is due to Boneh [3]. Our main contributions in this paper are twofold: on one hand, we show that the first bound $d < N^{\frac{1}{4}}$ is not accurate, and on the other hand, we can improve the Boneh bound from $d < \frac{1}{3}N^{\frac{1}{4}}$ to $d \leq \frac{1}{2.06\ldots}N^{\frac{1}{4}}$. Since many attacks on RSA based on the original Wiener attack, it is important to revisit this attack and provide an accurate analysis.

Our First Contribution. Based on the implementation of the Wiener algorithm and its execution, we have discovered that the Wiener attack fails for many values of $d < N^{\frac{1}{4}}$. This contradicts to the general belief about the Wiener attack where it has been reported that the Wiener attack works for all $d < N^{\frac{1}{4}}$ (see [1,4,13,17]). Obviously, to disprove this bound $d < N^{\frac{1}{4}}$, *one only needs to show one counterexample, i.e. a value of $d < N^{\frac{1}{4}}$ where the Wiener attack fails.* We do that in Sect. 4, where it is shown that the Wiener attack fails for a certain value of N and d with

$$d = \left\lfloor \frac{1}{2}N^{\frac{1}{4}} \right\rfloor + 1 < N^{\frac{1}{4}}.$$

Therefore, the bound $d < N^{\frac{1}{4}}$ for the Wiener attack *is not accurate* as it has been believed to date. At least, we can see that it fails at the halfway point of the range. This raises a natural question: *what is the correct bound for the Wiener attack?* And this comes to our second contribution.

Our Second Contribution. Boneh [3] provided the first and only rigorous proof which showed that the Wiener attack works for

$$d < \frac{1}{3} N^{\frac{1}{4}}.$$

The remaining question is whether this bound is the best bound for the Wiener attack. Additionally, we are wondering whether there exists another rigorous proof for a better bound. As the second contribution of this paper, we answer this question affirmatively by improving Boneh's bound.

Boneh's result does not say anything about the case $d \geq \frac{1}{3} N^{\frac{1}{4}}$. So the Wiener attack may work or it may fail for $d \geq \frac{1}{3} N^{\frac{1}{4}}$. Our first result already shows an instance where the Wiener attack fails at $d = \left\lfloor \frac{1}{2} N^{\frac{1}{4}} \right\rfloor + 1 \simeq \frac{1}{2} N^{\frac{1}{4}}$. This raises an open question: *does the Wiener attack work or fail in the following interval*

$$\frac{1}{3} N^{\frac{1}{4}} \leq d < \frac{1}{2} N^{\frac{1}{4}} ?$$

As the second contribution of this paper, using exactly the same setting as that of Boneh [3], we prove that the Wiener attack is always successful for all values of d in the larger interval

$$d \leq \frac{1}{\sqrt[4]{18}} N^{\frac{1}{4}} = \frac{1}{2.06...} N^{\frac{1}{4}}.$$

With this improvement of Boneh's bound from $d < \frac{1}{3} N^{\frac{1}{4}}$ to $d \leq \frac{1}{2.06...} N^{\frac{1}{4}}$, we show that the Wiener attack works for all value of d in the interval

$$\frac{1}{3} N^{\frac{1}{4}} \leq d \leq \frac{1}{2.06...} N^{\frac{1}{4}}.$$

Thus, the undecided interval has been narrowed down to

$$\frac{1}{2.06...} N^{\frac{1}{4}} < d < \frac{1}{2} N^{\frac{1}{4}}$$

and it is unknown if the Wiener attack fails or succeeds in this narrow interval. Nevertheless, we conjecture that our new bound $\frac{1}{2.06...} N^{\frac{1}{4}}$ is indeed *the best bound* for the Wiener attack. We conjecture that, for any $\frac{1}{2.06...} < \alpha \leq \frac{1}{2}$, there is always a value of d in the interval $\frac{1}{2.06...} N^{\frac{1}{4}} < d < \alpha N^{\frac{1}{4}}$ that makes the Wiener attack fail.

Our Experimental Results. In this paper, we show two experimental results. In Sect. 4, we show an example where *the Wiener attack fails* with

$$d = \left\lfloor \frac{1}{2} N^{\frac{1}{4}} \right\rfloor + 1 < N^{\frac{1}{4}},$$

this is *a counterexample* to disprove the first bound $d < N^{\frac{1}{4}}$. In Sect. 6, we show an example that *the Wiener attack works* with

$$d = \left\lfloor \frac{1}{\sqrt[4]{18}} N^{\frac{1}{4}} \right\rfloor = \left\lfloor \frac{1}{2.06...} N^{\frac{1}{4}} \right\rfloor,$$

this is *an illustration* to our new improved bound $d \leq \frac{1}{2.06...} N^{\frac{1}{4}}$.

Roadmap. The rest of this paper is organized as follows. The next section gives a brief introduction to the continued fractions. We revisit Boneh's version of Wiener's attack in Sect. 3 for clarity and completeness. In Sect. 4, we demonstrate our first experimental result showing an example that the Wiener attack fails at $d = \left\lfloor \frac{1}{2} N^{\frac{1}{4}} \right\rfloor + 1$. In Sect. 5, we give a new rigorous proof which shows that the Wiener continued fraction technique works for $d \leq \frac{1}{\sqrt[4]{18}} N^{\frac{1}{4}} = \frac{1}{2.06\dots} N^{\frac{1}{4}}$. Our new bound is verified experimentally in Sect. 6, where we show an example that the Wiener attack works with $d = \left\lfloor \frac{1}{\sqrt[4]{18}} N^{\frac{1}{4}} \right\rfloor$. Finally, we conclude our paper and discuss open problems in Sect. 7.

2   Preliminaries

In this section, we list several well-known results about continued fractions which can be found in [12,16].

A continued fraction expansion of a rational number $\frac{u}{v}$ is an expression of the form

$$\frac{u}{v} = x_0 + \cfrac{1}{x_1 + \cfrac{1}{\ddots + \cfrac{1}{x_n}}},$$

where the coefficient x_0 is an integer and all the other coefficients x_i for $i \geq 1$ are positive integers. The coefficients x_i are called the partial quotients of the continued fraction. Continued fraction expansion also exists for irrational numbers although it runs infinitely. In cryptography, finite continued fraction for rational numbers suffices our purpose.

There is a standard way to generate a unique continued fraction from any rational number. By the Euclidean division algorithm, one can efficiently determine all the coefficients $x_0, x_1, \dots, x_n$ of the continued fraction. For clarity, we present the following example to show how to construct the continued fraction for $\frac{2000}{2019}$.

By the Euclidean division algorithm, we have

$$2000 = 2019 \times \mathbf{0} + 2000$$
$$2019 = 2000 \times \mathbf{1} + 19$$
$$2000 = 19 \times \mathbf{105} + 5$$
$$19 = 5 \times \mathbf{3} + 4$$
$$5 = 4 \times \mathbf{1} + 1$$
$$4 = 1 \times \mathbf{4}$$

and thus, we can see that the coefficients $0, 1, 105, 3, 1, 4$ determined by the above Euclidean division algorithm become the coefficients for the continued fraction as follows,

$$\frac{2000}{2019} = 0 + \frac{2000}{2019} = 0 + \cfrac{1}{\frac{2019}{2000}} = 0 + \cfrac{1}{1 + \cfrac{19}{2000}} = 0 + \cfrac{1}{1 + \cfrac{1}{\frac{2000}{19}}}$$

$$= 0 + \cfrac{1}{1 + \cfrac{1}{105 + \cfrac{5}{19}}} = 0 + \cfrac{1}{1 + \cfrac{1}{105 + \cfrac{1}{\frac{19}{5}}}}$$

$$= 0 + \cfrac{1}{1 + \cfrac{1}{105 + \cfrac{1}{3 + \cfrac{4}{5}}}} = 0 + \cfrac{1}{1 + \cfrac{1}{105 + \cfrac{1}{3 + \cfrac{1}{\frac{5}{4}}}}}$$

$$= 0 + \cfrac{1}{1 + \cfrac{1}{105 + \cfrac{1}{3 + \cfrac{1}{1 + \cfrac{1}{4}}}}}.$$

Given the above continued fraction of $\frac{u}{v}$, by truncating the coefficients, we obtain $(n+1)$ approximations of $\frac{u}{v}$:

$$c_0 = x_0, \quad c_1 = x_0 + \frac{1}{x_1}, \quad c_2 = x_0 + \cfrac{1}{x_1 + \cfrac{1}{x_2}}, \dots, \quad c_n = x_0 + \cfrac{1}{x_1 + \cfrac{1}{\ddots + \cfrac{1}{x_n}}}.$$

The number c_j is called the jth *convergent* of the continued fraction and these convergents provide good approximations for $\frac{u}{v}$. To write the continued fraction expansion for a number $\frac{u}{v}$, we use the Euclidean division algorithm, which terminates in $O(\log(\max(u,v)))$ steps. As a result, there are $O(\log(\max(u,v)))$ number of convergents of $\frac{u}{v}$. Thus, the Wiener continued fraction technique runs very efficiently.

The convergents $c_0, c_1, \dots, c_n$ of the continued fraction of $\frac{u}{v}$ give good approximation to $\frac{u}{v}$, however, an approximation to $\frac{u}{v}$ is not always a convergent. The following classical theorem due to Legendre gives a sufficient condition for a rational number $\frac{a}{b}$ to be a convergent for the continued fraction of $\frac{u}{v}$.

Theorem 1 (The Legendre Theorem [14]). *Let $a \in \mathbb{Z}$ and $b \in \mathbb{Z}^+$ such that*

$$\left| \frac{u}{v} - \frac{a}{b} \right| < \frac{1}{2b^2}.$$

Then $\frac{a}{b}$ is equal to a convergent of the continued fraction of $\frac{u}{v}$.

The following Euler-Wallis Theorem gives us the recursive formulas to calculate the convergent sequence $\{c_i\}$ efficiently based on the coefficients x_0, $x_1, \ldots, x_n$.

Theorem 2 (The Euler-Wallis Theorem [12]). *For any $j \geq 0$, the jth convergent can be determined as $c_j = \frac{a_j}{b_j}$, where the numerator and the denominator sequences $\{a_i\}$ and $\{b_i\}$ are calculated as follows:*

$$a_{-2} = 0, \quad a_{-1} = 1, \quad a_i = x_i\, a_{i-1} + a_{i-2}, \quad \forall i \geq 0,$$
$$b_{-2} = 1, \quad b_{-1} = 0, \quad b_i = x_i\, b_{i-1} + b_{i-2}, \quad \forall i \geq 0.$$

Based on the Euler-Wallis Theorem, the following identity involving the numerator a_i and the denominator b_i of the convergent c_i can be easily obtained by mathematical induction.

Theorem 3. [12] *The numerator a_i and the denominator b_i of the convergent c_i satisfy the following identity*

$$b_i a_{i-1} - a_i b_{i-1} = (-1)^i, \quad \forall i \geq 0. \tag{1}$$

3 Boneh's Version of the Wiener Attack

In this section, for clarity and completeness, we recall here Boneh's version of the Wiener attack result [3]. Boneh provided the first and only rigorous proof which showed that the Wiener attack works for

$$d < \frac{1}{3} N^{\frac{1}{4}}.$$

Theorem 4 (The Wiener-Boneh Theorem [3]). *If the following conditions are satisfied*

(i) $q < p < 2q$
(ii) $0 < e < \phi(N)$
(iii) $ed - k\phi(N) = 1$
(iv) $d < \frac{1}{3} N^{\frac{1}{4}}$

then $\frac{k}{d}$ is equal to a convergent of the continued fraction of $\frac{e}{N}$.

Remark. Since $ed - k\phi(N) = 1$, we have $\gcd(k, d) = 1$. By the identity (1) in Theorem 3, we also have $\gcd(a_i, b_i) = 1$. Therefore, if $\frac{k}{d}$ is equal to a convergent of the continued fraction of $\frac{e}{N}$,

$$\frac{k}{d} = c_i = \frac{a_i}{b_i},$$

then we must have $k = a_i$ and $d = b_i$. In that case, using the equation $ed - k\phi(N) = 1$, we have $eb_i - a_i\phi(N) = 1$, and $\phi(N) = \frac{eb_i - 1}{a_i}$.

From here, we obtain

$$S = p + q = N - \phi(N) + 1,$$

and with $N = pq$, we can solve for p and q from the quadratic equation

$$x^2 - Sx + N = 0.$$

Algorithm 1. Factorisation Algorithm Based on Continued Fraction

---

Input: e, N

Output: (d, p, q) or $\perp$

1: Run the Euclidean division algorithm on input (e, N) to obtain the coefficients $x_0, x_1, \ldots, x_n$ of the continued fraction of $\frac{e}{N}$.

2: Use the Euler-Wallis Theorem to calculate the convergents

$$c_0 = \frac{a_0}{b_0}, c_1 = \frac{a_1}{b_1}, \ldots, c_n = \frac{a_n}{b_n}.$$

3: **for** $0 \leq i \leq n$ **do**

4:    **if** $a_i | (eb_i - 1)$ **then**

5:        $\lambda_i = \dfrac{eb_i - 1}{a_i}$ $\triangleright$ $\lambda_i = \phi(N)$ if $\frac{a_i}{b_i} = \frac{k}{d}$

6:        $S = N - \lambda_i + 1$ $\triangleright$ $S = p + q$ if $\lambda_i = \phi(N)$

7:        Find the two roots p' and q' by solving the quadratic equation

$$x^2 - Sx + N = 0$$

8:        **if** p' and q' are prime numbers **then**

9:            **return** $(d = b_i, p = p', q = q')$ $\triangleright$ Successfully factorise N

10:       **end if**

11:    **end if**

12: **end for**

13: **return** $\perp$ $\triangleright$ Fail to factorise N

In the Algorithm 1, we can see that if $\frac{k}{d}$ is equal to a convergent of the continued fraction of $\frac{e}{N}$ as asserted in Theorem 4, then the secret information p, q, d, k can be recovered from the public information (e, N). By the Euclidean division algorithm, we obtain $O(\log(N))$ number of convergents of the continued fraction of $\frac{e}{N}$, so the Wiener algorithm will succeed to factor N and output p, q, d, k in $O(\log(N))$ time complexity.

Our experiments confirm that the Wiener algorithm runs very efficiently. In Sects. 4 and 5, we use 1024-bit primes p and q, and with the Euclidean division algorithm, the continued fractions of $\frac{e}{N}$ give us less than 2000 convergents c_i.

4   An Experimental Result

In this section, we give an example where the Wiener attack fails with

$$d = \left\lfloor \frac{1}{2} N^{\frac{1}{4}} \right\rfloor + 1,$$

thus, showing that the bound $d < N^{\frac{1}{4}}$ is not accurate as it has been generally believed [1,4,13,17].

This result came as a total surprise to us. As we implemented the Wiener algorithm and run it, we found out that the Wiener attack failed for many values of $d < N^{\frac{1}{4}}$. The example here clearly shows that it fails at the halfway point of the range. This raises a natural question: what is the correct bound for the Wiener attack? Attempting to answer this question has been the motivation of this work, and hence *the quest for the exact bound*.

Below, we choose 1024-bit primes p and q which give 2047-bit modulus N. We set the private key

$$d = \left\lfloor \frac{1}{2} N^{\frac{1}{4}} \right\rfloor + 1$$

which is a 511-bit number and the corresponding public key e is 2047-bit. Using the Euclidean division algorithm, we determine the continued fraction expansion of $\frac{e}{N}$. This continued fraction has 1179 convergents: $c_0, c_1, \ldots, c_{1178}$. Using the Algorithm 1 to search through these 1179 convergents, we found no factorization of N, so the Wiener algorithm failed in this case.

Here are the experimental values:

$p = 1491527899\ 5477760590\ 2728010071\ 6980981660\ 1258222662$
$2431819289\ 1225141694\ 5753993233\ 4134597092\ 2789813803$
$2123071118\ 7456841568\ 6244681095\ 6494959013\ 6209617496$
$4856101327\ 5715997217\ 9803365696\ 1960828527\ 8759316539$
$7375676105\ 8838761560\ 3738626761\ 6351893514\ 2444493175$
$0194503087\ 8223260165\ 3356278700\ 2338989328\ 5059210806$
$959842047\ (1024\ \text{bits})$

$q = 9111167064\ 7390707425\ 7779057216\ 8580155934\ 8047103723$
$9509013689\ 9393941503\ 6663226117\ 3483046733\ 6435253791$
$0245424858\ 8231334271\ 0003745035\ 1560880167\ 0686028666$
$9368653851\ 4065809046\ 6070550773\ 1596277357\ 7225073326$
$8667388642\ 6946395521\ 3055868264\ 9615090699\ 8451255847$
$8563387800\ 1084724118\ 4269448761\ 8873870285\ 9133249777$
$21380459\ (1024\ \text{bits})$

$N =$1358955987 4499142355 7513414060 3539768425 5014057126
0741075421 2867822612 0805968144 4708819214 5518842119
9958881804 7937878622 4112295347 5325559673 5996725202
8633553360 3757756220 1871004594 8076611030 2567765384
0026153784 2770613729 4329327237 0569653405 5424667619
2238028495 4841783632 6958663905 5958512318 1193434612
0315768395 7219446440 1318651117 5563726203 4345904525
9443782456 6436078112 6077167607 7739231458 9205427377
2268437286 4735492393 2750716520 2984412539 2729934943
9305127634 2706564766 5583235029 4396813965 7917910935
3031271720 0339494884 0018966371 3447510835 9275849868
6562766142 9910164397 0677468356 5904851307 0086539066
0235916943 2359573 (2047 bits)

$e =$1330419030 5540874988 5376069329 7084174518 7260177538
5866925366 2997366672 3493599969 0390276038 0919368940
1864701342 9310242427 8833742509 7494436400 5403659294
0555161192 1972457828 7339053358 7614588496 6324498356
6363071098 8205134167 5000847275 0988164806 4636099774
1181379056 1319572282 3672568352 1298430680 1201814131
9604052114 8335594185 3173571813 7624310228 5349453986
0737412659 9608417423 2546667689 2033178326 5130304082
6314383724 2740893126 4550856662 5119551763 4091295935
2191957179 9876282943 3381372125 9047810743 6224521388
6861509236 7407065451 7584476965 4348997529 8178870165
9669410312 1497394053 8763499800 1901681249 3233425747
4891365832 5046931 (2047 bits)

$d = \left\lfloor \dfrac{1}{2}N^{\frac{1}{4}} \right\rfloor + 1 =$5398478203 0311651626 6068367829 8945738486 9044874575
7958435010 7981488386 1130096080 6180756651 2262828961
6340636130 6706635548 8922382801 5381181990 9555989039
3235 (511 bits)

$k =$5285114605 3829091397 9620556948 0145234187 5641719964
7496242061 4986547849 9915220055 9741796430 2523466970
5824394524 5600033207 6486525013 4460390163 5991230680
7438 (511 bits)

In the Algorithm 1, the continued fraction of $\frac{e}{N}$ has 1179 convergents c_i, so

$$n = 1178.$$

In line 4 of the Algorithm 1, there are only 2 values of i that $a_i \mid (eb_i - 1)$:

$$i = 1, \quad a_1 = 1, \quad b_1 = 1,$$

and

$$i = 3, \quad a_3 = 47, \quad b_3 = 48.$$

With these two cases: $i = 1$ and $i = 3$, the quadratic equation in line 7 of the Algorithm 1 does not produce prime number roots. So the Wiener algorithm fails in this example.

We can explain the reason for the Wiener algorithm fails in this example. This is because among 1179 convergents of the continued fraction of $\frac{e}{N}$, none of them is equal to $\frac{k}{d}$ as required in Theorem 4.

5   Improving Boneh's Bound on the Wiener Attack

By using the classical Legendre Theorem on continued fractions, Boneh provided the first rigorous proof [3] which showed that the Wiener attack works for

$$d < \frac{1}{3}N^{\frac{1}{4}}.$$

In this section, we establish an improved bound on the Wiener's attack. We extend the well-known Boneh's bound and show that the Wiener continued fraction technique works for a wider range, namely, for

$$d \le \frac{1}{\sqrt[4]{18}}N^{\frac{1}{4}} = \frac{1}{2.06...}N^{\frac{1}{4}}.$$

Below is our new theorem which is an improvement of the Wiener-Boneh Theorem (i.e., Theorem 4). Additionally, our new proof is also based on the Legendre Theorem.

Theorem 5. *If the following conditions are satisfied*

(i) $q < p < 2q$
(ii) $0 < e < \phi(N)$
(iii) $ed - k\phi(N) = 1$
(iv) $d \le \frac{1}{\sqrt[4]{18}}N^{\frac{1}{4}} = \frac{1}{2.06...}N^{\frac{1}{4}}$

then $\frac{k}{d}$ *is equal to a convergent of the continued fraction of* $\frac{e}{N}$. *Thus, the secret information* p, q, d, k *can be recovered from public information* (e, N) *in* $O(\log(N))$ *time complexity.*

Proof. As we want to use the Legendre Theorem (Theorem 1) to prove that $\frac{k}{d}$ is equal to a convergent of the continued fraction of $\frac{e}{N}$, we consider the following inequality

$$
\left| \frac{e}{N} - \frac{k}{d} \right| = \frac{|kN - ed|}{Nd} = \frac{|k(N - \phi(N)) - (ed - k\phi(N))|}{Nd}
$$
$$
= \frac{k(p + q - 1) - 1}{Nd} < \frac{k(p + q)}{Nd}.
$$

Since $ed - k\phi(N) = 1$ and $e < \phi(N)$, we have $k < d$. Therefore,

$$
\left| \frac{e}{N} - \frac{k}{d} \right| < \frac{p + q}{N}.
$$

It follows from $q < p < 2q$ that $1 < \sqrt{\frac{p}{q}} < \sqrt{2}$, and since the function $f(x) = x + \frac{1}{x}$ is increasing on $[1, +\infty)$, we have

$$
\frac{p + q}{N^{\frac{1}{2}}} = \sqrt{\frac{p}{q}} + \sqrt{\frac{q}{p}} < \sqrt{2} + \frac{1}{\sqrt{2}} = \frac{3}{\sqrt{2}}.
$$

Thus,

$$
p + q < \frac{3}{\sqrt{2}} N^{\frac{1}{2}}. \tag{2}
$$

It follows that

$$
\left| \frac{e}{N} - \frac{k}{d} \right| < \frac{\frac{3}{\sqrt{2}} N^{\frac{1}{2}}}{N} = \frac{3}{\sqrt{2} N^{\frac{1}{2}}}
$$

Finally, since $d \leq \frac{1}{\sqrt[4]{18}} N^{\frac{1}{4}}$, we have

$$
\left| \frac{e}{N} - \frac{k}{d} \right| < \frac{1}{2d^2}.
$$

By the Legendre Theorem (Theorem 1), $\frac{k}{d}$ is equal to a convergent of the continued fraction of $\frac{e}{N}$ and the theorem is proved. ∎

6   The Second Experimental Result

In Sect. 5, we improve the Boneh bound [3]:

$$
d < \frac{1}{3} N^{\frac{1}{4}}.
$$

We show that the Wiener continued fraction technique works for a wider range, namely, for

$$d \leq \frac{1}{\sqrt[4]{18}} N^{\frac{1}{4}} = \frac{1}{2.06...} N^{\frac{1}{4}}.$$

In this section, we provide an experimental result to support our new bound. We choose a private key $d = \left\lfloor \frac{1}{\sqrt[4]{18}} N^{\frac{1}{4}} \right\rfloor$ and show that the Wiener attack indeed works, which confirms our new bound.

Here, we select a 2048-bit modulus N. We set the private key $d = \left\lfloor \frac{1}{\sqrt[4]{18}} N^{\frac{1}{4}} \right\rfloor$ which is a 511-bit number. The corresponding public key e is 2048-bit.

Using the Euclidean division algorithm, we determine the continued fraction expansion of $\frac{e}{N}$. This continued fraction has 1219 convergents: $c_0, c_1, \ldots, c_{1218}$. We run the Wiener algorithm through these 1219 convergents. At the 289th convergent $c_{289} = \frac{a_{289}}{b_{289}}$, we found the correct factorization of the modulus N into two 1024-bit primes p and q. Hence, the Wiener algorithm is successful in this case which confirms our new bound in Theorem 5.

Here are the experimental values:

$p =$1753651555 7959285985 8389246962 5666004143 2631322905
    3792511376 1823387899 6863875472 8500338195 6106187059
    8979790786 3900938931 7295752778 9842328060 3224176903
    6697007530 6302349794 5882100113 2594934722 2701276857
    3702925327 3032617922 5592387182 1655023312 3781280062
    3318071860 0703325676 9316877525 0029640840 1329310468
    563365517 (1024 bits)

$q =$1302246063 5244450969 8486520987 6835312123 3825549540
    4590911663 0930183138 4524166515 2217429150 6917508540
    1229882549 1643140442 7317286012 5333646913 8593238275
    0954632799 2092626902 5564720911 8376898712 1336228332
    6412475983 8782926026 4681550732 7524640686 1898664920
    0982675880 5711531846 6818868729 5634599558 9465454245
    497973799 (1024 bits)

$N =$2283685835 3287668091 9203688162 8641577810 3964252589
2829513042 0474999022 9966219821 6666459658 1454018899
4842992237 6560732622 7548715380 4387435627 0300826321
1665057256 4937978011 1813943886 7926552494 0467869924
8547365003 8355720409 4262355848 3358418844 9224331698
6356990029 6911605460 6455811765 2232596722 1393273906
6967318845 7131381644 1207877832 1534284874 4792830245
0180559814 0668893320 3072001361 9079413832 5132168722
1421794347 4001731747 8227015966 3404029234 2194986951
9455164666 8806852454 0063123724 1365869202 7515557841
4144066123 2146905186 4313571125 6653677066 9381756925
3817941547 8954522854 7119685992 7901448206 0579354284
5523886372 6089083 (2048 bits)

$e =$1716081930 8904585327 7890161348 9791423576 2203050367
3463267958 5567058963 9956759654 2803490663 7374660531
6475059968 7461192166 4245059192 9370601129 3378320096
4337238276 6547546926 5356977528 0523991876 7190684796
2650929866 9049485976 1183156661 2687168184 7641670872
5889507391 9139366379 9018676640 7654053176 5577090231
6720982183 2859747419 6583443634 6658489531 6847817524
2470325739 2651850823 5172974203 8213894377 0358904660
5944230019 1228592937 2517345927 3262320732 4742303631
3243627441 4264865868 0285278401 0248376241 4082363751
8720861263 2105886502 3936481567 7633023698 7329249988
1142950825 6124902530 9574993383 3690395192 4035916501
5366161007 0010419 (2048 bits)

$d = \left\lfloor \dfrac{1}{\sqrt[4]{18}} N^{\frac{1}{4}} \right\rfloor =$5968166949 0793605552 2026899285 2191823920 0238114742
8873867437 0592596189 5174438877 8002365303 1793516493
8064621142 4818137141 6016184480 4216409734 3986334607
9123 (511 bits)

In the Algorithm 1, the continued fraction of $\frac{e}{N}$ has 1219 convergents c_i, and the 289th convergent c_{289} produces the correct factorization of the modulus N.

$$i = 289,$$

a_{289} =4484795282 8757963262 4661693174 9335120861 3264690597
1711725983 1381808371 6124351193 7219275062 5936785513
3802411458 7021923657 4897458445 0198267245 3098232091
5377

b_{289} =5968166949 0793605552 2026899285 2191823920 0238114742
8873867437 0592596189 5174438877 8002365303 1793516493
8064621142 4818137141 6016184480 4216409734 3986334607
9123

λ_{289} =2283685835 3287668091 9203688162 8641577810 3964252589
2829513042 0474999022 9966219821 6666459658 1454018899
4842992237 6560732622 7548715380 4387435627 0300826321
1665057256 4937978011 1813943886 7926552494 0467869924
8547365003 8355720409 4262355848 3358418844 9224331698
6356990029 6911605460 6455811765 2232596722 1393273906
6967318815 1541619712 0834182263 3957489849 4661203580
4493315230 2326589392 7714897548 0275215025 3355434091
9052234345 3034398192 3819078520 2100150082 4597489533
7713646790 3642819470 0565454009 6683766693 0332214401
0393547122 0606774068 2759176222 9259885575 1415357068
5823443304 8879748790 5633933631 4326822749 4155314376
6047414966 4749768

The quadratic equation in line 7 produces two correct prime roots p and q.
Hence, the Wiener algorithm is successful in this example.

We can see that the Wiener algorithm works because the convergent

$$c_{289} = \frac{a_{289}}{b_{289}} = \frac{k}{d}$$

as confirmed in our Theorem 5.

7 Conclusion

In this paper, we show a certain belief about the Wiener attack on the RSA
is not accurate. It has been a general belief that the Wiener attack works for
$d < N^{\frac{1}{4}}$ (see [1,4,13,17]), and on the converse, Steinfeld-Contini-Wang-Pieprzyk
[17] showed that Wiener's attack fails with an overwhelming probability for a
random choice $d \approx N^{\frac{1}{4}+\epsilon}$ for any positive number ϵ. Thus, as depicted in Fig. 1(i),

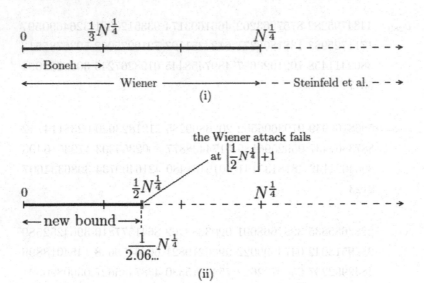

Fig. 1. (i) Old belief: Wiener attack works for $d < N^{\frac{1}{4}}$. Boneh's rigorous proof covers $d < \frac{1}{3}N^{\frac{1}{4}}$. (ii) Our research shows that Wiener attack fails at $d = \lfloor \frac{1}{2}N^{\frac{1}{4}} \rfloor + 1$. Our new rigorous proof covers $d \leq \frac{1}{\sqrt[4]{18}}N^{\frac{1}{4}} = \frac{1}{2.06...}N^{\frac{1}{4}}$.

the bound $d < N^{\frac{1}{4}}$ has since been believed to be the optimal bound for the Wiener attack.

On the contrary, in this paper, we show that the bound $d < N^{\frac{1}{4}}$ for the Wiener attack on the RSA is not accurate. We give an example where the Wiener attack fails with

$$d = \left\lfloor \frac{1}{2}N^{\frac{1}{4}} \right\rfloor + 1.$$

By using the Legendre Theorem on continued fractions, Boneh provided the first rigorous proof which showed that the Wiener attack works for

$$d < \frac{1}{3}N^{\frac{1}{4}}.$$

As depicted in Fig. 1(ii), in this paper, we improve Boneh's bound by showing that the Wiener continued fraction technique actually works for a wider range, namely, for

$$d \leq \frac{1}{\sqrt[4]{18}}N^{\frac{1}{4}} = \frac{1}{2.06...}N^{\frac{1}{4}}.$$

Our new result is supported by an experimental result where it is shown that the Wiener attack succeeds with $d = \left\lfloor \frac{1}{\sqrt[4]{18}}N^{\frac{1}{4}} \right\rfloor$.

It is an open problem to determine the exact optimal bound for the Wiener attack. Suppose that

$$d < \omega N^{\frac{1}{4}}$$

is this exact optimal bound, then by the two main results of this paper, it follows that

$$\frac{1}{\sqrt[4]{18}} \leq \omega \leq \frac{1}{2},$$

where $\sqrt[4]{18} = 2.06...$ We are yet to find the exact value of ω and we conjecture that $\omega = \frac{1}{\sqrt[4]{18}}$ (Fig. 2).

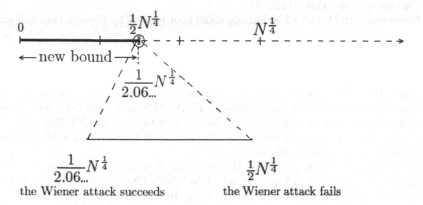

Fig. 2. Open problem. Undecided interval: it is unknown if the Wiener attack fails or succeeds in the interval $\frac{1}{\sqrt[4]{18}}N^{\frac{1}{4}} < d \leq \frac{1}{2}N^{\frac{1}{4}}$.

References

1. Bleichenbacher, D., May, A.: New attacks on RSA with small secret CRT-exponents. In: Yung, M., Dodis, Y., Kiayias, A., Malkin, T. (eds.) PKC 2006. LNCS, vol. 3958, pp. 1–13. Springer, Heidelberg (2006). https://doi.org/10.1007/11745853_1

2. Blömer, J., May, A.: A generalized wiener attack on RSA. In: Bao, F., Deng, R., Zhou, J. (eds.) PKC 2004. LNCS, vol. 2947, pp. 1–13. Springer, Heidelberg (2004). https://doi.org/10.1007/978-3-540-24632-9_1

3. Boneh, D.: Twenty years of attacks on the RSA cryptosystem. Not. Am. Math. Soc. **46**, 203–213 (1999)

4. Boneh, D., Durfee, G.: Cryptanalysis of RSA with private key d less than $N^{0.292}$. IEEE Trans. Inf. Theor. **46**, 1339–1349 (2000)

5. Bunder, M., Nitaj, A., Susilo, W., Tonien, J.: A new attack on three variants of the RSA cryptosystem. In: Liu, J.K., Steinfeld, R. (eds.) ACISP 2016. LNCS, vol. 9723, pp. 258–268. Springer, Cham (2016). https://doi.org/10.1007/978-3-319-40367-0_16

6. Bunder, M., Nitaj, A., Susilo, W., Tonien, J.: A generalized attack on RSA type cryptosystems. Theor. Comput. Sci. **704**, 74–81 (2017)

7. Bunder, M., Nitaj, A., Susilo, W., Tonien, J.: Cryptanalysis of RSA-type cryptosystems based on Lucas sequences, Gaussian integers and elliptic curves. J. Inf. Secur. Appl. **40**, 193–198 (2018)

8. Bunder, M., Tonien, J.: A new attack on the RSA cryptosystem based on continued fractions. Malays. J. Math. Sci. **11**, 45–57 (2017)
9. Coppersmith, D.: Small solutions to polynomial equations, and low exponent RSA vulnerabilities. J. Cryptology **10**, 233–260 (1997)
10. Dujella, A.: Continued fractions and RSA with small secret exponent. Tatra Mt. Math. Publ. **29**, 101–112 (2004)
11. Dujella, A.: A variant of wiener's attack on RSA. Computing **85**, 77–83 (2009)
12. Hardy, G., Wright, E.: An Introduction to the Theory of Numbers, 6th edn. Oxford University Press, Oxford (2008)
13. Herrmann, M., May, A.: Maximizing small root bounds by linearization and applications to small secret exponent RSA. In: Nguyen, P.Q., Pointcheval, D. (eds.) PKC 2010. LNCS, vol. 6056, pp. 53–69. Springer, Heidelberg (2010). https://doi.org/10.1007/978-3-642-13013-7_4
14. Legendre, A.M.: Essai sur la théorie des nombres. Duprat, An VI, Paris (1798)
15. Nassr, D.I., Bahig, H.M., Bhery, A., Daoud, S.S.: A new RSA vulnerability using continued fractions. In: Proceedings of IEEE/ACS International Conference on Computer Systems and Applications AICCSA, 2008, pp. 694–701 (2008)
16. Olds, C.D.: Continued fractions. New Mathematical Library, vol. 9. Mathematical Association of America, Washington (1963)
17. Steinfeld, R., Contini, S., Wang, H., Pieprzyk, J.: Converse results to the wiener attack on RSA. In: Vaudenay, S. (ed.) PKC 2005. LNCS, vol. 3386, pp. 184–198. Springer, Heidelberg (2005). https://doi.org/10.1007/978-3-540-30580-4_13
18. Verheul, E., van Tilborg, H.: Cryptanalysis of 'less short' RSA secret exponents. Appl. Algebra Eng. Commun. Comput. **8**, 425–435 (1997)
19. de Weger, B.: Cryptanalysis of RSA with small prime difference. Appl. Algebra Eng. Commun. Comput. **13**, 17–28 (2002)
20. Wiener, M.: Cryptanalysis of short RSA secret exponents. IEEE Trans. Inf. Theor. **36**, 553–558 (1990)

Function-Dependent Commitments
from Homomorphic Authenticators

Lucas Schabhüser[✉], Denis Butin, and Johannes Buchmann

Technische Universität Darmstadt, Darmstadt, Germany
{lschabhueser,dbutin,buchmann}@cdc.informatik.tu-darmstadt.de

Abstract. In cloud computing, delegated computing raises the security issue of guaranteeing data authenticity during a remote computation. In this context, the recently introduced function-dependent commitments (FDCs) are the only approach providing both fast correctness verification, information-theoretic input-output privacy, and strong unforgeability. Homomorphic authenticators—the established approach to this problem—do not provide information-theoretic privacy and always reveal the computation's result upon verification, thus violating output privacy. Since many homomorphic authenticator schemes already exist, we investigate the relation between them and FDCs to clarify how existing schemes can be supplemented with information-theoretic output privacy. Specifically, we present a generic transformation turning any structure-preserving homomorphic authenticator scheme into an FDC scheme. This facilitates the design of multi-party computation schemes with full information-theoretic privacy. We also introduce a new structure-preserving, linearly homomorphic authenticator scheme suitable for our transformation. It is the first both context hiding and structure-preserving homomorphic authenticator scheme. Our scheme is also the first structure-preserving homomorphic authenticator scheme to achieve efficient verification.

1 Introduction

Time-consuming computations are commonly outsourced to the cloud. Such infrastructures attractively offer cost savings and dynamic computing resource allocation. In such a situation, it is desirable to be able to verify the outsourced computation. The verification must be *efficient*, by which we mean that the verification procedure is significantly faster than verified computation itself. Otherwise, the verifier could as well carry out the computation by himself, negating the advantage of outsourcing. Often, not only the data owner is interested in the correctness of a computation; but also third parties, like insurance companies in the case of medical data. In addition, there are scenarios in which computations are performed over sensitive data. For instance, a cloud server may collect health data of individuals and compute aggregated data. Hence the requirement for efficient verification procedures for outsourced computing that are privacy-preserving, both for computation inputs and for computation results.

© Springer Nature Switzerland AG 2019
J. Jang-Jaccard and F. Guo (Eds.): ACISP 2019, LNCS 11547, pp. 399–418, 2019.
https://doi.org/10.1007/978-3-030-21548-4_22

Growing amounts of data are sensitive enough to require long-term protection. Electronic health records, voting records, or tax data require protection periods exceeding the lifetime of an individual. Over such a long time, complexity-based confidentiality protection is unsuitable because algorithmic progress is unpredictable. In contrast, *information-theoretic* confidentiality protection is not threatened by algorithmic progress and supports long-term security. Existing approaches address verifiability and confidentiality to various degrees.

Homomorphic authenticators [4] sometimes allow for efficient verification, keeping the computational effort of the verifier low. They fail to provide information-theoretic confidentiality. Some schemes offer so-called context hiding security, a form of input privacy. However, stronger privacy notions are not achieved.

Homomorphic commitments [6,19,23] can be used in audit schemes. In particular, Pedersen commitments [19] provide information-theoretic confidentiality. Homomorphic commitments however, lead to costly verification procedures.

Function-dependent commitments [22] (FDCs) are a generic construction for authentified delegated computing. Their core idea is as follows. First, commit to input values and to a function. Then, authenticate all inputs. Next, compute an authenticated commitment to the computation's result using homomorphic properties. FDCs combine the advantages of homomorphic authenticators and homomorphic commitments. They allow for information-theoretic input and output privacy as well as efficient verification. Compared to homomorphic authenticators they achieve a *hiding* property. The *context hiding* property of homomorphic authenticators guarantees that authenticators to the *output* of a computation do not leak information about the *input* of the computation (beyond what can be inferred from the result). The authenticator to the input, however, leaks information about the authenticated data. The hiding property of FDCs ensures that not even this is possible. In [22] an information-theoretically hiding FDC was combined with secret sharing for efficiently verifiable multi-party computation. Combining homomorphic authenticators with secret sharing can be instantiated by a straightforward composition, or by authenticating individual shares. The former leads to a loss of information-theoretic privacy, the latter requires all storage servers to perform computations on audit data. By contrast, FDC-based verifiable multi-party computation can be instantiated so that auditing only requires a single storage server. FDC-based verifiable multi-party computation thus provides not only privacy gains, but also efficiency improvements with respect to the classical variant using homomorphic authenticators.

For a detailed comparison to related work, see Sect. 5. There are various homomorphic authenticator schemes fine-tailored to specific scenarios. For FDCs, so far only one construction is known [22]. Adding the privacy properties of FDCs to known homomorphic authenticator schemes makes them suitable even when sensitive data are processed. In this paper, we show how to achieve this.

Contribution Overview. In this paper, we investigate the relation between homomorphic authenticators and FDCs. Our contribution is twofold.

First, we show how an FDC can be generically constructed from a *structure-preserving* homomorphic authenticator scheme, assuming the additional existence of a homomorphic commitment scheme and of a separate classical commitment scheme. We require the commitment space of the homomorphic commitment scheme to be a subset of the structure preserved by the homomorphic authenticator scheme. The message space of the classical commitment scheme allows labeled programs as admissible inputs, unlike the homomorphic commitment scheme. We show that if the two underlying commitment schemes are binding, then the resulting FDC inherits this bindingness. Furthermore, we prove that the output FDC inherits the unconditional hiding from the underlying homomorphic commitment scheme. The correctness of the output FDC is shown to follow from three assumptions on the input homomorphic authenticator scheme: authentication correctness, evaluation correctness and efficient verification. Regarding security, we prove that unforgeability is also inherited. This is done by showing that a simulator can forward adversary queries in the FDC security experiment to queries in the homomorphic authenticator experiment. The resulting forgery can be used to compute a forgery in the other experiment. For performance, we show that if the input scheme is succinct, respectively efficiently verifiable, then the output FDC is also succinct, respectively has amortized efficiency. Our transformation enables the use of certain existing homomorphic authenticator schemes in particularly privacy-sensitive settings. Applying this transformation enables information-theoretic output privacy. This allows third parties to verify the correct computation of a function without even needing to learn the result. In the full version [21] we show how every FDC can be transformed into a homomorphic authenticator scheme, showing that FDCs are at least as powerful schemes as homomorphic authenticators.

Second, we introduce a structure-preserving, linearly homomorphic authenticator scheme suitable for our transformation. All known structure-preserving homomorphic authenticator schemes are limited to linear functions. Our scheme is the first such construction to achieve constant-time verification (after a one-time pre-processing). It is also the first structure-preserving homomorphic authenticator scheme to be *context hiding*. This property ensures that a third-party verifier does not learn anything about the inputs to a computation beyond what it knows from the output of the computation. For simplicity, our scheme is limited to a single dataset. However, it can be extended to a multi-dataset scheme following a result by Fiore et al. [11]. Furthermore, our scheme is succinct. Authenticators consist of two elements of a cyclic group of prime order. The security of our construction relies on the hardness of the Double Pairing Assumption [1], which implies the Decisional Diffie–Hellman assumption with a tight security reduction.

The remainder of this paper is organized as follows. We first provide the necessary background on FDCs and homomorphic authenticators (Sect. 2). We then show how to construct FDCs from homomorphic commitments and structure-preserving homomorphic authenticators (Sect. 3). Next, we present a new instantiation for a context hiding, structure-preserving linearly homomorphic signature scheme (Sect. 4). Finally, we compare our work to the state of the art (Sect. 5).

2   Preliminaries

We first formalize the notion of homomorphic commitments.

Afterwards, we provide the terminology of labeled programs, on which the notions of unforgeability in this paper are based. We then describe FDCs and their properties. These include the classical hiding and binding properties of commitments, as well as further FDC-specific properties such as correctness, unforgeability, succinctness and amortized efficiency. Likewise, we recall definitions for homomorphic authenticators and their properties. Finally, we define structure-preserving signatures.

Commitment Schemes. Commitment schemes, particularly homomorphic commitment schemes, are a basic building block in cryptography. We provide the formalizations used in this work.

Definition 1 (Commitment Scheme). *A commitment scheme* Com *is a tuple of the following algorithms (*CSetup, Commit, Decommit*):*

CSetup(1^λ): *On input a security parameter λ, this algorithm outputs a commitment key* CK. *We implicitly assume that every algorithm uses this commitment key, leaving it out of the notation.*

Commit(m, r): *On input a message $m \in \mathcal{M}$ and randomness $r \in \mathcal{R}$, it outputs the commitment C and the decommitment d.*

Decommit(m, d, C): *On input a message $m \in \mathcal{M}$, decommitment d, and a commitment C, it outputs 1 or 0.*

Definition 2 (Homomorphic Commitment Scheme). *Let $\mathcal{F}$ be a class of functions. A commitment scheme* Com $=$ (CSetup, Commit, Decommit) *is $\mathcal{F}$-homomorphic if there exists an algorithm* CEval *with the following properties:*

CEval($f, C_1, \ldots, C_n$): *On input a function $f \in \mathcal{F}$ and a tuple of commitments C_i for $i \in [n]$, the algorithm outputs C^*.*

Correctness: *For every $m_i \in \mathcal{M}$, $r_i \in \mathcal{R}$, $i \in [n]$ with $(C_i, d_i) \leftarrow$ Commit(m_i, r_i) and $C^* \leftarrow$ CEval($f, C_1, \ldots, C_n$), there exists a unique function $\hat{f} \in \mathcal{F}$, such that* Decommit($f(m_1, \ldots, m_n), \hat{f}(m_1, \ldots, m_n, r_1, \ldots r_n), C^*$) $= 1$.

Labeled Programs. To accurately describe both correct and legitimate operations for homomorphic authenticators, we use *multi-labeled programs* similarly to Backes, Fiore, and Reischuk [5]. The basic idea is to append a function by several identifiers, in our case *input identifiers* and *dataset identifiers*. Input identifiers label in which order the input values are to be used. Dataset identifiers determine which authenticators can be homomorphically combined. The idea is that only authenticators created under the same dataset identifier can be combined. Intuitively, we need input identifiers to distinguish between messages. This allows restricting homomorphic evaluation to authenticators related to the same set of messages, leading to a stronger unforgeability notion.

Formally, a *labeled program* $\mathcal{P}$ consists of a tuple $(f, \tau_1, \ldots, \tau_n)$, where $f : \mathcal{M}^n \to \mathcal{M}$ is a function with n inputs and $\tau_i \in \mathcal{T}$ with $i \in [n]$ is a label for the ith input of f from some set $\mathcal{T}$. Given a set of labeled programs $\mathcal{P}_1, \ldots, \mathcal{P}_N$ and a function $g : \mathcal{M}^N \to \mathcal{M}$, they can be composed by evaluating g over the labeled programs, i.e. $\mathcal{P}^* = g(\mathcal{P}_1, \ldots, \mathcal{P}_N)$. This is an abuse of notation analogous to function composition. The identity program with label τ is given by $\mathcal{I}_\tau = (f_{id}, \tau)$, where $f_{id} : \mathcal{M} \to \mathcal{M}$ is the identity function. The program $\mathcal{P} = (f, \tau_1, \ldots, \tau_n)$ can be expressed as the composition of n identity programs $\mathcal{P} = f(\mathcal{I}_{\tau_1}, \ldots, \mathcal{I}_{\tau_n})$.

A *multi-labeled program* $\mathcal{P}_\Delta$ is a pair $(\mathcal{P}, \Delta)$ of the labeled program $\mathcal{P}$ and a dataset identifier Δ. Given a set of N multi-labeled programs with same dataset identifier Δ, i.e. $(\mathcal{P}_1, \Delta), \ldots, (\mathcal{P}_N, \Delta)$, and a function $g : \mathcal{M}^N \to \mathcal{M}$, a composed multi-labeled program $\mathcal{P}_\Delta^*$ can be computed, consisting of the pair $(\mathcal{P}^*, \Delta)$, where $\mathcal{P}^* = g(\mathcal{P}_1, \ldots, \mathcal{P}_N)$. Analogously to the identity program for labeled programs, we refer to a multi-labeled identity program by $\mathcal{I}_{(\tau, \Delta)} = ((f_{id}, \tau), \Delta)$.

Definition 3 (Well Defined Program). *A labeled program $\mathcal{P} = (f, \tau_1, \ldots, \tau_n)$ is well defined with respect to a list $L \subset \mathcal{T} \times \mathcal{M}$ if exactly one of the two following cases holds: First, there are messages $m_1, \ldots, m_n$ such that $(\tau_i, m_i) \in L \; \forall i \in [n]$. Second, there is an $i \in \{1, \ldots, n\}$ such that $(\tau_i, \cdot) \notin L$ and $f(\{m_j\}_{(\tau_j, m_j) \in L} \cup \{m_k'\}_{(\tau_k, \cdot) \notin L})$ is constant over all possible choices of $m_k' \in \mathcal{M}$.*

If f is a linear function, $\mathcal{P} = (f, \tau_1, \ldots, \tau_n)$, with $f(m_1, \ldots, m_n) = \sum_{i=1}^n f_i m_i$ fulfills the second condition if and only if $f_k = 0$ for all $(\tau_k, \cdot) \notin L$.

FDCs. Going beyond the basic functionalities of homomorphic commitments, the idea of FDCs was introduced by Schabhüser et al. [22]. In particular, this framework allows for a notion of unforgeability.

Definition 4 ([22]). *An FDC scheme for a class $\mathcal{F}$ of functions is a tuple of algorithms (*Setup, KeyGen, PublicCommit, PrivateCommit, FunctionCommit, Eval, FunctionVerify, PublicDecommit*):*

Setup(1^λ) *takes as input the security parameter λ and outputs public parameters* pp. *We implicitly assume that every algorithm uses these public parameters, leaving them out of the notation (except for* KeyGen*).*

KeyGen(pp) *takes the public parameters* pp *as input and outputs a secret-public key pair* (sk, pk).

PublicCommit(m, r) *takes as input a message m and randomness r and outputs commitment C.*

PrivateCommit(sk, m, r, Δ, τ) *takes as input the secret key* sk, *a message m, randomness r, a dataset Δ, and an identifier τ and outputs an authenticator A for the tuple (m, r, Δ, τ).*

FunctionCommit(pk, $\mathcal{P}$) *takes as input the public key* pk *and a labeled program* $\mathcal{P}$ *and outputs a function commitment F to $\mathcal{P}$.*

Eval($f, A_1, \ldots A_n$) *takes as input a function $f \in \mathcal{F}$ and a set of authenticators $A_1, \ldots, A_n$, where A_i is an authenticator for $(m_i, r_i, \Delta, \tau_i)$, for $i = 1, \ldots, n$. It computes an authenticator A^* using the A_i and outputs A^*.*

FunctionVerify(pk, A, C, F, Δ) *takes as input a public key* pk, *an authenticator A, a commitment C, a function commitment F, as well as a dataset identifier Δ. It outputs either 1 (accept) or 0 (reject).*

PublicDecommit(m, r, C) *takes as input message m, randomness r, and commitment C. It outputs either 1 (accept) or 0 (reject).*

The intuition behind FDC algorithms is as follows. FDCs allow for two different ways of committing to messages. One is just a standard commitment. This enables output privacy with respect to the verifier. The other way commits to a message under a secret key to produce an authenticator. These authenticators allow for homomorphic evaluation. Given authenticators to the input of a function, one can derive an authenticator to the output of a function. Additionally, one can commit to a function under a public verification key. This results in a function commitment. One can then check if a public commitment C matches an authenticator A (derived from a secret key) and a function commitment F (derived from a public key). As long as a cryptographic hardness assumption holds, such a match is only possible if A was obtained by running the evaluation on the exact function committed to via F.

As for classical commitments, we want our schemes to be *binding*. That is, after committing to a message, it should be infeasible to open the commitment to a different message. We describe the following security experiment between a challenger $\mathcal{C}$ and an adversary $\mathcal{A}$.

Definition 5 (Bindingness experiments $\mathbf{EXP}_{A,Com}^{Bind}(\lambda)$). *Challenger $\mathcal{C}$ runs* (sk, pk) $\leftarrow$ KeyGen(pp) *and gives* pk *to the adversary $\mathcal{A}$. $\mathcal{A}$ outputs the pairs (m, r) and (m', r'), with $m \neq m'$. If* PublicCommit(m', r') = PublicCommit(m, r) *the experiment outputs 1, else it returns 0.*

Definition 6 (Binding). *Using the formalism of Definition 5, an FDC is called* binding *if for any probabilistic polynomial-time (PPT) adversary $\mathcal{A}$, $\Pr[\boldsymbol{EXP}_{A,Com}^{Bind}(\lambda) = 1] = \mathsf{negl}(\lambda)$, where $\mathsf{negl}(\lambda)$ denotes any function negligible in the security parameter λ.*

The binding property for FunctionCommit is defined analogously.

Another important notion, targeting privacy, is the hiding property. Commitments are intended not to leak information about the messages they commit to. This is not to be confused with the context hiding property, where homomorphic authenticators to the output of a computation do not leak information about the inputs to the computation. Context hiding homomorphic authenticators do however leak information about the output.

Definition 7 (Hiding). *An FDC is called* computationally hiding *if the sets of commitments* $\{\mathsf{PublicCommit}(m, r) \mid r \overset{\$}{\leftarrow} \mathcal{R}\}$ *and* $\{\mathsf{PublicCommit}(m', r') \mid r' \overset{\$}{\leftarrow} \mathcal{R}\}$ *as well as* $\{\mathsf{PrivateCommit}(\mathsf{sk}, m, r, \Delta, \tau) \mid r \overset{\$}{\leftarrow} \mathcal{R}\}$ *and* $\{\mathsf{PrivateCommit}(\mathsf{sk}, m', r', \Delta, \tau) \mid r' \overset{\$}{\leftarrow} \mathcal{R}\}$ *have distributions that are indistinguishable for any PPT adversary* $\mathcal{A}$ *for all* $m \neq m' \in \mathcal{M}$. *An FDC is called* unconditionally hiding *if these sets have the* same *distribution respectively for all* $m \neq m' \in \mathcal{M}$.

An obvious requirement for an FDC is to be *correct*, i.e. if messages are authenticated properly and evaluation is performed honestly, the resulting commitment should be accepted. This is formalized in the following definition.

Definition 8 (Correctness). *An FDC achieves* correctness *if for any security parameter* λ, *any public parameters* $\mathsf{pp} \leftarrow \mathsf{Setup}(1^\lambda)$, *any key pair* $(\mathsf{sk}, \mathsf{pk}) \leftarrow \mathsf{KeyGen}(\mathsf{pp})$, *and any dataset identifier* $\Delta \in \{0, 1\}^*$, *the following properties hold:*

For any message $m \in \mathcal{M}$, *randomness* $r \in \mathcal{R}$, *label* $\tau \in \mathcal{T}$, *authenticator* $A \leftarrow \mathsf{PrivateCommit}(\mathsf{sk}, m, r, \Delta, \tau)$, *commitment* $C \leftarrow \mathsf{PublicCommit}(m, r)$, *and function commitment* $F_{\mathcal{I}} \leftarrow \mathsf{FunctionCommit}(\mathsf{pk}, \mathcal{I}_\tau)$, *where* $\mathcal{I}_\tau$ *is the labeled identity program, we have both* $\mathsf{PublicDecommit}(m, r, C) = 1$ *and* $\mathsf{FunctionVerify}(\mathsf{pk}, A, C, F_{\mathcal{I}}, \Delta) = 1$.

For any tuple $\{(A_i, m_i, r_i, \mathcal{P}_i)\}_{i \in [N]}$ *such that for* $C_i \leftarrow \mathsf{PublicCommit}(m_i, r_i)$, $F_i \leftarrow \mathsf{FunctionCommit}(\mathsf{pk}, \mathcal{P}_i)$, $\mathsf{FunctionVerify}(\mathsf{pk}, A_i, C_i, F_i, \Delta) = 1$, *and any function* $g \in \mathcal{F}$ *the following holds: There exists a function* $\hat{g} \in \mathcal{F}$, *that is efficiently computable from* g, *such that for* $m^* = g(m_1, \ldots, m_N)$, $r^* = \hat{g}(m_1, \ldots, m_N, r_1, \ldots r_N)$, $C^* \leftarrow \mathsf{PublicCommit}(m^*, r^*)$, $\mathcal{P}^* = g(\mathcal{P}_1, \ldots, \mathcal{P}_N)$, $F^* \leftarrow \mathsf{FunctionCommit}(\mathsf{pk}, \mathcal{P}^*)$, $A^* \leftarrow \mathsf{Eval}(g, A_1, \ldots, A_N)$,

$$\mathsf{FunctionVerify}(\mathsf{pk}, A^*, C^*, F^*, \Delta) = 1.$$

The security notion of FDCs is also based on *well defined programs* (see Definition 3). We introduce an experiment the attacker can run in order to generate a successful forgery and present a definition for unforgeability based on it.

Definition 9 (Forgery). *A forgery is a tuple* $(\mathcal{P}^*_{\Delta^*}, A^*, C^*)$ *such that*

$$\mathsf{FunctionVerify}(\mathsf{pk}, A^*, C^*, \mathsf{FunctionCommit}(\mathsf{pk}, \mathcal{P}^*), \Delta^*) = 1$$

holds and exactly one of the following conditions is met:

Type 1: *No message was ever committed under the data set identifier* Δ^*, *i.e. the list* L_{Δ^*} *of tuples* (τ, m, r) *was not initialized during the security experiment.*

Type 2: $\mathcal{P}^*_{\Delta^*}$ *is well defined with respect to list* L_{Δ^*} *and*

$$C^* \neq \mathsf{PublicCommit}(f(\{m_j\}_{(\tau_j, m_j, r_j) \in L_{\Delta^*}}), \hat{f}(\{(m_j, r_j)\}_{(\tau_j, m_j, r_j) \in L_{\Delta^*}})),$$

where f *is taken from* $\mathcal{P}^*$, *that is,* C^* *is not a commitment to the correct output of the computation.*

Type 3: $\mathcal{P}^*_{\Delta^*}$ *is not well defined with respect to* L_{Δ^*}.

To define unforgeability, we first describe the experiment $\mathbf{EXP}^{UF-CMA}_{\mathcal{A},FDC}(\lambda)$ between an adversary $\mathcal{A}$ and a challenger $\mathcal{C}$.

Definition 10 ($EXP^{UF-CMA}_{\mathcal{A},FDC}(\lambda)$ [22]).

Setup $\mathcal{C}$ *calls* $pp \xleftarrow{\$} \mathsf{Setup}(1^\lambda)$ *and gives* pp *to* $\mathcal{A}$.

Key Generation $\mathcal{C}$ *calls* $(sk, pk) \xleftarrow{\$} \mathsf{KeyGen}(pp)$ *and gives* pk *to* $\mathcal{A}$.

Queries $\mathcal{A}$ *adaptively submits queries for* (Δ, τ, m, r) *where* Δ *is a dataset,* τ *is an identifier,* m *is a message, and* r *is a random value.* $\mathcal{C}$ *proceeds as follows:*

If (Δ, τ, m, r) *is the first query with dataset identifier* Δ, *it initializes an empty list* $L_\Delta = \emptyset$ *for* Δ.

If L_Δ *does not contain a tuple* $(\tau, \cdot, \cdot)$, *that is,* $\mathcal{A}$ *never queried* $(\Delta, \tau, \cdot, \cdot)$, $\mathcal{C}$ *calls* $A \leftarrow \mathsf{PrivateCommit}(sk, m, r, \Delta, \tau)$, *updates the list* $L_\Delta = L_\Delta \cup (\tau, m, r)$, *and gives* A *to* $\mathcal{A}$.

If $(\tau, m, r) \in L_\Delta$, *then* $\mathcal{C}$ *returns the same authenticator* A *as before.*

If L_{Δ^*} *already contains a tuple* (τ, m', r') *for* $(m, r) \neq (m', r')$, $\mathcal{C}$ *returns* $\bot$.

Forgery $\mathcal{A}$ *outputs a tuple* $(\mathcal{P}^*_{\Delta^*}, A^*, C^*)$.

$EXP^{UF-CMA}_{\mathcal{A},FDC}(\lambda)$ *outputs* 1 *if the tuple returned by* $\mathcal{A}$ *is a forgery (Definition 9).*

Definition 11 (Unforgeability). *An FDC is unforgeable if for any PPT adversary* $\mathcal{A}$, $\Pr[EXP^{UF-CMA}_{\mathcal{A},FDC}(\lambda) = 1] = \mathsf{negl}(\lambda)$.

Regarding performance, we consider additional properties. *Succinctness* specifies a limit on the size of the FDCs, thus keeping the required bandwidth low when using FDCs to verify the correctness of an outsourced computation.

Definition 12 (Succinctness). *An FDC is succinct if, for fixed* λ, *the size of the authenticators depends at most logarithmically on the dataset size* n.

Amortized efficiency specifies a bound on the computational effort required to perform verifications.

Definition 13 (Amortized Efficiency). *Let* $\mathcal{P}_\Delta = (\mathcal{P}, \Delta)$ *be a multi-labeled program,* $m_1, \ldots, m_n \in \mathcal{M}$ *a set of messages,* $r_1, \ldots r_n \in \mathcal{R}$ *a set of randomness,* $f \in \mathcal{F}$ *be an arbitrary function, and* $t(n)$ *be the time required to compute* $f(m_1, \ldots, m_n)$. *An FDC achieves amortized efficiency if, for any public parameters* pp *and any* $(sk, pk) \xleftarrow{\$} \mathsf{KeyGen}(pp)$, *any authenticator* A, *any commitment* C, *and function commitment* F, *the time required to compute* $\mathsf{FunctionVerify}(pk, A, C, F, \Delta)$ *is* $t' = o(t(n))$. *Note that* A *and* F *may depend on* f *and* n.

Homomorphic Authenticators. Homomorphic authenticators and their properties of unforgeability, authentication correctness, evaluation correctness, succinctness, efficient verification, and context hiding have been formally defined in various works, e.g. [7] or in the more general setting of multi-key homomorphic authenticators in [11].

Pairings and Structure-Preserving Signatures. We formalize the definitions and assumptions related to pairings. These will be the main building block for our construction in Sect. 4. Structure-preserving signatures are also defined.

Definition 14 (Double Pairing Assumption in $\mathbb{G}_2$ (DBP$_2$, e.g. [1])). *Let* $\mathsf{bgp} = (p, \mathbb{G}_1, \mathbb{G}_2, \mathbb{G}_T, g_1, g_2, e) \stackrel{\$}{\leftarrow} \mathcal{G}(1^\lambda)$ *and* $R, Z \stackrel{\$}{\leftarrow} \mathbb{G}_2$. *Any PPT adversary* $\mathcal{A}$ *can produce* $(G_R, G_Z) \in \mathbb{G}_1^2 \backslash \{(1,1)\}$ *such that* $1 = e(G_R, R) \cdot e(G_Z, Z)$ *only with a probability negligible in* λ.

DBP$_2$ implies the DDH assumption in $\mathbb{G}_2$, and the reduction is tight [3].

Definition 15 (Structure-Preserving Signature [15]). *A structure - preserving signature scheme is a triple of PPT algorithms* $\mathsf{SPS} = (\mathsf{Gen}, \mathsf{Sign}, \mathsf{Verify})$:

The probabilistic key generation algorithm $\mathsf{Gen}(1^\lambda)$ *returns the secret/public key pair* $(\mathsf{sk}, \mathsf{pk})$, *where* $\mathsf{pk} \in \mathbb{G}^{n_{\mathsf{pk}}}$ *for some* $n_{\mathsf{pk}} \in \mathsf{poly}(\lambda)$. *We assume that* pk *implicitly defines a message space* $\mathcal{M} = \mathbb{G}^n$ *for some* $n \in \mathsf{poly}(\lambda)$.
The probabilistic signing algorithm $\mathsf{Sign}(\mathsf{sk}, M)$ *returns a signature* $\sigma \in \mathbb{G}^{n_\sigma}$ *for some* $n_\sigma \in \mathsf{poly}(\lambda)$.
The deterministic verification algorithm $\mathsf{Verify}(\mathsf{pk}, M, \sigma)$ *only consists of pairing product equations and returns* 1 *or* 0.

(Perfect Correctness.) for all $(\mathsf{sk}, \mathsf{pk}) \stackrel{\$}{\leftarrow} \mathsf{Gen}(1^\lambda)$ *and all messages* $M \in \mathcal{M}$ *and all* $\sigma \stackrel{\$}{\leftarrow} \mathsf{Sign}(\mathsf{sk}, M)$, *we have* $\mathsf{Verify}(\mathsf{pk}, M, \sigma) = 1$.

Libert et al. [16] adapted this to the scenario of homomorphic signatures. There, a signature scheme is structure-preserving if messages, signature components and public keys are elements of the group bgp.

3   FDCs from Homomorphic Authenticators

In this section, we discuss how to construct an FDC from (homomorphic) commitment schemes and structure-preserving homomorphic signatures schemes over the commitment space. We show how the properties of the resulting FDC depend on the underlying homomorphic signature scheme and commitment scheme.

Assume the homomorphic authenticator scheme $\mathsf{HAuth} = (\mathsf{HSetup}, \mathsf{HKeyGen}, \mathsf{Auth}, \mathsf{HEval}, \mathsf{Ver})$ is structure-preserving over some structure $\mathcal{X}$. Let Com be a homomorphic commitment scheme $\mathsf{Com} = (\mathsf{CSetup}, \mathsf{Commit}, \mathsf{Decommit}, \mathsf{CEval})$

with message space $\mathcal{M}$ and commitment space $\mathcal{C} \subset \mathcal{X}$. We also assume the existence of an ordinary commitment scheme $\mathsf{Com}' = (\mathsf{CSetup}', \mathsf{Commit}', \mathsf{Decommit}')$ with message space $\mathcal{F} \times \mathcal{T}^n$, so labeled programs are admissible inputs. One can always split up Ver into $(\mathsf{VerPrep}, \mathsf{EffVer})$ as follows.

$\mathsf{VerPrep}(\mathcal{P}, \mathsf{vk})$: On input a labeled program $\mathcal{P}$ and a verification key vk, the algorithm sets $\mathsf{vk}_\mathcal{P} = (\mathcal{P}, \mathsf{vk})$. It returns $\mathsf{vk}_\mathcal{P}$.

$\mathsf{EffVer}(\mathsf{vk}_\mathcal{P}, C, \sigma, \Delta)$: On input a concise verification key $\mathsf{vk}_\mathcal{P}$, a message C, an authenticator σ, and a dataset identifier $\Delta \in \{0,1\}^*$, the algorithm parses $\mathsf{vk}_\mathcal{P} = (\mathcal{P}, \mathsf{vk})$. It runs $b \leftarrow \mathsf{Ver}(\mathcal{P}, \mathsf{vk}, C, \sigma, \Delta)$ and returns b.

We now show how to construct an FDC.

$\mathsf{Setup}(1^\lambda)$ takes the security parameter λ as input. It runs $\mathsf{CK} \leftarrow \mathsf{CSetup}(1^\lambda)$, $\mathsf{CK}' \leftarrow \mathsf{CSetup}'(1^\lambda)$ as well as $\mathsf{pp}' \leftarrow \mathsf{HSetup}(1^\lambda)$. It sets $\mathsf{pp} = (\mathsf{CK}, \mathsf{CK}', \mathsf{pp}')$ and outputs pp. We implicitly assume that every algorithm uses these public parameters pp, leaving them out of the notation.

$\mathsf{KeyGen}(\mathsf{pp})$ takes the public parameters pp and runs $(\mathsf{sk}', \mathsf{ek}, \mathsf{vk}) \leftarrow \mathsf{HKeyGen}(\mathsf{pp})$. It sets $\mathsf{sk} = (\mathsf{sk}', \mathsf{ek})$, $\mathsf{pk} = (\mathsf{ek}, \mathsf{vk})$ and outputs the key pair $(\mathsf{sk}, \mathsf{pk})$.

$\mathsf{PublicCommit}(m, r)$ takes as input a message m and randomness r and runs $(C, d) \leftarrow \mathsf{Commit}(m, r)$. It outputs the commitment C.

$\mathsf{PrivateCommit}(\mathsf{sk}, m, r, \Delta, \tau)$ takes as input the secret key sk, a message m, randomness r, an identifier τ and a dataset identifier Δ. It runs $(C, d) \leftarrow \mathsf{Commit}(m, r)$, $A' \leftarrow \mathsf{Auth}(\mathsf{sk}, \tau, \Delta, C)$ and outputs $A = (A', \mathsf{ek})$.

$\mathsf{FunctionCommit}(\mathsf{pk}, \mathcal{P})$ takes as input the public key pk and a labeled program $\mathcal{P}$. It parses $\mathsf{pk} = (\mathsf{ek}, \mathsf{vk})$ and runs $\mathsf{vk}_\mathcal{P} \leftarrow \mathsf{VerPrep}(\mathcal{P}, \mathsf{vk})$. It chooses randomness $r_\mathcal{P} \overset{\$}{\leftarrow} \mathcal{R}$ uniformly at random and runs $(C_\mathcal{P}, d_\mathcal{P}) \leftarrow \mathsf{Commit}'(\mathcal{P}, r_\mathcal{P})$. It outputs the function commitment $F = (\mathsf{vk}_\mathcal{P}, C_\mathcal{P})$.

$\mathsf{Eval}(f, A_1, \ldots A_n)$ takes as input a function f and a set of authenticators $A_1, \ldots, A_n$. It parses $A_i = (A_i', \mathsf{ek}_i)$ for all $i \in [n]$, and runs $\hat{A} \leftarrow \mathsf{HEval}(f, \{A_i'\}_{i \in [n]}, \mathsf{ek}_1)$. It outputs $A^* = (\hat{A}, \mathsf{ek}_1)$.

$\mathsf{FunctionVerify}(\mathsf{pk}, A, C, F, \Delta)$ takes as input a public key pk, an FDC containing an authenticator A and a commitment C, a function commitment F as well as a dataset identifier Δ. It parses $F = (\mathsf{vk}_\mathcal{P}, C_\mathcal{P})$, and $A = (A', \mathsf{ek})$. It runs $b \leftarrow \mathsf{EffVer}(\mathsf{vk}_\mathcal{P}, C, A', \Delta)$ and outputs b.

$\mathsf{PublicDecommit}(m, r, C)$ takes as input message m, randomness r, and commitment C. It runs $(C, d) \leftarrow \mathsf{Commit}(m, r)$ as well as $b \leftarrow \mathsf{Decommit}(m, d, C)$ and outputs b.

We first look at the commitment properties — hiding and binding. In our transformation, these are inherited from the underlying commitment schemes.

Lemma 1. *The construction* FDC *is binding in the sense of Definition 6 if* Com *and* Com' *used in the construction are binding commitment schemes.*

Proof. Obviously, if Com is binding then PublicCommit is binding. We parse a function commitment as $F = (\mathsf{vk}_\mathcal{P}, C_\mathcal{P})$. Note that $C_\mathcal{P}$ is by assumption a binding commitment, thus FunctionCommit is also binding.

The hiding property of FDCs (Definition 7) is different from the context hiding property of homomorphic authenticators [7]. Context hiding guarantees that authenticators to the *output* of a computation do not leak information about the *inputs* to the computation. By contrast, the hiding property of FDCs guarantees that even authenticators to the inputs do not leak information about inputs to the computation. In [22], this property was used to combine an FDC with secret sharing to construct an efficient verifiable multi-party computation scheme. This privacy gain is one of the major benefits of FDCs over homomorphic authenticators when sensitive data are used as computation inputs.

Lemma 2. *If* Com *is (unconditionally) hiding, then* FDC *is unconditionally hiding in the sense of Definition 7.*

Proof. If Com is (unconditionally) hiding, then the probabilistic distributions over the sets $\{\mathsf{Commit}(m, r) \mid r \xleftarrow{\$} \mathcal{R}\}$ and $\{\mathsf{Commit}(m', r') \mid r' \xleftarrow{\$} \mathcal{R}\}$ are perfectly indistinguishable for all $m, m' \in \mathcal{M}$. This is independent of any $\tau \in \mathcal{T}$ and any $\Delta \in \{0,1\}^*$. Hence the probabilistic distributions over sets $\{\mathsf{Auth}(\mathsf{sk}, \Delta, \tau, C) \mid C \leftarrow \mathsf{Commit}(m, r), r \xleftarrow{\$} \mathcal{R}\}$ and $\{\mathsf{Auth}(\mathsf{sk}, \Delta, \tau, C') \mid C' \leftarrow \mathsf{Commit}(m', r'), r' \xleftarrow{\$} \mathcal{R}\}$ are perfectly indistinguishable for all $m, m' \in \mathcal{M}, \tau \in \mathcal{T}, \Delta \in \{0,1\}^*$. Since $\{\mathsf{Auth}(\mathsf{sk}, \Delta, \tau, C) \mid C \leftarrow \mathsf{Commit}(m, r), r \xleftarrow{\$} \mathcal{R}\} = \{\mathsf{PrivateCommit}(\mathsf{sk}, m, r, \Delta, \tau) \mid r \xleftarrow{\$} \mathcal{R}\}$ for all $m \in \mathcal{M}, \tau \in \mathcal{T}, \Delta \in \{0,1\}^*$ the probabilistic distributions over $\{\mathsf{PrivateCommit}(\mathsf{sk}, m, r, \Delta, \tau) \mid r \xleftarrow{\$} \mathcal{R}\}$ and $\{\mathsf{PrivateCommit}(\mathsf{sk}, m', r', \Delta, \tau) \mid r' \xleftarrow{\$} \mathcal{R}\}$ are also (perfectly) indistinguishable. The PublicCommit case is trivial.

Next, we investigate the homomorphic property of such an FDC. We can show that if the homomorphic authenticator scheme HAuth satisfies both correctness properties — authentication and evaluation, and furthermore supports efficient verification, then the transformed FDC is also correct.

Lemma 3. *If* HAuth *achieves authentication (see [7]), evaluation correctness (see [7]), and efficient verification (see [7]), then* FDC *is correct in the sense of Definition 8 with overwhelming probability.*

Proof. Let λ be any security parameter, $\mathsf{pp} \leftarrow \mathsf{Setup}(1^\lambda)$, $(\mathsf{sk}, \mathsf{pk}) \leftarrow \mathsf{KeyGen}(\mathsf{pp})$, and let $\Delta \in \{0,1\}^*$ be an arbitrary dataset identifier. Let $m \in \mathcal{M}$ be an arbitrary message and $r \in \mathcal{R}$ arbitrary randomness. We set $A \leftarrow \mathsf{PrivateCommit}(\mathsf{sk}, m, r, \Delta, \tau)$, $C \leftarrow \mathsf{PublicCommit}(m, r)$, $F_\mathcal{I} \leftarrow \mathsf{FunctionCommit}(\mathsf{pk}, \mathcal{I}_\tau)$, where $\mathcal{I}_\tau$ is the labeled identity program. Then we have $A = \mathsf{Auth}(\mathsf{sk}, \Delta, \tau, C)$. By the authentication correctness of HAuth, we know that $\mathsf{Ver}(\mathcal{I}_{\tau,\Delta}, \mathsf{vk}, C, \sigma) = 1$. Since HAuth achieves efficient verification, $\mathsf{EffVer}(\mathsf{vk}_{\mathcal{I}_\tau}, C, \sigma, \Delta) = 1$ with overwhelming probability. By construction, $\mathsf{FunctionVerify}(\mathsf{pk}, A, C, F_\mathcal{I}, \Delta) = 1$.

Let $\{m_i, \sigma_i, \mathcal{P}_i)\}_{i \in [N]}$ be any set of tuples (parsed as $\sigma_i = (r_i, A_i)$) such that for $C_i \leftarrow \mathsf{PublicCommit}(m_i, r_i)$, $F_i \leftarrow \mathsf{FunctionCommit}(\mathsf{pk}, \mathcal{P}_i)$, $\mathsf{FunctionVerify}(\mathsf{pk}, A_i, C_i, F_i, \Delta) = 1$. This implies $\mathsf{EffVer}(\mathsf{vk}_{\mathcal{P}_i}, C_i, \sigma_i, \Delta) = 1$, thus $\mathsf{Ver}(\mathcal{P}_{i,\Delta}, \mathsf{vk}, C_i, \sigma_i) = 1$ with overwhelming probability. Then let $m^* = g(m_1, \ldots, m_N)$, $r^* = \hat{g}(m_1, \ldots, m_N, r_1, \ldots r_N)$, $C^* \leftarrow \mathsf{PublicCommit}(m^*, r^*)$, $\mathcal{P}^* = g(\mathcal{P}_1, \ldots, \mathcal{P}_N)$, $F^* \leftarrow \mathsf{FunctionCommit}(\mathsf{pk}, \mathcal{P}^*)$, $A^* \leftarrow \mathsf{Eval}(f, A_1, \ldots, A_N)$, and $\sigma^* = (r^*, A^*)$. From the homomorphic property of Com, we have $C^* = \mathsf{CEval}(g, C_1, \ldots, C_N)$. By the evaluation correctness of HAuth we have $\mathsf{Ver}(\mathcal{P}^*, \mathsf{vk}, C^*, \sigma^*) = 1$. Thus $\mathsf{EffVer}(\mathsf{vk}_{\mathcal{P}^*}, C^*, \sigma^*, \Delta) = 1$ with overwhelming probability, due to the correctness of efficient verification. By construction, $\mathsf{FunctionVerify}(\mathsf{pk}, A^*, C^*, F^*, \Delta) = 1$.

We now look at the essential security property of an FDC — unforgeability. We show how an adversary that can break the security experiment for FDCs can be used to break the security experiment for homomorphic authenticators. A simulator can forward the queries used by the adversary in the FDC experiment as queries in the homomorphic authenticator experiment, and use the resulting forgery in the one experiment to compute a forgery in the other.

Lemma 4. *If* HAuth *is secure (see [7]), then* FDC *is unforgeable (Definition 11).*

Proof. Assume we have a PPT adversary $\mathcal{A}$ that can produce a successful forgery during the security experiment $\mathbf{EXP}_{\mathcal{A},\mathrm{FDC}}^{UF-CMA}$, we then show how a simulator $\mathcal{S}$ can use $\mathcal{A}$ to win the security experiment $\mathsf{HomUF} - \mathsf{CMA}_{\mathcal{A},\mathsf{HAuth}}$ (see [7]).

Setup. $\mathcal{S}$ gets pp' from the challenger of the experiment $\mathsf{HomUF} - \mathsf{CMA}_{\mathcal{A},\mathsf{HAuth}}$. It runs $\mathsf{CK} \leftarrow \mathsf{CSetup}(1^\lambda)$, $\mathsf{CK}' \leftarrow \mathsf{CSetup}'(1^\lambda)$. It sets $\mathsf{pp} = (\mathsf{CK}, \mathsf{CK}', \mathsf{pp}')$ and outputs pp to the adversary $\mathcal{A}$.

Key Generation. $\mathcal{S}$ receives $(\mathsf{ek}, \mathsf{vk})$ from the challenger of the experiment $\mathsf{HomUF} - \mathsf{CMA}_{\mathcal{A},\mathsf{HAuth}}$. It sets $\mathsf{pk} = (\mathsf{ek}, \mathsf{vk})$ and outputs pk to $\mathcal{A}$.

Queries. When $\mathcal{A}$ ask queries (Δ, τ, m, r), $\mathcal{S}$ computes $(C, d) \leftarrow \mathsf{Commit}(m, r)$ and queries (Δ, τ, C) to receive an authenticator σ. It sets $A = \sigma$ and replies to the query with the private commitment A. This is the exact same reply to a query in experiment $\mathbf{EXP}_{\mathcal{A},\mathrm{FDC}}^{UF-CMA}$.

Forgery. The adversary $\mathcal{A}$ returns a forgery $(\mathcal{P}_{\Delta^*}^*, m^*, r^*, A^*)$. $\mathcal{S}$ computes $(C^*, d^*) \leftarrow \mathsf{Commit}(m^*, r^*)$ and outputs $(\mathcal{P}_{\Delta^*}^*, C^*, A^*)$.

A type 1, 2, 3 forgery in experiment $\mathbf{EXP}_{\mathcal{A},\mathrm{FDC}}^{UF-CMA}$ corresponds to a forgery in experiment $\mathsf{HomUF} - \mathsf{CMA}_{\mathcal{A},\mathsf{HAuth}}$. Thus $\mathcal{S}$ produces a forgery with the same probability as $\mathcal{A}$.

We now analyze an FDC obtained by our transformation with respect to its efficiency properties. On the one hand we have succinctness, which guarantees that authenticators are short, so bandwidth requirements are low. On the other hand, we show how the FDC inherits amortized efficiency, i.e. efficient verification after a one-time preprocessing from the efficient verification of the underlying homomorphic authenticator scheme.

Lemma 5. *If HAuth is succinct (see [7]), then FDC is succinct (Definition 12).*

Proof. By assumption, HAuth produces authenticators whose size depends at most logarithmically on the data set size n. By construction, the output size of PrivateCommit and Eval thus depends at most logarithmically on n.

Lemma 6. *If HAuth is efficiently verifiable (see [7]), then FDC has amortized efficiency in the sense of Definition 13.*

Proof. Let $t(n)$ be the runtime of $f(m_1, \ldots, m_n)$. FunctionVerify parses a function commitment $F = (\mathsf{vk}_\mathcal{P}, C_\mathcal{P})$ and runs $\mathsf{EffVer}(\mathsf{vk}_\mathcal{P}, C, A, \Delta)$. By assumption, the runtime of EffVer is $o(t(n))$. Thus the runtime of FunctionVerify is also $o(t(n))$.

3.1 A New Structure-Preserving Homomorphic Signature Scheme

We now consider the special case of a single-dataset, structure-preserving homomorphic signature scheme. Obviously, our transformation also works for such a scheme. This can easily be seen by interpreting the underlying authenticator scheme as one where all algorithms are constant over all inputs $\Delta \in \{0,1\}^*$. This leads to a single dataset FDC. It is an immediate corollary of [11, Theorem 2] that a single dataset FDC can be transformed into a multi dataset FDC. On a high level, this transformation uses a keyed pseudorandom function that on input a dataset $\Delta \in \{0,1\}^*$ produces the keys $(\mathsf{sk}_\Delta, \mathsf{ek}_\Delta, \mathsf{vk}_\Delta)$ and then uses a conventional UF-CMA secure signature scheme to bind the dataset to the public keys by signing $\Delta \mid \mathsf{vk}_\Delta$. For details, see Fiore et al. [11]. In Sect. 4, we present such a single dataset structure-preserving homomorphic signature scheme.

4 A New Single-Dataset, Structure-Preserving Linearly Homomorphic Signature Scheme

We now describe a novel structure-preserving linearly homomorphic signature scheme SPHAuth for a single dataset. As we discussed in Sect. 3, this can be extended to a scheme for multiple datasets by standard methods. Our structure-preserving linearly homomorphic signature scheme is the first structure-preserving homomorphic signature scheme to achieve efficient verification, and the first context hiding. It achieves the latter even in an information-theoretic sense.

$\mathsf{HSetup}(1^\lambda)$: On input a security parameter λ, this algorithm chooses the parameter $n \in \mathbb{Z}$, a bilinear group $\mathsf{bgp} = (p, \mathbb{G}_1, \mathbb{G}_2, \mathbb{G}_T, g_1, g_2, e) \xleftarrow{\$} \mathcal{G}(1^\lambda)$ and the tag space $\mathcal{T} = [n]$. Additionally, it fixes a pseudorandom function $F : \mathcal{K} \times \{0,1\}^* \to \mathbb{Z}_p$. It outputs the public parameters $\mathsf{pp} = (n, F, \mathsf{bgp})$.

$\mathsf{HKeyGen}(\mathsf{pp})$: On input the public parameters pp, the algorithm chooses chooses $x_1, \ldots, x_n, y, z \in \mathbb{Z}_p$ uniformly at random. It sets $h_i = g_t^{x_i}$ for all $i \in [n]$, as well as $Y = g_2^y, Z = g_2^z$. Additionally the algorithm chooses a random seed $K \xleftarrow{\$} \mathcal{K}$ for the pseudorandom function F. It sets $\mathsf{sk} = (K, x_1, \ldots, x_n, y, z)$, $\mathsf{ek} = 0$, $\mathsf{vk} = (h_1, \ldots, h_n, Y, Z)$ and outputs $(\mathsf{sk}, \mathsf{ek}, \mathsf{vk})$.

$\mathsf{Auth}(\mathsf{sk}, \tau, M)$: On input a secret key sk, an input identifier τ, and a message $M \in \mathbb{G}_1$, the algorithm takes x, y from sk. It computes $s = F_K(\tau)$ and sets $S = g_1^s$, $\Lambda = \left(g_1^{x_\tau + s} \cdot M^y\right)^{\frac{1}{z}}$. It outputs $\sigma = (\Lambda, S)$.

$\mathsf{HEval}(f, \{\sigma_i\}_{i \in [n]}, 0)$: On input an function $f : \mathcal{M}^n \to \mathcal{M}$ and a set $\{\sigma_i\}_{i \in [n]}$ of authenticators, and an empty evaluation key, the algorithm parses $f = (f_1, \ldots, f_n)$ as a coefficient vector. It parses each σ_i as (Λ_i, S_i) and sets $\Lambda = \prod_{i=1}^n \Lambda_i^{f_i}$ and $S = \prod_{i=1}^n S_i^{f_i}$. It returns $\sigma = (\Lambda, S)$.

$\mathsf{Ver}(\mathcal{P}, \mathsf{vk}, M, \sigma)$: On input a labeled program $\mathcal{P}$, a verification key vk, a message $M \in \mathbb{G}_1$, and an authenticator σ, the algorithm parses $\sigma = (\Lambda, S)$. It checks whether $e(\Lambda, Z) = e(M, Y) \cdot \prod_{i=1}^n h_{\tau_i}^{f_i} \cdot e(S, g_2)$. If the equation holds, it outputs 1, otherwise it outputs 0.

This scheme $\mathsf{SPHAuth}$ is structure-preserving, as messages are taken from $\mathbb{G}_1$, public keys lie in $\mathbb{G}_2$ or $\mathbb{G}_T$ and authenticators lie in $\mathbb{G}_1$. An obvious requirement for this structure-preserving homomorphic signature scheme is to be correct. For homomorphic authenticators, two different notions of correctness are considered. One ensures that freshly generated authenticators obtained by running Auth verify correctly. The other correctness property ensures that any derived signature, obtained by running HEval verifies correctly w.r.t the correct labeled program $\mathcal{P}$.

Lemma 7. $\mathsf{SPHAuth}$ *satisfies authentication correctness (see [7]).*

Proof. For all public parameters $\mathsf{pp} \leftarrow \mathsf{HSetup}(1^\lambda)$, and key triple $(\mathsf{sk}, \mathsf{ek}, \mathsf{vk}) \leftarrow \mathsf{HKeyGen}(\mathsf{pp})$, we have $\mathsf{sk} = (x_1, \ldots, x_n, y, z)$, $\mathsf{ek} = 0$, $\mathsf{vk} = (h_1, \ldots, h_n, Y, Z)$. For any input identifier $\tau \in \mathcal{T}$, and any message $M \in \mathbb{G}_1$ we have $\sigma = (\Lambda, S)$ with $\Lambda = \left(g_1^{x_\tau + s} \cdot M^y\right)^{\frac{1}{z}}$ and $S = g_1^s$. We consider $\mathcal{P} = \mathcal{I}_\tau$ the identity program for label τ. During the computation of $\mathsf{Ver}(\mathcal{I}_\tau, \mathsf{vk}, M, \sigma)$, $e(\Lambda, Z) = e\left(\left(g_1^{x_\tau + s} \cdot M^y\right)^{\frac{1}{z}}, g_2^z\right) = e\left(g_1^{x_\tau + s} \cdot M^y, g_2\right) = e\left(g_1^{x_\tau}, g_2\right) \cdot e\left(g_1^s, g_2\right) \cdot e\left(M, g_2^y\right) = e(M, Y) \cdot h_\tau \cdot e(S, g_2)$. Thus $\mathsf{SPHAuth}$ satisfies authentication correctness with probability 1.

Lemma 8. $\mathsf{SPHAuth}$ *satisfies evaluation correctness (see [7]).*

Proof. We fix the public parameters $\mathsf{pp} \leftarrow \mathsf{HSetup}(1^\lambda)$, key triple $(\mathsf{sk}, \mathsf{ek}, \mathsf{vk}) \leftarrow \mathsf{HKeyGen}(\mathsf{pp})$, a function $g : \mathbb{G}_1^N \to \mathbb{G}_1$, given by its coefficient vector $(g_1, \ldots, g_N)$ and any set of program/message/authenticator triples $\{(\mathcal{P}_i, M_i, \sigma_i)\}_{i \in [N]}$ such that $\mathsf{Ver}(\mathcal{P}_i, \mathsf{vk}, M_i, \sigma_i) = 1$ for all $i \in [N]$. So in particular, for $\sigma_i = (\Lambda_i, S_i)$, $e(\Lambda_i, Z) = e(M_i, Y) \cdot h_{\mathcal{P}_i} \cdot e(S_i, g_2)$ For readability, we write $h_{\mathcal{P}_i} = \prod_{k=1}^n h_{\tau_{i,k}}^{f_{i,k}}$ with $\mathcal{P}_i = (f_{i,1}, \ldots, f_{i,n}, \tau_{i,1}, \ldots, \tau_{i,n})$. Let $M^* = \prod_{i=1}^N M_i^{g_i}$, $\mathcal{P}^* = g(\mathcal{P}_1, \ldots, \mathcal{P}_N)$, and $\sigma^* = \mathsf{HEval}(g, \{\sigma_i\}_{i \in [N]}, 0)$ (we have an empty evaluation key). We parse $\sigma^* = (\Lambda^*, S^*)$. Then $e(\Lambda^*, Z) = e\left(\prod_{i=1}^N \Lambda_i^{g_i}, Z\right) = \prod_{i=1}^N e(\Lambda_i, Z)^{g_i} = \prod_{i=1}^N (e(M_i, Y) \cdot h_{\mathcal{P}_i} \cdot e(S_i, g_2))^{g_i} = \prod_{i=1}^N e(M_i, Y)^{g_i} \cdot \prod_{i=1}^N h_{\mathcal{P}_i}^{g_i} \cdot \prod_{i=1}^N e(S_i, g_2)^{g_i} = e(\prod_{i=1}^N M_i^{g_i}, Y) \cdot h_{\mathcal{P}^*} \cdot e\left(\prod_{i=1}^N S_i^{g_i}, g_2\right) = e(M^*, Y) \cdot h_{\mathcal{P}^*} \cdot e(S^*, g_2)$. Thus $\mathsf{SPHAuth}$ satisfies evaluation correctness with probability 1.

Next, we show that SPHAuth is efficient with respect to both bandwidth (succinctness) and verification time (efficient verification).

Lemma 9. SPHAuth *is succinct (see [7]).*

Proof. An authenticator consist of 2 $\mathbb{G}_1$ elements and is thus independent of n.

Lemma 10. SPHAuth *allows for efficient verification (see [7]).*

Proof. We describe the algorithms (VerPrep, EffVer):

VerPrep($\mathcal{P}$, vk) : On input the labeled program $\mathcal{P} = (f, \tau_1, \ldots, \tau_n)$, with f given by its coefficient vector $(f_1, \ldots, f_n)$, the algorithm takes Y, Z from vk. For label τ_i it takes h_{τ_i} from vk. It computes $h_{\mathcal{P}} \leftarrow \prod_{i=1}^n h_{\tau_i}^{f_i}$ and outputs $\text{vk}_{\mathcal{P}} \leftarrow (h_{\mathcal{P}}, Y, Z)$. This is independent of the input size n.

EffVer($\text{vk}_{\mathcal{P}}, M, \sigma$): On input a concise verification key $\text{vk}_{\mathcal{P}}$, a message M, and an authenticator σ, the algorithm parses $\sigma = (\Lambda, S)$. It checks whether the following equation holds: $e(\Lambda, Z) = h_{\mathcal{P}} \cdot e(M, Y) \cdot e(S, g_2)$. If it does, it outputs 1, otherwise it outputs 0.

This obviously satisfies correctness. We can see that the runtime of EffVer is $\mathcal{O}(1)$, and is independent of the input size n. Thus, for large n, this scheme allows for efficient verification.

We now prove the unforgeability of our scheme. To this end, we first describe a sequence of games, allowing us to argue about different variants of forgeries. We show how any noticeable difference between the first two games leads to a distinguisher against the pseudorandomness of F. We then show how both a noticeable difference between the latter two games, as well as a forgery in the final game lead to a solver of the double pairing assumption.

Theorem 1. *If F is a pseudorandom function and the double pairing assumption holds in $\mathbb{G}_2$ (see Definition 14), then* SPHAuth *is unforgeable.*

Proof. We now provide the security reduction for the unforgeability of our scheme in the standard model. We define a series of games with the adversary $\mathcal{A}$ and we show that $\mathcal{A}$ wins, i.e. any game outputs 1, only with negligible probability. Following the notation of [7], we write $G_i(\mathcal{A})$ to denote that a run of game i with $\mathcal{A}$ returns 1. We use flag values bad_i, initially set to false. If, at the end of each game, any of these previously defined flags is set to true, the game simply outputs 0. Let Bad_i denote the event that bad_i is set to true during game i.

Game 1 is defined as the security experiment $\text{HomUF} - \text{CMA}_{\mathcal{A}, \text{MKHAuth}}(\lambda)$ between adversary $\mathcal{A}$ and challenger $\mathcal{C}$.

Game 2 is defined as Game 1, except that the keyed pseudorandom function F_K is replaced by a random function $\mathcal{R} : \{0, 1\}^* \to \mathbb{Z}_p$.

Game 3 is defined as Game 2, except for the following change. The challenger runs an additional check. It computes $\hat{\sigma} \leftarrow \text{HEval}(f, \{\sigma_i, \}_{i \in [n]}, 0)$ over the σ_i

given to the adversary $\mathcal{A}$ in answer to his queries. It parses $\hat{\sigma} = (\hat{\Lambda}, \hat{S})$. It parses the forgery $\sigma^* = (\Lambda^*, S^*)$. If $\hat{S} = S^*$ it sets $\mathsf{bad}_3 = \mathsf{true}$.

First, we show that for every PPT adversary $\mathcal{A}$ running Game 2, there exists a PPT distinguisher $\mathcal{D}$ such that $|\Pr[G_2(\mathcal{A})] - \Pr[G_1(\mathcal{A})]| \leq \mathsf{Adv}_{F,D}^{PRF}(\lambda)$.

Assume we have a noticeable difference $|\Pr[G_1(\mathcal{A})] - \Pr[G_2(\mathcal{A})]| \geq \epsilon$. Since the only difference between these games is the replacement of the pseudorandom function F by the random function $\mathcal{R}$, this immediately leads to a distinguisher $\mathcal{D}$ that achieves an advantage of ϵ against the pseudorandomness of F.

Now, we show that $\Pr[\mathsf{Bad}_3] = \mathsf{negl}(\lambda)$. The simulator $\mathcal{S}$ gets as input $\mathsf{bgp}, Z \in \mathbb{G}_2$. It simulates Game 3.

Setup. Simulator $\mathcal{S}$ chooses the parameter $n \in \mathbb{Z}$ and the tag space $\mathcal{T} = [n]$. It outputs the public parameters $\mathsf{pp} = (n, \mathsf{bgp})$.

KeyGen. Simulator $\mathcal{S}$ chooses $a_i, b_i \in \mathbb{Z}_p$ uniformly at random for all $i = 1, \dots, n$. It sets $h_i = g_t^{a_i} \cdot e(g_1, g_2)^{b_i}$. It chooses $y \in \mathbb{Z}_p$ uniformly at random and sets $Y = g_2^y$. It gives the verification key $\mathsf{vk} = (h_1, \dots, h_n, Y, Z)$ to $\mathcal{A}$.

Queries. When queried for (M, τ), simulator $\mathcal{S}$ sets $\Lambda = g_1^{b_\tau}$ as well as $S = g_1^{-a_\tau} \cdot M^{-y}$. Since a_τ, b_τ were chosen uniformly at random, the signature is correctly distributed.

Forgery. Let $(\mathcal{P}^*, M^*, \sigma^*)$ with $\sigma^* = (\Lambda^*, S^*)$ be the forgery returned by $\mathcal{A}$. $\mathcal{S}$ follows Game 3 to compute $\hat{\Lambda}, \hat{S}, \hat{M}$. Since σ^* is a successful forgery, we furthermore know that both $e(\Lambda^*, Z) = e(M^*, Y) \cdot \prod_{i=1}^n h_{\tau_i}^{f_i} \cdot e(S^*, g_2)$ and $e\left(\hat{\Lambda}, Z\right) = e\left(\hat{M}, Y\right) \cdot \prod_{i=1}^n h_{\tau_i}^{f_i} \cdot e\left(\hat{S}, g_2\right)$. Dividing the equations and considering that $\hat{S} = S^*$ since $\mathsf{bad}_3 = \mathsf{true}$, $e\left(\frac{\Lambda^*}{\hat{\Lambda}}, Z\right) = e\left(\frac{M^*}{\hat{M}}, Y\right)$ or alternatively $e\left(\frac{\Lambda^*}{\hat{\Lambda}}, Z\right) \cdot e\left(\left(\frac{\hat{M}}{M^*}\right)^y, g_2\right) = 1$ and we have found a solution to the double pairing problem. By definition, we have $M^* \neq \hat{M}$.

Now we consider the general case. The simulator $\mathcal{S}$ gets as input $\mathsf{bgp}, Z \in \mathbb{G}_2$. It simulates Game 3.

Setup. Simulator $\mathcal{S}$ chooses the parameter $n \in \mathbb{Z}$ and the tag space $\mathcal{T} = [n]$. It outputs the public parameters $\mathsf{pp} = (n, \mathsf{bgp})$.

KeyGen. Simulator $\mathcal{S}$ chooses $a_i, b_i \in \mathbb{Z}_p$ uniformly at random for all $i = 1, \dots, n$. It sets $h_i = g_t^{a_i} \cdot e(g_1, G_2)^{b_i}$. It chooses $y \in \mathbb{Z}_p$ uniformly at random and sets $Y = Z^y$. It gives the verification key $\mathsf{vk} = (h_1, \dots, h_n, Y, Z)$ to $\mathcal{A}$.

Queries. When queried for (M, τ) simulator $\mathcal{S}$ sets $\Lambda = g_1^{b_\tau} \cdot M^y$ as well as $S = g_1^{-a_\tau}$. Note that since a_τ, b_τ were chosen uniformly at random the signature is correctly distributed.

Forgery. Let $(\mathcal{P}^*, M^*, \sigma^*)$ with $\sigma^* = (\Lambda^*, S^*)$ be the forgery returned by $\mathcal{A}$. $\mathcal{S}$ follows Game 3 to compute $\hat{\Lambda}, \hat{S}, \hat{M}$. Since σ^* is a successful forgery, we furthermore know that both $e(\Lambda^*, Z) = e(M^*, Y) \cdot \prod_{i=1}^n h_{\tau_i}^{f_i} \cdot e(S^*, g_2)$ and $e\left(\hat{\Lambda}, Z\right) = e\left(\hat{M}, Y\right) \cdot \prod_{i=1}^n h_{\tau_i}^{f_i} \cdot e\left(\hat{S}, g_2\right)$.

Dividing the equations and using the identity $Y = Z^y$ yields $e\left(\frac{\Lambda^*}{\hat{\Lambda}}, Z\right) = e\left(\frac{M^*}{\hat{M}}, Z^y\right) \cdot e\left(\frac{S^*}{\hat{S}}, g_2\right)$ or alternatively $e\left(\frac{\Lambda^*}{\hat{\Lambda}} \cdot \left(\frac{\hat{M}}{M^*}\right)^y, Z\right) \cdot e\left(\frac{\hat{S}}{S^*}, g_2\right) = 1$

and we have found a solution to the double pairing problem. Since we have $\mathsf{bad}_3 = \mathsf{false}$ we know that $\hat{S} \neq S^*$.

Finally, we argue the privacy of SPHAuth. Intuitively, a homomorphic authenticator scheme is context hiding if it is infeasible to derive information about the inputs to a computation from an authenticator to the outcome of a computation (beyond what can be learned from the output itself). We show that for SPHAuth, this holds even against a computationally unbounded adversary.

Theorem 2. SPHAuth *is perfectly context hiding (see [7]).*

Proof. We show that SPHAuth is perfectly context hiding by comparing the distributions of homomorphically derived signatures to that of simulated signatures. First, in our case, the algorithm Hide is just the identity function. More precisely, we have $\mathsf{Hide}(\mathsf{vk}, M, \sigma) = \sigma$, for all possible verification keys vk, messages $M \in \mathbb{G}_1$ and authenticators σ. Thus we have HideVer = Ver, so correctness and unforgeability hold by Lemmas 7, and 8, and Theorem 1.

We show how to construct a simulator Sim that outputs signatures perfectly indistinguishable from the ones obtained by running Eval. Parse the simulator's input as $\mathsf{sk} = (K, x_1, \ldots, x_n, y, z)$, $\mathcal{P}_\Delta = (f, \tau_1, \ldots, \tau_n, \Delta)$. It computes $s_i = F_K(\tau_i)$. It sets $S' = g_1^{\sum_{i=1}^n s_i}$ and $\Lambda' = \left(g_1^{\sum_{i=1}^n (x_{\tau_i} + s_i)} \cdot M^y \right)^{\frac{1}{z}}$.

Let $\sigma_i \leftarrow \mathsf{Auth}(\mathsf{sk}, \tau_i, M_i)$, $\sigma^* \leftarrow \mathsf{HEval}(f, \{\sigma_i, \}_{i \in [n]}, 0)$. Parsing $\sigma^* = (\Lambda^*, S^*)$, we have by construction $S^* = S'$ and $\Lambda^* = \Lambda'$. Since these elements are identical, they are indistinguishable against a computationally unbounded distinguisher.

5 Related Work

Transforming Homomorphic Authenticators. Catalano et al. [9] showed a transformation for linearly homomorphic signatures. They introduced a primitive called *linearly homomorphic authenticated encryption with public verifiability* (LAEPuV), and how to obtain LAEPuV schemes from Paillier encryption and homomorphic signatures. Their work is restricted to the computational security of Paillier encryption. Our approach also allows for information-theoretic privacy.

Commitments. Commitment schemes (e.g. [19]) can add verifiability to secret sharing [19], multi-party computation [6], or e-voting [18]. In commitment-based audit schemes, authenticity is typically achieved by using a secure bulletin board [10], for which finding secure instantiations has been challenging so far. In [22], FDC schemes are introduced. Unlike previous commitment schemes, they allow for succinctness and amortized efficiency. Furthermore, FDCs support messages stored in datasets and thus enables a much more expressive notion of public verifiability and more rigorous definition of forgery. Besides, a secure bulletin board is not required. In this work, we investigate the relations between homomorphic authenticators and FDCs. In particular, we show how to construct FDCs from structure-preserving signatures. In [17], the notion of *functional commitments* is introduced. Their notion of function bindingness, however, is strictly weaker than our notion of adaptive unforgeability.

Homomorphic Authenticators. Homomorphic authenticators have been proposed both in the secret-key setting, as homomorphic MACs (e.g. [4,5,24]), and in the public-key setting as homomorphic signatures (e.g. [7,8,20]). In contrast, FDCs additionally consider information-theoretic privacy. Libert et al. [16] presented a structure-preserving, linearly homomorphic signature scheme. For structure-preserving homomorphic signatures, so far, only schemes limited to linear functions are known. Our construction in Sect. 4 is, however, the first such scheme to achieve efficient verification as well as the first to be context hiding.

Structure-Preserving Signatures. The notion of signatures to group elements consisting of group elements were introduced by Groth [13]. This property was later called *structure-preserving* [2]. Since then, various constructions have been proposed (e.g. [1,12,14]).

Acknowledgments. This work has received funding from the DFG as part of project S6 within the CRC 1119 CROSSING.

References

1. Abe, M., Chase, M., David, B., Kohlweiss, M., Nishimaki, R., Ohkubo, M.: Constant-size structure-preserving signatures: generic constructions and simple assumptions. In: Wang, X., Sako, K. (eds.) ASIACRYPT 2012. LNCS, vol. 7658, pp. 4–24. Springer, Heidelberg (2012). https://doi.org/10.1007/978-3-642-34961-4_3
2. Abe, M., Fuchsbauer, G., Groth, J., Haralambiev, K., Ohkubo, M.: Structure-preserving signatures and commitments to group elements. In: Rabin, T. (ed.) CRYPTO 2010. LNCS, vol. 6223, pp. 209–236. Springer, Heidelberg (2010). https://doi.org/10.1007/978-3-642-14623-7_12
3. Abe, M., Haralambiev, K., Ohkubo, M.: Signing on elements in bilinear groups for modular protocol design. IACR ePrint 2010, 133 (2010)
4. Agrawal, S., Boneh, D.: Homomorphic MACs: MAC-based integrity for network coding. In: Abdalla, M., Pointcheval, D., Fouque, P.-A., Vergnaud, D. (eds.) ACNS 2009. LNCS, vol. 5536, pp. 292–305. Springer, Heidelberg (2009). https://doi.org/10.1007/978-3-642-01957-9_18
5. Backes, M., Fiore, D., Reischuk, R.M.: Verifiable delegation of computation on outsourced data. In: ACM CCS, pp. 863–874. ACM (2013)
6. Baum, C., Damgård, I., Orlandi, C.: Publicly auditable secure multi-party computation. In: Abdalla, M., De Prisco, R. (eds.) SCN 2014. LNCS, vol. 8642, pp. 175–196. Springer, Cham (2014). https://doi.org/10.1007/978-3-319-10879-7_11
7. Catalano, D., Fiore, D., Nizzardo, L.: Programmable hash functions go private: constructions and applications to (homomorphic) signatures with shorter public keys. In: Gennaro, R., Robshaw, M. (eds.) CRYPTO 2015. LNCS, vol. 9216, pp. 254–274. Springer, Heidelberg (2015). https://doi.org/10.1007/978-3-662-48000-7_13

8. Catalano, D., Fiore, D., Warinschi, B.: Homomorphic signatures with efficient verification for polynomial functions. In: Garay, J.A., Gennaro, R. (eds.) CRYPTO 2014. LNCS, vol. 8616, pp. 371–389. Springer, Heidelberg (2014). https://doi.org/10.1007/978-3-662-44371-2_21

9. Catalano, D., Marcedone, A., Puglisi, O.: Authenticating computation on groups: new homomorphic primitives and applications. In: Sarkar, P., Iwata, T. (eds.) ASIACRYPT 2014. LNCS, vol. 8874, pp. 193–212. Springer, Heidelberg (2014). https://doi.org/10.1007/978-3-662-45608-8_11

10. Culnane, C., Schneider, S.A.: A peered bulletin board for robust use in verifiable voting systems. In: CSF, pp. 169–183. IEEE Computer Society (2014)

11. Fiore, D., Mitrokotsa, A., Nizzardo, L., Pagnin, E.: Multi-key homomorphic authenticators. In: Cheon, J.H., Takagi, T. (eds.) ASIACRYPT 2016. LNCS, vol. 10032, pp. 499–530. Springer, Heidelberg (2016). https://doi.org/10.1007/978-3-662-53890-6_17

12. Ghadafi, E.: How low can you go? short structure-preserving signatures for Diffie-Hellman vectors. In: O'Neill, M. (ed.) IMACC 2017. LNCS, vol. 10655, pp. 185–204. Springer, Cham (2017). https://doi.org/10.1007/978-3-319-71045-7_10

13. Groth, J.: Simulation-sound NIZK proofs for a practical language and constant size group signatures. In: Lai, X., Chen, K. (eds.) ASIACRYPT 2006. LNCS, vol. 4284, pp. 444–459. Springer, Heidelberg (2006). https://doi.org/10.1007/11935230_29

14. Jutla, C.S., Roy, A.: Improved structure preserving signatures under standard bilinear assumptions. In: Fehr, S. (ed.) PKC 2017. LNCS, vol. 10175, pp. 183–209. Springer, Heidelberg (2017). https://doi.org/10.1007/978-3-662-54388-7_7

15. Kiltz, E., Pan, J., Wee, H.: Structure-preserving signatures from standard assumptions, revisited. In: Gennaro, R., Robshaw, M. (eds.) CRYPTO 2015. LNCS, vol. 9216, pp. 275–295. Springer, Heidelberg (2015). https://doi.org/10.1007/978-3-662-48000-7_14

16. Libert, B., Peters, T., Joye, M., Yung, M.: Linearly homomorphic structure-preserving signatures and their applications. In: Canetti, R., Garay, J.A. (eds.) CRYPTO 2013. LNCS, vol. 8043, pp. 289–307. Springer, Heidelberg (2013). https://doi.org/10.1007/978-3-642-40084-1_17

17. Libert, B., Ramanna, S.C., Yung, M.: Functional commitment schemes: from polynomial commitments to pairing-based accumulators from simple assumptions. In: ICALP. LIPIcs, vol. 55, pp. 30:1–30:14, Dagstuhl (2016)

18. Moran, T., Naor, M.: Receipt-free universally-verifiable voting with everlasting privacy. In: Dwork, C. (ed.) CRYPTO 2006. LNCS, vol. 4117, pp. 373–392. Springer, Heidelberg (2006). https://doi.org/10.1007/11818175_22

19. Pedersen, T.P.: Non-interactive and information-theoretic secure verifiable secret sharing. In: Feigenbaum, J. (ed.) CRYPTO 1991. LNCS, vol. 576, pp. 129–140. Springer, Heidelberg (1992). https://doi.org/10.1007/3-540-46766-1_9

20. Schabhüser, L., Butin, D., Buchmann, J.: CHQS: publicly verifiable homomorphic signatures beyond the linear case. In: Su, C., Kikuchi, H. (eds.) ISPEC 2018. LNCS, vol. 11125, pp. 213–228. Springer, Cham (2018). https://doi.org/10.1007/978-3-319-99807-7_13

21. Schabhüser, L., Butin, D., Buchmann, J.: Function-dependent commitments from homomorphic authenticators. IACR ePrint 2019, 250 (2019)

22. Schabhüser, L., Butin, D., Demirel, D., Buchmann, J.: Function-dependent commitments for verifiable multi-party computation. In: Chen, L., Manulis, M., Schneider, S. (eds.) ISC 2018. LNCS, vol. 11060, pp. 289–307. Springer, Cham (2018). https://doi.org/10.1007/978-3-319-99136-8_16

23. Schabhüser, L., Demirel, D., Buchmann, J.: An unconditionally hiding auditing procedure for computations over distributed data. In: CNS, pp. 552–560. IEEE (2016)
24. Zhang, L.F., Safavi-Naini, R.: Generalized homomorphic MACs with efficient verification. In: AsiaPKC@AsiaCCS, pp. 3–12. ACM (2014)

Security Against Subversion
in a Multi-surveillant Setting

Geng Li, Jianwei Liu, and Zongyang Zhang[✉]

School of Cyber Science and Technology, Beihang University, Beijing, China
{ligeng,liujianwei,zongyangzhang}@buaa.edu.cn

Abstract. Mass surveillance attracts much of attentions nowadays. Evidences showed that some intelligence agencies try to monitor public's communication by unconventional methods, for example, providing users subverted cryptographic algorithms and compelling them to use. To address this new situation, researchers proposed a series of formal analyses and security definitions. However, current researches are restrictive as they only considered a single surveillant setting. In reality, there may exist multiple surveillants for different governments or manufacturers. This paper initializes the analysis of security against subversion in a multi-surveillant setting. We consider the case where users could only use subverted algorithms from different sources to achieve a subliminal communication. We introduce a new security notion that the transmission of a real message is "undetectable", which means all surveillants either think the users execute the subverted algorithms honestly to transmit an innocuous message, or consider users are using non-subverted algorithms. We present a concrete design and prove that it satisfies our security definition.

Keywords: Post-Snowden cryptography ·
Algorithm-substitution attack (ASA) · Message-transmission protocol

1 Introduction

The PRISM in 2013 showed that some agencies try to monitor a user's communication by providing corrupted algorithms with an underlying "backdoor". A typical example is Dual_EC_DRBG [4]. Designed by National Security Agency, Dual_EC_DRBG acts as a pseudorandom generator. After knowing a series of outputs of Dual_EC_DRBG, an attacker getting access to its backdoor can predict the subsequent outputs.

A series of studies considered about this new situation, where the implementations of cryptographic algorithms may diverge from their original security due to implanting of backdoors. To address this problem, researchers regarded the insecure implementations with backdoors as subversion, and proposed several security models to capture the actual security requirements, such as "kleptography" [14], surveillance-detection model [3], cryptography reverse firewall [10], self-guarding model [8], watchdog-based model [11] et al.

© Springer Nature Switzerland AG 2019
J. Jang-Jaccard and F. Guo (Eds.): ACISP 2019, LNCS 11547, pp. 419–437, 2019.
https://doi.org/10.1007/978-3-030-21548-4_23

Current researches are restrictive as they only considered a single surveillant setting. There is an implicit assumption that the surveillant is a single entity, despite there may exist several subverted algorithms (such as "decomposition and amalgamation" model proposed by Russell et al. [12]). However, it is quite possible for users to run several cryptographic algorithms from different sources to construct a single system in reality. In this case, perhaps multiple surveillants exist and all the algorithms are corrupted. This setting is reasonable, since each government and organization may have its own independent surveillant system and cryptographic standard, and different manufacturers producing backdoored devices may have their respective supervisors. We emphasize that different organizations may be independent, and it is impossible for them to collaborate to conduct surveillance.

We initialize the security analysis in the multi-surveillant setting and focus on a message-transmission protocol. We assume that users could run implementations from different surveillants to construct their system. Normally, we may just hope the message is private against all surveillants. It may seem not difficult to achieve this, as in the multi-surveillant setting every surveillant only knows part of the backdoors, and in previous studies [2,3,6], a subversion is usually considered to be secure against ones who do not know the backdoor.

However, a powerful surveillant may find that the ciphertexts deviate from the normal encrypted message traffic and mount an attack. For example, if a surveillant can decrypt ciphertexts with a backdoor, he may detect the messages are not sampled from a vaild distribution. So we expect something more. We want the transmission not only private but also undetectable to all surveillants. Every surveillant either thinks the users are invoking the normal algorithm without subversion, or consider the users are exactly using the subverted algorithm it presents but detects nothing about the subliminal communication. We aim to design a message-transmission protocol which transmits the message privately and achieves the undetectability above. We call a protocol satisfying such property a subliminal communication protocol.

To be more concrete, we follow the work [9] and introduce a next-message generator $\mathcal{M}(\tau)$. $\mathcal{M}(\tau)$ takes a state τ as its input, renews the state τ and outputs a legal message m, where m has no relationship to real transmitted message msg. $\mathcal{M}(\tau)$ is independent of both users and surveillants. Intuitively, a user transmits msg to the other by embedding msg into its output as in Fig. 1(a), but for each surveillant, a user's output in Fig. 1(a) is indistinguishable to either case in Fig. 1(b), where C is a non-subverted specification, and C_0 and C_1 are two implementations of C given by two independent surveillants, respectively. The formal definition will be presented in Sect. 3.

Our work has a subtle relationship with steganography, which aims to hide secure communication under innocent-looking messages. The subliminal communication is different to steganography in formal expression, as the actual cover objects in subliminal communication are ciphertexts of innocuous messages, whereas in steganography the cover objects are plaintexts. However, in a

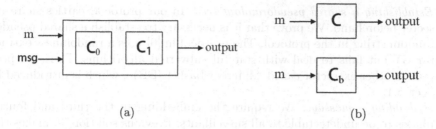

(a)   (b)

Fig. 1. An intuitive description for subliminal communication, $b \in \{0, 1\}$.

broad perspective, our scheme achieves the effect of steganography in hidding messages, even when surveillants are able to decrypt the ciphertexts.

This paper presents a concrete design of subliminal communication protocol in the multi-surveillant setting. We design a message-transmit protocol as a combination of a key-exchange protocol and a symmetric encryption scheme. In our protocol, two surveillants provide their implementations of the key-exchange and the encryption algorithms, respectively. Using techniques such as randomness extracting and messages embedding, two parties achieve a subliminal communication.

1.1 Our Contribution

Security Model in the Multi-surveillant Setting. We initialize the security analysis in the multi-surveillant setting. We consider the case where there are multiple implementations of cryptographic algorithms with backdoors, and the backdoors are managed by different surveillants. A user is allowed to run all the implementations to construct its system. Roughly speaking, a message-transmission protocol is secure if users can transmit their message in a subliminal method without any detection of abnormality by any surveillant.

A Subliminal Communication Protocol. We design a subliminal communication Protocol satisfying the above security. In our protocol both parties use implementations from different surveillants. Our protocol consists of four phases. In the key-exchange phase, two parties run a key-exchange protocol honestly and get a shared symmetric key. In the shared seed establishing phase, two parties extract a pseudorandom seed from the ciphertexts. In the subliminal key-exchange phase, two parties run the same key-exchange protocol subliminally and embed the transcripts into innocuous messages. In the subliminal communication phase, the sender embeds the ciphertext of a message into innocuous messages.

Our design is similar to the protocol in [9], but with two key differences. Firstly, in our protocol users need not get access to a non-subverted implementation but use multiple subverted implementations instead; secondly, subverted implementations are stateful, i.e., they can remember all the previous inputs and outputs. We mainly solve the following two problems:

- *Establishing a shared pseudorandom seed.* In our protocol, parties share no secret beforehand. We prove that it is necessary to establish a shared pseudo-random string in the protocol. The protocol in [9] uses a randomness extractor GT but fails to deal with stateful subverted algorithms. Thus, we propose another extractor called "different basket (DB)", which is introduced in Sect. 5.1.
- *Embedding a message.* We require the embedding in the third and fourth phases to be undetectable to all surveillants. Previous solution [9] makes the embedded message to be pseudorandom, thus, a surveillant cannot distinguish a ciphertext embedded with a message from a normal one. However, when all the cryptographic algorithms are subverted, such pseudorandomness is hard to achieve.
  Our protocol runs two kinds of implementations KE_0, KE_1, E_0, E_1 of the same key-exchange protocol KE and encryption scheme E. We use KE_1 and E_1 to generate embedded messages and E_0 to embed them into ciphertexts. Our embedding relies on the subverted implementation from one surveillant to cheat other surveillants. In this way, the embedding is undetectable to all surveillants.

1.2   Related Work

The security of maliciously subverted cryptographic algorithms is firstly analyzed by Young and Yung [13–16]. They proposed a new cryptographic model called "kleptography". In this model an adversary is permitted to compromise the security by designing an implementation of algorithms. They also designed concrete attack methods for common encryption and signature schemes.

In order to characterize a surveillant's behavior, Bellare, Paterson and Rogaway [3] presented algorithm substation attacks (ASAs). They summarized the attacks that maliciously substitutes an algorithm as subversion, and formalized security notions of symmetric encryption scheme against ASAs. Degabriele, Farshim and Poettering [6] introduced an "input-triggered attack", pointed out the weakness of the security model in [3] and proposed a new model to analyze the security in the subversion settings. With consideration of input-triggered attack, Bellare, Jaeger and Kane [2] improved the prior security model in [3] and present a stronger ASA, which can be stateless.

Russell et al. [11] proposed watchdog-based model. A watchdog is a probalistic polynomial-time algorithm which judges an algorithm to be correct or subverted by testing it as a blackbox. An attack is considered as successful if an implementation not only breaks the security but also passes any watchdog's test. Russell et al. [12] also proposed a model named "decomposition and amalgamation", where an algorithm is divided into several sub-algorithms. All the sub-algorithms together achieve the same functionality and security as the original algorithm, while they are under subversion risk, except that all sub-algorithms are working in the trusted amalgamation model.

Mironov and Stephens-Davidowitz [10] introduced the notion of a cryptographic reverse firewall (CRF). A CRF is a machine sitting at the boundary between a user's computer and the outside world, intercepting and modifying all the messages incoming and outcoming. A CRF has a special trust state. On the one hand, a CRF cannot be subverted. On the other hand, it is not a trusted module and can only access to public information. Dodis, Mironov and Stephens-Davidowitz [7] provided concrete designs of CRFs in a message-transmission protocol. Chen et al. [5] introduced the notion of malleable smooth projective hash function based on the smooth projective hash function (SPHF), and show how to generically construct CRFs via malleable SPHFs in a modular way for some widely used cryptographic protocols.

Fischlin and Mazaheri [8] proposed another defending strategy called self-guarding. Compared with detection-based solutions [3,11], it proactively thwarts attacks, and compared with CRFs it does not assume an online external party. They presented constructions for encryption schemes and signature schemes.

Horel et al. [9] proposed an analytical framework which is rather different to the previous studies. They considered the case where a surveillant provides a corrupted algorithm but a user can deal with it more actively. This means, a user can manage its implementation and query the subverted algorithm. Users try to cheat a surveillant by convincing it that they honestly execute the subverted algorithm and all the communicating message is under surveillance. However, the real message is transmitted in an undetectable way.

Organization. Section 2 introduces the main notations and preliminaries. Section 3 describes the multi-surveillant setting, and presents a formal definition of a subliminal communication protocol. Section 4 rebuts several previous methods in our setting and proposes some impossibility results. Section 5 constructs a subliminal communication protocol with a formal security proof.

2 Preliminary

2.1 Notations

When s is chosen uniformly random in a set $\mathcal{S}$, we write $s \xleftarrow{\$} \mathcal{S}$. Denote by U_ℓ a ℓ bit uniformly random string. We write the set $\{1, 2, \cdots, r\}$ simply by $[r]$. Let $\mathsf{poly}(x)$ represent a polynomial function of x. Let κ be a security parameter. A function $\mathsf{negl}(\kappa)$ is called negligible in κ if it vanishes faster than the inverse of any polynomial in κ. An algorithm $\mathsf{A}(x)$ is a probabilistic polynomial-time (PPT) algorithm if for any input, $\mathsf{A}(x)$ terminates at most $\mathsf{poly}(|x|)$ steps. If the algorithm A outputs y upon the input x, we write $y \leftarrow \mathsf{A}(x)$. We use $s_1 || s_2$ to denote the concatenation of two bit strings s_1 and s_2.

For two distributions $\mathcal{X} = \{X_\kappa\}$ and $\mathcal{Y} = \{Y_\kappa\}$ over set $\mathcal{S}$. We define statistical distance as $||\mathcal{X} - \mathcal{Y}||_s \overset{def}{=} \frac{1}{2} \sum_{\alpha \in \mathcal{S}} |\Pr[\alpha \in \mathcal{X}] - \Pr[\alpha \in \mathcal{Y}]|$. We define $\mathsf{Dist}_\mathsf{D}(\mathcal{X}, \mathcal{Y}) \overset{def}{=} |\Pr[\mathsf{D}(X_\kappa) = 1] - \Pr[\mathsf{D}(Y_\kappa) = 1]|$. If $\mathsf{Dist}_\mathsf{D}(\mathcal{X}, \mathcal{Y}) \leq \mathsf{negl}(\kappa)$ for all PPT algorithm D, we call $\mathcal{X}$ and $\mathcal{Y}$ are computational indistinguishable.

2.2   Ciphertext Pseudorandom Encryption and Key-Exchange Protocol

We borrow the idea of ciphertext pseudorandom (CPR) secure encryption in [1], and present our security definition for symmetric encryption as below.

Definition 1. *Let* $\mathsf{E} = (\mathsf{Gen}, \mathsf{Enc}, \mathsf{Dec})$ *be a symmetric encryption scheme, where* $\mathsf{Gen} : \{0,1\}^\kappa \to \{0,1\}^\ell$, $\mathsf{Enc} : \{0,1\}^p \times \{0,1\}^\ell \to \{0,1\}^q$, $\mathsf{Dec} : \{0,1\}^q \times \{0,1\}^\ell \to \{0,1\}^p$. *We say* E *satisfies ciphertext pseudorandom (CPR) security if for any* $m \in \{0,1\}^p$, $k \in \{0,1\}^\ell$, *and any PPT adversary* $\mathcal{A}$,

$$\mathsf{Adv}_{\mathsf{E},\mathcal{A}}^{\mathsf{CPR}}(\kappa) \overset{def}{=} \left| \Pr[\mathcal{A}(m, \mathsf{E}.\mathsf{Enc}(m,k)) = 1] - \Pr[\mathcal{A}(m, U_q) = 1] \right| \leq \mathsf{negl}(\kappa).$$

A CPR secure symmetric encryption scheme can be built from one-way functions [9].

We take the idea of pseudorandom key-exchange protocol in [9] and present Definition 2.

Definition 2. *Let* $\mathsf{KE} = (\Lambda_{0,1}, \Lambda_{1,1}, \cdots, \Lambda_{0,r}, \Lambda_{1,r}, \Lambda_{0,\mathsf{out}}, \Lambda_{1,\mathsf{out}})$ *be a two-party key-exchange protocol. For* $i \in [r]$, $\lambda_{1,0} = \bot$, $(\lambda_{0,i}, s_{0,i}) \leftarrow \Lambda_{0,i}(s_{0,i-1}, \lambda_{1,i-1})$, $(\lambda_{1,i}, s_{1,i}) \leftarrow \Lambda_{1,i}(s_{1,i-1}, \lambda_{0,i})$, $k^b \leftarrow \Lambda_{b,\mathsf{out}}(s_{b,r})$, *where* $\lambda_{b,i}$ *is the transcript and* $s_{b,i}$ *denotes the state. We say* KE *is pseudorandom if for any PPT adversary* $\mathcal{A}$,

$$\mathsf{Adv}_{\mathsf{KE},\mathcal{A}}^{\mathsf{PSE}}(\kappa) \overset{def}{=} \left| \Pr[\mathcal{A}(\{\lambda_{b,i}\}_{b\in\{0,1\}, i\in[r]}, k^b) = 1] - \Pr[\mathcal{A}(U, U_{|k^b|}) = 1] \right| \leq \mathsf{negl}(\kappa),$$

where U *is a uniform random string with the same length as* $\{\lambda_{b,i}\}_{b\in\{0,1\}, i\in[r]}$.

Most known key agreement protocols are pseudorandom, e.g., the classical protocol of Diffie and Hellman [9].

2.3   Watchdog-Based Test

We call an ideal algorithm "specification" and an algorithm used in practice "implementation". Watchdog-based test, proposed by Russell et al. [11], is used to recognize the implementation which diverges from its specification distinctly. A watchdog W is a PPT algorithm with access to the specification of an algorithm $\mathsf{F}_{\mathsf{spec}}$. It takes as input an algorithm implementation $\mathsf{F}_{\mathsf{impl}}$ as a blackbox, and judges whether it is an honest implementation. If for all the PPT W, an implementation $\mathsf{F}_{\mathsf{impl}}$ of its specification $\mathsf{F}_{\mathsf{spec}}$ satisfies,

$$\mathsf{Det}_{\mathsf{W}}^{\mathsf{F}_{\mathsf{impl}}}(\kappa) \overset{def}{=} \left| \Pr[\mathsf{W}^{\mathsf{F}_{\mathsf{impl}}}(1^\kappa) = 1] - \Pr[\mathsf{W}^{\mathsf{F}_{\mathsf{spec}}}(1^\kappa) = 1] \right| \leq \mathsf{negl}(\kappa),$$

then we say that the implementation is *algorithm-indistinguishable*.

3 Subliminal Communication in the Muti-surveillant Setting

3.1 Background

Normal Transmission Scheme. We design a normal transmission scheme as a combination of a key-exchange protocol and a symmetric encryption scheme. Concretely, let $E = (Gen, Enc, Dec)$ be a symmetric encryption scheme, and $KE = (\Lambda_{0,1}, \Lambda_{1,1}, \cdots, \Lambda_{0,r'}, \Lambda_{1,r'}, \Lambda_{0,out}, \Lambda_{1,out})$ be a r'-round key-exchange protocol. In a normal session, two parties P_0 and P_1 run as follows.

1. Both parties invoke KE, get a shared key k and parse k as $k_0 \| k_1$ of equal length
2. In round $i \in [1, 2, 3, \cdots]$:
   - P_0 gets a message $m_{0,i}$ and a ciphertext $c_{1,i}$. It decrypts the received ciphertext as $m'_{1,i} \leftarrow E.Dec(c_{1,i}, k_1)$ and sends $c_{0,i} \leftarrow E.Enc(m_{0,i}, k_0)$;
   - P_1 gets a message $m_{1,i}$ and a ciphertext $c_{0,i}$. It decrypts the received ciphertext as $m'_{0,i} \leftarrow E.Dec(c_{0,i}, k_0)$ and sends $c_{1,i} \leftarrow E.Enc(m_{1,i}, k_1)$.

Entities. Observe that surveillants may provide their implementations of the algorithms, respectively. We consider the following entities in our model:

1. B_0/B_1: surveillants who provide implementations E_b and KE_b of the specifications E and KE, $b \in \{0, 1\}$. E_b and KE_b may have their backdoor $\widetilde{BK}_{E_b}$ and $\widetilde{BK}_{KE_b}$. B_0 and B_1 are independent surveillants, having no collaboration.
2. W: a watchdog. It tests E_b and KE_b as blackboxes, judging whether they are correct implementations, with access to the specification E and KE.
3. P_0/P_1: two participants in protocol using the E_b and KE_b.

3.2 Security Model

We then present a formal definition of subliminal communication in the muti-surveillant setting. Our model borrows the ideas from [11] and [9]. Let msg denote the message that users intend to transmit. Following from [9], we assume the existence of a next-message generator $\mathcal{M}$. Based on the current state, it generates an innocuous message being indistinguishable to the usual transmission traffic.[1] For simplicity, we omit the update of the state and denote it by $m_{b,i} \leftarrow \mathcal{M}(\tau_{b,i})$.

Definition 3. *A subliminal communication protocol is a two-party protocol with two phases:*

- *Key-exchange phase:* $\Phi^{KE_0} = (\Phi_{0,1}^{KE_0}, \Phi_{1,1}^{KE_0}, \cdots, \Phi_{0,r'}^{KE_0}, \Phi_{1,r'}^{KE_0}, \Phi_{0,out}^{KE_0}, \Phi_{1,out}^{KE_0})$;

---

[1] In our model we expect the users to transmit msg under any cover message. $\mathcal{M}$ is independent of all users and surveillants, and generates messages with no extra requirement except looking innocent.

- *Communication phase:* $\Pi^{E_0,E_1,KE_1} = (\Pi_{0,1}^{E_0,E_1,KE_1}, \Pi_{1,1}^{E_0,E_1,KE_1}, \cdots, \Pi_{0,r}^{E_0,E_1,KE_1},$
$\Pi_{1,r}^{E_0,E_1,KE_1}, \Pi_{1,out}^{E_0,E_1,KE_1})$,

where $r', r \in \mathsf{poly}(\kappa)$ are the numbers of exchange-rounds. $\Phi_{b,i}^{KE_0}$ and $\Phi_{1,output}^{KE_0}$ are PPT algorithms with oracle access only to implementation KE_0. They cannot invoke other key-exchange algorithms. $\Pi_{b,i}^{E_0,E_1,KE_1}$ and $\Pi_{1,out}^{E_0,E_1,KE_1}$ are PPT algorithms with oracle access only to implementations E_0, E_1, KE_1. They cannot invoke other encryption or key-exchange algorithms. Party P_0 receives as input a message msg that is to be sent to P_1 in an undetectable fashion. The algorithms $\Phi_{b,i}^{KE_0}$ and $\Pi_{b,i}^{E_0,E_1,KE_1}$ are run by P_b. $\Phi_{b,out}^{KE_0}$ is run by P_b and outputs a shared key. $\Pi_{1,out}^{E_0,E_1,KE_1}$ is run by P_1 and outputs msg' at the end of the protocol.

Intuitively, our security goal is to transmit msg only using the cryptographic algorithms given by surveillants, making the surveillants either think that the users are transmitting innocuous messages by backdoored implementations or consider them just using non-subverted implementations. We present the syntax, correctness, and security of a subliminal communication protocol as below.

Syntax.

- The protocol Φ proceeds as follows.
  Set $\lambda_{1,0} \leftarrow \bot$. In each exchange-round $i \in [r']$ of Φ,
  1. P_0 runs $(\lambda_{0,i}, s_{0,i}) \leftarrow \Phi_{0,i}^{KE_0}(s_{0,i-1}, \lambda_{1,i-1})$, stores $s_{0,i}$, sends $\lambda_{0,i}$ to P_1.
  2. P_1 runs $(\lambda_{1,i}, s_{1,i}) \leftarrow \Phi_{1,i}^{KE_0}(s_{1,i-1}, \lambda_{0,i})$, stores $s_{1,i}$ and sends $\lambda_{1,i}$ to P_0.
  When Φ completes, both parties output the shared key $k \leftarrow \Phi_{b,out}^{KE_0}(s_{0,r'})$ and parse k as $k_0 \| k_1$ of equal length.
- The protocol Π proceeds as follows.
  Set $C_{1,0} \leftarrow \bot$, for $i \in [r]$,
  1. P_0 samples $m_{0,i} \leftarrow \mathcal{M}(\tau_{0,i})$, invokes $(C_{0,i}, \varsigma_{0,i}) \leftarrow \Pi_{0,i}^{E_0,E_1,KE_1}(\mathsf{msg}, m_{0,i}, k_0,$
     $C_{1,i-1}, \varsigma_{0,i-1})$, stores $\varsigma_{0,i}$ and sends $C_{0,i}$ to P_1.
  2. P_1 samples $m_{1,i} \leftarrow \mathcal{M}(\tau_{1,i})$, invokes $(C_{1,i}, \varsigma_{1,i}) \leftarrow \Pi_{1,i}^{E_0,E_1,KE_1}(m_{1,i}, k_1, C_{0,i},$
     $\varsigma_{1,i-1})$, stores $\varsigma_{1,i}$ and sends $C_{1,i}$ to P_0.
  In the end, P_1 computes $\mathsf{msg}' = \Pi_{1,out}^{E_0,E_1,KE_1}(\varsigma_{1,r})$.

Correctness. For any E_0, E_1, KE_0, KE_1 satisfying correctness and any message $\mathsf{msg} \in \{0,1\}^p$, if P_0 and P_1 run Φ^{KE_0} and Π^{E_0,E_1,KE_1} honestly, then $\mathsf{msg}' = \mathsf{msg}$ with probability $1 - \mathsf{negl}(k)$.

Security.

- *Algorithm-indistinguishability.* For any PPT algorithm W with oracle access to E_0, E_1, KE_0 and KE_1, for any $b \in \{0,1\}$, if the following holds

$$\mathsf{Det}_W^{KE_b,E_b}(\kappa) = \left| \Pr[W^{KE_b,E_b}(1^\kappa) = 1] - \Pr[W^{KE,E}(1^\kappa) = 1] \right| \le \mathsf{negl}(\kappa),$$

then we say E_0, E_1, KE_0 and KE_1 satisfy algorithm-indistinguishability.

– *Undetectability I.* For any implementations E_0, E_1, KE_0 and KE_1 satisfying algorithm-indistinguishability, and any hidden messages msg, if for $b \in \{0,1\}$, the following distributions are computationally indistinguishable:

$$(\text{Ideal}(\mathcal{M}); \widetilde{BK}_{E_b}, \widetilde{BK}_{KE_b}) \text{ and } (\text{Subliminal}_{\Phi,\Pi}(\text{msg}, \mathcal{M}); \widetilde{BK}_{E_b}, \widetilde{BK}_{KE_b}),$$

where $\widetilde{BK}_{E_0}, \widetilde{BK}_{E_1}, \widetilde{BK}_{KE_0}$, and $\widetilde{BK}_{KE_1}$ are backdoors for E_0, E_1, KE_0, KE_1, respectively, and $\text{Ideal}(\mathcal{M})$ and $\text{Subliminal}_{\Phi,\Pi}(\text{msg}, \mathcal{M})$ are shown in Fig. 2, then we say Φ^{KE_0} and Π^{E_0,E_1,KE_1} satisfy undetectability I for B_b.

– *Undetectability II.* For any implementations E_0, E_1, KE_0 and KE_1 satisfying algorithm-indistinguishability, any hidden messages msg, if for $b \in \{0,1\}$, the following distributions are computationally indistinguishable:

$$(\text{Subversion}_b(\mathcal{M}); \widetilde{BK}_{E_b}, \widetilde{BK}_{KE_b}) \text{ and } (\text{Subliminal}_{\Phi,\Pi}(\text{msg}, \mathcal{M}); \widetilde{BK}_{E_b}, \widetilde{BK}_{KE_b}),$$

where $\widetilde{BK}_{E_0}, \widetilde{BK}_{E_1}, \widetilde{BK}_{KE_0}$, and $\widetilde{BK}_{KE_1}$ are backdoors for E_0, E_1, KE_0, KE_1, respectively, and $\text{Subversion}_b(\mathcal{M})$ and $\text{Subliminal}_{\Phi,\Pi}(\text{msg}, \mathcal{M})$ are shown in Fig. 3, then we say Φ^{KE_0} and Π^{E_0,E_1,KE_1} satisfy undetectability II for B_b.

Definition 4 *(Security of a subliminal communication protocol). A subliminal communication protocol (Φ, Π) is secure in the two-surveillant setting, if for both B_0 and B_1, either undetectability I or undetectability II is satisfied.*

Ideal($\mathcal{M}$):	Subliminal$_{\Phi,\Pi}$(msg, $\mathcal{M}$)
$\lambda_{1,0} = \bot$	$\lambda_{1,0} = \bot$, $C_{1,0} = \bot$
for $i \in [r']$	for $i \in [r']$
$(\lambda_{0,i}, s_{0,i}) \leftarrow \text{KE}.\Lambda_{0,i}(s_{0,i-1}, \lambda_{1,i-1})$	$(\lambda_{0,i}, s_{0,i}) \leftarrow \Phi^{KE_0}_{0,i}(s_{0,i-1}, \lambda_{1,i-1})$
$(\lambda_{1,i}, s_{1,i}) \leftarrow \text{KE}.\Lambda_{1,i}(s_{1,i-1}, \lambda_{0,i})$	$(\lambda_{1,i}, s_{1,i}) \leftarrow \Phi^{KE_0}_{1,i}(s_{1,i-1}, \lambda_{0,i})$
$k_0 \| k_1 \leftarrow \text{KE}.\Lambda_{b'',\text{out}}(s_{b''}, r'), b'' \in \{0,1\}$	$k_0 \| k_1 \leftarrow \Phi^{KE_0}_{b'',\text{out}}(s_{b''}, r'), b'' \in \{0,1\}$
for $i \in [r]$	for $i \in [r]$
$m_{0,i} \leftarrow \mathcal{M}(\tau_{0,i})$	$m_{0,i} \leftarrow \mathcal{M}(\tau_{0,i})$
$m_{1,i} \leftarrow \mathcal{M}(\tau_{1,i})$	$m_{1,i} \leftarrow \mathcal{M}(\tau_{1,i})$
$C_{0,i} \leftarrow \text{E.Enc}(m_{0,i}, k_0)$	$(C_{0,i}, \varsigma_{0,i})$
$C_{1,i} \leftarrow \text{E.Enc}(m_{1,i}, k_1)$	$\leftarrow \Pi^{E_0,E_1,KE_1}_{0,i}(\text{msg}, m_{0,i}, k_0, C_{1,i-1}, \varsigma_{0,i-1})$
output:	$(C_{1,i}, \varsigma_{1,i})$
$((\lambda_{b',i})_{b' \in \{0,1\}, i \in [r']}, (C_{b',i})_{b' \in \{0,1\}, i \in [r]})$	$\leftarrow \Pi^{E_0,E_1,KE_1}_{1,i}(m_{1,i}, k_1, C_{0,i}, \varsigma_{1,i-1})$
	output:
	$((\lambda_{b',i})_{b' \in \{0,1\}, i \in [r']}, (C_{b',i})_{b' \in \{0,1\}, i \in [r]})$

Fig. 2. Definition of undetectability I. Ideal($\mathcal{M}$) denotes a normal communication based on specifications, and Subliminal$_{\Phi,\Pi}$(msg, $\mathcal{M}$) denotes the communication that users attempt to transmit msg based on subverted implementations.

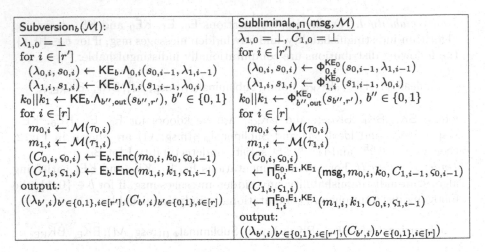

Fig. 3. Definition of undetectability II. Subversion$_b(\mathcal{M})$ denotes a communication based on subverted implementations KE$_b$ and E$_b$, and Subliminal$_{\Phi,\Pi}$(msg, $\mathcal{M}$) denotes the communication that users attempt to transmit msg based on subverted implementations.

4 Negative Results

We assume that subverted implementations are stateful, i.e., it remembers all previous inputs and outputs. In the meantime, we make a limitation that an implementation cannot collect extra information except its inputs.

Note that our design is based on a restriction that parties have no shared secret at the very beginning. In this case, we state that it is necessary to establish a secret seed in the protocol for embedding message.

Theorem 1. *For any subliminal communication protocol, if it does not establish a pseudorandom seed S between two parties, then there exists a subverted encryption algorithm to violate the correctness property.*

Proof. Intuitively, note that parties share no secret against subverted encryption algorithms. A subverted algorithm can generate ciphertexts which are embedded with a random string everytime in the same way to users' embedding. Hence, the subliminal channel is "blocked".

Concretely, assume that the parties transmit the message msg in a subliminal way without a shared pseudorandom seed. Suppose ciphertexts are generated by an algorithm $\sum^{E_b}(\text{msg}, k, m)$, where k is a shared key and m is an innocuous message. The subverted algorithm E_b can also invoke $\sum^E$. E_b generates $U_{|\text{msg}|}$, and outputs ciphertext as $C \leftarrow \sum^E(U_{|\text{msg}|}, k, m)$. Hence, all the ciphertexts are embedded with the message $U_{|\text{msg}|}$.

Horel et al. [9] proposed a method to establish a pseudorandom seed S. In their design, every bit in S is extracted based on two sequential ciphertexts generated by a *single* party. However, we stress that this method does not work when subverted algorithms are stateful, as a subverted algorithm may recover the extracted bit in the same way. This is formalized in Theorem 2. Therefore, S should be generated by *both* parties together. Whereas, if an implementation is allowed to collect extra information from other implementations, Theorem 2 still works. This is why we set the limitation that an implementation cannot collect extra information except its inputs.

Theorem 2. *If any bit in the seed S is extracted from outputs which are generated by a single algorithm F, then there exists a PPT adversary with only oracle access to F that distinguishes between S and a uniformly random string of the same length.*

Proof. Observe that parties share no secret before establishing S. Denote the algorithm that extracts any bit in S by EX. Then we design a PPT adversary $\mathcal{A}$ that invokes F and gets the outputs, and extracts the S from the outputs by running EX. Certainly, S is not random to $\mathcal{A}$.

5 Construction of Subliminal Communication Protocol

To achieve subliminal communication, we assume a pseudorandom key-exchange protocol $\mathsf{KE} = (\Lambda_{0,1}, \Lambda_{1,1}, \cdots, \Lambda_{0,r}, \Lambda_{1,r}, \Lambda_{0,\mathsf{out}}, \Lambda_{1,\mathsf{out}})$ as in Definition 2 and a CPR secure encryption scheme $\mathsf{E} = (\mathsf{Gen}, \mathsf{Enc}, \mathsf{Dec})$ as in Definition 1.

5.1 Establishing a Shared Seed

We define the extractor DB in Definition 5.

Definition 5. *Denote the ciphertext space of the encryption scheme E as $\mathcal{CS}$. We can judge whether $C_0 > C_1$ or not for any $C_0, C_1 \in \mathcal{CS}$. C_m is the median of $\mathcal{CS}$. A two-source extractor DB outputs 1 bit based on two ciphertexts:*

$$\mathsf{DB}(C_0, C_1) = \begin{cases} 0, & \text{if } C_0, C_1 \leq C_m \text{ or } C_0, C_1 > C_m; \\ 1, & \text{if } C_0 \leq C_m, C_1 > C_m \text{ or } C_1 \leq C_m, C_0 > C_m. \end{cases}$$

We improve the method in [9] by extracting a single random bit from ciphertexts generated by both communicating parties. In this way, together with the limitation that the subverted implementations must be approved by a watchdog, we can ensure that a seed extracted by DB is pseudorandom in subverted algorithms' view even if they are stateful. Next, we present Lemma 1.

Lemma 1. *Suppose that KE is a pseudorandom key-exchange protocol, and E is a CPR encryption scheme. KE' and E' are implementations of KE and E. For any PPT watchdog W, $\mathsf{Det}_W^{\mathsf{E}',\mathsf{KE}'}(\kappa) = \left|\Pr[W^{\mathsf{E},\mathsf{KE}}(1^\kappa) = 1] - \Pr[W^{\mathsf{E}',\mathsf{KE}'}(1^\kappa) = 1]\right| < \mathsf{negl}(\kappa)$. C_m is the median of the ciphertext space $\mathcal{CS}$ of E. For $m \in \{0,1\}^p$, $k_0'\|k_1'$ generated by KE', $C' \leftarrow \mathsf{E}'.\mathsf{Enc}(k_b', m)$ and any PPT algorithm $\mathcal{A}$, we have*

$$\left|\Pr[\mathcal{A}(k_{1-b}', m, \mathsf{R}(C')) = 1] - \Pr[\mathcal{A}(k_{1-b}', m, U_1) = 1]\right| < \mathsf{negl}(\kappa), \tag{1}$$

where $R(C')$ *is defined as:*

$$R(C') \stackrel{def}{=} \begin{cases} 0, & \text{if } C' \leq C_m; \\ 1, & \text{if } C' > C_m. \end{cases} \tag{2}$$

Proof. It is straightforward to see that if $k_0 \| k_1$ is generated by KE and $C \leftarrow$ E.Enc(m, k_b), then the Eq. (1) holds. Concretely,

$$\left| \Pr[\mathcal{A}(k_{1-b}, m, R(C)) = 1] - \Pr[\mathcal{A}(k_{1-b}, m, U_1) = 1] \right|$$
$$= \left| \Pr[\mathcal{A}(k_{1-b}, m, R(C)) = 1] - \Pr[\mathcal{A}(U_{|k_b|}, m, R(C)) = 1] + \Pr[\mathcal{A}(U_{|k_b|}, m, R(C)) = 1] \right.$$
$$\left. - \Pr[\mathcal{A}((U_{|k_b|}, m, U_1) = 1] + \Pr[\mathcal{A}(U_{|k_b|}, m, U_1) = 1] - \Pr[\mathcal{A}(k_{1-b}, m, U_1) = 1] \right|$$
$$\leq \left| \Pr[\mathcal{A}(k_{1-b}, m, R(C)) = 1] - \Pr[\mathcal{A}(U_{|k_b|}, m, R(C)) = 1] \right| + \left| \Pr[\mathcal{A}(U_{|k_b|}, m, R(C)) = 1] \right.$$
$$\left. - \Pr[\mathcal{A}(U_{|k_b|}, m, U_1) = 1] \right| + \left| \Pr[\mathcal{A}(U_{|k_b|}, m, U_1) = 1] - \Pr[\mathcal{A}(k_{1-b}, m, U_1) = 1] \right|$$
$$= 2\mathsf{Adv}_{\mathsf{KE},\mathcal{A}}^{\mathsf{PSE}}(\kappa) + \left| \Pr[\mathcal{A}(U_{|k_b|}, m, R(C)) = 1] - \Pr[\mathcal{A}(U_{|k_b|}, m, R(U_{|C|})) = 1] \right|$$
$$= 2\mathsf{Adv}_{\mathsf{KE},\mathcal{A}}^{\mathsf{PSE}}(\kappa) + \mathsf{Adv}_{\mathsf{E},\mathcal{A}}^{\mathsf{CPR}}(\kappa).$$

Assume that there exists such a PPT algorithm $\mathcal{A}$ that

$$\left| \Pr[\mathcal{A}(k'_{1-b}, m, R(C')) = 1] - \Pr[\mathcal{A}(k'_{1-b}, m, U_1) = 1] \right| \geq \frac{1}{\mathsf{poly}(\kappa)}.$$

Then we construct a watchdog W to distinguish $\{\mathsf{KE}^*, \mathsf{E}^*\} \in \{\{\mathsf{KE}, \mathsf{E}\}, \{\mathsf{KE}', \mathsf{E}'\}\}$ making use of $\mathcal{A}$ by following strategy. (1) Sample a plaintext $m \in \{0,1\}^p$ and generate keys $k_0^* \| k_1^*$ by KE^*; (2) $b' \stackrel{\$}{\leftarrow} \{0,1\}$, $C^* \leftarrow \mathsf{E}^*.\mathsf{Enc}(m, k_b^*)$, $r_0 \leftarrow R(C^*)$ and $r_1 \leftarrow U_1$; (3) Send $(k_{1-b}, m, r_{b'})$ to $\mathcal{A}$, and gets $\mathcal{A}$'s output b''; (4) If $b'' = b'$, output 1, else output 0. Then, we deduce that

$$\left| \Pr[\mathsf{W}^{\mathsf{E}',\mathsf{KE}'}(1^\kappa) = 1] - \Pr[\mathsf{W}^{\mathsf{E},\mathsf{KE}}(1^\kappa) = 1] \right| \geq \frac{1}{2 \cdot \mathsf{poly}(\kappa)} - \mathsf{negl}(\kappa),$$

which contradicts the algorithm-indistinguishability of $\{\mathsf{KE}', \mathsf{E}'\}$. It is sufficient to prove Lemma 1.

Theorem 3. *Let d be a polynomial. Suppose that the follows holds:*

- *KE is a pseudorandom key-exchange protocol and E is a CPR secure symmetric encryption scheme. KE_0 and E_0 are implementations of KE and E, respectively. For any PPT watchdog W, we have*

$$\mathsf{Det}_{\mathsf{W}}^{\mathsf{KE}_0, \mathsf{E}_0}(\kappa) = \left| \mathsf{W}^{\mathsf{KE}_0, \mathsf{E}_0}(1^\kappa) - \mathsf{W}^{\mathsf{KE}, \mathsf{E}}(1^\kappa) \right| < \mathsf{negl}(\kappa).$$

- *$k_0 \| k_1$ is generated by KE_0. For $i \in [d]$, $b \in \{0,1\}$, $m_{b,i} \leftarrow \mathcal{M}(\tau_{b,i})$, $C_{b,i} \leftarrow \mathsf{E}_0.\mathsf{Enc}(m_{b,i}, k_b)$.*
- *Let $S = \mathsf{BD}(C_{0,1}, C_{1,1}) \| \mathsf{BD}(C_{0,2}, C_{1,2}) \| \cdots \| \mathsf{BD}(C_{0,d}, C_{1,d})$.*

Denote all the innocuous plaintexts $\{m_{b',i}\}_{b' \in \{0,1\}, i \in [d]}$ by M, for any $b \in \{0,1\}$ and any PPT adversary $\mathcal{A}$, we have

$$\mathsf{Adv}_{S,\mathcal{A}}^{\mathsf{PSE}}(\kappa) \stackrel{def}{=} \left| \Pr[\mathcal{A}(k_b, M, S) = 1] - \Pr[\mathcal{A}(k_b, M, U_d) = 1] \right| < \mathsf{negl}(\kappa).$$

Proof. Parse S as $S_1||S_2||\cdots||S_d \leftarrow S$ where S_i is a bit. Define R as in Eq. (2). Following from Lemma 1, for $j \in [d]$, we have

$$\left|\Pr[\mathcal{A}(k_b, M, S_j) = 1] - \Pr[\mathcal{A}(k_b, M, U_1) = 1]\right|$$
$$= \left|\Pr[\mathcal{A}(k_b, M, \mathsf{R}(C_{b,j}) \oplus \mathsf{R}(C_{1-b,j})) = 1] - \Pr[\mathcal{A}(k_b, M, U_1) = 1]\right|$$
$$= \left|\Pr[\mathcal{A}(k_b, M, \mathsf{R}(\mathsf{E}_0.\mathsf{Enc}(m_{b,j}, k_b)) \oplus \mathsf{R}(C_{1-b,j})) = 1] - \Pr[\mathcal{A}(k_b, M, U_1) = 1]\right|$$
$$\leq \left|\Pr[\mathcal{A}(k_b, M, \mathsf{R}(C_{1-b,j})) = 1] - \Pr[\mathcal{A}(k_b, M, U_1) = 1]\right| < \mathsf{negl}(\kappa),$$

where the last in equation follows from Lemma 1. Due to the independence of the ciphertexts, we have $\mathsf{Adv}_{S,\mathcal{A}}^{\mathsf{PSE}}(\kappa) = \sum_{j=1}^{d} \left|\Pr[\mathcal{A}(k_b, M, S_j) = 1] - \Pr[(k_b, M, U_1) = 1]\right| < \mathsf{negl}(\kappa)$.

5.2   Embedding Random Strings

Next we discuss how to embed messages into ciphertexts based on a shared pseudorandom seed S. Note that S is merely unknown to the subverted algorithms but not random to an adversary accessing all the transmitted transcripts, so the thing is still not easy. Our method to embed a string str into a ciphertext is similar to the *biased-ciphertext attack* in [3]. Formally, we borrow the notations from [9] and present the embedding method in Algorithm 1.

Algorithm 1. Rejection sampler $\sum^{\mathsf{E},S}(\mathsf{str}, m, k)$

Public parameter: S (a d-bit seed)

Input: str is a v-bit string to be embedded, m is a plaintext and k is a ℓ-bit key.

1. Generate a q-bit ciphertext $C \leftarrow \mathsf{E}.\mathsf{Enc}(m, k)$.
2. If $\mathsf{H}(S||C||k) = \mathsf{str}$, then output C; else go to step 1.

Theorem 4. *Let* $\mathsf{H} : \{0,1\}^{d+q+\ell} \to \{0,1\}^v$ *be a hash function modeled as a random oracle.* E *is an encryption scheme with ciphertext space* $\{0,1\}^q$. $\sum^{\mathsf{E},S}$ *is defined as Algorithm 1. For any* $m \in \{0,1\}^p$ *and* $S \in \{0,1\}^d$, *the following properties hold:*

1. *Correctness: for any* $\mathsf{str} \in \{0,1\}^v$, $C = \sum^{\mathsf{E},S}(\mathsf{str}, m, k)$ *and* $\mathsf{str}' = \mathsf{H}(S||C||k)$, str' *equals* str.

2. *Security I: for* $\mathsf{str} \xleftarrow{\$} \{0,1\}^v$, *any* $k \in \{0,1\}^\ell$, $C' \leftarrow \sum^{\mathsf{E},S}(\mathsf{str}, m, k)$ *and* $C'' \leftarrow \sum^{\mathsf{E},U_d}(\mathsf{str}, m, k)$, *for any adversary* $\mathcal{A}$,
$$\mathsf{Adv}_{\sum,\mathcal{A}}^{\mathsf{SEC-I}}(\kappa) \stackrel{def}{=} \left|\Pr[\mathcal{A}(k, S, C') = 1] - \Pr[\mathcal{A}(k, S, C'') = 1]\right| < \mathsf{negl}(\kappa).$$

3. *Security II: for* $\mathsf{str} \xleftarrow{\$} \{0,1\}^v$, *any* $k \in \{0,1\}^\ell$, $C \leftarrow \mathsf{E}.\mathsf{Enc}(m, k)$, *and* $C'' \leftarrow \sum^{\mathsf{E},U_d}(\mathsf{str}, m, k)$, *for any adversary* $\mathcal{A}$,
$$\mathsf{Adv}_{\sum,\mathcal{A}}^{\mathsf{SEC-II}}(\kappa) \stackrel{def}{=} \left|\Pr[\mathcal{A}(k, C'') = 1] - \Pr[\mathcal{A}(k, C) = 1]\right| < \mathsf{negl}(\kappa).$$

4. *Security III: for* $k \xleftarrow{\$} \{0,1\}^\ell$, *any* $\mathsf{str} \in \{0,1\}^v$, $C' \leftarrow \sum^{\mathsf{E},S}(\mathsf{str}, m, k)$ *and* $C'' \leftarrow \sum^{\mathsf{E},U_d}(\mathsf{str}, m, k)$, *for any adversary* $\mathcal{A}$,
$$\mathsf{Adv}_{\sum,\mathcal{A}}^{\mathsf{SEC-III}}(\kappa) \stackrel{def}{=} \left|\Pr[\mathcal{A}(\mathsf{str}, S, C') = 1] - \Pr[\mathcal{A}(\mathsf{str}, S, C'') = 1]\right| < \mathsf{negl}(\kappa).$$

5. *Security IV: for* $k \stackrel{\$}{\leftarrow} \{0,1\}^{\ell}$, *str* $\in \{0,1\}^{v}$, $C \leftarrow \mathsf{E.Enc}(m,k)$ *and* $C'' \leftarrow$
$\sum^{\mathsf{E},U_d}(\text{str}, m, k)$, *for any adversary* $\mathcal{A}$,

$$\mathsf{Adv}_{\sum,\mathcal{A}}^{\mathsf{SEC-IV}}(\kappa) \stackrel{def}{=} \left| \Pr[\mathcal{A}(\text{str}, C'') = 1] - \Pr[\mathcal{A}(\text{str}, C) = 1] \right| < \mathsf{negl}(\kappa).$$

Proof. The correctness directly follows from the definition of Algorithm 1.

Security I: for randomness of str and randomness of the output of a hash function, we have $||(k, S, \text{str}) - (k, S, \mathsf{H}(S||C''||k))||_{\mathsf{s}} \leq \mathsf{negl}(\kappa)$. Apply $\sum^{\mathsf{E},S}(\cdot, m, k)$ on both str and $\mathsf{H}(S||C''||k)$, and the statistical distance can only decrease, hence $||(k, S, C') - (k, S, C'')||_{\mathsf{s}} \leq \mathsf{negl}(\kappa)$.

Security II: for randomness of str and randomness of the output of a hash function, we have $||(k, \mathsf{H}(U_d||C||k)) - (k, \text{str})||_{\mathsf{s}} \leq \mathsf{negl}(\kappa)$. Apply $\sum^{\mathsf{E},U_d}(\cdot, m, k)$ on both $\mathsf{H}(U_d||C||k)$ and str, and the statistical distance can only decrease, hence $||(k, C) - (k, C'')||_{\mathsf{s}} \leq \mathsf{negl}(\kappa)$.

Security III and Security IV follow from the security of a hash function. Due to page limit, readers are refered to the security analysis of biased-ciphertext attack in [3] for a similar proof.

5.3   Full Protocol

At first sight, our protocol is similar to the design in [9]. However, there are two significant differences. (1) In our design, parties in the protocol cannot get access to a non-subverted implementation of cryptographic algorithm, in other word, they can only make key-exchange by corrupted key-exchange protocols and encrypt messages using backdoored encryption implementations. (2) We define the subverted implementations to be stateful and they remember all the previous inputs. This increases the hardness of pseudorandom seed establishing because a subverted implementation may choose the current output adaptively according to the previous outputs. We deal with this problem by using the pseudorandom seed establishing method discussed in Sect. 5.1, which extracts every bit of the seed based on outputs of both parties. Therefore, the result still remains random even knowing all outputs of either side.

Our full protocol consists of four phases. In the key-exchange phase, two parties run the key-exchange protocol KE_0 honestly and get a shared symmetric key $k_0||k_1$. In the shared seed establishing phase, two parties run the encryption scheme E_0 honestly, and extract a pseudorandom seed S from the ciphertexts. In the subliminal key-exchange phase, two parties run the key-exchange protocol KE_1 subliminally and embed the transcripts into innocuous messages by $\sum^{\mathsf{E}_0,S}$. In the subliminal communication phase, the sender first encrypts the message msg using E_1, and then embeds the ciphertext into innocuous messages by $\sum^{\mathsf{E}_0,S}$.

Key-Exchange Phase Φ (Honestly Run KE_0)
Set $\lambda_{1,0} \leftarrow \bot$. For $i \in [r']$

- P_0 receives $\lambda_{1,i-1}$, runs $(\lambda_{0,i}, s_{0,i}) \leftarrow \mathsf{KE}_0.\Lambda_{0,i}(s_{0,i-1}, \lambda_{1,i-1})$ and sends $\lambda_{0,i}$ to P_1.
- P_1 receives $\lambda_{0,i}$, runs $(\lambda_{1,i}, s_{1,i}) \leftarrow \mathsf{KE}_0.\Lambda_{1,i}(s_{1,i-1}, \lambda_{0,i})$ and sends $\lambda_{1,i}$ to P_0.

At the end of the protocol, each party invokes $k \leftarrow \mathsf{KE_0}.\Lambda_{b,\mathsf{out}}(s_{b,r'})$, parse k as $k_0||k_1$ of equal length, and adds them into its state.

Communication Phase Π

(a) **Shared seed establishing phase**

For $i \in [d]$, P_b ($b \in \{0,1\}$) does:
- Run $m_{b,i} \leftarrow \mathcal{M}(\tau_{b,i})$ and send $C_{b,i} \leftarrow \mathsf{E_0}.\mathsf{Enc}(m_{b,i}, k_b)$ to P_{1-b}.
- Add the transcripts of all protocol messages into its updated state.
At the end of the d exchange-rounds, each party updates its state to contain the seed $S = \mathsf{BD}(C_{0,1}, C_{1,1})||\mathsf{BD}(C_{0,2}, C_{1,2})|| \cdots ||\mathsf{BD}(C_{0,d}, C_{1,d})$.

(b) **Subliminal key-exchange phase**

Let $p = \frac{u}{v}$, where u is the length of $\lambda_{b,i}$. This phase takes $r' \cdot p$ exchange-rounds. Set $\lambda_{1,0} \leftarrow \perp$.
For $j \in [r']$ and $b \in \{0,1\}$
- P_b generates the transcript in this round using $\mathsf{KE_1}$.
  if $b = 0$, $(\lambda_{0,j}, \varsigma_{0,j}) \leftarrow \mathsf{KE_1}.\Lambda_{0,j}(\varsigma_{0,j-1}, \lambda_{1,j-1})$;
  else, $(\lambda_{1,j}, \varsigma_{1,j}) \leftarrow \mathsf{KE_1}.\Lambda_{1,j}(\varsigma_{1,j}, \lambda_{0,j})$.
- P_b parses $\lambda_{b,j}$ into v-bit blocks $\lambda_{b,j} \rightarrow \lambda_{b,j}^1|| \cdots ||\lambda_{b,j}^p$.
- For $q \in [p]$, $i = d + (j-1)p + q$, P_b does:
  (1) Run $m_{b,i} \leftarrow \mathcal{M}(\tau_{b,i})$ and send $C_{b,i} \leftarrow \sum^{\mathsf{E_0},S}(\lambda_{b,i}^q, m_{b,i}, k_b)$ to P_{1-b}.
  (2) Renew the state to contain all the transcripts of protocol so far.
- At the end of the q exchange-rounds, P_{1-b} recovers $\lambda_{b,j}$ as
  $$\lambda_{b,j} \leftarrow \mathsf{H}(S||C_{b,d+(j-1)p+1}||k_b)|| \cdots ||\mathsf{H}(S||C_{b,d+(j-1)p+q}||k_b).$$
  and adds all the transcripts into its updated state.
At the end of the $r' \cdot p$ exchange-rounds, each party invokes $k^*||k' \leftarrow \mathsf{KE_1}.\Lambda_{b,\mathsf{out}}(\varsigma_{b,r'})$ and adds the subliminal secret key k^* into its state.

(c) **Subliminal communication phase**

This phase takes $t = \frac{\ell}{v}$ exchange-rounds.
P_0 computes $c^* \leftarrow \mathsf{E_1}.\mathsf{Enc}(msg, k^*)$, and parses c^* into v-bit blocks $c_1^*|| \cdots ||c_t^*$.
For $j \in [t]$, $i = d + r'p + j$
- P_0 invokes $m_{0,i} \leftarrow \mathcal{M}(\tau_{0,i})$ and $C_{0,i} \leftarrow \sum^{\mathsf{E_0},S}(c_j^*, m_{0,i}, k_0)$.
- P_1 invokes $m_{1,i} \leftarrow \mathcal{M}(\tau_{1,i})$ and $C_{1,i} \leftarrow \mathsf{E_0}.\mathsf{Enc}(m_{1,i}, k_1)$, and adds all the transcripts into its updated state.
After t exchange-rounds, P_1 does:
- $c^{**} \leftarrow \mathsf{H}(S||C_{0,d+r'p+1}||k_0)|| \cdots ||\mathsf{H}(S||C_{0,d+r'p+t}||k_0)$.
- Output $msg' \leftarrow \mathsf{E_0}.\mathsf{Dec}(k^*, c^{**})$.

It is straightforward to show the correctness of the above protocol.

5.4 Security Analysis

Theorem 5. *Assume* KE_0 *and* KE_1 *are two implementations of a pseudo-random key-exchange protocol* KE; E_0 *and* E_1 *are two implementations of a CPR secure encryption scheme* E. *All the implementations satisfy algorithm-indistinguishability defined in Sect. 2.3. Then the subliminal communication protocol* (Φ, Π) *in Sect. 5.3 satisfies the security in Definition 4.*

Proof (sketch). We use game sequence and define the following hybrids:

– HYBRID 0: Parties execute (Φ, Π) in Sect. 5.3.
– HYBRID 1: Exactly like HYBRID 0 except that the seed S in the shared seed establishing phase is replaced by a uniformly random string.
– HYBRID 2_X: Exactly like HYBRID 1 except that the KE_1 in the subliminal key-exchange phase is replaced by a non-subverted implementation KE.
– HYBRID 3_X: Exactly like HYBRID 2_X except that the $\lambda_{b,i}$ and $k^*\|k'$ in the subliminal key-exchange phase are replaced by uniformly random strings.
– HYBRID 4_X: Exactly like HYBRID 3_X except that the E_1 in the subliminal communication phase is replaced by a non-subverted implementation E.
– HYBRID 5_X: Exactly like HYBRID 4_X except that the c^* in the subliminal communication phase is replaced by a uniformly random string.
– HYBRID 2_Y: Exactly like HYBRID 1 except that the implementation KE_0 in the key-exchange phase Φ is replaced by the non-subverted algorithm KE.
– HYBRID 3_Y: Exactly like HYBRID 2_Y except that the secret keys $k_0\|k_1$ and $\lambda_{b,i}$ in the key-exchange phase Φ are replaced by uniformly random strings.
– HYBRID 4_Y: Exactly like HYBRID 3_Y except that the implementation E_0 in the communication phase Π is replaced by a non-subverted algorithm E.
– HYBRID 5_Y: Exactly like Ideal in Fig. 2 except that the $k_0\|k_1$ is replaced by $U_{2\ell}$.

We define the advantage of B_0 and B_1 in HYBRID N as

$$\mathsf{Adv}^N_{\mathsf{B}_0}(\kappa) \overset{def}{=} \Big| \Pr[\mathsf{B}_0(\mathsf{Subversion}_0(\mathcal{M}); \widetilde{\mathsf{BK}}_{\mathsf{E}_0}, \widetilde{\mathsf{BK}}_{\mathsf{KE}_0}) = 1]$$
$$- \Pr[\mathsf{B}_0(\mathsf{Subliminal}_{\Phi,\Pi}(\mathsf{msg}, \mathcal{M}); \widetilde{\mathsf{BK}}_{\mathsf{E}_0}, \widetilde{\mathsf{BK}}_{\mathsf{KE}_0}) = 1]\Big|,$$
$$\mathsf{Adv}^N_{\mathsf{B}_1}(\kappa) \overset{def}{=} \Big| \Pr[\mathsf{B}_1(\mathsf{Ideal}(\mathcal{M}); \widetilde{\mathsf{BK}}_{\mathsf{E}_1}, \widetilde{\mathsf{BK}}_{\mathsf{KE}_1}) = 1]$$
$$- \Pr[\mathsf{B}_1(\mathsf{Subliminal}_{\Phi,\Pi}(\mathsf{msg}, \mathcal{M}); \widetilde{\mathsf{BK}}_{\mathsf{E}_1}, \widetilde{\mathsf{BK}}_{\mathsf{KE}_1}) = 1]\Big|.$$

HYBRID 0 and HYBRID 1: Due to Security I and Security III in Theorem 4, we can design two PPT adversaries $\mathcal{A}_1$ and $\mathcal{A}_2$ that satisfy $\big|\mathsf{Adv}^0_{\mathsf{B}_0}(\kappa) - \mathsf{Adv}^1_{\mathsf{B}_0}(\kappa)\big| \leq \mathsf{Adv}^{\mathsf{SEC-I}}_{\Sigma, \mathcal{A}_1}(\kappa)/2$ and $\big|\mathsf{Adv}^0_{\mathsf{B}_1}(\kappa) - \mathsf{Adv}^1_{\mathsf{B}_1}(\kappa)\big| \leq \mathsf{Adv}^{\mathsf{SEC-III}}_{\Sigma, \mathcal{A}_2}(\kappa)/2$.

HYBRID 1 and HYBRID 2_X: We design a PPT watchdog W_1 that distinguishes $\{\mathsf{KE}, \mathsf{KE}_1\}$ based on B_0's output. W_1 receives its input $\mathsf{KE}^* \in \{\mathsf{KE}, \mathsf{KE}_1\}$ and samples $b' \overset{\$}{\leftarrow} \{0,1\}$. If $b' = 0$, W_1 generates $\mathsf{Subversion}_0(\mathcal{M})$, else it generates $\mathsf{Subliminal}_{\Phi,\Pi}(\mathsf{msg}, \mathcal{M})$ as HYBRID 1 except using KE^* in the subliminal key-exchange phase. W_1 sends the transcript to B_0 and gets B_0's output b''.

If $b'' = b'$, W_1 outputs 1, else W_1 outputs 0. Following from the algorithm-indistinguishability of KE_1 we have $\left| \mathsf{Adv}_{B_0}^1(\kappa) - \mathsf{Adv}_{B_0}^{2x}(\kappa) \right| \leq \mathsf{Det}_{W_1}^{KE_1}(\kappa)/2$.

HYBRID 2_X and HYBRID 3_X: We design a PPT adversary $\mathcal{A}_3$ that breaks the pseudorandomness of the key-exchange protocol KE based on B_0's output. $\mathcal{A}_3$ takes as input $(\{\lambda_{b,i}^*\}_{b\in\{0,1\},i\in[r]}, k^*) \in \{(\{\lambda_{b,i}\}_{b\in\{0,1\},i\in[r]}, k), (U, U_{|k|})\}$ and samples $b' \xleftarrow{\$} \{0,1\}$. If $b' = 0$, $\mathcal{A}_3$ generates $\mathsf{Subversion}_0(\mathcal{M})$, else $\mathcal{A}_3$ generates $\mathsf{Subliminal}_{\Phi,\Pi}(\mathsf{msg}, \mathcal{M})$ as HYBRID 2_X except that it embeds $(\{\lambda_{b,i}^*\}_{b\in\{0,1\},i\in[r]}, k^*)$ as the transcripts and the key in the subliminal key-exchange phase. $\mathcal{A}_3$ sends the transcript to B_0 and gets B_0's output b''. If $b'' = b'$, $\mathcal{A}_3$ outputs 1, else $\mathcal{A}_3$ outputs 0. Due to the pseudorandomness of KE, we have $\left| \mathsf{Adv}_{B_0}^{2x}(\kappa) - \mathsf{Adv}_{B_0}^{3x}(\kappa) \right| \leq \mathsf{Adv}_{KE,\mathcal{A}_3}^{PSE}(\kappa)/2$.

HYBRID 3_X and HYBRID 4_X: Similar to the analysis of HYBRID 1 and HYBRID 2_X, we have $\left| \mathsf{Adv}_{B_0}^{3x}(\kappa) - \mathsf{Adv}_{B_0}^{4x}(\kappa) \right| \leq \mathsf{Det}_{W_2}^{E_1}(\kappa)/2$.

HYBRID 4_X and HYBRID 5_X: Similar to the analysis of HYBRID 2_X and HYBRID 3_X, following from the CPR security of E, we have $\left| \mathsf{Adv}_{B_0}^{4x}(\kappa) - \mathsf{Adv}_{B_0}^{5x}(\kappa) \right| \leq \mathsf{Adv}_{E,\mathcal{A}_4}^{CPR}(\kappa)/2$.

HYBRID 5_X is only different to the distribution of $\mathsf{Subversion}_0(\mathcal{M})$ by using $\sum^{E_0, U_d}(U_v, m, k_b)$ instead of $E_0.\mathsf{Enc}(m, k_b)$ in the communication phase Π. Following from Security II in Theorem 4, we have $\mathsf{Adv}_{B_0}^{5x}(\kappa) \leq \mathsf{Adv}_{\Sigma, \mathcal{A}_5}^{SEC-II}(\kappa)$.

HYBRID 1 and HYBRID 2_Y: Similar to the analysis of HYBRID 1 and HYBRID 2_X, we have $\left| \mathsf{Adv}_{B_1}^1(\kappa) - \mathsf{Adv}_{B_1}^{2y}(\kappa) \right| \leq \mathsf{Det}_{W_3}^{KE_0}(\kappa)/2$.

HYBRID 2_Y and HYBRID 3_Y: Similar to the analysis of HYBRID 2_X and HYBRID 3_X, we have $\left| \mathsf{Adv}_{B_1}^{2y}(\kappa) - \mathsf{Adv}_{B_1}^{3y}(\kappa) \right| \leq \mathsf{Adv}_{KE,\mathcal{A}_6}^{PSE}(\kappa)/2$.

HYBRID 3_Y and HYBRID 4_Y: Similar to the analysis of HYBRID 1 and HYBRID 2_X, we have $\left| \mathsf{Adv}_{B_1}^{3y}(\kappa) - \mathsf{Adv}_{B_1}^{4y}(\kappa) \right| \leq \mathsf{Det}_{W_4}^{E_0}(\kappa)/2$.

HYBRID 4_Y and HYBRID 5_Y: The only difference lies in that in the communication phase Π, HYBRID 4_Y runs $\sum^{E, U_d}(\mathsf{str}, m, U_\ell)$ whereas HYBRID 5_Y runs $E.\mathsf{Enc}(m, U_\ell)$. Following from Security IV in Theorem 4 we have $\left| \mathsf{Adv}_{B_1}^{4y}(\kappa) - \mathsf{Adv}_{B_1}^{5y}(\kappa) \right| \leq \mathsf{Adv}_{\Sigma, \mathcal{A}_7}^{SEC-IV}(\kappa)/2$.

HYBRID 5_Y: Following from the pseudorandomness of the key-exchange protocol KE, we have $\mathsf{Adv}_{B_1}^{5y}(\kappa) \leq \mathsf{Adv}_{KE,\mathcal{A}_8}^{PSE}(\kappa)$. Hence, we have

$$\mathsf{Adv}_{B_0}^0(\kappa) \leq \left(\mathsf{Adv}_{\Sigma, \mathcal{A}_1}^{SEC-I}(\kappa) + \mathsf{Det}_{W_1}^{KE_1}(\kappa) + \mathsf{Adv}_{KE,\mathcal{A}_3}^{PSE}(\kappa) + \mathsf{Det}_{W_2}^{E_1}(\kappa) + \mathsf{Adv}_{E,\mathcal{A}_4}^{CPR}(\kappa) \right.$$
$$\left. + 2 \cdot \mathsf{Adv}_{\Sigma, \mathcal{A}_5}^{SEC-II}(\kappa) \right)/2 < \mathsf{negl}(\kappa),$$
$$\mathsf{Adv}_{B_1}^0(\kappa) \leq \left(\mathsf{Adv}_{\Sigma, \mathcal{A}_2}^{SEC-III}(\kappa) + \mathsf{Det}_{W_3}^{KE_0}(\kappa) + \mathsf{Adv}_{KE,\mathcal{A}_6}^{PSE}(\kappa) + \mathsf{Det}_{W_4}^{E_0}(\kappa) \right.$$
$$\left. + 2 \cdot \mathsf{Adv}_{KE,\mathcal{A}_8}^{PSE}(\kappa) + \mathsf{Adv}_{\Sigma, \mathcal{A}_7}^{SEC-IV}(\kappa) \right)/2 < \mathsf{negl}(\kappa).$$

It suffices to prove Theorem 5.

5.5   Further Discussion and Open Problems

For simplicity, in this paper we only consider the case where all surveillants provide subverted implementations of the same specifications, i.e., subverted implementations aim at achieving the same function. However, in reality, users could adopt implementations of different algorithms to achieve subliminal communication. We leave this as a future work.

In our model all surveillants have no cooperation, as different surveillants may stay in a hostile relationship. However, we could further consider the case where surveillants cooperate and communicate without leaking their backdoors. This will bring great difficulties for subliminal communication.

Acknowledgment. The work is supported partly by Beijing Natural Science Foundation (4182033) and National Cryptography Development Fund (MMJJ20180215). We sincerely thank anonymous reviewers for valuable comments, especially about the definition of cover message.

References

1. Bellare, M., Fuchsbauer, G., Scafuro, A.: NIZKs with an untrusted CRS: security in the face of parameter subversion. In: Cheon, J.H., Takagi, T. (eds.) ASIACRYPT 2016. LNCS, vol. 10032, pp. 777–804. Springer, Heidelberg (2016). https://doi.org/10.1007/978-3-662-53890-6_26
2. Bellare, M., Jaeger, J., Kane, D.: Mass-surveillance without the state: strongly undetectable algorithm-substitution attacks. In: ACM CCS, pp. 1431–1440 (2015)
3. Bellare, M., Paterson, K.G., Rogaway, P.: Security of symmetric encryption against mass surveillance. In: Garay, J.A., Gennaro, R. (eds.) CRYPTO 2014. LNCS, vol. 8616, pp. 1–19. Springer, Heidelberg (2014). https://doi.org/10.1007/978-3-662-44371-2_1
4. Bernstein, D.J., Lange, T., Niederhagen, R.: Dual EC: a standardized back door. In: Ryan, P.Y.A., Naccache, D., Quisquater, J.-J. (eds.) The New Codebreakers. LNCS, vol. 9100, pp. 256–281. Springer, Heidelberg (2016). https://doi.org/10.1007/978-3-662-49301-4_17
5. Chen, R., Mu, Y., Yang, G., Susilo, W., Guo, F., Zhang, M.: Cryptographic reverse firewall via malleable smooth projective hash functions. In: Cheon, J.H., Takagi, T. (eds.) ASIACRYPT 2016. LNCS, vol. 10031, pp. 844–876. Springer, Heidelberg (2016). https://doi.org/10.1007/978-3-662-53887-6_31
6. Degabriele, J.P., Farshim, P., Poettering, B.: A more cautious approach to security against mass surveillance. In: Leander, G. (ed.) FSE 2015. LNCS, vol. 9054, pp. 579–598. Springer, Heidelberg (2015). https://doi.org/10.1007/978-3-662-48116-5_28
7. Dodis, Y., Mironov, I., Stephens-Davidowitz, N.: Message transmission with reverse firewalls—secure communication on corrupted machines. In: Robshaw, M., Katz, J. (eds.) CRYPTO 2016. LNCS, vol. 9814, pp. 341–372. Springer, Heidelberg (2016). https://doi.org/10.1007/978-3-662-53018-4_13
8. Fischlin, M., Mazaheri, S.: Self-guarding cryptographic protocols against algorithm substitution attacks. In: CSF, pp. 76–90 (2018)
9. Horel, T., Park, S., Richelson, S., Vaikuntanathan, V.: How to subvert backdoored encryption: security against adversaries that decrypt all ciphertexts. In: ITCS (2019, to appear)
10. Mironov, I., Stephens-Davidowitz, N.: Cryptographic reverse firewalls. In: Oswald, E., Fischlin, M. (eds.) EUROCRYPT 2015. LNCS, vol. 9057, pp. 657–686. Springer, Heidelberg (2015). https://doi.org/10.1007/978-3-662-46803-6_22

11. Russell, A., Tang, Q., Yung, M., Zhou, H.-S.: Cliptography: clipping the power of kleptographic attacks. In: Cheon, J.H., Takagi, T. (eds.) ASIACRYPT 2016. LNCS, vol. 10032, pp. 34–64. Springer, Heidelberg (2016). https://doi.org/10.1007/978-3-662-53890-6_2

12. Russell, A., Tang, Q., Yung, M., Zhou, H.: Generic semantic security against a kleptographic adversary. In: ACM CCS, pp. 907–922 (2017)

13. Young, A., Yung, M.: The dark side of "Black-Box" cryptography or: should we trust capstone? In: Koblitz, N. (ed.) CRYPTO 1996. LNCS, vol. 1109, pp. 89–103. Springer, Heidelberg (1996). https://doi.org/10.1007/3-540-68697-5_8

14. Young, A., Yung, M.: Kleptography: using cryptography against cryptography. In: Fumy, W. (ed.) EUROCRYPT 1997. LNCS, vol. 1233, pp. 62–74. Springer, Heidelberg (1997). https://doi.org/10.1007/3-540-69053-0_6

15. Young, A., Yung, M.: The prevalence of kleptographic attacks on discrete-log based cryptosystems. In: Kaliski, B.S. (ed.) CRYPTO 1997. LNCS, vol. 1294, pp. 264–276. Springer, Heidelberg (1997). https://doi.org/10.1007/BFb0052241

16. Young, A., Yung, M.: Malicious cryptography: kleptographic aspects. In: Menezes, A. (ed.) CT-RSA 2005. LNCS, vol. 3376, pp. 7–18. Springer, Heidelberg (2005). https://doi.org/10.1007/978-3-540-30574-3_2

System and Network Security

Dimensionality Reduction and Visualization of Network Intrusion Detection Data

Wei Zong, Yang-Wai Chow[✉], and Willy Susilo

Institute of Cybersecurity and Cryptology,
School of Computing and Information Technology, University of Wollongong,
Wollongong, NSW, Australia
wz630@uowmail.edu.au, {caseyc,wsusilo}@uow.edu.au

Abstract. Nowadays, network intrusion detection is researched extensively due to increasing global network threats. Many researchers propose to incorporate machine learning techniques in network intrusion detection systems since these techniques allow for automated intrusion detection with high accuracy. Furthermore, dimensionality reduction techniques can improve the performance of machine learning models, and as such, are widely used as a pre-processing step. Nevertheless, many researchers consider machine learning techniques as a black box because of its complex intrinsic mechanism. Visualization plays an important role in facilitating the understanding of such sophisticated techniques because visualization is able to offer intuitive meaning to the machine learning results. This research investigates the performance of two dimensionality reduction techniques on network intrusion detection datasets. In addition, this work also demonstrates visualizing the resulting data in 3-dimensional space. The purpose of this is to possibly gain insight into the results, which can potentially aid in the improvement of machine learning performance.

Keywords: Dimensionality reduction · Machine learning ·
Network intrusion detection · Visualization

1 Introduction

The Internet is essential in daily life for almost everyone in contemporary society. Meanwhile, there has been extensive research conducted on Network Intrusion Detection Systems (NIDS) due to the increasing global threat of cyberattacks. Machine learning techniques have been proposed by cyber security experts as a promising solution for NIDS to combat cyberattacks. This is because machine learning can provide an automated approach to detecting intrusions with high accuracy [13].

To improve the intrusion detection performance of machine learning models, techniques for dimensionality reduction are widely used as one of the pre-processing steps [3,11]. Wang et al. [16] investigated different dimensionality

© Springer Nature Switzerland AG 2019
J. Jang-Jaccard and F. Guo (Eds.): ACISP 2019, LNCS 11547, pp. 441–455, 2019.
https://doi.org/10.1007/978-3-030-21548-4_24

reduction techniques and concluded that the autoencoder technique outperforms other dimensionality reduction techniques in certain situations. This technique has also been adopted for the purpose of network intrusion detection. As an example, the autoencoder technique was used in Javaid et al. [4] to learn new feature representation before using a soft-max regression for classification.

Although some machine learning models can provide adequate intrusion detection performances, the underlying reasons that affect accuracy are not usually analyzed. Furthermore, improvement of machine learning models usually rely on a time-consuming trial-and-error process due of the complex nature of machine learning mechanisms [7]. The reason for this is because machine learning is typically treated as a black box, and while the performance might be impressive, researchers may not know the theoretical link between a machine learning model and its performance [16].

Information visualization techniques can potentially bridge the gap between the performance of machine learning models and understanding factors that contribute to its performance. Visualization, whether in 2-dimensions (2D) or 3-dimensions (3D), also plays an important role in the cyber security domain [14]. In addition, previous work has shown that complex attack patterns in NIDS can be visualized in various forms [1,9]. Previous research in this area includes a visual approach to analyzing the characteristics of network intrusion detection datasets in 3D space [17]. Visualization makes these characteristics more comprehendible and intuitive, while they may be difficult to perceive when using traditional statistical data analysis alone [7].

In this paper, we first investigate the performance of two dimensionality reduction techniques on the benchmark NSL_KDD and UNSW-NB15 network intrusion datasets. The results show the relationship between the number of dimensions and the intrusion detection performance. This allows us to identify the number of dimensions that will give rise to good performance for different classifiers. We then implement a method to visualize the data in 3D, in order to observe patterns in the data and to gain a better understanding of the machine learning results. In this visual form, the data is more intuitive and potential insight can be gained to improve machine learning performance.

Our Contributions. This paper investigates and compares the performance of two dimensionality reduction techniques, namely, the principal component analysis and autoencoder techniques, for network intrusion detection using three different classifiers. The classifiers that were used in this study were the k-nearest neighbors classifier, the multi-layer perceptron classifier and the decision tree classifier. Results of our experiments show the relationship between the number of dimensions and the intrusion detection performance for the respective classifiers. This paper also demonstrates how visually presenting the results in 3D space can facilitate the intuitive identifying of patterns in the data. This can potentially provide useful insight that can be used to understand and improve machine learning performance, rather than relying on the usual trial-and-error process.

2   Background

2.1   Dimensionality Reduction

Dimensionality reduction is used in a number of areas, including for machine learning. The research presented in this paper investigates the use of two of these techniques for the purpose of network intrusion detection.

Principal Component Analysis (PCA) is a commonly used dimensionality reduction technique for projecting data onto new axes which are orthogonal to each other [5]. In PCA, the first principal component captures the largest variance, while the second principal component capture the largest variance among the remaining orthogonal directions, etc. Therefore, each principal component captures the largest variance excluding the preceding principal components. To project data into 3D space, an approach is to only use data from the first 3 principal components.

Autoencoder is a type of artificial neural network that can be used for dimensionality reduction. This is because it can automatically learn feature representation of the data. The autoencoder technique consists of an encoder and a decoder. When the number of nodes in the hidden layer are made smaller than the input nodes, autoencoder can learn a compressed presentation of the data. In this manner, autoencoder is capable of reducing the dimensions of the input data. Compared with other dimensionality reduction techniques, autoencoder may produce more favorable results in certain situations and can detect repetitive characteristics in datasets [16].

2.2   Network Intrusion Detection Datasets

Network intrusion detection datasets are important when it comes to validating the performance of NIDS. Benchmark datasets for NIDS, namely, KDD98, KDD CUP99 and NSL_KDD, are widely used in research to compare results of intrusion detection methods. These datasets categorize network attacks into different types, e.g., Denial of Service (DoS) attacks, probe attacks, Remote to Local (R2L) and User to Root (U2R) attacks. However, it has been contended that these datasets are outdated since they were proposed more than a decade ago. In addition, they contain some flaws which negatively affect the performance of NIDS [8]. To reflect contemporary cyber traffic, the UNSW-NB15 dataset was proposed [10]. In addition to normal connections, this dataset contains 9 types of network attacks, including worm and shellcode attacks. Although in this paper, we utilize NSL_KDD and UNSW-NB15 datasets for our experiments, our proposed approach can be applied to other network intrusion detection datasets.

2.3   Related Work

Dimensionality reduction techniques can improve the performance of machine learning models. Among various techniques, PCA and autoencoder are widely used to reduce the high number of dataset dimensions before classification.

Moustafa et al. [11] used the PCA technique to reduce the high dimension of the network intrusion datasets before classifying cyberattacks. de la Hoz Correa et al. [3] also used the PCA technique to select useful features and to remove noise in network intrusion data. Javaid et al. [4] used the autoencoder technique to learn a feature representation of the NSL_KDD dataset. Then, they used soft-max regression to do the classification and achieved competitive results. Wang et al. [16] compared autoencoder with other commonly used dimensionality reduction techniques, such as PCA and Isomap, on synthesized data and image datasets. Their study showed that results obtained from the use of autoencoder differed from other dimensionality reduction techniques, and concluded that the autoencoder technique is potentially suitable for detecting repetitive structures in datasets.

In the NIDS domain, machine learning approaches have been extensively studied as these are seen as promising solutions towards automating the detection of abnormal network connections with high accuracy [13]. For example, Lin et al. [6] considered the geometric relationship between data records and proposed a novel feature representation method. They then used a k-Nearest Neighbors (kNN) classifier to detect cyberattacks. Wang et al. [15] proposed a multi-step NIDS. They first divided the training set into subsets by fuzzy clustering. Subsequently, they trained an artificial neural network on each subset. Finally, the detection results were combined using a fuzzy aggregation module. Their method was reported to achieve high network intrusion detection performance. In addition, a two-stage approach for network intrusion detention has also been proposed, where different machine learning models can be used in the different stages [18]. An advantage of this approach is that it can deal with the extremely imbalanced characteristics of network intrusion datasets.

Although machine learning models can achieved satisfactory results, the underlying reasons affecting accuracy are still not well understood. As an example, Javaid et al. [4] demonstrated the competitive performance of their approach without analyzing the reasons for misclassification. Moustafa et al. [11] proposed a novel approach, called geometric area analysis based on trapezoidal area estimation for NIDS. Their approach effectively detected intrusions in the NSL_KDD and UNSW-NB15 datasets. However, they did not analyze misclassification in detail. It has been argued that without a comprehensive and intuitive understanding of the underlying reasons that cause misclassification, the improvement of machine learning models usually relies on a time-consuming trial-and-error process due to the complex nature of machine learning mechanisms [7].

Visualization techniques can be used to facilitate the development of machine learning models since these techniques can show characteristics that humans can understand intuitively. Rauber et al. [12] proposed to visualize relationships between learned representations of observations, and relationships between artificial neurons. They performed this projection using t-distributed Stochastic Neighbor Embedding (t-SNE), so that they could view the data in 2D space. In other work, Liu et al. [7] proposed a system for enabling users to perform visual analysis to help understand, diagnose and refine deep convolution neural networks.

Visualization approaches have also been proposed in the field of network intrusion detection. Angelini et al. [1] described a cyber security visualization system that can facilitate user awareness of cyber security statuses and events. McKenna et al. [9] showed a cyber security dashboard that can help experts understand global attack patterns. An approach to visualizing network intrusion datasets in 3D space was presented in Zong et al. [17]. Results of this approach demonstrated that it can be used to identify visual characteristics in the datasets, which can potentially contribute to improving detection performance of machine learning models in NIDS.

3   Proposed Approach

In this section, we describe the details of our proposed approach. In essence, the purpose of this work is to examine dimensionality reduction and visualization for network intrusion detection. For this, we investigated the relationship between the number of dimensions and intrusion detection performance. This allowed for the identification of a good value for dimension reduction that will produce reasonably good performance for different classifiers. We then implemented a method to visualize the data in 3D, in order to examine the intrusion detection results from the visual representation. The various stages involved in the overall process is depicted in Fig. 1.

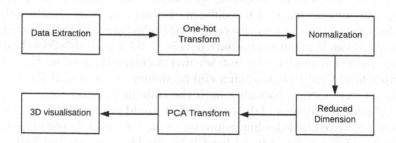

Fig. 1. Stages in the proposed approach.

The NSL_KDD and UNSW-NB15 network intrusion detection datasets were used in this study. The first step was to extract data from the original datasets. NSL_KDD and UNSW-NB15 are known as imbalanced datasets, because they contain minor classes that only occupy a relatively small proportion of the dataset, whereas the remainder of the dataset consists of major classes [18]. For example, worm attacks in the UNSW-NB15 occupy <1% of the dataset, similarly U2R attacks in the NSL_KDD only represents a minor portion of the dataset.

Methods to improve the intrusion detection performance of imbalanced datasets is to over-sample minor classes, to down-sample major classes, or both [2]. Therefore, in the data extraction stage, we extracted all minor classes from the dataset. Then, we randomly extracted other classes until a certain percentage, 30% in our experiments, of the dataset was extracted to establish our training set. Other than our training set, we also extracted data from the original training set which accounted for 10% of the data to establish a validation set. Since the training set includes all the minor classes, the minor classes in the validation set are repeated in the training set. However, other classes in the validation set are not repeated in the training set. In this way, we could use less computational power to achieve satisfactory detection results and the visual quality in 3D space was not adversely affected.

Subsequently, one-hot transform was applied to the categorical features in the datasets since the dimensionality reduction techniques adopted in our experiments, i.e. PCA and autoencoder, only operate on numeric data and are not suitable for categorical features. After one-hot transformation, only numeric data remains. It should be noted that, one-hot transform is applied to the training and test sets separately. Consequently, the training set may generate some features that do not exist in the test set and vice versa. This may happen because some categorical values may exist in only one set but not in both sets. To handle this situation, we only used features in the transformed training set. In this way, whenever the training set contains features that were missing in the test set, a value of zero would be used. On the other hand, if the test set contains some features that the training set did not contain, such features were ignored.

The next step was to normalize the data. Normalization was performed because the numeric range of the different features can vary significantly. For example, some features range between 0 to 100, while other features range from 0 to several million. Without normalization, this would negatively affect the dimensionality reduction results. The test set was normalized based on the training data. Specifically, only the maximum and minimum values of each feature in the training set were used to normalize both the training and test sets.

To examine the number of dimensions that would produce the best detection performance, we reduced the dimensions to a range of values. In our experiments, the number of dimensions ranged from 2 to 30. Then, we applied basic classifiers, such as k-nearest neighbors and decision trees to the data. The number of dimensions that gave rise to reasonably good performance for all classifiers was identified to be as the best value to use for dimensionality reduction.

Once this value was selected, dimensionality reduction was performed on the original data to transform the data into the specific number of dimensions. The PCA technique was then used to transform the data into 3D space in order to visualize the results. The reason why the PCA algorithm was used is because PCA transformation can be inversed. In this manner, when performing visual examination on certain areas of the data in 3D space, the data can be inversed and examined in higher dimension space. Thus, allowing us to adequately analyze the detection performance using the visual form.

4   Results and Discussion

In this section, we describe our experiment results. Experiments using the proposed approach were performed on both the UNSW-NB15 and NSL-KDD datasets. First, we present results of the dimensionality reduction study using the autoencoder and PCA techniques, respectively. We project the extracted data to lower dimension spaces, ranging from 2 to 30, to find the number of dimensions that produced reasonably good performance for all classifiers. The classifiers that were used in the experiments were the k-Nearest Neighbors (kNN) classifier, the Multi-Layer Perceptron (MLP) classifier and the Decision Tree (DT) classifier. Subsequently, we present examples of results that demonstrate observable visual characteristics, which were obtained by projecting the data with the best number of dimensions into a 3D visual space.

4.1   Results for the UNSW-NB15 Dataset

Figures 2(a)–(c) and 3(a)–(c), depict results of accuracy trends that were obtained when the three different classifiers were applied to the validation set for binary classification and multiclass classification, respectively. The difference between binary classification and multiclass classification is that in binary classification, network traffic instances were either classified as normal traffic or abnormal traffic. Whereas in multiclass classification, the machine learning model was used to classify all categories of network traffic (e.g., normal traffic, DoS attacks, worm attacks, U2R attacks, exploits, etc.).

From Figs. 2 and 3, we can see that accuracy trends in the kNN and MLP results are more stable than accuracy trends in the DT results. In general, accuracy increases with the number of dimension. It can also be seen that the performance of dimensionality reduction based on autoencoder outperforms PCA for the kNN and MLP classifiers, since they achieve higher accuracy results when autoencoder is used. However, for the DT classifier it is less obvious as to which dimensionality reduction technique is better. Overall, autoencoder performs better than PCA in relation to dimensionality reduction and accuracy. From the

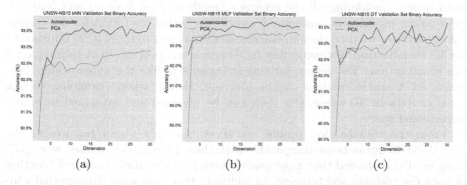

Fig. 2. UNSW-NB15 binary classification accuracy trends on the validation set using the (a) kNN classifier; (b) MLP classifier; (c) DT classifier.

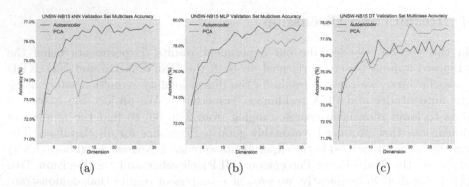

Fig. 3. UNSW-NB15 multiclass classification accuracy trends on the validation set using the (a) kNN classifier; (b) MLP classifier; (c) DT classifier.

figures, one can see that the trend is such that the intrusion detection accuracy typically increases as the dimensions increase, then remains relatively stable once the number of dimensions reaches a certain value.

From these results, our purpose is to find the number of dimensions at which all three classifiers perform reasonably well for both the autoencoder and PCA techniques. From Figs. 2 and 3, we can see that the value of 20 is a reasonable choice for the number of dimensions because at this value almost all classifiers are near their peak accuracy for PCA and autoencoder. To confirm our choice of the intrinsic number of dimensions, we also present results showing accuracy trends when experiments were conducted on the test set. This is shown in Figs. 4(a)–(c) and 5(a)–(c) for binary classification and multiclass classification, respectively.

From Figs. 4(a)–(c) and 5(a)–(c), it can be observed that although there is a greater degree of fluctuation, accuracy trends in the test set show similar characteristics to those in the validation set for both binary and multiclass classification. Overall, autoencoder still performs better than PCA for dimensionality reduction. In Fig. 5(c), there is an abrupt drop in accuracy when the number of dimensions is 18. This may be due to over-fitting of the DT classifier. Nevertheless, the other accuracy trends as shown in the figures are reasonable.

The value of 20 is still a reasonably good choice for the best number of dimensions, when considering all the accuracy trends in Figs. 4(a)–(c) and 5(a)–(c). Since in our experiments autoencoder performs better than PCA for dimensionality reduction, we used the autoencoder data that was reduced to 20 dimensions for 3D visualization. For projecting to 3D space, we used the PCA technique for the visualization. The reason for this is because unlike the autoencoder technique, PCA transformation can be inversed. Hence, when examining certain areas of data in 3D space, this data can be inversed and examined in higher dimensional space.

From the visualization results, we show that key visual features of the UNSW-NB15 datasets are comparable with those presented in related work [17]. Zong et al. [17] showed that most generic attacks are visually clustered together in both the training and test sets. In addition, there are some clusters that contain only normal connections in both the training and test sets. Their results

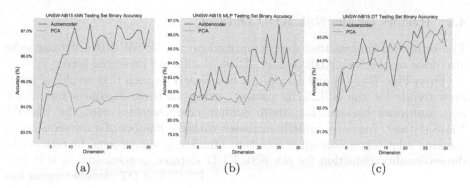

Fig. 4. UNSW-NB15 binary classification accuracy trends on the test set using the (a) kNN classifier; (b) MLP classifier; (c) DT classifier.

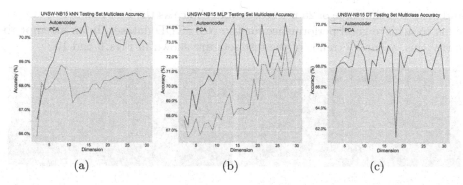

Fig. 5. UNSW-NB15 multiclass classification accuracy trends in testing set using the (a) kNN classifier; (b) MLP classifier; (c) DT classifier.

also showed that the main difficulty encountered by machine learning intrusion detection methods using the UNSW-NB15 dataset, comes from clusters where different categories of traffic are densely mixed. These three features can also be observed in our visualization experiment as shown in Fig. 6.

From the visual representations shown in Fig. 6(a) and (b), it can clearly be seen in the visual representation that most generic attacks are grouped together in the training and test sets. We can also find homogeneous clusters of normal connections in the training and test sets as shown in Fig. 6(c) and (d), respectively. In addition, Fig. 6(e) and (f) respectively show sections that contain a mixture of network traffic in the training and test sets. Despite the visualization results in our experiment differing from the results in [17], the visual features are similar. This affirms the validity of our 3D visualization results. An obvious visual characteristic of UNSW-NB15 is that the training set and the test set have similar characteristics in 3D space. This implies that the original data in the training and test sets are similar in nature. This characteristic is the reason why we can choose the best dimension that can produce relatively good results in both validation and test sets.

4.2   Results for the NSL_KDD Dataset

The same experiments that were performed on the UNSW-NB15 dataset were
also done on the NSL_KDD dataset. These results are presented here.

From Figs. 7(a)–(c) and 8(a)–(c), it can clearly be seen that results of accuracy trends for the NSL_KDD dataset, using all three classifiers for binary
and multiclass classification, share similar characteristics with the UNSW-
NB15 dataset. Accuracy initially increases with the number of dimensions, then
remains relatively stable after a certain number of dimensions. In relation to
dimensionality reduction for the NSL_KDD dataset, autoencoder is still better in terms of performance compared with PCA. The DT classifier again has
more fluctuations than the other two classifiers. Similar to the UNSW-NB15
dataset results, the kNN and MLP classifiers favor autoencoder when it comes
to reducing the dimensionality of data. Considering the results in Figs. 7(a)–(c)
and 8(a)–(c), the value of 25 is a reasonable choice as the best number of dimensions to achieve good performance for the NSL_KDD dataset. In an attempt to
verify this, accuracy trends of the test sets are shown in Figs. 9 and 10.

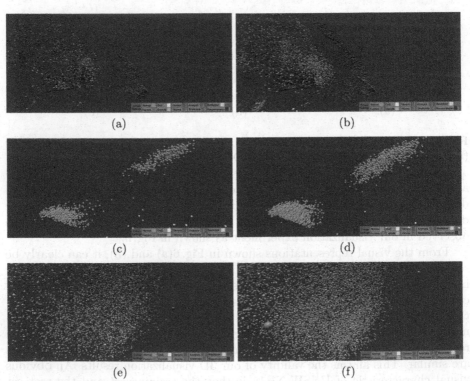

(a)   (b)

(c)   (d)

(e)   (f)

Fig. 6. 3D visualization results from the UNSW-NB15 dataset showing (a) clusters of
generic attacks in the training set; (b) clusters of generic attacks in the test set; (c) homogeneous clusters containing only normal connections in the training set; (d) homogeneous
clusters containing only normal connections in the test set; (e) clusters containing mixed
traffic in the training set; (f) clusters containing mixed traffic in the test set.

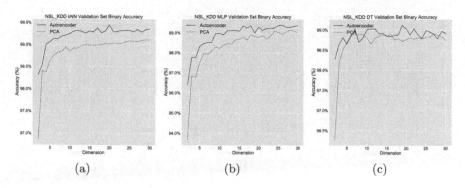

Fig. 7. NSL_KDD binary classification accuracy trends on the validation set using the (a) KNN classifier; (b) MLP classifier; (c) DT classifier.

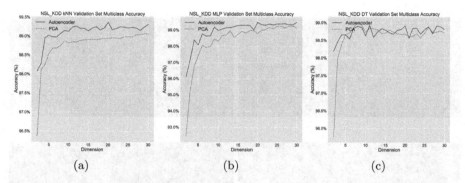

Fig. 8. NSL_KDD multiclass classification accuracy trends on the validation set using the (a) KNN classifier; (b) MLP classifier; (c) DT classifier.

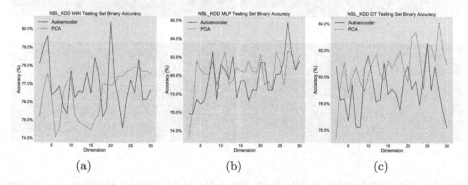

Fig. 9. NSL_KDD binary classification accuracy trends in the test set using the (a) kNN classifier; (b) MLP classifier; (c) DT classifier.

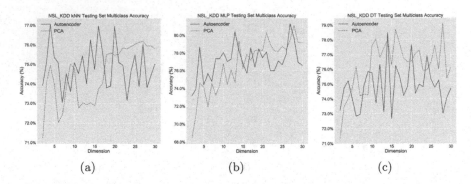

(a)   (b)   (c)

Fig. 10. NSL_KDD multiclass classification accuracy trends in the test set using the (a) kNN classifier; (b) MLP classifier; (c) DT classifier.

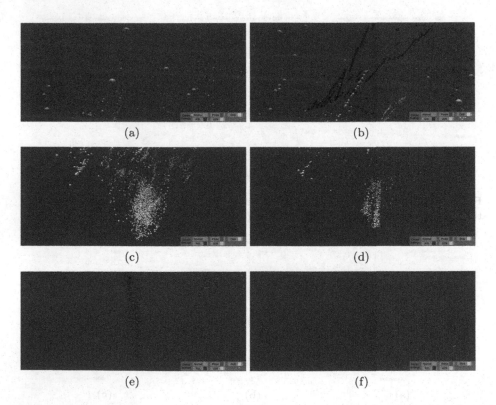

Fig. 11. 3D visualization results from the NSL_KDD dataset showing (a) various attacks in the training set; (b) previously unknown attacks in the test set; (c) homogeneous clusters of DoS attacks in the training set; (d) homogeneous clusters of DoS attacks in the test set; (e) clusters of probe attacks in the training set; (f) clusters of probe attacks in the test set.

As can be seen from the results in Figs. 9(a)–(c) and 10(a)–(c), the accuracy obtained from the NSL_KDD test data do not show obvious trends, because the values fluctuate wildly with respect to the number of dimensions. Hence, the best value for the number of dimensions that was selected in the validation set cannot be verified from results of the test set. Therefore, for the purpose of our experiment as long as the dimension was not too small, i.e. larger than 5, there was no significant difference in choosing the best number of dimensions. The reason why this situation occurs can be explained from the 3D visualization results. In particular, the difficulty in intrusion detection when using the NSL_KDD dataset lies in the fact that the test set contains previously unknown attacks [17]. In view of the accuracy trends in the validation set, we first reduce the number of dimensions to 25 using autoencoder and then use PCA to visualize the data. Examples of visualization results are shown in Fig. 11.

From visual inspection of the 3D visualization results in Fig. 11, we can see that there are attacks that only exist in the test set but are not in the training set. This can be seen when comparing the visual results in Fig. 11(a) and (b), as the attack characteristics in Fig. 11(b) contain previously unknown attacks when compared with Fig. 11(a). This difference is the main reason why there are obvious fluctuations in the results presented in Figs. 9 and 10. Consequently, for the NSL_KDD test set, no good value for the number of dimensions to produce optimal performance could be identified. This situation is different from the UNSW-NB15 dataset and shows that there are obvious differences in the datasets, which can easily be seen in the visual representation. From the visualization results, we can also find highly homogeneous clusters that contain the same type of network traffic in both the training and test sets. For example, it can be seen that both Fig. 11(c) and (d) contain clusters with only DoS attacks, and also Fig. 11(e) and (f) which show sections that contain mainly probe attacks. Similar visual characteristics in the NSL_KDD dataset have also been reported in Zong et al. [17].

5 Conclusion

This paper investigates the effects of two dimensionality reduction techniques on network intrusion detection datasets. The experiment results show that the autoencoder technique typically performs better than the PCA technique for both the UNSW-NB15 and NSL_KDD datasets. For UNSW-NB15 dataset, we were able to identify a specific number of dimensions at which the classifiers produced relatively good results in both the validation and test sets. This is likely due to high similarity between data in the training and test sets. On the other hand, we could not easily identify such a value for the NSL_KDD dataset, despite clear accuracy trends in the validation set. From visual inspection of the 3D visualization results, the reason for this is likely due to the fact that data in the training and test sets of the NSL_KDD dataset contain significant differences, e.g., previously unknown attacks which were not in the validation set are present in the test set. As such, this paper also demonstrates how 3D visualization can facilitate the understanding of intrusion detection results, as visual patterns in a dataset can be identified through visual inspection of the data.

References

1. Angelini, M., Prigent, N., Santucci, G.: PERCIVAL: proactive and reactive attack and response assessment for cyber incidents using visual analytics. In: Harrison, L., Prigent, N., Engle, S., Best, D.M. (eds.), 2015 IEEE Symposium on Visualization for Cyber Security, VizSec 2015, Chicago, IL, USA, 25 October 2015, pp. 1–8. IEEE Computer Society (2015)
2. Chawla, N.V., Bowyer, K.W., Hall, L.O., Kegelmeyer, W.P.: SMOTE: synthetic minority over-sampling technique. J. Artif. Intell. Res. **16**, 321–357 (2002)
3. de la Hoz Correa, E., de la Hoz Franco, E., Ortiz, A., Ortega, J., Prieto, B.: PCA filtering and probabilistic SOM for network intrusion detection. Neurocomputing **164**, 71–81 (2015)
4. Javaid, A.Y., Niyaz, Q., Sun, W., Alam, M.: A deep learning approach for network intrusion detection system. ICST Trans. Secur. Saf. **3**(9), e2 (2016)
5. Lakhina, A., Crovella, M., Diot, C.: Diagnosing network-wide traffic anomalies. In: Yavatkar, R., Zegura, E.W., Rexford, J. (eds.), Proceedings of the ACM SIG-COMM 2004 Conference on Applications, Technologies, Architectures, and Protocols for Computer Communication, Portland, Oregon, USA, 30 August–3 September 2004, pp. 219–230. ACM (2004)
6. Lin, W., Ke, S., Tsai, C.: CANN: an intrusion detection system based on combining cluster centers and nearest neighbors. Knowl. Based Syst. **78**, 13–21 (2015)
7. Liu, S., Wang, X., Liu, M., Zhu, J.: Towards better analysis of machine learning models: a visual analytics perspective. Vis. Inf. **1**(1), 48–56 (2017)
8. McHugh, J.: Testing intrusion detection systems: a critique of the 1998 and 1999 DARPA intrusion detection system evaluations as performed by Lincoln Laboratory. ACM Trans. Inf. Syst. Secur. **3**(4), 262–294 (2000)
9. McKenna, S., Staheli, D., Fulcher, C., Meyer, M.D.: BubbleNet: a cyber security dashboard for visualizing patterns. Comput. Graph. Forum **35**(3), 281–290 (2016)
10. Moustafa, N., Slay, J.: UNSW-NB15: a comprehensive data set for network intrusion detection systems (UNSW-NB15 network data set). In: 2015 Military Communications and Information Systems Conference, MilCIS 2015, Canberra, Australia, 10–12 November 2015, pp. 1–6. IEEE (2015)
11. Moustafa, N., Slay, J., Creech, G.: Novel geometric area analysis technique for anomaly detection using trapezoidal area estimation on large-scale networks. IEEE Trans. Big Data 1 (2018). https://doi.org/10.1109/TBDATA.2017.2715166
12. Rauber, P.E., Fadel, S.G., Falcão, A.X., Telea, A.C.: Visualizing the hidden activity of artificial neural networks. IEEE Trans. Vis. Comput. Graph. **23**(1), 101–110 (2017)
13. Sommer, R., Paxson, V.: Outside the closed world: on using machine learning for network intrusion detection. In: 31st IEEE Symposium on Security and Privacy, S&P 2010, 16–19 May 2010, Berleley/Oakland, California, USA, pp. 305–316. IEEE Computer Society (2010)
14. Staheli, D., et al.: Visualization evaluation for cyber security: trends and future directions. In: Whitley, K., Engle, S., Harrison, L., Fischer, F., Prigent, N. (eds.), Proceedings of the Eleventh Workshop on Visualization for Cyber Security, Paris, France, 10 November 2014, pp. 49–56. ACM (2014)

15. Wang, G., Hao, J., Ma, J., Huang, L.: A new approach to intrusion detection using artificial neural networks and fuzzy clustering. Expert Syst. Appl. **37**(9), 6225–6232 (2010)
16. Wang, Y., Yao, H., Zhao, S.: Auto-encoder based dimensionality reduction. Neurocomputing **184**, 232–242 (2016)
17. Zong, W., Chow, Y., Susilo, W.: A 3D approach for the visualization of network intrusion detection data. In: Sourin, A., Sourina, O., Rosenberger, C., Erdt, M. (eds.), 2018 International Conference on Cyberworlds, CW 2018, Singapore, 3–5 October 2018, pp. 308–315. IEEE (2018)
18. Zong, W., Chow, Y.-W., Susilo, W.: A two-stage classifier approach for network intrusion detection. In: Su, C., Kikuchi, H. (eds.) ISPEC 2018. LNCS, vol. 11125, pp. 329–340. Springer, Cham (2018). https://doi.org/10.1007/978-3-319-99807-7_20

DOCSDN: Dynamic and Optimal Configuration of Software-Defined Networks

Timothy Curry, Devon Callahan$^{(\boxtimes)}$, Benjamin Fuller, and Laurent Michel

University of Connecticut, Storrs, CT 06268, USA
{timothy.curry,devon.callahan,benjamin.fuller,laurent.michel}@uconn.edu

Abstract. Networks are designed with functionality, security, performance, and cost in mind. Tools exist to check or optimize individual properties of a network. These properties may conflict, so it is not always possible to run these tools in series to find a configuration that meets all requirements. This leads to network administrators manually searching for a configuration.

This need not be the case. In this paper, we introduce a layered framework for optimizing network configuration for functional and security requirements. Our framework is able to output configurations that meet reachability, bandwidth, and risk requirements. Each layer of our framework optimizes over a single property. A lower layer can constrain the search problem of a higher layer allowing the framework to converge on a joint solution.

Our approach has the most promise for software-defined networks which can easily reconfigure their logical configuration. Our approach is validated with experiments over the fat tree topology, which is commonly used in data center networks. Search terminates in between 1–5 min in experiments. Thus, our solution can propose new configurations for short term events such as defending against a focused network attack.

Keywords: Network configuration · Software Defined Networking · Reachability · Constraint programming · Optimization

1 Introduction

Network configuration is a crucial task in any enterprise. Administrators balance functionality, performance, security, cost, and other industry specific requirements. The resulting configuration is subject to periodic analysis and redesign due to red team recommendations, emerging threats, and changing priorities. Tools assist administrators with this complex task: existing work assesses network reachability [27], wireless conflicts [40], network security risk [46,52], and load balancing [48,51]. These tools assess the quality of a potential configuration. Unfortunately, current tools suffer from three limitations:

This is a U.S. government work and not under copyright protection in the U.S.;
foreign copyright protection may apply 2019
J. Jang-Jaccard and F. Guo (Eds.): ACISP 2019, LNCS 11547, pp. 456–474, 2019.
https://doi.org/10.1007/978-3-030-21548-4_25

1. Tools assess whether a single property is satisfied, making no recommendation if the property is not satisfied. This leaves IT personnel with the task of deciding how to change the network.
2. Tools assess networks with respect to an individual goal at a time. This means a change to satisfy a single property may break another property. There is no guidance for personnel on how to design a network that meets the complex and often conflicting network requirements.
3. Tools do not react to changing external information such as the publication of a new security vulnerability.

Our Contribution. This work introduces a new optimization framework that finds network configurations that satisfy multiple (conflicting) requirements. We focus on data center networks (DCN) that use software defined networking (SDN). Background on these settings is in Sect. 2. Our framework is called DocSDN (Dynamic and Optimal Configuration of Software-Defined Networks).

DocSDN searches for network configurations that simultaneously satisfy multiple properties. DocSDN is organized into layers that consider different properties. The core of DocSDN is a multistage optimization that decouples search on "orthogonal" concerns. The majority of the technical work is to effectively separate concerns so the optimization problems remain tractable. Our framework is designed to continually produce network configurations based on changing requirements and threats. It frees IT personnel from the complex question of how to satisfy multiple requirements and can quickly incorporate new threat information.

DocSDN focuses on achieving functional requirements (such as network reachability and flow satisfaction) and limiting security risk (such as isolating high risk nodes and nodes under denial of service attack). Naturally, other layers such as performance or cost can be incorporated. The search for a good configuration could be organized in many ways. State-of-the-art approaches assess different properties in isolation, frustrating search for a solution that satisfies all requirements. Ideally, a framework should search for a configuration that simultaneously satisfies all requirements. This extreme is unlikely to be tractable on all but the smallest networks. DocSDN mediates between these approaches separating the functional and security search problems but introducing a feedback loop between the two search problems based on *cuts*.

In the proposed organization the functional layer is "above" the security layer. Through the feedback loop, the security layer describes a problematic part of the network to the functional layer. The functional layer then refines its model and searches for a functional configuration that satisfies an additional *constraint*. This has the effect of blocking the problematic part of the configuration. Currently, the feedback signal is a pair of nodes that should not be proximate in the network. After multiple iterations the two layers jointly produce a solution that optimizes the SDN configuration both with respect to functionality and security risks.

DocSDN provides solutions of improving quality before the final solution. Thus, the network can be reconfigured once the objective improves on the current

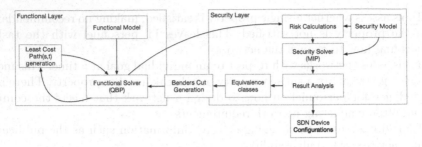

Fig. 1. DocSDN Framework. A layered decomposition that breaks down configuration synthesis into functional and security layers.

configuration by a large enough amount (to justify the cost/impact of reconfiguration).

The underlying optimization problems are NP-hard but optimization technology has seen tremendous advances in performance during the past few decades. Since 1991, mathematical programming solvers have delivered speedups of 11 orders of magnitude [8,17]. Hybrid techniques such as Benders decomposition [6,12,20,21] and column generation [3,19,31] (aka, Dantzig-Wolfe decomposition [14]) made it possible to solve huge problems thanks to on-demand generation of macroscopic variables and the dynamic addition of critical constraints. Large Neighborhood Search [47] further contributed to delivering high-quality solution within constrained time budgets.

These techniques are beginning to see adoption in network security. Yu et al. recently applied stochastic optimization with Bender's decomposition to assess network risk under uncertainty for IoT devices [52]. They used Bender's decomposition on a scenario-based stochastic optimization model to produce a parent problem that chooses a deployment plan while children are concerned with *choosing* the optimal nodes to serve the demands in individual scenarios. In comparison, our approach addresses *both functional and security requirements*. It relies on Bender's cuts from the security layer (child) to rule out vulnerable functional plans whose routing paths fail to adequately minimize risks and maximize served clients. We now briefly describe the framework (a formal description is in Sect. 3) and present an illustrative example.

Overview of DocSDN. Figure 1 presents an overview of the framework. The functional layer takes as input a *Functional Model* that describes the network including the physical topology, capacity, the allowable communication patterns and the demand requirements. Network reachability begins with a priming procedure that generates the k-least cost paths to the optimizer for each source/destination pair in the demand requirements. The objective for the functional layer is to find a logical topology (a collection of routed paths) that meets all demand requirements while favoring shorter length routing paths and load balancing. The program is formulated as quadratic binary program (QBP). The solution as determined by the functional layer is passed to the security layer.

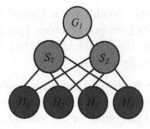

Fig. 2. Toy network example with a single gateway device G_1, two intermediate switches S_1 and S_2 and four hosts. We assume the switches are physically connected to all hosts.

The output of the functional layer and a *security model* are the input for the security layer. The current configuration is fed to a module that uses risk assessments for the individual network devices (obtained for example using a vulnerability database) to assess the overall risk of the entire configuration. In our current implementation this risk calculation is based on a simple risk propagation model where a path's risk is based on the risk of nodes on the path and close to the source and sink. The security layer can deploy firewalls and deep packet inspection as network defenses. Since these mechanisms affect route capacity, the security layer has a dual objective function: (1) maximizing the functional objective and (2) minimizing security risk. The security objective is formulated as a mixed integer program (*MIP*). When the security search completes, it proposes nodes to the functional layer that should be separated. As an example, a high value node with low risk may be placed in a different (virtual) LAN than a high risk node. These *Benders cuts* are designed to entice a better logical topology from a subsequent iteration in the functional layer. This feedback loop between the two layers can iterate multiple times. When no further cuts are available, the overall output is a set of configuration rules.

An Example Configuration. This section describes an application of our framework to automatically respond to a distributed denial of service (DDoS) attack. Current DDoS attacks demonstrate peak volume of 1 Tbps [29]. Many DDoS defense techniques require changes to the network behavior by rate limiting, filtering, or reconfiguring the network (see [23,24,37,43,53]). Recent techniques [15] leverage SDNs to react to DDoS attacks in a dynamic and flexible manner. We show how such a response would work in our framework using a toy network illustrated in Fig. 2. A more realistic network and the framework's response are described in Sect. 5. We stress that DDoS attacks are often short in timescale making human diagnosis and reaction costly or impractical. Consider a focused DDoS attack against a number of services in an enterprise but not the entirety of its publicly accessible address space. (The Great Cannon's attack against GreatFire targeted two specific Github repositories [35].) We assume a service hosted by H_1 is targeted, while services on H_2, H_3 and H_4 are not.

Recall, the functional layer establishes a logical topology (forwarding rules) while the security layer adds network defenses (packet inspection modules and firewall rules). We elide how the attack is detected and assume it increases the risk score for H_1 in the security model.

The First Iteration. The functional layer proposes a candidate configuration where G_1 routes all traffic intended for H_1 and H_2 to S_1 which then forwards the traffic and G_1 routes traffic intended for H_3 and H_4 to S_2 which then forwards the traffic. This is the first candidate solution presented to the security layer.

Since H_1 is high risk the security layer proposes a firewall at S_1 to block all port 80 traffic. This reduces risk at the cost of blocking all traffic to H_2. Of course, in real firewalls more fine-grained rules are possible, this simplified example is meant to illustrate a case where collateral damage to the functional objective is necessary to achieve the security objective. Since traffic is being blocked to a node with low risk, the security layer asks the functional layer to separate H_1 and H_2 so H_2 does not suffer.

Repeated Iterations. The functional layer now has a constraint that H_1 and H_2 should not be collocated in the network. As such, it proposes a new configuration with H_1 and H_3 under S_1 and H_2 and H_4 under S_2. This is then sent to the security layer. The security layer makes a similar assessment and proposes a firewall rule at S_2, finds this recommendation hurts functionality and requests separation of H_1 and H_3.

This process repeats with the functional layer proposing to collocate H_1 and H_4. The security layer similarly asks to separate H_1 and H_4. Finally, H_1 is segregated from all other nodes. This produces a configuration where H_1 is the only child of S_1. Note that having H_2, H_3 and H_4 under a single switch may hurt performance but the effect is less than blocking traffic to one of the nodes entirely. DocSDN can then output the candidate solution as high level SDN fragments (using a high-level language like Frenetic [16]).

Recovery. Importantly, when the DDoS abates, DocSDN automatically reruns with a changed risk for H_1, outputting a binary tree.

Organization. The rest of the work is organized as follows: Sect. 2 provides background on our application and discusses related work, Sect. 3 describes our framework and accompanying optimization models, Sect. 4 describes our experimental setup, Sect. 5 evaluates the framework and finally Sect. 6 concludes.

2   Background and Related Work

Data Center Networks (DCN) host, process and analyze data in financial, entertainment, medical, government and military sectors. The services provided by DCNs must be reliable, accurate and timely. Services provided by DCNs (and the corresponding traffic) are heterogeneous. The network must adapt to changing priorities and requirements while protecting from emerging threats. They scale to thousands of servers linked through various interconnects. Protocols used for these services are split roughly 60% web (HTTP/HTPS) and 40% file storage (SMB/AFS) [7]. The interdependence of device configurations make modifying any single configuration difficult and possibly dangerous for network health. A seemingly simple update can cause significant collateral damage and unintended consequences.

Simultaneously, the network fabric is changing with the advent of Software Defined Networking (SDN) [30]. SDNs are flexible and programmable networks that can adapt to emergent functional or performance requirements. Openflow [36] is a common open source software stack. Researchers have proposed high-level languages and compilers [5,16,28,44] that bridge the semantic gap between network administrators and the configuration languages used by SDN devices. These languages focus on *compositional* and *parametric* SDN software modules that execute specific micro-functions (e.g., packet forwarding, dropping, routing, etc.). The use of a high level language is prompted by a desire to be able to *select*, *instantiate* and *compose* SDN modules with guarantees.

Our framework is intended to be modular and allow integration of prior work on evaluating network configurations. As such there is a breadth of relevant work. Due to space constraints we focus on the most relevant works. In the conclusion we elaborate on the characteristics needed to integrate a prior assessment tool into our framework (see Sect. 6).

Measuring Network Risk. Known threats against computer systems are maintained by governments and industry. Common Vulnerabilities and Exposures (CVE) is a publicly available dictionary including an identifier and description of known vulnerabilities [13], CVE does not provide a severity score or priority ranking for vulnerabilities. The US National Vulnerability Database (NVD) [41] is provided by the US National Institute of Standards and Technology (NIST). The NVD augments the CVE, adding severity scores and impact ratings for vulnerabilities in the CVE.

There are many mechanisms for measuring the security risk on a network [10, 25,34,49,50]. Lippmann et al. present a network security model which computes risk based on a list of the most current threats [33]. This model implements a cycle of observe network state, compute risk, prioritize risk, and mitigate the risk.

This loop is often codified into an *attack graph* [22,26,46]. Attack graphs try to model the most likely paths that an attacker could use to penetrate a network. Attack Graphs often leverage one or more of the aforementioned vulnerability assessment tools as input, combined with a network topology and device software configurations to generate the graph. Current attack graph technologies provide recommendations to network administrators that effectively remove edges from the graph and trigger a re-evaluation of the utility for the attacker. To the best of our knowledge, current practice does not leverage network risk measurement into constraints used for the generation of new configurations.

Network Reachability. The expansion of SDN has aided the applicability of formal verification to computer networks. Prior to SDN, the lack of clear separation between the data and control plain created an intractable problem when considering a network of any scale. Bounded model checking using SAT and SMT solvers [4,54] can currently verify reachability properties in networks with several thousands of nodes.

Configuration Search. Constraint Programming (CP) was introduced in the late 1980s [45] and is used for scheduling [2], routing, and configuration problems. Large-scale optimization problems are often decomposed including Benders [12] and Dantzig-Wolfe [14]. *Soft constraints* or Lagrangian relaxation are used for over-constrained problems or when the problem is too computationally expensive. Stochastic optimization techniques have been used for many applications in resilience [9,39] and the underlying methodologies are a key part of this research. Prior work in configuration management with constraint programming [11,32] focused on connectivity or security. We are not aware of any work that balances these two objectives in a meaningful way.

3   Implementation

Figure 1 outlines the overall structure of the DocSDN framework. layer interconnections as well as their internals. The functional layer uses a mathematical optimization model that is fed to a quadratic mixed boolean programming (QBP) solver alongside an initial set of least-cost paths to be considered to service the required flows. The security layer receives the topology chosen by the functional layer and a security model to solve, with a mixed-integer programming (MIP) solver, the risk minimization problem. The output can result in low-risk flows being blocked as a consequence of deploying firewalls to mitigate high-risk flows. A result analysis module then produces *equivalence classes* that are sent back to the functional layer to request the separation of specific flows that should not share paths, with the goal of minimizing the collateral damage to low-risk flows. These equivalence classes generate additional constraints, known as Bender's cuts, that are added to the functional solver for a new iteration. The remainder of this section describes the major modules in Fig. 1.

3.1   Functional Layer

The mathematical optimization model in the functional layer is a quadratic mixed binary programming model. In constraint programming the four main components are Inputs, Variables, Constraints, and an Objective function. Inputs are below.

Inputs

$\mathcal{N}$ – the set of all network devices
$\mathcal{E}$ – the set of edges (pair of vertices) connecting network devices
$\mathcal{T}$ – the set of types of traffic to be routed
$\mathcal{F}$ – the set of $(s, t, T) \in \mathcal{N} \times \mathcal{N} \times \mathcal{T}$ tuples defining desired traffic flows of type
     T from source node s to sink node t.

$D(f) : \mathcal{F} \to \mathbb{R}$ – the actual demand for each flow $f \in \mathcal{F}$

$\mathcal{C} \subseteq 2^{\mathcal{N}}$ – a subset of sets of network devices

$\mathcal{R} \subseteq \mathcal{C} \times \mathcal{C}$ – pairs (c_1, c_2) of equivalence classes that segregate traffic from c_1 to c_2.

$\mathcal{P}$ – the set of all paths

$P(e) : \mathcal{E} \to \mathcal{P}$ – the set of all paths containing edge e

$P(n) : \mathcal{N} \to \mathcal{P}$ – the set of all paths containing node n

$P(c) : \mathcal{C} \to \mathcal{P}$ – the set of all paths containing a node in c

$N(p) : \mathcal{P} \to \mathcal{C}$ – the set of nodes appearing in path p

$P(s, t) : \mathcal{N} \times \mathcal{N} \to \mathcal{P}$ – the set of all paths $s \to t$

$cap(e) : \mathcal{E} \to \mathbb{R}$ – gives the capacity of an edge e.

Variables

$active_{p,T} \in \{0, 1\}$, – for every path $p \in \mathcal{P}$ and traffic type $T \in \mathcal{T}$, indicates whether path p carries traffic of type T

$flow_{p,T} \in \mathbb{R}_{\geq 0}$ – for every path $p \in \mathcal{P}$ and traffic type $T \in \mathcal{T}$, amount of flow of type T that is sent along path p

$equiv_{c,n} \in \{0, 1\}$ – does node $n \in \mathcal{N}$ appear in an active path together with a node in equivalence class c

$share_{c_1,c_2,n} \in \{0, 1\}$ – indicates whether node $n \in \mathcal{N}$ appears on any active path with nodes in classes $c_1, c_2 \in \mathcal{C}$. Namely,

$$share_{c_1,c_2,n} \Leftrightarrow n \in \left(\left(\cup_{p \in P(c_1):active_{p,*}} N(p) \right) \cap \left(\cup_{p \in P(c_2):active_{p,*}} N(p) \right) \right)$$

$active_{p,*} = 1$ if there is a type $T \in \mathcal{T}$ where $active_{p,T} = 1$

$load_n \in \mathbb{R}$ – the amount of flow that goes through node n

$loadObj$ – the sum of squares of all $load_n$ variables.

Constraints

$$\sum_{p \in P(e), T \in \mathcal{T}} flow_{p,T} \leq cap(e), \ \forall e \in \mathcal{E} \tag{1}$$

$$\sum_{p \in P(s,t)} flow_{p,T} \geq D(s, t, T), \ \forall(s, t, T) \in \mathcal{F} \tag{2}$$

$$active_{p,T} = 1 \to flow_{p,T} \geq 1, \forall(s, t, T) \in \mathcal{F}, p \in P(s, t) \tag{3}$$

$$\sum_{p \in P(s,t)} active_{p,T} = 1, \ \forall(s, t, T) \in \mathcal{F} \tag{4}$$

$$equiv_{c,n} = \bigvee_{p \in P(n) \cap P(c)} (active_{p,T}), \forall T \in \mathcal{T}, n \in \mathcal{N}, c \in \mathcal{C} \tag{5}$$

$$share_{c_1,c_2,n} = equiv_{c_1,n} \wedge equiv_{c_2,n}, \forall n \in \mathcal{N}, (c_1, c_2) \in \mathcal{R} \tag{6}$$

$$load_n = \sum_{p \in P(n), T \in \mathcal{T}} flow_{p,T}, \forall n \in \mathcal{N} \qquad (7)$$

Equation 1 enforces the edge capacity constraint to service the demand of all paths flowing through it. Equation 2 ensures that enough capacity is available to meet the demand of an (s, t, T) flow. Equation 3 ensures that some non-zero capacity is used if a specific path is activated (conversely, an inactive path can only have a 0 flow). Equation 4 states that a single path should be chosen to service a given flow $f \in \mathcal{F}$. Equations 5 define the auxiliary variables $equiv_{c,n}$ as true if and only if node $n \in \mathcal{N}$ appears on an active path sharing a node with the equivalence class $c \in \mathcal{C}$. Equation 6 defines an active path that shares at least one node with two classes. Finally, Eq. 7 defines the load of a node as the sum of the flows associated to active paths passing through node n.

Objective

$$\min \begin{pmatrix} \alpha_0 \sum_{p,T} len(p) * flow_{p,T} & + \\ \alpha_1 \sum_{(c_1,c_2) \in \mathcal{R}, n \in \mathcal{N}} (share_{c_1,c_2,n} - 1) + \\ \alpha_2 \sum_{n \in \mathcal{N}} (load_n)^2 & \end{pmatrix} \qquad (8)$$

The objective function 8 in this model is a weighted sum of three terms. The first term captures the total flows which are penalized by the length of the path used to dispatch those flows (such policies are codified in OSFP [38] and BGP practice [18]). The second term gives a unit credit each time equivalence classes on the segregation list $\mathcal{R}$ do not share a node. (Due to this term, the objective value of the final solution may change between iterations of the functional layer.) The third and final term contribute to a bias towards solutions that achieve load balancing thanks to the quadratic component which heavily penalizes nodes with large loads.

Solving the Functional Model. The functional model starts with empty sets $\mathcal{C}$ and $\mathcal{R}$ which are augmented with each iteration of the framework. New sets of nodes are added to $\mathcal{C}$ and new segregation rules are added to $\mathcal{R}$ (by the security layer). In the current implementation, least cost paths between pairs of nodes s, t are not generated "on demand". Instead, the generation is limited to the first best k such paths, for increasing values of k. This process will ultimately be improved to use column generation techniques [14].

3.2   Risk Calculation

After the functional layer finds an optimal solution, it passes this solution to the risk calculation procedure. This input is the set of active paths. This module calculates the effective risk to the network for each path and traffic type.

Inputs

$risk(n, T) : \mathcal{N} \times \mathcal{T} \rightarrow \mathbb{R}$ – the risk inherit to network device n for traffic of type T ($risk(n, T) \geq 1$)

$d_k(n) : \mathcal{N} \to 2^{\mathcal{N}}$ – the set of nodes at a distance at most k from n in the logical topology

Calculation

Given an *active* path $p \in \mathcal{P}$ with source s and sink t, the calculation proceeds by partitioning the set of nodes of the path into three segments: the nodes "close" to the source s, "close" to the sink t and the nodes "in between". Closeness is characterized by the function d_k and is meant to capture any connected node over the logical topology which sits no more that k hops away. Given this partition, $flowRisk(p, T)$ is:

$$flowRisk(p, T) = \sum_{i \in d_2(s) \cup d_2(t)} risk(i, T)^2 + \\ \sum_{i \in N(p) \setminus (d_2(s) \cup d_2(t))} risk(i, T)^2$$

We use $k = 2$ to model nodes on the same LAN. The rationale is to impart to source s and sink t risk resulting from *lateral movement* of attacks. All other nodes contribute to the overall path risk in proportion to the square of their own risks. We expect in most networks for $d_2(s)$ and $d_2(t)$ to include nodes not directly on the path (like nodes on the same LAN). The input path risk calculation $flowRisk(p, T)$ is modular and can be augmented using other risk calculation methods.

3.3 Security Layer

The mathematical optimization model in the security layer is a mixed integer programming model. We similarly present the inputs, variables, constraints, and objective for the security layer. Its inputs are given below. Also note that all the variables from the functional model are *constants*.

Inputs

$mem(n) : \mathcal{N} \to \mathbb{R}$ – the memory resources of SDN device n
$fwCost(T) : \mathcal{T} \to \mathbb{R}$ – the memory footprint for a firewall blocking traffic type T
$piCost$ – the memory footprint for a packet inspection post
$fwComp$ – the complexity footprint for adding a firewall
$piComp$ – the complexity footprint for adding a packet inspection post to the network
$penalty(p, T) : \mathcal{P} \times \mathcal{T} \to \mathbb{R}$ – the penalty for blocking a unit of flow of type T along path p
$rank(n, p) : \mathcal{N} \times \mathcal{P} \to \mathbb{Z}$ – the position of node n in path p
$flowRisk(p, T) : \mathcal{P} \times \mathcal{T} \to \mathbb{R}_{\geq 0}$ – above risk calculation

Variables

$fw_{n,T} \in \{0, 1\}$ – does a firewall block traffic type T at n
$pi_n \in \{0, 1\}$ – is there packet inspection at network device n

$fwOR_{n,T} \in \{0,1\}$ – is there a *block everything* or *block traffic of type* T firewall at network device n

$fwOP_{p,T} \in \{0,1\}$ – is there a firewall on path p

$rf_{p,T} \in [0,1]$ – risk factor for path $p \in P(s,t)$ servicing flow $(s,t,T) \in \mathcal{F}$

$RMfw_{p,n,T} \in [0,1]$ – used in the riskFactor calculation

$RMpi_{p,n,T} \in [0,1]$ – used in the riskFactor calculation

Constraints

$$fwOR_{n,T} = fw_{n,T} \vee fw_{n,*}, \forall n \in \mathcal{N}, T \in \mathcal{T} \tag{9}$$

$$\sum_{T \in \mathcal{T} \cup \{*\}} fwCost_T \cdot fw_{n,T} + piCost \cdot pi_n \leq mem_n, \forall n \in \mathcal{N} \tag{10}$$

$$fwOP_{p,T} = \bigvee_{n \in N(p)} (fwOR_{n,T}), \forall T \in \mathcal{T}, p \in \mathcal{P} : active_{p,T} \tag{11}$$

$$RMfw_{p,n,T} = 1 - (.5)^{rank(n,p)} \cdot fwOR_{n,T},$$
$$\forall p \in P(s,t), n \in N(p), (s,t,T) \in \mathcal{F} \tag{12}$$

$$RMpi_{p,n,T} = 1 - 0.1 \cdot (.5)^{rank(n,p)} \cdot pi_n,$$
$$\forall p \in P(s,t), n \in N(p), (s,t,T) \in \mathcal{F} \tag{13}$$

$$rf_{p,T} = \min \bigcup_{n \in N(p)} \{RMfw_{p,n,T}, RMpi_{p,n,T}\},$$
$$\forall T \in \mathcal{T}, p \in \mathcal{P} : active_{p,T} \tag{14}$$

Equation 9 is used to define the presence of a firewall that will block traffic of type T at a node n. Equation 10 ensures that the memory footprint in SDN node n for the deployment of the firewall and the packet inspection logic does not exceed the device memory. Equation 11 links the presence of a firewall that will block traffic of type T on a path with the presence of a firewall that will block traffic of type T on any node along the active path. Equation 12 defines the minimum risk factor associated to a firewall. The earlier on the path the firewall is deployed, the lower the risk. Equation 13 similarly defines the minimal risk. Equation 14 defines the composite risk factor.

Objective

$$\min \begin{pmatrix} \beta_0 \left(\sum_{n,T} fwComp \cdot fw_{n,T} + \sum_n piComp \cdot pi_n \right) + \\ \beta_1 \sum_n load_n \cdot pi_n + \\ \beta_2 \sum_{p,T} penalty(p,T) \cdot flow_{p,T} \cdot fwOP_{p,T} + \\ \beta_3 \sum_{p,T} flowRisk_{p,T} \cdot rf_{p,T} \end{pmatrix} \tag{15}$$

The objective function defined in Eq. 15 is a weighted sum of four distinct terms that focus on minimizing the network complexity based on security resources deployed, the load induced by inspection posts, the penalties incurred from dropping desirable flows due to firewall placement and finally the residual risk. This model is a classic mixed integer programming formulation.

3.4   Result Analysis

The result analysis module tries to generate cuts for the functional layer with the goal of improving both functionality and security. To generate cuts, this module will form equivalence classes of network nodes and pass back certain pairs of these classes, one at a time, to the functional layer. Each pair of classes describes a segregation rule, or a cut, to which to functional layer will adhere to as much as possible.

After the functional and security layers are re-optimized using the most recent cut, the result analysis module determines whether the cut was beneficial or harmful based on the objectives of each layer. If the cut is deemed to have been beneficial, we permanently keep it as a constraint, repopulate the cut queue, and continue the process.

If the cut is deemed to have been harmful, it is removed from the functional layer's constraint pool. Then the next cut in the queue will be passed back to the functional layer. If the cut queue is empty, the feedback mechanism terminates and we output the best solution found.

We note that since this process only provides pairs of nodes it is a heuristic. It may be necessary for many nodes to simultaneously be separated to arrive at a global optimum. This mechanism performed well in our experiments.

3.5   Layer Coordination

It is valuable to review how the layers coordinate. The functional layer sends to the security layer a set of paths that implements the routing within the network to serve the specified flows while satisfying a set of segregation requirements. The security layer first computes *risks* for these paths based on its knowledge of the traffic. The paths, their risk and the security model are then tasked with deploying packet inspection apparatus as well as firewalls within that logical topology to monitor the traffic and block threats (risky traffic). Once the security model is solved to optimality, an analysis can determine whether the proposed logical topology is beneficial or not (w.r.t. its objective) and even suggest further equivalence classes for network nodes as well as segregation rules to be sent back to the functional layer for another iteration. Fundamentally, the coordination signal boils down to additional equivalence classes to group nodes together with segregation rules to separate paths that include network nodes in "antagonistic" equivalence classes.

3.6   Outputs

When the set of potential cuts is empty, the proposed configuration can be parsed and translated into SDN language fragments to be deployed on the network devices in order to obtain the desired logical network topology put forth by our framework.

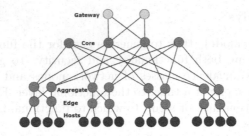

Fig. 3. Order 4 Fat-tree with 2 gateway switches at the top and 2 hosts per edge switch.

4   Experimental Setup

A fundamental component of our work is the separation of the physical and logical networks. Our framework has potential in applications where many different logical topologies are possible from a single physical topology. Physical topology is an input to our framework and the empirical evaluation is based on a popular topology: Fat-Tree [1].

The instance of Fat-Tree we use is shown in Fig. 3. The network design avoids bottlenecks through multiple equal capacity links between layers. This design uses four layers of switches: gateway, core, aggregate and edge. The edge switches serve as top-of-rack switches and are where our hosts connect.

Within our sample network, we consider having two main types of devices: switches/routers and hosts. In order to model traffic between internal and external entities we utilize two gateway switches which represent the boundary of our network. For generality we consider two traffic types (A and B) which could represent any type of traffic such as web and storage. We also classify traffic as internal and external, with external traffic traversing one of the gateways. We allow only half of our hosts to communicate with external sources by allowing them to connect to one of the two gateways. Further, all hosts are involved in internal communications. In this instance we have 16 hosts and we generated 60 flows, 44 of them being internal and 16 being external.

Additionally, our setup simulates an emergent vulnerability/active attack. We select two hosts that are highly vulnerable to, or being targeted on, a specific type of traffic, resulting in a significant increase in their risk for the corresponding type of traffic. In particular, this could represent at DDoS attack on these two hosts.

We run multiple experiments providing the framework increasing numbers of starting paths between source and destination (from the priming procedure) to determine the impact on the solution quality.

Our implementation was built in Python 3.6 using the Gurobi 8.1 optimization library [42]. The experiments were run on a machine running Ubuntu 18.04 and equipped with an Intel Core i9-8950HK processor operating at 2.90 GHz with a 12 MB Cache and 32 GB of physical memory.

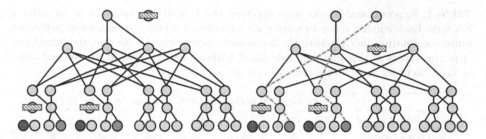

Fig. 4. Illustration of the Fat-Tree network after the first pass through both layers of
the framework (left) and the final configuration (right). Note: Firewalls are depicted
with rectangles, red nodes represent high risk nodes, green nodes represent nodes that
are initially blocked and recovered in the final configuration, utilizing the updated
routes shown in dashed lines. The modification of the logical topology allows for more
intelligent firewall placement balancing both functionality and security. (Color figure
online)

5   Evaluation/Results

We begin with the model's resolution on the above scenario using the 10 shortest
paths per source and destination pair to prime the optimization. We assume
equal demand for each of the 60 flows and two high risk hosts (in red in Fig. 4).
In each iteration the functional layer of the framework generates a candidate
topology and passes this solution to the security layer. The security layer then
calculates the network risk and deploys firewalls (represented with rectangles).

In the initial configuration, the gateway on the right serves both low risk
(shown in green) and high risk hosts (shown in red). Deploying a firewall on this
gateway significantly reduces the network risk and selected as optimal by the
security layer. Importantly, this results in collateral damage as flows to low risk
hosts are blocked. In total, the first iteration through the framework deploys 3
firewalls which block 12 flows, 8 of which are high risk.

Iteratively, the security layer proposes separation of these collateral nodes
from the high-risk nodes. The solution of the last framework iteration (493 candidates cuts are proposed, 40 prove beneficial) is shown on the right. This configuration routes all high risk flows through one core switch where a firewall is
now deployed. Meanwhile, all the low risk flows access the gateways through a
separate core switch.

Overall we conducted six experiments with this configuration modifying only
the number of paths ($\{10, 20, 30, 40, 50, 100\}$) being used to prime the functional
layer for each source-destination pair. Ultimately, this process will be dynamic
and use column-generation. Complete experimental results are shown in Table 1.
A few observations are in order:

- The overall objective reflects both the functional and security layers. The
  other objective rows refer to each layer objective individually. The network
  risk rows quantify the risks and their change as the optimization proceeds.

Table 1. Experimental results from applying the DocSDN framework to an order 4 Fat-tree. Each column refers to a separate experiment where the number of paths per source-destination pair given to the framework were varied. Note that the functional objective values in this table are calculated without the cut reward, the second term in Eq. 8, in order to facilitate comparisons across columns.

	10 paths	20 paths	30 paths	40 paths	50 paths	100 paths
Initial flows blocked	12	12	12	12	12	12
Final flows blocked	8	8	8	8	8	8
Initial functional objective	2012	2012	2012	2012	2012	2012
Final functional objective	2014	2014	2014	2015	2014	2015
Cut reward	−8450	−4260	−7210	−4900	−5540	−3840
Initial security objective	13735	13724	13729	13723	13696	13726
Final security objective	13356	13356	13356	13356	13356	13348
Initial network risk	10425	10414	10419	10413	10386	10416
Final network risk	11646	11646	11646	11646	11646	11638
Functional nodes explored	370	55	206	83	510	46
Security nodes explored	1922	1650	152	30	28	19
Beneficial cuts	40	20	34	23	26	18
Harmful cuts	453	70	237	81	68	74
Iterations needed	494	91	272	105	95	93
Time in model (s)	283	40	319	112	76	273

For instance, for the 10 paths benchmark, the risk degrades from 10425 to 11646 or 11.7% as a result of supporting an additional 4 good flows.

- The "nodes explored" rows indicate of the size of the branch and bound tree and remains quite modest throughout.
- Within each experiment we observe a meaningful search, as seen by numerous cuts sent back to the functional layer, to segregate high and low risk flows.
- All runs blocked all flows that contain a high risk host while preserving the low risk flows. All experiments delivered final configurations that preserved the same low-risk flows. We therefore hypothesize that a column-generation would quickly settle down and prove that no additional path can improve the quality of the solution. It is nonetheless interesting that adding more paths does not negatively impact the overall runtime.
- The objective functions of the functional and security layers use "scores" meant to ease the interplay between the two. Yet, it is wise to consult the *raw* properties of the solutions to appreciate the impact of the optimization. In particular, the number of flows blocked and the network risks. What is readily apparent is that improving functionality induces a slight degradation in the network risks, underlying the conflicting nature of the two objectives. The individual objective scores while moving in the correct direction are not to be viewed as stand alone metrics to determine solution quality but

rather inter layer communications indicating improvement or decline from a functional or security perspective.

- The objective scores vary across our experiments due to the stochasticity introduced by our heuristic-driven feedback module (see Sect. 3.4 for discussion). For instance, the functional objective in the 30 path experiment is slightly worse than it is in other runs, but this difference does not impact the number of serviced flows in the final configuration.
- The variance in time, iterations and number of cuts produced by each experiment is due to symmetries in the formulation. Solutions that are symmetric in the functional layer may not be symmetric in the security layer and induce slightly different solutions there. This is especially true for a Fat-tree network due to its built in redundancy/symmetry.
- Beneficial cuts reflects the number of segregation proposals from the security layers that are adopted by the functional layer (these cuts remove the current best feasible solution). harmful cuts are segregation proposals that do not "cut" the current best feasible solution or worsen the functional solution.

6   Conclusion

Our framework is portable with respect to network risk assessment. Since the risk calculation/analysis is decoupled from the optimization model, the framework can be combined with any procedure that calculates risk on a per path basis. Along with this procedure, the other requirements for implementing a different risk mechanism are (1) A way of evaluating how risk changes due to the deployment of network defenses and (2) The ability to propose candidate cuts that can be passed to the functional layer.

Our results show it is possible to effectively, automatically, and quickly find a network configuration that meets multiple conflicting properties. Our framework is modular, enabling integration of new desired properties. DocSDN will allow network administrators to effectively prioritize and choose their desired properties. The efficiency of DocSDN is enabled by the feedback/interplay between the functional and security optimization layers.

Acknowledgments. The authors thank the anonymous reviewers for their helpful insights. The authors would also like to thank Pascal Van Hentenryck, Bing Wang, Sridhar Duggirala and Heytem Zitoun for their helpful feedback and discussions. The work of T.C., B.F., and L.M. are supported by the Office of Naval Research, Comcast and Synchrony Financial. The work of D.C. is supported by the U.S. Army. The opinions in this paper are those of the authors and do not necessarily reflect the opinions of the supporting organizations.

References

1. Al-Fares, M., Loukissas, A., Vahdat, A.: A scalable, commodity data center network architecture. In: Proceedings of the ACM SIGCOMM 2008 Conference on Data Communication, SIGCOMM 2008, pp. 63–74. ACM, New York (2008)
2. Baptiste, P., Le Pape, C., Nuijten, W.: Constraint-Based Scheduling. Kluwer Academic Publishers (2001)
3. Barnhart, C., Johnson, E.L., Nemhauser, G.L., Savelsbergh, M.W.P., Vance, P.H.: Branch-and-price: column generation for solving huge integer programs. Oper. Res. **46**(3), 316–329 (1998)
4. Beckett, R., Gupta, A., Mahajan, R., Walker, D.: A general approach to network configuration verification. In: Proceedings of the Conference of the ACM Special Interest Group on Data Communication, pp. 155–168. ACM (2017)
5. Beckett, R., Mahajan, R., Millstein, T., Padhye, J., Walker, D.: Network configuration synthesis with abstract topologies. In: Proceedings of the 38th ACM SIGPLAN Conference on Programming Language Design and Implementation, pp. 437–451. ACM (2017)
6. Benders, J.F.: Partitioning procedures for solving mixed-variables programming problems. Numer. Math. **4**(1), 238–252 (1962)
7. Benson, T., Akella, A., Maltz, D.A.: Network traffic characteristics of data centers in the wild. In: Proceedings of the 10th ACM SIGCOMM Conference on Internet Measurement, IMC 2010, pp. 267–280. ACM, New York (2010)
8. Bixby, E.R., Fenelon, M., Gu, Z., Rothberg, E., Wunderling, R.: MIP: theory and practice — closing the gap. In: Powell, M.J.D., Scholtes, S. (eds.) CSMO 1999. ITIFIP, vol. 46, pp. 19–49. Springer, Boston, MA (2000). https://doi.org/10.1007/978-0-387-35514-6_2
9. Byeon, G., Van Hentenryck, P., Bent, R., Nagarajan, H.: Communication-Constrained Expansion Planning for Resilient Distribution Systems. ArXiv e-prints, January 2018
10. Cherdantseva, Y., et al.: A review of cyber security risk assessment methods for scada systems. Comput. Secur. **56**, 1–27 (2016)
11. Coatta, T., Neufeld, G.W.: Configuration management via constraint programming. In: CDS, pp. 90–101. IEEE (1992)
12. Codato, G., Fischetti, M.: Combinatorial Benders' cuts for mixed-integer linear programming. Oper. Res. **54**(4), 756–766 (2006)
13. MITRE Corporation. Common vulnerabilities and exposures, December 2018
14. Dantzig, G.B., Wolfe, P.: Decomposition principle for linear programs. Oper. Res. **8**(1), 101–111 (1960)
15. Fayaz, S.K., Tobioka, Y., Sekar, V., Bailey, M.: Bohatei: flexible and elastic DDoS defense. In: USENIX Security Symposium, pp. 817–832 (2015)
16. Foster, N., et al.: Frenetic: a network programming language. ACM SIGPLAN Not. **46**(9), 279–291 (2011)
17. Fourer, B.: Amazing solver speedups (2015). http://bob4er.blogspot.com/2015/05/amazing-solver-speedups.html
18. Gill, P., Schapira, M., Goldberg, S.: A survey of interdomain routing policies. ACM SIGCOMM Comput. Commun. Rev. **44**(1), 28–34 (2013)
19. Hijazi, H., Mak, T.W.K., Van Hentenryck, P.: Power system restoration with transient stability. In: Proceedings of the Twenty-Ninth AAAI Conference on Artificial Intelligence, AAAI 2015, pp. 658–664. AAAI Press (2015)
20. Hooker, J.N.: Logic-based Benders decomposition. Math. Program. **96**, 2003 (1995)

21. Hooker, J.N.: Logic-Based Methods for Optimization: Combining Optimization and Constraint Satisfaction. Wiley, Hoboken (2000)
22. Ingols, K., Lippmann, R., Piwowarski, K.: Practical attack graph generation for network defense. In: Annual Computer Security Applications Conference, pp. 121–130. IEEE (2006)
23. Ioannidis, J., Bellovin, S.M.: Pushback: router-based defense against DDoS attacks (2001)
24. Ioannidis, J., Bellovin, S.M.: Implementing pushback: router-based defense against DDoS attacks. In: NDSS, vol. 2 (2002)
25. Jansen, W.: Directions in Security Metrics Research. Diane Publishing (2010)
26. Kaynar, K.: A taxonomy for attack graph generation and usage in network security. J. Inf. Secur. Appl. **29**, 27–56 (2016)
27. Khurshid, A., Zhou, W., Caesar, M., Godfrey, P.: Veriflow: verifying network-wide invariants in real time. In: Proceedings of the First Workshop on Hot Topics in Software Defined Networks, pp. 49–54. ACM (2012)
28. Kim, H., Reich, J., Gupta, A., Shahbaz, M., Feamster, N., Clark, R.J.: Kinetic: verifiable dynamic network control. In: NSDI, pp. 59–72 (2015)
29. Kottler, S.: February 28th DDoS incident report, March 2018
30. Kreutz, D., Ramos, F.M.V., Verissimo, P.E., Rothenberg, C.E., Azodolmolky, S., Uhlig, S.: Software-defined networking: a comprehensive survey. Proc. IEEE **103**(1), 14–76 (2015)
31. Lam, E., Van Hentenryck, P.: A branch-and-price-and-check model for the vehicle routing problem with location congestion. Constraints **21**(3), 394–412 (2016)
32. Layeghy, S., Pakzad, F., Portmann, M.: SCOR: software-defined constrained optimal routing platform for SDN. CoRR, abs/1607.03243 (2016)
33. Lippmann, R.P., Riordan, J.F.: Threat-based risk assessment for enterprise networks. Lincoln Lab. J. **22**(1), 33–45 (2016)
34. Lippmann, R.P., Riordan, J.F., Yu, T.H., Watson, K.K.: Continuous security metrics for prevalent network threats: introduction and first four metrics. Technical report, Massachusetts Institute of Technology Lexington Lincoln Laboratory (2012)
35. Marczak, B., et al.: China's great cannon. Citizen Lab (2015)
36. McKeown, N., et al.: Openflow: enabling innovation in campus networks. ACM SIGCOMM Comput. Commun. Rev. **38**(2), 69–74 (2008)
37. Mirkovic, J., Reiher, P.: A taxonomy of DDoS attack and DDoS defense mechanisms. ACM SIGCOMM Comput. Commun. Rev. **34**(2), 39–53 (2004)
38. Moy, J.T.: OSPF: Anatomy of An Internet Routing Protocol. Addison-Wesley Professional, Boston (1998)
39. Nagarajan, H., Yamangil, E., Bent, R., Van Hentenryck, P., Backhaus, S.: Optimal resilient transmission grid design. In: PSCC, pp. 1–7. IEEE (2016)
40. Neves, P., et al.: The SELFNET approach for autonomic management in an NFV/SDN networking paradigm. Int. J. Distrib. Sensor Netw. **12**(2), 2897479 (2016)
41. NIST. National vulnerability database, December 2018
42. Gurobi Optimization Inc.: Gurobi optimizer reference manual (2015). http://www.gurobi.com (2014)
43. Peng, T., Leckie, C., Ramamohanarao, K.: Survey of network-based defense mechanisms countering the DoS and DDoS problems. ACM Comput. Surv. (CSUR) **39**(1), 3 (2007)
44. Reich, J., Monsanto, C., Foster, N., Rexford, J., Walker, D.: Modular SDN programming with Pyretic. Technical report of USENIX (2013)

45. Rossi, F., van Beek, P., Walsh, T.: Handbook of Constraint Programming (Foundations of Artificial Intelligence). Elsevier Science Inc., New York (2006)
46. Schneier, B.: Attack trees. Blog (1999)
47. Shaw, P.: Using constraint programming and local search methods to solve vehicle routing problems. In: Maher, M., Puget, J.-F. (eds.) CP 1998. LNCS, vol. 1520, pp. 417–431. Springer, Heidelberg (1998). https://doi.org/10.1007/3-540-49481-2_30
48. Skowyra, R., Lapets, A., Bestavros, A., Kfoury, A.: A verification platform for SDN-enabled applications. In: IEEE International Conference on Cloud Engineering (IC2E), pp. 337–342. IEEE (2014)
49. Stolfo, S., Bellovin, S.M., Evans, D.: Measuring security. IEEE Secur. Privacy 9(3), 60–65 (2011)
50. Stoneburner, G., Goguen, A.Y., Feringa, A.: SP 800-30. Risk management guide for information technology systems (2002)
51. Wang, R., Butnariu, D., Rexford, J., et al.: Openflow-based server load balancing gone wild. Hot-ICE 11, 12 (2011)
52. Yu, R., Xue, G., Kilari, V.T., Zhang, X.: Deploying robust security in internet of things. In: IEEE Conference on Computer and Network Security (2018)
53. Zargar, S.T., Joshi, J., Tipper, D.: A survey of defense mechanisms against distributed denial of service (DDoS) flooding attacks. IEEE Commun. Surv. Tutor. 15(4), 2046–2069 (2013)
54. Zhang, S., Malik, S.: SAT based verification of network data planes. In: Van Hung, D., Ogawa, M. (eds.) ATVA 2013. LNCS, vol. 8172, pp. 496–505. Springer, Cham (2013). https://doi.org/10.1007/978-3-319-02444-8_43

A Low Overhead Error Correction Algorithm Using Random Permutation for SRAM PUFs

Liang Zheng[1,2,3], Donglei Han[1,2,3], Zongbin Liu[1,3(✉)], Cunqing Ma[1,3], Lingchen Zhang[1,3], and Churan Tang[1,2,3]

[1] State Key Laboratory of Information Security,
Institute of Information Engineering, CAS, 100093 Beijing, China
{zhengliang,handonglei,liuzongbin,macunqing,zhanglingchen,
tangchuran}@iie.ac.cn
[2] School of Cyber Security, University of Chinese Academy of Sciences,
Beijing 100049, China
[3] Data Assurance and Communication Security Research Center, CAS,
Beijing, China

Abstract. Static Random Access Memory-based Physically Unclonable Function (SRAM PUF) is frequently used in cryptographic applications such as key generation and IP protection because of its low cost, simple operation and high security features. The stability of PUF response is susceptible to environmental noise, so it requires the assistance of error correction algorithms when used as a key or ID. However, the actual error correction capability of the theoretically selected Error Correcting Codes (ECC) is always lower than expected. In this paper, we explore the specific reasons why SRAM PUF cannot use the theoretically selected ECC algorithm directly. In addition, an efficient and concise preprocessing method for random permutation is proposed to disturb the original position of unstable bits in the SRAM PUF response, thus confusing its instability distribution. Our experimental results show that the processed SRAM PUFs can recover the response sequence stably without increasing ECC's error correction capability, which effectively saves the resource consumption of error correction circuit.

Keywords: SRAM PUF · Key generation · Error Correcting Codes · Non-uniform · Random permutation · Reed-Muller Codes

1 Introduction

The concept of Physically Unclonable Function (PUF) was first proposed by Pappu in 2001 [19]. As a kind of physical trust root, PUF provides the underlying physical trust foundation for information security applications [1,14]. PUF's departure point is that there are no two identical integrated circuits (ICs) in the real world. Even if the design is consistent, there will still be inevitable differences

© Springer Nature Switzerland AG 2019
J. Jang-Jaccard and F. Guo (Eds.): ACISP 2019, LNCS 11547, pp. 475–493, 2019.
https://doi.org/10.1007/978-3-030-21548-4_26

in the manufactured ICs, which are introduced randomly during the manufacturing process. For example, when the same electrical signal is transmitted on two completely symmetrical circuits, there are different transmission delays. Also, SRAM cells have different start-up values because of process variation including lithographic variations in effective feature size and random threshold voltages [9]. In general, the goal of PUF is to extract the randomness of these manufacturing differences as a unique 'physical fingerprint' of cryptographic devices, thus providing many new high-security solutions for key generation and storage [15], IP protection [8], entity authentication [2] and other aspects.

The PUF-generated key does not need to be stored digitally on the cryptographic device and is only extracted from the device's circuit when it is used. As a result, no secrets are stored on the device when the power is turned off, which will minimize the time the key appears in the cryptographic device. PUF also has low resource consumption, as the PUF-generated key can be extracted from existing circuits, or from some circuits constructed with a few inverters, combinational logic, etc. In addition, even if a PUF is destroyed by an attacker in a physical attack, the PUF will no longer be able to obtain the key, and the attacker naturally has difficulty obtaining it. Common PUFs at present include Arbiter PUF [24], Ring Oscillator PUF (RO PUF) [17], Glitch PUF [23], SRAM PUF [8–10,16,21] and Butterfly PUF [13], etc. Among these PUFs, SRAM PUF is popular for its low cost, simple operation and good stability.

SRAM memory consists of a number of SRAM cells, each of which can be considered to be made up of two cross-coupled inverters that are nominally identical, but the strength of its transistors varies in the actual manufacturing process. If this difference is obvious, the stronger inverter will quickly push the state of the SRAM cell to a steady state - 0 or 1, which is determined by the output of the inverter each time the SRAM is powered on. This start-up value is the embodiment of the inherent characteristics of the SRAM entity. Therefore, for an SRAM PUF, we challenge the addresses of some cells in SRAM, then the start-up value of cells corresponding to these addresses is the response of PUF.

When the influence of circuit noise on the SRAM PUF is greater than the impact of manufacturing differences, the response sequence will have some random flipping of unstable bits every time the power is turned on. In order to obtain a stable key, Error Correcting Codes (ECC) [22] are needed to correct these unstable bits. In a resource-constrained scenario, if there are too many unstable bits in SRAM PUF, the general ECC algorithm cannot be directly applied because the cost is too high. In [6], a preprocessing method for selecting SRAM cell addresses with stable bits by multiple power-on operations was proposed to remove most unstable bit addresses, but this method is not suitable for applications that cannot be powered on multiple times. An improved 8T-SRAM PUF with embedded latches was constructed in [11], which maintains the start-up values of SRAM cell by holding the value in the latches, however, this approach is highly complex.

Our Contributions. In this paper, we use the SRAM in the self-developed chip SSX1624 of SMIC 180 nm process to collect its start-up values as a test data set.

First, we explore the distribution of unstable bits in SRAM PUF response and find that the unstable bits tend to be clustered together, that is, there is a certain correlation between them. This phenomenon is inconsistent with the premise of using ECC algorithm, because if the response is divided into blocks for error correction, it is often required that the unstable bits are independent and uniformly distributed. Therefore, we propose a method using random permutation matrix to transform the SRAM PUF response position in order to confuse the non-uniformity of unstable bits and break up the correlation between them. Proved by our experiment with the existing error correction capability unchanged (same as the theoretically selected ECC algorithm), we can use Reed-Muller (1,5) Code to correct all the errors that could not be corrected before, greatly improving the success rate of error correction. This method is simple in operation and requires only a small consumption, it is suitable for some resource-constrained application scenarios and does not require multiple power-on operations.

In conclusion, our contributions are summarized as follows:

1. We analyze the reason why the error correction capability of theoretically selected ECC algorithm can not correct the unstable bits in SRAM PUF as expected, and prove it with experiments.
2. We propose a position transformation method for random permutation matrix, which is easy to operate and can greatly improve the success rate of error correction while the existing error correction capability remains unchanged.
3. We conduct a large number of data acquisition experiments on SRAM PUF on both the card reader and tablet collection platforms and obtain $200 \times 100 \times 768$-bit responses respectively. We not only compare the error correction results of the unstable bits of SRAM PUF before and after using our preprocessing method, but also evaluate the basic properties such as uniqueness and reliability of SRAM PUF.

Paper Outline. The rest of this paper is organized as follows. Section 2 introduces some basic concepts of SRAM PUF structure, PUF-based key generation scheme and Reed-Muller Codes. In Sect. 3, we describe the phenomenon of 'Non-Uniform SRAM PUF' and analyze the reasons for its occurrence. Section 4 proposes a preprocessing method for random permutation regarding ECC algorithm. We conduct detailed experimental analysis in Sect. 5. Finally, Sect. 6 concludes this paper and plans our future work.

2 Preliminaries

2.1 The Structure of SRAM PUF

The SRAM cell is composed of six MOSFETs (from M1 to M6) as shown in Fig. 1(a). Logically, it can also be considered as two cross-coupled inverters and two read-write control switches in Fig. 1(b), where each inverter consists of one n-MOS and one p-MOS transistors.

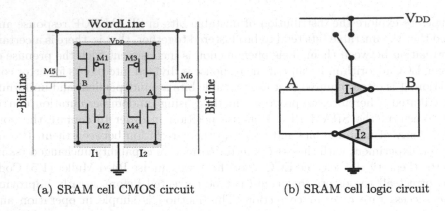

(a) SRAM cell CMOS circuit   (b) SRAM cell logic circuit

Fig. 1. Basic circuit structure of SRAM cell [14]

When reading and writing SRAM cells, we need to enable WL (WordLine) to make transistors M5, M6 conductive, at which time, we can read or write the cell through BL (BitLine). The SRAM cell is volatile, so when the SRAM power is cut off, the charge of the SRAM cell is lost instantaneously, and AB is "00". When the SRAM cell is powered on, because the inverter is in an unstable state, one of the inverters must be reversed once, that is, AB becomes "01" or "10". Ideally, whether AB is "01" or "10" is completely random and unbiased, but in fact, due to some uncontrollable factors in the manufacturing process, such as random fluctuations in dopant concentration, the threshold voltage of the transistor will be different, so that the value stored in a single SRAM cell tends to be a fixed value - 0 or 1 (we assume that the value of A is the output of SRAM cell, $A = \bar{B}$), forming a 0-biased or 1-biased memory cell. In this case, the tendency of start-up value of SRAM cell is stable. Each SRAM memory produces a unique and random binary response sequence, also known as the SRAM's 'fingerprint', which can be used as PUF.

However, if the difference between the two inverters is not obvious, the factor that determines the start-up value of the SRAM cell becomes circuit noise, that is, the influence of noise masks the manufacturing difference. When the SRAM cell is powered up each time, the start-up value is often not the same, and its tendency is not obvious. This is the noise source for the SRAM PUF's response.

2.2 The Key Generation Scheme Based on PUF

Since the PUF response is noisy and not completely evenly distributed, the PUF-based key generator usually needs to use a Fuzzy Extractor [4,12] or Helper Data Algorithm [3,16] to ensure that a stable secure key can be extracted from PUF. The Fuzzy Extractor consists of a Security Sketch based on ECC [22] and an Entropy Accumulator [5] to correct the error bits in PUF response sequence and compress enough entropy into a fixed-length key. Taking SRAM PUF as an example, a common PUF-based key generation scheme is shown in Fig. 2, which is mainly divided into an enrollment phase and a reconstruction phase [14]:

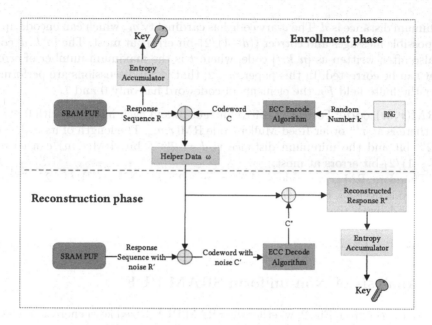

Fig. 2. PUF-based key enrollment and reconstruction process

(i) Enrollment phase: $R \to Generate(key, \omega)$. We can obtain the response sequence R by reading the start-up values of SRAM, and then generate a fixed-length secure key through an Entropy Accumulator, usually a Hash function. In addition, we perform ECC encoding on a random number k generated by Random Number Generator (RNG) to obtain a random codeword C. Then the helper data ω is calculated by R and C, i.e., $\omega = R \oplus C$. The selection of ECC algorithm is determined by the length of the response R and the number of errors that need to be corrected.

(ii) Reconstruction phase: $Recover(R', \omega) \to key$. The generated response R' is noisy when SRAM is powered on again. We first calculate the noisy codeword $C' = R' \oplus \omega = (R' \oplus R) \oplus C$, then C' is corrected to obtain C'' by using the ECC decoding algorithm which has sufficient error correction ability, $C'' = Correct(C') = C$. Finally, the recovered response is calculated: $R'' = \omega \oplus C'' = R \oplus (C \oplus C'') = R$.

2.3 Reed-Muller Codes

The Reed-Muller (RM) Codes are one of the oldest and simplest known linear block codes, which have been widely used. They were discovered by Muller in 1954 [18] and decoded by Reed in the same year [20]. Here we will introduce some basic concepts:

- **$[n, k, d]$-linear q-ary code** [8]: Given an error correction code $[n, k, d]$ over F_q, n is the encoding length, the codeword is n-tuples in F_q elements and its minimum distance is d. The q-ary code has cardinality q_k, which can encode up to q_k possible messages and correct $\lfloor (d-1)/2 \rfloor$-bit errors at most. The $[n, k, d]$ code is also often written as $[n, k, t]$ code, where t is the maximum number of errors that can be corrected. In this paper, $q = 2$, that is, all discussions are performed over the finite field F_2, the elements of codeword has only 0 and 1.

- **RM(r,m) code:** For each positive integer m and each integer r with $0 \le r \le m$, there is an rth order Reed-Muller Code RM(r,m). The length of its codeword is 2^m bit and the minimum distance is $d = 2^{m-r}$ bit. RM(r, m) can correct $\lfloor (d-1)/2 \rfloor$-bit errors at most.

Therefore, RM (r,m) code is a binary $[n = 2^m, k = \sum_{i=0}^{r} \binom{m}{i}, t = 2^{m-r-1}-1]$ linear code over F_2. For instance, the 1st-order RM(1,5) code is a binary [32,6,7] linear code with the codeword length of $n = 2^5 = 32$ bit and the dimension of $k = \binom{5}{0} + \binom{5}{1} = 6$ bit. The maximum number of error bits that can be corrected is $t = 2^{5-2} - 1 = 7$.

3   Analysis of Non-uniform SRAM PUF

As can be seen from Fig. 2, whether the SRAM PUF-based key generation scheme can stably recover key depends largely on the selection of ECC algorithm.

Assuming that the length of the SRAM PUF response sequence R is L bits and all bits are mutually independent, taking the original response sequence of the enrollment phase as a standard, the probability of having at most t unstable error bits in the response sequence generated during the reconstruction phase can be defined as P_{error} [8]:

$$P_{error} = \sum_{i=0}^{t} \binom{L}{i} \cdot e^i (1 - e)^{L-i} \tag{1}$$

where e represents the average bit error rate of the response sequence R.

The acceptable failure rate P_{fail} when we recover errors in PUF response can be expressed as:

$$P_{fail} = 1 - P_{error} = 1 - \sum_{i=0}^{t} \binom{L}{i} \cdot e^i (1 - e)^{L-i} \tag{2}$$

If the unstable error bits are also mutually independent, given the values of e and P_{fail}, t can be obtained through Formula (2), and then the appropriate ECC algorithm can be selected according to the value of t.

Usually, due to the excessive number of response bits required, the resource consumption will be too large if the error correction operation is directly performed on the entire response sequence. Therefore, we can divide the response sequence into blocks and then perform error correction separately. Assuming that the response sequence R can be divided into n blocks for error correction, each block has b bits, and the probability that unstable error bits in each block can be corrected is r. If the unstable error bits are mutually independent and evenly distributed, then the average bit error rate for each block is the same as the average bit error rate for the entire response sequence, which is equal to e. Therefore, the probability that the entire response sequence cannot be corrected is P'_{fail}:

$$P'_{fail} = 1 - r^n, n = L/b,$$

$$r = \sum_{i=0}^{t} \binom{b}{i} \cdot e^i (1-e)^{b-i} \tag{3}$$

We selected 200 chips with the same SRAM for testing, each chip collected 100 times through the card reader platform. According to statistics (detailed calculation in Sect. 5.2), the maximum average bit error rate is 2.28%, and the average Shannon entropy density is 0.998 bit. To ensure the availability of SRAM PUF and low resource consumption for error correction, we specify $e = 3\%$ and $P'_{fail} = 10^{-4}$. According to the security and correctness constraints of Fuzzy Extractor mentioned by Roel Maes in [14], we need at least a 704-bit SRAM PUF response sequence if we want to obtain a 128-bit full entropy stable key, and we need to use a [32,6,7] linear block code to ensure $P_{fail} \leq 10^{-4}$. Therefore, we finally decided to read the $32 \times 24 = 768$-bit response to ensure the security of the key. The response sequence is divided into $n = 24$ blocks and each block is $b = 32$ bit, the maximum number of error bits that can be corrected back in each block is 7.

However, according to our experimental results in Sect. 5.2, it is found that the [32,6,7] linear block code does not completely correct the error bits in all SRAM PUFs even if their average bit error rate is below 3%. We explored the causes of this phenomenon, as can be seen from the assumptions of Formula (3), there is a strong assumption in calculating P'_{fail} that the unstable error bits are mutually independent and evenly distributed, but we suspect that the distribution of unstable error bits may not be so uniform and have some correlation due to SRAM manufacturing process or environmental noise.

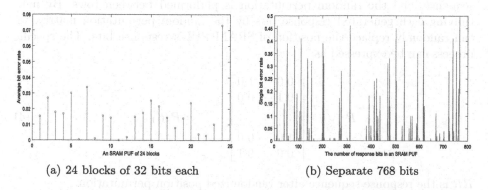

(a) 24 blocks of 32 bits each   (b) Separate 768 bits

Fig. 3. Statistics of bit error rate under different circumstances

We selected one of the SRAM PUFs for analysis and found that the average bit error rate of 24 blocks has a large gap, the smallest is 0 while the largest has reaches 0.073, this result is shown in Fig. 3(a). Furthermore, we also show the single bit error rate of 768-bit response of this SRAM PUF in Fig. 3(b). It can be found that many unstable error bits are clustered together, that is, if a certain bit of the SRAM PUF response is unstable and error-prone, the surrounding response bits are also more error-prone.

In addition, according to Pelgrom's model [7], there are inherent spatial correlation structures in the physical properties of semiconductor devices. Specifically, devices that are closely placed together have a higher correlation than devices that are separated by a larger distance. This also confirms the correctness of our experimental conclusion. This SRAM PUF's unstable error bits are more likely to cluster together, so we call it as 'Non-Uniform SRAM PUF'.

Obviously, it is not feasible to directly use the general theoretical ECC algorithm for such PUFs because its error correction effect is always lower than expected, so we will explore the solutions from the uniformity of unstable bits.

4   The Proposed Random Permutation Position Scheme

According to the above analysis, when using block error correction, such 'Non-Uniform SRAM PUF' will often result in some blocks having more unstable error bits than the maximum correctable error number t of ECC algorithm, and some blocks having fewer unstable error bits, so the phenomenon that the unstable bits cannot be corrected will occur. We can't help thinking that if the distribution of unstable bits can be disturbed so that the unstable bits originally concentrated together are dispersed between other stable bits, the whole response will become a sequence with more uniform distribution of unstable bits, that is, the number of unstable bits in each block will become average at this time.

Based on this idea, we decide to use a unit matrix with a random row transformation to disturb the position of SRAM PUF's response bits. The size of the matrix is $N \times N$ bits, where N is the number of bits in SRAM PUF response sequence, and the random permutation is performed between rows. By multiplying each generated response bits by the random permutation matrix, we can randomly replace the position of SRAM PUF's response bits. The specific process can be expressed as:

$$
R_{1 \times N} \cdot \begin{bmatrix} 0 & 0 & \cdots & 1 & 0 \\ 0 & 1 & \cdots & 0 & 0 \\ \vdots & \vdots & \ddots & \vdots & \vdots \\ 1 & 0 & \cdots & 0 & 0 \\ 0 & 0 & \cdots & 0 & 1 \end{bmatrix}_{N \times N} = RR_{1 \times N} \tag{4}
$$

RR is the response sequence after randomized position permutation.

The SRAM PUF-based key generation scheme can also be improved as shown in Fig. 4. Each SRAM PUF has the same random permutation matrix, which is generated and stored in advance. In enrollment phase, we perform a random position permutation matrix on the original response sequence R, then the key and helper data ω are obtained by using the response sequence RR after the permutation. In reconstruction phase, we still perform the same permutation process on the noisy response sequence R'. At this time, the concentrated position of the unstable error bits in SRAM PUF response has been broken up, so it is easier to successfully correct these error bits using the theoretically feasible ECC algorithm.

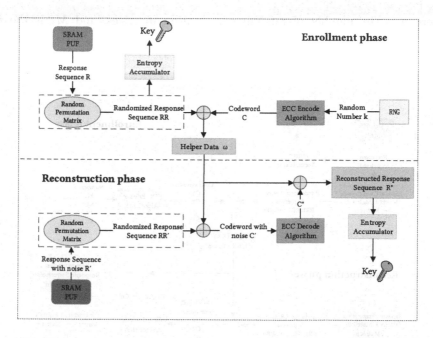

Fig. 4. Improved PUF-based key enrollment and reconstruction process

However, the above scheme is only applicable to some SRAM PUFs with low bit error rate. For SRAM PUFs with high error rate, if only one random permutation matrix is used, the effect of disturbing unstable positions may not be very good. Therefore, we have upgraded this scheme as shown in Fig. 5. Each SRAM PUF has n different random permutation matrices ($n \geq 3$).

In enrollment phase, the key is generated directly by the original response sequence R through the Entropy Accumulator. We perform n random position permutations on the original response R, then the corresponding n helper data are generated: $\omega 1, \omega 2, ..., \omega n$. These helper data are obtained by using different random numbers $k1, k2, ..., kn$, so they do not leak entropy to each other. In reconstruction phase, we also recover n response sequences $R1'', R2'', ..., Rn''$, where the bit position of these sequences are still randomly permuted. In order to successfully recover the key, these response sequences must be restored to the original bit position distribution. We can use the inverse of n random permutation matrices to complete, that is:

$$Ri''_{1 \times N} \cdot \left(\begin{bmatrix} 0 & 0 & \cdots & 1 & 0 \\ 0 & 1 & \cdots & 0 & 0 \\ \vdots & \vdots & \ddots & \vdots & \vdots \\ 1 & 0 & \cdots & 0 & 0 \\ 0 & 0 & \cdots & 0 & 1 \end{bmatrix}_{N \times N} \right)^{-1}_{i} = Mi_{1 \times N} \ (1 \leq i \leq n) \tag{5}$$

where n is the number of random permutation matrices, and Mi is the ith response sequence after recovering to the original bit position. By taking the value that occurs most frequently in Mi, namely Mode, as the final recovery response $M = Mode(M1, M2, .., Mn)$.

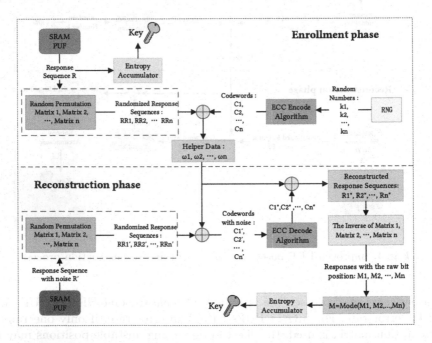

Fig. 5. Further upgrades for the PUF-based key enrollment and reconstruction process

This upgraded scheme effectively increases the success rate of key recovery. Even if the first random permutation matrix does not disturb the distribution of unstable bits well, the subsequent random permutation matrices can be remedied. Considering the resource and efficiency issues, we generally think that the value of n does not exceed 5.

5 Experiments and Results

The SRAM we used in the experiment comes from the self-developed low-power entity identification chip SSX1624, which adopts the SMIC 180 nm CMOS process. We collected the start-up values of the same address of SRAM memory in 200 chips at room temperature, and each chip was powered on 100 times with 768-bit responses collected each time. In addition, we used Near Field Communication (NFC) function from two different platforms for collection: OMNIKEY CardMan 5x21-CL Reader and SONY Xperia Z2 Tablet (SGP541).

5.1 Basic Properties of Our SRAM PUF

In general, we mainly evaluate the performance of a PUF from three aspects of uniqueness, reliability and randomness.

Uniqueness: can be measured by PUF's inter-distance, which is the average Hamming distance between responses obtained by applying the same challenge information to different PUF entities. The calculation of inter-distance is as follows:

$$\mu_{inter} = \sum_{i=1}^{N_{meas}} \sum_{j_1=1}^{N_{puf}-1} \sum_{j_2=j_1+1}^{N_{puf}} \frac{2 \cdot HD(R_{i,j_1}, R_{i,j_2})}{N \cdot N_{puf} \cdot (N_{puf} - 1) \cdot N_{meas}} \tag{6}$$

N_{puf} represents the number of PUF entities, N_{meas} represents the number of times each entity is measured, N represents the length of the response sequence. For the $j_1{}^{th}$ and $j_2{}^{th}$ PUF entities, R_{i,j_1} and R_{i,j_2} represent the response sequence obtained by the ith measurement respectively.

Reliability: can be measured by PUF's intra-distance, which is the average Hamming distance between responses obtained by applying the same challenge information to the same PUF entity multiple times. The calculation of intra-distance is as follows:

$$\mu_{intra} = \sum_{j=1}^{N_{puf}} \sum_{i_1=1}^{N_{meas}-1} \sum_{i_2=i_1+1}^{N_{meas}} \frac{2 \cdot HD(R_{i_1,j}, R_{i_2,j})}{N \cdot N_{puf} \cdot N_{meas} \cdot (N_{meas} - 1)} \tag{7}$$

Where, $R_{i_1,j}$ and $R_{i_2,j}$ represent the response sequences obtained by the $i_1{}^{th}$ and $i_2{}^{th}$ measurements respectively for the jth PUF entity.

Randomness: can be measured by the Shannon entropy of PUF's response sequence, and its calculation formula is:

$$H(R) = \sum_{j=1}^{N_{puf}} \sum_{i=1}^{N_{meas}} \frac{[-P(r_k = 0) \log_2 P(r_k = 0) - P(r_k = 1) \log_2 P(r_k = 1)]}{N_{puf} \cdot N_{meas}} \tag{8}$$

$P(r_k = 0)$ represents the probability that the element in the response sequence is '0'. Similarly, $P(r_k = 1)$ represents the probability that the element in the response sequence is '1'.

A good PUF should have an inter-distance close to 50%, an intra-distance close to 0 and as much entropy as possible. In our experiment, $N_{puf} = 200$, $N_{meas} = 100$, $N = 768$. The basic properties of our SRAM PUF on both reader and tablet collection platforms are summarized in Table 1.

Table 1. Statistics on the basic properties of SRAM PUF (room temperature)

Collection platform	Inter distance	Intra distance	Shannon entropy density per bit
OMNIKEY CardMan 5x21-CL Reader	49.99%	1.89%	0.999
SONY Xperia Z2 Tablet (SGP541)	48.58%	4.63%	0.998

It can be seen that the average inter-distance is close to 50% on two collection platforms, so our SRAM PUF has good uniqueness. The average intra-distance of the response collected by the card reader is 1.89%, while that collected by the tablet has reached 4.63%. This shows that the stability of SRAM PUF response obtained by different collection platforms is not the same. We speculate that this is related to the magnitude of the Radio Frequency (RF) current induced by NFC in different platforms. According to the Shannon entropy density, our SRAM PUF has very good randomness. In addition, we show the distribution of inter-distance and intra-distance under the card reader platform in Fig. 6, and it can be found that they generally follow a normal distribution.

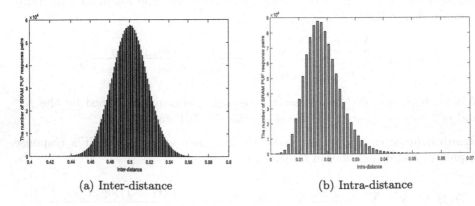

(a) Inter-distance   (b) Intra-distance

Fig. 6. SRAM PUF's inter-distance and intra-distance distributions

5.2 Error Correction Using General ECC Directly

Before error correction, we first describe our calculation method for "unstable error bits" as shown in Fig. 7. Suppose the length of the response sequence is N, N_{meas} response sequences are collected for the same SRAM, and R_i^j represents the ith bit of SRAM PUF response in the jth measurement. For the ith bit, we set the number of occurrences of '1' in the N_{meas} measurement as Num_i, and the ith bit of standard values obtained after judgment is denoted as S_i, there is

$$Num_i = \sum_{j=0}^{N_{meas}} R_i^j \Rightarrow \begin{cases} \geq 50, & S_i = 1 \\ < 50, & S_i = 0 \end{cases} \tag{9}$$

We take the standard values as a benchmark response sequence, which can be considered as the original response sequence during the enrollment phase, and then compare it with N_{meas} response sequences. The different bits are called unstable error bits E and the same bits are called stable bits, still marked as R. In Fig. 7, $N_{meas} = 100, N = 32$.

Bits serial number	1	2	3	4	......	29	30	31	32
1st	1	1	0	1	......	1	0	1	0
2nd	1	1	0	1	......	1	0	1	0
3rd	1	1	0	1	......	1	0	0	0
⋮		⋮		⋮			⋮		
97th	1	1	0	1	......	1	0	1	0
98th	1	1	0	1	......	0	1	0	0
99th	1	1	0	1	......	1	0	1	0
100th	1	1	0	0	......	0	0	1	0
Standard values	1	1	0	1	......	1	0	1	0
Unstable values	R	R	R	E	......	E	E	E	R

R − Stable bits   E − Unstable Error bits

Fig. 7. Schematic diagram of unstable error bits

In addition, the average error rate of response sequence can be calculated accordingly:

$$e = \sum_{i=0}^{N} \sum_{j=0}^{N_{meas}} \frac{R_i^j \oplus S_i}{N \cdot N_{meas}} \tag{10}$$

For the SRAM PUF data collected by the card reader with a maximum average error rate of less than 3%, we can see from the analysis in Sect. 3 that if the failure rate P'_{fail} of error correction is not more than 10^{-4}, a [32,6,7] linear block code is required. Considering the simple operation of RM Codes, we decided to use RM(1,5) Code, which has a 32-bit encoding length and can correct up to 7-bit errors. The 768-bit SRAM PUF response is divided into 24 blocks, each of which contains 32 bits. In the actual response recovery process, as long as the number of unstable error bits in each block does not exceed 7 bits, it can be considered that the original response can be successfully recovered using RM(1,5) Code.

Therefore, in 200 SRAM PUFs, we count that the number of 200 × 100 response sequences that can not be corrected back is 13, then $P'_{meas-fail} = 13/200 \times 100 = 6.5 \times 10^{-4} > 10^{-4}$. More specifically, we separately calculate the number of unstable error bits of 100×24 32-bit blocks per SRAM PUF, and display the maximum distribution of all SRAM PUFs in Fig. 8(a). We can see that there are already 6 SRAM PUFs with a maximum number of unstable error bits greater than 7, but the maximum number of most SRAM PUFs is no more than 5, which also indicates that the SRAM PUF response collected by the card reader is relatively stable. In addition, we select the worst stability of 200 SRAM PUFs for analysis, as can be seen from Fig. 8(b), there are 5 times of maximum unstable error bits greater than 7 bits in the 100 measurements of this SRAM PUF.

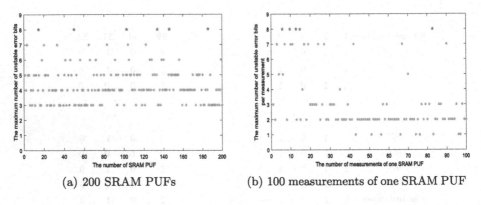

(a) 200 SRAM PUFs   (b) 100 measurements of one SRAM PUF

Fig. 8. Statistics of the maximum number of unstable error bits in SRAM PUF on card reader platform under different circumstances

In summary, if we directly use RM(1,5) Code for error correction, we cannot guarantee that the stable response can be successfully recovered with the theoretical failure rate p'_{fail}.

For the SRAM PUF response collected by the tablet, the maximum average bit error rate is 4.34% in our statistics. Similarly, we still use RM(1,5) Code for error correction and count that 200×100 response sequences cannot be corrected back is 7 times, that is, $P'_{meas-fail} = 3.5 \times 10^{-4}$. From Fig. 9(a), we can see that the maximum number of unstable bits per SRAM PUF is mostly between 5 and 7 bits, which proves that the stability of the response collected by the tablet is worse than that of the card reader. The distribution of 100 measurements of one of SRAM PUF is shown in Fig. 9(b).

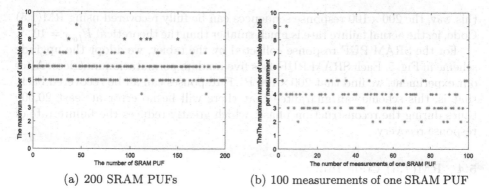

(a) 200 SRAM PUFs   (b) 100 measurements of one SRAM PUF

Fig. 9. Statistics of the maximum number of unstable error bits in SRAM PUF on tablet platform under different circumstances

5.3   Error Correction Using Random Permutation Position Scheme

Since the SRAM PUF response collected by the card reader has a small average bit error rate, we only need to use a 768×768 random permutation matrix for each SRAM PUF (using the improved method in Fig. 4), and the permutation process is operated by software. After the permutation is performed, we recount the maximum number of unstable bits in each SRAM PUF with 32-bit block units as shown in Fig. 10(a), and we find that it does not exceed 5 bits. Compared with Fig. 8(a), our scheme not only eliminates 8-bit unstable bits, but also averages 6-bit and 7-bit unstable bits into other blocks with smaller number of unstable bits. Figure 10(b) shows the unstable bit distribution of SRAM PUF with the worst stability, most of unstable bits are no more than 3 bits in 100 measurements, the unstable bits are greatly averaged compared with Fig. 8(b). In

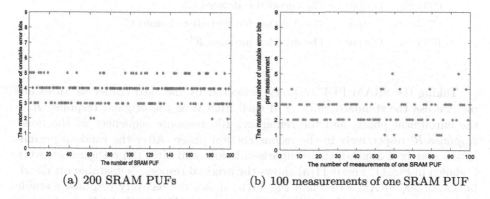

(a) 200 SRAM PUFs   (b) 100 measurements of one SRAM PUF

Fig. 10. Statistics of the maximum number of unstable error bits in SRAM PUF on card reader platform under different circumstances after the random permutation

this way, the 200×100 response sequences can be fully recovered using RM(1,5) Code, ie, the actual failure rate is much smaller than the theoretical $P'_{fail} = 10^{-4}$.

For the SRAM PUF response collected by the tablet, we adopt the upgrade scheme in Fig. 5. Each SRAM PUF uses five random permutation matrices. After our experiment, we find that 200×100 PUF responses can all be recovered back, that is, this scheme can guarantee that there will be no error at least 20,000 times during the reconstruction phase, which greatly reduces the failure rate of response recovery.

5.4   RM(1,5) Code Implementation and Error Correction Result

The RM(1,5) Code module contains two functions of encoding and decoding, and the specific functions of interface signals are listed in Table 2. We implemented our module on the Xilinx ZedBoard (device type: xc7z020clg484-1) Evaluation Platform. According to the synthesis report of Xilinx ISE 14.6 software, this module only uses 191 LUTs (Look Up Tables), 81 IOBs (Input/Output Blocks) and 1 BUFG (Global Clock Buffer).

Table 2. Descriptions of interface signals

Signal	Direction	Description
clk	Input	Clock signal
$rstn$	Input	Asynchronously reset signal, active low
$Start$	Input	Module operation start signal
$FunSel$	Input	Function select signal: 0 is encoding, 1 is decoding
$K[5:0]$	Input	Message K to be encoded
$C'[31,0]$	Input	Codeword C' to be decoded (corrected)
$Done$	Output	Module operation end signal
$C[31:0]$	Output	The encoded codeword C
$C''[31:0]$	Output	The decoded (corrected) codeword C''
$K'[5:0]$	Output	The decoded message K'

Taking the SRAM PUF response collected by the card reader as an example, we use the standard value S of each SRAM as the original response R in the enrollment phase, and the remaining 100 response sequences as the noisy response R' respectively in the reconstruction phase. After the random permutation matrix is applied, the comparison before and after the response recovery is shown in Fig. 11. Figure 11(a) shows the original response's unstable bit distribution of 200 SRAM PUFs and Fig. 11(b) shows the recovery response's stable bit distribution obtained after error correction of RM(1,5) Code. It can be seen that all the unstable bits (orange dots) have been corrected back. With a stable SRAM PUF response output, a stable key can be generated through an Entropy Accumulator.

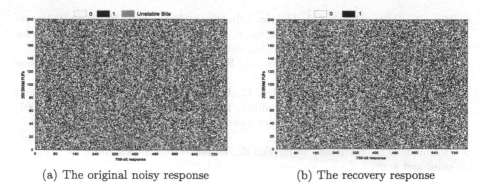

(a) The original noisy response   (b) The recovery response

Fig. 11. Comparison of the unstable bit distribution of SRAM PUF response on card reader platform before and after using RM(1,5) Code

6 Conclusion and Future Work

In this paper, we analyze the unstable bit distribution of 'Non-Uniform PUF' and the specific reasons why the error correction capability of ECC algorithm is always lower than expected. Moreover, a random permutation position scheme is proposed with simple operation and no additional error correction resources, which effectively saves the consumption of error correction circuit and has a wide range of application scenarios. Our experiments have proved the effectiveness and practicability of our scheme. In future work, we will evaluate and test the effectiveness of our method for SRAM PUF under different environments (temperature, voltage and aging, etc.).

References

1. Armknecht, F., Maes, R., Sadeghi, A.R., Standaert, F.X., Wachsmann, C.: A formal foundation for the security features of physical functions. In: 32nd IEEE Symposium on Security and Privacy, S&P 2011, vol. 9, no. 1, pp. 397–412 (2011)
2. Delvaux, J., Gu, D., Schellekens, D., Verbauwhede, I.: Secure lightweight entity authentication with strong PUFs: mission impossible? In: Batina, L., Robshaw, M. (eds.) CHES 2014. LNCS, vol. 8731, pp. 451–475. Springer, Heidelberg (2014). https://doi.org/10.1007/978-3-662-44709-3_25
3. Delvaux, J., Gu, D., Schellekens, D., Verbauwhede, I.: Helper data algorithms for PUF-based key generation: overview and analysis. IEEE Trans. CAD Integr. Circ. Syst. **34**(6), 889–902 (2015)
4. Dodis, Y., Reyzin, L., Smith, A.: Fuzzy extractors: how to generate strong keys from biometrics and other noisy data. In: Cachin, C., Camenisch, J.L. (eds.) EUROCRYPT 2004. LNCS, vol. 3027, pp. 523–540. Springer, Heidelberg (2004). https://doi.org/10.1007/978-3-540-24676-3_31
5. Dupuis, F., Fawzi, O., Renner, R.: Entropy accumulation. CoRR abs/1607.01796 (2016)

6. Eiroa, S., Castro-Ramirez, J., Martínez-Rodríguez, M.C., Tena, E., Brox, P., Baturone, I.: Reducing bit flipping problems in SRAM physical unclonable functions for chip identification. In: ICECS, pp. 392–395. IEEE (2012)

7. Friedberg, P., Cheung, W., Spanos, C.: Spatial variability of critical dimensions (2005)

8. Guajardo, J., Kumar, S.S., Schrijen, G.-J., Tuyls, P.: FPGA intrinsic PUFs and their use for IP protection. In: Paillier, P., Verbauwhede, I. (eds.) CHES 2007. LNCS, vol. 4727, pp. 63–80. Springer, Heidelberg (2007). https://doi.org/10.1007/978-3-540-74735-2_5

9. Holcomb, D.E., Burleson, W.P., Fu, K., et al.: Initial SRAM state as a fingerprint and source of true random numbers for RFID tags. In: Proceedings of the Conference on RFID Security, vol. 7, p. 1 (2007)

10. Intrinsic ID: WHITE PAPER-SRAM PUF: The Secure Silicon Fingerprint (2016). https://www.intrinsic-id.com/resources/white-papers/

11. Jang, J., Ghosh, S.: Design and analysis of novel SRAM PUFs with embedded latch for robustness. In: ISQED, pp. 298–302. IEEE (2015)

12. Kang, H., Hori, Y., Katashita, T., Hagiwara, M., Iwamura, K.: Performance analysis for PUF data using fuzzy extractor. In: Jeong, Y.-S., Park, Y.-H., Hsu, C.-H.R., Park, J.J.J.H. (eds.) Ubiquitous Information Technologies and Applications. LNEE, vol. 280, pp. 277–284. Springer, Heidelberg (2014). https://doi.org/10.1007/978-3-642-41671-2_36

13. Kumar, S.S., Guajardo, J., Maes, R., Schrijen, G.J., Tuyls, P.: The butterfly PUF: protecting IP on every FPGA. In: HOST, pp. 67–70. IEEE Computer Society (2008)

14. Maes, R.: Physically Unclonable Functions - Constructions, Properties and Applications. Springer, Heidelberg (2013). https://doi.org/10.1007/978-3-642-41395-7

15. Maes, R., van der Leest, V., van der Sluis, E., Willems, F.: Secure key generation from biased PUFs. In: Güneysu, T., Handschuh, H. (eds.) CHES 2015. LNCS, vol. 9293, pp. 517–534. Springer, Heidelberg (2015). https://doi.org/10.1007/978-3-662-48324-4_26

16. Maes, R., Tuyls, P., Verbauwhede, I.: Low-overhead implementation of a soft decision helper data algorithm for SRAM PUFs. In: Clavier, C., Gaj, K. (eds.) CHES 2009. LNCS, vol. 5747, pp. 332–347. Springer, Heidelberg (2009). https://doi.org/10.1007/978-3-642-04138-9_24

17. Maiti, A., Casarona, J., McHale, L., Schaumont, P.: A large scale characterization of RO-PUF. In: HOST, pp. 94–99. IEEE Computer Society (2010)

18. Muller, D.E.: Application of boolean algebra to switching circuit design and to error detection. Trans. I.R.E. Prof. Group Electron. Comput. 3(3), 6–12 (1954)

19. Pappu, R., Recht, B., Taylor, J., Gershenfeld, N.: Physical one-way functions. Science 297(5589), 2026–2030 (2002)

20. Reed, I.S.: A class of multiple-error-correcting codes and the decoding scheme. Trans. IRE Prof. Group Inf. Theory (TIT) 4, 38–49 (1954)

21. Selimis, G.N., et al.: Evaluation of 90nm 6T-SRAM as physical unclonable function for secure key generation in wireless sensor nodes. In: ISCAS, pp. 567–570. IEEE (2011)

22. Sun, K., Lao, Y., Liu, W., You, X., Zhang, C.: Application of LDPC codes on PUF error correction based on code-offset construction. In: ASICON, pp. 867–870. IEEE (2017)

23. Suzuki, D., Shimizu, K.: The glitch PUF: a new delay-PUF architecture exploiting glitch shapes. In: Mangard, S., Standaert, F.-X. (eds.) CHES 2010. LNCS, vol. 6225, pp. 366–382. Springer, Heidelberg (2010). https://doi.org/10.1007/978-3-642-15031-9_25

24. Tajik, S., et al.: Physical characterization of arbiter PUFs. In: Batina, L., Robshaw, M. (eds.) CHES 2014. LNCS, vol. 8731, pp. 493–509. Springer, Heidelberg (2014). https://doi.org/10.1007/978-3-662-44709-3_27

Practical Dynamic Taint Tracking
for Exploiting Input Sanitization Error
in Java Applications

Mohammadreza Ashouri$^{(\boxtimes)}$ (iD)

University of Potsdam, August-Bebel-Strasse 89, 14482 Potsdam, Germany
ashouri@uni-potsdam.de

Abstract. Errors in the sanitization of user inputs lead to serious security vulnerabilities. Many applications contain such errors, making them vulnerable to input sanitization exploits. Therefore, internet worms via exploiting vulnerabilities in applications infect hundreds of thousands of users in a matter of short time, causing hundreds of millions of dollars in damages. To successfully counter internet worm attacks, we need automatic detection and defense mechanisms. First, we need automatic detection mechanisms that can detect runtime attacks for vulnerabilities. A disclosure mechanism should be simple to deploy, resulting in few false positives and few false negatives.

In this paper we present Tainer, an automatic dynamic taint analysis framework to detect and generate exploits for sanitization based vulnerabilities for Java web applications. Particularly, our method is based on tracking the flow of taint information from untrusted input the application sensitive methods (such as console, file, network, database or another program). Our proposed framework is portable, quick, accurate, and does not need the source code of applications. We demonstrate the usefulness of the framework by detecting several zero-day actual vulnerabilities in popular Java applications.

1 Introduction

So far many tools have been created to detect security issues and hacking attacks for networks and software, and they can be divided into two main categories as follow:

1. Coarse-grained detectors, capable of detecting network anomalies such as the occurrence of port scanning or unusual activity in a specific IP or port.
2. Fine-grained detectors, capable of detecting the attacks based on suspicious activities within the application.

Coarse-grained detection mechanisms are prone to reporting many false positives and lack detailed and precise information about the vulnerabilities, intersoftware activities and methods of intrusion. Therefore, they cannot help much with finding application vulnerabilities and preventing the spread of malware

© Springer Nature Switzerland AG 2019
J. Jang-Jaccard and F. Guo (Eds.): ACISP 2019, LNCS 11547, pp. 494–513, 2019.
https://doi.org/10.1007/978-3-030-21548-4_27

based on such vulnerabilities. For example, a malware that attacks via web-based vulnerabilities such as SQL injection or Cross Site Scripting (XSS) sends its payload to the victim's machine through supposedly normal and authorized network requests. Consequently, it seems better to converge on fine-grained detectors that record fewer false positives and carry further details about vulnerabilities and the methods of invasion in hacking attacks [14].

For the implementation of fine-grained detectors several approaches have been proposed. However, most of them require application source code or special decompiling of application executable files. These approaches are often accompanied by numerous flaws (e.g., high false positives). Also, they are not popular among software developers due to the requirement for the understanding of security issues and similar problems. For instance, tools like FindBugs, PDM, Infer, Soot and Coverity are well-known static analyzers (which are also used to detect vulnerabilities) need to recompile the libraries or modify the source code of applications in order to perform the analysis [38]. Thus, it makes the analyzers impractical in many real work situations, especially for commercial applications whose merchants are naturally reluctant to publish their source code. Such limitations narrow down the areas where static analysis tools can be used and implemented, and this is true especially in the case of industrial applications.

Consequently, creating fine-grained detectors seems necessary in the implementation of defensive mechanisms. Such a tool should work with any application without requiring the source code; also its configuration and running process should be fast and straightforward even though we believe reaching this goal is not an easy job.

Except for some research regarding dynamic taint analysis for vulnerability detection in Java applications, the majority of near studies used static analysis which requires the source code of applications [2,32,40,47]. The main drawback of static analysis is high false positive rates [30]. Moreover, static analysis tools can only control for the existence of the sanitization functions and not evaluate their effectiveness [4]. Therefore, it confines the capability of static analysis to address the context-sensitiveness of sanitization errors. On the other hand, dynamic analysis systems seems to be more powerful and precise to evaluate applications responses to identify any sanitization errors and concerning security issues [20].

Regarding security vulnerabilities in applications, our assumption is there are security issues where inputs without being adequately sanitized from untrusted sources (such as keyboard, file, network or another program) go into sensitive sinks (such as console, file, network, database or another program). Hence, if we were able to identify such vulnerable data flows in applications, we can intuitively recognize applications vulnerabilities due to the lack of sanitization.

In this research, our primary objective is to introduce a framework which identifies untrusted data flows at runtime, reports applications vulnerabilities to users and generates concise exploits for the detected security issues. Hence, we introduce Tainer as a straightforward, portable and scalable framework which

works based on a dynamic taint tracking system to taint such data flows and
enables users to identify vulnerabilities and hacking attacks at runtime. More
precisely, Tainer works based on bytecode instrumentation (BCI) and runs on
all standard operating systems and hardware architectures. It also requires that
the runtime environment including JVM and the binary files of Java applications
be equipped with a taint propagation mechanism. This conservative approach
provides a high precision environment for monitoring the inter-application activities. Fortunately, Tainer needs no specialized/modified JVMs, and it works with
standard off-the-rack JVMs. Moreover, the framework is built on top of the ASM
framework[1] [29] which has a satisfactory performance at runtime.

Briefly, this work achieved the following contributions:

1. **Non-reliance on source code.** Tainer works based on bytecode instrumentation of applications' binaries, so it does not need the source code of
   applications. This feature makes the framework easy-to-use and more practical so that it can be employed in a wide variety of real-world applications
   including commercial software whose source code is not available.
2. **Detecting state-of-the-art vulnerabilities.** Despite similar works that
   often focus on old-fashioned and straightforward vulnerabilities, Tainer not
   only detects and exploits the classic techniques, i.e., SQL injection, Remote
   Command Execution (RCE) and XSS, but also it covers modern techniques
   such as EL injections, OGNL injection, and obfuscation methods in J2EE
   applications and MVC frameworks.
3. **Experimental validation.** During the study of the previous works, we realized that one of the major obstacles for preparing a precise evaluation is finding non-commercial Java datasets. Moreover, almost all of the similar studies
   for Java often used student project applications which cannot represent the
   complexities of real-world circumstances. However, in this work, we prepare a
   fairly extensive dataset of Java applications including Apache Struts, Spring
   Boot, Hibernate, Scala as a part of our experimental benchmark.
4. **The capability to modernize and upgrade by users.** Despite the similar works in which users only can use the already hard-coded specifications,
   Tainer is adjustable. In other words, users can customize and upgrade the
   specifications of Tainer based on their requirements, without struggling with
   code recompilation. Consequently, in our proposed framework, all of the data
   flow specifications and vulnerability patterns in Tainer are stored as separated
   plain text files out of the Tainer's kernel. Hence, users can actively engage in
   modernizing and enhancing our framework without getting stuck in low-level
   structures and compilation process.
5. **Portability.** Tainer runs with standard JVMs such as OpenJDK and Oracle's JDK on all standard operating systems. Hence, users can employ the
   framework to instrumented their local runtime environment without struggling with limited pre-instrumented versions of JVM.
6. **Automatic exploit generation.** We are conscious of the fact that having
   proof of concept (PoC) exploits is the best way to prove the presence of a vul-

---

[1] https://asm.ow2.io/.

nerability in an application. It also enables maintenance teams to construct and test the patches effectively. Once the vulnerability is being detected, Tainer begins to reproduce exploits based on the characteristics of vulnerable data flow such as vulnerability type, input format and other necessary information.

We have been evaluated Tainer with 15 popular and well-known Java projects that incorporated 6.65 million lines of code. We deliberately added some of the real-world projects such as Apache Struts, Spring framework, Hibernate, Scala as well as educational projects such as Webgoat to our test unit. The results of the experiments demonstrate that Tainer reports and generates a total of 155 potential security violations along with their exploits in our benchmarks, out of which 131 turned out to be actual security vulnerabilities.

2   Background

2.1   Taint Analysis

Taint analysis stays within the domain of information flow analyses. Essentially, the core idea of this process is tracking variables propagate throughout the application of analysis. To detect information flow vulnerabilities, entry points for external inputs in an application need to be identified. The external inputs could be data from any source outside an application that is not trusted. In other words, it must be determined where there is a crossing in the applications establishing a trust boundary. In a web application context, this is typically user input fetched from a web page form, but would also include, for example, HTTP header, URL parameters, data and cookies [43].

In taint analysis, the recognized entry points are called sources. The sources are marked as tainted, and the analysis tracks how these tainted objects propagate throughout the application. A tainted object rarely exclusively remains in the initially assigned object, and thus it propagates [7]. This means that it affects objects other than its original assignment. This can happen directly or indirectly. Directly in that, for instance, a tainted string object is assigned either partly or fully to a new object of some sort.

A tainted object in itself is not dangerous to an application. When a tainted object is used in a critical operation without suitable sanitization, vulnerabilities could appear. Sanitizing a object indicates to remove data or format it in such a way that it will not carry any data that could exploit the critical command in which it will be used [37]. An illustration is when querying a database with a tainted string, it could open for SQL injection if the string contains characters that either change the intended query or divided it into additional new queries. Adequate sanitization would eliminate the unwanted characters, eliminating the chance of unintended queries and essentially preventing SQL injection. Contrary to input data being assigned as sources, methods that execute crucial operations are called sinks in taint analysis. When a tainted object can be used within a sink, a successful taint analysis implementation will identify this as a vulnerability.

2.2 Dynamic Taint Analysis vs Static Taint Analysis

Taint analysis can be divided into two approaches, dynamic taint analysis and static taint analysis [44]. The dynamic taint analysis (DTA) approach analyzes the different executed paths in an application specific runtime environment, tracks the information flow between identified source to sink method, and controls how this kind of analysis is carried out. Static taint analysis is a method that analyses the application source code. This means that, finally, all possible execution paths can be covered in this type of analysis, whereas in a dynamic taint analysis context, only those paths included explicitly in the analysis are covered.

Checking properties for all possible executions paths makes static analysis time-consuming and likely to generate a large number of false positives and false negatives. However, static analysis seems to be the more cost-efficient with the ability to discover bugs at an initial phase of the software development life cycle. Dynamic analysis, on the other hand, is capable of detecting a indirect bug or vulnerability too complex for static analysis solely to unveil and can also be the more convenient method of testing which does not require the source code. A dynamic test, however, only finds bugs in the piece of the code that is executed.

DTA can be used in test case generation to generate input to test applications automatically. This is suitable for discovering how the behaviour of an application changes with various types of input to test applications automatically [3]. Such an analysis could be useful as a step in the development testing phase of a deployed application since this could also detect vulnerabilities that are implementation specific. DTA is also efficient because it requires to check only a single path, and it is accurate because the properties are verified on the real implementation and not on an abstracted version of the system [26]. DTA can also be used for malware analysis in revealing how information flows through a malicious software binary [8].

2.3 Java Bytecode Instrumentation

Compiled Java classes are collected in an intermediary class file format. A class file carries bytecodes, i.e. instructions that are represented by the Java virtual machine (JVM) [1]. JVM is a cross-platform execution environment that transforms Java bytecode into machine language and executes it. Even though the binary class file format is well-defined and programming bytecode methods by hand is feasible, there are some bytecode generation libraries prepared which can be used to assist with instrumenting the bytecode of existing classes, e.g., Javassist [9], ASM [29] and BCEL [11].

Instrumentation is a technique to modify the execution of an application at runtime without knowing or changing the application code itself [6]. This is feasible thanks to the Java Instrumentation API which is implemented by the JVM. This API is designed to manipulate code before it executes. Genuine use cases for Java instrumentation are, e.g., taint tracking, monitoring agents and event loggers. Using this technique makes it possible to introduce almost any changes to already deployed Java application by operating on its bytecode level which is interpreted by JVM at runtime, without modifying application's source code (since no need to re-compilation, re-assembly and re-deployment of an application) [21]. It is conducted through implementing an agent that makes it possible to transform every class loaded by the Class Loader before being used for the first time [15].

3   Methodology

Tainer operates based on Java application bytecode instrumentation technique. The instrumentation should be taken for both given Java applications and host JVM. Once the instrumentation process was done, the instrumented applications can run normally, without changing behaviour, under the instrumented JVM (Fig. 1).

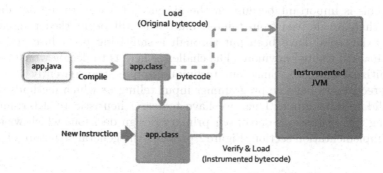

Fig. 1. Running an instrumented class inside of an instrumented JVM

For the instrumentation process, the following items should be taken:

- Sources: These methods return data input from untrusted input sources. For instance, methods that read HTML form input or read cookies stored from browsers, or parse HTTP parameters. All strings entering from sources must be marked tainted.
- Propagation: Data from sources usually are manipulated to form other strings such as queries, scripts, or file-system paths. Data that are acquired from tainted strings also need to be marked.
- Sinks: These are methods that use input or derivative of user input. They comprise of methods that execute some form of code, e.g., script or query, or methods which output data - namely presenting a new HTML page. Tainted data must be restricted from being used as a malicious input for sink methods.

Source and sink methods necessitate being specified once per libraries which applications use. In Tainer, we carefully specify and preserve some of the most useful source methods of Tomcat web server which enable the framework to inspect all HTTP(S) requests from client-side (such as POST, GET, and cookie). Moreover, we construct a precise large set of sensitive sinks (such as database executions, process management, file system, console, and operating system) for Java standard libraries and popular frameworks, e.g., Struts, Spring, Hibernate, which incorporate the most common sensitives methods in enterprise J2EE web applications. In order to track the taintedness of untrusted data, we associated a taint flag with every string. This taint flag is set when a data string is returned by a source method. We propagate this taint flag to strings that are derived from tainted strings through operations such as case conversion, concatenation. This method is the same for all standard operating systems which support Java. Needless to mention that Tainer instruments all standard versions of JVM.

3.1   Untainting

Once we have a mechanism to mark data tainted, we also need a way to untaint them. This is important because in the absence of a way to untaint data, all strings that are derived from tainted data will still be marked tainted. This includes data that have been put through a sanitizing procedure and should not be marked tainted anymore. The challenge here is to decide which methods are sanitizing methods. Since our technique applies transparently to existing Java bytecode, we have no programmer input telling us which methods sanitize and validate data input. Thus, we have to use a heuristic to determine this. Choosing this heuristic is one of our primary design decisions which we explain in the implementation section. Figure 2 presents the general structure of Tainer.

3.2   Dealing with Taint Errors

While instrumented J2EE applications run on an instrumented JVM, if malicious users or malware attempt to attack the applications, the following actions are carried out in Tainer (Fig. 3):

1. If data issued from one of the specified sources and reach one of the specified sink methods, the JVM taints the data flow and raises an exception indicating a runtime taint violation. Considering this is an exception, the application is unaware of this particular exception, and the application is not be caught unless it has a mechanism to deal with unknown runtime exceptions.
2. Tainer as a background process catches the exception, creates a new thread which we name it Vulnerability Analyzer (VA) and relinquishes the tainted flow to it.
3. The VA inspects the flow content with matching the tainted data with a set of regular expressions to find whether the flows contain malicious data. These regular expressions are collected as a set of plain text files in the Tainer path, and therefore users can upgrade them quickly. Listing 1.1 shows how the VA detects the no correctly sanitized data in a given tainted flow.

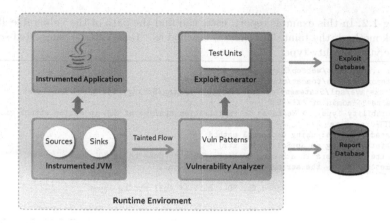

Fig. 2. Overview of the framework architecture

Listing 1.1. This piece of Java code demonstrates how the VA matches a given tainted data with XSS pattern. Example shown at the basic level

```
XSS_pattern=@"|(<(script|iframe|embed|frame|frameset|object|_
img|applet|body|html|style|layer|link|ilayer|meta|bgsound))";
Matcher XSSmatcher = pattern.matcher(XSS_pattern);
        boolean XSSfound = false;
        while (XSSmatcher.find()) {
                XSSfound = true;
                ...
```

4. The VA passes the tainted flows to the Exploit Generator (EG) along with guide information such as the path of the vulnerable file, HTTP method, vulnerability type, sink arguments, and then the EG begins to generate exploits. The EG works with the help of JUnit tests.

5. Ultimately, the Report Generator provides necessary information concerning the attack to users. The information includes the type vulnerability, data flow involving sources and sinks, and recommended solutions. These reports enable users (including software developers) to discern applications' vulnerabilities and leads them to patch security issues accurately. Listing 1.2 presents a sample generated report for SQL injection attack. Also, in Table 4 (appendix) we state some of the regular expressions which Tainer uses.

Fig. 3. Flowchart outlines the process of exploit generation from an inspected tainted flow in Tainer. For easier reading, the example is shown at the basic level.

Listing 1.2. In this example report, users can find the path of the vulnerable JSP file, the sink method, the taint data (here is labelled as "TaintValue"), suggested solution, and the vulnerability type.

```
+ Path: ../testunit/websep/login.jsp
+ Source=org/apache/tomcat/util/net/NloEndpoint$;
      Sink=java/sql/Statement.executeQuery(Ljava/lang/String;)Ljava/sql/ResultSet;
TaintValue=" 'admin or 'X'='X "
+ Vulnerability Type = > Weakness in sanitization against of SQL injection attack via the
      HTTP requests
+ Suggested Solution: using escapeSql method :
public static String escapeSql(String str)
Escapes the characters in a String to be suitable to pass to an SQL query.
-- Parameters: str - the string to escape, may be null

-- Returns: a new String, escaped for SQL, null if null string input

+ How to fix: www.owasp.org/index.php/Injection_Prevention_Cheat_Sheet_in_Java
```

4   Implementation

As we mentioned earlier, Tainer requires that Java applications and their runtime environment be equipped with taint propagation mechanism. Therefore, Tainer modifies the application class files through the Bytecode Instrumentation (BCI) [15], so we no need access to the application's source code. BCI gives a way to add code into the Java class file methods, either before the VM loads the class file or by redefining the class files on the fly [6]. Genuine use cases for BCI are monitoring agents, event loggers and taint trackers. Our framework instruments the bytecode instructions before loading by JVM.

For implementing bytecode instrumentation in our method, we used ASM [29] which is a widely adopted Java bytecode manipulation framework. The ASM provides methods for reading, write and transform such byte arrays by using higher level concepts than bytes, that means, through the API in the ASM library, we can analyze the class without reading the source code [42].

The ASM framework also is the de-facto standard for high-performance byte-code transformations, and it is used in many Java-based applications and frameworks including code analyzers (SonarJ, IBM AUS), ORM mappers (including Oracle TopLink and Berkley DB, ObjectWeb EasyBeans and Speedo), and scripting languages (BeanShell, Groovy and JRuby) [29].

Other libraries, such as BCEL [12] and SERP[2], are also available for bytecode instrumentation purposes; however, what sets ASM aside from the others is ASM has a small memory footprint and is relatively fast in comparison with other frameworks.

The following listings show a basic illustration of the sort of transformations that Tainer atop of ASM applies at the byte code level to support taint tracking – the changes made by the framework during the instrumentation. Please note that for easier reading the example is shown at the source level.

---

[2] http://serp.sourceforge.net/.

Listing 1.3. Sample class before the instrumentation

```
public class OtherClass{

  byte[] Key;

  OtherClass(int Len,byte[] Seed){

  Key=new byte[Len];
  Key=Seed;

  }
}
```

Listing 1.4. Sample class after the instrumentation

```
public class OtherClass{

  byte[] Key;
  byte[] Trace_Key;

  OtherClass(int Trace_Len,int Len,byte[] Trace_Seed,byte[] Seed){

  Key=new byte[Len];
  Trace_Key=new byte[Len];
  Key=Seed;
  Trace_Key=Seed;

  }
}
```

Users via source-sink specification can tell to Tainer which data flows must be considered for tracking tainting input data at runtime. The way of adding sources and sinks into the framework is rather straightforward. For instance, we extract and preserve source and sink methods of Java core libraries with the return type information in plain text files. As we stated before, these files can also be updated by users directly. In other words, users can customize the performance and tainting policy of the framework simply by modifying the source and sink files. In the following, we elaborate on the source and sink specification.

4.1   Source Methods

In this paper (because we focus on J2EE web applications) we attempt to check all HTTP(S) methods (e.g., POST, GET, HEAD, DELETE and PUT). Thus, we notice that if we intercept the Buffer of incoming HTTP requests of a Tomcat server, we can in fact inspect all client-side traffic coming to the J2EE applications on the server. Consequently, we define **NioBufferHandler** method as an untrusted data source for Tainer (Listing 1.5). Table 3 (appendix) represents some of the specified source and sink methods in the framework.

Listing 1.5. NioEndpoint.NioBufferHandler used for socket processing in Apache Tomcat web server

```
import org.apache.tomcat.util.net.NioEndpoint;
public NioEndpoint.NioBufferHandler(int readsize, int writesize, boolean direct)
```

4.2   Sink Methods

We carefully specify a large set of sink methods which are involved in security issues. The process of sink methods specification should be taken conservatively. Otherwise, Tainer has to taint a vast number of data flows which are not necessarily involved in actual attacks. No need to explain that tracking redundant flows imposes more overheads to the runtime performance. In addition to Java standard libraries, we consciously extract sink methods from popular frameworks (e.g., Apache Struts and Spring Boots). In order to extract these methods, we employ both our experience and the reported vulnerabilities from Common Vulnerabilities and Exposures (CVE)[3] and ExploitDB[4]. Table 1 shows the summary of specified sink methods for each project in our benchmark.

Table 1. Examples sinks in Tainer

Framework	Number of sinks
Spring Boots	178
Struts	142
JBoss Seam	12
Apache Turbine	12
Hibernate	5
AWS Java	3
Jenkins	3
JavaBeans	2

4.3   Automatic Exploit Generation

The Exploit Generator (EG) module in Tainer is responsible for performing security unit testing for the vulnerable data flows (the data flows that are identified by the Vulnerability Analyzer module.). Unit tests for the data flows are automatically constructed out of each JSP page and then evaluated by inputs which are generated via grammar-based attack string generator. The proposed tests, ensure that payload of a produced exploit works correctly with the target sink in the way it is intended to.

---

[3] https://cve.mitre.org.
[4] https://www.exploit-db.com.

Given the target sink method properties, the vulnerability type, the format and size of the parameters in the method (which is derived from the VA) are important metrics to set up the attack generator properly. Along with the grammar-based input generator, we also created a hashtable for the payloads inside of the EG module. Note that if the grammar-based input generator cannot provide any proper input to pass the tests, EG starts to pick an input from the payloads hashtable.

In this work, we have extracted 488 payloads for various web vulnerabilities from Exploit-DB.com. We also assumed that the source code of the input application is not accessible. Moreover, we implement test units based on BCI technique, which enables us to handle the bytecode of applications by our Java agent (which is built on the ASM framework). If a generated input passes the test unit, EG produces a concrete exploit via using CURL[5] (generated exploits are formed in bash files). Listing 1.6 shows an example exploit that is produced by Tainer for OGNL injection vulnerability in struts 2.3.12.

Listing 1.6. Exploit is produced for the OGNL injection vulnerability in struts 2.3.12

```
curl -i -s -k -X $'GET' \
  -H $'User-Agent: Mozilla/5.0' -H $'Content-Type:
    %{(#_=\'multipart/form-data\').(#dm=@ognl.OgnlContext@DEFAULT_MEMBER_ACCESS)._
  (#_memberAccess?(#_memberAccess=#dm):((#container=#context[\'com.opensymphony_
  .xwork2.ActionContext.container\']).(#ognlUtil=#container.getInstance(@com._
  opensymphony.xwork2.ognl.OgnlUtil@class)).(#ognlUtil.getExcludedPackageNames()_
  .clear()).(#ognlUtil.getExcludedClasses().clear()).(#context.setMemberAccess(#dm))))_
  .(#cmd=\'dir\').(#iswin....).(#ros.flush())}' \
  $'https://localhost:8080/benchmark/struts2/struts2-showcase-2.3.12/showcase.action'
```

5   Results and Discussion

In this section, we summarize the experiments we performed and describe the security violations we found with Tainer. We begin by outlining our benchmark applications and experimental setup, describe some representative vulnerabilities found by our analysis and interpret the impact of analysis features on precision.

While there is a decent number of industrial and open-source tools available for testing web application security, there are no stabilized benchmarks for comparing tools' effectiveness in J2EE application. The task of getting suitable benchmarks for our experiments was especially challenging by the fact that most J2EE applications are exclusive software, whose merchants are understandably reluctant to publish their code, not to mention the vulnerabilities found. At the same time, we did not want to focus on synthetic micro-benchmarks or student projects that lack the complexities fixed in real applications. While some tries have been made at forming synthetic benchmarks, we believe that real-life programs are much better suited for measuring security tools. Accordingly, we concentrate on a set of large, illustrative well-known applications, most of which are available on GitHub.

---

[5] https://curl.haxx.se.

Subject Applications. We assess Tainer with 15 Java projects including 13 J2EE applications as well as Kotlin and Scala that included 6.65 million lines of code. For instance, we assess Apache Struts which is a popular MVC framework that many web developers used for creating modern Java web applications [17]. We also consider some of the popular artificial vulnerable projects such as Webgoat for our benchmark [22].

Setup. We run Tainer along with the benchmark on a MacOSX machine with 32 GB memory and Intel Xeon W CPU with OpenJDK 8 installed. Discern that the traditional lines-of-code metric is slightly misrepresenting in the case of applications that use large libraries. Many of these benchmarks depend on massive libraries, so, while some of the applications code may be short, the full size of the applications executed at runtime is large.

Evaluation Methodology. In order to evaluate Tainer with our benchmark, we test the J2EE applications on Apache Tomcat 8. Then, we instrument the web server folder with the applications in one time and then we start attacking the benchmark. The attacks carried out accurately - namely through working with Kali Linux, Burp and Wfuzz[6], and in some cases like testing of Struts framework, we used the Metasploit framework[7].

5.1 Vulnerabilities Discovered

Our results in Table 2 reveals that Tainer reports a total of 155 potential security violations in our benchmarks, out of which 131 turned out to be actual security vulnerabilities, while 24 are false positives.

In the first view, it seems expanding the number of source and sink methods may have an actual impact on finding more vulnerable data flows and detecting more security issues. However, our results deny this view. For instance, the result of OGNL injection (e.g., in Spring project) demonstrates that including additional sinks to detect more vulnerabilities turns out as raising more false positive exceptions. In case of RCE attacks, because running operating system commands in Java is relatively confined to a few straightforward methods, and we have specified them elaborately; therefore, we have no false positive reports for RCE in our benchmark. We call this situation **"sinks interventions"** which causes performance overhead for Tainer and reduces the accuracy of the generated reports.

Another illustration is when injecting SQL commands to the database of a web application with a tainted string. While with the lack of proper input sanitization, SQL commands can propagate maliciously to database methods (such as **executeQuery**), the application may respond some information (including sensitive data) to the attacker via the **javax.servlet.jsp.print** method. In this case, the data flow from the user input to the **javax.servlet.jsp.print** method may be reported as a vulnerable flow, which in fact is **false positive**, because

---

[6] https://github.com/xmendez/wfuzz.
[7] https://github.com/rapid7/metasploit-framework.

Table 2. The number of tainted flows and related vulnerabilities in the benchmark

Project	Sinks	Tainted flows	Reported vulns	Exploits	False positives	KLOC
Spring	178	128	16	11	5	381
Struts 2	142	101	7	7	0	210
Scala	25	21	3	2	1	335
JBoss Seam	12	8	4	2	2	1188
Turbine	12	7	1	0	1	47
Hibernate	5	5	3	3	0	1085
Kotlin	4	4	1	1	0	934
AWS Java	3	2	1	1	0	2013
Jenkins	3	3	2	0	2	253
JavaBeans	2	2	1	1	0	6
Webgoat	0	80	31	28	3	175
Wavsep	0	67	43	37	6	19
Bodgeit	0	39	31	27	4	2
Insecure App	0	8	5	5	0	1
Puzzelmall	0	7	6	6	0	4
Total	386	482	155	131	24	6653

the actual vulnerable data flow ends in **executeQuery** along with non-sanitized malicious input. However, the false positive regarding sinks interventions can be easily eliminated, if users elaborately define sink methods for Tainer (e.g., by considering the properties of input applications).

5.2 Zero-Day Exploits for Struts

Regarding the zero-day vulnerabilities found by Tainer in the Struct framework, we first need to give a brief introduction about the OGNL injection vulnerability. Object graph navigation language (OGNL) is an open source language for Java which is developed presently as a part of the Apache. OGNL provides the set of object attributes and execution of various methods of Java classes. The evaluation of unvalidated OGNL expressions can grant an attacker access to modify system variables to execute command execution attacks on Apache servers [25]. Using OGNL could make it simplistic for hackers to execute Java code as Apache Struts uses OGNL for most of its processes [34].

In our benchmark, we evaluate Struts 1.3.x, 2.1.x, 2.3.x and 2.5.x. Tainer produces 7 zero-day exploits including 3 reflected XSS vulnerabilities and 4 OGNL injections in Struts 1.3.X and 2.3.X which they have not been reported publicly. However, it seems the vulnerabilities have been fixed in version 2.3.37 which is the latest release of Struts 2.3.x that contains the latest security fixes, released on 30 December 2018. We have informed these vulnerabilities to the Struts development team.

5.3   Validation of the Vulnerabilities

Not all security errors found by Tainer are surely exploitable in practice. The error may not correspond to a flow that can be taken dynamically, or it may not be possible to construct significant malicious input. Exploits might also be ruled out because of the unique configuration of an application. However, the configurations might change over time, potentially making exploits available. Moreover, practically all of the security errors we found can be repaired easily by modifying several lines of Java source code, so there is generally no reason not to fix them in practice. After we ran our analysis, we manually examined all the errors reported to ensure they represent security errors. Since our knowledge of the applications was not sufficient to ascertain that the errors we found were exploitable, to gain additional assurance, we manually grouped and tested each application's reported exploits to make sure the security leaks are rightly reported.

We obtained the exploits by searching the name and version of the applications on valid vulnerabilities databases such as National Vulnerability Database (NVD)[8], TrendMicro.com, and Metasploit. After ensuring the correctness of the exploits, we ran the exploits on the instrumented applications on our instrumented JVM (OpenJDK). Also, for being sure about the correctness of the results, we manually compare the affected sink methods pointed in each report with the corresponding methods in the source code of the exploits. Ultimately, we compared the exploit payloads with the content of the tainted flows in the Tainer generated reports.

6   Limitations and Future Works

There are several constraints to our approach that can be solved. For example, the source and sink specification should perform precisely; otherwise, the **sinks interventions** problem may happen. However, we consider adding a future extension to complete this process automatically, based on the runtime libraries used in applications.

Also, even though we prepare an extensive benchmark for the evaluation of Tainer, our benchmark still does not introduce all sorts of vulnerabilities that would usually are targets for dynamic taint analysis. For instance, certain features of web applications are not yet supported and consequently limit our coverage, e.g., unrestricted file upload [13] in which web forms that have inputs of type file require the user to select and upload an actual file from the local system. However, this issue can be addressed with further improvements in the framework.

Lastly, Tainer works within the constraint of the JVM, which means it is not able to track data flow through native code executing outside of but interacting with the JVM (e.g., The Java Native Interface (JNI)). JNI is a native programming interface which allows Java code running in a JVM to call and be called by

---

[8] https://nvd.nist.gov.

[31] native applications (e.g., applications which are implemented in separate .c files). Although using JNI in Java applications is not widely common (especially for standard J2EE applications), we consider resolving this concern in future extensions.

7 Related Works

Finding security vulnerabilities via DTA systems have been comprehensively studied. For instance, there are some system-wide tainting methods which work based on modifications to the operating system [46], or based on system calls invoked mostly in C and C++ languages [16,18,19,48]. However, our interception technique is based on Java bytecode instrumentation and JVM internals.

Vulnerability Analysis. There are plenty of research that analyzed server-side vulnerability detection. Generally, there are static analysis techniques (e.g., [33,35,40]), dynamic analysis methods (e.g., [21,23,28,32,46–48]), and hybrid techniques (such as [4,36]). Although Tainer uses some of these analysis methods to find vulnerabilities, the purpose of Tainer is different from these works as it creates exploits for the identified vulnerabilities.

Taint Tracking. LIFT [41] is designed by Qin et al. based on StarDBT, which distinctly reduces the taint analysis by eliminating for redundant data flow information whereas the problem of memory consumption has not been adequately addressed. DyTan [10] is a taint tracking system targeting x86 binaries that uses control flow tainting. However, this tool still presents the limitation of time overhead. Phosphor [5] is a general purpose taint tracking system for Java binaries that tracks taint object at runtime. However, this tool is not able to detect security vulnerabilities in data flows and create exploits. Also, due to its heavy instrumentation process, it suffers from significant time and runtime overhead. Also, it seems it has several inconsistencies in running with Oracle JDK and instrumenting of practical Java libraries (such as Apache Derby).

Moreover, Newsome et al. published TaintCheck [39] from Valgrind presents taint analysis for data flow for the disclosure of buffer overflow vulnerabilities. However, this tool has significant overhead and ignores the analysis for control flow. BitBlaze [45], DTA++ [27], and DECAF [24] attempt to implement a combination method of dynamic taint analysis and symbolic execution, so they better the path coverage of dynamic taint analysis. Although the above techniques have improved the performance of dynamic taint analysis, several problems are still not permanently resolved including the high memory and runtime overhead.

The closest work to our technique is Haldar [23]. This paper proposes a DTA system for identifying vulnerabilities in Java applications. More precisely, Haldar introduces a pre-made instrumented JVM which tested on WebGoat. However, this JVM is not capable to be upgraded to the newer versions. Also, users cannot specify the policies for tainted objects tracking (while Tainer works with all standard JVMs and allows users to independently specify their own tracking policies.). Presently, Haldar 's work does not include exploit generation for identified issues. Also, there is no information available concerning the description and quantity of detected vulnerabilities in their work.

8   Conclusion and Future Works

In this paper, we present Tainer as an accurate, scalable, and portable framework for Java applications which works based on dynamic taint tracking technique. Our proposed framework not only automatically identifies hacking attacks and security issues at runtime but also reproduces concerning reports and exploits to assist users in resolving vulnerabilities before being maliciously exploited. Our technique applies to the applications bytecodes and no need to the source code. Hence, Tainer can be helpful to design secure applications and enhance user security at the time of attacks. There is also a potential to utilize Tainer to detect security issues in Android apps with additional modifications. Lastly, in this work, we show that Tainer significantly exceeds prior work on the precision, portability, and scalability of vulnerability detection and automatic exploit generation for Java applications.

Appendix A

Table 3. Some of the specified source and sink methods in Tainer

Method	Description	Source	Sink
tomcat.util.net.NioBufferHandler.getReadBuffer	Read the buffer of Apache server	✓	-
org.apache.catalina.connector.Request.getStream	Return the input stream of a request	✓	-
javax.servlet.http.Part.getHeaderNames	Gets the header names	✓	-
org.eclipse.jetty.server.Request.getReader	Shows a Post form item	✓	-
java.lang.Runtime.exec	Execute the string command in a process	-	✓
java.sql.Statement.executeQuery	Execute a given SQL statement with JDBC	-	✓
java.net.URL.openConnection	Returns an HttpURLConnection object	-	✓
javax.servlet.jsp.JspWriter	Writes characters to stream or console	-	✓
org.apache.struts.action.ActionForward.setPath	Sets URI to which control should be forwarded	-	✓
ognl.OgnlReflectionProvider.getValue	Evaluate the provided OGNL expression	-	✓
util.TextParseUtil.ParsedValueEvaluator	Evaluate the value of OGNL value stack	-	✓
turbine.om.peer.BasePeer.executeQuery	Execute a given query in Apache Turbin	-	✓
org.hibernate.Session.createSQLQuery	Execute a given SQL statement in Hibernate	-	✓

Table 4. Some of the regular expressions used in the framework

Attack	Pattern
SQLi	$(?i)(.*)(//b) + SELECT(//b) + //s. * (//b) + FROM(/b) + //s. * (.*)$
	$(?i)(.*)(//b) + INSERT(//b) + //s. * (//b) + INTO(//b) + //s. * (.*)$
	$(?i)(.*)(//b) + UPDATE(//b) + //s. * (.*)$
	$(?i)(.*)(//b) + DELETE(//b) + //s. * (//b) + FROM(//b) + //s. * (.*)$
	$(?i)(.*)(//b) + DESC(//b) + (//w) * //s. * (.*)$
XSS	$(.*)" + lt + script + gt + "(.*)" + lt + bs + script + gt + "(.*)$
	$(.*)(" + javascript + "|" + vbscript + ")(.*)$
	$lt + htmlTags + "(.*)(//s + |/)(src|dynsrc|lowsrc|href)//s* = " + quote...$
	...

References

1. Aarniala, J.: Instrumenting Java bytecode. In: Seminar Work for the Compilerscourse, Department of Computer Science, University of Helsinki, Finland (2005)
2. AlBreiki, H.H., Mahmoud, Q.H.: Evaluation of static analysis tools for software security. In: 2014 10th International Conference on Innovations in Information Technology (INNOVATIONS), pp. 93–98. IEEE (2014)
3. Arzt, S., et al.: Flowdroid: precise context, flow, field, object-sensitive and lifecycle-aware taint analysis for android apps. ACM SIGPLAN Not. **49**(6), 259–269 (2014)
4. Balzarotti, D., et al.: Saner: composing static and dynamic analysis to validate sanitization in web applications. In: 2008 IEEE Symposium on Security and Privacy (SP 2008), pp. 387–401 (2008)
5. Bell, J.: Detecting, isolating, and enforcing dependencies among and within test cases. In: Proceedings of the 22nd ACM SIGSOFT International Symposium on Foundations of Software Engineering, pp. 799–802. ACM (2014)
6. Binder, W., Hulaas, J., Moret, P.: Advanced Java bytecode instrumentation. In: Proceedings of the 5th International Symposium on Principles and Practice of Programming in Java, pp. 135–144. ACM (2007)
7. Boonstoppel, P., Cadar, C., Engler, D.: RWset: attacking path explosion in constraint-based test generation. In: Ramakrishnan, C.R., Rehof, J. (eds.) TACAS 2008. LNCS, vol. 4963, pp. 351–366. Springer, Heidelberg (2008). https://doi.org/10.1007/978-3-540-78800-3_27
8. Brumley, D., Caballero, J., Liang, Z., Newsome, J., Song, D.: Towards automatic discovery of deviations in binary implementations with applications to error detection and fingerprint generation. In: USENIX Security Symposium, p. 15 (2007)
9. Chiba, S.: Javassist: Java bytecode engineering made simple. Java Dev. J. **9**(1), 30 (2004)
10. Clause, J., Li, W., Orso, A.: Dytan: a generic dynamic taint analysis framework. In: Proceedings of the 2007 International Symposium on Software Testing and Analysis, pp. 196–206. ACM (2007)
11. Dahm, M.: Byte code engineering. In: Cap, C.H. (ed.) JIT 1999. INFORMAT, pp. 267–277. Springer, Heidelberg (1999). https://doi.org/10.1007/978-3-642-60247-4_25
12. Dahm, M., van Zyl, J., Haase, E.: The bytecode engineering library (BCEL) (2003)
13. Dalton, M., Kozyrakis, C., Zeldovich, N.: Nemesis: preventing authentication & [and] access control vulnerabilities in web applications (2009)

14. Enck, W., et al.: TaintDroid: an information-flow tracking system for realtime privacy monitoring on smartphones. ACM Trans. Comput. Syst. (TOCS) **32**(2), 5 (2014)
15. Fan, N., Winslow, A.B., Wu, T.B., Yu, J.X.: Automatic deployment of Java classes using byte code instrumentation. US Patent 8,397,227, 12 March 2013
16. Feng, H.H., Kolesnikov, O.M., Fogla, P., Lee, W., Gong, W.: Anomaly detection using call stack information. In: 2003 Symposium on Security and Privacy, pp. 62–75. IEEE (2003)
17. Spring Framework: Spring framework. https://spring.io/?. Accessed Mar 2018
18. Gao, D., Reiter, M.K., Song, D.: Gray-box extraction of execution graphs for anomaly detection. In: Proceedings of the 11th ACM Conference on Computer and Communications Security, pp. 318–329. ACM (2004)
19. Giffin, J.T., Jha, S., Miller, B.P.: Detecting manipulated remote call streams. In: USENIX Security Symposium, pp. 61–79 (2002)
20. Godefroid, P., Levin, M.Y., Molnar, D.A.: SAGE: whitebox fuzzing for security testing. ACM Queue **55**(3), 40–44 (2012)
21. Goldberg, A., Haveland, K.: Instrumentation of Java bytecode for runtime analysis (2003)
22. Gupta, S., Gupta, B.B.: Detection, avoidance, and attack pattern mechanisms in modern web application vulnerabilities: present and future challenges. Int. J. Cloud Appl. Comput. (IJCAC) **7**(3), 1–43 (2017)
23. Haldar, V., Chandra, D., Franz, M.: Dynamic taint propagation for Java. In: 21st Annual Computer Security Applications Conference, pp. 9–pp. IEEE (2005)
24. Henderson, A.: DECAF: a platform-neutral whole-system dynamic binary analysis platform. IEEE Trans. Softw. Eng. **43**(2), 164–184 (2017)
25. Hu, A., Peng, G., Chen, Z., Zhu, Z.: A struts2 unknown vulnerability attack detection and backtracking scheme based on multilayer monitoring. In: Xu, M., Qin, Z., Yan, F., Fu, S. (eds.) CTCIS 2017. CCIS, vol. 704, pp. 383–396. Springer, Singapore (2017). https://doi.org/10.1007/978-981-10-7080-8_26
26. Ishrat, M., Saxena, M., Alamgir, M.: Comparison of static and dynamic analysis for runtime monitoring. Int. J. Comput. Sci. Commun. Netw. **2**(5), 615–617 (2012)
27. Kang, M.G., McCamant, S., Poosankam, P., Song, D.: DTA++: dynamic taint analysis with targeted control-flow propagation. In: NDSS (2011)
28. Kim, H.C., Keromytis, A.: On the deployment of dynamic taint analysis for application communities. IEICE Trans. Inf. Syst. **92**(3), 548–551 (2009)
29. Kuleshov, E.: Using the ASM framework to implement common Java bytecode transformation patterns. Aspect-Oriented Software Development (2007)
30. Li, L., Dong, Q., Liu, D., Zhu, L.: The application of fuzzing in web software security vulnerabilities test. In: 2013 International Conference on Information Technology and Applications, pp. 130–133 (2013)
31. Liang, S.: The Java Native Interface: Programmer's Guide and Specification. Addison-Wesley Professional, Boston (1999)
32. Livshits, B., Martin, M., Lam, M.S.: SecuriFly: runtime protection and recovery from web application vulnerabilities. Technical report (2006)
33. Livshits, V.B., Lam, M.S.: Finding security vulnerabilities in Java applications with static analysis. In: USENIX Security Symposium, vol. 14, p. 18 (2005)
34. Luszcz, J.: Apache struts 2: how technical and development gaps caused the equifax breach. Netw. Secur. **2018**(1), 5–8 (2018)
35. Medeiros, I., Neves, N., Correia, M.: DEKANT: a static analysis tool that learns to detect web application vulnerabilities. In: Proceedings of the 25th International Symposium on Software Testing and Analysis, pp. 1–11. ACM (2016)

36. Mongiovì, M., Giannone, G., Fornaia, A., Pappalardo, G., Tramontana, E.: Combining static and dynamic data flow analysis: a hybrid approach for detecting data leaks in Java applications. In: Proceedings of the 30th Annual ACM Symposium on Applied Computing, pp. 1573–1579. ACM (2015)
37. Naderi-Afooshteh, A., Nguyen-Tuong, A., Bagheri-Marzijarani, M., Hiser, J.D., Davidson, J.W.: Joza: hybrid taint inference for defeating web application SQL injection attacks. In: 2015 45th Annual IEEE/IFIP International Conference on Dependable Systems and Networks (DSN), pp. 172–183. IEEE (2015)
38. Newsome, J., Karp, B., Song, D.: Polygraph: automatically generating signatures for polymorphic worms. In: 2005 IEEE Symposium on Security and Privacy, pp. 226–241. IEEE (2005)
39. Newsome, J., Song, D.X.: Dynamic taint analysis for automatic detection, analysis, and signature generation of exploits on commodity software. In: NDSS, vol. 5, pp. 3–4. Citeseer (2005)
40. Pérez, P.M., Filipiak, J., Sierra, J.M.: LAPSE+ static analysis security software: vulnerabilities detection in Java EE applications. In: Park, J.J., Yang, L.T., Lee, C. (eds.) FutureTech 2011. CCIS, vol. 184, pp. 148–156. Springer, Heidelberg (2011). https://doi.org/10.1007/978-3-642-22333-4_17
41. Qin, F., Wang, C., Li, Z., Kim, H., Zhou, Y., Wu, Y.: LIFT: a low-overhead practical information flow tracking system for detecting security attacks. In: 2006 39th Annual IEEE/ACM International Symposium on Microarchitecture, MICRO-39, pp. 135–148. IEEE (2006)
42. Royer, M.E., Chawathe, S.S.: Java unit annotations for units-of-measurement error prevention. In: 2018 IEEE 8th Annual Computing and Communication Workshop and Conference (CCWC), pp. 816–822. IEEE (2018)
43. Schwartz, E.J., Avgerinos, T., Brumley, D.: All you ever wanted to know about dynamic taint analysis and forward symbolic execution (but might have been afraid to ask). In: 2010 IEEE Symposium on Security and Privacy (SP), pp. 317–331. IEEE (2010)
44. Shoshitaishvili, Y., et al.: SOK: (state of) the art of war: offensive techniques in binary analysis. In: 2016 IEEE Symposium on Security and Privacy (SP), pp. 138–157. IEEE (2016)
45. Song, D., et al.: BitBlaze: a new approach to computer security via binary analysis. In: Sekar, R., Pujari, A.K. (eds.) ICISS 2008. LNCS, vol. 5352, pp. 1–25. Springer, Heidelberg (2008). https://doi.org/10.1007/978-3-540-89862-7_1
46. Suh, G.E., Lee, J.W., Zhang, D., Devadas, S.: Secure program execution via dynamic information flow tracking. In: ACM SIGPLAN Notices, vol. 39, pp. 85–96. ACM (2004)
47. Stenzel, O.: Gradient index films and multilayers. The Physics of Thin Film Optical Spectra. SSSS, vol. 44, pp. 163–180. Springer, Cham (2016). https://doi.org/10.1007/978-3-319-21602-7_8
48. Xu, W., Bhatkar, S., Sekar, R.: Practical dynamic taint analysis for countering input validation attacks on web applications. Technical report SECLAB-05-04, Department of Computer Science, Stony Brook (2005)

AMOGAP: Defending Against Man-in-the-Middle and Offline Guessing Attacks on Passwords

Jaryn Shen[1], Timothy T. Yuen[2], Kim-Kwang Raymond Choo[3], and Qingkai Zeng[1(✉)]

[1] State Key Laboratory for Novel Software Technology, Nanjing University, Nanjing 210023, Jiangsu Province, China
jarynshen@gmail.com, zqk@nju.edu.cn
[2] Department of Interdisciplinary Learning and Teaching, University of Texas at San Antonio, San Antonio, TX 78249, USA
timothy.yuen@utsa.edu
[3] Department of Information Systems and Cyber Security, University of Texas at San Antonio, San Antonio, TX 78249, USA
raymond.choo@fulbrightmail.org

Abstract. Passwords are widely used in online services, such as electronic and mobile banking services, and may be complemented by other authentication mechanism(s) for example in two-factor or three-factor authentication systems. There are, however, a number of known limitations and risks associated with the use of passwords, such as man-in-the-middle (MitM) and offline guessing attacks. In this paper, we present AMOGAP, a novel text password-based user authentication mechanism, to defend against MitM and offline guessing attacks. In our approach, users can select easy-to-remember passwords, and AMOGAP converts currently-used salted and hashed password files into user tokens, whose security relies on the Decisional Diffie-Hellman (DDH) assumption, at the server end. In other words, we use a difficult problem in number theory (i.e., DDH problem), rather than a one-way hash function, to ensure security against offline password guessing attackers and MitM attackers. AMOGAP does not require any change in existing authentication process and infrastructure or incur additional costs at the server.

Keywords: Offline guessing attacks · MitM attacks · Password · DDH · Password-based authentication

1 Introduction

Despite their inherent weaknesses, passwords are still widely used as a standalone authentication mechanism or in combination with other systems (e.g., multi-factor authentication systems and biometric authentication systems). Passwords are likely to remain a dominant authentication mechanism in the foreseeable

© Springer Nature Switzerland AG 2019
J. Jang-Jaccard and F. Guo (Eds.): ACISP 2019, LNCS 11547, pp. 514–532, 2019.
https://doi.org/10.1007/978-3-030-21548-4_28

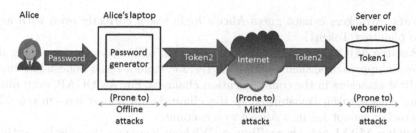

Fig. 1. Proposed AMOGAP

future due to low cost, ease of use, deployment and convenience. There is no perfect security or authentication mechanism; for example, there are also privacy concerns with regards to the potential abuse of biometric data in biometric authentication systems. In recent years, there have been a number of high profile incidents where user passwords were stolen [4,16,20,33], for example due to weaknesses or vulnerabilities in the systems that were exploited by attackers conducting man-in-the-middle (MitM) and offline guessing attacks [8,12,13]. In addition, servers that host salted and hashed password files have also been compromised by attackers or malicious insiders. Such files were then subjected to offline brute-force or statistical guessing attacks [18].

In this paper, we propose AMOGAP, a novel text password-based authentication scheme that will be able to counter the MitM and offline guessing attacks. Using AMOGAP (see Fig. 1), users can select easy-to-remember passwords as complex user tokens are stored at the server. Next, we will describe a scenario in which AMOGAP can be implemented.

Let Alice be an ordinary user in the system. When Alice logs into a web service, she inputs her password to the password generator, such as KYO [17] or Kamouflage [6], on her laptop. Then, the password generator outputs Alice's login token of the particular web service and submits this token to the server of that web service. Thus, there are two of Alice's tokens in the web server, namely: one that is transmitted from Alice's laptop to the server (i.e., Token2), and the token already stored in the server (i.e., Token1; generated when she first registered with the service). The authentication system of the web service authenticates Alice's login attempt by comparing both Token1 and Token2.

Our proposal comprises two schemes, namely: the basic AMOGAP (Scheme 1 in Fig. 2) and the advanced AMOGAP (Scheme 2 in Fig. 3) based on the Decisional Diffie-Hellman (DDH) assumption [14]. Both schemes are designed to achieve offline password guessing attack resilience. Furthermore, Scheme 1 can defeat an honest-but-curious MitM attacker and Scheme 2 can defeat an active MitM attacker. In summary, AMOGAP achieves the following properties:

- **Offline guessing attack resilience.** At the server side, AMOGAP converts currently-used salted and hashed password files into user tokens, and it does not require a change in the underpinning infrastructure or incur additional costs. Attackers cannot guess Alice's login token correctly even with access to plaintext Token1.

- **Passive MitM attack resilience.** Existing offline password guessing miti-gation approaches, such as those of [1,7,23], cannot resist honest-but-curious MitM attackers in the communication channels. For AMOGAP, even obtain-ing Alice's token transmitted in the channels, an honest-but-curious MitM attacker cannot log into Alice's web account.
- **Active MitM attack resilience.** Without changing the existing authenti-cation process, the advanced AMOGAP scheme (Scheme 2) can defeat active MitM attackers who interfere with the communication between Alice and the web server. Such interference (e.g., tampering, forging or replaying Alice's tokens transmitted in the channels) does not allow the attacker to imperson-ate either Alice or the web server to the other party.

Additionally, even if Alice exposes the data of the password generator on her lap-top, an offline attacker cannot guess Alice's password or her login token correctly. Many password generators, such as KYO [17] and Kamouflage [6], achieve this feature, so we do not list this functionality as one of the advantages of AMOGAP.

Based on the DDH assumption, we formally prove AMOGAP's security in defeating offline guessing attacks (Theorems 1 and 2), passive MitM attacks (Theorem 3), and active MitM attacks (Theorem 4–10).

The remainder of this paper is organized as follows: In the next two sections, we will respectively introduce the background and related work, and the threat model. Then, we describe our proposed AMOGAP schemes in Sect. 4 and analyze its security in Sect. 5. The extended AMOGAP scheme introduced in Sect. 6 is designed to facilitate a user to use other devices to log in his/her web account. Finally, the conclusion is presented in Sect. 7.

2 Background and Related Work

The number of incidents relating to password leakage is increasing [11], including those due to online guessing attacks, MitM attacks, and offline guessing attacks. It is relatively easy to protect passwords against online guessing attacks through deploying CAPTCHAs and restricting the number of authentication attempts before the account is locked [27]. As a result, unsurprisingly, the majority of the related work focuses on offline guessing attack resilience with less emphasis on MitM attacks.

2.1 Optimization of Algorithmic Primitives

Some work focuses on the algorithmic primitives, with the aim of increasing the time complexity or memory complexity required to perform brute-force attacks. The technique *key stretching* [22] makes short passwords have the same time complexity as long passwords. Similar to *key stretching*, based on the blowfish block cipher, *bcrypt* [28] adds the time complexity through increasing the number of iterations of the algorithm. *Balloon* [7] and *scrypt* [26] focus on increasing the memory complexity through parameterizing the memory usage of the algorithm so as to defeat offline attackers' special hardware such as the ASICs.

These techniques, however, only increase attackers' computational cost. Provided that attackers possess enough computing resources (e.g., using graphics processing units – GPUs, or cloud resources), these techniques will lose efficacy especially in statistical guessing attacks.

2.2 Decrease of Password Popularity

To resist offline statistical password guessing attacks [34], some approaches [23, 25, 30] focus on decreasing the use of popular or frequently-used passwords. The Count-min Sketch forbids users from selecting popular passwords through recording the popularity of the passwords in the system [30]. Telepathwords prevents users selecting weak passwords with four fixed constructive patterns of passwords [23].

All of these approaches, however, need users to change their passwords frequently if they select popular ones. Further, these approaches may recognize unpopular passwords as popular ones, then ask users to change their passwords unnecessarily [30]; or recognize weak passwords as unpopular ones, which is a false negative [23].

2.3 Password Sharing

Approaches such as Shamir's (k, n) scheme [31], Bounded Retrieval Model [10], and PolyPasswordHasher [9], think of a password as a secret, and convert the entire secret into fragmentary shares. Shamir's (k, n) scheme [31] divides a secret into n pieces, and reconstructs the secret by at least k pieces where $k < n$. The Bounded Retrieval Model [10] maps a password to lots of storage locations, the sum of these locations represents the hashed value of the password. PolyPasswordHasher [9] distributes (k, n) shares to protector accounts and needs at least k online protector accounts to reconstruct the secret. Others, such as Honeywords [21] and SAuth [24], rely on a hardened computer system. Honeywords [21] uses a separate honeychecker to judge a password is authentic or forged. SAuth [24] uses vouching web services: in order to log in a web service, a user needs not only a password of this service, but also the passwords of those vouching parties.

All of these methods, however, require a much forced hypothetical condition that attackers cannot access some computer system(s) or obtain some data. This hypothesis is impractical since attackers can also be malicious insiders or colluding with an insider.

2.4 Password Generators

Many password generators employ similar techniques as in Sect. 2.1 to protect passwords from offline guessing attacks on the client side [19, 29]. Kamouflage [6], for example, employs decoy databases to protect user passwords, so that it cannot be brute-forced on the client side. Similarly, KYO [17] is designed to defeat brute-forced attacks on the client side.

With a master password of a password generator on the client side, users can manage many passwords for their web accounts, so the passwords stored on the server side can be random and complicated. Hence, in a reasonable amount of time, offline guessing attackers cannot crack the salted and hashed password files on the server side any more. A password generator on the client side, however, cannot resist MitM attacks in communication channels.

2.5   Weaknesses Against MitM Attacks

The literature reviewed in the preceding subsections does not fully address MitM attacks on passwords. Some approaches make no mention of MitM attack resilience, and others consider MitM attacks out of scope. However, the potential of MitM attacks on passwords is actually a threat that needs to be addressed [15,32].

From the MitM attackers' perspective, the defenses mentioned above on both client and server sides are meaningless and ineffective. The most common case of an MitM attack on passwords deals with the *evil twin* Wi-Fi hotspot where unsuspecting users connect to what they believe is a legitimate Wi-Fi hotspot. In actuality, someone else has set this Wi-Fi for the purpose of eavesdropping on the users' online activities. Assume that Alice goes to a cafe and connects to the wireless network with her laptop. The cafe's official hotspot is named CoffeeWIFI, but an MitM attacker has set up a similarly named CoffeeWIFI-Guest. She inadvertently connects to the CoffeeWIFI-Guest through which the attacker can eavesdrop on her activities. If the web services do not employ TLS/SSL, the eavesdropper can obtain Alice's passwords, among other private information, for these web services through Wi-Fi signals no matter how complicated these passwords are.

Attackers do not always think about attacking the place where good defense is deployed. On the contrary, they prefer to attack those weaknesses. Hence, we should neither consider MitM attacks out of scope nor should take it for granted that attackers only occupy a very limited portion of computing resources and cannot compromise those hardened computer systems. There are many highly sophisticated MitM attacks in reality yet much of the existing research focuses only brute-force attacks as shown in the reviewed research. In MitM attacks, attackers may also circumvent the TLS/SSL validation and intercept transmitted passwords even though web services employ TLS/SSL [12,13,32,38]. Therefore, there is an inherent need to develop a stronger defense against MitM attacks.

For all the above reasons, we propose AMOGAP and anchor our hope on AMOGAP to fully defeat password attacks on Internet. The motivation of AMO-GAP is to defeat not only offline guessing attacks but also MitM attacks on passwords.

3   Threat Model

There are two main kinds of security threats on passwords for web accounts: offline guessing attacks and MitM attacks; the former takes place in the server or client side, and the latter takes place in communication channels on Internet. They are illustrated in Fig. 1. We take no account of online guessing attacks since we can deploy CAPTCHAs and limit the rate of online password guessing attempts [27].

On the server side, offline guessing attackers can obtain all the user tokens, and can launch offline guessing attacks including not only trawling guessing attacks [35] but also targeted guessing attacks [36]. We assume that offline guessing attackers can only obtain user tokens, but they cannot change these tokens. Such assumption is reasonable. Otherwise, attackers can always log into Alice's web account since they can arbitrarily change her token stored on the web server.

In the communication channels, MitM attackers can obtain all the transmitted messages. There are two types of MitM attackers: passive and active. Passive MitM attackers are honest but curious: they do not interfere with the communication. They only eavesdrop or sniff in channels. Meanwhile, active MitM attackers arbitrarily tamper, forge or replay messages in channels.

On the client side, we believe that the surrounding area is secure when Alice inputs her password to the password generator on her laptop (i.e., we omit shoulder snooping, key loggers, or hardware-based side channel attacks).

4   Proposed AMOGAP Secure Under DDH

We start by introducing the basic idea of our proposal, AMOGAP, whose security depends on the DDH assumption.

We first show the basic AMOGAP secure only against offline guessing attackers and passive MitM attackers, assuming messages cannot be interfered in channels (Scheme 1 in Fig. 2), and then proceed to explain how we can address tampering, forging or replaying messages in channels and achieve security against active MitM attackers (the advanced AMOGAP: Scheme 2 in Fig. 3).

In the basic AMOGAP (Scheme 1), we only employ a password generator KYO [17] on the client side and convert the currently-used salted and hashed password files into user tokens on the server side. All the tokens that Alice sends to the web server are plaintext, and the web server just keeps Alice's plaintext tokens. Such a scheme is exactly the same as the current password authentication technique in process and infrastructure, but it provides more security guarantees: besides defeating offline password guessing attackers, Scheme 1 can also defeat passive MitM attackers.

In the presence of active MitM attackers, however, we need to address a number of issues: How to securely transmit Alice's tokens to the web server? How to verify Alice's tokens in the web server? In addition to tampering and forging, how to prevent active MitM attackers from replaying Alice's tokens? At the same time, we cannot employ zero-knowledge proofs protocols [3] to solve

Alice   S

Registration Procedure

| Store: $PW(k, \sigma, \gamma)$ | $Token1(u,a,b) = (\mathcal{U}, g, g^{x_0})$ | Store: Token1 |
| $T(S, \mathcal{U}, k, \sigma_{S,\mathcal{U}})$ | | $= (\mathcal{U}, g, g^{x_0})$ |

The i-th Login Procedure

Input: ρ		
Output: x_{i-1}	$Token2(u,x,y,z) = (\mathcal{U}, x_{i-1}, g, g^{x_i})$	Verify: $a^x \overset{?}{=} b$
Store: $PW(k, \sigma', \gamma')$		Update: $b \leftarrow z$
$T(S, \mathcal{U}, k, \sigma'_{S,\mathcal{U}})$		

Fig. 2. Scheme 1: Basic AMOGAP against passive MitM attacks and offline attacks

these issues because zero-knowledge proofs involve at least 3 messages (i.e., Alice sends some function(s) to the web server; the server sends the challenge(s) back to Alice; Alice responds to the server), whereas there can only be 1 message in the user authentication procedure (i.e., Alice wants to log into her web account and sends her token to the web server). The advanced AMOGAP (Scheme 2) solves all the above issues without changing the existing authentication process and infrastructure or incurring additional costs on the server side.

4.1   Basic AMOGAP: Scheme 1

We introduce Scheme 1 in this subsection. Let g be a generator of a cyclic group $\mathbb{G}$ of prime order q, and $x_i \in \mathbb{Z}_q$, where the integer $i \geq 0$.

Registration Procedure. Assume Alice registers a web account on website S, and her user name is $\mathcal{U}$ and her password is ρ on S. The registration procedure proceeds as follows:

(1) Alice inputs her password ρ to the password generator in her laptop. The password generator generates Token1 for $\mathcal{U}$.
(2) $Token1(u, a, b) = (\mathcal{U}, g, g^{x_0})$, where x_0 is uniformly chosen from $\mathbb{Z}_q$ by the password generator.
(3) Token1 is sent to website S and stored in the server of S for user authentication in the future.
(4) The data S and $\mathcal{U}$ are important for authentication, so the password generator stores them in Alice's laptop.
(5) The data x_0 is pivotal for authentication, and the password generator does not store x_0 directly, x_0 will be recalled by ρ.

Login Procedure. Assume it is the i-th time ($i \geq 1$) that Alice logs into the web service on website S, and her user name is $\mathcal{U}$ and her password is ρ on S. The login procedure proceeds as follows:

(6) Alice inputs her password ρ to the password generator in her laptop. The password generator recalls x_{i-1} via ρ.

(7) Independent of x_{i-1}, x_i is uniformly chosen from $\mathbb{Z}_q$. The password generator generates $\text{Token2}(u, x, y, z) = (\mathcal{U}, x_{i-1}, g, g^{x_i})$.

(8) Token2 is sent to website S. The authentication system of S authenticates the login attempt through $\text{Token1}(u, a, b)$ and $\text{Token2}(u, x, y, z)$.

(9) If $a^x = b$, Alice logs into her account successfully, and goto next step. If $a^x \neq b$, the login attempt fails, and quit the login procedure.

(10) The authentication system of S updates Token1 according to Alice's Token2 in her i-th successful login. $\text{Token1}(u, a, b) = (u, y, z)$.

(11) The password generator updates the data in Alice's laptop so that ρ can recall x_i rather than x_{i-1} in the next time.

In Step (7) of the above login procedure, we can also select another generator g' and uniformly choose x_i from $\mathbb{Z}_{q'}$, where g' is a generator of group $\mathbb{G}'$ of prime order q'. Thus, $\text{Token2}(u, x, y, z) = (\mathcal{U}, x_{i-1}, g', (g')^{x_i})$. For simplicity, we fix y in Token2 and do not change the generator g in this paper.

Abnormal Changing Token1 Procedure. Consider an abnormal situation: Alice cannot use her password ρ to log into her web account on website S. In this situation, Alice has to enter her email address associated with her account into S. Then, S sends an email to Alice. The content in this email is a hyperlink, which redirects Alice to a webpage on S, for changing Token1. Such a process of changing Token1 is similar to the registration procedure.

4.2   Recall x_i ($i \geq 0$) via Password ρ

In Step (5), (6) and (11) of the above registration and login procedure, we do not directly store $x_i(i \geq 0)$ in the password generator on the client side, but recall x_i with the help of Alice's password ρ. This functionality is accomplished by many existing password generators, such as KYO [17] and Kamouflage [6]. In this paper, we think of KYO as an important component of AMOGAP. We briefly introduce the accomplishment of this functionality in this subsection. See more details in KYO [17].

KYO selects a seed $\sigma_{S,\mathcal{U}}$ to let $F_{\sigma_{S,\mathcal{U}}}(\rho) = x_i$ where $i \geq 0$, and selects a pair of σ and γ to let $F_\sigma(\rho) = \gamma$. KYO stores (k, σ, γ) into the file PW and stores $(S, \mathcal{U}, k, \sigma_{S,\mathcal{U}})$ into the file T in Alice's laptop.

When Alice inputs her password ρ to the password generator, KYO verifies ρ in the file PW. First, KYO finds a tuple in PW, (k, σ, γ), which satisfies $F_\sigma(\rho) = \gamma$. Then, KYO searches the tuples in the file T according to the index k in (k, σ, γ). After finding the tuple $(S, \mathcal{U}, k, \sigma_{S,\mathcal{U}})$ in T, KYO recalls x_i because $F_{\sigma_{S,\mathcal{U}}}(\rho) = x_i$. KYO builds such a function F that we can recall x_i via ρ and we need not store x_i in Alice's laptop.

KYO can freely change x_i to x_{i+1} without changing Alice's password ρ because it is easy to find a seed $\sigma'_{S,\mathcal{U}}$ and a pair of σ' and γ' to satisfy $F_{\sigma'_{S,\mathcal{U}}}(\rho) = x_{i+1}$ and $F_{\sigma'}(\rho) = \gamma'$. Similarly, Alice can freely change her password ρ to ρ' without changing x_i.

4.3   Advanced AMOGAP: Scheme 2

Scheme 1 can defeat the simplest MitM attack described in Sect. 2.5. It is already better than related work in which offline guessing attacks are addressed but not all MitM attacks are addressed. Scheme 1 cannot defeat active MitM attacks such as forging or replaying messages. Therefore, in this subsection, we describe Scheme 2 which addresses active MitM attacks (see Scheme 2 in Fig. 3).

We must solve active MitM attackers' interference in channels. The most common approach is to employ HTTPS with an authority-signed or self-signed certificate. An authority-signed certificate requires extra expense for website S, and Alice must be very careful because web browsers typically come pre-configured with many authorities' public keys and some of these authorities are just new companies whose trustworthiness is not yet established. A self-signed certificate is free for the owner of a web service, but it is insecure because the computer systems may be compromised on the server side.

In this paper, without secure channels, in order to resist active MitM attackers' interference, we introduce a simple approach as follows, which is not only provably secure, but also costless, applicable and practical.

Using ElGamal encryption scheme [14], Alice's private key and public key are K_1 and K_2, respectively. When registering her web account on website S, Alice fills in her email address and cellphone number on website S. Then S randomly generates a pair of asymmetric keys k_1^t and k_2^t of ElGamal, which are only temporarily effective in this registration session. S secretly sends k_2^t to Alice by out-of-band means such as Alice's email or short message service (SMS) of her cellphone. Alice receives k_2^t out of band and uses this temporary key k_2^t to encrypt her public key K_2 and sends Token1$(t, u, a, b, E_{K_1}(b), E_{k_2^t}(K_2))$ to S, where t is a timestamp and u, a, b are the same meaning as in Scheme 1. $E_{(\cdot)}(\cdot)$ denotes encryption, and the subscript is the encryption key. $D_{(\cdot)}(\cdot)$ denotes decryption, and the subscript is the decryption key. S decrypts $E_{k_2^t}(K_2)$ with another temporary key k_1^t: $K_2 = D_{k_1^t}(E_{k_2^t}(K_2))$, and simultaneously verifies both K_2 and b through the equation $b = D_{K_2}(E_{K_1}(b))$. The rigorous proof is in Theorem 5 (K_2 is unaltered) and Theorem 6 (b is not forged) in Sect. 5.

The whole authentication procedure of Scheme 2 is described as below.

Registration Procedure. Alice registers her web account $\mathcal{U}$ on website S.

1. Alice fills in her email and cellphone number on S. Then S generates a pair of temporary asymmetric key k_1^t and k_2^t, and sends k_2^t to Alice out of band.
2. Alice receives a temporary key k_2^t from S through email or SMS, and encrypts her public key K_2 with k_2^t: $E_{k_2^t}(K_2)$, then discards k_2^t.
3. The time when Alice registers her web account $\mathcal{U}$ on website S is marked as a timestamp t: $t = \tau_0$.
4. Alice sends Token1$(t, u, a, b, E_{K_1}(b), E_{k_2^t}(K_2))$ $=$ $(\tau_0, \mathcal{U}, g, g^{x_0}, E_{K_1}(g^{x_0}),$ $E_{k_2^t}(K_2))$ to S.
5. With k_1^t, S decrypts $E_{k_2^t}(K_2)$: $K_2 = D_{k_1^t}(E_{k_2^t}(K_2))$. S verifies Token1: If $b \neq D_{K_2}(E_{K_1}(b))$, registration fails, and cancel this registration procedure.

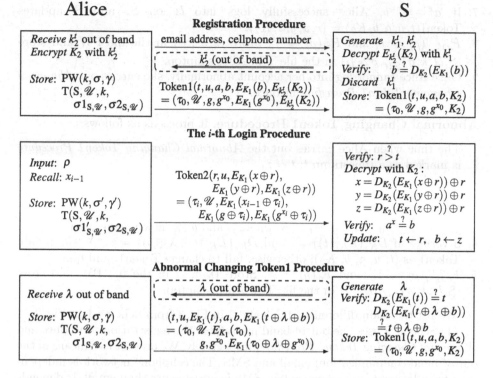

Fig. 3. Scheme 2: Advanced AMOGAP against active MitM attacks and offline attacks

6. If $b = D_{K_2}(E_{K_1}(b))$, then S discards k_1^t and stores $\text{Token1}(t, u, a, b, K_2) = (\tau_0, \mathcal{U}, g, g^{x_0}, K_2)$.
7. $F_{\sigma1\text{s},u}(\rho) = x_0$, $F_{\sigma2\text{s},u}(\rho) = K_1$, and $F_\sigma(\rho) = \gamma$. Store (k, σ, γ) in the file PW and store $(\text{S}, \mathcal{U}, k, \sigma1_{\text{s},\mathcal{U}}, \sigma2_{\text{s},\mathcal{U}})$ in the file T in Alice's laptop.

Login Procedure. Alice logs into $\mathcal{U}$ on S for the i-th time ($i \geq 1$).

1. Alice uses her password ρ to recall x_{i-1} and K_1 according to $F_{\sigma1\text{s},u}(\rho) = x_{i-1}$, $F_{\sigma2\text{s},u}(\rho) = K_1$, and $F_\sigma(\rho) = \gamma$.
2. The time when Alice logs into her web account $\mathcal{U}$ on website S is marked as a timestamp r: $r = \tau_i$.
3. Alice sends $\text{Token2}(r, u, E_{K_1}(x \oplus r), E_{K_1}(y \oplus r), E_{K_1}(z \oplus r)) = (\tau_i, \mathcal{U}, E_{K_1}(x_{i-1} \oplus \tau_i), E_{K_1}(g \oplus \tau_i), E_{K_1}(g^{x_i} \oplus \tau_i))$ to website S.
4. S verifies the timestamp in Token2. If $r \leq t$ (t is in Token1 stored on S), then login fails, and quit this login attempt.
5. With key K_2 and timestamp r, S decrypts $E_{K_1}(x \oplus r)$, $E_{K_1}(y \oplus r)$ and $E_{K_1}(z \oplus r)$ to x, y and z, respectively.
6. S authenticates Token2 with that previous stored Token1. If $a^x \neq b$, login fails, and quit this login attempt.

7. If $a^x = b$, Alice successfully logs into $\mathcal{U}$ on S, and S updates $\text{Token1}(t, u, a, b, K_2) = (r, u, y, z, K_2)$.
8. $F_{\sigma 1'_{\text{S},\mathcal{U}}}(\rho) = x_i$ and $F_{\sigma'}(\rho) = \gamma'$. Store (k, σ', γ') in the file PW and store $(\text{S}, \mathcal{U}, k, \sigma 1'_{\text{S},\mathcal{U}}, \sigma 2_{\text{S},\mathcal{U}})$ in the file T in Alice's laptop.
9. Once Alice cannot log into her account abnormally, she carries out *Abnormal Changing Token1 Procedure* at once.

Abnormal Changing Token1 Procedure. It proceeds as follows:

1. The time when Alice carries out the *Abnormal Changing Token1 Procedure* is marked as a timestamp t: $t = \tau_0$.
2. S sends a hyperlink directing a specific webpage on S and a random number λ to Alice's email address or cellphone number associated with $\mathcal{U}$.
3. Alice receives λ and sends $(t, u, E_{K_1}(t), a, b, E_{K_1}(t \oplus \lambda \oplus b)) = (\tau_0, \mathcal{U}, E_{K_1}(\tau_0), g, g^{x_0}, E_{K_1}(\tau_0 \oplus \lambda \oplus g^{x_0}))$ to S, where a and b are newly generated.
4. S verifies: if $D_{K_2}(E_{K_1}(t)) = t$ and $D_{K_2}(E_{K_1}(t \oplus \lambda \oplus b)) = t \oplus \lambda \oplus b$, update Token1 as (t, u, a, b, K_2); otherwise, fail to change Token1, and quit.
5. $F_{\sigma 1_{\text{S},\mathcal{U}}}(\rho) = x_0$, and $F_\sigma(\rho) = \gamma$. Store (k, σ, γ) in the file PW and store $(\text{S}, \mathcal{U}, k, \sigma 1_{\text{S},\mathcal{U}}, \sigma 2_{\text{S},\mathcal{U}})$ in the file T in Alice's laptop.

We list the main difference of Scheme 2 in Fig. 3 from Scheme 1 in Fig. 2:

(1) Scheme 2 uses one out-of-band message in the registration procedure and *Abnormal Changing Token1 Procedure*, respectively. We present two means of the out-of-band communication: email and SMS. The cellphone network is independent from Internet, so to some extent SMS is more secure than email. It depends on Alice and the website to decide to select which out-of-band means. Such out-of-band communication does not burden the user authentication mechanism anything because the current password authentication technique has widely used the out-of-band communication to help users with changing their passwords, which is similar with the *Abnormal Changing Token1 Procedure* in AMOGAP.

(2) Scheme 2 employs ElGamal encryption in transmitting Alice's tokens, and stores Alice's plaintext Token1 on the web server. K_1/K_2 and k_1^t/k_2^t denote two pairs of keys of ElGamal encryption that we employ in Scheme 2. For the sake of brevity and readability, we do not unfold the details of these keys.

(3) In the registration procedure, the main purpose of the out-of-band message (i.e., k_2^t) is to make Alice's public key K_2 be securely sent to the server side so that the authentication system on the server side can obtain an unaltered public key K_2. Therefore, once the web server obtains K_2, Scheme 2 discards k_1^t and k_2^t.

(4) Scheme 2 uses the timestamp to prevent replay attacks by active MitM attackers, but if Alice resets and calls back the clock time on her laptop (e.g., when she travels internationally) and cannot log into her web account caused by the timestamp, she can carry out the *Abnormal Changing Token1 Procedure* to replace her timestamp t in Token1 stored on the web server.

(5) In the *Abnormal Changing Token1 Procedure*, the out-of-band message (i.e., λ) prevents active MitM attackers replaying Alice's previous tokens in the login procedure and in the *Abnormal Changing Token1 Procedure*.

(6) Scheme 2 protects Alice's password from malicious attacks and stops attackers logging into Alice's web account, but it does not protect all the communication between Alice and the web server especially after Alice successfully logging into her account, which is out of scope.

(7) AMOGAP is a password-based user authentication mechanism, it is not a Password-based Authenticated Key Exchange (PAKE) protocol although it employs DDH assumption. Hence, we do not compare AMOGAP with PAKE protocols in this paper.

5   Security Analysis

In this section, we analyse the security of AMOGAP based on two assumptions.

Assumption 1. Any offline password guessing attacker or MitM attacker $\mathcal{A}$ is equivalent to a probabilistic polynomial-time (PPT) Turing machine [37].

Assumption 2 (DDH Assumption). The DDH problem is hard relative to a group-generation algorithm $\mathcal{G}$. For all probabilistic polynomial-time algorithms $\mathcal{A}$ there is a negligible function negl such that

$$|\Pr[\mathcal{A}(\mathbb{G}, q, g, g^x, g^y, g^z) = 1] - \Pr[\mathcal{A}(\mathbb{G}, q, g, g^x, g^y, g^{xy}) = 1]| \leq \mathsf{negl}(n),$$

where in each case the probabilities are taken over the experiment in which $\mathcal{G}(1^n)$ outputs $(\mathbb{G}, q, g)$, and then uniform $x, y, z \in \mathbb{Z}_q$ are chosen. (Note that when z is uniform in $\mathbb{Z}_q$, then g^z is uniformly distributed in $\mathbb{G}$.)

Lemma 1 (DL Problem) The discrete-logarithm problem is hard for all probabilistic polynomial-time algorithms.

Proof. If the discrete-logarithm problem is not hard to one PPT algorithm, according to Assumption 1, given (g^x, g^y, g^z), attackers can efficiently decide whether $g^z = g^{xy}$ by first taking the discrete $\log_g$ of g^x, and then comparing g^z with $(g^y)^x$. Thus, we deduce that DDH Assumption is false, which contradicts with Assumption 2. Therefore, the discrete-logarithm problem is hard.   □

Theorem 1. In Scheme 1, offline password guessing attackers cannot log into Alice's account after obtaining Token1 stored on the server side.

Proof. Offline password guessing attackers obtain Token1(u, a, b) in Scheme 1. If attackers want to log into Alice's account, they must obtain x s.t. $a^x = b$, where $a = g$ and $b = g^{x_{i-1}}$ ($i \geq 1$), which is the DL Problem. Therefore, attackers cannot obtain such x according to Assumption 1 and Lemma 1.   □

Theorem 2. In Scheme 1, given unlimited time, offline password guessing attackers cannot log into Alice's account with high probability even after obtaining Token1 stored on the server side.

Proof. Because attackers are given unlimited time, they are computationally unbounded, and they can obtain x s.t. $a^x = b$, where $a = g$ and $b = g^{x_{i-1}}$ $(i \geq 1)$ in Token1.

During the time for attackers computing $x = \log_g g^{x_{i-1}}$, however, Token1 is updated as long as Alice logs into her account, then attackers cannot use $x = x_{i-1}$ to log into Alice's account because $a^{x_{i-1}} \neq b$ where a and b are in the updated Token1. The probability is low that Alice does not log into her account in a large time span unless she discards her account.   □

Theorem 3. In Scheme 1, passive (honest-but-curious) MitM attackers cannot log into Alice's account after obtaining Alice's tokens transmitted in channels.

Proof. In Scheme 1, passive MitM attackers obtain Token1(u, a, b) or Token2(u, x, y, z) in channels.

(1) Attackers cannot log into Alice's account after obtaining Token1 according to Theorem 1.

(2) Token2$(u, x, y, z) = (\mathcal{U}, x_{i-1}, g, g^{x_i})$. The element $x = x_{i-1}$ is for Alice's i-th login attempt, attackers cannot use it to log into Alice's account next time. Next time, attackers must use x_i (i.e., Token2 $= (\mathcal{U}, x_i, \bigcirc, \bigcirc)$, where $\bigcirc$ denotes an undetermined element) to log into Alice's account, but they cannot obtain x_i from $y = g$ and $z = g^{x_i}$ according to Assumption 1 and Lemma 1.   □

All the theorems in Scheme 1 are also appropriate for Scheme 2 obviously. Consequently, within AMOGAP, passive MitM and offline guessing attackers cannot log into Alice's web account even if they obtain her tokens (Theorem 1 and 3). Given unlimited time, offline guessing attackers cannot log into Alice's web account with high probability (Theorem 2).

In Scheme 2, for conciseness, we use capital letters M and N to denote $E_{K_1}(b)$ and $E_{k_2^t}(K_2)$ in Token1, repectively; then (t, u, a, b, M, N) denotes Token1. Similarly, we use A, B and C to denote $E_{K_1}(x \oplus r)$, $E_{K_1}(y \oplus r)$ and $E_{K_1}(z \oplus r)$ in Token2, respectively; then Token2 is denoted as (r, u, A, B, C) in Scheme 2.

Lemma 2. ElGamal encryption scheme is CPA-secure.

Proof. Define an ElGamal encryption scheme: the public key $(\mathbb{G}, q, g, h)$, the private key $(\mathbb{G}, q, g, x)$, where $x \in \mathbb{Z}_q$, $h = g^x$, and the message space $\mathbb{G}$.

Given $m_b \in \mathbb{G}$ and $b \in \{0, 1\}$. The ciphertext $c_b = (u_b, v_b) = (g^y, h^y \cdot m_b) = (g^y, g^{xy} \cdot m_b)$, where $y \in \mathbb{Z}_q$. Let $v_b' = v_b \cdot m_b^{-1} = g^{xy}$. Then we have $(h, u_b, v_b') = (g^x, g^y, g^{xy})$, which is a DDH triplet. According to Assumption 2, we cannot distinguish g^{xy} from random elements in $\mathbb{G}$. Therefore, we cannot distinguish between c_0 and c_1.   □

Theorem 4. In Scheme 2, in the registration procedure, active MitM attackers cannot effectively forge Alice's encrypted messages $E_{k_2^t}(\cdot)$ from plaintext $(\cdot)$.

Proof. $E_{k_2^t}(\cdot)$ is the ciphertext of $(\cdot)$. It is the ElGamal encryption with a pair of secret keys k_1^t and k_2^t, therefore, it is CPA-secure according to Lemma 2.   □

Theorem 5. In Scheme 2, in the registration procedure, website S receives Alice's unaltered public key K_2.

Proof. In Scheme 2, Alice sends $\text{Token1}(t, u, a, b, M, N)$ to S in the registration procedure. If attackers do not tamper N, then $K_2 = D_{k_1^t}(N)$, completing the proof. Hence, we assume attackers tamper N.

Let $K_2^{ta} = D_{k_1^t}(N)$. On S, the verification for Alice's public key is $b = D_{K_2^{ta}}(M)$. In order to circumvent the verification, attackers have to tamper b and M s.t. $M = E_{K_1^{ta}}(b)$, where K_1^{ta} and K_2^{ta} are a pair of keys of ElGamal forged by attackers. Therefore, K_2^{ta} is not arbitrary. It is chosen by attackers; otherwise, it will be rejected by the verification procedure on S.

Since $K_2^{ta} = D_{k_2^t}(N)$, then $N = E_{k_2^t}(K_2^{ta})$. Therefore, N is the ciphertext of K_2^{ta}. According to Theorem 4, however, attackers cannot effectively forge the ciphertext (i.e., N) from the plaintext (i.e., K_2^{ta}), which contradicts with the initial assumption in the proof. □

Theorem 6. In Scheme 2, active MitM attackers cannot effectively forge Alice's encrypted messages $E_{K_1}(\cdot)$ from plaintext $(\cdot)$.

Proof. $E_{K_1}(\cdot)$ is the ciphertext of $(\cdot)$. It is the ElGamal encryption scheme with the private key K_1 and the public key K_2. K_1 is secret. K_2 is unaltered according to Theorem 5. Therefore, it is CPA-secure according to Lemma 2. □

Theorem 7. In Scheme 2, in the login procedure, active MitM attackers cannot log into Alice's account through reconstructing her previous tokens.

Proof. Assume attackers obtain all of Alice's past tokens, then they can decrypt all of the $\text{Token2}(r, u, A, B, C)$ to the plaintext (r, u, x, y, z) with key K_2. As a consequence, attackers accumulate g, x_0, g^{x_0}, x_1, g^{x_1}, x_2, g^{x_2}, etc. They, however, cannot reconstruct the plaintext of Token2 in the i-th login attempt to $(r, u, x_{i-1}, g, g^{x_j})$ and log in with $(r, u, x_j, g, \bigcirc)$ in the $(i+1)$-th login attempt, where $0 \leq j \leq i-1$. The reason is that attackers cannot use an old timestamp in a new Token2; if they use a new timestamp r, they cannot construct $\text{Token2}(r, u, A, B, C)$ s.t. $A = E_{K_1}(x \oplus r)$, $B = E_{K_1}(y \oplus r)$ and $C = E_{K_1}(z \oplus r)$ according to Theorem 6. □

Theorem 8. In Scheme 2, active MitM attackers cannot log into Alice's account through reconstructing Alice's token in the *Abnormal Changing Token1 Procedure*.

Proof. Alice's token is $(t, u, E_{K_1}(t), a, b, E_{K_1}(t \oplus \lambda \oplus b))$ in the *Abnormal Changing Token1 Procedure*.

(1) Attackers cannot effectively forge $E_{K_1}(t \oplus \lambda \oplus b)$ according to Theorem 6.

(2) Attackers cannot effectively replace $E_{K_1}(t \oplus \lambda \oplus b)$ with C in $\text{Token2}(r, u, A, B, C)$ which is previously sent by Alice in the login procedure, where $C = E_{K_1}(r \oplus z)$. The reasons are as follows. Because λ is generated by the server on S and attackers cannot tamper it, in order to circumvent the verification on

S and log into Alice's account next time, attackers have to reconstruct Alice's token to $(t_a, u, E_{K_1}(t_a), a, z, E_{K_1}(r \oplus z))$ s.t. $D_{K_2}(E_{K_1}(r \oplus z)) = t_a \oplus \lambda \oplus z$. Thus, $t_a = r \oplus \lambda$, but attackers cannot effectively forge $E_{K_1}(t_a)$ according to Theorem 6.

(3) Attackers cannot effectively replace $E_{K_1}(t \oplus \lambda \oplus b)$ with $E_{K_1}(t' \oplus \lambda' \oplus b')$ sent by Alice in the previous *Abnormal Changing Token1 Procedure*. The reasons are as follows. In order to log into Alice's account next time, attackers have to reconstruct Alice's token to $(t_a, u, E_{K_1}(t_a), a, b', E_{K_1}(t' \oplus \lambda' \oplus b'))$ s.t. $D_{K_2}(E_{K_1}(t' \oplus \lambda' \oplus b')) = t_a \oplus \lambda \oplus b'$. Thus, $t_a = t' \oplus \lambda \oplus \lambda'$. Attackers, however, cannot effectively forge $E_{K_1}(t_a)$ according to Theorem 6.

From (1)(2)(3) above, attackers cannot effectively reconstruct $E_{K_1}(t \oplus \lambda \oplus b)$ to circumvent the verification on S. Consequently, attackers cannot log into Alice's account through reconstructing her token in the *Abnormal Changing Token1 Procedure*. □

Theorem 9. In Scheme 2, even though Alice resets and calls back the clock time on her laptop, active MitM attackers cannot log into Alice's account through reconstructing her previous tokens.

Proof. Alice may need to reset and call back the clock time on her laptop when she travels internationally. As a consequence, she maybe need to carry out the *Abnormal Changing Token1 Procedure* due to a change in the timestamp.

According to Theorem 8, attackers cannot effectively tamper Alice's token in the *Abnormal Changing Token1 Procedure*. Therefore, in her next login attempt after the *Abnormal Changing Token1 Procedure*, attackers cannot effectively replace A in Token2(r, u, A, B, C) with previous ones whose timestamps are later than r. Therefore, they cannot effectively replace r in Token2 by later ones since attackers cannot forge A in effect according to Theorem 6. Consequently, attackers cannot effectively replace B and C in Token2 with previous ones whose timestamps are later than r. Recursively, attackers cannot effectively replace Alice's Token2 in her following login attempts. □

Theorem 10. In Scheme 2, in the login procedure, Alice can catch active MitM attackers' interception at the first moment.

Proof. Assume attackers intercept Alice's Token2(r, u, A, B, C) in her i-th login attempt.

(1) If attackers let Alice log in successfully in the i-th login attempt, then they cannot log into her account next time according to Theorem 6 and 7.
(2) If attackers use Alice's Token2 to log into her account, then Alice cannot log in abnormally and carries out the *Abnormal Changing Token1 Procedure* at once. As a consequence, she stops attackers' attempt at the first moment. □

Within the advanced AMOGAP (Scheme 2), active MitM attackers cannot log into Alice's account through tampering and forging (Theorems 5 and 6), replaying (Theorems 7, 8 and 9), or intercepting (Theorem 10) Alice's tokens. With respect to offline guessing attacks on the client side, that security is guaranteed by KYO [17].

6 Using Other Devices to Log in

Alice always login in her account on her laptop. It is the limitation of AMOGAP: we must store the data such as (k, σ, γ) and $(S, \mathcal{U}, k, \sigma 1_{S,\mathcal{U}}, \sigma 2_{S,\mathcal{U}})$ in Scheme 2 into Alice's laptop. This leads to the problem of portability. Alice may want to use other devices such as her work computer to log into her web account. PPSS [2] may solve this issue. With PPSS, Alice can secret-share the data among n on-line trustees. When she uses another device (e.g., her work computer) to log into her web account, she can recall her login token by sending/receiving messages to/from t $(t \leq n)$ on-line trustees. In this whole process, Alice just needs to input her password ρ to her work computer and does not expose her password to these trustees. The only premise is that Alice's work computer is secure (i.e., there is no shoulder snooping, key loggers, or hardware-based side channel attacks to her work computer).

7 Conclusion

In this paper, we presented a novel text password-based authentication scheme, AMOGAP. Allowing users to select easy-to-remember passwords, AMOGAP protects user passwords from MitM and offline guessing attacks; thus, preventing attackers from logging into users' web services. AMOGAP converts the widely-used salted and hashed passwords to user tokens on the server side, and employs a difficult problem in number theory (i.e., DDH) rather than a one-way hash function. As a text password-based authentication mechanism, AMOGAP does not change the existing authentication process. At the same time, it does not change the infrastructure or increase any burden on the server side though it provides much more robust security guarantees than existing related approaches. On the server side, AMOGAP makes the user tokens stored there valueless for offline guessing attackers. If AMOGAP is adopted, we expect a substantial decrease in the number of user passwords sold on the dark web [5]. In communication channels, AMOGAP makes it so that MitM attackers cannot cheat users or web servers. On the client side, AMOGAP employs a previous work KYO [17]; in order to eliminate its limitation on portability, AMOGAP also uses another previous work PPSS [2]. We rigorously proved the security of AMOGAP based on DDH assumption.

Future research includes extending and building AMOGAP on other hard problems, including those that are known to be resilience to quantum computing attacks, as well as implementing a prototype of the proposed scheme in a real-world setting.

Acknowledgement. This work has been partly supported by National NSF of China under Grant No. 61772266, 61572248, 61431008.

References

1. Alwen, J., Chen, B., Pietrzak, K., Reyzin, L., Tessaro, S.: Scrypt is maximally memory-hard. In: Coron, J.-S., Nielsen, J.B. (eds.) EUROCRYPT 2017. LNCS, vol. 10212, pp. 33–62. Springer, Cham (2017). https://doi.org/10.1007/978-3-319-56617-7_2
2. Bagherzandi, A., Jarecki, S., Saxena, N., Lu, Y.: Password-protected secret sharing. In: Proceedings of the 18th ACM Conference on Computer and Communications Security, pp. 433–444. ACM (2011)
3. Baum, C., Damgård, I., Larsen, K.G., Nielsen, M.: How to prove knowledge of small secrets. In: Robshaw, M., Katz, J. (eds.) CRYPTO 2016. LNCS, vol. 9816, pp. 478–498. Springer, Heidelberg (2016). https://doi.org/10.1007/978-3-662-53015-3_17
4. Bisson, D.: The 10 biggest data breaches of 2018... so far, July 2018. https://blog.barkly.com/biggest-data-breaches-2018-so-far
5. Blocki, J., Harsha, B., Zhou, S.: On the economics of offline password cracking. In: 2018 IEEE Symposium on Security and Privacy (SP), pp. 35–53 (2018)
6. Bojinov, H., Bursztein, E., Boyen, X., Boneh, D.: Kamouflage: loss-resistant password management. In: Gritzalis, D., Preneel, B., Theoharidou, M. (eds.) ESORICS 2010. LNCS, vol. 6345, pp. 286–302. Springer, Heidelberg (2010). https://doi.org/10.1007/978-3-642-15497-3_18
7. Boneh, D., Corrigan-Gibbs, H., Schechter, S.: Balloon hashing: a memory-hard function providing provable protection against sequential attacks. In: Cheon, J.H., Takagi, T. (eds.) ASIACRYPT 2016. LNCS, vol. 10031, pp. 220–248. Springer, Heidelberg (2016). https://doi.org/10.1007/978-3-662-53887-6_8
8. Callegati, F., Cerroni, W., Ramilli, M.: Man-in-the-middle attack to the HTTPS protocol. IEEE Secur. Priv. 7(1), 78–81 (2009)
9. Cappos, J., Torres, S.: PolyPasswordHasher: protecting passwords in the event of a password file disclosure. Technical report (2014). https://password-hashing.net/submissions/specs/PolyPassHash-v1.pdf
10. Di Crescenzo, G., Lipton, R., Walfish, S.: Perfectly secure password protocols in the bounded retrieval model. In: Halevi, S., Rabin, T. (eds.) TCC 2006. LNCS, vol. 3876, pp. 225–244. Springer, Heidelberg (2006). https://doi.org/10.1007/11681878_12
11. Wang, D., Cheng, H., Wang, P., Yan, J., Huang, X.: A security analysis of honeywords. In: Proceedings of the 25th Annual Network and Distributed System Security Symposium (2018)
12. D'Orazio, C.J., Choo, K.K.R.: A technique to circumvent SSL/TLS validations on iOS devices. Future Gener. Comput. Syst. 74, 366–374 (2017)
13. D'Orazio, C.J., Choo, K.K.R.: Circumventing iOS security mechanisms for APT forensic investigations: a security taxonomy for cloud apps. Future Gener. Comput. Syst. 79, 247–261 (2018)
14. ElGamal, T.: A public key cryptosystem and a signature scheme based on discrete logarithms. IEEE Trans. Inf. Theory 31(4), 469–472 (1985)
15. Gelernter, N., Kalma, S., Magnezi, B., Porcilan, H.: The password reset MitM attack. In: 2017 IEEE Symposium on Security and Privacy, pp. 251–267 (2017)
16. Grosse, E.: Gmail account security in Iran, September 2011. https://security.googleblog.com/2011/09/gmail-account-security-in-iran.html
17. Güldenring, B., Roth, V., Ries, L.: Knock Yourself Out: secure authentication with short re-usable passwords. In: Proceedings of the 22nd Annual Network and Distributed System Security Symposium (2015)

18. Hackett, R.: Yahoo raises breach estimate to full 3 billion accounts, by far biggest known, October 2017. http://fortune.com/2017/10/03/yahoo-breach-mail/
19. Halderman, J.A., Waters, B., Felten, E.W.: A convenient method for securely managing passwords. In: Proceedings of the 14th International Conference on World Wide Web, pp. 471–479. ACM (2005)
20. Heim, P.: Resetting passwords to keep your files safe, August 2016. blogs.dropbox.com/dropbox/2016/08/resetting-passwords-to-keep-your-files-safe/
21. Juels, A., Rivest, R.L.: Honeywords: making password-cracking detectable. In: Proceedings of the 20th ACM Conference on Computer and Communications Security, pp. 145–160. ACM (2013)
22. Kelsey, J., Schneier, B., Hall, C., Wagner, D.: Secure applications of low-entropy keys. In: Okamoto, E., Davida, G., Mambo, M. (eds.) ISW 1997. LNCS, vol. 1396, pp. 121–134. Springer, Heidelberg (1998). https://doi.org/10.1007/BFb0030415
23. Komanduri, S., Shay, R., Cranor, L.F., Herley, C., Schechter, S.E.: Telepathwords: preventing weak passwords by reading users' minds. In: USENIX Security Symposium, pp. 591–606 (2014)
24. Kontaxis, G., Athanasopoulos, E., Portokalidis, G., Keromytis, A.D.: SAuth: Protecting user accounts from password database leaks. In: Proceedings of the 20th ACM Conference on Computer and Communications Security, pp. 187–198 (2013)
25. Leininger, H.: Libpathwell 0.6.1 released (2015). https://blog.korelogic.com/blog/2015/07/31/libpathwell-0_6_1
26. Percival, C.: Stronger key derivation via sequential memory-hard functions. In: BSDCan 2009 (self-published), pp. 1–16 (2009)
27. Pinkas, B., Sander, T.: Securing passwords against dictionary attacks. In: Proceedings of the 9th ACM Conference on Computer and Communications Security, pp. 161–170. ACM (2002)
28. Provos, N., Mazieres, D.: A future-adaptable password scheme. In: USENIX Annual Technical Conference, FREENIX Track, pp. 81–91 (1999)
29. Ross, B., Jackson, C., Miyake, N., Boneh, D., Mitchell, J.C.: Stronger password authentication using browser extensions. In: USENIX Security, Baltimore, MD, USA, pp. 17–32 (2005)
30. Schechter, S., Herley, C., Mitzenmacher, M.: Popularity is everything: a new approach to protecting passwords from statistical-guessing attacks. In: USENIX Conference on Hot Topics in Security, pp. 1–8 (2010)
31. Shamir, A.: How to share a secret. Commun. ACM **22**(11), 612–613 (1979)
32. Shetty, R., Grispos, G., Choo, K.K.R.: Are you dating danger? An interdisciplinary approach to evaluating the (in) security of android dating apps. IEEE Trans. Sustain. Comput. (2017, in press). https://doi.org/10.1109/TSUSC.2017.2783858
33. Bernard, T.S., Hsu, T., Perlroth, N., Lieber, R.: Equifax says cyberattack may have affected 143 million in the U.S. September 2017. https://www.nytimes.com/2017/09/07/business/equifax-cyberattack.html
34. Wang, D., Cheng, H., Wang, P., Huang, X., Jian, G.: Zipf's law in passwords. IEEE Trans. Inf. Forensics Secur. **12**(11), 2776–2791 (2017)
35. Wang, D., Wang, P.: The emperor's new password creation policies: an evaluation of leading web services and the effect of role in resisting against online guessing. In: Pernul, G., Ryan, P.Y.A., Weippl, E. (eds.) ESORICS 2015. LNCS, vol. 9327, pp. 456–477. Springer, Cham (2015). https://doi.org/10.1007/978-3-319-24177-7_23

36. Wang, D., Zhang, Z., Wang, P., Yan, J., Huang, X.: Targeted online password guessing: an underestimated threat. In: Proceedings of the 2016 ACM SIGSAC Conference on Computer and Communications Security, pp. 1242–1254. ACM (2016)
37. Wu, L., Wang, J., Choo, K.K.R., He, D.: Secure key agreement and key protection for mobile device user authentication. IEEE Trans. Inf. Forensics Secur. 14(2), 319–330 (2019)
38. Yoo, C., Kang, B.T., Kim, H.K.: Case study of the vulnerability of OTP implemented in internet banking systems of South Korea. Multimed. Tools Appl. 74(10), 3289–3303 (2015)

MineAuth: Mining Behavioural Habits for Continuous Authentication on a Smartphone

Xiaojian Pang[1], Li Yang[2(✉)], Maozhen Liu[1], and Jianfeng Ma[1]

[1] School of Cyber Engineering, Xidian University, Xi'an 710071, China
Xiaojian_Pang@hotmail.com, maozhen840@foxmail.com,
jfma@mail.xidian.edu.cn
[2] School of Computer Science and Technology, Xidian University,
Xi'an 710071, China
yangli@xidian.edu.cn

Abstract. The increasing use of smartphones raises many concerns related to data security, as the loss of a smartphone could compromise sensitive data. Authentication on smartphones plays an important role in protecting users' data from attacks. However, traditional authentication methods cannot provide continuous protection for a user's data after the user has passed the initial authentication. In this paper, we present a novel continuous authentication approach called MineAuth based on the user's daily interactive behaviours with his/her smartphone. We construct interactive behaviours from data captured by the smartphone. We then propose a weighting-based time period frequent pattern mining algorithm called WeMine to mine user's frequent patterns to characterize the habits of mobile users. We build an authenticator using a one-class classification technique that only relies on the legitimate user data. We also develop a decision procedure to perform the task continuously. The entire process occurs on the smartphone, which provides better privacy guarantees to users and eliminates dependency on cloud connectivity. We also integrate our approach into the Android system and evaluate the performance of our approach. Our approach can achieve good performance. Additionally, it can achieve a high authentication accuracy of up to 98.3%. Regarding resource consumption, our approach consumes less than 0.4% of power while running for an entire day.

Keywords: Continuous authentication · Interactive behaviour · Frequent pattern · Privacy

1 Introduction

Recent developments in mobile internet have led to an explosion in the use of smartphones. Smartphones have become a personal computing platform for accessing and storing sensitive data. Among smartphone users, 92.8% tend to

© Springer Nature Switzerland AG 2019
J. Jang-Jaccard and F. Guo (Eds.): ACISP 2019, LNCS 11547, pp. 533–551, 2019.
https://doi.org/10.1007/978-3-030-21548-4_29

store their personal information on their mobile phones to facilitate their work and life [9]. Hence, there are many attacks aimed at smartphones. Securely and efficiently protecting people's sensitive data stored on smartphones has been a major concern for the public [17].

Authentication is a widely adopted mechanism for preventing unauthorized access to personal information stored on a user's smartphone. Unfortunately, traditional methods, such as PINs or pattern passwords, are easy to be guessed by attackers [21]. There are some other authentication methods, such as fingerprint- and face-based authentication that can slove the above problems, but these methods are one-time authentication methods [1,15]. These methods do not reauthenticate the user after the user has passed the initial authentication. They cannot provide continuous authentication during user operations. Therefore, it is highly desirable to enhance user's security with a continuous authentication method to authenticate the user during the user operations. A promising approach is the use of behavioural aspects of users' interactions with their smartphones.

Continuous authentication has been widely explored in recent years [4,5,7,8, 12,13,19,22,23]. These approaches can verify users' identity continuously based on behavioural aspects of users' interactions with their smartphones. However, such approaches suffer from the following drawbacks: (1) Many previous studies [1,5] require users to send their behaviour data to a remote server. However, we cannot guarantee that the data at the remote server will not be used illegally. (2) Some methods need root access privilege during data collection [4,5]. Once a smartphone has been rooted, major security risks arise. (3) Some approaches utilize touchscreen information to verify the user's identity. However, these approaches cannot withstand effectively simulated behavioural attacks, including shoulder peeks and offline training attacks [7,8]. (4) Many approaches utilize two-class machine learning algorithms to build authentication models, e.g., LSTM [1] and SVM [4]. These approaches need to collect enough data from the legitimate user and impostors; however, only data of legitimate users are usually available in practice.

Based on the above analysis, we propose a secure continuous authentication approach called MineAuth. We chose the seven representative modalities of Wi-Fi and Bluetooth connections, activity behaviour, location of the device, application usage patterns, and call and SMS behaviours to construct interactive behaviour. The reason for choosing these modalities is that they are common and can roughly distinguish among different users. In the remainder of the paper, these seven modalities will be referred to as WiFi, BLUETOOTH, ACTIVITY, LOCATION, APP, CALL and SMS, respectively. Additionally, we explore the applicability of interactive behaviour to continuous authentication. The rationale behind our approach is that the interactive behaviour of different users could reflect such users' behavioural habits, which may represent unique behavioural characteristics of individuals. In the course of the daily usage of a smartphone by a user, interactive data are collected from the smartphone. We construct interactive behaviour from these interactive data. We build an authenticator using a one-class classification technique that only relies on the legitimate user data. We then develop a decision procedure to perform the continuous authentication task. We also integrate our approach into the Android platform and evaluate the performance of our approach.

Our approach has the following 6 advantages compared with previous methods: (1) Continuous authentication. MineAuth can provide continuous authentication instead of one-time authentication when a user uses a smartphone. (2) Privacy protection. A user's behaviour data used by MineAuth are not shared with any entity, which reduces the risk of privacy breaches. (3) Generality. MineAuth does not require the root privilege on the smartphone to access biometric data. (4) High accuracy. MineAuth has a high accuracy of up to 98.3%. (5) Hard to forge. MineAuth constructs interactive behaviour using seven modalities, which increases the difficulty of forgery by an attacker. (6) Applicability. MineAuth builds an authenticator using a one-class method trained on the data only from the legitimate user. The key contributions of our work are as follows:

(1) We propose a continuous authentication approach called MineAuth that considers the user's daily interactive behaviour with his/her smartphone. Our approach continuously monitors the user's behaviour and verifies the user's identity accurately and efficiently. Additionally, our approach does not require users to share private data with any entity and protects the user's privacy.
(2) We present a weighting-based time period frequent pattern mining algorithm called WeMine to mine the user's habits and build a one-class authenticator so that the model can be trained solely on the samples from the legitimate user.
(3) We implement our approach on the Android platform. Additionally, we evaluate the performance and resource consumption of our approach. Our approach can achieve a high accuracy of up to 98.5% and less than 0.4% battery consumption.

2   Related Work

Continuous Authentication

With the enhancement of the computing and sensing capabilities of smartphones, researchers have started to exploit effective continuous authentication approaches. In previous studies, built-in sensors' data are the most commonly used modality for continuous authentication. There are several studies using built-in sensors, such as the touchscreen sensor [15,16], the location sensor [4] and the motion sensor [1]. In addition, some researchers focused on the interactive behaviours of users and utilized application usage [20] or web browsing [6] to build continuous authentication models. The above efforts reveal that both built-in sensor data and interaction data have considerable utility for continuous authentication.

Multimodal Data for Continuous Authentication

Because single-modality data contain limited identity information, using single-modality data to build an authenticator always results in low accuracy. Hence, some researchers proposed combining multimodal data to provide higher accuracy [4,15]. Fridman et al. [4] evaluated the performance of authentication models based on stylometry, application usage, web browsing, or GPS and obtained the best performance of a 0.05 equal error rate. Subsequently, the researchers tested the fusion of the four modalities, obtaining a 0.01 equal error rate, which illustrated that the application of multimodal data in an authenticator had an advantage over that of single-modality data.

Protection of Private Data

Most continuous authentication approaches collect a lot of private data about users and require users to share their private data with a remote server to verify users' identities [1], which results in leakage of private data. There are two ideas to protect private data used for continuous authentication. The first is to protect the private data by using cryptography. Safa et al. [14] proposed an implicit authentication approach with privacy protection, which first encrypts the collected multiple feature values using the homomorphic encryption algorithm and uploads them to the authentication server. The authentication server uses the average absolute deviation (AAD) and order preserving symmetric encryption (OPSE) [2] to calculate the total score of the encrypted feature values and determine whether the user is considered to be authenticated. Since the homomorphic encryption algorithm and OPSE can perform algebraic operations and sort operations in the case of data encryption, the authentication server cannot obtain the real feature values of the user, thereby implementing privacy protection. However, the computational complexity of this approach is too high, and the approach can only support numerical features. The second idea is to authenticate the user on the client side. Murmuria et al. [11] proposed an activity-based authentication model to authenticate the user. In this scheme, the data and the authentication model are stored on the smartphone, and the authentication model does not share any data with remote servers. However, this scheme only provided a preliminary experimental result, and the authentication accuracy was unsatisfactory.

One-Class and Two-Class Machine Learning Algorithms

One-class and two-class machine learning algorithms are most commonly used to build the continuous authentication model. The difference between these two algorithms is the application scenario. In the model building process, the one-class machine learning algorithm only uses the data of the legitimate user, while the two-class machine learning algorithm needs to use the data from both the legitimate user and illegitimate users. Although most existing schemes apply the two-class machine learning algorithm to construct an authentication model [4], this kind of authentication model can only identify the illegitimate users whose datasets have been collected and cannot identify an illegitimate user whose dataset has not been collected. In particular, the data collected from illegitimate users are very limited; thus, the one-class learning algorithm is more suitable for use in continuous authentication scenarios. Liu et al. [10] presented a smartphone authentication approach, which used a one-class SVM algorithm to build a continuous authentication model based on three modalities: user touch dynamics, movements, and power consumption. However, there is a high equal error rate 5% in the model, because the data used to build the model is not denoised.

To develop an efficient continuous authentication approach, we should make full use of the multimodal data and avoid leaking the privacy of the user. Moreover, an appropriate algorithm for the continuous authentication approach needs to be considered in practice.

3 Overview

3.1 Definitions

To simplify the presentation of our approach, we first define several related notions that we have used in our approach.

Interactive Action: This term refers to an action that occurs when the user uses the smartphone, which includes three modalities: Call, SMS and APP.

Context: This term refers to the relevant environment when an interactive action occurs, including a Wi-Fi connection, a Bluetooth connection, and location and activity statuses of the user. Assume that set $F = \{f_1, f_2, ..., f_m\}$ includes all context attributes, and $C_i = \{x_1, x_2, ..., x_k\}$ denotes the set of context attributes that records the relevant environment on the phone when an interactive action occurs, where $x_j \in F$, $j \in [1, k]$, and $k > 0$.

Interactive Behaviour: A user's interactive actions with the smartphone are associated closely with time and a volatile context. Hence, interactive behaviour is expressed as a tuple $B_i = <T_i, C_i, A_i>$, where T_i, C_i and A_i denote the time, context and interactive action, respectively. Behaviour dataset $R = \{B_1, B_2, ..., B_n\}$ denotes the set of interactive behaviours ordered by the time of occurrence.

Support: This term refers to the support of itemset P in set R, which is defined formally as $Support(P) = \frac{\sum_{i=1}^{n} count(P \subseteq B_i)}{|R|}$, with $count(P \subseteq B_i) = \{1 \ if P \subseteq B_i | 0 \ otherwise\}$, where B_i denotes an element of behaviour set R, and $|R|$ denotes the number of elements in set R. If the support of one interactive behaviour P is not less than the minimum support threshold assigned previously, then P is referred to as a frequent itemset and represents a behavioural habit of the user.

Behaviour Template: This term refers to the set of behavioural habits, formally expressed as $BP = \{P_i | Support(P_i) \geq minisupport\}$, where P_i denotes an interactive behaviour with support greater than the minimum support threshold $minisupport$.

Imitation Ability: This term refers to the ability of an attacker to imitate the legitimate user to generate similar interactive behaviours during an attack and is formally expressed as $IA(NormalData, AttackData) = \frac{|NormalData \cap AttackData|}{|AttackData|}$, where $NormalData$ and $AttackData$ denote the behaviour datasets of the legitimate user and the attacker, respectively.

3.2   Architecture

The architecture of MineAuth is shown in Fig. 1. MineAuth consists of five models: data collection, behaviour construction, behavioural habit mining, the authenticator and the decision maker. First, MineAuth collects user's behavioural data in using his/her smartphone. Then, We construct the interactive behaviour to generate the interactive behaviour dataset. Next, we use WeMine algorithm to mine the user's behavioural habits from the interactive behaviour dataset that represents only the legitimate user. We consider the mined behavioural habits as a behaviour template, as shown in Definition Sect. 3.1. We calculate the outlier score range between the behaviour template and the legitimate user behaviours to build a one-class authenticator. Once the model has been built, any incoming behaviour data are continuously verified. To make the authentication approach robust, we design a decision procedure by using an observation window that contains multiple interactive behaviours to make the authentication decision. The decision maker provides the result of authentication. If the current user is verified as the legitimate user, the user can keep accessing the data on the smartphone, and the user behaviour is added to the interactive behaviour dataset. However, if the current user fails authentication, MineAuth locks the smartphone and asks the user to authenticate using a strong authentication method, such as a password.

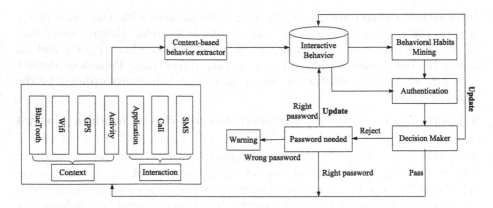

Fig. 1. Framework of MineAuth.

3.3   Threat Model

MineAuth is responsible for authenticating the current user based on the habits mined from the legitimate user's behavioural data. We assume that the behavioural data used to mine habits is all collected from the legitimate user. We also assume that the adversary can observe and learn the legitimate user's interactive behaviours continuously, and can also use the legitimate user's smartphone furtively. We consider an imitation attack that the adversary may cheat

MineAuth to achieve unauthorized access by imitating the legitimate user's interactive behaviours. The ability of each adversary to imitate a legitimate user varies from person to person. In order to quantify the degree of attack by the adversary, we mix legitimate user data and illegitimate user data to generate the adversary data. The percentage of legitimate user data in the adversary data indicates the imitation ability of the adversary, as shown in Definition Sect. 3.1.

4   Building Blocks

4.1   Data Collection

In our method, we develop a data collection application that can transparently collect the user's interactive behaviours. The collected data consist of seven modalities: WiFi, BLUETOOTH, ACTIVITY, LOCATION, APP, CALL, and SMS. We use the above seven modalities' data to construct the user's interactive behaviours for the following reasons: (1) The resulting description of the user's interactive behaviours is more detailed. These seven modalities describe three dimensions of interactive behaviour: time, context and interactive action. The APP, CALL and SMS modalities describe the user's interactive actions, and the WiFi, BLUETOOTH, ACTIVITY and LOCATION modalities describe the context of interactive actions. (2) This approach increases the difficulty of impostors imitating the legitimate user's behaviour. (3) The seven modalities' data are easily collected, and no special hardware or root privilege is needed.

4.2   Behaviour Construction

Behaviour construction consists of three models: location extraction, data fuzzification and the behaviour construction engine. First, we extract locations from Wi-Fi data using the location extraction approach to solve the problem of sparse GPS data. Next, we input the data collected into the data fuzzification model to fuzzy the APP and LOCATION data. Lastly, we use the behaviour construction engine to construct the user's interactive behaviour from the above data.

Location Extraction. Due to the small amount of collected GPS data, the location information of each user is unknown most of the time. In comparison to GPS data, the amount of Wi-Fi data collected by each user on his/her mobile phone is much larger and has a long duration. In practice, the coverage of Wi-Fi signals is very widespread, and Wi-Fi signals in a certain area are relatively stable, so the list of Wi-Fi signals can be used as the location label for the covered area. Motivated by this reasoning, we propose a simple algorithm called WFTL to convert Wi-Fi signals to location labels as shown in Algorithm 1.

First, the WFTL algorithm divides Wi-Fi data into several groups such that the Wi-Fi data in each group have the same timestamp. Next, the unique identifier BSSID of each Wi-Fi signal in a group is extracted to form the set BSSIDSet to identify the geographical location. All BSSIDSets are added to BSSIDSetList to record the user's movement trajectory. Due to limited coverage of a Wi-Fi

---

Algorithm 1. Algorithm for Extracting Location from Wi-Fi Data.

Input: rowWiFiData
Output: locationLabelMap
 1: **function** WFTL(rowWiFiData)
 2:     $locationLabelMap \leftarrow NULL$
 3:     $WiFiGroups \leftarrow rowWiFiData.groupby(rowWiFiData.Time)$
 4:     $bssidSetList \leftarrow WiFiGroups.extract(BSSID)$
 5:     **for** $bssidSet$ in $bssidSetListdo$ **do**
 6:         **if** $locationLabelMap.keys()! = NULL$ **then**
 7:             $newBssidSet \leftarrow bssidSet - locationLabelMap.keys()$
 8:             $oldBssidSet \leftarrow bssidSet - newBssidSet$
 9:             $locationLabel \leftarrow locationLabelMap[oldBssidSet]$
10:             $locationLabelMap.add(newBssidSet, locationLabel)$
11:         **else**
12:             $newLocationLabel \leftarrow createLocLabel(bssidSet)$
13:             $locationLabelMap.add(bssidSet, newLocationLabel)$
14:         **end if**
15:     **end for**
16:     **return** $locationLabelMap$
17: **end function**

---

signal, different Wi-Fi signal lists may be collected in the same area, so BSSID-Sets with the largest intersections should point to the same area, as shown in the 9th line in Algorithm 1. If there is no intersection between the current BSSID-Set and all of the keys in locationLabelMap, a new geographical location label newlocationLabel is generated, as shown in the 10th line in Algorithm 1. Finally, (BSSIDSet, newlocationLabel) is added as a mapping pair to locationLabelMap, and the updated locationLabelMap is returned.

Data Fuzzification. The number of unique items in the original data is too large to mine effective behavioural habits. Hence, we have to reduce the number of unique items. According to our observations, some interactive behaviours can be regarded as the same type of behaviour. For instance, assume that there are two different interactive behaviours generated by a user, < 9:06 am, Sunday, (N39.504, E118.586), Glory of the King > and < 9:15 am, Sunday, (N39.505, E118.587), PUBG Mobile >. Intuitively, these two interactive behaviours are completely different. However, if these two timestamps are mapped to the corresponding time period, i.e., 9 : 00 am-9 : 30 am, these two precise geographical coordinates are mapped to the corresponding location with an area range, i.e., some residential area, and these applications are classified as game applications, then these two different interactive behaviours can be mapped to the same behaviour after being fuzzified, which effectively helps mine the behaviour habits of each user. The focus here is on fuzzy processing of GPS data and application data.

(1) **Fuzzy processing of GPS data.** The format of the collected GPS data is the coordinate pair of longitude a and latitude b, i.e., (a, b). To map the

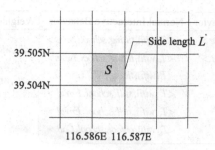

Fig. 2. Fuzzy processing of GPS data.

coordinate pair to a location with an area range, we use the intersecting latitude and longitude lines to form a fine-grained earth grid that divides the earth into numerous areas, e.g., s labelled in Fig. 2. All of the coordinate pairs in the range of the same area are marked as the same location. For example, as shown in Fig. 2, the span of longitude and latitude for each region s is set to 0.01 degrees, corresponding to 1–1.21 km^2. Region s can be regarded as a square with a side length $L = \sqrt{s}$ ranging from 1 to 1.1 km. Each coordinate pair (a, b) corresponds to a geographical location marked $LID = H(x||y)$, where $x = \lfloor 100 * a \rfloor$ and $y = \lfloor 100 * b \rfloor$, $H(\cdot)$ denotes a hash function, and $\lfloor \cdot \rfloor$ denotes rounding down the number inside the brackets.

(2) **Fuzzy processing of app data.** Fuzzy processing of app data maps the APP name to the APP category using an "APP Name–APP Category" mapping table. In this study, we first refer to the Google Play standard to define 17 application categories, as shown in Table 1. Next, according to Table 1, we classify approximately two thousand applications from the collected app data of all volunteers and construct an "APP Name–APP Category" mapping table.

Table 1. Categories of application software.

Audio	Browser	Utilities
Games	Launcher	Email
Photo&Video	News&Books	Map&Travel
System	PlayStore	Food&Drink
Health&Medical	Social Networking	Productivity
Education	Entertainment	Shopping&Payment

Interactive Behaviour Construction. The interactive behaviour construction process is illustrated in Fig. 4 using a simple example. First, MineAuth collects context data and interactive action data with a certain sampling frequency to obtain the original interactive behaviour, such

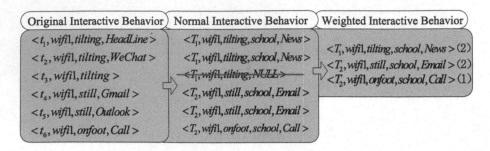

Fig. 3. Interactive behaviour construction process.

as $<t1, wifi1, tilting, Headlineapp>$. Next, MineAuth preprocesses the original interactive behaviours, including performing data fuzzification and location extraction, to obtain the general interactive behaviours, such as $<T1, wifi1, tilting, school, News>$. During preprocessing, the timestamp is mapped to the time period with a certain granularity, the GPS coordinate pair is mapped to the location label LID, and the application is mapped to the corresponding application category. If the GPS data do not exist, the list of collectable Wi-Fi signals is transformed to a location label $WFTLID$ to supplement the location information. In addition, MineAuth mainly focuses on interactive behaviours generated when the user uses the phone, so interactive behaviours without interactive action data are discarded during preprocessing.

Compared to the original interactive behaviours, general interactive behaviours are generalized and abstract and can express the essential characteristics of users' behaviour. In fact, it is almost impossible for a user to use the same application software at the point with the same coordinates at times with the same timestamp on different days because users do not think about objective information such as timestamps and coordinates. However, it is quite possible for a user to use application software belonging to the same category in the same area for the same time period on different days. Therefore, the general interactive behaviours are more conducive to mining behavioural habits on the phone.

Instead of repeating the general interactive behaviours, MineAuth compresses each general interactive behaviour into a weighted interactive behaviour and associates a weight with each weighted interactive behaviour, indicating the number of times it is repeated. In Fig. 3, six original interactive behaviours are processed to obtain only three weighted interactive behaviours, which not only reduces the use of the phone's storage but also improves the efficiency of the behavioural habit mining algorithm.

4.3 Behavioural Habit Mining

In our method, we partition the interactive behaviour dataset to two subsets: the training dataset and the validation dataset. We mine frequent patterns in the training dataset to characterize the habits of users, and build a one-class authenticator using validation dataset. The more details on building the authenticator is in Sect. 4.5. Mining frequent patterns on smartphones cannot be performed by the traditional frequent pattern mining algorithms because traditional algorithms need to consume significant computing resources on the phone. For example, using the Apriori algorithm to process user data collected on a smartphone takes several hours [23]. In addition, unbalanced occurrences of time, context and interactions also pose a challenge to traditional algorithms, potentially causing them to mine many invalid frequent patterns.

To solve the above problems, we propose a weighting-based time period frequent pattern mining algorithm called WeMine. Our algorithm is divided into two steps. First, the weighted interactive behaviour data are divided into several groups according to the time period. In a group, all interactive behaviours have occurred during the same time period. Therefore, in the subsequent mining algorithm, the interference of time is ignored. Next, we use the WeMiT algorithm [18] to mine frequent patterns in each group as the time period behavioural habits. The WeMiT algorithm can significantly reduce the running time. The WeMiT algorithm considers the number of repetitions of an interactive behaviour as its weight and compresses the repeated interactive behaviours into weighted interactive behaviours, as shown in Fig. 4. Since there are fewer weighted interactive behaviours, the running time of frequent pattern mining is significantly reduced. In particular, we use the weighted interactive behaviour dataset $R = \{B_1^{w_1}, B_2^{w_2}, ..., B_n^{w_n}\}$, where w_k is the weight of interactive behaviour B_k, and the definition of the support of itemset P in the weighted interactive behaviour dataset R is $\sum_{i=1}^{n} contain(B_i^{w_i}, P) * w_i$, where $contain(p, q) = \{1 \ if q \subseteq p | 0 \ otherwise\}$. Finally, the behavioural habits for each time period are combined to form the behavioural temple. It is worth noting that B_k denotes the interactive behaviour without the attribute of time.

4.4 Authentication

We build a one-class authenticator using the validation dataset from legitimate user. The steps of building authentictor as follows:

(1) We calculate the frequent pattern outlier score of each interactive behaviour in the validation dataset for behavioural temple mined from the training dataset. The definition of the frequent pattern outlier score FPOS is
$FPOS(B, T) = \frac{\sum_{X \subseteq B, X \in T} Support(X)}{|T|}$, where X denotes a frequent itemset belonging to the set of the corresponding time period behavioural temple T. $X \subseteq B$ signifies that X is a subset of interactive behaviour B, $Support(X)$ denotes the support of frequent itemset X, and $|T|$ denotes the number of frequent itemsets in T.
(2) We analyse the distribution of scores and find the range of scores for normal interactive behaviour to build the authenticator.

4.5   Decision Maker

After building the authenticator of the legitimate user's interactive behaviours, we use this model to verify whether the current interactive behaviour is normal. During the authentication process, we calculate the outlier score between the legitimate user's behavioural habits and the current interactive behaviour. If the outlier score is outside of the range of normal behaviour, then the current interactive behaviour is considered to be anomalous. Since a single behaviour is insufficient for determining the current user's identity, we use an observation window that contains mutiple interactive behaviours to improve the accuracy and robustness of authentication. If the number of anomalous behaviours is larger than the number of normal behaviours, then the current user is considered to be an impostor.

5   System Implementation and Evaluation

5.1   System Implementation

We integrate our approach into the Android system, and implement an application. The application consists of several modules: the data collection module, the interactive behaviour construction module, the authenticator and the decision-maker. The data collection module runs as a background thread that continuously records interactive data during routine smartphone usage. The interactive behaviour construction module aims to construct interactive behaviour from data collected to be used in the authenticator. The decision maker provides the authentication result by judging the validity of several consecutive interactive behaviours.

5.2   Evaluation Indicators

We use three standard metrics to report the performance of MineAuth:

Recall Rate (R): This metric refers to the percentage of true unauthorized accesses being detected among all the true unauthorized accesses in the dataset.

Precision Rate (P): This metric refers to the percentage of true unauthorized accesses among all the unauthorized accesses detected.

F1-score (F1): This metric refers to the harmonic mean of the recall rate and precision rate, defined as $F1 = \frac{2*P*R}{P+R}$.

5.3   Dataset

We collect interactive data from 33 users for 30 days. Table 2 shows the number of records in the data collected.

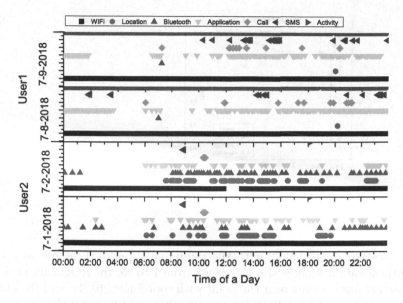

Fig. 4. Behaviour data collected from User1 and User2 for two days.

Figure 4 visually shows the differences in the behaviour data between the two users for two consecutive days. We observe that the distribution of the behaviour data varies significantly with the user, while the distributions of the behaviour data for the same user on consecutive days are similar. This finding also illustrates that the seven modalities we have chosen are reasonable.

Table 2. 33 random users' records from the collected dataset.

Sensor name	Num. of instance
WiFi	8,340,121
Bluetooth	10,234
GPS	72,509
Activity	135,009
APP	145,803
Call	9,234
SMS	7,509
All Data	8,720,419

5.4   Relating Usability to Minisupport and the Observation Window Size

As shown in Fig. 5, each curve represents the receiver operating characteristic (ROC) curve of MineAuth for a specific minimum support threshold and a specific authentication window size. Each point on the curve corresponds to an

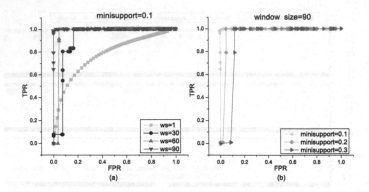

Fig. 5. ROC curves.

FPT threshold. In Fig. 5(a), with the minimum support threshold of 0.1 and the authentication window size increasing from 1 to 90, the ROC curve becomes increasingly more convex near the point with coordinates (0, 1), and the authentication accuracy of MineAuth increases to 98%, which shows the outstanding authentication performance of MineAuth. In Fig. 5(b), under the condition of the authentication window size being 90, it is clear that an increase of the minimum support threshold causes the ROC curve to gradually move away from the point with coordinates (0, 1), which indicates that the authentication accuracy of MineAuth decreases as the minimum support threshold increases. To ensure that MineAuth performs authentication well, according to this experiment, we set the minimum support threshold to 0.1 and the authentication window size to 90. In the following experiments, these two parameter values are valid, unless otherwise specified.

5.5   Comparison with Other Approaches

We experiment with three other popular one-class machine learning methods for authentication to explore our approach's effectiveness. The three one-class learning methods used in our experiments are as follows: (1) Isolation Forest (iForest), (2) Support Vector Machine (1-SVM), and (3) Local Outlier Factor (LOF). Here, we implement the above three one-class learning methods. We set the best parameter for iForest, 1-SVM and LOF [3]. For MineAuth, we set minisupport to 0.1.

Figure 6 shows the performance of the four methods from three aspects: precision rate, recall rate and F1-score. The best performance corresponds to a precision rate of 98.2%, a recall rate of 98.5%, and an F1-score of 98.3%, and was obtained by our MineAuth method. The result indicates that our approach is more effective for variable behaviour data than iForest,1-SVM and LOF.

Compared with iForest, 1-SVM and LOF, the reason that MineAuth obtains high accuracy is that can mine the associations between time, contexts and interactive actions that describe the temporal nature and contextual properties of user's habits. Conversely, iForest, 1-SVM and LOF algorithms do not consider the associated relation information and may thus perform poorly.

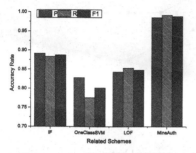
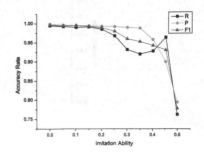

Fig. 6. Performance of related methods.   **Fig. 7.** Resilience to adversary imitation.

5.6   Resilience to Adversary Imitation

In the threat model, we assume the adversary can observe and learn the legitimate user's interactive behaviours for a long time. In this section, we design the following experiments to evaluate MineAuth's resilience to adversary imitation attack. In our experiments, we build several adversary samples with different imitation ability by combining the legitimate user's data and another user's data at various ratios. The imitation ability is selected from $\{0, 0.05, 0.1, 0.15, 0.2, 0.25, 0.3, 0.35, 0.4, 0.45, 0.5\}$. We only estimate the authentication accuracy under the condition that the imitation ability is not more than 0.5, because when the imitation ability exceeds 0.5, the number of legal behaviours is always larger than that of illegal behaviors, which directly leads to the system failing to properly authenticate the attacker.

According to Fig. 7, with the increase of the imitation ability, the recall rate shows a trend of first decreasing and then increasing, while the precision rate and F1-score decline steadily. We explain this phenomenon as follows: the increase of the imitation ability will interfere with MineAuth's authentication ability, resulting in lower recall rate and precision rate. With the further increase of the imitation ability, MineAuth chooses a lager outlier score range to identify more illegitimate behaviours, which causes the recall rate to rebound. Meanwhile, more legitimate behaviours will be misidentified as illegitimate behaviours, resulting in a continuous decrease in the precision rate, which causes F1 to exhibit a downward trend.

As shown in Fig. 7, when the imitation ability increases from 0 to 0.45, the performance of MineAuth is characterized by a recall rate of 96%, a precision rate of approximately 90% and an F1-score of 92%, which means that MineAuth can effectively resist adversary imitation.

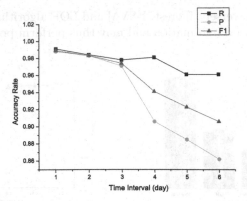

Fig. 8. Experiment analysing the impact of the time interval between the training data and the test data on MineAuth's authentication performance with different levels of imitation ability.

5.7 Response to User Behaviour Change

As is well known, users' behaviours are inconsistent and will change over a period of time. However, the quality of mined habits is affected by behavioural variability. Correspondingly, the accuracy of authentication will decrease. To explore the impact of behavioural change, we design the following experiments by varying the time intervals between training data and test data. For a given user, we use the user's 7-day behaviour data as the training data to mine the user's habits and use the data of the following 1 to 6 days as test data. The experimental results are shown in Fig. 8.

As shown in Fig. 8, with increasing time interval, the precision rate, recall rate and F1-score continue to decline. However, the F1-scores for six days are greater than 85%. According to the results, we can conclude that the user's behavioural habits will change over time, but the user's behaviour within a week is relatively stable. Hence, it is reasonable that we use 7-day behaviour data to mine behavioural habits. To improve performance in the scenario of behavioural change, one possible approach is to introduce some habit update strategies. We update the interactive behaviour dataset periodically to mine user's new habits.

5.8 Resource Consumption

Resource consumption is an important measure that determines whether our method can run on a smartphone. We evaluated the running time, the usage of CPU and memory, and the battery power consumption of MineAuth with tests performed on a Nokia 7 Plus smartphone with a 4 GHz processor and 6 GB of RAM, running Android 8.0.1. Table 3 shows the resource consumption of MineAuth running for one day.

We observe from Table 3 that the interactive behaviour construction module is the most time-consuming part; however, it takes only approximately 1.5 min to process the behaviour data generated over an entire day. It takes approximately 2310 ms to mine behaviour habits and build the authenticator. As the most active module, the decision maker needs to process interactive behaviour data in real time; however, doing so takes the least amount of time, and the total time required to process the behaviour data for the entire day is less than one second. The interactive behaviour construction module uses the largest amount of memory of approximately 75.10 Mbytes (an empty app needs approximately 46 Mbytes of memory resources), but this is not a sizeable burden for a typical mobile phone. The CPU usage of each module is almost the same at approximately 15.7%. In addition, MineAuth only needs less than 0.40% of power to operate for one day; such power consumption can be ignored. In summary, MineAuth can run efficiently on resource-constrained mobile devices without interfering with user's behaviour.

Table 3. Resource consumption of MineAuth running for one day.

Resource consumption	Behaviour construction	Habits mining & authenticator	Decision maker
Running time	87,759 ms	2310 ms	532 ms
Memory usage	75.10 MB	60.2 MB	50.99 MB
CPU usage	15.30%	16.10%	15.45%
Power consumption	0.35%	<0.01%	<0.01%

6 Conclusion

We present a novel continual authentication method called MineAuth. We also present a novel algorithm called WeMine to mine user's behavioural habits. We use a one-class classification technique to build an authenticator only using legitimate user's data. To make MineAuth robust and stable, we introduce an observation window mechanism. MineAuth runs completely on the smartphone, which provides better privacy guarantees to users. Regarding MineAuth's performance, MineAuth has a F1-score of 98.3%, and its power consumption is less than 0.4% over an entire day. Moreover, MineAuth can effectively resist attackers with an imitation ability of not more than 50%.

However, there are still some shortcomings in MineAuth. To improve the accuracy of MineAuth, we introduce an observation window mechanism. The larger the observation window is, the higher the accuracy, and the longer the time of making decision will be. How to chose a suitable size of the observation window is impotant to keep a balance between accuracy and the time of making decision. In future work, we will study an adaptive mechanism to select the observation window size according to different scenarios. In addition, in our system implementation, we store the user's data in clear text, and this may lead to a risk of leaving behavioural template exposed during authentication. A more secure way is to employ trust zone mechanism to store the user's data, and this also will be our future research focus.

Acknowledgements. We would like to thank the reviewers for their careful reading and useful comments. This work was supported by the National Natural Science Foundation of China (61671360, 61672415), the Key Program of NSFC-Tongyong Union Foundation under Grant (U1636209), the National Key Basic Research Program (2016YFB0801101, 2017YFB0801805), the Key Program of NSFC Grant 1010 (U1405255).

References

1. Amini, S., Noroozi, V., Pande, A., Gupte, S., Yu, P.S., Kanich, C.: DeepAuth: a framework for continuous user re-authentication in mobile apps. In: Proceedings of the 27th ACM International Conference on Information and Knowledge Management, pp. 2027–2035. ACM (2018)
2. Boldyreva, A., Chenette, N., Lee, Y., O'Neill, A.: Order-preserving symmetric encryption. In: Joux, A. (ed.) EUROCRYPT 2009. LNCS, vol. 5479, pp. 224–241. Springer, Heidelberg (2009). https://doi.org/10.1007/978-3-642-01001-9_13
3. Chen, Y., Shen, C., Wang, Z., Yu, T.: Modeling interactive sensor-behavior with smartphones for implicit and active user authentication. In: 2017 IEEE International Conference on Identity, Security and Behavior Analysis (ISBA), pp. 1–6. IEEE (2017)
4. Fridman, L., Weber, S., Greenstadt, R., Kam, M.: Active authentication on mobile devices via stylometry, application usage, web browsing, and GPS location. IEEE Syst. J. **11**(2), 513–521 (2017)
5. Gjoreski, H., Lustrek, M., Gams, M.: Accelerometer placement for posture recognition and fall detection. In: 2011 Seventh International Conference on Intelligent Environments, pp. 47–54. IEEE (2011)
6. Gomi, H., Yamaguchi, S., Tsubouchi, K., Sasaya, N.: Continuous authentication system using online activities. In: 2018 17th IEEE International Conference On Trust, Security And Privacy In Computing And Communications/12th IEEE International Conference On Big Data Science And Engineering (TrustCom/BigDataSE), pp. 522–532. IEEE (2018)
7. Khan, H.: Evaluating the efficacy of implicit authentication under realistic operating scenarios (2016)
8. Khan, H., Hengartner, U., Vogel, D.: Targeted mimicry attacks on touch input based implicit authentication schemes. In: Proceedings of the 14th Annual International Conference on Mobile Systems, Applications, and Services, pp. 387–398. ACM (2016)
9. Kim, Y., Oh, T., Kim, J.: Analyzing user awareness of privacy data leak in mobile applications. Mob. Inf. Syst. **2015** (2015)
10. Liu, X., Shen, C., Chen, Y.: Multi-source interactive behavior analysis for continuous user authentication on smartphones. In: Zhou, J., et al. (eds.) CCBR 2018. LNCS, vol. 10996, pp. 669–677. Springer, Cham (2018). https://doi.org/10.1007/978-3-319-97909-0_71
11. Murmuria, R., Stavrou, A., Barbara, D., Sritapan, V.: Your data in your hands: privacy-preserving user behavior models for context computation. In: 2017 IEEE International Conference on Pervasive Computing and Communications Workshops (PerCom Workshops), pp. 170–175. IEEE (2017)
12. Niinuma, K., Park, U., Jain, A.K.: Soft biometric traits for continuous user authentication. IEEE Trans. Inf. Forensics Secur. **5**(4), 771–780 (2010)

13. Patel, V.M., Chellappa, R., Chandra, D., Barbello, B.: Continuous user authentication on mobile devices: recent progress and remaining challenges. IEEE Signal Process. Mag. **33**(4), 49–61 (2016)
14. Safa, N.A., Safavi-Naini, R., Shahandashti, S.F.: Privacy-preserving implicit authentication. In: Cuppens-Boulahia, N., Cuppens, F., Jajodia, S., Abou El Kalam, A., Sans, T. (eds.) SEC 2014. IAICT, vol. 428, pp. 471–484. Springer, Heidelberg (2014). https://doi.org/10.1007/978-3-642-55415-5_40
15. Shen, C., Li, Y., Chen, Y., Guan, X., Maxion, R.A.: Performance analysis of multimotion sensor behavior for active smartphone authentication. IEEE Trans. Inf. Forensics Secur. **13**(1), 48–62 (2018)
16. Shen, C., Zhang, Y., Cai, Z., Yu, T., Guan, X.: Touch-interaction behavior for continuous user authentication on smartphones. In: 2015 International Conference on Biometrics (ICB). pp. 157–162. IEEE (2015)
17. Singh., R.: Your smart phone might be leaking your business information. https://www.entrepreneur.com/article/271417. Accessed 26 Feb 2016
18. Srinivasan, V., Moghaddam, S., Mukherji, A., Rachuri, K.K., Xu, C., Tapia, E.M.: MobileMiner: mining your frequent patterns on your phone. In: Proceedings of the 2014 ACM International Joint Conference on Pervasive and Ubiquitous Computing, pp. 389–400. ACM (2014)
19. Teh, P.S., Zhang, N., Teoh, A.B.J., Chen, K.: A survey on touch dynamics authentication in mobile devices. Comput. Secur. **59**, 210–235 (2016)
20. Voris, J., Song, Y., Ben Salem, M., Stolfo, S.: You are what you use: an initial study of authenticating mobile users via application usage. In: Proceedings of the 8th EAI International Conference on Mobile Computing, Applications and Services, pp. 51–61. ICST(Institute for Computer Sciences, Social-Informatics and Telecommunications Engineering) (2016)
21. Wang, D., Zhang, Z., Wang, P., Yan, J., Huang, X.: Targeted online password guessing: an underestimated threat. In: Proceedings of the 2016 ACM SIGSAC Conference on Computer and Communications Security, pp. 1242–1254. ACM (2016)
22. Xi, K., Hu, J., Han, F.: Mobile device access control: an improved correlation based face authentication scheme and its Java ME application. Concurr. Comput.: Pract. Exp. **24**(10), 1066–1085 (2012)
23. Zhu, J., Wu, P., Wang, X., Zhang, J.: SenSec: mobile security through passive sensing. In: 2013 International Conference on Computing, Networking and Communications (ICNC), pp. 1128–1133. IEEE (2013)

Symmetric Cryptography

Related-Key Boomerang Attacks
on GIFT with Automated Trail Search
Including BCT Effect

Yunwen Liu[1,3] and Yu Sasaki[2(✉)]

[1] Department of Mathematics, National University of Defence Technology,
Changsha, China
univerlyw@hotmail.com
[2] NTT Secure Platform Laboratories, Tokyo, Japan
yu.sasaki.sk@hco.ntt.co.jp
[3] imec-COSIC, KU Leuven, Leuven, Belgium

Abstract. In Eurocrypt 2018, Cid et al. proposed a novel notion called
the boomerang connectivity table, which formalised the switch property
in the middle round of boomerang distinguishers in a unified approach.
In this paper, we present a generic model of the boomerang connectivity
table with automatic search technique for the first time, and search for
(related-key) boomerang distinguishers directly by combining with the
search of (related-key) differential characteristics. With the technique,
we are able to find 19-round related-key boomerang distinguishers in the
lightweight block cipher GIFT-64 and GIFT-128. Interestingly, a transition that is not predictable by the conventional switches is realised
in a boomerang distinguisher predicted by the boomerang connectivity table. In addition, we experimentally extend the 19-round distinguisher by one more round. A 23-round key-recovery attack is presented
on GIFT-64 based on the distinguisher, which covers more rounds than
previous known results in the single-key setting. Although the designers of GIFT do not claim related-key security, bit positions of the key
addition and 16-bit rotations were chosen to optimize the related-key
differential bound. Indeed, the designers evaluated related-key differential attacks. This is the first work to present better related-key attacks
than the simple related-key differential attack.

Keywords: Boomerang connectivity table · GIFT · Automatic search

1 Introduction

Boomerang connectivity table (BCT) [7] is a novel technique proposed by Cid et
al. in Eurocrypt 2018 on analysing the middle rounds of boomerang distinguishers. Through the boomerang connectivity table of an S-box, the middle round
of a boomerang distinguisher through the S-box layer is described in a unified
model similar to differential cryptanalysis with the difference distribution table.

© Springer Nature Switzerland AG 2019
J. Jang-Jaccard and F. Guo (Eds.): ACISP 2019, LNCS 11547, pp. 555–572, 2019.
https://doi.org/10.1007/978-3-030-21548-4_30

As a result, previous methods [3,4,8] such as ladder switch and S-box switch are special cases of the boomerang transitions predicted by the BCT. Moreover, the boomerang connectivity table reveals new properties in the S-boxes such that new transitions can be derived which are not detectable by any previous methods.

Currently, automatic search has been widely adopted in finding distinguishers in cryptographic primitives, including differential characteristics, impossible differentials and many others [10,11]. The technique requires an explicit model on the propagation of the differences through a number of rounds, and solves the problem with an MILP (Mixed integer linear programming) or an SMT (Satisfiability module theory) solver. In the scenario of the boomerang attack, due to the lack of unified mathematical model for the middle round of the boomerang distinguishers before the BCT, one searches for differential characteristics in two parts of the encryption function separately, and concatenates them together by analysing the property in the middle round. In ToSC 2017, Cid et al. studied ladder switch for a boomerang attack of Deoxys, searching with an MILP model [6]. Whereas a general technique for the automatic search on boomerang distinguishers is still left unsolved.

In this paper, we propose the first model of the BCT theory with automatic search techniques, and merge it with the search for the related-key differential characteristics. By converting the boomerang connectivity table of an S-box into (vectorial) logical constraints, the propagations of differences through an S-box is completely modeled for the middle round of a boomerang distinguisher. As a result, we are able to search for boomerang distinguishers with a direct evaluation of the middle switches.

As an application, we construct boomerang distinguishers for a recently proposed block cipher GIFT. Proposed by Banik at CHES 2017 [1], GIFT is an improved version of the lightweight block cipher PRESENT [5] with a novel design strategy on the bit-shuffle layer. GIFT-64 and GIFT-128 support 64-bit and 128-bit block sizes, respectively, while both members support the 128-bit key size. With the optimisation on the diffusion of single-bit differences/masks, the number of rounds for GIFT-64 is largely reduced comparing with that of PRESENT. Shortly after the proposal of GIFT, Zhu et al. report a differential attack on 19-round of GIFT-64 based on a 12-round differential distinguisher under the single-key setting [14]. In addition, the security of the cipher against MITM attack and integral cryptanalysis has been studied as well [1,9]. As far as we know, there is few result on evaluating the cipher in the related-key model. Notice that the key schedule of the GIFT cipher is linear, the attacks under the related-key setting may penetrate more rounds, and reveal a better picture of its security.

Our second contribution is the first third-party security evaluation of the GIFT block cipher in the related-key setting. Based on the automatic search model developed for boomerang distinguishers, we obtain boomerang distinguishers for GIFT-64 (consisting of 28 rounds) and GIFT-128 (consisting of 40 rounds), both cover 19 rounds with two parts of 9-round encryptions and one middle part of 1 round. In addition, with an experimental approach, we extend the 19-round boomerang distinguisher of GIFT-64 to several 20-round ones, each with probability $2^{-62.6}$. Afterwards, a key-recovery attack is launched for GIFT-64 reduced to 23 rounds, with data complexity $2^{63.3}$ and time complexity 2^{96}. The attack covers about 82% of the entire construction, which well-illustrates the security margin of GIFT-64 in the related-key setting. In addition, we give a 21-round attack on GIFT-128 based on a 19-round boomerang distinguisher. The attack only reaches (52.5%) of the entire construction. Our analysis implies that the security margin of GIFT-128 is better than that of the smaller version. A comparison of our attacks with previous works is summarised in Table 1.

The rest of this paper is organised as follows. In Sect. 2, an overview of boomerang attacks and the BCT theory is given, as well as an description of the GIFT cipher. The mathematical description of the BCT table is converted into an automatic search model in Sect. 3, with applications to search for boomerang distinguishers in GIFT-64 and GIFT-128 in Sect. 4. We extend the boomerang distinguisher into a key-recovery attack for GIFT-64 in Sect. 5. Section 6 concludes the paper.

Table 1. A comparison of attacks on GIFT-64 and GIFT-128. DC stands for differential cryptanalysis; IC stands for integral cryptanalysis; MITM stands for meet-in-the-middle attack; RK-B stands for related-key boomerang attack.

	Type	#rd	Prob.	Attack #rd	Data	Time	cf.
GIFT-64 (28 rounds)	DC	13	2^{-62}	-	-	-	[13]
	DC	12	2^{-60}	19	2^{63}	2^{112}	[14]
	IC	10	2^{-63}	14	2^{63}	2^{97}	[1]
	MITM			15	2^{64}	2^{120}	[1]
	MITM			15		2^{112}	[9]
	RK-B	20	$2^{-62.6}$	23	$2^{63.3}$	$2^{126.6}$	This paper
GIFT-128 (40 rounds)	DC	18	-	23	2^{120}	2^{120}	[14]
	RK-B	19	$2^{-121.2}$	21	$2^{126.6}$	$2^{126.6}$	This paper

2 Preliminaries

2.1 Boomerang Attacks

Boomerang attack [12] is an effective cryptanalysis tool, especially for ciphers where the probabilities of the differential characteristics decrease exponentially with respect to the growth of rounds. As a result, the concatenation of two short characteristics may possess a better probability. The diagram of a (related-key) boomerang distinguisher can be illustrated as shown in Fig. 1(1).

The target cipher E is decomposed into two parts E_0 and E_1. Assume that a differential characteristic (α, β) with probability p is found for E_0, and (γ, δ)

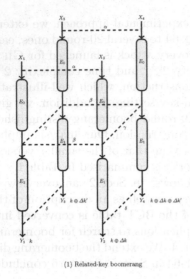 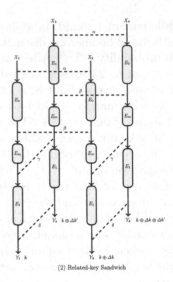

(1) Related-key boomerang   (2) Related-key Sandwich

Fig. 1. An illustration of a related-key boomerang (1) and a related-key sandwich (2).

with probability q for E_1. Then the probability of the boomerang distinguisher is

$$\Pr[E^{-1}(E(x) \oplus \delta) \oplus E^{-1}(E(x \oplus \alpha) \oplus \delta) = \alpha] = p^2 q^2.$$

The boomerang attack works in a chosen-plaintext and chosen-ciphertext model. In 2001, Biham et al. showed that it is possible to construct a rectangle attack [2] based on a boomerang distinguisher where only the chosen-plaintext setting is required. The technique exploits the fact that a pair of paired values $(x, x \oplus \alpha)$ and $(x', x' \oplus \alpha)$, $x, x' \in \{0,1\}^n$ satisfies the boomerang structure, i.e. $E(x) \oplus E(x') = \delta$ and $E(x \oplus \alpha) \oplus E(x' \oplus \alpha) = \delta$ with probability $p^2 q^2 2^{-n}$, thus may be generated after querying $p^{-1} q^{-1} 2^{n/2}$ chosen-plaintext pairs.

2.2 Boomerang Connectivity Table

The partition in the boomerang attack can be extended by decomposing the encryption function into three parts, where the middle round E_m contains many useful transitions. A number of observations and generalisations on boomerang attack focus on the margin of the decomposition with techniques such as S-box switch, boomerang switch and sandwich attack [4,8], see Fig. 1(2) for a diagram of a sandwich. Differential behaviours through the S-box are usually summarised in the precomputed table called differential distribution table (DDT). Those research results imply that the transitions of differences in the middle part of a boomerang distinguisher through the S-boxes differ from the prediction from the DDT. In Eurocrypt 2018, Cid et al. proposed a novel notion called boomerang connectivity table (BCT), which systematically characterised the propagation of differences and the corresponding probabilities.

Table 2. DDT of the GIFT S-box

$\Delta_i \backslash \Delta_o$	0	1	2	3	4	5	6	7	8	9	a	b	c	d	e	f
0	16	0	0	0	0	0	0	0	0	0	0	0	0	0	0	0
1	0	0	0	0	0	2	2	0	2	2	2	2	2	0	0	2
2	0	0	0	0	0	4	4	0	0	2	2	0	0	2	2	0
3	0	0	0	0	2	2	0	2	0	0	2	2	2	2	2	2
4	0	0	0	2	0	4	0	6	0	2	0	0	0	2	0	0
5	0	0	2	0	0	2	0	0	2	0	0	0	2	2	2	4
6	0	0	4	6	0	0	0	2	0	0	2	0	0	0	2	0
7	0	0	2	0	0	2	0	0	2	2	2	4	2	0	0	0
8	0	0	0	4	0	0	0	4	0	0	0	4	0	0	0	4
9	0	2	0	2	0	0	2	2	2	0	2	0	0	2	2	0
a	0	4	0	0	0	0	4	0	0	2	2	0	0	2	2	0
b	0	2	0	2	0	0	2	2	2	2	0	0	2	0	2	0
c	0	0	4	0	4	0	0	0	2	0	2	0	2	0	2	0
d	0	2	2	4	0	0	0	0	0	2	2	0	2	0	2	0
e	0	4	0	0	4	0	0	0	2	2	0	0	2	2	0	0
f	0	2	2	0	4	0	0	0	0	2	0	2	0	0	2	2

Table 3. BCT of the GIFT S-box

$\Delta_i \backslash \nabla_o$	0	1	2	3	4	5	6	7	8	9	a	b	c	d	e	f
0	16	16	16	16	16	16	16	16	16	16	16	16	16	16	16	16
1	16	0	0	0	0	2	2	0	2	2	2	2	2	0	0	2
2	16	0	4	4	0	8	4	4	0	2	2	0	0	2	2	0
3	16	0	0	0	0	2	2	0	2	0	0	2	2	2	2	2
4	16	4	4	10	4	8	8	6	0	2	0	0	0	2	0	0
5	16	0	2	0	4	2	0	0	2	0	0	4	2	2	2	4
6	16	4	8	6	4	8	4	10	0	0	2	0	0	0	2	0
7	16	0	2	0	4	2	0	0	2	2	2	4	2	0	0	4
8	16	0	0	8	16	0	0	8	0	0	8	0	0	0	0	8
9	16	2	0	2	0	0	2	2	2	0	2	0	0	2	2	0
a	16	8	4	4	0	0	4	4	0	2	2	0	0	2	2	0
b	16	2	0	2	0	0	2	2	2	2	0	0	2	0	2	0
c	16	4	4	8	4	0	0	4	2	0	2	0	2	0	2	0
d	16	2	2	0	4	0	0	0	0	2	6	0	0	2	0	6
e	16	4	0	4	4	0	4	8	2	2	0	0	2	2	0	0
f	16	2	2	0	4	0	0	0	0	2	0	6	0	0	2	6

Definition 1 (BCT [7]). *Let $S : \{0,1\}^n \to \{0,1\}^n$ be an invertible function. For input difference Δ_i and output difference ∇_o, the entry (Δ_i, ∇_o) in the boomerang connectivity table $T(\Delta_i, \nabla_o)$ of S is given by*

$$T(\Delta_i, \nabla_o) = \#\{x \in \{0,1\}^n \mid S^{-1}(S(x) \oplus \nabla_o) \oplus S^{-1}(S(x \oplus \Delta_i) \oplus \nabla_o) = \Delta_i\}.$$

The above definition implies an important feature that the middle round E_m does not require the squared probability p^2 or q^2 because the generation of a right quartet is the probabilistic event over 2^n possibilities. As an example, the DDT and BCT of the GIFT S-box are given in Tables 2 and 3.

The proposal of boomerang connectivity table enables an unified view on the behaviour of the boomerang distinguishers in the middle round(s). Apart from explaining previous results in the literature, the BCT table provides guidance in new improvements on boomerang attacks for certain ciphers.

2.3 The Specification of GIFT

Proposed by Banik *et al.* in CHES 2017, GIFT [1] is a lightweight block cipher which is a descendent of PRESENT [5]. The block size n of GIFT takes 64 bits or 128 bits, and the key size is 128 bits. We denote the corresponding ciphers by GIFT-64 and GIFT-128. One round of GIFT contains only an S-box layer (SubCells), a bit-shuffle (BitPerm) and a round-key injection (AddKey). The round function of GIFT-64 is depicted in Fig. 2.

Both versions of GIFT adopt the same 4-bit S-box that is different from the S-box in PRESENT.

$$S[16] = \{1, a, 4, c, 6, f, 3, 9, 2, d, b, 7, 5, 0, 8, e\}.$$

The bit permutation used in GIFT follows a new strategy called BOGI (Bad Output must go to Good Input) to overcome the existence of single active bit

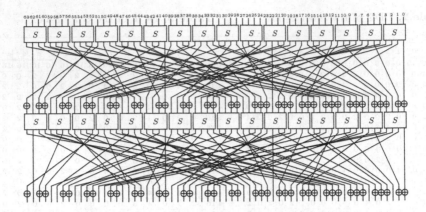

Fig. 2. Two rounds of the block cipher GIFT-64.

path in characteristics. The detail of the permutations can be found in the specification of the cipher [1].

The round keys are XORed to two bits of the 4-bit cells. An $s(= n/2)$-bit round key $RK = U\|V = k_1\|k_0 = u_{s-1}\cdots u_0\|v_{s-1}\cdots v_0$ is obtained from the key state. For GIFT-64, the 128-bit key state is updated as follows,

$$b_{4i+1} \leftarrow b_{4i+1} \oplus u_i, \quad b_{4i} \leftarrow b_{4i} \oplus v_i, i \in \{0, \cdots, 15\}.$$

For GIFT-128, $RK = U\|V = (k_5\|k_4)\|(k_1\|k_0) = u_{s-1}\cdots u_0\|v_{s-1}\cdots v_0$

$$b_{4i+2} \leftarrow b_{4i+2} \oplus u_i, \quad b_{4i+1} \leftarrow b_{4i+1} \oplus v_i, i \in \{0, \cdots, 31\}.$$

The 128-bit key state is updated as follows,

$$k_7\|k_6\|\cdots\|k_1\|k_0 \leftarrow (k_1 \ggg 2)\|(k_0 \ggg 12)\|\cdots\|k_3\|k_2.$$

The total number of rounds in GIFT-64 is 28, while the 128-bit version has 40 rounds.

Differential Property. The notable feature of GIFT is that the maximum differential probability for the S-box is $2^{-1.4}$, which is higher than 2^{-2} ensured by many other lightweight block ciphers. In fact, in Table 2, two entries have the value 6, which implies that the transition is satisfied with probability $6/16 \approx 2^{-1.4}$. This contributes relatively larger numbers in BCT, in particular it includes one non-trivial entry that is propagated with probability 1.

3   Automatic Search of (Related-Key) Boomerang Based on Boomerang Connectivity Table

In this section, we transform the mathematical description of the boomerang connectivity table into an automatic search model for boomerang distinguishers in block ciphers.

The boomerang connectivity table shares some similarity with difference distribution tables, therefore, it is possible to convert BCT tables into constraints, similar to several previous techniques for DDT tables when dealing with S-boxes in automatic search. As a typical technique which is proposed by Sun et al. [11], legal transitions of the differences are modeled as a convex hull and described by a set of linear inequalities. To include the probability information to the model, an additional variable can be allocated to represent the abstract binary logarithm of the probability. As a result, this will probably lead to an increased number of linear inequalities in the model of the Sbox. We notice that a BCT table often encompass more values than the corresponding DDT table, for instance, a differentially 4-uniform S-box may have entries being 6 in its BCT. As a result, it takes more conditions to accurately describe the propagation rules and the corresponding probabilities in a BCT than the corresponding DDT.

In the following, we propose an alternative method to model the BCT table of an S-box with boolean constraints. Assume that for an input difference Δ, there exist l possible output differences $\{\nabla_0, \ldots, \nabla_{l-1}\} = D_t(\Delta)$ where the BCT entries equal to t. We describe the transition $(x \to y)$ with the following logic expression, which evaluates to 1 when $x = \Delta$ and $y \in D_t(\Delta)$, otherwise 0.

$$(x = \Delta) \wedge ((y = \nabla_0) \vee \cdots \vee (y = \nabla_{l-1})) = (x = \Delta) \wedge (\bigvee_{\nabla \in D_t(\Delta)} (y = \nabla)).$$

In addition, a binary variable w_t is allocated to store the probability information for the BCT entry t. To be specific, when the difference transition is $(x \to y)$, we define w_t as

$$w_t = \bigvee_{\Delta} ((x = \Delta) \wedge (\bigvee_{\nabla \in D_t(\Delta)} (y = \nabla))).$$

From the expression, w_t evaluates to 1 if one of the possible transitions with BCT value being t is taken.

For instance, in the BCT table of the GIFT S-box (Table 3), when the BCT value t equals 10, there are two possible transitions, namely, $(4 \to 3)$ and $(6 \to 7)$. So we have

$$w_{10} = ((x = 4) \wedge (y = 3)) \vee ((x = 6) \wedge (y = 7)).$$

It means that if any of the two possible transitions is taken, the variable w_{10} evaluates to 1, which indicates a probability of 10/16 through the S-box.

It is clear that the number of clauses in describing an S-box depends on the nonzero entries of the BCT, corresponding to the variables w_t. In the case of the GIFT Sbox, the number of clauses is 7, where $t = 0, 2, 4, 6, 8, 10, 16$. Therefore, the transitions and their probabilities may be modeled with fewer conditions with our encoding method than before. This is beneficial especially when the number of rounds and the block size are large enough.

To search for a boomerang distinguisher in a block cipher E which is decomposed into three parts E_0, E_m, E_1, one first sets the conditions for valid difference transitions in E_0 and E_1 through the round functions. For the middle round E_m, the propagation through the S-box layer can be modelled with the encoding of BCT discussed above; and we take the linear layer into consideration to connect the characteristics in E_0 and E_1. The probability of the difference propagation through an Sbox can be deduced from the binary variables w_t, which is

$$\sum_t w_t * (t/16).$$

Take the abstract binary logarithm being its weight, and assume that the total weights of the characteristics in E_0, E_1 and E_m are W_0, W_1 and W_m, respectively. The weight of the boomerang is

$$2 * (W_0 + W_1) + W_m.$$

By optimising it, we can directly find a boomerang distinguisher with optimal probability in E.

Remark 1. With related-key differential characteristics, we are able to find related-key boomerang distinguishers. The distinguisher involves four different keys: k and $k \oplus \Delta k$ for a related-key differential characteristic in E_0, and $k \oplus \Delta k'$ and $k \oplus \Delta k \oplus \Delta k'$ in E_1, as shown in Fig. 1.

4   Automatic Search of Boomerang Distinguishers in GIFT

In this section, our aim is to apply the automatic search model to search for related-key boomerang distinguishers in GIFT-64 and GIFT-128.

Intuition: Why Boomerang Attacks Can Be Strong? We start with finding optimal related-key differential characteristics. Due to the design of the key schedule in GIFT-64, the first four round keys are independent of each other. Thus the number of active S-boxes can be 0 up to 3 rounds by canceling the plaintext difference with the first round key. Table 4 shows the minimum number of active S-boxes in related-key differential characteristics of GIFT-64 from 4 rounds.

Table 4. The minimum number of active S-boxes in related-key differential characteristics of GIFT-64.

#rounds	4	5	6	7	8	9	10	11	12	13	14	15	16	17	18	19
#AS	1	1	2	3	4	6	9	11	13	15	17	19	21	23	25	27

We observe that the number of active S-boxes slowly increases when the number of rounds is small, especially up to 8 rounds. In contrast, the number of active S-boxes rapidly increases when the number of rounds is large.

This is a typical case that the related-key boomerang distinguisher may have a much higher probability than the related-key differential characteristics covering the same number of rounds, by concatenating two short characteristics with high probabilities. Let p_i be the probability of the differential propagation in round i. Then the probability of the differential distinguisher for x rounds is denoted by $\prod_{r=0}^{x} p_i$. In contrast, the boomerang distinguisher basically concatenates two $x/2$-round trail by considering the squared probability, namely $\left(\prod_{r=0}^{x/2} p_i^2\right)^2$. From Table 4, when we increase the number of attacked rounds by 1, the boomerang distinguisher will involve 1 more active S-box with the squared probability and the differential distinguisher will involve 2 more active S-boxes with the normal probability. Those would give almost the same impact to the attack complexity. As a result, the boomerang distinguisher can be more efficient than the differential distinguisher because the boomerang distinguisher can include 3 blank rounds twice (in E_0 and in E_1) and the middle rounds E_m do not require the squared probability.

Finding Boomerang Distinguishers. In this section, we focus on boomerang distinguishers that divide the entire encryption into three parts E_0, E_m and E_1, denoted by $X + 1 + Y$ where X and Y stands for the number of round covered by the differential characteristics in E_0 and E_1, respectively. For instance, an optimal 4-round related-key differential characteristic in GIFT-64 has a probability of $2^{-1.4}$, and it is possible to find a related-key boomerang distinguisher covering 9 rounds with the form $4 + 1 + 4$, where the total probability of the boomerang distinguisher is $(2^{-1.4})^2 \times 1 \times (2^{-1.4})^2 = 2^{-5.6}$.

The strategy of finding boomerang distinguishers follows the theory of the boomerang connectivity table and the model of BCT tables in automatic search techniques. In order to find boomerang distinguishers automatically, our search techniques are based on the model of searching related-key differential characteristics and the translation of BCT table into a solver-friendly language with respect to SMT solvers as explained in Sect. 3.

The boomerang connectivity table of GIFT S-box is shown in Table 3. For each value in the table, we describe the constraints for valid difference transitions in BCT. For instance, for all the entries $(a \rightarrow b)$ taking the value 6, the constraint in SMTLIB-2 language is

```
(= w (bvor (bvand (= a #x2) (= b #x5))
(bvor (bvand (= a #x4) (bvor (= b #x5) (= b #x6)))
(bvor (bvand (= a #x6) (bvor (= b #x2) (= b #x5)))
(bvor (bvand (= a #x8) (bvor (= b #x3) (bvor (= b #x7)
                                  (bvor (= b #xb) (= b #xf)))))
(bvor (bvand (= a #xa) (= b #x1))
(bvor (bvand (= a #xc) (= b #x3))
(bvand (= a #xe) (= b #x7))
))))))),
```

where one of the transitions is taken if $w = 1$.

With the transitions of differences in boomerang distinguishers characterised, we execute the model of GIFT-64 for searching boomerang distinguishers with the form $X + 1 + X$, where $X = 4, 5, 6, 7, 8, 9, 10$. The probability of the optimal related-key boomerang distinguishers in GIFT-64 which takes the form $X + 1 + X$ can be found in the following Table 5.

Table 5. The probability of the optimal related-key boomerang distinguishers in GIFT-64 which takes the form $X + 1 + X$, with a comparison to the probability of the optimal related-key differential characteristics.

#rounds	9	11	13	15	17	19	21
Pr. of RK-boomerang	$2^{-5.6}$	$2^{-5.6}$	$2^{-13.6}$	$2^{-21.6}$	2^{-32}	$2^{-53.6}$	$2^{-79.2}$
Pr. of RK-differential	$2^{-13.4}$	$2^{-28.8}$	2^{-39}	2^{-50}	2^{-61}	2^{-78}	2^{-89}

It can be seen that the distinguishers cover up to 19 rounds of GIFT-64 with a probability larger than 2^{-64}, whereas the probability of the optimal 19-round differential characteristic might be much lower, given that 27 S-boxes are active. We actually searched for the maximum differential characteristic probability for 19 rounds, which was turned out to be 2^{-78}. In Fig. 3, we illustrate the comparison between the probabilities of related-key boomerangs and related-key differential characteristics.

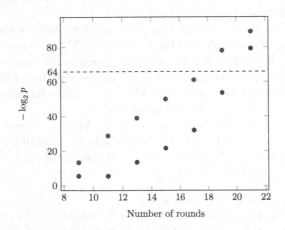

Fig. 3. The comparison between the probabilities of related-key boomerangs and related-key differential characteristics in GIFT-64. The probabilities are shown as the abstract binary logarithm $-\log_2(p)$.

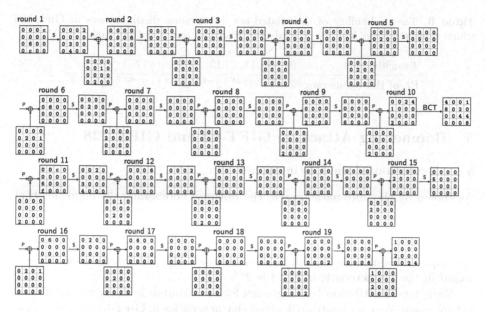

Fig. 4. A 19-round boomerang distinguisher with the form $X + 1 + X$ in GIFT-64, where $X = 9$. The probability is $2^{-58.6}$.

Note that we confirmed that the distinguisher does not reach 20 rounds even by relaxing the search space to $X + 1 + Y, X \neq Y$.

Details of the Detected Trail. In Fig. 4, we show the detail of a 19-round related-key boomerang distinguisher in GIFT-64. We concatenate two 9-round characteristics of probability $2^{-13.4}$. The transition in the middle round E_m has a probability of 2^{-5}, due to the propagation of differences in the BCT table. It is interesting to notice that the transitions $(1 \rightarrow 8)$ and $(4 \rightarrow 1)$ take advantage of the new properties predicted by the BCT than previous techniques of finding boomerang distinguishers.

Application to GIFT-128. Similarly, we are able to search for boomerang distinguishers in GIFT-128. Usually, the complexity of the problem is proportional to the size of constraints and variables. It is generally more difficult to find characteristics for ciphers with large block size. Therefore, we terminate the program and return the best found solution if necessary. Table 6 shows the probability of the best-found boomerang distinguishers up to 19-rounds for GIFT-128.

Table 6. The probability of the related-key boomerang distinguishers in GIFT-128 which takes the form $X + 1 + X$. Only the 19-round one is not optimal.

#rounds	9	11	13	15	17	19
Pr. of RK-boomerang	$2^{-13.6}$	2^{-24}	2^{-40}	$2^{-59.2}$	$2^{-83.2}$	$2^{-121.2}$

5   Boomerang Attack on GIFT-64 and GIFT-128

5.1   Extension of the Distinguisher

As shown by the automatic search, the optimal boomerang distinguisher that covers 19-round GIFT-64 has the probability $2^{-53.6}$, which is obtained by connecting two 9-round related-key characteristics of probability $2^{-13.4}$. The transition probability in the middle round is 1, which largely depends on the output and input differences in E_0 and E_1. For instance, the probability of the middle round in the characteristic in Fig. 4 is 2^{-5}.

We extend the 19-round distinguisher for more rounds by using an experimental approach. We enumerate all 9-round characteristics in GIFT-64 with probability $2^{-13.4}$. There are in total 120 such characteristics $\Omega_0, \cdots, \Omega_{119}$. We consider using $\Omega_i, i \in \{0, 1, \ldots, 119\}$ for the first 9 rounds of E_0 and $\Omega_j, j \in \{0, 1, \ldots, 119\}$ for the last 9 rounds of E_1. We have $14,400$ combinations. For each combination, the input and output differences for the middle part E_m are fixed, thus the connecting probability in the middle round(s) can be experimentally found. Notice that many characteristics share the same input and output differences. After removing the duplicated patterns, there are 16 distinct output differences from E_0 and 58 distinct input difference to E_1 (Table 7). Hence, the total number of patterns to be checked is reduced to $16 \times 58 = 928$.

For each of the patterns, we generate $2^{13} (= 8,192)$ random keys and state values to experimentally check the probability that the middle round is satisfied. The number of rounds for E_m is a parameter. When we set the number of rounds for E_m is 1, namely when the boomerang characteristic has the form $9 + 1 + 9$, we have 34 combinations such that the probability of the middle round is 1.

The experiment can be extended for boomerang distinguishers with the form $9 + Y + 9$, where the middle part contains $Y = 2, 3$ rounds. Only 10 combinations result in a probability larger than 2^{-10} when $Y = 2$, while all combinations have a probability lower than 2^{-15} for $Y = 3$. As a consequence, we are able to push the 19-round boomerang distinguisher for one round more, and obtain 20-round distinguishers with probability $2^{-62.6}$ as shown in Table 8.

5.2   Key Recovery Attacks

The boomerang distinguisher found above can be extended to a 23-round key-recovery attack against GIFT-64 by adding one round in the beginning and two rounds at the end.

Table 7. All distinct input and output differences of $\Omega_0, \cdots, \Omega_{119}$

ID	Output Diff from E_0	ID	Output Diff from E_0	ID	Output Diff from E_0	ID	Output Diff from E_0
01	0100040000000102	05	4000000010000201	09	0040000000120100	13	2010004000200000
02	0100040002000002	06	4000200000000201	10	0040002000020100	14	2010004000000010
03	0004000200002010	07	1000400000001020	11	0201000400020000	15	0400020000201000
04	0004000000012010	08	1000400020000020	12	0201000400000001	16	0400000001201000

ID	Input Diff to E_1	ID	Input Diff to E_1	ID	Input Diff to E_1	ID	Input Diff to E_1
01	0000600e00000006	16	000c0000d6000000	31	600c0000000c0000	46	000000600000600d
02	0000600f00000006	17	0000000c0000d600	32	600d0000000c0000	47	000000c00000600c
03	0000600e0000000c	18	0000000c0000f600	33	0000e60000006000	48	000000c00000600d
04	0000600f0000000c	19	0000000c0000e600	34	0000f60000006000	49	00c00000600c0000
05	0000600c00000006	20	0000000c0000c600	35	0000e6000000c000	50	00c00000600d0000
06	0000600d00000006	21	000000060000e600	36	0000f6000000c000	51	00c00000600e0000
07	0000600c0000000c	22	000000060000c600	37	0000c6000000c000	52	00c00000600f0000
08	0000600d0000000c	23	000000060000d600	38	0000d6000000c000	53	00600000600c0000
09	00060000e6000000	24	000000060000f600	39	0000c60000006000	54	00600000600d0000
10	00060000f6000000	25	600e000000060000	40	0000d60000006000	55	00600000600e0000
11	000c0000e6000000	26	600f000000060000	41	000000600000600e	56	00600000600f0000
12	000c0000f6000000	27	600e0000000c0000	42	000000600000600f	57	c600000060000000
13	00060000c6000000	28	600f0000000c0000	43	000000c00000600e	58	c6000000c0000000
14	00060000d6000000	29	600c000000060000	44	000000c00000600f	59	
15	000c0000c6000000	30	600d000000060000	45	00000060000000600c	60	

The linear layer in the last round does not impact to our attack. We omit in order to keep the description of the attack procedure as simple as possible. Note that the bit positions of the key injection need to change accordingly to the BitPerm operation. However, BitPerm is designed to be closed in each register in the bit-slice implementation. Namely, the first and the second bits of each S-box is XORed by the round key. Indeed, bit-positions $4i$ for $i = 0, 1, ..., 15$ move to bit-position $4j$ for $j = 0, 1, ..., 15$ and the same applies to bit-positions from $4i + 1$ to $4j + 1$.

The distinguisher covers the segment from round 2 to round 21. We prepare the plaintext quartets with the desired input difference at the first round, and perform 2-round partial decryptions on the ciphertexts under the guessed key. To produce the output difference as predicted, we need to make $Q = 2^n p_b^{-2}$ quartets, where n is the block size and p_b is the probability of the boomerang distinguisher. By birthday paradox, the quartets can be generated by making pairs between p_1 and p_2 as well as p_3 and p_4, separately. Each case requires $Q^{1/2}$ queries. After combining them, we get Q quartets with $2 \times (Q^{1/2} + Q^{1/2})$ queries in total, where a pair requires 2 queries. Unfortunately, a direct estimation of the data complexity turns out to exceed the total data available. Therefore, we need to utilise the input differences of the boomerang distinguishers in Table 8, and generate the required quartets with fewer queries. In the following, let the output difference be 0100040000000102.

The detail of the attack procedure is as follows.

Step 1: (Offline) We have SubCells, BitPerm and AddKey before the 20-round distinguisher. Since the round-key difference can be derived through the linear

Table 8. A 20-round boomerang distinguisher of the form $9 + 2 + 9$ by concatenating two 9-round characteristics with probability $2^{-13.4}$. The probability of the middle connection is $2^{-8.34}$. The difference nibbles $\mathtt{x} \in \{6, \mathtt{c}\}$, $\mathtt{y} \in \{\mathtt{c}, \mathtt{d}, \mathtt{e}, \mathtt{f}\}$, $(\mathtt{w}, \mathtt{z}) \in (2, 0), (0, 1)$. The key differences in the two middle rounds follow those in E_1.

Round	Characteristic	Key difference $k_7\ k_6\ \cdots\ k_1\ k_0$
0	00x00000600y0000	0040 0000 0000 0000 0004 0000 0008 0020
1	0000006000000000	0002 0200 0040 0000 0000 0000 0004 0000
2	0000000000000000	0001 0000 0002 0200 0040 0000 0000 0000
3	0000000000000000	0000 0000 0001 0000 0002 0200 0040 0000
4	0000000002000000	0010 0000 0000 0000 0001 0000 0002 0200
5	0000000000000060	8000 2000 0010 0000 0000 0000 0001 0000
6	0000000000000000	4000 0000 8000 2000 0010 0000 0000 0000
7	0000000000000000	0000 0000 4000 0000 8000 2000 0010 0000
8	0000000000020000	0004 0000 0000 0000 4000 0000 8000 2000
9	2010004000200000	2000 0002 0004 0000 0000 0000 4000 0000
10	2-round BCT	1000 0000 2000 0002 0004 0000 0000 0000
11	0000600d00000006	0400 0000 0000 0000 4000 0000 0010 0040
12	0000060000000000	0004 0400 0400 0000 0000 0000 4000 0000
13	0000000000000000	1000 0000 0004 0400 0400 0000 0000 0000
14	0000000000000000	0000 0000 1000 0000 0004 0400 0400 0000
15	0000020000000000	0100 0000 0000 0000 1000 0000 0004 0400
16	0000000000000600	0001 4000 0100 0000 0000 0000 1000 0000
17	0000000000000000	0400 0000 0001 4000 0100 0000 0000 0000
18	0000000000000000	0000 0000 0400 0000 0001 4000 0100 0000
19	0000000200000000	0040 0000 0000 0000 0400 0000 0001 4000
20	010004000w000z02	

key schedule, the difference after SubCells in the first round is known. When we choose plaintext, we choose the internal state values after SubCells in the first round to satisfy this difference. We then compute the inverse of SubCells offline to generate the plaintext.

Step 2: (Online) The goal of this step is to make $D = 2^{63.3}$ queries to generate $Q = 2^{126.6}$ quartets. With a probability of 2^{-64}, the encryptions with E_0 of the quartets match the intermediate difference γ, thus we can expect one right quartet satisfying the boomerang distinguisher. The procedure is shown below.

2.(a): At the beginning of the boomerang distinguisher, fix x to 6. Then the truncated differences is 00600000600y0000, where $\mathtt{y} \in \{\mathtt{c}, \mathtt{d}, \mathtt{e}, \mathtt{f}\}$. Notice that the difference on the 16-th and 17-th bit can take any value.

2.(b): Fix a plaintext value p_1 and take all four cases of the 16-th and 17-th bits. Query those 4 plaintexts to the oracle with key K.

2.(c): Compute p_2 by $p_2 = p_1 \oplus \alpha$. Then, make 4 queries to the oracle with $K^{\oplus}\Delta_k$ by testing all the four cases for the 16-th and 17-th bits.

2.(d): Generate $4 \times 4 = 16$ pairs from the above 8 queries.

2.(e): Repeat the process for $2^{59.3}$ different values of p_1 ($2^{62.3}$ queries in total) to generate $2^{63.3}$ pairs of p_1, p_2.

2.(f): Prepare the pairs between p_3 and p_4 analogously, with $2^{62.3}$ queries we generate $2^{63.3}$ pairs of p_3, p_4. By birthday paradox, we get Q quartets p_1, p_2, p_3, p_4 by combining the pairs p_1, p_2 and p_3, p_4.

Step 3: The differential propagation for the extended two rounds after the 20-round distinguisher is shown in Fig. 5.

Collect right quartet candidates where the outputs after 23-rounds of encryption have inactive nibbles at the 1st, 5th, 11th and 13th nibbles for both pairs of c_1, c_3 and c_2, c_4.

Step 4: Guess 8 key-bits at round 22 and 24 key-bits at round 23 for the partial decryption of the ciphertext quartets c_1, c_2, c_3, c_4, which leads to the middle states m_1, m_2, m_3, m_4 having the output difference from the 20-round distinguisher. The positions of the involved key-bits are shown in Fig. 5.

Step 5: Exhaustively search for the remaining $128 - 32 = 96$ bits of the key.

From the procedure of Step 2, the data complexity of the attack D is $2^{62.3} + 2^{62.3} = 2^{63.3}$ queries in total. After the filter by the ciphertext difference at Step 3, we obtain $Q \times 2^{-16-16} = 2^{94.6}$ right quartet candidates. At Step 4, we guess $8 + 24 = 32$ key bits and apply partial decryption for all $2^{94.6}$ candidates, it will take $2^{94.6} \times 2^{32} = 2^{126.6}$ 2-round decryptions. Step 4 involves 16 S-boxes and the probability that all the 16 S-boxes will behave as expected is 2^{-128} for each wrong guess. Hence, we expect the only 1 key survives after Step 4.

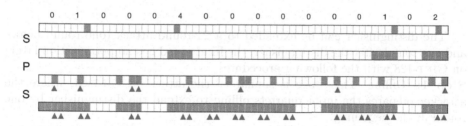

Fig. 5. The difference propagation in the final two rounds when the output difference of the boomerang is 0100040000000102. The blue triangles label the positions of the guessed key bits. (Color figure online)

5.3   21-Round Key Recovery on GIFT-128

Note that the optimal boomerang distinguisher we obtained in the previous section for GIFT-128 covers the same number of rounds as that of GIFT-64 even though the attacker can make queries up to 2^{128} plaintexts. Such inefficiency in GIFT-128 comes from the larger round key size. GIFT-128 injects 64 key bits in every round, which is double of the GIFT-64. This significantly improves the speed of differential diffusion, which only allows the attack up to the same number of rounds as GIFT-64.

We present the 21-round attack on GIFT-128 based on the 19-round boomerang distinguisher found in the previous section. Table 9 shows the 9-round differential characteristic used for the concatenation of the 19-round boomerang. The probability of the 19-round boomerang distinguisher is $2^{-121.2}$, where the middle round switch takes a probability of 2^{-2} as predicted by the BCT.

Table 9. A 9-round differential characteristic of probability $2^{-29.8}$ which can be extended into a 19-round boomerang distinguisher with the form $9+1+9$. The column of the key differences shows the values (k_5, k_4, k_1, k_0) for generating the differences used in round keys.

Round	Characteristic	Key difference (k_5 k_4 k_1 k_0)
0	000006000000e0000000000000000060	1000 0000 4000 0001
1	00000000000000000000000000000000	0008 0000 0000 0000
2	00000000000040000000000000000000	0000 1000 0010 4000
3	00000000000000000205000000000000	0000 0008 0000 0000
4	00000000000010000000200000000000	0400 0000 0004 0010
5	0000000000000000000000000000a0000	0002 0000 0000 0000
6	00000000000000000000002000000000	0000 0400 0100 0004
7	00000002000000000000000000000000	0000 0002 0000 0000
8	00000000040000000200000000000040	0100 0000 0040 0100
9	00200005021010000000000600404002	

The distinguisher can be extended to a 21-round attack (one round before and one round after the distinguisher, the final round has no permutation layer) on GIFT-128 with the following procedure.

Step 1: (Offline) This stage is similar to the attack on GIFT-64, where the attacker prepares the input quartets offline to extend the distinguisher by one round at the beginning.

Step 2: (Online) We make $2^{126.6}$ queries to generate $2^{249.2}$ quartets. With a probability of 2^{-128}, the encryptions with E_0 of the quartets match the intermediate difference γ, and it is sufficient to produce one right quartet satisfying the boomerang distinguisher.

2.(a): Take the difference 000006000000e0000000000000000060 at the beginning of the boomerang distinguisher.

2.(b): We need $2^{125.6}$ queries to generate $2^{124.6}$ pairs between p_1 and p_2. Similarly for p_3 and p_4.

2.(c): By birthday paradox, we get $2^{249.2}$ quartets p_1, p_2, p_3, p_4 by combining the pairs p_1, p_2 and p_3, p_4.

Step 3: Collect the outputs after 23-rounds of encryption. Guess 18 key-bits at round 21 for the partial decryption of the ciphertext quartets c_1, c_2, c_3, c_4, and

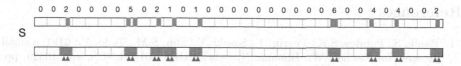

Fig. 6. The difference propagation in the final round when the output difference of the boomerang is 0020000502101000000000600404002. The blue triangles label the positions of the guessed key bits in 9 S-boxes with nonzero differences. (Color figure online)

we obtain the middle states m_1, m_2, m_3, m_4. The guessed key bits are located in those 9 S-boxes with a nonzero difference in the output difference as shown in Fig. 6. With the ciphertext filtering technique, we have a gain of 2^{92} since there are 23 nibbles with no difference after the S-box layer.

Step 4: Check the differences among the quartets of the middle states, if the difference match the boomerang distinguisher, the guessed key bits are the candidates for the right keys.

Step 5: The remaining $128 - 18 = 110$ bits of the key is recovered by an exhaustive search.

The data complexity of the attack is $2^{126.6}$. And the time complexity is $2^{126.6} \times 2^{18} \times 2^{-92} + 2^{110} \approx 2^{110}$ partial encryptions. Hence the bottleneck of the complexity is the memory accesses to $2^{126.6}$ queried data.

6 Conclusion

In this paper, we study the automatic search model of boomerang connectivity table and its applications. By converting the boomerang connectivity table into SMT language, we are able to directly model the propagations in boomerang distinguishers with an automatic search based on the search of differential characteristics. It enables us to find optimal switches in the middle round(s) which may not be predictable by previous techniques. As an application, our target is a recently proposed block ciphers family GIFT, and related-key boomerang distinguishers covering 19 rounds of GIFT-64 and GIFT-128 are found with the automatic search model. Moreover, we experimentally extended the 19-round distinguisher of GIFT-64 into a 20-round one, and launched a key-recovery attack against GIFT-64 reduced to 23 rounds. Our analysis shows that GIFT-64 seems to have a smaller security margin than that of GIFT-128.

Acknowledgement. The authors would like to thank the reviewers for their valuable comments. Yunwen Liu is supported by National Natural Science Foundation (No. 61672530, No. 61702537) and Research Fund KU Leuven grant C16/18/004.

References

1. Banik, S., Pandey, S.K., Peyrin, T., Sasaki, Y., Sim, S.M., Todo, Y.: GIFT: a small present. In: Fischer, W., Homma, N. (eds.) CHES 2017. LNCS, vol. 10529, pp. 321–345. Springer, Cham (2017). https://doi.org/10.1007/978-3-319-66787-4_16
2. Biham, E., Dunkelman, O., Keller, N.: The rectangle attack—rectangling the serpent. In: Pfitzmann, B. (ed.) EUROCRYPT 2001. LNCS, vol. 2045, pp. 340–357. Springer, Heidelberg (2001). https://doi.org/10.1007/3-540-44987-6_21
3. Biryukov, A., De Cannière, C., Dellkrantz, G.: Cryptanalysis of SAFER++. In: Boneh, D. (ed.) CRYPTO 2003. LNCS, vol. 2729, pp. 195–211. Springer, Heidelberg (2003). https://doi.org/10.1007/978-3-540-45146-4_12
4. Biryukov, A., Khovratovich, D.: Related-key cryptanalysis of the full AES-192 and AES-256. In: Matsui, M. (ed.) ASIACRYPT 2009. LNCS, vol. 5912, pp. 1–18. Springer, Heidelberg (2009). https://doi.org/10.1007/978-3-642-10366-7_1
5. Bogdanov, A., et al.: PRESENT: an ultra-lightweight block cipher. In: Paillier, P., Verbauwhede, I. (eds.) CHES 2007. LNCS, vol. 4727, pp. 450–466. Springer, Heidelberg (2007). https://doi.org/10.1007/978-3-540-74735-2_31
6. Cid, C., Huang, T., Peyrin, T., Sasaki, Y., Song, L.: A security analysis of deoxys and its internal tweakable block ciphers. IACR Trans. Symmetric Cryptol. 2017(3), 73–107 (2017)
7. Cid, C., Huang, T., Peyrin, T., Sasaki, Y., Song, L.: Boomerang connectivity table: a new cryptanalysis tool. In: Nielsen, J.B., Rijmen, V. (eds.) EUROCRYPT 2018. LNCS, vol. 10821, pp. 683–714. Springer, Cham (2018). https://doi.org/10.1007/978-3-319-78375-8_22
8. Dunkelman, O., Keller, N., Shamir, A.: A practical-time related-key attack on the KASUMI cryptosystem used in GSM and 3G telephony. J. Cryptol. 27(4), 824–849 (2014)
9. Sasaki, Y.: Integer linear programming for three-subset meet-in-the-middle attacks: application to GIFT. In: Inomata, A., Yasuda, K. (eds.) IWSEC 2018. LNCS, vol. 11049, pp. 227–243. Springer, Cham (2018). https://doi.org/10.1007/978-3-319-97916-8_15
10. Sasaki, Y., Todo, Y.: New impossible differential search tool from design and cryptanalysis aspects. In: Coron, J.-S., Nielsen, J.B. (eds.) EUROCRYPT 2017. LNCS, vol. 10212, pp. 185–215. Springer, Cham (2017). https://doi.org/10.1007/978-3-319-56617-7_7
11. Sun, S., Hu, L., Wang, P., Qiao, K., Ma, X., Song, L.: Automatic security evaluation and (related-key) differential characteristic search: application to SIMON, PRESENT, LBlock, DES(L) and other bit-oriented block ciphers. In: Sarkar, P., Iwata, T. (eds.) ASIACRYPT 2014. LNCS, vol. 8873, pp. 158–178. Springer, Heidelberg (2014). https://doi.org/10.1007/978-3-662-45611-8_9
12. Wagner, D.: The boomerang attack. In: Knudsen, L. (ed.) FSE 1999. LNCS, vol. 1636, pp. 156–170. Springer, Heidelberg (1999). https://doi.org/10.1007/3-540-48519-8_12
13. Zhou, C., Zhang, W., Ding, T., Xiang, Z.: Improving the MILP-based security evaluation algorithms against differential cryptanalysis using divide-and-conquer approach. https://eprint.iacr.org/2019/019.pdf
14. Zhu, B., Dong, X., Yu, H.: MILP-based differential attack on round-reduced gift. https://eprint.iacr.org/2018/390.pdf

Fast Chosen-Key Distinguish Attacks on Round-Reduced AES-192

Chunbo Zhu[1], Gaoli Wang[1(✉)], and Boyu Zhu[2]

[1] School of Computer Science and Software Engineering,
East China Normal University, Shanghai 200062, China
onehundredyear@163.com, glwang@sei.ecnu.edu.cn
[2] Department of Computer Science and Technology,
Nanjing University, Nanjing 210023, China
zhuzby@outlook.com

Abstract. The open-key attack is a very popular research topic in the symmetric-key community recently. In this paper, we focus on the security of AES-192 in one of its settings, namely the chosen-key setting. First, thanks to the linear relations between most of AES-192 subkeys, we construct an 8-round chosen-key distinguishers for it using the meet-in-the-middle idea and the SuperSbox technique. Then we turn this distinguisher into a key-recovery attack with a time complexity of one 8-round AES-192 encryption. Using the same approaches and with more efforts on exploiting the weak key schedule of this variant, 9-round chosen-key distinguishers is constructed and the master key is recovered afterwards at the cost of one 9-round AES-192 encryption. These results have been experimentally confirmed and two examples can be found in the appendix. While our work may not pose a threat to the security of AES-192 in a traditional way as those single-key recovery attacks do, we believe it do prove a non-trivial weakness in its key schedule to some extent and thus undermines its expectation as an ideal building block for hash functions.

Keywords: AES · Chosen-key distinguisher · Key recovery · Practical attacks

1 Introduction

Block ciphers are one of the most important primitives in Cryptography. They are not only a good tool for encryption, but also an important building block for some hash functions. In this context, AES [1] can be viewed as the most widely-used block cipher and the most popular component which many hash functions [2–5] are based on or mimic. Traditionally, researchers would investigate the security of AES or other block ciphers in the single secret-key setting where the randomly-generated key is unknown. However this classical approach has somehow become not so dominant since the rise of open-key model. Specifically, there are two kinds of open-key model, namely the known-key model and

© Springer Nature Switzerland AG 2019
J. Jang-Jaccard and F. Guo (Eds.): ACISP 2019, LNCS 11547, pp. 573–587, 2019.
https://doi.org/10.1007/978-3-030-21548-4_31

chosen-key model (or related-key model). Both of them focus on the study of security margin of block cipher applications, *e.g*, block-cipher based hash functions, where the key is known to the attacker, or at least under his control to some extent.

Just as its name suggests, the known-key model means the attacker knows the key. This concept is first introduced by Knudsen and Rijmen [6], based on which they propose two distinguishers for 7-round AES and a class of Feistel ciphers. Afterwards, [7] constructs an known-key distinguisher for 8-round AES with truncated differentials and SuperSbox technique, which is improved by [8] later on. At ASIACRYPT 2014, Gilbert [9] successfully extends an 8-round known-key distinguisher into a more intricate 10-round distinguisher by using a novel representation of AES, and hence presented for the first time a known-key distinguisher for full AES-128. Following this work, [10] further explores the limits of the known-key model with a focus on the AES. Apart from these efforts on the known-key attacks of AES, there is also a considerable number of researches dedicated to other block ciphers, such as Rijndael [11,12], SP-based Feistel ciphers [13,14] and some other constructions [15–17].

The chosen-key model (or related-key model), on the other hand, is more relaxed compared to the known-key model. Its main idea is to take advantage of the weakness in the key schedule by allowing the adversary to choose the relations of some subkeys (with unknown values) or just their values. The first scenario is initially considered by Biham [18] who calls these special subkeys related keys and the corresponding attack related-key attack. Later on, various researches show that this attack works more efficiently when combined with other kinds of attacks. These new results include related-key rectangle attacks [19,20], related-key differential attacks [21–23], and related-key impossible differential attacks [24,25]. As for the second scenario, there are relatively few results in the literature. At CRYPTO 2009, Biryukov *et al.* [22] introduce the first chosen-key distinguisher for full AES-256. Then, an 8-round chosen-key distinguisher for AES-128 and a 9-round one for AES-256 with low time complexity are proposed by Derbez *et al.* [26]. Later, [8] demonstrates that the complexity of this 8-round distinguisher [26] could be further reduced if the adversary considers several characteristics in parallel. At CRYPTO 2013, Fouque *et al.* [27] carry out a chosen-key attack on 9-round AES-128 through the structural evaluation of AES-128 and graph-based ideas, after which [29] introduces Constraint Programming (CP) models for solving a problem related to the chosen-key differential cryptanalysis of AES. Besides, there are also several works examining the security of Feistel-SP ciphers in this senario, such as [17,28].

Our Contributions. While there are several cryptanalyses proposed against AES-128 [8,26,27] and AES-256 [26] in the chosen-key setting, few work has been done on the 192-bit key version. Motivated by the desire to fill this blank, we construct a chosen-key distinguisher on AES-192 reduced to 8 rounds with the meet-in-the-middle idea and the SuperSbox technique. This distinguisher is later translated to a key-recovery attack with a time complexity of one 8-round AES-192 encryption. Using the same approaches, we manage to distinguish the 9-round AES-192 in the chosen-key setting and recover the master key at the

Table 1. Our results and best-known chosen-key distinguishers on AES

Algorithm	Rounds	Data	Time*	Memory	Reference
AES-128	7	–	2^8	2^8	[26]
	8	–	$2^{13.4}$	-	[8]
	9	–	2^{55}	2^{32}	[27]
AES-192	8	–	1	2^{16}	Section 3
	9	–	1	2^{16}	Section 4
AES-256	7	–	2^8	2^8	[26]
	8	–	2^8	2^8	[26]
	9	–	2^{24}	2^{16}	[26]

* The time complexity is measured by the unit of an equivalent encryption of a reduced-round of AES that the adversary can break.

cost of one 9-round AES-192 encryption. Both results have been experimentally confirmed on a single PC with Intel Core i5-4210M microprocessor and a memory of 8 GB. Specifically, the experimental result shows that it only takes 1.05 s to break the 8-round AES-192 and 1.14 s for the 9-round one.

Table 1 summarizes our attacks along with the previous best-known results on AES in chosen-key setting. The key factor of our success in breaking these two versions of round-reduced AES-192 with such a low time complexity is, we believe, the weakness in the key schedule of AES-192. This weakness is that, as [23] notes, when the expanded keys are viewed as a sequence of words, the key schedule of AES-192 applies non-linear transformations to every sixth word, whereas the key schedules of AES-128 and AES-256 apply non-linear transformations to every fourth word. This means the adversary can retrieve more information on the unknown subkeys from the subkeys he already knows and thus recovers the master key more quickly in the case of AES-192 than he would be able to do in the case of the other two AES variants.

Organization of the Paper. The rest of the paper is organized as follows. Section 2 recalls the description of AES block cipher and the previous known-key and chosen-key distinguishers on AES, and gives an account of the notations and definitions used throughout the paper. Afterwards, we show how to construct chosen-key distinguishers for 8-round and 9-round AES-192 in Sects. 3 and 4, respectively. Finally, Sect. 5 concludes this paper. As an additional note, we also refer the readers to Appendices A and B for two instantiated examples of our attacks.

2 Preliminaries

2.1 A Brief Description of AES

The Advanced Encryption Standard (AES) is a Substitution-Permutation Network [1], which supports three different key sizes, namely 128, 192 and 256.

The 128-bit internal state is treated as a byte matrix of size 4×4, each byte representing a value in $GF(2^8)$ that is defined via the irreducible polynomial $x^8 + x^4 + x^3 + x + 1$ over $GF(2)$. After applying a pre-whitening subkey addition modulo 2, the encryption procedure of AES runs a round function for N_r times, which depends on the key size, to update the state. For instance, $N_r = 10$ for AES-128, $N_r = 12$ for AES-192 and $N_r = 14$ for AES-256. Each round consists of the following 4 basic transformations:

- SubBytes(SB) applies an 8-bit SBox to each byte of the state in parallel.
- ShiftRows(SR) rotates the i-th row by i bytes to the left, where $i = 0, 1, 2, 3$.
- MixColumns(MC) multiplies each column of the state by a constant MDS matrix over $GF(2^8)$.
- AddRoundKey(AK) xors the state with the round subkey.

Note that we omit the MixColumns operation in the last round.

As regards the key schedule of AES, it transforms the master key into $N_r + 1$ 128-bit subkeys. For the sake of simplicity, we represented this subkey array in the form of $W[0, ..., 4 \times N_r + 3]$ where each word $W[\cdot]$ is composed of 32 bits. The length of master key is then denoted by N_k 32-bit words, e.g., $N_k = 4$ for AES-128, $N_k = 6$ for AES-192 and $N_k = 8$ for AES-256. The first N_k 32-bit words of $W[\cdot]$ is loaded with the master key, while the rest words of $W[\cdot]$ is generated in the following manner:

- For $i = N_k$ to $4 \times N_r + 3$, do
  - if $i \equiv 0 \mod N_k$, then $W[i] = W[i - N_k] \oplus SB(W[i - 1] \lll 8) \oplus RCON[i/N_k]$,
  - else if $N_k = 8$ and $i \equiv 4 \mod 8$, then $W[i] = W[i - 8] \oplus SB(W[i - 1])$,
  - otherwise $W[i] = W[i - 1] \oplus W[i - N_k]$,

where $RCON[\cdot]$ is an array of fixed constants and $\lll$ denotes left rotation. For complete details of AES, we refer to [1].

2.2   Definitions and Notation

In order to make the demonstration clear and concise, here we give an account of the definitions and notations utilized in this paper.

1. P and C denote the plaintext and the ciphertext respectively.
2. The numbering of the 16 state bytes starts with 0, from top to bottom and left to right.
3. $[a, b, c, d]^T$ denotes the transpose of the row vector $[a, b, c, d]$.
4. X_i denotes the internal state at the beginning of SB operation in the i-th round, where $0 \le i \le N_r - 1$.
5. Y_i denotes the state before SR transformations in the i-th round, where $0 \le i \le N_r - 1$.
6. Z_i denotes the state before MC transformations in the i-th round, where $0 \le i \le N_r - 1$.

7. W_i denotes the state before AK transformations in the i-th round, where $0 \leq i \leq N_r - 1$.
8. k_i represents the subkey of round i, where $0 \leq i \leq N_r - 1$.
9. k_{-1} represents the pre-whitening subkey.
10. u_i denotes an equivalent key of $MC^{-1}(k_i)$.
11. $\overline{w}_i$ denotes $Z_i \oplus u_i$.
12. $X_i[m]$ denotes the state byte in position m in round i. Same notations apply to $k_i[m]$, $k_{-1}[m]$, $P^j[m]$ as well.
13. $X_i[m-n]$ represents the state bytes positioned from m to n. Same notations apply to each $k_i[m-n]$ as well.
14. ΔX_i denotes the difference in a state X_i.
15. $\parallel$ denotes concatenation.

2.3   Chosen-Key Distinguisher

First, we briefly recall the definition of the chosen-key distinguisher in [26]. In this setting, the adversary is challenged to find a key and a pair of plaintexts whose difference is constraint in a predefined input space such that the ciphertext difference lies in another predefined subspace for the targeted permutation Q. Once he finds one, he constructs a so-called chosen-key distinguisher. Formally speaking, a chosen-key distinguisher has the following property:

Property 1. Given any two subspaces IN and OUT, a key k and a pair of messages (x, x') can verify a certain property of a permutation Q if $x \oplus x' \in IN$ and $Q(x) \oplus Q(x') \in OUT$.

Like other distinguishers, the main purpose of the chosen-key distinguisher is to distinguish the targeted permutation from an ideal one. So what is the general attack complexity to build a chosen-key distinguisher for an ideal permutation? Before answering this question, we'd like to introduce another similar distinguisher, known as the limited birthday distinguisher. Introduced by Gilbert and Peyrin [7], the limited birthday distinguisher aims to find a pair of messages satisfying the subspace constraints of Property 1. In other words, the chosen-key distinguisher has more freedom in the choice of key bits. However, [26] notes that this extra freedom does not contribute to the acquirement of the actual message pair that verifies the required property, which means the birthday paradox in the chosen-key seeting is as constraint as the one in the knowing-key setting. Therefore, [26] concludes the limited birthday distinguisher also applies in the chosen-key setting. Accordingly, the complexity of the chosen-key distinguisher for an ideal permutation, denoted by $C(IN, OUT)$, can be calculated by the same formula of the limited birthday distinguisher [7], which is:

$$C(IN, OUT) = max \left\{ min \left\{ \sqrt{2^n/IN}, \sqrt{2^n/OUT} \right\}, \frac{2^{n+1}}{IN \cdot OUT} \right\} \quad (1)$$

Where n represents the size of the input/output.

SuperSBox of AES in the Chosen-Key Setting. In this paper, we also utilize a popular cryptanalysis technique against AES-like permutations, which is named SuperSBox. The concept of SuperSBox is first introduced by Rijmen and Daemen in [30], where they regard the composition of SB ∘ AK(k) ∘ MC ∘ SB as a layer of column-wise applications of four 32-bit SuperSBoxes. It turns out that this technique is very useful in the known-key attacks when combined with the meet-in-the-middle technique since it can allow the attackers to break one more middle round of AES than they do previously without increasing the attack complexity. Then Derbez *et al.* [26] apply a twisted version of SuperSBox to the chosen-key attacks where the key is hidden from the adversary. Consequently, they denote this kind of SuperSBox, keyed by a 32-bit key k, by SuperSBox$_k$. Moreover, for the SuperSBox$_k$ in Fig. 1, they present the following interesting observation.

Observation 1 [26]. Let a, b be two bytes, and c be an AES-column. Given any 32-bit input and output differences Δ_{in} and Δ_{out} of a SuperSBox$_k$, where k is unknown, the following equations:

$$\begin{cases} SuperSBox_k(c) \oplus SuperSBox_k(c \oplus \Delta_{in}) = \Delta_{out} \\ SuperSBox_k(c) = [a, b, *, *]^T \end{cases} \tag{2}$$

has 2^{16} solutions for (c, k) with 2^{16} basic operations.

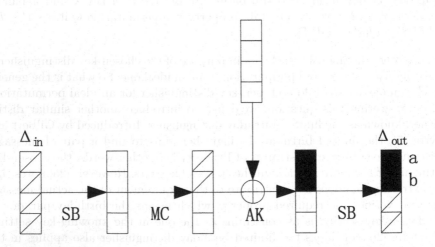

Fig. 1. SuperSBox of AES in the chosen-key setting: black bytes have known values and differences, hatched bytes have known differences and the remaining bytes have unknown values and differences

Proof. For the first two output bytes at the second SB layer are known, one can directly compute the corresponding two input bytes as well as their difference. After guessing the differences of the remaining two input bytes at this layer, the adversary propagates the differences backward to the output of the first SB layer. According to the differential properties of AES S-Box, there is one solution on average for each of the 6 unset bytes at both SB layers. Once the input and output of AK operation are known, the four bytes of k are also determined. Therefore, by iterating over the 2^{16} possible differences for the two unset bytes at the second SB layer which can be regarded as 2^{16} basic operations, one expects to find 2^{16} solutions.

3 Chosen-Key Distinguisher for 8-Round AES-192

This section describes a way to launch a chosen-key attack on AES-192 reduced to 8 rounds with the SuperSbox technique mentioned previously. The basic differential characteristic we employ covers the following transition:

$$4 \xrightarrow{R_0} 1 \xrightarrow{R_1} 4 \xrightarrow{R_2} 16 \xrightarrow{R_3} 16 \xrightarrow{R_4} 4 \xrightarrow{R_5} 1 \xrightarrow{R_6} 4 \xrightarrow{R_7} 4$$

Particularly, we focus on the middle rounds from round 1 to 5 which are depicted in Fig. 2. For all the intermediate states in Fig. 2, we hypothesize that the black bytes have known values and differences, the gray bytes have known values and zero differences, and the hatched bytes have known differences and unknown values. Besides, the bytes marked by '?' have unknown values and differences, while the remaining bytes have zero difference and unknown values. As for the subkeys, the bytes marked by black dots have known values, while the rest bytes don't.

Our strategy is to find enough solutions for these rounds and then filter them out through the outward transitions (namely round 0, round 6 and round 7). Due to the fact that the forward and backward transitions happen with a probability of 1, it requires only one solution for the middle rounds. In what follows, we will show how to find this solution in time 1.

We start by randomizing $\Delta Y_1[0]$, from which $\Delta X_2[0-3]$ is deduced. Then, ΔX_3 can be determined by guessing the values in the first column of X_2. From the backward direction, with the knowledge of $\Delta W_5[0]||W_5[0-3]||W_4[0-7]$, one is able to obtain $\Delta Y_4||Y_4[0, 3-5, 9, 10, 14, 15]$ as well as $k_4[0, 5]$. In consequence, the four SuperSBoxes between state X_3 and state Y_4, keyed by the four corresponding columns of k_3, satisfies the requirements of Observation 1. For $i \in \{0, 1, 2, 3\}$, we store all the 2^{16} elements for the i-th SuperSBox associated the i-th column of X_4 in list L_i. Then we can retrieve one element for each SuperSBoxes in time and memory 1 on average. More detailed, the adversary first randomly picks one element from L_1, L_2 and L_3, respectively. Then, he learns the value of $k_3[4-15]$. By the key schedule of AES-192, $u_2[0, 7]$ can be deduced, which leads to the determination of $\overline{w}_2[0, 7]$. With $\overline{w}_2[0, 7]$ and $X_3[1-4, 6, 7]$, one obtains $X_3[0, 5]$ by the MC operation. Afterwards, only one element in L_0 is expected to share the same value of $X_3[0, 5]$. At this point, we achieve a partial pair of internal states that conform to the transition from X_3 to Y_4.

While determining the values and differences of the intermediate states from round 1 to round 5, we also fix some bytes of k_2, k_3 and k_4 that are marked

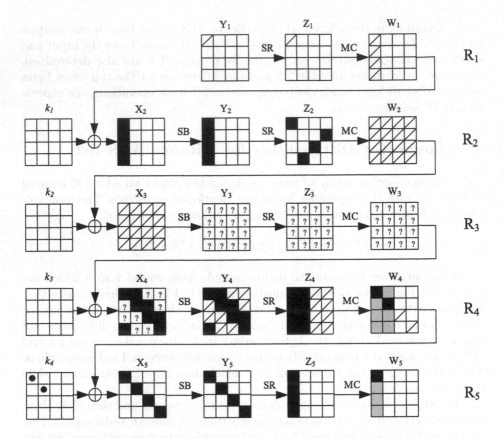

Fig. 2. The main part of the 8-round chosen-key distinguisher on AES-192

gray in Fig. 3. However, it is not sufficient to generate a compatible key with the knowledge of these subkey bytes. To solve this problem, we choose random values for the 2 bytes tagged by 1, namely $k_2[9]$ and $k_2[10]$. As there are four known bytes among the eight bytes in the third column of k_2 and u_2, it is not hard to estimate the bytes tagged by 2 by the MC transformation. Next, the bytes tagged by 3 and 4 are deduced by the key schedule. Again, the properties of MC enable us to compute the bytes tagged by 5, after which the byte tagged by 6 is known. Finally, the master key k can be recovered by inverting the key schedule.

To conclude, for AES-192 the complexity to find a triplet (m, m', k) verifying the pre-defined 8-round differential path is just 1. In terms of the freedom degrees, there are 16 bytes in the first message and 4 more bytes in the second message. Together with the additional 24 bytes in the key, one has 44 freedom degrees at the input. Considering the probability of the 8-round differential path is 2^{-144}, 26 freedom degrees are available for us. By using the method above, then, it only costs 18 of them to construct the distinguisher, which means a total of 2^{64} solutions is expected to be found. Indeed, we can get $2^{16 \times 3}$ solutions when

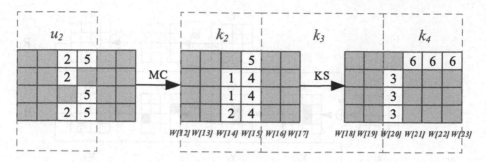

Fig. 3. The generation of a compatible key: gray bytes are known and the numbers indicate the order in which we guess or determine the bytes

connecting the elements from the four lists L_i. For each solution, there are 2^{16} compatible keys as we can randomly choose the values of the 2 bytes tagged by 1. It follows that there are at most 2^{64} triplets (m, m', k) that satisfies the 8-round path. Appendix A has provided one example and our C implementation can be found in [31].

4   Chosen-Key Distinguisher for 9-Round AES-192

In the case of the 9-round chosen-key distinguisher for AES-192, we consider the following differential characteristic:

$$12 \xrightarrow{R_0} 3 \xrightarrow{R_1} 2 \xrightarrow{R_2} 8 \xrightarrow{R_3} 16 \xrightarrow{R_4} 16 \xrightarrow{R_5} 4 \xrightarrow{R_6} 1 \xrightarrow{R_7} 4 \xrightarrow{R_8} 4.$$

Again, we split the attack into two parts. The first one, as shown in Fig. 4, is to collect enough solutions for the middle rounds from round 1 to round 6. The other one is to work as a filter that discard wrong solutions through the MC operation in the outward direction. In this attack, since the three transitions in the backward or forward direction happen with probability 1, only one solution is required for the middle rounds. Finally, one triplet (m, m', k) fulfilling the 9-round differential characteristic will be found. The major procedure is as follows.

First of all, we choose a random difference for the byte 4 of Z_1 so as to get $\Delta Z_1[5, 6] \| \Delta W_1[5, 6] \| \Delta X_2[5, 6]$. Then, by guessing the values of $X_2[5, 6]$ and $X_3[0-2, 12-15]$, we can propagate the difference to state X_4. In the meantime, $u_2[1, 14]$ is deduced. Next, we randomize the values of $\Delta W_6[0-4] \| W_6[0-4]$. Doing so, ΔY_5 can be computed.

Now, all the input and out differences of the four SuperSBoxes between X_4 and Y_5 are set. The next step is to guess two input or output byte values for each SuperSBox if one wants to utilize Observation 1 in the attack. This time, however, we make an adjustment. That is, we set the first two input bytes to random values, which means the first two columns of X_4 are known. Consequently, $u_3[0, 4, 6, 7]$ is determined.

As before, we build 4 lists $L_i (i \in \{0, 1, 2, 3\})$, each storing the 2^{16} values of the i-th column of k_4 and the i-th diagonal of X_4. After that, one retrieves 1

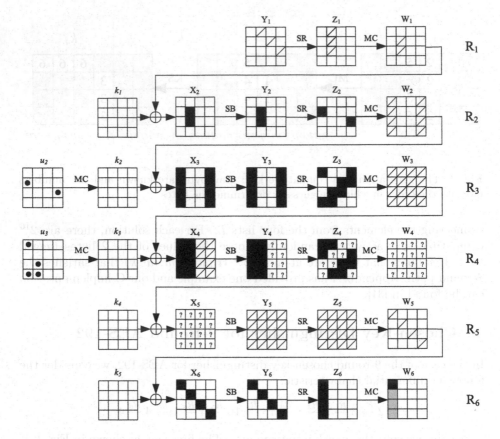

Fig. 4. The main part of the 9-round chosen-key distinguisher on AES-192

element from L_3. The knowledge of $k_4[12-15]$ and $u_3[6,7]$ allows us to compute $u_4[10,11]$. This imposes a 16-bit constraint on the elements of L_2 such that only one element will be left. Then, by the key schedule, $u_4[4,7]$ is deduced from $k_4[8-11]$ and $u_3[0,4]$. After filtering the elements of L_1, we are expected to find one $k_4[4-7]$ which can result in the same value of $u_4[4,7]$ as the one deduced above. Then, with the knowledge of $u_2[14]$ and $k_4[4-7]$, it is sufficient to compute $u_4[2]$. We also notice that $u_2[1]$ and $k_3[4-7]$ are already set in the previous steps. According to Observation 1, we then learn $u_3[11]$. With this subkey byte and $Z_3[11]$, one can be computed. As $X_4[8]$, $X_4[9]$ and $X_4[11]$ are known, the property of MC operation allows us to deduce $X_4[10]$. Finally, one looks up L_0 to retrieve the element which meets the constraints on $u_4[2]$ and $X_4[10]$. At this point, one solution is found.

The next step is to derive a valid key for this solution. As shown in Fig. 5, the grey bytes of subkeys are fixed on account of the previous steps. For the rest unknown bytes, we first set $k_3[9]$, tagged by 1, to random values. Using the properties of MC, the 4 bytes tagged by 2 in the third column of k_3 and u_3 can be linearly calculated. Then by the key schedule, one learns the bytes tagged by 3 and 4. Since $u_3[12, 13]$ is already known, 5 bytes in the last columns of k_3 and u_3 are determined. In that case, the probability that these 5 bytes verify the properties of MC is 2^{-8}. Therefore, after iterating the 2^8 possible values of $k_3[9]$, we expect to find one match and obtain $k_3[12]||u_3[14, 15]$. Once $k_3[12]$ is known, the adversary is able to deduce the bytes tagged by 6 and then retrieve the master key k.

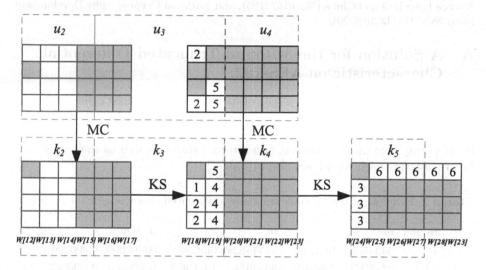

Fig. 5. The generation of a compatible key: gray bytes are known and the numbers indicate the order in which we guess or determine the bytes

Overall, the 9-round chosen-key distinguisher for AES-192 can be built with a complexity of one 9-round AES-192 encryption. When it comes to the freedom degrees, it can be calculated in the following manner. Undoubtedly, there are $16 + 12 + 24 = 52$ freedom degrees at the input, among which 26 are consumed by the 9-round pre-described differential path. Then, it calls for 24 freedom degrees to establish the 9-round distinguisher. As a result, 2^{16} solutions in total are expected to be found. To testify our result, we provide one triplet (m, m', k) in Appendix B. Our C implementation can be found in [31].

5   Conclusion

These days, many hash functions utilize part of AES or mimic its behaviors to construct their internal components under the assumption that the underlying block cipher is ideal. But the reality is that the security margin of AES is undermined when applied to a hash function in which its key is now at the control of the adversary. That's why it is important to do a thorough evaluation of AES in the chosen-key setting. By using the meet-in-the-middle idea, Super-Sbox technique and the available degrees of freedom in the key, we propose two chosen-key distinguish attack against 8-round and 9-round AES-192 with practical time complexities. However, it is far from enough. There are many works needed to be done in the future, such as extending the distinguishers to more rounds, or applying the efficient chosen-key attacks into the real world.

Acknowledgment. The authors would like to thank the anonymous reviewers for their helpful comments and suggestions. This work is supported by the National Natural Science Foundation of China (No. 61572125), and National Cryptography Development Fund (No. MMJJ20180201).

A   A Solution for the 8-Round Truncated Differential Characteristic on AES-192

The following is an example of a pair of messages (m, m') that conforms to the 8-rounds truncated differential characteristic for AES-192, where the master key is: eb7d63b4 e2ee9c50 e39dc9c6 cc9ccea1 98de6570 7bcef0c2. In detail, the lines in this array contain the values of two internal states as well as their difference before entering each round, see also in Table 2.

Table 2. Example of the 8-rounds truncated differential characteristic for AES-192

Round	m		m'		$m \oplus m'$	
P	3d345b2a	6f5f2afe	a4345b2a	6faf2afe	99000000	00f00000
	33a4f1f4	14e19f40	33a4fff4	14e19fe2	00000e00	000000a2
R_0	d649389e	8db1b6ae	4f49389e	8d41b6ae	99000000	00f00000
	d0393832	d87d51e1	d0393632	d87d5143	00000e00	000000a2
R_1	d3524655	2dd41bf0	0a524655	2dd41bf0	d9000000	00000000
	f205d52e	eb755c55	f205d52e	eb755c55	00000000	00000000
R_2	01010101	86bec013	03000002	86bec013	02010103	00000000
	dd86b296	92b092fd	dd86b296	92b092fd	00000000	00000000
R_3	994b2386	958f86c9	974c248f	9e849bdf	0e070709	0b0b1d16
	a20df3cc	1e80a57b	bd2ccdd3	3fbeba64	1f213e1f	213e1f1f
R_4	ee002b90	216d9fb2	8497bc62	5721beeb	6a9797f2	764c2159
	2871a4cb	2c1b6bce	5e8462fe	eaee2157	76f5c635	c6f54a99
R_5	d77355cc	2f40079b	527355cc	2f52079b	85000000	00120000
	fb71f372	695df49e	fb715272	695df452	0000a100	000000cc
R_6	ea7d6348	c23792c4	eb7d6348	c23792c4	01000000	00000000
	c1015534	2a74e9fc	c1015534	2a74e9fc	00000000	00000000
R_7	9fa433b7	1b8dff1a	43ca5d05	1b8dff1a	dc6e6eb2	00000000
	5130407f	955a5363	5130407f	955a5363	00000000	00000000
C	31533f91	899615e5	f0533f91	89961527	c1000000	000000c2
	848f3dd6	e6588415	848fb2d6	e6658415	00008f00	003d0000

B   A Solution for the 9-Round Truncated Differential Characteristic on AES-192

The following is an example of a pair of messages (m, m') that conforms to the 9-rounds truncated differential characteristic for AES-192, where the master key is: 33d481b7 61ba9ffd c8363e8b 4db50f1c 4f5f0d27 25508fcd. In detail, the lines in this array contain the values of two internal states as well as their difference before entering each round, see also in Table 3.

Table 3. Example of the 9-rounds truncated differential characteristic for AES-192

Round	m		m'		$m \oplus m'$	
P	1ff4a032	34fa0947	15f487e8	bb9d09b3	0a0027da	8f6700f4
	83221d49	efdff942	108fb349	efd995b4	93adae00	00066cf6
R_0	2c202185	554096ba	2620065f	da27964e	0a0027da	8f6700f4
	4b1423c2	a26af65e	d8b98dc2	a26c9aa8	93adae00	00066cf6
R_1	c80ed12b	0612af5f	6a0ed12b	06b7af5f	a2000000	00a50000
	13f86b4a	03dc7a56	13f8a24a	03dc7a56	0000c900	00000000
R_2	8d7a8a12	b3f71b31	a79f8a12	b3f71b31	2ae50000	00000000
	5026527f	50fa53e0	5026527f	50fa53e0	00000000	00000000
R_3	01010101	1e0db406	03000002	1e0db406	02010103	00000000
	4217e2ef	01010101	4217e2ef	02030000	00000000	03020101
R_4	1b023bc8	65e4d111	0a1a1dff	71cef218	11182637	142a2309
	03471883	00dfd5db	1568219b	37eac1d9	162f3918	37351402
R_5	ee7bcb90	216df456	8410ce62	57211006	6a6b05f2	764ce450
	e171a4fc	c9246bce	e784629b	0b562157	06f5c667	c2724a99
R_6	d709f932	2f405739	5209f932	2f525739	85000000	00120000
	3456f3ad	4d31a59e	345652ad	4d31a552	0000a100	000000cc
R_7	4f56f415	cd14153a	4e56f415	cd14153a	01000000	00000000
	29478607	fff0e139	29478607	fff0e139	00000000	00000000
R_8	948e1a8f	7f5330b3	d925b169	7f5330b3	4dababe6	00000000
	eb550e4c	78b94027	eb550e4c	78b94027	00000000	00000000
C	434a9744	d2e1aa06	544a9744	d2e1aa8c	17000000	0000008a
	217d3f93	398796cb	217d5593	39a196cb	00006a00	00260000

References

1. Daemen, J., Rijmen, V.: AES proposal: Rijndael. In: First Advanced Encryption Standard (AES) Conference (1998)
2. Rijmen, V., Barreto, P.S.L.M.: The whirlpool hashing function. Submitted to NESSIE, September 2000. Accessed May 2003. http://www.larc.usp.br/~pbarreto/WhirlpoolPage.html

3. Benadjila, R., et al.: SHA proposal: ECHO. Submission to NIST (updated) (2009)
4. Gauravaram, P., et al.: Grøstl - a SHA-3 candidate. Submission to NIST, Round 3 (2011)
5. Information Protection and Special Communications of the Federal Security Service of the Russian Federation. Gost r 34.11.2012 information technology cryptographic date security hash-functions (in English) (2012). http://tk26.ru/en/GOSTR3411-2012/GOST_R_34_11-2012_eng.pdf/
6. Knudsen, L.R., Rijmen, V.: Known-key distinguishers for some block ciphers. In: Kurosawa, K. (ed.) ASIACRYPT 2007. LNCS, vol. 4833, pp. 315–324. Springer, Heidelberg (2007). https://doi.org/10.1007/978-3-540-76900-2_19
7. Gilbert, H., Peyrin, T.: Super-Sbox cryptanalysis: improved attacks for AES-like permutations. In: Hong, S., Iwata, T. (eds.) FSE 2010. LNCS, vol. 6147, pp. 365–383. Springer, Heidelberg (2010). https://doi.org/10.1007/978-3-642-13858-4_21
8. Jean, J., Naya-Plasencia, M., Peyrin, T.: Multiple limited-birthday distinguishers and applications. In: Lange, T., Lauter, K., Lisoněk, P. (eds.) SAC 2013. LNCS, vol. 8282, pp. 533–550. Springer, Heidelberg (2014). https://doi.org/10.1007/978-3-662-43414-7_27
9. Gilbert, H.: A simplified representation of AES. In: Sarkar, P., Iwata, T. (eds.) ASIACRYPT 2014. LNCS, vol. 8873, pp. 200–222. Springer, Heidelberg (2014). https://doi.org/10.1007/978-3-662-45611-8_11
10. Grassi, L., Rechberger, C.: New and old limits for AES known-key distinguishers. IACR Cryptology ePrint Archive (2007). https://eprint.iacr.org/2017/255.pdf
11. Minier, M., Phan, R.C.-W., Pousse, B.: Distinguishers for ciphers and known key attack against Rijndael with large blocks. In: Preneel, B. (ed.) AFRICACRYPT 2009. LNCS, vol. 5580, pp. 60–76. Springer, Heidelberg (2009). https://doi.org/10.1007/978-3-642-02384-2_5
12. Sasaki, Y.: Known-key attacks on Rijndael with large blocks and strengthening ShiftRow parameter. In: Echizen, I., Kunihiro, N., Sasaki, R. (eds.) IWSEC 2010. LNCS, vol. 6434, pp. 301–315. Springer, Heidelberg (2010). https://doi.org/10.1007/978-3-642-16825-3_20
13. Sasaki, Y., Emami, S., Hong, D., Kumar, A.: Improved known-key distinguishers on Feistel-SP ciphers and application to Camellia. In: Susilo, W., Mu, Y., Seberry, J. (eds.) ACISP 2012. LNCS, vol. 7372, pp. 87–100. Springer, Heidelberg (2012). https://doi.org/10.1007/978-3-642-31448-3_7
14. Sasaki, Y., Yasuda, K.: Known-key distinguishers on 11-round Feistel and collision attacks on its hashing modes. In: Joux, A. (ed.) FSE 2011. LNCS, vol. 6733, pp. 397–415. Springer, Heidelberg (2011). https://doi.org/10.1007/978-3-642-21702-9_23
15. Dong, L., Wu, W., Wu, S., Zou, J.: Known-key distinguisher on round-reduced 3D block cipher. In: Jung, S., Yung, M. (eds.) WISA 2011. LNCS, vol. 7115, pp. 55–69. Springer, Heidelberg (2012). https://doi.org/10.1007/978-3-642-27890-7_5
16. NakaharaJr, J.: New impossible differential and known-key distinguishers for the 3D cipher. In: Bao, F., Weng, J. (eds.) ISPEC 2011. LNCS, vol. 6672, pp. 208–221. Springer, Heidelberg (2011). https://doi.org/10.1007/978-3-642-21031-0_16
17. Nikolić, I., Pieprzyk, J., Sokołowski, P., Steinfeld, R.: Known and chosen key differential distinguishers for block ciphers. In: Rhee, K.-H., Nyang, D.H. (eds.) ICISC 2010. LNCS, vol. 6829, pp. 29–48. Springer, Heidelberg (2011). https://doi.org/10.1007/978-3-642-24209-0_3
18. Biham, E.: New types of cryptanalytic attacks using related keys. J. Cryptol. 7(4), 229–246 (1994)

19. Biham, E., Dunkelman, O., Keller, N.: Related-key boomerang and rectangle attacks. In: Cramer, R. (ed.) EUROCRYPT 2005. LNCS, vol. 3494, pp. 507–525. Springer, Heidelberg (2005). https://doi.org/10.1007/11426639_30
20. Hong, S., Kim, J., Lee, S., Preneel, B.: Related-key rectangle attacks on reduced versions of SHACAL-1 and AES-192. In: Gilbert, H., Handschuh, H. (eds.) FSE 2005. LNCS, vol. 3557, pp. 368–383. Springer, Heidelberg (2005). https://doi.org/10.1007/11502760_25
21. Biryukov, A., Khovratovich, D.: Related-key cryptanalysis of the full AES-192 and AES-256. In: Matsui, M. (ed.) ASIACRYPT 2009. LNCS, vol. 5912, pp. 1–18. Springer, Heidelberg (2009). https://doi.org/10.1007/978-3-642-10366-7_1
22. Biryukov, A., Khovratovich, D., Nikolić, I.: Distinguisher and related-key attack on the full AES-256. In: Halevi, S. (ed.) CRYPTO 2009. LNCS, vol. 5677, pp. 231–249. Springer, Heidelberg (2009). https://doi.org/10.1007/978-3-642-03356-8_14
23. Jakimoski, G., Desmedt, Y.: Related-key differential cryptanalysis of 192-bit key AES variants. In: Matsui, M., Zuccherato, R.J. (eds.) SAC 2003. LNCS, vol. 3006, pp. 208–221. Springer, Heidelberg (2004). https://doi.org/10.1007/978-3-540-24654-1_15
24. Mala, H., Dakhilalian, M., Rijmen, V., Modarres-Hashemi, M.: Improved impossible differential cryptanalysis of 7-round AES-128. In: Gong, G., Gupta, K.C. (eds.) INDOCRYPT 2010. LNCS, vol. 6498, pp. 282–291. Springer, Heidelberg (2010). https://doi.org/10.1007/978-3-642-17401-8_20
25. Biham, E., Dunkelman, O., Keller, N.: Related-key impossible differential attacks on 8-round AES-192. In: Pointcheval, D. (ed.) CT-RSA 2006. LNCS, vol. 3860, pp. 21–33. Springer, Heidelberg (2006). https://doi.org/10.1007/11605805_2
26. Derbez, P., Fouque, P.-A., Jean, J.: Faster chosen-key distinguishers on reduced-round AES. In: Galbraith, S., Nandi, M. (eds.) INDOCRYPT 2012. LNCS, vol. 7668, pp. 225–243. Springer, Heidelberg (2012). https://doi.org/10.1007/978-3-642-34931-7_14
27. Fouque, P.-A., Jean, J., Peyrin, T.: Structural evaluation of AES and chosen-key distinguisher of 9-round AES-128. In: Canetti, R., Garay, J.A. (eds.) CRYPTO 2013. LNCS, vol. 8042, pp. 183–203. Springer, Heidelberg (2013). https://doi.org/10.1007/978-3-642-40041-4_11
28. Dong, X., Wang, X.: Chosen-key distinguishers on 12-round Feistel-SP and 11-round collision attacks on its hashing modes. IACR Trans. Symmetric Cryptol. **2016**, 13–32 (2016)
29. Gerault, D., Minier, M., Solnon, C.: Constraint programming models for chosen key differential cryptanalysis. In: Rueher, M. (ed.) CP 2016. LNCS, vol. 9892, pp. 584–601. Springer, Cham (2016). https://doi.org/10.1007/978-3-319-44953-1_37
30. Daemen, J., Rijmen, V.: Understanding two-round differentials in AES. In: De Prisco, R., Yung, M. (eds.) SCN 2006. LNCS, vol. 4116, pp. 78–94. Springer, Heidelberg (2006). https://doi.org/10.1007/11832072_6
31. Verification of chosen-key distinguishers on 8-round and 9-round AES-192 (2016). https://github.com/Crypt-CNS/AES_5-Round_Distinguishers/tree/Crypt-CNS-AES_8-and-9-Round_Distinguishers

A Highly Secure MAC from Tweakable Blockciphers with Support for Short Tweaks

Yusuke Naito[✉]

Mitsubishi Electric Corporation, Kamakura, Kanagawa, Japan
Naito.Yusuke@ce.MitsubishiElectric.co.jp

Abstract. Existing tweakable blockcipher (TBC)-based message authentication codes (MACs), in order to achieve full b-bit pseudorandom function (PRF) security, require a TBC with t-bit tweak and b-bit input block spaces such that $b \leq t$. An open problem from the previous works is to design a TBC-based MAC achieving the b-bit security even when $b > t$. We present PMAC3, a TBC-based MAC achieving the b-bit security as long as $b/2 \leq t$.

Keywords: MAC · PRF · BBB security · Tweakable blockcipher · Short tweak

1 Introduction

Message authentication code (MAC) is a fundamental symmetric-key primitive that provides the authenticity of messages. A number of MACs have been designed by using blockciphers via modes of operation, and most of them, e.g., [4,6,18], are secure pseudo-random functions (PRFs) up to $O(2^{b/2})$ blockcipher calls, using a blockcipher with b-bit blocks, which is so-called birthday-bound security. However, birthday-bound security becomes unreliable, when the block size is small, when large amounts of data are processed, or when a large number of connections need to be kept secure. Indeed, a plaintext of the CBC encryption using a 64-bit blockcipher is recovered within a few days [3]. For this reason, *beyond-birthday-bound* (BBB)-secure MACs have been designed.

BBB-Secure MACs. The first attempt to achieve BBB-security was made in ISO 9797-1 [10] (without proofs of security), where six CBC-type MACs are defined. Yasuda [19] proved that Algorithm 6 achieves BBB-security (security up to $O(2^{2b/3})$ blockcipher calls), and improved the MAC, where the number of blockcipher keys is reduced from 6 to 4. After that, several BBB-secure MACs have been proposed, e.g., PMAC_Plus [20], 1-k-PMAC_Plus [5] (security

© Springer Nature Switzerland AG 2019
J. Jang-Jaccard and F. Guo (Eds.): ACISP 2019, LNCS 11547, pp. 588–606, 2019.
https://doi.org/10.1007/978-3-030-21548-4_32

up to $O(2^{2b/3})$ blockcipher calls), F_r [7] and LightMAC_Plus2 [17] (security up to $O(2^{rb/(r+1)})$ queries for a parameter r).[1]

Another approach to achieve BBB-security is to use tweakable blockcipher (TBC). The advantage of TBC-based design over blockcipher-based one is that a highly efficient and full-bit (b-bit) secure MACs can be designed. TBC whose concept was introduced by Liskov et al. [11] is a generalization of classical block-cipher. A TBC takes a public input called tweak in addition to key and input block. The role of tweak is that a retweaking (changing a tweak) offers the same functionality as changing its secret key but should be less costly. A TBC can be either constructed in a generic way from a blockcipher through a mode of opera-tion e.g., [18], or as a dedicated design such as Deoxys-BC, Kiasu-BC, Joltik-BC [9] and SKINNY [1], following the so-called TWEAKEY framework [9].

Rogaway [18] proposed PMAC1, a TBC-based MAC that is a secure PRF up to $O(2^{b/2})$ TBC calls when using a TBC with a b-bit input-block space. Naito [16] proposed PMAC_TBC1k, a combination of PMAC1 and PMAC_Plus, and claimed that PMAC_TBC1k is a secure PRF up to $O(2^b)$ queries, using a TBC with a t-bit tweak space such that $b/2 \leq t$. List and Nandi [12] pointed out a glitch, and gave a valid proof for $b \leq t$. In PMAC_TBC1k, for each i-th message block M_i of b bits, M_i is input to the input block space and the counter value i is input to the tweak space (counter-based construction from PMAC1), and then the b-bit outputs are extended to $2b$ bits (PMAC_Plus's technique). The counter-based construction avoids a collision in inputs to TBC calls at distinct positions, and the PMAC_Plus's technique avoids the $O(2^{b/2})$ birthday attack, thus full b-bit security can be achieved by these techniques. List and Nandi [12] also proposed PMAC2x which extends the output length of PMAC_TBC1k from b to $2b$ bits without harming efficiency nor security, and PMACx which is a modifi-cation of PMAC_TBC1k with b-bit outputs. Minematsu and Iwata [15] reported a flaw of the security result, and List and Nandi [12] modified their propos-als so that the flaw is fixed. Iwata et al. [8] proposed ZMAC, a highly efficient MAC with PRF-security up to $O(2^{b/2+\min\{t,b\}/2})$ TBC calls. In ZMAC, both the input-block and (t-bit) tweak spaces are used to take message blocks. Hence, the number of TBC calls in ZMAC is roughly $(b+t)/b$ times less than previous TBC-based MACs. Instead of the counter-based construction in PMAC_TBC1k, ZMAC employs the XT(X) tweak extension [14] in order to use the tweak spaces: two secret maskings defined by the powering-up scheme [18] are applied to the input-block and tweak spaces for each TBC call. List and Nandi [13] proposed ZMAC+, a variant of ZMAC that supports variable-length outputs, while retain-ing the $O(2^{b/2+\min\{t,b\}/2})$-security.

Open Problem. Even when using a TBC with a short tweak space, i.e., $t < b$, the security proofs of the existing TBC-based MACs with BBB-security ZMAC

---

[1] When security depends on both the numbers of queries and message lengths, the security level is measured by the number of blockcipher calls performed in a MAC. When it depends on only the number of queries, the security level is measured by the number of queries.

and ZMAC+ hold, however, the security levels become less than the full b bit. For example, using Kiasu-BC (64-bit tweak and 128-bit input-block), these MACs are secure PRFs up to roughly 2^{96} TBC calls. On the other hand, in general, reducing a tweak size, a TBC becomes more compact, e.g., Kiasu-BC is more compact than Deoxys-BC (128 (or more)-bit tweak and 128-bit input-block). Hence, using a TBC with $t < b$, these MACs become more compact. This motivates us to design a TBC-based MAC with full-bit security even when using a TBC with $t < b$.

There are two reasons why these MACs do not achieve b-bit security when $t < b$. **(1)** The first reason is the XT(X) tweak extension that introduces the term $O(\sigma^2/2^{b+\min\{t,b\}})$ in the security bound where σ is the number of TBC calls. The term comes from a collision in inputs of $b + \min\{t,b\}$ bits to TBC calls at distinct positions, which yields an attack on XT(X); **(2)** The second reason is the internal state sizes. In the hashing phases of ZMAC and ZMAC+, a $2b$-bit value is defined by the PMAC_Plus's technique, and when $t < b$, the $b-t$ bits of the $2b$-bit value are truncated in order to obtain an input to a TBC in the finalization phase. By the truncation, the internal state sizes becomes $b + \min\{t,b\}$ bits, and by the birthday analysis on the internal state, the term $O(q^2/2^{b+\min\{t,b\}})$ is introduced in the security bound; Note that Iwata et al. [8] gave a comment that using the counter-based construction instead of the XT(X) tweak extension, the collision influence of the XT(X) tweak extension can be removed, that is, $O(\sigma^2/2^{b+\min\{t,b\}})$ is removed. However, the term $O(q^2/2^{b+\min\{t,b\}})$ remains in the security bound.

Our Contribution. In this paper, we present PMAC3, a TBC-based MAC with full b-bit security even when using a TBC with a short tweak space $t < b$. In order to achieve the b-bit security, the following two techniques are used. The first technique is the existing one, and the second technique is new. **(1)** In order to avoid the XT(X) tweak extension, the counter-based construction used in PMAC1 and PMAC_TBC1k is employed. The counter-based construction avoids an input collision arising in the XT(X) tweak extension, thus the term $O(\sigma^2/2^{b+\min\{t,b\}})$ can be avoided; **(2)** When $t < b$, in order to avoid the birthday analysis on the $(t + b)$-bit internal state, the internal state is extended to $(2t + b)$ bits (hence, the internal state consists of 3 lines: two t-bit lines and one b-bit line, and the name PMAC "3" comes from the number of lines), and this technique improves the birthday probability from $O(q^2/2^{b+\min\{t,b\}})$ to $O(q^2/2^{b+\min\{2t,b\}})$. By these techniques, PMAC3 is a secure PRF up to $O(2^{(b+\min\{2t,b\})/2})$ queries, and thus achieves the b-bit security when $b/2 \leq t$. For example, using Kiasu-BC that is a TBC with 64-bit tweak and 128-bit input-block spaces, PMAC3 is a secure PRF up to roughly 2^{128} queries. On the other hand, ZMAC and ZMAC+ are secure PRFs up to roughly 2^{96} TBC calls. In Table 1, PMAC3 is compared with existing TBC-based MACs, with respect to security bound and message-block length in bits for each TBC call. PMAC3 uses partial bits of the tweak space to take message blocks, and ZMAC and ZMAC+ use full bits of the tweak space,

Table 1. Comparison of TBC-based MACs. q is the number of queries. σ is the number of TBC calls defined by all queries. # bits/TBC shows lengths of message blocks for each TBC call. The parameter c is the counter size in PMAC3, and in PMAC3 the remaining $(b-c)$-bit tweak space of each TBC calls is used to take a message block. (this technique is introduced in ZMAC [8]).

Scheme [Ref.]	Security bound	# bits/TBC
PMAC1 [18]	$O(\sigma^2/2^b)$	b
PMAC_TBC1k [16]	$O(q/2^b)$ (only when $b \leq t$)	b
PMAC(2)x [12]	$O(q^2/2^{2b})$ (only when $b \leq t$)	b
ZMAC [8]	$O(\sigma^2/2^{b+\min\{t,b\}} + (q/2^b)^{3/2})$	$t+b$
ZMAC+ [13]	$O(q\sigma/2^{b+\min\{t,b\}} + q/2^b)$	$t+b$
PMAC3 [Ours]	$O(q^2/2^{b+\min\{2t,b\}})$	$(t-c)+b$

thereby PMAC3 is less efficient than ZMAC and ZMAC+ regarding the number of TBC calls. However, it achieves a higher level of security when $t < b$.

2   Preliminaries

Notation. Let λ be an empty string and $\{0,1\}^*$ the set of all bit strings. For an integer $a \geq 0$, let $\{0,1\}^a$ the set of all a-bit strings, $(\{0,1\}^a)^*$ the set of all bit strings whose lengths are multiples of a, and 0^a resp. 1^a the bit string of a-bit zeroes resp. ones. For an integer $a \geq 1$, let $[a] := \{1,2,\ldots,a\}$. For a non-empty set X, $x \xleftarrow{\$} X$ means that an element is chosen uniformly at random from X and is assigned to x. The concatenation of two bit strings X and Y is written as $X\|Y$ or XY when no confusion is possible. For integers $0 \leq i, a$ and $X \in \{0,1\}^a$, $\mathsf{msb}_i(X)$ resp. $\mathsf{lsb}_i(X)$ denotes the most resp. least significant i bits of X if $i \leq a$; $\mathsf{msb}_i(X) = \mathsf{lsb}_i(X) := 0^{i-a}\|X$ if $i > a$. For integers $a, i \geq 0$ with $a < 2^i$, let $\mathsf{str}_i(a)$ be the i-bit binary representation of a. For integers $a, b \geq 0$ and a bit string $X \in \{0,1\}^{a+b}$, $(L,R) \xleftarrow{a,b} X$ denotes the parsing into a-bit and b-bit strings, where $L = \mathsf{msb}_a(X)$ and $R = \mathsf{lsb}_b(X)$. For integers $a, b \geq 0$ and an ab-bit string M, $(M_1, M_2, \ldots, M_a) \xleftarrow{b} M$ denotes the parsing into b-bit strings, where $M = M_1\|M_2\|\cdots\|M_a$.

Let $GF(2^n)$ be the field with 2^n elements and $GF(2^n)^*$ the multiplication subgroup of this field which contains $2^n - 1$ elements. We interchangeably think of an element a in $GF(2^n)$ in any of the following ways: as an n-bit string $a_{n-1}\cdots a_1 a_0 \in \{0,1\}^n$ and as a formal polynomial $a_{n-1}\mathsf{x}^{n-1} + \cdots + a_1\mathsf{x} + a_0 \in GF(2^n)$. Hence we need to fix a primitive polynomial $a(\mathsf{x}) = \mathsf{x}^n + a_{n-1}\mathsf{x}^{n-1} + \cdots + a_1\mathsf{x} + a_0$. This paper uses a primitive polynomial with the property that the element $2 = \mathsf{x}$ generates the entire multiplication group $GF(2^n)^*$ of order $2^n - 1$. The primitive polynomials for $n = 64$ and $n = 128$ are e.g., $a(\mathsf{x}) = \mathsf{x}^{64} + \mathsf{x}^4 + \mathsf{x}^3 + \mathsf{x} + 1$ and $a(\mathsf{x}) = \mathsf{x}^{128} + \mathsf{x}^7 + \mathsf{x}^2 + \mathsf{x} + 1$.

Tweakable Blockcipher. A tweakable blockcipher (TBC) is a set of permutations indexed by a key and a public input called tweak. Let $\mathcal{K}$ be a key space, $\mathcal{TW}$ a tweak space, and b an input/output-block size. Through this paper, for a non-empty set $\mathcal{I}$ and an integer $t \geq 1$, $\mathcal{TW} := \mathcal{I} \times \{0,1\}^t$, a TBC is denoted by $\widetilde{E} : \mathcal{K} \times \mathcal{TW} \times \{0,1\}^b \to \{0,1\}^b$, and for $K \in \mathcal{K}$ and $(i, tw) \in \mathcal{TW}$, $\widetilde{E}(K, (i, tw), \cdot)$ is written as $\widetilde{E}_K^i(tw, \cdot)$.

In this paper, a security proof is given in the information theoretic model where the underlying keyed TBC is replaced with a tweakable random permutation (TRP). A tweakable permutation (TP) $\widetilde{P} : \mathcal{TW} \times \{0,1\}^b \to \{0,1\}^b$ is the set of b-bit permutations indexed by a tweak in $\mathcal{TW}$. Let $\widetilde{\mathsf{Perm}}(\mathcal{TW}, \{0,1\}^b)$ be the set of all TPs: $\mathcal{TW} \times \{0,1\}^b \to \{0,1\}^b$. Then a TRP is defined as $\widetilde{P} \xleftarrow{\$} \widetilde{\mathsf{Perm}}(\mathcal{TW}, \{0,1\}^b)$. The security goal of the underlying keyed TBC is tweakable pseudo-random-permutation (TPRP) security. TPRP-security is defined in terms of indistinguishability between a keyed TBC and a TRP. An adversary $\mathbf{A}$ has access to either the keyed TBC or a TRP, and returns a decision bit $y \in \{0,1\}$ after its interaction. An output of $\mathbf{A}$ with access to $\mathcal{O}$ is denoted by $\mathbf{A}^{\mathcal{O}}$. The TPRP-security advantage function of $\mathbf{A}$ is defined as

$$\mathbf{Adv}_{\widetilde{E}}^{\mathsf{tprp}}(\mathbf{A}) := \Pr\left[K \xleftarrow{\$} \mathcal{K}; \mathbf{A}^{\widetilde{E}_K} = 1\right] - \Pr\left[\widetilde{P} \xleftarrow{\$} \widetilde{\mathsf{Perm}}(\mathcal{TW}, \{0,1\}^b); \mathbf{A}^{\widetilde{P}} = 1\right],$$

where the probabilities are taken over $K, \widetilde{P}$ and $\mathbf{A}$. Note that using a keyed TBC $\widetilde{E}_K$ in a MAC, the TPRP-security advantage function of $\widetilde{E}$ is introduced in addition to the security bound of the MAC in the TRP model.

PRF-Security of MAC Using TRP. Through this paper, an adversary $\mathbf{A}$ is a computationally unbounded algorithm. Its complexity is solely measured by the number of queries made to its oracles. Let $F[\widetilde{P}]$ be a MAC function with τ-bit outputs using a TP $\widetilde{P} \in \widetilde{\mathsf{Perm}}(\mathcal{TW}, \{0,1\}^b)$, where τ is a positive integer.

The pseudo-random-function (PRF) security of $F[\widetilde{P}]$ is defined in terms of indistinguishability between the real and ideal worlds. In the real world, $\mathbf{A}$ has access to $F[\widetilde{P}]$, where $\widetilde{P} \xleftarrow{\$} \widetilde{\mathsf{Perm}}(\mathcal{TW}, \{0,1\}^b)$. In the ideal world, it has access to a random function $\mathcal{R}$, where $\mathsf{Func}(\{0,1\}^\tau)$ is the set of all functions from $\{0,1\}^*$ to $\{0,1\}^\tau$, and a random function is defined as $\mathcal{R} \xleftarrow{\$} \mathsf{Func}(\{0,1\}^\tau)$. After the interaction, $\mathbf{A}$ outputs a decision bit $y \in \{0,1\}$. The PRF-security advantage function of $\mathbf{A}$ is defined as $\mathbf{Adv}_{F[\widetilde{P}]}^{\mathsf{prf}}(\mathbf{A}) :=$

$$\Pr\left[\widetilde{P} \xleftarrow{\$} \widetilde{\mathsf{Perm}}(\mathcal{TW}, \{0,1\}^b); \mathbf{A}^{F[\widetilde{P}]} = 1\right] - \Pr\left[\mathcal{R} \xleftarrow{\$} \mathsf{Func}(\{0,1\}^\tau); \mathbf{A}^{\mathcal{R}} = 1\right],$$

where the probabilities are taken over $\widetilde{P}, \mathcal{R}$ and $\mathbf{A}$.

3   PMAC3: Specification and Security Bound

PMAC3 is a single key TBC-based mode of operation. It is designed to be parallelizable and a secure PRF up to $O(2^{b/2 + \min\{2t, b\}/2})$ queries, that is, full b-bit security as long as $b/2 \leq t$.

Parameters. Regarding the underlying TBC $\widetilde{E} : \mathcal{K} \times \mathcal{TW} \times \{0,1\}^b \to \{0,1\}^b$, the first tweak space is defined as $\mathcal{I} := \{0,1,2\}$, thus $\mathcal{TW} := \{0,1,2\} \times \{0,1\}^t$. Let the counter size c be an integer with $0 < c \leq t$, and the tag size τ an integer with $0 < \tau \leq b$. Let $r := t - c$ be the size of message blocks that are input to the second tweak spaces.

High-Level Structure. Firstly, a one-zero padding $\mathsf{ozp} : \{0,1\}^* \to (\{0,1\}^{b+r})^*$ is applied to an input message $M \in \{0,1\}^*$, where $\mathsf{ozp}(M) = M\|1\|0^z$ where $z = (b+r) - (|M| \bmod (b+r)) - 1$. Then, the hash function $\mathsf{PHASH3} : (\{0,1\}^{b+r})^* \to \{0,1\}^{b+2t}$ is performed. Finally, the finalization function: $\{0,1\}^{b+2t} \to \{0,1\}^\tau$ is performed. Regarding the underlying TBC having a key $K \in \mathcal{K}$, $\widetilde{E}_K$, the TBC with the first tweak 0, $\widetilde{E}_K^0$ is used in the hash function, and the TBCs with the first tweak 1 and with the first tweak 2, $\widetilde{E}_K^1$ and $\widetilde{E}_K^2$ are used in the finalization function.

Design Rationale. In PHASH3, in order to avoid a collision between inputs at distinct positions, a counter-based construction is employed: for an i-th message block M_i, the c-bit counter $\mathsf{str}_c(i)$ is input to the (second) tweak space of the TBC $\widetilde{E}_K^0$. If the counter size is less than the tweak size, i.e., $c < t$, the remaining r-bit tweak space is used to take a message block R_i. Hence, M_i consists of L_i (b bits) and R_i (r bits), and the i-th TBC output is defined as $C_i = \widetilde{E}_K^0(\mathsf{str}_c(i)\|R_i, L_i)$. After processing message blocks $M_1, \ldots, M_m$, m b-bit TBC outputs $C_1, \ldots, C_m$ are defined.

In order to avoid a birthday attack with $O(2^{b/2})$ queries, the PMAC_Plus's technique [20] is used, thus a $2b$-bit value (A, B) is defined from the m b-bit TBC outputs: the first b-bit value A is defined by XORing these outputs, $A = \bigoplus_{i=1}^m C_i$, and the remaining b-bit value B is defined by performing XOR operations and multiplications by 2 over $GF(2^b)^*$, $B = \bigoplus_{i=1}^m 2^{m-i+1} \cdot C_i$. Then, in order to achieve $O(2^{b/2+\min\{2t,b\}/2})$ security, PHASH3 returns a $2t + b$-bit hash value (A_1, A_2, B) such that all bits of A are used if $b/2 \leq t$: $A_1 = \mathsf{msb}_t(A) \oplus \bigoplus_{i=1}^m (0^c\|R_i)$; $A_2 = \mathsf{lsb}_t(A) \oplus \bigoplus_{i=1}^m (0^c\|R_i)$. Note that $A_1 = A_2$ if $b \leq t$. The checksum, $\bigoplus_{i=1}^m (0^c\|R_i)$ is applied to A_1 and A_2, in order to avoid an attack using a collision in TBC outputs (the collision is found with $O(2^{b/2})$ TBC calls by the birthday analysis). This technique was introduced in ZMAC [8]. If a collision occurs in the i-th TBC outputs C_i and other input blocks are the same, then the output collision offers a collision in the (A, B) values. If the checksum is absent, then a hash collision occurs and offers a distinguishing attack. On the other hand, using the checksum, since the i-th output collision implies that the corresponding R_i values are distinct, the corresponding pairs of (A_1, A_2) become distinct, thereby the output collision can be avoided (if R_i values are the same, the i-th outputs are defined by the same permutation, thus no output collision occurs).

Finally, in the finalization phase, in order to process all $2t + b$ bits of (A_1, A_2, B), a TBC is performed twice, where the input pair at the first resp.

second TBC call is (A_1, B) resp. (A_2, B). Then, the XOR of the TBC outputs becomes the tag: $T = \widetilde{E}_K^1(A_1, B) \oplus \widetilde{E}_K^2(A_2, B)$.

Algorithm 1. PMAC3

▶ Main Procedure PMAC3$[\widetilde{E}_K](M)$

1: $M^* \leftarrow \mathsf{ozp}(M);\ (A_1, A_2, B) \leftarrow \mathsf{PHASH3}[\widetilde{E}_K](M^*)$
2: $T_1 \leftarrow \widetilde{E}_K^1(A_1, B);\ T_2 \leftarrow \widetilde{E}_K^2(A_2, B);\ T \leftarrow T_1 \oplus T_2;\ \textbf{return } \mathsf{msb}_\tau(T)$

▶ Subroutine PHASH3$[\widetilde{E}_K](M^*)$

1: $M_1, \ldots, M_m \xleftarrow{b+r} M^*;\ A \leftarrow 0^b;\ B \leftarrow 0^b$
2: **for** $i = 1, \ldots, m$ **do**
3: $\quad (L_i, R_i) \xleftarrow{b,r} (M_i);\ C_i \leftarrow \widetilde{E}_K^0(\mathsf{str}_c(i)\|R_i, L_i);\ A \leftarrow A \oplus C_i;\ B \leftarrow 2 \cdot (B \oplus C_i)$
4: **end for**
5: $A_1 \leftarrow \mathsf{msb}_t(A) \oplus \left(\bigoplus_{i=1}^m (0^c\|R_i)\right);\ A_2 \leftarrow \mathsf{lsb}_t(A) \oplus \left(\bigoplus_{i=1}^m (0^c\|R_i)\right);\ \textbf{return}$
  (A_1, A_2, B)

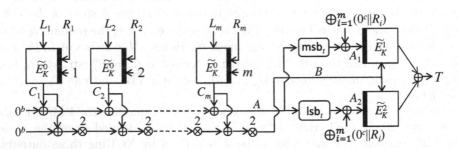

Fig. 1. PMAC3. $M_1, \ldots, M_m \xleftarrow{b+r} \mathsf{ozp}(M).$ $(L_i, R_i) \xleftarrow{b,r} (M_i).$ $\otimes$ is a multiplication over $GF(2^b)$.

Specification. The specification of PMAC3 is given in Algorithm 1 and Fig. 1.

Security Bound. The PRF-security bound of PMAC3 is given below.

Theorem 1. *Assume that $b \geq 2$ and $m \leq 2^b - 2$. Let $\mathbf{A}$ be an adversary making q queries. Then we have* $\mathbf{Adv}_{\mathsf{PMAC3}[\widetilde{P}]}^{\mathsf{prf}}(\mathbf{A}) \leq \frac{2q^2}{2^{b+\min\{2t,b\}}} + \frac{7q^3}{2^{2b+\min\{2t,b\}}}.$

4 Proof of Theorem 1

Without loss of generality, we assume that an adversary $\mathbf{A}$ is deterministic and makes no repeated query. This proof uses the following notations. For each $\alpha \in [q]$, values and variables defined at the α-th query are denoted by

---

Initialization

1: $\widetilde{P}^0 \xleftarrow{\$} \widetilde{\mathsf{Perm}}(\{0,1\}^t, \{0,1\}^b)$

2: $\forall V \in \{0,1\}^t, W \in \{0,1\}^b : \widetilde{P}^1(V, W) \leftarrow \perp, \widetilde{P}^2(V, W) \leftarrow \perp$

Main Game: Upon the α-th query M^α **do**

1: $(A_1^\alpha, A_2^\alpha, B^\alpha) \leftarrow \mathsf{PHASH3}[\widetilde{P}](M^\alpha)$

2: **if** $\left(\widetilde{P}^1(A_1^\alpha, B^\alpha) \neq\perp \text{ and } \widetilde{P}^2(A_2^\alpha, B^\alpha) \neq\perp \right)$ **then goto Case A**

3: **if** $\left(\widetilde{P}^1(A_1^\alpha, B^\alpha) \neq\perp \text{ and } \widetilde{P}^2(A_2^\alpha, B^\alpha) =\perp \right)$ **or** $\left(\widetilde{P}^1(A_1^\alpha, B^\alpha) =\perp \text{ and } \widetilde{P}^2(A_2^\alpha, B^\alpha) \neq\perp \right)$ **then goto Case B**

4: **if** $\left(\widetilde{P}^1(A_1^\alpha, B^\alpha) =\perp \text{ and } \widetilde{P}^2(A_2^\alpha, B^\alpha) =\perp \right)$ **then goto Case C**

5: **return** T^α

Fig. 2. Main game.

using the superscript character of α such as $A_1^\alpha, A_2^\alpha, B^\alpha$, etc, and the message length m at the α-th query is denoted by m_α. Let $\mathcal{M} := \{M^\alpha | \alpha \in [q]\}$ be the set of all queries. For distinct messages $M^\alpha, M^\beta \in \mathcal{M}$, let $I(M^\alpha, M^\beta) = \{I \in [\max\{m_\alpha, m_\beta\}] | M_i^\alpha \neq M_i^\beta\}$ be the set of indexes such that the corresponding message blocks are distinct, where if $m_\alpha < m_\beta$ then $M_i^\alpha := \lambda$ for $i = m_\alpha + 1, \ldots, m_\beta$ (and if $m_\alpha > m_\beta$ then $M_i^\beta := \lambda$ for $i = m_\beta + 1, \ldots, m_\alpha$). Let $\eta_i^m := 2^{m-i+1}$. For two variables C_i^α, C_j^β corresponding with distinct messages $M^\alpha, M^\beta \in \mathcal{M}$, we use the following three terms, same, distinct and independent, with respect to the relation between these variables.

- The i-th variable C_i^α and the j-th variable C_j^β are the same, denoted by $C_i^\alpha \stackrel{same}{=} C_j^\beta$ if the corresponding tweaks and input-blocks are the same, i.e., $(\mathsf{str}_c(i) \| R_i^\alpha, L_i^\alpha) = (\mathsf{str}_c(j) \| R_j^\alpha, L_j^\alpha)$. In this case, $C_i^\alpha = C_j^\beta = \widetilde{P}^0(\mathsf{str}_c(i) \| R_i^\alpha, L_i^\alpha)$.

- The i-th variable C_i^α and the j-th variable C_j^β are distinct, denoted by $C_i^\alpha \stackrel{dist}{\neq} C_j^\beta$, if the corresponding tweaks are the same and the input-blocks are distinct, i.e., $(\mathsf{str}_c(i) \| R_i^\alpha) = (\mathsf{str}_c(j) \| R_j^\beta)$ and $L_i^\alpha \neq L_j^\beta$. In this case, these variables are defined by the same RP $\widetilde{P}^0(\mathsf{str}_c(i) \| R_i^\alpha, \cdot)$ with distinct input-blocks, thus become distinct.

- The i-th variable C_i^α and the j-th variable C_j^β are independent, denoted by $C_i^\alpha \stackrel{ind}{\neq} C_j^\beta$, if the corresponding tweaks are distinct. In this case, these variables are defined by independent RPs, thus chosen independently.

4.1 Proof Strategy and Security Bound

This proof largely depends on the so-called game-playing technique [2]. In this proof, a TRP with tweak 0 ($\widetilde{P}^0$) is defined before starting the game, and TRPs

Case A:
1: if ¬bad then $\mathsf{bad}_A \leftarrow \mathsf{true}$
2: $T^\alpha \xleftarrow{\$} \{0,1\}^n$; $\boxed{T_1^\alpha \leftarrow \widetilde{P}^1(A_1^\alpha, B^\alpha); \ T_2^\alpha \leftarrow \widetilde{P}^2(A_2^\alpha, B^\alpha); \ T^\alpha \leftarrow T_1^\alpha \oplus T_2^\alpha}$

Case B: In the following procedure, $j_1 \neq j_2 \in [2]$, $\widetilde{P}^{j_1}(A_{j_1}^\alpha, B^\alpha) \neq \perp$ and $\widetilde{P}^{j_2}(A_{j_2}^\alpha, B^\alpha) = \perp$.

1: $T_{j_2}^\alpha \xleftarrow{\$} \{0,1\}^b$
2: if $T_{j_2}^\alpha \in \widetilde{P}^{j_2}(A_{j_2}^\alpha, *)$ then
3:    if ¬bad then $\mathsf{bad}_B \leftarrow \mathsf{true}$
4:    $\boxed{T_{j_2}^\alpha \xleftarrow{\$} \{0,1\}^b \backslash \widetilde{P}^{j_2}(A_{j_2}^\alpha, *)}$
5: end if
6: $\widetilde{P}^{j_2}(A_{j_2}^\alpha, B^\alpha) \leftarrow T_{j_2}^\alpha$; $T_{j_1}^\alpha \leftarrow \widetilde{P}^{j_1}(A_{j_1}^\alpha, B^\alpha)$; $T^\alpha \leftarrow T_1^\alpha \oplus T_2^\alpha$

Case C:
1: $T_1^\alpha \xleftarrow{\$} \{0,1\}^b$; $T_2^\alpha \xleftarrow{\$} \{0,1\}^b \backslash \widetilde{P}^2(A_2^\alpha, *)$
2: if $T_1^\alpha \in \widetilde{P}^1(A_1^\alpha, *)$ then
3:    $T_1^\alpha \xleftarrow{\$} \{0,1\}^b \backslash \widetilde{P}^1(A_1^\alpha, *)$; $T_2^\alpha \xleftarrow{\$} \{0,1\}^b$
4:    if $T_2^\alpha \in \widetilde{P}^2(A_2^\alpha, *)$ then
5:       if ¬bad then $\mathsf{bad}_C \leftarrow \mathsf{true}$
6:       $\boxed{T_2^\alpha \xleftarrow{\$} \{0,1\}^b \backslash \widetilde{P}^2(A_2^\alpha, *)}$
7:    end if
8: end if
9: $\widetilde{P}^1(A_1^\alpha, B^\alpha) \leftarrow T_1^\alpha$; $\widetilde{P}^2(A_2^\alpha, B^\alpha) \leftarrow T_2^\alpha$; $T^\alpha \leftarrow T_1^\alpha \oplus T_2^\alpha$

Fig. 3. Cases A, B and C. The boxed statements are removed in the ideal world.

with tweak 1 or 2 ($\widetilde{P}^1$ and $\widetilde{P}^2$) are realized by lazy sampling. Before starting the main game, for each of $i \in [2]$, all responses of $\widetilde{P}^i$ are not defined, that is, $\forall V \in \{0,1\}^t, W \in \{0,1\}^b : \widetilde{P}^i(V, W) = \perp$. When $\widetilde{P}^i(V, W)$ becomes necessary, it is defined as $\widetilde{P}^i(V, W) \xleftarrow{\$} \{0,1\}^b \backslash \widetilde{P}^i(V, *)$ if $\widetilde{P}^i(V, W) = \perp$; it is not updated otherwise. For $i = 1, 2$ and $V \in \{0,1\}^t$, let $\widetilde{P}^i(V, *) := \{\widetilde{P}^i(V, W) | W \in \{0,1\}^b \wedge \widetilde{P}^i(V, W) \neq \perp\}$ be the set of outputs of $\widetilde{P}^i$ with the tweak V.

The initialization and the main game are defined in Fig. 2. The initialization is performed before starting the main game. In the main game, three cases are considered, and these procedures are defined in Fig. 3. Let $\mathsf{bad} := \mathsf{bad}_A \vee \mathsf{bad}_B \vee \mathsf{bad}_C$.

- Case A is performed when inputs to both $\widetilde{P}^1$ and $\widetilde{P}^2$ are not new, i.e., $\exists \beta, \gamma \in [\alpha - 1]$ s.t. $(A_1^\alpha, B^\alpha) = (A_1^\beta, B^\beta)$ and $(A_2^\alpha, B^\alpha) = (A_2^\gamma, B^\gamma)$. When including the boxed statements, TRPs are simulated, and when removing the boxed statements, T^α is chosen uniformly at random from $\{0,1\}^b$.
- Case B is performed when an input to either $\widetilde{P}^1$ or $\widetilde{P}^2$ is not new, i.e., either

- $\exists \beta \in [\alpha - 1]$ s.t. $(A_1^\alpha, B^\alpha) = (A_1^\beta, B^\beta) \land \forall \gamma \in [\alpha - 1] \backslash \{\beta\} : (A_2^\alpha, B^\alpha) \neq (A_2^\gamma, B^\gamma)$, or
- $\exists \gamma \in [\alpha - 1]$ s.t. $(A_2^\alpha, B^\alpha) \neq (A_2^\beta, B^\beta) \land \forall \beta \in [\alpha - 1] \backslash \{\gamma\} : (A_1^\alpha, B^\alpha) = (A_1^\gamma, B^\gamma)$.

When including the boxed statement, TRPs are simulated: an output of $\widetilde{P}^{j_2}$, $T_{j_2}^\alpha$ is chosen uniformly at random from $\{0,1\}^b \backslash \widetilde{P}^{j_2}(A_{j_2}^\alpha, *)$. When removing the boxed statement, $T_{j_2}^\alpha$ is chosen uniformly at random from $\{0,1\}^b$, thereby T^α is chosen uniformly at random from $\{0,1\}^b$.

- Case C is performed when inputs to both $\widetilde{P}^1$ and $\widetilde{P}^2$ are new, i.e.,
  - $\forall \beta, \gamma \in [\alpha - 1] : (A_1^\alpha, B^\alpha) \neq (A_1^\beta, B^\beta) \land (A_2^\alpha, B^\alpha) \neq (A_2^\gamma, B^\gamma)$.

When including the boxed statement, the TRPs are simulated: for each $i \in [2]$, T_i^α is chosen uniformly at random from $\{0,1\}^b \backslash \widetilde{P}^i(A_i^\alpha, *)$. When removing the boxed statement, either T_1^α or T_2^α is chosen uniformly at random from $\{0,1\}^b$, thereby T^α is chosen uniformly at random from $\{0,1\}^b$.

Thus, the procedures with the boxed statements realize the real world, and the procedure without the boxed statements realize the ideal world.

By the fundamental lemma of game-playing [2], we have $\mathbf{Adv}^{\mathrm{prf}}_{F[\widetilde{P}]}(A) \leq$ $\Pr[\mathsf{bad}] \leq \Pr[\mathsf{bad_A}] + \Pr[\mathsf{bad_B}] + \Pr[\mathsf{bad_C}]$. In Subsect. 4.2, $\Pr[\mathsf{bad_A}]$ is upper-bounded, in Subsect. 4.3, $\Pr[\mathsf{bad_B}]$ is upper-bounded, and in Subsect. 4.4, $\Pr[\mathsf{bad_C}]$ is upper-bounded. Summing these upper-bounds (1) (7) (8) gives the one in Theorem 1.

4.2 Upper-Bounding $\Pr[\mathsf{bad_A}]$

$\mathsf{bad_A}$ occurs if and only if

Case A1: $\exists M^\alpha, M^\beta \in \mathcal{M}$ s.t. $A_1^\alpha = A_1^\beta \land A_2^\alpha = A_2^\beta \land B^\alpha = B^\beta$, or

Case A2: $\exists M^\alpha, M^\beta, M^\gamma \in \mathcal{M}$ s.t. $A_1^\alpha = A_1^\beta \land B^\alpha = B^\beta \land A_2^\alpha = A_2^\gamma \land B^\alpha = B^\gamma$,

where $\alpha, \beta, \gamma \in [q]$ are distinct. The following lemmas give the upper-bounds of the probabilities that Case A1 occurs and that Case A2 occurs.

Lemma 1 (Case A1). *For any distinct messages* $M^\alpha, M^\beta \in \mathcal{M}$ *where* $\alpha, \beta \in [q]$, $\Pr\left[A_1^\alpha = A_1^\beta \land A_2^\alpha = A_2^\beta \land B^\alpha = B^\beta\right] \leq \frac{4}{2^{b+\min\{2t,b\}}}$.

Lemma 2 (Case A2). *For any distinct messages* $M^\alpha, M^\beta, M^\gamma \in \mathcal{M}$ *where* $\alpha, \beta, \gamma \in [q]$, $\Pr[A_1^\alpha = A_1^\beta \land B^\alpha = B^\beta \land A_2^\alpha = A_2^\gamma \land B^\alpha = B^\gamma] \leq \frac{16}{2^{2b+\min\{2t,b\}}}$.

These upper-bounds give $\Pr[\mathsf{bad_A}] \leq$

$$\binom{q}{2} \cdot \frac{4}{2^{b+\min\{2t,b\}}} + \binom{q}{3} \cdot \frac{16}{2^{2b+\min\{2t,b\}}} \leq \frac{2q^2}{2^{b+\min\{2t,b\}}} + \frac{8/3 \cdot q^3}{2^{2b+\min\{2t,b\}}}. \quad (1)$$

Proof of Lemma 1. Let $M^\alpha, M^\beta \in \mathcal{M}$ be distinct messages and $m_\alpha \geq m_\beta$. In this proof, the probability $p_{A1} := \Pr[A_1^\alpha = A_1^\beta \land A_2^\alpha = A_2^\beta \land B^\alpha = B^\beta]$ is upper-bounded, which is the probability that the hash collision $\mathsf{PHASH3}[\widetilde{P}](M^\alpha) =$

PHASH3$[\widetilde{P}](M^\beta)$ occurs. The collisions $A_1^\alpha = A_1^\beta, A_2^\alpha = A_2^\beta, B^\alpha = B^\beta$ are of the forms

$$
\left.\begin{array}{c}
\displaystyle\bigoplus_{i=1}^{m_\alpha}\left(\mathsf{msb}_t\left(C_i^\alpha\right) \oplus \left(0^c\|R_i^\alpha\right)\right) = \displaystyle\bigoplus_{i=1}^{m_\beta}\left(\mathsf{msb}_t\left(C_i^\beta\right) \oplus \left(0^c\|R_i^\beta\right)\right), \\[3mm]
\displaystyle\bigoplus_{i=1}^{m_\alpha}\left(\mathsf{lsb}_t\left(C_i^\alpha\right) \oplus \left(0^c\|R_i^\alpha\right)\right) = \displaystyle\bigoplus_{i=1}^{m_\beta}\left(\mathsf{lsb}_t\left(C_i^\beta\right) \oplus \left(0^c\|R_i^\beta\right)\right), \\[3mm]
\displaystyle\bigoplus_{i=1}^{m_\alpha}\eta_i^{m_\alpha}\cdot C_i^\alpha = \displaystyle\bigoplus_{i=1}^{m_\beta}\eta_i^{m_\beta}\cdot C_i^\beta.
\end{array}\right\} \tag{2}
$$

Let $C_{j_1}^\alpha, C_{j_2}^\alpha$ be two variables that appear in (2). Using these variables, for some $v \in \{0,1\}$ and $w_1, w_2 \in GF(2^b)^*\backslash\{1\}$, the equations in (2) are written as

$$
\mathsf{msb}_t\left(v\cdot C_{j_1}^\alpha \oplus C_{j_2}^\alpha\right) = \delta_{A,1}^*, \ \mathsf{lsb}_t\left(v\cdot C_{j_1}^\alpha \oplus C_{j_2}^\alpha\right) = \delta_{A,2}^*, \ w_1\cdot C_{j_1}^\alpha \oplus w_2\cdot C_{j_2}^\alpha = \delta_B^*, \tag{3}
$$

respectively, where $\delta_{A,1}^* := A_1^\alpha \oplus A_1^\beta \oplus \mathsf{msb}_t(v \cdot C_{j_1}^\alpha \oplus C_{j_2}^\alpha)$, $\delta_{A,2}^* := A_2^\alpha \oplus A_2^\beta \oplus \mathsf{lsb}_t(v \cdot C_{j_1}^\alpha \oplus C_{j_2}^\alpha)$, and $\delta_B^* := B^\alpha \oplus B^\beta \oplus (w_1 \cdot C_{j_1}^\alpha \oplus w_2 \cdot C_{j_2}^\alpha)$.

Assume that the following conditions are satisfied:

- **(A1-1)** Fixing the variables in (2) except for $(C_{j_1}^\alpha, C_{j_2}^\alpha)$, $(\delta_{A,1}^*, \delta_{A,2}^*, \delta_B^*)$ in (3) is defined;
- **(A1-2)** $C_{j_1}^\alpha \overset{\mathrm{ind}}{\neq} C_{j_2}^\alpha$;
- **(A1-3)** Fixing the variables except for $(C_{j_1}^\alpha, C_{j_2}^\alpha)$, the system (3) without msb_t and lsb_t, i.e., the following one has a unique solution for $(C_{j_1}^\alpha, C_{j_2}^\alpha)$:
$v\cdot C_{j_1}^\alpha \oplus C_{j_2}^\alpha = \delta_A^*, \ w_1\cdot C_{j_1}^\alpha \oplus w_2\cdot C_{j_2}^\alpha = \delta_B^*$, where $\delta_A^* = A^\alpha \oplus A^\beta \oplus (v\cdot C_{j_1}^\alpha \oplus C_{j_2}^\alpha)$.

By the condition (A1-1), we have

$$
p_{A1} \leq \max_{\delta_{A,1}, \delta_{A,2}, \delta_B} \Pr\left[\begin{array}{c} \mathsf{msb}_t\left(v \cdot C_{j_1}^\alpha \oplus C_{j_2}^\alpha\right) = \delta_{A,1}, \ \mathsf{lsb}_t\left(v \cdot C_{j_1}^\alpha \oplus C_{j_2}^\alpha\right) = \delta_{A,2}, \\[2mm] w_1 \cdot C_{j_1}^\alpha \oplus w_2 \cdot C_{j_2}^\alpha = \delta_B \end{array}\right]
$$

$$
\leq 2^{b-\min\{2t,b\}} \cdot \underbrace{\max_{\delta_A, \delta_B} \Pr\left[v \cdot C_{j_1}^\alpha \oplus C_{j_2}^\alpha = \delta_A, \ w_1 \cdot C_{j_1}^\alpha \oplus w_2 \cdot C_{j_2}^\alpha = \delta_B\right]}_{S_{A1}}.
$$

By the conditions (A1-2), (A1-3), the system S_{A1} offers a unique solution for $(C_{j_1}^\alpha, C_{j_2}^\alpha)$. As these variables are chosen uniformly at random from $\{0,1\}^b\backslash\{C_{j_1}^\beta\}$ and $\{0,1\}^b\backslash\{C_{j_2}^\beta\}$, respectively, we have $p_{A1} \leq 2^{b-\min\{2t,b\}} \cdot \frac{1}{(2^b-1)^2} \leq \frac{4}{2^{b+\min\{2t,b\}}}$.

Hence, the remaining work is to show that the system (3) with the conditions (A1-1), (A1-2) and (A1-3) can be constructed. To show this, messages M^α, M^β are categorized into the following three types. We show that for the type-1, the system (3) cannot be constructed and $p_{A1} = 0$, and for each of the type-2 and type-3, the system can be constructed.

- **Type-1** $(m_\alpha = m_\beta \wedge |I(M^\alpha, M^\beta)| = 1)$ Let $I(M^\alpha, M^\beta) = \{I\}$, i.e., $(L_i^\alpha, R_i^\alpha) \neq (L_i^\beta, R_i^\beta)$. If the output collision, $C_i^\alpha = C_i^\beta$ occurs, then the corresponding tweaks are distinct, i.e., $(\mathsf{str}_c(i)\|R_i^\alpha) \neq (\mathsf{str}_c(i)\|R_i^\beta)$. Hence, $A_1^\alpha \oplus A_1^\beta = (0^c\|R_i^\alpha) \oplus (0^c\|R_i^\beta) \neq 0^b$, thus $p_{A1} = 0$. If $C_i^\alpha \neq C_i^\beta$, then $B^\alpha \oplus B^\beta = \eta_i^{m_\alpha} \cdot (C_i^\beta \oplus C_i^\alpha) \neq 0^b$, thus $p_{A1} = 0$.

- **Type-2** $(m_\alpha = m_\beta \wedge |I(M^\alpha, M^\beta)| \geq 2)$ Let $i_1, i_2 \in I(M^\alpha, M^\beta)$ with $i_1 \neq i_2$. In this case, $C_{i_1}^\alpha \overset{\text{ind}}{\neq} C_{i_2}^\alpha$, thus (A1-2) is satisfied. Using the variables, the system (2) is written as
  - $\mathsf{msb}_t(C_{i_1}^\alpha \oplus C_{i_2}^\alpha) = \delta_{A,1}^*$, $\mathsf{lsb}_t(C_{i_1}^\alpha \oplus C_{i_2}^\alpha) = \delta_{A,2}^*$, $\eta_{i_1}^{m_\alpha} \cdot C_{i_1}^\alpha \oplus \eta_{i_2}^{m_\alpha} \cdot C_{i_2}^\alpha = \delta_B^*$, where $\delta_{A,1}^*, \delta_{A,2}^*, \delta_B^*$ are defined as (3). Thus (A1-1) is satisfied. Fixing the variables except for $(C_{i_1}^\alpha, C_{i_2}^\alpha)$, the above system without msb_t and lsb_t offers a unique solution for $(C_{i_1}^\alpha, C_{i_2}^\alpha)$, and thus (A1-3) is satisfied. Hence, system (3) with (A1-1), (A1-2), (A1-3) can be constructed.

- **Type-3** $(m_\alpha > m_\beta)$ In this case, $m_\alpha \in I(M^\alpha, M^\beta)$ and $m_\alpha \neq 1$, thus $C_1^\alpha \overset{\text{ind}}{\neq} C_{m_\alpha}^\alpha$ and (A1-2) is satisfied. Using these variables, the system (2) is written as
  - $\mathsf{msb}_t(v \cdot C_1^\alpha \oplus C_{m_\alpha}^\alpha) = \delta_{A,1}^*$, $\mathsf{lsb}_t(v \cdot C_1^\alpha \oplus C_{m_\alpha}^\alpha) = \delta_{A,2}^*$, $w_1 \cdot C_1^\alpha \oplus \eta_{m_\alpha}^{m_\alpha} \cdot C_{m_\alpha}^\alpha = \delta_B^*$, where $\delta_{A,1}^*, \delta_{A,2}^*, \delta_B^*$ are defined as (3), and $(v, w_1) = (0, \eta_{m_\alpha}^{m_\alpha} \oplus \eta_1^{m_\beta})$ if $C_1^\alpha \overset{\text{same}}{=} C_1^\beta$; $(v, w_1) = (1, \eta_1^{m_\alpha})$ otherwise. Thus, (A1-1) is satisfied. Fixing the variables except for $(C_1^\alpha, C_{m_\alpha}^\alpha)$, the above system without msb_t and lsb_t offers a unique solution for $(C_1^\alpha, C_{m_\alpha}^\alpha)$, thus (A1-3) is satisfied. Hence, the system (3) with (A1-1), (A1-2), (A1-3) can be constructed.

$\square$

Proof of Lemma 2. Let $M^\alpha, M^\beta, M^\gamma \in \mathcal{M}$ be three distinct messages. In this proof, the probability $p_{A2} := \Pr[A_1^\alpha = A_1^\beta \wedge B^\alpha = B^\beta \wedge A_2^\alpha = A_2^\gamma \wedge B^\alpha = B^\gamma]$ is upper-bounded, where $A_1^\alpha = A_1^\beta$ and $B^\alpha = B^\beta$ are of the forms:

$$\left.\begin{array}{l} \displaystyle\bigoplus_{i=1}^{m_\alpha}\left(\mathsf{msb}_t\left(C_i^\alpha\right) \oplus \left(0^c\|R_i^\alpha\right)\right) = \bigoplus_{i=1}^{m_\beta}\left(\mathsf{msb}_t\left(C_i^\beta\right) \oplus \left(0^c\|R_i^\beta\right)\right) \\[4mm] \displaystyle\bigoplus_{i=1}^{m_\alpha}\eta_i^{m_\alpha} \cdot C_i^\alpha = \bigoplus_{i=1}^{m_\beta}\eta_i^{m_\beta} \cdot C_i^\beta, \end{array}\right\} \quad (4)$$

and $A_2^\alpha = A_2^\gamma$ and $B^\alpha = B^\gamma$ are of the forms:

$$\left.\begin{array}{l} \displaystyle\bigoplus_{i=1}^{m_\alpha}\left(\mathsf{lsb}_t\left(C_i^\alpha\right) \oplus \left(0^c\|R_i^\alpha\right)\right) = \bigoplus_{i=1}^{m_\gamma}\left(\mathsf{lsb}_t\left(C_i^\gamma\right) \oplus \left(0^c\|R_i^\gamma\right)\right) \\[4mm] \displaystyle\bigoplus_{i=1}^{m_\alpha}\eta_i^{m_\alpha} \cdot C_i^\alpha = \bigoplus_{i=1}^{m_\gamma}\eta_i^{m_\gamma} \cdot C_i^\gamma. \end{array}\right\} \quad (5)$$

Let $C_{j_1}^{x_1}, C_{j_2}^{x_2}, C_{j_3}^{x_3}, C_{j_4}^{x_4}$ be such that $x_1, x_2 \in \{\alpha, \beta\}$, $x_3, x_4 \in \{\alpha, \gamma\}$, $C_{j_1}^{x_1}, C_{j_2}^{x_2}$ appear in (4), and $C_{j_3}^{x_3}, C_{j_4}^{x_4}$ appear in (5). Using these variables, for some $v_2, v_4 \in$

$\{0,1\}$ and $w_1, w_2, w_3, w_4 \in GF(2^b)^* \backslash \{1\}$, (4), (5) are written as

$$\left.\begin{array}{ll}
\mathsf{msb}_t\left(C_{j_1}^{x_1} \oplus v_2 \cdot C_{j_2}^{x_2}\right) = \delta_{A,1}^*, & w_1 \cdot C_{j_1}^{x_1} \oplus w_2 \cdot C_{j_2}^{x_2} = \delta_{B,1}^*, \\
\mathsf{lsb}_t\left(C_{j_3}^{x_3} \oplus v_4 \cdot C_{j_4}^{x_4}\right) = \delta_{A,2}^*, & w_3 \cdot C_{j_3}^{x_3} \oplus w_4 \cdot C_{j_4}^{x_4} = \delta_{B,2}^*,
\end{array}\right\} \quad (6)$$

where $\delta_{A,1}^* := A_1^\alpha \oplus A_1^\beta \oplus \mathsf{msb}_t(C_{j_1}^{x_1} \oplus v_2 \cdot C_{j_2}^{x_2})$, $\delta_{B,1}^* := B^\alpha \oplus B^\beta \oplus (w_1 \cdot C_{j_1}^{x_1} \oplus w_2 \cdot C_{j_2}^{x_2})$, $\delta_{A,2}^* := A_2^\alpha \oplus A_2^\gamma \oplus \mathsf{lsb}_t(C_{j_3}^{x_3} \oplus v_4 \cdot C_{j_4}^{x_4})$, and $\delta_{B,2}^* := B^\alpha \oplus B^\gamma \oplus (w_3 \cdot C_{j_3}^{x_3} \oplus w_4 \cdot C_{j_4}^{x_4})$.

Assume that the following conditions are satisfied:

- **(A2-1)** Fixing the variables in (4) except for $(C_{j_1}^{x_1}, C_{j_2}^{x_2})$, $(\delta_{A,1}^*, \delta_{B,1}^*)$ in (6) are defined, and fixing the variables in (5) except for $(C_{j_3}^{x_3}, C_{j_4}^{x_4})$, $(\delta_{A,2}^*, \delta_{B,2}^*)$ in (6) are defined;
- **(A2-2)** At least three of $(C_{j_1}^{x_1}, C_{j_2}^{x_2}, C_{j_3}^{x_3}, C_{j_4}^{x_4})$ are distinct or independent;
- **(A2-3)** Fixing $(\delta_{A,1}^*, \delta_{B,1}^*)$, the top system in (6) without msb_t, i.e., the following one offers a unique solution for $(C_{j_1}^{x_1}, C_{j_2}^{x_2})$: $C_{j_1}^{x_1} \oplus v_2 \cdot C_{j_2}^{x_2} = \delta_{A,1}^{**}$ and $w_1 \cdot C_{j_1}^{x_1} \oplus w_2 \cdot C_{j_2}^{x_2} = \delta_{B,1}^*$, where $\delta_{A,1}^{**} := A^\alpha \oplus A^\beta \oplus (C_{j_1}^{x_1} \oplus v_2 \cdot C_{j_2}^{x_2})$;
- **(A2-4)** Fixing $\delta_{A,2}^*, \delta_{B,2}^*$, the bottom system in (6) without lsb_t, i.e., the following one offers a unique solution for $(C_{j_3}^{x_3}, C_{j_4}^{x_4})$: $C_{j_3}^{x_3} \oplus v_4 \cdot C_{j_4}^{x_4} = \delta_{A,2}^{**}$ and $w_3 \cdot C_{j_3}^{x_3} \oplus w_4 \cdot C_{j_4}^{x_4} = \delta_{B,2}^*$, where $\delta_{A,2}^{**} := A^\alpha \oplus A^\beta \oplus (C_{j_3}^{x_3} \oplus v_4 \cdot C_{j_4}^{x_4})$.

By the condition (A2-1), $p_{A2} \le$

$$\max_{\substack{\delta_{A,1}, \delta_{A,2}, \\ \delta_{B,1}, \delta_{B,2}}} \Pr \underbrace{\left[\begin{array}{l}
\mathsf{msb}_t\left(C_{j_1}^{x_1} \oplus v_2 \cdot C_{j_2}^{x_2}\right) = \delta_{A,1}, w_1 \cdot C_{j_1}^{x_1} \oplus w_2 \cdot C_{j_2}^{x_2} = \delta_{B,1} \\
\mathsf{lsb}_t\left(C_{j_3}^{x_3} \oplus v_4 \cdot C_{j_4}^{x_4}\right) = \delta_{A,2}, w_3 \cdot C_{j_3}^{x_3} \oplus w_4 \cdot C_{j_4}^{x_4} = \delta_{B,2}
\end{array}\right]}_{S_{A2,1}}.$$

By the condition (A2-2), the following two cases are considered.

- If three of $(C_{j_1}^{x_1}, C_{j_2}^{x_2}, C_{j_3}^{x_3}, C_{j_4}^{x_4})$ are distinct or independent (i.e., two of these variables are the same), then $p_{A2} \le 2^{b-\min\{2t,b\}} \cdot X_1$ where

$$X_1 = \max_{\substack{\delta_{A,1}', \delta_{A,2}', \\ \delta_{B,1}, \delta_{B,2}}} \Pr \underbrace{\left[\begin{array}{l}
C_{j_1}^{x_1} \oplus v_2 \cdot C_{j_2}^{x_2} = \delta_{A,1}', w_1 \cdot C_{j_1}^{x_1} \oplus w_2 \cdot C_{j_2}^{x_2} = \delta_{B,1} \\
C_{j_3}^{x_3} \oplus v_4 \cdot C_{j_4}^{x_4} = \delta_{A,2}', w_3 \cdot C_{j_3}^{x_3} \oplus w_4 \cdot C_{j_4}^{x_4} = \delta_{B,2}
\end{array}\right]}_{S_{A2,2}}.$$

By the conditions (A2-3), (A2-4), the top system in $S_{A2,2}$ offers a unique solution for $(C_{j_1}^{x_1}, C_{j_2}^{x_2})$, and the bottom one offers a unique solution for $(C_{j_3}^{x_3}, C_{j_4}^{x_4})$. These variables are chosen uniformly at random from at least $2^b - 2$ b-bit strings. We thus have $p_{A2} \le 2^{b-\min\{2t,b\}} \cdot \frac{1}{(2^b-2)^3} \le \frac{8}{2^{2b+\min\{2t,b\}}}$, assuming $2 \le b$.

- If all of $(C_{j_1}^{x_1}, C_{j_2}^{x_2}, C_{j_3}^{x_3}, C_{j_4}^{x_4})$ are distinct or independent, then $p_{A2} \le 2^{2(b-\min\{t,b\})} \cdot X_2$, where

$$X_2 = \max_{\substack{\delta_{A,1}', \delta_{A,2}', \\ \delta_{B,1}, \delta_{B,2}}} \Pr \underbrace{\left[\begin{array}{l}
C_{j_1}^{x_1} \oplus v_2 \cdot C_{j_2}^{x_2} = \delta_{A,1}', w_1 \cdot C_{j_1}^{x_1} \oplus w_2 \cdot C_{j_2}^{x_2} = \delta_{B,1} \\
C_{j_3}^{x_3} \oplus v_4 \cdot C_{j_4}^{x_4} = \delta_{A,2}', w_3 \cdot C_{j_3}^{x_3} \oplus w_4 \cdot C_{j_4}^{x_4} = \delta_{B,2}
\end{array}\right]}_{S_{A2,3}}.$$

By the conditions (A2-3), (A2-4), the top system in $S_{A2,3}$ offers a unique solution for $(C_{j_1}^{x_1}, C_{j_2}^{x_2})$, and the bottom one offers a unique solution for $(C_{j_3}^{x_3}, C_{j_4}^{x_4})$. These variables are chosen uniformly at random from at least $2^b - 2$ b-bit strings. We thus have $p_{A2} \leq 2^{2(b - \min\{t, b\})} \cdot \frac{1}{(2^b - 2)^4} \leq \frac{16}{2^{2(b + \min\{t, b\})}}$, assuming $2 \leq b$.

By the above upper-bounds, we have $p_{A2} \leq \max\left\{\frac{16}{2^{2(b + \min\{t, b\})}}, \frac{8}{2^{2b + \min\{2t, b\}}}\right\}$ $\leq \frac{16}{2^{2b + \min\{2t, b\}}}$.

Hence, the remaining work is to show that the system (6) with the conditions (A2-1), (A2-2), (A2-3), (A2-4) can be constructed. To show this, messages $M^\alpha, M^\beta, M^\gamma$ are categorized into the following 10 types. The types-1–5 are such that m_α is equal to m_β or m_γ. The types-6–8 are such that $m_\alpha \neq m_\beta = m_\gamma$. The remaining types-9–10 are such that $m_\alpha, m_\beta, m_\gamma$ are distinct. Hereafter, we show that for each of the types-1 and -2, the system (6) cannot be constructed and $p_{A2} = 0$, and for each of the types-3–10, the system (6) with the conditions (A2-1), (A2-2), (A2-3), (A2-4) can be constructed.

- **Type-1** $(m_\alpha = m_\beta \wedge |I(M^\alpha, M^\beta)| = 1)$ Let $I(M^\alpha, M^\beta) = \{I\}$, i.e., $(L_i^\alpha, R_i^\alpha) \neq (L_i^\beta, R_i^\beta)$. If the output collision, $C_i^\alpha = C_i^\beta$ occurs, then the corresponding tweaks are distinct, i.e., $\left(R_i^\alpha \| \mathsf{str}_c(i)\right) \neq \left(R_i^\beta \| \mathsf{str}_c(i)\right)$. Hence, $A_1^\alpha \oplus A_1^\beta = \left(0^c \| R_i^\alpha\right) \oplus \left(0^c \| R_i^\beta\right) \neq 0^b$, and $p_{A2} = 0$. If $C_i^\alpha \neq C_i^\beta$, then $B^\alpha \oplus B^\beta = \eta_i^{m_\alpha} \cdot \left(C_i^\beta \oplus C_i^\alpha\right) \neq 0^b$, thus $p_{A2} = 0$.

- **Type-2** $(m_\alpha = m_\gamma \wedge |I(M^\alpha, M^\gamma)| = 1)$ Since the calculations of A_1 and A_2 are symmetry by msb_t and lsb_t, this analysis is the same as the type-1, thus $p_{A2} = 0$.

- **Type-3** $(m_\alpha = m_\beta \neq m_\gamma \wedge |I(M^\alpha, M^\beta)| \geq 2)$ Let $i_1, i_2 \in I(M^\alpha, M^\beta)$ with $i_1 < i_2$. This analysis uses three variables $(C_{i_1}^\alpha, C_{i_2}^\beta, C_{m_x}^x)$, where $x = \alpha$ if $m_\alpha > m_\gamma$; $x = \gamma$ if $m_\alpha < m_\gamma$. $(C_{i_1}^\alpha, C_{i_2}^\beta, C_{m_x}^x)$ are independent or distinct. Thus (A2-2) is satisfied. Using the variables,
  - (4) is written as $\mathsf{msb}_t(C_{i_1}^\alpha \oplus C_{i_2}^\beta) = \delta_{A,1}^*$, $\eta_{i_1}^{m_\alpha} \cdot C_{i_1}^\alpha \oplus \eta_{i_2}^{m_\beta} \cdot C_{i_2}^\beta = \delta_{B,1}^*$, and
  - (5) is written as $\mathsf{lsb}_t(v_4 \cdot C_{i_1}^\alpha \oplus C_{m_x}^x) = \delta_{A,2}^*$, $w_4 \cdot C_{i_1}^\alpha \oplus \eta_{m_x}^{m_x} \cdot C_{m_x}^x = \delta_{B,2}^*$,

  where $\delta_{A,1}^*, \delta_{B,1}^*, \delta_{A,2}^*, \delta_{B,2}^*$ are defined as (6), and $(v_4, w_4) = (0, \eta_{i_1}^{m_\alpha} \oplus \eta_{i_1}^{m_\gamma})$ if $C_{i_1}^\alpha \overset{\text{same}}{=} C_{i_1}^\gamma$; $(v_4, w_4) = (1, \eta_{i_1}^{m_\alpha})$ otherwise. In this case, fixing the variables in (4) except for $(C_{i_1}^\alpha, C_{i_2}^\beta)$, $(\delta_{A,1}^*, \delta_{B,1}^*)$ can be defined, and fixing the variables in (5) except for $(C_{i_1}^\alpha, C_{m_x}^x)$, $(\delta_{A,2}^*, \delta_{B,2}^*)$ can be defined. Thus, (A2-1) is satisfied. Removing $\mathsf{msb}_t, \mathsf{lsb}_t$ and fixing the variables except for $(C_{i_1}^\alpha, C_{i_2}^\beta)$ and $(C_{i_1}^\alpha, C_{m_x}^x)$, the system from (4) offers a unique solution for $(C_{i_1}^\alpha, C_{i_2}^\beta)$, and the one from (5) offers a unique solution for $(C_{i_1}^\alpha, C_{m_x}^x)$, thus (A2-3) and (A2-4) are satisfied. Hence, the system (6) with (A2-1), (A2-2), (A2-3), (A2-4) can be constructed.

- **Type-4** $(m_\alpha = m_\gamma \neq m_\beta \wedge |I(M^\alpha, M^\gamma)| \geq 2)$ Since the calculations of A_1 and A_2 are symmetry by msb_t and lsb_t, this analysis is the same as the type-3, thus the system (6) with (A2-1), (A2-2), (A2-3), (A2-4) can be constructed.

- **Type-5** ($m_\alpha = m_\beta = m_\gamma \wedge |I(M^\alpha, M^\beta)| \geq 2 \wedge |I(M^\alpha, M^\gamma)| \geq 2$) In this case, by $I(M^\beta, M^\gamma) \neq \emptyset$ (since $M^\beta \neq M^\gamma$), there exist indexes $i_1, i_2 \in I(M^\alpha, M^\beta)$ and $i_3, i_4 \in I(M^\alpha, M^\gamma)$ such that $i_1 < i_2$, $i_3 < i_4$ (thus, $C^\beta_{i_1} \overset{\text{ind}}{\neq} C^\beta_{i_2}$ and $C^\gamma_{i_3} \overset{\text{ind}}{\neq} C^\gamma_{i_4}$), and at least three of $(C^\beta_{i_1}, C^\beta_{i_2}, C^\gamma_{i_3}, C^\gamma_{i_4})$ are distinct or independent.[2] Thus, (A2-2) is satisfied. Using these variables,
  - (4) is written as $\mathsf{msb}_t(C^\beta_{i_1} \oplus C^\beta_{i_2}) = \delta^*_{A,1}$, $\eta^{m_\alpha}_{i_1} \cdot C^\beta_{i_1} \oplus \eta^{m_\alpha}_{i_2} \cdot C^\beta_{i_2} = \delta^*_{B,1}$, and
  - (5) is written as $\mathsf{lsb}_t(C^\gamma_{i_3} \oplus C^\gamma_{i_4}) = \delta^*_{A,2}$, $\eta^{m_\gamma}_{i_3} \cdot C^\gamma_{i_3} \oplus \eta^{m_\gamma}_{i_4} \cdot C^\gamma_{i_4} = \delta^*_{B,2}$,

  where $\delta^*_{A,1}, \delta^*_{B,1}, \delta^*_{A,2}, \delta^*_{B,2}$ are defined as (6). In this case, fixing the variables in (4) except for $(C^\beta_{i_1}, C^\beta_{i_2})$, $(\delta^*_{A,1}, \delta^*_{B,1})$ are defined, and fixing the variables in (5) except for $(C^\gamma_{i_3}, C^\gamma_{i_4})$ $(\delta^*_{A,2}, \delta^*_{B,2})$ are defined. Thus (A2-1) is satisfied. Removing $\mathsf{msb}_t, \mathsf{lsb}_t$ and fixing the variables except for $(C^\beta_{i_1}, C^\beta_{i_2})$ and $(C^\gamma_{i_3}, C^\gamma_{i_4})$, the top system offers a unique solution for $(C^\beta_{i_1}, C^\beta_{i_2})$, and the bottom one offers a unique solution for $(C^\gamma_{i_3}, C^\gamma_{i_4})$. Thus (A2-3), (A2-4) are satisfied. Hence, the system (6) with (A2-1), (A2-2), (A2-3), (A2-4) can be constructed.

- **Type-6** ($m_\alpha < m_\beta = m_\gamma \wedge m_\beta \notin I(M^\beta, M^\gamma)$) Let $i \in I(M^\beta, M^\gamma)$ with $i \neq m_\beta$. This analysis uses variables $C^\beta_i, C^\gamma_i, C^\beta_{m_\beta}$ ($\overset{\text{same}}{=} C^\gamma_{m_\beta}$) that are independent or distinct. Thus, (A2-2) is satisfied. Using these variables,
  - (4) is written as $\mathsf{msb}_t(v_2 \cdot C^\beta_i \oplus C^\beta_{m_\beta}) = \delta^*_{A,1}$, $w_2 \cdot C^\beta_i \oplus \eta^{m_\beta}_{m_\beta} \cdot C^\beta_{m_\beta} = \delta^*_{B,1}$,
  - (5) is written as $\mathsf{lsb}_t(v_4 \cdot C^\gamma_i \oplus C^\beta_{m_\beta}) = \delta^*_{A,2}$, $w_4 \cdot C^\gamma_i \oplus \eta^{m_\beta}_{m_\beta} \cdot C^\beta_{m_\beta} = \delta^*_{B,2}$,

  where $(\delta^*_{A,1}, \delta^*_{B,1}, \delta^*_{A,2}, \delta^*_{B,2})$ are defined as (6), $(v_2, w_2) = (0, \eta^{m_\alpha}_i \oplus \eta^{m_\beta}_i)$ if $C^\alpha_i \overset{\text{same}}{=} C^\beta_i$; $(v_2, w_2) = (1, \eta^{m_\beta}_i)$ otherwise, and $(v_4, w_4) = (0, \eta^{m_\alpha}_i \oplus \eta^{m_\beta}_i)$ if $C^\alpha_i \overset{\text{same}}{=} C^\gamma_i$; $(v_4, w_4) = (1, \eta^{m_\beta}_i)$ otherwise. In this case, fixing the variables in (4) except for $(C^\beta_i, C^\beta_{m_\beta})$, $(\delta^*_{A,1}, \delta^*_{B,1})$ are defined, and fixing the variables in (5) except for $(C^\gamma_i, C^\beta_{m_\beta})$, $(\delta^*_{A,2}, \delta^*_{B,2})$ are defined. Thus (A2-1) is satisfied. Removing $\mathsf{msb}_t, \mathsf{lsb}_t$ and fixing the variables except for $(C^\beta_i, C^\beta_{m_\beta})$ and $C^\gamma_i, C^\beta_{m_\beta}$, the system from (4) offers a unique solution for $(C^\beta_i, C^\beta_{m_\beta})$, and the one from (5) offers a unique solution for $(C^\gamma_i, C^\beta_{m_\beta})$. Thus (A2-3) and (A2-4) are satisfied. Hence, the system (6) with (A2-1), (A2-2), (A2-3), (A2-4) can be constructed.

- **Type-7** ($m_\alpha < m_\beta = m_\gamma \wedge m_\beta \in I(M^\beta, M^\gamma)$) This analysis uses variables $(C^\beta_1, C^\gamma_1, C^\beta_{m_\beta}, C^\gamma_{m_\gamma})$, where ($C^\beta_1$ or C^γ_1), $C^\beta_{m_\beta}$, and $C^\gamma_{m_\beta}$ are distinct or independent (C^β_1 and C^γ_1 are any of the same, distinct or independent). Thus, (A2-2) is satisfied. Using the variables,
  - (4) is written as $\mathsf{msb}_t(v_2 \cdot C^\beta_1 \oplus C^\beta_{m_\beta}) = \delta^*_{A,1}$, $w_2 \cdot C^\beta_1 \oplus \eta^{m_\beta}_{m_\beta} \cdot C^\beta_{m_\beta} = \delta^*_{B,1}$,

---

[2] If $I(M^\alpha, M^\beta) = \{I_1, i_2\}$, $I(M^\alpha, M^\gamma) = \{I_3, i_4\}$ and $i_1 = i_3 < i_2 = i_4$, then by $M^\beta \neq M^\gamma$, $i_1 \in I(M^\beta, M^\gamma)$ or $i_2 \in I(M^\beta, M^\gamma)$. Thus, $C^\beta_{I_1}, C^\beta_{i_2}$ and $C^\gamma_{i_3}$ are distinct or independent, or $C^\beta_{i_1}, C^\beta_{i_2}$ and $C^\gamma_{i_4}$ are distinct or independent. Otherwise, there exist $i_1, i_2 \in I(M^\alpha, M^\beta)$ and $i_3, i_4 \in I(M^\alpha, M^\gamma)$ such that at least three of (i_1, i_2, i_3, i_4) are distinct, thus at least three of $(C^\beta_{i_1}, C^\beta_{i_2}, C^\gamma_{i_3}, C^\gamma_{i_4})$ are independent.

– (5) is written as $\mathsf{lsb}_t(v_4 \cdot C_1^\gamma \oplus C_{m_\beta}^\gamma) = \delta_{A,2}^*$, $w_4 \cdot C_1^\gamma \oplus \eta_{m_\beta}^{m_\beta} \cdot C_{m_\beta}^\gamma = \delta_{B,2}^*$,

where $(\delta_{A,1}^*, \delta_{B,1}^*, \delta_{A,2}^*, \delta_{B,2}^*)$ are defined as (6), $(v_2, w_2) = (0, \eta_1^{m_\alpha} \oplus \eta_1^{m_\beta})$ if $C_1^\alpha \overset{same}{=} C_1^\beta$; $(v_2, w_2) = (1, \eta_1^{m_\beta})$ otherwise, and $(v_4, w_4) = (0, \eta_1^{m_\alpha} \oplus \eta_1^{m_\beta})$ if $C_1^\alpha \overset{same}{=} C_1^\gamma$; $(v_4, w_4) = (1, \eta_1^{m_\beta})$ otherwise. In this case, fixing the variables in (4) except for $(C_1^\beta, C_{m_\beta}^\beta)$, $(\delta_{A,1}^*, \delta_{B,1}^*)$ can be defined, and fixing the variables in (5) except for $(C_1^\gamma, C_{m_\beta}^\gamma)$, $(\delta_{A,2}^*, \delta_{B,2}^*)$ can be defined. Thus (A2-1) is satisfied. Removing $\mathsf{msb}_t, \mathsf{lsb}_t$ and fixing the variables except for $(C_1^\beta, C_{m_\beta}^\beta)$ and $(C_1^\gamma, C_{m_\beta}^\gamma)$, the system from (4) offers a unique solution for $(C_1^\beta, C_{m_\beta}^\beta)$, and the one from (5) offers a unique solution for $(C_1^\gamma, C_{m_\beta}^\gamma)$. Thus (A2-3), (A2-4) are satisfied. Hence, the system (6) with (A2-1), (A2-2), (A2-3), (A2-4) can be constructed.

- **Type-8** $(m_\alpha > m_\beta = m_\gamma)$ Let $i \in I(M^\beta, M^\gamma)$. This analysis uses variables C_i^β, C_i^γ and $C_{m_\alpha}^\alpha$ that are distinct or independent. Thus (A2-2) is satisfied. Using the variables,
  – (4) is written as $\mathsf{msb}_t(v_2 \cdot C_i^\beta \oplus C_{m_\alpha}^\alpha) = \delta_{A,1}^*$, $w_2 \cdot C_i^\beta \oplus \eta_{m_\alpha}^{m_\alpha} \cdot C_{m_\alpha}^\alpha = \delta_{B,1}^*$,
  – (5) is written as $\mathsf{lsb}_t(v_4 \cdot C_i^\gamma \oplus C_{m_\alpha}^\alpha) = \delta_{A,2}^*$, $w_4 \cdot C_i^\gamma \oplus \eta_{m_\alpha}^{m_\alpha} \cdot C_{m_\alpha}^\alpha = \delta_{B,2}^*$,

  where $(\delta_{A,1}^*, \delta_{B,1}^*, \delta_{A,2}^*, \delta_{B,2}^*)$ are defined as (6), $(v_2, w_2) = (0, \eta_i^{m_\alpha} \oplus \eta_i^{m_\beta})$ if $C_i^\alpha \overset{same}{=} C_i^\beta$; $(v_2, w_2) = (1, \eta_i^{m_\beta})$ otherwise, and $(v_4, w_4) = (0, \eta_i^{m_\alpha} \oplus \eta_i^{m_\beta})$ if $C_i^\alpha \overset{same}{=} C_i^\gamma$; $(v_4, w_4) = (1, \eta_i^{m_\beta})$ otherwise. In this case, fixing the variables in (4) except for $(C_i^\beta, C_{m_\alpha}^\alpha)$, $(\delta_{A,1}^*, \delta_{B,1}^*)$ are defined, and fixing the variables in (5) except for $(C_i^\gamma, C_{m_\alpha}^\alpha)$, $(\delta_{A,2}^*, \delta_{B,2}^*)$ are defined. Thus (A2-1) is satisfied. Removing $(\mathsf{msb}_t, \mathsf{lsb}_t)$ and fixing the variables except for $(C_i^\beta, C_{m_\alpha}^\alpha)$ and $(C_i^\gamma, C_{m_\alpha}^\alpha)$, the system from (4) offers a unique solution for $(C_i^\beta, C_{m_\alpha}^\alpha)$, and the one from (5) offers a unique solution for $(C_i^\gamma, C_{m_\alpha}^\alpha)$. Thus (A2-3), (A2-4) are satisfied. Hence, the system (6) with (A2-1), (A2-2), (A2-3), (A2-4) can be constructed.

- **Type-9** $(m_\alpha \neq m_\gamma < m_\beta)$ This analysis uses variables C_1^α, $C_{m_x}^x$, C_2^β and $C_{m_\beta}^\beta$, where $x = \alpha$ if $m_\alpha > m_\gamma$; $x = \gamma$ if $m_\alpha < m_\gamma$. C_1^α, $(C_{m_x}^x$ or $C_2^\beta)$ and $C_{m_\beta}^\beta$ are independent, since $2 \leq m_x < m_\beta$ ($C_{m_x}^x$ and C_2^β are any of the same, distinct or independent). Thus (A2-2) is satisfied. Using the variables,
  – (4) is written as $\mathsf{msb}_t(v_2 \cdot C_2^\beta \oplus C_{m_\beta}^\beta) = \delta_{A,1}^*$, $w_2 \cdot C_2^\beta \oplus \eta_{m_\beta}^{m_\beta} \cdot C_{m_\beta}^\beta = \delta_{B,1}^*$,
  – (5) is written as $\mathsf{lsb}_t(v_4 \cdot C_1^\alpha \oplus C_{m_x}^x) = \delta_{A,2}^*$, $w_4 \cdot C_1^\alpha \oplus \eta_{m_x}^{m_x} \cdot C_{m_x}^x = \delta_{B,2}^*$,

  where $(\delta_{A,1}^*, \delta_{B,1}^*, \delta_{A,2}^*, \delta_{B,2}^*)$ are defined as (6), $(v_2, w_2) = (0, \eta_2^{m_\alpha} \oplus \eta_2^{m_\beta})$ if $C_2^\alpha \overset{same}{=} C_2^\beta$; $(v_2, w_2) = (1, \eta_2^{m_\beta})$ otherwise, and $(v_4, w_4) = (0, \eta_1^{m_\alpha} \oplus \eta_1^{m_\gamma})$ if $C_1^\alpha \overset{same}{=} C_1^\gamma$; $(v_4, w_4) = (1, \eta_1^{m_\alpha})$ otherwise. In this case, fixing the variables in (4) except for $(C_2^\beta, C_{m_\beta}^\beta)$, $\delta_{A,1}^*, \delta_{B,1}^*$ are defined, and fixing the variables in (5) except for $(C_1^\alpha, C_{m_x}^x)$, $\delta_{A,2}^*, \delta_{B,2}^*$ are defined. Thus (A2-1) is satisfied. Removing $\mathsf{msb}_t, \mathsf{lsb}_t$ and fixing the variables except for $(C_2^\beta, C_{m_\beta}^\beta)$ and $(C_1^\alpha, C_{m_x}^x)$, the system from (4) offers a unique solution for $(C_2^\beta, C_{m_\beta}^\beta)$, and the one from (5) offers a unique solution for $(C_1^\alpha, C_{m_x}^x)$. Thus (A2-3), (A2-4) are satisfied. Hence, the system (6) with (A2-1), (A2-2), (A2-3), (A2-4) can be constructed.

- **Type-10** ($m_\alpha \neq m_\beta < m_\gamma$) Since the calculations of A_1 and A_2 are symmetry, this analysis is the same as the type-9, thus the system (6) with (A2-1), (A2-2), (A2-3), (A2-4) can be constructed.

□

4.3 Upper-Bounding Pr[bad$_B$]

First, fix $\alpha \in [q]$ and upper-bound the probability that **A** sets bad$_B$ at the α-th query, i.e, for some distinct $j_1, j_2 \in [2]$, $\widetilde{P}^{j_1}(A^\alpha_{j_1}, B^\alpha) \neq \bot$, $\widetilde{P}^{j_2}(A^\alpha_{j_2}, B^\alpha) = \bot$ and bad$_B \leftarrow$ true.

The case where $j_1 = 1$ and $j_2 = 2$ is considered.

- $\widetilde{P}^1(A^\alpha_1, B^\alpha) \neq \bot$ implies $\exists \beta \in [\alpha - 1]$ s.t. $A^\alpha_1 = A^\beta_1 \wedge B^\alpha = B^\beta$, and
- $\widetilde{P}^2(A^\alpha_2, B^\alpha) = \bot \wedge$ bad$_B \leftarrow$ true implies $\exists \gamma \in [\alpha - 1]$ s.t. $A^\alpha_2 = A^\gamma_2 \wedge B^\alpha \neq B^\gamma \wedge T^\alpha_2 = T^\gamma_2$.

Note that by $B^\alpha = B^\beta$ and $B^\alpha \neq B^\gamma$, $\beta \neq \gamma$ is satisfied. Regarding the condition $T^\alpha_2 = T^\gamma_2$, since T^α_2 is chosen uniformly at random from $\{0,1\}^b$, fixing γ, the probability that the condition is satisfied is at most $1/2^b$. The remaining conditions $A^\alpha_1 = A^\beta_1$, $B^\alpha = B^\beta$ and $A^\alpha_2 = A^\gamma_2$ are considered in the following lemma.

Lemma 3. *For any distinct messages* $M^\alpha, M^\beta, M^\gamma \in \mathcal{M}$,
$$\Pr[A^\alpha_1 = A^\beta_1 \wedge B^\alpha = B^\beta \wedge A^\alpha_2 = A^\gamma_2] \leq \frac{8}{2^{b+\min\{2t,b\}}}.$$

Due to the lack of space, the proof is omitted but is basically the same as the proof of Lemma 2. The full proof is given in the full version of this paper. Hence, the probability that at the α-th query, **A** sets bad$_B$ is at most $\sum_{\beta,\gamma\in[\alpha-1] \text{ s.t. } \beta\neq\gamma} \frac{1}{2^b} \cdot \frac{8}{2^{b+\min\{2t,b\}}}$.

Regarding the case where $j_1 = 2$ and $j_2 = 1$, since the calculations of A_1 and A_2 are symmetry, this analysis is the same as the above one, thus the probability that at the α-th query, **A** sets bad$_B$ is at most $\sum_{\beta,\gamma\in[\alpha-1] \text{ s.t. } \beta\neq\gamma} \frac{1}{2^b} \cdot \frac{8}{2^{b+\min\{2t,b\}}}$.

Finally, we have

$$\Pr[\text{bad}_B] \leq 2 \cdot \binom{q}{3} \cdot \frac{8}{2^{2b+\min\{2t,b\}}} \leq \frac{8/3 \cdot q^3}{2^{2b+\min\{2t,b\}}}. \tag{7}$$

4.4 Upper-Bounding Pr[bad$_C$]

First, fix $\alpha \in [q]$ and upper-bound the probability that **A** sets bad$_C$ at the α-th query, i.e., $\widetilde{P}^1(A^\alpha_1, B^\alpha) = \bot$, $\widetilde{P}^2(A^\alpha_2, B^\alpha) = \bot$ and bad$_C \leftarrow$ true.

- $\widetilde{P}^1(A^\alpha_1, B^\alpha) = \bot \wedge$ bad$_C \leftarrow$ true implies $\exists \beta \in [\alpha - 1]$ s.t. $A^\alpha_1 = A^\beta_1 \wedge T^\alpha_1 = T^\beta_1$,
- $\widetilde{P}^2(A^\alpha_2, B^\alpha) = \bot \wedge$ bad$_C \leftarrow$ true implies $\exists \gamma \in [\alpha - 1]$ s.t. $A^\alpha_2 = A^\gamma_2 \wedge T^\alpha_2 = T^\gamma_2$.

Fix $\beta, \gamma \in [\alpha - 1]$. Regarding the conditions $T_1^\alpha = T_1^\beta$ and $T_2^\alpha = T_2^\gamma$, since T_1^α and T_2^α are chosen uniformly at random from $\{0, 1\}^b$, the probability that the conditions are satisfied is $1/2^{2b}$. In the following lemmas, the remaining conditions $A_1^\alpha = A_1^\beta$ and $A_2^\alpha = A_2^\gamma$ are considered.

Lemma 4. ($\beta = \gamma$) For any distinct messages $M^\alpha, M^\beta \in \mathcal{M}$,
$$\Pr[A_1^\alpha = A_1^\beta \wedge A_2^\alpha = A_2^\beta] \le \frac{2}{2^{\min\{2t,b\}}}.$$
($\beta \ne \gamma$) For any distinct messages $M^\alpha, M^\beta, M^\gamma \in \mathcal{M}$,
$$\Pr[A_1^\alpha = A_1^\beta \wedge A_2^\alpha = A_2^\gamma] \le \frac{4}{2^{\min\{2t,b\}}}.$$

Due to the lack of space, the proof is omitted but is basically the same as the proofs of Lemmas 1 and 2. The full proof is given in the full version of this paper. Hence, the probability that **A** sets bad$_C$ at the α-th query is at most
$$(\alpha - 1) \cdot \frac{1}{2^{2b}} \cdot \frac{2}{2^{\min\{2t,b\}}} + \frac{1}{2^{2b}} \cdot \sum_{\beta, \gamma \in [\alpha - 1] \text{ s.t. } \beta \ne \gamma} \frac{4}{2^{\min\{2t,b\}}}.$$
Finally, we have $\Pr[\mathsf{bad}_C] \le$

$$\binom{q}{2} \cdot \frac{2}{2^{2b+\min\{2t,b\}}} + \binom{q}{3} \cdot \frac{4}{2^{2b+\min\{2t,b\}}} \le \frac{q^2}{2^{2b+\min\{2t,b\}}} + \frac{2/3 \cdot q^3}{2^{2b+\min\{2t,b\}}}. \quad (8)$$

References

1. Beierle, C., et al.: The SKINNY family of block ciphers and its low-latency variant MANTIS. In: Robshaw, M., Katz, J. (eds.) CRYPTO 2016. LNCS, vol. 9815, pp. 123–153. Springer, Heidelberg (2016). https://doi.org/10.1007/978-3-662-53008-5_5

2. Bellare, M., Rogaway, P.: Code-based game-playing proofs and the security of triple encryption. IACR Cryptology ePrint Archive 2004/331 (2004)

3. Bhargavan, K., Leurent, G.: On the practical (in-)security of 64-bit block ciphers: collision attacks on HTTP over TLS and OpenVPN. In: CCS 2016, pp. 456–467. ACM (2016)

4. Black, J., Rogaway, P.: A block-cipher mode of operation for parallelizable message authentication. In: Knudsen, L.R. (ed.) EUROCRYPT 2002. LNCS, vol. 2332, pp. 384–397. Springer, Heidelberg (2002). https://doi.org/10.1007/3-540-46035-7_25

5. Datta, N., Dutta, A., Nandi, M., Paul, G., Zhang, L.: Single key variant of PMAC_Plus. IACR Trans. Symmetric Cryptol. **2017**(4), 268–305 (2017)

6. Iwata, T., Kurosawa, K.: OMAC: one-key CBC MAC. In: Johansson, T. (ed.) FSE 2003. LNCS, vol. 2887, pp. 129–153. Springer, Heidelberg (2003). https://doi.org/10.1007/978-3-540-39887-5_11

7. Iwata, T., Minematsu, K.: Stronger security variants of GCM-SIV. IACR Trans. Symmetric Cryptol. **2016**(1), 134–157 (2016)

8. Iwata, T., Minematsu, K., Peyrin, T., Seurin, Y.: ZMAC: a fast tweakable block cipher mode for highly secure message authentication. In: Katz, J., Shacham, H. (eds.) CRYPTO 2017. LNCS, vol. 10403, pp. 34–65. Springer, Cham (2017). https://doi.org/10.1007/978-3-319-63697-9_2

9. Jean, J., Nikolić, I., Peyrin, T.: Tweaks and keys for block ciphers: the TWEAKEY framework. In: Sarkar, P., Iwata, T. (eds.) ASIACRYPT 2014. LNCS, vol. 8874, pp. 274–288. Springer, Heidelberg (2014). https://doi.org/10.1007/978-3-662-45608-8_15

10. JTC1: ISO/IEC 9797-1:1999 Information technology—Security techniques—Message Authentication Codes (MACs)—Part 1: mechanisms using a block cipher (1999)
11. Liskov, M., Rivest, R.L., Wagner, D.: Tweakable block ciphers. In: Yung, M. (ed.) CRYPTO 2002. LNCS, vol. 2442, pp. 31–46. Springer, Heidelberg (2002). https://doi.org/10.1007/3-540-45708-9_3
12. List, E., Nandi, M.: Revisiting Full-PRF-Secure PMAC and using it for beyond-birthday authenticated encryption. In: Handschuh, H. (ed.) CT-RSA 2017. LNCS, vol. 10159, pp. 258–274. Springer, Cham (2017). https://doi.org/10.1007/978-3-319-52153-4_15
13. List, E., Nandi, M.: ZMAC+ - an efficient variable-output-length variant of ZMAC. IACR Trans. Symmetric Cryptol. **2017**(4), 306–325 (2017)
14. Minematsu, K., Iwata, T.: Tweak-length extension for tweakable blockciphers. In: Groth, J. (ed.) IMACC 2015. LNCS, vol. 9496, pp. 77–93. Springer, Cham (2015). https://doi.org/10.1007/978-3-319-27239-9_5
15. Minematsu, K., Iwata, T.: Cryptanalysis of PMACx, PMAC2x, and SIVx. IACR Trans. Symmetric Cryptol. **2017**(2), 162–176 (2017)
16. Naito, Y.: Full PRF-secure message authentication code based on tweakable block cipher. In: Au, M.-H., Miyaji, A. (eds.) ProvSec 2015. LNCS, vol. 9451, pp. 167–182. Springer, Cham (2015). https://doi.org/10.1007/978-3-319-26059-4_9
17. Naito, Y.: Blockcipher-based MACs: beyond the birthday bound without message length. In: Takagi, T., Peyrin, T. (eds.) ASIACRYPT 2017. LNCS, vol. 10626, pp. 446–470. Springer, Cham (2017). https://doi.org/10.1007/978-3-319-70700-6_16
18. Rogaway, P.: Efficient instantiations of tweakable blockciphers and refinements to modes OCB and PMAC. In: Lee, P.J. (ed.) ASIACRYPT 2004. LNCS, vol. 3329, pp. 16–31. Springer, Heidelberg (2004). https://doi.org/10.1007/978-3-540-30539-2_2
19. Yasuda, K.: The sum of CBC MACs is a secure PRF. In: Pieprzyk, J. (ed.) CT-RSA 2010. LNCS, vol. 5985, pp. 366–381. Springer, Heidelberg (2010). https://doi.org/10.1007/978-3-642-11925-5_25
20. Yasuda, K.: A new variant of PMAC: beyond the birthday bound. In: Rogaway, P. (ed.) CRYPTO 2011. LNCS, vol. 6841, pp. 596–609. Springer, Heidelberg (2011). https://doi.org/10.1007/978-3-642-22792-9_34

Short Papers

Short Papers

Witness Encryption with (Weak) Unique Decryption and Message Indistinguishability: Constructions and Applications

Dongxue Pan[1,2,3], Bei Liang[4(✉)] ⓘ, Hongda Li[1,2,3], and Peifang Ni[1,2,3]

[1] School of Cyber Security, University of Chinese Academy of Sciences, Beijing, China
[2] State Key Lab of Information Security, Institute of Information Engineering, Chinese Academy of Sciences, Beijing, China
{pandongxue,lihongda,nipeifang}@iie.ac.cn
[3] Data Assurance and Communication Security Research Center, CAS, Beijing, China
[4] Chalmers University of Technology, Gothenburg, Sweden
lbei@chalmers.se

Abstract. In this paper, we investigate WE scheme with the unique decryption and message indistinguishability, as well as its compelling applications. Our contributions are three-fold: *(i)* we first propose the notion of WE with MI and *weak* unique decryption, and give a construction based on public-coin differing-inputs obfuscation (diO), pseudorandom generator, and the Goldreich-Levin hard-core predicate; *(ii)* We show that our WE with MI and weak unique decryption can be used to construct a 4-round non-black-box honest-verifier zero-knowledge argument protocol; and *(iii)* We present a WE scheme with unique decryption and MI based on public-coin diO and weak auxiliary input multi-bit output point obfuscation (AIMPO). Moreover, we show that using our WE with unique decryption, we can get rid of the limitation of honest-verifier zero-knowledge property, thus yielding a 4-round non-black-box zero-knowledge argument.

Keywords: Witness encryption · Differing-inputs obfuscation · Unique decryption · Zero-knowledge

1 Introduction

Witness encryption (WE) is introduced by Garg *et al.* [10] (abbreviated as GGSW-WE) to define an encryption framework that allows to encrypt a message to an instance of an NP language L. The encryption algorithm takes as input an instance x along with a message m and produces a ciphertext CT. Any user who has knowledge of a witness w showing that x is in the language L (*i.e.*,

© Springer Nature Switzerland AG 2019
J. Jang-Jaccard and F. Guo (Eds.): ACISP 2019, LNCS 11547, pp. 609–619, 2019.
https://doi.org/10.1007/978-3-030-21548-4_33

$x \in L$) according to the relation $\mathcal{R}_L$, namely $(x,w) \in \mathcal{R}_L$, is able to decrypt the ciphertext CT and recover m. The soundness security requirement of WE states that, for any ciphertext created for an instance x that is not in the language L (*i.e.*, $x \notin L$), it must be hard for any polynomial-time attacker to distinguish between the encryptions of two messages with equal length.

Garg *et al.* [10] also gave a candidate construction of WE for the NP-complete Exact Cover problem using multilinear encodings system [9]. Afterwards, a plenty of works have investigated on how to construct WE schemes with various useful properties under reliable assumptions [1–3,5,7,8,11,14].

Message Indistinguishability. As Garg *et al.* [10] pointed out, there is a gap between the soundness security requirement and correctness property for GGSW-WE definition. Their correctness stipulates that given a ciphertext which is an encryption of a message m to an instance x (denoted as $Encrypt(x,m)$), and a valid witness w of x, the decryption algorithm can recover the message m correctly. Whereas, the soundness states that if $x \notin L$ then no polynomial-time attacker can decrypt. However, GGSW-WE definition is (intentionally) silent on the case when $x \in L$ but the attacker does not know any witness for the relation $\mathcal{R}_L$. Subsequently, Gentry *et al.* [11] gave a strengthened version of soundness security for WE, called *message indistinguishability*, which requires that the soundness property is entirely independent of whether $x \in L$ or not, namely, the encryptions of two messages with equal length are computationally indistinguishable no matter whether $x \in L$ or not. Gentry *et al.* [11] also provided two instantiations of WE with message indistinguishability based on multilinear maps in an asymmetric model of composite-order multilinear groups and prime-order multilinear groups respectively.

Unique Decryption. The unique decryption property of WE, introduced by Niu *et al.*, is to guarantee that a (possibly *invalid*) ciphertext c only can be decrypted to a unique message even if using different witnesses for $x \in L$. Niu *et al.* proposed a generic approach of using a weak auxiliary input multi-bit output point obfuscation (AIMPO) to convert a WE into one with unique decryption. Their core idea is to include a weak AIMPO of an specific function as part of the ciphertext besides the encryption c of message m under the WE scheme, which provides the certification that only one correct message hardwired in AIMPO can be recovered. The function is defined to output a string r on input m, where r is the random coins used to encrypt m to c, while on other inputs, output 0.

Motivation. Even though all of known constructions of WE and its variants are built upon the heavy tools, such as multilinear maps, iO, NIZK, or lattices, none of them focuses on constructing WE scheme achieving both the message indistinguishability property and the unique decryption property. This gives rise to the following question: *Is it possible to construct a WE scheme satisfying both the message indistinguishability (MI) property and the unique decryption property?*

Our Contributions. We summarize our contributions as follows.

- We first propose a notion of WE with *weak* unique decryption and MI. We call it weak in the sense that using different valid witnesses for $x \in L$ to decrypt a (possibly *invalid*) ciphertext c only can yield to an unique message if no decryption outputs the symbol $\bot$. We provide a witness encryption scheme with *weak* unique decryption and MI property based on public-coin diO, pseudorandom generator, and the Goldreich-Levin hard-core predicate.

- We show that our WE with *weak* unique decryption and MI property can be used to construct a 4-round non-black-box honest-verifier zero-knowledge argument protocol.
- Then we show how to build a witness encryption scheme with unique decryption and MI property based on public-coin diO and weak auxiliary input multi-bit output point obfuscation (AIMPO). Furthermore, we demonstrate that using our WE with unique decryption property, our 4-round argument given in Sect. 4.1 can get rid of the limitation of honest-verifier zero-knowledge property, thus yielding a 4-round non-black-box zero-knowledge argument.

2 Preliminaries

We use n to denote the security parameter. For a finite set $\mathcal{S}$, we use $y \leftarrow_R \mathcal{S}$ to denote that y is uniformly selected from $\mathcal{S}$. We use $[l]$ to denote the set $\{1, \cdots, l\}$. We write $negl(\cdot)$ to denote an unspecified negligible function, $poly(\cdot)$ an unspecified polynomial. We denote by $|a|$ the length of string a.

Definition 2.1 Hard-Core Predicate. *A polynomial-time-computable predicate written as $B : \{0,1\}^* \rightarrow \{0,1\}$ is called a hard-core of a function f if for every PPT algorithm A, every positive polynomial $p(\cdot)$, and all sufficiently large n:*

$$\Pr[A(F(U_n)) = B(U_n)] < 1/2 + 1/p(n),$$

where U_n is uniformly distributed over $\{0,1\}^n$. We call it unpredictability.

Theorem 2.1 Goldreich-Levin Hard-Core Predicate. *Let f be an arbitrary one-way function, and let g be defined by $g(x,r) = (f(x),r)$, where $|x| = |r|$. Let $b(x,r) = \langle x,r \rangle$ denote the inner product mod 2 of the binary vectors x and r. Then the predicate b is a hard-core of the function g [12].*

Definition 2.2 Hard-Core Function. *Let $h : \{0,1\}^* \rightarrow \{0,1\}^*$ be a polynomial-time-computable function satisfying $|h(x)| = |h(y)|$ for all $|x| = |y|$, and let $l(n) = |h(1^n)|$. The function h is called a hard-core of a function f if for every PPT algorithm D, every positive polynomial $p(\cdot)$, and all sufficiently large n:*

$$|\Pr[D((F(X_n), h(X_n)) = 1] - \Pr[D((F(X_n), R_l(n)) = 1] < 1/p(n),$$

where X_n and $R_l(n)$ are two independent random variables, the first uniformly distributed over $\{0,1\}^n$ and the second uniformly distributed over $\{0,1\}^{l(n)}$.

612   D. Pan et al.

We recall the definitions of public-coin differing-inputs obfuscation in [13]. The following is the definition of public-coin differing-inputs obfuscation for circuits, and the definition of public-coin differing-inputs obfuscation for turing machines is similar.

Definition 2.3 *Public-coin differing-inputs sampler for circuits* [13]. *An efficient non-uniform sampling algorithm $Sam = \{Sam_n\}$ is called a public-coin differing-inputs sampler for the parameterized collection of circuits $\mathcal{C} = \{\mathcal{C}_n\}$ if the output of Sam_n is distributed over $\mathcal{C}_n \times \mathcal{C}_n$ and for every efficient non-uniform algorithm $A = \{A_n\}$ there exists a negligible function $negl(\cdot)$ such that for all $n \in N$:*

$$\Pr_r[C_0(x) \neq C_1(x) : (C_0, C_1) \leftarrow Sam_n(r), x \leftarrow A_n(r)] \leq negl(n).$$

Definition 2.4 *Public-coin differing-inputs obfuscator for circuits* [13]. *An uniform PPT algorithm diO is a public-coin differing-inputs obfuscator for the parameterized collection of circuits $\mathcal{C} = \{\mathcal{C}_n\}$ if the following requirements hold:*

- *(functionality) For all security parameters $n \in N$, for all $C \in \mathcal{C}_n$, and for all input x we have that $\Pr[C'(x) = C(x) : C' \leftarrow diO(1^n, C)] = 1$.*
- *(security) For every public-coin differing-inputs samplers $Sam = \{Sam_n\}$, for the collection $\mathcal{C}$, every PPT distinguishing algorithm $\mathcal{T} = \{\mathcal{T}_n\}$, there exists a negligible function $negl(\cdot)$ such that for all security parameters $n \in N$:*

$$\left| \Pr\left[\begin{array}{c} \mathcal{T}_n(r, C') = 1 : (C_0, C_1) \leftarrow Sam_n(r) \\ C' \leftarrow diO(1^n, C_0) \end{array} \right] \right.$$
$$\left. - \Pr\left[\begin{array}{c} \mathcal{T}_n(r, C') = 1 : (C_0, C_1) \leftarrow Sam_n(r) \\ C' \leftarrow diO(1^n, C_1) \end{array} \right] \right| \leq negl(n),$$

where the probability is taken over r and the coins of diO and $\mathcal{T}_n$.

3 Witness Encryption with (Weak) Unique Decryption and Message Indistinguishability: Definitions and Constructions

Definition 3.1. *A witness encryption scheme with (weak) unique decryption and message indistinguishability for an NP language L with corresponding relation $\mathcal{R}_L$ consists of the following two polynomial-time algorithms:*

- ***Encryption.*** *The algorithm $Encrypt(1^n, x, m)$ takes as input a security parameter 1^n, an unbounded-length string x, and a message $m \in M$ for some message space M, and outputs a ciphertext CT.*
- ***Decryption.*** *The algorithm $Decrypt(CT, w)$ takes as input a ciphertext CT and an unbounded-length string w, and outputs a message m or the symbol $\perp$.*

These algorithms satisfy the following conditions:

- **Correctness.** *For any security parameter n, for any $m \in M$, and for any $x \in L$ such that $\mathcal{R}_L(x, w)$ holds, there exists a negligible function $negl(\cdot)$, such that:*

$$\Pr[Decrypt(Encrypt(1^n, x, m), w) = m] \geq 1 - negl(n).$$

- **Message Indistinguishability.** *For any $x \in L$ or $x \notin L$, for any PPT adversary A and messages $m_0, m_1 \in M$, there exists a negligible function $negl(\cdot)$, such that:*

$$\left| \Pr[A(Encrypt(1^n, x, m_0)) = 1] - \Pr[A(Encrypt(1^n, x, m_1)) = 1] \right| < negl(n).$$

- **Weak Unique Decryption.** *If w_1, w_2 satisfies $(x, w_1) \in \mathcal{R}_L, (x, w_2) \in \mathcal{R}_L$, then for any (possibly invalid) ciphertext CT, if the decryptions $Decrypt(CT, w_1) \neq \perp$ and $Decrypt(CT, w_2) \neq \perp$, it holds: $Decrypt(CT, w_1) = Decrypt(CT, w_2)$.*

- **Unique Decryption.** *If w_1, w_2 satisfies $(x, w_1) \in \mathcal{R}_L, (x, w_2) \in \mathcal{R}_L$, then for any (possibly invalid) ciphertext CT, $Decrypt(CT, w_1) = Decrypt(CT, w_2)$.*

3.1   Construction of WE with Weak Unique Decryption and MI

The goal in this subsection is to construct a WE scheme with weak unique decryption and MI (abbreviated as weak UWE). For MI of the weak UWE scheme, we use a public-coin diO for a specific function, which outputs the message m on input w such that $(x, w) \in \mathcal{R}$. To achieve the weak unique decryption property, we employ the idea of including the "encoded" function that outputs the random coins used to produce the encryption of a message under general WE, as part of the new ciphertext, but to achieve it without using weak AIMPO. First, we define the specific function as follows.

Definition 3.2 *Hiding-input point function with multi-bit output. Let L be a language in NP. $\mathcal{R}_L$ is the corresponding relation. Let φ be an instance such that for any PPT algorithm A, $\Pr[\mathcal{R}_L(x, w) = 1 : w \leftarrow A(\varphi)] < negl(n)$. Then, we call φ a hard problem for L and define hiding-input point function with multi-bit output as follows:*

$$I_{\varphi,y}(x) = \begin{cases} y, & if\ \mathcal{R}_L(\varphi, x) = 1 \\ 0, & otherwise \end{cases},$$

where $y \in \{0, 1\}^{poly(n)}$ and $poly(n)$ is a polynomial in n.

Let L be an NP language only consisting of hard problems and then any instance φ (no matter $\varphi \in L$ or not) is a hard problem for L. And let any instance φ be efficiently samplable without knowing any witness for $\varphi \in L$. Then with two public-coin diO algorithms $\mathcal{O}_1, \mathcal{O}_2$ for the function families $\{I_{\varphi,y}\}_{y \in \{0,1\}^n}, \{I_{\varphi,y}\}_{y \in \{0,1\}^{n^2}}$ respectively, a pseudorandom generator $G : \{0, 1\}^n \rightarrow \{0, 1\}^{poly(n)}$, and the Goldreich-Levin hard-core predicate, we show our construction of weak unique witness encryption as follows. We remark that details of the proofs of the theorems are omitted from this version due to page limit and can be found in the full version.

Construction 3.1. Weak unique witness encryption scheme for L.

- **Encrypt** $(1^n, \varphi, \cdot, \cdot)$: On input a message $m \in \{0,1\}^n$, it chooses random values $m_1, \cdots, m_n, r_1, \cdots, r_n \in \{0,1\}^n$ and $r_e \in \{0,1\}^*$, and computes

$$r = \langle m_1, r_1 \rangle, \cdots, \langle m_n, r_n \rangle, r_d = G(r).$$

Then it encrypts m as

$$CT = Encrypt(1^n, \varphi, m, (m_1, \cdots, m_n, r_1, \cdots, r_n, r_e))$$
$$= \mathcal{O}_1(I_{\varphi,m}; r_d), \mathcal{O}_2(I_{\varphi,(m_1,\cdots,m_n)}; r_e), r_1, \cdots, r_n$$
$$= CT_{0,1}, CT_{0,2}, CT_1, \cdots, CT_n.$$

- **Decrypt** $(1^n, \cdot, (\varphi, w))$: On input a ciphertext CT, it parses the ciphertext as

$$CT = (CT_{0,1}, CT_{0,2}, CT_1, \cdots, CT_n)$$

and runs $CT_0 = (CT_{0,1}, CT_{0,2})$ on w. If $CT_0(w) = (CT_{0,1}(w), CT_{0,2}(w)) \neq 0$, it parses $CT_0(w) = m', m_1', \cdots, m_n'$ and computes

$$r' = \langle m_1', CT_1 \rangle, \cdots, \langle m_n', CT_n \rangle, r_d' = G(r'), CT_{0,1}' = \mathcal{O}_1(I_{\varphi,m'}; r_d').$$

If $CT_{0,1}' = CT_{0,1}$, it outputs m', otherwise it outputs the symbol $\perp$.

Theorem 3.1. *Assuming L only consists of hard problems and any hard problem for L is efficiently samplable without knowing a witness, and there are public-coin differing-inputs obfuscation algorithms for the function family $\{I_{\phi,y}\}_{y \in \{0,1\}^{poly n}}$, where ϕ is a variable of the uniform distribution of hard problems for L. Additionally assuming the existence of pseudorandom generator and the Goldreich-Levin hard-core predicate is secure. Then, the Construction 3.1 is a weak unique witness encryption.*

3.2 Construction of WE with Unique Decryption and MI

We observe that according to our construction in Sect. 3.1, for an invalid ciphertext $\tilde{CT} = (\mathcal{O}_1(I_{\varphi,m}), \mathcal{O}_2(I_{\tilde{\varphi},\tilde{m}}), r_1, \ldots, r_n)$, it might occur that there exists two witnesses w_1, w_2 such that w_1 is a valid witness for both φ and $\tilde{\varphi}$ but w_2 is valid for φ and not valid for $\tilde{\varphi}$, then using w_1 to decrypt the ciphertext $\tilde{CT}$ will get m while using w_2 will fail, which demonstrates the gap between the definition of weak unique decryption and unique decryption.

Now we will construct a WE scheme with unique decryption and message indistinguishability (abbreviated as UWE). To achieve the unique decryption property, we extend the idea of Niu *et al.* [14] and include a weak AIMPO of function I_{m,r_d} as part of the ciphertext where r_d is the random coin used to produce $\mathcal{O}(I_{\varphi,m})$. The functionality of I_{m,r_d} is to output the random coin r_d on input point m and output 0 otherwise. Before giving our construction we first provide some basic definitions.

Definition 3.3 *Unpredictable distribution* [6]. *A distribution ensemble* $D = \{D_n = (Z_n, M_n, R_n)\}_{n \in N}$ *on triple of strings is unpredictable if no poly-size circuit family can predict* M_n *from* Z_n. *That is, for every poly-size circuit sequence* $\{C_n\}_{n \in N}$ *and for all large enough* n: $\Pr_{(z,m,r) \leftarrow_R D_n}[C_n(z) = m] \leq negl(n)$.

Definition 3.4 *Weak auxiliary input multi-bit output point obfuscation for unpredictable distributions* [14]. *A PPT algorithm* $\mathcal{MO}$ *is a weak auxiliary input multi-bit output point obfuscator of the circuit class* $\mathcal{C} = \{C_n = \{I_{m,r} | m \in \{0,1\}^n, r \in \{0,1\}^{poly(n)}\}\}$ *for unpredictable distributions if it satisfies:*

- *(functionality) For any* $n \in N$, *any* $I_{m,r} \in C_n$, *and any input* $x \neq m$, *it holds that* $\mathcal{MO}(I_{m,r})(x) = I_{m,r}(x)$ *and* $\Pr[\mathcal{MO}(I_{m,r})(m) \neq r] \leq negl(n)$, *where the probability is taken over the randomness of* $\mathcal{MO}$.
- *(polynomial slowdown) For any* $n \in N$, $I_{m,r} \in C_n$, $|\mathcal{MO}(I_{m,r})| \leq poly(|I_{m,r}|)$.
- *(secrecy) For any unpredictable distribution* $D = \{D_n = (Z_n, M_n, R_n)\}_{n \in N}$ *over* $\{0,1\}^{poly(n)} \times \{0,1\}^n \times \{0,1\}^{poly(n)}$, *it holds that for any PPT algorithm* A:

$$\Pr_{(z,m,r) \leftarrow_R D_n}[A(1^n, z, \mathcal{MO}(I_{m,r})) = m] \leq negl(n).$$

Let L be an NP language only consisting of hard problems. And let any instance φ be efficiently samplable without knowing any witness for $\varphi \in L$. Then with a public-coin diO algorithm $\mathcal{O}$ for the function families $\{I_{\varphi,y}\}_{y \in \{0,1\}^n}$, and a weak AIMPO algorithm $\mathcal{MO}$, we show our construction of unique witness encryption as follows.

Construction 3.2. Unique witness encryption scheme for L.

- **Encrypt** $(1^n, \varphi, \cdot, \cdot)$: On input a message $m \in \{0,1\}^n$, it chooses random values $r_d \in \{0,1\}^{poly(n)}$ and $r_e \in \{0,1\}^{poly(n)}$. Then it encrypts m as

$$CT = Encrypt(1^n, \varphi, m, (r_d, r_e)) = \mathcal{O}(I_{\varphi,m}; r_d), \mathcal{MO}(I_{m,r_d}; r_e) = CT_0, CT_1.$$

- **Decrypt** $(1^n, \cdot, (\varphi, w))$: On input a ciphertext CT, it parses $CT = CT_0, CT_1$, and runs CT_0 on w. If $CT_0(w) = m' \neq 0$, it runs CT_1 on m' and sets $r'_d = CT_1(m')$. Then it computes $CT'_0 = \mathcal{O}(I_{\varphi,m'}; r'_d)$. If $CT'_0 = CT_0$, it outputs m', otherwise it outputs the symbol $\perp$.

Theorem 3.2. *Let L be defined as above. Assuming that there are public-coin diO algorithms for the function family* $\{I_{\phi,y}\}_{y \in \{0,1\}^{poly n}}$, *where ϕ is a variable of the uniform distribution of hard problems for L. Additionally assuming the existence of weak AIMPO. Then, the Construction 3.2 is a unique witness encryption.*

4   Application

We first show how to use our weak UWE to construct a 4-round non-black-box honest-verifier zero-knowledge argument $\langle P, V \rangle$ for any NP language L. Then by replacing the weak UWE with UWE, we can get rid of the limitation of honest-verifier zero-knowledge property, thus yielding a 4-round zero-knowledge argument.

Definition 4.1 Interactive Proof System. *A pair of interactive Turing machines $\langle P, V \rangle$ is called an interactive proof system for a language L if machine V is polynomial-time and the following two conditions hold:*

- *Completeness: There exists a negligible function c such that for every $x \in L$,
  $\Pr[\langle P, V \rangle(x) = 1] > 1 - c(|x|)$;*
- *Soundness: There exists a negligible function s such that for every $x \notin L$ and every interactive machine B, it holds that $\Pr[\langle B, V \rangle(x) = 1] < s(|x|)$.*

$c(\cdot)$ is called the completeness error, and $s(\cdot)$ the soundness error.

If the soundness condition holds against computationally bounded provers, $\langle P, V \rangle$ is an interactive argument system. Let $View^P_{V(z)}(x)$ denote the view of V with auxiliary input z in the real execution of the protocol with P.

Definition 4.2 Honest-Verifier Zero-Knowledge Argument (HVZKA). *Let $\langle P, V \rangle$ be an interactive argument system for an NP language L. $\langle P, V \rangle$ is said to be honest-verifier zero-knowledge if there exists a PPT algorithm S such that $\{View^P_V(x)\}_{x \in L}$ and $\{S(x)\}_{x \in L}$ are computationally indistinguishable.*

Definition 4.3 Zero-Knowledge Argument (ZKA). *Let $\langle P, V \rangle$ be an interactive argument system for an NP language L. $\langle P, V \rangle$ is said to be zero-knowledge if for every PPT malicious verifier V^* there exists a PPT algorithm S such that the distributions $\{View^P_{V^*(z)}(x)\}_{x \in L, z \in \{0,1\}^*}$ and $\{S(x, z)\}_{x \in L, z \in \{0,1\}^*}$ are computationally indistinguishable.*

We use Barak's non-black-box simulation [4] and use $StatGen := \langle P_1, V_1 \rangle$ to denote the statement generation protocol in [4]. Let $\mathcal{H}_n$ be a family of collision-resistant hash functions $h \in \mathcal{H}_n$ such that $h : \{0,1\}^* \to \{0,1\}^n$ and let Com be a non-interactive statistically-binding commitment scheme for $\{0,1\}^n$.

Barak's Statement Generation Protocol in [4] $StatGen := \langle P_1, V_1 \rangle$**:**

1. V_1 sends a random $h \leftarrow \mathcal{H}$.
2. P_1 send a commitment $c = Com(0^n; r_c)$, where r_c is chosen randomly.
3. V_1 sends a random string $r \in \{0,1\}^n$

The transcript of the protocol is $\tau := (h, c, r)$. The language is defined as

$$L_1 = \{\tau := \langle h, c, r \rangle : \exists\, \sigma = (\Pi, r_c) \text{ such that } c = Com(h(\Pi); r_c) \wedge \Pi(c) = r\},$$

where (h, c, r) is sampled by $StatGen$.

4.1 Zero-Knowledge Protocols

For any NP language L, we first define a subset $L_{hard} \subseteq L$ as

$$L_{hard} = \{x : x \in L \wedge x \text{ is a hard problem for } L\}.$$

That is, L_{hard} consists of all the hard instances in L such that for any $x \in L_{hard}$ and for any PPT algorithm A, $\Pr[\mathcal{R}_L(x,w) = 1 : w \leftarrow A(x)] < negl(n)$.

For a (weak) UWE scheme related to L as constructed in Sect. 3, we can see that the correctness and (weak) unique decryption properties still hold as required while the message indistinguishability will hold for instances sampled from $(\{0,1\}^n \cap L_{hard}) \cup (\{0,1\}^n \backslash L)$. Fortunately, this condition is sufficient for our zero-knowledge protocol.

Let $\mathcal{H}_n$ and Com be defined as above. Let $Pre_n(\cdot)$ be a function that outputs the first n bits of its input. Then we modify the language L_1 as

$$L_2 = \{\tau := \langle h,c,r \rangle : \exists\, \sigma = (\Pi, r_c) \text{ s.t. } c = Com(h(\Pi); r_c) \wedge Pre_n(\Pi(c)) = r\},$$

where (h,c,r) is sampled by the prover and the verifier of our zero-knowledge protocol. Let $l = l(n) = |\tau|$ be the length of instances of L_2.

We define another NP language $L_{UWE} = \{(x,\tau) : x \in L \text{ Or } \tau \in L_2\}$ as follows.

$$L_{UWE} = \left\{ \begin{array}{l} (x,(h,c,r)) : \exists\, w \text{ s.t. } \mathcal{R}_L(x,w) = 1 \text{ Or} \\ \exists\, \sigma = (\Pi, r_c) \text{ s.t. } (c = Com(h(\Pi); r_c) \wedge Pre_n(\Pi(c)) = r) \end{array} \right\},$$

where (h,c,r) is sampled by the prover and the verifier, and the relation is $\mathcal{R}_{L_{UWE}}$.

$P(x,w)$		$V(x)$
	$\xleftarrow{\quad h \quad}$	select $h \in \mathcal{H}$
select $r_c \in \{0,1\}^*$,		
compute $c = Com(0^n; r_c)$	$\xrightarrow{\quad c \quad}$	select $r \in \{0,1\}^*$, $m \in \{0,1\}^n$
		set $\phi = (x, (h,c,r))$ as an instance
		of L', compute
compute m' with	$\xleftarrow{\;r, ct\;}$	$ct = WUWE.Enc(1^n, \phi, m)$
$WUWE.Dec(1^n, ct, (\phi, w))$	$\xrightarrow{\quad m' \quad}$	accept iff $m' = m$

Fig. 1. 4-round HVZKA protocol

Let $WUWE = (Enc, Dec)$ be a weak UWE scheme related to L_{UWE} as constructed in Sect. 3, then the message indistinguishability will hold for instances sampled from $(\{0,1\}^{n+l} \cap (L_{UWE})_{hard}) \cup (\{0,1\}^{n+l} \backslash (L_{UWE}))$. Now we show our 4-round protocol $\langle P, V \rangle$ for L.

The prover P and verifier V first execute Barak's generation protocol and obtain a transcript $\tau = (h, c, r)$. After executing the protocol $StatGen$ the prover

618   D. Pan et al.

and the verifier obtain an instance $(x, (h, c, r))$ of L_{UWE}. Notice that the prover has an input w such that $\mathcal{R}_L(x, w) = 1$, and thus the prover has an witness for $(x, (h, c, r)) \in L_{UWE}$. On the third round, besides a random string $r \in \{0, 1\}^n$, the verifier also sends a ciphertext $ct = WUWE.Enc(1^n, (x, (h, c, r)), m)$, where m is chosen randomly in $\{0, 1\}^n$. In the fourth round, the prover computes $m' = WUWE.Dec(1^n, ct, ((x, (h, c, r)), w))$ and sends m'. The verifier checks $m' = m$ and accepts $x \in L$ if the check succeeds. The detail of our zero-knowledge argument protocol is shown in Fig. 1.

Theorem 4.1. *Assuming the existence of collision-resistant hash function and the Construction 3.1 is a weak unique witness encryption scheme. Then, the construction in Fig. 1 is an honest-verifier zero-knowledge argument protocol.*

Theorem 4.2. *Assuming the existence of collision-resistant hash function and the Construction 3.2 is a unique witness encryption scheme. Then, by replacing the weak UWE scheme used in Fig. 1 with a UWE scheme, the construction is a zero-knowledge argument protocol.*

Acknowledgement. This work is supported by National Key R&D Program of China (No. 2017YFB0802500). This work is also partially supported by the Swedish Research Council (Vetenskapsrådet) through the grant PRECIS (621-2014-4845).

References

1. Abusalah, H., Fuchsbauer, G., Pietrzak, K.: Offline witness encryption. In: Manulis, M., Sadeghi, A.-R., Schneider, S. (eds.) ACNS 2016. LNCS, vol. 9696, pp. 285–303. Springer, Cham (2016). https://doi.org/10.1007/978-3-319-39555-5_16
2. Ananth, P., Jain, A., Naor, M., Sahai, A., Yogev, E.: Universal constructions and robust combiners for indistinguishability obfuscation and witness encryption. In: Robshaw, M., Katz, J. (eds.) CRYPTO 2016. LNCS, vol. 9815, pp. 491–520. Springer, Heidelberg (2016). https://doi.org/10.1007/978-3-662-53008-5_17
3. Arita, S., Handa, S.: Two applications of multilinear maps: group key exchange and witness encryption. In: ACM Workshop on Asia Public-key Cryptography (2014)
4. Barak, B.: How to go beyond the black-box simulation barrier. In: IEEE Symposium on Foundations of Computer Science (2001)
5. Bellare, M., Hoang, V.T.: Adaptive witness encryption and asymmetric password-based cryptography. In: Katz, J. (ed.) PKC 2015. LNCS, vol. 9020, pp. 308–331. Springer, Heidelberg (2015). https://doi.org/10.1007/978-3-662-46447-2_14
6. Bitansky, N., Paneth, O.: Point obfuscation and 3-round zero-knowledge. In: Cramer, R. (ed.) TCC 2012. LNCS, vol. 7194, pp. 190–208. Springer, Heidelberg (2012). https://doi.org/10.1007/978-3-642-28914-9_11
7. Brakerski, Z., Jain, A., Komargodski, I., Passelègue, A., Wichs, D.: Non-trivial witness encryption and null-iO from standard assumptions. In: Catalano, D., De Prisco, R. (eds.) SCN 2018. LNCS, vol. 11035, pp. 425–441. Springer, Cham (2018). https://doi.org/10.1007/978-3-319-98113-0_23
8. Derler, D., Slamanig, D.: Practical witness encryption for algebraic languages or how to encrypt under groth-sahai proofs. Des. Codes Crypt. 2, 1–23 (2018)

9. Garg, S., Gentry, C., Halevi, S.: Candidate multilinear maps from ideal lattices. In: Johansson, T., Nguyen, P.Q. (eds.) EUROCRYPT 2013. LNCS, vol. 7881, pp. 1–17. Springer, Heidelberg (2013). https://doi.org/10.1007/978-3-642-38348-9_1

10. Garg, S., Gentry, C., Sahai, A., Waters, B.: Witness encryption and its applications. In: ACM Symposium on Theory of Computing (2013)

11. Gentry, C., Lewko, A., Waters, B.: Witness encryption from instance independent assumptions. In: Garay, J.A., Gennaro, R. (eds.) CRYPTO 2014. LNCS, vol. 8616, pp. 426–443. Springer, Heidelberg (2014). https://doi.org/10.1007/978-3-662-44371-2_24

12. Goldreich, O., Levin, L.A.: A hard-core predicate for all one-way functions. In: ACM Symposium on Theory of Computing (1989)

13. Ishai, Y., Pandey, O., Sahai, A.: Public-coin differing-inputs obfuscation and its applications. In: Dodis, Y., Nielsen, J.B. (eds.) TCC 2015. LNCS, vol. 9015, pp. 668–697. Springer, Heidelberg (2015). https://doi.org/10.1007/978-3-662-46497-7_26

14. Niu, Q., Li, H., Huang, G., Liang, B., Tang, F.: One-round witness indistinguishability from indistinguishability obfuscation. In: Lopez, J., Wu, Y. (eds.) ISPEC 2015. LNCS, vol. 9065, pp. 559–574. Springer, Cham (2015). https://doi.org/10.1007/978-3-319-17533-1_38

Speeding up Scalar Multiplication on Koblitz Curves Using μ_4 Coordinates

Weixuan Li[1,2,3], Wei Yu[1,2(✉)], Bao Li[1,2], and Xuejun Fan[1,2,3]

[1] State Key Laboratory of Information Security,
Institute of Information Engineering, Chinese Academy of Sciences, Beijing, China
wxli13@is.ac.cn, yuwei_1_yw@163.com
[2] Data Assurance and Communication Security Research Center,
Chinese Academy of Sciences, Beijing, China
[3] School of Cyber Security, University of Chinese Academy of Sciences,
Beijing, China

Abstract. Koblitz curves are a special family of binary elliptic curves satisfying equation $y^2 + xy = x^3 + ax^2 + 1$, $a \in \{0, 1\}$. Scalar multiplication on Koblitz curves can be achieved with point addition and fast Frobenius endomorphism. We show a new point representation system μ_4 coordinates for Koblitz curves. When $a = 0$, μ_4 coordinates derive basic group operations—point addition and mixed-addition with complexities $7\mathbf{M} + 2\mathbf{S}$ and $6\mathbf{M} + 2\mathbf{S}$, respectively. Moreover, Frobenius endomorphism on μ_4 coordinates requires $4\mathbf{S}$. Compared with the state-of-the-art λ representation system, the timings obtained using μ_4 coordinates show speed-ups of 28.6% to 32.2% for NAF algorithms, of 13.7% to 20.1% for τNAF and of 18.4% to 23.1% for regular τNAF on four NIST-recommended Koblitz curves K-233, K-283, K-409 and K-571.

1 Introduction

Firstly proposed by Koblitz [5], Koblitz curves are a special family of binary elliptic curves, defined over binary fields $\mathbb{F}_{2^m}$ by equation $K_a : y^2 + xy = x^3 + ax^2 + 1, a \in \{0, 1\}$. NIST [4] recommended four Koblitz curves, K-233, K-283, K-409 and K-571, with $a = 0$, to satisfy different cryptographic security level requirements. The family of Koblitz curves draws a lot of interests, resulting from its compatibility with highly efficient computable Frobenius endomorphism $\tau P(x, y) = (x^2, y^2)$, for any point $P \in K_a$. Let $\mu = (-1)^{1-a}$, one can verify that τ satisfies the quadratic equation $\tau^2 P + 2P = \mu \tau P$. Therefore it is possible to replace doubling operations by Frobenius maps in scalar multiplication algorithms using Koblitz curves. Solinas [10] developed several radix-τ based scalar recoding algorithms, including τ *non-adjacent form*(NAF) and window τNAF algorithms.

This work is supported by the National Natural Science Foundation of China (No. 61872442, No. 61802401, No. 61502487) and the National Cryptography Development Fund (No. MMJJ20180216).

J. Jang-Jaccard and F. Guo (Eds.): ACISP 2019, LNCS 11547, pp. 620–629, 2019.
https://doi.org/10.1007/978-3-030-21548-4_34

In 2017, Kohel [6] proposed binary twisted μ_4-normal elliptic curves:

$$X_0^2 + bX_2^2 = X_1X_3 + aX_0X_2, X_1^2 + X_3^2 = X_0X_2, \tag{1}$$

with a $9\mathbf{M} + 2\mathbf{S}$ addition and a $2\mathbf{M} + 5\mathbf{S} + 2\mathbf{m}$ doubling formulas, where $\mathbf{m}$ represents a multiplication by a fixed constant that is related to curve parameters. The new form arises from a linear transformation of twisted Edwards curves in extended Edwards coordinates [2] over prime fields and has good reduction at characteristic 2. Besides efficient point operations resulted from inherited symmetries of twisted Edwards curves, another prominent advantage of twisted μ_4-normal curves is that they cover all the NIST-recommended binary elliptic curves. Inspired by his work, we modify the birational equivalence between binary Weierstrass and twisted μ_4-normal elliptic curves [6] to optimize the efficiency of Koblitz curves. In another respect, we may view twisted μ_4-normal form as a new coordinates representation system for Koblitz curves and exploit its point operations, especially Frobenius endomorphism, to improve the efficiency of protected and unprotected scalar multiplication.

Our Contributions. The purpose of this paper is to utilize μ_4 coordinates system to accelerate the performance of basic group operations on Koblitz curves. The new projective coordinates system and its group operation significantly speed up scalar multiplication algorithms.

- The full-addition formulas in μ_4 coordinates cost $7\mathbf{M} + 2\mathbf{S}$ or $8\mathbf{M} + 2\mathbf{S}$ for parameter $a = 0$ or $a = 1$. A mixed-addition $R = P + Q$ with P represented in affine μ_4 coordinates saves $1\mathbf{M}$, additionally. Besides a faster doubling formula that costs $2\mathbf{M} + 6\mathbf{S}$, we show that Frobenius endomorphism on μ_4 coordinates requires $4\mathbf{M}$. For completeness, we present a precise verification that Frobenius endomorphism satisfies the quadratic equation $\tau^2 P + 2P = (-1)^{1-a}\tau P$, for every point P on Koblitz curves.
- We investigate several scalar multiplication algorithms and give a theoretic analysis of how μ_4 coordinates system affects the performance of scalar multiplication. From the standpoint of efficiency, our work include NAF, τNAF, and window τNAF with window width $3, 4, 5, 6$. In consideration of protected execution to resist side-channel attacks, we analyze point multiplication based on regular τNAF expansion of scalars. The results are influenced by squaring to multiplication ratios(denoted as $\mathbf{S}/\mathbf{M}$) on different platforms. We assume that $\mathbf{S}/\mathbf{M}$ ratio ranges from 0 to 0.4.
- In the discussion of implementation issues, we test four NIST-recommended Koblitz curves: K-233, K-283, K-409 and K-571. From an efficiency standpoint, NAF and τNAF scalar multiplication gain considerably improvements when μ_4 coordinates system is implemented. Regular τNAF is also examined to take side-channel threats into account. Compared with λ coordinates, the timings obtained using μ_4 coordinates show a speed-up of 28.6% to 32.2% for NAF, of 13.7% to 20.1% for τNAF and of 18.4% to 23.1% for regular τNAF algorithms.

2   New Arithmetic on Koblitz Curves

The focus of this section is on Koblitz curves represented in projective μ_4 coordinates, and defined over binary fields $\mathbb{F}_{2^m}$ by equation

$$E_a : X_0^2 + X_2^2 = X_1 X_3 + a X_0 X_2, X_1^2 + X_3^2 = X_0 X_2 \qquad (2)$$

with $a \in \mathbb{F}_2$. It can be derived from Corollary 10 in [6] that any point $P(x_0, x_1, x_3)$ on affine part of E_a

$$x_0^2 + 1 = x_1 x_3 + a x_0, x_1^2 + x_3^2 = x_0$$

is isomorphic to Koblitz curves in affine coordinates $K_a / \mathbb{F}_{2^m} : y^2 + xy = x^3 + ax^2 + 1$, by rational polynomial $(x_0, x_1, x_3) \mapsto (x_1 + x_3, x_0 + x_1)$, and its inverse map $(x, y) \mapsto (x^2, x^2 + y, x^2 + x + y)$. With the above morphisms between E_a and K_a, one can derive an addition formula on E_a, as an analog to "chord-and-tangent" law on Koblitz forms. As a consequence of Theorem 4 in [6], the addition laws space of bidegree $(2, 2)$ for E_a is a 4-dimensional $\mathbb{F}_{2^m}$-linear space. Any two $\mathbb{F}_{2^m}$-linear independent elements in the addition laws space form a complete addition law system.

Based on Kohel's original paper [6] and conference slides (see http://iml.univ-mrs.fr/kohel/pub/eurocrypt_2017_slides.pdf), we generalize optimized group arithmetic for E_a.

2.1   Addition and Doubling Algorithms

Depending on different values of a, addition formulas for E_a.

Theorem 1. [6] *Let $E_a : X_0^2 + X_2^2 = X_1 X_3 + a X_0 X_2, X_1^2 + X_3^2 = X_0 X_2$, where $a \in \{0, 1\}$, be Koblitz curves in μ_4 coordinates. Then there exist $7\mathbf{M} + 2\mathbf{S}$ and $8\mathbf{M} + 2\mathbf{S}$ addition for E_0 and E_1 separately.*

The mixed-addition follows the same formulas as point addition, by specializing $Y_2 = 1$. So we have the following corollary.

Corollary 1. *Let $E_a : X_0^2 + X_2^2 = X_1 X_3 + a X_0 X_2, X_1^2 + X_3^2 = X_0 X_2$, where $a \in \{0, 1\}$, be Koblitz curves in μ_4 coordinates. Mixed-addition algorithm for E_a can be done in $6\mathbf{M} + 2\mathbf{S}$ when curve parameter $a = 0$, in $7\mathbf{M} + 2\mathbf{S}$ when $a = 1$.*

What we show below is doubling formula for Koblitz curves in μ_4 coordinates.

Theorem 2. [6] *Let $E_a : X_0^2 + X_2^2 = X_1 X_3 + a X_0 X_2, X_1^2 + X_3^2 = X_0 X_2$, where $a \in \{0, 1\}$, be Koblitz curves in μ_4 coordinates. Then there exists a $2\mathbf{M} + 6\mathbf{S}$ doubling algorithm for E_a.*

2.2 Frobenius Endomorphism

In cryptographic circles, Koblitz curves draw a lot of interests because point doublings can be replaced by the efficiently computable Frobenius automorphism $\tau : (x, y) \mapsto (x^2, y^2)$, leading to a more efficient scalar multiplication. If elements in binary fields are represented in normal bases, the cost of Frobenius map is negligible. What's more, for any point P on Koblitz curves K_a, the quadratic equation $\tau^2 P + 2P = \mu \tau P$ holds, where $\mu = (-1)^{1-a}$, $a \in \{0, 1\}$ is the curve parameter. This means that Frobenius map on P can be regarded as multiplying complex number $\frac{\mu + \sqrt{-7}}{2}$.

Similar techniques can be developed for E_a, taking advantages of the fact that squares are easily implemented by bit shifts if elements in $\mathbb{F}_{2^m}$ are represented in terms of a set of normal basis. Under this condition, for any point $P(X_0, X_1, X_2, X_3)$ in μ_4 coordinates, we call $\tau P = (X_0^2, X_1^2, X_2^2, X_3^2)$ Frobenius endomorphism of P on E_a. What's more, τ satisfies the following theorem.

Theorem 3. *Let $E_a : X_0^2 + X_2^2 = X_1 X_3 + a X_0 X_2, X_1^2 + X_3^2 = X_0 X_2$ be Koblitz curves in μ_4 coordinates, and $a \in \{0, 1\}$. Then the Frobenius map τ satisfies $\tau^2 P + 2P = (-1)^{1-a} \tau P$ for any point $P \in E_a$.*

Proof. For a point $P_E(X_0, X_1, X_2, X_3)$ on E_a, the corresponding point P_K on K_a is $\phi : (X_0, X_1, X_2, X_3) \mapsto (X_1 + X_3, X_0 + X_1, X_2)$. After operation by Frobenius map on K_a,

$$\tau : K_a \to K_a$$

$$(X_1 + X_3, X_0 + X_1, X_2) \mapsto (X_1^2 + X_3^2, X_0^2 + X_1^2, X_2^2)$$

we have τP_K. Then pullback the resulted point on K_a through $\phi^{-1} : (X_1^2 + X_3^2, X_0^2 + X_1^2, X_2^2) \mapsto ((X_1 + X_3)^4, (X_1 + X_3)^4 + (X_0 + X_1)^2 X_2^2, X_2^4, (X_1 + X_3)^4 + (X_0 + X_3)^2 X_2^2) = (X_0^2, X_1^2, X_2^2, X_3^2) = \tau P_E$. That is to say, the following diagram commutes:

$$
\begin{array}{ccc}
E_a & \xrightarrow{\ \phi\ } & K_a \\
{\scriptstyle \tau} \downarrow & & \downarrow {\scriptstyle \tau} \\
E_a & \xleftarrow[\ \phi^{-1}\ ]{} & K_a
\end{array}
$$

Therefore we can easily get a direct verification of this theorem.

2.3 Arithmetic Comparison

Taking the best known algorithms from [1], we present costs comparison of basic arithmetic between different representation systems for Koblitz curves to show the impact of μ_4 coordinates. The transformations between affine Koblitz curves and μ_4 coordinates take several field squares and multiplications, and is negligible compared with costly scalar multiplication process. As to affine form of E_a, we let the X_2-coordinate be 1, as commonly used in mixed-addition formulas. Table 1

Table 1. Comparison of point operations on koblitz curves with different coordinates

Coordinates	Addition	Mixed-addition	Doubling	τ-endomorphism
LD [7]	$13M + 4S$	$8M + 5S$	$3M + 5S$	$3S$
Lambda, $a = 0$ [9]	$11M + 2S$	$8M + 2S$	$3M + 4S$	$3S$
Lambda, $a = 1$ [9]	$11M + 2S$	$8M + 2S$	$3M + 5S$	$3S$
Twisted μ_4, $a = 0$ (this work)	$7M + 2S$	$6M + 2S$	$2M + 6S$	$4S$
Twisted μ_4, $a = 1$ (this work)	$8M + 2S$	$7M + 2S$	$2M + 6S$	$4S$

summarizes the complexity of basic point operations for Koblitz curves using LD coordinates, λ coordinates and μ_4 coordinates.

Although τ endomorphisms on μ_4 coordinates cost more $1S$ than that on lambda coordinates, they are still superior to the later one. One of the reasons is that a squaring is nearly free on $\mathbb{F}_{2^m}$ using normal basis, the other reason is benefiting from faster addition and doubling operations.

3   Scalar Multiplication

This section describes the most prominent accelerations for scalar multiplication algorithms on Koblitz curves in combination with τ endomorphisms, from both efficiency and simple side-channel resistance respect.

3.1 τ-Adic NAF

The existence of complex multiplication τ allows one viewing any integer as an element in the Euclidean ring $\mathbb{Z}[\tau]$. For scalar multiplication on Eq. 2, τ-adic non-adjacent form (τNAF) algorithm converts a scalar k into a finite sum of unsigned powers of τ: $k = \sum_{i=0}^{m} s_i \tau^i$, $s_i \in \{0, \pm 1\}$.

In [10], Solinas proposed an efficient reduced τNAF expansion for any integers of which the average Hamming weight is $\frac{m}{3}$, where m is the bit length of the scalar. To derive short representation, this algorithm first find an element ρ of as small norm as possible, such that $\rho \equiv k \mod (\tau^m - 1)/(\tau - 1)$. This process is easily implemented by modular reduction in $\mathbb{Z}[\tau]$. Then for a point P of E_a, $kP = \rho P$ and an on-the-fly right-to-left scalar multiplication based on τNAF expansion is derived. The recoding procedure is analogous to the derivation of k's binary representation, via modifying the process of dividing by 2 into dividing by τ during main iteration. τNAF computes multiplication by a m-bit scalar k by total complexity of m τ endomorphisms and $\frac{m}{3}$ mixed-addition. τ-adic NAF is particularly suitable for unknown point scalar multiplication, because it necessitates no precomputation and memory storage space, except intrinsic mathematical descriptions of curves themselves.

3.2 Window-ω τ-Adic NAF

In consideration of fixed-point scalar multiplication, with sufficient memory for storing a few multiples of the known point, a window-ω τNAF [10] is preferred for it decreases the amount of essential point additions, as shown in Algorithm 1. Let $\{U_k\}$ be a Lucas sequence w.r.t E_a that satisfies the following relation:

$$U_0 = 0, U_1 = 1, U_{k+1} = \mu U_k - 2U_{k-1}, \text{ for } k \geq 1,$$

and $\mu = (-1)^{1-a}$. Let $t_\omega = 2U_{\omega-1}U_\omega^{-1} \mod 2^\omega$. Deriving from the property of $\{U_k\}$, t_ω is viewed as the ω-th 2-adic approximation of τ, and satisfies $t_\omega^2 + 2 - \mu \cdot t_\omega \equiv 0 \mod 2^\omega$.

Let ϕ_ω be the ring homomorphism between $\mathbb{Z}[\tau]$ and $\mathbb{Z}/2^\omega\mathbb{Z}$,

$$\phi_\omega : \mathbb{Z}[\tau] \to \mathbb{Z}/2^\omega\mathbb{Z}$$
$$u_0 + u_1\tau \mapsto u_0 + u_1 t_\omega.$$

In light of [10], ϕ_ω preserves the congruent relationship, that is, each incongruent class in $\mathbb{Z}[\tau]$ corresponds to incongruent class under ϕ_ω in $\mathbb{Z}/2^\omega\mathbb{Z}$. Theorem 4 permits an easy precomputation of window-ω τNAF.

Theorem 4. $\{\pm 1, \pm 3, \cdots, \pm(2^{\omega-1} - 1)\}$ *are odd incongruent classes modulo* 2^ω. *Compute* $\alpha_i = i \mod \tau^\omega$, $i \in \{\pm 1, \pm 3, \cdots, \pm(2^{\omega-1} - 1)\}$, *then* α_i *are odd incongruent classes modulo* τ^ω.

Algorithm 1. Window-ω τ Non-adjacent Form

Data: ω; t_ω; $r_0 + r_1\tau \equiv k \mod \frac{\tau^m - 1}{\tau - 1}$

Result: $k = \sum_{i=0} u_i\tau^i$, $u_i \in \{0, \pm 1, \pm 3, \cdots, \pm(2^{\omega-1} - 1)\}$

Set $i \leftarrow 0$;

while $r_0 \neq 0$ *or* $r_1 \neq 0$ **do**

    if r_0 *is odd* **then**

        $u_i \leftarrow r_0 + r_1 t_\omega \mod 2^\omega$;

        $r_0 \leftarrow r_0 - u_i$

    else

        $u_i \leftarrow 0$

    end

    $i \leftarrow i + 1$, $r_0 \leftarrow r_1 + \frac{\mu r_0}{2}$, $r_1 \leftarrow \frac{-r_0}{2}$

end

Return $(\cdots, u_1, u_0)$

Algorithm 1 achieves further acceleration by representing a scalar k into a m-bit string $k = \sum_{i=0}^m u_i 2^i$, $u_i \in \{0, \pm 1, \pm 3, \cdots, \pm(2^{\omega-1} - 1)\}$, with average density $\frac{1}{\omega+1}$. [12] evaluated the total costs of optimal precomputation schemes for window-ω τNAF. It requires $2^{\omega-2} - 1$ mixed additions and two Frobenius maps when window width $\omega \geq 4$. When $\omega = 3$, only one Frobenius map τ is needed.

3.3   Regular τ-Adic Expansion Approach

Oliveira, Aranha, López and Henríguez [8] designed a regular window-ω τ-adic non-adjacent expansion, inspired by Joye and Tunstall's key idea [3] that any odd integer i in $[0, 2^{\omega+1})$ can be rewritten as $2^\omega + (-(2^\omega - i))$. Algorithm 2 achieves a constant-time regular τ-adic expansion for an integer, that is compatible with Frobenius endomorphism and provides efficient scalar multiplication algorithm against simple side-channel attacks.

Algorithm 2. Regular τ-Adic NAF Scalar Multiplication

Data: $r_0 + r_1\tau \equiv k \mod \frac{\tau^m - 1}{\tau - 1}$ with r_0 is odd; an elliptic point P
Result: $kP = \sum_{i=0}^m u_i\tau^i P$, $u_i \in \{-1, 1\}$
Set $Q \leftarrow \mathcal{O}, T \leftarrow P$;
while $r_0 \neq 0$ *or* $r_1 \neq 0$ **do**
  $u \leftarrow ((r_0 - 2r_1) \mod 4) - 2, r_0 \leftarrow r_0 - u$;
  if $u = 1$ **then**
  | $Q \leftarrow Q + T$
  else
  | $Q \leftarrow Q - T$
  end
  $T \leftarrow \tau T, r_0 \leftarrow r_1 + \frac{\mu r_0}{2}, r_1 \leftarrow \frac{-r_0}{2}$
end
Return Q

Assume an attacker is able to distinguish the process of τ multiplication and point addition, by detecting time consumption or other physical information. Algorithm 2 is simple side-channel attacks resistant. It recodes a scalar into a regular sequence of digits in $\{-1, 1\}$, and eliminates side-channel information that an attacker could gather. Because in each iteration both a point multiplication and a τ endomorphism are required. In the meanwhile, it is an on-the-fly algorithm and requires no pre-computation and storage, and particularly suitable for variant-scalar multiplication or restricted storage environments. In this setting, the total cost of the scalar multiplication using Algorithm 2 is m Frobenius endomorphisms and m additions on average.

3.4   Costs Comparison

We present theoretic complexity analysis of the above algorithms for Koblitz curves, based on different **S/M** ratios, in μ_4 coordinates and λ coordinates respectively. Platform constructions are influential to **S/M** ratios. Suppose that **S/M**= 0 or 0.2, as suggested by Bernstein and Lange [1] in characteristic 2 fields. Moreover, the authors of [11] proposed to employ the carry-less instruction in Intel processors, significantly accelerates field multiplication on binary fields. Under this circumstance **S/M** reaches 0.4 closely.

τNAF, window-ω τNAF and regular τNAF algorithms recode a m-bit scalar into a sequence digits of density $\frac{1}{3}$, $\frac{1}{\omega+1}$ and 1, respectively. Counting point operations during each scalar multiplication, Table 2 conclude the total costs for $a = 0$ Koblitz curves in terms of field multiplications of the above algorithms. It should be noted that the cost of precomputation scheme for window-ω τNAF is negligible compared with that of multiplying a large scalar. As a consequence, the data in Table 2 exclude precomputation costs.

Table 2. Complexity for m-bit scalar multiplications on $a = 0$ Koblitz curves

Algorithms	λ coordinates			μ_4 coordinates		
	S = 0M	S = 0.2M	S = 0.4M	S = 0M	S = 0.2M	S = 0.4M
NAF	$5.67m$M	$6.6m$M	$7.53m$M	$4m$M	$5.33m$M	$6.66m$M
τNAF	$2.67m$M	$3.4m$M	$4.13m$M	$2m$M	$2.93m$M	$3.86m$M
window-ω τNAF($\omega = 3$)	$2m$M	$2.7m$M	$3.4m$M	$1.5m$M	$2.4m$M	$3.3m$M
window-ω τNAF($\omega = 4$)	$1.6m$M	$2.28m$M	$2.96m$M	$1.2m$M	$2.08m$M	$2.96m$M
window-ω τNAF($\omega = 5$)	$1.33m$M	$2m$M	$2.66m$M	$1m$M	$1.87m$M	$2.73m$M
window-ω τNAF($\omega = 6$)	$1.14m$M	$1.80m$M	$2.45m$M	$0.86m$M	$1.72m$M	$2.57m$M
regular τNAF	$8m$M	$9m$M	$10m$M	$6m$M	$7.2m$M	$8.4m$M

It turns out that when $a = 0$, NAF algorithm in μ_4 coordinates saves 11.5%, 19.2% and 29.4% complexity compared with that in λ coordinates, when the S/M ratio is 0.4, 0.2 and 0. Similar results for τ-based NAF algorithm in μ_4 coordinates saves 6.5%, 13.8% and 25% when $a = 0$. As to window-ω τNAF, we select four typical window widths $\omega = 3, 4, 5$ and 6. Window width-3 τNAF algorithm in μ_4 coordinates saves 2.9%, 11.1% and 25% complexity compared with that in λ coordinates, when the S/M ratios are 0.4, 0.2 and 0. When window width is 4, if the S/M ratio is 0.4, it shows no efficiency difference between μ_4 coordinates and λ coordinates; if S/M ratio is 0.2, μ_4 coordinates system saves 8.7% complexity; if the cost of field squaring is neglected, the margin becomes 25%. When window width is larger than 5 and S/M ratio is no less than 0.2, window τNAF scalar multiplication on Koblitz curves using μ_4 coordinates is not as efficient as that in λ coordinates. From side-channel resistant standpoint, using μ_4 coordinates in regular τNAF algorithm saves 16% to 25% complexity compared that in λ coordinates, when the S/M ratio ranges from 0.4 to 0.

4   Implementation Results

To evaluate the performance of τ endomorphisms for Koblitz curves in μ_4 coordinates, we developed experiments on a 3.20 GHz Intel Core i5 processor in C++ programming language. The tests were compiled with Visual Studio 2013 on a 64-bit Windows 10 OS, using C programming language Miracl library for multi-precision arithmetic. Particularly, we ignored the scalar recoding procedures that turned an integer into a reduced τNAF representation chain.

We considered NIST-recommended Koblitz curves K-233, K-283, K-409 and K-571[4]. A remarkable common feature of these curves is that parameter $a = 0$ for all curves, under which condition the addition formula of μ_4 coordinates is considerably faster than that in λ coordinates. In this section, we test the practical efficiency of several algorithms for unprotected and protected scalar multiplication for Koblitz curves.

We run each algorithm 100000 times on K-233, K-283, K-409 and K-571 with a fixed elliptic point P and random scalars k, using μ_4 coordinates and λ coordinates separately. Table 3 reports the required average timings for radix-2 NAF scalar multiplication, in terms of clock cycles. Regardless of SPA-resistance and precomputation, it's shown that using μ_4 coordinates saves 28.6%, 29.3%, 30.7% and 32.2% timings compared with that using λ coordinates on K-233, K-283, K-409 and K-571. Besides, we also notice that using μ_4 coordinates when implementing τNAF scalar multiplication provides a speed-up of 13.7% to 20.1% on different security level Koblitz curves, as shown in Table 3. We report the timings obtained for regular τNAF using μ_4 coordinates and λ coordinates respectively. Protected algorithms requires considerable overheads. Experiments show that using μ_4 coordinates, when implementing regular τNAF scalar multiplication, provides a speed-up of 18.4%, 21.3%, 22.1% and 23.1% on K-233, K-283, K-409 and K-571 respectively.

Table 3. Timings of NAF scalar multiplication algorithms (in 10^3 clock cycles)

		K233	K283	K409	K571
NAF	μ_4 coordinates	1389	1982	5071	10279
	λ coordinates	1947	2805	7319	15167
τNAF	μ_4 coordinates	728	1046	2581	4892
	λ coordinates	844	1261	3122	6124
regular τNAF	μ_4 coordinates	1928	2771	6802	13724
	λ coordinates	2363	3523	8735	17849

5   Conclusion

We provide efficient arithmetic for Koblitz curves, by introducing μ_4 coordinates system. Particularly, we study its compatibility with Frobenious endomorphisms and improvements on unprotected and protected scalar multiplication algorithms. From both efficiency and security standpoint, we implement τ morphisms on NAF, τNAF and regular τNAF using μ_4 coordinates for NIST-recommended Koblitz curves K-233, K-283, K-409 and K-571. Compared with the state-of-the-art λ coordinates, the timings obtained show a speed-up of 28.6% to 32.2% for NAF algorithms, of 13.7% to 20.1% for τNAF and of 18.4% to 23.1% for regular τNAF scalar multiplications.

References

1. Bernstein, D.J.: Explicit-formulas database (2007)
2. Hisil, H., Wong, K.K.-H., Carter, G., Dawson, E.: Twisted Edwards curves revisited. In: Pieprzyk, J. (ed.) ASIACRYPT 2008. LNCS, vol. 5350, pp. 326–343. Springer, Heidelberg (2008). https://doi.org/10.1007/978-3-540-89255-7_20
3. Joye, M., Tunstall, M.: Exponent recoding and regular exponentiation algorithms. In: Preneel, B. (ed.) AFRICACRYPT 2009. LNCS, vol. 5580, pp. 334–349. Springer, Heidelberg (2009). https://doi.org/10.1007/978-3-642-02384-2_21
4. Kerry, C.F., Director, C.R.: FIPS PUB 186-4 federal information processing standards publication digital signature standard (DSS) (2013)
5. Koblitz, N.: CM-curves with good cryptographic properties. In: Feigenbaum, J. (ed.) CRYPTO 1991. LNCS, vol. 576, pp. 279–287. Springer, Heidelberg (1992). https://doi.org/10.1007/3-540-46766-1_22
6. Kohel, D.: Twisted μ_4-normal form for elliptic curves. In: Coron, J.-S., Nielsen, J.B. (eds.) EUROCRYPT 2017. LNCS, vol. 10210, pp. 659–678. Springer, Cham (2017). https://doi.org/10.1007/978-3-319-56620-7_23
7. López, J., Dahab, R.: Improved algorithms for elliptic curve arithmetic in $GF(2^n)$. In: Tavares, S., Meijer, H. (eds.) SAC 1998. LNCS, vol. 1556, pp. 201–212. Springer, Heidelberg (1999). https://doi.org/10.1007/3-540-48892-8_16
8. Oliveira, T., Aranha, D.F., López, J., Rodríguez-Henríquez, F.: Fast point multiplication algorithms for binary elliptic curves with and without precomputation. In: Joux, A., Youssef, A. (eds.) SAC 2014. LNCS, vol. 8781, pp. 324–344. Springer, Cham (2014). https://doi.org/10.1007/978-3-319-13051-4_20
9. Oliveira, T., López, J., Aranha, D.F., Rodríguez-Henríquez, F.: Lambda coordinates for binary elliptic curves. In: Bertoni, G., Coron, J.-S. (eds.) CHES 2013. LNCS, vol. 8086, pp. 311–330. Springer, Heidelberg (2013). https://doi.org/10.1007/978-3-642-40349-1_18
10. Solinas, J.A.: Efficient arithmetic on Koblitz curves. Des. Codes Crypt. **19**(2/3), 195–249 (2000)
11. Taverne, J., Faz-Hernndez, A., Aranha, D.F., Rodríguez-Henríquez, F., Hankerson, D., López, J.: Speeding scalar multiplication over binary elliptic curves using the new carry-less multiplication instruction. J. Crypt. Eng. **1**(3), 187 (2011)
12. Trost, W.R., Guangwu, X.: On the optimal pre-computation of window τ NAF for Koblitz curves. IEEE Trans. Comput. **65**(9), 2918–2924 (2016)

Constructing Hyperelliptic Covers for Elliptic Curves over Quadratic Extension Fields

Xuejun Fan[1,2,3(✉)], Song Tian[1,2,3,4(✉)], Bao Li[1,2,3], and Weixuan Li[1,2,3]

[1] School of Cyber Security, University of Chinese Academy of Sciences,
Beijing, China
[2] State Key Laboratory of Information Security,
Institute of Information Engineering, Chinese Academy of Sciences, Beijing, China
{fanxuejun,tiansong}@iie.ac.cn
[3] Data Assurances and Communications Security,
Institute of Information Engineering, Chinese Academy of Sciences, Beijing, China
[4] State Key Laboratory of Cryptology, Beijing, China

Abstract. Elliptic curves and hyperelliptic curves over finite fields are of great interest in public key cryptography. Using much smaller field for same security makes the genus 2 curves more competitive than elliptic curves. However, point counting algorithms for the Jacobians of genus 2 curves are not as efficient as what we have for elliptic curves. We give a method to generate genus 2 curves for which the point counting problems can be easily solved with efficient algorithms for elliptic curves. As an application, an example of a hyperelliptic curve whose order is a 256-bit prime is given. The method relies on the construction of a cover map from a hyperelliptic curve to an elliptic curve. Another important application of the construction is to generate the cover for the cover-decomposition attack on the discrete logarithm problems in elliptic curves.

Keywords: Hyperelliptic curve · Elliptic curve · Cover map · Point counting · Discrete logarithm problem

1 Introduction

The security of public-key cryptosystems relies on the hardness of hard problems such as discrete logarithm problem (DLP) and elliptic curve discrete logarithm problem (ECDLP). The ECDLP is the fundamental building block for elliptic curve cryptography and has been discussed for several decades [5].

Jacobians of hyperelliptic curves have been proposed for use in public key cryptography [6] and it is necessary to count the points on them efficiently. In ECC and HECC [1], the size of cipher-text space defined by the cardinality of the Jacobian is significant to measure the security level. Specifically, the cardinality should be a large prime times a small so-called cofactor c to avoid the Pohlig-Hellman attack [16]. For elliptic curves, there is a practical algorithm

© Springer Nature Switzerland AG 2019
J. Jang-Jaccard and F. Guo (Eds.): ACISP 2019, LNCS 11547, pp. 630–638, 2019.
https://doi.org/10.1007/978-3-030-21548-4_35

SEA to count the number of the rational points [9]. However, for doing this on hyperelliptic curves, no sub-exponential general algorithm is currently known except for some small sets of examples [4], which is an impediment to their use. An algorithm proposed by Gaudry and Harley [17] to compute the orders of the Jacobians of random hyperelliptic curves would run for about a week for a genus 2 curve defined over an 80-bit field. In 2003, Scholten [8] has proposed a way to count the orders of the Jacobians of the hyperelliptic curves of special type $y^2 = rx^6 + sx^4 + \sigma(s)x^2 + \sigma(r)$, where σ is the generator of the Galois group of a quadratic extension. Inspired by Scholten, we consider cover maps can help to count the orders of the Jacobians of hyperelliptic curves and the crucial point is to find the cover maps from some specific hyperelliptic curves to elliptic curves.

In this article, we construct cover maps from hyperelliptic curves of genus 2 to elliptic curves with prime orders over quadratic extension fields. The whole process is based on the results in [7,8,10]. The important fact about the cover map $\phi \colon H/\mathbb{F}_q \to E/\mathbb{F}_{q^2}$ is that the Weierstrass points of the hyperelliptic curve H lie over the 2-torsion points of the elliptic curve E (up to translation). Under the given restrictions, we can get a system of some equations whose solutions determine our cover maps. After many experiments over small fields, we give the special form of f in the equations of hyperelliptic curves $y^2 = f(x)$ that $f = (x - \alpha)(x - \alpha^q)(x - \alpha^{q^2})(x - \gamma)(x - \gamma^q)(x - \gamma^{q^2})$ with $(\alpha + \gamma)(\omega^q + \omega) = 2(\alpha\gamma + \omega^{q+1})$, which offers more specific scope of the hyperelliptic curves suitable for our algorithms. If the Jacobian J_H is simple, then $\#J_H(\mathbb{F}_q) = \#E(\mathbb{F}_{q^2})$, which is useful for calculating $\#J_H(\mathbb{F}_q)$. The experiment can begin with the hyperelliptic curve and aim at finding the corresponding elliptic curve E. Then SEA can be used to compute the cardinality of $E(\mathbb{F}_{q^2})$ to evaluate $\#J_H(\mathbb{F}_q)$ in polynomial running time as long as the cover map exists. At the end of the paper, we give an example over 128-bit field to show the efficiency of our algorithms.

Inspirited by Satoh [11], we can also use our algorithms to generate the required hyperelliptic curves. For example, if a hyperelliptic curve of which the Jacobian has prime order is required, we can randomly select an elliptic curve of prime order as the input of our algorithms. If we can construct the cover map successfully, the required hyperelliptic curve along with the order of its Jacobian can be given. Otherwise, we can select another elliptic curve. The whole process can be viewed as a probabilistic polynomial-time algorithm.

We can also use the cover maps to generate a cover for cover-decomposition attack on ECDLP. For many elliptic curves over finite fields, the fastest algorithms to solve the ECDLP are still generic algorithms. But there are also many families of elliptic curves, in particular those over finite non-prime fields, for which the ECDLP can be solved faster by other methods, such as summation polynomials and cover attacks. The cover attacks [3] aim at reducing the DLP in the group of the rational points of an elliptic curve over $\mathbb{F}_{q^n}$ to the DLP in the Jacobian of a curve C over $\mathbb{F}_q$. The main idea of cover attacks is Weil descent which was first introduced into cryptography by Frey [12]. The major difficulty of cover attacks lies in constructing the curve C, which was first solved by Gaudry, Hess and Smart (GHS) [13] over binary fields and generalized by Diem [2] in odd characteristic. To find an attack which applies to all composite degree extension fields, Joux and Vitse [15] combined the Weil descent with the decomposition attack. They used the GHS attack for the part of Weil descent, while the GHS attack can not produce a cover with small genus to make the whole attack work well when the elliptic curves have cofactor 2 over cubic extension fields. Tian et al. [10] used the result in [7] to overcome the limitation of the GHS attack. In ECC, the elliptic curves of prime orders are of great interest. Our cover maps can be used to transfer the DLP in the elliptic curve with prime order into the DLPs in the Jacobians of hyperelliptic curves which can be solved by decomposition attacks of Nagao [14]. The main difference between GHS and our method is that our algorithms aim at the elliptic curves of prime orders over quadratic extension fields and get curves of genus 2 as the resulting curves, while the GHS attacks can not obtain the curves of genus 2. The isogeny walk can extend the scope of curves vulnerable to our attack. Finally we count the number of isomorphic classes of E in specific form over small fields and find that our algorithm can yield hyperelliptic covers for all of these elliptic curves (Table 1).

Organization. The rest of the paper is organized as follows. In Sect. 2, we recall some basic results on cover maps and Jacobians. In Sect. 3, we give some important propositions and explain our algorithms in detail. In Sect. 4, we give an example over large finite fields. In Sect. 5, we give a conclusion.

2   Preliminaries

2.1   Cover Maps

Let $\phi : H \to E$ be a map from a curve of genus 2 to a curve of genus 1 and let ι_H be the hyperelliptic involution on H. The hyperelliptic involution ι_H can induce an involution ι_E on E such that $\phi \circ \iota_H = \iota_E \circ \phi$. Then the quotient map $\pi_H : H \to H^\iota = H/\langle \iota_H \rangle$ is ramified at 6 points $A_1, A_2, \cdots, A_6$, called the Weierstrass ramification points of H. And the quotient map $\pi_E : E \to E^\iota = E/\langle \iota_E \rangle$ is ramified at 4 points B_1, B_2, B_3, B_4, called ramification points of E over E^ι. There is also a map $\phi^\iota : H^\iota \to E^\iota$ such that $\pi_E \circ \phi = \phi^\iota \circ \pi_H$ [7]. Lemma 1 determines the ramification pattern of ϕ^ι over β_j. In Sect. 3, we will give slightly specific information about ϕ^ι.

Lemma 1. *Let $A_i, i = 1, 2, 3, 4, 5, 6$, be the Weierstrass ramification points of H and $B_j, j = 1, 2, 3, 4$, be the ramification points of E over E^ι. Let $\alpha_i \in H^\iota$ (resp. $\beta_j \in E^\iota$) be the image of A_i (resp. B_j) under π_H (resp. π_E) Then $(\phi^\iota)^{-1}(\beta_j)$ contains some of α_i with odd multiplicity and any other points of H^ι with even multiplicity for each j.*

2.2   The Equation of the Hyperelliptic Curve

Let $\mathbb{F}_q$ denote a finite field with q elements and $\overline{\mathbb{F}}_q$ an algebraic closure of $\mathbb{F}_q$. Then the unique subfield of $\overline{\mathbb{F}}_q$ with q^m elements, $\mathbb{F}_{q^m}$, is an extension field of $\mathbb{F}_q$. Assume that $\mathbb{F}_q$ has odd characteristic, then every genus 2 hyperelliptic curve

H over $\mathbb{F}_q$ can be represented by $y^2 = f(x)$, where $f \in \mathbb{F}_q[x]$ is a polynomial of degree 6 without multiple roots. We can have the following propositions.

Proposition 1. *If J_H is simple but not simple over $\mathbb{F}_{q^2}$, then $J_H/\mathbb{F}_{q^2}$ is isogenous to the product of two copies of elliptic curve $E/\mathbb{F}_{q^2}$ and $\#J_H(\mathbb{F}_q) = \#E(\mathbb{F}_{q^2})$.*

Let $P_1, ..., P_6$ be the Weierstrass points of H. According to Lemma 2.4 in [18], the 15 distinct divisor classes $e_{\{i,j\}} = [(P_i)+(P_j)-(\infty_1)-(\infty_2)](1 \leq i < j \leq 6)$ are the 15 points of order 2 on J_H. This will be used to prove Proposition 2.

Proposition 2. *Let H be a genus 2 hyperelliptic curve given by $y^2 = f(x)$ with f a polynomial of degree 6 in $\mathbb{F}_q[x]$. If the Jacobian J_H of H is simple but not simple over $\mathbb{F}_{q^2}$ and $\#J_H(\mathbb{F}_q)$ is odd, then f is either an irreducible polynomial or a product of two irreducible polynomials of degree 3.*

Proof. The proof is similar to that in [10]. We have already known that $\chi_H(T) = T^4 + \sigma T^2 + q^2$ with $\sigma = \#E(\mathbb{F}_{q^2}) - q^2 - 1$. Because $\#J_H(\mathbb{F}_q) = \chi_H(1)$ is odd, σ is odd. Then $T^6 \equiv 1 \mod(<2, \chi_H>)$, which means the 2-torsion points of J_H are all $\mathbb{F}_{q^6}$-rational. Hence f is a product of linear factors over $\mathbb{F}_{q^6}$, implying the degrees of the $\mathbb{F}_q$-irreducible factors of f must be factors of 6. So we only need to prove that the number of $\mathbb{F}_q$-irreducible factors of f is at most 2.

If $f = h_1 \cdots h_i (i \geq 3)$ had more than two $\mathbb{F}_q$-irreducible factors, then there would be a factor h_i of degree 2 or two factors h_j, h_k of degree 1. Let D defined by $\text{div}(h_i) = 2D$ or $\text{div}(h_j h_k) = 2D$. Then $[D]$ is an $\mathbb{F}_q$-rational point of order 2 on J_H, contradicting the condition that $\#J_H(\mathbb{F}_q)$ is odd.

3 Our Algorithms

We now provide algorithms to find the degree 2 cover map from hyperelliptic curves of genus 2 to elliptic curves of prime order. Assume that E is defined by $s^2 = g(t)$ with $g(t) \in \mathbb{F}_{q^2}[t]$ an irreducible polynomial of degree 3. Since $E(\mathbb{F}_{q^2})$ has no point of order 2, $g(t) = (t - \beta)(t - \beta^{q^2})(t - \beta^{q^4}), \beta \in \mathbb{F}_{q^6} \backslash \mathbb{F}_{q^2}$.

Under the existence of the cover map $\phi(x, y) = (\phi_1(x), \phi_2(x, y))$, it is easy to deduce a map $\phi_1 : \mathbb{P}^1 \to \mathbb{P}^1$. Assume that the preimages of ∞ under ϕ_1 is $\epsilon \neq \infty$, then the expression of ϕ_1 is $\phi_1(x) = \frac{a_2 x^2 + a_1 x + a_0}{(x-\epsilon)^2}$, where $a_0, a_1, a_2, \epsilon \in \mathbb{F}_{q^2}$ are the values to be determined. We further assume that $\epsilon \in \mathbb{F}_{q^2} \backslash \mathbb{F}_q$ and use the linear map $\tau(x) = \frac{ax+b}{cx+d}$ where $a, b, c, d \in \mathbb{F}_q$ with $ad - bc \neq 0$ to fix $\tau(\epsilon) = \omega \in \mathbb{F}_{q^2} \backslash \mathbb{F}_q$, a generator of $\mathbb{F}_{q^2}^*$. Then ϕ_1 can be written as $\phi_1(x) = \frac{a_2 x^2 + a_1 x + a_0}{(x-\omega)^2}$. We can also have $\phi_2(x, y) = \frac{\phi_1'(x)y}{\psi(x)}$ where $\phi_1'(x)$ is derivative of $\phi_1(x)$.

Next we will respectively discuss the algorithms according to the different forms of hyperelliptic curves. All of the computation are done in Magma.

3.1 f Is Irreducible

Now, we focus on case that H is defined by $y^2 = f(x)$ and $f \in \mathbb{F}_q[x]$ is an irreducible polynomial of degree 6, which can be factored over $\mathbb{F}_{q^6}$ into $f(x) = (x - \alpha)(x - \alpha^q) \cdots (x - \alpha^{q^5}), \alpha \in \mathbb{F}_{q^6}$. Notice that one can extract a bit of information from $\phi_1(x) \in \mathbb{F}_{q^2}[x]$. For example, if α is a root of f, then $\phi_1(\alpha^{q^2}) = \phi_1(\alpha)^{q^2}$. According to Lemma 1, we can deduce the ramification pattern in the first box in the following diagram. The ramification index of ϕ_1 at α^{q^i} is 1:

α	α^{q^2}	α^{q^4}	$\parallel$		α	α^{q^2}	α^{q^4}			α	α^{q^2}	α^{q}	
$\mathbb{P}^1$ α^q	α^{q^3}	α^{q^5}	ϵ $\parallel$	$\mathbb{P}^1$ α^{q^3}	α^{q^5}	α^q	ϵ		$\mathbb{P}^1$ γ	γ^{q^2}	γ^q	ϵ
$\downarrow$ $\downarrow$	$\downarrow$ $\downarrow$	$\downarrow$ $\parallel$		$\downarrow$ $\downarrow$	$\downarrow$	$\downarrow$ $\downarrow$			$\downarrow$ $\downarrow$	$\downarrow$ $\downarrow$	$\downarrow$	
$\mathbb{P}^1$ β	β^{q^2}	β^{q^4} ∞ $\parallel$		$\mathbb{P}^1$ β	β^{q^2}	β^{q^4} ∞			$\mathbb{P}^1$ β	β^{q^2}	β^{q^4} ∞	

Taking the first one as an example, we explain how to compute the ϕ_1 and $f(x)$ from a given $E : s^2 = (t - \beta)(t - \beta^{q^2})(t - \beta^{q^4})$.

First we examine the existence of the hyperelliptic curves, with simple Jacobian over $\mathbb{F}_q$, split Jacobian over $\mathbb{F}_{q^2}$ and $\#J_H(\mathbb{F}_q)$ prime, which can be mapped into $E/\mathbb{F}_{q^2}$. And then, we choose the element $\varepsilon \in \mathbb{F}_{q^6}$ such that the 6 elements $\varepsilon, \varepsilon^q, \cdots, \varepsilon^{q^5}$ form a normal basis for $\mathbb{F}_{q^6}$ over $\mathbb{F}_q$. So

$$\alpha_i = \alpha^{q^i} = x_1 \varepsilon^{q^i} + x_2 \varepsilon^{q^{i+1}} + \cdots + x_6 \varepsilon^{q^{i+5}} \in \mathbb{F}_{q^6} \quad i \in \{0, 1, \cdots, 5\},$$

$$a_i = x_{i+7}(\varepsilon + \varepsilon^{q^2} + \varepsilon^{q^4}) + x_{i+10}(\varepsilon^q + \varepsilon^{q^3} + \varepsilon^{q^5}) \in \mathbb{F}_{q^2} \quad i \in \{0, 1, 2\},$$

where $x_1, \cdots, x_{12} \in \mathbb{F}_q$ are the unknown values that should be determined to find out the hyperelliptic curves. The diagram implies the following two equations:

$$a_2 \alpha_i^2 + a_1 \alpha_i + a_0 - \beta(\alpha_i - \omega)^2 = 0, \quad i = 0, 1. \tag{1}$$

By using the scalar restriction approach on the equations, we can get a system of 12 equations of degree 3 whose Groebner basis is easy to compute. We can then obtain an ideal of dimension 0 generated by the equations and compute the points on the zero-dimensional scheme. The solutions of the equations are what we need to get the expressions of the cover maps and hyperelliptic curves.

Finally, we substitute t with $t = \phi_1(x)$ in the equation of E and get $s^2 = \frac{y^2 g(a_2)}{(x-\omega)^6}$. So $g(a_2)$ must be a square in $\mathbb{F}_{q^2}$ to get $\phi_2(x, y)$.

3.2 f Is Reducible

In this work, we discuss the algorithms with reducible f. Then by Proposition 2, it can be factored over $\mathbb{F}_{q^6}$ into $f(x) = (x-\alpha)(x-\alpha^q)(x-\alpha^{q^3})(x-\gamma)(x-\gamma^q)(x-\gamma^{q^3}), \alpha, \gamma \in \mathbb{F}_{q^3} \setminus \mathbb{F}_q$. So we can get the corresponding map, the second box in the above diagram. The whole process is similar to the case that f is irreducible with a few differences on the expression of α_i and the restricted equations

$$a_2\alpha_0^2 + a_1\alpha_0 + a_0 - \beta(\alpha_0 - \omega)^2 = 0, \quad a_2\gamma_0^2 + a_1\gamma_0 + a_0 - \beta(\gamma_0 - \omega)^2 = 0. \quad (2)$$

Using the scalar restriction on (2), we can get a system of 12 equations in 12 variables, generating an ideal of dimension 3. More information about the hyperelliptic curves should be extracted to reduce the number of the free variables and thus reduce the dimension of the final ideal. The following proposition serves to give specific forms of the hyperelliptic curves and reduce the time complexity.

Proposition 3. *Let H be a genus 2 hyperelliptic curve which is given by $y^2 = f(x)$ with f a polynomial of degree 6 in $\mathbb{F}_q[x]$. If H has split Jacobian $J_H/\mathbb{F}_{q^2} \sim E^2/\mathbb{F}_{q^2}$ with $\#J_H(\mathbb{F}_q)$ a prime and the degree of the cover map $\phi\colon H/\mathbb{F}_q \to E/\mathbb{F}_{q^2}$ is 2. Then the corresponding cover map can be computed only if f is of the form:*

$$f(x) = (x - \alpha)(x - \alpha^q)(x - \alpha^{q^2})(x - \gamma)(x - \gamma^q)(x - \gamma^{q^2}),$$

where $(\alpha + \gamma)(\omega^q + \omega) = 2(\alpha\gamma + \omega^{q+1})$ and ω is the generator of $\mathbb{F}_{q^2}^*$, $\alpha, \gamma \in \mathbb{F}_{q^3} \backslash \mathbb{F}_q$.

Proof. The ramification index of ϕ_1 at ω is 2. By the Riemann-Hurwitz formula, there must be another point c_0 where the ramification index of ϕ_1 is 2. So we get an equation $\phi_1(c_0) = t_0$ with a double root $c_0 = -\frac{2a_0 + a_1\omega}{2a_2\omega + a_1}$. Let $\tau : \mathbb{P}^1 \to \mathbb{P}^1$ be an involution over $\mathbb{F}_{q^2}$, then $\tau(x) = \frac{x+b}{cx-1}$ or $\frac{b}{x}(b, c \in \mathbb{F}_{q^2})$. Since $\tau(\omega) = \omega \in \mathbb{F}_{q^2} \backslash \mathbb{F}_q$, we have $b, c \in \mathbb{F}_q$ such that $c\omega^2 - 2\omega - b = 0$. So $c = \frac{2}{\omega + \omega^q}$ with $\omega + \omega^q \neq 0$ and $b = -c\omega\omega^q$. Combine $c\omega^2 - 2\omega - b = 0$ with $\phi_1(x) = \phi_1(\tau(x))$, we have $a_0 = 0$ and $a_1 + (2\omega - c\omega^2)a_2 = 0$. Combine them with the original restriction of $\phi_1\colon \phi_1(\alpha) = \phi_1(\gamma), \alpha \neq \gamma$, we can obtain $\alpha + b = c\gamma\alpha + \gamma$, where we substitute b, c with $c = \frac{2}{\omega + \omega^q}$ and $b = -c\omega\omega^q$ and get $(\alpha + \gamma)(\omega^q + \omega) = 2(\alpha\gamma + \omega^{q+1})$.

3.3 Statistical Results

Elliptic curves with same j-invariant are in the same isomorphism class. We count the number of the isomorphism classes that have hyperelliptic covers by our algorithms in some small fields. Let $Total$ be the number of $j(E) \neq 0, 1728$ when $E/\mathbb{F}_{q^2}$ is of the form $y^2 = (x - \beta)(x - \beta^{q^2})(x - \beta^{q^4}), \beta \in \mathbb{F}_{q^6}$. Let $Cover_1$ (resp. $Cover_2$) be the number of $j(E)$ that E has hyperelliptic covers through the algorithms with irreducible(resp. reducible) f.

Table 1. Number of isomorphism classes that have hyperelliptic covers by algorithms.

q	3	5	7	11	13	17	19	23	29	31	37
$Total$	3	8	16	40	56	96	121	176	280	320	456
$Cover_1$	1	4	4	7	8	11	12	16	20	20	24
$Cover_2$	3	8	16	40	56	96	121	176	280	320	456

From the table, we give a conjecture that all of the isomorphic classes of E in the form of $y^2 = (x - \beta)(x - \beta^{q^2})(x - \beta^{q^4}), \beta \in \mathbb{F}_{q^6}$ can have hyperelliptic covers by our algorithms for $\deg(\phi(x)) = 2$ and reducible f.

4   Example for $\deg(\phi) = 2$ and f is Reducible

Let q be the prime $2^{128} + 51$. Define the $\mathbb{F}_{q^2} = \mathbb{F}_q[\omega]$ with $\omega^2 + 2816727792924429$ $820226788263398674201450\omega + 110523335847250297425127553909826919399 = 0$. The elliptic curve

$E/\mathbb{F}_{q^2} : y^2 = x^3 + (172239620323233229419247395322935747591\omega + 70947195208414$

$1740544987103049080544)x^2 + (1340031173633824376141694586626415343\omega + 31472$

$24343228202505589545427683265133032)x + 24655036166390622523367731749491238$

$9706\omega + 16498221100558043623778785181136278805,$

whose order $\#E(\mathbb{F}_{q^2})$ is a 256-bit prime $1157920892373161954235709850086879$ $0788814017019678814379425906599409911016\overline{9459}$, can be covered by hyperelliptic curve

$H/\mathbb{F}_p : y^2 = x^6 + 306311310527212692259946066199443128485x^5 + 19394319184883$

$12656977711696432153006177x^4 + 31479713569582744121573609868345470882 8x^3 +$

$127930997360388525283702304567680577582x^2 + 33088624320475722625912703713$

$756545590x + 1515420720404195609723640073121371191 74$

The cover map is given by $\phi(x, y) = (\phi_1(x), \phi_2(x, y))$, where

$$\phi_1(x) = \frac{x^2 + 29567739429855780381390627507299503045x}{(x - \omega)^2},$$

$$\phi_2(x, y) = \frac{779296648487209380138032677580337393110\omega}{deno}y +$$
$$\frac{24174705507821788204881789177793817367 6}{deno}y$$

with $deno = x^3 + 340282366920938463463374607431768211504\omega x^2 + (1758287$ $6288548644432208734327570237408 6\omega + 8712359379187571187991945702287453310)x + 1586998874066213581308321990001964899 29\omega + 640075049601737413$ $11415206434389648547.$

According to Proposition 1, we have $\#J_H(\mathbb{F}_q) = \#E(\mathbb{F}_{q^2})$. One can check that the point $[D] = (x^2 + 1509136575337276119058433927686398598536x + 19200$ $46855118857897474205032387441744 03, 15852961356456345819398481105434 84$ $83327x + 8988758595694470625856802147394851610 9, 2)$ in $J_H(\mathbb{F}_q)$ has order $\#E(\mathbb{F}_{q^2})$.

5 Conclusion

In the article, we discuss a new method to compute the cover maps from the hyperelliptic curves of genus 2 to the elliptic curves with prime orders. To conduct the experiments successfully, we give some important lemmas and propositions first. And then we explain different algorithms according to the different forms of equations of hyperelliptic curves. As an application, we give examples in relatively large fields. Under the existences of the cover maps, we can use them to generate hyperelliptic covers in cover-decomposition attacks in some specific cases. We can also use the algorithms to evaluate the orders of the Jacobians of hyperelliptic curves in polynomial time, which can be generalized to generating the required hyperelliptic curves. It should be improved that our algorithms only apply to a particular part of elliptic curves and hyperelliptic curves, but the method is still very useful in the ECC and HECC.

Acknowledgement. We thank the anonymous reviewers for their helpful comments. This work was supported by the National Natural Science Foundation of China (No. 61802401, No. 61772515 and No. 61872442).

References

1. Cohen, H., et al.: Handbook of Elliptic and Hyperelliptic Curve Cryptography. CRC Press, Boca Raton (2005)
2. Diem, C.: The GHS attack in odd characteristic. J. Ramanujan Math. Soc. **18**(1), 1–32 (2003)
3. Diem, C., Scholten, J.: Cover Attacks-a Report for the AREHCC Project. Preprint, October 2003
4. Frey, G., Rück, H.G.: A remark concerning m-divisibility and the discrete logarithm in the divisor class group of curves. Math. Comput. **62**, 865–874 (1994)
5. Galbraith, S.D., Gaudry, P.: Recent progress on the elliptic curve discrete logarithm problem. Des. Codes Cryptogr. **78**(1), 51–72 (2016)
6. Koblitz, N.: Hyperelliptic cryptosystems. J. Cryptol. **1**(3), 139–150 (1989)
7. Kuhn, R.M.: Curves of genus 2 with split Jacobian. Trans. Am. Math. Soc. **307**(1), 41–49 (1988)
8. Scholten, J.: Weil Restriction of an Elliptic Curve over a Quadratic Extension. Preprint (2003). http://homes.esat.kuleuven.be/~jscholte/weilres.pdf
9. Schoof, R.: Counting points on elliptic curves over finite fields. J. Théor. Nombres Bordeaux **7**(1), 219–254 (1995)
10. Tian, S., Li, B., Wang, K.P., Yu, W.: Cover attacks for elliptic curves with cofactor two. Des. Codes Cryptogr. **86**, 1–18 (2018)
11. Satoh, T.: Generating genus two hyperelliptic curves over large characteristic finite fields. In: Joux, A. (ed.) EUROCRYPT 2009. LNCS, vol. 5479, pp. 536–553. Springer, Heidelberg (2009). https://doi.org/10.1007/978-3-642-01001-9_31
12. Frey, G.: How to Disguise an elliptic curve (weil descent). In: Talk at the 2nd Elliptic Curve Cryptography Workshop (ECC) (1998)
13. Gaudry, P., Hess, F., Smart, N.P.: Constructive and destructive facets of weil descent on elliptic curves. J. Cryptol. **15**(1), 19–46 (2002)

14. Nagao, K.: Decomposition attack for the Jacobian of a hyperelliptic curve over an extension field. In: Hanrot, G., Morain, F., Thomé, E. (eds.) ANTS 2010. LNCS, vol. 6197, pp. 285–300. Springer, Heidelberg (2010). https://doi.org/10.1007/978-3-642-14518-6_23

15. Joux, A., Vitse, V.: Cover and decomposition index calculus on elliptic curves made practical. In: Pointcheval, D., Johansson, T. (eds.) EUROCRYPT 2012. LNCS, vol. 7237, pp. 9–26. Springer, Heidelberg (2012). https://doi.org/10.1007/978-3-642-29011-4_3

16. Pohlig, S., Hellman, M.: An improved algorithm for computing discrete logarithms over GF(p) and its cryptographic significance. IEEE Trans. Inf. Theory **24**, 106–110 (1978)

17. Gaudry, P., Harley, R.: Counting points on hyperelliptic curves over finite fields. In: Bosma, W. (ed.) ANTS 2000. LNCS, vol. 1838, pp. 313–332. Springer, Heidelberg (2000). https://doi.org/10.1007/10722028_18

18. Mumford, D.: Tata lectures on Theta II: Progress in Mathematics. Springer, Berlin (1984)

Secure and Compact Elliptic Curve Cryptosystems

Yaoan Jin and Atsuko Miyaji[✉]

Graduate School of Engineering, Osaka University, Suita, Japan
jin@cy2sec.comm.eng.osaka-u.ac.jp, miyaji@comm.eng.osaka-u.ac.jp

Abstract. Elliptic curve cryptosystems (ECCs) are widely used because of their short key size. They can ensure enough security with shorter keys, and use less memory space to reduce parameters. Hence, an elliptic curve is typically used in embedded systems. The dominant computation of an ECC is scalar multiplication $Q = kP, P \in E(\mathbb{F}_q)$. Thus, the security and efficiency of scalar multiplication are paramount. To render secure ECCs, complete addition formulae can be employed for a secure scalar multiplication. However, this requires significant memory and is thus not suitable for compact devices. Several coordinates exist for elliptic curves such as affine, Jacobian, projective. The complete addition formulae are not based on affine coordinates and thus require considerable memory. In this study, we achieved a compact ECC by focusing on affine coordinates. In fact, affine coordinates are highly advantageous in terms of memory but require many **if statements** for scalar multiplication owing to exceptional points. We improve the scalar multiplication and reduce the limitations for input k. Furthermore, we extend the affine addition formulae to delete some exceptional inputs for scalar multiplication. Our compact ECC reduces memory complexity up to 26 % and is much more efficient compared to Joye's RL 2-ary algorithm with the complete addition of formulae when the ratio I/M of computational complexity of inversion (I) to multiplication (M) is less than 7.2.

Keywords: Elliptic curve scalar multiplication ·
Side channel attack (SCA) · Exception-free addition formulae

1 Introduction

Elliptic curve cryptosystems (ECCs) are widely used because of their short key size. They can ensure enough security with shorter keys, and use less memory space to reduce parameters. Hence, an elliptic curve is typically used in embedded systems [1]. The dominant computation of ECCs is scalar multiplication $Q = kP, P \in E(\mathbb{F}_q)$. Thus, the security and efficiency of scalar multiplication is paramount.

Studies regarding secure elliptic curve scalar multiplication algorithms can be divided into two. One pertains to prior studies regarding efficient secure

© Springer Nature Switzerland AG 2019
J. Jang-Jaccard and F. Guo (Eds.): ACISP 2019, LNCS 11547, pp. 639–650, 2019.
https://doi.org/10.1007/978-3-030-21548-4_36

scalar multiplication [6–8,10]. The other pertains to efficient coordinates with addition formulae. Several coordinates for elliptic curves exist such as affine, Jacobian, and projective. Although it appears that we need to only combine efficient secure scalar multiplication with efficient coordinates, it is in fact not that simple because some scalar multiplications require branches to apply the addition formulae. For example, in the case of affine or Jacobian coordinates, both doubling and addition formulae exist for two inputs of P and Q [4]. That is, when the scalar multiplication algorithm employs addition formulae in affine or Jacobian coordinates, we need to versify whether the two input points are equal. In fact, not only the condition $P = Q$ but also other points such as $\mathcal{O} + P$, $P - P$, and $2P = \mathcal{O}$ become exceptional inputs. Hence, researchers have investigated on complete addition formulae [5,11,13], which can compute for any two input points. Further, new methods have been proposed by combining a powering ladder with complete addition formulae to protect the elliptic curve scalar multiplication from side channel attack (SCA) [12].

Complete addition formulae operate well to exclude such branches. However, complete addition formulae are not efficient from the memory and computational standpoints. Particularly, complete addition formulae are not based on affine coordinates and thus require significant memory.

In this study, we achieved a compact ECC by focusing on affine coordinates. In fact, affine coordinates are highly advantageous in terms of memory but requires many if statements for scalar multiplication owing to exceptional points. We adopt two approaches. First, we analyze a scalar multiplication with the input point and scalar k in detail by assigning three notions of generality of k, secure generality, and executable coordinate. Subsequently, we demonstrate that the Montgomery ladder [8], Joye's LR 2-ary algorithm [7], and Joye's RL 2-ary algorithm [7] satisfy the secure generality but that Joye's double-add algorithm [6] does not satisfy secure generality. Further, we verify coordinates that becomes executable. Subsequently, we improve Joye's RL 2-ary algorithm [7] to reduce the limitations for input k. Further, we extend the affine addition formulae to delete some exceptional inputs for scalar multiplication. Subsequently, we propose a new scalar multiplication by combining our improved Joye's RL 2-ary algorithm to our extended affine addition formulae. We enhance the efficiency of our method by 2-bit scanning using the affine double and quadruple formulae (DQ) [9], that can compute both $2P$ and $4P$ simultaneously with only one inversion computation. Finally, our compact ECC reduces memory complexity by 36% and is more efficient compared to Joye's RL 2-ary algorithm with complete addition formulae when the ratio of inversion to multiplication is less than 7.2.

This paper is organized as follows. We first introduce the related work in Sect. 2. In Sect. 3, we analyze a scalar multiplication from the point of input scalar k in detail assigning three new notions. Subsequently, we propose a variant of the affine addition formulae in Sect. 4. We improve Joye's RL 2-ary algorithm to reduce the limitations for input k and coordinates in Sect. 5. We compare our scalar multiplication with the affine formulae to previous scalar multiplication algorithms with complete addition formulae in Sect. 6. We conclude our work in Sect. 7.

2 Related Work

The related studies regarding secure elliptic curve scalar multiplication algorithms can be divided into two. One pertains to prior studies regarding efficient scalar multiplication [6–8,10] and the other pertains to efficient complete addition formulae [5,11,13]. Some scalar multiplications require branches to apply the addition formulae. Complete addition formulae operate well to exclude such branches. However, complete addition formulae are not efficient from the memory and computational standpoints. We focus on right-to-left (RL) algorithm in this paper.

2.1 Scalar Multiplication

Montgomery ladder scanning scalar from MSB to LSB without dummy computations can compute scalar multiplications regularly [8]. Thus, in the Montgomery ladder, the security issue depends on the addition formulae of the elliptic curve. If we utilize addition formulae on affine or Jacobian coordinates, branches to avoid additions on two inputs exist, such as $P + P$, $P - P$, and $\mathcal{O} + P$, and the doubling of P with $2P = \mathcal{O}$. Branches results in SCA. Hence, upon implementation, we should use "if statements" carefully. Meanwhile, if we utilize complete addition formulae [11], then we exclude "if statements" but sacrifice memory and computational efficiency [12].

As for Joye's double-add algorithm, Algorithm 1, by scanning a scalar from LSB to MSB [6], the same discussion as the above holds. Furthermore, for regular right-to-left (RL) m-ary, Algorithm 2 are proposed in [7]. In this m-ary algorithm, the same discussion as that of the Montgomery ladder holds. It is noteworthy that both the regular LR m-Ary and RL m-Ary algorithms are suitable for scalar multiplications with m-Ary representation. The regular 2-Ary algorithms are improved from Algorithm 2 by assuming that the MSB of the input scalar is always '1' in [7]. However, they can not compute scalar multiplications correctly when the scalar begins with '0'. All of these ladders are regular and without dummy computations. They perform equally well compared to Montgomery ladder mentioned before.

2.2 Complete Elliptic Curve Addition Formulae

Izu and Takagi proposed the x-only differential addition and doubling formulae [5], which proved to be exceptional only if both input coordinates of x and z are 0 [12]. These addition formulae are applied to the Montgomery ladder, in which after the computation of the x-coordinate, the y-coordinate can be recovered by the formula of Ebeid and Lambert [3].

Renes, Costello, and Batina proposed complete addition formulae for prime order elliptic curves [11]. Based on the theorems of Bosma and Lenstra [2], the complete addition formulae for an elliptic curve $E(\mathbb{F}_p)$ can be obtained without points of order two. $E(\mathbb{F}_p)$ with prime order excludes the points of order two, thus, we can use the complete addition formulae on $E(\mathbb{F}_p)$. The authors also mentioned that if the complete addition formulae were used in an application, their efficiency could be improved based on specific parameters and further computation. However, they are still costly.

Table 1 summarizes the addition formulae including the complete addition formulae, where M, S, I, and A are the costs for one field multiplication, square, inversion and addition, respectively; further, ma and mb are the costs for multiplication to a and b, respectively,

Assuming that $S = 0.8M$ and ignoring the computational complexity of ma, mb, and A, the computational complexity of ADD + DBL in complete addition is $24M$. Subsequently, the computational complexity of ADD + DBL in affine is more efficient than that in complete addition or Jacobian when $I < 8.8M$ or $I < 8.2M$. Meanwhile, the computational complexity of ADD + DBL in Jacobian is always more efficient than that in complete addition by $11.2M$.

Table 1. Computational complexity of elliptic curve addition formulae

Method	Conditions	ADD	DBL	Memory
x-only addition [5]	Either x or z-coordinate is not 0	$8M + 2S$	$5M + 3S$	10
Complete addition [11]	$2 \nmid \#E(\mathbb{F}_p)$	$12M + 3ma + 2mb + 23A$	$12M + 3ma + 2mb + 23A$	15
Affine	-	$2M + S + I$	$2M + 2S + I$	5
Jacobian	-	$12M + 4S$	$2M + 7S$	8

3   Exceptional Inputs in Scalar Multiplication

This section analyzes two algorithms (Algorithms 1–2) with input scalar $k = \sum_{i=0}^{\ell-1} k_i 2^i$ (in binary) and point P from the following three aspects: generality of k, secure generality, and executable coordinate.

3.1   Generality of k

We define the *generality* of k as follows. The scalar multiplication should compute kP for $\forall k \in [0, N-1]$, where $N \in \{0,1\}^\ell$ is the order of P. Subsequently, it includes a case where the MSB of k is zero ($k_{\ell-1} = 0$). We say that a scalar multiplication satisfies the generality if it can operate for any $k \in [0, N-1]$ with ($k_{\ell-1} = 0$) or ($k_{\ell-1} = 1$). Let us investigate whether Algorithms 1–2 satisfy the generality of input scalar k. The Joye's double-add algorithm (Algorithm 1) can operate for any input scalar $k \in [0, N-1]$. It is obvious that Algorithm 1 can compute kP correctly when $k_{\ell-1} = 1$. Algorithm 1 scans the scalar from the right and reads "0"s at the end if $k_{\ell-1} = 0$. The "0"s read at the end does not change the value saved in $R[0]$ that is the correct computation result. In summary, Algorithm 1 can compute kP correctly with any input scalar $k \in [0, N-1]$.

Joye's RL m-ary algorithm satisfies the generality, implying that it can compute kP for any input $k \in \{0,1\}^{\ell}, k \in [0, N-1]$. This proof will be given in the final version. We herein focus on the case of $m = 2$, which is shown in Algorithm 2.

Algorithm 1. Joye's double-add algorithm [6]	**Algorithm 2.** Joye's RL 2-ary algorithm [7]
Input: $P \in E(\mathbb{F}_p), k = \sum_{i=0}^{\ell-1} k_i 2^i$	**Input:** $P \in E(\mathbb{F}_p), k = \sum_{i=0}^{\ell-1} k_i 2^i$
Output: kP	**Output:** kP
Uses: $R[0], R[1]$	**Uses:** $A, R[1], R[2]$
1: $R[0] \leftarrow \mathcal{O}$	**Initialization**
2: $R[1] \leftarrow P$	1: $R[1] \leftarrow \mathcal{O}, R[2] \leftarrow \mathcal{O}, A \leftarrow P$
3: **for** $i = 0$ to $\ell - 1$ **do**	**Main Loop**
4: $\quad R[1-k_i] \leftarrow 2R[1-k_i] + R[k_i]$	2: **for** $i = 0$ to $\ell - 2$ **do**
5: **end for**	3: $\quad R[1+k_i] \leftarrow R[1+k_i] + A, A \leftarrow 2A$
6: **return** R[0]	4: **end for**
	Aggregation and Final correction
	5: $A \leftarrow (k_{\ell-1} - 1)A + R[1] + 2R[2]$
	6: $A \leftarrow A + P$
	7: **return** A

3.2 Secure Generality

We define the notion of the *secure generality* added to the generality as follows: If a scalar multiplication can compute kP regularly without dummy operations satisfying generality for $k \in [0, N-1]$, where $N \in \{0,1\}^{\ell}$ is the order of P, then we say that such an algorithm satisfies the *secure generality*.

Algorithm 2 executes the same computations of addition and doubling without any dummy operations for every bit of scalar yielding a point P and a scalar $k \in \{0,1\}^{\ell}$. It is regular without dummy operations for any k, and thus satisfies secure generality. Algorithm 1 also executes the same computations of addition and doubling without any dummy operations until the final input bit of a scalar $k \in \{0,1\}^{\ell}$. Its final step in the main loop becomes a dummy operation when processing $k_{\ell-1} = 0$. In fact, Algorithm 1 reads "0"s at the end if $k_{\ell-1} = 0$. Subsequently, the computation $R[1] \leftarrow 2R[1] + R[0]$ becomes a dummy operation, thus, we can know whether the scalar begins with "0" by changing the value of $R[1]$. If the result does not change, then the MSB of the scalar is "0". Thus, Algorithm 1 does not satisfy secure generality at the k_{l-1}.

3.3 Executable Coordinate

Let us define the notion of a coordinate to a scalar multiplication algorithm. If the coordinate can be executed for an algorithm for $\forall k \in \{0,1\}^{\ell}$, we say that a coordinate is *executable coordinate* for the algorithm. This notion is important because even if an algorithm satisfies secure generality, we must choose an executable coordinate.

Let us investigate the executable coordinates in Algorithm 1. Algorithm 1 requires addition or doubling formulae with $\mathcal{O}$. This is why neither the affine nor Jacobian coordinate is executable.

Let us investigate Algorithm 2. Algorithm 2 contains exceptional inputs k. $R[1]$ and $R[2]$ are initialized as $\mathcal{O}$ in Step 2 and A is initialized as P in Step 4. In the main loop, $\mathcal{O} + P$ appears independent of k in Step 6. It is obvious that $\mathcal{O} + P$, $P + P$, and $-P + P$ are computed when $k = 1, 2, 0$ in the final correction, respectively. In summary, Algorithm 2 has to compute addition with $\mathcal{O}$ independent to k, $P + P$ if $k = 2$, $P - P$ if $k = 0$. Neither the affine nor Jacobian coordinate can compute all of $\mathcal{O} + P$, $\mathcal{O} + 2P$, $2P + 2P$, $P + P$, and $-P + P$. Meanwhile, the complete addition formulae [11] are executable coordinates. As shown in Sect. 2, we must sacrifice computational and memory complexity if we use the complete addition formulae.

We herein focus on Algorithm 2 as it satisfies the secure generality of k, and improve it such that it can be used for the affine coordinate that requires a small memory. It is noteworthy that our idea can be applied to Algorithm 1 easily and that Jacobian coordinate is also executable for our new Algorithms 7–8.

4   Variants of Affine Addition Formulae

Affine addition formulae are advantageous because of less memory usage. The computational cost, however, depends on the ratio of inversion to the multiplication cost, where $t(A + A) = 2M + S + I$ and $t(2A) = 2M + 2S + I$.

Algorithm 3. Affine addition formula	**Algorithm 4.** Affine doubling formula
Input: $P = (x_1, y_1)$ and $Q = (x_2, y_2)$	**Input:** $P = (x_1, y_1)$
Output: $P, P + Q$	**Output:** $P, 2P$
1: $t_0 \leftarrow (x_2 - x_1)^{-1}$	1: $t_0 \leftarrow 3x_1^2 + a$
2: $y_2 \leftarrow y_2 - y_1$	2: $t_1 \leftarrow (2y_1)^{-1}$
3: $t_0 \leftarrow t_0 y_2$	3: $t_0 \leftarrow t_0 t_1$
4: $y_2 \leftarrow t_0^2 - x_1 - x_2$	4: $t_1 \leftarrow t_0^2 - 2x_1$
5: $x_2 \leftarrow (x_1 - y_2)t_0 - y_1$	5: $t_2 \leftarrow (x_1 - t_1)t_0 - y_1$
6: **return** $(x_1, y_1), (y_2, x_2)$	6: **return** $(x_1, y_1), (t_1, t_2)$

The detailed algorithms are shown in Algorithms 3 and 4. It is noteworthy that both Algorithms 3 and 4 can retain the value of the input point of P, which can be used continually for the next input. Affine addition formulae have *exceptional points*. $\mathcal{O}$ can not be represented explicitly, while it is described as a point at infinity. Thus, affine addition formulae cannot compute $\mathcal{O} + P = \mathcal{O}$,

$P - P = \mathcal{O}$, or $2P = \mathcal{O}$. The addition formula cannot compute $P + P$, which can only be computed by the doubling formula. When implementing affine addition formulae, branches are required to avoid such exceptional points. We want to fully utilize affine addition formulae because they reduce memory. Scalar multiplications should satisfy the generality of k in Sect. 3, and thus suitable for any $k \in [0, N - 1]$, where the order of P is N, which includes a special case of $k = 0$. Algorithm 2 satisfies the secure generality but the affine coordinate is not executable on them. Thus, we extend the affine addition formulae. The corresponding operations are shown in Algorithms 5 and 6, which can compute $P - P = \mathcal{O}$ and $2P = \mathcal{O}$ when $E(\mathbb{F}_p)$ does not include a point $(0, 0)$. For example, $E(\mathbb{F}_p)$ without two-torsion points, including the prime order elliptic curve on the Weierstrass form satisfy the condition. It is noteworthy that both Algorithms 5 and 6 retain the value of the input point of P similarly as Algorithms 3 and 4. Let us explain our idea of the extended affine addition formulae. The inversion of $a \pmod{p}$ can be computed by the extended Euclidean algorithm, $Ecd(a, p)$, or Fermat's little theorem, $Fermat(a, p) = a^{p-2} \pmod{p}$. Interestingly, both algorithms can operate and output 0 even if $a = 0$; that is, both are executable for a special input of "0". Therefore, we compute $\frac{1}{x_2 - x_1}$ and $\frac{1}{2y_1}$ from Algorithms 3 and 4 in the beginning and execute the remaining parts. Subsequently, the results for the ordinary inputs of P, Q are the same as those of Algorithms 3 and 4, respectively. Furthermore, the results for the exceptional inputs of $P - P$ and $2P = \mathcal{O}$ can be given as $(0, 0)$, which is assumed as $\mathcal{O} = (0, 0)$.

Algorithm 5. Extended affine addition	**Algorithm 6.** Extended affine doubling
Input: $P = (x_1, y_1)$ and $Q = (x_2, y_2)$	**Input:** $P = (x_1, y_1)$
Output: $P, P + Q$	**Output:** $P, 2P$
1: $t_0 \leftarrow (x_2 - x_1)^{-1}$	1: $t_0 \leftarrow 3x_1^2 + a,\ t_1 \leftarrow (2y_1)^{-1}$
2: $y_2 \leftarrow y_2 - y_1$	2: $t_4 \leftarrow y_1^2,\ t_2 \leftarrow 8x_1 t_4$
3: $x_2 \leftarrow x_2 - x_1$	3: $t_3 \leftarrow t_0^2 - t_2,\ t_2 \leftarrow t_1^2$
4: $t_1 \leftarrow (x_2 + 2x_1)x_2$	4: $t_3 \leftarrow t_3 t_2,\ x_1 \leftarrow x_1 - t_3$
5: $x_2 \leftarrow y_1 x_2$	5: $t_0 \leftarrow t_0 x_1,\ t_4 \leftarrow 2t_4$
6: $t_2 \leftarrow (y_2^2 t_0 - t_1)t_0$	6: $t_0 \leftarrow (t_0 - t_4)t_1$
7: $t_1 \leftarrow ((x_1 - t_2)y_2 - x_2)t_0$	7: $x_1 \leftarrow x_1 + t_3$
8: **return** $(x_1, y_1), (t_2, t_1)$	8: **return** $(x_1, y_1), (t_3, t_0)$

Remark 1. Neither Algorithm 3 nor 4 can output $P - P = (0, 0)$ or $2P = (0, 0)$, even if an inversion of $x_2 - x_1$ or $2y_1$ is computed by the Euclidean algorithm or Fermat's little theorem.

Theorem 1. *Let $E(\mathbb{F}_p)$ be $y^2 = x^3 + ax + b,\ b \neq 0 \pmod{p}$, meaning that point $(0, 0)$ is not on $E(\mathbb{F}_p)$. P, Q are points on $E(\mathbb{F}_p)$. By setting $(0, 0)$ as $\mathcal{O}$, the extended addition formula can compute the addition of P and Q correctly if $P \neq Q$ $(P \neq \mathcal{O}, Q \neq \mathcal{O})$, $P - P = \mathcal{O}$, and $\mathcal{O} + \mathcal{O}$. The extended doubling formula can compute the doubling of P correctly for any point on $E(\mathbb{F}_p)$.*

Proof. We can transform formulae (1) (2) to the extended affine addition formula by extracting the factor of $\frac{1}{X_2 - X_1}$. When computing $P - P$, the inversion of zero must be computed. By the extended Euclidean algorithm, or Fermat's little theorem, we obtain zero for the inversion of zero. This demonstrates that by our affine addition formula, we can compute $P - P$:

$$X_3 = 0, Y_3 = 0 \tag{1}$$

This implies $P - P = (0,0)$. Further, we regard $(0,0)$ as $\mathcal{O}$. Subsequently, our variant of affine addition formula computes $P - P = \mathcal{O}$ correctly. Further, it is clear that $\mathcal{O} + \mathcal{O} = \mathcal{O}$ can be computed correctly. We should emphasize that extracting the factor of $\frac{1}{x_2 - x_1}$ does not affect the addition of other points because the factor $\frac{1}{x_2 - x_1}$ will become zero only when computing $P - P$ and $\mathcal{O} + \mathcal{O}$, and in the other situation, extracting the factor of $\frac{1}{x_2 - x_1}$ is always safe. The computational cost of Algorithm 5 is $6M + S + I$ and uses the memory of seven.

We can transform formulae (3) (4) to the extended affine doubling formula by extracting $\frac{1}{y_1}$. When computing $2P = \mathcal{O}$, where P is of zero y-coordinate, the inversion of zero will be zero. Subsequently, we can compute $2P = (0,0)$ by our affine doubling formula. Further, we regard $(0,0)$ as $\mathcal{O}$, implying that our variant of the affine doubling formula can compute $2P = \mathcal{O}$ correctly when the point $(0,0)$ is not on $E(\mathbb{F}_p)$. Further, extracting the factor of $\frac{1}{2y_1}$ does not affect the doubling of other points. The y-coordinate of P becomes zero only when $2P = \mathcal{O}$. The variant of the affine doubling formula is exception-free, implying that it can compute the doubling of all points on $E(\mathbb{F}_p)$, where the point $(0,0)$ is not on it. The computational cost of Algorithm 6 is $4M + 4S + I$ and uses the memory of seven.

It is noteworthy here that the original affine addition formulae cannot compute $P - P = \mathcal{O}$, $P + \mathcal{O} = P$, and $2P = \mathcal{O}$, while our extended affine addition formulae can compute $P - P$ and $2P = \mathcal{O}$ correctly. The Jacobian and projective addition formulae compute $P - P = \mathcal{O}$ and $2P = \mathcal{O}$ correctly. Thus, both coordinates become "executable coordinates" in our Algorithms 7–8. This implies that if our scheme perform well on the affine addition formulae to compute scalar multiplications, it can be extended to the Jacobian addition formulae or projective addition formulae easily and will perform better.

5   Secure and Efficient Elliptic Curve Scalar Multiplication

We propose memory-efficient algorithms that can avoid SCA by combining Algorithm 2 with the original and our extended affine addition formulae. It is noteworthy that the original affine coordinate is not executable for Algorithm 2 because the addition formula excludes $P + P$, $P + \mathcal{O}$, and $P - P$ and the doubling formula excludes $2P$ with a two-torsion point P. We improve Algorithm 2 to avoid these exceptional inputs such that the original and extended affine coordinates become executable for Algorithm 2.

We also enhance the efficiency of our method by two-bit scanning using the affine double and quadruple formulae (DQ-formula) [9], which can compute both $2P$ and $4P$ simultaneously with only one inversion computation, denoted by $\{2P, 4P\} \leftarrow DQ(P)$. Thus, the computational cost of obtaining both $2P$ and $4P$ in the affine coordinate is $t(\{2P, 4P\} \leftarrow P) = 8M + 8S + I$. Our primary idea to apply the DQ-formulae is by adjusting the length of the scalar by padding "0" in front of the scalar to guarantee no processing required for the remaining bits after a two-bit scanning. Using our adjusting idea, the processing of the remaining bits does not depend on the odd or even length of the input scalar k.

Algorithm 7. New 2-ary RL powering ladder

Input: $P \in E(\mathbb{F}_p)$
  $k = \sum_{i=0}^{\ell-1} k_i 2^i, k \in [0, N]$
Output: kP
Uses: A, A[0], R[0], R[1]
Initialization
1: $R[0] = -P$
2: $R[1] = P$
3: $A \leftarrow 2P$
4: $R[k_0] \leftarrow R[k_0] + A$
Main Loop
5: **for** $i = 1$ to $\ell - 1$ **do**
6:   $R[k_i] \leftarrow R[k_i] + A$
7:   $A \leftarrow 2A$
8: **end for**
Final Correction
9: $R[k_0] \leftarrow R[k_0] - P$
10: $A \leftarrow -A + R[0] + 2R[1]$
11: **return** A

Algorithm 8. New two-bit 2-ary RL powering ladder

Input: $P \in E(\mathbb{F}_p)$
  $k = \sum_{i=0}^{\ell-1} k_i 2^i, k \in [0, N]$
Output: kP
Uses: A, A[0], R[0], R[1]
Initialization
1: $R[0] = -P$
2: $R[1] = P$
3: $\{A, A[1]\} \leftarrow DQ(P) = \{2P, 4P\}$
4: $R[k_0] \leftarrow R[k_0] + A$
Main Loop
5: **for** $i = 1$ to $\ell - 1$ **do**
6:   $R[k_i] \leftarrow R[k_i] + A$
7:   $R[k_{i+1}] \leftarrow R[k_{i+1}] + A[1]$
8:   $\{A, A[1]\} \leftarrow DQ(A[1])$
9:   $i = i + 2$
10: **end for**
Final Correction
11: $R[k_0] \leftarrow R[k_0] - P$
12: $A \leftarrow -A + R[0] + 2R[1]$
13: **return** A

First, we improve Algorithm 2 to the new 2-ary RL Algorithm 7, and combine with two-bit scanning to obtain the new two-bit 2-ary RL Algorithm 8. Algorithms 7 and 8 consist of three parts: initialization, main loop and final correction. Compared to Algorithm 2, we change the initialization of $R[.]$ to avoid the exceptional initialization of $\mathcal{O}$ and the exceptional computation $\mathcal{O} + P$ in the main loop. The initialization of $R[.]$ causes $R[1] + 2R[2] = \mathcal{O}$ to be added to the final result in the aggregation of Algorithm 2. The initialization of $R[.]$ causes $R[0] + 2R[1] = P$ to be added to the final result in the final Step of our algorithms. Thus, we avoid the exceptional computations in the original final correction $A \leftarrow A + P$ of Algorithm 2. Steps 3 and 4 of Algorithms 7 and 8 help to avoid the exceptional computations of $P + P$ or $P - P$ if A is initialized as P. The final correction adjusts the excess computations in Steps 3 and 4 in Algorithms 7 and 8. We adjust the length of k to be even by padding "0" in front of input scalar k, and thus verify whether two-bit scanning can operate in Algorithm 8.

Next, we explain the affine coordinates (ordinary and our extended version) that is used in Algorithms 7 and 8. The original affine coordinate is used in Step 1–9 of Algorithm 7 and Steps 1–11 of Algorithm 8. Our extended affine formulae are used in Step 10 of Algorithm 7 and Step 12 of Algorithm 8. Our Algorithms 7 and 8 satisfy generality of k, and execute the same computations of addition and doubling without any dummy operations.

Theorem 2 proves that Algorithms 7–8 avoid all exceptional computations of affine addition formulae when $k \in [0, N - 3]$.

Theorem 2. *Let $E/\mathbb{F}_p$ be an elliptic without two-torsion points. Let $E(\mathbb{F}_p) \ni P \neq \mathcal{O}$ be an elliptic curve point, whose order is $N \in \{0, 1\}^\ell$. Then, Algorithms 7 and 8 can compute kP correctly for input $k \in [0, N - 3]$.*

Proof. We prove that all three parts exclude the exceptional computations of affine addition formulae, which are additions of $P \pm P$ and $\mathcal{O} + P$, and doubling of $2P = \mathcal{O}$. The doubling of $2P = \mathcal{O}$ does not appear in the algorithms because of $E(\mathbb{F}_p)$ without two-torsion points. Thus, we only focus on the exceptional additions.

In the initialization, $R[0]$ and $R[1]$ initialized as $(P_x, -P_y)$ and (P_x, P_y) are "odd" scalar points such as $(2t + 1)P, t \in \mathbb{Z}$. A initialized as $((2P)_x, (2P)_y)$ is an "even" scalar point such as $2tP, t \in \mathbb{Z}$. It is obvious that $R[0] \leftarrow -P + 2P$ or $R[1] \leftarrow P + 2P$ in Step 4 is computed correctly by the addition formula if $N \neq 3$.

In the main loop, it is noteworthy that (1) $A \neq \mathcal{O}$ because of $E(\mathbb{F}_p)$ without two-torsion points and A always increases as an "even" scalar point until $2^{\ell-l}P, 2^{\ell-1} < N$ when loop processing $k_{\ell-2}$. A increases to an "odd" scalar point at the end of loop. (2) Until loop processing $k_{\ell-2}$, $R[0] \neq \mathcal{O}$ is always updated as an "odd" scalar point and with a smaller scalar than A. (3) Until loop processing $k_{\ell-2}$, $R[1] \neq \mathcal{O}$ is also always updated as an "odd" scalar point. If $k = \{1\}^\ell$, $R[1]$ is always with a larger scalar than A and becomes $(2^{\ell-1} + 1)P, (2^{\ell-1} + 1) \leq N$. It also occurs when $k = N - 1$ or $k = N - 2$, so we excludes these two cases. Otherwise, $R[1]$ is with a smaller scalar than A in the main loop. In summary, $R[0], R[1], A[1] \neq \mathcal{O}$ are scalar points of P whose scalars are never over N until loop processing $k_{\ell-2}$. Therefore, the "odd" scalar point can never be the same point as the "even" scalar point. The computations in the main loop exclude the exceptional computations of affine.

In the final correction, $R[k_0] \neq \mathcal{O}$ is an "odd" scalar point and $-P = (N-1)P$ is an "even" scalar point. Step 11 computes $P - P$ only when $k_0 = 0$. However we can always put an '0' in front of k to avoid this. If $k = 0$, Step 12 computes the exceptional computation, $P - P$. Our extended affine addition formula can be used here because $E(\mathbb{F}_p)$ without two-torsion points excludes point $(0, 0)$.

The same proof can be shown in the two-bit scanning version.

6   Efficiency and Memory Analysis

We analyze the computational and memory complexity of Algorithms 2, 7 and 8, which are shown in Table 2. The memory complexity counts the number of $\mathbb{F}_p$ elements including the memory used in the addition formulae. The total computational complexity of Algorithm 2 with complete addition is $(\ell+1)24M$, if we ignore the computational complexity of ma, mb and A. Assuming the ratio of $S = 0.8M$, Algorithms 7 and 8 are more efficient than Algorithm 2 with complete addition if $\frac{I}{M} < 8.8$ and $\frac{I}{M} < 9.3$. Algorithm 8 is more efficient than Algorithm 7 if $\frac{I}{M} > 7.2$. In summary, if $9.3 > \frac{I}{M} > 7.2$, Algorithm 8 is the most efficient. If $\frac{I}{M} < 7.2$, Algorithm 7 is the most efficient.

As for memory complexity, Algorithms 7 and 8 can reduce that of Algorithm 2 with complete addition by 26% and 16%, respectively.

Table 2. Comparison analysis

	Computational cost	Memory
Algorithm 2 + Complete addition [11]	$(\ell+1)(24M + 6ma + 4mb + 46A)$	19
Algorithm 7 + Affine	$(6.4\ell + 18.8)M + (2\ell + 4)I$	14
Algorithm 8 + Affine	$(10\ell + 33.2)M + \frac{3\ell + 12}{2}I$	16

7   Conclusion

We proposed two new secure and compact elliptic curve scalar multiplication Algorithms 7 and 8 by combining Affine coordinates to Joye's regular RL 2-ary algorithm. Our primary ideas were to exclude the exceptional computations of $\mathcal{O} + P$, $P - P = \mathcal{O}$ and $P + P$ in the addition formulae from Joye's regular RL 2-ary algorithm and extend the Affine coordinates to compute $P - P = \mathcal{O}$ and $2P = \mathcal{O}$ by introducing a point $(0,0)$ as $\mathcal{O}$ when an elliptic curve $E(\mathbb{F}_p) \not\ni (0,0)$. Algorithm 8 combined two-bit scanning to further improve the efficiency. Consequently, Algorithms 7 and 8 were more efficient than Algorithm 2 with complete addition if $\frac{I}{M} < 8.8$ and $\frac{I}{M} < 9.3$. Further, Algorithms 7 and 8 could reduce the memory of Algorithm 2 with complete addition by 26% and 16%, respectively.

Acknowledgement. This work is partially supported by Microsoft Research Asia, CREST (JPMJCR1404) at Japan Science and Technology Agency, Project for Establishing a Nationwide Practical Education Network for IT Human Resources Development, Education Network for Practical Information Technologies, and Innovation Platform for Society 5.0 at MEXT.

References

1. Afreen, R., Mehrotra, S.: A review on elliptic curve cryptography for embedded systems. arXiv preprint arXiv:1107.3631 (2011)
2. Bosma, W., Lenstra, H.W.: Complete systems of two addition laws for elliptic curves. J. Number Theory **53**(2), 229–240 (1995)
3. Ebeid, N., Lambert, R.: Securing the elliptic curve montgomery ladder against fault attacks. In: 2009 Workshop on Fault Diagnosis and Tolerance in Cryptography (FDTC), pp. 46–50. IEEE (2009)
4. Goundar, R.R., Joye, M., Miyaji, A., Rivain, M., Venelli, A.: Scalar multiplication on Weierstraß elliptic curves from Co-Z arithmetic. J. Cryptogr. Eng. **1**(2), 161 (2011)
5. Izu, T., Takagi, T.: A fast parallel elliptic curve multiplication resistant against side channel attacks. In: Naccache, D., Paillier, P. (eds.) PKC 2002. LNCS, vol. 2274, pp. 280–296. Springer, Heidelberg (2002). https://doi.org/10.1007/3-540-45664-3_20
6. Joye, M.: Highly regular right-to-left algorithms for scalar multiplication. In: Paillier, P., Verbauwhede, I. (eds.) CHES 2007. LNCS, vol. 4727, pp. 135–147. Springer, Heidelberg (2007). https://doi.org/10.1007/978-3-540-74735-2_10
7. Joye, M.: Highly regular m-Ary powering ladders. In: Jacobson, M.J., Rijmen, V., Safavi-Naini, R. (eds.) SAC 2009. LNCS, vol. 5867, pp. 350–363. Springer, Heidelberg (2009). https://doi.org/10.1007/978-3-642-05445-7_22
8. Joye, M., Yen, S.-M.: The montgomery powering ladder. In: Kaliski, B.S., Koç, K., Paar, C. (eds.) CHES 2002. LNCS, vol. 2523, pp. 291–302. Springer, Heidelberg (2003). https://doi.org/10.1007/3-540-36400-5_22
9. Le, D.P., Nguyen, B.P.: Fast point quadrupling on elliptic curves. In: Proceedings of the Third Symposium on Information and Communication Technology, pp. 218–222. ACM (2012)
10. Miyaji, A., Mo, Y.: How to enhance the security on the least significant bit. In: Pieprzyk, J., Sadeghi, A.-R., Manulis, M. (eds.) CANS 2012. LNCS, vol. 7712, pp. 263–279. Springer, Heidelberg (2012). https://doi.org/10.1007/978-3-642-35404-5_20
11. Renes, J., Costello, C., Batina, L.: Complete addition formulas for prime order elliptic curves. In: Fischlin, M., Coron, J.-S. (eds.) EUROCRYPT 2016. LNCS, vol. 9665, pp. 403–428. Springer, Heidelberg (2016). https://doi.org/10.1007/978-3-662-49890-3_16
12. Susella, R., Montrasio, S.: A compact and exception-free ladder for all short Weierstrass elliptic curves. In: Lemke-Rust, K., Tunstall, M. (eds.) CARDIS 2016. LNCS, vol. 10146, pp. 156–173. Springer, Cham (2017). https://doi.org/10.1007/978-3-319-54669-8_10
13. Wroński, M.: Faster point scalar multiplication on short Weierstrass elliptic curves over Fp using twisted Hessian curves over Fp2. J. Telecommun. Inf. Technol. (2016)

A Quantitative Study of Attribute Based Correlation in Micro-databases and Its Effects on Privacy

Debanjan Sadhya[1]([✉]) [iD] and Bodhi Chakraborty[2] [iD]

[1] ABV-Indian Institute of Information Technology and Management Gwalior,
Gwalior 474015, India
debanjan@iiitm.ac.in
[2] Indian Institute of Information Technology Allahabad, Allahabad 211015, India
rs166@iiita.ac.in

Abstract. Preserving the privacy associated with publicly released micro-databases is an active area of research since an adversary can mine sensitive information about the database respondents from them. The work in this paper establishes a working model for quantitatively estimating the attribute based correlation present among multiple micro-databases. In this study, we have introduced an information-theoretic metric termed as *Correlation Degree* (ρ) which estimates the amount of correlated information present among two micro-databases and accordingly assigns a cumulative score in the range $[0, 1]$. The design of our proposed metric is based on the fact that correlation among multiple datasets exists due to the presence of both overlapping and implicitly dependent attributes. We have also established a functional association between ρ and the general notion of privacy during the execution of an adversarial *linking attack*. Finally, we have empirically validated our work by estimating the value of ρ and the resulting privacy loss for the *Adult* micro-database on the backdrop of two well-established privacy preservation models.

Keywords: Privacy · Micro-database · Attribute based correlation · Linking attacks

1 Introduction

Databases which contain specific information about their respondents are termed as micro-databases. Based upon the nature of the data which they represent, micro-database attributes can be divided into three categories: *Identifiers*, *Key attributes (or quasi-identifiers)* and *Confidential (sensitive) attributes* [8]. Identifiers are those attributes which unambiguously identify the respondents. Typical examples of these in micro-databases include 'SSN' and 'passport number'. These attributes are either removed or encrypted before distribution due to the high privacy risks associated with them. Key attributes are those properties which can

© Springer Nature Switzerland AG 2019
J. Jang-Jaccard and F. Guo (Eds.): ACISP 2019, LNCS 11547, pp. 651–659, 2019.
https://doi.org/10.1007/978-3-030-21548-4_37

be linked or combined with external sources or databases to re-identify a respondent. Typical examples of such attributes include 'age', 'gender' and 'address'. Sensitive attributes contain the most critical data of the users; maintaining their confidentiality is the primary objective of any database security scheme. Prime examples of these attributes include 'medical diagnosis' and 'political affiliation'.

Accumulating personalized information in some central storage facility poses great risks for the individuals participating in the data collection process. Although there are well-defined policies and guidelines to restrict the types of publishable data, they are regularly circumvented in practical data sharing scenarios. As a direct consequence, the likelihood of an adversary in retrieving critical information about any targeted individual from micro-databases remains alarmingly high. The primary technique that the adversary employs for this task is related to the usage of the key attributes/quasi-identifiers. Herein, the adversary tries to correlate between the key attributes of multiple databases in which an individual had provided his/her data. These type of attacks are commonly known as *linking attacks* or *statistical de-anonymization attacks* [6]. Prominent examples of such attacks include re-identifying the sensitive medical record of William Weld (governor of Massachusetts) by joining it with public voter databases [10], de-anonymization of individual DNA sequences [5], privacy breaches owing to AOL search data [3], and de-anonymization of Netflix subscribers by correlating it with the Internet Movie Database (IMDb) [6].

The work in this paper is primarily concerned with quantitatively estimating the amount of attribute based correlated information which is present among two micro-databases. For achieving such objectives, we initially model a generic micro-database along with the associated private and public attributes. Subsequently, we introduce a metric termed *Correlation Degree* (ρ) for capturing the extent of inter-database correlation. The intuition behind developing ρ is the fact that correlation among multiple micro-databases exists due to the presence of overlapping attributes, as well as implicitly dependent attributes. Our proposed metric incorporates both of these factors, thereby making it a very practical measure. Moreover, we have established an information theoretic relationship of ρ with the associated privacy levels of the database respondents during an adversarial *linking attack*. This fundamental association formally connects the abstract notions of privacy and attribute based correlation involving micro-databases. Furthermore, we have estimated the overall privacy loss (due to linking attacks) by finding the difference between the initial and final levels of privacy. Importantly, this strategy provides an effective way for estimating the privacy loss during linking attacks irrespective of the mechanism utilized for executing any domain-specific attack.

2 Theoretical Model Development

This section describes the theoretical models which characterize a generic micro-database and the associated privacy criteria. These analytic models would serve as the basis for developing our proposed metric.

2.1 Micro-database Model

We start by defining the notations for two micro-databases DB^1 and DB^2 consisting of n observations (we will refer to the properties of the first and second databases with superscripts ^{1} and ^{2} respectively). Let K^1 and K^2 denote the number of attributes in the two databases; also let $\mathcal{K}^1$ and $\mathcal{K}^2$ be the sets representing these attributes. Let $X_{\mathcal{K}^1}$ and $X_{\mathcal{K}^2}$ denote the random variables representing the attribute values of the two databases respectively. Furthermore, let $(\mathcal{K}^1_{pub}, \mathcal{K}^1_{prv})$ and $(\mathcal{K}^2_{pub}, \mathcal{K}^2_{prv})$ represent public and private attributes in the two databases respectively. Hence by design, $(\mathcal{K}^1_{pub} \cup \mathcal{K}^1_{prv}) = \mathcal{K}^1$, $(\mathcal{K}^1_{pub} \cap \mathcal{K}^1_{prv}) = \emptyset$, $(\mathcal{K}^2_{pub} \cup \mathcal{K}^2_{prv}) = \mathcal{K}^2$ and $(\mathcal{K}^2_{pub} \cap \mathcal{K}^2_{prv}) = \emptyset$. We denote their corresponding random variables by $X_{\mathcal{K}^1_{pub}}$, $X_{\mathcal{K}^1_{prv}}$, $X_{\mathcal{K}^2_{pub}}$ and $X_{\mathcal{K}^2_{prv}}$ respectively.

2.2 Privacy Model

The privacy of an individual remains intact if the disclosure of the associated public attributes provides no additional information (in relation to that available in the initial stage) about the corresponding private attributes. Let's assume that some generic private ($\mathcal{K}_{prv}$) and public ($\mathcal{K}_{pub}$) attributes are correlated by a joint probability distribution function $p_{(\mathcal{K}_{prv}, \mathcal{K}_{pub})}(y, x)$ where $\forall (y, x) | y \in \mathcal{K}_{prv}$ and $x \in \mathcal{K}_{pub}$. Under such conditions, the privacy ($\mathcal{P}$) can be expressed as [8] -

$$\mathcal{P} = H(X_{\mathcal{K}_{prv}} | X_{\mathcal{K}_{pub}}) \tag{1}$$

In Eq. (1), $H(X_{\mathcal{K}_{prv}} | X_{\mathcal{K}_{pub}})$ denotes the conditional entropy (equivocation) of the private data ($X_{\mathcal{K}_{prv}}$) given some associated public data ($X_{\mathcal{K}_{pub}}$). Although there are other well-defined privacy metrics, we would use this information theoretic notion in our work since it best suits our holistic model.

3 Correlation Degree (ρ)

This is the main section of our work wherein we define our proposed metric. We also establish its formal relationship with the notion of privacy.

3.1 Metric Formulation

Correlation between multiple databases can occur via two distinct mechanisms - the existence of identical attributes and the presence of implicit dependencies between separate attributes. For modeling the first case, we assume that some of the attributes from both the databases overlap. This assumption is practical since real-world micro-databases normally contains interrelated attributes. The second case concerning the presence of correlation among distinct attributes is more subtle. A majority of practical micro-databases consisting of disjoint attribute set are implicitly correlated. For instance, 'height' and 'weight' of an individual are directly related to each other via the BMI measure. We denote such attributes by the set $\mathcal{K}_c$. Evidently, $\mathcal{K}_c \subseteq (\mathcal{K}^1 \cup \mathcal{K}^2)$. Conversely, we assume two attributes to be uncorrelated (i.e., generated from stochastically independent distributions) if they do not fall into any of the two aforementioned categories. If the value of n (records) is large enough, the existence of these attributes can be empirically justified if their mutual information equals zero. Let the number of correlated attributes be denoted by K°, and the attributes themselves be represented by a set $\mathcal{K}^\circ$. Thus $1 \leq K^\circ \leq (K^1 + K^2)$ and $\mathcal{K}^\circ = \{(\mathcal{K}^1 \cap \mathcal{K}^2) \cup \mathcal{K}_c\}$. Let the random variable representing $\mathcal{K}^\circ$ be denoted by $X_{\mathcal{K}^\circ}$. Subsequently, we construct an intermediate database DB° by merging only the correlated attributes of DB^1 and DB^2.

Now we devise a method for measuring the extent of correlated information between DB^1 and DB^2. Let the number of respondents whose records are contained in both DB^1 and DB^2 be denoted by N. As such, the total correlated information present in DB° is $H(X_{\mathcal{K}^\circ})$. One important point to note here concerns the dependency of $H(X_{\mathcal{K}^\circ})$ on the uniqueness of the records in DB°. The presence or absence of any particular record is implicitly reflected on the probability distributions of the associated attributes. Subsequently, the information contained in the resulting distributions is captured by the entropy of the correlated attributes. Based on these observations, we define a parameter *Correlation Degree* (ρ) as the ratio of correlated information present in DB° to the overall information present in the two databases.

Definition 1. *The Correlation Degree (ρ) between two micro-databases DB^1 and DB^2 is defined as:*

$$\rho = \frac{H(X_{\mathcal{K}^\circ})}{H(X_{\mathcal{K}^1}, X_{\mathcal{K}^2})} \tag{2}$$

where $H(X_{\mathcal{K}^\circ})$ represents the entropy of only the correlated attributes and $H(X_{\mathcal{K}^1}, X_{\mathcal{K}^2})$ denotes the joint entropy between all the attributes of the two databases.

Since ρ is defined over both the private and public attributes, the applicability of this metric substantially increases for practical micro-databases (where correlation among both the type of attributes exists). Noticeably, a similar measure δ in the range $[-1, 1]$ and characterized by a local threshold δ_0 has been previously defined for differential private settings [12]. However in contrast to our study, that work focused on determining the correlation present between individual records. Furthermore, our metric is set in the range $[0, 1]$, which can be easily verified by computing its lower and upper bounds respectively. To summarize, the value of ρ quantitatively represents the amount by which two databases are correlated. A higher value of ρ indicates the presence of a significant amount of correlated information between the two databases, and vice-versa.

3.2   Linking Attacks and Privacy

Now we formally state the association of attribute based correlation with the obtainable privacy levels during a linking attack. Our general strategy in establishing this relationship is to initially estimate the individual privacy levels of each micro-database and subsequently evaluate the left-over privacy after an adversary links the two databases via their correlated attributes. We finally compute the loss in privacy by finding the difference between the initial and final privacy levels. Noticeably, the overall privacy corresponding to the two micro-databases is obtained by aggregating the individual privacy levels.

The initial privacy associated with DB^1 and DB^2 (in isolation) is directly related to the entropy of the associated private variables. These fundamental privacy levels are also the maximum possible since an adversary initially possesses no public information via which he/she can gain knowledge about any sensitive information of the database respondents. Let us denote this quantity by $\mathcal{P}_I$. Thus:

$$\mathcal{P}_I = H(X_{\mathcal{K}^1_{prv}}) + H(X_{\mathcal{K}^2_{prv}}) \tag{3}$$

The final privacy after a linking attack depends on the amount of attribute based correlated information which is present among the two micro-databases. Hence for estimating this quantity, we initially state the formal association between privacy and Correlation Degree.

Theorem 1. *For two micro databases DB^1 and DB^2, the overall privacy ($\mathcal{P}$) is related to the Correlation Degree (ρ) via the following identity -*

$$\mathcal{P} = H(X_{\mathcal{K}^1_{prv}}, X_{\mathcal{K}^\circ}) + H(X_{\mathcal{K}^2_{prv}}, X_{\mathcal{K}^\circ}) \\ - 2 \times \rho \times H(X_{\mathcal{K}^1}, X_{\mathcal{K}^2}) \tag{4}$$

where, $H(X_{\mathcal{K}^1_{prv}}, X_{\mathcal{K}^\circ})$ and $H(X_{\mathcal{K}^2_{prv}}, X_{\mathcal{K}^\circ})$ are the joint entropy between the correlated attributes and the private attributes of DB^1 and DB^2 respectively.

Proof. The public source of data which we consider the adversary possesses in this scenario is the correlated information present between DB^1 and DB^2. As discussed previously in Sect. 3.1, the joint correlation between the two micro-databases is captured by the random variable $X_{\mathcal{K}^\circ}$. Based on this premise, the privacy for DB^1 and DB^2 can be defined by modifying Eq. (1) as -

$$\mathcal{P}^1 = H(X_{\mathcal{K}^1_{prv}}|X_{\mathcal{K}^\circ}) \text{ and } \mathcal{P}^2 = H(X_{\mathcal{K}^2_{prv}}|X_{\mathcal{K}^\circ}) \tag{5}$$

The values of $\mathcal{P}^1$ and $\mathcal{P}^2$ in Eq. (5) can be further expressed as -

$$\mathcal{P}^1 = H(X_{\mathcal{K}^1_{prv}}, X_{\mathcal{K}^\circ}) - H(X_{\mathcal{K}^\circ}) \text{ and } \mathcal{P}^2 = H(X_{\mathcal{K}^2_{prv}}, X_{\mathcal{K}^\circ}) - H(X_{\mathcal{K}^\circ}) \tag{6}$$

Substituting the value of $H(X_{\mathcal{K}^\circ})$ from Eq. (2) in Eq. (6) we get,

$$\mathcal{P}^1 = H(X_{\mathcal{K}^1_{prv}}, X_{\mathcal{K}^\circ}) - \rho \times H(X_{\mathcal{K}^1}, X_{\mathcal{K}^2}) \\ \mathcal{P}^2 = H(X_{\mathcal{K}^2_{prv}}, X_{\mathcal{K}^\circ}) - \rho \times H(X_{\mathcal{K}^1}, X_{\mathcal{K}^2}) \tag{7}$$

The privacy levels $\mathcal{P}^1$ and $\mathcal{P}^2$ represent the leftover entropy of the private attributes of DB^1 and DB^2 after the adversary observes their joint correlated information. Thus by adding the values of $\mathcal{P}^1$ and $\mathcal{P}^1$, we prove Theorem 1.   □

The quantity $\mathcal{P}$ essentially represents the remaining privacy after an adversary executes attribute based linking involving the two micro-databases. Let us denote this final privacy level by $\mathcal{P}_F$. Thus for our case, $\mathcal{P}_F = \mathcal{P}$. The resulting loss in privacy $(\mathcal{L})$ can be estimated by computing the difference between the initial and final privacy levels, viz. $\mathcal{L} = \mathcal{P}_I - \mathcal{P}_F$. Hence substituting the values of $\mathcal{P}_I$ and $\mathcal{P}_F$, we get -

$$\mathcal{L} = H(X_{\mathcal{K}^1_{prv}}) + H(X_{\mathcal{K}^2_{prv}}) - \left\{ H(X_{\mathcal{K}^1_{prv}}, X_{\mathcal{K}^\circ}) + H(X_{\mathcal{K}^2_{prv}}, X_{\mathcal{K}^\circ}) - 2 \times H(X_{\mathcal{K}^\circ}) \right\}$$
(8)

The maximum value of ρ $(\rho = 1)$ corresponds to the fact that all the attributes between DB^1 and DB^2 are correlated. For such a case, $H(X_{\mathcal{K}^\circ}) = H(X_{\mathcal{K}^1}, X_{\mathcal{K}^2})$, and accordingly $\mathcal{P}_F = H(X_{\mathcal{K}^1}, X_{\mathcal{K}^2}) + H(X_{\mathcal{K}^1}, X_{\mathcal{K}^2}) - 2 \times H(X_{\mathcal{K}^1}, X_{\mathcal{K}^2}) = 0$. Hence due to the presence of maximum possible correlation, the final privacy decreases to the lower bound of zero and the corresponding $\mathcal{L}$ attains the maximum value of $\mathcal{P}_I$. Alternatively, the minimum value of ρ $(\rho = 0)$ translates to the presence of no correlated attributes; hence $H(X_{\mathcal{K}^\circ}) = 0$. Correspondingly, $\mathcal{P}_F = H(X_{\mathcal{K}^1_{prv}}) + H(X_{\mathcal{K}^2_{prv}})$, and $\mathcal{L} = 0$. This observation hence indicates that there is no loss in privacy if correlated information is not present between the databases. Thus, Eq. (8) quantitatively captures the notion of 'loss in privacy' when an adversary performs an attribute based linking attack between two micro-databases. This privacy loss can also be understood as a direct consequence of the *information amplification attack* performed by the adversary [2]. For our model, the abstract notion of *additional information* is accurately captured by conditional entropy (as described by Eq. (1)). Subsequently, $\mathcal{L}$ naturally accounts for the loss in privacy due to the amount of sensitive/critical information gained by the adversary.

4   Experimental Results

We perform various experiments related to our model and subsequently analyze the associated results. Noticeably, we have utilized the popular privacy models of k-anonymity [11] and l-diversity [4] for sanitizing the utilized database. We have implemented these models on the popular ARX tool [7], which is used for anonymizing sensitive data. The general settings of ARX which we kept fixed during the entire process were - *suppression limit* $= 0\%$, *aggregate function* = geometric mean, *utility measure* = loss, and *individual attribute weights* $= 0.5$.

4.1   Database

In our empirical study, we have considered the *Adult* dataset of UCI machine learning repository [1]. This dataset was extracted from the 1994 US Census database, and comprises of 15 numeric and categorical attributes corresponding to 32561 individual records. For our work, we have selected a subset of 30163

Table 1. Attribute categorization for the Adult_Education and Adult_Employment datasets.

Dataset	Type	Notation	Attribute name
Adult_Education	Identifier	-	fnlwgt
	Quasi-identifier/public	$\mathcal{K}_{pub}^1$	age, sex, native-country, race, education
	Sensitive/private	$\mathcal{K}_{prv}^1$	$\emptyset$
Adult_Employment	Identifier	-	fnlwgt
	Quasi-identifier/public	$\mathcal{K}_{pub}^2$	age, sex, native-country, marital-status, workclass, occupation
	Sensitive/private	$\mathcal{K}_{prv}^2$	salary

records after eliminating rows which contained missing information. Furthermore, we have partitioned all the attributes of the Adult dataset into two overlapping sets for creating two sub-datasets: *Adult_Education* and *Adult_Employment*.

The detailed categorization policy for the attributes of both these datasets is presented in Table 1. The policy itself is based on the understandings of the authors and previous related works [9]. In terms of the notations defined in Sect. 3.1, $\mathcal{K}_c = \{$education, salary$\}$, and $\mathcal{K}^\circ = \{$sex, age, native-country, education, salary$\}$. Furthermore, $H(X_{\mathcal{K}_{prv}^1}, X_{\mathcal{K}^\circ}) = H(X_{\mathcal{K}^\circ})$ since $\mathcal{K}_{prv}^1 = \emptyset$, and $H(X_{\mathcal{K}_{prv}^2}, X_{\mathcal{K}^\circ}) = H(X_{\mathcal{K}^\circ})$ since $\mathcal{K}_{prv}^2 \subset \mathcal{K}^\circ$.

4.2 Correlation Degree and Privacy Loss

Our objective in this simulation is to quantitatively estimate the values of Correlation Degree (ρ) and privacy loss ($\mathcal{L}$) before and after the application of the sanitization models. For both the micro-datasets, we compute ρ through Eq. (2) and the corresponding privacy loss via Eq. (8). The values of these two metrics along with the other associated parameters are presented in Table 2. As noticeable, the value of ρ among the two original datasets is 0.746, which is relatively high. This result accordingly signifies that there exists a large amount of correlated information among the two datasets. However, ρ decreases to 0.372 after the implementation of the sanitization mechanisms on the two datasets. The privacy loss also correspondingly reduces from 0.8096 to 0.0024, thereby indicating that the original level of privacy has been approximately preserved. All of these results empirically corroborate the role of the sanitization models in reducing

Table 2. Values of *Correlation Degree* and *Privacy Loss* for the Adult_Education and Adult_Employment datasets

Database status	$H(X_{\mathcal{K}^\circ})$	$H(X_{\mathcal{K}^1}, X_{\mathcal{K}^2})$	Correlation degree (ρ)	Privacy loss ($\mathcal{L}$)
Original	10.29	13.78	0.746	0.8096
Sanitized	5.13	5.7	0.372	0.0024

the amount of correlated information present among multiple micro-databases. Alternatively, we can infer that the risk of adversarial linking attacks diminishes after sanitization due to the decreases in the value of ρ.

5   Conclusion

Presence of correlated information among micro-databases is the primary cause for adversarial linking attacks. In our work, we have introduced an information theoretic metric termed as *Correlation Degree* (ρ) which quantitatively measures the amount of correlated information that is present among micro-database attributes. Our proposed parameter is postulated over the fact that inter-database correlation exists due to the presence of overlapping and implicitly dependent attributes. Importantly, the definition of ρ can be utilized for measuring the correlation extent even after the application of a generic sanitization scheme. Moreover, we have formally quantified the overall privacy loss ($\mathcal{L}$) after the execution of the (in)famous attribute based linking attacks. Hence our model would directly facilitate data publishers in analyzing the privacy risks associated with micro-databases prior to their publication phase.

References

1. Blake, C., Merz, C.: UCI repository of machine learning databases (1998). http://archive.ics.uci.edu/ml/datasets/Adult
2. Datta, A., Sharma, D., Sinha, A.: Provable de-anonymization of large datasets with sparse dimensions. In: Degano, P., Guttman, J.D. (eds.) POST 2012. LNCS, vol. 7215, pp. 229–248. Springer, Heidelberg (2012). https://doi.org/10.1007/978-3-642-28641-4_13
3. Hansell, S.: AOL removes search data on vast group of web users. Technical report, New York Times, August 2006
4. Machanavajjhala, A., Kifer, D., Gehrke, J., Venkitasubramaniam, M.: L-diversity: privacy beyond k-anonymity. ACM Trans. Knowl. Discov. Data **1**(1), 1–52 (2007)
5. Malin, B., Sweeney, L.: How (not) to protect genomic data privacy in a distributed network: using trail re-identification to evaluate and design anonymity protection systems. J. Biomed. Inform. **37**(3), 179–192 (2004)
6. Narayanan, A., Shmatikov, V.: Robust de-anonymization of large sparse datasets. In: Proceedings of the 2008 IEEE Symposium on Security and Privacy, SP 2008, pp. 111–125. IEEE Computer Society, Washington, DC (2008)
7. Prasser, F., Kohlmayer, F.: Putting statistical disclosure control into practice: the ARX data anonymization tool. In: Gkoulalas-Divanis, A., Loukides, G. (eds.) Medical Data Privacy Handbook, pp. 111–148. Springer, Cham (2015). https://doi.org/10.1007/978-3-319-23633-9_6
8. Sankar, L., Rajagopalan, S.R., Poor, H.V.: Utility-privacy tradeoffs in databases: an information-theoretic approach. IEEE Trans. Inf. Forensics Secur. **8**(6), 838–852 (2013)
9. Sondeck, L.P., Laurent, M., Frey, V.: Discrimination rate: an attribute-centric metric to measure privacy. Ann. Telecommun. **72**, 11–12 (2017)

10. Sweeney, L.: Statement before the privacy and integrity advisory committee of the department of homeland security. Technical report, Department of Homeland Security, June 2005
11. Sweeney, L.: K-anonymity: a model for protecting privacy. Int. J. Uncertain. Fuzziness Knowl.-Based Syst. **10**(5), 557–570 (2002)
12. Zhu, T., Xiong, P., Li, G., Zhou, W.: Correlated differential privacy: hiding information in non-IID data set. IEEE Trans. Inf. Forensics Secur. **10**(2), 229–242 (2015)

Tagging Malware Intentions by Using Attention-Based Sequence-to-Sequence Neural Network

Yi-Ting Huang[1]([⊠]), Yu-Yuan Chen[2], Chih-Chun Yang[2], Yeali Sun[2], Shun-Wen Hsiao[3] [ID], and Meng Chang Chen[1,4] [ID]

[1] Institute of Information Science, Academia Sinica, Taipei, Taiwan
ythuang@iis.sinica.edu.tw
[2] Information Management, National Taiwan University, Taipei, Taiwan
[3] Management Information Systems, National Chengchi University,
Taipei, Taiwan
[4] Research Center of Information Technology Innovation, Academia Sinica,
Taipei, Taiwan

Abstract. Malware detection has noticeably increased in computer security community. However, little is known about a malware's intentions. In this study, we propose a novel idea to adopt sequence-to-sequence (seq2seq) neural network architecture to analyze a sequence of Windows API invocation calls recording a malware at runtime, and generate tags to describe its malicious behavior. To the best of our knowledge, this is the first research effort which incorporate a malware's intentions in malware analysis and in security domain. It is important to note that we design three embedding modules for transforming Windows API's parameter values, registry, a file name and URL, into low-dimension vectors to preserve the semantics. Also, we apply the attention mechanism [10] to capture the relationship between a tag and certain API invocation calls when predicting tags. This will be helpful for security analysts to understand malicious intentions with easy-to-understand description. Results demonstrated that seq2seq model could mostly find possible malicious actions.

Keywords: Malware analysis · Dynamic analysis · seq2seq neural network

1 Introduction

A malware, such as virus, Internet worm, trojan horse, and botnet, has been a main challenge in computer security, because it may disrupt infected network service, destroy software or data, steal sensitive information, or take control of the host. Thus, malware detection and malware classification have been widely investigated [1–5, 9].

Anti-virus products have primarily concerned with malware individual signatures to detect a malware. However, more recently, with the development of obfuscation techniques and the prevailing access to open source tools, it has been easy to create variants of a malware so that it has been greatly increase the number of malwares. Thus, rather than detecting malware individual signatures, we shifted our attention to analyze malware behavior. If malicious characteristics can be caught, they can be the

© Springer Nature Switzerland AG 2019
J. Jang-Jaccard and F. Guo (Eds.): ACISP 2019, LNCS 11547, pp. 660–668, 2019.
https://doi.org/10.1007/978-3-030-21548-4_38

basis of malware detection. This approach will increase the effectiveness of malware detection and decrease the operating cost of it.

As far as we know, there is no benchmark for malicious characteristics, because it is a challenge to examine the infected systems, system logs and malware binaries, and understand any possible intention. Windows APIs, an access to system resources, can be another resource to reveal malware behavior when a malware is executing. Thus, we will hook the Windows API functions at the virtualization layer to intercept the targeted malware at the runtime and record its invoked API calls.

In this paper, we propose a neural sequence-to-sequence (seq2seq) model, which analyzes a sequence of Windows API invocation calls, and labels subsequences of Windows API invocation calls with tags. These tags can be used to explain malicious intentions of a malware. This study will lead to a better understanding of malware characteristics in malware analysis. This paper makes the following contributions:

- We apply a neural network model, which predicting one or more tags, to describe malicious intentions of a malware.
- We propose approaches for transforming a Windows API invocation call into a numeric vector (embedding).

2 System Design

In this paper, our goal is to employ neural network technology to construct an automatic malware tagging system by analyzing a large set of malware samples. When given a malware sample, the system can output a list of tags which can truly capture the essence of the series of activities performed by the malicious program.

Figure 1 depicts the overall architecture of the model. The model consists of an embedding layer and an attention-based seq2seq model. Because the execution traces generated from the dynamic malware behavior profiling system are text files, we need to transform the plaintext representations of the API invocation calls into vectorized representations. Thus, an embedding layer, consisting of API function name embedding, parameter value embedding and return value embedding, takes a variable-length execution trace $x = \{x_1, ..., x_m\}$ as the input and outputs a sequence of embedding vectors $x' = \{x'_1, ... x'_m\}$. Some parameter types may have numerous categorical values, such as Registry. It is compute-inefficient to model them all in one-hot encoding format. Thus, Three embedding modules – registry value embedding, library name embedding, and URL embedding – are proposed, and will be explained.

A sequence-to-sequence (a.k.a. encoder-decoder) model is a neural network architecture which consists of an encoder and a decoder. Long Short-Term Memory (LSTM) [7] is used for sequence processing from a sequential input. A bi-directional encoder $BiLSTM_{encoder}$ processes a sequence of variable-length embedding vector $x' = \{x'_1, ... x'_m\}$ from forward and backward simultaneously, and outputs a series of vector representation $h = \{h_1, ..., h_m\}$. A decoder $LSTM_{decoder}$ is conditioned on the output h from the encoder to generate a hidden state d_j. One key component of the model is to connect subsequences of API invocation calls to an individual tag. For example, a code subsequence directly reflects the operation of self-propagation, i.e., tag "*worm*." Hence, we use an attention mechanism to establish such relationships. We would like to pay special **attention** to the relevant subsequence as we tag. The decoder at each time step focuses on a different part of the input trace to gather the semantics information in order to generate proper tag. This attention weights are computed by the current hidden state d_j from the decoder and all hidden state h_i from the encoder. With the attention weights, we can obtain a weighted summarization a_j of the hidden vectors from the encoder. A new representation $\hat{d}_j$ is the concatenation a_j and d_j for calculate the probability distribution over tags. Finally, a linear layer projects the new presentation $\hat{d}_j$ into a prediction layer, and a *softmax* layer computes the tag distribution. The predicated tag y_j is the target class with the highest probability. More details can be found in [10].

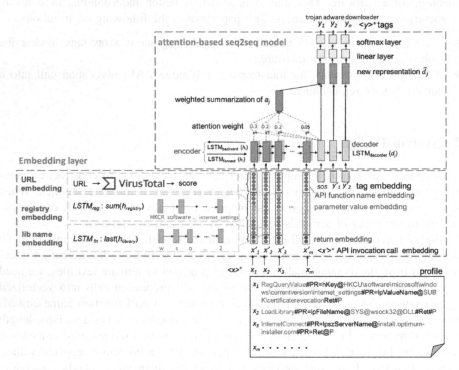

Fig. 1. When given a profile which contains $x_1...x_m$, the proposal system transforms a profile $x = \{x_1...x_m\}$ into embedding vector $x'_1...x'_m$, and predicts a list of tags $y = \{y_1...y_n\}$ by capturing the relations between each tag y_j and input sequence $x = \{x_1...x_m\}$.

2.1   The Embedding Layer

The goal of the embedding layer is to produce a fixed-size vector as the corresponding embedding x' when given a Windows API invocation call x. An API invocation call x_i consists of an API function name w_i, one or more parameter values v_i, none or one return value ret_i. Each element, x_i, is transformed as an embedding x'_i as a concatenation of a function name embedding w_i', parameter embeddings v_i' and a return embedding ret_i'. Each element learns its identical weighted embedding matrix E.

$$x_i' = concate\left(E_w w_i, concate_k^{|pr|}(E_k v_{ik}), E_{ret} ret_i\right) \tag{1}$$

where $E_w \in R^{e_w \times |w|}, E_k \in R^{e_k \times |k|}, E_{ret} \in R^{e_{ret} \times |ret|}$ are function name, parameter, and return embedding matrices; e_w, e_k, and e_{ret} are embedding sizes respectively.

We focus on three resources and propose respective approaches to transform a parameter value into a low-dimension vector while preserving the semantics. The rest of input values, including API function names, the other parameter values, and the return value are initialized by drawing samples from a uniform distribution within Xavier initializer [6] and learn their own embedding matrices as well.

Registry Value Embedding. In Windows system, registry contains important configuration information for the operating system, services, applications and user settings. Therefore, registry-related operations are important in malicious behavior analysis and the parameter values are especially critical. The Windows registry is a hierarchical database which includes keys, subkeys and values. The structure of registry keys is similar to that of folders in the file system and they are referenced with a syntax similar to Window's path, using backslashes to indicate levels of hierarchy. Thus, we construct a registry value embedding module to tokenize keys with a backslash, '\', and then use a LSTM unit referred to as the $LSTM_{reg}$ to transform a key denoted by $key = \{key_1, ..., key_n\}$ into hidden vectors $h_{key1}...h_{keyn}$. All hidden vectors are then summed to a registry representation v_{reg}. For example, key "$HKCU\backslash software\backslash microsoft\backslash windows\backslash currentversion\backslash internet\_settings$" contains six tokens - "$HKCR$", "$software$", "$microsoft$", "$windows$", "$currentversion$" and "$internet\_settings$." Each token is an input to the LSTM unit. The output hidden vectors constitute the registry key representation, i.e., $h_{HKCU\backslash software\backslash microsoft\backslash windows\backslash currentversion\backslash internet\_settings} = h_{HKCR} + h_{software} + h_{microsoft} + h_{windows} + h_{currentversion} + h_{internet\_settings}$. Therefore, we could preserve the hierarchical relation between tokens and have a fixed and consistent embedding dimension regardless of the number of keys.

File Name Embedding. From our analysis of malware operations, malwares often code file names where the spellings deform some familiar regular names to obfuscate the intent, e.g., "$2dvaai32.dll$" vs. "$advapi32.dll$". There are also file names which comprise a file name and a random number, e.g., "$tsu08c6ec63.dll$" and "$tsu0ac63fe4.dll$". Some file names are generated from a hash value, e.g. "$518ca2bf37e13.dll$". In other words, any possible combinations for a file name are enormous and unpredictable. Here, we separate the file name into a sequence of character strings $\{c_1, ..., c_n\}$ and input each character string to a $LSTM_{fn}$ unit one by one and obtain the corresponding hidden vectors $\{h_{c1}, ..., h_{cn}\}$. The last hidden state h_{cn} is considered as file name representation v_{lib}. For example, a file name "$wsock32$", can be split into a series of characters, $\{w, s, ..., 2\}$. Each letter is an input to the $LSTM_{fn}$ unit. They are transformed into the associated hidden vectors, i.e., $h_{wsock32} = \{h_w, h_s, ..., h_2\}$ and h_2 can be considered as the file name representation for '$wsock32$'. The merit of the proposed LSTM unit is that it can capture the similarities between purposely obfuscated file names or different variations of the same file name while treating each individually.

URL Embedding. Malware programs often include codes that visit remote malicious web sites in background and gain control of a computer system without being detected. However, it is difficult to literally distinguish whether a URL is malicious or not. Nonetheless, we consider URLs are important part of the information about the program's operations. Specifically, we make use of the URL reports from *VirusTotal*[1] which give the result of the ratio of number of antivirus engines that detected a scanned URL is malicious or not. This ratio is used as the score for embedding URL. For instance, a URL, *"install.optimum-installer.com"*, got six over sixty-six. Since the score is a real number, the associated embedding E_{URL} is an identity matrix of 1×1.

3 Evaluation

3.1 Dataset

To capture the essentials of the execution behavior of a malware program, we used an automated dynamic malware behavior profiling and analysis system based on Virtual Machine Introspection (VMI) technique [8]. We carefully-selected 28 Windows API calls, shown in Table 1. A malware sample may create or fork one or more processes. An execution trace is generated per process. Some distinct malwares with the same intent have slightly different parameter values, such as the user-profile folders, *"user's Desktop"* and *"user's Documents"*, depending on the version of operating systems or their executable strategy. To reduce this noise, values relevant to file directory and registry key are symbolized, details in [2]. Also, a trace is reformatted and present a Windows API call line by line, as a profile illustrated in Fig. 1.

We collected 19,987 malware profiles from 11,939 samples, acquired from NCHC's OWL[2] project. Since a few profiles contained too many API calls or too few ones, we excluded the samples whose number of API calls were smaller than 10, or larger than 300. The final dataset includes 14,677 profiles from 9,666 samples.

In order to compile a set of tags which are descriptive terms to help users quickly grasp the characteristics of a malware program, we crawled labels from *VirusTotal* in April, 2018. The labels were changed to lowercase and tokenized by delimiters, "\|!|\| \)|\/|\]|@|:|·|/|\ |_|\-|." Only the first and second tokens are considered. We manually build an alias table for the tokens with same meaning. For example, *"troj"* and *"trj,"* are the abbreviations of *"trojan."* Seventy-six tags are compiled, shown in Table 2. We relabeled the tags for each malware sample. If a sample has any child process file, it is labeled with the same tags as the main process. We also sorted tags in descending order by counting occurrences in order to control the variance from the order of tags. We hope a tag with a highly frequent occurrence could be predicted first.

---

[1] https://www.virustotal.com.
[2] https://owl.nchc.org.tw.

We randomly divide the dataset into a training set (80%), a development set (10%), and a testing set (10%). Distributions of the three sets are then validated by F-test until none of them have no significant difference. We report results on the testing set.

Table 1. Summary of Windows API function name and parameter types used in this study.

Category	API function name	Parameter type
Registry	RegCreateKey, RegDeleteKey, RegSetValue, RegDeleteValue, RegOpenCurrentUser[+], RegEnumValue, RegQueryValue	hKey, lpSubKey, lpValueName
Process	CreateProcess, CreateRemoteThread, CreateThread, TerminateProcess, ExitProcess[*], OpenProcess[+], WinExec[+]	lpApplicationName, dwCreationFlags, uExitCode
Network	InternetOpen[+], WinHttpConnect, InternetConnect, WinHttpOpen[+], WinHttpOpenRequest[+], WinHttpReadData[+], WinHttpSendRequest[+], WinHttpWriteData[+], GetUrlCacheEntryInfo[+], HttpSendRequest[+]	lpszServerName, pswzServerName, nServerPort
Library	LoadLibrary	lpFileName
File	CopyFile, CreateFile, DeleteFile	lpFileName, lpExistingFileName, lpNewFileName, dwCreationDisposition, dwDesiredAccess, dwShareMode

[*]Only "ExitProcess" has no return value.
[+]Its associated parameter values are not considered.

Table 2. Seventy-six tags are collected.

Categories	Tags
Type or family	Adware, backdoor, bot, browsermodifier, bundler, ddos, game, grayware, networm, PUP[*], ransom, riskware, rootkit, spyware, trojan, virus, worm
Behavior	Autorun, binder, browserhijacker, clicker, crypt, dialer, dns, downloader, dropper, fakealert, fakeav, filecryptor, fileinfetor, flooder, fraudtool, hacktool, infostealer, installer, joke, keylog, lockscreen, memscan, monitor, packed, prochollow, procinject, virtool, webfilter
Route of infection	Air, email, im, p2p, patch, pdf, proxy, sms, uds
Programming lang.	Autoit, bat, html, js, php, vb
Other	Android, apt, avt, constructor, exploit, FAT[*], fca, hllp, iframe, irc, keygen, MBR[*], MSIL[*], password, PE[*], rat

[*]These tags are changed to uppercase in order to be understood easily.

3.2 Experimental Settings

We set the LSTM hidden unit size to 256 and the number of layers of LSTMs to 2 in both the encoder and the decoder. Optimization is performed using Adam optimizer, with an initial learning rate of 0.0002 for the encoder, and 2.5 for the decoder. Training runs for 600 epochs. We start halving the learning rate at epoch 300, and decay it per 100 epoch. The mini-batch size is set at 16. Dropout with probability is 0.1.

Two baselines and three input variations are examined to answer two questions: (1) is the seq2seq model suitable for our task? (2) Can the return embedding or the parameter embedding help models to predict tags? We reproduced Convolutional Neural Network (CNN) [11] and Multi-label Multi-class Classification (MLC) as baselines. Both models use the proposed embedding layer. While the CNN has three convolution layers (256, 192, 64) with an average pooling layer, MLC has the same encoder as the proposed system. Lastly, both connect to a dense layer and a sigmoid layer.

For each model, three input variations – only API function names, add the associated return values, and add the corresponding parameter values – were evaluated. To ensure that performance is not simply due to an increase in the number of model parameters, we keep the total size of the embedding layer fixed to 256. The size of the return embedding and the parameter embedding are set to 2 and 50 respectively, and the size of the function name embedding is set to bring the total size to 256.

Recall are preferably used as our metric because it means malicious patterns could be mostly found, which could help security analysis. Precision is also reported.

3.3 Results

Table 3 presents the results among different models and input settings. The results showed an obvious effect of models on recall and precision. With respect to recall, the predictions from the seq2seq models relatively approximated the ground truth. On the other hand, regarding to precision, the percentage of tags from the MLC models correctly predicted was highest, but the average number of predictions was much less than the number of ground truth (7.41). We compared the predicted tags from the MLC models against that from the seq2seq models. It showed that 84% of tags from the MLC models and 52% from the seq2seq models were the same.

Table 3. Experiment result between different models.

Model	Input setting	Recall	Precision	|Predicted tags|
CNN	API name	42.72%	69.32%	4.47
	API name + return	40.35%	72.27%	4.06
	API name + parameter + return	40.82%	69.63%	4.30
MLC	API name	45.50%	72.39%	4.46
	API name + return	44.66%	74.10%	4.34
	API name + parameter + return	46.40%	72.10%	4.63
seq2seq	API name	**57.10%**	53.02%	7.92
	API name + return	56.25%	52.39%	7.86
	API name + parameter + return	**57.18%**	53.05%	7.88

For each model, three input variants had slightly different and inconsistent results except for the seq2seq models. For seq2seq, considering all of input settings, including API function names, parameter values, and return values, had minor better performance than only considering API function names. It was surprised the performance was worse when considering API function names and return values. It implies we could analyze malware without knowing it was successful or not. We anticipate the tagging is related to attack intention, rather than the successfulness of the API call invocation.

4   Conclusion

In this paper, we present a novel neural seq2seq model to analyze Windows API invocation calls and predict tags to label a malware's intentions. Results showed that the seq2seq model, with all of input values, API function names, the associated return values, and the corresponding parameters, could find mostly possible malicious characteristics with respect to the number of prediction and the high ratio of correctly predicted tags to ground truth. This can help security experts to understand any potential malicious intentions with easy-to-understand description.

Acknowledgements. This work was supported by MOST107-2221-E-004-003-MY2.

References

1. Athiwaratkun, B., Stokes, J.W.: Malware classification with LSTM and GRU language models and a character-level CNN. In: 2017 IEEE International Conference on Acoustics, Speech and Signal Processing, pp. 2482–2486. IEEE, New Orelans (2017)
2. Chiu, W.J.: Automated malware family signature generation based on runtime API call sequence. Master thesis. National Taiwan University, Taiwan (2018)
3. Dahl, G.E., Stokes, J.W., Deng, L., Yu, D.: Large-scale malware classification using random projections and neural networks. In: Acoustics, Speech and Signal Processing, pp. 3422–3426. IEEE, Vancouver (2013)
4. Egele, M., Scholte, T., Kirda, E., Kruegel, C.: A survey on automated dynamic malware-analysis techniques and tools. ACM Comput. Surv. **44**(2), 6 (2012)
5. Gandotra, E., Bansal, D., Sofat, S.: Malware analysis and classification: a survey. J. Inf. Secur. **5**, 56–64 (2014)
6. Glorot, X., Bengio, Y.: Understanding the difficulty of training deep feedforward neural networks. In: Thirteenth International Conference on Artificial Intelligence and Statistics, pp. 249–256 (2010)
7. Hochreiter, S., Schmidhuber, J.: Long short-term memory. Neural Comput. **9**(8), 1735–1780 (1997)
8. Hsiao, S.W., Sun, Y.S., Chen, M.C: Virtual machine introspection based malware behavior profiling and family grouping. arXiv preprint arXiv:1705.01697 (2017)
9. Huang, W., Stokes, J.W.: MtNet: a multi-task neural network for dynamic malware classification. In: Detection of Intrusions and Malware, and Vulnerability Assessment, pp. 399–418. Springer, Cham (2016)

10. Luong, M.T., Pham, H., Manning, C.D.: Effective approaches to attention-based neural machine translation. In: Proceedings of Conference on Empirical Methods in Natural Language Processing, pp. 1412–1421. Lisbon, Portugal (2015)
11. Zhou, B., Khosla, A., Lapedriza, A., Oliva, A., Torralba, A.: Learning deep features for discriminative localization. In: Proceedings of the IEEE Conference on Computer Vision and Pattern Recognition, pp. 2921–2929. (2016)

A Novel Semi-supervised Adaboost Technique Based on Improved Tri-training

Dunming Li[✉], Jenwen Mao, and Fuke Shen[✉]

East China Normal University, Shanghai, China
18721070085@163.com, 52141201007@stu.ecnu.edu.cn, fkshen@ecnu.edu.cn

Abstract. With the development of the network, network attacks become more frequent and serious, so network security is becoming more and more important. Machine learning has been widely used for network traffic detection, but traditional supervised learning does not perform good in the case of a small amount of labeled data and a large amount of unlabeled data. And this situation exists in a large number in practical applications, so research on semi-supervised algorithms is necessary. The Tri-training algorithm is a semi-supervised learning algorithm with strong generalization ability, which can effectively improve the accuracy of detection. In this paper, we improve the traditional Tri-training algorithm and combine the ensemble learning algorithm to generate the final hypothesis by estimating the confidence of unlabeled data. Experiments show that the improvement of the Tri-training is effective, and a better detection rate is achieved. The proposed system performs well in network traffic detection. Even in the case where the training data set has only a small amount of tagged data, the system can achieve a good detection rate and a low false positive rate. On the NSL-KDD data set, the system performs best in terms of accuracy and algorithm time consumption. On the Kyoto data set, the system achieves a good balance between accuracy and time cost.

Keywords: Tri-training · Semi-supervised · Machine learning · Ensemble learning · Network security

1 Introduction

Due to the security risks brought by the rapid development of the network, intrusion detection systems have attracted much attention. A common method of intrusion detection is to extract statistical features to represent traffic and then apply machine learning (ML) techniques for classification. Early uses of ML algorithms can generally be divided into two categories, namely classification (or supervised learning) [1] and clustering (or unsupervised learning) [2]. Compared with obtaining labeled data, obtaining an unlabeled training process is easy, fast and inexpensive. Traditional supervised learning cannot train classifiers with

© Springer Nature Switzerland AG 2019
J. Jang-Jaccard and F. Guo (Eds.): ACISP 2019, LNCS 11547, pp. 669–678, 2019.
https://doi.org/10.1007/978-3-030-21548-4_39

better generalization ability, so more and more researchers are studying semi-supervised learning [3].

Erman et al. proposed a hybrid method called semi-supervised learning [4], which mixes a small amount of labeled data into a large amount of unlabeled data to generate a training set for the clustering algorithm. Wang et al. [5] added constraints in the clustering process, and used labeled data after clustering. By combining constraints in the clustering process, the accuracy and purity of clustering can be significantly improved. Li et al. [6] proposed a traffic classification method based on cooperative training semi-supervised clustering. It is found that the performance of the Co-training semi-supervised clustering algorithm is better than K-means clustering, DBSCAN and double-layer semi-supervised clustering, which has higher overall accuracy, and the accuracy and recall metric are also better. Co-training is a very classic method in semi-supervised machine learning, but there are still some important issues that need to be addressed (for example, two feature subsets are approximate enough and redundant).

Goldman and Zhou proposed an improved collaborative algorithm [11]. The main disadvantages of collaborative training are the time-consuming cross-validation and strict rules of classification algorithm and data. After, Zhou and Li proposed Tri-training algorithm for solving common training problems [12]. The method avoids the explicit measurement of the label confidence of each learner. Li et al. [7] proposed a new semi-supervised SVM algorithm (TSVM). It applies Tri-training to improve the SVM. Semi-supervised SVM uses a large amount of unlabeled data to iteratively modify the classifier. Tri-training can improve the classification accuracy of the SVM, increase the difference of the classifier, and finally the accuracy of the classifier will be higher. Yuan et al. [8] combines Tri-training methods and Adaboost algorithm. The Tri-training bootstrap sample was replaced by three different Adaboost algorithms to create diversity. It is a very good balance between execution time and detection rate and false positive rate. Xu et al [9] showed that Tri-training has the same performance as supervised learning in the absence of sufficient labeled data. Tri-training is a way to make models more general and versatile, but the noise introduced by the error labeled may offset the benefits of Tri-training. For this, we have improved Tri-training. We measured our experimental results in terms of accuracy, precision, recall, f-measure and detection time.

The contributions of this paper are as follows:

(1) We propose improved Tri-training algorithm. Confidence filtering for unlabeled data to remove some mislabeled data, and the error estimate takes into account the confidence of the unlabeled data, and the confidence of the unlabeled data is assigned as a weight for each unlabeled example, further reducing the potential negative impact.
(2) We reduce time costs by using decision tree algorithm as weak classifiers, the time cost of our model is much lower than the previous work.
(3) We proposed a semi-supervised Adaboost model based on improved Tri-training to solve the problem of poor balance between detection rate and

false positive rate. The accuracy of our model is higher and the false rate is lower.

The structure of this paper is organized as follows: Sect. 2 introduces the improved Tri-training algorithm and the semi-supervised detection model. Results and performance evaluation are shown in Sect. 3. Finally, conclusions and future improvements are presented in Sect. 4.

2 Algorithm and Model

2.1 Improved Tri-training

We denote L and U as the set of labeled and the set of unlabeled, and H_i represents the set of classifier other than the classifier h_i. The three classifiers are first trained from L, during each learning iteration, H_i checks the unlabeled data set U for each sample x_j, comprehensively calculates the probability that the sample belongs to each traffic class, and then selects the maximum probability as confidence of the sample. We use the labeled result of the unlabeled data on the companion set H_i as the confidence of the unlabeled data, then add the unlabeled data with confidence to the companion set to redefine each classifier, and iteratively calculate the confidence of each unlabeled data. If the number of classifications voted for a particular labeled exceeds a preset threshold θ, the unlabeled example and the newly assigned tag of the unlabeled example are copied into the new labeled set. Nigam et al. [13] reduced the negative impact when the underlying distribution was not fully captured by assigning weights to each unlabeled example. In our method we use the confidence of new labeled data as the weight of each new labeled data, further reducing the potential negative impact.

According to Angluin and Laird [14], assuming the size of the training data is denoted as m, the noise rate is denoted as η, then error rate (e) satisfies the following relationship in the worst case:

$$m = \frac{c}{e^2(1-2\eta)^2} \tag{1}$$

In Eq. 1, c is constant. By modifying Eq. 1, the classifier's classification ability is defined as the utility function u is:

$$u = \frac{c}{e^2} = m(1-2\eta)^2 \tag{2}$$

On the original labeled set, the size of the training data is m_0, the noise rate is η_0, the error rate is e_0, m_0 can be rewritten as a weighted value $W_0 = \sum_{j=0}^{m_0} 1$. During the t-th iteration, the labeled error rate of on the new labeled data set is defined as $e_{i,t}$, so the weighted error value that is incorrectly labeled is $e_{i,t}W_{i,t}$. The weighted $W_{i,t} = \sum_{j=0}^{m_{i,t}} w_{i,t,j}$, and $w_{i,t,j}$ is the predictive confidence of H_i on x_j in $L_{i,t}$, $m_{i,t}$ is the size of $L_{i,t}$, and $L_{i,t}$ is the labeled training set with weight after the t-th iteration. Therefore the noise rate ($\eta_{i,t}$) of the t-th iteration in $L \cup L_{i,t}$ can be estimated as:

$$\eta_{i,t} = \frac{\eta_0 W_0 + e_{i,t} W_{i,t}}{W_0 + W_{i,t}} \tag{3}$$

Replace the η in the Eq. 2, and m is replaced by $W_{i,t} + W_0$. The utility of classifier h_i in the t-th iterative classifier is:

$$u_{i,t} = (W_{i,t} + W_0)(1 - 2\frac{\eta_0 W_0 + e_{i,t} W_{i,t}}{W_0 + W_{i,t}})^2 \tag{4}$$

Similarly, the utility of classifier h_i in the (t-1)-th iterative classifier is:

Algorithm 1. Semi-Supervised AdaBoost model based on Improved Tri-training algorithm

1: **for** $i \in (1..3)$ **do**
2:      S_i=BootstrapSample(L); h_i=learn(L); $e_{i,0}$=0.5; $w_{i,0}$=0; l_i=0
      t=0
3: **while** $h_i changes(i \in 1..3)$ **do**
4:      $t = t + 1$
5:      **for** $i \in (1..3)$ **do**
6:          $L_{i,t} = \phi$; update=FALSE; $e_{i,t} = MeasureError(H_i, L)$
7:          **if** $e_{i,t} < e_{i,t-1}$ **then**
8:              $U_{i,t} = SubSampled(U, \frac{e_{i,t-1} W_{i,t-1}}{e_{i,t}})$
9:              **for** $x \in U_{i,t}$ **do**
10:                 **if** $Confidence(H_i, x) > \theta$ **then**
11:                     $L_{i,t} = L_{i,t-1} \cup (x, H_i)$; $w_{i,t} = w_{i,t-1} + Confidence(H_i, x)$
12:                 **if** $l_i = 0$ **then**
13:                     $l_i = [\frac{e_{i,t}}{e_{i,t-1} - e_{i,t}} + 1)]$
14:                 **if** $l_i < |L_{i,t}|$ **then**
15:                     **if** $e_{i,t-1} W_{i,t-1} > e_{i,t} W_{i,t}$ **then**
16:                         update=TRUE
17:      **for** $i \in (1..3)$ **do**
18:          **if** update=TRUE **then**
19:              $h_i = learn(L \cup L_{i,t})$; $e_{i,t-1} = e_{i,t}$; $l_i = |L_{i,t}|$
20: **Output:** $h(x) = \arg\max_{y \in label} \sum_i^{h_i(x)=y} 1$.

$$u_{i,t-1} = (W_{i,t-1} + W_0)(1 - 2\frac{\eta_0 W_0 + e_{i,t-1} W_{i,t-1}}{W_0 + W_{i,t-1}})^2 \tag{5}$$

The Eq. 2 shows that the utility u is inversely proportional to error rate e in the worst case. Therefore, in order to reduce e, the utility of h_i should be increased in the learning iterations ($u_{i,t} > u_{i,t-1}$), thus the constraint condition can be obtained by Eqs. 4 and 5 is that $W_{i,t} > W_{i,t-1}$ and $e_{i,t-1}W_{i,t-1} > e_{i,t}W_{i,t}$. Which can be summarized by

$$\frac{e_{i,t}}{e_{i,t-1}} < \frac{W_{i,t}}{W_{i,t-1}} < 1 \tag{6}$$

Algorithm 1 shows the pseudo-code of our improved Tri-training. Tri-training uses the majority vote of ensemble learning to avoid the complex and time-consuming process of collaborative training to generate learning hypotheses, but the introduced noise may cause errors in the unlabeled data, reduce the accuracy of experiment, and using a large amount of unlabeled data will make the model worse. We use confidence to filter unlabeled data and add confidence to each unlabeled data as a weight, which can reduce the impact of mislabeled data on the model, and improve accuracy. Because some of the unlabeled data is filtered, iterative data and time loss will be reduced.

2.2 Semi-supervised Model

Mousavi et al. demonstrate that decision trees algorithm can be easily classified and can handle noise (one of the main problems with network traffic) and has an advantage in implementation and time complexity. Akhil et al. proposed that decision trees algorithm is a simple and interpretable framework [15], and is not very sensitive to dimensions. For our proposed algorithm, we choose the decision trees as a weak classifier. In this paper, we propose a semi-supervised Adaboost decision trees model based on the improved Tri-training algorithm. Adaboost is

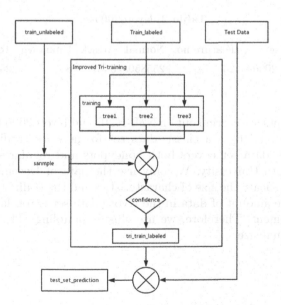

Fig. 1. Semi-supervised Adaboost model based on improved Tri-training algorithm

one of the ensemble learning methods [10]. Compared with bagging, Adaboost focuses on the misclassification training sample of the former classifier. A simple flow chart of the semi-supervised algorithm is shown in Fig. 1. In detail, three Adaboost decision trees models are trained from the labeled data sets, and then the unlabeled data is labeled according to the improved Tri-training algorithm, and the unlabeled data with a confidence greater than Θ are added to the labeled data sets to generate the final model.

3   Experiments

We use weka3.8 to perform our experiments. All experiments are carried out on a sever of Intel(R) Core(TM) i5-6300HQ CPU @2.30 GHZ.

3.1   Evaluation Index and Datasets

There are various ways to determine the performance of the classifier, we use the following performance indicators: Accuracy, Precision, Recall, F-Measure.

Table 1. NSL-KDD.

Data set	Feature no.	Normal	Dos	R2L	U2R	Probe	Total
NSL-KDD	42	9710	7458	2887	67	2421	22543

Table 2. Kyoto2006+.

Data set	Feature no.	Normal	Attack	Unknown	Total
Kyoto2006+	24	255850	3451	8	259309

All experiments are carried out on NSL-KDD and Kyoto2006+ data sets. The NSL-KDD data set [16] is a classic data set for network traffic classification. Kyoto2006+ [17] data set covers both honeypots and regular servers that are deployed at Kyoto University. We only use the data of December 10th, 2015. Tables 1 and 2 indicate the size of characteristics and the traffic type in two data sets. Because the amount of data in the Kyoto data set is too large to meet the memory requirement. Therefore, we use cluster sampling. The test set size is 10% of the original size.

Table 3. Accuracy and time of different algorithm in 20% ratio of labeled and unlabeled data sets

Data set	Algorithm	Adaboost (DT)	SVM	NaiveBayes	Decision trees	Random forest	BP
Koyto	Accuracy (%)	95.52	**99.96**	89.88	93.39	97.12	Overrun
	Time (ms)	(5247,55)	(279359,168713)	(3436,1468)	**(2713,16)**	(54545,2163)	Overrun
NSL-KDD	Accuracy (%)	**96.08**	92.03	72.53	92.03	95.14	94.06
	Time (ms)	(2860,118)	(1658,256)	(7221,3949)	**(1295,24)**	(8275,3114)	(932289,4080)

3.2   Performance Evaluation and Analysis

In experiment, the size of the unlabeled data set is 10% of the test set size, the size of the labeled data set is 20%, 40%, 60%, 80% of the unlabeled data sets size.

In our improved Tri-training algorithm, We tested the impact of different weak classifiers on the model. Table 3 shows the results. The first number of time results represents training time and the second number represents detection time. We have bolded the best results. Obviously, the accuracy of Decision trees is close to the best results, but it is much lower in time cost than other algorithms, and combined with the ensemble learning algorithm, the accuracy is increased by 4% and the detection time is only increased by 0.1s. Therefore, we chose Adaboost (Decision trees) (or Adaboost (DT)) as the weak classification of our model.

Table 4. False rate of different θ with different ratios of labeled

Data set	θ	0.1	0.2	0.3	0.4	0.5	0.6	0.7	0.8	0.9
NSL-KDD	False rate(80%)	2.62	2.62	2.62	2.62	2.77	2.56	2.51	2.57	2.59
	False rate (60%)	3.25	3.25	3.31	3.03	3.03	2.99	2.91	2.97	2.97
	False rate (40%)	3.94	3.94	3.94	4.02	3.80	3.59	3.48	3.75	3.75
	False rate (20%)	5.47	5.47	5.08	5.21	4.93	5.36	3.92	4.05	4.05
	False rate (average)	3.82	3.82	3.74	3.72	3.63	3.625	**3.2**	3.335	3.34
Kyoto	False rate(80%)	2.72	2.72	2.72	2.72	2.72	2.74	2.74	3.04	3.04
	False rate (60%)	3.99	3.99	3.99	3.99	3.97	2.89	2.94	6.37	5.89
	False rate (40%)	6.98	6.98	6.98	6.98	6.98	0.84	0.78	1.93	1.93
	False rate (20%)	9.25	9.25	9.25	9.25	9.25	8.01	4.48	7.55	9.57
	False rate (average)	5.735	5.735	5.735	5.735	5.73	3.62	**2.735**	4.723	5.11

In the algorithm we mentioned that the new labeled instance here needs to satisfy the condition that the confidence is greater than threshold θ. We tested the effect of different θ values on the improved Tri-training algorithm. The results is shown as Table 4. False rate equals 1 minus accuracy. We have proved that the algorithm is not sensitive to θ. Even if θ is small, the false rate of the experiment is also very low. We also calculated the average of the false rate, Table 4 shows that the average of false rate is lowest when $\theta = 0.7$. So we use $\theta = 0.7$ as our final threshold.

Table 5. Results for 20% ratio of labeled and unlabeled data sets

Data set	Model	Accuracy	Precision	Recall	F-measure	Time (ms)
NSL-KDD	Co-training	89.8	89	88	88.9	(4648,742)
	TSVM	92.1	93.5	92.9	92.5	(2127,228)
	Tri-training (Adaboost)	95.5	95.5	94.9	95.2	(3393,151)
	Improved Tri-training (Adaboost)	**96.1**	**96.0**	**95.7**	**95.9**	**(2941,130)**
Kyoto	Co-training	80	80	79	80	(5755,639)
	TSVM	**97.6**	**97.8**	**97.6**	**97.7**	(485072,46176)
	Tri-training (Adaboost)	90.1	91.5	90.9	90.5	(6625,61)
	Improved Tri-training (Adaboost)	95.5	96.0	95.7	95.7	**(5257,35)**

To evaluate our model, We compare our model with Co-training clustering algorithm, Tri-training SVM algorithm (or TSVM) and Tri-training (Adaboost) algorithm. Table 5 shows the results. On the NSL-KDD data set, our model achieved the best results. On the Kyoto data set, TSVM achieved the best results, but the training time was one hundred times of the training time of our model. The detection time of TSVM is one thousand times of the detection time of our model, and the accuracy is only 2% higher than our model. Compared with Tri-training (Adaboost), we used the same weak classifier, but we improved the Tri-training algorithm. For our model eliminates the effects of mislabeled data, it has achieved good results in terms of precision, recall and f-measure. Time cost has also decreased because of the reduced iterative data size.

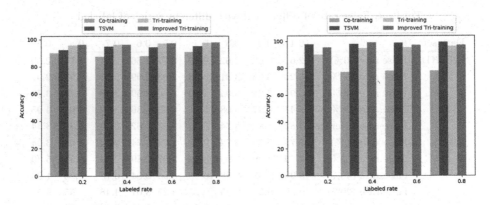

Fig. 2. Accuracy of different algorithms in different labeled rates.

We tested all results of the different ratios of labeled and unlabeled data sets in different data sets. We use the different labeled data sets with ratios of 20%, 40%, 60% and 80%. Figure 2 shows the accuracy of the different algorithms. And Table 6 shows the detection time of the different algorithms. Our model has achieved very good or better results in different scales in different data sets. At the same time, the detection time is also lower, and the attack traffic can be detected more quickly, which is especially important for attack detection. We also find that when the labeled rate is 40%, the error rate of our model is only 0.78. After removing the data of the error labeled, the trained model is more in line with the real situation. These results show that our model is very competitive with other models. Compared with Tri-training (Adaboost), our model improves accuracy, precision, recall, f-measure, and reduces detection time. These results also show that our improvement on the Tri-training algorithm is effective.

Table 6. Detection time of different algorithms in different labeled rates.

Data set	Model	0.2	0.4	0.6	0.8
NSL-KDD	Co-training (ms)	725	1038	934	921
	TSVM (ms)	204	218	218	218
	Tri-training (Adaboost)(ms)	126	128	143	137
	Improved Tri-training (Adaboost)(ms)	130	126	151	132
Kyoto	Co-training (ms)	868	584	794	892
	TSVM (ms)	46176	50085	48041	54185
	Tri-training (Adaboost) (ms)	61	59	61	63
	Improved Tri-training (Adaboost) (ms)	35	33	19	29

4 Conclusion

Our paper improved the traditional Tri-training algorithm and proves that we are effective in improving the Tri-trainings by comparing the results of different basic classifiers. And proposed a Semi-supervised Adaboost decision trees model based on improved algorithm. In the experiment, we used different sizes of tag data sets. Even if the labeled data set is small, our classifier can achieve low false positive rate and good detection rate. When using only 561 labeled examples and 2252 unlabeled examples, we can classify test sets of size 22543 with an accuracy of 96.1% in the NSL-KDD data set and 95.5% in the Kyoto data set. Theoretical analysis and experiments show that compared with the published semi-supervised detection algorithm based on sample data sets, our proposed algorithm is competitive and achieves better results regardless of the number of labeled data.

Our future work will focus on different data sets to test our algorithm and improve our algorithm. Improved Tri-training is an algorithm that can make good use of generalization ability. Currently, there are only three classifiers. So we will also focus on more classifiers, and the balance of accuracy and time will be future research goals.

References

1. Shang-fu, G., Chun-lan, Z.: Intrusion detection system based on classification. In: 2012 IEEE International Conference on Intelligent Control, Automatic Detection and High-End Equipment, pp. 78–83. IEEE (2012)
2. Mazel, J., Casas, P., Labit, Y., et al.: Sub-space clustering, inter-clustering results association & anomaly correlation for unsupervised network anomaly detection. In: International Conference on Network and Service Management. IEEE (2011)
3. Zhu, X.J.: Semi-supervised learning literature survey. Technical report 1530, Department of Computer Sciences, University of Wisconsin at Madison, Madison, WI, December 2007
4. Erman, J., Mahanti, A., Arlitt, M., et al.: Semi-supervised network traffic classification. In: SIGMETRICS, pp. 369–370 (2007)
5. Wang, Y., Xiang, Y., Zhang, J., et al.: A novel semi-supervised approach for network traffic clustering. In: International Conference on Network and System Security. IEEE (2011)
6. Li, X., Qi, F., Kun Yu, L., et al.: High accurate Internet traffic classification based on co-training semi-supervised clustering. In: International Conference on Advanced Intelligence and Awarenss Internet. IET (2010)
7. Li, K., et al.: A novel semi-supervised SVM based on tri-training. J. Comput. 5(4), 47–51 (2010)
8. Yuan, Y., Kaklamanos, G., Hogrefe, D.: A novel semi-supervised Adaboost technique for network anomaly detection. In: ACM International Conference on Modeling, Analysis and Simulation of Wireless and Mobile Systems, pp. 111–114. ACM (2016)
9. Xu, G., Zhao, J., Huang, D.: An improved social spammer detection based on tri-training. In: IEEE International Conference on Big Data. IEEE (2017)
10. Liu, X., Dai, Y., Zhang, Y., et al.: A preprocessing method of AdaBoost for mislabeled data classification. In: Control and Decision Conference, pp. 2738–2742. IEEE (2017)
11. Goldman, S., Zhou, Y.: Enhancing supervised learning with unlabeled data. In: ICML, pp. 327–334 (2000)
12. Zhou, Z.H., Li, M.: Tri-training: exploiting unlabeled data using three classifiers. IEEE Trans. Knowl. Data Eng. 17(11), 1529–1541 (2005)
13. Nigam, K., McCallum, A.K., Thrun, S., et al.: Text classification from labeled and unlabeled documents using EM. Mach. Learn. 39(2–3), 103–134 (2000)
14. Angluin, D., Laird, P.: Learning from noisy examples. Mach. Learn. 2(4), 343–370 (1988)
15. Jabbar, M.A., Samreen, S.: Intelligent network intrusion detection using alternating decision trees. In: 2016 International Conference on Circuits, Controls, Communications and Computing (I4C), pp. 1–6. IEEE (2016)
16. Lippmann, R., Haines, J.W., Fried, D.J., et al.: The 1999 DARPA off-line intrusion detection evaluation. Comput. Netw. 34(4), 579–595 (2000)
17. Sangkatsanee, P., Wattanapongsakorn, N., Charnsripinyo, C.: Practical real-time intrusion detection using machine learning approaches. Comput. Commun. 34(18), 2227–2235 (2011)

Automated Cash Mining Attacks
on Mobile Advertising Networks

Woojoong Ji[1]([✉]), Taeyun Kim[1], Kuyju Kim[2], and Hyoungshick Kim[1]

[1] Sungkyunkwan University, Suwon, Republic of Korea
{woojoong,taeyun1010,hyoung}@skku.edu
[2] AhnLab, Seongnam, Republic of Korea
kuyju.kim@ahnlab.com

Abstract. Rewarded advertisements are popularly used in the mobile advertising industry. In this paper, we analyze several rewarded advertisement applications to discover security weaknesses, which allow malicious users to automatically generate in-app activities for earning cash rewards on advertisement networks; we call this attack *automated cash mining*. To show the risk of this attack, we implemented automated cashing attacks on four popularly used Android applications (`Cash Slide`, `Fronto`, `Honey Screen` and `Screen Stash`) with rewarded advertisements through reverse engineering and demonstrated that all the tested reward apps are vulnerable to our attack implementation.

1 Introduction

In rewarded advertisement services, the most important security issue is the detection of (artificially created) fraudulent user engagement activities that have no intention of generating value for the advertiser [6]. Recently, there have been few studies [2,3] that analyze the potential security risks in this domain. Cho et al. [2] demonstrated that six Android advertising networks were vulnerable to automated click fraud attacks through the Android Debug Bridge (ADB).

In this paper, we extend Cho et al's attack model of relying on automated input sequences at the user interface level into a more sophisticated attack called *automated cash mining*, which allows an attacker to automatically generate in-app activities at the network packet level. This is a significant advancement from previous studies [2,3] that merely showed potential weaknesses in rewarded advertisement applications.

To show the feasibility of our attack, we analyzed four popularly used reward apps (`Cash Slide`, `Fronto`, `Honey Screen` and `Screen Stash`) by reverse engineering and packet analysis, and we found that all tested reward apps are vulnerable to automated cash mining attacks.

2 Mobile Advertising Network

To provide a better understanding of automated cash mining attacks, we first present the typical model of a mobile advertising network for reward applications.

© Springer Nature Switzerland AG 2019
J. Jang-Jaccard and F. Guo (Eds.): ACISP 2019, LNCS 11547, pp. 679–686, 2019.
https://doi.org/10.1007/978-3-030-21548-4_40

In the advertising network model, there are four main entities: (1) publisher, (2) advertising network, (3) advertiser and (4) reward app.

A publisher (i.e., app developer) develops a reward app with the SDK library for an advertising network and releases it to users. Advertisers can add new advertisements to the advertising network when they want. The reward app can periodically fetch a list of advertisements from the advertising network via its SDK library incorporated in the app itself. In general, the advertising network manages publishers and advertisers as a moderator in this model.

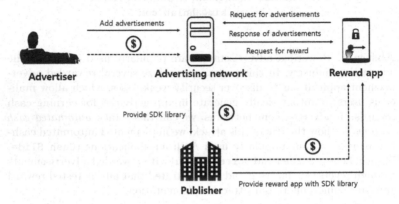

Fig. 1. Business model of advertising networks with reward apps.

Whenever a user watches advertisements on the reward app, the app then reports the user engagement activities referred to as *'impressions'* to the advertising network. This reporting process is triggered by sending a request message for a reward from the reward app to the advertising network. Consequently, the user would be rewarded for performing such activities within the reward app. For this rewarding process, advertisers pay money to the advertising network depending on the number of impressions they receive; the advertising network pays money to the publishers; and a publisher finally pays money to its reward app users. This process is depicted in Fig. 1.

3   Automated Cash Mining Attack

Our goal is to generate network traffic that emulates a real reward app. To artificially generate reward request messages for automated cash mining attacks, we must know how a reward app interacts with its advertising network. Therefore, we carefully analyzed the network messages exchanged between a target reward app and its advertising network server by a web debugging proxy.

From our traffic analysis of the four reward apps tested (Cash Slide, Fronto, Honey Screen and Screen Stash), we found that reward apps' request messages generally include an *authentication code* to verify the authenticity of reward messages. The authentication code is *newly* calculated every time in a *secret* function f (e.g., encryption or cryptographic hash function) with a reward app's internal parameters such as advertisement identifier, user identifier, timestamp, reward amount, etc. to prevent replay attacks. Therefore, to implement automated cash mining attacks, the most challenging task is to analyze how such an authentication code is computed in a function f, which is internally implemented in each reward app. To achieve this, we examined the procedure of authentication code generation in each reward app through reverse engineering.

If we are able to compute authentication codes with the internal parameters of a reward app, we can systemically generate reward request messages containing valid authentication codes.

4   Implementation

To perform automated cash mining attacks, we need to intentionally craft reward request messages to deceive a victim advertising network. Therefore, we first analyze the structure of network messages used in genuine reward apps and then generate reward request messages based on our analysis results.

4.1   Analysis of Network Messages

To generate reward request messages, it is necessary to analyze the messages exchanged between the advertising network and the reward app. To analyze the HTTPS traffic, we used *Fiddler* (https://www.telerik.com/fiddler) to mount a man-in-the-middle attack. In practice, there are several methods (e.g., certificate pinning [5]) to prevent man-in-the-middle attacks on HTTPS but all the tested reward apps failed to prevent our traffic analysis.

There are two types of advertisements in reward apps: (1) advertisements that have a reward and (2) advertisements that do not have a reward. After receiving a request to deliver the current advertisement list to the reward app, the advertising network server responds with the requested advertisement list in JavaScript Object Notation (JSON) format.

We found that the reward amounts can be changed dynamically depending on the type of advertisement (e.g., some advertisements do not have a reward at all). Therefore, to maximize their gain, attackers must first obtain the information about the reward amount for each advertisement so that they can selectively generate request messages only for advertisements with a (high) reward. For reward apps, it is essential to maintain up-to-date reward amount information for advertisements. In the reward apps on Android, such information is typically stored on a system cache and/or a database file. We experimentally observed that a request message for new advertisements would be generated in most reward apps when they are restarted after erasing the system cache and database file for advertisements. Therefore, in a reward app, we can try to analyze the structure of the request message for new advertisements by intentionally erasing the system cache and database file and restarting the app itself. If we completely analyze the structure of the request message for new advertisements, we can also generate the request message based on our analysis results and send the message to obtain the information about advertisements. Thus, we can selectively generate request messages only for advertisements with rewards to boost the efficiency of automated cash mining attacks.

4.2 Analysis of Authentication Code Computation

As explained in Sect. 3, in reward apps, the authentication code is typically used to verify the integrity and authenticity of reward messages. For example, in Cash Slide, *key* and *ts* are used to compute the authentication code. Cash Slide calculates a *key* value by combining the user's name (*c_nickname*) and timestamp for the purpose of preventing replay attacks. The *ts* field provides the timestamp that is used when generating the *key* value. As a result of the analysis, we discovered that only the *key* and *ts* fields are periodically refreshed, and the rest of the fields are always fixed. Hence, the attacker only needs to dynamically calculate the *key* and *ts* fields to make valid request messages.

Therefore, we need to analyze the reward apps' codes for computing authentication codes and reimplement them to automatically generate valid reward request messages. To achieve this, we analyzed the APK files of each reward app. We note that Android apps are written in Java, and they are compiled to Java byte code and then translated into the Dalvik executable (DEX) format [4]. Using an APK extractor, we first extracted a target reward app's APK file from the app and then converted the extracted APK file into JAR files. Next, we used a decomplier (e.g., *JD-decompiler*) to decompile the JAR files and analyze the decompiled source codes. In the decompiled source codes, we can find a few candidate functions using text keyword matching (e.g., crypto, key and AES).

```
public static String a = "1a2b3c4d5e6f7g8h9i1j2k3l4m5n6o7p";
public static String b = "1a2b3c4d5e6f7g8h";
...
try
{
  Object abc = new javax/crypto/spec/SecretKeySpec;
  ((SecretKeySpec)abc).<init>(a.getBytes(), "AES");
  Object def = b;
  def = Cipher.getInstance("AES/CBC/PKCS5PADDING");
      ...
  abc = ((Cipher)def).doFinal(paramString.getBytes());
}
...
```

Fig. 2. Function for authentication code computation in Cash Slide.

To identify the candidate functions, we used dynamic analysis tools (*Frida*, https://www.frida.re/ and *AppMon*, https://dpnishant.github.io/appmon/) to analyze how an authentication code is computed by using a cryptographic algorithm (e.g., AES or MD5) with its parameters. To use *Frida* and *AppMon* on an Android smartphone, the smartphone must be rooted. However, none of the apps tested had any anti-rooting mechanisms.

Among the apps tested, two apps (`Cash Slide` and `Fronto`) only used an encryption algorithm to compute authentication codes. The remaining apps (`Honey Screen` and `Screen Stash`) only used a cryptographic hash function (e.g., MD5) instead. Figure 2 shows the decompiled code for computing authentication codes in `Cash Slide`. From this code, we can see that AES in CBC mode with PKCS5 padding algorithm with the hard-coded encryption key and initial vector is used to compute authentication codes.

4.3   Generation of Messages to Mimic Reward Apps

The overall process of our automated cash mining attack is as follows:

1. Send a request message to obtain information about the advertisement (e.g., advertisement's identifier, user identifier, timestamp and reward amount).
2. Send reward request messages periodically for advertisements with a (high) reward.

The reward request messages that will be sent to the advertising network can be easily generated using Request to Code [1], which is a `Fiddler` extension.

After making such a request, we use the advertisement identifier and other information of advertisements with rewards from the list to automatically calculate authentication codes.

5   Experiments

We analyzed four popularly used reward apps (`Cash Slide`, `Fronto`, `Honey Screen` and `Screen Stash`) and implemented automated cash mining attacks to generate *valid* reward request messages to mimic the messages generated by human users using those reward apps. To evaluate the performance of our attack implementations, we created log files to record the response messages from the advertising network. We demonstrate that our implementation of automated cash mining attacks can be used to obtain rewards from reward apps in an automated manner, and we confirmed that there were only a few defense mechanisms in the four reward applications that we investigated. We also discovered that it is possible to implement automated cash mining attacks to financially damage real-world mobile advertising networks with all four reward apps. The detailed experiment results are explained in the following sections.

5.1 Data Protection

We analyzed the features that the developers used to protect their data, such as hash and cryptographic functions. As shown in Table 1, two of the four apps used AES encryption but the encryption keys and IV vector values were stored in plaintext form in the APK files. As a result, malicious users can easily access these values. In addition, we found that both the encryption keys and the IV vector values were fixed, and they were not changed following encryption. Attackers can decrypt the encrypted messages by obtaining the encryption keys and IV vector values that the app uses to encrypt messages.

Table 1. Security mechanisms used in reward apps.

| Application | Data protection | | Reward policy | Defense mechanisms | | | |
	Encryption	Hash	Fixed reward	Rooting check	Hooking check	TLS certificate	Code obfuscation
Cash Slide	✓	✗	✓	✗	✗	✗	✓
Fronto	✓	✗	✓	✗	✗	✗	✓
Honey Screen	✗	✓	✗	✗	✗	✗	✓
Screen Stash	✗	✓	✗	✗	✗	✗	✓

✓=used; ✗=not used

As shown in Table 1, the two remaining apps used the MD5 hash function instead of AES encryption, and the hash function was applied to one of the fields in the message. Since the hash function is not an encryption method, the attackers can generate the same output by analyzing the input value through source code analysis.

5.2 Reward Policy

Many reward applications have mechanisms to protect themselves. The reward apps have reward policies, such as a time limit to request a reward or verification of a reward. We analyzed the reward polices of the four reward apps. As shown in Table 1, in two of the four apps, the users receive a fixed amount of rewards. For the other two apps, the attackers can change the reward value. In this case, the attackers can obtain more rewards than the intended amount of rewards since they can manipulate the reward value.

5.3 Defense Mechanisms

In all the apps we tested, we found that there is no proper defense mechanism (e.g., anti-debugging) except simple code obfuscation to hide package/class/variable names. Therefore, we can effectively analyze the procedures to compute the authentication code by tracing crypto APIs with *Frida*.

Another straightforward defense solution is to limit the number of reward request messages in a specific time interval. However, `Cash Slide` did not limit the number of request attempts. Another defense mechanism is to limit the number of request attempts within a fixed time interval, but automated cash mining attacks can still be financially damaging over long periods of time.

5.4   Attack Results

To show the feasibility of an automated cash mining attack, we performed the attack for a total of three days using the vulnerabilities discovered against the four reward apps (see Table 2).

Table 2. Results of performing *automated cash mining* attacks on reward apps

| Application | Normal user(Avg.) | | Attacker | | Time interval | Reward manipulation |
	Amount of reward	Number of reward	Amount of reward	Number of reward		
Cach Slide	$0.04	27	$127.84	28,533	Unlimited time	✗ $0.005
Fronto	$0.06	21	$0.56	70	25m	✗ $0.009
Honey Screen	$0.04	23	$0.6	21	40m	✓ ($0.005 → $0.03)
Screen Stash	$0.02	16	$0.52	19	40m	✓ ($0.005 → $0.03)

✓=possible ✗=not possible

When normal users use the four reward apps without launching an automated cash mining attack for three days, they can receive an average of $0.04 (Cash Slide), $0.06 (Fronto), $0.04 (Honey Screen) and $0.02 (Screen Stash) for each app. Hence, the reward app in which the users can receive the highest reward is Fronto with $0.06, and the reward app in which the users can receive the lowest reward is Screen Stash with $0.02. Additionally, the number of advertisements with rewards displayed on the lock screen within three days was 27 (Cash Slide), 21 (Fronto), 23 (Honey Screen) and 16 (Screen Stash) on average for each reward app. Cash Slide displayed the most number of such advertisements (27 times), and Screen Stash displayed the least (16 times).

When launching automated cash mining attacks to show the security weakness of reward apps, we were able to earn $127.84 (Cash Slide), $0.56 (Fronto), $0.6 (Honey Screen) and $0.52 (Screen Stash), respectively, for each of the four reward apps within one day. For Honey Screen and Screen Stash, the amount of rewards in reward request messages can be modified even though the maximum allowable value is $0.03. This is six times higher than the default reward value ($0.005) while the amount of rewards for Cash Slide and Fronto were fixed to $0.005 and $0.009, respectively. In the case of Cash Slide, however, the most serious financial damage occurred because we can generate reward request messages without any limitation.

To test how effectively the automated cash mining attack obtains rewards, we compared the case when a normal user uses the app for three days with the case when the automated cash mining attack is launched. Compared to the case of a normal user, the amount of rewards received for three days increased by 3,196 times, 9.3 times, 15 times, 26 times when the automated cash mining attack was launched. Further, compared to the case of a normal user, the number of advertisements with rewards increased by 1,057 times, 3.3 times, 0.9 times, 1.2 times during the same time period. As a result, we confirmed that we could obtain rewards with 0.9 times to 1,057 times more efficiency using automated cash mining attack.

6   Conclusion

In this paper, we analyzed the security flaws present in mobile advertising networks. We introduced automated cash mining attacks to automatically generate in-app activities at the network packet level. While previous studies [2,3] have only demonstrated the feasibility of automated attacks by emulating human click behaviors at the UI level, we implemented the first *fully automated* and working tool that is capable of generating reward request messages in a massive manner.

In our attack experiments, we found that all tested adverting networks failed to detect our automated cash mining attacks. This could be explained from the economic incentives of a security failure in current mobile adverting network models. We expect that in automated cash mining attacks, the advertisers incur the financial losses rather than the advertising networks. To make matters worse, the success of automated cash mining attacks is not a loss in an advertising network but rather a profit. Because of this disincentive, we surmise that adverting networks might not be sufficiently motivated to detect automated cash mining attacks. To fix this problem, we suggest that the interaction between adverting networks and reward applications should be audited and monitored regularly by an external third party in order to properly regulate adverting networks.

Acknowledgments. This work was supported in part by NRF of Korea (NRF-2017K1A3A1A17092614) and the ICT Consilience Creative support program (IITP-2019-2015-0-00742).

References

1. Fiddler Extension (Requset to Code). http://www.chadsowald.com/software/fiddler-extension-request-to-code. Accessed 28 Feb 2019
2. Cho, G., Cho, J., Song, Y., Choi, D., Kim, H.: Combating online fraud attacks in mobile-based advertising. EURASIP J. Inf. Secur. **2016**(1), 2 (2016)
3. Crussell, J., Stevens, R., Chen, H.: Madfraud: investigating ad fraud in android applications. In: Proceedings of the 12th Annual International Conference on Mobile Systems, Applications, and Services (2014)
4. Enck, W., Octeau, D., McDaniel, P., Chaudhuri, S.: A study of android application security. In: Proceedings of the 20th USENIX Security Symposium (2011)
5. Evans, C., Palmer, C.: Certificate pinning extension for HSTS (2011). https://tools.ietf.org/html/draft-evans-palmer-hsts-pinning-00
6. Immorlica, N., Jain, K., Mahdian, M., Talwar, K.: Click fraud resistant methods for learning click-through rates. In: Deng, X., Ye, Y. (eds.) WINE 2005. LNCS, vol. 3828, pp. 34–45. Springer, Heidelberg (2005). https://doi.org/10.1007/11600930_5

Author Index